Lecture Notes in Computer Science 1000

Edited by G. Goos, J. Hartmanis and J. van Leeuwen

Advisory Board: W. Brauer   D. Gries   J. Stoer

Springer
Berlin
Heidelberg
New York
Barcelona
Budapest
Hong Kong
London
Milan
Paris
Santa Clara
Singapore
Tokyo

Jan van Leeuwen (Ed.)

Computer Science Today

Recent Trends and Developments

 Springer

Series Editors

Gerhard Goos, Karlsruhe University, Germany

Juris Hartmanis, Cornell University, NY, USA

Jan van Leeuwen, Utrecht University, The Netherlands

Volume Editor

Jan van Leeuwen
Department of Computer Science, Utrecht University
Padualaan 14, 3584 CH Utrecht, The Netherlands

Cataloging-in-Publication data applied for

Die Deutsche Bibliothek - CIP-Einheitsaufnahme

Computer science today : recent trends and developments / Jan
van Leeuwen (ed.). - Berlin ; Heidelberg ; New York ;
Barcelona ; Budapest ; Hong Kong ; London ; Milan ; Paris ;
Tokyo : Springer, 1995
  (Lecture notes in computer science ; 1000)
  ISBN 3-540-60105-8
NE: Leeuwen, Jan van [Hrsg.]; GT

CR Subject Classification (1991): A.1

ISBN 3-540-60105-8 Springer-Verlag Berlin Heidelberg New York

© Springer-Verlag Berlin Heidelberg 1995
Printed in Germany

Typesetting: Camera-ready by author
SPIN 10485993   06/3142 – 5 4 3 2 1 0   Printed on acid-free paper

Preface

This volume of the series *Lecture Notes in Computer Science* (and *Lecture Notes in Artificial Intelligence*) marks a truly unique and festive moment: it is the *1000th* volume that is appearing in the series.

To commemorate the special occasion, this volume presents a unique collection of expository papers on major themes that are representative for computer science 'today'. The papers were written by leading experts and teams in the computer science area with a very specific goal in mind, namely to demonstrate the scope and stature of the field today and give an impression of some of the chief motivations and challenges for tomorrow's computer science.

The series was founded in 1973 on the initiative of Klaus Peters and his wife Alice Peters, who were the responsible editors within Springer-Verlag at the time for the mathematics and economics-oriented publishing activities. The successful Lecture Notes in Mathematics (published since 1964) and Lecture Notes in Economics and Mathematical Systems (published since 1968, initially as Lecture Notes in Operations Research and Mathematical Economics and later as Lecture Notes in Operations Research and Mathematical Systems) were the leading examples for the series. It was first named 'Lecture Notes in Computer Science' in an internal Springer memo of Walter Kaufmann-Bühler to Klaus Peters dated January 23, 1973.

Gerhard Goos, who had become an editor of the Lecture Notes in Economics and Mathematical Systems in 1972, was asked to become editor of the new series and shortly later, on the invitation by Alice Peters in March 1973, Juris Hartmanis joined as series editor as well. With the strategic support of the Advisory Board, Goos and Hartmanis have directed the series since. Under their editorial rule, the series developed into the exceedingly valuable collection of volumes that it is today, indispensable for the practicing scientist in any branch of computer science or related discipline.

It is extremely interesting and educational to look again at the first one-hundred volumes that appeared in the series Lecture Notes in Computer Science and to see how they reflect the gradual formation of computer science as a science through the 1970s in Europe and in the world. There were influential lecture notes from conferences, schools and advanced courses on compiler construction, complexity theory, distributed systems, net theory, operating systems, optimization methods, program construction, programming languages and their implementation, and software engineering, to mention just a few of the volumes. Conferences like the International Colloquium on Automata, Languages and Programming (ICALP, starting at Volume 14) and the Symposium on Mathematical Foundations of Computer Science (MFCS, starting at Volume 28) were among the first to record their proceedings in the Lecture Notes series.

From the very beginning, course notes such as Sheila Greibach's "Theory of Program Structures: Schemes, Semantics, Verification" (Volume 36), monographs like Robin Milner's "A Calculus of Communicating Systems" (Volume 92), selected Ph.D. theses like Joost Engelfriet's (Volume 20) and Samuel Fuller's

(Volume 31), language documents like "Towards a Formal Description of ADA" (Volume 98) and manuals like Volume 6 on EISPACK (with an extension in Volume 51) were included in the series. The best known 'Lecture Note' from those times undoubtedly is Volume 18: Jensen and Wirth's "PASCAL – User Manual and Report". Volume 100 appeared in 1981, eight years after the series was started. It was the proceedings of the 6th International Workshop on Graph-Theoretic Concepts in Computer Science (WG).

Computer science developed tremendously throughout the 1980s. The ever increasing computational and information-processing capabilities of computers were recognized in all disciplines and led to many 'computational sciences' and the beginnings of present-day information technology. The development of personal computers and workstations on the one hand, and of attractive and powerful software tools and user-interfaces on the other, made the techniques of computer science available to the entire community. It placed enormous demands on the field, requiring both theory and practice to advance with giant leaps.

One consequence of this development was that it triggered an enormous advance in the design of intelligent systems, leading to many new challenges in, e.g., conceptual modeling and formal methods. In 1987 it was decided to devote a special subseries within the Lecture Notes series to Artificial Intelligence, and Jörg Siekmann was asked to be the series editor for this area, starting with Volume 345 in 1988. In the second half of 1993, starting with Volume 764, Jaime G. Carbonell joined to become the second series editor of the Lecture Notes in Artificial Intelligence. To date, over 120 volumes have appeared in the subseries. I joined Goos and Hartmanis as series editor of the Lecture Notes in Computer Science in 1994, starting at Volume 850.

It is instructive to look at the past one-hundred volumes of the Lecture Notes in Computer Science as well, by way of comparison. Volume 900, the proceedings of the 12th Annual Symposium on Theoretical Aspects of Computer Science (STACS'95), appeared in January 1995. Again the Lecture Notes series reflects the massive, new developments in the computer science field. There are volumes devoted to conferences and workshops on algorithms, artificial life, bio-computing, cooperative work, computational geometry, computer-aided verification, constraint programming, cryptography, databases, functional programming, high-performance computing and networking, intelligent agents, learning, object-oriented programming, parallel programming, program construction, reasoning systems, systems engineering and telematics, to mention just a few of the subject areas. Every volume represents a wealth of scientific information, easily accessible and quickly disseminated for study and reference. In turn, the Lecture Notes in Computer Science continue to be a chief instrument in the development of computer science worldwide.

In 1973, the year in which the Lecture Notes in Computer Science started, Donald E. Knuth (*American Scientist* 61 (1973) p. 708) wrote:

> "One of my mathematician friends told me he would be willing to recognize computer science as a worthwhile field of study, as soon as it contains 1000 deep theorems. This criterion should obviously be changed to in-

clude algorithms as well as theorems [$\cdots$]. But even so it is clear that computer science today does not measure up to such a test, if "deep" means that a brilliant person would need many months to discover the theorems or the algorithms. Computer science is still too young for this [in 1973]."

It is clear that computer science passed the criterion years ago but, to quote Donald Knuth (personal correspondence, February 27, 1995) again, it seems that the appearance of the 1000th volume of the Lecture Notes in Computer Science is as good a time as any to celebrate the obvious fact that computer science has come of age. Juris Hartmanis (e-mail correspondence, June 18, 1995) formulated it like this:

"[$\cdots$] it is a haunting coincidence that LNCS has reached its 1000th volume at this time. To me it has a deeper significance, as if a period of exciting growth has reached a major milestone in the achievements of computer science and the recognition of its impact. This is the time when the Worldwide Web has gained so much visibility and prominence that the Information Superhighway is recognized by politicians as a vital issue and e-mail addresses are given out for the White House. This visibility of computer science is not built on its deepest achievements, but it is proof of the recognition and awareness that computing and communications are changing our societies very fundamentally and, by implication, that computer science is the catalyst for this process."

It is thus only fitting that we have entitled the anniversary volume: *Computer Science Today*.

Volume 1000 was designed to give a broad view of the achievements and challenges of modern computer science. Stated in this way, it is clear that not even 1000 pages would have been sufficient to give an adequate overview of the field. Besides, many of the Lecture Notes routinely contain the text of invited lectures and surveys that give in-depth accounts of many specialized themes already! As editor of Volume 1000 I have selected a number of themes which have struck me as being particularly representative for the kind of concerns in present day computer science, from algorithms to software technology to multimedia and ethical issues. I am very grateful to all colleagues who have responded to the invitation to contribute to the volume and give an exposition of their area of interest and expertise, or just of an exciting new development in the computer science field. Without exception, the support for making this volume a truly unique one has been overwhelming. I thank each and every author for the contribution to this volume and for the non-trivial amount of time that they have all given to the preparation of their paper for this volume.

The present landmark in the history of the Lecture Notes in Computer Science series could only be reached because of the unfailing support of the publisher, Springer-Verlag. Special thanks are due to the in-house Computer Science editors of Springer-Verlag who have been responsible for the series: Alice Peters from the beginning of the series until 1978, Gerhard Rossbach from 1978 until

1985, and Hans Wössner from 1985 until 1991, with substantial support by Ingeborg Mayer as associate editor from 1976 onward. In 1991 Alfred Hofmann joined Springer-Verlag and assumed the responsibility for the series, with editorial assistance in the past two years by Simone Reutner. Angelika Bernauer-Budiman has served as production editor for the series since 1981 and supervised the production of more than 900 volumes. I am very grateful to my colleague series editors, Gerhard Goos and Juris Hartmanis, and especially to Alfred Hofmann for their help and advice during the preparation of this very special volume in the series Lecture Notes in Computer Science.

While a new 'millennium' in the series is presenting itself and new challenges of the electronic age must be met, we hope that this volume will lead the reader to reminisce about the impact of computer science and to contemplate the many challenges that must be met in the future.

Utrecht, September 1995   Jan van Leeuwen

Lecture Notes in Computer Science

Series Editors

Gerhard Goos studied mathematics at the Freie Universität Berlin and the Universität Erlangen where he received his Dr.rer.nat. in 1965. After five years at the Technische Universität München, he joined the Universität Karlsruhe as the founding chair of the Informatics Department. From 1983 to 1991 he served as director of the Institute for System Technology and then as member of the Board of the GMD, the German National Laboratory for Computer Science. His research interests center on software engineering and compiler technology. He served as chairman of IFIP Working Group 2.4 (on System Programming Languages) from 1981 to 1984, and he is a trustee of the International Computer Science Institute (ICSI) at Berkeley since its foundation in 1986. Goos is known in Germany for his textbooks *Informatik, eine einführende Übersicht* (2 volumes, 1971, with F.L. Bauer, now in its 4th edition) and internationally for *Compiler Construction* (1983, with W.M. Waite). He is a series editor of Springer-Verlag's Lectures Notes in Computer Science and an editor of the journals Informatik-Spektrum, Informatik-Forschung und Entwicklung, Formal Aspects of Computing, and Software – Concepts and Tools.

Juris Hartmanis was born in Riga (Latvia) and studied physics at the Philips University in Marburg, Germany, where he received his Cand.Phil. degree in 1949. He received his M.A. in mathematics from the University of Kansas in 1951 and his Ph.D. from the California Institute of Technology in 1955. After teaching mathematics at Cornell and Ohio State Universities he joined the GE Research Laboratory in Schenectady, NY in 1958 and was quickly initiated in computer science research. In 1965 he joined Cornell University as the founding chair of the Computer Science Department. Hartmanis has been at Cornell since, except for his sabbatical leaves at the GMD in Bonn, MSRI in Berkeley and the Max-Planck-Institut für Informatik in Saarbrücken. His research interests center on theory of computation and computational complexity. Hartmanis is a member of the National Academy of Engineering, foreign member of the Latvian Academy of Sciences, Fellow of the American Academy of Arts and Sciences, the New York State Academy of Sciences, and the American Association for the Advancement of Science, and Charter Fellow of the ACM. In 1993 Hartmanis was awarded with R.E. Stearns the ACM Turing Award, and in 1995 he received a Dr.h.c. from the Universität Dortmund and the Golden Bolzano Medal awarded by the Academy of Sciences of the Czech Republic. He is editor of the Springer-Verlag Lecture Notes in Computer Science, the Journal of Computer and System Sciences, the SIAM Journal on Computing, the Journal for Universal Computer Science, and The Chicago Journal of Theoretical Computer Science.

Jan van Leeuwen studied mathematics at Utrecht University, where he received his M.Sc. degree in 1969. He continued in a research position in applied mathematics, specializing in the 'informatics' of that time: programming theory, computability, and automata and formal language theory. After obtaining his Ph.D. at Utrecht University in 1972, he went to the US and immersed himself in the many different aspects of computer science. He held positions in computer science at the University of California at Berkeley, the State University of New York at Buffalo (NY), and the Pennsylvania State University. In 1977 he was appointed at Utrecht University again, to head the newly formed Department of Computer Science. He is a Full Professor of Computer Science at Utrecht University since 1982 and presently serving as Dean of the Faculty of Mathematics and Computer Science. Jan van Leeuwen has published extensively on the design and analysis of algorithms, from datastructuring and computational geometry to parallel and distributed algorithms. His interests cover a wide spectrum of research in algorithms and formal methods for computing and other fields that are amenable to theoretical modeling and analysis. He is a member of the International Panel of BRICS (Aarhus, DK) and has served as chair/organizer or program committee member of many conferences and workshops on algorithms. He was a consulting editor for the Addison-Wesley Publishing Company (Europe) from 1981 to 1991, managing editor of the 2-volume *Handbook of Theoretical Computer Science* (now also in a Japanese translation), served on the editorial boards of Information and Computation, the SIAM Journal on Computing, and Theoretical Computer Science, and edited or co-edited the following Lecture Notes in Computer Science: Volumes 85, 312, 344, 486, 505/506, 790, 855, and 1000. He became a series editor of the Springer-Verlag Lecture Notes in Computer Science in 1994.

Contents

Verification and Reasoning

Intelligent Systems

Multimedia and Hypermedia

Contributors to Volume 1000

The following authors, in alphabetical order, have contributed to this anniversary volume of the Lecture Notes in Computer Science.

L.M. Adleman	B. Monien
P.K. Agarwal	A. Mulkers
R. Anderson	S. Nakano
A. Anuchitanukul	R. Needham
Z. Bai	J. Nievergelt
Th. Beth	T. Nishizeki
G. Brassard	A. Nückel
M. Broy	P.A. Pevzner
M. Bruynooghe	V. Pratt
D.C.A. Bulterman	N.J. Radcliffe
E.M. Clarke	S. Rajsbaum
M. Codish	W. Reisig
D. Day	Th. Römke
J. Demmel	A. Ruhe
R. Diekmann	E. Sandewall
J. Dongarra	F.B. Schneider
J.-O. Eklundh	U.-P. Schroeder
R. Feldmann	M. Sharir
D. Garlan	M. Shaw
R. Gasser	H.T. Siegelmann
D. Gries	G. Smolka
M. Gu	L. Snyder
S. Hannenhalli	L. Steels
D. Harel	R. Steinmetz
L. Hardman	P.D. Surry
M. Herlihy	M. Tokoro
S. Jha	T.E. Uribe
Th. Käppner	H. van der Vorst
A. Klappenecker	C.J. van Rijsbergen
R. Klasing	M.Y. Vardi
M. Li	P. Vitányi
R. Lüling	G. Vossen
Z. Manna	J. Wiedermann
F. Mäser	C. Wirth
H. Maurer	D. Wood
W.F. McColl	R.R. Yager
K. Menzel	X. Zhou
T. Minkwitz	

A Quantum Jump in Computer Science

Gilles BRASSARD*

Université de Montréal, Département d'informatique et de recherche opérationnelle
C. P. 6128, Succursale Centre–Ville, Montréal (Québec), CANADA H3C 3J7
email: brassard@iro.umontreal.ca

Abstract. Classical and quantum information are very different. Together they can perform feats that neither could achieve alone. These include quantum computing, quantum cryptography and quantum teleportation. This paper surveys some of the most striking new applications of quantum mechanics to computer science. Some of these applications are still theoretical but others have been implemented.

1 Introduction: the Qubit

Classical and quantum information are very different. Classical information can be read, copied and transcribed into any medium; it can be transmitted and broadcast, but it cannot travel faster than the speed of light. Quantum information cannot be read or copied without disturbance, but in some instances it appears to propagate instantaneously or even backward in time. In principle—and sometimes also in practice—the two kinds of information can perform together several feats that neither could achieve alone. These include quantum computing, quantum cryptography and quantum teleportation.

Quantum mechanics has the potential to bring about a spectacular revolution in computer science. Even though current-day computers use quantum-mechanical effects in their operation, for example through the use of transistors, they are still very much classical computing devices. A supercomputer is not fundamentally different from a purely mechanical computer that could be built around simple relays: their operation can be described in terms of classical physics and they can simulate one another in a straightforward manner, given sufficient storage. All deterministic classical single-processor models of computation are computationally equivalent to the classical Turing machine up to polynomial factors. In contrast, computers could in principle be built to profit from genuine quantum phenomena that have no classical analogue, sometimes providing exponential speed-up compared to classical computers even if the classical computer is allowed to be probabilistic and to make occasional mistakes. Quantum information is also at the core of other phenomena that would be impossible to achieve in a purely classical world, such as unconditionally secure distribution of secret cryptographic material.

* This essay was written while the author was on sabbatical leave at the University of Wollongong, Australia; Research supported in part by NSERC and FCAR.

At the heart of it all is the quantum bit, or *qubit*, a word coined by Schumacher. A classical bit can take either value 0 or value 1. Nothing in between is allowed. According to quantum mechanics, a qubit can be in linear *superposition* of the two classical states. If we denote the classical states by $|0\rangle$ and $|1\rangle$, then a qubit can be in state

$$|\Psi\rangle = \alpha|0\rangle + \beta|1\rangle$$

for arbitrary complex numbers α and β subject to $|\alpha|^2 + |\beta|^2 = 1$. The coefficients α and β are called the *amplitudes* of $|0\rangle$ and $|1\rangle$, respectively. A qubit is best visualized as a point on the surface of a unit sphere whose North and South poles correspond to the classical values. This is not at all the same as taking a value *between* 0 and 1 as in classical analogue computing.

In general, qubits cannot be measured reliably. The simplest measurement on $|\Psi\rangle = \alpha|0\rangle + \beta|1\rangle$ consists of asking it to choose between the two classical states. In this case, the qubit *collapses* onto $|0\rangle$ with probability $|\alpha|^2$ and onto $|1\rangle$ with complementary probability $|\beta|^2$, and all additional information about the original superposition is lost irreversibly. Other measurements are also possible, but the more information you obtain about $|\Psi\rangle$, the more you risk spoiling it. Even though there is a continuum of possible quantum states of a single qubit, these states cannot all be distinguished reliably from each other: no measurement can extract more than one expected bit of information from any given qubit and even this much is not always possible. It is this manifestation of Heisenberg's uncertainty principle that makes quantum computing challenging but it also makes quantum cryptography possible.

2   Two Qubits Are More Than Twice Better Than One

We begin with a simple example that illustrates the difference between classical and quantum information. A *trine* is a qubit that can be either in state $|0\rangle$, $\frac{1}{2}|0\rangle + \frac{\sqrt{3}}{2}|1\rangle$ or $\frac{1}{2}|0\rangle - \frac{\sqrt{3}}{2}|1\rangle$, each possibility being equally likely [1]. From the point of view of classical information theory, a trine encodes $\log_2 3 \approx 1.585$ bits of information. However, the best possible measurement on a trine can do no better than rule out one of the three possibilities, leaving one bit of uncertainty about the original state of the qubit. Thus, it is not possible to extract more than $(\log_2 3) - 1 \approx 0.585$ bit of classical information from any given trine. Suppose now that you are presented with two trines that are guaranteed to be identical. Peres and Wootters have discovered that there is a measurement that can extract $\frac{\sqrt{2}}{3}\left(1 + \log_2(17 + 12\sqrt{2})\right) - \frac{3}{2} \approx 1.369 > 2 \times 0.585$ bits of information from both trines combined [31]. Thus it is possible in some cases to extract more than twice as much information from two *identical* qubits than from either one alone! This has no counterpart in classical information theory.

---

[1] If the qubit is implemented by the polarization of a photon such that $|0\rangle$ and $|1\rangle$ are encoded by vertical and horizontal polarizations, respectively, the three trine states correspond to a polarization that is either vertical, $+30°$ or $-30°$ from the horizontal.

3   Quantum Computing

Can computers simulate physics? This question was the topic of Feynman's keynote address at the 1981 Workshop on Physics of Computation [23]. This would hardly have been an original question had he not asked more specifically if physics can be simulated *efficiently* by *classical* computers. He gave reasons to believe the answer is negative. Today, we know that Feynman's intuition was correct—provided factoring is genuinely difficult for classical computers. Specifically, Shor [32], building on work of Deutsch and Jozsa [17], Bernstein and Vazirani [9] and Simon [33], has discovered how to factor arbitrarily large integers in polynomial time on a quantum computer. Thus, any efficient simulation of physics on a classical computer would yield an efficient classical algorithm for factoring. See also Berthiaume and Brassard [10] for early oracle results.

The concept of quantum computing evolved from the work of Benioff [2], Feynman [23, 24] and Deutsch [16] in the first half of the 1980s. In a classical probabilistic calculation, it is possible to program the computer to select one of several possible computation paths according to the laws of probability. In any specific instance of the calculation, however, only one of the potential paths is actually taken, and what-could-have-happened-but-did-not has no influence whatsoever on the actual outcome. In a quantum computer, all potential computation paths are taken simultaneously. More precisely, just as a qubit can be in linear superposition of states $|0\rangle$ and $|1\rangle$, a quantum computer can be in linear superposition of having followed several different alternatives simultaneously. What makes quantum computation so powerful—and mysterious—is that the possible paths that would yield the same result *interfere*, a notion that has no analogue in classical computation. This interference can be constructive or destructive, much as in Young's celebrated double-slit experiment. This allows for the reinforcement of the probability of obtaining desired results while at the same time reducing or even annihilating the probability of spurious results. This happens because the amplitude of reaching any given state is the sum of the amplitudes of reaching this state by all possible computation paths. Because amplitudes can be negative (even complex), the amplitude of reaching an undesirable result from one path can be cancelled by the amplitude of reaching it from another path. In the words of Feynman, "somehow or other it appears as if the probabilities would have to go negative" [23].

As a simple illustration of the phenomenon of quantum interference, consider a one-qubit quantum register whose possible classical states are $|0\rangle$ and $|1\rangle$. We have seen that it can be in any state of the form $|\Psi\rangle = \alpha|0\rangle + \beta|1\rangle$, where $|\alpha|^2 + |\beta|^2 = 1$. Consider the quantum algorithm given in Fig. 1. Note that this algorithm does *not* say that we begin by measuring state $|\Psi\rangle$ to decide classically which path to follow: we want the program to exhibit interesting behaviour when state $|\Psi\rangle$ is already in quantum superposition before the call.

If we start in state $|\Psi\rangle = |0\rangle$, a call on QCF produces the quantum superposition of $|0\rangle$ and $|1\rangle$ with amplitudes $+\sqrt{2}/2$ and $-\sqrt{2}/2$, respectively. In other words, the result is $|\Psi\rangle = \frac{\sqrt{2}}{2}(|0\rangle - |1\rangle)$. If we start in state $|\Psi\rangle = |1\rangle$, on the other

procedure QCF

$\textbf{if } |\Psi\rangle = |0\rangle \textbf{ then } |\Psi\rangle \leftarrow \begin{cases} |0\rangle \text{ with amplitude } +\sqrt{2}/2 \\ |1\rangle \text{ with amplitude } -\sqrt{2}/2 \end{cases}$

$\textbf{if } |\Psi\rangle = |1\rangle \textbf{ then } |\Psi\rangle \leftarrow \begin{cases} |0\rangle \text{ with amplitude } +\sqrt{2}/2 \\ |1\rangle \text{ with amplitude } +\sqrt{2}/2 \end{cases}$

Fig. 1. Quantum coin flipping algorithm

hand, a call on QCF results in $|\Psi\rangle = \frac{\sqrt{2}}{2}(|0\rangle + |1\rangle)$. In either case, an immediate measurement of $|\Psi\rangle$ would yield either $|0\rangle$ or $|1\rangle$ with probability 50% since $|\sqrt{2}/2|^2 = |-\sqrt{2}/2|^2 = 1/2$. In other words, if we start the computer in either classical state, call QCF once and observe the result, we have implemented a fair coin toss. This is at best useful for classical probabilistic computing.

Consider now what happens if we call QCF twice *without observing the result between calls*. Say we start in state $|\Psi\rangle = |1\rangle$. The first call produces $|\Psi\rangle = \frac{\sqrt{2}}{2}(|0\rangle + |1\rangle)$, as we have just seen. The second call transforms the $|0\rangle$ component of this state into $\frac{\sqrt{2}}{2}(|0\rangle - |1\rangle)$ and the $|1\rangle$ component into $\frac{\sqrt{2}}{2}(|0\rangle + |1\rangle)$, so that the net result is

$$|\Psi\rangle = \frac{\sqrt{2}}{2}\left(\frac{\sqrt{2}}{2}(|0\rangle - |1\rangle) + \frac{\sqrt{2}}{2}(|0\rangle + |1\rangle)\right)$$
$$= \frac{1}{2}(|0\rangle - |1\rangle + |0\rangle + |1\rangle) = |0\rangle.$$

Similarly, if we start with $|\Psi\rangle = |0\rangle$ and apply QCF twice, we end up in state $|\Psi\rangle = -|1\rangle$. Thus, if we observe the result of two successive calls on QCF starting with the computer in a classical state, we find that it has switched to the logical negation of its original state. Because the first call on QCF completely randomizes either classical input if the output is observed, yet the second call produces a deterministic result that depends on the initial input if no observation is made between calls, Hayes suggested the following analogy: "It is as if we had invented a machine that first scrambles eggs and then unscrambles them". [2] It is slightly more challenging to find a quantum algorithm whose effect, when composed with itself, is to transform $|1\rangle$ into $|0\rangle$ and $|0\rangle$ into $|1\rangle$, rather than $-|1\rangle$, but this can be done: it is known as the *square root of not*. Try it!

To see more clearly the quantum interference at work, consider again what happens if we start in state $|1\rangle$ and make two calls on QCF. Thinking classically, there are four possible computation paths of the form $|a\rangle \rightarrow |b\rangle \rightarrow |c\rangle$, where

---

[2] The magic disappears if we implement quantum bits of memory with the polarization of single photons using an arbitrary coding scheme such as representing $|0\rangle$ with vertically polarized photons and $|1\rangle$ with horizontally polarized photons: in this case, algorithm QCF performs a simple polarization rotation by 45 degrees. But don't worry: more subtle uses of quantum interference, such as those used for quantum factorization, cannot be explained away so easily with classical thinking.

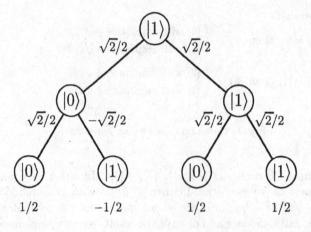

Fig. 2. The computation tree of two calls on QCF starting with $|\Psi\rangle = |1\rangle$

$|a\rangle = |1\rangle$ is the classical state before the first call, $|b\rangle$ is the classical state between the two calls and $|c\rangle$ is the classical state after the second call: $|1\rangle \rightarrow |0\rangle \rightarrow |0\rangle$, $|1\rangle \rightarrow |0\rangle \rightarrow |1\rangle$, $|1\rangle \rightarrow |1\rangle \rightarrow |0\rangle$ and $|1\rangle \rightarrow |1\rangle \rightarrow |1\rangle$. See Fig. 2. The amplitude of path $|1\rangle \rightarrow |0\rangle \rightarrow |1\rangle$, for example, is $\frac{\sqrt{2}}{2} \times (-\frac{\sqrt{2}}{2}) = -^1/_2$ because the amplitude of going from $|1\rangle$ to $|0\rangle$ is $\sqrt{2}/2$ and the amplitude of going back from $|0\rangle$ to $|1\rangle$ is $-\sqrt{2}/2$. (The amplitude of any given path is the product of the amplitudes along that path, much like probabilities multiply along each path in probabilistic algorithms.) Similarly, the amplitude of the three other paths is $+^1/_2$.

If there were no interference, the probability of following any given path would be the square of the magnitude of its amplitude, which in this case is $|\pm ^1/_2|^2 = ^1/_4$ for each path. Thus each path would be followed with equal probability and the end result would be equally likely to be $|0\rangle$ or $|1\rangle$. But what really happens is that the two paths ending in $|0\rangle$ interfere constructively: their amplitudes add up to produce $^1/_2 + ^1/_2 = 1$. By contrast, the two paths ending in $|1\rangle$ interfere destructively: their amplitudes add up to produce $-^1/_2 + ^1/_2 = 0$. The net result is that $|0\rangle$ is observed with certainty. There were two paths leading to $|1\rangle$ and each would have nonzero probability of being taken if we thought classically, yet they cancel each other out and $|1\rangle$ is never observed.

Although the above example is exceedingly simple, it illustrates the basic principle behind the design of quantum algorithms. The trick is to program the computer so that the computation paths that yield undesirable results interfere destructively whereas the "good" computation paths interfere constructively. Of course, interesting algorithms for the quantum computer are not restricted to working on a single qubit of memory. We saw already that two identical trines are more than twice as useful as a single trine. Similarly, a quantum register made out of n qubits can be exponentially more powerful than a single qubit. This is because the qubits in a quantum register do not have to be independent from

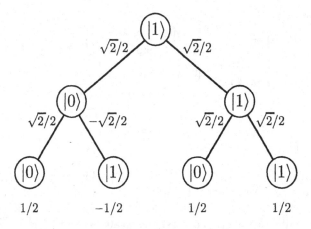

Fig. 2. The computation tree of two calls on QCF starting with $|\Psi\rangle = |1\rangle$

$|a\rangle = |1\rangle$ is the classical state before the first call, $|b\rangle$ is the classical state between the two calls and $|c\rangle$ is the classical state after the second call: $|1\rangle \rightarrow |0\rangle \rightarrow |0\rangle$, $|1\rangle \rightarrow |0\rangle \rightarrow |1\rangle$, $|1\rangle \rightarrow |1\rangle \rightarrow |0\rangle$ and $|1\rangle \rightarrow |1\rangle \rightarrow |1\rangle$. See Fig. 2. The amplitude of path $|1\rangle \rightarrow |0\rangle \rightarrow |1\rangle$, for example, is $\frac{\sqrt{2}}{2} \times (-\frac{\sqrt{2}}{2}) = -1/2$ because the amplitude of going from $|1\rangle$ to $|0\rangle$ is $\sqrt{2}/2$ and the amplitude of going back from $|0\rangle$ to $|1\rangle$ is $-\sqrt{2}/2$. (The amplitude of any given path is the product of the amplitudes along that path, much like probabilities multiply along each path in probabilistic algorithms.) Similarly, the amplitude of the three other paths is $+1/2$.

If there were no interference, the probability of following any given path would be the square of the magnitude of its amplitude, which in this case is $|\pm 1/2|^2 = 1/4$ for each path. Thus each path would be followed with equal probability and the end result would be equally likely to be $|0\rangle$ or $|1\rangle$. But what really happens is that the two paths ending in $|0\rangle$ interfere constructively: their amplitudes add up to produce $1/2 + 1/2 = 1$. By contrast, the two paths ending in $|1\rangle$ interfere destructively: their amplitudes add up to produce $-1/2 + 1/2 = 0$. The net result is that $|0\rangle$ is observed with certainty. There were two paths leading to $|1\rangle$ and each would have nonzero probability of being taken if we thought classically, yet they cancel each other out and $|1\rangle$ is never observed.

Although the above example is exceedingly simple, it illustrates the basic principle behind the design of quantum algorithms. The trick is to program the computer so that the computation paths that yield undesirable results interfere destructively whereas the "good" computation paths interfere constructively. Of course, interesting algorithms for the quantum computer are not restricted to working on a single qubit of memory. We saw already that two identical trines are more than twice as useful as a single trine. Similarly, a quantum register made out of n qubits can be exponentially more powerful than a single qubit. This is because the qubits in a quantum register do not have to be independent from

procedure QCF

$$\textbf{if } |\Psi\rangle = |0\rangle \textbf{ then } |\Psi\rangle \leftarrow \begin{cases} |0\rangle \text{ with amplitude } +\sqrt{2}/2 \\ |1\rangle \text{ with amplitude } -\sqrt{2}/2 \end{cases}$$

$$\textbf{if } |\Psi\rangle = |1\rangle \textbf{ then } |\Psi\rangle \leftarrow \begin{cases} |0\rangle \text{ with amplitude } +\sqrt{2}/2 \\ |1\rangle \text{ with amplitude } +\sqrt{2}/2 \end{cases}$$

Fig. 1. Quantum coin flipping algorithm

hand, a call on QCF results in $|\Psi\rangle = \frac{\sqrt{2}}{2}(|0\rangle + |1\rangle)$. In either case, an immediate measurement of $|\Psi\rangle$ would yield either $|0\rangle$ or $|1\rangle$ with probability 50% since $|\sqrt{2}/2|^2 = |-\sqrt{2}/2|^2 = {}^1/_2$. In other words, if we start the computer in either classical state, call QCF once and observe the result, we have implemented a fair coin toss. This is at best useful for classical probabilistic computing.

Consider now what happens if we call QCF twice *without observing the result between calls*. Say we start in state $|\Psi\rangle = |1\rangle$. The first call produces $|\Psi\rangle = \frac{\sqrt{2}}{2}(|0\rangle + |1\rangle)$, as we have just seen. The second call transforms the $|0\rangle$ component of this state into $\frac{\sqrt{2}}{2}(|0\rangle - |1\rangle)$ and the $|1\rangle$ component into $\frac{\sqrt{2}}{2}(|0\rangle + |1\rangle)$, so that the net result is

$$|\Psi\rangle = \frac{\sqrt{2}}{2}\left(\frac{\sqrt{2}}{2}(|0\rangle - |1\rangle) + \frac{\sqrt{2}}{2}(|0\rangle + |1\rangle)\right)$$
$$= \frac{1}{2}(|0\rangle - |1\rangle + |0\rangle + |1\rangle) = |0\rangle.$$

Similarly, if we start with $|\Psi\rangle = |0\rangle$ and apply QCF twice, we end up in state $|\Psi\rangle = -|1\rangle$. Thus, if we observe the result of two successive calls on QCF starting with the computer in a classical state, we find that it has switched to the logical negation of its original state. Because the first call on QCF completely randomizes either classical input if the output is observed, yet the second call produces a deterministic result that depends on the initial input if no observation is made between calls, Hayes suggested the following analogy: "It is as if we had invented a machine that first scrambles eggs and then unscrambles them".[2] It is slightly more challenging to find a quantum algorithm whose effect, when composed with itself, is to transform $|1\rangle$ into $|0\rangle$ and $|0\rangle$ into $|1\rangle$, rather than $-|1\rangle$, but this can be done: it is known as the *square root of not*. Try it!

To see more clearly the quantum interference at work, consider again what happens if we start in state $|1\rangle$ and make two calls on QCF. Thinking classically, there are four possible computation paths of the form $|a\rangle \rightarrow |b\rangle \rightarrow |c\rangle$, where

---

[2] The magic disappears if we implement quantum bits of memory with the polarization of single photons using an arbitrary coding scheme such as representing $|0\rangle$ with vertically polarized photons and $|1\rangle$ with horizontally polarized photons: in this case, algorithm QCF performs a simple polarization rotation by 45 degrees. But don't worry: more subtle uses of quantum interference, such as those used for quantum factorization, cannot be explained away so easily with classical thinking.

one another: they can be *entangled*. In general, an n–qubit quantum register can be in an arbitrary linear superposition of all 2^n classical states:

$$|\Psi\rangle = \sum_{x \in \{0,1\}^n} \alpha_x |x\rangle$$

with the restriction that $\sum_{x \in \{0,1\}^n} |\alpha_x|^2 = 1$. If this quantum register is measured in the sense that it is asked to assume a classical value, the formula is much the same as with a single qubit: the register collapses onto some classical n–bit string x, and each possible such x is obtained with probability $|\alpha_x|^2$.

To understand the notion of entanglement, consider a two-qubit quantum register. Suppose at first that each qubit is independently in state $\frac{\sqrt{2}}{2}|0\rangle + \frac{\sqrt{2}}{2}|1\rangle$. The register is then in a state $|\Psi\rangle$ that can be represented by the *product* of two such states. By this we mean that amplitudes are multiplied but the product of classical states denotes their concatenation: $|0\rangle|1\rangle$ is the same as $|01\rangle$, a classical state for a two-qubit quantum register. Continuing our example,

$$|\Psi\rangle = \left(\tfrac{\sqrt{2}}{2}|0\rangle + \tfrac{\sqrt{2}}{2}|1\rangle\right) \left(\tfrac{\sqrt{2}}{2}|0\rangle + \tfrac{\sqrt{2}}{2}|1\rangle\right)$$
$$= \tfrac{1}{2}(|00\rangle + |01\rangle + |10\rangle + |11\rangle).$$

This is not a very interesting state. If it is asked to assume a classical value, each of the four possible classical two-bit strings is obtained with equal probability $|1/2|^2 = 1/4$. This is exactly the same as saying that each of the two qubits, when measured, yields an independent random bit: the two qubits are not entangled.

Consider now a more interesting state for our quantum register.

$$|\widehat{\Psi}\rangle = \tfrac{\sqrt{2}}{2}(|00\rangle + |11\rangle) \tag{1}$$

This time, if the register is asked to assume a classical value, we observe either $|00\rangle$ or $|11\rangle$, each with probability $|\sqrt{2}/2|^2 = 1/2$, but we never observe $|01\rangle$ nor $|10\rangle$. The two qubits are entangled: the register cannot be represented as a product of two independent qubits. To see why this is remarkable, consider what happens if we perform a *partial* measurement. Let us say that we measure only the first qubit of the register. The outcome is equally likely to be $|0\rangle$ or $|1\rangle$. Similarly, the second qubit would have been equally likely to yield $|0\rangle$ or $|1\rangle$ had we measured *it* instead. But now that we have measured the first qubit, the outcome of a subsequent measurement on the second qubit is determined: it will yield the same value as the first. In other words, measuring one qubit can have an instantaneous effect on the state of another. This is as if we had a pair of *magic coins*: the outcome of either coin is not determined until it *or its twin* has been flipped. This works no matter how far apart the two qubits (or coins) are, which troubled Einstein very much indeed when he discovered a similar quantum phenomenon with Podolsky and Rosen 60 years ago [20]: he later called it "spooky action at a distance" [3] (*spukhafte Fernwirkungen*) in a letter to Born. Such states were subsequently observed in the laboratory.

---

[3] Although qubits appear to communicate instantaneously with one another, this phenomenon cannot be used to send a signal faster than light.

The relevance of entangled states to computing is best illustrated by the following example, which is due to Vazirani and inspired by Simon. Consider a function $h : \{0,1\}^n \to \{0,1\}^m$ and a quantum computer equipped with $n + m$ qubits of quantum register. Program your quantum computer to transform $|x, 0\rangle$ into $|x, h(x)\rangle$, where $x \in \{0,1\}^n$ and 0 denotes the all-zero m–bit vector. Now, prepare your quantum register in the following initial state

$$|\Psi_0\rangle = \sum_{x \in \{0,1\}^n} 2^{-n/2} |x, 0\rangle .$$

If you run your quantum computer on that state, the resulting state will be

$$|\Psi_1\rangle = \sum_{x \in \{0,1\}^n} 2^{-n/2} |x, h(x)\rangle .$$

In general, this is an entangled state that cannot be expressed as a product of the states of $n + m$ qubits. The first thing to notice is that you have computed the value of $h(x)$ for exponentially many different values of x in the time it would have taken to compute it on a single input with a classical computer. This phenomenon, known as *quantum parallelism*, is at the core of all speed-ups offered by quantum computing. Unfortunately, quantum mechanics severely restricts the information you can extract from $|\Psi_1\rangle$. In particular, it would be pointless to measure it in the way we have seen so far: if you ask $|\Psi_1\rangle$ to assume a classical value, it will simply collapse onto a pair $|x, h(x)\rangle$ for a randomly chosen $x \in \{0,1\}^n$ and you will be none the wiser since you could just as easily have obtained this with a classical probabilistic computer. Instead, measure only the last m qubits of the register. As they collapse to a random value y in the image of h (with probabilities that depend on the number of preimages), entanglement causes the first n qubits to collapse to an equally-weighted superposition of all preimages of y under h. The resulting state is

$$|\Psi_2\rangle = \sum_{x \in h^{-1}[y]} \frac{1}{\sqrt{\#h^{-1}[y]}} |x, y\rangle .$$

For the cryptographically-minded, this is a way to generate collisions[4] out of an arbitrary hashing function h. But don't get too excited because, once again, the collision thus obtained cannot be extracted in general from the state $|\Psi_2\rangle$ of the quantum register. If you measure the first n qubits of your register now, you obtain a random preimage x of the random image y you had previously observed. This is pointless because you could produce the same result by first choosing x randomly and then computing $y = f(x)$. Thus, state $|\Psi_2\rangle$ encodes precious information, but you cannot get at it by a direct measurement. How tantalizing!

This is where quantum *interference* enters the game. Under some conditions on the type of function h considered, Simon [33] has discovered how to massage state $|\Psi_2\rangle$ in a way that interference patterns allow us subsequently to measure useful information that efficiently yields a collision with high probability.

---

[4] A *collision* is a pair of distinct values $x_1, x_2 \in \{0,1\}^n$ such that $h(x_1) = h(x_2)$.

Although his condition on h is somewhat unnatural, Simon's result is of great theoretical importance because he has also proved (assuming h is given by a black box) that no classical computer could find collisions on such functions in less than exponential time with better than an exponentially small probability of success, even if the classical algorithm is probabilistic and not required to return a correct answer with certainty. This was the first convincing argument that quantum computers can be exponentially faster than classical probabilistic computers. (It was known previously that quantum computers can be exponentially faster than classical deterministic computers [17] and that they can be somewhat faster than classical probabilistic computers [9].)

Shor's algorithm for the efficient factorization of large integers on the quantum computer follows a similar line of attack, but with some Fourier transforms and some number theory thrown in [32]. The details are beyond the scope of this essay. Note however that Ekert and Jozsa have written a particularly lucid account of Shor's algorithm [22]. You should also read Coppersmith's algorithm for approximating Fourier transforms on the quantum computer [15].

Before you run off and start writing your own quantum algorithms, you must be warned about a crucial restriction on such algorithms that is imposed by the laws of quantum mechanics. Clearly we must require that if classical state $|x\rangle$ leads to superposition $\sum \alpha_i |x_i\rangle$ then $\sum |\alpha_i|^2 = 1$ so that the probabilities sum up to 1 if an observation is made. For example, $|\sqrt{2}/2|^2 + |\pm \sqrt{2}/2|^2 = 1$ in algorithm QCF. By analogy with classical probabilistic algorithms, you may think this is the only restriction on quantum algorithms. Wrong! Quantum mechanics requires the operation of the computer to be *unitary*. This means that if X is the set of all possible classical states of the computer so that a general quantum state $|\Psi\rangle$ is represented by a column vector of amplitudes $|\Psi\rangle = (\alpha_x)_{x \in X}$, and if matrix U describes the program in the sense that the state that follows $|\Psi\rangle$ after one step is $U|\Psi\rangle$, then quantum mechanics requires that the inverse of U be its own conjugate transpose.

In the case of a one-bit computer, we could represent $|0\rangle$ as $\binom{1}{0}$ and $|1\rangle$ as $\binom{0}{1}$. In general, $\alpha|0\rangle + \beta|1\rangle$ is represented as $\binom{\alpha}{\beta}$. With this notation, consider

$$U = \frac{\sqrt{2}}{2} \begin{bmatrix} 1 & 1 \\ -1 & 1 \end{bmatrix} \text{ and } \widehat{U} = \frac{1}{2} \begin{bmatrix} 1-i & 1+i \\ 1+i & 1-i \end{bmatrix}.$$

The reader is invited to verify that both these matrices are unitary, that U corresponds to algorithm QCF from Fig. 1 and that $\widehat{U}$ solves the square root of not riddle: $\widehat{U}^2|0\rangle = |1\rangle$ and $\widehat{U}^2|1\rangle = |0\rangle$.

Unitarity is not an easy constraint to work with. In particular, unitary operations must be reversible, which forces us to rethink the way we program. Fortunately, it has been proved by Bennett [3] that reversibility is not a serious handicap when it comes to efficient classical computation, so that polynomial-time quantum computers are at least as powerful as their classical counterpart. As we have seen, there are good reasons to believe that they are in fact significantly more powerful.

This is all very well in theory, but how realistic are quantum computers from a technological point of view? Actual implementation of quantum computing offers formidable challenges such as the need to keep quantum *coherence* for a macroscopic amount of time. The difficulty is that coherent superpositions are very fragile: they spontaneously turn into incoherent statistical mixtures—which are unsuitable for quantum parallelism—because of residual interactions with the environment. Consequently, quantum information disappears gradually from the computer. Moreover, the coherence time decreases with the number of qubits involved [34], so that the larger the problem you want to solve, the less time you have to tackle it! Landauer has pointed out the additional problem that quantum computation may be susceptible to spontaneous reversals, which would unpredictably cause the computation to go backwards [27]. (Landauer's argument applies to a "pure" quantum computer of the kind advocated by Deutsch [16] but it may not be relevant if a classical computer is used to "drive" a quantum register, which would be sufficient to implement Shor's quantum factoring algorithm.) Yet another difficulty is that of error correction despite early work by Peres [30] and more recent work by Berthiaume, Deutsch and Jozsa [11]: in classical digital computing, discrete states are continuously snapped back onto the proper voltages for 0 and 1, but no similar process is available for quantum computing even if the intended states have discrete amplitudes. Consequently, the computer may slowly drift away from its intended state.

Nevertheless, the prospect for experimental quantum computing became less remote when DiVincenzo discovered that universal quantum computers can be built of two-input quantum gates [18], which may greatly simplify the technology required to build them. Similar constructions were also obtained by Barenco and by Sleator and Weinfurter. (It is well-known that two-input gates are universal for classical computation but the same was not obvious for quantum computation because we saw that it has to be unitary—and therefore reversible—and universal classical reversible gates need at least three inputs.) In fact, the natural quantum extension of the classical exclusive-or gate—also known as "controlled-not"—is universal for quantum computation, if supplemented by simple operations on single qubits. Theoreticians as well as experimental physicists are feverishly at work trying to realize basic quantum computing gates. Lloyd was an early pioneer with his "potentially realizable quantum computer" [28]. Domokos, Raimond, Brune and Haroche are working on a prototype of the quantum exclusive-or gate based on atomic interferometry and microwave cavities capable of trapping single photons [19]. Similar cavity QED ideas were suggested by Sleator and Weinfurter. Another promising approach, which involves trapped ions, was proposed theoretically by Cirac and Zoller; in recent experiments, Monroe and Wineland have built a quantum exclusive-or gate prototype that works at least 70% of the time. See also [1, 22] for implementation proposals.

I do not know if quantum computers will forever remain a dream, but it may be easier to begin with a special-purpose quantum factorization device. This would be a delightful return of history as the very first electronic computer ever built—the Colossus—was also a special-purpose cryptanalytic device.

4   Time For Another Paradigm Shift

In his seminal 1936 paper, Turing insisted that any reasonable model of computation should be physically realizable and he argued that such was the case with what was to become known as the Turing machine. In the early days of computational complexity, it was suggested that a problem should be considered *tractable* if and only if it can be solved in polynomial time on a deterministic Turing machine. This obeyed Turing's paradigm because Turing machines can be implemented in the real world. Moreover, the notion seemed robust because it does not depend on the specifics of the Turing machine: it is invariant on the type of computer used, *provided we stick to single-processor deterministic computers*. It was soon realized, however, that the restriction to deterministic computation was unacceptable: there is strong evidence that probabilistic machines can solve more problems in polynomial time, especially but not necessarily if we tolerate an arbitrarily small error probability. Since probabilistic machines can also be implemented in the real world, it was in keeping with Turing's spirit to extend the notion of tractability accordingly.

The time is ripe for yet another paradigm shift. Because we live in a quantum-mechanical world, it is no longer possible to accept the thesis according to which the definition of tractability should take account only of computations performed on computers whose operation is restricted by the laws of classical physics, perhaps with the mere addition of true randomness. Quantum computation is an important formal notion, distinct from and with as much claim to physical realism as classical deterministic and probabilistic computation. The fact that no quantum computer has yet been built should not be considered more fundamental an issue than that no classical computers existed when Turing set forth his model of computation. I strongly believe that the class of problems that can be solved efficiently on a quantum computer with arbitrarily small error probability is the best concept yet put forward to model the notion of what is computationally tractable by a physically realizable device.

When I expressed those views [13] in my response to Hartmanis's Turing Award paper (in which he had said that "There is a strong effort to define and prove the *feasible* limits of computation, but even here the basic model of computation is not questioned"), Hartmanis responded "The exploration [of quantum computing] deserves our best effort. At the same time, a theoretical model alone is not going to change the limits of feasible computations. [...] Its relevance still depends on the possibility of implementing it." [26] Although he is obviously correct from a practical point of view—knowing Shor's algorithm won't help you factor large numbers if you can't build the device—I must disagree from a theoretical standpoint. In my opinion, the theoretical notion of feasible computation should be modelled on our understanding of the physical world, not on our technological abilities. After all, the classical Turing machine itself is an idealization that cannot be built in practice even not taking account of the unbounded tape: any real implementation of a Turing machine would have nonzero probability of making a mistake. Does this discredit the model? I think not.

5   Quantum Cryptography

Shor's breakthrough has two spectacular consequences. We saw already that one is the answer to Feynman's question: physics cannot be simulated efficiently on classical computers assuming factoring is classically hard. The other consequence is that much of classical cryptography will crumble if and when a quantum computer is built. (Of course, "classical" is used here to mean non-quantum, and it includes secret-key and public-key cryptography on the same footing, just as "classical physics" lumps together Newton's mechanics with Einstein's relativity.) This is because the security of a significant proportion of cryptography in use today depends directly or indirectly on the presumed difficulty of either factoring or extracting discrete logarithms, and Shor has also discovered how to extract discrete logarithms in polynomial time on a quantum computer [32]. Secret key cryptosystems such as the DES have not yet been shown to be efficiently breakable by quantum computers, but they become vulnerable if their keys are exchanged with public-key techniques, which is often the case. A direct quantum cryptanalysis of the DES would be an interesting academic exercise even though this cryptosystem may have fallen into disuse before quantum computers become available. At the very least, this would be as much fun as writing a program to break Enigma on a contemporary classical supercomputer.

The security of information-theoretic based cryptosystems such as the one-time-pad would not be compromised by the availability of a quantum computer, provided the long keys they need to operate are transmitted securely. Thus quantum mechanics has the potential to be the nemesis of most of contemporary cryptography but ironically it also offers salvation thanks to quantum cryptography [4, 7, 12], which exploits the impossibility to measure quantum information reliably. When information is encoded with non-orthogonal quantum states, any attempt from an eavesdropper to access it necessarily entails a probability of spoiling it irreversibly, which can be detected by the legitimate users. Using protocols that I have designed with Bennett, building on earlier work of Wiesner, this phenomenon can be exploited to implement a key distribution system that is provably secure even against an eavesdropper with unlimited computing power. This is achieved by the exchange of very tenuous signals that consist on the average of one-tenth of one photon per pulse. Thanks to further work in collaboration with Crépeau and others [6, 14], quantum techniques may also assist in the achievement of subtler cryptographic goals, such as protecting private information while it is being used to reach public decisions. Ekert suggested the use of entanglement as an alternative approach to quantum cryptography [21]. Quantum cryptography provides a typical example of the thesis presented in the opening paragraph of this essay: it is provably impossible to achieve the benefits of quantum cryptography using only classical information if no restrictions are assumed on the eavesdropper's computing power and technology.

In the early days of quantum cryptography, more than 15 years ago, the topic was thought of as science fiction even by the researchers directly involved in developing it. Today, several prototypes have been built, including one that is fully operational over 30 kilometres of ordinary optical fibre [29], and encouraging experiments on quantum key distribution under Lake Geneva (23 kilometres) have just been completed [25]. The reason why quantum cryptography went from science fiction to science fact in such a short time is not due to a technological breakthrough: rather it is because we discovered how to make reasonable use of quantum mechanics for cryptographic purposes.

Perhaps the same fate awaits quantum computing. Perhaps quantum computing as we conceive it today will forever remain beyond available technology, yet perhaps we shall think of new, more reasonable ways to harness the strange properties of quantum mechanics for computing purposes.

6   Quantum Teleportation

Quantum information cannot be measured in general, but it can be *teleported* from one place to another [5]. This provides an intriguing theoretical application for spatially separated entangled qubits such as those described by Equation (1). Assume Alice and Bob share a pair of entangled qubits and let Alice be given a "mystery" particle that holds an unknown qubit. What should she do if she wishes Bob to have the mystery qubit instead of her? Surely, she cannot measure the particle to learn the information, which she could then transmit to Bob over a classical channel: any such attempt would be almost certain to spoil the information irreversibly. Instead, she makes the particle interact in the proper way with her share of the entangled pair. As a result, Bob's share instantaneously becomes a replica of the mystery qubit up to rotation. At the same time Alice's mystery particle loses its information but she obtains two purely random bits of classical information that tell her which rotation Bob should perform on his replica to match the original: she must communicate these two bits to Bob over a classical channel because Bob's replica remains indistinguishable from a purely random qubit until he has performed the required rotation.

This process cannot be used to transmit information faster than light between Alice and Bob (thank goodness!), but it can be argued that all the information that was present in the mystery particle is transmitted instantaneously—except for two (random!) bits that need to chug along at the speed of light. If needed, imperfect stores of spatially separated entangled qubit pairs can be *purified* by local transformations and exchange of classical information [8]. Quantum teleportation and purification provide an example that is even more convincing than quantum cryptography for the thesis according to which classical and quantum information can benefit from one another.

Although the teleportation of people is still very far away [;-)], experiments are under way to teleport the state of single qubits. In fact, a few quantum gates for the exclusive-or would be sufficient to implement teleportation. Conversely, quantum teleportation could be a useful tool to move information around in a quantum computer and to transmit quantum information for quantum cryptographic purposes. Thus we see that it all fits together.

Acknowledgements

Charles H. Bennett initiated me to the wonders of quantum mechanics years ago. I have benefited from further stimulating discussions with too many people to list them all here. Among them, André Berthiaume, Paul Bratley, Claude Crépeau, David DiVincenzo, Artur Ekert, Nicolas Gisin, Sophie Laplante, Ueli Maurer, Pierre McKenzie, David Mermin, Asher Peres, Jean–Michel Raimond, Neil Stewart and William Wootters have contributed directly to the writing of this essay. I am grateful to the Natural Sciences and Engineering Research Council of Canada for the freedom and funding that came with my E. W. R. Steacie Memorial Fellowship. Quantum teleportation was born of this fellowship.

References

1. Barenco, A., D. Deutsch, A. Ekert and R. Jozsa, "Conditional quantum dynamics and logic gates", *Physical Review Letters*, Vol. 74, 1995, pp. 4083 – 4086.
2. Benioff, P., "Quantum mechanical Hamiltonian models of Turing machines", *Journal of Statistical Physics*, Vol. 29, no. 3, 1982, pp. 515 – 546.
3. Bennett, C. H., "Logical reversibility of computation", *IBM Journal of Research and Development*, Vol. 17, 1973, pp. 525 – 532.
4. Bennett, C. H., F. Bessette, G. Brassard, L. Salvail and J. Smolin, "Experimental quantum cryptography", *Journal of Cryptology*, Vol. 5, no. 1, 1992, pp. 3 – 28.
5. Bennett, C. H., G. Brassard, C. Crépeau, R. Jozsa, A. Peres and W. K. Wootters, "Teleporting an unknown quantum state via dual classical and Einstein–Podolsky–Rosen channels", *Physical Review Letters*, Vol. 70, no. 13, 29 March 1993, pp. 1895 – 1899.
6. Bennett, C. H., G. Brassard, C. Crépeau and M.–H. Skubiszewska, "Practical quantum oblivious transfer", in *Advances in Cryptology – CRYPTO '91 Proceedings*, J. Feigenbaum (editor), Lecture Notes in Computer Science, Vol. 576, Springer-Verlag, Berlin, 1992, pp. 351 – 366.
7. Bennett, C. H., G. Brassard and A. Ekert, "Quantum cryptography", *Scientific American*, October 1992, pp. 50 – 57. Reprinted in *The Computer in the 21st Century*, Scientific American, Inc., 1995, pp. 164 – 171.
8. Bennett, C. H., G. Brassard, B. Schumacher, J. Smolin and W. K. Wootters, "Purification of noisy entanglement, and faithful teleportation via noisy channels", manuscript, 1995.
9. Bernstein, E. and U. Vazirani, "Quantum complexity theory", *Proceedings of the 25th Annual ACM Symposium on Theory of Computing*, 1993, pp. 11 – 20.
10. Berthiaume, A. and G. Brassard, "Oracle quantum computing", *Journal of Modern Optics*, Vol. 41, no. 12, 1994, pp. 2521 – 2535.
11. Berthiaume, A., D. Deutsch and R. Jozsa, "The stabilisation of quantum computations", *Proceedings of the Third Workshop on Physics and Computation — PhysComp '94*, Dallas, November 1994, IEEE Computer Society Press, 1994, pp. 60 – 62.
12. Brassard, G., "Cryptology column — Quantum cryptography: A bibliography", *Sigact News*, Vol. 24, no. 3, 1993, pp. 16 – 20.
13. Brassard, G., "Time for another paradigm shift", *Computing Surveys*, Vol. 27, no. 1, 1995, pp. 19 – 21.

14. Brassard, G., C. Crépeau, R. Jozsa and D. Langlois, "A quantum bit commitment scheme provably unbreakable by both parties", *Proceedings of the 34th Annual IEEE Symposium on Foundations of Computer Science*, 1993, pp. 362–371.
15. Coppersmith, D., "An approximate Fourier transform useful in quantum factoring", IBM T. J. Watson Research Report RC 19642, Yorktown Heights, NY 10598, USA, 12 July 1994.
16. Deutsch, D., "Quantum theory, the Church–Turing principle and the universal quantum computer", *Proceedings of the Royal Society*, London, Vol. A400, 1985, pp. 97–117.
17. Deutsch, D. and R. Jozsa, "Rapid solution of problems by quantum computation", *Proceedings of the Royal Society*, London, Vol. A439, 1992, pp. 553–558.
18. DiVincenzo, D. P., "Two-bit gates are universal for quantum computation", *Physical Review A*, Vol. 51, 1995, pp. 1015–1022.
19. Domokos, P., J.–M. Raimond, M. Brune and S. Haroche, "A simple cavity-QED two-bit universal quantum logic gate: principle and expected performances", *Physical Review A*, to appear.
20. Einstein, A., B. Podolsky and N. Rosen, "Can quantum-mechanical description of physical reality be considered complete?", *Physical Review*, Vol. 47, 1935, pp. 777–780.
21. Ekert, A., "Quantum cryptography based on Bell's theorem", *Physical Review Letters*, Vol. 67, no. 6, 5 August 1991, pp. 661–663.
22. Ekert, A. and R. Jozsa, "Shor's quantum algorithm for factorising numbers", *Review of Modern Physics*, to appear.
23. Feynman, R. P., "Simulating physics with computers", *International Journal of Theoretical Physics*, Vol. 21, nos. 6/7, 1982, pp. 467–488.
24. Feynman, R. P., "Quantum mechanical computers", *Optics News*, February 1985. Reprinted in *Foundations of Physics*, Vol. 16, no. 6, 1986, pp. 507–531.
25. Gisin, N., personal communication, 18 May 1995.
26. Hartmanis, J., "Response to the essays 'On computational complexity and the nature of computer science'", *Computing Surveys*, Vol. 27, no. 1, 1995, pp. 59–61.
27. Landauer, R., "Is quantum mechanically coherent computation useful?", in *Proceedings of the Drexel-4 Symposium on Quantum Nonintegrability—Quantum Classical Correspondence*, D. H. Feng and B.–L. Hu (editors), International Press, 1995.
28. Lloyd, S., "A potentially realizable quantum computer", *Science*, Vol. 261, 17 September 1993, pp. 1569–1571.
29. Marand, C. and P. D. Townsend, "Quantum key distribution over distances as long as 30 km", *Optics Letters*, Vol. 20, 15 August 1995.
30. Peres, A., "Reversible logic and quantum computers", *Physical Review A*, Vol. 32, 1985, pp. 3266–3276.
31. Peres, A. and W. K. Wootters, "Optimal detection of quantum information", *Physical Review Letters*, Vol. 66, no. 9, 4 March 1991, pp. 1119–1122.
32. Shor, P. W., "Algorithms for quantum computation: Discrete logarithms and factoring", *Proceedings of the 35th Annual IEEE Symposium on Foundations of Computer Science*, 1994, pp. 124–134.
33. Simon, D., "On the power of quantum computation", *Proceedings of the 35th Annual IEEE Symposium on Foundations of Computer Science*, 1994, pp. 116–123.
34. Unruh, W. G., "Maintaining coherence in quantum computers", *Physical Review A*, Vol. 51, February 1995, pp. 992–997.

Artificial Life and Real World Computing

Luc Steels[1] and Mario Tokoro[2]

[1]Artificial Intelligence Laboratory, Vrije Universiteit Brussel
Visiting: Sony Computer Science Laboratory, Tokyo
E-mail: steels@arti.vub.ac.be
[2]Keio University, Tokyo and
Sony Computer Science Laboratory, Tokyo
E-mail: mario@csl.sony.co.jp

Abstract. The paper motivates the use of biological mechanisms in the construction of artificial systems by pointing to the growing need for open complex real world computing in distributed networked computers, software agents and intelligent autonomous robots. It then discusses in some more detail trends in this last application area, focusing in particular on how new complexity may be generated.

1   Introduction

There is a great urgency for computer scientists to learn more about biology, and this for various reasons.

1. *The growth of open systems.* In the past, computer systems and programs have been designed and programmed under the assumption that they could act as closed systems, which are not changed once they are put into practice. But today users interact with networks of computers that operate as global loosely-coupled systems. The network has become the computer. The Internet with services like the World Wide Web is the most dramatic illustration. A network is by its very nature open and distributed. Users demand that it is in operation at all times. New applications or releases of applications, new hardware, new interconnections, extensions to standards, etc. need to be added without closing down systems. The computing environment is therefore becoming a truly open system and is in this sense becoming like ecologies or human societies which constantly adapt, change, and expand [50]. It suggests that biological mechanisms which regulate the operation of ecologies are relevant for managing (or rather self-organising) distributed computer systems.

2. *The growth of complexity.* Evolutions in networking and the growing need for complex applications make the digital world come closer in terms of complexity to the biological world. We are beginning to feel the limitations of the engineering approach which requires that all interactions and possible contexts of a system are understood at design time. Nature has managed to arrive at very complex systems in other ways, using mechanisms like genetic evolution by natural selection, self-organisation, adaptation, etc. It is conceivable that similar mechanisms may become essential to push up the complexity of human artifacts

or to get artifacts that do not depend so critically on knowing *a priori* the context of use. Recent research in genetic algorithms and evolutionary computing [16] has already shown how that could be done.

3. *Coping with the real world.* The computing power and the sensor and actuator technology is becoming available to have very close interactions with the real world, as needed for robotics, real-time process control, or visual and auditive human-computer interaction [48]. However despite many efforts, the capacity of artificial systems to cope with the real world is far below that of biological systems. Here again the study and incorporation of biological mechanisms may provide a clue on how to proceed further. Such a direction is taken for example in recent work on neural networks [22].

4. *Autonomy.* Software agents, robotic agents, and other long-lived applications require continuous operation without constant overseeing and intervention by humans. It appears that building autonomous computer systems will require an understanding of the concept of autonomy as found in biology [23]. Autonomy means more than the ability to act independently. It implies that the system makes up its own laws as it adapts to changing environments and that it can protect itself against security violations or the self-interest of others.

5. *Cognition.* Artificial intelligence is still an open problem for computer science, despite many advances mostly centering around the concept of knowledge representation and (symbolic) problem solving [35]. Also the need for artificial intelligence is still growing, not only for applications like expert systems but also for software agents. Software agents are mobile programs that partly carry their own data. They do tasks like resource discovery, i.e. the search the exponentially growing World Wide Web information resources. In some cases these agents act as representatives of humans and therefore need mentalistic attributes like beliefs and commitments [37]. The key question, that is far from understood, is how a system can *become* intelligent, rather than being programmed or fed knowledge by a human analyst to yield an instance of frozen intelligence. Biological organisms build up their cognitive capabilities in a developmental process and through learning. The same approach may be necessary for artificial systems.

For all these issues and novel applications, the fundamental question is the growth and management of complexity. Nature has found ways to form sustainable ecosystems with millions of complex entities interacting in a harmonious way. It is doing so using mechanisms that are only partially understood but that are in any case very different from those now used to build artificial systems. This suggests that if we can understand and use these mechanisms we may be able to address technological challenges which are now beyond reach.

This idea has been underlying a new subfield of computer science known as *artificial life* [17]. This field brings together scientists coming from many areas, mostly biology, physics and mathematics and of course also computer science. It has spawned its own regular conferences ([21], [51]), and journals ([1],[34]) and hopes to contribute both to the practice of computing and to the understanding of the fundamental mechanisms underlying complexity in the natural world.

We believe that the approaches currently being investigated in artificial life research are not just possible avenues of fascinating research but necessary to develop the real world computing systems of the future. The tendency towards open systems, growing complexity, real world interfacing, autonomy and cognitive capabilities, is undeniably present and in some cases urgently requires solutions. The area that has so far mostly confronted the issues is the domain of intelligent autonomous robotic agents because here the challenges of handling real world computing in open environments is so prominent that no agents can be built without these challenges. Hence we focus in this paper on this topic.

2   Intelligent Autonomous Robotic Agents

One of the key areas where artificial life meets real world computing is in the development of autonomous robotic agents. These efforts build further on the extensive work on computer-based robotics since the early days of artificial intelligence and computing [27]. Many difficult issues like real-time computing, signal processing, real world vision, actuator control, planning, etc. have been studied in great depth and partially resolved. There is now a real robotics industry which manufactures increasingly more complex robots. But artificial life research studies robotics from a quite different angle. The goal is to investigate how robots could act like *intelligent autonomous agents* [47], [44].

The term *agent* suggests that the robot should be capable to act independently and without constant human supervision. The term *autonomy* implies that the robot is responsible for making and abiding to its own laws (Greek: *autos* self *nomos* law), in other words that it is capable to bootstrap itself while remaining viable in the world [40]. The term *intelligent* is more difficult to define. But there is some consensus that it implies being well adapted by the exploitation of representations of the environment [45]. This definition deviates from the Turing definition of intelligence, which is based on the ability to hold a conversation indistinguishable from a human, or from the classical AI definition that a system is intelligent if it can be attributed knowledge level descriptions [26]. Some autonomous agents researchers have positioned themselves polemically in opposition to this knowledge-based orientation [32].

When surveying work done so far, one can clearly see a number of trends emerging (see [41] for a more extended review). First of all there is an insistence on building real robots [6]. Simulation work, which formed the main core of earlier investigations, particularly in AI, is seen as avoiding the main issues, which are: how to cope with massive amounts of data coming from real and therefore noise-intensive sensors, how to cope with the unpredictabilities of a real open world, how to act under the constraints of real time performance, how to deal with imprecise actuation. The robots that are being built with great enthusiasm by researchers in the field make use of the miniaturisation of electronics so that experimentation can proceed reasonably fast and at low cost. More recently, there has been a trend towards more complexity with efforts to build humanoids [7].

Second a number of behavior-oriented architectures have been proposed to address the issue how real-time response and reactivity can be achieved. Behavior-oriented means that each module can take care of one particular behavior with a high degree of autonomy. All behaviors operate in parallel and each one has direct access to sensing and effecting as needed to cope with its task. For example, there are behavioral modules for low level primitives like obstacle avoidance or forward movement, as well as more complex modules that may rely on sets of other behaviors. An example of a behavior-oriented architecture is the subsumption architecture developed by Brooks and his associates [6]. The subsumption architecture uses augmented finite state machines as the building blocks of a behavioral module and assumes inhibition links (subsumption relations) between behavioral modules. Other architectures have their roots in cybernetics and control theory. They assume that behavioral modules are dynamical systems that use self-organising principles for their coordination [40].

All these ideas are strongly technology-inspired. The biological orientation begins to be felt in a third trend, which is to view autonomous robots as animals in the sense that they exist within a particular ecosystem and are subjected to ecological pressures. The robots have to cope with conflicts, dangers, management of depleting resources, competitors, etc. They struggle for their own survival as they carry out tasks. This point of view has been worked out in some detail by the ethologist David McFarland [23] and has lead to the construction of various robotic ecosystems in which robots evolve under pressure.

Fig. 1 depicts an example of such an ecosystem built at the VUB AI lab in Brussels. It is typical for the ones now found in research environments. It contains a set of robots, built with Lego Technics, PC-compatible microprocessors and dedicated electronics. It also contains a charging station and parasites in the form of lamps that take away energy from the charging station. The robots detect the charging station using phototaxis and can recharge themselves by sliding into it. The parasites take away energy from the global ecosystem but can be dimmed by pushing against the boxes in which they are housed. A struggle for survival develops in which robots have to work to obtain energy. They are in competition with each other but also must cooperate to cope with the parasites.

The mechanisms used to realise the robotic behavior in this ecosystem were first identified by ethologists in higher animals. They involve the use of motivational states, trade-offs between cue strength and motivation in determining the tendency for a particular behavior, balancing between altruistic and selfish behavior, etc. [43]. These robotic systems are models for real world environments in which robots will similarly have to divide their time between worrying about survival and executing various tasks.

3   Origins of Behavioral Complexity

Against this background, the key problem in autonomous agents research, namely how robotic agents may develop their own behavioral repertoire, has been attacked in a number of different ways. We summarise work on four different approaches which have all been strongly inspired by biological mechanisms. These

Fig. 1. Overview of a robotic ecosystem built at the VUB AI laboratory in Brussels. The robots can recharge themselves by going to a charging station. Each robot is in competition with other robots and with parasites which also take energy away.

approaches are mutually compatible. Research on each approach is still in its infancy.

3.1 Genetic Evolution

The first explanation for the origin of complexity in the biological world was given by Darwin's theory of evolution by natural selection. Darwin hypothesized that there is a representation of how the structure and functioning of an organism is to be built, the genome, and that this representation is copied from parents to offspring. The copying process may produce a variant which will be kept in the population if the resulting organism (the phenotype) has a better chance of survival or eliminated if the organism is not viable or does not produce offspring. Darwin's theory has since been dramatically confirmed, particularly with the discovery of the physical implementation of the genetic representation in the form of DNA molecules.

Several computer scientists have been inspired by this mechanism to look for ways in which new algorithms could be derived automatically. The success has been dramatic. It has been possible to evolve algorithms by copy, mutation and recombination operations on procedural representations which sometimes take the form of bitstrings [11] and sometimes that of programs in higher level languages like LISP [16]. An initial set of solutions is randomly generated, each solution is tested, and the members of the set that better approach the desired computational function are kept for the next generation whereas others are weeded out. This technique has lead to the new field of evolutionary computation which has now its own conferences and journals. A deeper discussion is found in the paper by Radcliffe in this volume.

The application of these ideas to the development of autonomous agents is however not straightforward. Genetic evolution works on large populations and requires a long time due to the incremental step-wise nature of the mechanism. Evolutionary computation methods also require that the fitness criteria can be identified in advance whereas in natural evolution these criteria are implicit in the environment. Evolutionary techniques in autonomous agents research have been tried so far by conducting the evolution in simulated environments and then porting a viable solution to the real robot operating in a real environment. The simulated environment must capture the essential properties of the target environment which often requires detailed simulations of the physics, the operations of sensors and actuators, the dynamics of interaction between robots and the environment, etc.

Intriguing results with a software simulation approach were obtained for example by Sims [38] who evolved artificial creatures in simulated environments (fig.2). The creatures have an internal dynamical network structure that governs the movement of their parts in reaction to environmental conditions. A representation of this structure is subjected to genetic evolution and the creatures are tested out in an artificial environment often in competition with other creatures. The approach has also been tried for real robots. For example, Nolfi, et.al. [24] report evolutionary experiments on simulated models of the Khepera and then successfully transported it to the real robot. Other researchers [9], [36] go one step further because they conduct evolutionary experiments directly in real environments, each time testing new control programs on the same robot body.

Fig. 2. Examples of artificial creatures evolved in simulated environments. The physics of the real world is simulated and neural networks are evolved by selecting over variants whose phenotypes win in a competition.

3.2   Adaptation

A second explanation for the origin of behavioral complexity that has a long history of work focuses on the adaptation and learning of an organism which neurobiologists hypothesise as taking place by the change of connections in networks of neurons. The concept of a neural network dates from research in the fifties and sixties on abstract neurophysiological models and its application to the construction of autonomous agents is a very active research area [2]. This approach is strongly related to biological cybernetics, and neuroethology [5].

A neural network consists of a set of nodes linked together in a network. Each node receives input from a set of nodes and sends activation as output to another set of nodes. Some inputs could come immediately from sensors. Some outputs are linked with actuators. The links between nodes are weighted. When the sum of the weighted inputs to a node exceeds a threshold, activation propagates to the output nodes. There are many variants of neural networks, depending on the type of propagation and the adaptation mechanism that is used for changing the weights [15]. Neural networks can be generalised so that they become a model for studying dynamical systems in general. This topic is discussed in more detail in the paper by Siegelmann in this volume.

The application of neural network techniques to the construction of robotic agents is non-trivial and very few hard results have been reported so far. Usually a single neural network (even with multiple layers) is not enough to build a complete robotic agent. More structure is needed in which different neural networks can be hierarchically combined. Consequently, several architectures and associated programming languages have been proposed for building and experimenting with neural networks on robots. One of the best worked out examples is reported by Lyons and Arbib [18].

Another problem is that neural networks require a supervisor that provides reinforcement signals [12] or a series of examples over which the generalisation process (which may take a long time) can operate. For a robot roaming around in the real world there is in general no such a supervisor available, nor are there sufficient examples and sufficient time. Also the global search space for an agent is too big to start from zero with neural network techniques. Much more initial structure must typically be encoded which is sometimes difficult to express in network terms. So far the best results have been obtained when there is already an initial structure (for example derived using a genetic algorithm [14]) and neural network techniques are then used for further adaptation.

3.3   Development

A third intriguing avenue of research focuses on the development of behavioral complexity through a developmental process. Only in the case of lower level animals can one say that the neural network which results from genetic evolution completely determines how it will behave. In other cases, and particularly in humans, there is a complex staged developmental process as first emphasised by Piaget. Steels has obtained some recent results based on the idea that there is a representation (called a bene by analogy with a gene) of the dynamics underlying specific behavior. One bene may for example prescribe that a certain quantity (such as the behavioral intensity of forward movement) should follow in a reverse direction another quantity (for example the sensed energy level in the batteries). This has the effect that the speed of forward movement will increase as the battery decreases. Benes undergo variation and selection just like benes. Development is then analogous to genetic evolution. Starting from an initial set of benes, a variation is tried and this variation is kept in the pool when it has a positive effect on the viability of the agent. The introduction of a new bene may give a discontinuous qualitative change in behavior which looks like a discovery if it is beneficial to the agent. There is no supervisor nor a prior series of examples, as in the case of neural networks.

Fig. 3. shows an example which is to be seen in the context of the ecosystem described earlier (fig 1.). The agent starts from a regular cycle in which it is going to the charging station and then recharging based on a bene that pushes the forward speed up as the battery level goes down. Because the agent slides through the charging station at a too high speed it does not fully recharge its batteries. At timestep 100 a new bene is introduced which pushes the forward speed down in the same direction as the battery level. The effect of the two benes together is at first surprising. The agent now slows down before going into the charging station and therefore gets to recharge longer. After a while it has in fact slowed down so much that it is able to halt inside the charging station and thus get a guaranteed supply of energy.

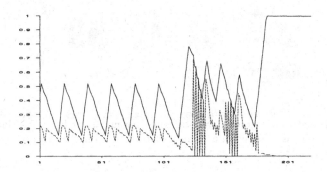

Fig. 3. The top graph plots the energy level the bottom graph the forward speed of a robot. There is a regular cycle with two activities: recharging and seeking the charging station. A new bene is added after 100 time steps. The robot now slows down while moving in the charging station and thus ensures itself after some cycles of eternal life.

3.4   Self-organisation

Finally there is some work going on inspired by recent advances in dynamical systems theory. It is known that complex dynamical systems can spontaneously exhibit order or move to regimes of chaos for certain parameter regions [31], [8]. Autonomous agents become dynamical systems as soon as several of them are together in the same environment or when their internals are viewed as networks of dynamically behaving elements (as is the case of neural networks or behavior-oriented process networks). This implies that self-organisation and evolution towards chaos may be observed, sometimes unexpectedly.

One prototypical example of self-organisation is the formation of paths in ant societies [29]. The temporary structure in this case is a chemical pheromone gradient deposited in the environment. Ants are attracted to the pheromone and therefore have a tendency to aggregate along the path. Ants deposit the pheromone as they are carrying food back to the nest and are therefore responsible for the pheromone gradient in the first place. The pheromone dissipates so that it will disappear gradually when the food source is depleted. The ants operate uniquely on local information of the pheromone gradient. Only the observer sees the global path. The phenomenon has been shown in simulation studies [10] and recently on physical robots [4]. Other experiments, such as those by Mataric [19], have shown that aggregation, the collection of objects in a pile, formation of a connected structure, etc. can all be achieved using completely distributed self-organising mechanisms (see fig.5).

Fig. 4. Aggregation of a group of robots from experiments conducted by Mataric. This flocking behavior is achieved in a completely distributed fashion rather than through a central coordinator.

As another example of complexity due to systems dynamics, Steels [46] reports experiments in which there is spontaneous cluster formation in groups of identical robots within the ecosystem discussed earlier (fig 2.). Starting from identical but adaptive parameter settings, one group of robots adapts in such a way that it 'works' significantly more than the other group. This clustering phenomenon appears to be related to the clustering that spontaneously occurs in globally coupled maps and is seen as an explanation of many other self-organising phenomena in biology such as cell differentiation [13].

The area of autonomous agents research has already produced a number of important steps in understanding how biological mechanisms may be used for developing artifacts that operate in open real-world environments:

- Agent architectures have been proposed that handle parallelism and real-time constraints. Almost all of them assume a behavior-oriented as opposed to hierarchical organisation.
- Researchers have begun to focus on the problem of resource constraints (time, space, energy) and have built robotic ecosystems in which agents compete and cooperate.
- Several mechanisms for the generation and management of complexity have been proposed: evolution by variation and selection, adaptation by weight changes, step-wise development, and self-organisation in dynamical systems.

All researchers active in the field however agree that this is only the beginning and another decade of research could easily pass before robotic agents with some degrees of autonomy and intelligence are a reality. For certain problems such as the origin of symbols and hence symbol grounding there are only very tentative proposals [49].

4   Software Agents

The different issues posed by autonomous robotic agents are also relevant for other areas of computing and consequently some of the same mechanisms may apply. This is particularly the case for software agents and their underlying foundation, namely open distributed operating systems.

It is foreseeable that in the future traditional programs will give way to software agents, which are mobile programs that carry part of their own data as they navigate on computational networks. Software agents have partial autonomy, their own responsibility, and finite resources. Some simple forms of software agents already operate on the network, such as the Netcrawler which builds up a progressive indexing of topics and web-pages [30].

Software agents will hit very similar issues as robotic agents when they go into full-scale operation:

1. Resource constraints: As there are more and more agents traveling over the network, the problem of storing, transmitting and running agents based on resources provided by foreign hosts will become pressing. Agents therefore will be subjected to the same resource constraints as robotic agents.
2. Autonomy: Computer viruses, computer crimes, and the tendency of some companies to monopolise open research results for their own profits illustrates that not everybody in the digital community has benevolent intentions. Software agents will need to defend their own self-interest for security reasons and the self-interests of their owners.
3. Human-computer interaction: As software agents penetrate all activities of daily life, the smooth interaction with human users through voice, visual recognition, tactile sensing, computer animation, natural language communication, etc. will become essential and common. This will put extreme demands on the capability to interpret the world through sensors that deliver continuous signals and to respond under severe time constraints, just like robots.
4. Dynamics: Groups of software agents form a dynamical system and will therefore be subjected to phenomena like self-organisation and chaos. For example, it might well happen that electronic commerce carried out by software agents causes economic crashes of the sort already seen on electronically driven financial markets.

Many of these issues have hardly been addressed and unfortunately software agent applications are being released without fully understanding all the possible ramifications. But there is already some intriguing work going on using the artificial life techniques discussed earlier on. For example, Tom Ray [33] has developed a system called Tierra in which an agent takes the form of a program that can make a copy of itself. The copy process occasionally makes mistakes thus causing variants to be produced. The selectionist criteria amount to limitations in time and space and the occasional action of a 'reaper' which will blindly eliminate new programs. Ray has shown that within this computational environment different forms of copy-programs originate spontaneously, including parasites that use part of the programs of others to copy themselves. Ray is currently engaged in the construction of a distributed version of this system (called NetTierra) in which agents will also be mobile and thus can exploit the computational resources on other sites to enhance their distribution in the total population. These experiments are important preliminary steps to learn how new functionality may emerge in software agents independently of designed intentions, to investigate the security issues involved in evolving autonomous software entities, etc.

There are also a number of attempts focusing on (i) incorporating the notion of *utility* (or *reward* or *gain*), (ii) incorporating the notion of *survivability*, and (iii) incorporating *security* and *self-maintenance* into each module. What makes those attempts different from conventional views is that those are all necessary for each *individual* software module, agent, and not for the system as a whole, as we cannot predefine the ever-changing whole system in the open system settings.

The direct implementation of the notion of utility is the incorporation of an accounting mechanism (as a server) to charge for usage and a book keeping mechanism (as a client) to record the charges (or price lists) of services provided by different servers to each agent. The ecological and therefore evolutionary view of utility has also been studied through game theoretic approaches [20], [3], and applied to multi agent systems settings [such as [25]]. The same problem has also been attacked from a complex systems viewpoint [[28]].

The first step in implementing the notion of *survivability* is the incorporation of *time* (or a clock) to each agent. This gives the analogy to the body clock of biological individuals. By using a clock, each agent can make temporal (and timely) decisions to get out of critical situations. An example of incorporating time into a programming language in order to minimize agent's loss and to survive is reported in [39].

The infrastructures for executing and migrating agents as well as for communication among agents are yet another important issue. The continuous operation and the adaptation to application changes are two fundamental features that such infrastructures must provide. A real-time distributed operating system called Apertos [52] are one of the candidates. It has incorporated the *meta-objects* architecture that has enabled a very small kernel and dynamic changes of operating systems components without halting the system.

5 Conclusion

The paper surveyed work going on under the banner of 'artificial life' research. We identified a set of common issues, which mostly center on the problem how new complexity may arise or can be managed in a distributed fashion. We also identified some areas in computing where these issues are prominently present and where the techniques coming from artificial life research may be most fruitfully applied. These areas include intelligent autonomous robotic agents and software agents. The notion of agents, borrowing from many ideas from biological systems and human individuals, is one of the key issues in future man-made systems and will be needed to build a technology that can interface to the real world in which we live and that is harmoniously integrated with sustainable ecosystems.

Many very difficult issues remain in this exciting research domain. The newly formed interdisciplinary connections between computer science on the one hand and biology and complex dynamical systems research on the other hand will undoubtedly yield important new discoveries and hopefully also a future technology that may be more in harmony with the natural ecosystems now inhabiting our planet.

6   Acknowledgement

Luc Steels worked on this paper while visiting the Sony Computer Science Laboratory in Tokyo and is strongly indebted to Toshi Doi and Mario Tokoro for creating a great research environment and providing the opportunity to work in it. Chisato Numaoka from Sony CSL and Peter Stuer from the VUB AI lab contributed in getting the digitised pictures. The VUB group is financed by the Belgian Federal government FKFO project on emergent functionality (NFWO contract nr. G.0014.95) and the IUAP project (nr. 20) CONSTRUCT.

References

1. *Artificial Life Journal*, Vol 1, 1994-5. The MIT Press, Cambridge, Ma.
2. Arbib, M.A. and A.R. Hanson (eds.) (1987), *Vision, Brain, and Cooperative Computation*. The MIT Press, Cambridge, Ma.
3. Axelrod, R., (1984), *The Evolution of Co-operation*, Basic Books, Inc., 1984.
4. Beckers, R., O.E. Holland and J.L. Deneubourg (1994), From local actions to global tasks: Stigmergy and collective robotics. In: *Proc. Alife IV*. The MIT Press/Bradford Books, Cambridge Ma.
5. Beer, R.D. (1990), *Intelligence as Adaptive Behavior: An Experiment in Computational Neuroethology*. Academic Press, Cambridge Ma.
6. Brooks, R. (1986), A robust layered control system for a mobile robot. *IEEE Journal of Robotics and Automation* 2(1), pp. 14-23.
7. Brooks, R. (1994), Coherent behavior from many adaptive processes. In: Cliff, D. et al. (eds.) (1994), *From Animals to Animats 3*. The MIT Press, Cambridge, Ma., p. 22-29.
8. Cohen, J. and I. Stewart (1994), *The Collapse of Chaos*. London: Viking Press.
9. Cliff, D., I. Harvey, and P. Husbands (1993), Explorations in evolutionary robotics. *Adaptive Behavior* 2(1), 71-104.

10. Deneubourg, J-L. and S. Goss (1990), Collective patterns and decision making. *Ecology, Ethology and Evolution* Vol 1, pp. 295-311.
11. Holland, J.H. (1975), *Adaptation in Natural and Artificial Systems.* The University of Michigan Press, Ann Arbor, Michigan.
12. Kaelbling, L., Littman and Moore (1995), An overview of reinforcement learning. In: Steels, L. (1995), *The Biology and Technology of Intelligent Autonomous Agents.* NATO ASI Series. Springer-Verlag, Berlin.
13. Kaneko, K. (1994). Relevance of dynamic clustering to biological networks. *Physica D* 75 (1994) 55-73.
14. Kitano, H. (1990), Designing neural networks using genetic algorithms with graph generation system. *Complex Systems* 4(4).
15. Kosko, B. (1992), *Neural Networks and Fuzzy Systems. A Dynamical Systems Approach to Machine Intelligence.* Prentice Hall, Englewood Cliffs, NJ.
16. Koza, J. (1992), *Genetic Programming.* The MIT Press, Cambridge, Ma.
17. Langton, C.G. (1989), *Artificial Life.* Santa Fe Institute Studies in the Sciences of Complexity. Proc. Vol VI. Addison-Wesley, Reading, Ma.
18. Lyons, D.M., and M.A. Arbib (1989), A formal model of computation for sensory-based robotics. *IEEE Trans. on Robotics and Automation* 5, pp. 280-293.
19. Mataric, Maja J. (1995), Issues and approaches in design of collective autonomous agents. *Robotics and Autonomous Systems Journal.* Vol 15.
20. Maynard-Smith, J. (1982), *Evolution and the Theory of Games.* Cambridge Univ. Press, Cambridge UK.
21. Meyer, J-A., and S.W. Wilson (1991), From Animals to Animats. *Proc. First International Conference on Simulation of Adaptive Behavior.* The MIT Press, Cambridge, Ma.
22. McClelland, J.L. and D.E. Rumelhart (eds.) (1986), *Explorations in Parallel Distributed Processing.* The MIT Press, Cambridge, Ma.
23. McFarland, D. and T. Boesser (1994), *Intelligent Behavior in Animals and Robots.* The MIT Press, Cambridge, Ma.
24. Nolfi, S., D. Floreano, O. Miglino and F. Mondada (1994), How to evolve autonomous robots: Different approaches in evolutionary robotics. In: *Proc. Alife IV.* The MIT Press, Cambridge, Ma., pp. 190-197.
25. Matsubayashi, K. and Tokoro, M. (1994), A collaboration strategy for repetitive encounters, *Proc. of Modeling Autonomous Agents in a Multi-Agent World Conference* (MAAMAW'94), August 1994.
26. Newell, A. (1982), The knowledge level. *Artificial Intelligence Journal* Vol 18, pp. 87-127.
27. Nilsson, N. (ed.) (1984), *Shakey the Robot.* SRI AI center, Technical Note 323.
28. Numaoka, C. and Takeuchi, A. (1992), Collective choice of strategic type, *Proc. of International Conference on Simulation of Adaptive Behavior* (SAB'92), December 1992.
29. Pasteels, J.M. and J-L Deneubourg (1987), *From Individual to Collective Behaviour in Social Insects.* Birkhäuser, Basel.
30. Pinkerton, B. (1994), Finding what people want: Experiences with the Web-Crawler. In: *Proc. First WWW Conference.* Cern, Geneva.
31. Prigogine, I. and I. Stengers (1984), *Order Out of Chaos.* Bantam Books, New York.
32. Pfeifer, R. and P. Verschure (1992), Distributed adaptive control: A paradigm for designing autonomous agents. In: *Proc. First European Conference on Artificial Life.* The MIT Press, Cambridge, Ma., pp. 21-30.

33. Ray, T. (1992), An approach to the synthesis of life. In: *Artificial Life II*. Proc. Workshop on Artificial Life Held February, 1990 in Santa Fe, New Mexico. pp. 325-371.
34. SAB. *Simulation of Adaptive Behavior Journal*. The MIT Press, Cambridge, Ma.
35. Shapiro, S.C. (1992), *Encyclopedia of Artificial Intelligence*. Second Edition. John Wiley and Sons, Inc. New York.
36. Shibata, T. and T. Fukuda (1993), Coordinative balancing in evolutionary multi-agent robot systems. In: *Proc. First European Conference on Artificial Life*. The MIT Press, Cambridge, Ma., p. 990-1003.
37. Shoham, Y. (1993), Agent-oriented programming. *Artificial Intelligence Journal*.
38. Sims, K. (1991), Interactive evolution for computer graphics. *Computer Graphics* vol. 25. nr 4. pp. 319-328.
39. Takashio, K. and Tokoro, M. (1992), DROL: An object-oriented programming language for distributed real-time systems, *Proc. of ACM OOPSLA '92*, October 1992. pp. 276-294.
40. Smithers, T. (1995), Are autonomous agents information processing systems? In: Steels, L. and R. Brooks (eds.) (1995), *The 'artificial life' route to 'artificial intelligence'. Building situated embodied agents*. Lawrence Erlbaum Associates, New Haven.
41. Steels, L. (1994), The artificial life roots of artificial intelligence. *Artificial Life Journal* 1(1), pp. 89-125.
42. Steels, L. (1994a), A case study in the behavior-oriented design of autonomous agents. In: *Proc. Simulation of Adaptive Behavior Conference*. Brighton. The MIT Press, Cambridge, Ma.
43. Steels, L. (1994b), Emergent functionality through on-line evolution. In: *Proc. 4th Artificial Life Conference*. The MIT Press, Cambridge, Ma.
44. Steels, L. (ed.) (1995), *The Biology and Technology of Intelligent Autonomous Agents*. NATO ASI Series. Springer-Verlag, Berlin.
45. Steels, L. (ed.) (1995b), When are robots intelligent autonomous agents? *Journal for Robotics and Autonomous Systems*, Vol 15.
46. Steels, L. (1995), Intelligence: dynamics and representation. In: Steels, L. (ed.) (1995), *The Biology and Technology of Intelligent Autonomous Agents*. NATO ASI Series. Springer-Verlag, Berlin.
47. Steels, L. and R. Brooks (eds.) (1995), *The 'artificial life' route to 'artificial intelligence'. Building situated embodied agents*. Lawrence Erlbaum Associates, New Haven.
48. Takeuchi, A. and K. Nagao. (1993), Communicative facial displays as a new conversational modality. *Proc. ACM/IFIP Inter-CHI*. Amsterdam, pp. 187-193.
49. Tani, J. and N. Fukumura (1995), Embedding a grammatical description in deterministic chaos: an experiment in recurrent neural learning. *Biol. Cybernetics* 72, 365-370.
50. Tokoro, M. (1993), The society of objects. *Addendum to the Oopsla 93 Proc.* Reprinted in *ACM OOPS Messenger* Vol 5(2). April 1994.
51. Varela, F.J. and P. Bourgine (eds.) (1992), Toward a practice of autonomous systems. *Proc. First European Conference on Artificial Life*. The MIT Press, Cambridge, Ma.
52. Yokote, Y. (1992) The Apertos Reflective Operating System: The Concept and its Implementation, *Proc. of ACM OOPSLA '92,* October 1992. pp. 414-434.

Recurrent Neural Networks

Hava T. Siegelmann

Faculty of Industrial Engineering and Management
Technion (Israel Institute of Technology), Haifa 32000 Israel
iehava@ie.technion.ac.il

Abstract. Neural networks have attracted much attention lately as a powerful tool of automatic learning. Of particular interest is the class of recurrent networks which allow for loops and cycles and thus give rise to dynamical systems, to flexible behavior, and to computation. This paper reviews the recent findings that mathematically quantify the computational power and dynamic capabilities of recurrent neural networks. The appeal of the network as a possible standard model of analog computation also will be discussed.

1 Introduction

Although much of the inspiration for artificial neural networks has come from neuroscience, their main use is in engineering. Networks are able to approximate input-output mapping, to learn from examples, and to adapt to new environments. The networks are thus of great use as automatic learning tools and as adaptive and optimal controllers. Much effort has been directed towards practical applications, including, for example, those for explosion detection in airport security, signature verification, and financial and medical time-series prediction [24, 39, 38]). The networks also are popular in applications to vision, speech processing, robotics, signal processing, and many other fields (see [12],[35],[21],[28]). Some applications have been very successful; others have been less so. Despite the plethora of applications, one of the deficiencies of the neural networks arena has been the lack of basic foundations explaining the computational power and capabilities of this useful model. The work to be described in this paper was begun as an initial attempt to explicate the computational basis of neural networks.

We will begin with a review of the neural architectures. These consist of simple processors, or "neurons," each of which computes a scalar real-valued function of its input. The scalar value produced by a neuron is, in turn, broadcast to the successive neurons involved in a given computation. It is possible to classify neural networks according to their architecture. The simplest form of neural network is a *feedforward* network. Such networks consist of multiple layers, where the input of each layer is the output of the preceding one. The interconnection graph is acyclic, and thus the response time of a network to an input is the constant number of layers of which it consists. Because it supports no memory, the feedforward network cannot provide a computational model. On the other hand, it is useful in approximating functions, and some theory has been developed around it (see, e.g., [3, 4, 6, 7, 15, 16, 20, 37, 36]). If one wants

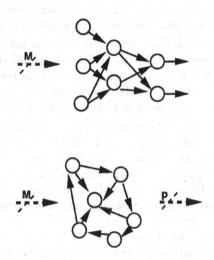

Fig. 1. Feedforward (above) and Recurrent Networks (below)

to have a computational model, one must incorporate memory into the computation, and thus allow the system to evolve for a flexible amount of time. The *recurrent* neural network models have this property. They have no concept of "layers"; instead, feedback loops are supported by and give rise to a dynamical system. Endowed with loops, the recurrent neural networks are capable of approximating a large class of dynamical systems and non-stationary series [12]. They also are capable of computation.

Until recently, very little was known about the computability of neural networks. Most of the previous work on recurrent neural networks has focused on networks of infinite size (e.g., [11, 8, 9, 13, 40, 25]). Because these models contain an unbounded number of neurons, however, they cannot really explain the true power of their networks. They provide not only infinite memory (a fair resource), but they become infinite automata. Perhaps it is more appropriate to consider computational models which include a finite number of neurons, but still allow for growing memory by allowing, for example, for growing precision in the neurons.

Almost no previous work has addressed computability by finite networks, however. The classic result of McCulloch and Pitts in 1943 [22] (and Kleene [18]) showed how to implement Boolean gates by threshold networks, and therefore how to simulate finite automata by such networks. The first computational model that combined a finite number of neurons and infinite precision was introduced by Pollack [27]. He proved his model to be universal in power. Each neuron in his model computed a second-order polynomial or the threshold function; his model did not allow for first-order polynomials, as is common in neural networks, nor did it allow for any continuous activation function. Continuity, however, is an important requirement when one wants to model physical systems with neural networks. It is hard to imagine many natural systems where any two arbitrary close numbers can be well discerned, as they are by the threshold function.

This paper will concentrate on *continuous* recurrent networks; it will describe recent findings that reveal and mathematically quantify the computational power and dynamic capabilities of these networks. Most of the theory to be presented here was conducted jointly with Eduardo Sontag (e.g., [31, 33, 32]), and has already triggered much other work (e.g., [19, 17, 23, 10, 34]).

Another appeal of recurrent neural networks, in addition to their being computationally powerful engineering tools, is that these networks allow for real constants and compute over real numbers. They do not constrain to finite precision as do regular computers. We can delineate these features and demonstrate their usefulness in modeling nature. In natural analog systems, certain real numbers that correspond to values of resistances, capacities, physical constants, and so forth, may not be directly measurable – indeed may not even be computable real numbers – but they affect the "macroscopic" behavior of the system. For instance, imagine a spring/mass system. The dynamical behavior of this system is influenced by several real-valued constants, such as frequency. On any finite time interval, one could replace these constants by rational numbers and observe the same qualitative behavior, but the long-term infinite-time characteristics of the system depend on the true precise real values. Our theory promotes recurrent networks as a standard representative of analog computation [32].

The model closest to ours is perhaps the model of real-number-based computation introduced by Blum, Shub and Smale (see, e.g., [5]). Similarly to Pollack's processors, those of Blum and his colleagues compute either polynomials or the threshold function. In contradiction to the neural network philosophy, they also allow for memory registers that contain the real values. In neural networks, there are no memory registers; rather, the state of the network is revealed in the dynamic flow of information. The BSS model is an interesting mathematical model of computation over real numbers. Our model, although similar to the BSS model in its use of real numbers, is neural-based and simpler. Importantly, our model also better models analog computation.

1.1   The Model

As mentioned earlier, our model concerns recurrent neural networks. Unlike feed-forward networks, recurrent networks allow for the modeling of series with changing statistics [12], and can execute computation rather than approximation only.

Recurrent networks consist of a finite number of neurons. The *activation value*, or *state*, of each processor is updated at times $t = 1, 2, 3, \ldots$, according to a function of the activations (x_j) and inputs (u_j) at time $t-1$, and a set of real coefficients —also called *weights*— (a_{ij}, b_{ij}, c_i). More precisely, each processor's state is updated by an equation of the type

$$x_i(t+1) = \sigma \left(\sum_{j=1}^{N} a_{ij} x_j(t) + \sum_{j=1}^{M} b_{ij} u_j(t) + c_i \right) , \quad i = 1, \ldots, N \qquad (1)$$

where N is the number of processors, M is the number of external input signals, and σ is a "sigmoid-like" function. In our model, σ is a very simple sigmoid, namely the saturated-linear function:

$$\sigma(x) := \begin{cases} 0 & \text{if } x < 0 \\ x & \text{if } 0 \leq x \leq 1 \\ 1 & \text{if } x > 1 . \end{cases} \qquad (2)$$

As part of the description, we assume that we have singled out a subset of p out of the N processors, say $x_{i_1}, \ldots, x_{i_p}$; these are the p *output processors*, and they are used to communicate the outputs of the network to the environment. Thus a network is specified by the data (a_{ij}, b_{ij}, c_i), together with a subset of its processors.

Note that our model is highly homogeneous and extremely simple, in the sense that each neuron computes the composition of two simple functions: affine combination and the simple saturated-linear activation function. Various others models of recurrent networks currently in use are more complicated than ours. Models that emphasize learning use the classical sigmoid function $\frac{1}{1+e^{-x}}$ or other smooth functions. Biological models allow for heterogeneous networks; and in engineering applications, there has been a tendency towards more complicated neurons in order to "make the networks more powerful computationally."

It has been shown in [32] that if one allows multiplications in addition to only linear operations in each neuron – that is, if one considers instead what are often called *high order* neural networks – the computational power does not increase. Further, and perhaps more surprising, is that no increase in computational power (up to polynomial time) can be achieved by letting the activation function be other than the simple saturated linear function in Equation 2. Also, no increase in computational power results even if the activation functions are not necessarily identical in the different processors. Thus, the simple model in Equation 2 is both computationally strong and encompasses all "reasonable" analog networks.

1.2   The Computational Power

Recurrent networks turn out to be *rich enough* to exhibit behavior that is not captured by digital computation, while still being amenable to useful theoretical analysis. That is, they compute functions (or equivalently, accept binary languages) which are not computable by Turing Machines. However, they are not too strong, because the imposition of resource constraints still results in a *nontrivial reduction of computational power* [32].

In particular, if exponential computation time is allowed, for each binary language — including non-computable ones — there is a network that accepts it. In polynomial time, the networks accept exactly the language class P/poly; that is, the same class of languages recognized by the Turing Machines that consult sparse oracles. The class P/poly includes all P and, moreover, some non-recursive sets, such as a unary encoding of the halting problem. Still, this class contains only a very small fraction of all languages.

The correspondence between the networks and P/poly will be a consequence of the following equivalence of networks and Boolean circuits. A *Boolean circuit* is a directed acyclic graph of gates that are labeled by one of the Boolean functions AND, OR, or NOT. A *family of circuits* C is a set of circuits

$$\{c_n, n \in \mathbb{N}\} \ .$$

These have sizes $S_C(n)$; that is, numbers of gates in the circuits, $n = 1, 2, \ldots$, which are assumed to be monotone nondecreasing functions. If $L \subseteq \{0, 1\}^+$, we say that the language L is *computed by the family* C if the characteristic function of

$$L \bigcap \{0, 1\}^n$$

is computed by c_n, for each $n \in \mathbb{N}$.

The qualifier "nonuniform" serves as a reminder that there is no requirement that circuit families be recursively described. We have shown in [32] that recurrent neural networks, although "uniform" in the sense that they have an unchanging physical structure, share exactly the same power as nonuniform families of circuits.

For functions $T : \mathbb{N} \to \mathbb{N}$ and $S : \mathbb{N} \to \mathbb{N}$ on natural numbers, let NET (T) be the class of all functions computed by neural networks in *time* $T(n)$ —that is, recognition of strings of length n is in time at most $T(n)$— and let CIRCUIT (S) be the class of functions computed by nonuniform families of circuits of *size* $S(n)$ —that is, circuits for input vectors of length n have size at most $S(n)$. We have shown in [32] that if F is such that $F(n) \geq n$, then

$$\text{NET } (F(n)) \subseteq \text{CIRCUIT } (\text{Poly}(F(n)))$$

and

$$\text{CIRCUIT } (F(n)) \subseteq \text{NET } (\text{Poly}(F(n))) \ .$$

In other words, not only are networks and circuits equivalent, but they are *polynomially equivalent* for resource constraints in the computational time of the networks and the size of the circuits.

It must be emphasized that, in contradiction to the nonuniform family of circuits, our networks have a fixed structure. The networks are built up of a finite number of processors, whose number *does not increase* with the length of the input. There is a small number of input channels (just two in our main result), into which inputs are presented sequentially. We assume that the structure of the network, including the values of the interconnection weights, does not change in time, but rather remains constant. What changes in time are the activation values, or outputs of each processor, which are used in the next iteration (A synchronous update model is used.). In this sense our model is "uniform" in contrast with certain models used in the past (e.g., [13]) that allow the number of units to increase over time and often even allow the structure to change, depending on the length of inputs being presented. Ours is the first uniform model that has been proven to be nonuniformly strong.

1.3   Linear Precision Suffices

Because recurrent neural networks are defined with unbounded precision, one could think, naively, that infinite precision is required to fully describe their computation; however, we know that this is not the case. We actually have proved that "linear precision suffices" [32]; that is, up to the qth step of the computation, only the first $O(q)$ bits in both weights and activation values of the neurons influence the result.

This property of being indifferent to small changes in the internal value, where "small" is measured as a function of the computation time, can be interpreted as a weak property of robustness. This robustness includes changes in the precise form of the activation function, in the weights of the network, and even an error in the update. In the classical model of (digital) computation, in contrast to in our model, this type of robustness cannot even be properly defined.

1.4   Connecting to Classical Computability

One may wonder about the connection between these computationally powerful recurrent neural networks and classical computability. We have proved [33] that the classical Turing Model is a subset of the recurrent networks. If one restricts attention [33] to networks whose interconnection weights are all rational numbers, then one obtains a model of computation that is polynomially related to Turing Machines. In particular, we proved that given any multi-tape Turing Machine, one can simulate it in real time by some network with rational weights, and of course the converse simulation in polynomial time is obvious. We counted and found [33] a network that is made up of 886 neurons and computes all partial recursive functions.

In the Turing model, to get the P/poly power, one has to add nonuniformity or sparse oracles; both additions seem superficial. The neural network framework, on the other hand, is both natural and elegant: a change in the weights from rational numbers to real numbers is all that is needed to change the power of the system from that of a Turing Machine to the class P/poly.

Two questions arise from considering Turing Machines as a subset of recurrent networks. First, what is the essence of the difference between rational and real numbers that causes such a discrepancy in computational power? Second, are there some networks whose computational power is between P and P/poly? We have indeed shown [2] that the equivalences between neural networks and either 'Turing Machines' (P) or 'Turing Machines with polynomial advice' (P/poly) constitute only two special cases of the computational picture spanned by the neural networks. To do this, we recruited a tool from information theory, the Kolmogorov characterization [1].

Kolmogorov complexity is a measure of the information contained in an individual object. We used a variant of Kolmogorov characterization to measure the information encoded in numbers; this variant takes into account computation efficiency. We then defined rational numbers, real numbers and an infinite hierarchy in the real numbers (between rationals and "total-reals") in terms of their *resource-bounded Kolmogorov complexity* [2]. In this way, we were able to reveal an infinite hierarchy of computational classes associated with neural networks that have weights of increasing Kolmogorov characterization; the hierarchy lies between Turing Machines and Turing Machines with polynomial advice.

Now that we have described the background and advantages of our recurrent network model, we will focus on the mathematical basis of the model. In the following sections, we will provide precise definitions of the main results, and then highlight the proofs of the Turing Machine simulation of rational networks and of the circuit simulation of the general model.

2   Basic Definitions

We consider synchronous networks as in Equation 1. These networks can be represented as dynamical systems whose state at each instant is a real vector $x(t) \in \mathbb{R}^N$. The ith coordinate of this vector represents the activation value of the ith processor at time t. In matrix form, the equations are

$$x^+ = \sigma(Ax + Bu + c) \tag{3}$$

for suitable matrices A, B and vector c.

Given a system of equations such as (3), an initial state $x(1)$, and an infinite input sequence

$$u = u(1), u(2), \ldots \;,$$

one can define iteratively the state $x(t)$ at time t, for each integer $t \geq 1$, as the value obtained by recursively solving the equations. This gives rise, in turn, to a sequence of output values, by restricting attention to the output processors.

To define what we mean by a network recognizing a language

$$L \subseteq \{0, 1\}^+ \;,$$

a *formal network*, a network which adheres to a rigid encoding of its input and output has been defined. Formal networks have two binary input lines. The first of these is a *data line*, and it is used to carry a binary input signal; when no signal is present, it defaults to zero. The second is the *validation line*, and it indicates when the data line is active; it takes the value "1" while the input is present there and "0" thereafter. We use "D" and "V" to denote the contents of these two lines, respectively, so

$$u(t) = (D(t), V(t)) \in \{0, 1\}^2$$

for each t. The initial static state $x(1)$ is zero, that is,

$$\sigma(A0 + B0 + c) = \sigma(c) = 0 .$$

There are also two output processors, which also take the role of data and validation lines and are denoted $O_d(t)$ and $O_v(t)$, respectively.

The convention of using two input lines allows us to have all external signals be binary; of course many other conventions are possible and would give rise to the same results, for instance, one could use a three-valued input, say with values $\{-1, 0, 1\}$, where "0" indicates that no signal is present, and ± 1 are the two possible binary input values.

We now encode each word

$$\alpha = \alpha_1 \cdots \alpha_k \in \{0, 1\}^+$$

as follows. Let

$$u_\alpha(t) = (V_\alpha(t), D_\alpha(t)) , \quad t = 1, \ldots ,$$

where

$$V_\alpha(t) = \begin{cases} 1 & \text{if } t = 1, \ldots, k \\ 0 & \text{otherwise} , \end{cases}$$

and

$$D_\alpha(t) = \begin{cases} \alpha_k & \text{if } t = 1, \ldots, k \\ 0 & \text{otherwise} . \end{cases}$$

Given a formal network $\mathcal{N}$, with two inputs as above, we say that a word α is *classified in time* τ if the following property holds: the output sequence

$$y(t) = (O_d(t), O_v(t))$$

produced by u_α when starting from $x(1) = 0$ has the form

$$O_d = \underbrace{0 \cdots 0}_{\tau-1} \eta_\alpha 000 \cdots , \quad O_v = \underbrace{0 \cdots 0}_{\tau-1} 1000 \cdots ,$$

where $\eta_\alpha = 0$ or 1.

Let $T : \mathbb{N} \to \mathbb{N}$ be a function on natural numbers. We say that the language $L \subseteq \{0, 1\}^+$ is *recognized in time* T by the formal network $\mathcal{N}$, provided that each word $\alpha \in \{0, 1\}^+$ is classified in time $\tau \leq T(|\alpha|)$, and η_α equals 1 when $\alpha \in L$, and η_α equals 0 otherwise.

We can similarly define a network that computes binary functions rather than one that accepts languages only.

Now that we have defined the input-output mappings associated with recurrent networks, we are ready to provide the specific theorems of our model.

3   Turing Machine Equivalence of Rational Nets

If the weights are rational numbers, the network is equivalent in power to the Turing Machine model [31]. Two different I/O conventions are suggested in [33]: in the first, input lines and output neurons are used, and in the second, the discrete input and the output are encoded as the state of two fixed neurons. The results for each convention are formally stated as follows.

3.1   Theorems

Theorem 1. *Let $\phi : \{0,1\}^* \to \{0,1\}^*$ be any partial recursive function. Then, there exists a network $\mathcal{N}$, with input lines, that computes ϕ. Furthermore, if there is a Turing Machine (with one input tape and several work tapes) that computes $\phi(\omega)$ (ω is an input string) in time $T(\omega)$, then some network $\mathcal{N}$ computes $\phi(\omega)$ in time $O\left(T(\omega) + |\omega|\right)$.*

Theorem 2. *Let M be a Turing Machine computing $\phi : \{0,1\}^* \to \{0,1\}^*$ in time T. Then there exists a network $\mathcal{N}$, without inputs, such that the following properties hold: For each $\omega \in \{0,1\}^*$, assume that $\mathcal{N}$ is started in the initial state*

$$\xi(\omega) = (\delta[\omega], 0, \ldots, 0) \in \mathbb{Q}^N,$$

where $\delta : \{0,1\}^* \to [0,1]$ is defined by $\delta(\omega_1 \omega_2 \cdots \omega_n) = \sum_{i=1}^{n} \frac{2\omega_i + 1}{4^i}$. Then, if $\phi(\omega)$ is undefined, the second coordinate $\xi(\omega)_2^t$ of the state after t steps is identically equal to zero, for all t. If instead $\phi(\omega)$ is defined, then

$$\xi(\omega)_2^t = 0, \quad \text{for } t = 0, \ldots, T(w)-1, \quad \xi(\omega)_2^{T(w)} = 1 \quad \text{and} \quad \xi(\omega)_1^{T(w)} = \delta[\phi(\omega)].$$

Furthermore, all weights in $\mathcal{N}$ are simple, non-periodic, and bounded rationals.

In both theorems, the size of $\mathcal{N}$ is fixed, independent of the running time T.

3.2   Proofs

The proof of the first theorem relies on the second one and on the observation that given an input string, the network can encode it in linear time as the initial state in the second theorem, and output the result as given in the second theorem through the output neurons.

We now highlight the main part of the proof of the second theorem. We start with a 2-stack machine; this model is obviously equivalent to a 1-tape (standard) Turing Machine ([14]). Formally, a 2-stack machine consists of a finite control and two binary stacks, unbounded in length. Each stack is accessed by a read-write head, which is located at the top element of the stack. At the beginning of the computation, the binary input sequence is written on stack_1. The machine at every step reads the top element of each stack as a symbol $\alpha \in \{0, 1, \#\}$ (where $\#$ means that the stack is empty), checks the state of the control ($s \in \{1, 2, \ldots |S|\}$), and executes the following operations:

1. Makes one of the following manipulations for each stack:
   (a) Pops the top element.
   (b) Pushes an extra element on the top of the stack (either 0 or 1).
   (c) Does not change the stack.
2. Changes the state of the control.

When the control reaches a special state, called the "halting state," the machine stops. Its output is defined as the binary sequence on one predefined stack. Thus, the I/O map, or function, computed by a 2-stack machine is defined by the binary sequences on stack$_1$ before and after the computation.

3.3 Encoding the Stacks

Assume we were to encode a binary stream $\omega = \omega_1\omega_2\cdots\omega_n$ into the number

$$\sum_{i=1}^{n} \frac{\omega_i}{2^i}.$$

Such a value could be held in a neuron since it ranges in $[0,1]$. However, there are a few problems with this simple encoding. First, one cannot differentiate between the strings "β" and "$\beta\cdot 0$", where '·' denotes the concatenation operator. Second, even when assuming that each binary string ends with 1, the continuity of the activation function σ makes it impossible to retrieve the most significant bit (in radix 2) of a string in a constant amount of time. (For example, the values .100000000000 and .011111111111111 are almost indistinguishable by a network, although they represent very different stack values.) In summary, given streams of binary input signals, one does not want them to be encoded on a continuous range, but rather to have gaps between valid encoding of the strings. Such gaps would enable a quick decoding of the number by means of an operation requiring only finite precision, or equivalently, by reading the most significant bit in some representation in a constant amount of time. On the other hand, if we choose some set of "numbers with gaps" to encode the different binary strings, we have to assure that various manipulations on these numbers during the computation leave the stack encoding in the same set of "numbers with gaps."

As a solution, the encoding of stacks is chosen to be as follows. Read the binary elements in each stack from top to bottom as a binary string $\omega = \omega_1\omega_2\cdots\omega_n$. Now, encode this string into the number

$$\sum_{i=1}^{n} \frac{2\omega_i + 1}{4^i}.$$

This number ranges in $[0,1)$, but not every value in $[0,1)$ appears. If the string started with the value 1, then the associated number has a value of at least $\frac{3}{4}$, and if it started with 0, the value is in the range $[\frac{1}{4}, \frac{1}{2})$. The empty string is encoded into the value 0. The next element in the stack restricts the possible value further.

The set of possible values is not continuous and has "holes." Such a set of values "with holes" is a Cantor set. Its self-similar structure means that bit shifts preserve the "holes." The advantage of this approach is that there is never a need to distinguish between two very close numbers in order to read the most significant digit in the base-4 representation.

3.4 Stack Operations

We next demonstrate the usefulness of our encoding of the stacks.

1. **Reading the Top:** Assume that a stack has the value $\omega = 1011$, that is, that it is encoded by the number $q = .3133_4$ (this number is to be read in base 4). As discussed above, the value of q is at least $\frac{3}{4}$ when the top of the stack is 1, and at most $\frac{1}{2}$ otherwise. The linear operation

$$4q - 2$$

transfers this range to at least 1 when the top element is 1, and to at most 0 otherwise. Thus, the function $\mathrm{top}(q)$

$$\mathrm{top}\,(q) = \sigma(4q - 2)$$

provides the value of the top element.

2. **Push to Stack:** Pushing 0 onto the stack $\omega = 1011$ changes the value into $\omega = 01011$. In terms of the encoding, $q = .3133_4$ is transferred into $q = .13133_4$. That is, the suffix remains the same and the new element is entered into the most significant location. This is easily done by the operation

$$\frac{q}{4} + \frac{1}{4}$$

(which is equivalent to $\sigma(\frac{q}{4} + \frac{1}{4})$ given that $q \in [0, 1)$). Pushing the value 1 onto the stack can be implemented by $\frac{q}{4} + \frac{3}{4}$.

3. **Pop Stack:** Popping a stack transfers $\omega = 1011$ into 011, or the encoding from $q = .3133_4$ to $.133_4$. When the top element is known, the operation

$$4q - (2\,\mathrm{top}\,(q) + 1)$$

(or equivalently $\sigma(4q - (2\,\mathrm{top}\,(q) + 1))$) has the effect of popping the stack.

4. **Non-empty Stack:** The predicate "Non-empty" indicates whether the stack w is empty or not, which means in terms of the encoding, whether $q = 0$ or $q \geq .1_4$. This can be decided by the operation

$$\sigma(4q)\,.$$

3.5   General Construction of the Network

From the above discussion, we construct a network architecture that has three neurons per stack. One neuron holds the stack encoding (q), one holds $top(q)$, and one indicates whether the stack is empty. In addition, the architecture has a few neurons that represent the finite control (this is the old McCulloch and Pitts result [41]) and a set of neurons which take their input both from the stack-reading neurons and from the finite-control neurons and "decide" the next step.

The above encoding results in a Turing Machine simulation that requires four steps of the network for each step of the Turing Machine. To achieve a "step per step" simulation, a more sophisticated encoding is required. This encoding relies upon a Cantor set with a specific size of gaps. As a special case, we simulated a universal two-stack machine via a network of size 886; this is the network that computes any partial recursive function.

4   General Networks and Boolean Circuits

The above section dealt with neural networks using rational weights. When real constants are allowed, the networks compute the class P/poly. Recall that NET $(T(n))$ is the class of languages recognized by formal networks (with real weights) in time $T(n)$ and that CIRCUIT $(S(n))$ is the class of languages recognized by (nonuniform) families of circuits of size $S(n)$. The main theorem is as follows [32]:

Theorem 3. *Let F be so that $F(n) \geq n$. Then,* NET $(F(n)) \subseteq$ CIRCUIT $(\text{Poly}(F(n)))$, *and* CIRCUIT $(F(n)) \subseteq$ NET $(\text{Poly}(F(n)))$.

More precisely, we prove the following two facts. For each function $F(n) \geq n$:

- CIRCUIT $(F(n)) \subseteq$ NET $(nF^2(n))$.
- NET $(F(n)) \subseteq$ CIRCUIT $(F^3(n))$.

We now sketch the proof.

For the first direction, we have shown a network architecture such that for any family of circuits there is some weight assignment to the network so that the network computes the same function as the family does. The time of computation is square the size of the circuit. The main idea is to encode the whole circuit family in a real number and to fix this number as a weight of the network. The network then operates as follows:

1. It receives input and measures the length of the input.
2. It retrieves the circuit description from the real weight.
3. While having the circuit description and the input, it simulates the circuit.

The encoding should be easy to retrieve and any Cantor line encoding will do. For example, we can encode a circuit as a finite sequence over the alphabet $\{0, 2, 4, 6\}$, as follows:

- In this example, the encoding of each level i starts with the letter 6. Levels are encoded successively, starting with the bottom level and ending with the top one.
- At each level, gates are encoded successively. The encoding of a gate g consists of three parts—a starting symbol, a 2-digit code for the gate type, and a code to indicate which gate feeds into it:
  - It starts with the letter 0.
  - A two-digit sequence $\{42, 44, 22\}$ denotes the type of the gate, $\{\text{AND, OR, NOT}\}$ respectively.
  - If gate g is in level i, then the input to g is represented as a sequence in $\{2, 4\}^{w_{i-1}}$, such that the jth position in the sequence is 4 if and only if the jth gate of the $(i-1)$th level feeds into gate g.

Example 1. The circuit c_1 in Figure 2 is encoded as

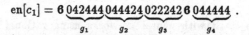

$$\text{en}[c_1] = \mathbf{6}\ \underbrace{042444}_{g_1}\ \underbrace{044424}_{g_2}\ \underbrace{022242}_{g_3}\ \mathbf{6}\ \underbrace{044444}_{g_4}\ .$$

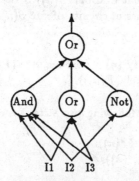

Fig. 2. Circuit c_1

For instance, the NOT gate corresponds to the subsequence "022242": It starts with the letter 0, followed by the two digits "22," denoting that the gate is of type NOT, and ends with "242," which indicates that only the second input feeds into the gate.   □

The other direction of the theorem states that networks can be simulated by circuits. At first glance this statement seems almost trivial: If a nonuniform family of circuits is such a strong function, why would it not be able to easily simulate a finite neural network? Recall, however, that the inclusion should be in polynomial time, and thus if the network computes in polynomial time it has to be simulated by a polynomial size Boolean circuit. The network may include weights that are real numbers specifiable by infinitely many bits, and thus the activations of the neurons may take real values as well. How are we to simulate these real values with Boolean circuits of polynomial size?

We now need a new and important observation:

Lemma 4. *Let $\mathcal{N}$ be a network as in Equation 2. Define by q-Truncation($\mathcal{N}$) a network which updates by*

$$x_i^+ = q\text{-Truncation } [\sigma(\sum_{j=1}^{N} a_{ij}^q x_j + \sum_{j=1}^{M} b_{ij}^q u_j + c_i^q)] ,$$

where q-Truncation means the operation of truncating after q bits, and for which all weights are also truncated at q bits. Then q-Truncation($\mathcal{N}$) computes like $\mathcal{N}$ in the first q computational steps.

This is the lemma referred to above as the "linear precision suffices"; it is proven by numerical analysis techniques. The lemma has various consequences. Here, we use it only to complete the proof of Theorem 3: Given input of length n, a network that computes it in polynomial time equivalently to the original $\mathcal{N}$ has weights of polynomial length only. This network can be simulated easily by a Boolean circuit of polynomial size.

5   Discussion

The natural extension of the network model is to endow it with stochasticity. A model of stochastic networks that corresponds to von-Neumann's model of unreliable Boolean feedforward networks was introduced in [29]. In this model, the neurons may apply randomness that can be modeled by additional input of independent identically distributed binary sequences (IID). Stochastisity with exact known parameters seems to have the potential of increasing the computational power of the underlying deterministic process. We found, however, that the stochasticity of von Neumann's type does not affect the computational power of recurrent neural networks.

Motivated by having a very large class of analog networks and dynamical systems that are computationally stronger than the Turing Model, but with no more power than the recurrent neural network, we promoted the simple neural network model as a standard model for analog computation. We formulated it as an analog of the Church-Turing thesis of digital computation: "Any reasonable analog computer will have no more power (up to polynomial time) than the recurrent neural network."

In [30], a chaotic dynamical system that is computationally equivalent to the recurrent neural network model was presented. This system, called "the analog shift map," is an almost classical chaotic dynamical system. It is also associated with the analog computation models suggested in this paper (and hence the term 'analog'). More than that, it is a mathematical formulation that is conjectured to describe idealized physical phenomena. To the extent that the analog shift map does describe idealized physical phenomena, the same is true for neural networks. In this case, neural networks have two important advantages: they are both mathematically strong and meaningful.

Our model, even if not viewed as a general standard analog model, may have an interesting consequence. That is, it may be thought of as a possible answer to Penrose's recent claim [26] that the standard model of computing is not appropriate for modeling true biological intelligence. Penrose argues that physical processes, evolving at a quantum level, may result in computations which cannot be incorporated in Church's Thesis. It is interesting to point out that the recurrent neural network does allow for non-Turing power while keeping track of computational constraints, and thus embeds a possible answer to Penrose's challenge within the framework of classical computer science.

In this section, we have speculated about possible implications of recurrent models, in general, and of our model, in particular. The accuracy of these speculations remains to be demonstrated, but should not detract attention from the primary intent of this paper, and of our work: the work described in this paper constitutes the rigorous mathematical foundation of the recurrent neural network model. This model is particularly interesting because of its popularity in engineering applications of automatic learning and time series prediction; and because it can model natural biological systems. To us as computer scientists, it is especially interesting mathematically, as it allows for unbounded (analog) precision while still being bounded in processing elements and having no long-term memory registers.

References

1. J. L. Balcázar, J. Díaz, and J. Gabarró. *Structural Complexity*, volume I and II. EATCS Monographs in Theoretical Computer Science, Springer-Verlag, Berlin, 1988-1990.
2. J. L. Balcázar, R. Gavaldà, H.T. Siegelmann, and E. D. Sontag. Some structural complexity aspects of neural computation. In *8th Ann. IEEE conf. on Structure in Complexity Theory*, pages 253-265, San Diego, CA, May 1993.
3. A.R. Barron. Neural net approximation. In *Proc. Seventh Yale Workshop on Adaptive and Learning Systems*, pages 69-72, Yale University, 1992.
4. E.B. Baum and D. Haussler. What size net gives valid generalization? *Neural Computation*, 1:151-160, 1989.
5. L. Blum, M. Shub, and S. Smale. On a theory of computation and complexity over the real numbers: NP completeness, recursive functions, and universal machines. *Bull. A.M.S.*, 21:1-46, 1989.

6. G. Cybenko. Approximation by superpositions of a sigmoidal function. *Math. Control, Signals, and Systems*, 2:303–314, 1989.

7. J.A. Franklin. On the approximate realization of continuous mappings by neural networks. *Neural Networks*, 2:183–192, 1989.

8. S. Franklin and M. Garzon. Neural computability. In O. M. Omidvar, editor, *Progress In Neural Networks*, pages 128–144. Ablex, Norwood, NJ, 1990.

9. M. Garzon and S. Franklin. Neural computability. In *Proc. 3rd Int. Joint Conf. Neural Networks*, volume II, pages 631–637, 1989.

10. C.L. Giles, B.G. Horne, and T. Lin. Learning a class of large finite state machines with a recurrent neural network. *Neural Networks*, 1995. In press.

11. R. Hartley and H. Szu. A comparison of the computational power of neural network models. In *Proc. IEEE Conf. Neural Networks*, pages 17–22, 1987.

12. S. Haykin. *Neural Networks: A Comprehensive Foundation.* IEEE Press, New York, 1994.

13. J.W. Hong. On connectionist models. *On Pure and Applied Mathematics*, 41, 1988.

14. J.E. Hopcroft and J.D. Ullman. *Introduction to Automata Theory, Languages, and Computation.* Addison-Wesley Publishing Company, Inc., Reading, MA, 1979.

15. K. Hornik. Approximation capabilities of multilayer feedforward networks. *Neural Networks*, 4:251–257, 1991.

16. K. Hornik, M. Stinchcombe, and H. White. Universal approximation of an unknown mapping and its derivatives using multilayer feedforward networks. *Neural Networks*, 3: 551–560, 1990.

17. J. Kilian and H.T. Siegelmann. On the power of sigmoid neural networks. In *Proc. Sixth ACM Workshop on Computational Learning Theory*, Santa Cruz, July 1993.

18. S. C. Kleene. Representation of events in nerve nets and finite automata. In C.E. Shannon and J. McCarthy, editors, *Automata Studies*, pages 3–41. Princeton Univ. Press, 1956.

19. P. Koiran, M. Cosnard, and M. Garzon. Computability with low-dimensional dynamical systems. *Theoretical Computer Science*, 132:113–128, 1994.

20. W. Maass, G. Schnitger, and E.D. Sontag. On the computational power of sigmoid versus boolean threshold circuits. In *Proc. 32nd Ann. IEEE Symp. Foundations of Computer Science*, pages 767–776, 1991.

21. M. Matthews. On the uniform approximation of nonlinear discrete-time fading-memory systems using neural network models. Technical Report Ph.D. Thesis, ETH No. 9635, E.T.H. Zurich, 1992.

22. W. S. McCulloch and W. Pitts. A logical calculus of the ideas immanent in nervous activity. *Bull. Math. Biophys*, 5:115–133, 1943.

23. C.B. Miller and C.L. Giles. Experimental comparison of the effect of order in recurrent neural networks. *International Journal of Pattern Recognition and Artificial Intelligence*, 7(4):849–872, 1993. Special Issue on Neural Networks and Pattern Recognition, editors: I. Guyon , P.S.P. Wang.

24. J. Moody, A. Levin, and S. Rehfuss. Predicting the U. S. index of industrial production. *Neural Network World*, 3(6):791–794, 1993.

25. P. Orponen. On the computational power of discrete Hopfield nets. A. Lingas, R. Karlsson, S. Carlsson (Eds.), Automata, Languages and Programming, Proc. 20th Intern. Symposium (ICALP'93), Lecture Notes in Computer Science, Vol. 700, Springer-Verlag, Berlin, 1993, pp. 215-226.

26. R. Penrose. *The Emperor's New Mind.* Oxford University Press, Oxford, 1989.

27. J. B. Pollack. *On Connectionist Models of Natural Language Processing.* PhD thesis, Computer Science Dept, Univ. of Illinois, Urbana, 1987.

28. M. M. Polycarpou and P.A. Ioannou. Identification and control of nonlinear systems using neural network models: Design and stability analysis. Technical Report 91-09-01, Department of EE/Systems, USC, Los Angeles, Sept 1991.

29. H. T. Siegelmann. On the computational power of probabilistic and faulty neural networks. In S. Abiteboul, E. Shamir (Eds.), *Automata, Languages and Programming*, Proc. 21st Intern. Symposium (ICALP 94), *Lecture Notes in Computer Science*, Vol. 820, Springer-Verlag, Berlin, 1994, pp. 23-33.

30. H. T. Siegelmann. Computation beyond the Turing limit. *SCIENCE*, 268(5210): 545-548, April 1995.

31. H. T. Siegelmann and E. D. Sontag. Turing computability with neural nets. *Appl. Math. Lett.*, 4(6):77-80, 1991.

32. H. T. Siegelmann and E. D. Sontag. Analog computation via neural networks. *Theoretical Computer Science*, Vol. 131: 331-360, 1994.

33. H. T. Siegelmann and E. D. Sontag. On computational power of neural networks. *J. Comp. Syst. Sci*, 50(1):132-150, 1995. Previous version appeared in *Proc. Fifth ACM Workshop on Computational Learning Theory*, pages 440-449, Pittsburgh, July 1992.

34. H.T. Siegelmann, B.G. Horne, and C.L. Giles. Computational capabilities of recurrent narx neural networks. Technical Report UMIACS-TR-95-12 and CS-TR-3408, Institute for Advanced Computer Studies, University of Maryland, College Park, Maryland, 1995.

35. E.D. Sontag. Neural nets as systems models and controllers. In *Proc. Seventh Yale Workshop on Adaptive and Learning Systems*, pages 73-79, Yale University, 1992.

36. M. Stinchcombe and H. White. Approximating and learning unknown mappings using multilayer feedforward networks with bounded weights. In *Proceedings of the International Joint Conference on Neural Networks, IEEE*, Vol. 3, pages 7-16, 1990.

37. H.J. Sussmann. Uniqueness of the weights for minimal feedforward nets with a given input-output map. *Neural Networks*, 5: 589-593, 1992.

38. V. Tresp, J. Moody, and W.R. Delong. Neural network modeling of physiological processes. In T. Petsche, M. Kearns, S. Hanson, and R. Rivest, editors, *Computational Learning Theory and Natural Learning Systems - vol. 2*. MIT Press, Cambridge MA, 1993: 363-378.

39. J. Utans, J. Moody, S. Rehfuss, and H. T. Siegelmann. Selecting input variables via sensitivity analysis: Application to predicting the U. S. business cycle. In *IEEE Computational Intelligence in Financial Engineering Conference*, New York, April 1995: 118-122.

40. D. Wolpert. A computationally universal field computer which is purely linear. Technical Report LA-UR-91-2937, Los Alamos National Laboratory, 1991.

41. W. Pitts W.S. McCulloch. A logical calculus of ideas immanent in nervous activity. *Bulletin of Mathematical Biophysics*, 5:115-133, 1943.

Scalable Computing

W. F. McColl

Programming Research Group, Oxford University Computing Laboratory, Wolfson Building, Parks Road, Oxford OX1 3QD, England

Abstract. Scalable computing will, over the next few years, become the normal form of computing. In this paper we present a unified framework, based on the BSP model, which aims to serve as a foundation for this evolutionary development. A number of important techniques, tools and methodologies for the design of sequential algorithms and programs have been developed over the past few decades. In the transition from sequential to scalable computing we will find that new requirements such as universality and predictable performance will necessitate significant changes of emphasis in these areas. Programs for scalable computing, in addition to being fully portable, will have to be efficiently universal, offering high performance, in a predictable way, on any general purpose parallel architecture. The BSP model provides a discipline for the design of scalable programs of this kind. We outline the approach and discuss some of the issues involved.

1   Introduction

For fifty years, sequential computing has been the normal form of computing. From the early proposal of von Neumann [5] to the present day, sequential computing has grown relentlessly, embracing new technologies as they have emerged and discarding them whenever something better came along. Today it is a huge global industry. The two parts of that industry, hardware and software, are quite different. Most sequential hardware has a life span of a few years. New technologies continually offer new ways of realising the same basic design in a form which is cheaper, more powerful, or both. In contrast, sequential software systems often take many years to develop, and are expected to last for a very long time, preferably for ever.

The key reason for the spectacular success of sequential computing has been the widespread, almost universal, adoption of the basic model proposed by von Neumann. To see why this happened it is necessary to go back further, to the work of Turing [20]. In his theoretical studies, Turing demonstrated that a single general purpose sequential machine could be designed which would be capable of efficiently performing any computation which could be performed by a special purpose sequential machine. Stated more concisely, he demonstrated that efficient universality was achievable for sequential computations. Around 1944,

---

* This work was supported in part by ESPRIT Basic Research Project 9072 - GEPP-COM (Foundations of General Purpose Parallel Computing).

von Neumann produced his proposal for a general purpose sequential computer which captured the principles of Turing's work in a practical design. The design, which has come to be known as the "von Neumann computer", has served as the basic model for almost all sequential computers produced from the late 1940s to the present time. The stability and universality provided by the von Neumann model has permitted and encouraged the development of high level languages and compilers. These, in turn, have created a large and diverse software industry producing portable applications software which will run with high performance on any sequential computer.

For sequential computing, the von Neumann model has given the two parts of the computing industry what they require to succeed. The hardware industry is provided with a focus for its technological innovation, and the confidence that, since the model is stable, software companies will find that the time and effort involved in developing software can be justified. The software industry meanwhile sees the stability of the model as providing a basis for the high level, cost-effective development of applications software, and also providing a guarantee that the software thus produced will not become obsolete with the next technological change.

Since the earliest days of sequential computing it has been clear that, sooner or later, sequential computing would be superseded by parallel computing. This has not yet happened, despite the availability of numerous parallel machines and the insatiable demand for increased computing power. In this paper we will argue that the evolution to parallel computing can now take place, and will do so over the next few years. We will show that all of the essential requirements for such a transition can now be satisfied. In particular, we will present the BSP model and will argue that it can play a unifying role analogous to that which the von Neumann model has played in the development of sequential computing.

2   Architectures

Parallel computing is not new. For many years, academic research groups and, more recently, companies, have been producing parallel computers and trying to persuade people to write parallel software for them. On most of the early parallel systems, the global communications networks were very poor and scalable performance could only be achieved by designing algorithms and programs which carefully exploited the particular architectural features of the machine. Besides being tedious and time consuming in most cases, this approach typically produced software which could not be easily adapted to run on other machines.

Over the last few years the situation has improved. For a variety of technological and economic reasons, the various classes of parallel computer in use (distributed memory machines, shared memory multiprocessors, clusters of workstations) have become more and more alike. The economic advantages of using standard commodity components has been a major factor in this convergence. Other influential factors have been the need to efficiently support a global address space on distributed memory machines for ease of programming, and the need to replace buses by networks to achieve scalability in shared memory multi-processors. These various pressures have acted to produce a rapid and significant evolutionary restructuring of the parallel computing industry.

There is now a growing consensus that for a combination of technological, commercial, and software reasons, we will see a steady evolution over the next few years towards a "standard" architectural model for scalable parallel computing. It is likely to consist of a collection of (workstation-like) processor-memory pairs connected by a communications network which can be used to efficiently support a global address space. Both message passing and shared memory programming styles will be efficiently supported on these architectures. As with all such successful models, there will be plenty of scope for the use of different designs and technologies to realise such systems in different forms depending on the cost and performance requirements sought.

The simplest, cheapest, and probably the most common architectures will be based on clusters of personal computers. The next Intel microprocessor, currently referred to as the P6, will be the first high volume, commodity microprocessor for the personal computer market with hardware support for multiprocessing. In a couple of years, very low cost multiprocessor personal computers will be available, along with very low cost networking technologies and software allowing these to be assembled into clusters for high performance computing. At the other end of the spectrum, there will continue to be a small group of companies producing very large, very powerful and very expensive parallel systems for those who require those computing resources. At present, a good example of a company operating in this end of the market is Cray Research. The CRAY T3D is a very powerful distributed memory architecture based on the DEC Alpha microprocessor. In addition to offering extremely high bandwidth global communications, it has several specialised hardware mechanisms which enable it to efficiently support parallel programs which execute in a global address space [2]. The mechanisms include hardware barrier synchronisation and direct remote memory access. The latter permits each processor to get a value directly from any remote memory location in the machine, and to put a value directly in any remote memory location. This is done in a way which avoids the performance penalties normally incurred in executing such operations on a distributed memory architecture, due to processor synchronisation and other unnecessary activities in the low level systems software. The companies which compete at the top end of the market will, as today, focus their attention not only on highly optimised architectural design, but also on new, and perhaps expensive, technologies which can offer increased performance. For example, some might use optical technologies to achieve more efficient global communications than could be achieved with VLSI systems.

The implementation of a global address space on a distributed memory architecture requires an efficient mechanism for the distributed routing of put and get requests, and of the replies to get requests, through the network of processors. A number of efficient routing and memory management techniques have been developed for this problem, see e.g. [13, 21, 22]. Consider the problem of packet routing on a p-processor network. Let an *h-relation* denote a routing problem where each processor has at most h packets to send to various processors in the network, and where each processor is also due to receive at most h packets from other processors. Here, a packet is one word of information, such as e.g. a real number or an integer. Using two-phase randomised routing one can, for example, show that every $(\log p)$-relation can be realised on a p processor hypercube in $O(\log p)$ steps. In [9] a simple and practical randomised method of routing h-relations on an optical communications system is described. The optical system is physically realistic and the method requires only $O(h + \log p \log \log p)$ steps. In [18] a simple and very efficient protocol for routing h-relations using only the total-exchange primitive is described.

The process of architectural convergence which was described above brings with it the hope that we can, over the next few years, establish scalable parallel computing as the normal form of computing, and begin to see the growth of a large and diverse global software industry for scalable computing similar to that which currently exists for sequential computing. The main goal of that industry will be to produce scalable software which will run unchanged, and with high performance, on any architecture, from a cheap multiprocessor PC to a large parallel supercomputer. The next major step towards this goal is to develop a foundation for the architecture independent programming of this emerging range of scalable parallel systems. The BSP approach described in this paper provides just such a foundation. It offers the prospect of achieving both scalable parallel performance and architecture independent parallel software, and provides a framework which permits the performance of parallel and distributed systems to be analysed and predicted in a precise way.

3   The BSP Model

In architectural terms, the BSP model is essentially the standard model described above. A *bulk synchronous parallel (BSP) computer* [13, 21] consists of a set of processor-memory pairs, a global communications network, and a mechanism for the efficient barrier synchronisation of the processors. There are no specialised broadcasting or combining facilities, although these can be efficiently realised in software where required [23]. The model also does not deal directly with issues such as input-output or the use of vector units, although it can be easily extended to do so. If we define a time step to be the time required for a single local operation, i.e. a basic operation (such as addition or multiplication) on locally held data values, then the performance of any BSP computer can be characterised by three parameters: p = number of processors; l = number of time steps for barrier synchronisation; g = (total number of local operations performed by all processors in one second)/(total number of words delivered by the communications network in one second). [There is also, of course, a fourth parameter, the number of time steps per second. However, since the other parameters are normalised with respect to that one, it can be ignored in the design of algorithms and programs.]

The parameter l corresponds to the network latency. The parameter g corresponds to the frequency with which remote memory accesses can be made without affecting the total time for the computation; in a machine with a higher value of g one must make remote memory accesses less frequently. More formally, g is related to the time required to realise h-relations in a situation of continuous message traffic; g is the value such that an h-relation can be performed in $h \cdot g$ time steps. Any scalable parallel system can be regarded as a BSP computer, and can be benchmarked accordingly to determine its BSP parameters l and g. The BSP model is therefore not prescriptive in terms of the physical architectures to which it applies. Every scalable architecture can be viewed by an algorithm designer or programmer as simply a point (p, l, g) in the space of all BSP machines.

The use of the parameters l and g to characterise the communications performance of the BSP computer contrasts sharply with the way in which communications performance is described for most distributed memory architectures on the market today. A major feature of the BSP model is that it lifts considerations of network performance from the local level to the global level. We are thus no longer particularly interested in whether the network is a 2D array, a butterfly or a hypercube, or whether it is implemented in VLSI or in some optical technology. Our interest is in global parameters of the network, such as l and g, which describe its ability to support remote memory accesses in a uniformly efficient manner.

In the design and implementation of a BSP computer, the values of l and g which can be achieved will depend on the capabilities of the available technology and the amount of money that one is willing to spend on the communications network. As the computational performance of machines continues to grow, we will find that to keep l and g low it will be necessary to continually increase our investment in the communications hardware as a percentage of the total cost of the machine. In asymptotic terms, the values of l and g one might expect for various p processor networks are: ring $[l = O(p), g = O(p)]$, 2D array $[l = O(p^{1/2}), g = O(p^{1/2})]$, butterfly $[l = O(\log p), g = O(\log p)]$, hypercube $[l = O(\log p), g = O(1)]$. These asymptotic estimates are based entirely on the degree and diameter properties of the corresponding graph. In a practical setting, the channel capacities, routing methods used, VLSI implementation etc. would also have a significant impact on the actual values of l and g which could be achieved on a given machine. New optical technologies may offer the prospect of further reductions in the values of l and g which can be achieved, by providing a more efficient means of non-local communication than is possible with VLSI.

For many of the current VLSI-based networks, the values of g and l are very similar. If we are interested in the problem of designing improved networks and routing methods which reduce g then perhaps the most obvious approach is to concentrate instead on the alternative problem of reducing l. This strategy is suggested by the following simple reasoning: If messages are in the network for a shorter period of time then, given that the network capacity is fixed, it will be possible to insert messages into the network more frequently. In the next section we will see that, in many cases, the performance of a BSP computation is limited much more by g than by l. This suggests that in future, when designing networks and routing methods it may be advantageous to accept a significant increase in l in order to secure even a modest decrease in g. This raises a number of interesting architectural questions which have not yet been explored. The work in [18] contains some interesting initial ideas in this direction. It is also interesting to note that the characteristics of many optical communication systems (slow switching, very high bandwidth) are very compatible with this alternative approach.

A BSP computer operates in the following way. A computation consists of a sequence of S parallel *supersteps* $s(i)$, $0 \leq i < S$, where each superstep consists of a sequence of steps, followed by a barrier synchronisation at which point any remote memory accesses take effect. During a superstep, each processor can perform a number of computation steps on values held locally at the start of the superstep, and send and receive a number of messages corresponding to remote get and put requests. The time for superstep $s(i)$ is determined as follows. Let the work w be the maximum number of local computation steps executed by any processor during $s(i)$, let h_{out} be the maximum number of messages sent by any processor during $s(i)$, and h_{in} be the maximum number of messages received by any processor during $s(i)$. The time for $s(i)$ is then at most $w + \max\{h_{out}, h_{in}\} \cdot g + l$ steps. The total time required for a BSP computation is easily obtained by adding the times for each of the S supersteps. This will produce an expression of the form $W + H \cdot g + S \cdot l$ where W, H, S will typically be functions of n and p. In designing an efficient BSP algorithm or program for a problem which can be solved sequentially in time $T(n)$ our goal will, in general, be to produce an algorithm requiring total time $W + H \cdot g + S \cdot l$ where $W(n,p) = T(n)/p$, $H(n,p)$ and $S(n,p)$ are as small as possible, and the range of values for p is as large as possible. In many cases, this will require that we carefully arrange the data distribution so as to minimise the frequency of remote memory references.

4 BSP Algorithm Design

To illustrate a number of the important issues in BSP algorithm design we will consider several computational problems involving matrices.

4.1 Dense Matrix-Vector Multiplication

In this section we consider the problem of multiplying an $n \times n$ matrix M by an n-element vector v on p processors, where M, v are both dense. In [3], the BSP cost of this problem, for both sparse and dense matrices, was theoretically and experimentally analysed. The BSP algorithm which we now describe was shown there. Its complexity is $n^2/p + (n/p^{1/2}) \cdot g + l$. [Throughout this paper we will omit the various small constant factors in such formulae.]

For dense M and $p \leq n$, the standard n^2 sequential algorithm can be adapted to run on a p processor BSP machine as follows. The matrix elements are initially distributed uniformly across the p processors, with each processor holding an $n/p^{1/2} \times n/p^{1/2}$ submatrix of M. [In [3] this is referred to as a "block-block" distribution.] The vectors u and v are also uniformly distributed across the machine, with n/p elements of u, and n/p elements of v, allocated to each processor. In the first superstep, each processor gets the set of all $n/p^{1/2}$ vector elements v_j for which it holds an $m_{i,j}$. The cost of this step is $(n/p^{1/2}) \cdot g + l$. In the second superstep, each processor k computes $u_i^k = \sum_{a \leq j < a+n/p^{1/2}} m_{i,j} \cdot v_j$ for each of the $n/p^{1/2}$ subrows of M which it holds, and sends the partial sum u_i^k to the processor which holds u_i. The time required for this step is $n^2/p + (n/p^{1/2}) \cdot g + l$. In the third and final superstep, each processor computes the value of each of its vector elements u_i by adding the $p^{1/2}$ values u_i^k which it receives. The time required for this final step is $n/p^{1/2} + l$.

An input-output complexity argument, similar to those in [1, 11], can be used to show that for any BSP algorithm which computes $u = M \cdot v$, if $W(n,p) = n^2/p$ then $H(n,p) \geq n/p^{1/2}$. Noting that the n^2 sequential computation cost is itself optimal we see that the above method is in a strong sense a best possible BSP algorithm for this problem. It simultaneously achieves the optimal computation cost $W(n,p) = n^2/p$, the optimal communication cost $H(n,p) \cdot g = (n/p^{1/2}) \cdot g$ and the optimal synchronisation cost $S(n,p) \cdot l = l$. Other matrix distributions, such as the "block-grid" distribution [3], also give these bounds. [The block-grid distribution is defined as follows. Let $PROC(r,c)$, $0 \leq r, c < p^{1/2}$, denote the p processors. The matrix elements $m_{i,j}$, $0 \leq i, j < n$, are uniformly distributed across the processors, with $m_{i,j}$ allocated to $PROC(i \textbf{ div } (n/p^{1/2}), j \bmod p^{1/2})$.]

4.2   Matrix Multiplication

We now consider the problem of multiplying two $n \times n$ dense matrices A, B on p processors. For $p \leq n^2$, the standard n^3 sequential algorithm can be adapted to run on a p processor BSP machine as follows. Each processor computes an $(n/p^{1/2}) \times (n/p^{1/2})$ submatrix of $C = A \cdot B$. To do so it will require $n^2/p^{1/2}$ elements from A and the same number from B. If A and B are both distributed uniformly across the p processors, with each processor holding n^2/p of the elements from each matrix, then the total time required for this algorithm will be $n^3/p + (n^2/p^{1/2}) \cdot g + l$.

We now describe a more efficient BSP implementation of the standard n^3 algorithm, due to the author and L. G. Valiant. Its BSP complexity is $n^3/p + (n^2/p^{2/3}) \cdot g + l$. As in the previous algorithm we begin with A, B distributed uniformly but arbitrarily across the p processors. At the end of the computation, the n^2 elements of C should also be distributed uniformly across the p processors. Let $s = n/p^{1/3}$ and $A[i,j]$ denote the $s \times s$ submatrix of A consisting of the elements $a_{\hat{i},\hat{j}}$ where $\hat{i} \textbf{ div } s = i$ and $\hat{j} \textbf{ div } s = j$. Define $B[i,j]$ and $C[i,j]$ similarly. Then we have $C[i,j] = \sum_{0 \leq k < p^{1/3}} A[i,k] \cdot B[k,j]$. Let $PROC(i,j,k)$, $0 \leq i, j, k < p^{1/3}$, denote the p processors.

In the first superstep each processor $PROC(i,j,k)$ gets the set of elements in $A[i,j]$ and those in $B[j,k]$. The cost of this step is $(n^2/p^{2/3}) \cdot g + l$. In the second superstep $PROC(i,j,k)$ computes $A[i,j] \cdot B[j,k]$ and sends each one of the $n^2/p^{2/3}$ resulting values to the unique processor which is responsible for computing the corresponding value in C. The cost of this step is $n^3/p + (n^2/p^{2/3}) \cdot g + l$. In the final superstep, each processor computes each of its n^2/p elements of C by adding the $p^{1/3}$ values received for that element. The cost of this step is $n^2/p^{2/3} + l$.

An input-output complexity argument can also be used to show that for any BSP implementation of the standard n^3 sequential algorithm, if $W(n,p) = n^3/p$ then $H(n,p) \geq n^2/p^{2/3}$. The above algorithm is therefore a best possible BSP implementation of the standard n^3 method in the sense that it simultaneously achieves the optimal values for $W(n,p)$, $H(n,p)$ and $S(n,p)$.

4.3   LU Decomposition

Many static computations can be conveniently modeled by directed acyclic graphs, where each node corresponds to some simple operation, and the arcs correspond to inputs and outputs. Let C_n denote the directed acyclic graph which has n^3 nodes $v_{i,j,k}$, $0 \leq i,j,k < n$, and arcs from $v_{i,j,k}$ to $v_{i+1,j,k}$, $v_{i,j+1,k}$ and $v_{i,j,k+1}$ where those nodes exist. In [14] it is shown that the LU decomposition of an $n \times n$ non-singular matrix A can be computed (without pivoting) using the following set of definitions: For all $0 \leq k \leq i, j < n$,

$$u_{k,k,k} = a_{k,k,k-1}$$
$$l_{i,j,k} = a_{i,j,k-1}/u_{i,j,k} \text{ if } j = k, \text{ and } l_{i,j-1,k} \text{ otherwise.}$$
$$u_{i,j,k} = a_{i,j,k-1} \text{ if } i = k, \text{ and } u_{i-1,j,k} \text{ otherwise.}$$
$$a_{i,j,k} = a_{i,j,k-1} - (l_{i,j,k} \cdot u_{i,j,k})$$

where $a_{i,j,-1} = a_{i,j}$. These definitions can be directly translated into a directed acyclic graph which is a subgraph of C_n. Therefore, to produce a BSP algorithm for LU decomposition it is sufficient to schedule C_n for a p processor BSP computer. We can do this by partitioning C_n into $p^{3/2}$ subgraphs, each of which is isomorphic to $C_{n/p^{1/2}}$.

Let $s = n/p^{1/2}$ and $C^{\hat{i},\hat{j},\hat{k}}$, $0 \leq \hat{i},\hat{j},\hat{k} < p^{1/2}$, denote the subset of s^3 nodes $v_{i,j,k}$ in C_n where $i \text{ div } s = \hat{i}$, $j \text{ div } s = \hat{j}$ and $k \text{ div } s = \hat{k}$. The following simple schedule for C_n requires $3p^{1/2} - 2$ supersteps: During superstep $s(t)$, each $C^{\hat{i},\hat{j},\hat{k}}$ for which $\hat{i} + \hat{j} + \hat{k} = t$ is computed by one of the p processors, with no two of them computed by the same processor. From the structure of C_n it is clear that during a superstep, each processor will receive n^2/p values, send n^2/p values, and perform $n^3/p^{3/2}$ computation steps. The total time required for the BSP implementation of any computation which can be modeled by C_n, such as LU decomposition, is therefore at most $n^3/p + (n^2/p^{1/2}) \cdot g + p^{1/2} \cdot l$.

4.4   Solution of a Triangular Linear System

Let A be an $n \times n$ non-singular, lower triangular matrix, and b be an n-element vector. The linear system $A \cdot x = b$ can be solved by back substitution using the recurrence $x_i = (b_i - \sum_{1 \leq j < i} a_{i,j} \cdot x_j)/a_{i,i}$ for $0 \leq i < n$. As in the case of LU decomposition, we can produce an efficient BSP implementation of back substitution by realising the computation as a directed acyclic graph and then scheduling the graph. Let D_n denote the directed acyclic graph which has n^2 nodes $v_{i,j}$, $0 \leq i, j < n$, and arcs from $v_{i,j}$ to $v_{i+1,j}$ and $v_{i,j+1}$ where those nodes exist. The back substitution recurrence above can be reformulated into the following set of definitions: For all $0 \leq j \leq i < n$,

$$t_{i,i} = (b_i - t_{i,i-1})/a_{i,i}$$
$$t_{i,j} = a_{i,j} \cdot r_{i,j} + t_{i,j-1} \text{ if } i > j$$
$$r_{i,i} = t_{i,i}$$
$$r_{i,j} = r_{i-1,j} \text{ if } i > j$$
$$x_i = t_{i,i}$$

where $t_{i,-1} = 0$. These definitions can be directly translated into a directed acyclic graph which is a subgraph of D_n. The graph D_n can be scheduled for a p processor BSP computer in a very similar manner to that used for C_n. In this case, we partition D_n into p^2 subgraphs, each of which is isomorphic to $D_{n/p}$.

Let $s = n/p$ and $C^{\hat{i},\hat{j}}$, $0 \leq \hat{i}, \hat{j} < p$, denote the set of nodes $v_{i,j}$ in D_n where $i \text{ div } s = \hat{i}$ and $j \text{ div } s = \hat{j}$. The following simple schedule for D_n requires $2p-1$ supersteps: During superstep $s(t)$, each $C^{\hat{i},\hat{j}}$ for which $\hat{i} + \hat{j} = t$ is computed by one of the p processors, with no two of them computed by the same processor. From the structure of D_n it is clear that during a superstep, each processor will receive n/p values, send n/p values, and perform n^2/p^2 computation steps. The total time required for the BSP implementation of any computation which can be modeled by D_n, such as back substitution, is therefore at most $n^2/p + n \cdot g + p \cdot l$.

In some situations, using more processors in a BSP architecture will actually *increase* the runtime. For example, consider a BSP architecture based on a ring, with $l = g = p$. The runtime of our BSP algorithm for the solution of an $n \times n$ triangular linear system will be $n^2/p + np + p^2$. This runtime is minimised when $p = n^{1/2}$. Increasing the number of processors beyond this value will increase the runtime.

4.5   Sparse Matrix-Vector Multiplication

We now return to the problem of computing $u = M \cdot v$. Our interest now is in the case where the matrix M is sparse. Sparse matrix-vector multiplication is a problem of fundamental importance in scientific computing. It is at the heart of many supercomputing applications which use iterative methods to solve very large linear systems. To enable the multiplication to be performed repeatedly with no additional data redistribution we require that the result vector $u = M \cdot v$ should be distributed across the parallel machine in the same way as the input vector v, i.e. the processor holding v_i at the start of the computation should hold u_i at the end of the computation.

Let $C(r,d)$ denote the adjacency matrix of the directed r-ary, d-dimensional hypercube graph. The nodes of this graph form a d-dimensional grid of $n = r^d$ points which are numbered lexicographically. Each node has directed arcs to itself and to its immediate neighbours in each dimension. For the purposes of discussion we will consider just four $n \times n$ sparse matrices. Three of the four are instances of $C(r,d)$. They are: 2D-MESH $= C(n^{1/2}, 2)$, 3D-MESH $= C(n^{1/3}, 3)$ and HYPERCUBE $= C(2, \log n)$. Matrices of this kind are often used to model finite-difference operators in the solution of partial differential equations [3]. The fourth matrix has a random structure in which each row and each column contains four nonzeros. We will refer to it as the EXPANDER matrix. [Note. The value four is not particularly significant. We could have chosen any small integer value greater than one.]

The theoretical and experimental analysis in [3] shows that, compared with random data distributions, matrix-based distributions such as block-grid can offer some reductions in the BSP communication cost $H(n,p)$ of most sparse matrix-vector multiplication problems. It also shows that in many cases, much more significant reductions in $H(n,p)$ can be achieved by using a data distribution based on an efficient decomposition of the underlying graph. For example, the nodes of the 2D-MESH graph can be partitioned into p regions, each of which corresponds to a 2D-MESH on n/p nodes. The corresponding data distribution for matrix elements gives a BSP algorithm for $u = M \cdot v$, where M is the 2D-MESH matrix, with total cost $n/p + (n^{1/2}/p^{1/2}) \cdot g + l$. The same approach, applied to the 3D-MESH matrix, gives a BSP algorithm with total cost $n/p + (n^{2/3}/p^{2/3}) \cdot g + l$ and, applied to the HYPERCUBE matrix, gives a BSP algorithm with total cost $(n \log n)/p + ((n \log p)/p) \cdot g + l$. In each case we minimise the communication cost of the algorithm by partitioning the nodes of the graph into p equal sized subsets in a way which minimises the number of arcs between different subsets. Lower bounds on the efficiency of such partitions can be derived from known isoperimetric inequalities in graph theory, see e.g. [4].

For the EXPANDER matrix, the best upper bound which we have is the trivial one, $n/p + (n/p) \cdot g + l$, which can be obtained by randomly distributing the matrix elements. Techniques similar to those in [12] can be used to show that for the EXPANDER matrix there is no partition of the nodes into p equal sized subsets which gives a value for $H(n,p)$ which is less than the trivial n/p. Therefore, for the EXPANDER matrix, $u = M \cdot v$ is an inherently non-local problem.

5   BSP Programming

Although we have described the BSP computer as an architectural model, one can also view bulk synchrony as a programming discipline. The essence of the BSP approach to parallel programming is the notion of the superstep, in which communication and synchronisation are completely decoupled. A "BSP program" is simply one which proceeds in phases, with the necessary global communications taking place between the phases. This approach to parallel programming is applicable to all kinds of parallel architecture: distributed memory architectures, shared memory multiprocessors, and networks of workstations. It provides a consistent, and very general, framework within which to develop portable software for scalable computing.

Since the early 1980s, message passing based on synchronised point-to-point communication has been the dominant programming approach in the area of parallel computing. What are the advantages of BSP programming over message passing? On heterogeneous parallel architectures, in which the individual nodes are quite varied, the answer is probably that there is not a lot to be gained from the BSP approach. On homogeneous distributed memory architectures with low capacity global communications, the two approaches will be broadly similar in terms of the efficiency which can be achieved. On shared memory architectures and on modern distributed memory architectures with powerful global communications, synchronised message passing is likely to be less efficient than BSP programming, where communication and synchronisation are decoupled. This will be especially true on those modern distributed memory architectures which have hardware support for non-blocking direct remote memory access (1-sided communications). Message passing systems based on pairwise, rather than barrier, synchronisation also suffer from having no simple analytic cost model for performance prediction, and no simple means of examining the global state of a computation for debugging. Comparing it to message passing, the BSP approach offers (a) a higher level of abstraction for the programmer, (b) a cost model for performance analysis and prediction which is simpler and compositional, and (c) more efficient implementations on many machines.

Some message passing systems provide primitives for various specialised communication patterns which arise frequently in message passing programs. These include broadcast, scatter, gather, complete exchange, reduction, scan etc. These standard communication patterns also arise frequently in the design of BSP algorithms. It is important that such structured patterns can be conveniently expressed and efficiently implemented in any BSP programming language, in addition to the more primitive operations such as put and get which generate arbitrary and unstructured communication patterns. The efficient implementation of broadcasting and combining on a BSP architecture is discussed in [23].

Data parallelism is an important niche within the field of scalable computing. A number of interesting programming languages and elegant theories have been developed in support of the data parallel style of programming, see e.g. [19]. The BSP approach, as outlined in this paper, aims to offer a more flexible and general style of programming than is provided by data parallelism. The two approaches are not, however, incompatible in any fundamental way. For some applications, the increased flexibility provided by the BSP approach may not be required and the more limited data parallel style may offer a more attractive and productive setting for parallel software development, since it frees the programmer from having to provide an explicit specification of the various scheduling and memory management aspects of the parallel computation. In such a situation, the BSP cost model can still play an extremely important role in terms of providing an analytic framework for performance prediction of the data parallel program.

In Figure 1 we give a pseudocode version of the BSP algorithm for dense matrix-vector multiplication, where the data distribution is defined to be block-grid. For simplicity we assume that n is a multiple of p, and that p is a perfect square. The assumption of such an ideal match between problem size and machine size is, of course, unrealistic in practice. It does however permit us to give a clear and concise description of the main points of the BSP algorithm and its implementation, without having to give all of the technical details required for the general case. The various non-standard constructs used in the pseudocode are informally described in Figure 2.

Given integers *ndivp*, *sqrtp*.

```
const p = sqrtp^2;
const n = ndivp*p;
const b = n/sqrtp;
const side = 0 .. n-1;
var amem : array [side,side] of real with blocksize [b,b];
view A[i,j] = amem[i,b*(j mod sqrtp)+(j div sqrtp)];
var vmem : array [side,(0 .. sqrtp)] of real with blocksize [ndivp,sqrtp+1];
view v[i] = vmem[i,0];
view vsums[i,j] = vmem[i,j];
par for (i ← 0, b .. n-1 ; j ← 0 .. sqrtp-1)
      at A[i,j];
      const jgroup = j, j+sqrtp .. n-1;
      var t : real;
      get v[k] for k ← jgroup;
      seq for bi ← i .. i+b-1
            t := 0.0;
            seq for bj ← jgroup
                  t := t+A[bi,bj]*v[bj];
            put t in vsums[bi,j+1];
par for k ← 0, ndivp .. n-1
      at v[k];
      seq for w ← k .. k+ndivp-1
            v[w] := 0.0;
            seq for x ← 1 .. sqrtp
                  v[w] := v[w]+vsums[w,x];
```

Fig. 1. *BSP pseudocode for an $n \times n$ matrix vector product on p processors.*

var A : **array** $[(1 .. c*r),(1 .. d*s)]$ **of real with blocksize** $[r,s]$;

> Declares a two-dimensional array A of size $c \cdot r \times d \cdot s$, in which the elements of A are to be partitioned into $c \cdot d$ contiguous blocks, each of size $r \times s$. The storage for each complete block will be allocated on a single processor-memory pair, i.e. a block will not be split across two or more memory modules. The arrangement of the various complete blocks will be made so as to uniformly distribute them across the set of memory modules in the machine.

get $v[i]$ **for** $i \leftarrow 1 .. m$;

> Get a local copy of the variables $v[1], v[2], \ldots, v[m]$ for use in the operations of the next superstep. If variable $v[i]$ is already held locally then the **get** $v[i]$ operation has no effect. [There is an implicit barrier synchronisation after any sequence of **get** statements.] Within a superstep, any attempt to access a value which is not held locally will result in a run-time error.

put u **in** v;

> Put the value of the local variable u in the remote variable v. [This remote write will be completed by the end of the current superstep.]

at v;

> Execute this parallel thread on the processor-memory pair to which the variable v has been allocated. The inclusion of an **at** declaration in a thread is optional.

Fig. 2. Notations used in the BSP pseudocode.

6   BSP Programming Languages

We noted above that the BSP model was not prescriptive in terms of the physical architectures to which it applies. It is also not prescriptive in terms of the programming languages and programming styles to which it applies. In this section we briefly describe a number of the programming languages and libraries which are currently available to support BSP programming, and some which are currently under development.

The PVM message passing library [8] is widely implemented and widely used. The MPI message passing interface [16] is more elaborate. It supports blocking and non-blocking point-to-point communication and a number of collective communications (broadcast, scatter, gather, reduction etc.). Although neither of these libraries is directly aimed at supporting BSP programming, they can be used for that purpose.

The Oxford BSP Library [17] consists of a set of subroutines which can be called from standard sequential languages such as Fortran and C. The core of the Library consists of just six routines: bsp_start, bsp_finish, bsp_sstep, bsp_sstep_end, bsp_fetch and bsp_store. The first two are for process management, the next two are for barrier synchronisation, and the last two are for communication. Higher level operations such as broadcast and reduction are also available. The Library supports a static SPMD style of BSP programming. It has been implemented on a large number of machines and is being used by a growing community of applications developers to produce source codes which run unchanged and efficiently on a wide variety of parallel and distributed systems. Generic versions of the Library are freely available by ftp to run on any homogeneous parallel UNIX machine with at least one of: PVM, PARMACS, TCP/IP, or System V Shared Memory primitives. Highly optimised native implementations have been produced for the IBM SP1/SP2, the SGI Power Challenge, the CRAY T3D and other machines. Some preliminary benchmarking studies have also been carried out for these systems, to estimate the values of l and g which a programmer using the native implementation should expect.

GPL is a new programming language for scalable computing. It is being developed at Oxford by the author and Quentin Miller as part of ESPRIT Project 9072 - GEPPCOM (Foundations of General Purpose Parallel Computing). The first prototype compiler is currently operational. A preliminary description of some of the ideas behind this work can be found in [15]. The language is designed to permit the efficient, high level programming of static and dynamic BSP computations, and to permit the performance of those programs to be accurately analysed and predicted. The notations used in the pseudocode example above are similar in style to those of GPL. The language is procedural, explicitly parallel and strongly-typed. It allows the programmer to explicitly control scheduling, synchronisation, memory management, combining and other properties of a program which may be crucial to achieving efficient, scalable and predictable performance while retaining portability. For example, if run on a BSP architecture, the program will have access to constants G, P and L corresponding to the BSP parameters of the machine. The program can use these to optimise the computation. In a multiuser system, the constants might be supplied by the operating system at run time. [At some point in the future of BSP computing it may also become customary for applications programs to assist in optimising resource allocation on multiuser multiprocessors by indicating to the operating system the p, g and l resources that it could efficiently utilise (or cope with!). For example, the dense matrix-vector multiplication code in the previous section might contain a declaration indicating $p_{max} = n$, $g_{max} = n/p^{1/2}$ and $l_{max} = n^2/p$ in some way.] As with any language for high performance programming, a key requirement of the GPL language and its implementations is that there should be an accurate cost model which will be applicable to any implementation of the language. With a reliable cost model of this kind, the programmer will be able to make appropriate design decisions to achieve the highest possible performance.

Split-C [7] is a parallel extension of C which supports efficient access to a global address space on current distributed memory architectures. Like GPL, it aims to support careful engineering and optimisation of portable parallel programs by providing a cost model for performance prediction. The language extension is based on a small set of global access primitives and simple memory management declarations which support both bulk synchronous and message driven styles of parallel programming.

BSP-L [6] is an experimental BSP programming language under development at Harvard. The language is being used to explore the effectiveness of various constructs which might be added to conventional languages such as Fortran and C to support BSP programming. An important objective of this work is to reach a much better understanding of the issues involved in designing optimising compilers and efficient run time systems for programming languages based on the BSP model.

7 Challenges

The study of BSP program design has only recently begun. In contrast to sequential computing, we do not yet have well developed techniques, tools and methodologies for dealing with the specification, refinement, transformation, verification, modularity, reusability, fault tolerance, and other important aspects of BSP programs. Nor do we have a blueprint for the development of a high performance operating system for multiuser BSP computers. These, and many other problems, remain challenges for the future of scalable computing.

References

1. A. Aggarwal, A. K. Chandra, and M. Snir. Communication complexity of PRAMs. *Theoretical Computer Science*, 71:3–28, 1990.
2. R. H. Arpaci, D. E. Culler, A. Krishnamurthy, S. G. Steinberg, and K. Yelick. Empirical evaluation of the CRAY-T3D: A compiler perspective. In *Proc. 22nd Annual International Symposium on Computer Architecture*, June 1995.
3. R. H. Bisseling and W. F. McColl. Scientific computing on bulk synchronous parallel architectures. Technical Report 836, Dept. of Mathematics, University of Utrecht, December 1993. Short version appears in Proc. 13th IFIP World Computer Congress. Volume I (1994), B. Pehrson and I. Simon, Eds., Elsevier, pp. 509-514.
4. B. Bollobás. *Random Graphs*. Academic Press, 1985.
5. A. W. Burks, H. H. Goldstine, and J. von Neumann. *Preliminary discussion of the logical design of an electronic computing instrument. Part 1, Volume 1*. The Institute of Advanced Study, Princeton, 1946. Report to the U.S. Army Ordnance Department. First edition, 28 June 1946. Second edition, 2 September 1947. Also appears in *Papers of John von Neumann on Computing and Computer Theory*, W. Aspray and A. Burks, editors. Volume 12 in the Charles Babbage Institute Reprint Series for the History of Computing, MIT Press, 1987, 97-142.
6. T. Cheatham, A. Fahmy, D. C. Stefanescu, and L. G. Valiant. Bulk synchronous parallel computing - a paradigm for transportable software. In *Proc. 28th Hawaii International Conference on System Science*, January 1995.
7. D. E. Culler, A. Dusseau, S. C. Goldstein, A. Krishnamurthy, S. Lumetta, T. von Eicken, and K. Yelick. Parallel programming in Split-C. In *Proc. Supercomputing '93*, pages 262–273, November 1993.
8. A. Geist, A. Beguelin, J. Dongarra, W. Jiang, R. Manchek, and V. Sunderam. *PVM: Parallel Virtual Machine - A Users' Guide and Tutorial for Networked Parallel Computing*. MIT Press, Cambridge, MA, 1994.
9. M. Gereb-Graus and T. Tsantilas. Efficient optical communication in parallel computers. In *Proc. 4th Annual ACM Symposium on Parallel Algorithms and Architectures*, pages 41–48, 1992.

10. A. M. Gibbons and P. Spirakis, editors. *Lectures on Parallel Computation*, volume 4 of *Cambridge International Series on Parallel Computation*. Cambridge University Press, Cambridge, UK, 1993.

11. J. W. Hong and H. T. Kung. I/O complexity: The red-blue pebble game. In *Proc. 13th Annual ACM Symposium on Theory of Computing*, pages 326–333, 1981.

12. G. Manzini. Sparse matrix vector multiplication on distributed architectures: Lower bounds and average complexity results. *Inform. Process. Lett.*, 50(5):231–238, June 1994.

13. W. F. McColl. General purpose parallel computing. In Gibbons and Spirakis [10], pages 337–391.

14. W. F. McColl. Special purpose parallel computing. In Gibbons and Spirakis [10], pages 261–336.

15. W. F. McColl. BSP programming. In G. E. Blelloch, K. M. Chandy, and S. Jagannathan, editors, *Specification of Parallel Algorithms. Proc. DIMACS Workshop, Princeton, May 9-11, 1994*, volume 18 of *DIMACS Series in Discrete Mathematics and Theoretical Computer Science*, pages 21–35. American Mathematical Society, 1994.

16. Message Passing Interface Forum. MPI: A message-passing interface standard. Technical report, May 1994.

17. R. Miller. A library for bulk-synchronous parallel programming. In *Proc. British Computer Society Parallel Processing Specialist Group workshop on General Purpose Parallel Computing*, December 1993. A revised and extended version of this paper is available by anonymous ftp from ftp.comlab.ox.ac.uk in directory /pub/Packages/BSP along with the Oxford BSP Library software distribution.

18. S. Rao, T. Suel, T. Tsantilas, and M. Goudreau. Efficient communication using total-exchange. In *Proc. 9th International Parallel Processing Symposium*, 1995.

19. D. Skillicorn. *Foundations of Parallel Programming*, volume 6 of *Cambridge International Series on Parallel Computation*. Cambridge University Press, Cambridge, UK, 1994.

20. A. M. Turing. On computable numbers, with an application to the Entscheidungsproblem. *Proceedings of the London Mathematical Society. Series 2*, 42:230–265, 1936. Corrections, *ibid.*, 43 (1937), 544-546.

21. L. G. Valiant. A bridging model for parallel computation. *Communications of the ACM*, 33(8):103–111, 1990.

22. L. G. Valiant. General purpose parallel architectures. In J. van Leeuwen, editor, *Handbook of Theoretical Computer Science : Volume A, Algorithms and Complexity*, pages 943–971. North Holland, 1990.

23. L. G. Valiant. A combining mechanism for parallel computers. In F. Meyer auf der Heide, B. Monien, and A. L. Rosenberg, editors, *Parallel Architectures and Their Efficient Use*. Proceedings of the First Heinz Nixdorf Symposium, Paderborn, November 1992. Lecture Notes in Computer Science, Vol. 678, Springer-Verlag, Berlin, 1993, pages 1–10.

Efficient Use of Parallel & Distributed Systems: From Theory to Practice *

Burkhard Monien,[1] Ralf Diekmann,[1] Rainer Feldmann,[1]
Ralf Klasing,[1] Reinhard Lüling,[1] Knut Menzel,[1]
Thomas Römke,[2] Ulf-Peter Schroeder,[1]

[1] Department of Computer Science, University of Paderborn, Germany
[2] Paderborn Center for Parallel Computing (PC²),
University of Paderborn, Germany **

Abstract. This article focuses on principles for the design of efficient
parallel algorithms for distributed memory computing systems. We describe the general trend in the development of architectural properties
and evaluate the state-of-the-art in a number of basic primitives like
graph embedding, partitioning, dynamic load distribution, and communication which are used, to some extent, within all parallel applications.
We discuss possible directions for future work on the design of *universal
basic primitives*, able to perform efficiently on a broad range of parallel
systems and applications, and we also give certain examples of specific
applications which demand specialized basic primitives in order to obtain
efficient parallel implementations. Finally, we show that *programming
frames* can offer a convenient way to encapsulate algorithmic know-how
on applications and basic primitives and to offer this knowledge to non-
specialist users in a very effective way.

1 Introduction

Parallel processing has clearly become a key economic and strategic issue. This is
illustrated by the fact that parallel computers have reached the business market
and by the increasing number of applications in need of this new technology. All
prospective studies agree that high performance computers (HPC) will be based
on parallel architectures in the future [55]. The architectural developments of
HPC systems tend towards systems connecting standardized processors by communication networks of high bandwidth. Strong efforts are put into developing
standards for parallel programming environments which show first results with
the construction of PVM (Parallel Virtual Machine) and the definition of MPI

* This work was partly supported by the EC Esprit Basic Research Action Nr. 7141
(ALCOM II), the EC Human Capital and Mobility Project "Efficient Use of Par-
allel Computers: Architecture, Mapping and Communication", and the DFG Son-
derforschungsbereich 1511 "Massive Parallelität: Algorithmen, Entwurfsmethoden,
Anwendungen".
** WWW: http://www.uni-paderborn.de/fachbereich/AG/monien/index.html

(Message Passing Interface). Fundamental improvements in the design of efficient mechanisms for *basic primitives* like *data placement, dynamic load balancing*, and *communication* could be achieved. Such primitives are used in special instantiations in nearly all parallel programs and efficient solutions for them enable efficient implementations of a large number of applications on distributed memory message passing systems [45].

Considering the current situation, two trends can be observed raising new challenges for future developments:

Irregularly Structured Problems: The current knowledge on basic primitives is sufficient to support the development of efficient parallelizations of many existing sequential algorithms. Regularities of the communication structure can be used to find highly efficient mapping and load balancing strategies. Unfortunately, many of the most advanced sequential algorithms work on highly irregular and sometimes even dynamic data structures. Adaptive solution methods in finite element simulations, for example, use error estimators to refine their underlying data structure at points of special interest. The refinement steps occur unpredictable in time and space. Another example can be found in tree search algorithms where sophisticated cut operations lead to trees of very irregular structure.

Granularity of Parallel Systems: The basic design principle of today's massively parallel computing systems (MPPs) is distributed memory message passing. Existing MPPs differ mainly in the computational power of their nodes and the communication capacity of their interconnection network. The *granularity* of a parallel computing systems can be defined as the relation between the average communication bandwidth of a single processor and its floating point performance (Byte/Flop). The range of granularities found in today's MPPs is broad and it can be expected that the differences will increase as local area networks (LAN) connecting workstations by relatively low-bandwidth communication links will be used as parallel computing platforms in the near future (a number of development projects aim in this direction, the Berkeley NOW Project [48] and the SUN S3.mp [49] are two representatives of these).

Within this article we will give an overview of basic primitives like mapping, load distribution, partitioning, communication, and others which are preconditions for the design of efficient parallel algorithms.

Considering the trends described above, it is necessary to develop basic primitives that are adaptable to the specific granularities of parallel systems and the detailed characteristics of applications. Machine characteristics are usually provided by the operating systems, application characteristics can be provided via parameters by the user. The question of how to automatically extract relevant application parameters is currently unsolved and an active research topic. We call a basic primitive *universal* if it performs efficiently on parallel architectures of different granularity and if it is able to take application characteristics into account. The integration of such primitives into operating systems of parallel machines will simplify the development of efficient and portable parallel software. Nevertheless, there is a tradeoff between the universality of a primitive and its efficiency for a special application. The highest efficiency can, in general, only be reached by specialized primitives. Especially for irregularly structured and dynamic problems like those mentioned above, a number of questions concerning load distribution are still unsolved.

In the following, we will describe the existing techniques for basic primitives and name a number of problems to be solved in order to face the challenges arising from the trends listed above. In Section 2, we will describe some aspects of the state-of-the-art in the areas of *load distribution* and global *communication*. Based on existing techniques we will present some ideas on how to realize universal methods and name a number of general open research problems. Section 3 describes some applications which make use of basic primitives but also cause difficult problems which are currently unsolved. We will show that in some cases specific solutions to load distribution or communication have to be developed. Finally, Section 4 describes a methodology to provide algorithmic knowledge on applications as well as basic primitives to non-experts.

2   Basic Primitives

Basic primitives form an intermediate layer between the operating system of a parallel machine and the application program. They provide functionality for data and process allocation and complex communication protocols like broadcasting, gossiping, and synchronization. Global variables or virtual shared memory which are also partly supported by basic primitives are not considered here.

Basic primitives are very important for the realization of efficient parallel application programs. In recent years, a large number of theoretical and experimental results concerning task mapping and global communication have been published. Most of the work was motivated by practical applications with different requirements which led to a large variety of specialized basic primitives. This is especially true for the problem of mapping program structures onto parallel systems. In the following, we distinguish between *static mapping methods* which are applied before program execution while taking into account information extracted from the application program and *dynamic mapping methods* which are applied during runtime based on accumulated information. Dynamic methods are often used in conjunction with static methods to improve the balancing quality during runtime if more information on the dynamic behavior of an application is available.

Static and dynamic methods are highly dependent on the underlying parallel architecture. To be able to perform theoretical investigations, abstract models of parallel architectures are necessary. Such models have to be as simple as possible but still should express the most important characteristics. Popular examples which take different characteristics into account are the *LogP* model and the *Distributed Memory Model (DMM)* [39]. The *LogP*-model describes the architectural properties of a parallel system by parameters L, for an upper bound on the communication latency, o, for the overhead of injecting a message into the network, g, for the gap between two consecutive message injections, and P, as the number of processors. The DMM describes a parallel computing system by a simple graph with processors as nodes and communication links as edges. It ignores details like message startup times but implicitly contains information on message latency and communication bandwidth (as those can be extracted from the interconnection topology).

In the following, we discuss static and dynamic methods for the load distribution problem as well as some communication primitives.

2.1   Static Load Distribution

Graph Embedding: If the DMM is used for a description of the underlying parallel computing systems, the load distribution problem can be viewed as a graph embedding problem which is to map a guest graph G (the process graph of an application with edges expressing communication demands) onto a host graph H (the processor graph with edges representing the communication resources) assigning each process to a processor and each communication demand in G to a path in H. There exist several well-known cost measures to rate the quality of an embedding (e.g. *load, dilation, congestion*). The *load* of a host node is the number of guest nodes assigned to it. Edge-*dilation* and edge- or node-*congestion* measure the embedding of edges. The dilation is the maximum distance in H an edge of G has to be routed, the congestion is the maximum number of edges from G routed via an arbitrary edge (or node) in H.

Besides an equal load on all processors, minimizing the edge dilation is the primary goal in most of the theoretical work dealing with embeddings. A number of excellent results on mapping popular graphs onto each other were obtained in recent years and research in this area is still ongoing. Bhatt et al. [8] described embeddings of arbitrary binary trees into hypercubes. An alternative construction with smaller dilation was described in [46]. A significant result about embeddings of 2-dimensional grids into hypercubes was obtained by Chan [9]. For a number of further interesting results we refer the reader to [7, 27, 30, 42, 43]. Detailed surveys can be found in [35, 47]. The most relevant results have been put into practice by implementing special mapping tools and incorporating them into operating systems for parallel computers [38, 53]. Using these tools allows a hardware-topology independent implementation of parallel applications which is a basic step towards developing portable parallel software.

New developments in interconnection architectures result in new constraints on the quality of mapping algorithms. With the establishment of dedicated routing networks and the introduction of message pipelining techniques like wormhole routing, the edge dilation plays a minor role. From a practical point of view, the edge-congestion is of larger importance and determines the overall efficiency of an embedding. The development of mapping techniques considering congestion is an interesting research field which raises a large number of currently unsolved problems.

Most of the theoretical work on embeddings considers structured (regular) graphs like grids, hypercubes, trees, etc. An increasing number of applications demand methods dealing with irregular graphs. Meshes resulting from numerical simulation (finite element meshes) or image processing, for example, are highly irregular and do not fit into any of the theoretically defined graph classes. Unfortunately, the general graph embedding problem is intractable, it is *NP*-complete, and efficient heuristics considering load, dilation, and congestion do not exist. A solution, at least from the practical point of view, can be delivered by reducing the problem to the *graph partitioning* problem. We describe this approach in the next section.

The embedding problem becomes even more complex, if it has to be applied in a dynamic way. Adaptive methods in numerical simulation result in dynamically changing graphs, which have to be embedded during runtime of the application. This so-called *dynamic re-embedding problem* will be described in Section 3.2 in more detail. Additional effort has to be put into developing parallel methods for graph embedding and partitioning because these problems occur either as preprocessing and have to be executed quickly, or during runtime of a parallel application. A first parallel approach for embedding grids into grids is presented in [52].

Graph Partitioning: The graph partitioning problem can be viewed as a relaxation of the embedding problem to settings where dilation is no longer considered and congestion only to some extent. The partitioning problem describes the task of clustering an application graph into a number of equal-sized parts (as many as there are processors) minimizing the number of edges crossing the partition boundaries (the *cut-size*). A mapping of clusters to nodes of the processor graph is not considered.

The general *k*-partitioning problem can again be relaxed to the recursive application of a number of bisection steps where the graph is split into two parts minimizing the cut-size. The main advantage of the partitioning problem compared to embedding is the fact that for a number of popular graphs, optimal bisections are known or at least tight bounds do exist [44]. For the general problem, very efficient heuristics exist [16, 22] which can be used to find approximate solutions to the embedding problem. These heuristics are used in many practical applications to map data or processes onto parallel systems [26, 28, 54].

The existing bisection heuristics are divided into *global* (or *construction*) and *local* (or *improvement*) heuristics [26]. Besides special techniques for special applications (e.g. partitioning of FEM meshes [15]), the most powerful global techniques are *Inertial-*, *Spectral-*, and *Geometric*-Partitioning [16, 22, 26, 29] especially if they are combined with edge-contraction schemes [28, 34]. The most efficient local methods are the Kernighan-Lin heuristic (KL) and the *Helpful-Set* heuristic (HS) [16]. Both methods are based on the principle of local search with sophisticated neighborhood relations. Best results can be obtained by a combination of powerful global heuristics determining initial solutions with powerful local methods used as additional "clean-up" [28].

Most of the existing partitioning heuristics minimize the cut-size. First attempts have been made to take the number of hops, i.e. the dilation, into account, if the clustered graph is mapped onto a hypercube network [26, 29]. This is a first step towards considering architectural parameters of the target machine and further work is needed in this direction.

Other new directions of work are motivated by the *LogP* model. Considering this model, the minimization of the cut-size may not always lead to optimal solutions if the message startup time dominates the communication costs. In this case, it may be much more efficient to minimize the degree of the cluster graph, thus reducing the overall startup times. Future work should be done to develop universal algorithms taking the parameters of the *LogP* model into account.

2.2 Dynamic Load Distribution

The *dynamic load distribution problem* has to be solved, if load packets (processes or data packets) are not initially available but generated dynamically during runtime in an unpredictable way. The task of a load distribution algorithm is to assign these dynamically generated load items onto the processor network.

The load distribution problem has a number of variations depending on the special characteristic of the application. We distinguish load distribution algorithms according to the way they take communication dependencies between load packets into account and according to the way packets are treated during runtime, i.e. whether they can be migrated after an initial placement or not.

Two load distribution problems which do not allow any migration of load packets are the *dynamic mapping* and the *dynamic embedding* problem. Whereas the dynamic mapping problem treats all load packets independently and places them as they are generated, dynamic embedding methods take communication dependencies into account. The latter problem has been analyzed theoretically for dynamically growing trees as guest graphs and hypercube-like host graphs [36, 51]. The practical relevance of the techniques used in these papers is limited as locality is not considered.

Dynamic load distribution algorithms for *uncoupled* load packets (i.e. load packets without any communication interaction between each other) that are allowed to be migrated during runtime are used in a large number of applications [45]. The two basic problems which are considered here are the *load balancing* problem and the *load sharing* problem. The load balancing problem typically arises if the load packets have to be balanced according to some cost measure. As an example one might consider different priorities assigned to load packets (jobs). In this case it is necessary to assign the workload onto the processors in such a way that all processors work on jobs with highest priority, thus the overall workload has to be balanced according to this measure. The load sharing problem does not consider the relative load of any two processors but aims at providing some load to all processors during runtime. Due to their general nature, load balancing and load sharing methods can be found in most application programs implemented on parallel systems.

Despite this large knowledge on load balancing and sharing, the theoretical foundation of these methods is still very weak. Some attempts have been made to overcome this problem using simplified models. The so-called *token distribution problem* can be regarded as an abstraction of the load balancing problem. In this setting, the overall load is assumed to be fixed. The task is to balance the workload in a minimal number of communication steps. A large number of results for different graphs and various specific settings have been found. For an overview and references of other results see [24]. The analysis of practical load balancing algorithms is an active research area. Up to know, only very few results are available [3, 37]. Improvements in this area, combined with a better understanding of the applications' requirements can lead to new, more universal algorithms. This is extremely important as most methods used today are tailored to a special application on a fixed parallel system.

Recently, a first attempt towards a universal load distribution method for the dynamic mapping problem was made. In this method a processor that needs to place a load packet asks a number of k randomly chosen other processors for their load and relays the task to the one with the minimal load. Considering the amount of work associated with each task as constant, the question is how to find an optimal number of k for a given application (described by the total number of tasks to be placed) and a given hardware characteristic. Thus, the tradeoff between the balancing quality and the time for getting k sets of load information has to be optimized.

The asymptotic properties of this algorithm were investigated recently by Azar et al. [2]. They showed that, compared to a random placement ($k = 1$), even the case of $k = 2$ results in an exponential decrease of the maximum load on a single processor (more precisely, they showed that the most heavily loaded processor receives $log\ log\ n/log\ k + \Theta(1)$ packets with high probability, if n is the number of packets). Adler et al. [1] extended the result to cases where more than one task can be placed in each time step. An algorithm to compute the best k for a given n and known hardware characteristic was described in [14]. Knowing optimal values for k, it is possible to incorporate this knowledge into the runtime environment of a parallel system allowing optimal mapping decisions with respect to the architecture and the application.

2.3   Communication

A number of communication problems in networks have been considered. Among the most important ones are the routing of information (resp. permutations), sorting [35], and, generally, the dissemination of information. We concentrate on the most frequently studied problems connected with the dissemination of information in networks: *broadcasting, accumulation, and gossiping.* For *broadcasting,* one processor has some piece of information and has to distribute it as soon as possible to all processors in the network. For *accumulation,* all processors have a piece of information and the problem consists of collecting all the pieces of information in a single processor. For *gossiping,* all processors have a piece of information and the problem is to make all the pieces of information known to all processors as soon as possible.

In the basic communication model, a *communication algorithm* consists of a sequence of *communication rounds*. The rules describing what can happen in one communication round are defined by the *communication mode*. The *cost measure* usually considered is the number of rounds of the communication algorithm. Detailed surveys about the most frequently studied communication problems and models of communication can be found in [19, 20, 32].

So far, most of the work has been focussed on the *standard (one-way or two-way) communication mode*, where in each round messages can be sent to exactly one neighbor in the network. An overview of the main results in this area is contained in [32].

The most practically oriented communication modes are the *vertex- and edge-disjoint paths* modes [33] where, each round, the processors can communicate via vertex- or edge-disjoint paths. These communication modes can actually be implemented on several existing parallel architectures. Optimal accumulation and broadcast algorithms in these communication modes have been derived. Tight upper and lower bounds for gossiping in common interconnection networks like hypercubes, cube-connected cycles, butterfly networks, and grids have also been achieved. Finally, a direct relationship between the gossip complexity and the vertex- or edge-bisection width of the considered graph has been established. Closely related to the gossip problem in the vertex- or edge-disjoint paths mode is the investigation of the size of planar and non-planar realizations of permutation networks for special sets of permutations which are of high practical relevance. Such classes of special permutations are, for example, the shifts of power 2 or the Fibonacci shifts as investigated in [31].

In the future, the existing theoretical and experimental results on classical switching techniques will have to be extended to include new network structures (e.g. hierarchical networks), to embrace new message passing standards (e.g. ATM), and to consider new technologies (e.g. optical networks) and routing algorithms (e.g. compact-, deflection-, all-optical-, or wormhole routing). The question of fault-tolerance in larger, hierarchical, and unstable networks will obtain increasing importance.

3   Applications

Basic primitives as they are available today and described above offer solutions for a broad range of applications. Considering the trend towards highly irregular and dynamic data structures, new and more sophisticated basic primitives for load distribution purposes have to be developed. In the following, we describe two application areas that require such methods and present some concrete open questions for further research.

3.1   Tree-Structured Problems

Tree search algorithms have been shown to be very effective for a large number
of applications in operations research and artificial intelligence. Due to the exponential growth of the tree in many applications, parallel search algorithms can
lead to substantial improvements in these areas. Therefore, the parallelization
of tree search algorithms is an important question that has gained considerable
attention over the last few years. In the following, we will consider the search in
OR trees and game trees (AND-OR trees) as two examples for tree-structured
search problems. There exist a number of algorithms for both kind of searches.
Popular examples are "best-first branch & bound" (B&B) for the OR tree search
and the α-β algorithm for the game tree search.

Common to both algorithms is that they build dynamically growing trees
during their runtime. These trees have to be mapped onto the processors of a
parallel computing system. Thus, a dynamic load distribution problem has to be
solved. In parallel B&B every processor keeps a local heap with its subproblems
ordered according to their bounds. These subproblems can be solved independently of each other. The load balancing has to make sure that the tops of the
heaps contain relevant subproblems at all processors. This is done by weighting
the subproblems according to their bound function value and then balancing
the work load in such a way that the best subproblems at all processors have
almost equal bounds. Using some sophisticated load balancing strategies, it is
then possible to achieve large speedups for hard optimization problems even on
architectures of up to 1024 processors [57]. There is a tradeoff between work
load and communication costs necessary to balance the work. In addition, the
load balancing policy has a strong impact on the number of nodes evaluated by
the parallel algorithm compared to those evaluated by the sequential one. It is
possible that processors explore nodes of the tree that would never be explored
in the sequential case. In this case, we say that *search overhead* arises.

The situation is even more challenging in α-β search: In contrast to B&B,
there are strong dependencies between the nodes of the search tree since the value
of any inner node is defined to be the maximum over the values of its successors.
Thus, an inner node cannot be solved unless its successors are solved. Moreover,
the search of a single successor may result in a bound for the inner node allowing
to cut off the other successors because they are known to be irrelevant for the final
result. This is meaningful for any parallel game tree search algorithm because
a parallel search of the successors may result in very large search overhead. In
addition, as a consequence of these cutoffs the search trees are irregular and their
size is unpredictable. The load balancing method, again, has a strong impact on
the work done by the parallel algorithm. There is a tradeoff between work load
and search overhead. To reduce the search overhead the so-called *Young Brothers
Wait Concept (*YBWC*)* has been introduced in [17]. It is based on the concept
that the successors of a node may not be searched in parallel unless the first
successor is already evaluated. Thus, idle processors may stay idle instead of
searching possibly irrelevant subtrees. However, the YBWC poses a challenging
task to the load balancing algorithm: Only a single node is active whenever any

node on the leftmost path is evaluated. Repeated redistribution of work load is necessary at these synchronization nodes. Here, a workstealing algorithm [3] provides very good results.

As for B&B, there is again a tradeoff between work load and communication costs of the load balancing. In parallel α-β search there is another tradeoff between search overhead and communication costs completing the tradeoff triangle. The sequential α-β algorithm uses a hash table containing previously computed results. This table is used to detect transpositions of moves and to avoid searches in irrelevant subtrees. In a parallel environment, local hash tables perform poorly. Thus, a distributed hash table has to be implemented. The accesses to the distributed hash table have to be done by routing messages between processors. Thus, frequent access to the hash table decreases the search overhead but increases the communication costs. Accessing the table only rarely results in small communication costs. The search overhead, however, increases.

In [18], the integration of these techniques into a chess program is described. It was found out that the methods lead to very good results if the basic primitives (load balancing and simulation of a global hash table) are highly optimized for the underlying machines. It can be expected for the future, when more and more advanced search techniques will be used, that the search trees become very sparse and left-weighted. Since these search trees will have to be searched with the YBWC or anything similar in effect, the load balancing problems will become still more involved. There will also be the need for a faster emulation of global memory. This will allow a more frequent access to the distributed hash table, which significantly reduces the search overhead. Moreover, large databases providing perfect play in the endgame may be cached into the distributed memory and accessed in a way similar to the transposition table access. Using a fast emulation of global memory, the chess program will then be able to direct its play from the late middle game into favorable endgames.

Load distribution problems which are tailored to the special characteristic of the application problem also arise for the solution of combinatorial optimization problem using Branch & Cut techniques. The success of these techniques is mainly based on powerful cutting plane algorithms. Such an algorithm can limit the number of nodes in the branching tree considerably. Now, the most time demanding step consists of repeated solutions of linear programs. In general, a parallelization of the method that assigns nodes of the branching tree to single processing elements cannot effectively utilize all processing elements of a massively parallel computer. Therefore, algorithms have to be developed that solve linear programming problems in parallel. First attempts have been made in this direction [25] but it is a very difficult task to achieve high efficiencies with algorithms solving large sparse systems of linear equations.

3.2 Mesh-Based Problems

In this section, we consider applications from the fields of numerical simulation (finite element methods and comparable techniques [59]) and parallel computer graphics (raytracing and radiosity methods [41, 50, 56]). Common to such applications is the underlying mesh-type data structure. Two basic problems have to be faced: The first is the generation of the mesh, the second is the distribution of the mesh onto the parallel architecture.

The problem of generating sufficiently accurate meshes is a very crucial step in both areas. Especially for certain numerical methods the meshes should contain as few elements as possible and approximate the domain as well as possible. Additionally, there are strong conditions on the shape of individual elements influencing the numerical efficiency considerably [23]. Automatically generating high quality meshes in complex domains is currently an unsolved problem. The importance of this problem is highlighted by the estimation that "the US industry would be able to save up to 75% of their budget spent for FEM simulations if automatic mesh generators were available"[11]. The problem becomes even more involved as in future applications the mesh generation would have to consider parallel solvers (i.e. it should generate "partitionable" meshes) and adaptivity (i.e. possibilities to refine the mesh). In addition it is supposed to run in parallel itself.

The parallelization of an algorithm based on a mesh-type data structure is done by data distribution using domain decomposition (DD) techniques [15]. The mesh is split into as many subdomains as there are processors. Techniques to partition and map the mesh can to some extent be based on universal basic primitives. For the most advanced parallel solution algorithms, however, the application structure as well as the algorithmic structure of the solvers have to be considered. We will see this in the following.

Numerical Simulation: Currently, the most efficient parallel solvers in the area of FEM are adaptive multigrid methods (MG) or adaptive preconditioned conjugate gradient methods (PCG). Unfortunately, there is a tradeoff between the efficiency of numerical solvers and the utilization of parallel machines. The most advanced preconditioning methods stipulate strong conditions on the quality of domain decompositions and adaptive refinement techniques cause difficult load balancing problems. Graph partitioning methods used to calculate decompositions have to consider not only load distribution and communication requirements but also the shape of subdomains. Important measures are in this case the *aspect ratio* of subdomains, which can be expressed by the ratio between the size of the largest inner circle (or ball) to the smallest outer circle (or ball), and the *convexity* of a domain [15]. The shape of subdomains can be one of the main determining factors for the convergence behavior of a parallel PCG, thus influencing the numerical efficiency considerably.

Especially in case of instationary problems (e.g. in computational fluid dynamics), adaptive methods are the best possibility for reducing computational complexity and obtaining best numerical efficiency [5]. Using error estimators, regions of the domain are identified where the solution is not exact enough and the convergence is very slow. Mesh refinement is then used to increase the convergence behavior locally. Considering instationary problems the problematic regions may move or change. In this case, the error estimators can also give hints where to coarsen the mesh preserving both numerical efficiency and proper convergence.

In case of parallel simulations, such adaptive methods cause a very complex combination of mapping and load balancing problems. Directly after a refinement or coarsening, the decomposition has to be balanced again, taking the locations of elements into account (i.e. newly generated elements cannot be moved to arbitrary processors but should reside in the neighborhood of other elements). First theoretical investigations show that even very simple cases of mapping refining graphs are very hard. Heuristics solving the problem have to be efficient in both their solution quality and their computation time and they have to run in parallel.

Computer Graphics: From the field of computer graphics we consider the photorealistic animation of 3D scenes. Techniques based on the simulation of light energy distributions are characterized by high computational complexity and extraordinary memory requirements which lead to problems in data management and load distribution. To overcome these problems, the data has to be accessed using a shared memory approach or all the data has to be distributed among the processors. In the latter case the distribution can either be done according to the objects' geometric position (cells, octtrees) or according to memory paging techniques [6, 41, 56]. However, as raytracing and radiosity compute the global illumination of scenes, the major problem is that each processing node needs to have access to a significant part of the scene. The resulting load distribution problems have to be solved either by using static methods in a preprocessing step or by applying dynamic strategies during runtime [37, 41]. As raytracing fulfills the coherence properties, load balancing strategies used in this context have to take these geometric properties into account. However, dynamic load distribution strategies provide a powerful mechanism in case the load of processing nodes varies during the computation which is in particular given if interactions with the scene are allowed as it is the case in "Virtual Reality" applications [21, 58].

Future applications of image generation demand for highest quality animation of complex 3D scenes. To meet online or even realtime requirements, scalable parallelization strategies have to be developed which allow the effective use of large MPPs. Therefore, research has to focus on the improvement of load balancing strategies following the previously mentioned conditions. Additionally, work has to be done to efficiently provide shared memory on MPPs, because for many computer graphics applications it is advantageous to enable all processors the access of a common memory.

4   Programming Frames

As the programming of parallel computing architectures is fundamentally different from that of sequential systems, new ways have to be found to transfer know-how on efficient parallel algorithms to the development of application programs. A possible way for this can be the development of libraries of basic algorithms, data structures, and *programming frames* (templates). As the LEDA system for the sequential case [40], each of these approaches provides non-expert users with tools to program and exploit parallel machines efficiently.

Some attempts have already been made to provide knowledge on specific parallel applications or basic primitives [4, 10, 12, 13] by use of programming frames. Programming frames as we understand them here are parallel programs that can be parameterized in a very general way. It is, for example, possible to take sequential functions or complete sequential programs as parameters for a programming frame. So-called *basic frames* contain knowledge on universal basic primitives that can be customized for a special application or target machine. Problem dependent frames contain the harness for a parallel program in a special application area. As an example, consider a frame for a parallel branch & bound application. This frame has at least three parameters, one for each of the branching and bounding algorithms and one for the target system. A user of this frame has to specify these sequential functions and will get an efficient application program. Special know-how on load balancing and distributed termination detection being necessary for parallel branch & bound, is already integrated into the frame. Using universal basic primitives it is also possible to adapt this frame to the special characteristics of the target machine using the parameters of the target system. Thus, all details of the parallel implementation are hidden. Programming frames used in this way are a direct consequence of universal basic primitives as they basically rely on universal primitives and make them usable in a very general sense.

Until now, none of the existing approaches has been designed to provide frameworks for several algorithms and for different target machines at the same time and none of them has led to a standardization. Thus, active research is necessary to accumulate and generalize algorithmic know-how on application problems and to develop universal basic primitives which can be incorporated into programming frames.

References

1. M. Adler, S. Chakrabarti, M. Mitzenmacher, L. Rasmussen: Parallel Randomized Load Balancing. *Proc. 27th Annual ACM Symp. on Theory of Computing (STOC '95)*, 1995.
2. Y. Azar, A.Z. Broder, A.R. Karlin, E. Upfal: Balanced Allocations. *Proc. 25th Annual ACM Symp. on Theory of Computing (STOC '93)*, pp. 593-602, 1993.
3. R. Blumofe, C.E. Leiserson: Scheduling Multithreaded Computations by Work Stealing. *Proc. 35th Annual IEEE Symp. on Foundations of Computer Science (FOCS '94)*, pp. 356-368, 1994.
4. R. Barret, M. Berry, T. Chan, J. Demmel, J. Donato, J. Dongarra, V. Eijkhout, R. Pozo, C. Romine, H. van der Vorst: *TEMPLATES for the Solution of Linear Systems: Building Blocks for Iterative Methods.* Tech. Rep., CS-Dept., Univ. of Tennessee, 1993. WWW: http://www.netlib.org/templates/templates.ps

5. F. Bornemann, B. Erdmann, R. Kornhuber: Adaptive Multilevel Methods in Three Space Dimensions. *Int. J. on Num. Meth. in Engineering* (36), pp. 3187-3203, 1993.
6. J. Buriánek, A. Holeček, K. Menzel, J. Přikryl, J. Žára: Load Balancing for Parallel Environment on Virtual Walls. accepted for the *Winter School of Computer Graphics and CAD Systems*, Pilsen, Czech Republic, 1995.
7. S. Bhatt, F. Chung, J. Hong, T. Leighton, B. Obrenic, A. Rosenberg, E. Schwabe: Optimal Emulations by Butterfly-like Networks. *J. of the ACM*, to appear. (A preliminary version, Optimal Simulations by Butterfly Networks, appeared in: *Proc. 20th ACM Symp. on Theory of Computing (STOC '88)*, pp. 192-204, 1988.)
8. S. Bhatt, F. Chung, T. Leighton, A. Rosenberg: Efficient Embeddings of Trees in Hypercubes. *SIAM J. on Computing*, Vol. 21, No. 1, pp. 151-162, 1992. (A preliminary version, Optimal Simulations of Tree Machines, appeared in *Proc. 27th IEEE Symp. on Foundat. of Computer Science (FOCS '86)*, pp. 274-282, 1986.)
9. M.Y. Chan: Embedding of Grids into Optimal Hypercubes. *SIAM J. on Computing*, Vol. 20, No. 5, pp. 834-864, 1991.
10. M. Cole: *Algorithmic Skeletons: Structured Management of Parallel Computation.* PhD, Research Monographs in Par. and Distr. Computing, MIT Press.
11. *The CUBIT Mesh Generation Research Project,* Sandia National Lab 1995, WWW: http://www.cs.sandia.gov/HPCCIT/cubit.html
12. M. Danelutto, R. Di Meglio, S. Orlando, S. Pelagatti, M. Vanneschi: A Methodology for the Development and the Support of Massively Parallel Programs. *J. on Future Generation Computer Systems (FCGS)*, Vol. 8, 1992.
13. J. Darlington, A.J. Field, P.G. Harrison, P.H.J. Kelly, D.W.N. Sharp, Q. Wu: Parallel Programming Using Skeleton Functions. *Proc. of Par. Arch. and Lang. Europe (PARLE '93)*, Lecture Notes in Computer Science No. 694, Springer-Verlag, 1993.
14. T. Decker, R. Diekmann, R. Lüling, B. Monien: Towards Developing Universal Dynamic Mapping Algorithms. *Proc. 7th IEEE Symp. on Parallel and Distributed Processing (SPDP '95)*, 1995, to appear.
15. R. Diekmann, D. Meyer, B. Monien: Parallel Decomposition of Unstructured FEM-Meshes. *Proc. Workshop on Parallel Algorithms for Irregularly Structured Problems (IRREGULAR '95)*, Lecture Notes in Computer Science, Springer-Verlag, 1995, to appear.
16. R. Diekmann, B. Monien, R. Preis: *Using Helpful Sets to Improve Graph Bisections.* Tech. Rep. tr-rf-94-008, Univ. of Paderborn, 1994, and: DIMACS Series in Discrete Mathematics and Theoretical Computer Science, AMS, 1995, to appear.
17. R. Feldmann, B. Monien, P. Mysliwietz, O. Vornberger: Distributed Game-Tree Search. *ICCA Journal*, Vol. 12, No. 2, pp. 65-73, 1989.
18. R. Feldmann: *Game Tree Search on Massively Parallel Systems.* Doctoral Thesis, University of Paderborn, Germany, 1993.
19. P. Fraigniaud, E. Lazard: Methods and problems of communication in usual networks. *Discrete Applied Mathematics*, Vol. 53, No. 1-3, pp. 79-133, 1994.
20. P. Fraigniaud: *Vers un principe de localité pour les communications dans les réseaux d'interconnection.* Habilitation Thesis, ENS Lyon, 1994.
21. W. Furmanski: *SuperComputing and Virtual Reality.* Presented at the Meckler Conference *Virtual Reality '92*, San Jose, Ca, 23-25 Sept, 1992.
22. A. George, J.R. Gilbert, J.W.H. Liu (ed.): *Graph Theory and Sparse Matrix Computations.* The IMA Volumes in Math. and its Appl. No. 56, Springer-Verlag, 1993.
23. P.L. George: *Automatic Mesh Generation.* John Wiley & Sons, 1993.
24. B. Ghosh, F.T. Leighton, B. Maggs S. Muthukrishnan, C.G. Plaxton, R. Rajaraman, A.W. Richa, R.E. Tarjan, D. Zuckerman: Tight Analyses of Two

Local Load Balancing Algorithms. *Proc. 27th Annual ACM Symp. on Theory of Computing (STOC '95)*, pp. 548-558, 1995.

25. A. Gupta, V. Kumar: *A Scalable Parallel Algorithm for Sparse Matrix Factorization*. Tech. Rep. TR 94-19, Dept. of Comp. Science, Univ. of Minnesota, 1994.

26. S.W. Hammond: *Mapping Unstructured Grid Computations to Massively Parallel Computers*. Tech. Rep. 92.14, RIACS, NASA Ames Research Center, 1992.

27. R. Heckmann, R. Klasing, B. Monien, W. Unger: Optimal Embedding of Complete Binary Trees into Lines and Grids. *Proc. 17th Int. Workshop on Graph-Theoretic Concepts in Computer Science (WG '91)*, Lecture Notes in Computer Science No. 570, Springer-Verlag, pp. 25-35, 1991.

28. B. Hendrickson, R. Leland: *The Chaco User's Guide*. Tech. Rep. SAND93-2339, Sandia National Lab., Nov. 1993.

29. B. Hendrickson, R. Leland: An Improved Spectral Graph Partitioning Algorithm for Mapping Parallel Computations. *SIAM J. on Scientific Computing*, Vol. 16, No. 2, pp. 452-469, 1995.

30. M. C. Heydemann, J. Opatrny, D. Sotteau: Embeddings of Hypercubes and Grids into de Bruijn Graphs. *J. of Parallel and Distributed Computing*, Vol. 23, pp. 104-111, 1994.

31. J. Hromkovič, K. Loryś, P. Kanarek, R. Klasing, W. Unger, H. Wagener: On the Sizes of Permutation Networks and Consequences for Efficient Simulation of Hypercube Algorithms on Bounded-Degree Networks. *Proc. 12th Symp. on Theoretical Aspects of Computer Science (STACS '95)*, Lecture Notes in Computer Science No. 900, Springer-Verlag, pp. 255-266, 1995.

32. J. Hromkovič, R. Klasing, B. Monien, R. Peine: *Dissemination of information in interconnection networks (broadcasting and gossiping)*. In: F. Hsu, D.-Z. Du (ed.): *Combinatorial Network Theory*, Kluwer Academic Pub., 1995, to appear.

33. J. Hromkovič, R. Klasing, W. Unger, H. Wagener: Optimal Algorithms for Broadcast and Gossip in the Edge-Disjoint Path Modes. *Proc. 4th Scandinavian Workshop on Algorithm Theory (SWAT '94)*, Lecture Notes in Computer Science No. 824, Springer-Verlag, pp. 219-230, 1994.

34. G. Karypis, V. Kumar: *A Fast and High Quality Multilevel Scheme for Partitioning Irregular Graphs*. Techn. Rep. 95-035, Dept. of Comp. Science, University of Minnesota, 1995.

35. F.T. Leighton: *Introduction to Parallel Algorithms and Architectures*. Morgan Kaufmann Publishers, 1992.

36. T. Leighton, M. Newman, A. Ranade, E. Schwabe: Dynamic Tree Embedding in Butterflies and Hypercubes. *Proc. 1st Annual ACM Symp. on Parallel Algorithms and Architectures (SPAA '89)*, pp. 224-234, 1989.

37. R. Lüling, B. Monien: A Dynamic Distributed Load Balancing Algorithm with Provable Good Performance. *Proc. 5th Annual ACM Symp. on Parallel Algorithms and Architectures (SPAA '93)*, pp. 164-173, 1993.

38. E. Ma, D.G. Shea: The Embedding Kernel on the IBM Victor Multiprocessor for Program Mapping and Network Reconfiguration. *Proc. 2nd IEEE Symp. on Parallel and Distributed Processing (SPDP '90)*, 1990.

39. B.M. Maggs, L.R. Matheson, R.E. Tarjan: Models of Parallel Computation: A Survey and Sythesis. *Proc. 28th Hawaii Int. Conference on System Sciences (HICSS-28)*, Vol. 2, pp. 61-70, 1995.

40. K. Mehlhorn, S. Näher: LEDA, a Library of Efficient Data Types and Algorithms. *Proc. 14th Int. Symp. on Mathem. Foundations of Computer Science (MFCS '89)*, Lecture Notes in Computer Science No. 379, Springer-Verlag, pp. 88-106, 1989.

41. K. Menzel: *Parallel Rendering Techniques for Multiprocessor Systems.* SSCG, Spring School on Computer Graphics, Bratislava, Slovakia, 1994, Comenius University Press, pp. 91-103, 1994.

42. Z. Miller, I.H. Sudborough: Compressing Grids into Small Hypercubes. *NETWORKS*, Vol. 24, pp. 327-358, 1994.

43. B. Monien: Simulating binary trees on X-trees. *Proc. 3rd Annual ACM Symp. on Parallel Algorithms and Architectures (SPAA '91)*, pp. 147-158, 1991.

44. B. Monien, R. Diekmann, R. Lüling: Communication Throughput of Interconnection Networks. *Proc. 19th Int. Symp. on Mathematical Foundations of Computer Science (MFCS '94)*, Lecture Notes in Computer Science No. 841, Springer-Verlag, pp. 72-86, 1994.

45. B. Monien, R. Feldmann, R. Klasing, R. Lüling: Parallel Architectures: Design and Efficient Use. *Proc. 10th Symp. on Theoretical Aspects of Computer Science (STACS '93)*, Lecture Notes in Computer Science No. 665, Springer-Verlag, pp. 247-269, 1993.

46. B. Monien, I.H. Sudborough: Simulating Binary Trees on Hypercubes. *Proc. Aegean Workshop on Computing (AWOC '88)*, Lecture Notes in Computer Science No. 319, Springer-Verlag, pp. 170-180, 1988.

47. B. Monien, I.H. Sudborough: Embedding one Interconnection Network in Another. *Computing Suppl.* 7, pp. 257–282, 1990.

48. *The Berkeley NOW Project.* WWW: http://now.cs.berkeley.edu/

49. A. Nowatzyk: The S3.mp Interconnect System and TIC Chip. in: *Hot Interconnects 93*, Stanford CA, August 1993.

50. W. Purgathofer, M. Feda: Progressive Refinement Radiosity on a Transputer Network. *Proc. 2nd Eurographics Workshop on Rendering*, Barcelona, Spain, 1991.

51. A. Ranade: Optimal Speedup for Backtrack Search on a Butterfly Network. *Proc. 3rd Annual ACM Symp. on Parallel Algorithms and Architectures (SPAA '91)*, pp. 40-48, 1991.

52. T. Römke, M. Röttger, U.-P. Schroeder, J. Simon: On Efficient Embeddings of Grids into Grids in Parix. *Proc. EURO-PAR '95*, Lecture Notes in Computer Science, Springer-Verlag, 1995, to appear.

53. M. Röttger, U.-P. Schroeder, J. Simon: Implementation of a Parallel and Distributed Mapping Kernel for PARIX. *Int. Conference and Exhibition on High-performance Computing and Networking (HPCN Europe '95)*, Lecture Notes in Computer Science No. 919, Springer-Verlag, pp. 781-786, 1995.

54. H.D. Simon: Partitioning of Unstructured Problems for Parallel Processing. *Computing Systems in Engineering* (2), pp. 135-148, 1991.

55. L. Smarr, C.E. Catlett: Metacomputing. *Comm. of the ACM* 35(6), pp. 45-52, 1992.

56. W. Stürzlinger, C. Wild: Parallel Visibility Computations for Parallel Radiosity. *Parallel Processing*, pp. 405-413, 1994.

57. S. Tschöke, R. Lüling, B. Monien: Solving the Traveling Salesman Problem with a Distributed Branch-and-Bound Algorithm on a 1024 Processor Network. *Proc. 9th Int. Parallel Processing Symp. (IPPS '95)*, pp. 182-189, 1995.

58. A.J. West, T.L.J. Howard et al.: *AVIARY: A Generic Virtual Reality Interface for Real Applications.* Virtual Reality Systems, 1992.

59. O.C. Zienkiewicz: *The finite element method.* McGraw-Hill, 1989.

Experimental Validation of Models of Parallel Computation

Lawrence Snyder

University of Washington, Computer Science & Engineering, Seattle WA 98195-2350,
USA

Abstract. The right model of parallel computation must possess various
properties including accurately predicting the behavior of real programs
on physical computers. It is argued that this property must be tested experimentally. Three experiments are reviewed supporting the hypothesis
that the CTA machine model and the Phase Abstractions programming
model predict accurately for real programs on physical computers. Data
for ten MIMD computers is reported. Additionally, basic concepts connected with models of computation are reviewed, and several recently
developed parallel models are critiqued.

1 Introduction

For a decade and a half researchers have focused on formulating a model of
parallel computation suitable for analyzing and designing parallel algorithms,
but the right model remains elusive. The "right" model will, like the RAM model,
capture all and only the significant capabilities and costs of parallel computation,
relegating everything else to "details." Predictions based on the "right" model
will be accurate for real programs executed on physical computers. Moreover,
the "right" model will focus our attention on the critical issues of parallelism,
rather than on some simplifying assumption which, when exploited to the limit,
produces ludicrous results.

The most crucial property of a "right" model—that its predictions be accurate for real programs executed on physical computers—is a requirement that
can and must be demonstrated experimentally. There is little prospect of establishing this property by logical argument from abstract principles, since no
formal characterization exists of either real programs on physical computers.
But, in the absence of evidence that it makes accurate predictions, what serious
interest can there be in either the model, or algorithms developed with it?

Of course, there are numerous problems demonstrating the "accurate predictions" requirement experimentally. First, the condition contains several universal quantifiers which inhibit any direct test: The predictions are to apply to
all programs and *all* physical computers in a broad class. For each program, the
prediction is to be accurate for *all* inputs for *all* numbers of processors, etc. Second, "accurate" is not a binary property, but is a qualitative term, mandating a
certain degree of interpretation. Third, programs must be written in a language,
with a particular syntax, semantics, compiler, run-time system, etc. Since the

model is only an abstraction and the language is the medium for expressing the abstraction's properties, features of the language's implementation may affect the predictions. For example, a poor compiler might introduce unnecessary overheads that "perturb" the predictions. This complicates the evaluation of a model's properties. It is little wonder that parallel models are routinely proposed without support for their predictive capabilities.

But, the fact that it is challenging does not mean the problem is impossible. Indeed, the presence of so many universal quantifiers implies that negative outcomes are extremely valuable. A conceptually simple methodology can yield such evidence: Write programs based on the model, predict properties of the programs using the model, e.g. execution time, run the programs, and observe whether the properties are as predicted. Positive outcomes each yield one data point supporting the predictive qualities of the model. But negative outcomes imply a failure in the model's predictive abilities, contradicting one or more of the universal quantifiers. This can motivate revising or discarding the model. Thus, negative outcomes provide important information to the researcher. Even positive outcomes are for the community a welcome substitute for the fond opinions of the model's inventors.

The PRAM model provides a convenient case to illustrate the use of negative evidence [26]. There exist computations that can be programmed using the PRAM model for which predictions can be made, and for which the "observed" performance on physical computers contradicts that prediction. Specifically, finding the maximum of P integers is predicted to have $O(\log\log P)$ execution time on P processors [33], but the "observed" performance is $\Omega(\log P \log\log P)$ on P processors, contradicting the prediction, assuming a factor of $\log P$ exceeds acceptable accuracy [2]. Thus, the PRAM does not fulfill the "accurate predictions" requirement. Indeed, it is not actually necessary to run this experiment on a physical computer. The simple fact that the PRAM's unit-cost random-access memory cannot be physically implemented is sufficient information to reason through the impossibility of any program realizing certain predictions of the model [2]. We conclude that the PRAM is not the "right" parallel model.

Realistic models are much more difficult to validate, since they actually require experimentation. The goal of this paper is to introduce the concept of experimental validation and to review some of the evidence accumulated over the past decade for the CTA parallel machine model, and its performance-transparent programming model, Phase Abstractions. The experimental evidence will support the hypothesis that these two models fulfill the "right" model's predictive requirement across a wide variety of MIMD architectures. In the process of presenting this evidence, basic concepts of models of computation will be reviewed, other models will be critiqued, and the CTA and Phase Abstractions will be argued to have additional favorable properties. From the presentation there is an implied challenge to other researchers: Provide experimental validation if your model is intended to be practical.

2   Machine and Programming Models

In the formulation of a parallel model of computation, it is rational to be guided by the success of sequential computing. This observation, however, seems too quickly to have motivated researchers to focus on the von Neumann or RAM model of sequential computation. True, the RAM is a critical component in the success of modeling sequential computation, but it is not the only component. The programming model is also critical:

- A *machine model* defines the behavior of an execution engine in sufficient detail that programmers can determine which among alternative solutions is best, i.e. it allows reliable performance estimates.[1]
- A *programming model* extends a machine model with an additional set of abstractions that raise the conceptual level of programming while incurring "known" costs.

Thus, the machine model is essentially an abstract device that executes programs, while the programming model can be thought of as a more abstract device that executes programs formulated at a higher level [32].

The von Neumann machine is an example machine model, of course, but there are many. Also modeling sequential computation, but with different costs, is the Database Machine Model—a RAM attached to one or more disks with free (internal) computation and the primary (time) cost being the transfer of a track between the processor and a disk. We call the sequential programming model presented in languages like Fortran, C, Pascal, Ada, etc. and widely used for algorithm design and scientific programming, the *imperative-procedural* model [32]. The object oriented model, as presented in languages like SmallTalk, C++, Eiffel, etc., illustrates that there are alternative ways to extend the von Neumann machine model.

The machine model describes a computational device and establishes the parameters of performance. Thus, the von Neumann machine can be described as executing a sequence of instructions one after another with the instruction's operands being fetched by their address in unit-time from a flat, randomly accessed memory, etc. One can predict performance accurately enough to choose between alternative solutions—a long sequence of instructions takes more time to execute than a shorter sequence of instructions—but it is not possible to make predictions in terms of physical units (seconds) or even certain logical units (clock ticks). To be machine-independent, i.e. predict independent of hardware implementation, a model must characterize only those features common to a whole range of physical implementations.

A machine model, which in principle could be physically implemented, typically describes computation at too low a level for convenient programming and

---

[1] I tried describing the RAM's role as a "type architecture" [26] and Valiant proposed "bridging model" [34], but "machine model" prevails as the term with widest currency.

algorithm design. After all, the von Neumann machine does not have arrays, re-cursion, etc. which algorithm designers routinely use. Why do we presume they are available? Because they are useful abstractions and can be implemented on the machines modeled by the RAM for a "known" cost. Abstractions with these properties form the programming model.

The programming model raises the conceptual level by defining a standard set of facilities that can be presumed to be available. In the imperative-procedural (i-p) model, for example, the programmer is presented with arrays, control struc-tures, procedures, parameter evaluation, naming and scoping, etc. Further, the facilities have "known" costs in the sense that programmers can have a rough idea how expensive the facilities are to use, and that the costs are reasonably independent of which physical machine runs the program. In the i-p model, the facilities can be compiled about as efficiently as if they were custom-designed by the programmer working at the machine-level, so they are interpreted as having a small constant cost, which is generally ignored in algorithm design. Facilities in other programming models, e.g. object oriented, are often much more expensive, making them less suitable for algorithm design and high performance computing.

One valuable feature of the imperative-procedural (i-p) model that is not typical of other programming models will be called *performance transparency*. That is, the von Neumann machine model is still exposed in the i-p programming model and can be used as if working at the machine level. Thus, one can postulate data structures, e.g. AVL trees, defined directly in the machine model, i.e. with explicit reference to memory locations, pointers, etc., and use them with other parts of the i-p model as if they were primitive. This enables programmers to focus closely on performance.

Thus, it is accurate to say that the success with algorithm design and machine-independent programming for sequential computers is due to the application of the von Neumann machine model in combination with the imperative-procedural model programming.[2] For parallel computing we seek the analogous concepts, a machine model and a programming model with performance transparency suit-able for algorithm design and machine-independent programming.

3   The CTA Machine Model

The CTA[3] machine model was formulated [26] as a practical alternative to the unit-cost shared memory models of the Paracomputer [25] and the PRAM. Schwartz, recognizing inadequacies in the Paracomputer model, had already in-troduced the Ultracomputer model as a realistic alternative from a VLSI and architectural perspective. But from a programming and algorithm design view

---

[2] The RAM model has well known shortcomings [4], and a variety of alternatives, e.g. accounting for memory hierarchy, have been proposed. Though it is entirely appropriate to remedy a model's weaknesses, the RAM is effective as is for almost all applications. Since no parallel model is known to have even a fraction of the applicability of the RAM , it will be regarded here as an ideal for which to strive.

[3] Mnemonic for Candidate Type Architecture.

point it was not adequate, so the CTA was proposed as a *candidate* machine model. Though perhaps not perfect, there seems little need for significant change even after a decade. Indeed, recent proposals [7] have by their similarity highlighted certain strengths of the CTA.

The CTA [26] is an abstract parallel computer which, though widely known, is defined here to assist with comparison to other models:

> The CTA is composed of a set of P von Neumann machines, the *processors*, connected by a sparse network of unspecified topology, the *communication network*, and linked to an additional distinguished von Neumann machine, the *controller*, by a common, narrow channel. (See Figure 1)

The fact that the processors are von Neumann machines implies they execute instructions stored in their local memories referenced by their own program-counters. Thus, the CTA is an MIMD model in Flynn's taxonomy. Another consequence is that the processors can reference their own local memories in unit time. The CTA model further stipulates that a processor's reference to nonlocal data requires a *latency* of λ time units to be filled, where λ is assumed to be "large," i.e. $\lambda \gg 1$. "Sparse" means that the node degree of the network is constant. The processors execute asynchronously. The controller, which can be thought of as orchestrating the computation, uses its narrow connection to the processors to assist with common global operations like barrier synchronizations, eurekas, broadcasts (of limited size data), peek/poke to processors, possibly reduce and scan, etc.

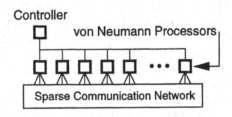

Fig. 1. The CTA machine model.

There are two parameters of the CTA, P, the number of processors and λ, the latency of interprocessor communication. Both parameters are thought to be given for each physical computer. Latency, in particular, is a quantity that must be used with care. It expresses the time observed by a processor to fill a nonlocal reference to data, and will typically measure a maximum distance, conflict-free memory-to-memory transfer. ("Conflict-free" excludes both network contention and internal-to-the-processor "conflicts" such as bus contention, cache misses, etc.) This "worst best case" number could be known exactly for any machine, but because the parallel machines modeled by the CTA can differ so dramatically from each other, and because the goal is to provide a basis for formulating machine independent computations, all that should be relied upon is that λ will be large, meaning 2, 3, perhaps 4 or more digits. This forces programmers and algorithm designers to attend to the matter of locality, i.e. how to arrange computations so references to local data are maximized, and the time-consuming references to nonlocal data are minimized. This imprecision about λ is essential, for reasons explained momentarily.

4   Discussion of the CTA

Like the von Neumann model, the CTA is a machine. It seems almost too obvious to mention, but the advantage of a machine for modeling computation rather than, say, a set of parameters, is that a machine "runs," and so it embodies more information than do abstract quantities. For example, it has not been asserted in print how long the CTA takes to synchronize, but one might estimate the time within limits, based on the fact that a mechanism involving the controller was alluded to: It may be assumed to take longer than unit time, since some protocol involving the processors is required, but probably no longer than a processor-processor communication, which involves another protocol. This estimate—more than one, no more than a neighbor reference—is probably as accurate as possible considering the diversity of machines, and it contains information. It implies that synchronization is not "free", but neither should it be considered as expensive as if implemented within the communication network. Such inferences are expected, and they save having to exhaustively enumerate every property that might ultimately be of interest [32].

Although the CM-5 and T3D are recent machines having controllers, the controller's purpose is not so much to model a physical device—no MIMD machine had one when the CTA was proposed—as to encapsulate certain global capabilities that should be provided in hardware. There was some hope of influencing architects, but the main motive was to focus programmers and algorithm designers on structuring parallel computations into phases and exploiting standard global operations that could receive hardware assistance, and therefore be fast. Identifying operations like synchronization, broadcast, parallel prefix, etc. explicitly in a computation, rather than burying them in a custom implementation in the program, allows the best machine specific solution to be used, either hardware or software. These will always be faster than general solutions, since they can exploit specific characteristics of the object machine.

Contrast this with the LogP model [7], whose similarity to the CTA is considerable, but which has no controller. An early application of LogP, therefore, was to prove time bounds for broadcast implemented in the communication network [12]. There are difficulties with the predictive properties of these results, discussed momentarily, but assuming programmers use the solutions directly in their programs, they obscure the fact that the intended computation is conceptually primitive. The compiler is not likely to recognize, unless told, that the implementation achieves the effect of broadcast, and thus will be unable to generate code for the best machine specific solution. This foregoes opportunities to exploit special purpose hardware (CM-5), or even if the broadcast must be done by software using the network, to exploit network properties (some routers have broadcast tags) or avoid network idiosyncrasies (pipelining might penalize a particular sending schedule). The CTA, by using the controller to identify such operations as primitive, adopts a higher level of abstraction favoring machine-independence.

Consider the LogP prediction embodied in the broadcast result just referred to, which essentially states that optimal broadcast in the network is achieved with a fanout tree whose node degree is determined by the relative values of latency, overhead and gap [12]. The critical quantity is "latency, L, the *maximum* delay associated with delivering a message" [7]. Worstcase delay can be a huge number, due to effects such as contention.[4] Contention is not only an observed property of practical computers, but for machines like the Intel Paragon and MIT J machine it is fundamental [5].[5] Using the given definitions, the result predicts for machines with huge L values (and moderate o and g) that broadcast is optimal when one processor sends to the other processors, i.e. the tree is the star. But such machines most certainly would benefit from a multilevel, lower degree tree, which would follow from a different definition of L, perhaps even λ's definition. Thus, we have another example where a model fails to predict accurately, though this time by being too pessimistic.

Precision and parameters are important issues, to which we now turn.

Worrying that the definition of L might also affect other predictions of the model, and recognizing that broadcast is not likely to saturate the network, one is tempted to save the prediction by reinterpreting L. But, other forms of broadcast, e.g. All-to-all and Continuous, are also expressed in terms of L [12], and for these contention is a concern. The problem is that with four parameters it is impossible to make accurate predictions at the machine-cycle level. Even simple computations like broadcasts require quantification of multiple properties of communication. Should more parameters be added to LogP? This would be in accord with the widely held view that "more parameters make better models," but this view seems to me to ignore the apparently necessary trade-off between generality and precision.

Machine models, which, like the RAM, are intended to generalize over a large range of implementations, must be restricted to universal properties and fundamental characteristics. Performance models, widely used in architectural design to search for optimum points in a design space, are extensively parameterized and capable of cycle-level predictions because the range of variability is restricted. This allows quantification of critical properties, and a precise specification of

---

[4] Indeed, adaptive networks with probabilistic livelock freedom, such as Chaos networks [13], have no worstcase bound on message delay because of contention, implying LogP cannot model computers with PLF networks even though they work well [3] and may soon be used in commercial systems.

[5] The so-called "finite capacity constraint" of the LogP model, that no more than $\lceil L/g \rceil$ messages be in flight per processor, is not limiting since these constructive lower bounds are for permutations.

parameter interactions,[6] but at the cost of limited applicability.

The CTA seeks to model MIMD computation generally. The objective is to provide a reliable abstraction to guide the design of machine-independent parallel computations. Precision sufficient to analyze performance at the machine cycle level is neither a goal nor possible.[7] Rather, the CTA like the RAM provides a general description of the basic phenomenon that is suitable for comparing alternative solutions.

5   Phase Abstractions Programming Model

The Phase Abstractions programming model [28, 29, 9, 1] provides standard programming concepts that extend the CTA in a performance-transparent way. The emphasis is on mechanisms to encapsulate locality. "Phase Abstractions" refers to two groups of programming concepts: the XYZ programming levels and ensembles.

The XYZ *programming levels* [28, 9] recognize that a parallel computation is expressed using three levels of specification:

Process (X) level, the composition of instructions,
Phase (Y) level, the composition of processes,
Problem (Z) level, the composition of phases.

Processes are simply threads of execution, phases correspond to our informal notion of parallel algorithm, and the problem level captures the idea of a parallel computation solving an entire application. Observe that the XYZ programming levels extend the CTA in the sense that they describe specification for the principal components of the CTA model: Processes (X) specify the behavior of processors, phases (Y) specify the behavior of the parallel "engine," i.e. the processors collectively with their communication network, and the problem (Z) specifies the behavior of the controller. Viewed in the ZYX order, the programming levels present a "top-down" definition of a parallel computation.

An *ensemble*—a set with a partitioning—is the fundamental structuring concept for a phase or parallel algorithm. A partition of an ensemble is a *section*. Three types of ensembles—data, code and port ensembles—are used in defining phases:[8]

---

[6] For parameters to be meaningful, their relationships to other parameters must be understood. Since parameters quantify aspects of physical devices, they may not be independent, i.e. not permitted to assume arbitrary values with respect to each other. For example, in the LogP model, L varies with machine size, implying that L and P are not independent. Dependence limits certain uses of the parameters. For example, fixing L and allowing P to vary for purposes of asymptotic analysis raises questions of interpretation, since there are at most finitely many values of P defined for any L.

[7] One can study algorithms in detail by adding *assumptions for analysis*, e.g. "assume $L \leq c\lambda$ is maximum message delay;" these describe the applicability of the results without limiting the model.

[8] This explanation is somewhat simplified by the "one per section" restrictions [32].

Data ensemble, a partitioning of a data structure.
Code ensemble, a partitioning of a set of process instances, one per section.
Port ensemble, a partitioning of a graph, one vertex per section.

To form a phase, the ensembles must have the same partitioning. The ensembles are then fused to become a phase, where corresponding sections are combined to form one unit of logical concurrency. Specifically, the process in each section of the code ensemble executes with local data from the corresponding sections of the data ensembles, and communicates with neighbor processes defined by the adjacencies to the vertex in the corresponding port ensemble.

To illustrate the phase abstractions concepts and to prepare for subsequent experiments, consider the Phase Abstractions formulation of the SIMPLE fluid dynamics computation, which models fluid under pressure in a sphere [15].[9] The problem (Z) level logic is given by the pseudocode:

```
begin real err,t; real array A, P, ..., R [1..n, 1..n];
    Phase (Y) and Process (X) declarations here;
    INITIALIZE(A, P, ..., R);
    while  err > 10**-6 do
        t := DELTA(A, P, ..., R);
        HYDRO(A, P, ..., R);
        HEAT(A, P, ..., R);
        ENERGY1(A, P, ..., R);
        err := ENERGY2(A, P, ..., R);
        end;
    OUTPUT(R);
end.
```

These instructions are logically executed by the controller. The capitalized words are phases, e.g. DELTA() computes the size of the time step which includes finding the maximum over some arrays. Thus, the Z level program orchestrates the invocation of parallel algorithms. Once started, the concurrent execution takes place on the parallel engine, and a phase logically runs to completion before the next phase begins.

The phases are built from ensembles, as is illustrated in the HEAT phase, Figure 2. The array ensembles are partitioned arrays, suitable for storage in the memories of the CTA's processors. (The details of allocation, e.g. by blocks or rows, are specified by the language semantics.) A process or thread will execute on each section of data, e.g. a process called Heat() applies to subarrays, and the collection of these processes form the code ensemble. Finally, to propagate information a process such as Heat() must exchange values with its four nearest neighbors, which is expressed as a partitioned mesh, i.e. the port ensemble. Figure 2 also illustrates one unit of logical concurrency.

Thus, the Phase Abstractions programming model presents a rather standard programming system—program text imperatively executing on data structures

---

[9] The details of this widely studied benchmark, developed at Lawrence Livermore National Labs [6], are not essential for the present discussion [15].

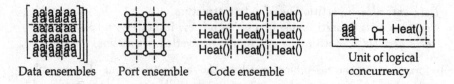

Data ensembles   Port ensemble   Code ensemble   Unit of logical concurrency

Fig. 2. The Phase Abstractions formulation of the HEAT() phase.

with the added requirements that the data structures be partitioned, separate (possibly different) program segments execute concurrently on each data partition, these segments communicate with their neighbors as defined by a graph, and the overall sequencing of these parallel algorithms is logically orchestrated with one parallel computation following another to solve a problem [9, 1].

6   Phase Abstractions Discussion

The most fundamental property of Phase Abstractions is that an s-ary partitioning represents a specification of s-way logical concurrency, where s is a variable. Thus, the model enforces an adaptivity that ranges from sequential computation, $s=1$, to the typical one-process-per-processor case, $s = P$, to the finest grain of one logical processor per data point, $s = n$. This allows the compiler to respond to the peculiarities of physical machines, since some computers are more efficient with a few large processes, e.g. to avoid "heavy-weight" context switching, while others "prefer" many small processes, e.g. to support latency hiding [32]. Though potentially there are computations that do not admit such broad variability, our experience has been the opposite: Most computations admit particularly elegant parallel solutions that can be scaled over a wide range, though possibly not for every integral value of s.

Contrast this, for example, with a "virtual processor" approach, where computation is defined at the finest grain possible, i.e. $s = n$ in our terms, and the physical processors are multiplexed when the logical concurrency exceeds the physical concurrency [11]. As has been explained [30], the widely accepted assumption that virtual process specification is ideal because "excess parallelism" can always be removed overlooks the compiler difficulties in performing this operation in general. Compilers can be successful in the simple cases, e.g. the ZPL compiler, described below, automatically changes granularity for a restricted version of the Phase Abstraction model, but generally programmers alone know how best to adapt to the available concurrency. Whether defined by programmer or compiler, the Phase Abstractions model requires that this form of scaling be known for every program.

The Phase Abstractions framework provides extensive variability:

– Phases are said to be "SIMD" when all processes of a code ensemble execute the same exact sequence of instructions, they are "SPMD" (single program, multiple data) when they are defined by instances of one process, and they are "MIMD" when they are defined by instances of multiple processes.

- Shared memory can be expressed by taking the port ensemble to be a complete graph. Of course, since the CTA model recognizes a performance difference between referencing local and nonlocal values, and since it has a sparse communication network, it follows that some costs will be incurred to realize shared memory. (The costs are made explicit when the designer of a shared memory language explains how the complete graph is to be implemented with the sparse network.) Phase abstractions does not prohibit shared memory, it simply connects its costs with the CTA's "reality."
- Though data parallel computations like SIMPLE above will tend to have all processes in a code ensemble be instances of the same source code, the model is MIMD, and thus permits the processes to be different. For example, a pipelined computation

$$P_1 \rightarrow P_2 \rightarrow P_3 \rightarrow \cdots \rightarrow P_k$$

would be represented with a different P_i in each section of the code ensemble, probably different data structures in each section of the data ensemble, and a line graph for a port ensemble. Scaling to more sections would probably introduce null processes, i.e. no benefit from additional parallelism would be expressed, and scaling smaller would likely combine multiple processes into one section. Other paradigms are also expressible.

Phase Abstractions is performance transparent with respect to the CTA, so it can be logically extended in ways analogous to the RAM.

Notice that the programmer might see Phase Abstractions as stating how to compose a parallel computation from primitive parts, whereas a compiler writer will see it as a description of how to decompose a parallel computation into its parts for code generation. Either view is correct, of course. Indeed, if the language designer sees how to automatically construct the ensembles from the program text, then the language can be implicitly parallel, as ZPL is. If this is not generally possible then some degree of explicit parallelism will be required. Algorithm designers will always chose to be explicit, since the roles of P, s and n are critical to their analysis.

7   Methodology

As the introduction noted, a model's most important quality, "accurate predictions for real programs executed on physical computers," requires experimental validation. Though the RAM was never validated in this sense, presumably because it was developed contemporaneously with the concept of "machine-independent model of computation," our daily experience with sequential computing continually adds more evidence of its effectiveness [32]. It is reasonable to expect daily experience to be the main evidence supporting a parallel model's effectiveness, too, but how is this process bootstrapped? Programmers would want to know that a model works before using it. Further, the practical application of a model requires considerable support—a language, compiler, run-time systems for one or more parallel machines, libraries, programming tools such as debuggers, etc.—before it is ready for use. One is, perhaps, reluctant to embark on so much software development without some assurance that the model is not flawed. Accordingly, we do not seek an air-tight test that the parallel model "accurately predicts" in any absolute sense, since this is not possible even for the RAM. Rather, we seek evidence suggestive enough to attract sustained interest of our skeptical colleagues, and persuasive enough to justify the continued efforts towards implementing the model for daily application.

Recall that in broad outline, the plan is to develop programs based on the model, i.e. the CTA as extended transparently by the Phase Abstractions model, to predict properties of the programs based on the CTA, to run the programs on physical computers and to observe whether the predictions are accurate. Even this simplistic approach was cited for numerous difficulties: multiple universal quantifiers, "accuracy" as a qualitative term, and "perturbations" by the language and other system components used to instantiate the computation. To deal with some of these (and others not yet mentioned), a related methodology will be used for Experiment 1. For this, two concepts must be introduced.

Observe that MIMD parallel computers are *extensional* in the sense that when restricted to a single processor, they are von Neumann machines, and so the remainder of the parallel computer, the other processors, the communication network, possibly a controller, etc. all extend a sequential machine. (A bit-serial SIMD machine, e.g. CM-1, is not extensional in this sense [27].) This means first that the RAM model will be taken as accurate within one processor, and second that the focus for the CTA validation will be on issues external to a single processor.

"Any" machine or programming model is machine-independent in the sense that programs written using it can execute on "any" computer. As with Turing machines, this assertion is true simply because a layer of software implementing the capabilities of the models can be "interposed between" the hardware and a program. Thus, the issue is not machine-independence *per se*, for that is immediate, but rather the expense of the software layer. Call this software the *insulation layer* and its cost *insulation*. To the extent that insulation is significant for some computers, i.e. time, memory or other resources are required but not accounted for in the model(s), then their predictions for these resources will be inaccurate. If the insulation layer is "thin" or nonexistent, the machine model accurately describes the hardware, but if it is "thick," the model is quite distinct from the implementing hardware. As noted in Section 2, the von Neumann and imperative-procedural model(s) require little insulation.

Containing insulation is fundamental to accurate prediction. A software layer is *logically* required for all features of a machine or programming model that do not explicitly exist in the physical hardware, and thus they *logically* imply insulation. But three considerations reduce the need for an insulation layer. First, features like the CTA's controller encapsulate computation in such a way that they need not be explicitly implemented. Thus, if a machine has a controller it performs the controller's operations, and if not, the operations, but not the controller performing them, will be implemented. In neither case is insulation incurred for the controller. Second, compilers may translate the model's features onto physical hardware without an insulation layer, e.g. linear arrays incur essentially no insulation. Third, even when software is introduced to implement an abstraction, if it is "essential" to the computation, i.e. would be implemented for a machine-specific solution, then that software cost is also not insulation. Procedures might be an example from the i-p model, while locking might be another from transaction models. In summary, insulation can be avoided with artful model design, compilers or abstractions so powerful they would be implemented even if not available.

There are two senses in which we expect the model to predict the behavior of computations as they would run on physical machines:[10]

- A model *consistently predicts* if the best among a set of alternative solutions in the model is the best among the implementations of those alternatives customized to a physical machine.
- A model *completely predicts* if the best solution in the model performs as well when implemented on the machine as the best solution customized to the machine.

Notice that both forms of prediction are comparative. Consistent prediction is essential for algorithm designers and programmers as they choose among alternatives, and is closely related to insulation. Complete prediction assures that the model is sufficient to cover all aspects of a broad class of machines. For example, an "SIMD model" might be said to predict incompletely (for MIMD computers) if its predictions can be improved upon by exploiting MIMD hardware; an experiment with Dataparallel C would be interesting in this regard [10].

Though consistent prediction appears to be somewhat easier to test experimentally than complete prediction, they both require that one identify "best" implementations. Producing "best" programs for a series of machines would not only be time consuming, but more worrisome it would be extremely difficult to defend them as best. So, using the extensional property of parallel computers, we bound the performance of the "best" implementations by the "perfect" parallel program for each machine, i.e. the parallel program that achieves P-fold improvement over the sequential program with P processors.[11]

This idealized linear speedup cannot exist for the "real" programs considered here. There are certainly subcomputations that are inherently sequential, and other parts, such as aggregation and broadcast that can benefit from parallelism, but not linearly. And, linear speedup ignores the fact that as P increases,

---

[10] These and other concepts treated here can obviously be formalized mathematically once a sufficient quantity of data is amassed to indicate that the model is promising.

[11] This is perfect performance in the model, but it is not in reality because of characteristics like "cache effects" that can lead to slightly superlinear speedup. Cache effects do occur. However, we accept P-ary speedup as perfect, since these effects are small, and are usually not observed because they effectively reduce the other costs of parallelism such as communication.

the grain size, i.e. the number of data items allocated to a section, diminishes. This means there is less "work" with which to amortize such parallel costs as communication, and so the departure from linear will increase with diminishing grain size. The "best" program will differ from the "perfect" program for all of these reasons. The CTA/PA program will differ from the "perfect" program for all of these reasons *plus* the cost of insulation introduced by the models. Both programs will depart from linear, but by amounts that cannot be known.

8   Validation Experiment 1: Insulation

For the first experiment, conducted by Calvin Lin, the SIMPLE computation was implemented in the CTA/PA [15]. SIMPLE is a 2400 line Fortran benchmark developed at Lawrence Livermore Laboratories [6] which has been extensively studied in the parallel computation setting. The principal data structures are two dimensional arrays of floating point numbers. The problem level logic, shown previously in pseudocode, invokes five phases in the main (timed) iteration. The principal data motions are an aggregation/broadcast tree[12] (DELTA, ENERGY2), a 4-nearest-neighbor mesh (HEAT) and 6-neighbor mesh (HYDRO, ENERGY1).

Lin wrote a program in C and pseudocode that realized the SIMPLE computation according to the precepts of the CTA/PA models. Thus, for example, the arrays were converted to variably-scaled ensembles with a block partitioning. This approach eliminated the perturbation affects of a language. This program was then hand-translated for a sampling of the MIMD parallel machines then available. This translation was achieved primarily using macros to customize the procedure calls to library routines for the target machine. No optimizations were performed. The translated programs were executed on MIMD machines for various numbers of processors and a single problem size of 1680 points. Absolute speedup for a give number of processors was computed by dividing the execution time into the execution time for the program specialized to sequential execution on one processor of the parallel machine.

The MIMD machines examined represented the major architectural approaches to parallel computer design at the time: The Sequent Symmetry has a shared memory implemented by a snooping bus; the NCube N/7 and the Intel iPSC/2 have distributed memory using hypercube interconnections; the BBN Butterfly has a shared memory implemented by a memory interconnect network; and the Transputer was a distributed memory computer with T800s in a 2D mesh [15].

The results are shown in Figure 3. The succinct summary of the results is

- The CTA/PA SIMPLE program delivered at least $P/2$ speedup on all experiments on all machines.

The speedup numbers are clustered reasonably tightly, indicating that the observed performance was reasonably consistent across platforms. Most of these

---

[12] These are controller functions, of course, but none of the machines used in the experiments had controllers, so in each case a custom solution for that architecture was implemented.

machines have large λ values, though the Symmetry has $\lambda \approx 3$, possibly explaining why it achieves the best performance.

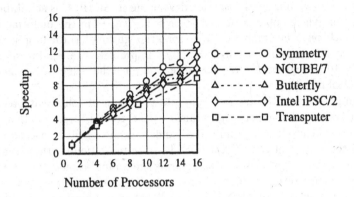

Fig. 3. SIMPLE on five parallel architectures.

Reasoning as follows, we claim these numbers imply the insulation of the CTA/PA models must be small: Thick insulation would add large overhead to the computation producing long execution times for the experiments on one or more machines for one or more values of P yielding small observed speedups, or possibly slowdowns. Since all factors preventing perfect speedup—inherent sequentiality, less-than-linear speedups, diminishing grain size, and insulation— collectively reduce the performance from "perfect" by strictly less than 50% in all cases, the overhead component must be small. If the overhead is small, the insulation layer must be "thin," and the features of the models can be efficiently implemented by these physical computers.

This methodology is indirect. It is possible that there is only a negligible performance difference between "perfect" and the hypothesized "best" program for each machine, and so essentially all of the observed cost should be assigned to the CTA/PA program's use of the model, i.e. assigned as the insulation cost. For some observers, a strictly-less-than-50% insulation cost may be quite acceptable. For them, the model is accurate, and the small insulation cost is proved within the limits of the experiment. But, if essentially all the observed cost were insulation, those believing overhead should be only grudgingly incurred might disagree. Fortunately, there are external reasons to believe the opposite, that the CTA/PA program approximates the hypothesized best: Rogers [24] formulated a performance model for SIMPLE eliminating any chance of near "perfect" speedup, the CTA/PA program is as fast or faster than other versions by other authors who have worked more directly from the original Fortran, etc. [15]. A wide perfect-best gap and a narrow best-CTA/PA gap seem the most likely explanation, which supports the claim of complete prediction and little insulation for the CTA/PA.

Obviously, the conclusion applies only to SIMPLE on these machines. It must be acknowledged that had the experiment used a different computation or different machines, it is possible that the results could be significantly different. But SIMPLE is representative of many scientific and engineering applications, which was the original motivation for developing it. SIMPLE is small, but it is not a kernel. The computers include representatives from the main families of MIMD machines. The number of processors, though small, is the largest number common to all available machines. Finally, the problem size is quite small, but this tends to strengthen the results, since it implies that there is relatively less parallel slackness [34].

An important qualitative fact supports the claim of consistent prediction, and justifies attaching more significance to the results, perhaps, than might at first be evident: In performing the hand-translations little mechanism was required to implement the CTA/PA model of computation on these machines, since much of the attention was to structuring the computation properly, and this tended to reduce rather than introduce code. Thus, the observed performance is the result of adding a little software, rather than much software lightly used. A small insulation layer implies a nearly direct implementation of the model, with little distortion that could lead to inconsistent prediction. Since the same mechanisms needed for SIMPLE will implement the CTA/PA for any program on these machines, little insulation can be presumed more generally, i.e. SIMPLE is effectively a general representative.

In summary, Experiment 1 indirectly supports the claims that the CTA/PA incurs little insulation and predicts completely for MIMD machines. Details of the implementation further support the small insulation claim, and suggest the CTA/PA predicts consistently.

9 Validation Experiment 2: Shared Memory Hardware

As noted in the introduction, though accurate predictions support a model, inaccurate predictions expose weaknesses that can motivate a revision. It is sensible, therefore, to formulate difficult tests that stress the model. If it passes the tests one develops confidence, and if it fails one learns something. The shared memory hardware test, which the CTA/PA passes, illustrates this approach.

The CTA postulates that scalable parallel computers have large λ values for two reasons that are unrelated to whether the machines have special hardware to support shared memory:

- Memories must be physically distributed, meaning distinct processors have distinct (possibly overlapping) access paths to a given memory location, and
- Performance derives from giving each processor local access to a portion of the memory.

Thus, the CTA/PA focuses on costs common to both shared or distributed memory computers. The shared memory model requires the imposition of a global addressing structure, enforcement of some form of memory consistency, etc., but these can be implemented in either hardware or software (insulation). Thus, shared memory computers simply include more hardware support for the shared memory model than do distributed memory computers. But, of course, if this hardware provides a significant performance advantage for these computers, then CTA/PA model programs should exploit it.

For the CTA/PA to predict completely for shared memory MIMD machines, programs written in the model must run as fast as programs customized to the hardware. Programs written in a shared memory model could serve as the "customized" programs, since, presumably, they would express the computation in a form that effectively uses the shared memory hardware. Thus, the claim is

> The CTA/PA predicts completely for MIMD shared memory computers if CTA/PA programs run as fast as shared memory model programs on shared memory computers.

If the conclusion is affirmative, then this is forceful evidence for the generality of the model, since the CTA/PA is also effective on distributed memory computers.

In a series of experiments conducted by Ton Ngo, the question of the CTA/PA ability to predict completely for shared memory machines was tested [22]. Two applications were selected: a molecular dynamics simulation (Water from the SPLASH benchmark suite) and LU Decomposition. The programs were thought to illustrate effective use of shared memory multiprocessors, and they were written by others. CTA/PA programs for these problems were written by Ngo based on the precepts of the models, again using C and pseudocode. No optimizations were performed. The hand-translated programs were run for a series of problem sizes ($n=200$, 300, 512 for LUD and $n=96$, 288, 512 for Water) on a set of five shared memory multiprocessors: Sequent Symmetry, BBN Butterfly, University of Illinois' Cedar, Kendall Square KSR-1, and Stanford University's DASH [23].

The shared memory model programs were taken to be the "best" on the implementing hardware, making this setting different from Experiment 1, since both programs for the relative comparison were available. The results generally support the claim, though they cannot be as succinctly described as in Experiment 1.

- LU Decomposition: For four of the five machines, the CTA/PA program ran significantly faster than the shared memory model program, with the advantage ranging from approximately 10% to more than 500%. For the Sequent Symmetry, both programs approximated linear speedup for all data points, except for $P=16$, where the shared memory program was faster, but by less than 10% for the examined problem sizes.
- Molecular Dynamics: For four of the five machines, the performance of the two programs were comparable, being within a few percent of one another except for 3 or 4 points with somewhat larger differences. For the Stanford DASH, the shared memory program was consistently better than the CTA/PA program independently of the number of processors or problem size, and by a significant amount. For example, the CTA was able to achieve only about 75% of DASH's performance for P=32 and n=512.

Space precludes presenting complete details of this large data set [22, 23].

Interpreting the results, the vast majority of data supports the claim. The CTA/PA program is either faster or within a few percent of the performance of the shared memory model program.[13] The molecular dynamics program on the DASH, the one case where the shared memory program was consistently superior, comes from the SPLASH suite of benchmarks, i.e. the program was written for the DASH. The DASH's programming model is not quite the shared memory model, but rather is a "relaxed consistency model," meaning that with programmer assistance the memory is allowed to violate strict sequential consistency as an assist to hiding latency. This may explain why Water was faster on the DASH, but not on any of the other architectures, and why LU decomposition, which was not customized for any particular machine, was not superior on the DASH. A more likely explanation is that Water exhibits a substantial amount of computation that can exploit read sharing, and so benefits especially well from the DASH's caching and invalidation mechanisms.

Various features were included by the architects of these shared memory computers to facilitate the execution of shared memory model programs, but for only one machine and one program was there a significant performance advantage over the CTA/PA. The original claim—that the CTA/PA model predicts completely for shared memory MIMD computers—is supported by the data. For the cases examined CTA/PA programs generally perform well on shared memory machines, both in an absolute sense, and when compared to programs written in the shared memory model.

It would be interesting to see data on the opposite experiment—predicting completely for distributed memory machines—for languages such as Linda, NESL, functional languages, etc., that opt not to encourage locality in the programming model.

10   Validation Experiment 3: Language "Perturbation"

A parallel model that has been validated along the lines presented so far can be of use to algorithm designers since they, like the experimenters, can access it through pseudocode. But programmers will access the model through the medium of a programming language. In implementing the programming model, the language and compiler can introduce more insulation than has already been accounted for in earlier experiments. Thus, the persistent concern that the predictive qualities of the models will be "perturbed" by the language. It is critical that a direct, essentially insulation-free implementation of the CTA/PA model

---

[13] No optimizations were allowed to assure that the hand-translation did not accidently introduce code improvements that could not be implemented by a compiler. This was perhaps excessively conservative, since it is clear that the slight loss in performance was due in most instances chiefly to a literal implementation of message passing [22], which is well within compiler technology to remove; see Methodology. Accordingly, cases where the CTA/PA performance approximated the shared memory model program to within a few per cent were considered equal.

be created if the model, and the algorithms developed with it, are to receive daily application.

In concept a language need only provide a means of expressing the components of Phase Abstractions—data, code and port ensembles, and the X, Y and Z programming levels—and the compiler need only identify these components and translate them onto physical hardware analogously to the way Lin and Ngo hand-translated the pseudocode. What complicates this simple approach is that one prefers the most convenient language possible to simplify the programmer's task. Convenience, however, can conflict with effective compilation, since often the less one expresses explicitly the more convenient the language, but the harder the compiler's task in generating insulation-free code. In the present setting the issue reduces to: Must a programmer explicitly give the Phase Abstractions components, or can a compiler automatically extract them by analysis from programs where they only exist implicitly?

At present no language provides access to the full Phase Abstractions model by means of implicit programming facilities. (No full language with explicit facilities has as yet been implemented, either.) However, a new array language, ZPL [18], implements a portion of the CTA/PA model, and provides an opportunity to measure the insulation for a language implementing a subset of the model.

ZPL [18, 19] is an array language, meaning that although scalar computations typical of i-p languages can be written, convenience and high performance are achieved by writing array expressions. Thus, A+1 increments all elements of an array A, and sin(A) computes the sine of each of its elements. The concept of "region" allows programmers to compute over subarrays. ZPL has the usual arithmetic and logical operators, the usual control structures and recursion, global operations such as reduce and scan, and a variety of concepts like "boundary" that assist with programming scientific computations [19]. For example, Figure 4 gives the ZPL program for the Jacobi computation [18].

Interpreted as a language for the CTA/PA model, ZPL is restrictive in the following ways:

- Data Ensembles: ZPL uses only one type of data ensemble, dense rectangular arrays with block partitionings, where the number and structure of the blocks are set at run time.
- Port Ensembles: The ZPL operators induce essentially three types of communication (nearest neighbor, aggregation/broadcast trees, and wrap-around communication) leading to one port ensemble that is the union of the three graphs.
- Code Ensembles: The single thread of control is compiled into a single process that implements the array operations on the blocks of the arrays allocated to a single section. This process is replicated in each section to define the code ensemble.

The ensembles are fused into a single phase whose invocation can be thought of as the only instruction of the Z level program.

The experiment, conducted by Lin and others, concerned the costs introduced by the language and the compiler [20]. Two programs, SIMPLE (500 lines) and

```
1   program Jacobi;
2   /*              Jacobi Iteration
3                                                          */
4   config var     N: integer = 512;
5                  delta: real = 0.000001;
6
7   region         R = [1..N, 1..N];          -- Declarations
8   var            A, Temp: [R] real;
9                  err: real;
10
11  direction      north = [-1, 0];
12                 east  = [ 0, 1];
13                 west  = [ 0,-1];
14                 south = [ 1, 0];
15
16  procedure Jacobi();
17  begin
18    [R]            A := 0.0;                  -- Initialization
19    [north of R]   A := 0.0;
20    [east of R]    A := 0.0;
21    [west of R]    A := 0.0;
22    [south of R]   A := 1.0;
23
24    [R]            repeat                     -- Body
25                     Temp := (A@north+A@east
26                             +A@west+A@south)/4.0;
27                     err := max\ abs(A-Temp);
28                     A := Temp;
29                   until err < delta;
30  end;
```

Fig. 4. The Jacobi computation in ZPL [31].

the Jacobi iteration (30 lines), were written in ZPL, and compared to programs hand-translated from C with pseudocode. Since the parallel computers used in Experiment 1 were no longer available 3 years later (a compelling argument for machine-independent programming), the comparisons were performed on the Intel Paragon, a distributed memory machine with a mesh topology, and the KSR-2, a shared memory machine based on a ring-of-rings structure.

The figures [20] indicate essentially identical performance for the Jacobi computation on both machines, and for SIMPLE on the Intel Paragon. The ZPL SIM-PLE was approximately 10% slower on the KSR-2 in some tests. These results represent the compiler's initial performance, essentially without optimizations. Optimizations are steadily being added, and it is likely that SIMPLE would now perform as well as the hand-translated pseudocode. Additionally, it has been shown [21] that certain computations with little or no communication exhibited linear speedup on the Paragon and Cray T3D, which with reasoning analogous to that used in Experiment 1, implies that ZPL is introducing little insulation.

A thorough study of the amount of insulation incurred by the language and compiler must await the completion of a full language implementing the CTA/PA model. *Advanced ZPL* is such a language.[14] However, these results are encouraging, since ZPL is already sufficient to program many scientific and engineering computations.

11 Summary

The general problem of experimentally validating a model of parallel computation has been studied. The specific problems of validating the CTA machine model and the Phase Abstractions programming model have served as illustrations of the methodology. The data is necessarily limited because of the considerable effort required to perform experiments across diverse parallel platforms. Nevertheless, data on ten parallel architectures running the CTA/PA model were reported here.

The experiments investigate the CTA/PA's effectiveness for making accurate predictions for real programs executing on physical computers. The concepts of insulation, extension, complete and consistent prediction, as well as experimental methodologies were introduced. Experiment 1 showed indirectly that the CTA/PA introduces little insulation for SIMPLE on a range of MIMD machines, and it was argued this result applies to other programs. Experiment 2 showed directly that the CTA/PA generally predicts completely for shared memory MIMD machines. Experiment 3 indicated that the ZPL language can implicitly define a subset of the CTA/PA model properties, and still introduce little additional insulation. Related experiments for other models were suggested.

Validation experiments beyond those presented here have also been conducted for the CTA/PA models [16, 17]. With the completion of the ZPL compiler, language based comparisons have been performed [21]. Finally, there has been some application of the CTA/PA model by scientists and engineers [14, 8], which constitute the beginnings of the "daily experience" validation.

References

1. G. Alverson, W. Griswold, D. Notkin, L. Snyder, "A flexible communication abstraction," *Supercomputing 90,* pp. 584–593, 1990.
2. R. Anderson, L. Snyder, "A comparison of shared and nonshared models," *Proc. of IEEE* 79(4):480–487, 1991.
3. K. Bolding, L. Snyder, "Mesh and torus chaotic routing," *Advanced Research in VLSI*, MIT Press, pp. 333–347, 1992.

---

[14] Advanced ZPL is the new name of the language formerly known as Orca C. The name was changed to avoid continued confusion with the Orca distributed computing project.

4. L. Carter, "The RAM model," TR RC 16319, IBM Watson Research Lab, 1990.
5. D. Chinn, F. Leighton, M. Tompa, "Minimal adaptive routing on the mesh with bounded queue size," *Sixth ACM SPAA*, pp. 354–363, 1994.
6. W. Crowley, C. Hendrickson, T. Luby, "The SIMPLE code," TR UCID-17715, Lawrence Livermore Laboratory, 1978.
7. D. Culler et al., "LogP: towards a realistic model of parallel computation," *ACM SIGPlan Symp. PPoPP*, pp. 1–12, 1993.
8. M. Dikaiakos, C. Lin, D. Manoussaki, "The portable parallel implementation of two novel mathematical biology algorithms in ZPL," *Ninth ACM Int'l Supercomputing*, 1995.
9. W. Griswold, G. Harrison, D. Notkin, L. Snyder, "Scalable abstractions," *Fifth Dist. Mem. Comp. Conf.*, IEEE, pp. 1008–1016, 1990.
10. P. Hatcher et al., "Data-parallel programming," *IEEE Trans. Par. Distrib. Syst.* 2(3):377–383, 1991.
11. W. Hillis, G. Steele, "Data parallel algorithms," *CACM* 29(12):1170–1183, 1986.
12. R. Karp, A. Sahay, E. Santos, K. Schauser, "Optimal broadcast and summation in the LogP model," *Fifth ACM SPAA*, pp. 142–153, 1993.
13. S. Konstantinidou, L. Snyder, "The chaos router," *IEEE Trans. on Computers* 43(12):1386–1397, 1994.
14. E Lewis, C. Lin, L. Snyder, G. Turkiyyah, "A portable parallel N-body solver," *Seventh SIAM Conf. on Parallel Proc. for Scientific Comp.*, pp. 331–336, 1995.
15. C. Lin, L. Snyder, "A portable implementation of SIMPLE," *Int'l J. of Par. Prog.* 20(5):363–401, 1991.
16. C. Lin, *The portability of parallel programs across MIMD computers*, PhD Dissertation, University of Washington, 1992.
17. C. Lin, L. Snyder, "Accommodating polymorphic data decompositions in explicitly parallel programs," *Eighth Int'l Parallel Proc. Symp.*, pp. 68–74, 1994.
18. C. Lin, L. Snyder, "ZPL: an array sublanguage." In U. Banerjee et al. (Eds.) *Lecture Notes in Computer Science*, Vol. 768, Springer-Verlag, pp. 96–114, 1994.
19. C. Lin, *ZPL language reference manual*, UW CSE TR 94-10-06, 1994.
20. C. Lin, L. Snyder, "SIMPLE performance results in ZPL." In K. Pingali et al. (Eds.) *Lecture Notes in Computer Science*, Vol. 892, Springer-Verlag, pp. 361–375, 1994.
21. C. Lin et al., "ZPL vs. HPF: A comparison of performance," UW CSE Technical Report, 1994.
22. T. Ngo, L. Snyder, "On the influence of programming models," *Scalable High Perf. Computing Conf.*, IEEE, pp. 284–291, 1992.
23. T. Ngo, L. Snyder, "Data locality on shared memory computers," UW TR 93-06-08, 1993.
24. A. Rogers, *Compiling for locality of reference*, PhD dissertation, Cornell, 1990.
25. J. Schwartz, "Ultracomputers," *ACM ToPLaS* 2(4):484–521, 1980.
26. L. Snyder, "Type architecture, shared memory and the corollary of modest potential," *Annual Review of CS*, I:289–317, 1986.
27. L. Snyder, "A taxonomy of synchronous parallel machines," *Int'l Conf. on Parallel Proc.*, Penn State, pp. 281–285, 1988.
28. L. Snyder, "The XYZ abstraction levels." In D. Gelernter et al. (Eds.) *Lang. Compilers for Parallel Comp.*, MIT Press, pp. 470–489, 1990.
29. L. Snyder, "Applications of the 'phase abstractions'." In J. Saltz and P. Mehrotra (Eds.) *Lang. Compilers and Run-time Environ. for Dist. Mem. Mach.*, Elsevier, pp. 79–102, 1992.

30. L. Snyder, "A practical parallel programming model," *AMS DIMACS Series in Disc. Math and Theoretical CS* 18:143–160, 1994.
31. L. Snyder, "ZPL programmer's guide," UW TR 94-12-02, 1994.
32. L. Snyder, "Foundations of practical parallel languages." In J. Ferrante and A. Hey (Eds.) *Portability and Perform. for Parallel Proc.*, John Wiley & Sons, pp. 1–19, 1994.
33. L. Valiant, "Parallelism in comparison problems," *SIAM J. Comp.* 4(3):348–355, 1975.
34. L. Valiant, "A bridging model for parallel computation," *CACM* 33(8):103–111, 1990.

Quo Vadetis, Parallel Machine Models?

Jiří Wiedermann*

Institute of Computer Science
Academy of Sciences of the Czech Republic
Pod vodárenskou věží 2, 182 07 Prague 8
Czech Republic
e–mail: wieder@uivt.cas.cz

Abstract. The practice of parallel computing seems to be in a crisis. Parallel computing has not become a common matter as it was expected some time ago. Some people are up in arms accusing computer science for not being sufficiently prepared for the advent of parallel computing and for not offering immediate remedies for the current situation. The present paper tries to recapitulate the relevant developments within the field of abstract parallel machine models by explaining its motivations, achievements and recent trends. We see a continuous interplay between the internal needs of the theory and the response to technological achievements. The parallel computing crisis and possible ways to resolve it are explained.

1 Introduction

By the end of the nineteen sixties a popular opinion emerged stating that computer users were facing the so–called *software crisis*. The main argument was that the progress in the field of software, as dictated by user requirements, was not sufficient in relation to the progress in the field of hardware. This has lead to the mobilization of a research effort in computer science that has concentrated on the identification and solution of the underlying theoretical problems. In the course of time, increasingly better ways of designing and producing both software and hardware have been developed. On the other hand, it has also been recognized and accepted that some of the related problems are indeed very complex, due to their nature and the fact that the original aims and ideas concerning their solution are in need of modification.

Some twenty-five years later, the software crisis has somehow been forgotten. This has happened essentially because one accepts the current situation of computer science as a standard one, both in theory and in practice.

From the viewpoint of the present paper the previous crisis can be appropriately considered as a *sequential* software (or computing) crisis. Nowadays it appears that history is about to repeat itself — this time in a parallel setting. Again the recent practical experience with parallel computing has been a disappointment. It clearly does not fulfill the original expectations. Moreover, the

* This research was supported by GA ČR Grant No. 201/95/0976 "HYPERCOMPLEX."

way out of this *parallel computing crisis* has been sought again in the realm of theoretical computer science.

This time, however, the theory seemed to be better prepared for such a situation. The study of parallel computing has traditionally been an integral part of computer science which has started its development almost simultaneously with the study of sequential computing. Yet, despite the sizeable body of respective knowledge for practical purpose, only a little of it has appeared to be of some immediate practical use. Did computer science fail, as some people believe [9], in this particular case? Did it develop in the wrong way? How is it reacting to the current situation in the practice of parallel computation?

It is the purpose of the present paper to provide some answers to the previous questions, by explaining the development within the field of (abstract) parallel machine models which are at the hard core of the respective theoretical background of parallel computing. To understand this development, its motivations, achievements, and recent trends, both the internal needs of the theory and the reactions to the technological achievements will be described.

First, in order to have some firm basis for comparing the qualitative and quantitative achievements of parallel computing, Section 2 will very briefly recapitulate the recent view of the field of sequential machine models.

In Section 3 we shall introduce the class of idealized parallel machine models. It has undergone a stormy development during the seventies. The development was mostly "curiosity driven". It was motivated primarily by theoretical questions related to finding the best possible ways of making use of parallelism.

By the beginning of the nineteen eighties it was clear that the idealized parallel machine models could not be realized in practice, because they neglect fundamental physical laws which relate to information transfer and processing. The respective development will be described in Section 4.

The impact of criticism against the idealized machine models on the further development of the theory of parallel machine models is discussed in the next two sections. In Section 5 the models of scalable parallel machines are reviewed. These are the models that strictly obey the basic physical laws and are therefore physically feasible.

Finally, in Section 6 the class of realistic parallel machine models is mentioned. These models are the subject of intensive current research, and their development is dominated by the possibilities and limits of current technologies.

Section 7 presents conclusions drawn from previous lessons. The moral is: the situation, both in theory and practice, of parallel computing is hardly surprising and there is no one and nothing to be blamed for it. Similar to the first software crisis, things are developing in a natural way, and some time is needed before the crisis disappears.

2   Sequential Machine Models

To understand and appreciate the advantages and benefits of parallel machine models, it is appropriate to compare their computational power and efficiency with that of sequential models. With these models we have more than fifty years of practical experience, and during the past thirty years complexity theory has accumulated a large body of knowledge about them.

The foundations of the complexity theory of sequential computations as we know them today, have been essentially determined at the beginning of the nineteen seventies. For our purpose, the greatest methodological discovery from that time was the fact that machine models exist with respect to which the definition of certain basic complexity classes is *invariant*. These classes are all comprising the hierarchy of fundamental complexity classes

$$LOG \subseteq NLOG \subseteq PTIME \subseteq NPTIME \subseteq PSPACE \subseteq EXPTIME \dots$$

The previous observation means that the definition of the above complexity classes is machine-independent w.r.t. the machine models from a certain class of machines. Following van Emde Boas [19], this machine class is nowadays known as *the first machine class* denoted as C_1. C_1 consists of Deterministic Turing Machines (DTMs) and of all other models that can simulate a DTM and that can be simulated by a DTM in polynomial time and in linear space. In this definition the linear space simulation can be different from polynomial time simulation.

It follows from classical results within complexity theory that all possible variants of DTMs which differ in number and dimensionality of their tapes, number of tape heads, RAMs and RASPs with logarithmic costs, to name only the most common machines, are members of the first machine class.

Intuitively, the first machine class should represent the class of ordinary sequential machine models.

3   Idealized Models of Parallel Machines

The idea of parallel computation, realized by machines that are parallel analogues of known sequential machines, has been around ever since the appearance of sequential machine models. As a result, the first theoretical models of parallel machines began to emerge by the beginning of the nineteen seventies.

All models of parallel machines known today are generalizations of models from the first machine class. Understandably, these early models — that can be appropriately termed *idealized parallel machine models* — were not influenced by technological constraints, since no real parallel computers except perhaps some experimental machines, existed. Rather, the aim was to exploit the rich design space for parallel machines and to single out the prospective machine models whose computational efficiency would surpass that of the models from the first machine class. Also, scientists were interested n determining the limits of parallelism with the help of these models.

When it comes to the design of a parallel machine model, two basic ideas come to mind. The new parallel computer can be built either from a set of sequential computers ("processors") which will cooperate in a suitable way, or the new parallel computer will look like a sequential computer. This computer will, however, be able to work with composite objects (for example, vectors) rather than with single atoms.

In the first case, several questions arise immediately: what should be the computational power of the individual processors? Clearly it can vary from that of Boolean gates via that of finite automata and neurons, to the full computing power of RAM-like processors. Even other parallel machines can serve as processors. Could these processors work in a synchronous manner? The next question could concern the mechanism of cooperation among processors. Should they communicate via a fixed interconnection network? If so, what would be its best topology? Should this network remain fixed during the computation, or would there be some advantage from its modifiable topology? Alternatively, would it be better to communicate via a common global memory? How will access conflicts be resolved then?

In the second case, one could ask what the composite objects should look like. Is it enough to consider only Boolean vectors or vectors with integer components or perhaps only 'long' integers?

What about nondeterminism in parallel computing: is it necessary to achieve the maximal efficiency of parallel machines, or is parallelism alone enough?

Last but not least, the questions relating to finding the right complexity measures, and assigning to them suitable costs come into play. In complexity theory, all of the above questions have been raised and answered.

Surprisingly and fortunately for this theory, it appeared that most of the resulting models, although wildly varying in their architectural features, possess about the same computational efficiency. For most of these models it has been proven that *parallel time* (of these models) is polynomially equivalent to *sequential space* (of the first class machines). The respective proofs are constructive via mutual simulations of the parallel and the sequential machines involved.

The above property of parallel machines is nowadays known as the *Parallel Computation Thesis* (PCT). The respective class of parallel machine models that satisfy this thesis is known as *the second machine class* denoted as C_2 [19].

Out of the great competition of all possible second class machines, the model of the *Parallel RAM* (PRAM) seems to achieve the greatest popularity. This is especially true among the designers of parallel algorithms, and also among the critics of idealized parallel machines (see Section 4 and 6). This machine model is very close to our intuitive ideas about how parallel computations can be performed, at least "mentally", as Papadimitriou [13] has put it nicely. A PRAM consists of several independent sequential processors, each with its own private memory. They communicate with one another through a global memory. In one unit of time each processor can read one global or local memory location, execute a single RAM operation, and write into one global or local memory location. PRAMs can be further classified according to the restrictions of the global memory accesses [11].

For an exhaustive overview of both the first and the second machine class models and for the related theoretical background one should see the excellent survey by van Emde Boas [19]. Now we have to discuss the importance of the above research and the results for complexity theory.

First of all, the above results demonstrate that the concept of parallelism as embodied by the PCT is very robust indeed: to a large extent it does not depend on particular parallel machine models. One advantage is that it makes the underlying theory machine-independent. On the other hand, it also leaves the freedom to study certain concrete problems on one's favorite model as well as making the results transferable to other models.

Second, the PCT enables an alternative characterization of certain fundamental complexity classes. E.g., denoting by //PTIME the class of problems solvable on the second class machines in (parallel) polynomial time, the PCT translates into the statement that //PTIME=PSPACE. It is amusing to observe that it follows from the previous equality that we do not know for sure whether $C_1 \neq C_2$, since in theory we do not know whether PTIME$\neq$PSPACE.

Nevertheless, the last equality, in fact, says that the second class machines are quite *time-efficient* indeed, as they can solve PSPACE–complete (and hence also NPTIME–complete) problems in polynomial time. It follows from the respective simulation proofs (simulating a polynomially space-bounded Turing machine by a polynomially time-bounded PRAM, say) that the price to be paid for such an efficiency is high. Unfortunately, no better simulation is known than the one requiring an exponential number of processors.

Third, the respective research has lead to the definition of a new complexity class whose investigation is presently at the center of the current parallel complexity theory. This class was discovered while trying to specify the class of problems that would be especially suitable for the parallel solution within C_2. Contrary to PTIME, the whole class //PTIME appears to be infeasible, due to its equality to PSPACE. Therefore, the class NC has been (roughly) defined as the class of problems that are solvable in polylogarithmic time (i.e., in time $O(\log^k n)$ for any k fixed) and simultaneously with only a polynomial number of processors on any C_2 machine. This clearly captures the main benefits of parallelism. For an affordable price (polynomial number of processors) one can obtain a substantial speedup (polylogarithmic time). Thus, the class NC can be viewed as the class of problems that admit an efficient parallel solution within C_2. It contains many important algorithms. Among them there are, for example, the basic arithmetic operations, transitive closure and the Boolean matrix multiplication, the computation of the determinant, the rank or inverse of a matrix, integer sorting, etc. [11].

Clearly NC$\subseteq$PTIME (since sequential simulation of one parallel step of an NC computation requires only polynomial time, and there is a polylogarithmic number of such steps to be simulated). We do not know whether NC=PTIME. The positive answer to this question would mean that all problems within PTIME (or P, the class of problems which are considered to be *sequentially feasible*) would also be *efficiently parallelizable* (within C_2). The least likely candidates from PTIME for membership in NC are the *P–complete problems* (cf. [11]).

It is possible to introduce a hierarchy within the class NC [10]. For instance, circuits with unbounded fan–in and fan–out of polynomial size and of constant depth present a very attractive class of computing devices that are the subjects of a very vivid recent research. The practical importance of NC algorithms will be discussed in Section 6.

4   The Physical Limitations of Parallel Machines

Soon after the appearance of the first models from C_2, results pointing to physical infeasibility of the related models appeared. These result are specifying that it is impossible to build realistic parallel machine models whose asymptotic performance would match the theoretical performance of the C_2 machines.

These results have been inspired by recent (in those times) progress in computer technology — namely by VLSI (Very Large Scale Integration) technology. The miniaturization and the density of computing elements on a single chip have approached their limits when the size of semiconductor elements, their switching time, the length and the thickness of wires started to play a crucial role in the performance of resulting devices [12]. On such a technological scale, one must at least count with the finite speed of signal propagation along the wires and on a certain lower bound on the minimal volume that any processor must occupy. Under such assumptions, no matter how tightly we pack n processors into a spherical body, its diameter would be of the order of $n^{1/3}$. This means that there must be processors about this distance apart and thus, the communication between any such pair of processors will take time proportional to $n^{1/3}$.

This observations immediately learns that in reality an exponential number of processors (as in the proof of PSPACE$\subseteq$//PTIME) cannot be activated in polynomial time, and unless PTIME=PSPACE, the Parallel Computation Thesis cannot be fulfilled by any real machine. From this point of view the class NC is also not well-defined. Thus, the class C_2 seems to be doomed to remain just a class of mathematical objects with a computational behaviour that cannot be realized in practice.

Under similar assumptions as above, it has even been proved that asymptotically any reasonable parallel machine of time complexity $T(n)$ can be simulated by a multitape TM in time $T^8(n)$ [5]. Thus, w.r.t. the first machine class at most a *polynomial asymptotical speedup* can be achieved.

The understanding that, in order to be realistic, the models of parallel machines must faithfully reflect the basic physical laws has brought the respective theory to a reevaluation of its results and goals.

First of all, in the theory of machine models the class C_2 has started to play a similar role as the completeness results do in the field of algorithms design. The membership of some machine model in this class can be interpreted as an *infeasibility result* for the model at hand. Nevertheless, this does not mean that the respective parallel algorithms, especially in the class NC, have entirely lost their value. They still present a valuable reservoir of basic ideas, tricks and techniques that can be used in the design of parallel algorithms for realistic models of parallel computers (see the discussion in Section 6).

Subsequently, a new field of research within the parallel machine models has been open, targeting the design and study of *realistic parallel machine models*. On the one hand, they should be physically feasible and on the other hand, they should still be substantially faster than sequential machines, albeit not necessarily in the asymptotic sense.

The respective development will be discussed in the next two sections.

5 Scalable Parallel Machines

Scalable parallel machines are abstract machine models that take into consideration the ultimate impact of fundamental physical limitations, as was already mentioned in the previous section. Thus, their performance must be tightly related to the performance of realistic, physically buildable machines that must obviously obey the restrictions resulting from physical laws.

A family $\mathcal{F}$ of abstract computational devices $\{\mathcal{F}\}_{n \geq 1}$, where each $\mathcal{F}_n$ is capable of processing any input of size n is called *scalable* if there exists a physical realization $\mathcal{R} = \{\mathcal{R}_n\}_{n \geq 1}$ of $\mathcal{F}$ such that for each n the maximal duration of any computational step (measured in any real unit of time) on $\mathcal{R}_n$ does not depend on n.

Intuitively, the notion of scalability captures the requirement that parallel machines of arbitrary size (i.e., those capable to process arbitrary long inputs) can be considered, and that their physical realization that will preserve their time complexity measure will always exist.

Examples of scalable machines include cellular automata [2], systolic machines [25], space machines [8] and multitape or multihead TMs [27].

Surprisingly, the RAM with a logarithmic cost criterion is not scalable, The reason is that access to its first $S(n)$ registers of size $O(\log S(n))$ each requires time in the order of $\Omega(\sqrt{S(n)} \log S(n))$ (when the memory is laid down in the two-dimensional plane), and it cannot be done in time $O(log S(n))$ as the logarithmic cost criterion assumes.

It has been shown that communication structures used in the design of second class machines — hypercubes, binary trees, cube-connected cycles, butterflies, etc. ([18]), are not scalable. Despite the low topological diameter of the respective graphs, in any physical realization of them in two dimensions, there will always appear an edge of length of at least $\Omega(\sqrt{n}/\log n)$. This destroys the assumption on unit cost of communication along the edges of the underlying graphs [21]. This is true even for random graphs with a low diameter [22].

The conclusion from all of the negative results above is that practically the only scalable structures are the *orthogonal meshes*. Other similar scalable graph structures like tridiagonal or hexagonal meshes can be emulated in real-time on orthogonal meshes. Presently there is a common consensus that mesh–connected architectures may be the ultimate solution for interconnecting the extremely large computer complexes of the future [21], [2].

The computational efficiency of scalable parallel machines in relation to classes $\mathcal{C}_1$ and $\mathcal{C}_2$ has been investigated in [24], [25]. A so–called *parallel Tur-*

ing machine (PTM) has been proposed as a representative of the respective scalable machines.

This machine looks like a nondeterministic multitape TM. However, its computational behaviour is different. Initially, the machine starts in the initial configuration as any TM. When, during its computation the PTM enters a configuration from which $d > 1$ next moves are possible, it multiplies the number of its finite control units (inclusively the respective heads) and creates d identical "copies" of them (so–called processors of a PTM). Then each of the d processors executes a different move from altogether d different moves that are to be performed, *still working on the same tape contents*. Further on each processor behaves independently. Combinatorial arguments can demonstrate that during a computation of length $T(n)$ at most a polynomial number (in $T(n)$) of different processors can emerge.

Thus, starting with a single processor a PTM can repeatedly create new processors that all compute over the same tapes. An input is accepted when all processors enter into accepting states.

The author of this model has shown that a single–tape PTM is scalable (or, as he has expressed it, is *physically feasible*: in real-time it can simulate any VLSI–like circuit obeying the physical laws and vice versa). It is linearly time-equivalent to any scalable machine model that we have mentioned in this section. From the computational point of view, it can serve as a joint representative of all these models.

The key idea of the discovery of the true computational power of PTMs, and hence of all other similar devices, lies in making use of their limited polynomial parallelism for processing not just a single input but of *a sequence of inputs*. It appears that the main difference between these machines and the first class machines is that the former can be programmed to process any sequence of inputs (of the same size to the same problem) in a *pipelined manner*. For this purpose the machines must be equipped with an input mechanism which ensures that after reading, for example, the k–th bit of an input the k–th bit of the *next input* can be read for all of $1 \leq k \leq n$. Thus, several inputs in parallel can be read at the same time. Moreover, there must be some output mechanism that prints the results which correspond with individual inputs. The PTM equipped with such an input and output mechanism is called a *pipelined PTM*.

For such machines, the *period* of a computation can be defined as the time elapsed between starting the reading of the i–th input and printing the corresponding answer (as usual, we take the maximum over all inputs of the given length).

Let PERIOD($F(n)$) be the class of all problems that can be solved by a pipelined single–tape PTM within the period of $F(n)$, let PPERIOD be the class of all problems that can be solved on the same machine with a polynomial period. In [24] it was shown that PPERIOD=PSPACE, i.e., polynomially space-bounded computations of TMs are equivalent with polynomially period-bounded computations of single–tape pipelined PTMs. This may be appropriately called the *pipelined computation thesis*. From the parallel computation thesis it follows that PPERIOD=//PTIME. Thus, the class of computational devices that are equivalent to single–tape pipelined PTMs (i.e., the class of scalable machines) is in a interesting way, via the period of the computation, polynomially related to both the first and the second machine class. In [25] the respective machine class satisfying the pipelined computation thesis is also called the class of *weakly parallel machines*.

As a matter of fact it has been shown in [25] that, while a nonpipelined version of a single–tape PTM belongs to $\mathcal{C}_1$, the nonpipelined version of a multitape PTM does not belong neither to $\mathcal{C}_1$ (it is not linearly space-equivalent to a TM), nor to $\mathcal{C}_2$ (since it can achieve at most a polynomial speedup w.r.t. a DTM). The latter machine is also not scalable.

For an overview of all known results about PTMs see [25].

6   Realistic Models of Parallel Machines

Both the second machine class and the class of weakly parallel machines have been developed, and are still under development primarily because of questions in complexity theory. The situation is rather different with the so–called *realistic machine models* of parallel computers. They emerged primarily by the beginning of the nineteen nineties as a direct reaction of complexity theory to the challenge of the parallel computing crisis mentioned in the introduction.

There is one early honorable exception — the so–called *Array Processing Machine* (APM) that was developed in 1984 by van Leeuwen and Wiedermann. Its development was inspired by existing array (or vector) processors and the aim was to design a parallel machine model that would play a similar role in $\mathcal{C}_2$ as the RAM does in $\mathcal{C}_1$. In [20] it is shown that the APM with a unit cost measure does belong to $\mathcal{C}_2$. Nevertheless, with the proper cost measure that would reflect the lengths of vectors to be processed, the APM starts to be a realistic model of vectorized parallel computers that make an intensive use of pipelining in realizing the vector operations. With the latter cost measure, until now the APM seems to be the only realistic model of parallel computers oriented towards vector processing.

The design of all realistic machine models is influenced by existing real computers. They try to capture the main *complexity features* (performance characteristics) of the real model rather than their architectural features. This is because the possible design space for parallel machines is too large, as is explained in Section 3. Therefore, there is a consensus that a single architecture for a computational model of realistic parallel computers like it is the case with RAMs in the first machine class cannot exist. By concentrating merely on complexity features the desired effect stating that the resulting models are to a large extend machine independent has been achieved. Moreover, the resulting models of realistic parallel machines are usually not scalable and, therefore, are not amenable to an asymptotical analysis with respect to the increasing number of processors.

One class of realistic parallel machine models that seems to cover the wide spectrum of existing parallel machines is based on the notion of PRAM (see its description in Section 3). The PRAM is transformed into a model of a parallel computer which in practice consists of a few hundred or thousand of nodes, each containing a powerful processor and a sizeable memory (a full RAM in our terms), interconnected by a point–to–point network with limited bandwidth (not arbitrary many messages can be sent or received by processors in parallel) and with a significant latency and overhead in communication (it takes some non trivial time to establish, realize and complete the communication among selected processors). For this purpose, the PRAM is equipped with additional explicit operations that make the operations of real machines that were neglected in PRAMs apparent. It is no longer assumed that the processors of a PRAM work in a synchronous manner. The synchronization must be done "manually" at times as it is required by the parallel algorithm. The mechanism for interprocessor communication is not specified. Its only requirement is that it must have the capability to realize, in a direct or indirect way, the transfer of information among any pair (or set) of processors. However, this operation is not for free. There is a special fee counted for establishing and/or finishing the connection and a special cost to be charged for transfer time. Also, there are restrictions on how many massages can be exchanged in parallel.

The resulting model is in fact a (multi)parametrized model. The parameters are essentially the complexity characteristics of the above mentioned communication primitives. The number of available processors is also included among the parameters. The algorithms are designed not only to work for any values of the parameters (or at least for parameter within a certain range), but to optimize their performance w.r.t. the above parameters. For optimal parallel algorithms of this type it is important to always find a proper balance between the amount of work spent by computations within individual processors and the required communication costs, while always making the maximal use of available parallelism within all relevant restrictions. The complexity of the resulting algorithms is expressed in terms of the respective parameters as well.

For concrete parallel machines these parameters take concrete values. Thus the expected performance of each algorithm can be determined. When the machines are not scalable, we usually do not know the asymptotic behaviour of some parameters and therefore, the asymptotic analysis of algorithms does not make much sense for such machines.

Since more factors than in the case of sequential algorithms must be taken into consideration, the design of parallel algorithms for realistic parallel machines is by an order of magnitude a more demanding intellectual task. It is here where one has to make use of the previous knowledge of PRAM or NC algorithms. This requires knowledgeable programmers with the proper theoretical background and it is therefore very important that the respective theory starts to be regularly included into the respective university curricula (contrary to some opposite proposals [9]).

Valiant's *Bulk Synchronized Parallel Computer* [17], or the *LogP* parallel computer proposed by Culler *et al.* [7] can serve as typical representatives of the above mentioned realistic machine models.

Defining (and accepting) a unique "bridging model" of a parallel computer (as Valiant has put it in [17]) will create a common platform for an independent development of both parallel software and parallel hardware. In this way it is hoped that the current parallel computing crisis will be overcome.

The other class of realistic parallel computers that are considered in the literature is inspired by the previous class of scalable machines. The idea is to consider "almost scalable" machines that are created by two–dimensional orthogonal square meshes of processors. Usually full RAMs are considered in the place of processors. With the exception of outer processors, each RAM is connected with its four neighbors. Each of n processors is addressable by a pair (i, j) that determines the position of processor within the mesh. What makes the resulting computer non–scalable is the fact that the size of internal processor's memory grows with the size of the mesh, since each processor must be able to store at least its address that is of size $\Theta(\log n)$. While this asymptotically violates the scalability, since the area of the resulting mesh computer grows faster than the number of its processors, in practice the respective machines can be considered scalable in a relatively large scope. This is because within the existing technology the speed of internal processor computations exceeds by far the overall time of message-transfers (including all communication overheads) between neighboring processors. The discrepancy between the respective times is so large that it even leaves room for sizeable internal processor memories. Roughly, the size of internal memory can grow as long as the corresponding memory access time is less than the total communication time. For a detailed discussion of the related issues see [2].

To make maximal use of the parallelism of mesh–connected parallel computers, special parallel algorithms tailored to the underlying mesh architecture must be designed [15]. Nevertheless, there is again a theoretical approach that in practice makes the mesh–connected computers more versatile than one might think at the first sight. The idea is to design efficient algorithms simulating any n processor PRAM on an n–node mesh. This will enable efficient realization of PRAM programs on meshes. Clearly, due to the mesh diameter, an $\Omega(\sqrt{n})$ lower bound applies to the simulation of any single PRAM operation. Therefore the simulated PRAM programs will be slowed down by the same factor. Fortunately, it appears that in many cases the optimal or almost optimal slowdown is achievable (cf. [14]). The underlying algorithms are quite complicated, often probabilistic or randomized ones.

To illustrate the main related problem, note that by a few PRAM operations one can, in constant time, realize an arbitrary permutation of variables stored in the PRAM processors (one variable per processor). On a mesh-connected computer this translates into the problem of correctly routing all the respective variables from their home processors to their target processors. Clearly, this requires at least $\Omega(\sqrt{n})$ moves. To achieve this bound schemes using only local information available in individual processors, and minimizing the delays and contentions when more messages need to pass through a given processor must be devised. In general one must consider even more complicated instances of the previous situation when in each processor there are initially several variables, and each processor is a target of several variables. Despite of a quite intensive research no definitive solutions to such problems have been found so far.

Though a slowdown of order $\Theta(\sqrt{n})$ seems to be quite high in the case of NC algorithms, it can still lead to algorithms that are of sublinear time complexity, and therefore, supersede the sequential computations. This again brings further support to the study of idealized parallel machine models and to the design of the corresponding efficient parallel algorithms.

The computational efficiency of a similar parallel model as above that, however, has a simpler topological structure and consists of less efficient processors, has been studied in [26]. Here a so-called *ring Turing machine* (essentially a ring network of Turing machines communicating via message exchanges) has been proposed. Its efficiency has been investigated w.r.t. its ability to simulate nondeterministic computations. It has been shown that within a certain range, the speed up proportional to the number of processors can be achieved.

For an other recent parallel machine model that, from our point of view, seems to be somewhere between realistic, scalable and idealized machine models, see [6].

Looking for efficient simulations of PRAMs on realistic parallel machines seems to be one of the most promising trends in the respective theory [1]. Assigning the real cost as induced by such simulations to PRAM operations, would turn the resulting PRAM model into a realistic model, while preserving its conceptual simplicity that makes it suitable for the design and analysis of parallel algorithms. In doing so, attention should be paid to the problems of simulating PRAMs on realistic models of parallel machines with a fixed number of processors. This would correspond to the most common situation in practice. When compared to the complexity of the best sequential algorithms the corresponding parallel algorithms on such machines should ideally attain a speedup proportional to the number of processors.

7   Conclusions

Nowadays many long-term research projects have been focused on "high performance computing," or "affordable parallel computing" as the current technical jargon for realistic parallel computing seems to be. If the respective research has to substantially contribute to the solution of the current parallel computing crisis, the ideas and aims of various projects should converge towards certain similar solutions. Nevertheless, this is to be expected, since all projects start from the same knowledge basis represented by the present achievements in parallel machine theory (as illustrated also in this paper) and in the related theoretical computer science disciplines. Moreover, there is already a consensus concerning the available research space in which the solution should be sought and how it should look like (the ideas from Section 6).

There is a part of machine theory that already thinks about the future of computing. It is occupied by futuristic models of computing machines that are based on principles whose validity is plausible but for which no real machines exist so far. The quantum computers [4], neural or analog computers [16], molecular computers [3], adiabatic computers [23] and others can serve as examples of such machines. In the presence of no relevant technical constraints, it is to be expected that, so far and again, the theory of only idealized models is being developed similarly as in the case of early days of parallel machine theory. Perhaps one day we will find ourselves in a "quantum computing crisis". Then, we should not be too surprised since we already know that this is the natural way in which things develop. We should rather be pleased because at that time we shall know that the parallel computing crisis is over.

References

1. Adler, M., Byers, J. W., Karp, R. M.: Scheduling Parallel Communication: The h-relation problem. In: J. Wiedermann, P. Hájek (Eds.), *Mathematical Foundations of Computer Science 1995*, 20th Int. Symposium (MFCS'95), Lecture Notes in Computer Science, Vol. 969, Springer-Verlag, Berlin, 1995, pp. 1–20.

2. Bilardi, G., Preparata, F. P.: Horizons of Parallel Computing. TR No. CS–93–20, Dept of Computer Science, Universita di Padova, May 1993.

3. Birge, R.R.: Protein–Based Computers. *Scientific American*, March 1995, pp. 66–71.

4. Brassard, G.: A Quantum Jump in Computer Science. This volume.

5. Chazelle, B., Monier, L.: A Model of Computation for VLSI with Related Complexity Results. *JACM* 32 (1985) 573–588.

6. Chlebus, B. S., Czumaj, A., Gasieniec, L., Kowaluk, M., Plandowski, W.: Parallel Alternating–Direction Access Machine. *Proceedings of Abstracts of ALTEC IV International Workshop*, Charles University, Prague, March 1995.

7. Culler, D., Karp, R., Patterson, D., Sahay, A., Schauser, K.E., Santos, E., Subramonian, R., von Eicken, T.: LogP: Towards a Realistic Model of Parallel Computation. In: *Proc. 4th Annual ACM Symposium on Principles and Practice of Parallel Programming* (PPOPP'93), May 1993, California, USA.

8. Feldman, Y., Shapiro, E.: Spatial Machines: a More Realistic Approach to Parallel Computing. *CACM* 35:10 (1992) 61–73.

9. Furht, B.: Parallel Computing: Glory and Collapse. *COMPUTER*, November 1994, pp. 74–75.

10. Johnson, D.S.: A Catalog of Complexity Classes. In: J. van Leeuwen (Ed.), *Handbook of Theoretical Computer Science*, Vol. A, Elsevier Science Publishers, Amsterdam, 1990, pp. 67–161.

11. Karp, R.M., Ramachandran, V.: Parallel Algorithms for Shared–Memory Machines. In: J. van Leeuwen (Ed.), *Handbook of Theoretical Computer Science*, Vol. A, Elsevier Science Publishers, Amsterdam, 1990, pp. 869–941.

12. Mead, C., Conway, L.: *Introduction to VLSI Systems*. Addison–Wesley Publ. Comp., Reading, MA, 1980.

13. Papadimitriou, Ch. H.: *Computational Complexity*. Addison–Wesley Publ. Comp., Reading, MA, 1994.

14. Pietracaprina, A., Pucci, G., Sibeyn, J.F.: Constructive Deterministic PRAM Simulation on a Mesh–Connected Computer. TR–93–059, International Computer Science Institute, Berkeley, CA, Oct. 1993.

15. Sibeyn, J.F., Kaufmann, M.: Solving Cheap Graph Problems on Meshes. In: J. Wiedermann, P. Hájek (Eds.), *Mathematical Foundations of Computer Science 1995*, 20th Int. Symposium (MFCS'95), Lecture Notes in Computer Science, Vol. 969, Springer-Verlag, Berlin, 1995, pp. 412–422.

16. Siegelmann, H.T.: Recurrent Neural Networks. This volume.

17. Valiant, L.G.: A Bridging Model for Parallel Computation. *CACM* 33:8 (1990) 103–111.

18. Valiant, L.G.: General Purpose Parallel Architectures. In: J. van Leeuwen (Ed.), *Handbook of Theoretical Computer Science*, Vol. A, Elsevier Science Publishers, Amsterdam, 1990, pp. 943–971.

19. van Emde Boas, P.: Machine Models and Simulations. In: J. van Leeuwen (Ed.), *Handbook of Theoretical Computer Science*, Vol. A, Elsevier Science Publishers, Amsterdam, 1990, pp. 1–66.

20. van Leeuwen, J., Wiedermann, J.: Array Processing Machines: An Abstract Model. *BIT* 27 (1987) 25–43.

21. Vitányi, P.: Locality, Communication, and Interconnect Length in Multicomputers. *SIAM J. Comput.*17:4 (1988) 659–672.

22. Vitányi, P.: Multiprocessor Architectures and Physical Laws. In: *Proc. PhysComp94*, IEEE Computer Society Press, 1994.

23. Vitányi, P.: Physics and the New Computation. In: J. Wiedermann, P. Hájek (Eds.), *Mathematical Foundations of Computer Science 1995*, 20th Int. Symposium (MFCS'95), Lecture Notes in Computer Science, Vol. 969, Springer-Verlag, Berlin, 1995, pp. 106–128.

24. Wiedermann, J.: Parallel Turing Machines. Tech. Rep. RUU–CS–84–11, Dept. of Computer Science, Utrecht University, Utrecht, 1984.

25. Wiedermann, J.: Weak Parallel Machines: A New Class of Physically Feasible Parallel Machine Models. In: I.M. Havel, V. Koubek (Eds.), *Mathematical Foundations of Computer Science 1992*, 17th Int. Symposium (MFCS'92), Lecture Notes in Computer Science, Vol. 629, Springer Verlag, Berlin, 1992, pp. 95–111.

26. Wiedermann, J.: Fast Sequential and Parallel Simulation of Nondeterministic Computations. *Computers and Artificial Intelligence* 13:6 (1994) 521–536.

27. Wiedermann, J.: Five New Simulation Results on Turing Machines. Technical Report V–631, Institute of Computer Science, Prague, 1995.

Templates for Linear Algebra Problems *

Zhaojun Bai[1], David Day[1], James Demmel[2], Jack Dongarra[3], Ming Gu[2],
Axel Ruhe[4], and Henk van der Vorst[5]

[1] Department of Mathematics, University of Kentucky, Lexington, KY 40506
[2] Computer Science Division and Department of Mathematics, University of
California, Berkeley, CA 94720
[3] Computer Science Department, University of Tennessee, Knoxville, TN 37996, and
Oak Ridge National Laboratory, Mathematical Science Section, Oak Ridge, TN 37831
[4] Dept. of Computing Science, Chalmers University of Technology, S-41296 Göteborg
[5] Department of Mathematics, Utrecht University, NL-3584 CH Utrecht

Abstract. The increasing availability of advanced-architecture computers is having a very significant effect on all spheres of scientific computation, including algorithm research and software development in numerical linear algebra. Linear algebra –in particular, the solution of linear systems of equations and eigenvalue problems – lies at the heart of
most calculations in scientific computing. This paper discusses some of
the recent developments in linear algebra designed to help the user on
advanced-architecture computers.
Much of the work in developing linear algebra software for advanced-
architecture computers is motivated by the need to solve large problems
on the fastest computers available. In this paper, we focus on four basic
issues: (1) the motivation for the work; (2) the development of standards
for use in linear algebra and the building blocks for a library; (3) aspects
of templates for the solution of large sparse systems of linear algorithm;
and (4) templates for the solution of large sparse eigenvalue problems.
This last project is under development and we will pay more attention
to it in this paper.

1 Introduction and Motivation

Large scale problems of engineering and scientific computing often require solutions of linear algebra problems, such as systems of linear equations, least squares
problems, or eigenvalue problems. There is a vast amount of material available
on solving such problems, in books, in journal articles, and as software. This
software consists of well-maintained libraries available commercially or electronically in the public-domain, other libraries distributed with texts or other books,

* This work was made possible in part by grants from the Defense Advanced Research
  Projects Agency under contract DAAL03-91-C-0047 administered by the Army Re-
  search Office, the Office of Scientific Computing U.S. Department of Energy un-
  der Contract DE-AC05-84OR21400, the National Science Foundation Science and
  Technology Center Cooperative Agreement No. CCR-8809615, and National Science
  Foundation Grant No. ASC-9005933.

individual subroutines tested and published by organizations like the ACM, and yet more software available from individuals or electronic sources like Netlib [21], which may be hard to find or come without support. So although many challenging numerical linear algebra problems still await satisfactory solutions, many excellent methods exist from a plethora of sources.

But the sheer number of algorithms and their implementations makes it hard even for experts, let alone general users, to find the best solution for a given problem. This has led to the development of various on-line search facilities for numerical software. One has been developed by NIST (National Institute of Standards and Technology), and is called GAMS (Guide to Available Mathematical Software) [7]; another is part of Netlib [21]. These facilities permit search based on library names, subroutines names, keywords, and a taxonomy of topics in numerical computing. But for the general user in search of advice as to which algorithm or which subroutine to use for her particular problem, they offer relatively little advice.

Furthermore, many challenging problems cannot be solved with existing "black-box" software packages in a reasonable time or space. This means that more special purpose methods must be used, and tuned for the problem at hand. This tuning is the greatest challenge, since there are a large number of tuning options available, and for many problems it is a challenge to get any acceptable answer at all, or have confidence in what is computed. The expertise regarding which options, or combinations of options, is likely to work in a specific application area, is widely distributed.

Thus, there is a need for tools to help users pick the best algorithm and implementation for their numerical problems, as well as expert advice on how to tune them. In fact, we see three potential user communities for such tools:

- The "HPCC" (High Performance Computing and Communication) community consists of those scientists trying to solve the largest, hardest applications in their fields. They desire high speed, access to algorithmic details for performance tuning, and reliability for their problem.
- Engineers and scientists generally desire easy-to-use, reliable software, that is also reasonably efficient.
- Students and teachers want simple but generally effective algorithms, which are easy to explain and understand.

It may seem difficult to address the needs of such diverse communities with a single document. Nevertheless, we believe this is possible in the form of *templates*.

A template for an algorithm includes

1. A high-level description of the algorithm.
2. A description of when it is effective, including conditions on the input, and estimates of the time, space or other resources required. If there are natural competitors, they will be referenced.
3. A description of available refinements and user-tunable parameters, as well as advice on when to use them.

4. Pointers to complete or partial implementations, perhaps in several languages or for several architectures (each parallel architecture). These implementation expose those details suitable for user-tuning, and hide the others.
5. Numerical examples, on a common set of examples, illustrating both easy cases and difficult cases.
6. Trouble shooting advice.
7. Pointers to texts or journal articles for further information.

In addition to individual templates, there will be a *decision tree* to help steer the user to the right algorithm, or to a subset of possible algorithms, based on a sequence of questions about the nature of the problem to be solved.

Our goal in this paper is to outline a set of templates for systems of linear equations and eigenvalue problems. The main theme is to explain how to use iterative methods.

The paper is organized as follows. Section 2 discusses related work. Section 3 describes the work we have done on templates for sparse linear systems. Section 4 described our taxonomy of eigenvalue problems and algorithms, which we will use to organize the templates and design a decision tree. Section 4.1 discusses notation and terminology. Sections 4.2 through 4.7 below describe the decision tree in more detail. Section 4.8 outlines a chapter on accuracy issues, which is meant to describe what accuracy one can expect to achieve, since eigenproblems can be very ill-conditioned, as well as tools for measuring accuracy. Section 4.9 describes the formats in which we expect to deliver both software and documentation. This paper is a design document. We encourage feedback, especially from potential users.

2   Related Work

Many excellent numerical linear algebra texts [43, 25, 30, 11, 33] and black-box software libraries [36, 24, 1] exist. A great deal of more specialized software for eigenproblems also exists, see e.g. [31, 4] for surveys on the subject.

A book of templates, including software, has already been written for iterative methods for solving linear systems [6], although it does not include all the ingredients mentioned above. In particular, it discusses some important advanced methods, such as preconditioning, domain decomposition and multigrid, relatively briefly, and does not have a comprehensive set of numerical examples to help explain the expected performance from each algorithm on various problem classes. It has a relatively simple decision tree to help users choose an algorithm. Nevertheless, it successfully incorporates many of the features we wish to have.

The linear algebra chapter in Numerical Recipes [32] contains a brief description of the conjugate gradient algorithm for sparse linear systems and the eigensystem chapter only contains the basic method for solving dense standard eigenvalue problem. All of the methods and available software in the recipes, except the Jacobi method for symmetric eigenvalue problem, are simplified versions of algorithms in the EISPACK and LAPACK. Beside on disk, the software in the recipes are actually printed line by line in the book.

2.1   Dense Linear Algebra Libraries

Over the past twenty-five years, we have been involved in the development of several important packages of dense linear algebra software: EISPACK [36, 24], LINPACK [16], LAPACK [1], and the BLAS [28, 19, 18]. In addition, we are currently involved in the development of ScaLAPACK [8], a scalable version of LAPACK for distributed memory concurrent computers. In this section, we give a brief review of these packages—their history, their advantages, and their limitations on high-performance computers.

EISPACK EISPACK is a collection of Fortran subroutines that compute the eigenvalues and eigenvectors of nine classes of matrices: complex general, complex Hermitian, real general, real symmetric, real symmetric banded, real symmetric tridiagonal, special real tridiagonal, generalized real, and generalized real symmetric matrices. In addition, two routines are included that use singular value decomposition to solve certain least-squares problems.

EISPACK is primarily based on a collection of Algol procedures developed in the 1960s and collected by J. H. Wilkinson and C. Reinsch in a volume entitled *Linear Algebra* in the *Handbook for Automatic Computation* series [44]. This volume was not designed to cover every possible method of solution; rather, algorithms were chosen on the basis of their generality, elegance, accuracy, speed, or economy of storage. Since the release of EISPACK in 1972, thousands of copies of the collection have been distributed worldwide.

LINPACK LINPACK is a collection of Fortran subroutines that analyze and solve linear equations and linear least-squares problems. The package solves linear systems whose matrices are general, banded, symmetric indefinite, symmetric positive definite, triangular, and tridiagonal square. In addition, the package computes the QR and singular value decompositions of rectangular matrices and applies them to least-squares problems.

LINPACK is organized around four matrix factorizations: LU factorization, Cholesky factorization, QR factorization, and singular value decomposition. The term LU factorization is used here in a very general sense to mean the factorization of a square matrix into a lower triangular part and an upper triangular part, perhaps with pivoting.

LINPACK uses column-oriented algorithms to increase efficiency by preserving locality of reference. By column orientation we mean that the LINPACK codes always reference arrays down columns, not across rows. This works because Fortran stores arrays in column major order. Thus, as one proceeds down a column of an array, the memory references proceed sequentially in memory. On the other hand, as one proceeds across a row, the memory references jump across memory, the length of the jump being proportional to the length of a column. The effects of column orientation are quite dramatic: on systems with virtual or cache memories, the LINPACK codes will significantly outperform codes that are not column oriented. We note, however, that textbook examples of matrix algorithms are seldom column oriented.

Another important factor influencing the efficiency of LINPACK is the use of the Level 1 BLAS; there are three effects.

First, the overhead entailed in calling the BLAS reduces the efficiency of the code. This reduction is negligible for large matrices, but it can be quite significant for small matrices. The matrix size at which it becomes unimportant varies from system to system; for square matrices it is typically between $n = 25$ and $n = 100$. If this seems like an unacceptably large overhead, remember that on many modern systems the solution of a system of order 25 or less is itself a negligible calculation. Nonetheless, it cannot be denied that a person whose programs depend critically on solving small matrix problems in inner loops will be better off with BLAS-less versions of the LINPACK codes. Fortunately, the BLAS can be removed from the smaller, more frequently used program in a short editing session.

Second, the BLAS improve the efficiency of programs when they are run on nonoptimizing compilers. This is because doubly subscripted array references in the inner loop of the algorithm are replaced by singly subscripted array references in the appropriate BLAS. The effect can be seen for matrices of quite small order, and for large orders the savings are quite significant.

Finally, improved efficiency can be achieved by coding a set of BLAS [18] to take advantage of the special features of the computers on which LINPACK is being run. For most computers, this simply means producing machine-language versions. However, the code can also take advantage of more exotic architectural features, such as vector operations. Further details about the BLAS are presented in Section 2.3.

LAPACK LAPACK [14] provides routines for solving systems of linear equations, least-squares problems, eigenvalue problems, and singular value problems. The associated matrix factorizations (LU, Cholesky, QR, SVD, Schur, generalized Schur) are also provided, as are related computations such as reordering of the Schur factorizations and estimating condition numbers. Dense and banded matrices are handled, but not general sparse matrices. In all areas, similar functionality is provided for real and complex matrices, in both single and double precision.

The original goal of the LAPACK project was to make the widely used EIS-PACK and LINPACK libraries run efficiently on shared-memory vector and parallel processors, as well as RISC workstations. On these machines, LINPACK and EISPACK are inefficient because their memory access patterns disregard the multilayered memory hierarchies of the machines, thereby spending too much time moving data instead of doing useful floating-point operations. LAPACK addresses this problem by reorganizing the algorithms to use block matrix operations, such as matrix multiplication, in the innermost loops [3, 14]. These block operations can be optimized for each architecture to account for the memory hierarchy [2], and so provide a transportable way to achieve high efficiency on diverse modern machines. Here we use the term "transportable" instead of "portable" because, for fastest possible performance, LAPACK requires that highly optimized block matrix operations be already implemented on each machine. In other words, the correctness of the code is portable, but high performance is not—if we limit ourselves to a single Fortran source code.

LAPACK can be regarded as a successor to LINPACK and EISPACK. It has virtually all the capabilities of these two packages and much more besides. LAPACK improves on LINPACK and EISPACK in four main respects: speed, accuracy, robustness and functionality. While LINPACK and EISPACK are based on the vector operation kernels of the Level 1 BLAS, LAPACK was designed at the outset to exploit the Level 3 BLAS —a set of specifications for Fortran subprograms that do various types of matrix multiplication and the solution of triangular systems with multiple right-hand sides. Because of the coarse granularity of the Level 3 BLAS operations, their use tends to promote high efficiency on many high-performance computers, particularly if specially coded implementations are provided by the manufacturer.

ScaLAPACK The ScaLAPACK software library extends the LAPACK library to run scalably on MIMD, distributed memory, concurrent computers [8, 9]. For such machines the memory hierarchy includes the off-processor memory of other processors, in addition to the hierarchy of registers, cache, and local memory on each processor. Like LAPACK, the ScaLAPACK routines are based on block-partitioned algorithms in order to minimize the frequency of data movement between different levels of the memory hierarchy. The fundamental building blocks of the ScaLAPACK library are distributed memory versions of the Level 2 and Level 3 BLAS, and a set of Basic Linear Algebra Communication Subprograms (BLACS) [17, 20] for communication tasks that arise frequently in parallel linear algebra computations. In the ScaLAPACK routines, all interprocessor communication occurs within the distributed BLAS and the BLACS, so the source code of the top software layer of ScaLAPACK looks very similar to that of LAPACK.

The interface for ScaLAPACK is similar to that of LAPACK, with some additional arguments passed to each routine to specify the data layout.

2.2   Target Architectures

The EISPACK and LINPACK software libraries were designed for supercomputers used in the 1970s and early 1980s, such as the CDC-7600, Cyber 205, and Cray-1. These machines featured multiple functional units pipelined for good performance [26]. The CDC-7600 was basically a high-performance scalar computer, while the Cyber 205 and Cray-1 were early vector computers.

The development of LAPACK in the late 1980s was intended to make the EISPACK and LINPACK libraries run efficiently on shared memory - vector supercomputers and RISC workstations. The ScaLAPACK software library will extend the use of LAPACK to distributed memory concurrent supercomputers.

The underlying concept of both the LAPACK and ScaLAPACK libraries is the use of block-partitioned algorithms to minimize data movement between different levels in hierarchical memory. Thus, the ideas for developing a library for dense linear algebra computations are applicable to any computer with a hierarchical memory that (1) imposes a sufficiently large startup cost on the movement of data between different levels in the hierarchy, and for which (2) the cost of a context switch is too great to make fine grain size multithreading worthwhile. Our target machines are, therefore, medium and large grain size advanced-architecture computers. These include "traditional" shared memory, vector supercomputers, such as the Cray Y-MP and C90, and MIMD distributed memory concurrent supercomputers, such as the Intel Paragon, the IBM SP2 and Cray T3D concurrent systems.

Future advances in compiler and hardware technologies in the mid to late 1990s are expected to make multithreading a viable approach for masking communication costs. Since the blocks in a block-partitioned algorithm can be regarded as separate threads, our approach will still be applicable on machines that exploit medium and coarse grain size multithreading.

2.3 The BLAS as the Key to Portability

At least three factors affect the performance of portable Fortran code.

1. **Vectorization.** Designing vectorizable algorithms in linear algebra is usually straightforward. Indeed, for many computations there are several variants, all vectorizable, but with different characteristics in performance (see, for example, [15]). Linear algebra algorithms can approach the peak performance of many machines—principally because peak performance depends on some form of chaining of vector addition and multiplication operations, and this is just what the algorithms require. However, when the algorithms are realized in straightforward Fortran 77 code, the performance may fall well short of the expected level, usually because vectorizing Fortran compilers fail to minimize the number of memory references—that is, the number of vector load and store operations.

2. **Data movement.** What often limits the actual performance of a vector, or scalar, floating-point unit is the rate of transfer of data between different levels of memory in the machine. Examples include the transfer of vector operands in and out of vector registers, the transfer of scalar operands in and out of a high-speed scalar processor, the movement of data between main memory and a high-speed cache or local memory, paging between actual memory and disk storage in a virtual memory system, and interprocessor communication on a distributed memory concurrent computer.

3. **Parallelism.** The nested loop structure of most linear algebra algorithms offers considerable scope for loop-based parallelism. This is the principal type of parallelism that LAPACK and ScaLAPACK presently aim to exploit. On shared memory concurrent computers, this type of parallelism can sometimes be generated automatically by a compiler, but often requires the insertion of compiler directives. On distributed memory concurrent computers, data must be moved between processors. This is usually done by explicit calls to message passing routines, although parallel language extensions such as Coherent Parallel C [22] and Split-C [10] do the message passing implicitly.

The question arises, "How can we achieve sufficient control over these three factors to obtain the levels of performance that machines can offer?" The answer is through use of the BLAS. There are now three levels of BLAS:

Level 1 BLAS [28]: for vector operations, such as $y \leftarrow \alpha x + y$
Level 2 BLAS [19]: for matrix-vector operations, such as $y \leftarrow \alpha Ax + \beta y$
Level 3 BLAS [18]: for matrix-matrix operations, such as $C \leftarrow \alpha AB + \beta C$.

Here, A, B and C are matrices, x and y are vectors, and α and β are scalars.

The Level 1 BLAS are used in LAPACK, but for convenience rather than for performance: they perform an insignificant fraction of the computation, and they cannot achieve high efficiency on most modern supercomputers.

The Level 2 BLAS can achieve near-peak performance on many vector processors, such as a single processor of a CRAY X-MP or Y-MP, or Convex C-2 machine. However, on other vector processors such as a CRAY-2 or an IBM 3090 VF, the performance of the Level 2 BLAS is limited by the rate of data movement between different levels of memory.

The Level 3 BLAS overcome this limitation. This third level of BLAS performs $O(n^3)$ floating-point operations on $O(n^2)$ data, whereas the Level 2 BLAS perform only $O(n^2)$ operations on $O(n^2)$ data. The Level 3 BLAS also allow us to exploit parallelism in a way that is transparent to the software that calls them. While the Level 2 BLAS offer some scope for exploiting parallelism, greater scope is provided by the Level 3 BLAS, as Table 1 illustrates.

Table 1. Speed in Mflop/s of Level 2 and Level 3 BLAS operations on a CRAY C90

(all matrices are of order 1000; U is upper triangular)

Number of processors:	1	2	4	8	16
Level 2: $y \leftarrow \alpha Ax + \beta y$	899	1780	3491	6783	11207
Level 3: $C \leftarrow \alpha AB + \beta C$	900	1800	3600	7199	14282
Level 2: $x \leftarrow Ux$	852	1620	3063	5554	6953
Level 3: $B \leftarrow UB$	900	1800	3574	7147	13281
Level 2: $x \leftarrow U^{-1}x$	802	1065	1452	1697	1558
Level 3: $B \leftarrow U^{-1}B$	896	1792	3578	7155	14009

3   Templates for Sparse Linear Solvers

The 'Templates' for the solution of large sparse linear systems consists of a collection of iterative methods together with a manual for algorithmic choices, instructions, and guidelines [6]. In contrast to the dense matrix case, there is no single iterative method that can solve any given sparse linear system in reasonable time and with reasonable memory requirements. In principle, many of the described methods solve a given system in at most n iteration steps, where n is the order of the linear system. Not only does this assume exact arithmetic, also one does not want to do as many as n iteration steps for large systems. A major problem with iterative solution methods is that their speed of convergence depends on certain properties of the linear system, and these properties are often unknown in practice. This makes it difficult to make the right selection for a method. For many very large linear systems iterative systems are at this moment the only possible choice; there is hardly an alternative. Therefore, it is necessary for the users for the users to have a meaningful variety of iterative methods available, and this is what Templates provides. The potential user is guided into the world of iterative methods, and only a minimum of linear algebra knowledge is assumed. With the information provided in [6] the user can build high quality software at several levels of sophistication, depending on requirements and goals.

The starting point in Templates is the presentation of a selection of iteration methods in a very simple form, which closely follows the algorithmic descriptions in the original references. There is no monitoring of convergence behavior, and there are no precautions against numerical problems.

In this form the iteration schemes consist of one or two matrix vector products, a couple of inner-products and a few vector updates. The algorithms also allow for some form of preconditioning, which means that in each step a linear system $Mz = r$ has to be solved, where M has to be specified by the user. All these operations are pretty well understood, and it is easy to see how the algorithms work. Although possible numerical complications are ignored, these basic iteration Templates may be used for simple computational experiments in order to get familiarized with the basic iteration methods and their mutual differences. The user is given extensive advice in the manual on how to expand the basic codes to reliable software for practical problems.

We believe that Templates in its present form is a good move in the process of educating and helping non-experts in understanding, and in the usage of iterative methods. Since the formulation is intentionally kept simple, it reveals the algorithmic essentials, and it shows where the major computational effort is going to be spent. The Matlab codes facilitate the user to play with the algorithms for relatively small but representative linear systems on workstations or even PC's, and help to develop some feeling for the potential usefulness of each of the methods. Together with the manual the chosen formulations provide the non-expert with a low-level entrance to the field. This approach has received approval recently in some new textbooks [39, 40].

The formulations and the notations have been chosen so that differences and similarities between algorithms are easily recognized. In this respect they provide simple and easy to code algorithms, that can serve as a yardstick with which other implementations can be compared. Templates provides codes in Fortran, Matlab, and C. The codes are equivalent for each algorithm, and the only differences in outputs may be attributed to the respective computer arithmetic. This usage of Templates makes it easier to compare and to present results for iteration methods in publications. It is easier now to check results which have been obtained through these standardized codes.

As an example of how Templates is intended to function, we discuss the algorithm for the preconditioned Conjugate Gradient method for the iterative solution of the linear system $Ax = b$, with A a symmetric positive definite matrix:

Compute $r_0 = b - Ax_0$ for some initial guess $x^{(0)}$
for $i = 0, 1, 2, ...$
    solve $Mz^{(i-1)} = r^{(i-1)}$
    $\rho_{i-1} = r^{(i-1)^T} z^{(i-1)}$
    if $i = 1$
        $p^{(1)} = z^{(0)}$
    else
        $\beta_{i-1} = \rho_{i-1}/\rho_{i-2}$
        $p^{(i)} = z^{(i-1)} + \beta_{i-1} p^{(i-1)}$
    endif
    $q^{(i)} = Ap^{(i)}$
    $\alpha_i = \rho_{i-1}/p^{(i)^T} q^{(i)}$
    $x^{(i)} = x^{(i-1)} + \alpha_i p^{(i)}$
    $r^{(i)} = r^{(i-1)} - \alpha_i q^{(i)}$
    check convergence; continue if necessary
end

In order to make the code useful for a specific problem class, the user has to provide a subroutine that computes Ap, for a given vector p. In Templates such code is not specified, but the user is given instructions on how to exploit sparsity of the given matrix A [6], and by well-chosen examples it is shown how to code the matrix vector product for specific data storage formats. The following sparse matrix storage formats are discussed at some length:

1. Compressed Row Storage
2. Compressed Column Storage
3. Block Compressed Row Storage
4. Compressed Diagonal Storage
5. Jagged Diagonal Storage
6. Skyline Storage

For example, in **Compressed Row Storage** format subsequent nonzeros of the matrix rows are put in contiguous memory locations. In this case we create 3 vectors: one for the floating point nonzero entries of A (**val**), the other two with integers (**col_ind, row_ptr**). The **row_ptr** vector stores the locations in the **val** vector that start a row; the **col_ind** vector stores the column indexes of the elements in the **val** vector. The matrix vector product should then look like

```
for i = 1, n
    q(i) = 0
    for j = row_ptr(i), row_ptr(i + 1) - 1
        q(i) = q(i) + val(j) × p(col_ind(j))
    end
end
```

Also suggestions are supplied for coding this on parallel computers. For some algorithms also code has to be provided that generates $A^T p$, and this is given much attention.

Similarly, the user has to provide a subroutine that solves the equation $Mz = r$ for given right-hand side r. In this respect M is called the preconditioner and the choice for an appropriate preconditioner is left to the user. The main reason for this is that it is very difficult, if not impossible, to predict what a good preconditioner might be for a given problem of which little else is known besides the fact that A is symmetric positive definite. In [6] an overview is given of possible choices and semi-code for the construction of some popular preconditioners is provided, along with instructions and examples on how to code them for certain data-storage formats. A popular preconditioner that is often used in connection with the Conjugate Gradient method is the Incomplete Cholesky preconditioner. If we write the matrix A as $A = L + D + L^T$ (L is strictly lower diagonal, D is diagonal), then a simplified form of the preconditioner can be written as $M = (L + D_C)D_C^{-1}(D_C + L^T)$, and in [6] formulas are given for the computation of the elements of the diagonal matrix D_C. Since the factor L is part of A, the coding for the preconditioner is not too complicated.

The other operations (inner-products and vector updates) in the algorithm are coded, in the Fortran codes, as BLAS operations. On most modern computers these BLAS are standard available as optimized kernels, and the user needs not to be concerned with these vector operations.

So, if the user wants to have transportable code, then he only needs to focus on the matrix vector product and the preconditioner. However, there is more that the user might want to reflect on. In the standard codes only a simple stopping criterion is provided, but in [6] a lengthy discussion is provided on different possible termination strategies and their merits. Templates for these strategies have not yet been provided since the better of these strategies require estimates for such quantities as $\|A\|$, or even $\|A^{-1}\|$, and we do not know about convenient algorithms for estimating these quantities (except possibly for the symmetric positive definite case). This is in contrast with dense systems, for which efficient estimators are available. As soon as a reliable estimating mechanisms for these norms become known then a template can be added.

The situation for other methods, for instance Bi-CG, may be slightly more complicated. Of course the standard template is still simple but now the user may be facing (near) break-down situations in actual computing. The solution for this problem is quite complicated, and the average user may not be expected to incorporate this easily and is referred to more professional software at this moment. A template for a cure of the break-downs would be very nice but is not planned as yet.

Also the updating for the residual vector $r^{(i)}$ and the approximate solution $x^{(i)}$ may suffer from problems due to the use of finite precision arithmetic. This may result into a vector $r^{(i)}$ that differs significantly from $b - Ax^{(i)}$, whereas these vectors should be equal in exact arithmetic. Recently, good and reliable strategies have been suggested [34], and these are easily incorporated into the present Templates.

At the moment the linear systems templates for iterative methods form a good starting point for the user for the construction of useful software modules. It is anticipated that in future updates, templates will be added for algorithmic details, such as reliable vector updating, stopping criteria, and error monitoring. It is also conceivable that templates will be provided that help the user to analyze the convergence behavior, and to help get more insight in characteristics of the given problem. Most of these aspects are now covered in the Templates book, in the form of guidelines and examples. The Templates book [6] gives an abundance of references for more background and for all kinds of relevant details.

4   Templates for Solution of Eigenvalue Problems

To guide our eigenvalue template design, we need to have a model of what the reader wants. We expect that a non-expert user confronted with an eigenvalue problem would be willing to supply

- as few facts as necessary about the operator or operators whose spectral information is desired,
- the kind of spectral information desired (including accuracy), and
- the kind of computer available to solve it (perhaps).

In return, the user would want

- the software to solve the problem,
- an estimate of how long it will take to solve, and
- a way to assess the accuracy (perhaps).

In the (likely) case that no single best algorithm exists, the user would want a list of reasonable alternatives and a discussion of the tradeoffs in time, space and accuracy among them. For example, it might be reasonable to use a dense algorithm on a sparse problem if high accuracy is desired, the problem is not too large, and/or the problem is to be solved just once. Much of our effort will center on educating the user as to which facts must be supplied to make a decision. To this end we categorize available methods along five (mostly independent) axes:

1. Mathematical Properties of the Problem,
2. Desired Spectral Information,
3. Problem Representation,
4. Available Transformations, and
5. Costs (including dependence on accuracy, computer type).

Ideally, the user would supply a "coordinate" for each of these five axes, thus uniquely identifying a problem class for which we could identify a "best algorithm," software implementing it, a performance model to predict its execution time, and a method to assess the accuracy.

Realistically, only a few regions of this five-dimensional space are populated with interesting or useful algorithms, and we expect to have a more decision-tree like approach to guide the user's expectations. The next five subsections are organized corresponding to one possible decision tree. The first "level" of the tree distinguishes problems according to their mathematical properties. The second level asks for desired spectral information, and so on.

This is not the only way to organize the decision tree. For example, a different user may wish to specify the desired spectral information later, in order to get a list of all possible algorithms relevant to her problem. Indeed, the actual internal organization of the tree may more resemble a lattice, since the some basic algorithms will be used many times in slightly different ways. Nonetheless, we believe these five axes are a good organizational tool for us to make sure we have covered all interesting cases, or at least limit the scope of what we want in an organized way. At this point, we invite suggestions as to the scope of our proposed project, whether we have left anything important out, or included something of lesser importance. Briefly, we only want to include a problem type if there is significant demand, and exploiting its special features confers *significant* performance or accuracy advantages over using a more general purpose algorithm. We want to keep the project small enough to come out with a reference book of at most two hundred pages (or the equivalent in html) within 2 years.

4.1 Notation

Matrix Pencil: We will talk mostly about eigenproblems of the form $(A - \lambda B)x = 0$. $A - \lambda B$ is also called a *matrix pencil*. λ is an indeterminate in this latter expression, and indicates that there are two matrices which define the eigenproblem. A and B need not be square.

Eigenvalues and Eigenvectors: For almost all fixed scalar values of λ, the rank of the matrix $A - \lambda B$ will be constant. The discrete set of values of λ for which the rank of $A - \lambda B$ is lower than this constant are the *eigenvalues*. Let $\lambda_1, ..., \lambda_k$ be the discrete set of eigenvalues. Some λ_i may be infinite, in which case we really consider $\mu A - B$ with eigenvalue $\mu_i = 0$. Nonzero vectors x_i and y_i such that

$$Ax_i = \lambda_i Bx_i \quad y_i^H A = \lambda_i y_i^H B,$$

are called a *right eigenvector* and a *left eigenvector*, respectively, where A^T is the transpose of A and A^H is its conjugate-transpose. The word *eigenvector* alone will mean right eigenvector.

Since there are many kinds of eigenproblems and associated algorithms, we propose some simple top level categories to help classify them. The ultimate decision tree presented to the reader will begin with easier concepts and questions about the eigenproblem in an attempt to classify it, and proceed to harder questions. For the purposes of this overview, we will use rather more advanced categories in order to be brief but precise. For background, see [23, 25, 12].

Regular and Singular Pencils: $A - \lambda B$ is regular if A and B are square and $det(A - \lambda B)$ is not identically zero for all λ; otherwise it is singular.

Regular pencils have well-defined sets of eigenvalues which change continuously as functions of A and B; this is a minimal requirement to be able to compute the eigenvalues accurately, in the absence of other constraints on A and B. Singular pencils have eigenvalues which can change *discontinuously* as functions of A and B; extra information about A and B, as well as special algorithms which use this information, are necessary in order to compute meaningful eigenvalues. Regular and singular pencils have correspondingly different *canonical forms* representing their spectral decompositions. The *Jordan Canonical Form* of a single matrix is the best known; the *Kronecker Canonical Form* of a singular pencil is the most general. More will be discussed in section 4.3 below.

Self-adjoint and Non-self-adjoint Eigenproblems: We abuse notation to avoid confusion with the very similar but less general notions of Hermitian and non-Hermitian: We call an eigenproblem $A - \lambda B$ is *self-adjoint* if 1) A and B are both Hermitian, and 2) there is a nonsingular X such that $XAX^H = \Lambda_A$ and $XBX^H = \Lambda_B$ are real and diagonal. Thus the finite eigenvalues are real, all elementary divisors are linear, and the only possible singular blocks in the Kronecker Canonical Form represent a common null space of A and B. The primary source of self-adjoint eigenproblems is eigenvalue problems in which B is known to be positive definite; in this case $A - \lambda B$ is called a *definite pencil*. These properties lead to generally simpler and more accurate algorithms. We classify the singular value decomposition (SVD) and its generalizations as self-adjoint, because of the relationship between the SVD of A and the eigendecomposition of the Hermitian matrix $\begin{bmatrix} 0 & A \\ A^H & 0 \end{bmatrix}$.

It is sometimes possible to change the classification of an eigenproblem by simple transformations. For example, multiplying a skew-Hermitian matrix A (i.e., $A^H = -A$) by the constant $\sqrt{-1}$ makes it Hermitian, so its eigenproblem becomes self-adjoint. Such simple transformations are very useful in finding the best algorithm for a problem.

Many other definition and notation will be introduced in section 4.3.

4.2 $\boxed{\text{Level 1 of Decision Tree}}$ Mathematical Properties

We will first list what we plan to include in the first round of the project, and then what we plan *not* to include.

What we plan to include The following description is very terse. The user will see a more extended description of each problem, including common synonyms.

1. Hermitian eigenproblem $A - \lambda I$
2. Non-Hermitian eigenproblem $A - \lambda I$
3. Generalized definite eigenproblem $A - \lambda B$, where $A = A^H$, $B = B^H > 0$
4. Generalized Hermitian eigenproblem $A - \lambda B$, where $A = A^H$, $B = B^H$
5. Generalized non-Hermitian eigenproblem $A - \lambda B$, where $B = B^H > 0$
6. Generalized non-Hermitian Eigenproblem $A - \lambda B$
7. Quadratic $\lambda^2 A + \lambda B + C$ or higher degree $\Sigma \lambda^i A_i$ eigenvalue problems
8. Singular Value Decomposition (SVD) of a single general matrix A
9. Generalized SVD of A and B
10. Other eigenvalue problems

Note that this list does include all the possible variations hinted at in the previous section; these will appear as the user traverses the tree. For example, there will be cross references to other, better algorithms in cases for which simple transformations permit their use. Here are some examples:

- Under "Hermitian eigenproblem $A - \lambda I$": If $A = BB^H$, the user will be advised to consider the SVD of B.
- Under "Generalized Hermitian eigenproblem": If $A = A^H$ and $B = B^H$, and the user knows real constants α and β such that $\alpha A + \beta B$ is positive definite, the user will be advised to consider the definite eigenproblem $A - \lambda(\alpha A + \beta B)$.
- Under "Non-Hermitian eigenproblem $A - \lambda I$": If $B = \alpha S A S^{-1}$ is Hermitian for known, simple α and S, the user will be advised to consider the eigenproblem for B.
- Under "SVD of A": If $A = BC^{-1}$, the user will be advised to consider the quotient SVD of B and C.
- Under "Quadratic $\lambda^2 A + \lambda B + C$ or higher degree $\Sigma \lambda^i A_i$ eigenvalue problems", the user will be advised to consider the linearization of problem to a matrix pencil eigenvalue problem.
- Under "Other eigenvalue problems", the user will see some other related eigenvalue problems, such as
  - Updating eigendecompositions
  - Polynomial zero finding
  - Rank revealing QR decomposition

What we plan not to include Some of them we may include, provided there is sufficient demand. Mostly, we would limit ourselves to literature references.

- There is a variety of "non-linear" eigenproblems which can be linearized in various ways and converted to the above problems
  1. Rational problems $A(\lambda)$
  2. General nonlinear problems $A(\lambda)$
  3. Polynomial system zero finding

- The SVD can be used to solve a variety of least squares problems, and these may best be solved by representing the SVD in "factored" form. These factored SVD algorithms are somewhat complicated and hard to motivate without the least squares application, but there are a great many least squares problems, but including too many of them (beyond references to the literature) would greatly expand the scope of this project. The same comments apply to the generalized SVD, of which there are even more variations.
- Eigenproblems from systems and control. There is a large source of eigenproblems, many of which can be reduced to finding certain kinds of spectral information about possibly singular pencils $A - \lambda B$. These problems arise with many kinds of special structures, many of which have been exploited in special packages, some of them can be solved by general algorithms. For example, solutions of Riccati equations are often reduced to eigenproblems. A comprehensive treatment of these problems would greatly expand the scope of the book, but including some treatment seems important.
- Structured singular value problems, also called μ-analysis by its practitioners These problems must generally be solved by optimization techniques, and indeed NP-completeness results exist for some of them. We believe that the algorithms in our proposed book would be called within inner loops for these optimization algorithms, and we should simply refer to the literature for this application. The same comment applies for other optimization problems based on eigenvalues (e.g. finding the nearest unstable matrix).
- Generalized singular value decompositions of more than two matrices
- Computing matrix functions like $\exp(A)$ or $\exp(A)x$, or for multivariate eigenvalue problems $A(\lambda, \mu)$, whose solutions are typically continua.

4.3   Level 2 of Decision Tree   Desired Spectral Information

For each eigenproblem, the user must choose which spectral information is desired. The available choices differ depending on the mathematical properties of the problem. In general, the more information the user desires, the more it will cost.

Self-adjoint Eigenproblems We first consider the n-by-n Hermitian matrix A, which has n real eigenvalues $\lambda_1 \leq \lambda_2 \leq \cdots \leq \lambda_n$. When computing eigenvalues, the following choices are possible:

1. All the eigenvalues, to some specified accuracy.
2. Eigenvalues λ_i for some specified set of subscripts $i \in \mathcal{I}$, including the special cases of the largest m eigenvalues λ_{n-m+1} through λ_n, and the smallest m eigenvalues λ_1 through λ_m. Again, the desired accuracy may be specified.
3. All the eigenvalues within a given subset of the real axis, such as the interval $[\alpha, \beta]$. Again, the desired accuracy may be specified.
4. Certain number of eigenvalues closest to a given value μ.

For each of these possibilities, the user can also compute the corresponding eigen-vectors (in this case left and right eigenvectors are equal). For the eigenvalues that are clustered together, the user may choose to compute the associated *invariant subspace*, i.e. the space spanned by the corresponding eigenvectors, since in this case the individual eigenvectors can be very ill-conditioned, while the invariant subspace may be less so.

The spectral information one can request from a singular value decomposi-tion is similar, except that there are left and right singular vectors and singular subspaces, corresponding to eigenvectors and invariant subspaces. Common re-quests might include the numerical rank, the null space, and the range space. In order to compute these the user must supply a tolerance $\tau > 0$, which will deter-mine which singular values are considered to be nonzero or zero. Methods can differ greatly depending on whether there is a gap between the singular values larger than τ and those smaller, and whether the user wants an approximate or precise answer.

Self-adjoint matrix pencils $A - \lambda B$, where A and B are n-by-n and Hermitian, and can be simultaneously diagonalized by a congruence, are quite similar. The case $B = I$ corresponds to the standard Hermitian eigenproblem just discussed. $A - \lambda B$ has $k \leq n$ real eigenvalues which we denote $\lambda_1 \leq \lambda_2 \leq \cdots \leq \lambda_k$. If B is nonsingular, $k = n$. The user may request similar subsets of eigenvalues as described above, as well as right and/or left eigenvectors. If the pencil is non-singular, the user may request *right or left deflating subspaces*, which are generalizations of invariant subspaces [37]. If $A - \lambda B$ is a singular pencil, the common null-space of A and B can also be computed, as well as the deflating subspaces of the regular part.

Just as the SVD of A is closely related to the eigendecomposition of $A^H A$, the QSVD corresponds to the matrix pencil $A^H A - \lambda B^H B$. The case $B = I$ corresponds to the usual SVD.

Table 2 spells out the possible decompositions which display all the infor-mation the user could want. We use terminology which will apply to the non-Hermitian problem too. "Schur" form refers to the simplest decomposition pos-sible with complex unitary transformations. (Real orthogonal matrices are also possible, if the original data is real; we leave out the real case for ease of expo-sition.) "Jordan-Schur" form refers to the most detailed decomposition possible with unitary transformations; this form reduces the matrix or matrices to "stair-case" form [41], wherein all the sizes of Jordan blocks are immediately available, and some more detailed invariant (or deflating [37] or reducing [42]) subspaces are computed. "Jordan" form, which typically requires non-unitary transformations and so can be very ill-conditioned to compute, is the most detailed decompo-sition. Jordan form is usually called Weierstrass form for regular pencils, and Kronecker form for singular pencils. Q and Z matrices in the table are unitary, S matrices are general nonsingular, Λ is real and diagonal, Σ is real, diagonal, and nonnegative, T matrices are upper triangular, and T_S matrices are in upper triangular staircase form.

The decompositions may also be written with A and B isolated on the left-hand-side, for example $A = Q\Lambda Q^H$ instead of $Q^H AQ = \Lambda$. The reason for writing these decompositions as they are shown, is that they can be *partial decompositions*, if only $k < n$ of the eigenvalues or singular values are of interest to the user. In this case the central matrices (Λ, Λ_A, Λ_B Σ, Σ_A, Σ_B T_A, T_B, $T_{S,A}$ and T_{S_B}) will be k-by-k, and the outer matrices (Q, Z and S) will be n-by-k.

Table 2. The Possible "Eigendecompositions" of Self-adjoint Eigenproblems

Problem Type	"Schur"	"Jordan-Schur"	"Jordan"
$A - \lambda I$	$Q^H AQ = \Lambda$	same as Schur	same as Schur
$A - \lambda B$	$Q^H AZ = T_A$	$Q^H AZ = T_{S,A}$	$S^H AS = \Lambda_A$
	$Q^H BZ = T_B$	$Q^H BZ = T_{S,B}$	$S^H BS = \Lambda_B$
SVD of A	$Q^H AZ = \Sigma$	same as Schur	same as Schur
QSVD of A, B	$Q^H AS = \Sigma_A$	same as Schur	same as Schur
	$Z^H BS = \Sigma_B$	same as Schur	same as Schur

In addition to these decompositions, the user may request *condition numbers* for any of the computed quantities (eigenvalues, means of eigenvalue clusters, eigenvectors, invariant/deflating/reducing subspaces) [27, 38, 13]. Given computed values for eigenvalues, eigenvectors, and/or subspaces, the user may also request an *a posteriori* error bound based on a computed residual.

Non-self-adjoint Eigenproblems An n-by-n non-Hermitian matrix has n eigenvalues, which can be anywhere in the complex plane. A non-self-adjoint regular pencil has from 0 to n eigenvalues, which can be anywhere in the extended complex plane. Thus some of the choices in the self-adjoint case do not apply here. Instead, the following choices of spectral information are possible:

1. All the eigenvalues.
2. All the eigenvalues in some specified region of the complex plane, such as
   - The peripheral eigenvalues (when the spectrum is seen as a set in the complex plane), such as the 10 rightmost eigenvalues.
   - Eigenvalues in a given compact region, such as the unit disk.
   - Eigenvalues in a given unbounded region, such as the left half plane, or (a region around) the imaginary axis.

As before, the desired accuracy of the eigenvalues may be specified. For each of these choices, the user can also compute the corresponding (left or right) eigenvectors, or Schur vectors. Since the eigenvalues of a non-Hermitian matrix can be very ill-conditioned, it is sometimes hard to find all eigenvalues within a given region with certainty. For eigenvalues that are clustered together, the user may choose to estimate the mean of the cluster, or even the ϵ-*pseudospectrum*, the smallest region in the complex plane which contains all the eigenvalues of all matrices B differing from the given matrix A by at most ϵ: $\|A - B\| \le \epsilon$. The user may also choose to compute the associated invariant (or deflating or reducing) subspaces (left or right) instead of individual eigenvectors. However, due to the potential ill-conditioning of the eigenvalues, there is no guarantee that the invariant subspace will be well-conditioned.

A singular pencil has a more complicated eigenstructure, as defined by the Kronecker Canonical Form, a generalization of the Jordan Canonical Form [23, 41]. Instead of invariant or deflating subspaces, we say a singular pencil has reducing subspaces.

Table 3 spells out the possibilities. In addition to the notation used in the last section, U matrices denote generalized upper triangular (singular pencils only), U_S matrices are generalized upper triangular in staircase form (singular pencils only), J is in Jordan form, and K is in Kronecker form. As before, these can be partial decompositions, when Q, Z, S_L and S_R are n-by-k instead of n-by-n.

Table 3. The Possible "Eigendecompositions" of Non-self-adjoint Eigenproblems

Problem Type	"Schur"	"Jordan-Schur"	"Jordan"
$A - \lambda I$	$Q^H AQ = T$	$Q^H AQ = T_S$	$S^{-1}AS = J$
$A - \lambda B$, regular	$Q^H AZ = T_A$ $Q^H BZ = T_B$	$Q^H AZ = T_{S,A}$ $Q^H BZ = T_{S,B}$	$S_L^{-1}AS_R = J_A$ $S_L^{-1}BS_R = J_B$
$A - \lambda B$, singular	$Q^H AZ = U_A$ $Q^H BZ = U_B$	$Q^H AZ = U_{S,A}$ $Q^H BZ = U_{S,B}$	$S_L^{-1}AS_R = K_A$ $S_L^{-1}BS_R = K_B$

In addition to these decompositions, the user may request condition numbers for any of the computed quantities (eigenvalues, means of eigenvalue clusters, eigenvectors, invariant/deflating/reducing subspaces). Given computed values for eigenvalues, eigenvectors, and/or subspaces, the user may also request an a posteriori error bound based on a computed residual.

4.4   Level 3 of Decision Tree   Problem Representation

First we discuss the *type* of individual matrix or operator entries. The simplest distinction is between *real* and *complex* data. The issues are speed (real arithmetic is faster than complex), storage (real numbers require half the storage of complex numbers), code complexity (some algorithms simplify greatly if we can do complex arithmetic), and stability (real arithmetic can guarantee complex conjugate eigenvalues of real matrices). The distinction between *single* and *double* precision, which clearly affects space, will be discussed again as an accuracy issue.

Given the type of individual operator entries, we must distinguish the overall structure of the operator. Here is our list. Two letter abbreviations (like GE) refer to matrix types supported by LAPACK [1, Table 2.1].

- Dense matrices
  - General (GE)
  - Hermitian, with only upper or lower half defined (SY or HE)
  - Hermitian, packed into half the space (SP or HP)
- Matrices depending systematically on $O(n)$ data.
  - Band matrices
    * Bidiagonal matrices, stored as two arrays (BD)
    * Tridiagonal matrices, stored as two or three arrays (ST, GT)
    * Wider band matrices (GB, SB, HB)
    * Band matrices with bulges ("look ahead" matrices)
  - Arrow, Toeplitz, Hankel, Circulant, and Companion matrices
  - Diagonal + rank-1 matrices, band + low rank matrices
- Sparse matrices, or those depending less systematically on $o(n^2)$ data. It turns out that the relevant classification is by the operations that can be performed on the operators represented, not the details of the representation. This will be clearer in Section 4.5.
  - can solve the linear system $(A - \mu B)x = b$
  - Matrix-vector multiplication possible $y = Ax$ (and $y = A^H x$) (this includes, for example, "dense" integral operators which have fast algorithms for performing $y = Ax$.)
  - under SVD or GSVD, possible to factor $AA^H - \lambda BB^H$ or $A^H A - \lambda B^H B$, or $\begin{bmatrix} 0 & A \\ A^H & 0 \end{bmatrix} - \lambda \begin{bmatrix} I & 0 \\ 0 & B^H B \end{bmatrix}$, perhaps shifted

There are many more special structures, often arising from control theory, such as unitary orthogonal matrices represented by their Schur parameters. Until we hear of a large demand for such problems, we do not plan to include them, other than as literature references. For the same reason we also do not plan to include algorithms for quaternion matrices, or matrices with rational entries, which are more properly included in the domain of symbolic computation.

4.5   Level 4 of Decision Tree   Available Operations

The choice between different methods very much depends on which of these operations one has available at a reasonable cost. We list the major ones in decreasing order of power:

- For those methods, which do not generally require user tuning for accuracy and reliability and has predictable cost and performance.
  - Some special matrices, such as bidiagonals or diagonal + rank-1 matrices, have special algorithms designed especially for them. Many good implementations are available [1].

- Similarity transformations $S^{-1}AS$ can be applied to matrices A of reasonable size, stored as two dimensional arrays, or in a dense band structure. (For pencils $A - \lambda B$, we would use equivalence transformations $S_L^{-1}AS_R - \lambda S_L^{-1}BS_R$ instead). Many of these algorithms have good implementations available [1]. Some of them (such as sign function based algorithms [5]) are currently being implemented. When good "black-box" implementations exist, they will not be described in detailed templates. We will however indicate when they are to be preferred over the iterative methods, which are the main theme of this collection.
- For those methods, which generally require user tuning
  - Multiplication of a vector x by a shifted-and-inverted operator, $y = (A - \mu I)^{-1}x$ or $y = (A - \mu B)^{-1}Bx$ for a given vector x, lets us quickly compute the eigenvalues closest to the shift μ. This operation may be implemented with an explicit triangular factorization

$$A - \mu B = PLU$$

    e.g. as a part of an FEM (finite element method) package, but any other implementation may also be used, such as those based on multigrid or more specialized methods. It is also possible to use an iterative solver which only uses multiplication by A (or A and B) internally, but this may not be superior to other methods discussed below.
  - If the shift μ is restricted, say to 0, then we will be restricted to efficiently finding eigenvalues closest to zero, and will need more iterations to find any but the few smallest eigenvalues.
  - If only B is factorizable, e.g. if $B = I$, so that we can only multiply vectors by AB^{-1}, we will be restricted to efficiently finding the *peripheral* eigenvalues, i.e. those eigenvalues near the "edges" of the spectrum, when the spectrum is seen as a set in the complex plane.

If, in a special purpose method, it is possible to multiply a vector by A^H in addition to A, or possibly $y = (A - \mu I)^{-H}x$ or $y = B^H(A - \mu B)^{-H}x$, depending on the situation, then a broader, more powerful class of algorithms are available.

Sometimes it is significantly cheaper to apply the operator to a set of vectors rather than just 1 vector at a time. This can happen because of memory hierarchy effects. There are algorithms to exploit this behavior. The worst case is when the only operation we can perform is multiplication of a vector by A (and possibly B). But algorithms are available in this case too.

Not only the matrix-vector operations but also the vector algebra needs special consideration. In all the algorithms that we will consider, only two different vector operations have to be applied to vectors of length n, dot products and the addition of a multiple of one vector to another, **axpy** to use terminology from the BLAS. These operations may be implemented on distributed processors in a way that is appropriate for the application or the computer at hand. In some cases a vector is not even represented as an array of numbers, but stands for a function represented in e.g. a finite element or wavelet basis. Then user-supplied routines for dot products and axpy will replace the basic vector operations in our templates.

4.6   Basic Iterative Algorithms

The following basic algorithms for sparse eigenproblems will be included.

- Simultaneous iteration methods
- Arnoldi methods
- Lanczos methods
- Davidson methods
- Refinement methods
- Trace minimization (self-adjoint case only)

This list is not exhaustive, and we are actively looking for other algorithms. Also, some common methods may classified in several ways. For example, simultaneous iteration and block-Arnoldi with an immediate restart are identical. These categories are not meant to be mutually exclusive, but to be helpful to the user. We will include some older but commonly used methods, just to be able to advise the user to use more powerful alternatives, and for experimental purposes.

Arnoldi and Lanczos methods are Krylov subspaces-based techniques. These methods may converge very fast in combination with shifted-and-inverted operators, which means that $(A - \mu I)^{-1}$ has to be used in matrix vector products in each iteration step. If only approximations for $(A - \mu I)^{-1}$ are available then Davidson's method can be used as an acceleration technique for the inexact shift-and-invert operations. Approximations for $(A - \mu I)^{-1}$ can be computed from a preconditioner for $A - \mu I$ or by a few steps of a (preconditioned) iterative method [35].

Trace minimization is suitable for self-adjoint problems, and uses optimization techniques like conjugate gradients to find the k smallest eigenvalues.

There is unfortunately no simple way to identify the best algorithm and choice of options to the user. The more the user discovers about the problem (such as approximate eigenvalues), the better a choice can be made. In the common situation where the user is solving a sequence of similar problems, this is quite important.

There is also unfortunately no inexpensive way to provide a guarantee that all eigenvalues in a region have been found, when the problem is not self-adjoint. For Hermitian eigenvalue problems by factoring certain translations of A by the identity, it is possible to guarantee that all eigenvalues in a region have been found. In the non-Hermitian case, this same task is accomplished by a vastly more expensive technique called a Nyquist plot (i.e. compute the winding number). However, depending on the problem, there are methods to help increase one's confidence that all eigenvalues have been found.

4.7   Cost Issues

As stated above, the user would ideally like a simple formula, or perhaps a program, that would predict the running time as a function of a few simple facts about the problem to be solved, and the computer to be used to solve it. This implies that we need performance models for all the algorithms we provide. Realistically, for some dense algorithms we will be able to give operation counts, dependent on the size and mathematical properties of the problem to be solved, the information desired by the user, and perhaps some rough properties of the operator, like the clustering of the spectrum. For sparse problems, we can do the same for the inner loop of the iteration, counting operations like matrix-factorizations, matrix-vector multiplies, dot products, saxpys, and so on.

For particular machines, we can provide Matlab scripts to actually estimate running times in terms of a few machine parameters like megaflop rate (for the 3 levels of BLAS), number of processors and communication costs (for parallel machines), matrix dimension, layout (on parallel machines), information desired by the user, and so on. There are two basic approaches to producing such performance models (hybrids are possible too). The first is *intrinsic*, which uses operation counts plus simpler models for the costs of each operation (BLAS operations and communication), and the second is *extrinsic*, which simply does curve fitting of benchmark runs. Intrinsic models are more difficult to produce, may be less accurate in certain extreme cases, but are more flexible and illuminating than extrinsic models.

4.8   Accuracy Issues

As usual in numerical linear algebra, we will use the backward error analysis model to assess the accuracy of the results. We will first give perturbation theorems that tell how much a perturbation of the data, in this case matrix elements, will change the results, eigenvalues, singular values and vectors. We will also provide a posteriori methods to measure the backward error for computed solutions.

In the simplest cases, the perturbation theorems give a bound for the perturbation of the eigenvalues as a multiple of the perturbation of the matrix elements. The multiplier is called a *condition number*. For eigenvectors we also need information about the distance between the different eigenvalues, as well as the angles between left and right eigenvectors. In degenerate cases, the best we can get is an asymptotic series, possibly involving fractional powers of the perturbation.

We will discuss what to do when a simple condition number based bound is not practical. If we do not have good bounds for individual eigenvectors, then a better conditioned invariant (or deflating or reducing) subspace of higher dimension may be available. We can also derive a bound for the norm of the resolvent and find *pseudospectra*.

For iterative algorithms *a posteriori* methods are used to compute the backward error, often using computed residuals. It is possible to compute, or at least estimate, the residual during the computation as part of monitoring for convergence.

We will show when stronger results as e.g. small relative error bounds for small eigenvalues exist. This is of importance, specially when an ill conditioned matrix comes from the discretization of a well conditioned continuous problem.

4.9   Format of Results

As stated earlier in this section, the user would ideally want to be asked a few questions about his or her problem, and in return get a summary of the right algorithm to use, a pointer to corresponding software, and performance and accuracy predictions. In addition to the conventional book format in which such information could be presented, we plan to explore the use of a hypertext interface to let the user browse through the information and traverse the underlying decision tree. Both "black boxes" as in LAPACK and "templates" will be possible recommendations at the bottom of the decision tree. Black boxes will be briefly described, but not in sufficient detail to reproduce a good implementation (which is why they are black boxes!). Templates will be made available in pseudocode, Matlab, and Fortran, as they were in the prior Templates book. If there is strong feeling that C, C++, or Fortran 90 should also be used, we would like to hear it (but note that we do not have the resources to recode LAPACK in Fortran-90 or C++, although wrappers are possible). We hope to assemble a set of test cases, and evaluate the algorithms we suggest on these test cases. The test cases should demonstrate both typical and extreme behaviors of the algorithms.

References

1. E. Anderson,   Z. Bai,   C. Bischof,   J. Demmel,   J. Dongarra,   J. Du Croz,
   A. Greenbaum, S. Hammarling, A. McKenney, S. Ostrouchov, and D. Sorensen.
   LAPACK Users' Guide, Release 2.0. SIAM, Philadelphia, 1995. 324 pages. URL
   http://www.netlib.org/lapack/lug/lapack_lug.html.
2. E. Anderson and J. Dongarra. Results from the initial release of LAPACK. Techn.
   Rep. LAPACK working note 16, Computer Science Department, University of Tennessee, Knoxville, TN, 1989.
3. E. Anderson and J. Dongarra. Evaluating block algorithm variants in LAPACK.
   Techn. Rep. LAPACK working note 19, Computer Science Department, University
   of Tennessee, Knoxville, TN, 1990.
4. Z. Bai. Progress in the numerical solution of the nonsymmetric eigenvalue problem,
   1993. To appear in *J. Num. Lin. Alg. Appl.*
5. Z. Bai and J. Demmel. Design of a parallel nonsymmetric eigenroutine toolbox,
   Part I. In *Proc. 6th SIAM Conference on Parallel Processing for Scientific Computing*. SIAM, 1993. Long version: UC Berkeley Comp. Sc. Rep. all.ps.Z via anonymous ftp from tr-ftp.cs.berkeley.edu, directory pub/tech-reports/csd/csd-92-718.
6. R. Barrett, M. Berry, T. Chan, J. Demmel, J. Donato, J. Dongarra, V. Eijkhout,
   V. Pozo, Romime C., and H. van der Vorst.   *Templates for the solution of*

linear systems: Building blocks for iterative methods. SIAM, 1994. URL http://www.netlib.org/templates/templates.ps.

7. R. Boisvert. The architecture of an intelligent virtual mathematical software repository system. *Mathematics and Computers in Simulation*, 36:269–279, 1994.

8. J. Choi, J. J. Dongarra, R. Pozo, and D. W. Walker. ScaLAPACK: A scalable linear algebra library for distributed memory concurrent computers. In *Proc. 4th Symposium on the Frontiers of Massively Parallel Computation*, pages 120–127. IEEE Computer Society Press, 1992.

9. J. Choi, J. J. Dongarra, and D. W. Walker. The design of scalable software libraries for distributed memory concurrent computers. In J. J. Dongarra and B. Tourancheau, editors, *Environments and Tools for Parallel Scientific Computing*. Elsevier Science Publishers, 1993.

10. D. E. Culler, A. Dusseau, S. C. Goldstein, A. Krishnamurthy, S. Lumetta, T. von Eicken, and K. Yelick. Introduction to Split-C: Version 0.9. Techn. Rep. Computer Science Division – EECS, Univ. of California, Berkeley, CA, February 1993.

11. J. Cullum and R. A. Willoughby. *Lanczos algorithms for large symmetric eigenvalue computations.* Birkhaüser, Basel, 1985. Vol.1, Theory, Vol.2. Program.

12. J. Demmel. Berkeley Lecture Notes in Numerical Linear Algebra. Mathematics Department, University of California, 1993. 215 pages.

13. J. Demmel and B. Kågström. The generalized Schur decomposition of an arbitrary pencil $A - \lambda B$: Robust software with error bounds and applications. Parts I and II, *ACM Trans. Math. Soft.*, 19(2), June 1993.

14. J. Demmel. LAPACK: A portable linear algebra library for supercomputers. In *Proc. 1989 IEEE Control Systems Society Workshop on Computer-Aided Control System Design*, December 1989.

15. J. J. Dongarra. Increasing the performance of mathematical software through high-level modularity. In *Proc. Sixth Int. Symp. Comp. Methods in Eng. & Applied Sciences, Versailles, France*, pages 239–248. North-Holland, 1984.

16. J. J. Dongarra, J. R. Bunch, C. B. Moler and G. W. Stewart. LINPACK Users' Guide. SIAM Press, 1979.

17. J. J. Dongarra. LAPACK Working Note 34: Workshop on the BLACS. Computer Science Dept. Technical Report CS-91-134, University of Tennessee, Knoxville, TN, May 1991.

18. J. J. Dongarra, J. Du Croz, S. Hammarling, and I. Duff. A set of level 3 basic linear algebra subprograms. *ACM Trans. Math. Softw.*, 16(1):1–17, 1990.

19. J. J. Dongarra, J. Du Croz, S. Hammarling, and R. Hanson. An extended set of Fortran basic linear algebra subroutines. *ACM Trans. Math. Softw.*, 14(1):1–17, March 1988.

20. J. J. Dongarra and R. A. van de Geijn. LAPACK Working Note 37: Two-dimensional basic linear algebra communication subprograms. Computer Science Department, University of Tennessee, Knoxville, TN, October 1991.

21. J. Dongarra and E. Grosse. Distribution of mathematical software via electronic mail. *Communications of the ACM*, 30(5):403–407, July 1987. URL http://www.netlib.org/.

22. E. W. Felten and S. W. Otto. Coherent parallel C. In G. C. Fox, editor, *Proc. 3rd Conference on Hypercube Concurrent Computers and Applications*, pages 440–450. ACM Press, 1988.

23. F. Gantmacher. *The Theory of Matrices, Vol. II (transl.).* Chelsea, New York, 1959.

24. B. S. Garbow, J. M. Boyle, J. J. Dongarra, and C. B. Moler. *Matrix Eigensystem Routines - EISPACK Guide Extension*, Lecture Notes in Computer Science, Vol. 51. Springer-Verlag, Berlin, 1977.

25. G. Golub and C. Van Loan. *Matrix Computations*. Johns Hopkins University Press, Baltimore, MD, 2nd edition, 1989.

26. R. W. Hockney and C. R. Jesshope. *Parallel Computers*. Adam Hilger Ltd., Bristol, UK, 1981.

27. T. Kato. *Perturbation Theory for Linear Operators*. Springer-Verlag, Berlin, 2 edition, 1980.

28. C. Lawson, R. Hanson, D. Kincaid, and F. Krogh. Basic Linear Algebra Subprograms for Fortran usage. *ACM Trans. Math. Soft.*, 5:308–323, 1979.

29. A. Packard, M. Fan, and J. Doyle. A power method for the structured singular value. In *IEEE Conf. on Decision and Control*, pages 2132–2137, 1988.

30. B. Parlett. *The Symmetric Eigenvalue Problem*. Prentice Hall, Englewood Cliffs, NJ, 1980.

31. B. Parlett. The software scene in the extraction of eigenvalues from sparse matrices. *SIAM J. Sci. Stat. Comp.*, 5:590–604, 1984.

32. W.H. Press, B.P. Flannery, S.A. Teukolsky, and W.T. Vetterling. *Numerical Recipes in C*. Cambridge University Press, Cambridge, UK, 1991.

33. Y. Saad. *Numerical methods for large eigenvalue problems*. Manchester University Press, 1992.

34. G. Sleijpen and H. van der Vorst. Reliable updated residuals in hybrid Bi-CG methods. Preprint 886, Utrecht University, the Netherlands, 1994. to appear in Computing.

35. G. Sleijpen and H. van der Vorst. A Jacobi-Davidson iteration method for linear eigenvalue problems. Preprint 856 (revised), Utrecht University, the Netherlands, 1995 . to appear in SIMAX.

36. B. T. Smith, J. M. Boyle, J. J. Dongarra, B. S. Garbow, Y. Ikebe, V. C. Klema, and C. B. Moler. *Matrix Eigensystem Routines - EISPACK Guide*, Lecture Notes in Computer Science, Vol. 6. Springer-Verlag, Berlin, 1976.

37. G. W. Stewart. Error and perturbation bounds for subspaces associated with certain eigenvalue problems. *SIAM Review*, 15(4):727–764, Oct 1973.

38. G. W. Stewart and J.-G. Sun. *Matrix Perturbation Theory*. Academic Press, New York, 1990.

39. C. Überhuber. Computer-Numerik, Part 1 and 2, Springer-Verlag, Berlin, 1995.

40. A.J. van der Steen (ed). Aspects of Computational Science. NCF, Den Haag, the Netherlands, 1995.

41. P. Van Dooren. The computation of Kronecker's canonical form of a singular pencil. *Lin. Alg. Appl.*, 27:103–141, 1979.

42. P. Van Dooren. Reducing subspaces: Definitions, properties and algorithms. In B. Kågström and A. Ruhe, editors, *Matrix Pencils*, pages 58–73. Lecture Notes in Mathematics, Vol. 973, Proceedings, Springer-Verlag, Berlin, 1983.

43. J. H. Wilkinson. *The Algebraic Eigenvalue Problem*. Oxford University Press, Oxford, 1965.

44. J. Wilkinson and C. Reinsch. *Handbook for Automatic Computation: Volume II - Linear Algebra*. Springer-Verlag, New York, 1971.

45. P. Young, M. Newlin, and J. Doyle. Practical computation of the mixed μ problem. In *Proc. American Control Conference*, pages 2190–2194, 1994.

The ART behind IDEAS

Thomas Beth, Andreas Klappenecker,* Torsten Minkwitz,** and Armin Nückel

Institut für Algorithmen und Kognitive Systeme
Universität Karlsruhe, Fakultät für Informatik
D-76128 Karlsruhe, Germany
e-mail: EISS_Office@ira.uka.de

Abstract. The IDEAS design system is an innovative algorithm engineering environment. It can be employed to derive correct and efficient software or hardware implementations from algebraic specifications using the advanced formal method ART. Several case studies for some algorithm engineering tasks are discussed in this article to demonstrate the feasibility of this system.

1 Introduction

IDEAS is the acronym (*I*ntelligent *D*esign *E*nvironment for *A*lgorithms and *S*ystems) for an innovative algorithm engineering tool that has been built during a long term research project at the authors' institution, incorporating modern techniques of informatics, mathematics, computer algebra, and engineering. In contrast to traditional CAE-tools, like software compilers or hardware description languages (HDLs) or so-called Silicon Compilers and synthesis tools, in IDEAS the problem specification is stated in terms of mathematical expressions, which are the natural application descriptions by the user. Subsequently, using the methodology of *A*bstract *R*epresentation *T*heory (ART), a type refinement is carried out to take into account the requirements of a given implementation technology according to the semantics of the application. The basic idea is to generate and optimize implementations by well-chosen mathematical operations in relation to the algebraic problem specification. This leads to an alternative approach to algorithm engineering. In several case studies the feasibility of such an intelligent design environment, the strength of the approach and the power of the system IDEAS is demonstarated.

1.1 The IDEAS Design Flow

What is the basic difference between the traditional top-down or bottom-up approach and the sketched IDEAS design flow presented here? Following the

* This research was supported by DFG under project Be 887/6-2.
** This research was supported by DFG through the Graduiertenkolleg "Beherrschbarkeit komplexer Systeme".

IDEAS approach, the terms *problem, specification, algorithm,* and *implementation* become quite well-defined algebraic notions. Since user defined specifications are done using traditional mathematical data structures, such as number domains, vector spaces, matrix algebras, polynomial rings, permutation groups and ordered sets, modelling the data structure means specializing the ADT by introducing operational semantics in the specificated domain itself. Obviously, the specification may be changed during the design process. At first glance, this seems improper, because the specification is describing the problem. The unusual idea, however, is to introduce operations on the specification itself, i.e. combining it with the process of modeling ab initio. The engineering tool is used to generate algorithms, which are correct with respect to the specification in the semantics of the given model. Optimization then becomes a rewriting problem of the specification. Summarizing, one can quote several advantages of the algebraic algorithm design approach:

- availability of deep mathematical knowledge,
- correctness by automatic algebraic transformations,
- efficiency by modularization and parallelization,
- reusability through ADT's

The design environment IDEAS is to our knowledge the first fully operational implementation (cf. Fig. 1) of such a system. The strength of the environment relying on the fact that both the knowledge representation and the transformations on the specifications are provided by modern Computer Algebra Systems. The implementation of the features of IDEAS, making it an intelligent design environment, are briefly sketched in the following sections. They have become possible due to the increased capabilities of the underlying Computer Algebra packages during the last decade.

1.2   The Principle of ART

The theoretical background of this approach, ART (Abstract Representation Theory) is based on the thought that problems should be specified in the most adequate data structure. Elementary datatypes that have been studied thoroughly in the past are boolean logic and finite state automata. For problem specifications of this type, quite efficient tools exist to optimize the specification before the actual implementation. However, if a problem is best and most naturally stated in terms of linear equations, it doesn't seem to make sense to first refine down to the level of boolean logic and then try to optimize at this level, since important information is lost.

The development of the theory was initiated by the observation that algorithm engineering for restricted problem classes in signal processing is based on a limited number of data types and design principles [1]. It became clear that there is a strong relationship between symmetries and fast implementation of a system matrix A [20, 19].

The *cyclic shift property* of the Discrete Fourier Transform (DFT) can be described in these terms of symmetries. If P denotes the cyclic shift, which e.g.

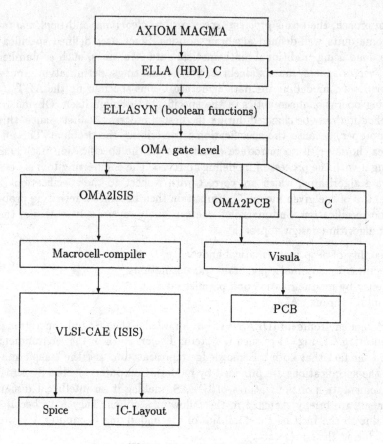

Fig. 1. The structure of IDEAS

naturally occurs as the phase shift operator in many models of specification (cf. section 4), and F denotes the Fourier tranfom matrix, then the following equation holds:

$$FP = QF,$$

where Q denotes the diagonal matrix $\operatorname{diag}(1, \omega, \omega^2, \ldots, \omega^{n-1})$. This property, which has many applications in position invariant pattern analysis, is an example of a *symmetry*, which offers itself to be reformulated in terms of representation theory.

Recall that for any finite group G, a linear representation of G in a vector space V is a homomorphism ρ from the group G into the group of invertible matrices of automorphisms $GL(V)$ of V. A *symmetry* of a matrix A is defined by a pair of representations ρ, σ with:

$$A\rho(g) = \sigma(g)A \qquad \forall g \in G,$$

where ρ is a permutation representation and σ is fully decomposed (thus of block diagonal form). If A is invertible, then $A\rho(g)A^{-1} = \sigma(g)$, and it is called a *decomposition matrix* of the permutation representation.

If a matrix has a symmetry, then the transform has obviously strong structural properties, which can be used to derive fast algorithms by modularization (block diagonal structure) or parallelization as a consequence of an induced tensor structure. The objective is the computation of a matrix describing a change of base, such that A can be rewritten as product of factors in a sparse form. As we shall show below, representation theory is a powerful tool to construct such suitable base change matrices. In order to explain the construction mechanism, some basic notions from representation theory are needed.

Recall that a representation $\rho : G \to GL(V)$ is called *irreducible*, if V is non-zero and if no vector subspace of V is stable under G, except 0 and V. Here, a vector space is called *stable*, if it is invariant under the action of G. For two irreducible representations $\rho : G \to GL(V)$ and $\sigma : G \to GL(W)$ Schur's Lemma [22] states in particular that a linear mapping $f : V \to W$ intertwining these representations, i.e. satisfying $\rho \circ f = f \circ \sigma$, is zero, if σ and ρ are not isomorphic, or otherwise is a scalar multiple of the identity.

Now if T_ρ is any decomposition matrix of a permutation representation, then an extension of Schur's Lemma shows that there is a matrix E with $ET_\rho = A$, such that E is block diagonal (up to a permutation) with blocks corresponding to homogeneous components of ρ. A homogeneous component of a representation ρ consists of all irreducible subrepresentation of ρ from one isomorphism class of irreducible representations of the group G. This enforces modularization and tensor product factorization. With a constructive method to compute a factorized decomposition matrix T_ρ with sparse factors at hand [20], using the equation $ET_\rho = A$, IDEAS constructs a fast algorithm to multiply with A. To give an impression of the notions used in this constructive process, the next section will provide a specific case study.

2   Case Study: Fast Cosine Transform

Here, in an application, we demonstrate that we have a method to produce a factorization of the transform matrix into sparse factors as an improved implementation from a specification given by the linear transform and a symmetry. A detailed explanation would require a thorough understanding of representation theory.

2.1   Preliminaries

The Discrete Cosine Transform (DCT) is well known from signal processing applications. Especially, this transform on eight points is at the heart of the well-known JPEG/MPEG compression family, the construction of a fast algorithm to carry out the DCT is an important task. An IDEAS generated solution improving the straight forward implementations is given in this case study. The DCT is given by:

$$x(n) = C_o(n)\sqrt{\frac{2}{N}} \sum_{k=0}^{N-1} C(k) \cos\left(\frac{k(n+1/2)\pi}{N}\right), \qquad n = 0, \ldots, N-1,$$

where $C_o(n) = 1/\sqrt{2}$, if $n = 0$, and 1 otherwise.

The DCT matrix of size 8×8 turns out to be a decomposition matrix of the dihedral group D_8 on 8 points (thus it has a symmetry), which can be written as a permutation group in the following form:

$$D_8 \cong \langle (1,3,5,7,8,6,4,2), (1,2)(3,4)(5,6)(7,8) \rangle,$$

resembling the invariance of the DCT with respect to 2-step reflected shifts and local swapping. As mentioned before, another decomposition matrix for the group D_8 can be constructed that differs only by a block diagonal matrix E as another factor. A factorized base change matrix is constructed using a recursive procedure along a chain of normal subgroups (cf.[2, 19]).

2.2   A Fast Discrete Cosine Transform Algorithm

The dihedral group in its usual permutation group presentation leads naturally to a permutation representation. In representation theory a key notion is that of an induced representation. Roughly speaking, the induction operation extends a 'small' representation of a subgroup to a 'bigger' representation of the whole group. The dimension of the representation vector space increases by a factor of $|\text{group}|/|\text{subgroup}|$, producing a block structure of this order. Permutation representations are always induced from representations of smaller groups, namely from the 1-representation of the stabilizer. More formally, this can be stated as follows:

$$\langle (1,3,5,7,8,6,4,2), (1,2)(3,4)(5,6)(7,8) \rangle \cong \text{Ind}_{\text{Stab}(D_8,1)}^{D_8}(1).$$

First Step. The dihedral group D_8 contains a normal subgroup D_4 of prime index that contains the stabilizer of D_8 :

$$D_4 \cong \langle (3,2)(5,4)(7,6), (1,5)(7,2)(8,4) \rangle$$

Now a procedure called *induction recursion* can be applied, which is based on the identity:

$$\text{Ind}_{\text{Stab}(D_8,1)}^{D_8}(1) \cong \text{Ind}_{D_4}^{D_8}\left(\text{Ind}_{\text{Stab}(D_8,1)}^{D_4}(1)\right).$$

This means that the induction operator can be factored, which leads to a factorization of the decomposition matrix. There are always four factors, typically of the form:

$$T = (T_1 \otimes 1)B(1 \otimes T_2)P,$$

where T_1 is a decomposition matrix of the factor group D_8/D_4, B is a block diagonal matrix with images of irreducible representations of the group D_8 as blocks, T_2 is a decomposition matrix of $D_4 \cong \langle(1,2,3,4),(1,4)(2,3)\rangle$, and P is simply a permutation.

Since the factor group $\mathbb{Z}_2 \cong D_8/D_4$ is abelian, the decomposition matrix is simply given by the Fourier matrix (cf. section 3.1)

$$T_1 := \begin{pmatrix} 1 & 1 \\ 1 & -1 \end{pmatrix}.$$

The matrix T_2 is determined by recursion, and the matrix B is given by a solution of a system of linear equations.

Second Step. The dihedral group D_4 contains $\mathbb{Z}_2 \times \mathbb{Z}_2 \cong \langle(2,4),(1,3)\rangle$ as a normal subgroup. Again, induction recursion can be applied. This time the identity

$$\mathrm{Ind}_{\mathrm{Stab}(D_4,1)}^{D_4}(1) \cong \mathrm{Ind}_{\mathbb{Z}_2 \times \mathbb{Z}_2}^{D_4}\left(\mathrm{Ind}_{\mathrm{Stab}(D_4,1)}^{\mathbb{Z}_2 \times \mathbb{Z}_2}(1)\right)$$

is used, leading again to a factorization of the form

$$T_2 = (T_1' \otimes 1)B'(1 \otimes T_2')P',$$

where the matrices are of size 4×4. The matrix T_2' is a decomposition matrix for $\mathbb{Z}_2 \times \mathbb{Z}_2$ with permutation representation $\langle(1,2)\rangle$ and is determined via recursion. The matrices T_1', B', and P' are like T_1, B, and P respectively execpt of smaller degree (cf. the similar approach in section 5).

Last Step. Since permutation groups of degree 2 always have the Fourier matrix DFT_2 as a decomposition matrix, this one is taken from a library. In the end, one has obtained a factorized decompostion matrix T. A fast algorithm to multiply with DCT_8 follows immediately. To learn about the details of computing B and B' consult [20].

2.3 VLSI Implementation

The previous section gave an impression of the "internal life" of IDEAS. The user from the outside is simply requested to provide a matrix together with its symmetry and gets a fast algorithm as a result of the ART approach. For the DCT_8 the system automatically produced an algorithm which uses 14 multiplications instead of 64. In view of the regularity, this compares preferably in gate count and chip size with the 13 multiplications of handoptimized algorithms [12], which economizes on multiplications at the cost of additions. The algorithm is stated as a list of matrices in a computer algebra system. The IDEAS system translates this representation to the high-level Hardware Description Language ELLA. Using the LOCAM synthesis tools a gate level description can be generated. The step from the gate level description to the geometry is done with the help of the VLSI-CAE system ISIS (cf. Fig. 1). Sequential programs (C-syntax) are generated by the use of ordinary software compilers for this purpose.

3 Case Study: Algebraic Discrete Fourier Transform

In this case study techniques for compiling and optimizing Algebraic Discrete Fourier Transforms (ADFTs) [1, 4] are dicussed. ADFT is based on the so-called Modular Polynomial Transformations (MPTs), providing a common generalization of the Diskrete Fourier Transform and Chinese Remainder Technique [8].

Both transformations are of high demand for high speed applications in coding theory [17, 6], cryptography [15, 13] and signal processing [1, 7].

3.1 Preliminaries

Denote by $a = (a_0, \ldots, a_{n-1})$ an input vector over a field $\mathbb{F}$. It will be convenient to repeat this vector as a signal polynomial, namely as $a(x) = \sum_{i=0}^{n-1} a_i x^i$. Assume that the characteristic of $\mathbb{F}$ does not divide the signal length n. The polynomial $x^n - 1$ can be decomposed in disjoint, irreducible, monic factors

$$x^n - 1 = \prod_{i=1}^{m} p_i(x) \in \mathbb{F}[x].$$

The *Modular Polynomial Transform* (MPT) to the factors $(p_i)_{i=1}^m$ of a signal polynomial $a(x)$ is defined as the set of polynomial remainders

$$MPT_{(\mathbb{F}, x^n-1)}(a(x)) = (B_1(x), \ldots, B_m(x)),$$

where $B_l(x) \equiv a(x) \bmod p_l(x)$. As a direct consequence of the Chinese remainder theorem it follows that the Modular Polynomial Transform is invertible. The intrinsic parallel structure of an MPT is illustrated in Figure 2, allowing a fast multiplication of degree n polynomials in $O(n^{1+\epsilon})$ or $O(n \log n)$ time rather than $O(n^2)$ [8].

The Modular Polynomial Transform with respect to the factor basis $(x - \omega^i)_{i=1}^n$ is important, because it computes the Discrete Fourier Transform of the same length if the n-th roots ω^i of unity are contained in $\mathbb{F}$. Otherwise it implicitly computes the Discrete Fourier Transform via the Algebraic Discrete Fourier Transform. For this it is necessary to represent all results of the MPT in a common field extension.

The irreducible factors $p_i(x)$ of $x^n - 1$ can be viewed as minimal polynomials of several extension fields of $\mathbb{F}$. Each zero of the polynomials $p_i(x)$ is some root of unity. In the case where $\mathbb{F}$ is the field of rationals, all quotient fields $\mathbb{Q}[x]/\langle p_i(x) \rangle$ can be viewed as subfields of the cyclotomic field $\mathbb{Q}[x]/\langle \phi_n(x) \rangle$, where ϕ_n is the n-th cyclotomic polynomial.

In the case where $\mathbb{F}$ is of characteristic p the situation is somewhat different. The usual cyclotomic polynomial $\phi_n(x) \in \mathbb{Q}[x]$ may be reducible over $\mathbb{F}$, and the situation may appear that some quotient fields are isomorphic. In this case, it suffices to work with one of the isomorphic fields, saving further computations after a local change of base to so-called normal bases. Recall that an $\mathbb{F}_p$-basis

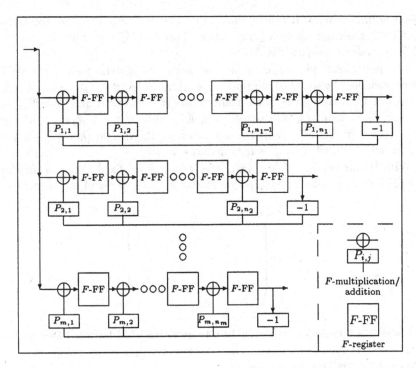

Fig. 2. The structure of Modular Polynomial Transforms over finite fields

of the form $(\alpha, \alpha^{p^1}, \alpha^{p^2}, \ldots, \alpha^{p^{n-1}})$ is called a *normal basis* of $\mathbb{F}_{p^n}$. Two normal bases $(\alpha, \alpha^{p^1}, \ldots, \alpha^{p^{n-1}})$ and $(\beta, \beta^{p^1}, \ldots, \beta^{p^{n-1}})$ are called *dual* iff

$$\sum_{i=0}^{n-1}(\beta_i \alpha_j)^{q^i} = \delta_{i,j}$$

holds. Moreover, if the two dual bases coincide, then the normal basis is called a *self-dual*.

3.2   The Algebraic Discrete Fourier Transform

Suppose that $\mathbb{F}$ is a field with a characteristic not dividing n. Denote by ω a primitive n-th root of unity and by $\mathbb{E}$ the Galois extension $\mathbb{F}(\omega)$. Furthermore, let DFT_N^n be the DFT-matrix (ω^{ij}) of size $n \times n$, where each coefficient is represented with respect to a normal base N of the field extension $\mathbb{E}/\mathbb{F}$. The ADFT is defined by the matrix that is obtained from the (ω^{ij}) matrix by projecting each coefficient ω^{ij} onto its first component with respect to the normal base B.

In this section an algorithm to compute the ADFT via the MPT is described. In a first step the $MPT_{(\mathbb{F}, x^n-1)}(a(x))$ is used to compute the remainders B_i. Then the different fields $\mathbb{F}/\langle p_i(x)\rangle$ are injected into the common field $\mathbb{E}$. Afterwards, a second base change is applied to represented the results with respect to a joint normal base N. It can be shown that the resulting transform computes the ADFT spectrum up to a permutation. Therefore, it is possible to use the MPT in order to compute the ADFT.

The multiplications required in the feedback shift registers realizing the MPT can be visualised by so-called multiplication matrices. Let $\beta \in \mathbb{F}_{p^n}$ be a primitive element of $\mathbb{F}_{p^n}^*$, then there is an isomorphism (the so-called dlog) $\phi : \mathbb{F}_{p^n}^* \to [1, \ldots, p^n - 1]$, mapping each element $b \in \mathbb{F}_{p^n}^*$ to a value $i \in \mathbb{Z}_{p^n-1}$ with the property: $b = \beta^i$. Let M_β denote the associated matrix with the property $b \cdot M_\beta = b \cdot \beta$ for all $b \in \mathbb{F}$, where $b \cdot \beta$ is regarded as a vector.

With the knowledge of M_β, gate level networks for fixed elements may be compiled. If $p(x)$ is the defining polynomial of $\mathbb{F}$, then M_β is of the form:

$$M_\beta = \begin{pmatrix} 0 & 1 & 0 & \ldots & 0 \\ \vdots & \ddots & \ddots & \ldots & \vdots \\ \vdots & & \ddots & 1 & 0 \\ 0 & & \ldots & 0 & 1 \\ -p_{n-1} & \ldots & \ldots & -p_1 & -p_0 \end{pmatrix} \quad (1)$$

Using this knowledge, it is clear how to generate VLSI layouts based on the method of algebraic compilation: The diagonal of 1's represent a shift operator followed by a feedback set of taps p_i.

3.3   VLSI Implementations

All the outputs of the computer algebra system, for which in this case AXIOM [16] was used, are sent to a parser and an HDL code generator. Together with commercial synthesis tools, a CMOS layout has been generated. Figure 3 shows an MPT layout for MPT($\mathbb{F}_{2^4}, x^7 - 1$) reflecting the factorization of $x^7 - 1$ which is $(x + 1)(x^3 + x + 1)(x^3 + x^2 + 1)$. In the next case study it is shown that architectural information is already available at the algebraic level and can be used to improve geometries.

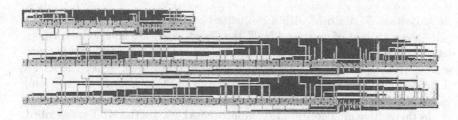

Fig. 3. Layout of the MPT of the polynomial $x^7 - 1$ is characterized by the factorization $(x + 1)(x^3 + x + 1)(x^3 + x^2 + 1)$.

It is possible to choose one of the most suitable normal bases with respect to the number of operations necessary to compute the base changes, refer also [14]. Figure 4 gives some results for different MPTs and bases. Thus only by some change of bases, a major reduction of the hardware was achieved. A similar transformation as described in the example can be computed with 4 additions and 2 multiplications. This completes the section on MPT, describing the use of computer algebra for compiling and optimizing these kinds of algorithms.

transform		additions		multiplications	
field	length	min	max	min	max
$\mathbb{F}_2$	3	1	1	-	-
$\mathbb{F}_4$	7	6	6	-	-
$\mathbb{F}_3$	4	2	2	1	4
$\mathbb{F}_3$	8	4	4	2	7
$\mathbb{F}_3$	16	24	24	7	14
$\mathbb{F}_5$	6	2	4	1	7
$\mathbb{F}_5$	12	4	8	3	14

Fig. 4. Some results of optimization.

4 Case Study: Fast Wavelet Transform

Wavelets are special orthogonal functions ψ which are localized having some oscillations. As such they can be chosen adapted to a certain waveform, giving high correlations with a signal. However, under the modelling paradigm of 1.1 such waveforms, such as noises or cracks on records, or ultrasound signatures, will be squeezed or spread and delayed in signal space. Therefore, the wavelet base of the model signal space is generated by dilation and translation from the *mother wavelet* ψ.

4.1 Preliminaries

Wavelet bases are special orthonormal bases of the space of square integrable functions $L^2(\mathbb{R})$ given by a family of wavelets of the form

$$\psi_{j,n}(x) = 2^{-j/2}\,\psi(2^{-j}x - n), \qquad j, n \in \mathbb{Z}.$$

A closer look at the construction of wavelet bases reveals an elegant way to derive the Fast Wavelet Transform (FWT) algorithm [10, 18].

A natural starting point for the construction is a *multiresolution analysis*, that is, in particular, a ladder of approximation subspaces

$$\{0\} \subset \cdots \subset V_2 \subset V_1 \subset V_0 \subset V_{-1} \subset V_{-2}\cdots \subset L^2(\mathbb{R}),$$

where for each $j \in \mathbb{Z}$ the subspace V_j is spanned by an orthonormal basis $\{2^{-j/2} \varphi(2^{-j}x - n) \mid j, n \in \mathbb{Z}\}$. The space V_0 is invariant under integer translations. The function φ is called *scaling function*.

The different approximation spaces are connected by the following dilation property:

$$f(x) \in V_j \iff f(2x) \in V_{j+1}.$$

Therefore, the scaling function φ fulfills a dilation equation:

$$\varphi(x) = \sqrt{2} \sum_{n \in \mathbb{Z}} h_n \, \varphi(2x - n), \qquad \text{with suitable} \quad h_n \in \mathbb{C}. \tag{2}$$

An orthonormal wavelet can be derived from the scaling function φ as follows:

$$\psi(x) = \sqrt{2} \sum_{n \in \mathbb{Z}} g_n \, \varphi(2x - n), \tag{3}$$

where $g_n = (-1)^n \, \overline{h_{k-n}}$, and k is an odd integer. The equations (2) and (3) play a key role in the construction of the FWT, which will be explained in the next section.

The hierarchic structure of a multiresolution analysis resembles that of the subgroup chain when deriving linear systems with symmetry. The techniques of the first case study are not applicable however, because the underlying vector spaces are not finite dimensional. Nevertheless, structural properties are used again to derive the fast algorithm.

4.2   The Fast Wavelet Transform Algorithm

Assume that the input signal s is already in an approximation space, say V_{-1}. Then this signal s can be represented as a sequence of "sample values"

$$(\ldots, \langle \varphi_{-1,n-1} \mid s \rangle, \langle \varphi_{-1,n} \mid s \rangle, \langle \varphi_{-1,n+1} \mid s \rangle, \ldots), \tag{4}$$

where $\varphi_{j,n}(x) = 2^{-j/2} \varphi(2^{-j}x - n)$, with respect to the orthonormal basis of V_{-1}. Denote by W_0 the orthogonal complement of V_0 in V_{-1}. The space W_0 comprises the "details" of V_{-1} missing in V_0. It can be shown that the integral translates of ψ constitute a basis for W_0.

The FWT realizes the change of base from V_{-1} to $V_0 \oplus W_0$. Substituting the integral translates of the scaling function $\varphi(x)$ in equation (2) and of the wavelet $\psi(x)$ in the equation (3), leads to an elementary decomposition step of the FWT:

$$\langle \varphi_{0,m} \mid s \rangle = \sum_{n \in \mathbb{Z}} \overline{h_{n-2m}} \, \langle \varphi_{-1,n} \mid s \rangle,$$

$$\langle \psi_{0,m} \mid s \rangle = \sum_{n \in \mathbb{Z}} \overline{g_{n-2m}} \, \langle \varphi_{-1,n} \mid s \rangle.$$

In other words, an elementary decomposition step can be visualized in matrix form as follows:

$$
\begin{pmatrix}
\ddots & \ddots & \ddots & \ddots & \ddots & & & \\
& \cdots & \bar{h}_0 & \bar{h}_1 & \bar{h}_2 & \bar{h}_3 & \cdots & \\
& & \cdots & \bar{h}_0 & \bar{h}_1 & \bar{h}_2 & \bar{h}_3 & \cdots \\
& & & & \ddots & \ddots & \ddots & \ddots \\
& \ddots & \ddots & \ddots & \ddots & & & \\
& \cdots & \bar{g}_0 & \bar{g}_1 & \bar{g}_2 & \bar{g}_3 & \cdots & \\
& & \cdots & \bar{g}_0 & \bar{g}_1 & \bar{g}_2 & \bar{g}_3 & \cdots \\
& & & & \ddots & \ddots & \ddots & \ddots
\end{pmatrix}
\tag{5}
$$

The design process for a VLSI implementation of an elementary decomposition step is sketched in the following sections.

4.3 VLSI Implementation

Input signals in signal processing applications are often associated with the rational sequence data type. From an algorithmic point of view, the FWT convolves in one decomposition step the rational input sequence with the sequences $(\bar{h}_{-n})_{n \in \mathbb{Z}}$ and $(\bar{g}_{-n})_{n \in \mathbb{Z}}$ and then drops every second sample in the resulting two sequences. Consider the sequence (h_n) corresponding to the Daubechies wavelet of order two [9]:

$$
h_0 := \frac{1 + \sqrt{3}}{8}, \quad h_1 := \frac{3 + \sqrt{3}}{8}, \quad h_2 := \frac{3 - \sqrt{3}}{8}, \quad h_3 := \frac{1 - \sqrt{3}}{8}.
\tag{6}
$$

The objective of this section is to derive an architecture for an elementary decomposition step of the FWT using internally symbolic arithmetic and delivering fixed point arithmetic.

At first glance, an obvious solution is to approximate the coefficients (h_n) numerically, for example as follows:

$$
h_0 := 0.3415064, \quad h_1 := 0.5915064, \quad h_2 := 0.1584936, \quad h_3 := -0.0915064.
$$

Integral coefficients are obtained after a suitable normalization. The multiplication with integer constants can be realized with shifts, additions, and subtractions. When IDEAS is provided with these coefficients, the system generates an elementary decomposition step with 26 adders and subtractors in total for a twenty bit resolution.

Following our comments about application driven re-modelling (cf. 1.1), alternatively, the specification can be re-written to take advantage of the specific arithmetic structure of the coefficients in (6). It is possible to specify the coefficients as elements of the field extension $\mathbb{Q}(\sqrt{3})$ instead of the rational domain.

Using the isomorphism $\mathbb{Q}(\sqrt{3}) \cong \mathbb{Q}[x]/\langle x^2 - 3 \rangle$, the coefficients (6) can be expressed as follows:

$$(h_0, h_1, h_2, h_3) = \left(\frac{1+x}{8}, \frac{3-x}{8}, \frac{3+x}{8}, \frac{1-x}{8} \right) \qquad \mathrm{mod}\,(x^2 - 3).$$

At first sight nothing is gained. However, conjugacy can be used to reduce hardware, using similar techniques as in the ADFT in section 3.2.

The automorphism $\sqrt{3} \mapsto -\sqrt{3}$ of the Galois group $\mathrm{Gal}(\mathbb{Q}(\sqrt{3})/\mathbb{Q})$ maps the coefficient sequence (h_n) onto the "mirrored" sequence (h_{3-n}). Up to change of sign, this conjugated sequences coincides with the sequence (g_n), which is given by $g_n = (-1)^n h_{3-n}$. Thus, the redundancy involved in the symbolic polynomial computation can be used to avoid effort for the computation of the convolution with (g_n). In order to transform the results from $\mathbb{Q}[x]/\langle x^2 - 3 \rangle$ to the fixed point format, numerical approximations to the roots of the minimal polynomial $x^2 - 3$ are subsituted for x.

Using the methods of the preceeding case study, IDEAS optimizes the polynomial bases to minimize the necessary operations. Depending on the algebraic structure, geometric information is derived in order to place and route the basic cells, implementing additions, subtractions, and circuits multiplying signal values with constants, etc. The current implementation of IDEAS produced a layout for one decomposition step based on 15 adders and subtractors. A part of the layout is shown in Figure 5. The placement and routing information is detected on the algebraic level. Due to the close integration of Computer Algebra Systems, ELLA, and ISIS, it is possible to use this geometric information for the generation of architectures.

5   Future Technology: Quantum Gates

The newly emerging fields of Quantum Computing as described in the contribution by Brassard in this volume presents a most natural area of applications for the IDEAS design tool, as we shall show in this last case study.

5.1   Preliminaries

The state space of a Quantum Computer can be viewed as a Hilbert space $\mathcal{H}$ of kets $|\psi\rangle$, the dual space of which is formed by the bras $\langle\varphi|$ with respect to the hermitian form $\langle .|. \rangle$. Since proper computational states are those kets $|\psi\rangle$ for which $\langle\psi|\psi\rangle = 1$, the dynamics of the Quantum Arithmetical Logical Unit (QALU) is necessarily given by unitary transforms on $\mathcal{H}$, which for practical reasons as well as for complexity aspects afford representations of small degree. Without loss of generality we therefore assume that the state transition functions of a QALU are matrices $U \in \mathcal{U}(N)$ the unitary group of degree N. A computation c links an initial state $|\psi\rangle \in \mathcal{H}$ with the final state $|\varphi\rangle = U_c|\psi\rangle$ weighted with the amplitude $a_{\varphi \to \psi} = \langle\varphi|\psi\rangle$ via the state transition matrix U_c associated with c. If U_c can be written as a product $U_c = U_{t_l} \ldots U_{t_1}$ with $U_{t_i} \in \mathcal{G}$ from a given

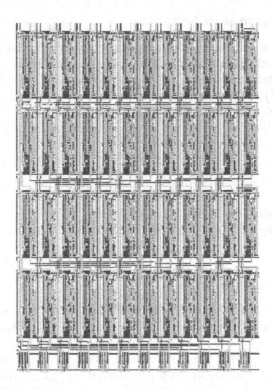

Fig. 5. Fast Wavelet Transform in a 12 bit realization. A part of the layout is shown. The full circuit is based on 4806 transistors and needs 1.544 mm² area with respect to a 1μ dual metal CMOS process.

set $\mathcal{G}$ of computational primitives of so-called quantum gates, the number l is the length of the computation. In this sense complexity issues can canonically be related to word problems in $\mathcal{U}(N)$ w.r.t. the generating set $\mathcal{G}$.

5.2   Quantum Parallelism

What is more, not only sequential computations can be expressed in this manner by forming products, but the concept of true parallelism comes very natural by considering the tensor space $\mathcal{H} \otimes \mathcal{H}'$ which is physically constructed by quantum interference coupling of the two separate QALU's with state spaces $\mathcal{H}$ (resp. $\mathcal{H}'$) by entanglement (*Verschränkung*, so-called by E. Schrödinger). Its state vectors are given by the tensors $|\psi, \xi\rangle := |\psi\rangle \otimes |\xi\rangle$ with $\psi \in \mathcal{H}, \xi \in \mathcal{H}'$. On this space the unitary transforms of the form $W = U \otimes V \in \mathcal{U}(NN')$ with $U \in \mathcal{U}(N), V \in \mathcal{U}(N')$ resemble fully parallel computations as for the Kronecker product of transforms we have $U \otimes V = (U \otimes I_{N'}) \cdot (I_N \otimes V)$, cf. section 2.2. The the meaning in quantum micro code of e.g. $U \otimes I \in \mathcal{U}(NN')$ is: "Apply the unitary transform to all kets $|\psi, \xi\rangle \in \mathcal{H} \otimes \mathcal{H}'$ simultaneously by altering the left part amplitudes according to U and leave the right part unchanged."

5.3   Superposition at its best

With this trick we can automatically generate an algorithm for producing an coherent equidistribution of all 2^n states in one quantum register consisting of n entangled 2-state systems $\mathcal{H}_i$, $i \in [1 : n]$, whose base in given by the kets $\{|\varepsilon_i\rangle \mid \varepsilon_i \in \{0,1\}\}$. The n-fold tensor space $\mathcal{H} = \mathcal{H}_1 \otimes \cdots \otimes \mathcal{H}_n$ of dimension 2^n consists of all kets $|\psi\rangle = \sum_{i=1}^{n} \sum_{\varepsilon_i=0}^{1} \alpha_{\varepsilon_1, \varepsilon_2, \ldots, \varepsilon_n} |\varepsilon_1, \varepsilon_2, \ldots, \varepsilon_n\rangle$. Starting from the initial ket $|0, \ldots, 0\rangle$ the n-th Hadamard-Walsh transformation $W_n = W_1 \otimes W_1 \otimes \ldots \otimes W_1$ with (cf. equation 2.2)

$$W_1 = \frac{1}{\sqrt{2}} T_1 = \frac{1}{\sqrt{2}} \begin{pmatrix} 1 & 1 \\ 1 & -1 \end{pmatrix} \tag{7}$$

produces the desired final state $|\psi_{equ}\rangle = 2^{-n/2} \sum_{i=1}^{n} \sum_{\varepsilon_i=0}^{1} |\varepsilon_1, \varepsilon_2, \ldots, \varepsilon_n\rangle$ in n parallel steps by applying W_1 successively to each of the n two-state systems $\mathcal{H}_i$.

5.4   Conditional Commands

Having produced a coherent superposition of all possible 2^n states equally "amply" computation can start on these simultaneously. For this different transforms U_k may have to be applied to different orthogonal states φ_k for $U \in [1 : n]$. The transform $U_{cond} = \sum_k |\varphi_k\rangle\langle\varphi_k| \otimes U_k$ resembles the conditional CASE-operator. The matrix U_{cond} has the form of a block matrix $\text{diag}(U_1, U_2, \ldots, U_k, \ldots)$, therefore representing a decomposition matrix for a subgroup of $\mathcal{U}(N)$ thus closing the loop to section 1.2 invoking the principles of ART in a most natural way.

5.5   Applying IDEAS: Automatic compilation and implementation

With these computational primitives, i.e., sequential, parallel, conditional composition, translated into unitary groups and therefore to the theory of Lie algebras, the IDEAS tools and paradigm provide a natural solution to the engineering task transforming the problem specification given by an initial /final state relationship $\langle\varphi|\psi\rangle$ for all $\varphi, \psi \in \mathcal{H}$ into the group-theoretic problem: To factor the matrix $U = (\langle\varphi|\psi\rangle)_{\varphi,\psi}$ with respect to the generating set $\mathcal{G}$. In other words, automatic compilation from a problem specification to a computation process will be possible. While a most general gate has been proposed by several authors [21, 11] resembling the basic primitive of a Boolean Horner scheme $(a, b, c) \rightarrow (a, b, (a \cdot b) \oplus c))$ on basis of which any Boolean polynomial presented in Ring-Normalform (i.e. the often called RM-Normalform) can be implemented, the IDEAS environment can be made to translate such unitary computations and compile them from a physically and practically feasible set $\mathcal{G}$ of generating customised gates adapted to efficient computational tasks as investigated recently by Beth, Blatt, Zoller & Weinfurter [3].

5.6   From Unitary Transforms to Layout: IDEAS all along

In implementing the unitary transform W_n, given as example in section 5.3, we have shown that is suffices to apply the basic transform

$$W_1 = \frac{1}{\sqrt{2}} \begin{pmatrix} 1 & 1 \\ 1 & -1 \end{pmatrix} \tag{8}$$

on each Qbit $|\varepsilon_1\rangle$. A "Quantum" standard cell for this purpose has been known since more than a century, the so-called "Mach-Zehnder interferometer" acting on photons [21]. It can easily be build from beam splitters, phase shifters and mirrors cf. Figure 6.

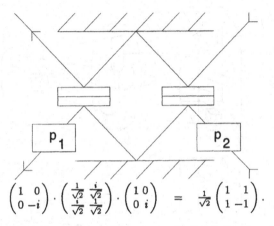

$$\begin{pmatrix} 1 & 0 \\ 0 & -i \end{pmatrix} \cdot \begin{pmatrix} \frac{1}{\sqrt{2}} & \frac{i}{\sqrt{2}} \\ \frac{i}{\sqrt{2}} & \frac{1}{\sqrt{2}} \end{pmatrix} \cdot \begin{pmatrix} 1 & 0 \\ 0 & i \end{pmatrix} = \frac{1}{\sqrt{2}} \begin{pmatrix} 1 & 1 \\ 1 & -1 \end{pmatrix}.$$

Fig. 6. The Mach Zehnder configuration: A standard cell for Quantum Computing $(p_1 = -\frac{\pi}{2}, p_2 = \frac{\pi}{2})$ and the corresponding $\mathcal{U}_2$ description of the experimental configuration is shown

6   Conclusion

We have demonstrated the power and applicability of the modern algorithm and system design environment IDEAS, which resembles the new representation theoretic approach ART to the problem of automatic engineering algorithm giving correct and efficient implementation for computations in hardware and software. It has been shown that the concept of manipulating Abstract Data Types by proper tools of Computer Algebra is feasible, especially if the categories of mathematical structures presented by the user have a rich and intrinsic structural theory, such as those many areas which can be described by the classical language of today's modern math. By detecting symmetries in the problems presented and formalising congruence classes of patterns in the abstract data types, the algebraic approach not only allows the automatic generation of fast

algorithms for solving problems in the model domains. What is more, it provides
the opportunity of re-modeling the semantics of the model algebra according to
symmetries detected in the algorithm development process. A surprising result
of this type has been obtained when the IDEAS approach was applied to the
design of molecular robotics [5], as a consequence of which also an improvement
on the control of an ultra-large milling machine was achieved. The latter example shows in a nutshell that the approach sketched here has opened a completely
new and promising road to solve wider classes of problems by the use of problem
adapted description languages. The ART behind IDEAS therefore has developed
beyond the Art of Computer Programming towards an art of integrated problem
solving.

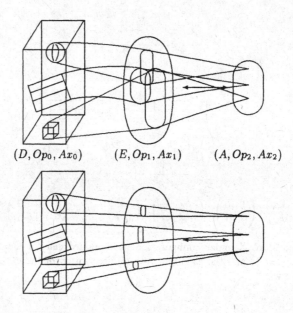

$$(D, Op_0, Ax_0) \qquad (E, Op_1, Ax_1) \qquad (A, Op_2, Ax_2)$$

Fig. 7. Unsuitable description languages (upper picture) induce bad class formation in
the model datatype due to inproper semantics. While in the lower picture a problem
adapted modelling by a suitable semantic comes with "good" description languages.

Acknowledgements

We thank Volker Baumgarte, Sebastian Egner, Rüdiger Ganz, Willi Geiselmann,
Dieter Gollmann, Martin Indlekofer, Kai Rohrbacher, Michael Vielhaber, and
Otto Wohlmuth for their contributions to the IDEAS pilot system. The support
by DFG, MWF (formally MWK) Baden-Würtemberg, WM Baden Würtemberg,
INMOS, DRA (formerly RSRE), and Racal-Redac is gratefully acknowledged,
which made the implementation of the IDEAS pilot system possible.

References

1. T. Beth. *Verfahren der schnellen Fourier-Transformation.* Teubner-Verlag, 1984.
2. T. Beth. Generating Fast Hartley Transforms – another application of the Algebraic Discrete Fourier Transform. In *Proc. Int. Sym. Signals, Systems, and Electronics ISSSE 89*, pages 688–692. Union Radio Scientifique International, 1989.
3. T. Beth, R. Blatt, P. Zoller, and H. Weinfurter. Engineering quantum gates. In preparation, 1995.
4. T. Beth, W. Fumy, and R. Mühlfeld. Zur Algebraische Diskreten Fourier Transformation. *Arch. Math.*, 40:238–244, 1983.
5. T. Beth, J. Müller-Quade, and A. Nückel. IDEAS - Intelligent Design Environment for Algorithms and Systems. In M. E. Welland and J. K. Gimzewski, editors, *Ultimate Limits of Fabrication and Measurement*, pages 49–57. Kluwer, 1995.
6. R. Blahut. *Theory & Practice of Error-Control Codes.* Addison-Wesley Publ. Comp., Reading, MA, 1983.
7. R. Blahut. *Fast algorithms for Digital Signal Processing.* Addison-Wesley Publ. Comp., Reading, MA, 1985.
8. B. Buchberger, Collins G. E., and Loos R. *Computer Algebra.* Springer-Verlag, Berlin, 1982.
9. I. Daubechies. Orthonormal bases of compactly supported wavelets. *Comm. Pure Appl. Math.*, 41:909–996, 1988.
10. I. Daubechies. *Ten Lectures on Wavelets.* CBMS-NSF Reg. Conf. Series Appl. Math., SIAM, 1992.
11. D. P. DiVincenzo. Two-bit gates are universal for quantum computation. *Physical Review A*, 51(2), 1995.
12. E. Feig and S. Winograd. Fast algorithms for the Discrete Cosine Transform. *IEEE Trans. on Signal Processing*, pages 2174–2193, 1992.
13. W. Fumy and H. P. Rieß. *Kryptographie.* Oldenburg, 1988.
14. W. Geiselmann. *Algebraische Algorithmenentwicklung am Beispiel der Arithmetik in endlichen Körpern.* Dissertation, Universität Karlsruhe, 1993.
15. D. Gollmann. *Algorithmenentwurf in der Kryptographie.* Bibliographisches Inst., Mannheim, 1994.
16. R. D. Jenks and R. S. Sutor. *Axiom: the scientific computation system.* Springer-Verlag, Berlin, 1992.
17. F. J. MacWilliams and N. J. A. Sloane. *The Theory of Error-Correcting Codes.* North-Holland Publ. Comp., Amsterdam, 1977.
18. S. G. Mallat. A theory for multiresolution signal decomposition: the wavelet representation. *IEEE Trans. Pattern Anal. Mach. Intell.*, 11(7):674–693, Juli 1989.
19. T. Minkwitz. *Algorithmensynthese für lineare Systeme mit Symmetrie.* Dissertation, Universität Karlsruhe, 1993.
20. T. Minkwitz. Algorithms explained by symmetries. In E. W. Mayr and C. Puech, editors, *STACS 95, Proc. 12th Annual Symposium*, volume 900 of *Lecture Notes in Computer Science*, pages 157–167. Springer-Verlag, Berlin, 1995.
21. M. Reck and A. Zeilinger. Experimental realization of any discrete unitary operator. *Physical Review Letters*, 73(1), 1994.
22. J. P. Serre. *Linear Representations of Finite Groups.* Grad. Texts in Math. **42**. Springer-Verlag, 1977.

Algorithmic Number Theory and Its Relationship to Computational Complexity

Leonard M. Adleman

Department of Computer Science
University of Southern California
Los Angeles, California, 90089
adleman@cs.usc.edu

Abstract. Though algorithmic number theory is one of man's oldest intellectual pursuits, its current vitality is perhaps unrivaled in history. This is due in part to the injection of new ideas from computational complexity. In this paper, a brief history of the symbiotic relationship between number theory and complexity theory will be presented. In addition, some of the technical aspects underlying 'modern' methods of primality testing and factoring will be described .

1 Introduction: *History of the two central problems - primality and factoring.*[1]

It all began a little over 2000 years ago. That's when Eratosthenes of Alexandria invented the sieve (and yes - this is the same Eratosthenes who measured the circumference of the earth). The sieve was apparently the first recorded method for testing primality (and factoring - at least square free factoring). Unfortunately, things did not progress rapidly from there. It was only around 1200 that Leonardo Pisano (also known as Leonardo Fibonacci) improved the method - noting that one could stop sieving when one reached the square root of the number of interest. Remarkably, this remained the fastest method known for both factoring and primality testing until 1974 when R. Sherman Lehman [Leh74] demonstrated that factoring could be done in time $O(n^{1/3})$. After Fibonacci, the problems began to attract the interest of mathematical heavyweights including Fermat, Euler, Legendre and most importantly Gauss. In 1801 Gauss published *Disquisitiones Arithmeticae* [Gau86]. He was intensely interested in primality testing and factoring as the following (now famous) quote shows:

> *The problem of distinguishing prime numbers from composite numbers and of resolving the latter into their prime factors is known to be one of the most important and useful in arithmetic. It has engaged the industry*

---

[1] This essay records the impressions which have guided the author and is not intended to be a complete historic account. For more on the history of the problems in this section, see for example [Dic71],[WS91]. A preliminary, more extensive version of this paper was presented at the 35th Annual IEEE Symposium on Foundations of Computer Science.

*and wisdom of ancient and modern geometers to such an extent that
it would be superfluous to discuss the problem at length.... Further, the
dignity of the science itself seems to require that every possible means be
explored for the solution of a problem so elegant and so celebrated.*

- Carl Friedrich Gauss.
Disquisitiones Arithmeticae (1801)
(translation: A. A. Clarke [Gau86])

Gauss was the first (that I know of) to realize that primality and factoring
were different problems and that one could hope to prove the compositeness
of a number without factoring it. Gauss gave two algorithms which he said
would 'prove rewarding to lovers of arithmetic'[2]. Gauss' algorithms are indeed
rewarding if you happen to like incredibly brilliant ideas; however, you may feel
less rewarded if you look at their complexity: strictly exponential.

Unfortunately for algorithmic number theory, Gauss was too good and he
created a schism which to this day is not fully repaired. In *Disquisitiones Arithmeticae*, Gauss laid the foundations for the development of number theory as
'pure math'. He was the first to use algebraic extensions of the rationals. His
proof of the quadratic reciprocity law spurred the search for generalizations,
ultimately leading to the development of class field theory. He (and Euler, Legendre, Dirichlet and Riemann) set analytic number theory going. Unfortunately,
everyone ran off to follow these various paths and computational number theory
suffered. In addition, perhaps because Gauss had used his computational ability to build large tables of primes and this led to his (and Legendre's) 'prime
number conjecture' (later the De la Vallée Poussin/Hadamard theorem), it led
researchers who followed to view computational number theory as an instrument
for experimentation -a microscope into the world of numbers which allowed for
the development and testing of conjectures. It served (and continues to serve)
that purpose well, but what was lost for over one hundred years was what Gauss
apparently understood - that primality testing and factoring were intrinsically
beautiful problems and that this alone was reason to study them.

Gauss was followed by a large number of talented researchers in algorithmic number theory, including[3]: K. Reuschle (1856), F. Landry (1869), E. Lucas
(1875), F. Proth (1876) , T. Pepin (1877), P. Seelhoff (1885), F. Cole (1903),
D.N. Lehmer (1909), J. Morehead (1909), A. Western (1909), H. Pocklington
(1910), R. Powers (1911) , M. Kraïchik (1911), E. Fauquembergue (1912), D.H.

---

[2] These lines are followed by: 'It is in the nature of the problem that *any* method
will become more prolix as the numbers get larger. Nevertheless, in the following
methods the difficulty increases rather slowly,...". These and other comments from
Disquisitiones Arithmeticae lead me to suspect that if Gauss had had a free weekend
sometime to think about all this, complexity theory would have begun a century and
a half earlier than it did.

[3] The dates are provided in some cases to indicate the period when these researchers
were active.

Lehmer (1926), R. Robinson (1954), M. Morrison, H.C. Williams, J. Brillhart, J.L. Selfridge, D. Shanks, S. Wagstaff, M.C Wunderlich. Researchers like Pocklington in the early part of this century were already aware of the distinction between polynomial and exponential time and of the value of randomness in computation. Lucas and D.H. Lehmer developed efficient methods for testing the primality of numbers of special form (e.g. Mersenne numbers, Fermat numbers). Seelhoff, Kraïchik, Lehmer, Powers, Morrison, Brillhart and others made important contributions to factoring. These 'pioneers' left a legacy of powerful ideas for those who would follow.

In the 1930's the second major thread in the story of algorithmic number theory began to develop - in the form of mathematical logic and recursive function theory. In the hands of Gödel, Turing, Kleene, and Church, a new aesthetic began to emerge: algorithmic aspects of problems were intrinsically interesting - whether or not you ever did any computation (one can't program the undecidability of arithmetic). This point of view can be seen in the well-known letter which Gödel sent to Von Neumann. In addition, to foreshadowing the NP=P question, Gödel also wrote:

> It would be interesting to know, for example, what the situation is with the determination if a number is a prime, and in general how much we can reduce the number of steps from the method of simply trying(,) for finite combinatorial problems

- Kurt Gödel
Letter to J. Von Neumann, 1956
(translation: J. Hartmanis [Ha89])

It is unlikely that Gödel cared to test numbers for primality. Rather, his interest seemed clearly to be in the intrinsic complexity of the primality problem. This kind of thinking led to the development of our field. In the late 1960's and early 1970's, the very gifted first generation of complexity theorists (naming names here would be too risky) put the central notions of polynomial time, NP and the rest in place.

It is in this setting that what I consider to be a renaissance in algorithmic number theory began. I should reiterate that as of 1973 the fastest factoring algorithm known and the fastest primality algorithm know were still due to Fibonacci. The rapid changes that followed, particularly in primality testing, are not attributable (at least not directly) to the advent of the electronic computer nor to any major breakthroughs in number theory but, rather, to the acceptance of the new aesthetic that algorithmic problems are interesting in their own right and that the correct way to proceed was by 'counting steps'.

This new point of view was powerful. It said that you could tell whether an algorithm was good or bad - not by trying a benchmark factorization or primality test - but by analyzing the algorithm's complexity. To some extent this was a license to steal. Young researchers in the field like Gary Miller, Vaughan Pratt, and myself - could go to the number theorists, look at their very clever algorithms, then 'cut and paste' their ideas together into new algorithms which to them often seemed useless because they did not factor numbers or test primality very well, but to us with our new aesthetic seemed important.

The first example of this was Pratt's 1974[4][Pra75] proof (based on work of Lucas nearly one hundred years earlier) that the primes were in NP. This is a perfect example of a non-result - from the point of view of the previous aesthetic. Many computational number theorists viewed it as entirely obvious [5] and of course no one could claim it was useful. However, in the new complexity theoretic aesthetic it was an important result. Pratt had culled an idea from the many currents in the literature and 'said' that this one idea must be important since it allowed for a better complexity result than was known before. We will see shortly, how important this idea was. But it is clear that without complexity theory there was no result at all.

Pratt's result was followed by a string of others, all made possible by the complexity theoretic point of view (and the hundreds of years of deep ideas by the number theorists). In 1975, Complexity theory received its first dividend. Solovay and Strassen [SS77] (and later Miller [Mil76] and Rabin [Rab80]) showed that the composites were in R (random polynomial time). While Gill [Gil77] had begun a theoretical study of the use of randomness in computation a few year prior, it was this result that made randomness a central feature in complexity theory. So the ancient problem still had something new to give.

This result was then followed by what I think of as one of the most beautiful in the field - Miller's 1975 proof that on the assumption of the Extended Riemann Hypothesis, primality is in P [Mil76]. This landmark result also marked the beginning of a new trend - the use of deep, modern mathematics in algorithmic number theory. This trend has continued in the years since.

Next came the second dividend for complexity theory - the RSA public key cryptosystem in 1977 [RSA78]. After 2000 years we could finally see that primality was 'easy' and factoring was 'hard' - and likely to stay that way for a long time. While Diffie and Hellman [DH76] had earlier produced the idea of a public key cryptosystem, it was this use of the two central problems in algorithmic number theory that provided an incarnation and led to the development of one of the primary subdisciplines of theoretical computer science.

In addition, the RSA system shook algorithmic number theory (and to some extent all of number theory) out of its 2000 plus years of isolation and made it into the stuff of popular culture:

"I'm really not into computers, Jay. I don't know much. I do know the key to the code was the product of two long prime numbers, each about a hundred digits, right?"

"Yes, that's correct. It's called the RSA cryptosystem."

---

[4] The years given for this and other discoveries are not necessarily those of the publication of the relevant papers, but my own best recollections of when the discoveries actually occurred

[5] This is not speculation, I have discussed this and related issues with number theorists on numerous occasions.

"Right, for Rivest, Shamir and Adleman from MIT. That much I know. I also understand that even using a sophisticated computer to decipher the code it would take forever," she recalled. *"Something like three point eight billion years for a two-hundred-digit key, right?"*

"That's exactly correct. All of the stolen information was apparently tapped from the phone lines running from the company offices to your house. Supposedly no one except Mike had the decoding key, and no one could figure it out unless he passed it along, but there has to be a bug in that logic somewhere" he said, loosening his dark green silk tie. *"Vee, it's much warmer than I thought. Would you mind if I removed my jacket?"*

"Of course not. You're so formal," she remarked ....

- Harlequin American Romance
Sunward Journey by Katherine Coffaro.

Three years later in 1980 came the result of Adleman, Pomerance and Rumely [APR83]: a 'near polynomial time' deterministic primality test. There exists a $c \in N_{>0}$ such that the actual running time of their algorithm is:

$$O((\log n)^{c \log \log \log n})$$

This result is also of interest sociologically since the authors collectively represented the experimental, the complexity theoretical and the 'pure' mathematical traditions - which in my mind bodes well for the eventual healing of the schism referred to earlier. It is also worth remarking that, when implemented (as done for example by Cohen and Lenstra), this algorithm actually has the pleasant added feature of being the fastest primality testing algorithm in practice.

Next came the lovely 1986 result of Goldwasser and Kilian [GK86] (only a little over a decade after Pratt). They resurrected the idea of Pratt and mixed it with René Schoof's [Sch85] and Hendrik Lenstra's [Len87] new idea of using elliptic curves. Goldwasser and Kilian proved that assuming an old conjecture due to Cramér [Cra36], primality was in R (random polynomial time). This was followed by the result of Adleman and Huang [AH92] who replaced the elliptic curves with the Jacobian's of hyperelliptic curves and proved that, without hypothesis, primality was in R. Some technical aspects of this development are informally described in the next section. To the extent one accepts randomness in computation, this completes the long quest for an efficient primality test. To the extend that one insists on determinism, the search goes on.

I have said much less about developments in factoring during this period. That's because the recent progress here has not been as pronounced. Perhaps this is because the problem is intractable and not much progress can be expected. Most of the progress that has occurred has been through consolidation of ideas going back to Gauss and Legendre. Primarily through the efforts of Seelhoff, Kraichik, Lehmer, Powers and finally Morrison and Brillhart [MB75] in 1975, it became clear that the single really important idea in factoring was 'smoothness'. Recall that a number is 'smooth' iff all of its prime factors are 'small'. This is the fundamental insight that 2000 years of effort brought forth. It led to the first subexponential factoring algorithm and recently has been exploited by Pollard and a host of other researchers to produce the so-called 'number field sieve' [LL93], the fastest method currently known. I will describe some of the technical aspects of these developments in the following section.

In the past year a very interesting development has occurred which suggests that the symbiosis between number theory and complexity theory continues. And that Physics may also have a part to play. Peter Shor [Sho94] has produced a striking result: factoring can be done in polynomial time on a quantum Turing machine. This result in some ways resembles those of Solovay and Strassen and of Rivest, Shamir and Adleman: an interesting theoretical notion made tangible by use of algorithmic number theory. The result is new and needs further analysis, but assuming that everything (including the physics) holds together, it suggests that primality and factoring may play an even greater role in the future than they have in the past.

In closing, let me say that I have concentrated here on primality and factoring, but algorithmic number theory is much larger than that. An extensive list of open problems can be found in [Adl94],[AM94].

2   Primality Testing and Factoring

Below are two algorithms which will prove rewarding to lovers of arithmetic.

2.1   How to Test Primality

In this subsection I will give an informal description of the ideas that led from Pratt [Pra75] to Goldwasser and Kilian [GK86] to Adleman and Huang [AH92] and resulted in the proof that Primality is in R (random polynomial time).

Consider the following proof that 11 is prime:

(1) $(4 - 1, 11) = 1$.
(2) $4^5 = 1024 \equiv 1 \bmod 11$.
(3) 5 is prime.

Assume 11 is not prime. Then there exists a prime $p \leq \sqrt{11} < 4$ which divides 11. (1) implies that the order of 4 in Z/pZ^* is not 1. (2) implies that the order of 4 in Z/pZ^* divides 5. (3) implies that the order of 4 in Z/pZ^* is exactly 5 which is impossible since $p < 4$.

If we had omitted (3) above, we would still have produced a proof that *if* 5 *is prime then* 11 *is prime*. Such a proof can be though of as a *reduction* of the proof of primality of 11 to the proof of primality of 5. This idea of reducing the proof of primality of one number to that of another number is central to the algorithms discussed here. The seeds of this idea can be found in Pratt.

For all sufficiently large primes p, is there always a reduction of the proof of primality of p to the proof of primality of $\frac{p-1}{2}$? The answer is yes. Can a computer generate such a reduction quickly (i.e. in random polynomial time)? Again the answer is yes. One (not particularly efficient) way for the computer to proceed is as follows:

(1) Pick $a \in Z_{>0}^{<p}$ at random until an a is found such that $(a-1, p) = 1$ and:
(2) $a^{\frac{p-1}{2}} \equiv 1 \bmod p$.

If such an a is found, then, as above, a reduction of the proof of primality of p to the proof of primality of $\frac{p-1}{2}$ is easily generated. Since GCD and modular exponentiation can be done in deterministic polynomial time and since for sufficiently large p, satisfactory a's are 'abundant' (i.e. for all primes $p > 2$, $\frac{p-3}{2}$ of the positive integers $a < p$ are such that $(a-1, p) = 1$ and $a^{\frac{p-1}{2}} \equiv 1 \bmod p$), we can expect that when p is sufficiently large (in this case $p > 3$ will do) the computer will quickly choose an appropriate a and hence generate the desired reduction.

Returning to the example above, we have a reduction of the proof of primality of 11 to the proof of primality of 5. We could now recurse and obtain a reduction of the proof of primality of 5 to the proof of primality of 2. Assuming that we have a direct proof that 2 is prime, we then have a proof that 11 (and also 5) is prime. Can recursing with this type of reduction yield a random polynomial time algorithm for proving primality? The answer is no, because for most primes p, the order of Z/pZ^* is not 2 times a prime. Reducing the proof of primality of 13 to the proof of primality of 6 works, but is not very useful.

Goldwasser and Kilian realized that there was a way to circumvent this problem by using groups other than Z/pZ^*. Their idea had been foreshadowed in the work of Lenstra [Len87] on integer factoring and their method makes use of elliptic curves. A computer can generate a Goldwasser-Kilian type reduction (essentially) as follows:

(0) Pick $a, b \in Z/pZ$ at random until a pair is found such that $f(x) = x^3 - ax + b$ has no multiple roots and such that the number n of rational points on the elliptic curve associated with $y^2 - f(x)$ is even (such can be done in random polynomial time, including (thanks to Schoof [Sch85]) the calculation of n).
(1) Compute a pair $s, t \in Z/pZ$ such that $v = <s, t>$ is on the curve.

(v does not have order 1)

(This is because an affine point cannot be the identity in the group of rational points on the elliptic curve.)

(2) $n/2 * v$ is the identity in the group associated with the curve.

(the order of v is divisible by $n/2$)

Modifying the arguments above, it is possible to show that for all sufficiently large primes p, if such a point v is found, then a reduction of the proof of primality of p to the proof of primality of $m = n/2$ has been generated. Further, from the Riemann hypothesis for finite fields (as proved by Weil) m will always be approximately half as big as p. However, like the previous reduction, a Goldwasser-Kilian type reduction is useful only if m is prime.

Can recursing with Goldwasser-Kilian type reductions yield a random polynomial time algorithm for primality testing? For this to be the case, it would be necessary that for all sufficiently large primes p, the number of rational points on a randomly chosen elliptic curve defined over Z/pZ would be 2 times a prime with high probability. By the Riemann hypothesis for finite fields, the number n of rational points on an elliptic curve defined over Z/pZ must always be between $p + 1 - 2\sqrt{p}$ and $p + 1 + 2\sqrt{p}$. Unfortunately, this interval is too small. Current knowledge does not allow us to rule out the possibility that there are infinitely many primes p for which there are no n's in the interval of the correct form. For such primes, there would be no 'useful' Goldwasser-Kilian type reductions at all. For this reason whether the Goldwasser-Kilian method yields a random polynomial time test for primality remains an open question.

Goldwasser and Kilian (using estimates of Heath-Brown [Hea78]) did succeed in demonstrating that their method 'works' for 'most' primes. That is, except for a small (but perhaps infinite) set of 'bad' primes, successive Goldwasser-Kilian type reductions will in polynomial time with high probability produce a proof of primality.

The Adleman Huang method begins by replacing the elliptic curves in the Goldwasser-Kilian approach by the Jacobians of curves of genus 2. A computer can in random polynomial time generate a reduction of the new type (essentially) as follows:

(0) Pick $f \in Z/pZ[x]$ of degree 6 at random until one is found such that f has no multiple roots. Calculate the number n of rational points on the Jacobian of the curve associated with $y^2 - f(x)$.

(1) Compute a pair $s, t \in Z/pZ$ with $t \neq 0$ such that $< s, t >$ is on the curve and let $v = \phi(< s, t >) - \phi(< s, -t >)$ (where ϕ is an embedding of the curve into the Jacobian)

   (v does not have order 1)

   (By construction, v cannot be the identity in the group of rational points on the Jacobian of the curve.)

(2) $n * v$ is the identity in the group of rational points on the Jacobian of the curve.)

   (the order of v is divisible by n)

   ($n/2$ is no longer important in this variation.)

Again by a modification of earlier arguments, it is possible to show that for all sufficiently large primes p, if such a point v is found then a reduction of the proof of primality of p to the proof of primality of n is easily generated. However, as before, the reduction is useful only if n is prime.

The new method carries with it some 'good news' and some 'bad news'. The good news: with 'high probability' n will be prime. That is: there is a constant $c \in Z_{>0}$ such that for sufficiently large primes p, at least $1/\log^c p$ of the f's chosen as above give rise to a Jacobian with a prime number of points.

It follows from this good news that there exists a random polynomial time algorithm for reducing the primality of p to a new prime n.

The bad news: n will always be much larger than p. Thus the new 'reductions' actually make the problem harder! Again by Weil's Riemann hypothesis for finite fields n must always be between $p^2 - 4p^{1.5} + 6p - 4p^{.5} + 1$ and $p^2 + 4p^{1.5} + 6p + 4p^{.5} + 1$. Hence n will be approximately p^2.

Fortunately there is a way to overcome the bad news. If we are trying to prove the primality of p and we have successfully produced a sequence of reductions of the new type (a sequence of 3 reductions is enough) then we have reduced the proof of primality of p to the proof of primality of a new (much larger) prime q. Since the new method uses randomness in selecting curves, there are in fact many different primes q which might arise. But the (generalized) Goldwasser-Kilian method produces primality proofs for all primes with a small set of exceptions. It turns out that with 'high probability', the q's which the new method produces can be proven to be prime using the (generalized) Goldwasser-Kilian method. Thus by combining the two methods a proof that p is prime will be obtained.

Put still less formally, the problem with the (generalized or ungeneralized) Goldwasser-Kilian method was that if p was one of the rare 'bad' primes, then there is no way to produce a proof of primality. The new method lets one 'randomize'. That is, one can use the new method to reduce the proof of primality for p to the proof of primality of a new prime q which is, roughly speaking, chosen at random. Consequently q is unlikely to be 'bad' and so the (generalized) Goldwasser-Kilian method can be used to prove the primality of q thus completing the proof of primality of p.

2.2   How to Factor an Integer

In this subsection I will give an informal description of how an old idea - smoothness - yields the fastest current factoring algorithm: the 'number field sieve'.

To begin with a number is smooth iff all of its prime factors are 'small'. $6960096 = 2^5 * 3^2 * 11 * 13^2$ is smooth. $69600970 = 2 * 5 * 6047 * 1151$ is not (6047 and 1151 are prime). The idea of using smoothness in factoring appears to be due to Gauss and Legendre. In *Disquisitiones Arithmeticae* [Gau86] Gauss has the following example of applying his method to factoring 997331. Basically, he squares numbers (near $\sqrt{997331}$) and takes their residues mod 997331. He keeps only those with smooth residues:

$$999^2 \equiv 2 * 5 * 67$$

$994^2 \equiv -5 * 11 * 13^2$
$706^2 \equiv -2^{-1} * 3^3 * 17$
$575^2 \equiv -3^{-1} * 4^2 * 11 * 31$
$577^2 \equiv 3^{-1} * 4^2 * 7 * 13$
$578^2 \equiv 3^{-1} * 7 * 19 * 37$
$299^2 \equiv -2 * 3 * 4^2 * 5 * 11^{-1} * 29$
$301^2 \equiv -2^4 * 3^2 * 5 * 11^{-1}$

He then combines these congruences to find small quadratic residues mod 997331:

For example $994^2 * 299^2 \equiv 2 * 3 * 4^2 * 5^2 * 13^2 * 29$ so that $174 = 2 * 3 * 29$ is a quadratic residue mod 997331.

He then uses these small quadratic residues to restrict potential divisors and it is here that he has apparently made his first and only wrong move. What he apparently should have done, as about one and three-quarters centuries of research by Seelhoff, Kraïchik, Lehmer, Powers, Morrison, Brillhart and others would finally reveal, was to use **Gaussian** elimination (mod 2) to obtain a congruence of squares. For example:

$$994^2 * 301^2 \equiv 2^4 * 3^2 * 5^2 * 13^2$$

or in other words:

$$(994 * 301)^2 \equiv (4 * 3 * 5 * 13)^2$$

Now obtaining such congruences is tantamount to factoring (as Gauss and Legendre knew, by the way). One now takes $\gcd(997331, 994*301-4*3*5*13) = 7853$. This is a non trivial prime factor of 997331 (the other one is 127). So the algorithm became:

1. Input n.
2. Choose random $r \in Z_{>1}^{\leq n}$.
3. Calculate $r^2 \bmod n = a$, if a is smooth - i.e. all prime factors are less than an appropriate bound B - keep it.
4. Once (approximately) B such r have been kept, use Gaussian elimination mod 2 on the exponents to build a congruence of squares $x^2 \equiv y^2 \bmod n$
5. Calculate $\gcd(x - y, n)$, it will be a nontrivial factor of n about half the time (or more).

One easily argues heuristically (a rigorous proof requires more work) that there exists a $\delta \in \Re_{>0}$ such the algorithm has expected running time:

$$L_n[1/2, \delta + o(1)]$$

where for all $n, \gamma, \delta \in \Re_{>0}$, with $n > e$

$$L_n[\gamma, \delta] = exp(\delta(\log n)^\gamma (\log \log n)^{1-\gamma})$$

This argument uses the following central fact about smooth numbers:

Theorem Canfield, Erdös and Pomerance *For all $n, \alpha, \beta, \gamma, \delta \in \Re_{>0}$ with $\alpha > \gamma$ and $n > e$, the number of $L[\gamma, \delta + o(1)]$ smooth numbers less than $L[\alpha, \beta + o(1)]$ is*

$$n/L[\alpha - \gamma, (\beta(\alpha - \gamma)/\delta) + o(1)]$$

For example, the above theorem implies that when $B = L_n[1/2, 1/\sqrt{2} + o(1)]$, the probability that a numbers less than n is B-smooth is essentially $1/B$.

So the effort since that time has been to use smoothness more efficiently. One can get a better factoring algorithm by improving one of the following:

- The function implicit in the $o(1)$ in the exponent - this is not interesting theoretically but can make actual implementations faster.
- The constant δ which is of limited theoretical interest but has a significant impact on actual implementations.
- The constant γ which is of interest theoretically and practically.
- The big prize - the shape of the function itself - e.g. to find a polynomial time algorithm.

Four has not been done. If a polynomial time algorithm exists, I suspect it will need a better idea than smoothness. However, recently Pollard [LL93] has come up with an idea for improving γ. Many researchers have contributed and the resulting algorithm, 'the number field sieve', has (heuristic) expected running time:

$$L_n[1/3, \delta + o(1)]$$

where the best currently known δ is approximately 1.90 due to Coppersmith [Cop90].

Here is how the number field sieve works. A positive integer n is given. One finds an irreducible polynomial $f \in Z[y]$ of degree d and an $m \in Z$ such that $f(m) \equiv 0 \bmod n$. Basically , this is done by choosing an m of appropriate size (chosen to optimize the running time) at random and then defining the coefficients of f to be the digits of n when written base m. Then working simultaneously in Q and the number field $L = Q[y]/(f)$, one seeks 'double smooth pairs' $< r, s > \in Z \times Z$ such that r and s are relatively prime and both $rm + s$ and $N_Q^L(ry + s) = r^d f(-s/r)$ are 'smooth' in Z (i.e. have no prime factors greater than some predetermined 'smoothness bound' B). In the simplest case where O_L, the ring of integers of L, is a PID then from such a double smooth pair we have:

$$rm + s = \prod_{i=1}^{z} p_i^{e_i}$$

where $p_1, p_2, ..., p_z$ are the primes less than B. And:

$$ry + s = \prod_{i=1}^{v} \epsilon_i^{f_i} \prod_{i=1}^{w} \wp_j^{g_j}$$

where $\epsilon_1, \epsilon_2, ...\epsilon_v$ is a basis for the units of O_L and $\wp_1, \wp_2, ..., \wp_w \in O_L$ are generators of the (residue class degree one) prime ideals of norm less than B.

Since there is a homomorphism ϕ from O_L to $Z/(n)$ induced by sending $y \mapsto m$, the above equations give rise to the congruence:

$$\prod_{i=1}^{z} p_i^{e_i} \equiv \prod_{i=1}^{v} \phi(\epsilon_i)^{f_i} \prod_{i=1}^{w} \phi(\wp_j)^{g_j}$$

One collects sufficiently many such double smooth pairs and puts the corresponding congruences together using linear algebra on the exponents to create a congruence of squares of the form:

$$(\prod_{i=1}^{z} p_i^{e'_i})^2 \equiv (\prod_{i=1}^{v} \phi(\epsilon_i)^{f'_i} \prod_{i=1}^{w} \phi(\wp_j)^{g'_j})^2$$

One now proceeds as before.

Of course when O_L is not a PID complications arise. But these can be overcome rather efficiently and the resulting algorithm is the most efficient (both in theory and in practice) currently known.

Acknowledgments

This research was supported by the National Science Foundation under grant CCR-9214671. This paper is a revision of [Adl94].

References

[Adl94] L. M. Adleman. Algorithmic number theory - the complexity contribution. In *Proc. 35th Annual IEEE Symposium on Foundations of Computer Science*, IEEE Computer Society, 1994, pp. 88-113.

[AH92] L. M. Adleman and Ming-Deh Huang. Primality testing and two dimensional Abelian varieties over finite fields, *Lecture Notes in Mathematics*, Vol. 1512, Springer-Verlag, 1992.

[AM94] L. M. Adleman and K. S. McCurley. Open problems in number theoretic complexity, II. In L.M. Adleman, M-D. Huang (Eds.), *Algorithmic Number Theory*, Proc. First Int. Symposium (ANTS-I), Lecture Notes in Computer Science, Vol. 877, Springer-Verlag, 1994, pp. 291-322.

[APR83] L. M. Adleman, C. Pomerance, and R. Rumely. On distinguishing prime numbers from composite numbers. *Annals of Mathematics*, 117:173-206, 1983.

[Cop90] D. Coppersmith. Modifications to the number field sieve. Techn. Rep. RC16264, IBM TJ Watson Research Center, Yorktown Heights, NY, 1990.

[Cra36] H. Cramer. On the order of magnitude of the difference between consecutive prime numbers. *Acta Arithmetica*, 2:23-46, 1936.

[DH76] W. Diffie and M. E. Hellman. New directions in cryptography. *IEEE Transactions on Information Theory*, 22:644-654, 1976.

[Dic71] L. E. Dickson. *History of the Theory of Numbers*, volume 1. Chelsea Books, New York, 1971.

[Gau86] C. F. Gauss. *Disquisitiones Arithmeticae*. Springer-Verlag, New York, 1986. Reprint of the 1966 English translation by Arthur A. Clarke, S.J., Yale University Press, revised by William C. Waterhouse. Original 1801 edition published by Fleischer, Leipzig.

[Gil77] J. Gill. Computational complexity of probabilistic Turing machines. *SIAM Journal of Computing*, 4:675495, 1977.

[GK86] S. Goldwasser and J. Kilian. Almost all primes can be quickly certified. In *Proc. 18th Annual ACM Symposium on Theory of Computing*, ACM Press, New York, 1986, pp. 316-329,

[Ha89] J. Hartmanis. Gödel, von Neumann and the P=?NP problem, *Bulletin of the EATCS* Nr 38, 1989, pp. 101-107.

[Hea78] D. R. Heath-Brown. Almost-primes in arithmetic progressions and short intervals. *Mathematical Proc. of the Cambridge Philosophical Society*, 83:357-375, 1978.

[Leh74] R. Sherman Lehman. Factoring lerge integers. *Math. Comp.* 18:637-646. 1974.

[Len87] H. W. Lenstra, Jr. Factoring integers with elliptic curves. *Annals of Mathematics*, 126:649-673, 1987.

[LL93] A. K. Lenstra and H. W. Lenstra, Jr. (Eds.), *The development of the number field sieve*. Lecture Notes in Mathematics, Vol. 1554, Springer-Verlag, 1993.

[MB75] M. Morrison and J. Brillhart. A method of factoring and the factorization of F7. *Mathematics of Computation*, 29:183-205, 1975.

[Mil76] G. L. Miller. Riemann's Hypothesis and tests for primality. *Journal of Computer and System Sciences*, 13:300-317, 1976.

[Pra75] V. Pratt. Every prime has a succinct certificate. *SIAM Journal of Computing*, 4:214-220, 1975.

[Rab80] M. 0. Rabin. Probabilistic algorithm for testing primality. *Journal of Number Theory*, 12:128-138, 1980.

[RSA78] R. Rivest, A. Shamir, and L. M. Adleman. A method for obtaining digital signatures and public key cryptosystems. *Communications of the ACM*, 21:120-126, 1978.

[Sch85] R. Schoof. Elliptic curves over finite fields and the computation of square roots modulo p. *Mathematics of Computation*, 44:483-494, 1985.

[Sho94] P. W. Shor. Algorithms for quantum computation: discrete logarithms and factoring. In *Proc. 35th Annual IEEE Symposium on Foundations of Computer Science*, IEEE Computer Society, 1994, pp. 124-134.

[SS77] R. Solovay and V. Strassen. A fast Monte-Carlo test for primality. *SIAM Journal of Computing*, 6:84-85, 1977.

[WS91] H.C. Williams and J.O. Shallit. Factoring integers before computers. In *Proceedings of Symposium in Applied Mathematics*, pages 1-51, 1991.

Edge-Coloring Algorithms

Shin-ichi Nakano, Xiao Zhou and Takao Nishizeki

Graduate School of Information Sciences

Tohoku University, Sendai 980-77, Japan

Abstract. The edge-coloring problem is one of the fundamental problems on graphs, which often appears in various scheduling problems like the file transfer problem on computer networks. In this paper, we survey recent advances and results on the classical edge-coloring problem as well as the generalized edge-coloring problems, called the f-coloring and fg-coloring problems. In particular we review various upper bounds on the minimum number of colors required to edge-color graphs, and present efficient algorithms to edge-color graphs with a number of colors not exceeding the upper bounds.

1 A survey of the edge-coloring problem

1.1 A history of the edge-coloring problem

The edge-coloring problem is one of the fundamental problems on graphs. A graph $G = (V, E)$ is an ordered pair of vertex set V and edge set E. An edge in E joins two vertices in V. Throughout the paper we let $n = |V|$ and $m = |E|$. The edge-coloring problem is to color all edges of a given graph with the minimum number of colors so that no two adjacent edges are assigned the same color. Fig. 1 illustrates an edge-coloring of a graph with four colors. A set of edges which are not adjacent each other is called a *matching*. Since each set of edges colored with the same color is a matching, an edge-coloring of a graph is indeed a partition of E to matchings.

We now historically review the edge-coloring problem. The edge-coloring problem was posed in 1880 in relation with the well-known four-color conjecture: every map could be colored with four colors so that any neighboring countries have different colors. It took more than 100 years to prove the conjecture affirmatively in 1976 with the help of computers since it was posed in 1852. The first paper that dealt with the edge-coloring problem was written by Tait in 1889 [10]. In the paper Tait proved that the four-color problem is equivalent with the problem of edge-coloring every planar 3-connected cubic graph with three colors. The minimum number of colors needed to edge-color G is called the *chromatic index* $\chi'(G)$ of G. The maximum degree of graph G is denoted by $\Delta(G)$ or simply by Δ. Obviously $\chi'(G) \geq \Delta(G)$ since all edges incident to the same vertex must be assigned different colors. König [20] proved that every bipartite graph can be edge-colored with exactly $\Delta(G)$ colors, that is $\chi'(G) = \Delta(G)$. Shannon [30] proved that every graph can be edge-colored with at most $3\Delta(G)/2$ colors, that is $\chi'(G) \leq 3\Delta(G)/2$. Vizing [32] proved that $\chi'(G) \leq \Delta(G) + 1$ for every simple graph. A few other upper bounds on $\chi'(G)$ have been known [2,14,17,27].

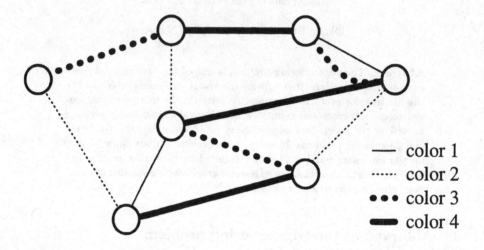

Fig. 1. An edge-coloring of a graph with four colors.

According to the rapid progress of computers, the research on computer algorithms has become active with emphasis on the efficiency and complexity, and efficient algorithms have been developed for various graph problems. However, Holyer [18] proved that the edge-coloring problem is NP-complete, and hence it is very unlikely that there is a polynomial time algorithm for solving the problem [1]. Hence a good approximation algorithm would be useful. Approximation algorithms are evaluated by the approximation ratio and the complexity. The polynomial time algorithm having the best approximate ratio so far was given by Nishizeki and Kashiwagi [27], whose approximation ratio is asymptotically 1.1. Gabow *et al.* [12] gave the most efficient algorithm which edge-colors a simple graph G with at most $\Delta(G) + 1$ colors in $O(m\sqrt{n\log n})$ time. Furthermore sequential and parallel algorithms have been obtained for various classes of graphs, such as bipartite graphs [8,11], planar graphs [6,7,12], series-parallel graphs [29,31,38,42,43], partial k-trees [4,36,37,40], degenerated graphs and bounded-genus graphs [39].

On the other hand, various generalizations of edge-coloring have been introduced and investigated. In 1970's Hilton and de Werra obtained many notable results on "equitable and edge-balanced colorings" in which each color appears at each vertex uniformly [16,34,35]. In 1980's Hakimi and Kariv studied the following f-coloring problem. An f-coloring of a graph G is a coloring of edges of

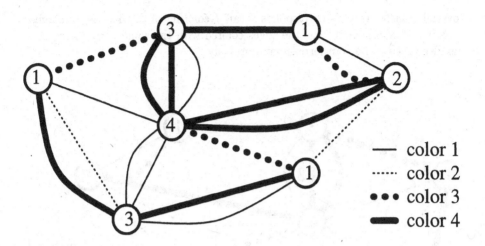

Fig. 2. An f-coloring of a graph with four colors.

G such that each color appears at each vertex $v \in V$ at most $f(v)$ times [15]. Fig. 2 depicts an f-coloring with four colors where numbers in circles mean $f(v)$ for vertices v. An ordinary edge-coloring is a special case of an f-coloring in which $f(v) = 1$ for every vertex $v \in V$. The minimum number of colors needed to f-color G is called the f-chromatic index $\chi'_f(G)$ of G. Since deciding the chromatic index of G is NP-complete [18], deciding the f-chromatic index of G is also NP-complete in general. On the other hand, various upper bounds on $\chi'_f(G)$ have been known [15,23,39].

The file transfer problem on computer networks introduced by Coffman *et al.*[5] is related to the edge-coloring problem. The file transfer problem is modeled as follows. Each computer v has a limited number $f(v)$ of communication ports. For each pair of computers there are a number of files which are transferred between the pair of computers. In such a situation the problem is how to schedule the file transfers so as to minimize the total time for the overall transfer process. The general problem is NP-complete since the simple version of the problem can be reduced to the edge-coloring problem. Coffman *et al.* obtained simple approximate algorithms for the file transfer problem. The file transfer problem in which each file has the same length is formulated as an f-coloring problem for a graph as follows. Vertices of the graph correspond to nodes of the network, and edges correspond to files to be transferred between the endpoints. Such a graph G describes the file transfer demands. Assume that each computer v has $f(v)$ communication ports, and transferring any file takes an equal amount of time. Under these assumptions, the schedule to minimize the total time for the overall transfer process corresponds to an f-coloring of G with the minimum number of colors. Note that the edges colored with the same color correspond to files that can be transferred simultaneously.

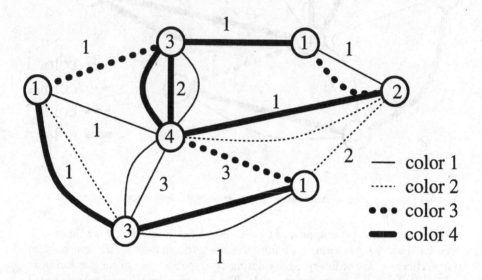

Fig. 3. An fg-coloring of a graph with four colors.

For some cases of the file transfer problem on computer networks, we must often consider the capacity of channels. An f-coloring is generalized to an fg-coloring so as to treat such a file transfer problem with channel constraints [24]. The capacity of a channel between vertices v and w is denoted by $g(vw)$. An fg-coloring of G is a coloring of edges such that each vertex v has at most $f(v)$ edges colored with the same color and each set $E(vw)$ of multiple edges contains at most $g(vw)$ edges colored with the same color. Fig. 3 depicts an fg-coloring with four colors, where numbers next to multiple edges $E(vw)$ mean $g(vw)$. The minimum number of colors needed to fg-color G is called the fg-chromatic index $\chi'_{fg}(G)$ of G. Several upper bounds on χ'_{fg} have been known [24,25].

1.2 Definitions

In this paper we deal with so-called *multigraphs* which may have multiple edges but have no selfloops. A graph in which at most one edge joins any pair of vertices is called a *simple* graph. $G = (V, E)$ denotes a graph with vertex set V and edge set E. We denote the degree of vertex v by $d(G, v)$ or simply by $d(v)$, and the *maximum degree* of G by $\Delta(G) = \max_{v \in V} d(v)$. An edge joining vertices v and w is denoted by vw. $E(vw)$ is the set of multiple edges joining vertices v

and w, and $p(vw)$ is the cardinality of the set $E(vw)$, that is $p(vw) = |E(vw)|$.
We write $H \subseteq G$ if H is a subgraph of G. $V(H)$ denotes the set of vertices of
H, and $E(H)$ denotes the set of edges of H. We use $\lfloor x \rfloor$ for the largest integer
not greater than x, and $\lceil x \rceil$ for the smallest integer not smaller than x.

A *bipartite graph* $G = (V_1, V_2, E)$ is a graph whose vertex set can be partitioned into two sets V_1 and V_2 so that $e \in V_1 \times V_2$ for each edge $e \in E$.

The class of *k-trees* is defined recursively as follows:

(a) A complete graph with k vertices is a k-tree.

(b) If $G = (V, E)$ is a k-tree and k vertices $v_1, v_2, \cdots v_k$ induce a complete
    subgraph of G, then $G' = (V \cup \{w\}, E \cup \{wv_i | 1 \le i \le k\})$ is a k-tree where
    w is a new vertex not contained in G.

(c) All k-trees can be formed with rules (a) and (b).

A graph is a *partial k-tree* if it is a subgraph of a k-tree. Thus partial k-trees are
simple graphs.

A *planar graph* is a simple graph which can be embedded in the plane so that
no two edges intersect geometrically except at a vertex to which they are both
incident.

The *genus* $g(G)$ of a simple graph G is the minimum number of handles
which must be added to a sphere so that G can be embedded on the resulting
surface. Of cource, $g(G) = 0$ if and only if G is planar.

Let s be a positive integer. A simple graph G is *s-degenerate* if the vertices
of G can be ordered $v_1, v_2, \cdots, v_n$ so that $d(v_i, G_i) \le s$ for each i, $1 \le i \le n$,
where $G_0 = G$ and $G_i = G - \{v_1, v_2, \cdots, v_{i-1}\}$. That is, G is s-degenerate
if and only if G can be reduced to the trivial (or degenerate) graph K_1 by the
successive removal of vertices having degree at most s. Obviously a partial k-tree
is k-degenerate, and a planar graph is 5-degenerate.

The *arboricity* of a simple graph G, denoted by $a(G)$, is the minimum number
of edge-disjoint forests into which G can be decomposed.

The *thickness* of a simple graph G, denoted by $\theta(G)$, is the minimum number
of planar subgraphs whose union is G.

2   Edge-coloring

2.1   Edge-colorings of multigraphs

Every bipartite multigraph G can be edge-colored with $\Delta(G)$ colors, that is
$\chi'(G) \le \Delta(G)$ [20]. On the other hand, clearly $\chi'(G) \ge \Delta(G)$. Therefore $\chi'(G) = \Delta(G)$. One can easily prove the inequality $\chi'(G) \le \Delta(G)$ above using a technique
of "switching an alternating path." The proof immediately yields an algorithm
to edge-color a bipartite graph G with $\Delta(G)$ colors in time $O(mn)$. There exists
a more efficient algorithm which, based on the divide and conquer, edge-colors
a bipartite multigraph in time $O(m \log m)$ [8].

Vizing [32] obtained the following upper bound on the chromatic index of
multigraphs:

$$\chi'(G) \le \max_{v,w \in V} \{d(w) + p(vw)\}.$$

On the other hand, Shannon [30] proved that the following upper bound holds:

$$\chi'(G) \le \left\lfloor \frac{3}{2}\Delta(G) \right\rfloor.$$

Shannon's proof immediately yields an algorithm to edge-color a multigraph G with $\lfloor \frac{3}{2}\Delta(G) \rfloor$ colors in time $O(m(\Delta(G) + n))$.

There is another upper bound on the chromatic index of multigraphs [2]:

$$\chi'(G) \le \max\left\{ l(G), \left\lfloor \frac{5\Delta(G)+2}{4} \right\rfloor \right\},$$

where

$$l(G) = \max_{H \subseteq G, |V(H)| \ge 3} \left\lceil \frac{|E(H)|}{\left\lfloor \frac{|V(H)|}{2} \right\rfloor} \right\rceil.$$

Clearly at most $\left\lfloor \frac{|V(H)|}{2} \right\rfloor$ edges of $|E(H)|$ edges in subgraph H can be colored with the same color. Therefore $l(G)$ is a lower bound on $\chi'(G)$: $\chi'(G) \ge l(G)$.

Furthermore the following better upper bounds are known [14, 17, 27]:

$$\chi'(G) \le \max\left\{ l(G), \left\lfloor \frac{7\Delta(G)+4}{6} \right\rfloor \right\},$$

$$\chi'(G) \le \max\left\{ l(G), \left\lfloor \frac{9\Delta(G)+6}{8} \right\rfloor \right\} \quad \text{and}$$

$$\chi'(G) \le \max\left\{ l(G), \left\lfloor \frac{11\Delta(G)+8}{10} \right\rfloor \right\}.$$

An algorithm using colors no more than Vizing's upper bound has the approximation ratio 2 since

$$\max_{v,w \in V} \{d(w) + p(vw)\} \le 2\chi'(G).$$

The algorithm using colors no more than Shannon's upper bound has the approximation ratio 3/2 since

$$\left\lfloor \frac{3}{2}\Delta(G) \right\rfloor \le \frac{3}{2}\chi'(G).$$

Furthermore Nishizeki and Kashiwagi's algorithm using colors no more than $\max\{l(G), \lfloor (11\Delta + 8)/10 \rfloor\}$ has the asymptotic approximation ratio 1.1 since

$$\max\left\{ l(G), \left\lfloor \frac{11\Delta(G)+8}{10} \right\rfloor \right\} \le \frac{11\chi'(G)+8}{10}.$$

Table 1. Sequential algorithms.

Classes of graphs	Time	Colors	Refs.
Simple graph	$O(m\sqrt{n}\log n)$	$\Delta + 1$	[12]
Multigraph	$O(m(\Delta + n))$	$1.1\chi' + 0.8$	[27]
Bipartite multigraph	$O(m\log m)$	Δ	[8]
Series-parallel multigraph	$O(m\log m)$	χ'	[42]
Partial k-tree	$O(n)$	χ'	[36]
Planar graph $(\Delta \geq 9)$	$O(n\log n)$	Δ	[6]
Planar graph $(\Delta \geq 19)$	$O(n)$	Δ	[7]
Genus $g \geq 1$ $(\Delta \geq 2\lfloor(5 + \sqrt{48g+1})/2\rfloor$	$O(n^2)$	Δ	[39]
Genus $g \geq 1$ $(\Delta \geq \lceil(9 + \sqrt{48g+1})^2/8\rceil$	$O(n\log n)$	Δ	[39]
Degeneracy s $(\Delta \geq 2s)$	$O(n^2)$	Δ	[39]
Degeneracy s $(\Delta \geq \lceil(s+2)^2/2\rceil - 1)$	$O(n\log n)$	Δ	[39]
Arboricity a $(\Delta \geq 4a - 2)$	$O(n^2)$	Δ	[39]
Arboricity a $(\Delta \geq \lceil(a+2)^2/2\rceil - 1)$	$O(n\log n)$	Δ	[39]
Thickness θ $(\Delta \geq 12\theta - 2)$	$O(n^2)$	Δ	[39]
Thickness θ $(\Delta \geq \lceil(3\theta+2)^2/2\rceil - 1)$	$O(n\log n)$	Δ	[39]

Table 2. NC parallel algorithms.

Classes of graphs	Parallel time	Operations	Colors	Refs.
Bipartite multigraph	$O(\log^3 n)$	$O(m)$	Δ	[21]
Series-parallel multigraph	$O(\log n)$	$O(n\Delta)$	χ'	[43]
Partial k-tree	$O(\log n)$	$O(n)$	χ'	[37]
Planar graph $(\Delta \geq 9)$	$O(\log^3 n)$	$O(n\log^3 n)$	Δ	[6]
Planar graph $(\Delta \geq 19)$	$O(\log^2 n)$	$O(n\log^2 n)$	Δ	[7]
Genus $g \geq 1$ $\Delta \geq \lceil(9 + \sqrt{48g+1})^2/8\rceil$	$O(\log^3 n)$	$O(n\log^3 n)$	Δ	[39]
Degeneracy s $(\Delta \geq \lceil(s+2)^2/2\rceil - 1)$	$O(\log^3 n)$	$O(n\log^3 n)$	Δ	[39]
Arboricity a $(\Delta \geq \lceil(a+2)^2/2\rceil - 1)$	$O(\log^3 n)$	$O(n\log^3 n)$	Δ	[39]
Thickness θ $(\Delta \geq \lceil(3\theta+2)^2/2\rceil - 1)$	$O(\log^3 n)$	$O(n\log^3 n)$	Δ	[39]

On the other hand, Goldberg [14] posed a conjecture that for every odd integer $k \geq 5$

$$\chi'(G) \leq \max\left\{l(G), \left\lfloor\frac{k\Delta(G) + (k-3)}{k-1}\right\rfloor\right\}.$$

Furthermore Goldberg [14] and Seymour [28] posed a conjecture that every multigraph G satisfies

$$\chi'(G) \leq \max\{l(G), \Delta(G) + 1\}.$$

Especially for series-parallel multigraph G it is known [22,29] that

$$\chi'(G) = \max\{l(G), \Delta(G)\},$$

and that there exists an algorithm to decide $\chi'(G)$ in linear time and find an edge-coloring of G with $\chi'(G)$ colors in time $O(m \log m)$ [42,43].

2.2   Edge-colorings of simple graphs

Vizing [32] proved that every simple graph G can be edge-colored with $\Delta(G)+1$ colors, that is,

$$\chi'(G) \leq \Delta(G) + 1.$$

Since $\chi'(G) \geq \Delta(G)$, every simple graph G can be edge-colored with either $\Delta(G)$ or $\Delta(G) + 1$ colors. His proof depends on a technique of "shifting a fan." The proof immediately yields an $O(mn)$ time algorithm to edge-color a simple graph G with $\Delta(G) + 1$ colors. There exist more efficient edge-coloring algorithms for simple graphs. The most efficient one takes time $O(m\sqrt{n \log n})$ [12].

The following results are known for planar graphs G. If $2 \leq \Delta(G) \leq 5$ then $\chi'(G) = \Delta(G)$ or $\Delta(G)+1$. If $\Delta(G) \geq 8$ then $\chi'(G) = \Delta(G)$. It is open whether there exists a planar graph G with $6 \leq \Delta(G) \leq 7$ such that $\chi'(G) = \Delta(G) + 1$. For the case $\Delta(G) \geq 8$ there is an $O(n^2)$ time algorithm for edge-coloring a planar graph G with $\Delta(G)$ colors [31]. Furthermore for the case $\Delta(G) \geq 9$ there is a more efficient algorithm of time-complexity $O(n \log n)$ [6].

There are efficient algorithms to edge-color various classes of graphs G with $\chi'(G)$ colors if $\Delta(G)$ is large. These sequential algorithms together with others are listed in Table 1, and NC parallel algorithms in Table 2. It has not been known whether there is an NC parallel algorithm to edge-color any simple graph G with $\Delta(G) + 1$ colors [19].

3 f-coloring

The *vertex-capacity* f is any function from the vertex set V to the natural numbers. An *f-coloring* of a graph G is a coloring of the edges of G such that each vertex v has at most $f(v)$ edges colored with the same color. The minimum number of colors needed to f-color G is called the *f-chromatic index* of G, and is denoted by $\chi'_f(G)$. Fig. 2 depicts an f-coloring with four colors, and $\chi'_f(G) = 4$ since there exists a vertex v such that $f(v) = 1$ and $d(v) = 4$. Hakimi and Kariv obtained the following upper bound on $\chi_f(G)$:

$$\chi'_f(G) \leq \max_{v,w \in V} \left\lceil \frac{d(v) + p(vw)}{f(v)} \right\rceil.$$

This upper bound is a generalization of Vizing's bound for the ordinary edge-coloring because an ordinary edge-coloring is a special case of an f-coloring in which $f(v) = 1$ for every vertex $v \in V$. Their proof uses an extended version of switching an alternating path and shifting a fan. The proof immediately yields an $O(m^2)$ time algorithm to find an f-coloring of G with a number of colors not exceeding the upper bound. Furthermore the time complexity was improved to $O(m\sqrt{m}\log m)$ [26]. The following upper bound on $\chi'_f(G)$ is also known [23]:

$$\chi'_f(G) \leq \max\left\{l_f(G), \left\lceil\frac{9\Delta_f(G)+6}{8}\right\rceil\right\}$$

where

$$l_f(G) = \max_{H\subseteq G, |V(H)|\geq 3}\left\lceil\frac{|E(H)|}{\left\lceil\frac{\sum_{v\in V(H)} f(v)}{2}\right\rceil}\right\rceil$$

and

$$\Delta_f(G) = \max_{v\in V}\left\lceil\frac{d(v)}{f(v)}\right\rceil.$$

Note that $l_f(G)$ and $\Delta_f(G)$ are trivial lower bounds on $\chi'_f(G)$. Furthermore an algorithm is known to find an f-coloring of G with a number of colors not exceeding the upper bound above in time $O(m^2)$ [23]. This algorithm has the asymptotic approximation ratio 9/8.

Since both the ordinary edge-coloring problem and the f-coloring problem are NP-complete, the theory of NP-completeness immediately implies that there exists a polynomial-time reduction of the f-coloring problem to the ordinary edge-coloring problem plausibly through SAT. Recently a very simple reduction of the f-coloring problem to the ordinary edge-coloring problem was found [41].

4 fg-coloring

The *edge-capacity* g is any function from the pairs of vertices $V \times V$ to the natural numbers. An fg-*coloring* of G is a coloring of the edges of G such that at most $f(v)$ edges incident to v are colored with the same color for each vertex $v \in V$ and at most $g(vw)$ multiple edges joining v and w are colored with the same color for each pair of vertices v and w. The minimum number of colors needed to fg-color G is called the fg-*chromatic index* of G, and is denoted by $\chi'_{fg}(G)$. The fg-chromatic index of G in Fig. 3 is four. The following upper bound on $\chi'_{fg}(G)$ has been known [25]:

$$\chi'_{fg}(G) \leq \left\lfloor\frac{3}{2}\Delta_{fg}(G)\right\rfloor,$$

where

$$\Delta_{fg}(G) = \max\left\{\Delta_f(G), \Delta_g(G)\right\},$$

$$\Delta_f(G) = \max_{v\in V}\left\lceil\frac{d(v)}{f(v)}\right\rceil,$$

and

$$\Delta_g(G) = \max_{vw\in E}\left\lceil\frac{p(vw)}{g(vw)}\right\rceil.$$

Note that $\Delta_f(G)$, $\Delta_g(G)$ and $\Delta_{fg}(G)$ are trivial lower bounds on $\chi'_{fg}(G)$. This upper bound is a generalization of Shannon's bound [30] for the ordinary edge-coloring. An $O(m^2)$ time algorithm to fg-color G with a number of colors not exceeding $\lfloor \frac{3}{2}\Delta_{fg}(G)\rfloor$ has been known [25]. Since

$$\left\lfloor \frac{3}{2}\Delta_{fg}(G)\right\rfloor \leq \frac{3}{2}\chi'_{fg}(G),$$

this algorithm has the approximation ratio $3/2$.

One may assume without loss of generality that $g(vw) \leq \max\{f(v), f(w)\}$ for any pair of vertices $v, w \in V$. Then the following upper bound holds for the fg-chromatic index $\chi'_{fg}(G)$ [24]:

$$\chi'_{fg}(G) \leq \max_{v,w\in V} \left\lceil \frac{d(v)}{f(v)} + \frac{p(vw)}{g(vw)}\right\rceil.$$

Although one may assume that $g(vw) \leq \min\{f(v), f(w)\}$, we assume as above since the bound would increase when g decreases. This upper bound is a generalization of Vizing's upper bound [32] for the ordinary edge-coloring and Hakimi and Kariv's [15] upper bound for the f-coloring. The proof for this upper bound is constructive, and immediately yields an $O(m^2)$ time algorithm to fg-color a given graph with a number of colors not exceeding the upper bound above. Since

$$\max_{v,w\in V} \left\lceil \frac{d(v)}{f(v)} + \frac{p(vw)}{g(vw)}\right\rceil \leq 2\chi'_{fg}(G),$$

this algorithm has the approximation ratio 2.

References

1. Aho, A. V., Hopcroft, J. E., Ullman, J. D.: *The Design and Analysis of Computer Algorithms.* Addison-Wesley, Reading, MA (1974).
2. Andersen, L.: On edge colorings of graphs. *Math. Scand.* **40** (1977) 161-175.
3. Arnborg, S., Proskurowski, A.: Linear time algorithms for NP-hard problems restricted to partial k-trees. *Discrete Appl. Math.* **23** (1989) 11-24.
4. Bodlaender, H. L.: Polynomial algorithms for graph isomorphism and chromatic index on partial k-trees. *Journal of Algorithms* **11** (1990) 631-643.
5. Coffman, Jr, E. G., Garey, M. R., Johnson, D. S., LaPaugh, A. S.: Scheduling file transfers. *SIAM J. Comput.* **14** (1985) 744-780.
6. Chrobak, M., Nishizeki, T.: Improved edge-coloring algorithms for planar graphs. *Journal of Algorithms* **11** (1990) 102-116.
7. Chrobak, M., Yung, M.: Fast algorithms for edge-coloring planar graphs. *Journal of Algorithms* **10** (1989) 35-51.
8. Cole, R., Hopcroft, J.: On edge coloring bipartite graphs. *SIAM J. Comput.* **11** (1982) 540-546.
9. Ehrenfeucht, A., Faber, V., Kierstead, H. A.: A new method of proving theorems on chromatic index. *Discrete Mathematics* **52** (1984) 159-164.
10. Fiorini, S., Wilson, R. J.: *Edge-Colouring of Graphs*, Pitman, London (1977).

11. Gabow, H. N., Kariv, O.: Algorithms for edge coloring bipartite graphs. *SIAM J. Comput.* **11** (1982) 117-129.

12. Gabow, H. N., Nishizeki, T., Kariv, O., Leven, D., Terada, O.: Algorithms for edge-coloring graphs. *Tech. Rep.* TRECIS-8501, Tohoku Univ. (1985).

13. Garey, M. R., Johnson, D. S.: *Computers and Intractability: A Guide to the Theory of NP-Completeness*. W. H. Freeman & Co., San Francisco (1979).

14. Goldberg, M. K.: Edge-colorings of multigraphs: recoloring techniques. *Journal of Graph Theory* **8** (1984) 122-136.

15. Hakimi, S. L., Kariv, O.: On a generalization of edge-coloring in graphs. *Journal of Graph Theory* **10** (1986) 139-154.

16. Hilton, A. J. W., de Werra, D.: Sufficient conditions for balanced and for equitable edge-colorings of graphs. *O. R. Working paper 82/3*, Dépt. of Math., École Polytechnique Fédérate de Lausanne, Switzerland (1982).

17. Hochbaum, D. S., Nishizeki, T., Shmoys, D. B.: A better than "best possible" algorithm to edge color multigraphs. *Journal of Algorithms* **7** (1986) 79-104.

18. Holyer, I. J.: The NP-completeness of edge colourings. *SIAM J. Comput.* **10** (1980) 718-720.

19. Karloff, H. J., Shmoys, D. B.: Efficient parallel algorithms for edge-coloring problems. *Journal of Algorithms* **8** (1987) 39-52.

20. König, D., Über Graphen und iher Anwendung auf Determinantentheorie und Mengenlehre. *Math. Ann.* **77** (1916) 453-465.

21. Lev, G. F., Pippenger, N., Valiant, L. G.: A fast parallel algorithm for routing in permutation networks, *IEEE Trans. Comput.*, **30** (1981) 93-100.

22. Marcotte, O.: Exact edge-coloring of graphs without prescribed minors. *DIMACS Series in Discrete Mathematics and Theoretical Computer Science* **1** (1990) 235-249.

23. Nakano, S., Nishizeki, T., Saito, N.: On the f-coloring of multigraphs. *IEEE Trans. Circuits and Syst.* **CAS-35** (1988) 345-353.

24. Nakano, S., Nishizeki, T., Saito, N.: On the fg-coloring of graphs. *Combinatorica* **10** (1990) 67-80.

25. Nakano, S., Nishizeki, T.: Scheduling file transfers under port and channel constraints. *International Journal of Foundation of Computer Science* **4** (1993) 101-115.

26. Nakano, S., Nishizeki, T.: Approximation algorithms for the f-edge-coloring of multigraphs. *Trans. of Japan SIAM* **3** (1993) 279-307 (in Japanese).

27. Nishizeki, T., Kashiwagi, K.: On the 1.1 edge-coloring of multigraphs. *SIAM J. Disc. Math.* **3** (1990) 391-410.

28. Seymour, P. D.: On multicolouring of cubic graphs, and conjecture of Fulkerson and Tutte. *Proc. London Math. Soc.* **38** (1979) 423-460.

29. Seymour, P. D.: Colouring series-parallel graphs. *Combinatorica* **10** (1990) 379-392.

30. Shannon, C. E.: A theorem on coloring the lines of a network. *J. Math. Phys.* **28** (1949) 148-151.

31. Terada, O., Nishizeki, T.: Approximate algorithms for the edge-coloring of graphs. *Trans. IEICE Japan* **J65-D** (1982) 1382-1389 (in Japanese).

32. Vizing, 2. G.: On an estimate of the chromatic class of a p-graph. *Discret Analiz* **3** (1964) 25-30 (in Russian).

33. Vizing, V. G.: The chromatic class of a multigraph. *Kibernetica(Kief)* **3** (1965) 29-39.

34. de Werra, D.: Some results in chromatic scheduling. *Zeitschrift fur Oper. Res.* **18** (1974) 167-175.

35. de Werra, D.: A few remarks on chromatic scheduling. *in Combinatorial Programming: Methods and Applications*, ed. Roy, B., D. Reidel Pub. Comp., Dordrecht-Holland (1975) 337-342.

36. Zhou, X., Nakano, S., Nishizeki, T.: A linear algorithm for edge-coloring partial k-tree. Th. Lengauer (Ed.), *Algorithms - ESA'93*, Proc. First Annual European Symposium, Lect. Notes in Comp. Sci., Vol. 726, Springer-Verlag (1993) 409-418.

37. Zhou, X., Nakano, S., Nishizeki, T.: A parallel algorithm for edge-coloring partial k-tree. in: E.M. Schmidt, S. Skyum (Eds.), *Algorithm Theory – SWAT '94*, Proc. 4th Scand. Workshop on Algorithm Theory, Lect. Notes in Comp. Sci., Vol. 824, Springer-Verlag (1994) 359-369.

38. Zhou, X., Nakano, S., Suzuki, H., Nishizeki, T.: An efficient algorithm for edge-coloring series-parallel multigraphs. in: I. Simon (Ed.), *LATIN'92*, Proc. 1st Latin American Symposium on Theoretical Informatics, Lect. Notes in Comp. Sci., Vol. 583, Springer-Verlag (1992) 516-529.

39. Zhou, X., Nishizeki, T.: Edge-coloring and f-coloring for various classes of graphs. in: D-Z. Du, X-S. Zhang (Eds.), *Algorithms and Computation*, Proc. 5th In. Symposium (ISAAC'94), Lect. Notes in Comp. Sci., Vol. 834, Springer-Verlag (1994) 199-207.

40. Zhou, X., Nishizeki, T.: Optimal parallel algorithms for edge-coloring partial k-trees with bounded degrees. *Trans. IEICE Japan* **E78-A** (1995) 463-469.

41. Zhou, X., Nishizeki, T.: Simple reductions of f-coloring to edge-colorings. *Proc. of First Ann. Int. Comput. and Combinatorics Conf., Lect. Notes in Comp. Sci.*, Springer-Verlag, to appear.

42. Zhou. X., Suzuki, H., Nishizeki, T.: A linear algorithm for edge-coloring series-parallel multigraphs. *Journal of Algorithms*, to appear.

43. Zhou, X., Suzuki, H., Nishizeki, T.: Sequential and parallel algorithms for edge-coloring series-parallel multigraphs. *Proc. of the Third Conference on Integer Programming and Combinatorial Optimization* (1993) 129-146.

Towards a Computational Theory of Genome Rearrangements

Sridhar Hannenhalli[*,1] and Pavel A. Pevzner[*,†,1]

Department of Computer Science and Engineering[*]
Institute for Molecular Evolutionary Genetics[†]
The Pennsylvania State University
University Park, PA 16802

Abstract. Analysis of genome rearrangements in molecular biology started in the late 1930's, when Dobzhansky and Sturtevant published a milestone paper presenting a rearrangement scenario with 17 inversions for the species of *Drosophila*. However, until recently there were no computer science results allowing a biologist to analyze genome rearrangements. The paper describes combinatorial problems motivated by genome rearrangements, surveys recently developed algorithms for genomic sequence comparison and presents applications of these algorithms to analyze rearrangements in herpes viruses, plant organelles, and mammalian chromosomes.

1   Introduction

In the late 1980's Jeffrey Palmer and colleagues discovered a remarkable and novel pattern of evolutionary change in plant organelles. They compared the mitochondrial genomes of *Brassica oleracea* (cabbage) and *Brassica campestris* (turnip), which are very closely related (many genes are 99% - 99.9% identical). To their surprise, these molecules, which are almost identical in *gene* sequences, differ dramatically in gene *order* (Fig. 1). This discovery and many other studies in the last decade convincingly proved that genome rearrangements is a common mode of molecular evolution. Every study of genome rearrangements involves solving a combinatorial "puzzle" to find a shortest series of *rearrangements* to transform one genome into another. (Three such rearrangements "transforming" cabbage into turnip are shown in Fig. 1.) In cases of genomes consisting of small number of "conserved blocks", Palmer and his co-workers were able to find the most parsimonious scenarios for rearrangements. However, for genomes consisting of more than 10 blocks, exhaustive search over all potential solutions is far beyond the possibilities of "pen-and-pencil" methods.

With the advent of large-scale DNA mapping and sequencing, the number of *genome comparison* problems similar to the one presented in Fig. 1 is rapidly

---

[1]This work is supported by NSF Young Investigator Award, NSF grant CCR-9308567, NIH grant 1R01 HG00987 and DOE grant DE-FG02-94ER61919. Authors' E-mail addresses: *hannenha@cse.psu.edu* and *pevzner@cse.psu.edu*.

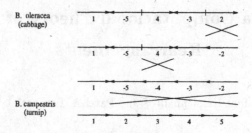

Figure 1: "Transformation" of cabbage into turnip

growing in different areas, including evolution of plant cpDNA (Raubeson and Jansen, 1992, Hoot and Palmer, 1994) and mtDNA (Palmer and Herbon, 1988, Fauron and Havlik, 1989), animal mtDNA (Hoffman et al., 1992, Sankoff et al., 1992), virology (Koonin and Dolya, 1993, Hannenhalli et al., 1995), *Drosophila* genetics (Whiting et al., 1989) and comparative physical mapping (Lyon, 1988). Genome comparison has certain merits and demerits as compared to classical *gene* comparison: genome comparison ignores actual DNA sequences of genes while gene comparison ignores gene order. The ultimate goal would be to combine merits of both genome and gene comparison in a single algorithm. However, until recently, studies of genome rearrangements were based on heuristic methods and there were no algorithms to analyze gene orders in molecular evolution.

A computational approach based on comparison of gene orders versus traditional comparison of DNA sequences was pioneered by Sankoff (see Sankoff et al., 1990, 1992 and Sankoff, 1992). Genome rearrangements provide a multitude of challenges for computer scientists; see Kececioglu and Sankoff, 1993 and Pevzner and Waterman, 1995 for a review of open combinatorial problems motivated by genome rearrangements. Rearrangements in mitochondrial, chloroplast, viral and bacterial DNA can be modeled by a combinatorial problem of sorting by reversals described below.

The order of genes in two arbitrary organisms is represented by permutations $\pi = (\pi_1 \pi_2 \ldots \pi_n)$ and $\sigma = (\sigma_1 \sigma_2 \ldots \sigma_n)$. A *reversal* $\rho(i,j)$ of an interval $[i,j]$, is the permutation

$$\begin{pmatrix} 1 & 2 & \ldots & i-1 & i & i+1 & \ldots & j-1 & j & j+1 & \ldots & n \\ 1 & 2 & \ldots & i-1 & j & j-1 & \ldots & i+1 & i & j+1 & \ldots & n \end{pmatrix}$$

Clearly $\pi \cdot \rho(i,j)$ has the effect of reversing the order of genes $\pi_i \pi_{i+1} \ldots \pi_j$ and transforms $(\pi_1 \ldots \pi_{i-1} \pi_i \ldots \pi_j \pi_{j+1} \ldots \pi_n)$ into $(\pi_1 \ldots \pi_{i-1} \pi_j \ldots \pi_i \pi_{j+1} \ldots \pi_n)$.

Given permutations π and σ, the *reversal distance problem* is to find a series of reversals $\rho_1, \rho_2, \ldots, \rho_t$ such that $\pi \cdot \rho_1 \cdot \rho_2 \cdots \rho_t = \sigma$ and t is minimum (Fig. 2a). We call t the *reversal distance* between π and σ. *Sorting* π *by reversals* is the problem of finding the reversal distance, $d(\pi)$, between π and the identity permutation $(12 \ldots n)$.

Reversals generate the *symmetric group* S_n. Given an arbitrary permutation

π from S_n we seek a shortest product of *generators* $\rho_1 \cdot \rho_2 \cdots \rho_t$ that equals π. Even and Goldreich, 1981 show that given a set of generators of a permutation group and a permutation π, determining the shortest product of generators that equals π is NP-hard. Jerrum, 1985 proves that the problem is PSPACE-complete, and that it remains so, when restricted to generator sets of size two. In our problem, the generator set is the set of all possible reversals. However, Kececioglu and Sankoff conjectured that sorting by reversals is NP-complete.

Gates and Papadimitriou, 1979 study a similar *sorting by prefix reversals* problem (also known as the *pancake flipping problem*): given an arbitrary permutation π, find $d_{pref}(\pi)$, which is the minimum number of reversals of the form $\rho(1, i)$ sorting π. They are concerned with bounds on the *prefix reversal diameter* of the symmetric group, $d_{pref}(n) = \max_{\pi \in S_n} d_{pref}(\pi)$. They show that $d_{pref}(n) \leq \frac{5}{3}n + \frac{5}{3}$ (see also Győri and Turan, 1978), and that for infinitely many n, $d_{pref}(n) \geq \frac{17}{16}n$. See Aigner and West, 1987 and Amato et al., 1989 for related combinatorial problems.

What makes it hard to sort a permutation? In the very first computational studies of genome rearrangements Watterson et al., 1982 and Nadeau and Taylor, 1984 introduced the notion of *breakpoint* and noticed some correlations between the reversal distance and the number of breakpoints. (In fact, Sturtevant and Dobzhansky, 1936 implicitly discussed these correlations 60 years ago!) Below we define the notion of breakpoint.

Let $i \sim j$ if $|i - j| = 1$. Extend a permutation $\pi = \pi_1 \pi_2 \ldots \pi_n$ by adding $\pi_0 = 0$ and $\pi_{n+1} = n + 1$. We call a pair of elements (π_i, π_{i+1}), $0 \leq i \leq n$, of π an *adjacency* if $\pi_i \sim \pi_{i+1}$, and a *breakpoint* if $\pi_i \not\sim \pi_{i+1}$. As the identity permutation has no breakpoints, sorting by reversals corresponds to eliminating breakpoints. An observation that every reversal can eliminate *at most* 2 breakpoints immediately implies that $d(\pi) \geq \frac{b(\pi)}{2}$, where $b(\pi)$ is the number of breakpoints in π. Based on the notion of breakpoint, Kececioglu and Sankoff, 1993 found an approximation algorithm for sorting by reversals with performance guarantee 2. They also devised efficient bounds, solving the reversal distance problem optimally or almost optimally for n ranging from 30 to 50. This range covers the biologically important case of mitochondrial genomes.

However, the estimate of reversal distance in terms of breakpoints is very inaccurate. Bafna and Pevzner, 1993 showed that there exists another parameter (size of a maximum cycle decomposition of the breakpoint graph) which estimates reversal distance with much greater accuracy. In the following section we introduce breakpoint graph of a permutation, which is a key notion in the analysis of genome rearrangements. Section 3 states the duality theorem which leads to polynomial algorithm for sorting signed permutations by reversals. Section 4 discusses the links between genome rearrangements and comparative physical mapping. Sections 5 and 6 deal with rearrangements in multi-chromosomal genomes. Finally, section 7 presents the biological applications of the described techniques.

2   Breakpoint Graph

The *breakpoint graph* of a permutation π is an edge-colored graph $G(\pi)$ with $n+2$ vertices $\{\pi_0, \pi_1, \ldots, \pi_n, \pi_{n+1}\} \equiv \{0, 1, \ldots, n, n+1\}$. We join vertices π_i and π_{i+1} by a *black* edge for $0 \le i \le n$. We join vertices π_i and π_j by a *gray* edge if $\pi_i \sim \pi_j$ (Fig. 2b).

A *cycle* in an edge-colored graph G is called *alternating* if the colors of every two consecutive edges of this cycle are distinct. In the following by cycles we mean alternating cycles. Consider a *cycle decomposition* of $G(\pi)$ into a *maximum* number $c(\pi)$ of edge-disjoint alternating cycles. For the permutation π in Fig. 2b $c(\pi) = 7$ since $G(\pi)$ can be decomposed into seven cycles $(1, 2, 1)$, $(10, 11, 10)$, $(11, 12, 11)$, $(8, 9, 7, 6, 8)$, $(8, 5, 4, 7, 8)$, $(3, 5, 6, 4, 3)$ and $(0, 1, 10, 9, 2, 3, 0)$. Bafna and Pevzner, 1993 showed that the maximum cycle decomposition provides a better bound for the reversal distance:

Theorem 1 *For a permutation π of order n, $d(\pi) \ge n + 1 - c(\pi)$.*

Using theorem 1 Bafna and Pevzner, 1993 devised an approximation algorithm for sorting by reversals with performance guarantee 1.75. They also proved the *Gollan conjecture* on the *reversal diameter* $d(n) = \max_{\pi \in S_n} d(\pi)$ of the symmetric group S_n of order n. Gollan conjectured that $d(n) = n - 1$ and that only one permutation γ_n, and its inverse, γ_n^{-1} require $n-1$ reversals to be sorted. The *Gollan* permutation, in one-line notation, is defined as follows:

$$\gamma_n = \begin{cases} (3, 1, 5, 2, 7, 4, \ldots, n-3, n-5, n-1, n-4, n, n-2), & n \text{ even} \\ (3, 1, 5, 2, 7, 4, \ldots, n-6, n-2, n-5, n, n-3, n-1), & n \text{ odd} \end{cases}$$

Theorem 2 *The reversal diameter of the symmetric group of order n is $n - 1$. For every n, γ_n and γ_n^{-1} are the only permutations that require $n - 1$ reversals to be sorted.*

Bafna and Pevzner, 1993 further studied the problem of *expected* reversal distance $E(n)$ between two random permutations of order n, and demonstrated that reversal distance between two random permutations is very close to the reversal diameter of the symmetric group:

Theorem 3 $E(n) \ge \left(1 - \frac{4.5}{\log n}\right) n$

This result indicates that reversal distance provides a good separation between related and non-related sequences in molecular evolution studies.

3   Duality Theorem for Signed Permutations

Finding a maximum cycle decomposition is a difficult problem. Fortunately in biologically more relevant case of *signed permutations*, this problem is trivial.

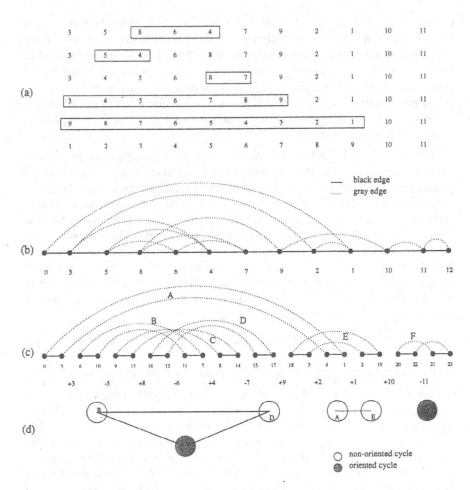

Figure 2: (a) Optimal sorting of a permutation (3 5 8 6 4 7 9 2 1 10 11) by 5 reversals and (b) breakpoint graph of this permutation; (c) Transformation of a signed permutation into an unsigned permutation π and the breakpoint graph $G(\pi)$; (d) Interleaving graph H_π with two oriented and one unoriented component.

Genes are *directed* fragments of DNA and sequence of n genes in a genome is represented by a *signed* permutation on $\{1, \ldots n\}$ with $+$ or $-$ sign associated with every element of π. For example, a gene order for *B. oleracea* presented in Fig. 1 is modeled by a signed permutation $(+1 - 5 + 4 - 3 + 2)$. In the signed case, every reversal of fragment $[i, j]$ changes *both* the order and the signs of the elements within that fragment (Fig. 1). We are interested in the minimum number of reversals $d(\pi)$ required to transform a signed permutation π into the identity signed permutation $(+1 + 2 \ldots + n)$.

Bafna and Pevzner, 1993 noted that the concept of breakpoint graph extends naturally to signed permutations and devised an approximation algorithm for sorting signed permutations by reversals with performance ratio 1.5. For signed permutations the bound $d(\pi) \geq n + 1 - c(\pi)$ approximates the reversal distance extremely well for both simulated (Kececioglu and Sankoff, 1994) and biological data (Bafna and Pevzner, 1995a, Hannenhalli et al., 1995). This intriguing performance raises a question whether the theorem 1 overlooked another parameter (in addition to the size of a maximum cycle decomposition) that would allow closing the gap between $d(\pi)$ and $n + 1 - c(\pi)$. Hannenhalli and Pevzner, 1995a revealed another "hidden" parameter (number of *hurdles* in π) making it harder to sort a signed permutation and showed that

$$n + 1 - c(\pi) + h(\pi) \leq d(\pi) \leq n + 2 - c(\pi) + h(\pi) \tag{1}$$

where $h(\pi)$ is the number of *hurdles* in π. Below we define the notion of hurdle.

Let $\vec{\pi}$ be a *signed* permutation of $\{1, \ldots, n\}$, *i.e.* a permutation with "$+$" or "$-$" sign associated with each element (Fig. 2c). Define a transformation from a signed permutation $\vec{\pi}$ of order n to an (unsigned) permutation π of $\{1, \ldots, 2n\}$ as follows. To model the signs of elements in $\vec{\pi}$ replace the positive elements $+x$ by $2x - 1, 2x$ and negative elements $-x$ by $2x, 2x - 1$ (Fig. 2c). We call the unsigned permutation π, the *image* of the signed permutation $\vec{\pi}$. In the breakpoint graph $G(\pi)$, elements $2x - 1$ and $2x$ are joined by both black and gray edges for $1 \leq x \leq n$. We define the breakpoint graph $G(\vec{\pi})$ of a signed permutation $\vec{\pi}$ as the breakpoint graph $G(\pi)$ with these $2n$ edges excluded. Observe that in $G(\vec{\pi})$ every vertex has degree 2 (Fig. 2c) and therefore the breakpoint graph of a signed permutation is a collection of disjoint cycles. Denote the number of such cycles as $c(\vec{\pi})$. We observe that the identity signed permutation of order n maps to the identity (unsigned) permutation of order $2n$, and the effect of a reversal on $\vec{\pi}$ can be mimicked by a reversal on π thus implying $d(\vec{\pi}) \geq d(\pi)$. In the rest of this section, π is an image of a signed permutation. A reversal $\rho(i, j)$ on π is *legal* if i is odd and j is even. Notice that any reversal on a signed permutation corresponds to a legal reversal on its image and vice versa. In the following, by reversal we mean legal reversal.

We say that reversal $\rho(i, j)$ *acts* on black edges (π_{i-1}, π_i) and (π_j, π_{j+1}) in $G(\pi)$. We call $\rho(i, j)$ a *reversal on a cycle* if the black edges (π_{i-1}, π_i) and (π_j, π_{j+1}) belong to the *same* cycle in $G(\pi)$. Every reversal increases $c(\pi)$ by at most 1, *i.e.* $c(\pi\rho) - c(\pi) \leq 1$ (Bafna and Pevzner, 1993). A gray edge g is *oriented* if for a reversal ρ acting on two black edges incident to g, $c(\pi\rho)-c(\pi) = 1$ and *unoriented* otherwise. A cycle in $G(\pi)$ is *oriented* if it has an oriented gray edge and unoriented otherwise. Gray edges (π_i, π_j) and (π_k, π_t) in $G(\pi)$ are *interleaving* if the intervals $[i, j]$ and $[k, t]$ overlap but neither of them contains the other. Cycles C_1 and C_2 are *interleaving* if there exist interleaving gray edges $g_1 \in C_1$ and $g_2 \in C_2$. See Fig. 2c for examples.

Let C_π be the set of cycles in the breakpoint graph of a permutation π. Define an *interleaving* graph $H_\pi(C_\pi, \mathcal{I}_\pi)$ of π with the edge set $\mathcal{I}_\pi = \{(C_1, C_2) : C_1$ and C_2 are interleaving cycles in $\pi\}$ (Fig. 2d). The vertex set of H_π is partitioned into *oriented* and *unoriented* vertices (cycles in C_π). A connected component of H_π is *oriented* if it has at least one oriented vertex and *unoriented* otherwise. In the following we use the terms edge of π, cycle in π and component of π instead of (more accurate) terms edge of $G(\pi)$, cycle in $G(\pi)$ and component of $H(\pi)$. A connected component U of π corresponds to the set of integers $\bar{U} = \{i : \pi_i \in C \in U\}$ representing the set of positions of the permutation belonging to cycles of U. For a set of integers U define $U_{min} = \min_{u \in U} u$ and $U_{max} = \max_{u \in U} u$.

Let $\prec$ be a partial order on a set P. An element $x \in P$ is called a *minimal element* in $\prec$ if there is no element $y \in P$ with $y \prec x$. An element $x \in P$ is the *greatest* in $\prec$ if $y \prec x$ for every $y \in P$. Let $\mathcal{U}$ be a collection of sets of integers. Define a partial order on $\mathcal{U}$ by the rule $U \prec W$ iff $[U_{min}, U_{max}] \subset [W_{min}, W_{max}]$ for $U, W \in \mathcal{U}$. We say that a set $U \in \mathcal{U}$ *separates* sets U' and U'' if there exists $u \in U$ such that $U'_{max} < u < U''_{min}$. A *hurdle for the set* $\mathcal{U}$ is defined as an element U in $\mathcal{U}$ which is either a minimal hurdle or the greatest hurdle where a *minimal hurdle* is a minimal element in $\prec$ and the *greatest hurdle* satisfies the following two conditions (i) U is the greatest element in $\prec$ *and* (ii) U does not separate any two elements in $\mathcal{U}$. A hurdle $K \in \mathcal{U}$ *protects* a non-hurdle $U \in \mathcal{U}$ if deleting K from $\mathcal{U}$ transforms U from a non-hurdle into a hurdle (*i.e.* U is not a hurdle in $\mathcal{U}$ and U is a hurdle in $\mathcal{U} \setminus K$). A hurdle in $\mathcal{U}$ is a *superhurdle* if it protects a non-hurdle in $\mathcal{U}$.

Define a collection of sets of integers $\mathcal{U}_\pi = \{\bar{U} : U$ is an unoriented component of permutation $\pi\}$ and let $h(\pi)$ be the overall number of hurdles for the collection $\mathcal{U}_\pi$. Permutation π is called a *fortress* if it has an odd number of hurdles and all these hurdles are superhurdles. Define

$$f(\pi) = \begin{cases} 1, & \text{if } \pi \text{ is a fortress} \\ 0, & \text{otherwise} \end{cases}$$

For a signed permutation $\vec{\pi}$ with the image π we define $c(\vec{\pi}) = c(\pi)$, $h(\vec{\pi}) = h(\pi)$ and $f(\vec{\pi}) = f(\pi)$.

Theorem 4 *(Hannenhalli and Pevzner, 1995a) For a signed permutation $\vec{\pi}$, $d(\vec{\pi}) = n + 1 - c(\vec{\pi}) + h(\vec{\pi}) + f(\vec{\pi})$.*

Based on theorem 4, Hannenhalli and Pevzner, 1995a devised an $O(n^4)$ algorithm for sorting signed permutations by reversals.

4   Sorting by Reversals and Comparative Physical Mapping

Since sorting by reversals as well as other genome rearrangements problems is believed to be NP-hard, most of the efforts in analyzing gene orders were directed towards approximation algorithms. A polynomial algorithm for sorting signed permutations by reversals raises a hope to find a polynomial algorithm for sorting (unsigned permutations) by reversals. Taking into account that all attempts to prove NP-hardness of sorting by reversals did not lead to a success yet, Hannenhalli and Pevzner, 1995b tried to devise an efficient algorithm for sorting by reversals.

Define a *block* of π as an interval $\pi_i \ldots \pi_j$ containing no breakpoints, *i.e.* (π_k, π_{k+1}) is an adjacency for $0 \le i \le k < j \le n+1$. Define a *strip* of π as a maximal block, *i.e.* a block $\pi_i \ldots \pi_j$ such that (π_{i-1}, π_i) and (π_j, π_{j+1}) are breakpoints. A strip of 1 element is called a *singleton*, a strip of 2 elements is called a *2-strip*, a strip with more than 2 elements is called a *long* strip. It turns out that singletons pose the major challenge in sorting by reversals.

A reversal $\rho(i, j)$ *cuts* a strip $\pi_k \ldots \pi_l$ if either $k < i \le l$ or $k \le j < l$. A reversal cutting a strip separates elements which are consecutive in the identity permutation. Therefore it is natural to expect that for every permutation π there exists an (optimal) sorting π by reversals which does not cut strips. This, however, is false. Permutation 3412 requires three reversals if we do not cut strips, yet it can be sorted with two: $3412 \to 1432 \to 1234$. Kececioglu and Sankoff conjectured that every permutation has an optimal sorting by reversals which does not cut *long* strips. Hannenhalli and Pevzner, 1995b proved this conjecture, thus demonstrating that major problem in sorting by reversals is posed by singletons and 2-strips.

Theorem 5 *For every (unsigned) permutation there exists an optimal sorting by reversals that never cuts long strips.*

Permutations without singletons are called *singleton-free* permutations. The difficulty in analyzing such permutations is posed by an alternative, *"to cut or not to cut"* 2-strips. A characterization of a set of 2-strips *"to cut"* (Hannenhalli and Pevzner, 1995b) leads to a polynomial algorithm for sorting singleton-free permutations and to a polynomial algorithm for sorting permutations with a small number of singletons. The algorithm can be applied to analyze rearrangement scenarios derived from comparative physical maps.

Biologists derive gene orders either by sequencing entire genomes or by comparative physical mapping. Sequencing provides information about directions of genes and allows one to represent a genome by a signed permutation. However, sequencing of entire genomes is still expensive and, at the moment, complete genomic sequences are known only for relatively short viral and organelle DNA. As a result, most of currently available experimental data on gene orders are based on comparative physical maps. Physical maps usually do not provide information about directions of genes and, therefore lead to representation of a genome as an *unsigned* permutation π. Biologists implicitly try to derive a signed permutation from this representation by assigning a positive (negative) sign to increasing (decreasing) strips of π. Theorem 5 provides a theoretical substantiation for such a procedure in the case of long strips. At the same time, for 2-strips this procedure might fail to find an optimal rearrangement scenario. Hannenhalli and Pevzner, 1995b described a new algorithm fixing this problem.

Since the identity permutation has no breakpoints, sorting by reversals corresponds to eliminating breakpoints. From this perspective it is natural to expect that for every permutation there exists an optimal sorting by reversals that never increases the number of breakpoints (*strong Kececioglu-Sankoff conjecture*). Hannenhalli and Pevzner, 1995b proved this conjecture by using the characterization theorem for singleton-free permutations and the duality theorem for signed permutations.

Theorem 6 *For every (unsigned) permutation π there exists an optimal sorting of π by reversals that never increases the number of breakpoints.*

The proof of the strong Kececioglu-Sankoff conjecture immediately leads to significant reduction in the running time of the computer program for sorting by reversals developed by Kececioglu and Sankoff, 1993.

5   Multi-Chromosomal Genomes

When Brothers Grimm described a transformation of a man into a mouse in the fairy tale "Puss N Boots" they could hardly anticipate that two centuries later human and mouse will be the most genetically studied mammals. Man-mouse comparative physical mapping started 20 years ago and currently more than 1300 pairs of homologous genes are mapped in these species. As a result, biologists found that the related genes in man and mouse are not chaotically distributed over the genomes but form "conserved blocks" instead. Current comparative mapping data indicate that both human and mouse genomes are combined from approximately 150 blocks which are "shuffled" in human as compared to mouse (Copeland et al., 1993). Shuffling of blocks happens quite rarely (roughly once in a million years) thus making it possible to reconstruct a rearrangement scenario of human-mouse evolution. In the pioneering paper, Nadeau and Taylor, 1984 estimated that surprisingly few genomic rearrangements (178 ± 39) happened since the divergence of human and mouse 80 million years ago. However, their analysis is non-constructive and no *rearrangement scenario* for man-mouse evolution has been suggested yet. The problem is complicated by the fact that rearrangements in multi-chromosomal genomes include inversions, translocations, fusions and fissions of chromosomes and form rather complex set of operations. Below we present the combinatorial formulation of the problem.

In the model we consider, every *gene* is represented by an *identification* number (positive integer) and an associated *sign* ("+" or "-") reflecting the *direction*

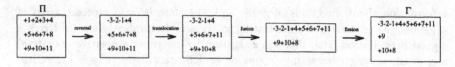

Figure 3: Evolution of genome Π into genome Γ

of the gene. A *chromosome* is defined as a *sequence* of genes while a *genome* is defined as a *set* of chromosomes. Given two genomes Π and Γ, we are interested in a most parsimonious scenario of *evolution* of Π into Γ, *i.e.* the shortest sequence of rearrangement events (defined below) to transform Π into Γ. In the following we assume that Π and Γ contain the same set of genes. Fig. 3 illustrates 4 rearrangement events transforming one genome into another.

Let $\Pi = \{\pi(1), \ldots, \pi(N)\}$ be a genome consisting of N chromosomes and let $\pi(i) = (\pi(i)_1 \ldots \pi(i)_{n_i})$, n_i being the number of genes in the ith chromosome. Every chromosome π can be viewed either from "left to right" (*i.e.* as $\pi = (\pi_1 \ldots \pi_n)$) or from "right to left" (*i.e.* as $-\pi = (-\pi_n \ldots -\pi_1)$) leading to two equivalent representations of the same chromosome. From this perspective a 3-chromosomal genome $\{\pi(1), \pi(2), \pi(3)\}$ is equivalent to $\{\pi(1), -\pi(2), \pi(3)\}$ or $\{-\pi(1), -\pi(2), -\pi(3)\}$, *i.e.* the *directions* of chromosomes are irrelevant. Four most common elementary rearrangement events in multi-chromosomal genomes are *reversals*, *translocations*, *fusions* and *fissions* defined below.

Let $\pi = (\pi_1 \ldots \pi_n)$ be a chromosome and $1 \leq i \leq j \leq n$. A *reversal* $\rho(\pi, i, j)$ *on a chromosome* π rearranges the genes *inside* $\pi = (\pi_1 \ldots \pi_{i-1}\pi_i \ldots \pi_j \pi_{j+1} \ldots \pi_n)$ and transforms π into $(\pi_1 \ldots \pi_{i-1} - \pi_j \ldots - \pi_i \pi_{j+1} \ldots \pi_n)$. Let $\pi = (\pi_1 \ldots \pi_n)$ and $\sigma = (\sigma_1 \ldots \sigma_m)$ be two chromosomes and $1 \leq i \leq n+1, 1 \leq j \leq m+1$. A *translocation* $\rho(\pi, \sigma, i, j)$ exchanges genes *between* two chromosomes π and σ and transforms them into chromosomes $(\pi_1 \ldots \pi_{i-1}\sigma_j \ldots \sigma_m)$ and $(\sigma_1 \ldots \sigma_{j-1}\pi_i \ldots \pi_n)$ with $(i-1) + (m-j+1)$ and $(j-1) + (n-i+1)$ genes respectively. We denote $\Pi \cdot \rho$ as the genome obtained from Π as a result of a rearrangement (reversal or translocation) ρ. Given genomes Π and Γ, the *genomic sorting* problem is to find a series of reversals and translocations $\rho_1, \ldots, \rho_t$ such that $\Pi \cdot \rho_1 \cdots \rho_t = \Gamma$ and t is minimum. We call t the *genomic distance* between Π and Γ. *Genomic distance* problem is the problem of finding the genomic distance $d(\Pi, \Gamma)$ between Π and Γ.

We distinguish between *internal* reversals which do not involve ends of the chromosomes (*i.e.* the reversals $\rho(\pi, i, j)$ of a n-gene chromosome with $1 < i \leq j < n$) and *prefix* reversals involving ends of the chromosomes (*i.e.* either $i = 1$ or $j = n$). Also note that a translocation $\rho(\pi, \sigma, n+1, 1)$ concatenates the chromosomes π and σ resulting in a chromosome $\pi_1 \ldots \pi_n \sigma_1 \ldots \sigma_m$ and an *empty* chromosome $\emptyset$. This special translocation leading to a reduction in the number of (non-empty) chromosomes is known in molecular biology as a *fusion*. The translocation $\rho(\pi, \emptyset, i, 1)$ for $1 < i < n$ "breaks" a chromosome π into two chromosomes $(\pi_1 \ldots \pi_{i-1})$ and $(\pi_i \ldots \pi_n)$. This translocation leading to an increase in the number of (non-empty) chromosomes is known as a *fis-*

sion. A translocation is *internal* if it is neither a fusion, nor a fission. Fusions and fissions are rather common in mammalian evolution, for example the only difference in the overall genome organization of human and chimpanzee is the fusion of chimpanzee chromosomes 12 and 13 into human chromosome 2. See Bafna and Pevzner,1995b for another (relatively rare) type of rearrangement called *transpositions*.

Kececioglu and Ravi, 1995 made the first attempt to analyze rearrangements of multi-chromosomal genomes by devising an approximation algorithm for genomes evolving by internal reversals and internal translocations. Hannenhalli, 1995 devised a polynomial algorithm for the case when only internal translocations are allowed. All these algorithms address the case when both genomes contain the same number of chromosomes. This is a serious limitation since different organisms (in particular human and mouse) have different number of chromosomes. From this perspective, every realistic model of genome rearrangements should include fusions and fissions. It turns out that fusions and fissions present a major difficulty in analyzing genome rearrangements: the problem of devising an *approximation* algorithm for genome rearrangements with reversals/translocations/fusions/fissions was raised by Kececioglu and Ravi, 1995. Hannenhalli and Pevzner, 1995c proved the duality theorem for multi-chromosomal genomes which computes the genomic distance in terms of seven parameters reflecting different combinatorial properties of sets of strings. Based on this result they found an polynomial algorithm for this problem.

The idea of the analysis is to concatenate N chromosomes of Π and Γ into permutations π and γ, respectively, and to mimic genomic sorting of Π into Γ by sorting π into γ by reversals. The difficulty with this approach is that there exists $N!2^N$ different concatenates for Π and Γ and only some of them, called *optimal concatenates*, mimic an *optimal* sorting of Π into Γ. Hannenhalli and Pevzner, 1995c introduced the techniques called *flipping* and *capping* of chromosomes allowing one to find an optimal concatenate. Below we describe the construction leading to duality theorem for so-called co-tailed genomes.

For a chromosome $\pi = (\pi_1 \ldots \pi_n)$, the numbers $+\pi_1$ and $-\pi_n$ are called *tails* of π. Note that changing the direction of a chromosome does not change the set of its tails. Tails in a N-chromosomal genome Π comprise the set $T(\Pi)$ of $2N$ tails. Genomes Π and Γ are *co-tailed* if $T(\Pi) = T(\Gamma)$. For co-tailed genomes internal reversals and translocations are sufficient for genomic sorting (*i.e.* prefix reversals, fusions and fissions can be ignored). For chromosomes $\pi = (\pi_1 \ldots \pi_n)$ and $\sigma = (\sigma_1 \ldots \sigma_m)$ denote $(\pi_1 \ldots \pi_n \sigma_1 \ldots \sigma_m)$ by $\pi + \sigma$ and $(\pi_1 \ldots \pi_n - \sigma_m \ldots - \sigma_1)$ by $\pi - \sigma$. Given an ordering of chromosomes $(\pi(1), \ldots, \pi(N))$ in a genome Π and a *flip* vector $s = (s(1), \ldots, s(N))$ with $s(i) \in \{-1, +1\}$ one can form a *concatenate* of Π as a permutation $\Pi(s) = s(1)\pi(1) + \ldots + s(N)\pi(N)$ on $\sum_{i=1}^{N} n_i$ elements. Depending on the choice of a flip vector there exists 2^N concatenates of Π for each of $N!$ orderings of chromosomes in Π. If an order of chromosomes in a genome Π is fixed we call Π an *ordered* genome.

In this section we assume w.l.o.g. that $\Gamma = (\gamma_1, \ldots, \gamma_N)$ is an (ordered) genome and $\gamma = \gamma_1 + \ldots + \gamma_N$ is the identity permutation. We denote $d(\Pi) \equiv d(\Pi, \Gamma)$ and call a problem of genomic sorting of Π into Γ simply a *sorting of a genome* Π.

Let π be a concatenate of $\Pi = (\pi(1), \ldots, \pi(N))$. Every tail of $\pi(i)$ corresponds to two vertices of π, exactly one of which is a boundary (either leftmost or rightmost) vertex among the vertices of the chromosome $\pi(i)$ in the concatenate π. We extend the term *tail* to denote such vertices in $G(\pi)$. An edge in a breakpoint graph $G(\pi)$ of a concatenate π is *interchromosomal* if it connects vertices in different chromosomes of Π and *intrachromosomal* otherwise. A component of π is *interchromosomal* if it contains an interchromosomal edge and *intrachromosomal* otherwise.

Every interchromosomal black edge in $G(\pi)$ connects two tails. Let $b_{tail}(\Pi)$ be the number of interchromosomal black edges in $G(\pi)$. and $c_{tail}(\Pi)$ be the number of cycles of $G(\pi)$ containing tails. Define $b(\Pi) = b(\pi) - b_{tail}(\pi)$ and $c(\Pi) = c(\pi) - c_{tail}(\pi)$. Notice that $b(\Pi)$ and $c(\Pi)$ do not depend on the choice of concatenate.

Consider the set of intrachromosomal unoriented components $\mathcal{IU}_\pi$ in H_π. Hurdles, superhurdles and fortresses for the set $\mathcal{IU}_\pi$ are called *knots, superknots* and *fortresses-of-knots* respectively. Let $k(\Pi)$ be the overall number of knots in a concatenate π of Π. Define $f(\Pi) = 1$ if π is a fortress-of-knots and $f(\Pi) = 0$ otherwise. Clearly, $b(\Pi)$ and $c(\Pi)$, $k(\Pi)$ and $f(\Pi)$ do not depend on the choice of a concatenate π.

Theorem 7 *For co-tailed genomes* Π *and* Γ, $d(\Pi, \Gamma) \equiv d(\Pi) = b(\Pi) - c(\Pi) + k(\Pi) + f(\Pi)$.

6   Generalized Duality Theorem

We now turn to the general case when genomes Π and Γ might have different sets of tails and different number of chromosomes. Let Π and Γ be two genomes with M and N chromosomes respectively. W.l.o.g. assume that $M \leq N$ and extend Π by $N - M$ empty chromosomes. As a result $\Pi = \{\pi(1), \ldots, \pi(N)\}$ and $\Gamma = \{\gamma(1), \ldots, \gamma(N)\}$ contain the same number of chromosomes.

Let $\{cap_0, \ldots, cap_{2N-1}\}$ be a set of $2N$ distinct positive integers (called *caps*) which are different from genes of Π (or equivalently, Γ). Let $\hat{\Pi} = \{\hat{\pi}(1), \ldots, \hat{\pi}(N)\}$ be a genome obtained from Π by adding caps to the ends of each chromosome, *i.e.* $\hat{\pi}(i) = (cap_{2(i-1)}, \pi(i)_1, \ldots, \pi(i)_{n_i}, cap_{2(i-1)+1})$. Note that every reversal/translocation in Π corresponds to an *internal* reversal/translocation in $\hat{\Pi}$.

Every sorting of Π into Γ induces a sorting of $\hat{\Pi}$ into a genome $\hat{\Gamma} = \{\hat{\gamma}(1), \ldots, \hat{\gamma}(N)\}$ (called *capping* of Γ), where

$$\hat{\gamma}(i) = ((-1)^j cap_j, \hat{\gamma}(i)_1, \ldots, \hat{\gamma}(i)_{m_i}, (-1)^{k+1} cap_k)$$

for $0 \leq j, k \leq 2N - 1$. Clearly, genomes $\hat{\Pi}$ and $\hat{\Gamma}$ are co-tailed and $T(\hat{\Pi}) =$

$T(\hat{\Gamma}) = \bigcup_{i=0}^{2N-1} (-1)^i cap_i$. There exists $(2N)!$ different cappings of Γ, each capping defined by the distribution of $2N$ caps of $\hat{\Pi}$ in $\hat{\Gamma}$. Denote the set of $(2N)!$ cappings of Γ as $\boldsymbol{\Gamma}$. The following theorem (Hannenhalli and Pevzner, 1995c) leads to an algorithm for computing genomic distance which is polynomial in the number of genes but exponential in the number of chromosomes N.

Theorem 8 $d(\Pi, \Gamma) = \min_{\hat{\Gamma} \in \boldsymbol{\Gamma}} b(\hat{\Pi}, \hat{\Gamma}) - c(\hat{\Pi}, \hat{\Gamma}) + k(\hat{\Pi}, \hat{\Gamma}) + f(\hat{\Pi}, \hat{\Gamma})$

Let $\hat{\pi}$ and $\hat{\gamma}$ be arbitrary concatenates of (ordered) cappings $\hat{\Pi} = (\hat{\pi}(1), \ldots, \hat{\pi}(N))$ and $\hat{\Gamma} = (\hat{\gamma}(1), \ldots, \hat{\gamma}(N))$. Let $G(\hat{\Pi}, \hat{\Gamma})$ be a graph obtained from $G(\hat{\pi}, \hat{\gamma})$ by deleting all tails (vertices of $G(\hat{\pi}, \hat{\gamma})$) of genome $\hat{\Pi}$ (or equivalently, $\hat{\Gamma}$) from $G(\hat{\pi}, \hat{\gamma})$. Different cappings $\hat{\Gamma}$ correspond to different graphs $G(\hat{\Pi}, \hat{\Gamma})$. Graph $G(\hat{\Pi}, \hat{\Gamma})$ has $2N$ vertices corresponding to caps, gray edges incident on these vertices completely define the capping $\hat{\Gamma}$. Therefore, deleting these $2N$ gray edges transforms $G(\hat{\Pi}, \hat{\Gamma})$ into a graph $G(\Pi, \Gamma)$ which does not depend on capping $\hat{\Gamma}$ (Fig. 4a,b,c,d).

Graph $G(\Pi, \Gamma)$ contains $2N$ vertices of degree 1 corresponding to $2N$ caps of Π (called Π-*caps*) and $2N$ vertices of degree 1 corresponding to $2N$ tails of Γ (called Γ-*tails*). Therefore, $G(\Pi, \Gamma)$ is a collection of cycles and $2N$ paths, each path starting and ending with a black edge. A path is a $\Pi\Pi$-*path* ($\Gamma\Gamma$-*path*) if it starts and ends with Π-caps (Γ-tails) and a $\Pi\Gamma$-*path* if it starts with a Π-cap and ends with a Γ-tail. A vertex in $G(\Pi, \Gamma)$ is a $\Pi\Gamma$-*vertex* if it is a Π-cap in a $\Pi\Gamma$-path and a $\Pi\Pi$-*vertex* if it is Π-cap in a $\Pi\Pi$-path. $\Gamma\Pi$- and $\Gamma\Gamma$-vertices are defined similarly (see Fig. 4d). Let $p(\Pi, \Gamma)$ be the number of $\Pi\Pi$-paths (or equivalently, $\Gamma\Gamma$-paths) in $G(\Pi, \Gamma)$.

Define $b(\Pi, \Gamma)$ as the number of black edges in $G(\Pi, \Gamma)$ and $c(\Pi, \Gamma)$ as the overall number of cycles and paths in $G(\Pi, \Gamma)$. We define the notions of interleaving cycles/paths, oriented and unoriented components, etc. in the graph $G(\Pi, \Gamma)$ in a usual way by making no distinction between cycles and paths in $G(\Pi, \Gamma)$. We say that a vertex π_j is *inside* a component U of π if $j \in [\bar{U}_{min}, \bar{U}_{max}]$. An intrachromosomal component for genomes Π and Γ is called a *real* component if it has neither a Π-cap nor a Γ-tail inside.

For genomes Π and Γ define $\mathcal{RU}(\Pi, \Gamma)$ as the set of real components and $\mathcal{IU}(\Pi, \Gamma)$ as the set of intrachromosomal components (as defined by the graph $G(\Pi, \Gamma)$). Clearly $\mathcal{RU}(\Pi, \Gamma) \subseteq \mathcal{IU}(\Pi, \Gamma)$. Hurdles for the set $\mathcal{RU}(\Pi, \Gamma)$ are called *real-knots*. Let RK be the set of real-knots (*i.e.* hurdles for the set $\mathcal{RU}(\Pi, \Gamma)$) and K be the set of knots (*i.e.* hurdles for the set $\mathcal{IU}(\Pi, \Gamma)$). A knot from the set $K \setminus RK$ is a *semi-knot* if it does not contain a $\Pi\Pi$- or $\Gamma\Gamma$-vertex inside. Denote the number of real-knots and semi-knots for genomes Π and Γ as $r(\Pi, \Gamma)$ and $s(\Pi, \Gamma)$, respectively.

The following theorem gives a tight estimate for genomic distance in terms of five parameters (see Hannenhalli and Pevzner, 1995c for duality theorem in full strength).

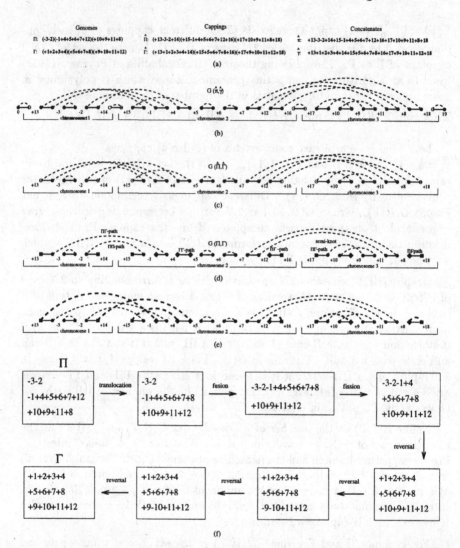

Figure 4: (a) Genomes Π and Γ, cappings $\hat{\Pi}$ and $\hat{\Gamma}$ and concatenates $\hat{\pi}$ and $\hat{\gamma}$. (b) Graph $G(\hat{\pi}, \hat{\gamma})$. Tails are shown as white circles. (c) Graph $G(\hat{\Pi}, \hat{\Gamma})$ is obtained from $G(\hat{\pi}, \hat{\gamma})$ by deleting the tails. Caps are shown as white circles. (d) Graph $G(\Pi, \Gamma)$ with 4 cycles and 6 paths ($c(\Pi, \Gamma) = 10$). Π-caps are shown as boxes while Γ-tails are shown by diamonds. For genomes Π and Γ, $b(\Pi, \Gamma) = 15$, $r(\Pi, \Gamma) = 0$, $p(\Pi, \Gamma) = 1$, $s(\Pi, \Gamma) = 1$ and $d(\Pi, \Gamma) = 15 - 10 + 1 + 0 + \lceil \frac{1}{2} \rceil = 7$. (e) Graph $G(\hat{\Pi}, \hat{\Gamma})$ corresponding to an optimal capping of $\hat{\Gamma} = (+13 + 1 + 2 + 3 + 4 - 15)(-14 + 5 + 6 + 7 + 8 + 18)(+17 + 9 + 10 + 11 + 12 + 16)$. Added gray edges are shown by thick dashed lines. (f) optimal sorting of Π into Γ with seven rearrangements.

Theorem 9

$$b(\Pi, \Gamma) - c(\Pi, \Gamma) + p(\Pi, \Gamma) + r(\Pi, \Gamma) + \lceil \frac{s(\Pi, \Gamma)}{2} \rceil \le d(\Pi, \Gamma) \le$$

$$b(\Pi, \Gamma) - c(\Pi, \Gamma) + p(\Pi, \Gamma) + r(\Pi, \Gamma) + \lceil \frac{s(\Pi, \Gamma)}{2} \rceil + 1$$

7 Applications

As was mentioned already, physical maps usually do not provide information about directions of genes and thus lead to representation of a genome as an *unsigned* permutation π. Hannenhalli and Pevzner, 1995b devised an algorithm *Reversal_Sort* which might guide a biologist in the choice of the desired degree of resolution of the constructed physical maps. Low-resolution physical maps usually contain many singletons and, as a result, rearrangement scenarios for such maps are hard to analyze. *Reversal_Sort* runs in polynomial time if the number of singletons is $O(\log n)$. It suggests biologists that $O(\log n)$ singletons is the desired trade-off of resolution for cross-hybridization physical mapping in molecular evolution studies. If the number of singletons is large, a biologist might choose additional experiments (*i.e.* sequencing of some areas) to resolve the ambiguities in gene directions. Below we describe a few applications of *Reversal_Sort*.

Kececioglu and Sankoff, 1993 described a family of lower and upper bounds for reversal distance and implemented a program based on these bounds and sparse linear programming. The program performs remarkably well on animal mitochondrial DNA (mtDNA), in particular Kececioglu and Sankoff, 1993 report computing a most parsimonious rearrangement scenario for yeast *S. pombe* versus human mtDNA containing 19(!)reversals. However, for a more complicated case of flatworm *Ascaris suum* versus human mtDNA their program did not find the reversal distance (although they found the scenario containing 27 reversals and provided a lower bound of 25 reversals). Since *Ascaris suum* mtDNA extensively rearranged as compared to human mtDNA, the reversal distance between corresponding permutations is close to reversal distance between "random" permutations. *Reversal_Sort* finds an optimal scenario with 26 reversals even without branch-and-bound optimization of the code.

Another complicated case of rearrangements was discovered by Fauron and Havlik, 1989 who compared maize mitochondrial genomes of normal type (N) and cytoplasmic male sterile type (T). They came to the conclusion that at least 30 different reversals/deletions/insertions of genes have occurred during the course of evolution. *Reversal_Sort* found that the differences in gene orders of these genomes can be explained by just 17 reversals (this optimal sorting by reversals ignores potential deletions and insertions of genes).

An extremely complicated case of rearrangements in green algae was recently discovered by Boudreau et al., 1994 . They constructed a physical map of

Chlamydomonas moewusii versus *Chlamydomonas reinhardtii* with 84 genes/exons
(27 singletons, 10 2-strips and 9 long strips) indicating that ancestral bacterial
operons that characterize the chloroplast genome organization of land plants
have been disrupted before the emergence of the genus *Chlamydomonas*. A
most parsimonious rearrangement scenario for *Chlamydomonas moewusii* versus *Chlamydomonas reinhardtii* includes 34 reversals and represents the most
complicated known case of rearrangements in organelles. The running time of
Reversal_Sort on this example was 24 hours on DEC-Alpha. In the further
development of this project Boudreau and Turmel, 1995 constructed a physical
map of *Chlamydomonas gelatinosa* versus *Chlamydomonas reinhardtii*. In this
case Boudreau et al., 1995 were able to limit the number of singletons to just 4
and the running time of *Reversal_Sort* was just three minutes on DEC-Alpha.

Bafna and Pevzner, 1995a and Hannenhalli and Pevzner, 1995c applied the
developed genome rearrangement algorithms to analyze evolution of mammalian
chromosomes. The large number of conserved segments in the maps of man and
mouse suggest that multiple chromosomal rearrangements have occurred since
the divergence of lineages leading to humans and mice. Nadeau and Taylor,
1984 estimate of 178 ± 39 rearrangements in man-mouse evolution survived a
ten-fold increase in the amount of the comparative man/mouse mapping information; the new estimate based on the latest data (Copeland et al., 1993)
changed little compared to Nadeau and Taylor, 1984. However, these estimates
are non-constructive. Recently Hannenhalli and Pevzner, 1995c constructed a
most parsimonious rearrangement scenario of man-mouse evolution which closely
fits the Copeland et al., 1993 estimate.

Extreme conservation of genes on X chromosomes across mammalian species
provides an opportunity to study evolutionary history of X chromosome independently of the rest of the genomes thus reducing computational complexity of the
problem. According to Ohno's law (Ohno, 1967) gene content of X chromosomes
is assumed to have remained the same throughout mammalian development in
the last 125 million years. However, the order of genes on X chromosomes has
been disrupted several times, even though synteny has been almost completely
conserved. Our analysis of the latest data on comparative man/mouse mapping
demonstrates that in order to explain the evolutionary history of X chromosomes, a larger than previously postulated (Davisson, 1987, Lyon, 1988) number
of rearrangements are required (Bafna and Pevzner, 1995a).

Of course, gene orders for just two genomes are hardly sufficient to delineate a correct rearrangement scenario. Comparative gene mapping has made
possible the generation of comparative maps for 28 species representing different
mammalian orders (O'Brien and Graves, 1991). However, the resolution of these
maps is significantly lower than the resolution of human-mouse map. Since the
conventional comparative physical mapping is very laborious and time consuming, one can hardly expect that the tremendous efforts involved in obtaining the
human-mouse map will be repeated for other mammalian genomes. However,
newly developed experimental technique called *chromosome painting* allows one

to derive gene order without actually building an accurate "gene-based" map! In the past, the applications of chromosome painting were limited to primates (Jauch et al., 1992) and the attempts to extend this approach to other mammals were not successful because of DNA sequence diversity between distantly related species. Very recently, an improved version of chromosome painting, called *ZOO-FISH* that is capable of detecting homologous chromosome fragments in distant mammalian species was developed (Scherthan et al., 1994). Recently, Rettenberg et al., reported a successful completion of the human-pig chromosome painting project. In a relatively inexpensive experiment Rettenberg et al., 1995 identified 47 conserved blocks common to human and pigs and used these data for analyzing human-pig evolution. The success of the human-pig chromosome painting project indicates that gene orders of many mammalian species can be generated with ZOO-FISH inexpensively thus providing invaluable new source of data to attack a 100-years old problem of mammalian evolution with a new *constructive* approach versus previous ones based on the statistics of point mutations.

Acknowledgments

We are indebted to Vineet Bafna and Eugene Koonin for many helpful discussions and suggestions.

References

[1] M. Aigner and D. B. West. Sorting by insertion of leading element. *Journal of Combinatorial Theory*, 45:306–309, 1987.

[2] N. Amato, M. Blum, S. Irani, and R. Rubinfeld. Reversing trains: A turn of the century sorting problem. *Journal of Algorithms*, 10:413–428, 1989.

[3] V. Bafna and P. Pevzner. Genome rearrangements and sorting by reversals. In *34th Annual IEEE Symposium on Foundations of Computer Science*, pages 148–157, 1993. (to appear in SIAM J. Computing).

[4] V. Bafna and P. Pevzner. Sorting by reversals: Genome rearrangements in plant organelles and evolutionary history of X chromosome. *Mol. Biol. and Evol.*, 12:239–246, 1995a.

[5] V. Bafna and P. Pevzner. Sorting by transpositions. In *Proc. 6th Annual ACM-SIAM Symposium on Discrete Algorithms*, pages 614–623, 1995b.

[6] E. Boudreau. 1995 (personal communication).

[7] E. Boudreau, C. Otis, and M. Turmel. Conserved gene clusters in the highly rearranged chloroplast genomes of *chlamydomonas moewusii* and *chlamydomonas reinhardtii*. *Plant Molecular Biology*, 24:585–602, 1994.

[8] N. G. Copeland, N. A. Jenkins, D. J. Gilbert, J. T. Eppig, L. J. Maltals, J. C. Miller, W. F. Dietrich, A. Weaver, S. E. Lincoln, R. G. Steen, L. D. Steen, J. H. Nadeau, and E. S. Lander. A genetic linkage map of the mouse: Current applications and future prospects. *Science*, 262:57–65, 1993.

[9] M. Davisson. X-linked genetic homologies between mouse and man. *Genomics*, 1:213–227, 1987.

[10] S. Even and O. Goldreich. The minimum-length generator sequence problem is NP-hard. *Journal of Algorithms*, 2:311–313, 1981.

[11] C. Fauron and M. Havlik. The maize mitochondrial genome of the normal type and the cytoplasmic male sterile type T have very different organization. *Current Genetics*, 15:149–154, 1989.

[12] W. H. Gates and C. H. Papadimitriou. Bounds for sorting by prefix reversals. *Discrete Mathematics*, 27:47–57, 1979.

[13] E. Györi and E. Turan. Stack of pancakes. *Studia Sci. Math. Hungar.*, 13:133–137, 1978.

[14] S. Hannenhalli. Polynomial algorithm for computing translocation distance between genomes. In *Combinatorial Pattern Matching, Proc. 6th Annual Symposium (CPM'95)*, Lecture Notes in Computer Science, pages 162–176. Springer-Verlag, Berlin, 1995.

[15] S. Hannenhalli, C. Chappey, E. Koonin, and P. Pevzner. Scenarios for genome rearrangements: Herpesvirus evolution as a test case. In *Proc. 3rd Intl. Conference on Bioinformatics and Complex Genome Analysis*, pages 91–106, 1995.

[16] S. Hannenhalli and P. Pevzner. Transforming cabbage into turnip (polynomial algorithm for sorting signed permutations by reversals). In *Proc. 27th Annual ACM Symposium on the Theory of Computing*, 1995a. (to appear).

[17] S. Hannenhalli and P. Pevzner. To cut ... or not to cut (applications of comparative physical maps in molecular evolution). Technical Report: CSE-94-074, Department of Computer Science and Engineering, The Pennsylvania State University, 1995b.

[18] S. Hannenhalli and P. Pevzner. Transforming men into mice (polynomial algorithm for genomic distance problem). In *36th Annual IEEE Symposium on Foundations of Computer Science*, 1995c. (to appear).

[19] R. J. Hoffmann, J. L. Boore, and W. M. Brown. A novel mitochondrial genome organization for the blue mussel, *Mytilus edulis*. *Genetics*, 131:397–412, 1992.

[20] S. B. Hoot and J. D. Palmer. Structural rearrangements including parallel inversions within the chloroplast genome of anemone and related genera. *Journal of Molecular Evolution*, 38:274–281, 1994.

[21] A. Jauch, J. Wienberg, Stanyon, N. Arnold, S. Tofanelli, T. Ishida, and T. Cremer. Reconstruction of genomic rearrangements in great apes gibbons by chromosome painting. *Proc. Natl. Acad. Sci.*, 89:8611–8615, 1992.

[22] M. Jerrum. The complexity of finding minimum-length generator sequences. *Theoretical Computer Science*, 36:265–289, 1985.

[23] J. Kececioglu and R. Ravi. Of mice and men: Evolutionary distances between genomes under translocation. In *Proc. 6th Annual ACM-SIAM Symposium on Discrete Algorithms*, pages 604–613, 1995.

[24] J. Kececioglu and D. Sankoff. Exact and approximation algorithms for the inversion distance between two permutations. In *Combinatorial Pattern Matching, Proc. 4th Annual Symposium (CPM'93)*, volume 684 of *Lecture Notes in Computer Science*, pages 87–105. Springer-Verlag, Berlin, 1993. (Extended version has appeared in Algorithmica, 13: 180-210, 1995.).

[25] J. Kececioglu and D. Sankoff. Efficient bounds for oriented chromosome inversion distance. In *Combinatorial Pattern Matching, Proc. 5th Annual Symposium (CPM'94)*, volume 807 of *Lecture Notes in Computer Science 807*, pages 307–325. Springer-Verlag, Berlin, 1994.

[26] E. V. Koonin and V. V. Dolja. Evolution and taxonomy of positive-strand RNA viruses: implications of comparative analysis of amino acid sequences. *Crit. Rev. Biochem. Molec. Biol.*, 28:375–430, 1993.

[27] M. F. Lyon. X-Chromosome Inactivation and the Location and Expression of X-linked Genes. *Am. J. Hum. Genet.*, 42:008–016, 1988.

[28] J. H. Nadeau and B. A. Taylor. Lengths of chromosomal segments conserved since divergence of man and mouse. *Proc. Natl. Acad. Sci. USA*, 81:814–818, 1984.

[29] S. O'Brien and J. Graves. Report of the committee on comparative gene mapping in mammals. *Cytogenet. Cell Genet.*, 58:1124–1151, 1991.

[30] S. Ohno. *Sex chromosomes and sex-linked genes*. Springer, Heidelberg, 1967.

[31] J. D. Palmer and L. A. Herbon. Plant mitochondrial DNA evolves rapidly in structure, but slowly in sequence. *Journal of Molecular Evolution*, 27:87–97, 1988.

[32] P.A. Pevzner and M.S. Waterman. Open combinatorial problems in computational molecular biology. In *3rd Israel Symposium on Theory of Computing and Systems*, pages 158–163. IEEE Computer Society Press, 1995.

[33] L. A. Raubeson and R. K. Jansen. Chloroplast DNA evidence on the ancient evolutionary split in vascular land plants. *Science*, 255:1697–1699, 1992.

[34] G. Rettenberger, C. Klett, U. Zechner, J. Kunz, W. Vogel, and H. Hameister. Visualization of the conservation of synteny between humans and pigs by hetereologous chromosomal painting. *Genomics*, 26:372–378, 1995.

[35] D. Sankoff. Edit distance for genome comparison based on non-local operations. In *Combinatorial Pattern Matching, Proc. 3rd Annual Symposium (CPM'92)*, volume 644 of *Lecture Notes in Computer Science*, pages 121–135. Springer-Verlag, Berlin, 1992.

[36] D. Sankoff, R. Cedergren, and Y. Abel. Genomic divergence through gene rearrangement. In *Molecular Evolution: Computer Analysis of Protein and Nucleic Acid Sequences*, chapter 26, pages 428–438. Academic Press, 1990.

[37] D. Sankoff, G. Leduc, N. Antoine, B. Paquin, B. F. Lang, and R. Cedergren. Gene order comparisons for phylogenetic inference: Evolution of the mitochondrial genome. *Proc. Natl. Acad. Sci. USA*, 89:6575–6579, 1992.

[38] H. Scherthan, T. Cremer, U. Arnason, H. Weier, A. Lima de Faria, and L. Fronicke. Comparative chromosomal painting discloses homologous segments in distantly related mammals. *Nature Genetics*, 6:342–347, April 1994.

[39] A. H. Sturtevant and T. Dobzhansky. Inversions in the third chromosome of wild races of *drosophila pseudoobscura*, and their use in the study of the history of the species. *Proc. Nat. Acad. Sci.*, 22:448–450, 1936.

[40] G. A. Watterson, W. J. Ewens, T. E. Hall, and A. Morgan. The chromosome inversion problem. *Journal of Theoretical Biology*, 99:1–7, 1982.

[41] J. Whiting, M. Pliley, J. Farmer, and D. Jeffery. In situ hybridization analysis of chromosomal homologies in *Drosophila melanogaster* and *Drosophila virilis*. *Genetics*, 122:99–109, 1989.

Algebraic Topology and Distributed Computing
A Primer

Maurice Herlihy[1] and Sergio Rajsbaum[2]

[1] Computer Science Department
Brown University, Providence, RI 02912
herlihy@cs.brown.edu ***
[2] Digital Equipment Corporation, Cambridge Research Lab
One Kendall Square, Cambridge, MA 02139
rajsbaum@crl.dec.com[†]

Abstract. Models and techniques borrowed from classical algebraic topology have recently yielded a variety of new lower bounds and impossibility results for distributed and concurrent computation. This paper explains the basic concepts underlying this approach, and shows how they apply to a simple distributed problem.

1 Introduction

The problem of coordinating concurrent processes remains one of the central problems of distributed computing. Coordination problems arise at all scales in distributed and concurrent systems, ranging from synchronizing data access in tightly-coupled multiprocessors, to allocating data paths in networks. Coordination is difficult because modern multiprocessor systems are inherently *asynchronous*: processes may be delayed without warning for a variety of reasons, including interrupts, pre-emption, cache misses, communication delays, or failures. These delays can vary enormously in scale: a cache miss might delay a process for fewer than ten instructions, a page fault for a few million instructions, and operating system pre-emption for hundreds of millions of instructions. Coordination protocols that do not take such delays into account run the risk that if one process is unexpectedly delayed, then the remaining processes may be unable to make progress.

Recently, techniques and models borrowed from classical algebraic topology have yielded a variety of new lower bounds for coordination problems. This paper is an attempt to explain the basic concepts and techniques underlying these results. We are particularly interested in making the mathematical concepts accessible to the Computer Science community. Although these concepts are

*** Research partly supported by ONR N00014-91-J-4052, ARPA Order 8225.
[†] On leave from Instituto de Matemáticas, U.N.A.M., México. Part of this work was done while visiting the Laboratory for Computer Science, MIT. Partly supported by DGAPA Projects.

abstract, they are elementary, being fully covered in the first chapter of Munkres' standard textbook [18].

Our discussion focuses on a class of problems called *decision tasks*, described in Section 2. In Section 3, we show how decision tasks can be modeled using *simplicial complexes*, a standard combinatorial structure from elementary topology. In Section 4, we review the notion of a *chain complex*, which provides an algebraic vocabulary for describing the topological properties of simplicial complexes. In Section 5, we show how these combinatorial and algebraic notions can be applied to prove a variety of lower bounds for a well-known problem in distributed computing, the *k-set agreement* task [7].

2   Model

A set of $n + 1$ sequential threads of control, called *processes*, communicate by applying operations to objects in shared memory. Examples of shared objects include message queues, read/write variables, test-and-set variables, or objects of arbitrary abstract type. Processes are asynchronous: they run at arbitrarily varying speeds. Up to t processes may fail. Because the processes are asynchronous, a protocol cannot distinguish a failed process from a slow process.

To distill the notion of a distributed computation to its simplest interesting form, we focus on a simple but important class of problems called *decision tasks*. We are given a set of $n + 1$ sequential processes $P_0, \ldots, P_n$. Each process starts out with a private *input value*, typically subject to task-specific constraints. The processes communicate for a while, then each process chooses a private *output value*, also subject to task-specific constraints, and then halts.

Decision tasks are intended to model "reactive" systems such as databases, file systems, or flight control systems. An input value represents information entering the system from the outside world, such as a character typed at a keyboard, a message from another computer, or a signal from a sensor. An output value models an effect on the outside world, such as an irrevocable decision to commit a transaction, to dispense cash, or to launch a missile.

Perhaps the simplest example of a decision task is *consensus* [9]. Each process starts with an input value and chooses an output value. All output values must agree, and each output value must have been some process's input value. If the input values are boolean, the task is called *binary consensus*. The consensus task was originally studied as an idealization of the transaction commitment problem, in which a number of database sites must agree on whether to commit or abort a distributed transaction.

A natural generalization of consensus is *k-set agreement* [7]. Like consensus, each process's output value must be some process's input value. Unlike consensus, which requires that all processes agree, k-set agreement requires that no more than k distinct output values be chosen. Consensus is 1-set agreement.

A program that solves a decision task is called a *protocol*. A protocol is *t-resilient* if any non-faulty process will finish the protocol in a fixed number of steps, regardless of failures or delays by up to t other processes. A protocol is *wait-free* if it tolerates failures or delay by all but one of the processes.

3   Combinatorial Structures

Formally, an initial or final state of a process is a *vertex*, $\mathbf{v} = \langle P_i, v_i \rangle$, a pair consisting of a process id and a value (either input or output). A set of $d+1$ mutually compatible initial or final process states is modeled as a *d-dimensional simplex*, (or *d*-simplex). A simplex is *properly colored* if each vertex is labeled with a distinct process id. The complete set of possible initial (or final) process states is represented by a set of properly colored simplexes, closed under containment, called a *simplicial complex* (or complex). The *dimension* of $\mathcal{C}$ is the dimension of a simplex of largest dimension in $\mathcal{C}$. Where convenient, we use superscripts to indicate dimensions of simplexes and complexes. The k-th *skeleton* of a complex, $skel^k(\mathcal{C}^n)$, is the subcomplex consisting of all simplexes of dimension k or less. The set of process ids associated with simplex S^n is denoted by $ids(S^n)$, and the set of values by $vals(S^n)$. S^m is a (proper) *face* of S^n if the vertexes of S^m are a (proper) subset of the vertices of S^n. If $\mathcal{K}$ and $\mathcal{L}$ are complexes, a *simplicial map* $\phi : \mathcal{K} \to \mathcal{L}$ carries vertexes of $\mathcal{K}$ to vertexes of $\mathcal{L}$ so that simplexes are preserved.

It is often convenient to visualize vertexes, simplexes, and complexes as point sets in Euclidian space. A vertex is simply a point, and an n-simplex is the convex hull of $n+1$ affinely-independent[5] vertexes. A complex is represented by a set of (geometric) simplexes arranged so that that each pair of simplexes intersects either in a common face, or not at all. The point set occupied by such a complex is called its *polyhedron*. Although we use this geometric interpretation for illustrations and informal discussions, we do not use it in our formal treatment.

A *decision task* for $n + 1$ processes is given by an *input complex* $\mathcal{I}$, an *output complex* $\mathcal{O}$, and a map Δ carrying each input n-simplex of $\mathcal{I}$ to a set of n-simplexes of $\mathcal{O}$. This map associates with each initial state of the system (an input n-simplex) the set of legal final states (output n-simplexes). It is convenient to extend Δ to simplexes of lower dimension: when $n - t \leq m < n$, $\Delta(S^m)$ is the set of legal final states in executions where only the indicated $m + 1$ processes take steps.

For example, the input complex for binary consensus is constructed by assigning independent binary values to $n+1$ processes. We call this complex the *binary n-sphere*, because its polyhedron is homeomorphic to an n-sphere (exercise left to the reader). The output complex consists of two disjoint n-simplexes, corresponding to decision values 0 and 1. Figure 1 illustrates the input and output complexes for two-process binary consensus.

As an example of an interesting output complex, consider the *renaming task* [1], in which each process is given a unique input name taken from a large name space, and must choose a unique output name taken from a much smaller name space. Figure 2 shows the output complex for the three-process renaming task

---

[5] $\mathbf{v}_0, \ldots, \mathbf{v}_n$ are affinely independent if $\mathbf{v}_1 - \mathbf{v}_0, \ldots, \mathbf{v}_n - \mathbf{v}_0$ are linearly independent.

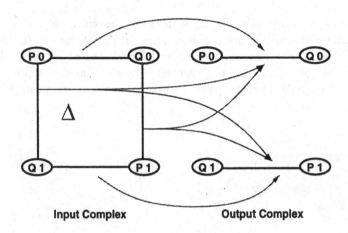

Fig. 1. Input and Output Complexes for 2-Process Consensus

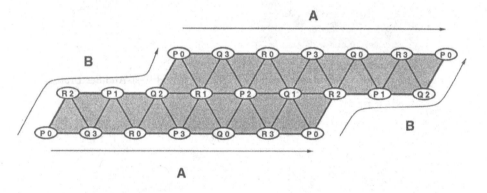

Fig. 2. Output Complex for 3-Process Renaming with 4 Names

using four output names. Notice that the two edges marked A are identical, as are the two edges marked B. By identifying these edges, we can see that this complex has a polyhedron homeomorphic to a torus.

At the end of a protocol, the process's *local state* is its view of the computation: its input value followed by the sequence of operations (including arguments and results) applied to shared objects. It is convenient to view a process as executing a protocol for a fixed number of steps, and then choosing its output value by applying a task-specific *decision map* δ to its local state.

We can treat any protocol as an "uninterpreted" protocol simply by treating each process's local state as its decision value (i.e., omitting the task-specific decision map δ). This uninterpreted protocol itself defines a complex $\mathcal{P}$, called its *protocol complex*. Each vertex **v** in this complex is labeled with a process id and a local state such that there exist some execution of the protocol in which process $id(\mathbf{v})$ finishes the protocol with local state $val(\mathbf{v})$. A simplex

$T^m = (\mathbf{t}_0, \ldots, \mathbf{t}_m)$ is in this complex if there is an execution of the protocol in which each process $id(\mathbf{t}_i)$ finishes the protocol with local state $val(\mathbf{t}_i)$ (i.e., the vertexes of any simplex are compatible local states). For an input simplex S^m, let $\mathcal{P}(S^m)$ be the subcomplex of $\mathcal{P}$ generated by executions in which only the processes in $ids(S^m)$ take steps, starting with input values from $vals(S^m)$.

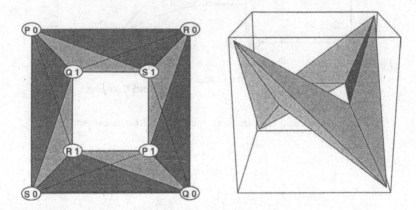

Fig. 3. Two Views of Protocol Complex for Single-Round Test-And-Set Protocol

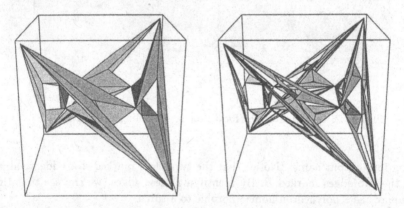

Fig. 4. Protocol Complexes for Multi-Round Test-And-Set Protocols

For example, consider a system in which asynchronous processes communicate by applying *test-and-set*[6] operations to shared variables. Figure 3 shows two views of the protocol complex for a a four-process one-round protocol in which processes P and Q share one test-and-set variable, and R and S share another. Both variables are initialized to 0, and each process executes a single test-and-set

---

[6] Recall that *test-and-set* atomically writes a 1 to a variable and returns the variable's previous contents.

operation and halts. This complex consists of four tetrahedrons, corresponding to the four possible outcomes of the two test-and-set operations. The left-hand side shows a schematic view of the complex, where each vertex is labeled with a process id and the result of the operation, while the right-hand side shows the same complex in three-dimensional perspective. Figure 4 shows two more protocol complexes for protocols in which the processes respectively iterate two and three-round test-and-set protocols, using fresh, 0-initialized variables for each round.

What does it mean for a protocol to solve a decision task? Recall that a process chooses a decision value by applying a decision map δ to its local state when the protocol is complete. Expressed in our terminology, a protocol solves a decision task $\langle \mathcal{I}, \mathcal{O}, \Delta \rangle$ if and only if there exists a simplicial map $\delta : \mathcal{P} \to \mathcal{O}$ such that for all $S^m \in \mathcal{I}$, and all $T^m \in \mathcal{P}(S^m)$, $\delta(T^m) \in \Delta(S^m)$, for $n - t \leq m \leq n$. This definition is just a formal way of stating that every execution of the protocol must yield an output value assignment permitted by the decision task. This might seem like a roundabout way to formulate such an obvious property, but it has an important and useful advantage. We have moved from an operational notion of a decision task, expressed in terms of computations unfolding in time, to a purely combinatorial description.

We are now ready to describe our strategy for proving impossibility results. To show that a decision task has no protocol in a given model of computation, it is enough to show that no decision map δ exists. Because decision maps are simplicial, they preserve topological structure. If we can show that a class of protocols generates protocol complexes that are "topologically incompatible" with the task's output complex, then we have established impossibility.

4   Algebraic Structures

So far, our model is entirely combinatorial. To analyze the topological structure of simplicial complexes, however, we now need to introduce some algebraic concepts. Our discussion closely follows that of Munkres [18, Section 1.13], which the reader is encouraged to consult for more details.

Let $\mathcal{K}$ be an n-dimensional simplicial complex, and $S^q = (s_0, \ldots, s_q)$ a q-simplex of $\mathcal{K}$. An *orientation* for S^q is an equivalence class of orderings on $s_0, \ldots, s_q$, consisting of one particular ordering and all even permutations of it. For example, an orientation of a 1-simplex (s_0, s_1) is just a direction, either from s_0 to s_1, or vice-versa. An orientation of a 2-simplex (s_0, s_1, s_2) can be either "clockwise," as in (s_0, s_1, s_2), or "counterclockwise," as in (s_0, s_2, s_1) (see Figure 5). By convention, simplexes are oriented in increasing subscript order unless explicitly stated otherwise.

A *q-chain* of $\mathcal{K}$ is a formal sum of oriented q-simplexes: $\sum_{i=0}^{\ell} \lambda_i \cdot S_i^q$, where each λ_i is an integer, and the S_i^q range over the q-simplexes of $\mathcal{K}$. When writing chains, we typically omit q-simplexes with zero coefficients, unless they are all zero, when we simply write 0. We write $1 \cdot S^q$ as S^q and $-1 \cdot S^q$ as $-S^q$. We identify $-S^q$ with S^q having the opposite orientation. The q-chains of $\mathcal{K}$ form a free Abelian group $C_q(\mathcal{K})$, called the q-th *chain group* of $\mathcal{K}$. For technical reasons, it is convenient to define $C_{-1}(\mathcal{K})$ to be the (infinite cyclic) group of integers under addition.

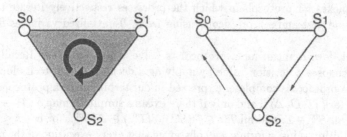

Fig. 5. An Oriented Simplex and its Boundary

Let $S^q = (\mathbf{s}_0, \ldots \mathbf{s}_q)$ be an oriented q-simplex. Define $face_i(S^q)$, the ith face of S^q, to be the $(q-1)$-simplex $(\mathbf{s}_0, \ldots, \hat{\mathbf{s}}_i, \ldots, \mathbf{s}_q)$, where circumflex denotes omission. The *boundary* operator $\partial_q : C_q(\mathcal{K}) \to C_{q-1}(\mathcal{K})$, $q > 0$, is defined on simplexes:

$$\partial S^q = \sum_{i=0}^{q} (-1)^i \cdot face_i(S^q),$$

and extends additively to chains: $\partial(\alpha_0 + \alpha_1) = \partial\alpha_0 + \partial\alpha_1$. The zero-dimensional boundary operator[7] $\partial_0 : C_0(\mathcal{K}) \to C_{-1}(\mathcal{K})$ is defined by $\partial_0(\mathbf{s}) = 1$, for each vertex $\mathbf{s}$. The boundary operator has the important property that applying it twice causes chains to vanish:

$$\partial_{q-1}\partial_q \alpha = 0. \tag{1}$$

The boundary operator is illustrated in Figure 5. Henceforth, we usually omit subscripts from boundary operators.

We illustrate these concepts with an example. Let $S^2 = (\mathbf{s}_0, \mathbf{s}_1, \mathbf{s}_2)$ be an oriented 2-simplex (a "solid" triangle), and $\dot{S}^1$ the complex of its proper faces (a "hollow" triangle). The complex $\dot{S}^1$ includes three 0-simplexes (vertexes): $\mathbf{s}_0$, $\mathbf{s}_1$, and $\mathbf{s}_2$, and three 1-simplexes: $S_i^1 = face_i(S^2)$, $0 \le i \le 2$. The boundaries for each of these simplexes are shown in Figure 7. The 0-th chain group of $\dot{S}^1$, $C_0(\dot{S}^1)$, is generated by the $\mathbf{s}_i$, meaning that all 0-chains have the form

$$\lambda_0 \cdot \mathbf{s}_0 + \lambda_1 \cdot \mathbf{s}_1 + \lambda_2 \cdot \mathbf{s}_2,$$

where the λ_i are integers. The first chain group, $C_1(\dot{S}^1)$, is generated by the S_i^1, and all 1-chains have the form

$$\lambda_0 \cdot S_0^1 + \lambda_1 \cdot S_1^1 + \lambda_2 \cdot S_2^1,$$

---

[7] Munkres [18] calls this operator an *augmentation*, and denotes it by ϵ.

where the S_0^1 each have standard orientation. Since $\dot{S}^1$ contains no simplexes of higher dimension, the higher chain groups are trivial.

A q-chain α is a *boundary* if $\alpha = \partial\beta$ for some $(q+1)$-chain β, and it is a *cycle* if $\partial\alpha = 0$. The boundary chains form a group $B_q(\mathcal{K}) = im(\partial_{q+1})$, and the cycles form a group $Z_q(\mathcal{K}) = ker(\partial_q)$. Equation 1 implies that $B_q(\mathcal{K})$ is a subgroup of $Z_q(\mathcal{K})$, and their quotient group is called the qth *homology group*:[8]

$$H_q(\mathcal{K}) = Z_q(\mathcal{K})/B_q(\mathcal{K}).$$

Informally, homology groups measure the extent to which a complex has holes. Any non-zero element of $H_q(\mathcal{K})$ is a q-cycle but not a q-boundary, corresponding to the intuitive notion of a q-dimensional "hole". Conversely, if $H_q(\mathcal{K}) = 0$ (the trivial single-element group), then every q-cycle is a q-boundary, so $\mathcal{K}$ has no "holes" of dimension q. $H_0(\mathcal{K}) = 0$ if and only if $\mathcal{K}$ is connected. If $H_q(\mathcal{K}) = 0$ for every q, we say that $\mathcal{K}$ is *acyclic*.

For example, $H_0(\dot{S}^1)$ is trivial, because $\dot{S}^1$ is connected. $H_1(\dot{S}^1)$ is non-trivial: the chain ∂S^2 is a cycle (because $\partial\partial S^2 = 0$), but not a boundary (because S^2 is not a simplex of $\dot{S}^1$). It can be shown that $H_1(\dot{S}^1)$ is infinite cyclic, generated by the equivalence class of ∂S^2 [18, 31.8].

The *chain complex* $C(\mathcal{K})$ is the sequence of groups and homomorphisms $\{C_q(\mathcal{K}), \partial_q\}$. Let $C(\mathcal{K}) = \{C_q(\mathcal{K}), \partial_q\}$ and $C(\mathcal{L}) = \{C_q(\mathcal{L}), \partial_q'\}$ be chain complexes for simplicial complexes $\mathcal{K}$ and $\mathcal{L}$. A *chain map* ϕ is a family of homomorphisms.

$$\phi_q : C_q(\mathcal{K}) \to C_q(\mathcal{L}),$$

that commute with the boundary operator: $\partial_q' \circ \phi_q = \phi_{q-1} \circ \partial_q$. (In dimension -1, ϕ_{-1} is just the identity map.) Chain maps thus preserve cycles and boundaries.

Recall that a simplicial map from $\mathcal{K}$ to $\mathcal{L}$ carries vertexes of $\mathcal{K}$ to vertexes of $\mathcal{L}$ so that every simplex of $\mathcal{K}$ maps to a simplex of $\mathcal{L}$. Any simplicial map ϕ induces a chain map $\phi_\#$ from $C(\mathcal{K})$ to $C(\mathcal{L})$: when $\phi(S^q)$ is of dimension q, $\phi_\#(S^q) = \phi(S^q)$, otherwise $\phi_\#(S^q) = 0$. Note, however, that not all chain maps are induced by simplicial maps. Henceforth, we abuse notion by omitting subscripts and sharp signs from chain maps. In this paper, we define chain maps by giving their values on simplexes (the chain group generators) and extending additively.

If $\phi, \psi : C(\mathcal{K}) \to C(\mathcal{L})$ are chain maps, then a *chain homotopy* from ϕ to ψ is a family of homomorphisms

$$D_q : C_q(\mathcal{K}) \to C_{q+1}(\mathcal{L}),$$

such that

$$\partial_{q+1}' D_q + D_{q-1} \partial_q = \phi_q - \psi_q.$$

Very roughly, if two chain maps are homotopic, then one can be deformed into the other; see Munkres [18] for intuitive justification for this definition.

---

[8] Strictly speaking, these are the *reduced* homology groups [18, p.71].

Definition 1. An *acyclic carrier* from $\mathcal{K}$ to $\mathcal{L}$ is a function Σ that assigns to each simplex S^q of $\mathcal{K}$ a non-empty subcomplex of $\mathcal{L}$ such that (1) $\Sigma(S^q)$ is acyclic, and (2) if S^p is a face of S^q, then $\Sigma(S^p) \subseteq \Sigma(S^q)$.

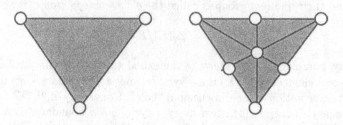

Fig. 6. The Complex $\mathcal{S}^2$ and a Subdivision

For example, a *subdivision* of a complex is an acyclic carrier. Informally, a complex is subdivided by partitioning each component simplex into smaller simplexes, as illustrated in Figure 6. Here, the acyclic carrier maps the 2-simplex S^2 to the entire subdivided complex, and each face S_i^1 to the corresponding subdivided face. While every subdivision is an acyclic carrier, an acyclic carrier need not be a subdivision.

A homomorphism $\phi : C_q(\mathcal{K}) \to C_q(\mathcal{L})$ is *carried* by Σ if each simplex appearing with a non-zero coefficient in $\phi(S^m)$ is in the subcomplex $\Sigma(S^m)$.

Theorem 2 [Acyclic Carrier Theorem]. *Let Σ be an acyclic carrier from $\mathcal{K}$ to $\mathcal{L}$.*

(1) *If ϕ and ψ are two chain maps from $C(\mathcal{K})$ to $C(\mathcal{L})$ that are carried by Σ, then there exists a chain homotopy of ϕ to ψ that is also carried by Σ.*

(2) *There exists a chain map from $C(\mathcal{K})$ to $C(\mathcal{L})$ that is carried by Σ.*

A proof of this theorem can be found in Munkres's text [18, 13.3]. The following lemma is an immediate consequence of the definitions.

Lemma 3. *If $\phi, \psi : C(\mathcal{K}) \to C(\mathcal{L})$ are both carried by Σ, and for each S^q in $\mathcal{K}$, $q = \dim(S^q) = \dim(\Sigma(S^q))$, then $C_{q+1}(\Sigma(S^q)) = 0$, $D_i = 0$ for all i, and ϕ and ψ are equal chain maps.*

Returning to our example, the rotation map $\rho : \dot{S}^1 \to \dot{S}^1$ defined by $\rho(\mathbf{s}_i) = \mathbf{s}_{i+1 \bmod 3}$ induces a chain map $\rho : C(\dot{S}^1) \to C(\dot{S}^1)$, shown in Figure 7. To verify that ρ is a chain map, it suffices to check that $\rho(\partial S_i^1) = \partial \rho(S_i^1)$. The identity map $\iota : \dot{S}^1 \to \dot{S}^1$ also induces a chain map $\iota : C(\dot{S}^1) \to C(\dot{S}^1)$. We now show that ι and ρ are chain homotopic, by displaying both an acyclic carrier Σ, and an explicit chain homotopy D. $\Sigma(\mathbf{s}_i)$ is the complex consisting of $S_{i-1 \bmod 3}^1$ and its vertexes, and $\Sigma(S_i^1)$ is the subcomplex of $\dot{S}^1$ containing S_i^1, $\rho(S_i^1)$, and their vertexes. Both ι and ρ are carried by Σ, and both $\Sigma(\mathbf{s}_i)$ and $\Sigma(S_i^1)$ are acyclic

	s_0	s_1	s_2	S_0^1	S_1^1	S_2^1
∂	1	1	1	$s_2 - s_1$	$s_2 - s_0$	$s_1 - s_0$
ρ	s_1	s_2	s_0	$-S_1^1$	$-S_2^1$	S_0^1
D	$-S_2^1$	$-S_0^1$	S_1^1	0	0	0
ϕ	s_0	s_1	s_2	$S_0^1 + \partial S^2$	$S_1^1 - \partial S^2$	$S_2^1 + \partial S^2$

Fig. 7. Maps used in Extended Example

(being contractible). The chain homotopy D is given in Figure 7. It is easily verified that

$$(D\partial + \partial D)(S) = (\iota - \rho)(S).$$

Although every simplicial map induces a chain map, some chain maps are not induced by any simplicial map. Consider the chain map ϕ given in Figure 7. Notice that $\phi(\partial S^2) = 4 \cdot \partial S^2$, so this map "wraps" the triangle boundary around itself four times, something no simplicial map could do. This map is not chain homotopic to ι or ρ, which "wrap around" only once.

5   An Application

Recall that in the k-set agreement task [7], each process is required to choose some process's input value, and the set of values chosen should have size at most k. We first give a theorem specifying an algebraic property that prevents a protocol from solving k-set agreement, and then we apply this theorem to a variety of different models of computation. The arguments presented here are taken from Herlihy and Rajsbaum [13].

Theorem 4. *Let S^ℓ be a simplex each of whose vertexes is labeled with a distinct input value, and $\mathcal{S}^\ell$ the complex of its faces. Let Π be a protocol, $\mathcal{P}$ its protocol complex, and δ its decision map. If there exists an acyclic carrier Σ from $\mathcal{S}^\ell$ to $\mathcal{P}$ such that*

$$vals(\delta(\Sigma(S))) = vals(S) \tag{2}$$

for all simplexes S in $\mathcal{S}^\ell$, then Π cannot solve k-set agreement for $k \leq \ell$.

Proof. Let $\pi : C(\mathcal{O}) \to C(\mathcal{S}^\ell)$ be the chain map induced by the simplicial map sending $\langle P_i, v_j \rangle$ to the vertex of $\mathcal{S}^\ell$ with value v_j. The acyclic carrier theorem guarantees a chain map $\sigma : C(\mathcal{S}^\ell) \to C(\mathcal{P})$ carried by Σ. By slight abuse of notation, let δ be the chain map induced by the (simplicial) decision map δ. We have:

$$C(\mathcal{S}^\ell) \xrightarrow{\sigma} C(\mathcal{P}) \xrightarrow{\delta} C(\mathcal{O}) \xrightarrow{\pi} C(\mathcal{S}^\ell)$$

Let $\phi : C(\mathcal{S}^\ell) \to C(\mathcal{S}^\ell)$ be the composition of σ, δ, and π. Let Φ be the acyclic carrier from $\mathcal{S}^\ell$ to itself, $\Phi(S^i) = \mathcal{S}^i$, and ι the identity chain map on $\mathcal{S}^\ell$. Thus ι is carried by Φ. Equation 2 implies that Φ is an acyclic carrier also for ϕ.

Because $\dim(S^i) = i = \dim(\Phi(S^i))$, Lemma 3 implies that the two maps are equal. Therefore $\iota(S^\ell) = \phi(S^\ell) = S^\ell$.

Assume for contradiction that $k \leq \ell$. In each execution, however, no more than ℓ values are chosen, implying that π reduces the dimension of every ℓ-simplex. The chain map π thus sends every ℓ-simplex to the 0 chain, so $\pi \circ \delta \circ \sigma(S^\ell) = \phi(S^\ell) = 0$, a contradiction. $\square$

We now show how to apply Theorem 4. Consider a model in which processes communicate by reading and writing shared variables. For any wait-free protocol, Herlihy and Shavit [14] showed that $\mathcal{P}(S^m)$ is acyclic for every input simplex S^m, $0 \leq m \leq n$. Let S^n be an input simplex where each vertex has a distinct input. The map Σ_{WF} that assigns to each face S^m of S^n the protocol subcomplex $\mathcal{P}(S^m)$ is an acyclic carrier. The only input values read or written in any execution in $\mathcal{P}(S^m)$ are the values from S^m, so each process must decide some value from $vals(S^m)$, and therefore Σ_{WF} satisfies the conditions of Theorem 4.

Corollary 5. *There is no wait-free read/write n-consensus protocol [4, 14, 20].*

For t-resilient protocols, a similar argument shows:

Corollary 6. *There is no t-resilient read/write t-consensus protocol.*

Although read/write memories are important from a theoretical point of view, modern multiprocessor architectures provide a variety of more powerful synchronization primitives, including test-and-set, fetch-and-add, compare-and-swap, and load-linked/store-conditional operations. How do these primitives affect the ability to solve k-set agreement? One way to classify these synchronization primitives is by *consensus number* [11, 16]: how many processes can solve consensus using such primitives. For example, test-and-set has consensus number 2, meaning that protocols using read, write, and test-and-set operations can solve consensus for two processes, but not three.

There is a direct connection between an object's consensus number and the homology of its protocol complexes. Consider a system in which processes share both read/write variables and objects that allow any c processes to reach consensus. Using shared objects that solve consensus among c processes, Herlihy and Rajsbaum [12] showed that it is possible to solve k-set agreement for $k = \lceil (n + 1)/c \rceil$ (via an easy protocol, left to the reader), but for no lower value of k. In other words, for any protocol complex $\mathcal{P}$ in this model, $\mathcal{P}(S^n)$ has no holes of dimension less than $\lceil (n + 1)/c \rceil - 1$ (i.e., these low-order homology groups are trivial). This result is illustrated by the protocol complexes of Figures 3 and 4: here, $n = 3$ and $c = 2$. Each of these complexes has non-trivial homology in dimension $\lceil 4/2 \rceil - 1 = 1$, but trivial homology in dimension $\lceil 4/2 \rceil - 2 = 0$ (being connected). More generally, at one extreme, when $c = 1$, $\mathcal{P}(S^n)$ is acyclic [14]. For higher consensus numbers, however, the complex may have holes. If the consensus number is low, then holes appear only in higher dimensions, but as the consensus number grows, the holes spread into increasingly lower dimensions. Finally, when $c = n + 1$, the protocol complex may become disconnected.

Let S^j be an input simplex, where $j = \lceil (n+1)/c \rceil - 1$, and $\mathcal{S}^j$ its complex of faces. These observations about the homology of the protocol complex can be exploited to construct an acyclic carrier Σ_c from $\mathcal{S}^j$ to $\mathcal{P}$. This carrier does not directly satisfy Equation 2, because $\Sigma_c(S)$ may include processes not in $ids(S)$. Nevertheless, it is possible to modify the decision values of the processes in $ids(\Sigma_c(S)) - ids(S)$ so as to satisfy Equation 2 (see [12] for details).

Corollary 7. *There is no wait-free ($\lceil (n+1)/c \rceil - 1$)-set agreement protocol if processes share read/write variables and objects with consensus number c [12].*

This result can be further generalized by including objects that allow any m processes to solve j-set agreement, a task we call (m, j)-consensus. There is an acyclic carrier from ℓ-simplexes of $\mathcal{I}$ to $\mathcal{P}$, for $\ell \leq J(n+1)$, where

$$J(u) = j \left\lfloor \frac{u}{m} \right\rfloor + \min\{j, u \bmod m\} - 1. \tag{3}$$

By a similar argument:

Corollary 8. *There is no wait-free $(n+1, J(n+1) - 1)$-consensus protocol if processes share a read/write memory and (m, j)-consensus objects.*

Finally, we turn our attention to synchronous models. Chaudhuri, Herlihy, Lynch, and Tuttle [8] considered a model in which $n+1$ processes communicate by sending messages over a completely connected network. Computation in this model proceeds in a sequence of rounds. In each round, processes send messages to other processes, then receive messages sent to them in the same round, and then perform some local computation and change state. Communication is reliable, but up to t processes can fail by stopping in the middle of the protocol, perhaps after sending only a subset of their messages. Let $\mathcal{P}_r$ be the protocol complex after r rounds. In the *Bermuda Triangle* construction, Chaudhuri et al. identified an acyclic carrier from an ℓ-simplex S^ℓ to $\mathcal{P}_r$, for $r < \lfloor t/\ell \rfloor$, satisfying Equation 2.

Corollary 9. *There is no t-resilient $(n+1, k)$-consensus protocol that takes fewer than $\lfloor t/k \rfloor + 1$ rounds in the synchronous fail-stop message-passing model [8].*

6   Related Work

In 1985, Fischer, Lynch, and Paterson [9] showed that the consensus task has no 1-resilient solution in a system where asynchronous processes communicate by exchanging messages. In 1988, Biran, Moran, and Zaks [3] gave a graph-theoretic characterization of a class of tasks that could be solved in asynchronous message-passing systems in the presence of a single failure.

Herlihy and Shavit [14] were the first to use simplicial complexes to model decision tasks, and to formulate properties of decision tasks in terms of simplicial homology. They showed that the protocol complex for every wait-free read/write protocol is simply connected with trivial homology (i.e., it has no holes). They also give a complete characterization of tasks that have a wait-free solution in read/write memory [14, 15]. Herlihy and Rajsbaum [12] showed that if read/write variables are augmented by more powerful shared objects than read/write registers, then the protocol complexes may have holes (non-trivial homology), but only in the higher dimensions.

The k-set agreement task was first proposed by Soma Chaudhuri [7] in 1989, along with a conjecture that it could not be solved in asynchronous systems. In 1993, three independent research teams, Borowsky and Gafni [4], Herlihy and Shavit [14], and Saks and Zaharoglou [20] proved this conjecture correct.

Attiya, Bar-Noy, Dolev, Koller, Peleg, and Reischuk [1] showed that in asynchronous systems, the renaming task has a solution if the output name space is sufficiently large, but they were unable to demonstrate the existence of a solution for a range of smaller output name spaces. In 1993, Herlihy and Shavit [14] showed that the task has no solution for these smaller name spaces.

Most of the technical content this paper is adapted from Herlihy and Rajsbaum [13], which simplifies the impossibility results of [14] by eliminating the need for certain continuous arguments. Attiya and Rajsbaum [2] take a different approach, proving a number of results about wait-free read/write memory by extending the simplicial model with a combinatorial notion called a "divided image".

In an intriguing recent development, Gafni and Koutsoupias [10] have shown that it is undecidable whether a wait-free read/write protocol exists for three-process tasks, using an argument based on the impossibility of computing the protocol complex's fundamental group, a topological invariant related to the first homology group.

7   Conclusions

We believe that these techniques and models, borrowed from classical algebraic topology, represent a promising new approach to the theory of distributed computing. Because these notions come from a mature branch of mainstream mathematics, the terminology (and to a lesser degree, the notation) is largely standardized, and the formalisms have been thoroughly debugged. Most importantly, however, this model makes it possible to exploit the extensive literature that has accumulated in the century since Poincaré and others invented modern algebraic topology.

We close with a brief summary of some open problems. The problem of classifying the computational power of objects for wait-free computation has attracted the attention of many researchers [5, 6, 16, 17, 19]. We have seen that the protocol complexes for different kinds of objects share certain topological properties: read/write complexes have no holes, set-agreement complexes have no holes below a certain dimension, and so on. It is intriguing to speculate whether some kind of topological classification of protocol complexes might yield a useful computational classification of objects.

We believe the time is ripe to apply these techniques to other tasks, to other models that make different timing or failure assumptions, as well as to long-lived objects that service repeated requests. Finally, most of the results surveyed here are impossibility results; little is known about the complexity of solvable problems in most models.

Acknowledgments

We are grateful to Hagit Attiya, Prasad Chalasani, Alan Fekete, Michaelangelo Grigni, Somesh Jha, Shlomo Moran, Lyle Ramshaw, Amber Settle, Lewis Stiller, Mark Tuttle, and David Wittenberg for their comments.

References

1. H. Attiya, A. Bar-Noy, D. Dolev, D. Peleg, and R. Reischuk. Renaming in an asynchronous environment. *Journal of the ACM*, 37(3):524–548, July 1990.
2. H. Attiya and S. Rajsbaum. A combinatorial topology framework for wait-free computability. Preprint.
3. O. Biran, S. Moran, and S. Zaks. A combinatorial characterization of the distributed tasks which are solvable in the presence of one faulty processor. In *Proceedings 7th Annual ACM Symposium on Principles of Distributed Computing*, pages 263–275, August 1988.
4. E. Borowsky and E. Gafni. Generalized FLP impossibility result for t-resilient asynchronous computations. In *Proceedings 25th Annual ACM Symposium on Theory of Computing*, pages 206–215, May 1993.
5. E. Borowsky, E. Gafni, and Y. Afek. Consensus power makes (some) sense! In *Proceedings 13th Annual ACM Symposium on Principles of Distributed Computing*, pages 363–373, August 1994.
6. T Chandra, V. Hadzilacos, P. Jayanti, and S. Toueg. Wait-freedom vs. t-resiliency and the robustness of wait-free hierarchies. In *Proceedings 13th Annual ACM Symposium on Principles of Distributed Computing*, pages 334–343, August 1994.
7. S. Chaudhuri. Agreement is harder than consensus: Set consensus problems in totally asynchronous systems. In *Proceedings 9th Annual ACM Symposium On Principles of Distributed Computing*, pages 311–234, August 1990.
8. S. Chaudhuri, M.P. Herlihy, N. Lynch, and M.R. Tuttle. A tight lower bound for k-set agreement. In *Proceedings 34th annual IEEE Symposium on Foundations of Computer Science*, pages 206–215, October 1993.
9. M. Fischer, N.A. Lynch, and M.S. Paterson. Impossibility of distributed commit with one faulty process. *Journal of the ACM*, 32(2):374–382, April 1985.
10. E. Gafni and E. Koutsoupias. 3-processor tasks are undecidable. In *Proceedings 14th Annual ACM Symposium on Principles of Distributed Computing*, August 1995.
11. M.P. Herlihy. Wait-free synchronization. *ACM Transactions on Programming Languages and Systems*, 13(1):123–149, January 1991.
12. M.P. Herlihy and S. Rajsbaum. Set consensus using arbitrary objects. In *Proceedings 13th Annual ACM Symposium on Principles of Distributed Computing*, August 1994.

13. M.P. Herlihy and S. Rajsbaum. Algebraic spans. In *Proceedings 14th Annual ACM Symposium on Principles of Distributed Computing*, August 1995.

14. M.P. Herlihy and N. Shavit. The asynchronous computability theorem for *t*-resilient tasks. In *Proceedings 25th Annual ACM Symposium on Theory of Computing*, pages 111–120, May 1993.

15. M.P. Herlihy and N. Shavit. A simple constructive computability theorem for wait-free computation. In *Proceedings 26th Annual ACM Symposium on Theory of Computing*, pages 243–252, May 1994.

16. P. Jayanti. On the robustness of Herlihy's hierarchy. In *Proceedings 12th Annual ACM Symposium on Principles of Distributed Computing*, pages 145–158, August 1993.

17. J. Kleinberg and S. Mullainathan. Resource bounds and combinations of consensus objects. In *Proceedings 12th Annual ACM Symposium on Principles of Distributed Computing*, pages 133–145, August 1993.

18. J.R. Munkres. *Elements Of Algebraic Topology*. Addison Wesley, Reading MA, 1984. ISBN 0-201-04586-9.

19. G. Peterson, R. Bazzi, and G. Neiger. A gap theorem for consensus types. In *Proceedings 13th Annual ACM Symposium on Principles of Distributed Computing*, pages 344–354, August 1994.

20. M. Saks and F. Zaharoglou. Wait-free *k*-set agreement is impossible: The topology of public knowledge. In *Proceedings 25th Annual ACM Symposium on Theory of Computing*, pages 101–110, May 1993.

Differential BDDs*

Anuchit Anuchitanukul, Zohar Manna and Tomás E. Uribe

Computer Science Department
Stanford University
Stanford, California 94305
{anuchit|manna|uribe}@cs.stanford.edu

Abstract. We present a class of Ordered Binary Decision Diagrams, Differential BDDs (ΔBDDs), and transformations *Push-up* ($\uparrow$) and *Delta* (δ) over them. In addition to the ordinary node-sharing in normal BDDs, isomorphic substructures can be collapsed further in ΔBDDs and their derived classes, forming a more compact representation of boolean functions. The elimination of isomorphic substructures coincides with the repetitive occurrences of small components in many applications of BDDs. The reduction is potentially exponential in the number of nodes and proportional to the number of variables, while operations on ΔBDDs remain efficient.

1 Introduction

Binary Decision Diagrams (BDDs) [1] are a representation of boolean functions widely accepted as an important tool in many applications. Ordered Binary Decision Diagrams (OBDDs) [9] are BDDs with canonical forms and efficient manipulation algorithms, which make them the standard representation used in most applications of BDDs.

Many problems in digital system design, verification, optimization of combinatorial circuits, and test pattern generation, can be formulated as a sequence of operations on boolean functions. With the demand to apply OBDDs to increasingly larger problems, close attention has been paid to efficient implementation techniques [8], as well as refinements that improve speed and save memory. These include complement edges [19] and attributed edges [22] that have been shown to reduce the size of the graphs in many practical cases.

Numerous other variations of the basic OBDD idea have been proposed to suit the needs of particular applications. These include zero-suppressed BDDs [21], multi-terminal BDDs [14], multi-valued BDDs [16], edge-valued BDDs [18], BDD trees [20], functional BDDs [3, 5], generalized branching tests [17], domain transformations [6], BMDs [12], and first-order BDDs [23], among others.

---

* This research was supported in part by the National Science Foundation under grant CCR-92-23226, the Advanced Research Projects Agency under NASA grant NAG2-892, the United States Air Force Office of Scientific Research under grant F49620-93-1-0139, and the Department of the Army under grant DAAH04-95-1-0317.

We define and analyze a new class of BDDs, called Differential BDDs (ΔBDDs), and explore two transformations over them, Push-up ($\uparrow$) and Delta (δ). These transformations have the potential to significantly reduce the size of the graphs, while preserving canonicity and allowing for efficient operations.

We present efficient algorithms for manipulating the general class of $\uparrow^n \Delta$BDDs, derived from ΔBDDs by n push-up transformations. $\uparrow\Delta$BDDs (when $n = 1$) coincide with the class of BDDs with "variable shifter" attributed edges proposed by Minato et. al. [22], who show that they can produce more compact circuit representations.

Some BDD variants, such as extended BDDs [15, 2] and IBDDs [7], can give a polynomial-size representation of functions for which OBDDs are always exponential in the number of variables, but lose canonicity and efficiency of operations. The graph-driven BDDs of [24] retain canonicity and efficiency of most operations, but require finding a background oracle graph suitable for all the functions of interest. Similar results apply to the domain transformations of [6]. While our proposed variants cannot achieve such reductions, we believe that they are simple and general-purpose enough to be combined with many of the varieties of BDDs mentioned above to achieve further gains.

For a survey of BDDs and their applications, see [11]; a collection of recent BDD work, including further variants and refinements, is [4].

2   BDDs, OBDDs, and ΔBDDs

A Binary Decision Diagram (BDD) over a set of variables $\mathcal{V}$ is a directed acyclic graph (DAG) with two leaf nodes, *true* and *false* (also identified as **1** and **0**), where each internal node is labeled with a variable in $\mathcal{V}$ and has two outgoing edges, labeled 0 and 1. The successors of a node v are denoted by $S(v, 1)$ and $S(v, 0)$. A BDD defines the boolean function over $\mathcal{V}$ evaluated by following the unique path from the root to a leaf that chooses at each node the edge given by the value of the corresponding variable.

A BDD is *reduced* if (a) no two distinct internal nodes have the same label and the same successors, and (b) the successors of each node are distinct (no redundant tests). Every BDD has an equivalent reduced form.

In an *Ordered* BDD, there can be an edge from a node labeled with x_1 to a node labeled with x_2 only if $x_1 \prec x_2$ for a fixed total order $\prec$ over $\mathcal{V}$. Given such an order, the reduced OBDD representation of a boolean function f is *canonical*: there is exactly one reduced OBDD that represents f. Thus, we can identify a boolean function f with the corresponding root node. OBDDs are *shared* when a set of functions is represented with a single multi-rooted graph. An efficient implementation will maintain exactly one node (or pointer) for each distinct boolean function, so function equivalence can be tested in constant time.

The fixed order on the variables also allows implementing all the usual operations on boolean formulas with a complexity polynomial in the size of the argument OBDDs (see Section 5). The main practical concern, then, is the *size* of the OBDDs created for a particular task: as long as OBDDs remain small, operations remain efficient. In this, the particular variable ordering chosen can have a dramatic effect, in some cases determining if the OBDD size is linear or exponential in the number of variables (see [11]).

2.1 ΔBDDs

In a *Differential* BDD (ΔBDD), each node is labeled by an integer that represents a *displacement* in the fixed variable order. The label of a node v, $L(v)$, represents the difference between the index of the variable associated with v (a function of the path traversed so far) and that of its predecessors. For the leaf nodes, $L(false) = L(true) = 0$.

The value of the boolean function represented by a node v evaluated on a vector $\mathbf{x} = [x_1, \ldots, x_m]$ is defined as in the BDD case, except that the variable x_i branched upon at each node is given by the sum i of the node labels encountered so far. The label of the root node is the index of the first variable on which the BDD depends, and the sum of all labels on any path must be less than or equal to the total number of variables. As with reduced OBDDs, we require that any two internal nodes with the same label and the same successors be identical.

Fig. 1 shows the transition from an OBDD to a ΔBDD.[2] In the intermediate graph, variable labels are replaced by the corresponding displacement. For example, the label $L(vh) = 2$ is the distance between x_1 and x_3. The ΔBDD is the reduced form of this graph. The nodes $\{va, vb, vc, vd\}$ are merged into $v5$, $\{ve, vf\}$ into $v4$, and $\{vg, vh\}$ into $v3$. We may drop the 0 and 1 annotations on the edges and assume that the left and right branches of a node v always lead to its successors $S(v, 0)$ and $S(v, 1)$, respectively.

The ΔBDD representation can sometimes yield more nodes than the corresponding OBDD. Fig. 2 demonstrates such a case. In general, we have:

Proposition 1. *ΔBDDs have the following properties:*

1. *(Canonicity) Given a fixed variable ordering, each boolean function has a unique representation (canonical form) as a ΔBDD.*
2. *For a fixed variable ordering, the reduction in size when moving from an OBDD to a ΔBDD is potentially exponential: if n is the number of nodes in an OBDD, then (in the best case) the number of nodes of a ΔBDD representing the same boolean function can be $O(\log n)$. As a function of the number of variables m, the reduction is at best a factor of m.*
3. *In the worst case, the increase in the number of nodes is a factor of n^2 in the number of nodes n, and a factor of m in the the number of variables m.*

Proof Outline: It is easy to show that for any ΔBDD there is exactly one OBDD with the same ordering that represents the same boolean function. From the canonicity of OBDDs, we conclude that ΔBDDs are canonical as well.

---

[2] For clarity, the figures use multiple copies of the leaf nodes; reduced OBDDs will share the unique copy of each.

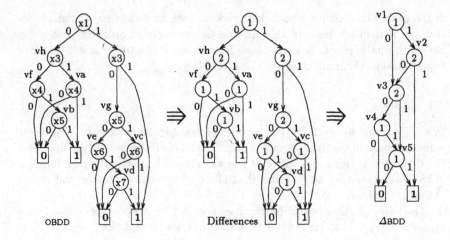

Fig. 1. From OBDD to ΔBDD

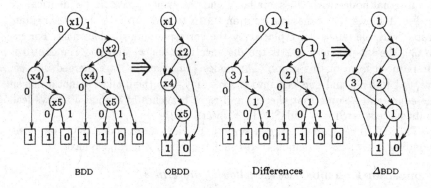

Fig. 2. A bad case for ΔBDDs

We can easily show that two distinct OBDD nodes labeled with the same variable are never reduced to a single ΔBDD node. With m variables, at most m nodes can be collapsed into one, so the reduction is at best a factor of m.

Exponential reduction occurs in the cases where (a) the left and right subgraphs of every OBDD node are isomorphic, and (b) if x_k is the label of a node in the left subgraph then the corresponding node in the right subgraph is labeled by x_{k+c} for some large enough c (e.g., bigger than the index of any label in the left subgraph). In these cases, the left and right subgraphs will be merged together repeatedly when translated into ΔBDDs, and the size of the ΔBDD will be $O(\log n)$.

The only case where an OBDD node is expanded into several ΔBDD nodes is when it has predecessors labeled with different variables: one extra node may be needed for each such label. There are at most n^2 pairs of nodes and predecessors, so the ΔBDD size increase is $O(n^2)$ in the worst case. The factor of m bound follows from the fact that there are at most m different labels.   ■

Boolean operations on ΔBDDs can be computed in time polynomial in the size of the BDDs; the operations and their analysis are a special case of the general algorithms described in Section 5.

We now show that for any OBDD we can find a unique ΔBDD of the same size (but that does *not*, in general, represent the same function). Since both representations are canonical, we conclude that the average ΔBDD and OBDD sizes are equal, for a given variable ordering.

Proposition 2. *Given an ordered set of variables $\mathcal{V}$, there is a one-to-one mapping between the sets of OBDDs and ΔBDDs over $\mathcal{V}$, such that each ΔBDD is mapped to an OBDD with the same size and structure (i.e., isomorphic up to relabeling of nodes).*

Proof Outline: Assume without loss of generality that the variable indices decrease from the root to the leaves. To construct an OBDD from a ΔBDD, start from the leaves and move upward, adding to each node label the larger of the labels of its two successors. At the end, change each label n to x_n. To check that the result is an OBDD, we show that no duplicate nodes are created, by induction on the structure of the subgraphs, using the fact that there are no duplicate nodes in the original ΔBDD. This construction is reversible, so the one-to-one correspondence follows.   ■

In the next section we introduce the $\uparrow$ transformation, which is applied to ΔBDDs to produce $\uparrow\Delta$BDDs. These inherit the potentially exponential reduction property and polynomial-time boolean operations, but are guaranteed to have no more nodes than the corresponding OBDD.

3   The $\uparrow$ Transformation

The *Push-up* ($\uparrow$) transformation takes a DAG with n labels on each node[3] and pushes one of the labels back through the incoming edges, into the predecessors of the node.

A binary DAG with n-ary labels, $\mathcal{G} = (\mathcal{N}, S, L)$, is a set of nodes $\mathcal{N}$, a successor function $S : \mathcal{N} \times \{0, 1\} \mapsto \mathcal{N}$, and a labeling function L that maps each node $v \in \mathcal{N}$ to an n-tuple label $L(v) = [d_0, \ldots, d_{n-1}]$. For each node $v \in \mathcal{N}$, we write $d(v, j)$ for the j-th component of the label of v. Given a binary DAG with n-ary labels $\mathcal{G}$, the transformation $\uparrow_i$ (or simply $\uparrow$ if $i = 0$) transforms $\mathcal{G}$ in two steps:

---

[3] Or, alternatively, an n-ary label in each node; this distinction will always be clear from context.

1. Relabel each node v with $[d_0, \ldots, d_{i-1}, d_{i+1}, \ldots, d_{n-1}, d_{s0}, d_{s1}]$, where $d_{s0} = d(S(v,0),i)$ and $d_{s1} = d(S(v,1),i)$. If v has no successor (i.e., it is a sink node), then $d_{s0} = d_{s1} = 0$.

2. Merge all the nodes with the same successors and the same label.

The result is a binary DAG with labels of length $n+1$ that represents $\mathcal{G}$. From now on, we focus on the case where $i = 0$, $\uparrow$. Fig. 3 shows the result of applying $\uparrow$ once ($\uparrow \Delta$BDD) and twice ($\uparrow^2 \Delta$BDD) to a ΔBDD. The nodes in each dashed box are merged into one node on the right. Unlike OBDDs and ΔBDDs, where a function is represented by a single node, in $\uparrow \Delta$BDDs a function is identified by a node *and* an integer, which is the by-product of the $\uparrow$ transformation.

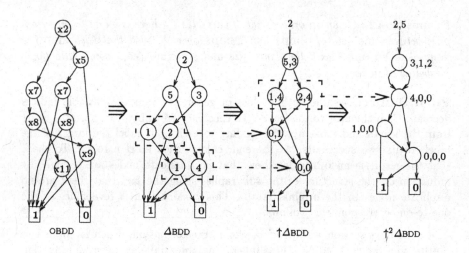

Fig. 3. Push-up transformation

In general, if $\mathcal{C}$ is a class of BDDs, then $\uparrow\mathcal{C}$ is the class of BDDs obtained from a push-up operation on the elements of $\mathcal{C}$.

Proposition 3. *Each application of $\uparrow$ to a class of BDDs has the following properties:*

1. *The number of nodes for each BDD is reduced up to a factor of m, where m is the number of variables.*
2. *Canonicity is preserved.*

Proof. The factor of m reduction is clear when we observe that no new nodes are created and that the labels of two collapsed nodes can differ only in their first element. For the canonicity property, observe that the $\uparrow$ transformation is reversible. Therefore, two different BDDs cannot be transformed into the same graph. If the original class is canonical, so is the derived class. ∎

Furthermore, we will see in Section 5 that boolean operations on the derived class of BDDs remain polynomial in the size of the component BDDs.

Even though the $\uparrow$ transformation offers a best-case reduction of m, it introduces one additional label per node. Therefore, to save memory the following condition must hold:

$$\frac{n_{elim}}{n} > \frac{1}{1 + \frac{|l|}{|dx|}}, \text{ where :}$$

- n is the total number of nodes before the transformation.
- n_{elim} is the number of nodes eliminated by the transformation.
- $|l|$ is the total bit-length of all the labels and pointers associated with each node before the transformation. For example, for OBDDs and ΔBDDs, $|l| = \log(m) + 2b$, where m is the number of variables and b is the bit-length of a pointer.
- $|dx|$ is the number of bits needed to hold the additional label for each node, which should, in fact, be $\log(m)$.

Two main arguments support using the $\uparrow$ transformation:

1. $|dx|$ is usually small since there is usually not a large number of variables. On the other hand, $|l|$ is relatively large since pointers could be 32- or 64-bit long. Thus, $1 + |l|/|dx|$ will usually be of the order of $5, 6, 7, 8 \ldots$, and we only need to eliminate a small fraction of nodes to save space.
2. Some unused bits may be used to hold the additional label. For example, if a word in the system is 32 bits long, but we only need 16 bits per label (*i.e.*, there are fewer than 65,536 variables), then we should apply $\uparrow$ and keep the additional label in the unused bits. If this is the case, $\uparrow$ will never increase memory usage, since it will never increase the number of nodes.

We also need to consider the space overhead in the *result cache* (see Section 5): each node in a cache entry will have an extra integer associated with it. However, this cache is usually of a fixed size, and the overhead incurred is proportional to it; alternatively, the absolute cache size can be held constant, at the expense of some efficiency loss. As above, no extra space is needed if the new label can be fitted into the existing words. Note that the *unique table* causes no additional storage overhead if its entries are pointers back to the original nodes.

4 $\uparrow \Delta$BDDs

Starting with $\uparrow \Delta$BDDs, $\uparrow^n \Delta$BDDs are guaranteed to have no more nodes than the corresponding OBDDs:

Proposition 4. *The number of nodes in a* $\uparrow \Delta$BDD *is always less than or equal to the number of nodes in an* OBDD *for the same boolean function with the same variable ordering.*

Proof Outline: We can show that each node in an OBDD is translated into at most one node in a ↑ΔBDD by induction on the structure of subgraphs. In the inductive case, consider any OBDD node v with successors $S(v, 0)$ and $S(v, 1)$. By the induction hypothesis, both $S(v, 0)$ and $S(v, 1)$ are translated into unique ↑ΔBDD nodes v'_0 and v'_1. Therefore, the node v is translated into the unique node v' such that v'_0 and v'_1 are the successors of v', and whose label is uniquely determined by the labels of v, $S(v, 0)$ and $S(v, 1)$. ∎

Recalling the analysis in the previous section, this property means that space savings relative to OBDDs can be more frequently obtained, even when accounting for the extra node label. The reduction in the number of nodes is potentially exponential, since the possible savings in the original ΔBDD are retained.

In applications such as combinational circuit representation, eliminating isomorphic structures in the BDD representation is a significant advantage. Many circuits contain identical components that cause their OBDD representation to have substructures that differ only in variable labeling (the input signals to each component). If the relative variable positions in each component are the same, the substructures will be collapsed into a single ↑ΔBDD. Note that partitioned and hierarchical representations facilitate such structure sharing.

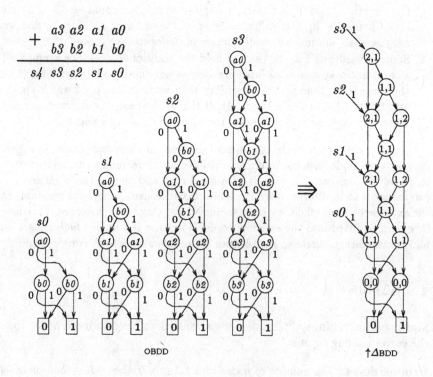

Fig. 4. OBDD and ↑ΔBDD for a 4-bit adder (suboptimal variable ordering)

Fig. 4 shows the $\uparrow\!\Delta\text{BDD}$ representation of a four-bit adder. The two operands are $[a_3, a_2, a_1, a_0]$ and $[b_3, b_2, b_1, b_0]$, and the variable ordering is $[a_0, b_0, \ldots, a_3, b_3]$. This ordering is not the optimal one for standard OBDDs, which is in fact the reverse one. Under the optimal ordering, the OBDD size is linear in the number of bits, as opposed to the quadratic case of Fig. 4. However, the $\uparrow\!\Delta\text{BDD}$ produces a minimal-size (linear) BDD for both orderings.[4] This example suggests that $\uparrow\!\Delta\text{BDDs}$ can give some extra flexibility in choosing good orderings, an important problem in the practical use of BDDs.

The BDDs with "variable shifter" edges presented by Minato *et. al.* [22] are an alternate presentation of $\uparrow\!\Delta\text{BDDs}$, where the two node labels are associated with the outgoing edges rather than the node itself.

5   Boolean Operations

We now present the main algorithm used to efficiently compute boolean operations on $\uparrow\!\Delta\text{BDDs}$ and derived classes. As in [8], we can implement all binary operations using a single operator, $ite(f, g, h)$, which takes as input the BDD representation of boolean functions f, g, h and returns that of the function

$$ite(f, g, h)(\mathbf{x}) \overset{\text{def}}{=} \text{if } f(\mathbf{x}) \text{ then } g(\mathbf{x}) \text{ else } h(\mathbf{x}) \ .$$

OBDDs are based on the *Shannon expansion* of boolean functions:[5] for any function f,

$$f \equiv \text{if } x \text{ then } f_x \text{ else } f_{\overline{x}},$$

where f_x and $f_{\overline{x}}$ are the *restrictions* of f (also called *cofactors*) when the variable x is assigned the value 0 or 1, respectively. Given procedures to compute f_x and $f_{\overline{x}}$, the *ite* function can be implemented recursively as follows:

$$ite(f, g, h) = assemble\ (x, ite(f_x, g_x, h_x), ite(f_{\overline{x}}, g_{\overline{x}}, h_{\overline{x}}))\ ,$$

where x is the first variable in the fixed ordering appearing in f, g or h, and $assemble(x, f_1, f_2)$ returns the unique OBDD node labelled with x that has f_1 and f_2 as its right and left successors. To ensure the uniqueness of each OBDD, *assemble* checks a hash table, called the *unique table*, for the existence of such a node before creating a new one. If $f_1 = f_2$, then *assemble* returns f_1, avoiding the redundant test on x.

Choosing x to be the smallest of all variables in f, g, h makes the operations f_x and $f_{\overline{x}}$ particularly easy to compute: if x labels the root node of f, we follow the left or right successor; otherwise, f does not depend on x, and the operation is the identity. In the remainder of this section, we reserve f_x and $f_{\overline{x}}$ for such restriction operations (*i.e.*, under an extra assumption on f and x); the general restriction algorithm is described in Section 5.2.

---

[4] For the optimal ordering, the $\uparrow\!\Delta\text{BDD}$ is still smaller (see Section 7).

[5] Some BDD variants [3, 5, 12] use other expansions, but the push-up transformation should be compatible with most.

In the case of $\uparrow\Delta$BDDs, a boolean function f is identified by a pair $\langle o, N \rangle$, for an integer o, which we call the *offset* of f, and a node N. The constant functions *true* and *false* have an offset of 0. We need to define an appropriate *assemble* function, as well as redefining the operators $f_x, f_{\overline{x}}$ for an integer offset x.

When computing *ite*, we take x to be the smallest offset of the three arguments. If f is the function $\langle o, N \rangle$ for an offset o and a node N, then

$$f_x = \langle o, N \rangle_x = \begin{cases} \langle o - x, N \rangle & \text{if } x < o \\ \langle r, S(N, 1) \rangle & \text{if } x = o \end{cases}$$

where r is the second label of N, and $S(N, 1)$ is the right descendant. The case of $f_{\overline{x}}$ is analogous. These operations are illustrated in Fig. 5. Note that the resulting BDD should be interpreted relative to the offset x in all cases.

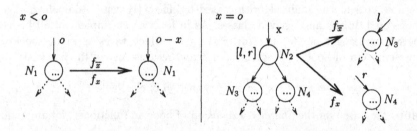

Fig. 5. $f_x, f_{\overline{x}}$ for $\uparrow\Delta$BDDs

The recursive calls to *ite* return two functions, $f_1 = \langle o_r, N_r \rangle$ and $f_2 = \langle o_l, N_l \rangle$, which are combined with x to produce the final result as follows:

$$assemble(x, \langle o_r, N_r \rangle, \langle o_l, N_l \rangle) = \begin{cases} \langle o_r + x, N_r \rangle & \text{if } f_1 = f_2 \\ \langle x, N' \rangle & \text{otherwise} \end{cases}$$

where N' is the node labeled with $[o_l, o_r]$ whose left and right successors are N_l and N_r respectively.

Like [8], we use a second hash table, the *result table*, to avoid multiple evaluations of *ite* on each triple $\langle f_1, f_2, f_3 \rangle$. Furthermore, triples can be normalized so that equivalent operations (including those equivalent modulo some initial offset) are mapped to a single table entry. We assume a good implementation of the hash tables where operations, on average, can be done in constant time. Let n_a, n_b, n_c be the size, in nodes, of the arguments, and m be the number of variables over which the functions range. There are $n_a n_b n_c m$ unique tuples to be evaluated, so the complexity of the algorithm is $O(n_a n_b n_c m)$.

Although the algorithm seems to have a higher complexity than that for normal OBDDs, which is $O(n'_a n'_b n'_c)$ in the sizes of the corresponding OBDDs, this is not a disadvantage. First, recall that the graphs are usually larger for

OBDDs. Second, there is a one-to-one (but not always onto) mapping from each evaluation tuple $\langle f_1, f_2, f_3 \rangle$ to a tuple $\langle v_1, v_2, v_3 \rangle$ where v_1, v_2, v_3 are nodes in the OBDD arguments. This means that the number of recursive calls to *ite* for $\uparrow \Delta$BDDs is less than or equal to the number of recursive calls for OBDDs that represent the same boolean functions. In essence, switching to $\uparrow \Delta$BDDs will never introduce any unnecessary computation.

This implementation is compatible with further refinements such as the use of complement edges for constant-time negation [19, 8].

5.1 $\uparrow^n \Delta$BDDs

In the general case of $\uparrow^n \Delta$BDDs, n push-up operations have been done. A function f is now identified by a pair $\langle l, N \rangle$, where l is a tuple of length n, called the *tag* of f, and N is a BDD node with a label of length $n + 1$. The first element of the tag l is again called the *offset* of f, and comes from the root of the original ΔBDD. The constant functions *true* and *false* have an all-zero tag.

Assume that the $n + 1$ components of each node label are marked indicating if they come from the left or right successor in the push-up operation[6]. We can do the same for the components of each function tag. Let o be the offset of f; we write $[o : l]$ for the tag of f. Assuming $x \leq o$, f_x is defined as follows:

$$f_x = \langle [o : l], N \rangle_x = \begin{cases} \langle [(o - x) : l], N \rangle & \text{if } x < o \\ \langle l', S(N, 1) \rangle & \text{if } x = o \end{cases}$$

where l' is obtained by appending the elements of l that are marked as coming from the right with the corresponding elements in the label of N. The $f_{\overline{x}}$ operation is defined analogously.

We also need to construct the $\uparrow^n \Delta$BDD obtained from branching on an offset x, leading to the functions (relative to this offset) $f_1 = \langle l_1, N_1 \rangle$ and $f_2 = \langle l_2, N_2 \rangle$. We interleave the elements of l_1 and l_2 and then split the resulting list into two parts: the first, l, of length $n - 1$, and the second, l', of length $n + 1$. Then

$$assemble(x, \langle l_1, N_1 \rangle, \langle l_2, N_2 \rangle) = \langle [x : l], N' \rangle,$$

where N' is the node with l' as its label, and N_1 and N_2 as its right and left successors.

The *ite* operation is now defined exactly as before, again choosing x to be the smallest offset. Note that in all cases $f = assemble(x, f_x, f_{\overline{x}})$, and that in the differential cases f_x and $f_{\overline{x}}$ give a result relative to the offset x.

5.2   Restriction

Another important BDD operation is the general restriction operation. Given a boolean function $f(x_1, \ldots, x_n)$, this operation fixes a variable x_j to be equal

---

[6] In our notation, if n is even, the left components are in the odd-numbered positions (starting from 0); if n is odd, the reverse applies.

to c, for $c \in \{0, 1\}$, yielding a function of $n-1$ variables that we write as $restrict(f, j, c)$.

Restriction is used to "quantify" over boolean variables, and is commonly used, for example, in model checking of finite-state systems [13]. $\exists x_j f$ is identified with $restrict(f, j, 0) \vee restrict(f, j, 1)$, while $\forall x_j f$ is $restrict(f, j, 0) \wedge restrict(f, j, 1)$. Restriction can be computed efficiently for $\uparrow\Delta$BDDs in a way similar to standard OBDDs. We define the procedure recursively: let o be the offset (the first element of the tag) of f. If $j < o$, the restriction is the identity:

$$restrict(f, j, 1) = restrict(f, j, 0) = f .$$

If $j = o$,

$$restrict(f, j, 1) = add\_offset(j, f_j) \quad \text{and} \quad restrict(f, j, 0) = add\_offset(j, f_{\bar{j}}),$$

where $add\_offset(j, f)$ adds j to the offset of f. If $j > o$, we recurse on the left and right cofactors and then put the result back together:

$$restrict(f, j, X) = assemble(o, restrict(f_o, j - o, X), restrict(f_{\bar{o}}, j - o, X)) .$$

6   The δ Transformation

There are variations of the $\uparrow$ transformation that also exploit regularity in the graph to reduce the number of nodes. One such variation is the *Delta* (δ) transformation. As demonstrated in Fig. 6, the δ transformation takes a DAG with at least two integer labels per node, computes the difference between two of the labels, pushes one of the two labels up and keeps the difference.

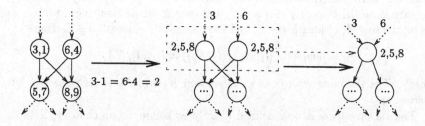

Fig. 6. δ transformation

Fig. 7 shows the application of δ to an entire $\uparrow\Delta$BDD. Like the $\uparrow$ transformation, δ preserves the essential properties of canonicity and efficient manipulation, and gives a best-case reduction proportional to the number of variables. $\delta\uparrow\Delta$BDDs also have the property that all OBDD nodes with the same successors are collapsed into a single $\delta\uparrow\Delta$BDD node.

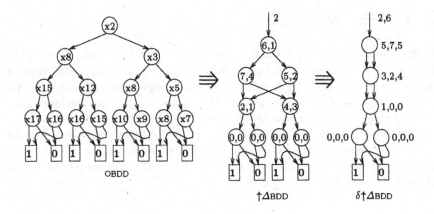

Fig. 7. From OBDD to $\delta\uparrow\Delta$BDD

It is easy to adapt the previous algorithms to a class of BDDs derived by a δ transformation. Fig. 8 describes the computation of the immediate restriction functions, f_x and $f_{\bar{x}}$, for $\delta\uparrow\Delta$BDDs. Fig. 8 also describes the construction of $assemble(x, f_1, f_2)$ for $f_1 \neq f_2$; if $f_1 = f_2$, then x is added to the first element of the tag of f_1 and the resulting pair is returned. Given f_x, $f_{\bar{x}}$ and $assemble$, the ite and $restrict$ operations are defined exactly as in Section 5.

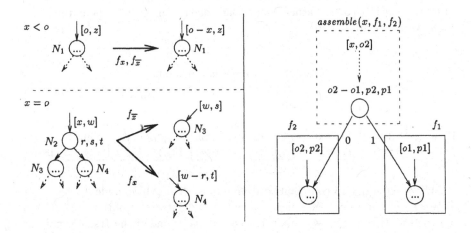

Fig. 8. $f_x, f_{\bar{x}}$ and $assemble(x, f_1, f_2)$ for $\delta\uparrow\Delta$BDDs

7   Experimental Results

Table 1 shows the number of OBDD nodes needed to build the representation of a 128-bit adder, together with the percentage of nodes *removed* by ΔBDD variants for 4 different variable orderings. In this example, the δ transformation does not improve the size of the BDD representation; a second push-up transformation increases the node savings for the two best variable orderings. Note that even ΔBDDs display the more dramatic reductions, for the two worst orders. In most cases, the representation for each individual output bit has the same size across the BDD variants; the savings come from *sharing* among the BDD representation of the 128 output functions (see Section 4).

Table 1. Nodes for 128-bit adder (and % OBDD nodes removed)

Order	OBDD	ΔBDD	$\uparrow\Delta$BDD	$\delta\uparrow\Delta$BDD	$\uparrow^2\Delta$BDD
optimal	1,538	2,048 (-33%)	1,154 (25%)	1,154 (25%)	1,025 (33%)
sub-1	3,647	4,839 (-33%)	3,314 (9%)	3,314 (9%)	3,056 (16%)
sub-2	196,737	5,587 (97%)	3,058 (98%)	3,058 (98%)	3,057 (98%)
sub-3	388,888	206,618 (47%)	201,862 (48%)	201,732 (48%)	201,477 (48%)

Of the satisfiability and verification problems discussed in [25], ΔBDDs and their variants were most useful in problems where OBDDs already had some success. Table 2 presents results for problems *not* generally amenable to BDD encoding, which yielded the smallest reductions: random satisfiability problems and multiplication circuits. Note, however, that the savings increase when a set of multipliers is encoded, rather than a single one (3- through 8-bits, in this case; input variables are shared).

Table 2. Hard problems for OBDDs

Problem	OBDD	ΔBDD	$\uparrow\Delta$BDD	$\delta\uparrow\Delta$BDD	$\uparrow^2\Delta$BDD
random1	3,033	4,024 (-33%)	2,909 (4%)	2,908 (4%)	2,789 (8%)
random2	3,480	4,604 (-32%)	3,382 (3%)	3,278 (6%)	3,268 (6%)
mult.8	134,401	134,700 (0%)	130,295 (3%)	128,678 (4%)	129,337 (4%)
mult.3–8	188,820	162,960 (14%)	155,632 (18%)	151,470 (20%)	154,313 (18%)

For other standard combinational circuits, such as ALUs, node savings were between 45% and 80%, of which a second δ and $\uparrow$ transformation contributed up to 10%. However, it was often the case that for one of the transformations the number of nodes remained essentially the same.

Our implementation followed [8] (see Section 5) and included complement edges. The $\uparrow\Delta$BDD, $\delta\uparrow\Delta$BDD, and $\uparrow^2\Delta$BDD variants were generally slower than the original OBDDs, due to the overhead in hash-table and *ite* operations caused by the extra labels. However, in most BDD applications it is space, not time, that presents the main limitation. The time overhead was never more than a factor of 3 (and can be reduced by a more careful implementation), and was offset by the smaller BDD sizes in the cases where the best savings were obtained.

A number of boolean functions, including multipliers, have an exponential-size OBDD (in the number of variables m) for *any* ordering of the variables [10]. Since the $\uparrow$ and δ transformations can only reduce the OBDD size by a factor of m, these problems will still be intractable. However, we hope that the δ and $\uparrow$ transformations can also be used to improve the efficiency of the BDD variants specialized to have small representations for these cases [6, 24].

8   Conclusion

The $\uparrow$ and δ transformations on ΔBDDs are general-purpose techniques to reduce the number of nodes in a class of BDDs, potentially reducing memory usage and speeding up operations. These techniques present a trade-off between the number of nodes and the number of labels per node, but we show that there can be a net gain. The transformations can be performed until the space required to hold the extra labels offsets the space saved by the reduction of nodes. In some environments, such as a machine with long words, unused bits can be utilized to store additional labels.

ΔBDDs give some measure of abstraction over the identity of particular boolean variables. The best space savings occur when representing related functions over different sets of variables. It would be interesting to investigate if these properties can be exploited in particular applications, such as symbolic model checking [13], including new encoding and variable ordering methods.

Acknowledgements

We thank Anca Browne, Nikolaj Bjørner, Henny Sipma, Mark Stickel and Howard Wong-Toi for their helpful comments.

References

1. AKERS, S. Binary decision diagrams. *IEEE Transactions on Computers 6*, 27 (June 1978), 509–516.

2. ASHAR, P., GHOSH, A., AND DEVADAS, S. Boolean satisfiability and equivalence checking using general binary decision diagrams. In *IEEE International Conf. on Computer Design: VLSI in Computers and Processors* (1991), pp. 259–264.

3. BANI-EQBAL, B. Exclusive normal form of boolean circuits. Tech. Rep. UMCS-92-4-1, Department of Computer Science, University of Manchester, 1992.

4. BECKER, B., BRYANT, R., COUDERT, O., AND MEINEL, C., Eds. *Report on the Third Workshop on Computer Aided Design and Test* (Feb. 1995). http://www.informatik.uni-trier.de/Design_and_Test/.

5. BECKER, B., DRECHSLER, R., AND THEOBALD, M. OKFDDs versus OBDDs and OFDDs. In *International Colloquium on Automata, Languages and Programming* (July 1995), LNCS. To appear.

6. BERN, J., MEINEL, C., AND SLOBODOVÁ, A. Efficient OBDD-based boolean manipulation in CAD beyond current limits. In 32nd *Design Automation Conf.* (1995).

7. BITNER, J., JAIN, J., ABADIR, M., ABRAHAM, J., AND FUSSELL, D. Efficient algorithmic computation using indexed BDDs. In 24th *Intl. Symposium on Fault-Tolerant Computing* (1994), pp. 266–275.

8. BRACE, K. S., RUDELL, R. L., AND BRYANT, R. E. Efficient implementation of a BDD package. In 27th *Design Automation Conf.* (1990), pp. 40–45.

9. BRYANT, R. E. Graph-based algorithms for Boolean function manipulation. *IEEE Trans. on Computers 35*, 8 (Aug. 1986), 677–691.

10. BRYANT, R. E. On the complexity of VLSI implementations and graph representations of Boolean functions with application to integer multiplication. *IEEE Trans. on Computers 40*, 2 (Feb. 1991), 205–213.

11. BRYANT, R. E. Symbolic Boolean manipulation with ordered binary-decision diagrams. *ACM Computing Surveys 24*, 3 (Sept. 1992), 293–318.

12. BRYANT, R. E., AND CHEN, Y.-A. Verification of arithmetic circuits with Binary Moment Diagrams. In 32nd *Design Automation Conf.* (June 1995). To appear.

13. BURCH, J., CLARKE, E., MCMILLAN, K., DILL, D., AND HWANG, L. Symbolic modelchecking: 10^{20} states and beyond. *Information and Computation 98*, 2 (June 1992), 142–170.

14. CLARKE, E. M., MCMILLAN, K., ZHAO, X., FUJITA, M., AND YANG, J. Spectral transforms for large Boolean functions with applications to technology mapping. In 30th *Design Automation Conf.* (June 1993).

15. JEONG, S., PLESSIER, B., HACHTEL, G., AND SOMENZI, F. Extended BDD's: Trading off canonicity for structure in verification algorithms. In *IEEE Intl. Conf. on Computer-Aided Design* (1991), pp. 464–467.

16. KAM, T. Y. K., AND BRAYTON, R. K. Multi-valued decision diagrams. Technical Report UCB/ERL M90/125, University of California, Berkeley, Dec. 1990.

17. KARPLUS, K. Using if-then-else DAGs for multi-level logic minimization. In *Advance Research in VLSI* (1989), C. Seitz, Ed., MIT Press, pp. 101–118.

18. LAI, Y.-T., AND SASTRY, S. Edge-valued binary decision diagrams for multi-level hierarchical verification. In 29th *Design Automation Conf.* (1992), pp. 608–613.

19. MADRE, J., AND BILLON, J. Proving circuit correctness using formal comparison between expected and extracted behaviour. In 25th *Design Automation Conf.* (June 1988), pp. 205–210.

20. MCMILLAN, K. L. Hierarchical representations of discrete functions, with application to model checking. In *Proc. 6th Intl. Conf. on Computer-Aided Verification* (June 1994), vol. 818 of *LNCS*, Springer-Verlag, pp. 41–54.

21. MINATO, S. Zero-supressed BDDs for set manipulation in combinatorial problems. In 30th *Design Automation Conf.* (1993), pp. 272–277.

22. MINATO, S., ISHIURA, N., AND JAJIMA, S. Shared binary decision diagram with attributed edges for efficient boolean function manipulation. In 27th *Design Automation Conf.* (1990), pp. 52–57.

23. POSSEGA, J., AND LUDÄSCHER, B. Towards first-order deduction based on Shannon graphs. In *Proc. 16th German Conf. on AI (GWAI-92)* (1992), vol. 671 of *LNAI*, Springer-Verlag, pp. 67–76.

24. SIELING, D., AND WEGENER, I. Graph driven BDDs—a new data structure for boolean functions. *Theoretical Comput. Sci. 141*, 2 (Apr. 1995).

25. URIBE, T. E., AND STICKEL, M. E. Ordered binary decision diagrams and the Davis-Putnam procedure. In *Proc. 1st Intl. Conf. on Constraints in Computational Logics* (Sept. 1994), vol. 845 of *LNCS*, pp. 34–49.

Algorithmic Techniques for Geometric Optimization*

Pankaj K. Agarwal[1] and Micha Sharir[2,3]

[1] Department of Computer Science
Box 90129, Duke University, Durham, NC 27708-0129, USA.
[2] School of Mathematical Sciences
Tel Aviv University, Tel Aviv 69978, ISRAEL.
[3] Courant Institute of Mathematical Sciences
New York University, New York, NY 10012, USA.

Abstract. We review the recent progress in the design of efficient algorithms for various problems in geometric optimization. The emphasis in this survey is on the techniques used to attack these problems, such as parametric searching, geometric alternatives to parametric searching, prune-and-search techniques for linear programming and related problems, and LP-type problems and their efficient solution.

1 Introduction

In this survey we describe several techniques that have lead to efficient algorithms for a variety of geometric optimization problems. We also list many applications of these techniques, and discuss some of them in more detail. The first technique that we present is the *parametric searching* technique. Although restricted forms of parametric searching already existed earlier [49, 57, 58], the parametric searching in its full generality was proposed by Megiddo in the late 1970's and the early 1980's [87, 88]. The technique was originally motivated by so-called *parametric optimization* problems in combinatorial optimization, and did not receive much attention by the computational geometry community until the late 1980's. In the last seven years, though, it has become one of the major techniques for solving geometric optimization problems efficiently. We outline the technique in detail in Section 2, first exemplifying it on the *slope selection problem* [36], and then presenting various extensions of the technique.

Despite its power and versatility, parametric searching has certain drawbacks, which we discuss below. Consequently, there have been several recent attempts to replace parametric searching by alternative techniques, including *randomization* [11, 33, 79], *expander graphs* [16, 70, 71, 72], *geometric cuttings* [12, 22], and

---

*Pankaj Agarwal has been supported by National Science Foundation Grant CCR-93–01259, an NYI award, and by matching funds from Xerox Corp. Micha Sharir has been supported by NSF Grants CCR-91-22103 and CCR-93-11127, by a Max-Planck Research Award, and by grants from the U.S.-Israeli Binational Science Foundation, the Israel Science Fund administered by the Israeli Academy of Sciences, and the G.I.F., the German-Israeli Foundation for Scientific Research and Development.

matrix searching [50, 51, 52, 53, 55]. We mention these alternative techniques in Section 3.

Almost concurrently with the development of the parametric searching technique, Megiddo devised another ingenious technique for solving linear programming and several related optimization problems [89, 90]. This technique, now known as *decimation* or *prune-and-search*, was later refined and extended by Dyer [41], Clarkson [30], and others. The technique can be viewed as an optimized version of parametric searching, in which certain special properties of the problem allows one to improve further the efficiency of the algorithm. For example, it yields linear-time deterministic algorithms for *linear programming* and for several related problems, such as the *smallest enclosing ball* problem, when the dimension is fixed. (However, the dependence of the running time of these algorithms on the dimension is at least exponential.) We present the technique and its applications in Section 4. Section 5 enumerates many recent applications of the techniques reviewed so far.

In the past decade, *randomized algorithms* have been developed for a wide variety of problems in computational geometry and in other fields; see, e.g., the books by Mulmuley [96] and by Motwani and Raghavan [95]. In particular, Clarkson [31] and Seidel [103] gave randomized algorithms for linear programming, whose expected time is linear in any fixed dimension, which are much simpler than their earlier deterministic counterparts, and the dependence of their running time on the dimension is better (though still exponential). Additional significant progress was made about four years ago, when new randomized algorithms for linear programming were obtained independently by Kalai [68], and by Matoušek et al. [86, 110] (these two algorithms are essentially dual versions of the same technique). The expected number of arithmetic operations performed by these algorithms is 'subexponential' in the input size, and is still linear in any fixed dimension, so they constitute an important step toward the still open goal of obtaining strongly-polynomial algorithms for linear programming. (Recall that the polynomial-time algorithms by Khachiyan [73] and Karmarkar [69] are not strongly polynomial, as the number of arithmetic operations performed by these algorithms depends on the size of coefficients of the input constraints.) This new technique is presented in Section 6. The algorithm in [86, 110] is formulated in a general abstract framework, which fits not only linear programming but many other problems. Such 'LP-type' problems are also reviewed in Section 6, including the connection, recently noted by Amenta [19, 20], between abstract linear programming and 'Helly-type' theorems.

2 Parametric Searching

2.1 Outline of the Technique

The parametric searching technique of Megiddo [87, 88] can be described in the following general terms (which are not as general as possible, but suffice for our purposes). Suppose we have a decision problem $\mathcal{P}(\lambda)$ that depends on a real parameter λ, and is *monotone* in λ, meaning that if $\mathcal{P}(\lambda_0)$ is true for some λ_0, then $\mathcal{P}(\lambda)$ is true for all $\lambda < \lambda_0$. Our goal is to find the maximum λ for which

$\mathcal{P}(\lambda)$ is true, assuming such a maximum exists. Suppose further that $\mathcal{P}(\lambda)$ can be solved by a (sequential) algorithm $A_s(\lambda)$ whose input is a set of data objects (independent of λ) and λ, and whose control flow is governed by comparisons, each of which amounts to testing the sign of some low-degree polynomial in λ. Megiddo's technique then runs A_s 'generically' at the unknown optimum λ^*. Whenever A_s reaches a branching point that depends on some comparison with an associated polynomial $p(\lambda)$, it computes all the roots of p and runs (the standard, non-generic version of) A_s with the value of λ equal to each of these roots. The outputs of these runs of A_s confine λ^* to an interval between two adjacent roots, which then enables the generic A_s to determine the sign of $p(\lambda^*)$, thereby resolving the comparison and allowing the generic execution to proceed. As this generic computation advances, the interval known to contain λ^* keeps shrinking as a result of resolving further comparisons, and, at the end, either the interval becomes a singleton, which is thus the desired λ^*, or else λ^* can be shown to be equal to its upper endpoint. (A third possibility is that the algorithm finds λ^* 'accidentally', during one of its comparison-resolving steps.)

If A_s runs in time T_s and makes C_s comparisons, then the cost of the procedure just described is $O(C_s T_s)$, and is thus generally quadratic in the original complexity. To speed up the execution, Megiddo proposes to implement the generic algorithm by a parallel algorithm A_p (under Valiant's *comparison model* of computation [115]). If A_p uses P processors and runs in T_p parallel steps, then each parallel step involves at most P *independent* comparisons; that is, we do not need to know the output of such a comparison to be able to execute other comparisons in the same 'batch'. We can then compute the roots of all the polynomials associated with these comparisons, and perform a binary search to locate λ^* among them, using (the non-generic) A_s at each binary step. The cost of simulating a parallel step of A_p is thus $O(P + T_s \log P)$, for a total running time of $O(PT_p + T_p T_s \log P)$. In most cases, the second term dominates the running time. The technique has been generalized further in [10, 37, 112, 113].

2.2 An Example: The Slope Selection Problem

As an illustration, consider the *slope selection* problem, which we formulate in a dual setting, as follows: We are given a set L of n nonvertical lines in the plane, and an integer $1 \le k \le \binom{n}{2}$, and we wish to find an intersection point between two lines of L that has the k-th smallest x-coordinate. (We assume, for simplicity, *general position* of the lines, so that no three lines are concurrent, and no two intersection points have the same x-coordinate.) We are thus seeking the k-th leftmost vertex of the *arrangement* $\mathcal{A}(L)$ of the lines in L; see [45, 108] for more details concerning arrangements. (The name of the problem comes from its primal setting, where we are given a set of n points and a parameter k as above, and wish to determine a segment connecting two input points that has the k-th smallest slope among all such segments.)

The parameter that we seek is the x-coordinate λ^* of the vertical line passing through the desired vertex, and the decision step is to compare λ^* with a given λ, that is, to determine how many vertices of $\mathcal{A}(L)$ lie to the left of (or on) the line $x = \lambda$. If we denote this number by k_λ, then we have $\lambda^* < \lambda$ (resp. $\lambda^* > \lambda$,

$\lambda^* = \lambda$) if and only if $k_\lambda > k$ (resp. $k_\lambda < k$, $k_\lambda = k$).

Let $(\ell_1, \ell_2, \ldots, \ell_n)$ denote the sequence of lines in L sorted in the decreasing order of their slopes, and let $(\ell_{\pi(1)}, \ell_{\pi(2)}, \ldots, \ell_{\pi(n)})$ denote the sequence of these lines sorted by their intercepts with $x = \lambda$. An easy observation is that two lines ℓ_i, ℓ_j, with $i < j$, intersect to the left of $x = \lambda$ if and only if $\pi(i) > \pi(j)$. In other words, the number of intersection points to the left of $x = \lambda$ can be counted, in $O(n \log n)$ time, by counting the number of *inversions* in the permutation π [78]: Construct a balanced binary tree T storing the lines of L in its leaves, in the decreasing slope order $\ell_1, \ldots, \ell_n$, by adding the lines one after the other, in the order $\ell_{\pi(1)}, \ldots, \ell_{\pi(n)}$. When a line ℓ_q is added, count the number of lines that are already present in T and have a larger index, and add up these counts, to obtain the total number of inversions. Since the insertion of a line can be done in $O(\log n)$ time, the whole decision procedure takes $O(n \log n)$ time. Any parallel sorting algorithm, which runs in $O(\log n)$ time using $O(n)$ processors [15], can count the number of inversions within the same time and processor bounds. (Notice that the construction of T itself does not involve any comparison that depends on the value of λ, and so need not be performed at all in the generic execution.) Plugging these algorithms into the parametric searching paradigm, we obtain an $O(n \log^3 n)$-time algorithm for the slope selection problem.

2.3   Improvements and Extensions

Cole [35] observed that in certain applications of parametric searching, including the slope selection problem, the running time can be improved to $O((P + T_s)T_p)$, as follows. Consider a parallel step of the above generic algorithm. Suppose that, instead of invoking the decision procedure $O(\log n)$ times in this step, we call it only $O(1)$ times, say, three times. This will determine the outcome of 7/8 of the comparisons, and will leave 1/8 of them unresolved. Suppose further that each of the unresolved comparisons can influence only a constant (and small) number of (say, two) comparisons executed at the next parallel step. Then 3/4 of these comparisons can still be simulated generically with the currently available information. This modified scheme mixes the parallel steps of the algorithm, since it forces us to perform together new comparisons and yet unresolved old comparisons. Nevertheless, Cole shows that, if carefully implemented, the number of parallel steps of the algorithm increases only by a constant factor, which leads to the improvement stated above. An ideal setup for Cole's improvement is when the parallel algorithm is described as a circuit (or network), each of whose gates has a constant fan-out.

Cole's idea improves the running time of the slope selection algorithm to $O(n \log^2 n)$. Later, Cole et al. [36] gave an optimal $O(n \log n)$-time solution. They observe that one can compare λ^* with a value λ that is 'far away' from λ^*, in a faster manner, by counting inversions only approximately. This approximation is progressively refined as λ approaches λ^* in subsequent comparisons. Cole et al. show that the overall cost of $O(\log n)$ calls to the approximating decision procedure is only $O(n \log n)$, so this also bounds the running time of the whole algorithm. This technique was subsequently simplified in [22]. Chazelle et al. [24] have shown that the algorithm of [36] can be extended to compute, in

$O(n \log n)$ time, the k-th leftmost vertex in an arrangement of n line segments.

Multi-dimensional parametric searching. The parametric searching technique can be extended to higher dimensions in a natural manner. Suppose we have a decision problem $\mathcal{P}(\lambda)$ as above, but now λ varies in $\mathbb{R}^d$. Assume also that the set Λ of points at which the answer of $\mathcal{P}(\lambda)$ is true is a convex region. We wish to compute the lexicographically largest point λ^* for which $P(\lambda)$ is true. Let A_s be, as above, an algorithm that solves $\mathcal{P}(\lambda_0)$ at any given λ_0, and can also compare λ_0 with λ^* (lexicographically). As above, we run A_s generically at λ^*. Each comparison depending on λ now amounts to evaluating the sign of some d-variate polynomial $p(\lambda_1, \ldots, \lambda_d)$.

First consider the case when p is a linear function of the form $a_0 + \sum_{1 \le i \le d} a_i \lambda_i$, such that $a_d \ne 0$. Consider the hyperplane $h : \lambda_d = -(a_0 + \sum_{i=1}^{d-1} a_i \lambda_i)/a_d$, and let h^+, h^- be the two open halfspaces bounded by h. Evaluating the sign of $p(\lambda^*)$ is equivalent to determining whether λ^* lies in h, h^+, or h^-. We solve this problem by considering the following more general problem: Let h be a k-flat in $\mathbb{R}^d$, and let $\hat{h}$ be the vertical d-hyperplane erected on h. If Λ intersects $\hat{h}$, we wish to return the lexicographically largest point of $\Lambda \cap \hat{h}$. Otherwise, we wish to determine which of the two open half-spaces bounded by $\hat{h}$ contains Λ. Inductively, assume that we have an algorithm $A_d^{(k-1)}$ that can solve this problem for any $(k-1)$-dimensional flat. Notice that $A_d^0 = A_s$, and that $k = d$ corresponds to the original problem. By running $A_d^{(k-1)}$ generically, such that λ varies over $\hat{h}$, one can determine whether Λ intersects $\hat{h}$, and, if not, determine which of the two halfspaces contains Λ. The details of this algorithm can be found in [13, 34, 81, 98]. Recently, Toledo [114] showed how to handle nonlinear polynomials, using Collins' cylindrical algebraic decomposition scheme [35].

3   Alternatives Approaches to Parametric Searching

Despite its power and versatility, the parametric searching technique, nevertheless, has some shortcomings:

(i) Parametric searching requires the design of an efficient parallel algorithm for the generic version of the decision procedure. This is not always easy, and it often tends to make the overall solution quite complicated and impractical.

(ii) The generic algorithm requires exact computation of the roots of the polynomials whose signs determine the outcome of the comparisons made by the algorithm. Such computation is possible, using standard computational algebra techniques, but it is often a time-consuming step.

(iii) Finally, from an aesthetic point of view, the execution of an algorithm based on parametric searching may appear to be somewhat chaotic, and its behavior is often difficult to explain in terms of the geometry of the problem.

These shortcomings have led several researchers to look for alternative approaches to parametric searching for geometric optimization problems. Roughly speaking, parametric searching effectively conducts an implicit binary search over a set $\Lambda = \{\lambda_1, \ldots, \lambda_t\}$ of 'critical values' of the parameter λ, to locate the optimum λ^* among them. (For example, in the slope selection problem, the critical values are the $\Theta(n^2)$ x-coordinates of the vertices of the arrangement $\mathcal{A}(L)$.) The power of the technique stems from its ability to generate only a small number of critical values during the search.

There are alternative ways of generating a small number of critical values in certain special cases. For example, one can use randomization: Suppose we know that λ^* lies in some interval $I = [\alpha, \beta]$. If we can randomly choose an element $\lambda_0 \in I \cap \Lambda$, where each item is chosen with probability $1/|I \cap \Lambda|$, then it follows that, with high probability, the size of $I \cap \Lambda$ will shrink significantly by performing just a few comparisons with the randomly chosen elements. Proceeding along these lines, Matoušek [79] gave a very simple algorithm for the slope selection problem, which runs in $O(n \log n)$ expected time. Other randomized techniques in geometric optimization will be mentioned in Section 5.

This randomized approach can be derandomized, without affecting the asymptotic running time, using standard techniques, such as *expanders* and *geometric partitionings*. Ajtai and Megiddo [16] gave an efficient parallel linear programming algorithm based on expanders, and later Katz [70] and Katz and Sharir [71, 72] applied expanders to solve several geometric optimization problems, including the slope selection problem. Brönniman and Chazelle [22] used geometric partitionings (also known as *cuttings*), to obtain a simpler $O(n \log n)$-time deterministic algorithm for the slope selection problem.

An entirely different approach to parametric searching was proposed by Frederickson and Johnson [50, 51, 52, 53], which is based on searching in *sorted matrices*. It is applicable in cases where the set Λ of candidate critical values for the optimum parameter λ^* can be stored in an $n \times n$ matrix A, each of whose rows and columns is sorted. The size of the matrix is too large for explicit binary search through its elements, so an implicit search is needed. This is done in a logarithmic number of iterations. In each stage, we have a collection of submatrices of A. We decompose each matrix into four submatrices, and run the decision procedure on the median value of the smallest elements in each submatrix, and on the median value of the largest elements in each submatrix. It is shown in [50, 52, 53] that this allows us to discard many submatrices, so that the number of matrices only roughly doubles at each stage, and the final number of matrices is only $O(n)$. This implies that the technique can be implemented with only $O(\log n)$ calls to the decision procedure and with only $O(n)$ other constant-time operations. The technique, when applicable, is both efficient and simple, as compared with standard parametric searching.

4   Prune-and-Search Technique

Like parametric searching, the *prune-and-search* (or *decimation*) technique also performs an implicit binary search over the finite set of candidate values for λ^*, but, while doing so, it also tries to eliminate input objects that can be determined not to affect the value of λ^*. Each phase of the technique eliminates a constant fraction of the remaining objects, so that, after a logarithmic number of steps, the problem size becomes a constant, and the problem can be solved in a final, brute-force step. The overall cost of the resulting algorithm remains proportional to the cost of a single pruning stage. The prune-and-search technique was originally introduced by Megiddo [89, 90], in developing an $O(2^{2^d}n)$-time algorithm for linear programming with n constraints in $\mathbb{R}^d$, but was later applied to many other geometric optimization problems (see Section 5). We illustrate the technique by describing Megiddo's two-dimensional linear programming algorithm.

We are given a set $H = \{h_1, \dots, h_n\}$ of n halfplanes and a vector c, and we wish to minimize cx over the *feasible region* $K = \bigcap_{i=1}^n h_i$. Without loss of generality, assume that $c = (0, 1)$. Let L denote the set of lines bounding the halfplanes of H, and let L^+ (resp. L^-) denote the subset of lines $\ell_i \in L$ whose associated halfplane h_i lies below (resp. above) ℓ_i. The algorithm pairs up the lines of L into disjoint pairs (ℓ_1, ℓ_2), $(\ell_3, \ell_4), \dots$, such that the lines in a pair either both belong to L^+ or both belong to L^-. The algorithm computes the intersection points of the lines in each pair, and chooses the median, x_m, of their x-coordinates. Let x^* denote the x-coordinate of the optimal point in K (if such a point exists). The algorithm then uses a linear-time decision procedure that compares x_m with x^*. If $x_m = x^*$ we stop, since we have found the optimum. Suppose that $x_m < x^*$. If (ℓ, ℓ') is a pair of lines, such that they both belong to L^-, and such that their intersection point lies to the left of x_m, then we can discard the line with the smaller slope from any further consideration, because that line is known to pass below the optimal point of K. All other cases can be treated in a fully symmetric manner, so we have managed to discard about $n/4$ lines. The running time of this pruning step is $O(n)$.

We have thus computed, in $O(n)$ time, a subset $H' \subseteq H$ of about $3n/4$ constraints such that the optimal point of $K' = \bigcap_{h \in H'} h$ is the same as that of K. We now apply the whole procedure once again to H', and keep repeating this, for $O(\log n)$ stages, until either the number of remaining lines falls below some small constant, in which case we solve the problem by brute force (in constant time), or the algorithm has hit x^* 'accidentally', in which case it stops right away. (We omit here the description of the decision procedure, and of handling cases in which K is empty or unbounded; see [45, 89, 90] for details.) It is now easy to see that the overall running time of the algorithm is $O(n)$.

This technique can be extended to higher dimensions, although it becomes more complicated, and requires recursive invocations of the algorithm on subproblems in lower dimensions. It yields a deterministic algorithm for linear programming that runs in $O(C_d n)$ time. The original algorithm of Megiddo gives $C_d = 2^{2^d}$, which was improved by Clarkson [30] and Dyer [41] to 3^{d^2}. Using randomization techniques, a number of simpler randomized algorithms have been developed for the problem [31, 43, 103, 117], with a better dependence on d, of which the best expected running time, $O(d^2 n + d^{d/2+O(1)} \log n)$, is due to Clarkson [31]. By derandomizing the algorithms in [31, 43], one can obtain $d^{O(d)}n$-time deterministic algorithms for linear programming in $\mathbb{R}^d$ [13, 26]. In Section 6, we will describe further improved randomized algorithms, due to Kalai [68] and to Matoušek et al. [86] (see also [110]), with subexponential expected running time.

5   Applications

In this section we briefly survey many geometric applications of parametric searching and its variants, and of the prune-and-search technique. Numerous nongeometric optimization problems have also benefited from these techniques (see [14, 34, 50, 59, 98] for a sample of such applications). Although the common theme of all the problems mentioned below is that they can be solved efficiently using parametric-searching and prune-and-search techniques, each of them requires a specific, and often fairly sophisticated, approach, involving the design of efficient sequential and parallel algorithms for solving the appropriate decision steps.

5.1   Facility Location Problems

A typical facility location problem is: Given a set D of n demand points in the plane, and a parameter p, we wish to find p supply objects (points, lines, segments, etc.), so that the maximum (Euclidean) distance between each point of D and its nearest supply object is minimized. Instead of minimizing this L_∞-norm, one can ask for the minimization of the L_1 or the L_2 norm of those 'deviations'. If p is considered as part of the input, most facility location problems are known to be NP-hard, even when the supply objects are points in the plane [94]. However, for fixed values of p, most of these problems can be solved in polynomial time. In this subsection we review efficient algorithms for some special cases of these problems.

p-center. Here we wish to compute the smallest real value r^* and a set S of p points, such that the union of disks of radius r^* centered at the points of S cover the given planar point set D. The decision problem is to determine, for a given radius r, whether D can be covered by the union of p disks of radius r. The decision problem for the 1-center is thus to determine whether D can be covered by a disk of radius r, which can be done in $O(\log n)$ parallel steps using $O(n)$ processors. This yields an $O(n \log^3 n)$-time algorithm for the 1-center problem. Using the prune-and-search paradigm, one can, however, solve the 1-center problem in linear time [41].

There is a trivial $O(n^3)$-time algorithm for the 2-center problem [40], which was improved by Agarwal and Sharir [10] to $O(n^2 \log^3 n)$, and then by Hershberger [61] to $O(n^2 \log^2 n)$. Matoušek [79] gave a simpler $O(n^2 \log^2 n)$ algorithm by replacing parametric searching by randomization. The best near-quadratic solution is due to Jaromczyk and Kowaluk [66], and runs in $O(n^2 \log n)$ time. A major progress on this problem was made recently by Sharir [107], who gave an $O(n \log^9 n)$-time algorithm, by combining the parametric searching technique with several additional tricks, including a variant of the matrix searching algorithm of Frederickson and Johnson [52]. See also [21, 39, 48, 74, 92, 93] for other results on p-center problems.

p-line-center. Here we wish to compute the smallest real value w^* such that D can be covered by the union of p strips of width w^*. For $p = 1$, this is the classical *width* problem, which can be solved in $O(n \log n)$ time [62]. For $p = 2$, Agarwal and Sharir [10] (see also [8]) gave an $O(n^2 \log^5 n)$-time algorithm. The running time was improved to $O(n^2 \log^4 n)$ by Katz and Sharir [72] and by Glozman et al. [55], using expander graphs and the matrix searching technique, respectively; see also [67].

Segment-center. Given a segment e, we wish to find a translated and rotated copy of e such that the maximum distance from this copy to the points of D is minimized. This problem was originally considered in [64], where an $O(n^4 \log n)$ algorithm was given. An improved solution, based on parametric searching, with $O(n^2 \alpha(n) \log^3 n)$ running time, was later obtained in [4]. The best known solution, due to Efrat and Sharir [47], runs in time $O(n^{1+\varepsilon})$, for any $\varepsilon > 0$; it is also based on parametric searching, but uses a deeper combinatorial analysis of the problem structure.

5.2 Proximity Problems

Diameter. Given a set S of n points in $\mathbb{R}^3$, we wish to compute the *diameter* of S, that is, the maximum distance between two points of S. A very simple $O(n \log n)$ expected-time randomized algorithm (which is worst-case optimal) was given by Clarkson and Shor [33], but no optimal deterministic algorithm is known. The best known deterministic solution is due to Brönniman et al. [23], and runs in $O(n \log^3 n)$ time. It is based on parametric searching, and uses some interesting derandomization techniques. See also [25, 85, 104] for earlier close-to-linear time algorithms based on parametric searching.

Closest line pair. Given a set L of n lines in the $\mathbb{R}^3$, we wish to compute a closest pair of lines in L. Independently, Chazelle et al. [25] and Pellegrini [99] gave parametric-searching based algorithms for this problem, whose running time is $O(n^{8/5+\varepsilon})$, for any $\varepsilon > 0$. If we are interested in computing a pair with the minimum vertical distance, the running time can be improved to $O(n^{4/3+\varepsilon})$ [99].

Selecting distances. Let S be a set of n points in the plane, and let $1 \le k \le \binom{n}{2}$ be an integer. We wish to compute the k-th smallest distance between a pair of points of S. The decision problem is to compute, for a given real r, the sum $\sum_{p \in S} |D_r(p) \cap (S - \{p\})|$, where $D_r(p)$ is the disk of radius r centered at p. (This sum is twice the number of pairs of points of S at distance $\le r$.) Agarwal et al. [2] gave an $O(n^{4/3} \log^{4/3} n)$ expected-time randomized algorithm for the decision problem, which yielded an $O(n^{4/3} \log^{8/3} n)$-time algorithm for the distance selection problem. Goodrich [56] derandomized this algorithm. Katz and Sharir [71] gave an expander-based $O(n^{4/3} \log^{3+\varepsilon} n)$-time algorithm for this problem, for any $\varepsilon > 0$. See also [102].

Minimum Hausdorff distance between polygons. Let P and Q be two polygons with m and n edges, respectively. The problem is to compute the *minimum Hausdorff distance under translation* between P and Q in the Euclidean metric. The Hausdorff distance is one of the common ways of measuring the resemblance between two sets P and Q [63]; it is defined as

$$H(P,Q) = \max \left\{ \max_{a \in P} \min_{b \in Q} d(a,b), \ \max_{a \in Q} \min_{b \in P} d(a,b) \right\},$$

and we wish to compute $\min_v \; H(P+v, Q)$. The problem has been solved in [12], using parametric searching, in $O((mn)^2 \log^3(mn))$ time, which is significantly faster than the previously best known algorithm of [17]. See [27, 28] for other parametric-searching based results on this problem.

5.3 Statistical Estimators and Related Problems

Plane fitting. Given a set S of n points in $\mathbb{R}^3$, we wish to fit a plane h through S so that the maximum distance between h and the points of S is minimized. This is the same problem as computing the *width* of S, which is considerably harder than the two-dimensional variant mentioned above. Chazelle et al. [25] gave an algorithm that is based on parametric searching and runs in time $O(n^{8/5+\varepsilon})$, for any $\varepsilon > 0$ (see also [1] for an improved bound). By replacing parametric searching with randomization, and by applying a more involved combinatorial analysis of the problem structure, Agarwal and Sharir [11] obtained the currently best solution, which runs in $O(n^{3/2+\varepsilon})$ expected time, for any $\varepsilon > 0$. See also [75, 84, 111, 116] for other results on hyperplane fitting.

Circle fitting. Given a set S of n points in the plane, we wish to fit a circle C through S, so that the maximum distance between C and the points of S is minimized. This is equivalent to finding an annulus of minimum width that contains S. This problem was initially solved in [44], by a quadratic-time algorithm, which was improved, using parametric searching, to $O(n^{17/11+\varepsilon})$, for any $\varepsilon > 0$ [1]. Using randomization and an improved analysis, this can be improved to $O(n^{3/2+\varepsilon})$ time, for any $\varepsilon > 0$ [11]. Finding an annulus of minimum area that contains S is a simpler problem, since it can be formulated as an instance of linear programming in $\mathbb{R}^4$, and can thus be solved in $O(n)$ time [90].

Center points. Given a set S of n points in the plane, we wish to determine a point $\sigma \in \mathbb{R}^2$, such that any halfplane containing σ also contains at least $\lfloor n/3 \rfloor$ points of S. (It is known that such σ always exists [45].) Cole et al. [37] gave an $O(n \log^3 n)$-time algorithm for computing σ, using multi-dimensional parametric searching. Using the prune-and-search paradigm, Matoušek [80] gave an $O(n \log^3 n)$-time algorithm for computing the set of all center points. Recently, Jadhav and Mukhopadhyay [65] gave a linear-time algorithm for computing a center point, using a direct and elegant technique.

For computing a center point in three dimensions, near-quadratic algorithms were developed in [37, 97]. Clarkson et al. [32] gave an efficient algorithm for computing an approximate center point.

Ham-sandwich cuts. Let $A_1, \dots, A_d$ be d point sets in $\mathbb{R}^d$. A *ham-sandwich cut* is a hyperplane that simultaneously bisects all the A_i's. The ham-sandwich theorem (see, e.g., [45]) guarantees the existence of such a cut.

Several prune-and-search algorithms have been proposed for computing a ham-sandwich cut in the plane. For the special case when A_1 and A_2 are linearly separable, Megiddo [91] gave a linear time algorithm. Modifying his algorithm, Edelsbrunner and Waupotitsch [46] gave an $O(n \log n)$-time algorithm when A_1 and A_2 are not linearly separable. The running time was then improved to linear

by Lo and Steiger [77]. Efficient algorithms for higher dimensions are given by
Lo et al. [76].

5.4   Placement and Intersection

Polygon placement. Let P be a polygonal object with m edges, and let Q be a
closed planar polygonal environment with n edges. We wish to find the largest
similar copy of P (under translation, rotation, and scaling) that can be placed
inside Q. Sharir and Toledo [109] gave an $O(m^3 n^2 2^{\alpha(mn)} \log^3 mn \log \log mn)$-
time algorithm, using parametric searching. If both P and Q are convex and
rotations are not allowed, then the problem can be solved in $O(m + n \log^2 n)$
time [112]. See also [29] for related results.

A special case of this problem is the so called *biggest-stick* problem, where,
given a simple polygon Q, we wish to find the longest segment that can be placed
inside Q. A randomized algorithm with expected-time $O(n^{3/2+\varepsilon})$, for any $\varepsilon > 0$,
is given in [11].

Intersection of polyhedra. Given a set $\mathcal{P} = \{P_1, \ldots, P_m\}$ of m convex polyhedra
in $\mathbb{R}^d$, with a total of n facets, do they have a common intersection point?
Reichling [105] gave an $O(\log m \log n)$-time prune-and-search algorithm for $d = 2$, and later extended his approach to $d = 3$ [106]. Using multi-dimensional
parametric searching, his approach can be generalized to higher dimensions.

5.5   Query Type Problems

Agarwal and Matoušek [5] gave a general technique, based on parametric searching, to answer *ray-shooting queries* (where we wish to preprocess a given set of
objects in $\mathbb{R}^d$, so that the first object hit by a query ray can be computed efficiently). This technique, further elaborated in [6, 9], has yielded fast algorithms
for several related problems, including hidden surface removal, nearest neighbor searching, computing convex layers, and computing higher-order Voronoi
diagrams; see [5, 6, 7, 100] for some of these results. Using multi-dimensional
parametric searching, Matoušek presented in [81] efficient algorithms for *linear
optimization queries*, where we wish to preprocess a set H of halfspaces in $\mathbb{R}^d$
into a linear-size data structure, so that, given a query linear objective function
c, we can efficiently compute the vertex of $\bigcap H$ that minimizes c. See [3, 7, 81]
for additional applications of multi-dimensional parametric searching for query
type problems.

6   Abstract Linear Programming

In this section we present an abstract framework that captures both linear programming and many other geometric optimization problems, including computing smallest enclosing balls (or ellipsoids) of finite point sets in $\mathbb{R}^d$, computing largest balls (ellipsoids) in convex polytopes in $\mathbb{R}^d$, computing the distance
between polytopes in d-space, general convex programming, and many other
problems. Sharir and Welzl [110] and Matoušek et al. [86] (see also Kalai [68])
presented a randomized algorithm for optimization problems in this framework,
whose expected running time is linear in terms of the number of constraints

whenever the dimension d is fixed. More importantly, the running time is 'subexponential' for many of the LP-type problems, including linear programming. To be more precise, what is measured here is the number of primitive operations that the algorithm performs on the constraints (see below for details). This is the first subexponential 'combinatorial' bound for linear programming (a bound that counts the number of arithmetic operations and is independent of the bit complexity of the input), and is a first step toward the major open problem of obtaining a strongly polynomial algorithm for linear programming.

6.1   An Abstract Framework

Let us consider optimization problems specified by pairs (H, w), where H is a finite set, and $w : 2^H \to \mathcal{W}$ is a function with values in a linearly ordered set $(\mathcal{W}, \leq)$; we assume that $\mathcal{W}$ has a minimum value $-\infty$. The elements of H are called *constraints*, and for $G \subseteq H$, $w(G)$ is called the *value of G*. Intuitively, $w(G)$ denotes the smallest value attainable for certain objective function while satisfying all the constraints of G. The goal is to compute a minimal subset B_H of H with the same value as H (from which, in general, the value of H is easy to determine), assuming the availability of three basic operations to be specified below.

Such a minimization problem is called *LP-type* if the following two axioms are satisfied:

Axiom 1.   (*Monotonicity*) For any F, G with $F \subseteq G \subseteq H$, we have
$$w(F) \leq w(G)$$

Axiom 2.   (*Locality*) For any $F \subseteq G \subseteq H$ with $-\infty < w(F) = w(G)$ and any $h \in H$,
$$w(G) < w(G \cup \{h\}) \Rightarrow w(F) < w(F \cup \{h\}).$$

Linear programming is easily shown to be an LP-type problem, if we set $w(G)$ to be the vertex of the feasible region which minimizes the objective function and which is lexicographically smallest (this definition is important to satisfy Axiom 2), and if we define $w(G)$ in an appropriate manner to handle empty or unbounded feasible regions.

A *basis* B is a set of constraints with $-\infty < w(B)$, and $w(B') < w(B)$ for all proper subsets B' of B. For $G \subseteq H$, if $-\infty < w(G)$, a *basis of G* is a minimal subset B of G with $w(B) = w(G)$. (For linear programming, a basis is a minimal set of halfspace constraints such that the minimal vertex of their intersection is some prescribed vertex.) A constraint h is *violated by G*, if $w(G) < w(G \cup \{h\})$, and it is *extreme in G*, if $w(G - \{h\}) < w(G)$. The *combinatorial dimension* of (H, w), denoted as $\dim(H, w)$, is the maximum cardinality of any basis. We call an LP-type problem *basis regular* if for any basis with $|B| = \dim(H, w)$ and for any constraint h, every basis of $B \cup \{h\}$ has exactly $\dim(H, w)$ elements. (Clearly, linear programming is basis-regular, where the dimension of every basis is d.)

We assume that the following primitive operations are available.

(*Violation test*) '*h* is violated by *B*', for a constraint h and a basis B, tests whether h is violated by B or not.

(*Basis computation*) '`basis(B, h)`', for a constraint h and a basis B, computes a basis of $B \cup \{h\}$.

(*Initial basis*) An initial basis B_0 with exactly $\dim(H, w)$ elements is available.

For linear programming, the first operation can be done in $O(d)$ time, by substituting the coordinates of the vertex $w(B)$ into the equation of the hyperplane defining h. The second operation can be regarded as a dual version of the pivot step in the simplex algorithm, and can be implemented in $O(d^2)$ time. The third operation is also easy to implement.

We are now in position to describe the algorithm. Using the initial-basis primitive, we compute a basis B_0 and use the following recursive algorithm to compute B_H.

```
function procedure SUBEX_lp(H,C);          /* H: n constraints in R^d;
    if H = C then                              /* C ⊆ H: a basis;
        return C                               /* returns a basis of H.
    else
        choose a random h ∈ H − C;
        B := SUBEX_lp(H − {h}, C);
        if h is violated by B then             /* ⇔ v_B ∉ h
            return SUBEX_lp(H, basis(B,h))
        else
            return B;
```

A simple inductive argument shows the expected number of primitive operations performed by the algorithm is $O(2^\delta n)$, where $n = |H|$ and $\delta = \dim(H, w)$ is the combinatorial dimension. However, using a more involved analysis, which can be found in [86], one can show that basis-regular LP-type problems can be solved with an expected number of at most $e^{2\sqrt{\delta \ln((n-\delta)/\sqrt{\delta})} + O(\sqrt{\delta} + \ln n)}$ violation tests and basis computations. This is the 'subexponential' bound that we alluded to.

6.2 Linear Programming

We are given a set H of n halfspaces in $\mathbb{R}^d$. We assume that the objective vector is $c = (1, 0, 0, \ldots, 0)$, and the goal is to minimize cx over all points in the common intersection $\bigcap_{h \in H} h$. For a subset $G \subseteq H$, define $w(G)$ to be the lexicographically smallest point (vertex) of the intersection of halfspaces in G.

As noted above, linear programming is a basis-regular LP-type problem, with combinatorial dimension d, and violation tests and basis changes operations can be implemented in time $O(d)$ and $O(d^2)$, respectively. In summary, we obtain a randomized algorithm for linear programming, which performs $e^{2\sqrt{d \ln(n/\sqrt{d})} + O(\sqrt{d} + \ln n)}$ expected number of arithmetic operations. Combining this algorithm with Clarkson's randomized linear programming algorithm mentioned in Section 4, the expected number of arithmetic operations can be reduced to $O(d^2 n) + e^{O(\sqrt{d \log d})}$.

Matoušek [82] has given examples of abstract LP-type problems of combinatorial dimension d and with $2d$ constraints, for which the above algorithm requires $\Omega(e^{\sqrt{2d}}/\sqrt[4]{d})$ primitive operations. Hence, in order to obtain a better bound on the performance of the algorithm for linear programming, one should aim to exploit additional properties of linear programming; this is still open.

6.3 Smallest Enclosing Ball and Related Problems

In Section 5.1 we mentioned that the smallest enclosing ball (i.e., disk) of a set of n points in the plane can be computed in linear time. In higher dimensions, one can solve this problem by an $d^{O(d)} n$-time algorithm [13, 26, 42]. It can be shown that the smallest enclosing ball problem is an LP-type problem, with combinatorial dimension $d+1$. It is, however, not basis-regular, and a naive implementation of the basis-changing operation may be quite costly (in d). Nevertheless, Gärtner [54] showed that this operation can be performed in this case using expected $e^{O(\sqrt{d})}$ arithmetic operations. Hence, the expected running time of the algorithm is $O(d^2 n) + e^{O(\sqrt{d \log d})}$.

There are several extensions of the smallest enclosing ball problem. They include: (i) computing the smallest enclosing ellipsoid of a point set [26, 42, 101, 117], (ii) computing the largest ellipsoid (or ball) inscribed inside a convex polytope in $\mathbb{R}^d$ [54], (iii) computing a smallest ball that intersects (or contains) a given set of convex objects in $\mathbb{R}^d$, and (iv) computing a smallest volume annulus containing a given planar point set. All these problems are known to be LP-type, and thus can be solved using the above algorithm. However, not all of them run in subexponential expected time because they are not basis regular.

6.4 Distance Between Polytopes

We wish to compute the Euclidean distance $d(\mathcal{P}_1, \mathcal{P}_2)$ between two given closed polytopes $\mathcal{P}_1$ and $\mathcal{P}_2$. If the polytopes intersect, then this distance is 0. If they do not intersect, then this distance equals the maximum distance between two parallel hyperplanes separating the polytopes; such a pair of hyperplanes is unique, and they are orthogonal to the segment connecting two points $a \in \mathcal{P}_1$ and $b \in \mathcal{P}_2$ with $d(a, b) = d(\mathcal{P}_1, \mathcal{P}_2)$. It is shown by Gärtner [54] that this problem is LP-type, with combinatorial dimension at most $d + 2$ (or $d + 1$, if the polytopes do not intersect). It is also shown there that the primitive operations can be performed with expected $e^{O(\sqrt{d})}$ arithmetic operations. Hence, as above, the expected number of arithmetic operations is $O(d^2 n) + e^{O(\sqrt{d \log d})}$.

6.5 Extensions

Recently, Chazelle and Matoušek [26] gave a deterministic algorithm for solving LP-type problems in time $O(\delta^{O(\delta)} n)$, provided an additional axiom holds (together with an additional computational assumption). Still, these extra requirements are satisfied in many natural LP-type problems. Matoušek [83] investigates the problem of finding the best solution, for abstract LP-type problems, which satisfies all but k of the given constraints.

Amenta [18] considers the following extension of the abstract framework: Suppose we are given a family of LP-type problems (H, w_λ), monotonically parameterized by a real parameter λ; the underlying ordered value set $\mathcal{W}$ has a maximum element $+\infty$ representing *infeasibility*. The goal is to find the smallest λ for which (H, w_λ) is feasible, i.e. $w_\lambda(H) < +\infty$. See [19, 20] for related work.

6.6 Abstract Linear Programming and Helly-type Theorems

In this subsection we describe an interesting connection between Helly-type theorems and LP-type problems, as originally noted by Amenta [18].

Let $\mathbf{K}$ be an infinite collection of sets in $\mathbb{R}^d$, and let t be an integer. We say that $\mathbf{K}$ satisfies a *Helly-type* theorem, with *Helly number* t, if the following holds: If $\mathcal{K}$ is a finite subcollection of $\mathbf{K}$ with the property that every subcollection of t elements of $\mathcal{K}$ has a nonempty intersection, then $\bigcap \mathcal{K} \neq \emptyset$. (The best known example of a Helly-type theorem is Helly's theorem itself [60], which applies for the collection $\mathbf{K}$ of all convex sets in $\mathbb{R}^d$, with the Helly number $d + 1$.) Suppose further that we are given a collection $\mathcal{K}(\lambda)$, consisting of n sets $K_1(\lambda), \ldots, K_n(\lambda)$ that are parametrized by some real parameter λ, with the property that $K_i(\lambda) \subseteq K_i(\lambda')$, for $i = 1, \ldots, n$ and for $\lambda \leq \lambda'$, and that, for any fixed λ, the family $\{K_1(\lambda), \ldots, K_n(\lambda)\}$ admits a Helly-type theorem, with Helly number t. Our goal is to compute the smallest λ for which $\bigcap_{i=1}^{n} K_i(\lambda) \neq \emptyset$, assuming that such a minimum exists. Amenta proved that this problem can be transformed to an LP-type problem, whose combinatorial dimension is at most t.

As an illustration, consider the smallest enclosing ball problem. Let $P = \{p_1, \ldots, p_n\}$ be the given set of n points in $\mathbb{R}^d$, and let $K_i(\lambda)$ be the ball of radius λ centered at p_i, for $i = 1, \ldots, n$. Since the K_i's are convex, the collection in question has Helly number $d + 1$. It is easily seen that the minimal λ for which the $K_i(\lambda)$'s have nonempty intersection is the radius of the smallest enclosing ball of P.

There are several other examples where Helly-type theorems can be turned into LP-type problems. They include (i) computing a line transversal to a family of translates of some convex objects in the plane, (ii) computing a smallest homothet of a given convex set that intersects (or contains, or is contained in) every member in a given collection of n convex sets in $\mathbb{R}^d$, and (iii) computing a line transversal to certain families of convex objects in 3-space. We refer the reader to [19, 20] for more details and for additional examples.

References

[1] P. Agarwal, B. Aronov, and M. Sharir, Computing lower envelopes in four dimensions with applications, *Proc. 10th ACM Symp. Comput. Geom.*, 1994, pp. 348–358.

[2] P. Agarwal, B. Aronov, M. Sharir, and S. Suri, Selecting distances in the plane, *Algorithmica* 9 (1993), 495–514.

[3] P. Agarwal, A. Efrat, and M. Sharir, Vertical decomposition of shallow levels in 3-dimensional arrangements and its applications, *Proc. 11th ACM Symp. Comput. Geom.*, 1995, 39–50.

[4] P. Agarwal, A. Efrat, M. Sharir, and S. Toledo, Computing a segment-center for a planar point set, *J. Algorithms* 15 (1993), 314–323.

[5] P. Agarwal and J. Matoušek, Ray shooting and parametric search, *SIAM J. Comput.* 22 (1993), 794–806.

[6] P. Agarwal and J. Matoušek, Range searching with semialgebraic sets, *Discr. Comput. Geom.* 11 (1994), 393–418.

[7] P. Agarwal and J. Matoušek, Dynamic half-space range searching and its applications, *Algorithmica* 14 (1995), 325–345.

[8] P. Agarwal and M. Sharir, Off line dynamic maintenance of the width of a planar point set, *Comput. Geom. Theory Appls.* 1 (1991), 65–78.

[9] P. Agarwal and M. Sharir, Ray shooting among convex polytopes in three dimensions, *SIAM J. Comput.*, to appear.

[10] P. Agarwal and M. Sharir, Planar geometric location problems, *Algorithmica* 11 (1994), 185–195.

[11] P. Agarwal and M. Sharir, Efficient randomized algorithms for some geometric optimization problems, *Proc. 11th ACM Symp. Comput. Geom.*, 1995, pp. 326–335.

[12] P. Agarwal, M. Sharir, and S. Toledo, New applications of parametric searching in computational geometry, *J. Algorithms* 17 (1994), 292–318.

[13] P. Agarwal, M. Sharir, and S. Toledo, An efficient multi-dimensional searching technique and its applications, Tech. Rept. CS-1993-20, Dept. Comp. Sci., Duke University, 1993.

[14] R. Agarwala and D. Fernández-Baca, Weighted multidimensional search and its applications to convex optimization, *SIAM J. Comput.*, to appear.

[15] M. Ajtai, J. Komlós, and E. Szemerédi, Sorting in $c \log n$ parallel steps, *Combinatorica*, 3 (1983), 1–19.

[16] M. Ajtai and N. Megiddo, A deterministic $poly(\log \log N)$-time N-processor algorithm for linear programming in fixed dimension, *Proc. 24th ACM Symp. Theory of Comput.*, 1992, pp. 327–338.

[17] H. Alt, B. Behrends, and J. Blömer, Approximate matching of polygonal shapes, *Proc. 7th ACM Symp. Comput. Geom.*, 1991, pp. 186–193.

[18] N. Amenta, Finding a line transversal of axial objects in three dimensions, *Proc. 3rd ACM-SIAM Symp. Discr. Algo.*, 1992, pp. 66–71.

[19] N. Amenta, Helly-type theorems and generalized linear programming, *Discr. Comput. Geom.* 12 (1994), 241–261.

[20] N. Amenta, Bounded boxes, Hausdorff distance, and a new proof of an interesting Helly-type theorem, *Proc. 10th ACM Symp. Comput. Geom.*, 1994, pp. 340–347.

[21] R. Bar-Yehuda, A. Efrat, and A. Itai, A simple algorithm for maintaining the center of a planar point-set, *Proc. 5th Canad. Conf. Comput. Geom.*, 1993, pp. 252–257.

[22] H. Brönnimann and B. Chazelle, Optimal slope selection via cuttings, *Proc. 6th Canad. Conf. Comput. Geom.*, 1994, pp. 99–103.

[23] H. Brönnimann, B. Chazelle, and J. Matoušek, Product range spaces, sensitive sampling, and derandomization, *Proc. 34th IEEE Symp. Found. of Comp. Sci.*, 1993, pp. 400–409.

[24] B. Chazelle, H. Edelsbrunner, L. Guibas, and M. Sharir, Algorithms for bichromatic line segment problems and polyhedral terrains, *Algorithmica* 11 (1994), 116–132.

[25] B. Chazelle, H. Edelsbrunner, L. Guibas, and M. Sharir, Diameter, width, closest line pair, and parametric searching, *Discr. Comput. Geom.* 10 (1993), 183–196.

[26] B. Chazelle and J. Matoušek, On linear-time deterministic algorithms for optimization problems in fixed dimensions, *Proc. 4th ACM-SIAM Symp. Discr. Algo.*, 1993, pp. 281–290.

[27] P. Chew, D. Dor, A. Efrat, and K. Kedem, Geometric pattern matching in d-dimensional space, *Proc. 3rd European Symp. Algo.*, 1995, to appear.

[28] P. Chew and K. Kedem, Improvements on geometric pattern matching problems, *Proc. 3rd Scand. Work. Algo. Theory*, 1992, pp. 318–325.

[29] P. Chew and K. Kedem, A convex polygon among polygonal obstacles: Placement and high-clearance motion, *Comput. Geom. Theory Appls.* 3 (1993), 59–89.

[30] K. Clarkson, Linear Programming in $O(n \cdot 3^{d^2})$ time, *Inform. Process. Lett.* 22 (1986), 21–24.

[31] K. Clarkson, Las Vegas algorithms for linear and integer programming when the dimension is small, *J. ACM* 45 (1995), 488–499.

[32] K. Clarkson, D. Eppstein, G. Miller, C. Sturtivant, and S.-H. Teng, Approximating center points with iterated Radon points, *Proc. 9th ACM Symp. Comput. Geom.*, 1993, pp. 91–98.

[33] K. Clarkson and P. Shor, Applications of random sampling in computational geometry, II, *Discr. Comput. Geom.* 4 (1989), 387–421.

[34] E. Cohen and N. Megiddo, Maximizing concave functions in fixed dimension, in *Complexity in Numeric Computation* (P. Pardalos, ed.), World Scientific, 1993.

[35] R. Cole, Slowing down sorting networks to obtain faster sorting algorithms, *J. ACM* 31 (1984), 200–208.

[36] R. Cole, J. Salowe, W. Steiger, and E. Szemerédi, Optimal slope selection, *SIAM J. Comput.* 18 (1989), 792–810.

[37] R. Cole, M. Sharir, and C. Yap, On k-hulls and related problems, *SIAM J. Comput.* 16 (1987), 61–77.

[38] G. Collins, Quantifier elimination for real closed fields by cylindrical algebraic decomposition, in *Second GI Conf. on Automata Theory and Formal Languages*, Lecture Notes in Comp. Sci., 33, Springer-Verlag, 1975, pp. 134–183.

[39] Z. Drezner, On the rectangular p-center problem, *Naval Res. Logist. Quart.*, 34 (1987), 229–234.

[40] Z. Drezner, The P-center problem: Heuristics and optimal algorithms, *J. Oper. Res. Soc.* 35 (1984), 741–748.

[41] M. Dyer, On a multidimensional search technique and its application to the Euclidean one-center problem, *SIAM J. Comput.* 15 (1986), 725–738.

[42] M. Dyer, A class of convex programs with applications to computational geometry, *Proc. 8th ACM Symp. Comput. Geom.*, 1992, pp. 9–15.

[43] M. Dyer and A. Frieze, A randomized algorithm for fixed-dimensional linear programming, *Math. Prog.* 44 (1989), 203–212.

[44] H. Ebara, N. Fukuyama, H. Nakano and Y. Nakanishi, Roundness algorithms using the Voronoi diagrams, *First Canad. Conf. Comput. Geom.*, 1989.

[45] H. Edelsbrunner, *Algorithms in Combinatorial Geometry*, Springer-Verlag, Heidelberg, 1987.

[46] H. Edelsbrunner and R. Waupotitsch, Computing a ham-sandwich cut in two dimensions, *J. Symb. Comput.* 2 (1986), 171–178.

[47] A. Efrat and M. Sharir, A near-linear algorithm for the planar segment center problem, *Discr. Comput. Geom.*, to appear.

[48] A. Efrat, M. Sharir and A. Ziv, Computing the smallest k-enclosing circle and related problems, *Comput. Geom. Theory Appls.* 4 (1994), 119–136.

[49] M. Eisner and D. Severance, Mathematical techniques for efficient record segmentation in large shared databases, *JACM* 23 (1976), 619–635.

[50] G. Frederickson, Optimal algorithms for tree partitioning, *Proc. 2nd ACM-SIAM Symp. Discr. Algo.*, 1991, pp. 168–177.

[51] G. Frederickson and D. Johnson, The complexity of selection and ranking in $X + Y$ and matrices with sorted columns, *J. Comp. Syst. Sci.* 24 (1982), 197–208.

[52] G. Frederickson and D. Johnson, Finding the k-th shortest paths and p-centers by generating and searching good data structures, *J. Algorithms* 4 (1983), 61–80.

[53] G. Frederickson and D. Johnson, Generalized selection and ranking: sorted matrices, *SIAM J. Comput.* 13 (1984), 14–30.

[54] B. Gärtner, A subexponential algorithm for abstract optimization problems, *Proc. 33rd IEEE Symp. Found. of Comp. Sci.*, 1992, pp. 464–472.

[55] A. Glozman, K. Kedem, and G. Shpitalnik, On some geometric selection and optimization problems via sorted matrices, *Proc. 4th Workshop Algo. and Data Struct.*, 1995, to appear.

[56] M. Goodrich, Geometric partitioning made easier, even in parallel, *Proc. 9th ACM Symp. Comput. Geom.*, 1993, pp. 73–82.

[57] D. Gusfield, Sensitivity analysis for combinatorial optimization, Tech. Rept. UCB/ERLM80/22, Univ. of California, Berkeley, 1980.

[58] D. Gusfield, Parametric combinatorial computing and a problem in program module allocation, *JACM* 30 (1983), 551–563.

[59] D. Gusfield, K. Balasubramanian, and D. Naor, Parametric optimization of sequence alignment, *Algorithmica* 12 (1994), 312–326.

[60] E. Helly, Über systeme von abgeschlossenen Mengen mit gemeinschaftlichen Punkten, *Monaths. Math. und Physik* 37 (1930), 281–302.

[61] J. Hershberger, A faster algorithm for the two-center decision problem, *Inform. Process. Lett.* 47 (1993), 23–29.

[62] M. Houle and G. Toussaint, Computing the width of a set, *IEEE Trans. Pattern Anal. Mach. Intell.* PAMI-10 (1988), 761–765.

[63] D. Huttenlocher and K. Kedem, Efficiently computing the Hausdorff distance for point sets under translation, *Proc. 6th ACM Symp. Comput. Geom.*, 1990, pp. 340–349.

[64] H. Imai, D.T. Lee, and C. Yang, 1-Segment center covering problems, *ORSA J. Comput.* 4 (1992), 426–434.

[65] S. Jadhav and A. Mukhopadhyay, Computing a centerpoint of a finite planar set of points in linear time, *Proc. 9th ACM Symp. Comput. Geom.*, 1993, pp. 83–90.

[66] J. Jaromczyk and M. Kowaluk, An efficient algorithm for the Euclidean two-center problem, *Proc. 10th ACM Symp. Comput. Geom.*, 1994, pp. 303–311.

[67] J. Jaromczyk and M. Kowaluk, The two-line center problem from a polar view: A new algorithm, *Proc. 4th Workshop Algo. Data Struct.*, 1995.

[68] G. Kalai, A subexponential randomized simplex algorithm, *Proc. 24th ACM Symp. Theory of Comput.*, 1992, pp. 475–482.

[69] N. Karmarkar, A new polynomial-time algorithm for linear programming, *Combinatorica* 4 (1984), 373–395.

[70] M. Katz, Improved algorithms in geometric optimization via expanders, *Proc. 3rd Israeli Symp. Theory of Comput. & Syst.*, 1995.

[71] M. Katz and M. Sharir, Optimal slope selection via expanders, *Inform. Process. Lett.* 47 (1993), 115–122.

[72] M. Katz and M. Sharir, An expander-based approach to geometric optimization, *Proc. 9th ACM Symp. Comput. Geom.*, 1993, pp. 198–207.

[73] L.G. Khachiyan, Polynomial algorithm in linear programming, *U.S.S.R. Comput. Math. and Math. Phys.* 20 (1980), 53–72.

[74] M. Ko and R. Lee, On weighted rectilinear 2-center and 3-center problems, *Info. Sci.* 54 (1991), 169–190.

[75] N. Korneenko and H. Martini, Hyperplane approximation and related topics, in *New Trends in Discrete and Computational Geometry*, (J. Pach, ed.), Springer-Verlag, 1993, 163–198.

[76] C.-Y. Lo, J. Matoušek, and W. Steiger, Algorithms for ham-sandwich cuts, *Discr. Comput. Geom.* 11 (1994), 433–452.

[77] C.-Y. Lo and W. Steiger, An optimal-time algorithm for ham-sandwich cuts in the plane, *Proc. 2nd Canad. Conf. Comput. Geom.*, 1990, pp. 5–9.

[78] D. Knuth, *The Art of Computer Programming, Vol. 3: Sorting and Searching*, Addison-Wesley, Reading, MA, 1973.

[79] J. Matoušek, Randomized optimal algorithm for slope selection, *Inform. Process. Lett.* 39 (1991), 183–187.

[80] J. Matoušek, Computing the center of planar point sets, in *Computational Geometry: Papers from the DIMACS Special Year* (J. Goodman, et al., eds.), AMS, Providence, RI, 1991, 221–230.

[81] J. Matoušek, Linear optimization queries, *J. Algorithms* 14 (1993), 432–448.

[82] J. Matoušek, Lower bounds for a subexponential optimization algorithm, *Random Struct. & Algo.* 5 (1994), 591–607.

[83] J. Matoušek, On geometric optimization with few violated constraints, *Proc. 10th ACM Symp. Comput. Geom.*, 1994, pp. 312–321.

[84] J. Matoušek, D. Mount, and N. Netanyahu, Efficient randomized algorithms for the repeated median line estimator, *Proc. 4th ACM-SIAM Symp. Discr. Algo.*, 1993, pp. 74–82.

[85] J. Matoušek and O. Schwarzkopf, A deterministic algorithm for the three-dimensional diameter problem, *Proc. 25th ACM Symp. Theory of Comput.*, 1993, pp. 478–484.

[86] J. Matoušek, M. Sharir, and E. Welzl, A subexponential bound for linear programming and related problems, *Algorithmica*, to appear.

[87] N. Megiddo, Combinatorial optimization with rational objective functions, *Math. Oper. Res.* 4 (1979), 414–424.

[88] N. Megiddo, Applying parallel computation algorithms in the design of serial algorithms, *J. ACM* 30 (1983), 852–865.

[89] N. Megiddo, Linear time algorithms for linear time programming in R^3 and related problems, *SIAM J. Comput.* 12 (1983), 759–776.

[90] N. Megiddo, Linear programming in linear time when the dimension is fixed, *J. ACM* 31 (1984), 114–127.

[91] N. Megiddo, Partitioning with two lines in the plane, *J. Algorithms* 6 (1985), 403–433.

[92] N. Megiddo, The weighted Euclidean 1-center problem, *Math. Oper. Res.* 8 (1983), 498–504.

[93] N. Megiddo, On the ball spanned by balls, *Discr. Comput. Geom.* 4 (1989), 605–610.

[94] N. Megiddo and K. Supowit, On the complexity of some common geometric location problems, *SIAM J. Comput.* 13 (1984), 182–196.

[95] R. Motwani and P. Raghavan, *Randomized Algorithms*, Cambridge University Press, New York, 1995.

[96] K. Mulmuley, *Computational Geometry: An Introduction Through Randomized Algorithms*, Prentice Hall, New York, 1993.

[97] N. Naor and M. Sharir, Computing the center of a point set in three dimensions, *Proc. 2nd Canad. Conf. Comput. Geom.*, 1990, pp. 10–13.

[98] C. Norton, S. Plotkin, and E. Tárdos, Using separation algorithms in fixed dimensions, *J. Algorithms* 13 (1992), 79–98.

[99] M. Pellegrini, Incidence and nearest-neighbor problems for lines in 3-space, *Proc. 8th ACM Symp. Comput. Geom.*, 1992, pp. 130–137.

[100] M. Pellegrini, Repetitive hidden-surface-removal for polyhedral scenes, *Proc. 3rd Workshop Algo. Data Struct.*, 1993, pp. 541–552.

[101] M. Post, Minimum spanning ellipsoids, *Proc. 16th ACM Symp. Theory of Comput.*, 1984, pp. 108–116.

[102] J. Salowe, L_∞-interdistance selection by parametric search, *Inform. Process. Lett.* 30 (1989), 9–14.

[103] R. Seidel, Low dimensional linear programming and convex hulls made easy, *Discr. Comput. Geom.* 6 (1991), 423–434.

[104] E. Ramos, Intersection of unit-balls and diameter of a point set in $\mathbb{R}^3$, manuscript, 1993.

[105] M. Reichling, On the detection of a common intersection of k convex objects in the plane, *Inform. Process. Lett.*, 29 (1988), 25–29.

[106] M. Reichling, On the detection of a common intersection of k convex polyhedra, in *Comput. Geom. & its Appl.*, Lecture Notes in Comp. Sci., 333, Springer-Verlag, 1988, pp. 180–186.

[107] M. Sharir, A near-linear algorithm for the planar 2-center problem, submitted to *Discr. Comput. Geom.*

[108] M. Sharir and P. Agarwal, *Davenport-Schinzel Sequences and Their Geometric Applications*, Cambridge University Press, Cambridge-New York-Melbourne, 1995.

[109] M. Sharir and S. Toledo, Extremal polygon containment problems, *Comput. Geom. Theory Appls.* 4 (1994), 99–118.

[110] M. Sharir and E. Welzl, A combinatorial bound for linear programming and related problems, *Proc. 9th Symp. Theo. Asp. Comp. Sci.*, (1992), pp. 569–579.

[111] A. Stein and M. Werman, Finding the repeated median regression line, *Proc. 3rd ACM-SIAM Symp. Discr. Algo.*, 1992, pp. 409–413.

[112] S. Toledo, *Extremal Polygon Containment Problems and Other Issues in Parametric Searching*, M.Sc. Thesis, Tel Aviv University, Tel Aviv, 1991.

[113] S. Toledo, Approximate parametric search, *Inform. Process. Lett.* 47 (1993), 1–4.

[114] S. Toledo, Maximizing non-linear convex functions in fixed dimensions, in *Complexity of Numerical Computations* (P. Pardalos, ed.), World Scientific, 1993.

[115] L. Valiant, Parallelism in comparison problems, *SIAM J. Comput.* 4 (1975), 348–355.

[116] K. Vardarajan and P. Agarwal, Linear approximation of simple objects, *Proc. 7th Canad. Conf. Comput. Geom.*, 1995, to appear.

[117] E. Welzl, Smallest enclosing disks (balls and ellipsoids), in *New Results and New Trends in Computer Science* (H. Maurer, ed.), Lecture Notes in Comp. Sci., 555, 1991, Springer-Verlag, pp. 359–370.

All the Needles in a Haystack: Can Exhaustive Search Overcome Combinatorial Chaos?

Jürg Nievergelt, Ralph Gasser, Fabian Mäser, Christoph Wirth

Department of Computer Science, ETH Zürich
CH-8092 Zürich, Switzerland

Abstract. For half a century since computers came into existence, the goal of finding elegant and efficient algorithms to solve "simple" (well-defined and well-structured) problems has dominated algorithm design. Over the same time period, both processing and storage capacity of computers have increased roughly by a factor of 10^6. The next few decades may well give us a similar rate of growth in raw computing power, due to various factors such as continuing miniaturization, parallel and distributed computing. If a quantitative change of orders of magnitude leads to qualitative changes, where will the latter take place? Many problems exhibit no detectable regular structure to be exploited, they appear "chaotic", and do not yield to efficient algorithms. Exhaustive search of large state spaces appears to be the only viable approach. We survey techniques for exhaustive search, typical combinatorial problems that have been solved, and present one case study in detail.

1 The Scope of Search Techniques

The concept of search plays an ambivalent role in computer science. On one hand, it is one of the fundamental concepts on which computer science is built, perhaps as fundamental as computability or complexity: any problem whatsoever can be seen as a search for "the right answer". On the other hand, despite its conceptually clear algorithmic nature, the problem domain "search" has not developed as rich a theory as, for example, algorithm complexity. When discussing search, a dozen unrelated techniques come to mind, ranging from binary search to fashionable trends such as neural nets or genetic algorithms.

The field of artificial intelligence has, at times, placed search at the center of its conceptual edifice. For example in the dichotomy of "search" versus "knowledge" as complementary or competing techniques to achieve "intelligent" behavior. Although the distinction between "search" and "knowledge" has an intuitive appeal ("where is it?" as opposed to "there it is!"), it is difficult to pin down. At the implementation level, it is often reduced to a distinction between a data structure (the "knowledge" of how data is organized, e.g. a binary search tree) and its access algorithms, e.g. the operation "find". The efficiency trade-off between knowledge and search turns merely into issues of preprocessing time and query time.

A discussion of search in general, independently of any specific problem, leads to four main concepts:

1. **State space, or search space.** The given problem is formalized by defining an appropriate set of "states" that represent possible configurations we may encounter along our way from the initial problem statement to a solution. In interesting search problems, this set has a rich structure, and hence is called a "space". The structure typically includes an adjacency relation to express the constraint that in a single step, we can only go from the current state to an adjacent state. Thus the state space is often modeled as a graph with directed or undirected edges. Various functions may be defined on the state space or on the set of edges, such as exact or approximate values to be optimized, and exact or estimated costs of going from one state to another.

2. **Goal, or search criterion.** This can vary widely with respect to both quantity and quality: from a single desired state to an exhaustive enumeration of all the states in the space; and from accepting only exact matches, or globally optimum states, to approximate matches, local optima, or heuristic values with unknown error bounds.

3. **Search algorithm**, a framework for specifying a class of possible traversals of the state space. Examples: greedy, gradient, or hill-climbing techniques, where each step is taken with the sole criterion of an immediate gain, regardless of past history or future consequences; or backtrack, a systematic enumeration of all states that meet given constraints. The direction of search can vary: from a given initial state to goal states, or, if the latter are known but paths leading to them are unknown, from the goal states back towards the initial state. Bidirectional search [Pohl 71] and other combinations are of interest.

4. **Data structures** used to organize the chosen search, such as: remember what part of the state space has been visited, find one's way to yet unexplored regions, store the collected information. A stack for depth-first search (DFS) and a queue for breadth-first search (BFS) are the most prominent examples, but combinations of these two and other structures, such as union-find, frequently occur.

The first two concepts, state space and goal, lend themselves to a rough but meaningful characterization of most search algorithms into the four categories described below, depending on whether:

- the state space has a regular structure to be exploited, such as a total order, or not, i.e. its only known structures are irregular, "random",
- the search goal is exact or approximate.

Regular structure, exact goal. Typical table-look-up techniques in a totally ordered space, such as binary search or interpolation search. Iterative techniques for finding zeros or minima of functions with special properties, such as Newton iteration or Fibonacci search for the minimum of a unimodal function. When the state space is a Cartesian product of totally ordered domains, such as d-dimensional Euclidean space, fast search techniques still apply in many cases.

Regular structure, approximate goal. Includes approximate pattern-matching algorithms, typically in 1 dimension (strings) or 2 (pictures).

Irregular structure, exact goal. The domain of exhaustive search techniques, such as sieves, backtrack, DFS, BFS, or reverse search for systematic enumeration of a state space, or retrograde analysis of of combinatorial puzzles and games.

Irregular structure, approximate goal. The domain of heuristic search. Includes greedy, gradient or hill-climbing techniques to find a local optimum. Along with enhancements to escape local minima to continue the search for better ones, without ever knowing whether a global optimum has been found. Includes simulated annealing, genetic algorithms, neural nets, tabu search.

This paper is about the class of search problems we call "state space of irregular structure, exact goal". Almost by definition, these problems can only be approached by techniques called "exhaustive search". Exhaustive search algorithms visit the entire state space in the worst case, and a significant fraction on the average. For any state not visited ("pruned"), a rigorous argument guarantees that visiting it would not change the result. This class includes dynamic programming, branch-and-bound, and alpha-beta evaluation of game trees — search algorithms that make extensive use of bounds to prune the search space.

At the risk of oversimplification we venture some comments about the relative importance of each of the four aspects mentioned above from a programmer's point of view.

1. Designing an effective state space is the first and foremost step! The main point to remember is that, in constructing a state space, the designer has the greatest opportunity to bring problem-specific knowledge to bear on the efficiency of the search techniques. This is the domain of conceptual clarity, common sense, and mathematics. Representations that exploit symmetry to avoid redundancy; heuristics that detect good candidates early without wasting time analysing poor candidates; theorems that preclude solutions from lying in certain subspaces, or assert lower or upper bounds on the value or cost of solutions, can turn a search problem from infeasible to trivial.

2. The goal is rarely under control of the programmer — it is given by the problem statement. It may be useful, however, to gather experience by first relaxing the goal, so as to reach a partial objective soon.

3. The choice of search algorithm, i.e. the class of traversals of the space that are considered, is often predetermined by characteristics of the problem. Available choices have clear consequences. Among forward searches, for example, DFS requires less temporary storage for its stack than BFS does for its queue, hence BFS may be impractical for a large problem. As another example, a backward search such as retrograde analysis is feasible only if all the goal states can be listed efficiently, i.e., an enumeration problem is solved first. Thus, it cannot be argued that one exhaustive search technique dominates others across the board. This situation is in contrast to heuristic search, where each of several fashionable paradigms (simulated annealing,

neural nets, genetic algorithms, etc.) can often be used interchangeably, and each has its proponents who proclaim it a superior general-purpose search technique.

4. Data structures are the key to program optimization in the small. A good implementation often saves a constant factor but is hardly decisive.

2   Emerging Achievements of Exhaustive Search

Exhaustive search is truly a creation of the computer era. Although the history of mathematics records amazing feats of paper-and-pencil computation, as a human activity, exhaustive search is boring, error-prone, exhausting, and never gets very far anyway. As a cautionary note, if any is needed, Ludolph van Ceulen died of exhaustion in 1610 after using regular polygons of 2^{62} sides to obtain 35 decimal digits of π — they are engraved on his tombstone.

With the advent of computers, "experimental mathematics" became practical: the systematic search for specific instances of mathematical objects with desired properties, perhaps to disprove a conjecture or to formulate new conjectures based on empirical observation. Number theory provides a fertile ground for the team "computation + conjecture", and Derrick Lehmer was a pioneer in using search algorithms such as sieves or backtrack in pursuit of theorems whose proof requires a massive amount of computation [Lehmer 53, Lehmer 64]. We make no attempt to survey the many results obtained thanks to computer-based mathematics, but merely recall a few as entry points into the pertinent literature:

- the continuing race for large primes, for example Mersenne primes of form $2^p - 1$
- the landmark proof of the "Four-Color Theorem" by Appell and Haken [Appell 77]
- recent work in Ramsey theory or cellular-automata [Horgan 93].

The applications of exhaustive search to which we refer in more detail is the esoteric field of games and puzzles. Because their rules and objectives are simple and rigorously defined, and progress can be quantified, games and puzzles have long been embraced by game theory [von Neumann 43, Berlekamp 82] and artificial intelligence (AI) communities as ideal testing environments. Chess was long regarded as the "drosophila of artificial intelligence", and if four decades of experimentation with chess-playing machines has taught us anything at all, it must be the amazing power of massive search to amplify the effect of a meager amount of game-specific positional knowledge. It has become evident that brute-force search suffices to play chess at a level of skill exceeded by at most a few hundred humans.

We are not concerned with heuristic game-playing in this paper, we are interested in "solving" games and puzzles by exhaustive search of their state spaces. Games successfully solved include Qubic [Patashnik 80], Connect-4 [Allen 89], Go-Moku [Allis 94], and Merrils or Nine Men's Morris [Gasser 94, Gasser 95].

[Allis 94] surveys the state of the art and lists all games known to have been solved. Exhaustive search has also been applied to puzzles, which can be considered to be one-player games. For the Rubik's cube there is an algorithm by Thistlethwaite which provably solves any position in at most 52 moves, while a recently introduced algorithm seemingly solves any position in at most 21 moves [Kociemba 92].

Sam Loyd's 15-puzzle (15 tiles sliding inside a 4 by 4 matrix) has so far resisted complete solution, although interesting mathematical results have been obtained. [Wilson 74] shows that the state space decomposes into two independent subspaces. When generalized to an $n \times n$ puzzle, finding optimal solution is NP-complete [Ratner 90], whereas non-optimal strategies are polynomial [Sucrow 92]. But as is often the case, such mathematical results for general n give little or no hint on how to approach a specific instance, say $n = 4$. Experience shows that improved lower bounds are the single most effective step towards efficient search, since they prune larger subspaces. Instead of the standard Manhattan distance bound, more informed bounds have been developed, e.g.: linear-conflict [Hansson 92], or fringe and corner databases [Culberson 94]. With further improved bounds, [Gasser 95] discovered positions requiring 80 moves to solve and proved that no position requires more than 87 moves to solve. This gap between upper and lower bound remains a challenge.

Returning to two-person games, there have been long-standing efforts to solve parts of games, typically endgames, where there is little hope of solving the entire game, now or perhaps ever. The motivation for this may come from attempts to improve the strength of heuristics game-playing programs. During their forward search, these use heuristic evaluation functions to assess the value of a position, and such functions are necessarily approximations of unknown quality. If exact values are available not only at the leaves, but already further up in the game tree thanks to a precomputed minimax evaluation, this has two desirable consequences. First, exact values have a beneficial effect on the quality of the "minimax-mix" of heuristic values. Second, longer endgames can be played perfectly, i.e. such as to guarantee an outcome of at least the game-theoretic value. We are aware of two endgame databases that were computed with this goal as primary motivation:

- *Checkers*: An 8×8 checkers project is headed by Jonathan Schaeffer [Schaeffer 92]. His group has computed all 7-piece positions and is working on 8 and 9 piece positions. Their databases contain about $1.5 \cdot 10^{11}$ positions. A workstation cluster (25-90 machines) and a BBN TC2000 allow an average of 425 million positions to be computed per day [Lake 94].
- *Awari*: Victor Allis first computed Awari endgame databases for use in his playing program Lithidion [Allis 94]. We have extended this work and now have all $5.5 \cdot 10^8$ positions with 22 or fewer stones at our disposal (T. Lincke).

Last but not least, the problem domain that spearheaded the drive to explore the limits of exhaustive search, and that gives us the clearest measure of progress, is chess endgames. [Stroehlein 70] started the race. For a summary of early results see [Herik 86]. Ken Thompson computed many four and five piece chess databases, which have been released on two compact disks [Thompson 91, Thompson 92]. Lewis Stiller used a Connection Machine CM-2 to compute six-piece chess databases, each of which consists of up to 6'185'385'360 positions [Stiller 91]. Grandmaster John Nunn's books tellingly entitled "Secrets of Rook Endings", "Secrets of Pawnless Endings", and "Secrets of Minor Piece Endings" [Nunn 92-95] is the first attempt to interpret such databases for human consumption.

Although a direct comparison of different enumeration problems is not easy, due to their state spaces of different structure and varying connectivity, it is striking that at present, the size of state spaces of various solved problems, including Merrils, is of the order of 10^{10} positions. The empirical fact that the raw size of the state space is the dominant parameter that affects complexity might be explained by the observation that the structure of all these spaces shows no regularity — they appear to be random graphs. Without predictable regularity to exploit, all exhaustive searches look like random walks in a random graph. Thus, the most telling indicator of complexity is the size of the space, and its connectivity is second.

3   The Role of Exhaustive Search: Speculation

After this brief presentation of a small niche of computer science and the work of a few researchers who have been driven by curiosity more than by any other motivation, let us ask some basic questions: What can we learn from dozens of case studies of exhaustive search reported since computers became available a few decades ago? Why keep computers busy for days or months exhaustively traversing the state space of some puzzle whose solution is merely a matter of curiosity? What contribution, if any, can we expected from further experiments based on exhaustive search?

These questions are hard to answer. Brute-force solutions are not "elegant" from a mathematical point of view. Their cryptical assertions such as "the game of Merrils is a draw", reached after producing Gigabytes of data, cannot be checked without computer. Neither algorithms nor results can be presented in a "user-friendly" manner. Attempts to extract rules from a data base of positions, in order to distinguish won, lost, and drawn positions, have not been very successful. If done automatically, e.g. by finding predicates and producing a decision tree, one obtains huge trees and predicates for which humans lack intuition [Gasser 95]. The answer that no simpler description exists fails to satisfy players. They prefer a simple, intuitive rule that allows exceptions to an unmotivated, impractical rule that claims perfection. Extracting rules from a database in such a way that players can understand it requires a huge effort by a top expert, as shown by Grandmaster Nunn's books [Nunn 92-95].

So why waste computer time to "solve" games in a way that has little or no interest to game players? One answer is undoubtedly the same as for the question "why climb Mount Everest?": to prove that it can be done. But we are intrigued by a second answer: exhaustive search in large state spaces is a very general approach to combinatorial problems of any kind, and promises to be increasingly important. Why? For decades, computer scientists have focused attention on problems that admit efficient algorithms. Algorithms whose running time grows no faster than some polynomial of low degree in the size of the input data still dominate textbooks on algorithms. In contrast, problems that appear not to admit polynomial time algorithms, specifically, NP-complete or NP-hard problems, are often considered mere objects for a theorem, but dismissed as "intractable" from an algorithmic point of view.

But efficient algorithms can only be found for selected, relatively simple problems, whereas the world of applications is not simple. Most problems of practical importance, if they can be approached by computation at all, call for compute-intensive methods. Accordingly, the attitude towards "intractable" problems began to change. First, researchers relaxed the goal of exact or optimal solutions and sought efficient approximation algorithms. Second, one noticed that not all "intractable problems" are equally intractable. There appear to be many problems where the average, or typical, instance is relatively easy to solve, and only the worst-case instances are computationally very demanding. The venerable traveling salesman problem (TSP) may be an example. In tsplib [Reinelt 95], a collection of TSP benchmark problems that serves as a yardstick of progress, the currently largest provably optimal solution involves 7397 cities. This progress could hardly have been expected a decade ago, when the largest instance of a TSP known to have been solved had 318 cities [Lawler 85].

In view of the fact that exhaustive search occasionally does succeed in solving surprisingly large instances of NP-complete problems, it is time to reconsider identifying "NP-complete" with "intractable". But whereas computer scientists feel they know everything worth knowing about sorting and binary search, we know little about how to organize large state spaces for effective exhaustive search. Judging from the experience that the resources needed to complete a given exhaustive search can rarely be predicted, we are still in the process of learning the basics. And for sharpening our tools, the well-defined "micro worlds" of games and puzzles, with state spaces of any size we feel challenged to tackle, are well suited. Playful experiments provide moving targets that let us explore the shifting boundary of feasible brute-force problem-solving.

It is common knowledge that the raw computing power available has increased spectacularly over the past three or four decades — easily a factor of 10^6 with respect to both: processing speed and memory capacity. Whereas "super computers" around 1960 offered Kiloflops to Megaflops and memories of size 10 to 100 KiloBytes, today's top-of-the-line machines are in the range of Gigaflops to Teraflops and 10 to 100 GigaBytes. What is less well known, perhaps controversial but certainly arguable, is that there are reasons to expect similar rates of growth in raw computing power over the coming few decades. A number of independent factors can be listed in support of such a prediction. The physical limits of current technologies have not yet been reached — Moore's "doubling law" is still in force; new technologies, such as optical storage devices, are only in the beginning stages of their potential development; last but not least, parallel and distributed computing are bound to increase in popularity with the continuing price drop of hardware. As a portent of trends we mention that, at the 1995 World computer chess championship a program Star Socrates participated, running on an Intel Paragon with 1800 processors.

We hasten to emphasize the phrase "raw computing power"! Whereas the asymptotic complexity analysis of efficient (polynomial-time) algorithms tells us with amazing accuracy what we can and cannot compute with given resources of time and memory, it is far from clear what additional problems can be solved by brute-force techniques with a millionfold increase of raw computing power. It is easy to demonstrate a problem where such a boost does not even suffice to go from a problem of size n to the same problem of size $n + 1$. But whereas problems like evaluating Ackermann's function are contrived by theoreticians, we observe the same phenomenon in empirical settings. To return to the example of computer chess: the 1800 processor monster Paragon came second to World Champion "Fritz" competing on a personal computer.

One expects a quantitative change of six orders of magnitude to lead to qualitative changes, but we don't know ahead of time where the latter will take place. This is particularly true for many problems such as combinatorial optimization that exhibit no detectable regular structure to be exploited. Their state spaces appear to be "chaotic", they allow no description briefer than an exhaustive enumeration of all states, and thus do not yield to efficient algorithms. Whatever progress has been made in this field owes a lot to tinkerers who apply great ingenuity to attack intriguing toy problems. Let us describe some of these.

4   State Spaces, their Size and Structure

Although one often talks about "the state space of a problem", this terminology is misleading. A problem does not come with "its state space" — rather, the problem solver must design a state space that models the problem adequately. A given problem may have many plausible state spaces that differ greatly in size, in structure, and ease of understanding.

In most cases, designing a state space, understanding its structure, and finding a good representation for it is by far the most important ingredient of an efficient search. Properties of the state space decide whether there exist invariants, bounds, symmetries that serve to "prune", i.e. avoid visiting, large parts of the state space. As a well-known illustration, consider the problem: is it possible to cover all the squares of an amputated chess board that is missing two diagonally opposite squares with dominoes, such that each domino covers two vertically or horizontally adjacent squares? A plausible state space might consists of all partial covers, with the initial state "no dominoes" and final states that leave no room to place any additional domino. But a simple parity argument suffices to answer "no", even if the problem is generalized to $n \times n$ chess boards, avoiding search altogether: Diagonally opposite corners are of the same color, thus the amputated chess board has an unequal number of white and black squares, and cannot possibly be covered by dominoes each of which covers one white and one black square.

As an example of how a well-designed state space and representation supports intuition and human problem solving, consider the following graphical presentation of an introductory problem discussed in many artificial intelligence textbooks, called "cannibals and missionaries". Three cannibals and three missionaries wish to cross a river in a two-person boat. The cannibals insist on never being left in a minority on either river bank, for fear of being converted by a majority of missionaries. A minority of zero cannibals is ok, of course - converting the empty set is no threat.

A few sentences should suffice to explain the space depicted below. A problem state consists primarily of the pair (C_L, M_L) of cannibals and missionaries on the left bank, where the team starts. Thus we consider a matrix $0 \leq C_L \leq 3$, $0 \leq M_L \leq 3$. The constraint "$C_L = 0$ or $C_L \geq M_L$" rules out three entries. But the same matrix can also be labeled with the complement (C_R, M_R) , and the constraint "$C_R = 0$ or $C_R \geq M_R$" rules out three more entries. The problem state contains an additional bit, namely, whether the boat is on the left or right shore. This bit flips at every move, so we take care of it by distinguishing odd moves and even moves. Odd moves start from the left bank and thus decrease (C_L, M_L) in one of 5 ways shown by arrows. Even moves start from the right bank and decrease (C_R, M_R) as shown by arrows in the opposite direction. Visual inspection quickly reveals that there is only one way to cross the barrier that separates the initial state from the goal state. Under the constraint of alternating between moves towards the upper left and moves back towards the lower right, the "N-shaped" pattern shown in bold arrows is unique. It is easy to extend these critical three steps to a solution consisting of 11 moves. This concise visual representation of the state space supports intuition and saves a lot of trial-and-error.

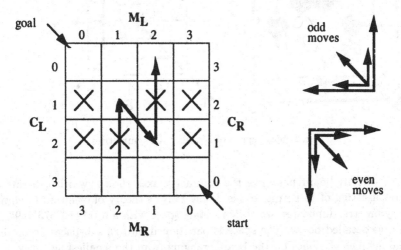

Fig. 1. State space and operators of the "Cannibals and missionaries" puzzle

The two examples of state spaces shown above are not typical. The first one is an extreme case where an invariant defined on the state space prunes the entire space, thus making search unnecessary. The second problem can be solved only by searching, but the state space is so tiny that even unsystematic search will soon find a solution. The examples do illustrate, however, the two basic steps in designing a state space. They become increasingly important the more challenging the problem: a rigorous, understandable definition of the state space, and the effectiveness of invariants in pruning the search.

As an example of a state space that taxes the state of the art, consider the game of Merrils (Nine Men's Morris, Muehle, Moulin) solved in [Gasser 95]. The board position below gives a hint of the complexity of the game. Two players White and Black alternate in first placing, then sliding, and ultimately jumping one stone of their own color. During the 18-ply (ply = a move by either player) opening, each player places his 9 stones on any unoccupied point among the 24 playable points of the board. During the midgame, each player slides one of his stones from its current location to an adjacent point. During the endgame, when at least one player has exactly three stones left, that player may jump, i.e. move any one of his stones to any unoccupied point. At all times, when a player "closes a mill", i.e. gets three of his stones in a row along adjacent points, he may remove an opponent's stone. That player loses who first cannot move or has fewer than three stones left. For Merrils players: the position below is a mutual "Zugzwang", i.e. the player to move loses against optimal play: White to move loses in 74 plys, Black in 60 plys.

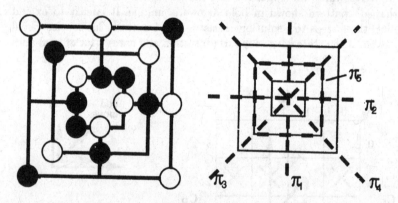

Fig. 2. State space of Merrils with symmetries

The Merrils board possesses the symmetry axes shown, which generate a group consisting of 16 permutations. Using Polya's theory of counting to elimi-nate symmetric duplicates, we obtain a state space with a total of 7'673'759'269 states, as detailed below. The space is partitioned into 28 subspaces according to the number of stones on the board, ranging from the smallest subspace 3-3 to the largest subspace 8-7, with over 10^9 positions. Part of the structure of the space is shown in the diagram at right, which illustrates the information flow among the subspaces. For example, a position with 9 white and 8 black stones transfers, after capture of a stone, either into an 8-8 or a 9-7-position. Thus the value of a 9-8 position is deduced from values of 8-8 and 9-7 positions, as explained in section 5.

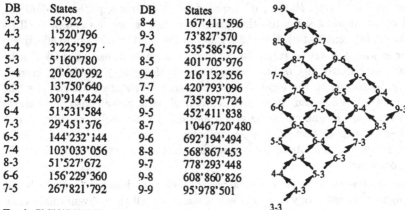

DB	States	DB	States
3-3	56'922	8-4	167'411'596
4-3	1'520'796	9-3	73'827'570
4-4	3'225'597 ·	7-6	535'586'576
5-3	5'160'780	8-5	401'705'976
5-4	20'620'992	9-4	216'132'556
6-3	13'750'640	7-7	420'793'096
5-5	30'914'424	8-6	735'897'724
6-4	51'531'584	9-5	452'411'838
7-3	29'451'376	8-7	1'046'720'480
6-5	144'232'144	9-6	692'194'494
7-4	103'033'056	8-8	568'867'453
8-3	51'527'672	9-7	778'293'448
6-6	156'229'360	9-8	608'860'826
7-5	267'821'792	9-9	95'978'501

Total: 7'673'759'269 states

Fig. 3. State space of Merrils: size and structure

5   Exhaustive Search Techniques

The literature on search uses an abundance of terminology to refer to the same few basic concepts and to techniques that differ only with respect to details. At the risk of oversimplification, let us single out a few fundamental ideas and their relation to each other, and point out modifications that capture a great variety of exhaustive search techniques.

The state space is a graph, directed or undirected, with possibly a host of other givens: initial states and goal states, functions defined on vertices (states) or edges, and constraints of the most varied kind. "Exhaustive" refers to the fact that we lack a priori information for excluding any subspace, hence the first requirement of an exhaustive search is a graph traversal algorithms capable of visiting all the states. Depth-first search (DFS) is the prime candidate. Its simple logic: "keep going as long as you see anything new, and when that is not possible, back up as far as necessary and proceed in a new direction", can be traced to the myth of Theseus traversing the Minotaur's labyrinth with the help of a thread held by Ariadne. This thread, called a stack in computer jargon, is obviously a key data structure for backing up. The myth does not tell us in detail sufficient to a programmer how Theseus kept track of the subspace already visited. It is instructive to investigate whether Theseus would have needed a chalk to guarantee visiting every cave in the labyrinth, and if not, what properties of the labyrinth and what algorithm guarantee an exhaustive traversal.

Whether or not a chalk is needed to mark states already visited is a major issue for the space complexity of the search. The chalk marks require memory proportional to the size of the graph, and that is typically much more than the other memory requirements. In realistic computations, the graph is rarely present in its entirety. Rather, its required parts are recomputed on demand, based on the usual assumption that given any state s, we can compute all its neighbors (adjacent states). But the totality of the chalk marks would effectively require storing the entire graph. In contrast, Ariadne's thread or stack can be expected to require only a diminishing fraction of memory — ideally, storage space proportional to the logarithm of the number of states. An entry in the stack used in DFS is usually a small amount of data. Since consecutive states in the stack are neighbors in the graph and differ little, only the difference is stored, not the entire state. In game terminology, two consecutive positions differ by one move, and the former is obtained by playing the reverse move from the later position.

Backtrack is one important special case of DFS that does not require a chalk. Although the terminology of search is not standard, all the conventional examples of backtrack show a state space given explicitly as a tree. If the Minotaur's labyrinth is a tree, Theseus will see nodes visited earlier only along the path from his current position to the root. Since these are momentarily marked by the thread, they need no chalk mark. The only assumption Theseus needs is that all the edges that emanate from a node are ordered, from first to last: when he backs up along edge i he will next plunge deeper into the labyrinth along edge $i + 1$, if it exists.

Problems may admit additional assumptions that define a subgraph T of the state space that is a spanning tree, or a spanning forest of trees. Since "spanning" means that T reaches every state, a backtrack search on T becomes a space-saving DFS of the entire state space. An interesting example is "reverse search" [Avis 92], which has been used to exhaustively enumerate all configurations in a variety of combinatorial problems, including: vertices of polyhedra, triangulations, spanning trees, topological orderings. The idea is to use greedy local optimization algorithms as can be found for most problems. A greedy algorithms g is a mapping $g : S \rightarrow S$ from the state space into itself. The trajectories of g are free of cycles, so they form a forest. Each fix point of g, i.e. each sink of a g-trajectory, is the root of one tree. If it is possible to efficiently enumerate all these roots as an initialization step, then a backtrack search starting from each root becomes an exhaustive enumeration of the entire space. Backtracking can even dispense with a stack, because the function g always points to the predecessor of any node.

Whereas DFS, in the image of the labyrinth, is a policy for quickly penetrating as deeply as possible, its cautious partner breadth-first search (BFS) can be likened to a wave propagating through the labyrinth at equal speed in all directions. The memory cost of maintaining the wave front is significant, since all states in the front must be stored in their entirety. Combinations of DFS and BFS can be used to shape the wave front and to focus the search in a promising direction, an aspect often used in heuristic search.

The traversals above respect locality to various extents. DFS, while advancing and when backing up, always steps from one state to an adjacent state. BFS also moves to an adjacent state whenever it expands the wave front, and although states within the front need not be adjacent, they obey some locality in that they are concentric from the root. In contrast, other "traversals" sequence the states "at random", ignoring the graph structure of a space. There are two reasons for such a counter-intuitive approach.

First, there are situations where we expect little or no pruning of the space will occur at search time, and we are resigned to visit all states without exception, in arbitrary order. For many challenging problem classes, the effort required to solve one instance is comparable to solving all instances in the class. One suspects, for example, that determining the value of the initial position in chess requires knowing the value of very many chess positions — the one instance "initial position" is comparable in difficulty to the class "all positions".

Second, every state has some internal representation, and these representations can be considered to be integers, or can be mapped to integers in an invertible way: given the integer, the state can be reconstructed. Such unique identifiers are called Goedel numbers in honor of the famous logician who used this technique to prove incompleteness theorems of mathematical logic. When states are identified with integers, the easiest way to list them all is from smallest to largest, even if the numerical order of the Goedel numbers has no relation to the graph structure.

Such chaotic traversals of the space have become standard, under the name of retrograde analysis, for solving games and puzzles (recall examples in section 2). Pick any state of Merrils, for example, such as the one labeled "Black to move loses" in the picture at left. Without any further information we can construct an arbitrary predecessor state by "unplaying" a White move and labeling it "White to move wins". Backing up a won position is somewhat more elaborate, as the picture at right shows. Thus, starting from known values at the leaves of a game tree, repeated application of such minmax operations eventually propagates correct values throughout the entire space.

Using retrograde analysis, the midgame and endgame state space of Merrils detailed in section 4, with 7.7 Billion positions, was calculated over a period of three years by a coalition of computers.

6   Case Study: Merrils and its Verification

Although the retrograde analysis mentioned above is the lion's share of a huge calculation, the case study of Merrils is not yet finished. The total state space of Merrils is roughly double this size, because the same board position represents two entirely different states depending on whether it occurs during the opening,

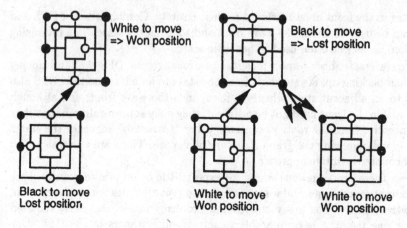

White to move
=> Won position

Black to move
=> Lost position

Black to move
Lost position

White to move
Won position

White to move
Won position

Fig. 4. Backing up lost and won positions

while stones are being placed on the board, or during the mid- or endgame, while stones slide or jump.

It is interesting to compare the two state spaces: opening vs. midgame and endgame. The two spaces are superficially similar because each state is identified with a board position, most of which look identical in both spaces. The differences between the board positions that arise in the opening and the midgame are minor: the opening space contains states where a player has fewer than 3 stones, but lacks certain other states that can arise in the midgame. Thus, the two spaces are roughly of equal size, but their structure is entirely different. Whereas the midgame space contains many cycles, the opening space is a directed acyclic graph (dag) of depth exactly 18. If symmetries were ignored, the fanout would decreases from 24 at the root of this dag to about 7 at the leaves (not necessarily exactly 7 because of possible captures). Taking symmetries into account, the dag becomes significantly slimmer — for example, there are only four inequivalent first moves out of 24 possible.

The limited depth and fanout of the opening space suggests a forward search may be more efficient than a backward search. This is reinforced by the fact that the goal is not to determine the value of all positions that could arise in the opening, but to prove the conjecture that Merrils is a draw under optimal play by both parties. Thus, the effective fanout of the dag is further decreased by best-first heuristics. By first investigating moves known or guessed to be good, one can often prove the hoped-for result without having to consider poor moves. Experienced Merrils players know that at most one or two mills will be closed during a well-played opening. Thus one aims to prove the draw by opening play limited to reaching three midgame databases only: 9-9, 9-8, and 8-8.

The forward search chosen replaces the dag by a tree many of whose nodes represent the same state. For reasons of program optimization whose intricate, lengthy justification we omit, two auxiliary data structures supported this search. A database of opening positions at depth 8 plies, and a hash table of positions at 14 plies. Thus, whenever the same 14th-ply-state is reached along different move sequences (transpositions), all but the first search finds the correct value already stored. This is illustrated in the following picture of a tree constricted at the 14th ply.

The draw was proven with two minmax evaluations using the well-known alpha-beta algorithm [Knuth 75]. One search proves that White, the first player to move, has at least a draw. The second search proves that Black has at least a draw. The effectiveness of alpha-beta is demonstrated by the fact that, of roughly 3.5 million positions at the 8 ply level, only 15'513 had to be evaluated to prove that White can hold the draw, and only 4'393 to prove that Black can hold the draw (the second player, Black, appears to have a small edge in Merrils). All others are pruned, i.e. can be eliminated as inferior without having been generated. This forward search took about 3 weeks of total run time on a Macintosh Quadra 800.

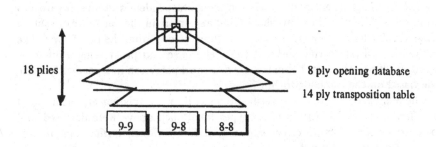

Fig. 5. Analyzing the opening: a deep but narrow forward search

How credible is the cryptic result "Merrils is a draw", obtained after three years of computation on a variety of machines that produced 10 Giga-Bytes of data? We undertook a most thorough verification of this result. Not because the Merrils draw is vital, but because the scope of this question greatly exceeds this particular problem.

Computer-aided proofs are becoming more important in mathematics and related branches of science — for example, they were essential for the four-color theorem, Ramsey theory or cellular-automata [Horgan 93]. A common objection raised against computer proofs is that they cannot be understood, nor their correctness conclusively established by humans. Thus we took Merrils as a challenge to investigate the general issues and approaches to the problem of verifying computer proofs.

Computer-aided proofs typically lead to complex software packages, long run-times, and much data — three major sources of diverse errors. The latter fall into three categories:

1. *Software errors*: These may occur in the algorithms programmed for the specific problem, or in the system software and tools used (compilers, linkers,

library programs). Although the latter errors are beyond the programmer's
direct control, he must be vigilant, because software that handles everyday
tasks reliably is often untested on files larger than usual.

2. *Hardware errors*: The much-debated recent bug in the Pentium microprocessor is a reminder that even arithmetic can't be relied on. Other hardware
is even less reliable. It is not uncommon for a bit to be flipped on the disk,
especially if the data is unused for long periods. This may be caused by
cosmic radiation, electric or magnetic fields.

3. *Handling errors*: Long computations are seldom run without interruption.
Thus, the user gets involved in many error-prone chores such as move data
to different disks, compressing files or resuming computation on a different
platform.

Hardware and handling errors are easiest to detect. Consistency checks at
run-time or thereafter will uncover handling errors and non-recurring hardware
glitches. Redoing the entire computation using independent system software and
compiler on a different machine should find any errors in the hardware or system
software. This leaves software errors stemming directly from the proof code. The
best method of uncovering these, is to develop a second proof using a different
algorithm. If no other algorithm is known, a third party can independently write
code based on the same algorithm.

The Merrils databases were verified repeatedly with different algorithms and
on different machines. Errors of all types mentioned above were detected and
corrected until no further errors surfaced. A first series of verifications merely
checked that the values stored with the positions are locally consistent. The
game-theoretic value of any position p must be the min or max of the values of the
successors of p. Although local consistency everywhere is a strong endorsement,
it does not guarantee correctness, as the following example shows.

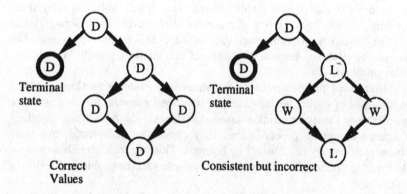

Fig. 6. Locally consistent values in cycles are not necessarily correct

The diagram at left shows a subspace all of whose positions are drawn (D).

If the 5 positions that contain a cycle of length 4 are alternatingly labeled loss (L) and win (W) for the player to move, as shown at right, everything is locally consistent. It is incorrect, however, because in Merrils, as in many games, endless repetition is declared a draw. This error, moreover, can propagate upwards and infect all predecessor positions.

Thus, a second series of verifications used as additional information the length of the shortest forced sequence that realizes the game-theoretic value of any position. When considering the position attributes: 0 = loss in 0 moves (terminal position), 1 = win in 1 move, 2 = loss in 2 moves, ..., 255 = draw (cycle), in addition to the game-theoretic value, the cycle with positions labeled L, D, L, D is no longer locally consistent and the error is detected.

The entire verification was run on an Intel Paragon parallel computer with 96 processors, at the rate of about 50'000 positions verified per second. The largest database (8-7, 1'072'591'519 positions) required 400 minutes.

7   Projects and Outlook

In an attempt to explore the possibilities and limits of exhaustive search, we pursue a number of other problems that span a variety of applications and techniques. The following snapshots of ongoing projects illustrate the potential breadth of exhaustive search (see also [Nievergelt 93]).

7.1   Using Heuristics to Trade Accuracy for Space and Time: Pawn endings in chess (C. Wirth)

An irritating feature of many exhaustive search computations is the fact that the program will search large subspaces where human insight could tell at a glance that nothing will be found. Such expert knowledge is frequently found in problem domains that admit natural visualizations, where humans' powerful visual pattern recognition ability let's us say "this doesn't look right", even if we are unable to say exactly why. And if we can't rigorously formulate an invariant, and prove its validity, chances are intuition will mislead us once in a while.

Because of the irregular structure characteristic of state spaces for which we use exhaustive search, it is not easy to formulate pruning insight in such a way that a program can act on it. As a test field for experiments, we have chosen King and Pawn chess endgames. There is much expert knowledge about this domain, explained in excellent books, and there are databases of exact values to compare against when there are only a few Pawns on the board.

The peculiar difficulty of King (K) and Pawn (P) endgames comes from the fact that Pawns can be promoted to any other piece: Queen (Q), Rook (R), Bishop (B), Knight (N). Thus an exhaustive analysis of KP endgames with a total of p Ps potentially calls upon all endgames with 2 Ks and p pieces of the right color. But the vast majority of KP endgames are decided soon after (or even before) a P promotion, because the material balance typically changes drastically - one party has a Q, the other does not. Thus, storing all the support databases of other piece endgames is an extremely expensive overhead when compared to their rare use.

We are experimenting with simple and often safe heuristics of the type: In a KP endgame, if Black promotes a P to a Q, and within x plies can prevent White from promoting one of its Ps, Black wins. This particular heuristic has well-known exceptions, such as when a White P on the seventh rank ensures a draw. Thus it is supplemented by other heuristics that, jointly, capture elementary chess lore about KP endgames.

The reduction in the size of state spaces and compute time effected by heuristics that obviate the need for support databases is drastic indeed, as the following examples show. KPPKP stands for the state space of endgames where White has 2 Ps and Black has 1 P.

State spaces		Pawns only	
KK + 2 pieces:	350 M states	KPKP:	4.5 M states
KK + 3 pieces:	100 G states	KPPKP:	250 M states
KK + 4 pieces:	30 T states	KPPKPP:	3 G states

Comparisons of exact databases with simple heuristics for KPKP combined with a 2-4 ply search on P promotion have shown that the latter contain about 2.5% errors. This is merely one data point along the trade-off curve between accuracy on one hand, and space and time on the other. Improved heuristics, larger databases, more forward search at the fringe of P promotion are just some of the parameters to play with in an attempt to push exhaustive search beyond the boundaries wherein exact calculation is feasible.

7.2 Enumeration of Maximally Elastic Graphs (A. Marzetta)

We study weighted graphs that can be embedded in Euclidean space in such a way as to preserve an edge's weight as distance between its two endpoints. Such questions arise in a variety of layout problems. In automatic graph drawing, for example, vertices are to be placed in the plane so as to approximate desired pairwise distances. The analogous 3-d problem arises in the distance geometry approach to molecular modeling, where edge weights are approximate distance measurements. The concept of elastic embeddability [Nievergelt 95] is designed to deal with distances subject to error. Elastic graphs are related to generically rigid graphs known in structural engineering. In particular, maximally elastic graphs are the same as minimally rigid (isostatic) graphs [Tay 95]. Although graphs isostatic in the plane are well understood, the analogous problem in 3 or more dimensions has generated interesting conjectures that might be settled by a search for counter examples.

7.3 Primes in Intervals of Fixed Length (R. Gasser, J. Waldvogel)

Although the distribution of prime numbers has been studied empirically and theoretically for centuries, it remains an inexhaustible source of interesting conjectures to be attacked by search. Let $\Pi(x)$ denote the number of primes $\leq x$. It follows from the prime number theorem: $\Pi(x) \sim x/\ln x$, that the average density of primes decreases with increasing x. Specifically, let $R(x) = \max(\Pi(y + x) - \Pi(y))$, where the maximum is over all $y \geq 0$, denote the maximally possible number of primes in an interval $(y, y + x]$ of length $x > 0$. Thus one might expect $R(x) \leq \Pi(x)$. But although the average decreases, the peak densities do not — surprisingly, they even increase in places. Using sieve techniques, [Gasser, Waldvogel 95] prove, among other results, that for all $x, 10 < x < 1416$, $R(x) < \Pi(x)$ as expected. But $x = 3250$ is the first known counter example where $R(x) > \Pi(x)$. Apparently, the densest clusters of primes in an interval of fixed length x occur starting at huge values of y.

7.4   Quo Vadis Exhaustive Search?

Brute-force techniques, as the name reveals, have never been considered elegant instruments in a computer scientist's toolbox. When used by novice programmers, the computer science community would automatically assume, often correctly, that an algorithms expert could obviously have designed a much more efficient program. But brute-force techniques have survived as a research niche for half century because a few top experts have always been intrigued by this unconventional approach to problem solving. And the complexity of problems solved has slowly but steadily grown in proportion to the power of available hardware.

The question is whether exhaustive search will remain a niche, used primarily for exotic topics such as games or number theory, or become a mainstream approach to a wide variety of applications. Instead of answering this question, let us close with one argument against and one in favor of an expanded role.

As stated in section 1, the effectiveness or "intelligence" of a search procedure is due mostly to problem-specific knowledge, not to differences between one or another general-purpose search procedure. But to the extent that a search uses properties specific to one problem to prune the state space, it becomes less of a brute-force technique by definition. From this point of view, exhaustive search applies to problems we do not yet understand well, and is forever being replaced by selective search as knowledge advances.

The argument for a more important role of brute-force techniques consist of two simple observations. We will never run out of problems whose structure we understand so poorly that exhaustive search is the only available approach. Second, computer science will continue to be technology-driven as it has been for decades; raw computing power will continue to increase, in particular with increased use of distributed and parallel computation. Thus the issue will always be present whether or not newly available raw power can solve new problems.

In any case, brute-force techniques are part of the computer science culture. Basic techniques of exhaustive search belong in introductory courses on algorithms and data structures along with the more traditional polynomial-time algorithms.

References

[Allen 89] J. D. Allen, A Note on the Computer Solution of Connect-Four, in: *Heuristic Programming in Artificial Intelligence* 1: *the First Computer Olympiad* (eds. D.N.L. Levy and D.F. Beal), Ellis Horwood, Chichester, England. 1989, pp. 134–135.

[Allis 94] L.V. Allis, *Searching for Solutions in Games and Artificial Intelligence*, Doctoral dissertation, University of Limburg, Maastricht, (1994).

[Appell 77] K. Appell and W. Haken, The Solution of the Four-Color-Map Problem, *Scientific American* (Oct. 1977) 108–121.

[Avis 92] D. Avis and K. Fukuda, *Reverse Search for Enumeration*, Report, U. Tsukuba. Discrete Applied Math. (1992) (to appear).

[Berlekamp 82] E. Berlekamp, J.H. Conway and R.K. Guy, *Winning Ways for your Mathematical Plays*, Academic Press, London, 1982.

[Culberson 94] J. Culberson and J. Schaeffer, *Efficiently Searching the 15-Puzzle*, internal report, University of Alberta, Edmonton, Canada, 1994.

[Gasser 90] R. Gasser, Applying Retrograde Analysis to Nine Men's Morris, in: *Heuristic Programming in Artificial Intelligence* 2: *the Second Computer Olympiad* (eds. D.N.L. Levy and D.F. Beal), Ellis Horwood, Chichester, England. 1990, pp. 161–173.

[Gasser 91] R. Gasser, Endgame Database Compression for Humans and Machines, in: *Heuristic Programming in Artificial Intelligence* 3: *the Third Computer Olympiad* (eds. H.J. van den Herik and L.V. Allis), Ellis Horwood, Chichester, England. 1990, pp. 180–191.

[Gasser 94] R. Gasser, J. Nievergelt, Es ist entschieden: Das Muehlespiel ist unentschieden, *Informatik Spektrum* 17:5 (1994) 314–317.

[Gasser 95] R. Gasser, *Harnessing Computational Resources for Efficient Exhaustive Search*, Doctoral dissertation, ETH Zürich, 1995.

[Gasser, Waldvogel 95] R. Gasser, J. Waldvogel, Primes in Intervals of Fixed Length, in preparation (1995).

[Hansson 92] O. Hansson, A. Mayer and M. Yung, Criticizing Solutions to Relaxed Models Yields Powerful Admissible Heuristics, *Information Sciences* 63 (1992) 207–227.

[Herik 86] H.J. van den Herik and I.S. Herschberg, A Data Base on Data Bases, *ICCA Journal* 9:1 (1986) 29.

[Horgan 93] J. Horgan, The Death of Proof, *Scientific American* (1993) 74–82.

[Knuth 75] D. E. Knuth and R. W. Moore, An analysis of Alpha-Beta Pruning, *Artificial Intelligence* 6 (1975) 293–326.

[Kociemba 92] H. Kociemba, Close to God's Algorithm, *Cubism for Fun* 28 (1992) 10–13.

[Korf 85] R.E. Korf, Depth-first Iterative Deepening, An Optimal Admissible Tree Search, *Artificial Intelligence* 27 (1985) 97–109.

[Lake 94] R. Lake, J. Schaeffer and P. Lu, *Solving Large Retrograde Analysis Problems Using a Network of Workstations*, internal report, University of Alberta, Edmonton, Canada, 1994.

[Lawler 85] E.L. Lawler, J.K. Lenstra, A.H.G. Rinnooy Kan, D.B. Shmoys, *The Traveling Salesman Problem — A Guided Tour of Combinatorial Optimization*, Wiley, 1985.

[Lehmer 53] D. H. Lehmer, The Sieve Problem for All-Purpose Computers, *Mathematical Tables and Aids to Computation* 7 (1953) 6–14.

[Lehmer 64] D. H. Lehmer, The Machine Tools of Combinatorics, in: E. F. Beckenbach (ed.), *Applied Combinatorial Mathematics*, Wiley, 1964, Chapter 1, pp. 5–31.

[Levy 91] D. Levy, Nine Men's Morris, *Heuristic Programming in Artificial Intelligence 2: the Second Computer Olympiad* (eds. D.N.L. Levy and D.F. Beal), Ellis Horwood, Chichester, England. 1991, 55–57.

[Nievergelt 93] J. Nievergelt, Experiments in Computational Heuristics, and their Lessons for Software and Knowledge Engineering, *Advances in Computers*, Vol 37 (M. Yovits, ed.), Academic Press. 1993, pp. 167–205.

[Nievergelt 95] J. Nievergelt, N. Deo, Metric Graphs Elastically Embeddable in the Plane, *Information Processing Letters* (1995) (to appear).

[Nunn 92-95] J. Nunn, *Secrets of Rook Endings 1992, Secrets of Pawnless Endings 1994, Secrets of Minor Piece Endings*, to appear 1995, Batsford Ltd. UK.

[Patashnik 80] O. Patashnik, Qubic: 4 × 4 × 4 Tic-Tac-Toe, *Mathematics Magazine* 53:4 (1980) 202–216.

[Pearl 84] J. Pearl, *Heuristics*, Addison-Wesley Publ. Comp., Reading, MA, 1984.

[Pohl 71] I. Pohl, Bi-Directional Search, *Machine Intelligence*, Vol. 6 (eds. B. Metzler and D. Michie), American Elsevier, New York. 1971, pp. 127–140.

[Ratner 90] D. Ratner and M. Warmuth, Finding a Shortest Solution for the $(N \times N)$-Extension of the 15-Puzzle is Intractable, *J. Symbolic Computation* 10 (1990) 111–137.

[Reinelt 95] G. Reinelt, "TSPLIB", available on the Worldwide Web (WWW), http://www.iwr.uni-heidelberg.de/iwr/comopt/soft/TSPLIB95/TSPLIB.html

[Schaeffer 92] J. Schaeffer, J. Culberson, N. Treloar, B. Knight, P. Lu and D. Szafron, A World Championship Caliber Checkers Program, *Artificial Intelligence* 53 (1992) 273–289.

[Stiller 91] L. Stiller, Group Graphs and Computational Symmetry on Massively Parallel Architecture, *The Journal of Supercomputing* 5 (1991) 99–117.

[Stroehlein 70] T. Stroehlein, *Untersuchungen ueber Kombinatorische Spiele*, Doctoral thesis, Technische Hochschule München, München, 1970.

[Sucrow 92] B. Sucrow, *Algorithmische und Kombinatorische Untersuchungen zum Puzzle von Sam Loyd*, Doctoral thesis, University of Essen, 1992.

[Tay 95] S. Tay, J. Nievergelt, A Minmax Relationship between Embeddable and Rigid Graphs, in preparation (1995).

[Thompson 86] K. Thompson, Retrograde Analysis of Certain Endgames, *ICCA Journal* 9:3 (1986) 131–139.

[Thompson 91] K. Thompson, Chess Endgames Vol. 1, *ICCA Journal* 14:1 (1991) 22.

[Thompson 92] K. Thompson, Chess Endgames Vol. 2, *ICCA Journal* 15:3 (1992) 149.

[von Neumann 43] J. von Neumann, O. Morgenstern, *Theory of Games and Economic Behavior*, Princeton Univ. Press, Princeton, NJ, 1953.

[Wells 71] M. Wells, *Elements of Combinatorial Computing*, Pergamon Press, Oxford, 1971.

[Wilson 74] R.M. Wilson, Graph Puzzles, Homotopy, and the Alternating Group, *J. Combinatorial Theory*, Series B: 16 (1974) 86–96.

Fundamental Limitations on Search Algorithms: Evolutionary Computing in Perspective

Nicholas J. Radcliffe[a,b] & Patrick D. Surry[a,b]
{njr,pds}@quadstone.co.uk

[a]Quadstone Ltd, 16 Chester Street, Edinburgh, EH3 7RA, UK
[b]Department of Mathematics, University of Edinburgh, The Kings Buildings, EH9 3JZ, UK

Abstract. The past twenty years has seen a rapid growth of interest in stochastic search algorithms, particularly those inspired by natural processes in physics and biology. Impressive results have been demonstrated on complex practical optimisation problems and related search applications taken from a variety of fields, but the theoretical understanding of these algorithms remains weak. This results partly from the insufficient attention that has been paid to results showing certain fundamental limitations on universal search algorithms, including the so-called "No Free Lunch" Theorem. This paper extends these results and draws out some of their implications for the design of search algorithms, and for the construction of useful representations. The resulting insights focus attention on tailoring algorithms and representations to particular problem classes by exploiting domain knowledge. This highlights the fundamental importance of gaining a better theoretical grasp of the ways in which such knowledge may be systematically exploited as a major research agenda for the future.

1 Overview

The last two decades has seen increasing interest in the application of stochastic search techniques to difficult problem domains. Strong biological metaphors led to the development of several schools of evolutionary computation, including work on genetic algorithms and classifier systems (Holland, 1975), evolution strategies (Rechenberg, 1973, 1984; Baeck & Schwefel, 1993), evolutionary programming (Fogel *et al.*, 1966) and genetic programming (Koza, 1991). Physical analogues provided both the motivation and theoretical framework for the method of simulated annealing (Kirkpatrick *et al.*, 1983). Other randomised methods, such as tabu search (Glover, 1986) and a variety of stochastic hill climbers and related search techniques have also attracted much interest.

Although some theoretical progress has been made in the study of stochastic search techniques, most attention has focused on the artificial situation of arbitrary ("blackbox") search problems. Despite occasional warnings from various researchers (Vose & Liepins, 1991; Radcliffe, 1992, 1994; Wolpert & Macready, 1995) a great deal of research seems oblivious to the fact that in such a situation there is no scope for distinguishing any of these biased sampling methods from enumeration—random or fixed— as we demonstrate below. There are exceptions to this, for example the convergence results for simulated annealing which exploit knowledge of the problem domain (e.g. Laarhoven & Aarts, 1989, Shapiro *et al.*, 1994) but much effort continues to be devoted to the "general" case, (Vose, 1992; Goldberg, 1989c, 1989a, 1989b). While such studies lead to elegant mathematics, and provide occasional insights into stochastic search, their practical utility in guiding—or even making contact with—practitioners tackling real search problems remains to be demonstrated.

This paper explicitly demonstrates these fundamental limitations on search algorithms, and highlights the necessity of theory incorporating knowledge of the problem domain of interest. Much interest in this topic has been aroused lately as awareness has grown of the so-called "No Free Lunch Theorem" (Wolpert & Macready, 1995), which—broadly—states that if a sufficiently inclusive class of problems is considered, no search method can outperform an enumeration. This paper discusses the consequences of this and other fundamental limitations on search for the practical design of stochastic search algorithms, particularly evolutionary algorithms, and emphasizes that there are many possible improvements that are *not* strongly limited by the theorems.

A more accessible and general form of the No Free Lunch Theorem is first presented, based on arguments put forward previously (Radcliffe, 1992, 1994). Strictly, this result shows that over the ensemble of all representations of one space with another, all algorithms (in a rather broad class) perform identically on any reasonable measure of performance. This has as an immediate corollary the No Free Lunch Theorem, and provides an interesting context for the "minimax" results given in Wolpert & Macready (1995).

Having proved the main results, attention turns to a discussion of their implications. First, issues concerning searches that re-sample points previously visited are discussed. After this, representational issues are discussed and restricted problem classes are considered in two stages. The first focuses on the case in which some unspecified representation is used which is known—in an appropriately defined sense—to fit the problem class well, and it is shown that different algorithms can be expected to perform differently in these cases. The second focuses on how knowledge concerning the structure of some class of functions under consideration can be used to choose an effective algorithm (consisting of a representation, a set of move operators and a sampling strategy). In particular, the critical rôle of representation in determining the potential efficacy of search algorithms is once again highlighted.

Finally, an agenda for future research is set forward, focusing on integrating the restrictions stated herein with the wide scope for theory incorporating domain-specific knowledge. The authors draw attention to what they feel are important unanswered questions concerning performance measurement, comparison of families of stochastic algorithms and difficulty of real-world problem domains, and suggest a new methodology for comparing search algorithms.

2   Terminology

2.1   Search Space Concepts

Before formulating theorems about search, it will be useful to introduce some terminology, to reduce the scope for misinterpretation. A search problem will be taken to be characterised by a *search space, S*—the set of objects over which the search is to be conducted—and an *objective function, f*, which is a mapping from S to the space of *objective function values,* $\mathcal{R}$, i.e.

$$f : \mathcal{S} \longrightarrow \mathcal{R}. \tag{1}$$

Although the most familiar situation arises when $\mathcal{R} = \mathbf{R}$ (the set of real numbers) and the goal is minimisation or maximisation of f, it is not necessary to require this for present purposes. For example, $\mathcal{R}$ could instead be a vector of objective function values, giving rise to a multicriterion optimisation.

Note that the set of all mappings from $\mathcal{S}$ to $\mathcal{R}$ is denoted $\mathcal{R}^{\mathcal{S}}$, so $f \in \mathcal{R}^{\mathcal{S}}$.

2.2 Representation

The issue of selecting an appropriate representation is central to search, as arguments in this paper will once again confirm. The present section gives a formal definition of a representation space, but further motivation for concentrating on representation as an issue is given in section 5.

A *representation of* $\mathcal{S}$ will be taken to be a set $\mathcal{C}$ (the *representation space*, or the space of *chromosomes*) of size at least equal to $\mathcal{S}$, together with a *surjective* function g (the *growth function*) that maps $\mathcal{C}$ onto $\mathcal{S}$:

$$g : \mathcal{C} \longrightarrow \mathcal{S}. \tag{2}$$

(Surjectivity is simply the requirement that g maps at least one point in $\mathcal{C}$ to each point in $\mathcal{S}$.) The set of surjective functions from $\mathcal{C}$ to $\mathcal{S}$ will be denoted $\mathcal{S}_{>}^{\mathcal{C}}$, so $g \in \mathcal{S}_{>}^{\mathcal{C}} \subset \mathcal{S}^{\mathcal{C}}$.

If $\mathcal{C}$ and $\mathcal{S}$ have the same size, then g is clearly invertible, and will be said to be a *faithful representation.*

Objective function values will also be associated with points in the representation space $\mathcal{C}$ through composition of f with g,

$$f \circ g : \mathcal{C} \longrightarrow \mathcal{R} \tag{3}$$

being given by

$$f \circ g(x) \triangleq f(g(x)). \tag{4}$$

The relationship between $\mathcal{C}$, $\mathcal{S}$ and $\mathcal{R}$ is shown in figure 1.

2.3 Sequences

Given any set $\mathcal{A}$, $\mathbb{S}(\mathcal{A})$ will be used to denote the set of all finite sequences over $\mathcal{A}$, including the empty sequence $\langle \rangle$, i.e.:

$$\mathbb{S}(\mathcal{A}) \triangleq \left\{ \langle a_1, a_2, \ldots, a_n \rangle \mid a_i \in \mathcal{A}, 1 \leq i \leq n \right\}. \tag{5}$$

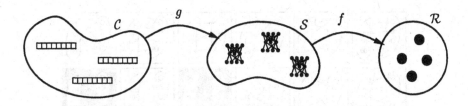

Fig. 1. The *growth function* g maps the *representation space* $\mathcal{C}$ onto the *search space* S, which is mapped to the space of *objective function values* $\mathcal{R}$ by the *objective function* f. If g is invertible, the representation is said to be *faithful*.

2.4 Permutations

Most of the "work" in the following theorems is achieved by using a permutation, i.e. a re-labelling of the elements of one of the spaces (usually $\mathcal{C}$). A permutation of a set $\mathcal{A}$ is a relabelling of the elements of the set, i.e. an *invertible* mapping

$$\pi : \mathcal{A} \longrightarrow \mathcal{A}. \tag{6}$$

The set of all permutations of $\mathcal{A}$ objects will be denoted $\mathcal{P}(\mathcal{A})$. The changes to a faithful representation of a search space S by a representation space $\mathcal{C}$ under all possible permutations of the elements of $\mathcal{C}$ are shown in figure 2.

2.5 Search Algorithms

For the purposes of the present paper, a *deterministic search algorithm* will be defined by a function which, given a sequence of points $\langle x_i \rangle$, with each $x_i \in \mathcal{C}$, and the corresponding sequence of objective function values for those points under the composed objective function $f \circ g$, generates a new point $x_{n+1} \in \mathcal{C}$. Thus, a search algorithm is defined by a mapping A

$$A : \mathsf{S}(\mathcal{C}) \times \mathsf{S}(\mathcal{R}) \longrightarrow \mathcal{C}. \tag{7}$$

The first point in the search sequence $\langle A_i \rangle \in \mathsf{S}(\mathcal{C})$ associated with the algorithm defined by A is

$$A_1 \triangleq A(\langle\rangle, \langle\rangle), \tag{8}$$

with subsequent points being recursively defined by

$$A_{n+1} \triangleq A(\langle A_i \rangle_{i=1}^n, \langle f \circ g(A_i) \rangle_{i=1}^n). \tag{9}$$

A *stochastic search algorithm* will be taken to be exactly the same as a deterministic search algorithm except that it also uses a seed for a pseudo-random number generator used to influence its choice of the next point x_{n+1}. Formally, a stochastic search algorithm is then defined by a mapping A' of the form

$$A' : \mathsf{S}(\mathcal{C}) \times \mathsf{S}(\mathcal{R}) \times \mathbb{Z} \longrightarrow \mathcal{C}. \tag{10}$$

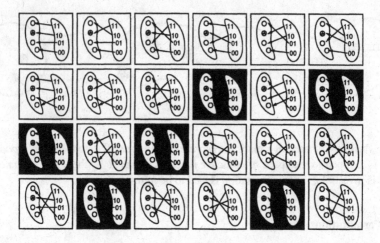

Fig. 2. This figure shows the 4! invertible mappings between a representation space $\mathcal{C}$ (in this case binary strings) and an arbitrary search space $\mathcal{S}$ of the same size. Note that 1/4 of the mappings (each shown in grey) map the global optimum (shown with a star) to the string 00.

(The seed is of course a constant, the same at every application of A'.) This process is illustrated in figures 3 and 4.

Note that a stochastic search algorithm is perfectly at liberty to ignore the given seed, and in this sense will be taken to include the case of a deterministic search algorithm. Because of this, results derived for the stochastic case also apply to the deterministic case. These definitions of algorithm are certainly broad enough to include all familiar classes of stochastic search algorithms as actually used (e.g. hill climbers, evolutionary algorithms, simulated annealing, tabu search). The issue of "insisting" on use of a representation is discussed further in section 5.

We shall abuse the notation slightly by identifying a search algorithm with the function that defines it, i.e. the search algorithm defined by the mapping A will also be denoted A.

Note particularly that in both cases, the sequence of points $\langle x_i \rangle$ is *not* assumed to be non-repeating except when this is explicitly stated. Further, search algorithms will always be assumed to run until they have searched the entire representation space $\mathcal{C}$, though performance measures will be at liberty use only some smaller number of function values (such as the first N).

2.6   Valid Search Sequence in $\mathcal{S}$

It will sometimes be convenient to refer to a *valid search sequence* in $\mathcal{S}$ in the context of some representation $g \in \mathcal{S}_{\leq}^{\mathcal{C}}$ and some non-repeating search algorithm A. A valid search sequence is simply one that can be generated as the image under g of a (non-repeating) search sequence in $\mathcal{C}$. For example, if $\mathcal{C}$ contains one more element that $\mathcal{S}$, each (complete) valid search sequence in $\mathcal{S}$ contains one member of $\mathcal{S}$ twice and all others exactly once.

$$A_2 = A(\langle A_1 \rangle, \langle f \circ g(A_1) \rangle, k)$$

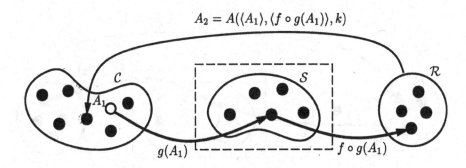

Fig. 3. The first point in the search is determined by the algorithm and the seed, $A_1 = A(\langle\rangle, \langle\rangle, k)$. The next point, A_2 is determined by these values together with the new information $f \circ g(A_1)$. Note that the algorithm has no information about the point $g(A_1)$ in S which was used to generate the observed function value: this is entirely controlled by the representation g.

2.7 Performance Measures

All the results below will refer rather cavalierly to "arbitrary performance measures", so it will be useful to make clear exactly what the assumed scope of such a performance measure actually is. A performance measure for a search algorithm will be taken to be any measure that depends only on the sequence of objective function values of the images under g of the points in C chosen by the algorithm. Formally, a performance measure μ will be taken to be any function

$$\mu : S(\mathcal{R}) \longrightarrow \mathcal{M} \qquad (11)$$

where $\mathcal{M}$ is any set used to measure the "quality" of some sequence of objective function values. Thus, abusing the notation further, we will define the performance of an algorithm A to be

$$\mu(A) \stackrel{\triangle}{=} \mu(\langle f \circ g(A_i)\rangle). \qquad (12)$$

There is an important distinction between algorithms that revisit points in C and those that do not. The performance measures defined here exclude those that can distinguish between objective function values deriving from newly visited points in C and points previously visited. Rather, we regard the non-revisiting algorithm derived from an algorithm that *does* revisit points in C as a different algorithm with potentially different performance.

We will also consider the performance of an algorithm over an (unordered) set of functions. By an *overall performance measure* we will mean any measure of the quality of a collection of sequences of objective function values. Given that two different objective functions may generate the same sequence of values, this collection will, in general,

$$A_3 = A(\langle A_1, A_2 \rangle, \langle f \circ g(A_1), f \circ g(A_2) \rangle, k)$$

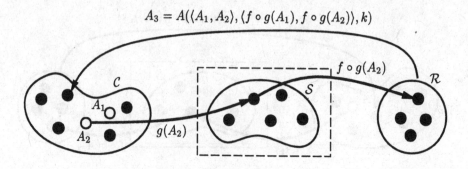

Fig. 4. The next point in the search is simply obtained by iterating the mapping. Notice that if $f \circ g(A_2) = f \circ g(A_1)$, the algorithm cannot "know" whether or not it visited a new point in S (i.e. whether $g(A_2) = g(A_1)$).

be a multiset (bag) of such sequences (i.e. sequences may appear more than once in the collection). Notice also that the collection is taken to be *unordered,* so that an overall performance measure is insensitive to the order in which the functions are presented. A simple example of such an overall performance measure is the average number of function evaluations required to find a global optimum.

3 No Free Lunch Theorems

The first task in formulating limitations on search is to define what it means for two algorithms to be *isomorphic.* Very simply, the idea is that two algorithms are isomorphic if one can be obtained from the other by a permutation of the representation space. This is what the following definition says.

Definition (Isomorphism for search algorithms). Let A and B be non-repeating stochastic search algorithms with an objective function $f \in \mathcal{R}^S$, a growth function $g \in \mathcal{S}_>^C$ and (fixed) seeds k_A and k_B respectively. Then A and B will be said to be *isomorphic with respect to f and g* if and only if there exists a permutation $\pi \in \mathcal{P}(C)$ such that

$$\langle g(A_i) \rangle = \langle g \circ \pi(B_i) \rangle. \tag{13}$$

∎

The idea of isomorphism between search algorithms is important because the following results will demonstrate that isomorphic algorithms perform equally in some extremely strong senses.

Theorem (Isomorphism for non-repeating algorithms). *Let A and B be non-repeating stochastic search algorithms using the same objective function f and the same representation space C. Then for every representation $g \in \mathcal{S}_>^C$, A and B are isomorphic with respect to f and g.*

Proof. Let g, g' be two different growth functions in $\mathcal{S}_{>}^{\mathcal{C}}$. Clearly, A must visit a different sequence of points in $\mathcal{S}$ under g and g'. (This may be clarified by looking again at figures 3 and 4. Since the first point, A_1, chosen by A is independent of the growth function, it is easy to see inductively that if A visited the same sequence of points in $\mathcal{S}$ under g and g', then g and g' would in fact be equal, as every point in $\mathcal{C}$ will eventually be visited by a non-terminating, non-repeating algorithm.) This shows that any valid search sequence in $\mathcal{S}$ under some $g \in \mathcal{S}_{>}^{\mathcal{C}}$ defines that g uniquely (for the algorithm A). Conversely each growth function g defines a unique search sequence in $\mathcal{S}$, namely $\langle g(A_i) \rangle$.

It is thus clear that for every $g \in \mathcal{S}_{>}^{\mathcal{C}}$, yielding search sequence $\langle g(A_i) \rangle$, there exists a $g' \in \mathcal{S}_{>}^{\mathcal{C}}$ such that $\langle g'(B_i) \rangle = \langle g(A_i) \rangle$. Further, it is easy to see that some permutation $\pi \in \mathcal{P}(\mathcal{C})$ exists such that $g' = g \circ \pi$—specifically, $\pi(B_i) = A_i$, which is a permutation of $\mathcal{C}$ since both $\langle A_i \rangle$ and $\langle B_i \rangle$ are non-repeating enumerations of $\mathcal{C}$. This is exactly the permutation required to demonstrate isomorphism of A and B with respect to f and g.

□

Theorem (Isomorphic algorithms perform equally over permutations of $\mathcal{C}$). *Let A and B be stochastic search algorithms that are isomorphic with respect to some objective function $f \in \mathcal{R}^{\mathcal{S}}$ and some set of growth functions $\mathcal{G} \subset \mathcal{S}_{>}^{\mathcal{C}}$ that is closed under permutation of $\mathcal{C}$. Then their overall performance on the ensemble of search problems defined by all growth functions in $\mathcal{G}$ is identical, regardless of the performance measure chosen.*

Proof. For any valid search sequence $\langle g(A_i) \rangle \in \mathbb{S}(\mathcal{S})$, we can find a permutation $\pi \in \mathcal{P}(\mathcal{C})$ such that $\langle g \circ \pi(B_i) \rangle = \langle g(A_i) \rangle$ from the definition of isomorphism. By symmetry, the converse is also true, so every search sequence in $\mathcal{S}$ generated by either algorithm is also generated by the other. Since it was shown in the proof of the previous theorem that different growth functions define different search sequences, this suffices to show that the set of search sequences in $\mathcal{S}$ generated by $\mathcal{G}$ is the same for the two algorithms, so their performance over $\mathcal{G}$ must be equal.

□

Perhaps the most interesting consequence of this theorem is that if the entire ensemble of representations in $\mathcal{S}_{>}^{\mathcal{C}}$ is considered, the only factor that differentiates algorithms is the frequency with which they revisit points. This is because, over this ensemble of representations, visiting one new point is no different from visiting any other.

Corollary (Overall Performance Measures). *Consider search algorithms in which the representation space $\mathcal{C}$ is the same as the search space $\mathcal{S}$. The overall performance of all search algorithms that do not revisit points in $\mathcal{C}$ on the ensemble of search problems defined by all objective functions in $\mathcal{R}^{\mathcal{S}}$ is identical, regardless of the overall performance measure chosen.*

■

Proof. For all functions in $\mathcal{R}_{>}^{\mathcal{S}}$, the result follows directly from the theorems by a trivial relabelling (figure 5) where we take $\mathcal{S} = \mathcal{R}$, f to be the identity mapping and $\mathcal{G}$ to be the set of all functions from $\mathcal{S}$ to $\mathcal{R}$. Similarly, for any set of functions surjective onto a subset of $\mathcal{R}$, the theorem still clearly holds taking $\mathcal{R}$ as the given subset of $\mathcal{R}$. Since the set of all functions in $\mathcal{R}^{\mathcal{S}}$ is clearly just the union over such surjective subsets, we have the required result.

■

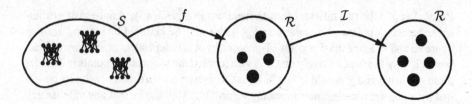

Fig. 5. The relabelling above, with $\mathcal{I}$ as the identity mapping, establishes that all iso-morphic algorithms have identical overall performance over all functions in $\mathcal{R}^S$ against any overall performance measure. If f is not surjective, the problem has to be reformulated using the image $f(S)$ in place of $\mathcal{R}$ for the theorem to apply directly, but since the theorem applies to each such image, it clearly also applies to their union.

The foregoing corollary is a minor generalisation of the "No Free Lunch" Theorem (Wolpert & Macready, 1995).

Corollary (Mean Performance of Isomorphic Algorithms). *The mean performance of all isomorphic search algorithms is identical over the set of all functions in $\mathcal{R}^S$ for any chosen performance measure.*

Proof. This follows immediately from the previous corollary.   □

Wolpert & Macready (1995) conjecture that there may be what they term "minimax" distinctions between pairs of algorithms. Here they have in mind "head-to-head" comparisons on a "function-by-function" basis, where, for example (their Appendix B), one algorithm (A) might outperform another (B) on some performance measure more often than the reverse is the case. This is clearly true, as table 1 shows. Notice, however, that such comparisons may be non-transitive, i.e. given a third algorithm C, it might be that case that

$$(C > B \text{ and } B > A) \not\Rightarrow C > A, \tag{14}$$

where $>$ means "outperforms" in the minimax sense described above. An example of exactly this situation, where $C > B$ and $B > A$ but $A > C$ is also shown in the table.

Corollary (Enumeration). *No non-repeating search algorithm can outperform enumeration over the ensemble of problems defined by $\mathcal{R}^S$.*

Proof. This is also immediate from the theorem, noting that no search can sample any proportion of the search space faster than enumeration.   □

4   Search Algorithms that Revisit Points

Before considering representational issues in more detail—which is the main theme of this paper—it is first useful to consider the implications of the restrictions of the earlier theorems to non-revisiting searches. In the form that they state the No Free Lunch

Function $f((1,2,3))$	Time to Minimum A	B	C	Winner A vs. B	Winner B vs. C	Winner C vs. A
(0,0,0)	1	1	1	tie	tie	tie
(0,0,1)	1	1	2	tie	B	A
(0,1,0)	1	2	1	A	C	tie
(0,1,1)	1	3	2	A	C	A
(1,0,0)	2	1	1	B	tie	C
(1,0,1)	2	1	3	B	B	A
(1,1,0)	3	2	1	B	C	C
(1,1,1)	1	1	1	tie	tie	tie
Overall winner				B	C	A

Table 1. Consider all functions from $S = \{1,2,3\}$ to $R = \{0,1\}$ and three search algorithms A, B and C, each of which simply enumerates S. In particular, take $\langle A_i \rangle = \langle 1,2,3 \rangle$, $\langle B_i \rangle = \langle 2,3,1 \rangle$ and $\langle C_i \rangle = \langle 3,1,2 \rangle$. The table lists all eight functions in R^S and compares the algorithms pairwise with respect to the particular performance measure 'number of steps to find a global minimum'. This illustrates the "minimax" distinction conjectured by Wolpert & Macready (1995), but also shows that this is non-transitive. Indeed, the overall performance of each algorithm is identical, regardless of what overall performance measure is chosen. (Columns 2, 3 and 4 are permutations of each other, illustrating this.)

Theorem, Wolpert & Macready only consider algorithms that do not revisit points already considered, and seem to regard the issue of revisiting as a trivial technicality. In fact, most searches do not have this property, and it is worth noting that there are good reasons for this. Perhaps the most obvious is finite memory of real computers, but this is not the most important explanation. For while there are undoubtedly searches carried out for which it would be impossible today to store every point visited, as main memory sizes increase, this becomes ever less of an issue. At the very least it is typically feasible to store a much larger history than even most population-based algorithms choose to do. Much more significant is the time needed to process large amounts of data—even merely to perform a check against every point so far evaluated requires, at best, log time. Depending on the details of the algorithm, other functions may take even longer. As an example, ranking schemes used in some genetic algorithms (Baker, 1987) require their populations to be sorted.

Because most algorithms used do revisit points, there is the potential, in principle, to improve real search techniques without reference to the particular problem being tackled. It should be clear that the kinds of performance measures relevant in this case concern the average number of points sampled, *including* points visited multiple times, to reach a solution of a certain quality, or the total "wall-clock" time to achieve the same goal. (Indeed, this "best-so-far" graph as a function of the number of function evaluations is precisely the graph shown in most empirical papers on stochastic search.) Thus, for example, when Whitley (1989) and Davis (1991) advocate barring duplicates in the population, it is perfectly possible that this will indeed prove beneficial over an entire ensemble of problems $\mathcal{R}^S$. The suggested benefits of enforcing uniqueness of solutions are that it leads to more accurate sampling (with respect to target sampling rates, Grefenstette & Baker, 1989), increases diversity in the population and makes better use of the limited "memory" that the population represents. On the other hand, there is a clear cost associated with maintaining uniqueness, in that it requires checking each new (tentative) solution generated. The point here is not *whether* enforcing uniqueness *does* improve evolutionary search in general, but that in principal it *could* do so. The same applies to any change that affects the diversity in the population, and which is therefore likely to affect the frequency with which points are revisited.

5 Representations and Algorithms

This paper has concentrated rather heavily on representational aspects of search, and in doing so has established some rather powerful, general results. However, the motivation for focusing on representation goes far beyond this. For present purposes, we shall ignore the almost philosophical debate about whether it is *possible* to perform a search without a representation, and simply accept that a search may be conducted "directly" in the search space, by-passing the representational issue. Nevertheless, it is important to emphasize that the representation is *not* being introduced in order to facilitate storage (or coding) of solutions on a computer or any other device, which we regard as an auxiliary issue. The "point" of our representation is that we assume that move operators are actually formulated (defined!) in the representation space $\mathcal{C}$, rather than the search space $\mathcal{S}$, and that some benefit is potentially conferred by this.

Consider the concrete example of a three-dimensional euclidean space $\mathcal{S}$ and the choice of representations between cartesian coordinates (x, y, z) and spherical polars (r, θ, ϕ). We would consider the representation used by an algorithm to be defined *not* by the coordinate system in which the points in $\mathcal{S}$ were stored in a computer (whether in terms of high-level language constructs or actual discretised bit-patterns in memory chips), but rather by whether the move operators manipulate polar or cartesian components. There are clearly problems for which each representation has advantages. For example, the polar representation might be expected to offer benefits in spherically symmetric problems.

It should further be pointed out that representation is often given an even more significant rôle than the central one discussed above (Hart *et al.*, 1994). Davis (1991), for example, has long used devices such as "greedy decoders" to map a "chromosome" manipulated by a genetic algorithm to the solution that it represents. While this can formally be viewed as a radically different kind of search, in which the search objects are really "hints" or starting points for a full local search, the more intuitive picture of a particularly complex growth function has some merit. Of course, fascinating new issues arise in this context, as there is typically no particular reason to suppose that the decoder is surjective (indeed, it would almost defeat its motivation if it were!), nor even that it can generate points of interest (such as global optima) for *any* input. Moreover, the decoder may well contain a stochastic element, further complicating matters. There is a need to try to generalise our theories of search to begin to accommodate some of these less conventional, but manifestly powerful, complex representations.

Returning to more prosaic representations, consider two different algorithms A and B, operating on the same problem f from $\mathcal{R}^S$ and using the same representation space $\mathcal{C}$, but with different growth functions $g, g' \in \mathcal{S}^{\mathcal{C}}$. It is clear that there are some situations in which even though $A \neq B$, and $g \neq g'$, the differences "cancel out" so that they perform the same search. (Indeed, an obvious case arises when the algorithms are isomorphic, and $g' = g \circ \pi$ for some suitable permutation π.) This might lead us to suspect that there is a *duality* between representations and algorithms, so that any change that can be effected by altering the representation could equally be achieved by a corresponding alteration to the algorithm, and any change made to the algorithm could equally be effected by a corresponding change to the representation. In fact, it has been shown (Radcliffe, 1994) that while the first of these statements is true, the second is not, in the general case of algorithms that are allowed to revisit points, or if the stochastic element is not "factored out" by fixing the seed. The duality—if that it be—is only partial.

If, for example, we consider a canonical genetic algorithm (say the Simple Genetic Algorithm—Goldberg, 1989c), but allow either one-point or uniform crossover, then there is clearly no change of representation that transforms one of these algorithms into the other, either over all possible seeds for the random number generator, or even for a particular seed when revisiting effects are considered. Moreover, there is no reason to assume that their performance over the class of all representations in $\mathcal{S}^{\mathcal{C}}_{\lesssim}$ (or indeed, all objective functions $f \in \mathcal{R}^S$) will be the same. In terms of the theorems described earlier, this merely amounts to the observation that revisiting algorithms are not, in general, isomorphic. However, this formally trivial statement has rather strong practical implications given that, as noted earlier, establishing whether a point has been previously sampled requires significant computational effort.

Despite the fact that more power is available by changing the algorithm than from merely changing the representation, the separation between representation and search algorithm remains extremely valuable. In section 6 we shall examine how good representations can be exploited and constructed.

6   Restricted Problem Classes

One of Wolpert and Macready's central messages, and one with which the authors agree strongly, is that if algorithms are to outperform random search, they must be matched to the search problem at hand. ("If no domain-specific knowledge is used in selecting an appropriate representation, the algorithm will have no opportunity to exceed the performance of an enumerative search"—Radcliffe, 1994.) It will be useful to consider the implications of the limitations on search algorithms from the theorems in two stages. First, consideration will be given to what can be expected if it is known that the representation used does—in an appropriately defined sense—"match" some restricted problem class under consideration (section 6.1). These considerations apply even if nothing more than this is known. After this case has been discussed, the focus will turn to how knowledge of a problem class can be harnessed to select algorithms that might be expected to perform well (section 6.2).

6.1   Assuming a Good Representation

It will first be useful to formalise what is meant by a "good" representation. The following definition is suggested.

Definition (Good representation, relative algorithmic performance). Let A be a search algorithm that can be applied to a set of search problems defined by $\mathcal{R}^S$, using a representation space $\mathcal{C}$. Let $\mathcal{D}$ be a (proper) subset of $\mathcal{R}^S$ (a problem "domain"). Then a representation $g \in S_>^{\mathcal{C}}$ will be said to be a *good* representation for $\mathcal{D}$ with respect to some performance measure μ if and only if A achieves better average performance with respect to μ on problems in $\mathcal{D}$ than on problems in the whole of $\mathcal{R}^S$.

Similarly, algorithm B will be said to be better than algorithm A over $\mathcal{D}$, with representation g, if it achieves a better average performance over $\mathcal{D}$ with respect to μ.

■

This is clearly a rather minimalist definition of "good", but it will serve the present purpose. In particular, the notion of a quality of a representation is interesting in the context of "representation-independent" algorithms, (effectively algorithms that can be instantiated for any specified representation g—Radcliffe & Surry, 1994b, 1994a). These are discussed in section 6.2.

Focusing once more on evolutionary algorithms, the kinds of representation spaces that are typically used are high dimensional

$$\mathcal{C} = \mathcal{C}_1 \times \mathcal{C}_2 \times \cdots \times \mathcal{C}_n \tag{15}$$

and the operators used normally manipulate the components of members of $\mathcal{C}$ to some extent independently. The "ideal" representation that we probably typically have in mind is one that induces a linearly separable mapping $f \circ g$ from $\mathcal{C}$ to $\mathcal{R}$, (Mason, 1993) so that

$$f \circ g((c_1, c_2, \ldots, c_n)) = \sum_{i=1}^{n} \phi_i(c_i) \tag{16}$$

for some functions

$$\phi_i : \mathcal{C}_i \longrightarrow \mathcal{R}. \tag{17}$$

While we would expect that most reasonable evolutionary algorithms would outperform enumeration in such circumstances, using any reasonable performance measure, ironically, we would *not* expect an evolutionary algorithm to compare well with simple hill climbers in this case. In particular, any greedy hill climber will have optimal performance against typical performance measures on such problems. The territory in which we actually expect sophisticated adaptive search schemes to excel is some intermediate *régime* between random representations and completely linearly separable (i.e. non-epistatic) ones.

6.2 Implications for Tackling Problem Classes

The observations above provide a motivation for considering ways in which both good representations and good algorithms can be designed and recognised for particular problem classes. In the case of representations, some preliminary steps have been taken, including work by Davidor (1990), Kauffman (1993) and Radcliffe & Surry (1994a), and from a different perspective, there is an extensive literature on deception, a particular form of linear non-separability (Goldberg, 1989a, 1989b; Whitley, 1991; Das & Whitley, 1991; Grefenstette, 1992; Louis & Rawlins, 1993). All of these examine some form of questions about what precisely "some degree of linear separability" means, how it can be measured and how it may be exploited by algorithms.

One approach that seems particularly fruitful to the authors is to measure properties of representations over well-defined problem classes, and then to seek to construct a theory of how such measured properties can be exploited by algorithms. In Radcliffe & Surry (1994a), we measured the variance of objective function value for four different representations for the travelling sales-rep problem (TSP) as a function of schema order to obtain the graph shown in figure 6. (A schema—or forma—fixes certain components of a member of $\mathcal{C}$, with order measuring the number of such fixed components.) The lower variance for the "corner" representation indicates that objective function value is more nearly linearly separable with respect to the components of this representation than is the case with the other representations. Although the four representations are all highly constrained, well-defined move operators were specified solely in terms of manipulations of $\mathcal{C}$: this is what is meant by representation-independent move operators. We were therefore able to compare the performance of identical algorithms with these four representations over a range of problem instances. The results, as expected, indicated that on standard performance metrics, most of the algorithms used worked better with the lower variance representations than their higher variance counterparts. This suggests strongly that developing further measurements of representation quality, together with further ways of characterising representation-independent operators (such as the notions of respect, assortment and transmission, developed by Radcliffe, 1991, 1994) and a theory linking those together, is an urgent task.

7 Outlook

We have provided in this paper a formal demonstration of various fundamental limitations on search algorithms, with particular reference to evolutionary algorithms. These results establish clearly the central rôle of representation in search, and point to the importance of developing a methodology for formalising, expressing and incorporating domain knowledge into representations and operators, together with a theory to underpin this.

The results demonstrate the futility of trying to construct universal algorithms, or universal representations. For example, neither "binary" nor gray coding (Caruana & Schaffer, 1988) can be said to be superior, either to each other or to any other representation, without reference to a particular problem domain. One immediate practical consequence of this should be a change of methodology regarding test suites of problems and comparative studies. Rather than developing a fixed (small) suite of problems

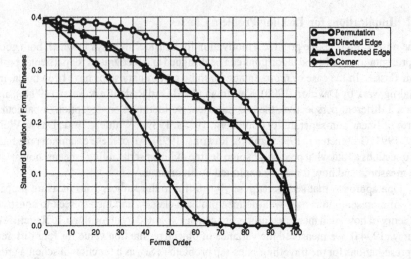

Fig. 6. The graph shows the mean standard deviation of tour length as a function of schema (forma) order for each of four representations of the TSP. These particular results are from a single problem instance generated using 100 samples drawn from 100 randomly generated schemata at each order shown, though the graph would look nearly identical if averaged sensibly over all 100-city TSPs.

for refining algorithms and representations, we believe that a significantly more useful approach consists of developing algorithms for a well-specified *class* of problems. The idea would be to refine algorithms using any small, randomly chosen subset of problems from this class, but to compare performance only against different randomly selected problem instances from the same class. We believe that a move towards this philosophy of comparative studies would allow the development of much more systematic insights.

The issues discussed in this paper seem to the authors central to gaining greater understanding of search methods, yet the questions that they raise receive remarkably little attention within the research community. On this basis, we conclude by suggesting some of the key open questions that we see.

– Given a class of problems about which we have partial knowledge, how can that knowledge be formalised in a way useful to constructing representations algorithms? Ideas from forma analysis (Radcliffe, 1991, 1994) offer some directions here, but there is clearly vastly more to be done.
– Can the quality of a representation be measured in any useful way?
– What kinds of predictive models of performance (if any) can be built given a well-defined problem domain, representation and algorithm?
– What performance metrics for algorithms are useful, given the limitations imposed by the theorems?

- Can we develop a useful methodology for determining appropriate parameters for a stochastic algorithm, given a representation and problem domain?
- Given an algorithm, can we determine the structure of the fitness landscape induced by the representation and move operators that is (implicitly) exploited by that algorithm? (What is a genetic algorithm *really* "processing"?) Such insights might allow us to build more powerful models of landscapes (Jones, 1994).

Acknowledgements

The authors would like to thank Bill Macready and David Wolpert for their comments on a draft of this paper. The ensuing discussion established that we had misunderstood their notion of "minimax" distinctions, and allowed us to refine our ideas in this area and establish their conjecture.

References

T. Bäck and H.-P. Schwefel, 1993. An overview of evolutionary algorithms for parameter optimisation. *Evolutionary Computation*, 1(1):1–24.

J. E. Baker, 1987. Reducing bias and inefficiency in the selection algorithm. In *Proceedings of the Second International Conference on Genetic Algorithms*. Lawrence Erlbaum Associates (Hillsdale).

R. A. Caruana and J. D. Schaffer, 1988. Representation and hidden bias: Gray vs. binary coding for genetic algorithms. In *Proceedings of the 5th International Conference on Machine Learning*. Morgan Kaufmann (Los Altos).

R. Das and D. Whitley, 1991. The only challenging problems are deceptive: Global search by solving order-1 hyperplanes. In *Proceedings of the Fourth International Conference on Genetic Algorithms*, pages 166–173. Morgan Kaufmann (San Mateo).

Y. Davidor, 1990. Epistasis variance: Suitability of a representation to genetic algorithms. *Complex Systems*, 4:369–383.

L. Davis, 1991. *Handbook of Genetic Algorithms*. Van Nostrand Reinhold (New York).

L. J. Fogel, A. J. Owens, and M. J. Walsh, 1966. *Artificial Intelligence Through Simulated Evolution*. Wiley Publishing (New York).

F. Glover, 1986. Future paths for integer programming and links to artificial-intelligence. *Computers and Operations Research*, 13(5):533–549.

D. E. Goldberg, 1989a. Genetic algorithms and Walsh functions: Part I, a gentle introduction. *Complex Systems*, 3:129–152.

D. E. Goldberg, 1989b. Genetic algorithms and Walsh functions: Part II, deception and its analysis. *Complex Systems*, 3:153–171.

D. E. Goldberg, 1989c. *Genetic Algorithms in Search, Optimization & Machine Learning*. Addison-Wesley (Reading, Mass).

J. J. Grefenstette and J. E. Baker, 1989. How genetic algorithms work: A critical look at intrinsic parallelism. In *Proceedings of the Third International Conference on Genetic Algorithms*. Morgan Kaufmann (San Mateo).

J. J. Grefenstette, 1992. Deception considered harmful. In *Foundations of Genetic Algorithms 2*, pages 75–91. Morgan Kaufmann (San Mateo, CA).

W. Hart, T. Kammeyer, and R. Belew, 1994. The role of development in genetic algorithms. To appear in Foundations of Genetic Algorithms 3.

J. H. Holland, 1975. *Adaptation in Natural and Artificial Systems.* University of Michigan Press (Ann Arbor).

T. Jones, 1994. A model of landscapes. Technical Report, Santa Fe Institute.

S. A. Kauffman, 1993. *The origins of order: self-organization and selection in evolution.* Oxford University Press (New York).

S. Kirkpatrick, C. D. Gelatt, and M. P. Vecchi, 1983. Optimisation by simulated annealing. *Science*, 220(4598):671–680.

J. R. Koza, 1991. Evolving a computer to generate random numbers using the genetic programming paradigm. In *Proceedings of the Fourth International Conference on Genetic Algorithms*, pages 37–44. Morgan Kaufmann (San Mateo).

S. J. Louis and G. J. E. Rawlins, 1993. Pareto optimality, GA-easiness and deception. In S. Forrest, editor, *Proceedings of the Fifth International Conference on Genetic Algorithms.* Morgan Kaufmann (San Mateo, CA).

A. J. Mason, 1993. Crossover non-linearity ratios and the genetic algorithm: Escaping the blinkers of schema processing and intrinsic parallelism. Technical Report Report No. 535b, School of Engineering, University of Auckland.

N. J. Radcliffe and P. D. Surry, 1994a. Fitness variance of formae and performance prediction. Technical report, To appear in Foundations of Genetic Algorithms 3.

N. J. Radcliffe and P. D. Surry, 1994b. Formal memetic algorithms. In Terence C. Fogarty, editor, *Evolutionary Computing: AISB Workshop*, pages 1–16. Springer-Verlag, Lecture Notes in Computer Science 865.

N. J. Radcliffe, 1991. Equivalence class analysis of genetic algorithms. *Complex Systems*, 5(2):183–205.

N. J. Radcliffe, 1992. Non-linear genetic representations. In R. Männer and B. Manderick, editors, *Parallel Problem Solving from Nature 2*, pages 259–268. Elsevier Science Publishers/North Holland (Amsterdam).

N. J. Radcliffe, 1994. The algebra of genetic algorithms. *Annals of Maths and Artificial Intelligence*, 10:339–384.

I. Rechenberg, 1973. *Evolutionstrategie—Optimierung technischer Systeme nach Prinzipien der biologischen Evolution.* Frommann-Holzboog (Stuttgart).

I. Rechenberg, 1984. The evolution strategy. a mathematical model of darwinian evolution. In E. Frehland, editor, *Synergetics—from Microscopic to Macroscopic Order*, pages 122–132. Springer-Verlag (New York).

J. Shapiro, A. Prügel-Bennett, and M. Rattray, 1994. A statistical mechanical formulation of the dynamics of genetic algorithms. In T. C. Fogarty, editor, *Evolutionary Computing: AISB Workshop*, pages 17–27. Springer-Verlag, Lecture Notes in Computer Science 865.

P. J. M. van Laarhoven and E. H. L. Aarts, 1989. *Simulated Annealing: Theory and Applications.* D. Reidel Publishing Company.

M. D. Vose and G. E. Liepins, 1991. Schema disruption. In *Proceedings of the Fourth International Conference on Genetic Algorithms*, pages 237–243. Morgan Kaufmann (San Mateo).

M. D. Vose, 1992. Modelling simple genetic algorithms. In D. Whitley, editor, *Foundations of Genetic Algorithms 2.* Morgan Kaufmann (San Mateo, CA).

D. Whitley, 1989. The GENITOR algorithm and selection pressure: Why rank-based allocation of reprodutive trials is best. In *Proceedings of the Third International Conference on Genetic Algorithms*, pages 116–121. Morgan Kaufmann (San Mateo).

L. D. Whitley, 1991. Fundamental principles of deception. In G. J. E. Rawlins, editor, *Foundations of Genetic Algorithms*, pages 221–241. Morgan Kaufmann (San Mateo).

D. H. Wolpert and W. G. Macready, 1995. No free lunch theorems for search. Technical Report SFI–TR–95–02–010, Santa Fe Institute.

Mathematical System Models as a Basis of Software Engineering*

Manfred Broy

Institut für Informatik, Technische Universität München,
Arcisstr. 21, D–80290 München, Germany

Abstract. We give mathematical system models as a basis for system specification, system development by refinement, and system implementation. It provides a simple homogeneous mathematical and logical foundation of software and systems engineering. We treat mathematical concepts of refinement through levels of abstraction and complementing system views as they are used in software engineering. The goal is to give a coherent and simple mathematical basis.

1 Introduction

Software engineering comprises methods, description techniques and development processes for the development of large software systems. The full framework of a software engineering method (such as for instance SSADM, see Downs et al. [9], or Cleanroom Software Engineering, see Mills et al. [16]) contains a large amount of complex and highly interconnected information. Traditionally, this information is provided by so called reference manuals and rationals providing an often strange mixture of ideology, technical explanation, experience reports and ad hoc hints. Mostly, the meaning of the proposed description techniques remains partially unclear and so does their relationships.

We claim that it is possible to give a much more precise presentation of software engineering techniques. We show that this can be done without too much overhead by providing a mathematical basis in little more than ten pages.

Our general goal is to give a comprehensive mathematical foundation of the models and notions used and needed in software engineering (see Booch [2], Coad and Yourdan [6], De Marco [7], Denert [8]) but keeping the mathematics as simple as possible. We describe a compositional system model that covers the main modeling issues dealt with in systems and software engineering.

1.1 Informal Survey of System Modeling Notions

An *interactive system* interacts with its environment by exchanging *messages*. The messages are exchanged through *input* and *output channels*. The causal

---

* This work was carried out within the Project SysLab, supported by Siemens Nixdorf and by the Deutsche Forschungsgemeinschaft under the Leibniz program. It is based on results worked out in the Sonderforschungsbereich 342 "Werkzeuge und Methoden für die Nutzung paralleler Rechnerarchitektur".

relationship between the input and output messages determines the *black box behavior* of a system also called its *interface*. Formally, this behavior is described by a *black box specification* also called an *interface specification*. By such a specification the behavior of a system may be specified uniquely for every pattern of input behavior given by its environment or the specification may leave some freedom. In the latter case we speak of *underspecification* or in the case of an operational system also of *nondeterminism*.

The behavior of a system may depend on the *timing* of its input messages. Also the timing of the output messages may be an important property of a system. Therefore we are interested in a specification technique that allows us to specify systems with timed and time dependent behaviors. For the description of the black box view of a system we use a logic based specification language.

When constructing an *implementation* of a system, we are not only interested in its black box behavior, but also in its internal structure. We speak of a *glass box view* of a system. Under its glass box view, a system may either be a *state machine* with a central state which we understand, in general, as a centralized nondistributed unit[1] or it may be a *distributed system* consisting of a family of *subsystems* called *components*. In a distributed system the only way the components interact is again by exchanging messages. However, also for a distributed system, a state view is possible by including all states of its components. This leads to a *distributed state*.

The messages and states of a system are mathematical elements of appropriately chosen carrier sets. They might be described by axiomatic specification techniques or by classical description techniques for *data models* as proposed in software engineering such as the widely used *entity/relationship* techniques.

A system (especially a distributed system) carries out a *process* that may depend on the behavior of the environment. Such a process consists of all the *actions* carried out by the system. Elementary actions of an interactive system consist in sending and receiving messages. The description of representative instances of such processes may help to understand the interactions of a system.

In the development of a system, we describe it and its parts at several *levels of abstraction*. Through the development, seen as a pure top down approach, we take into account more and more specific details and change the models such that they come closer to the structure required by system implementations finally leading to a *software architecture*. This process of system development is also called *refinement*. The notion of refinement is formalized by a refinement relation which is a mathematical relation between system specifications.

We consider, among others, the following types of refinement relations for system development:

- *black box refinement* (also called *property refinement*),
- *interface refinement*,
- *glass box refinement*.

---

[1] In this oversimplified view we include shared state systems with parallelism as nondistributed systems.

Glass box refinement aims at the design and implementation phase of a system. It may be classified into:

- *state space refinement,*
- *refinement by distribution.*

The corresponding refinement relations form the mathematical basis for the generation of logical verification conditions that have to be proved to show the correctness of the respective refinement steps.

1.2   Overall Organization of the Paper

In the following we define mathematical models capturing all the notions introduced informally in the introduction. We start by defining a mathematical system model which allows to model distributed systems in a hierarchical manner. Then we treat the notion of refinement and of complementing system views.

In our descriptions of system views and concepts, one goal is uniformity. We describe every system concept by a syntactic and a semantic part. In the syntactic part we define families of identifiers with additional sort information about them. In the semantic part, we associate mathematical elements with the introduced name spaces.

Our work is based on Broy [3], Focus [10], Broy [4], Broy [5] and Rumpe et al. [18]. An application of mathematical models to a specific software engineering method is shown in Hußmann [13] (see also Hußmann [14]) by treating the British development method SSADM.

2   The Mathematical System Model

In this section we introduce a mathematical model for interactive and distributed systems and define a number of fundamental aspects and views.

2.1   Data Models

A *data model* is used to model the data occurring in an information processing system. It consists of a syntactic and a semantic part. The syntactic part consists of a *signature* $\Sigma = (S, F)$. S denotes a set of *sorts* and F denotes a set of *function symbols*. For each of these function symbols, a functionality is predefined by a mapping

$$\text{fct} : F \to S^+$$

that associates with every function symbol its sequence of domain and range sorts. Thus, the syntactic part provides a name space with sort information.

Given a signature $\Sigma = (S, F)$, a Σ-algebra A consists of a carrier set s^A for every sort $s \in S$ and of a function

$$f^A : s_1^A \times \ldots \times s_n^A \to s_{n+1}^A$$

for every function symbol $f \in F$ with $\text{fct}(f) = <s_1 \dots s_{n+1}>$. A *sorted set* of identifiers is a set of identifiers X with a function

$$\text{Sort} : X \to S$$

that associates a sort with every identifier in X. By X^A we denote the set of all valuations which are mappings v that associate an element $v(x) \in \text{Sort}(x)^A$ with every identifier $x \in X$.

An *entity/relationship model* consists of a syntactic and a semantic part. Its syntactic part consists of a pair (E, R) where E is a sorted set of identifiers called *entities* and R is a set of identifiers called *relationships* for which there exists a function

$$\text{Sort} : R \to E \times E$$

The pair (E, R) is also called entity/relationship data model. A semantic model B of an entity/relationship model assigns a set e^B to each entity identifier $e \in E$ for which we have

$$e^B \subseteq \text{sort}(e)^A$$

and r^B is a *relation*

$$r^B \subseteq e^B \times e^B$$

A semantic model B is also called an *instance* of an entity/relationship data model. It is a straightforward step to include attributes into our concept of entity/relationship techniques. The set of all instances of an entity relationship model is called the *entity/relationship state space* (see Hettler [12] for an intensive treatment of this subject). Note that this definition already includes a simple integrity constraint namely that every element occurring in a relation is also an element of the involved entity. Note, moreover, how easy it is in this formalization to combine entity/relationship models with axiomatic specification techniques (see Wirsing [19]).

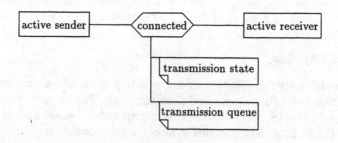

Fig. 1. Entity/relation diagram for the transmission medium with the entities *active sender* and *active receiver*, the relationship *connected* and two attributes

In Fig. 1 we show a simple entity/relationship diagram defining a data model for a transmission medium. It is a part of a message switching system which will be used as an example throughout the paper.

2.2 Communication Histories

Systems cooperate and interact by exchanging messages over channels. Given a sort of messages M, by

$$\text{Str } M$$

we denote the sort of *timed streams*. A timed stream is represented by a mapping

$$s : \mathbb{N} \backslash \{0\} \rightarrow (M^A)^\star$$

A stream denotes a *communication history* of a channel. We work with a discrete model of time and assume that our time is devided into an infinite sequence of time intervals. $s(i)$ represents the sequence of messages communicated in the ith time interval. Given a stream s, by

$$s|_k$$

we denote the restriction of the timed stream s to the first k time interval represented by $[1 : k]$. For every sequence of messages $m \in (M^A)^\star$ and every timed stream s of sort Str M we denote by

$$<m>^\frown s$$

the stream with the sequence m as its first element (the sequence of messages communicated in the first time interval) followed by the stream s.

Given a sorted set of identifiers X for channels, a communication history for these channels is denoted by a function Val that associates a stream Val(c) of sort Str Sort(c) with every channel $c \in X$. The set of these communication histories for the sorted set of identifiers X is denoted by

$$\vec{X}$$

B $X^{A\star}$ we denote the set of mappings m that associate a sequence $m(c) \in (s^A)^\star$ with every channel $c \in X$ of sort $s = \text{Sort}(c)$. For every $m \in X^{A\star}$ that assigns a sequence of messages to every channel and every $x \in \vec{X}$ we denote by $<m>^\frown x$ the communication history for the channels in X with

$$(<m>^\frown x)(c) = <m(c)>^\frown x(c)$$

for every channel $c \in X$.

2.3 Black Box System Models

A *black box system model* is given by a syntactic and a corresponding semantic interface. The syntactic interface consists of two sets of sorted identifiers I and O, denoting the sets of input and output channels with fixed sorts of messages communicated through them.

A black box behavior of a component with the syntactic interface (I, O) is modeled by a function

$$f : \vec{I} \rightarrow P(\vec{O})$$

(by $P(M)$) we denote the powerset over the set M) such that the output at time point k depends only on the input received till time point k. This is expressed by the following axiom of *well-timedness* (for all $i, j \in \vec{I}$):

$$i|_k = j|_k \Rightarrow f(i)|_k = f(j)|_k$$

A behavior f is called *deterministic*, if $f(i)$ contains exactly one element for every input history i. It is called consistent, if it contains a deterministic behavior.

The set of all black box behaviors with input channels I and output channels O is denoted by

$$I \rhd O.$$

Note that the set $I \rhd O$ provides the syntactic interface of a system and every element in $I \rhd O$ provides a semantic interface.

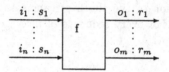

Fig. 2. Graphical representation of a syntactic interface with input channels $i_1, \ldots, i_n$ and output channels $o_1, \ldots, o_m$ and their respective sorts $s_1, \ldots, s_n$ and $r_1, \ldots, r_n$

2.4 State Transition Models

A state transition model is given by a nondeterministic state machine M with input and output. It consists of

- a state sort $s \in S$,
- an input set of sorted identifiers I,
- an output set of sorted identifiers O,
- a transition relation $\delta : s^A \times I^{A\star} \to P(s^A \times O^{A\star})$,
- a set $\sigma_0 \subseteq s^A$ of initial states.

With every state transition model we associate for every state $\sigma \in s^A$ a behavior

$$f_\sigma^M \in I \rhd O$$

by the following equation (let $i \in I^{A\star}$, $x \in \vec{I}$):

$$f_\sigma^M(<i>^\frown x) = \{<o>^\frown z : z \in f_{\tilde{\sigma}}^M(x) \wedge (\tilde{\sigma}, o) \in \delta(\sigma, i)\}$$

This is a recursive definition of the function f^M, but since the recursion is guarded its mathematical treatment is straightforward.

Fig. 3 gives a graphical representation of a system state view as it is often used in software engineering methods.

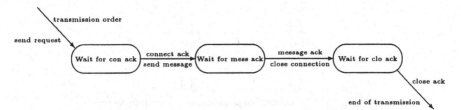

Fig. 3. State transition view of the sender, input messages are written above and output messages below the arrows

2.5   Distributed Systems

A distributed system $N = (C, I_0, O_0)$ consists of a set C of components that interact by exchanging messages over channels. Its syntax is given by

- the syntactic external interface of sorted input channels I_0 and output channels O_0,
- the set C of identifiers for components and a mapping that associates with each component identifier $c \in C$ a set of input channels I_c and a set of output channels O_c.

We require that all sets of output channels of the components in N are pairwise disjoint and disjoint to the set I_0 of input channels of the component and that $I_0 = H(N) \setminus \bigcup_{c \in C} O_c$. By $H(N)$ we denote the set of all channels of the system:

$$H(N) = I_0 \cup O_0 \cup \bigcup_{c \in C} (I_c \cup O_c)$$

The components and channels of a system form a data flow net. Fig. 4 gives an example of a graphical representation of a system by a data flow diagram. This provides a structural view of the system. For modeling dynamic systems where the number of components and channels changes over time, we need a more sophisticated mathematical model, of course.

The glass box semantics of the distributed system N is given by a mapping B that associates a behavior $B(c) \in I_c \rhd O_c$ with every component $c \in C$. A computation of the distributed system is a family of timed streams $x \in \overrightarrow{H(N)}$ such that

$$x|_{O_c} \in B(c)(x|_{I_c}) \text{ for all } c \in C$$

By $U(N)$ we denote the set of all computations of the distributed system N.

The black box behavior $B(N) \in I_0 \rhd O_0$ of the distributed system N with syntactic interface (I_0, O_0) is specified by (for all input histories $i \in \overrightarrow{I_0}$):

$$B(N)(i) = \{x|_{O_0} : x \in U(N) \wedge x|_{I_0} = i\}$$

$B(N)$ allows us to abstract away the distribution structure of the system N and to extract its black box behavior, its interface behavior.

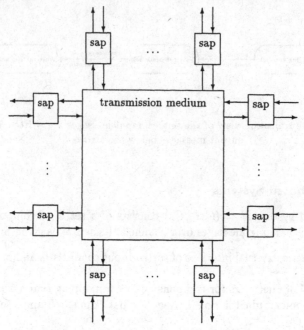

Fig. 4. A data flow diagram that gives a structural system view of a message transmission system with several service access points (saps)

2.6   Processes

For a distributed system N we have introduced its set of computations $U(N)$. In a computation we give for each channel a communication history by a stream. A process is a more detailed description of the run of a system N.

A process for an input i can be represented as a special case of a distributed system $\tilde{N} = (\tilde{C}, \tilde{I}, \tilde{O})$ with syntactic interface $(\tilde{I}, \tilde{O})$. For a process we assume an input $i \in \tilde{I}^A$ such that in the computation of $\tilde{N}$ for input i every channel (also those in $\tilde{I}$) contains exactly one message and the data flow graph associated with $\tilde{N}$ is acyclic and each component of P is deterministic. Then every channel denotes exactly one event of sending and receiving a message component $\tilde{c} \in \tilde{C}$ of the system $\tilde{N}$ denoting a process, represents one action. In this model of a process an action is a component that receives one input message on each of its input lines and produces one output message on each of its output channels. If there is a channel (an event) from an action a_1 to an action a_2 then a_1 is called *causal* for a_2.

This idea of modeling a process by a specific distributed system is similar to the concept of occurrence nets as introduced to represent concurrent processes that are runs of Petri-nets (see Reisig [17]).

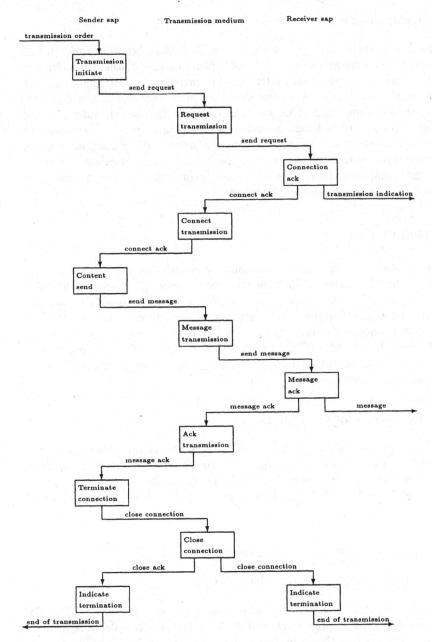

Fig. 5. Process description of a transmission scenario

2.7 Complete System Models

A complete hierarchical system model is given by a black box view consisting of a syntactic and semantic interface and of a glass box view consisting of either a corresponding state transition system or of a corresponding distributed system for it. In the latter case we require that each of its component is a complete hierarchical system again. This yields hierarchical distributed systems. Since we can associate a black box behavior to every state transition system and every distributed system, we can associate a behavior to every component in the hierarchy if the nesting is finite. A complete system is called *interface consistent*, if for each component its glass box behavior is consistent with (or a refinement of, see below) its given semantic interface.

3   Refinement

Large complex systems cannot be developed by considering all its complex properties in one step. Following the principle, not to cover more than one difficulty at a time, refinement allows us to add complexity to system models stepwise in a controlled way. All approaches to software engineering work with a formal or an informal concept of refinement.

We formalize the idea of refinement with the help of refinement relations in the sequel. A refinement relation is formally a mathematical relation between mathematical system models.

3.1 Refinement of Data Models

A data model given by a Σ-algebra A can be refined by adding sorts and function symbols to the signature and respectively carrier sets and functions. A more general notion of *refinement* is obtained by renaming the signature $\Sigma = (S, F)$ into a signature $\tilde{\Sigma} = (\tilde{S}, \tilde{F})$ by a *signature morphism*. It is given by a pair of functions

$$\sigma_1 : S \to \tilde{S}, \sigma_2 : F \to \tilde{F}$$

where $\tilde{\Sigma} = (\tilde{S}, \tilde{F})$ is the refined signature and for all $f \in F$:

$$\text{fct } \tilde{f} = \sigma_1(\text{fct } f)$$

where the mapping σ_1 is extended to sequences of sorts elementwise. This determines the syntactic part of refinement. A $\tilde{\Sigma}$-algebra $\tilde{A}$ is called a *refinement* of the Σ-algebra A, if there are functions

$$\alpha_s : \sigma_1(s)^{\tilde{A}} \to s^A, \varrho_s : s^A \to P(\sigma_1(s)^{\tilde{A}})$$

for every sort $s \in S$ such that for every data element $a \in s^A$ we have:

$$\{\alpha_s(\tilde{a}) : \tilde{a} \in \varrho_s(a)\} = \{a\}$$

and for all functions $f \in F$ with $\text{fct}(f) = <s_1 \ldots s_{n+1}>$ we have for all data elements $a_1 \in s_1^A, \ldots, a_n \in s_n^A$:

$$\alpha_{s_{n+1}}(\sigma_2(f)^{\tilde{A}}(\tilde{a}_1, \ldots, \tilde{a}_n)) = f^A(a_1, \ldots, a_n)$$

for all $\tilde{a}_1 \in \varrho_{s_1}(a_1), \ldots, \tilde{a}_n \in \varrho_{s_n}(a_n)$. This is the classical notion of data refinement, where all abstract elements are represented by concrete elements. This way we obtain a refinement notion for state machines and also for entity/relationship models (for a detailed treatment of this aspect see Hettler [12]).

3.2   Refinement of Communication Histories

The refinement concept for general data models can be carried over to a refinement concept for communication histories. This is an advantage of the incorporation of communication histories as mathematical elements into our system model. Given a pair of functions

$$\alpha : \vec{X}_1 \to \vec{X}_0, \varrho : \vec{X}_0 \to P(\vec{X}_1)$$

a sorted set C_1 of identifiers is called a *communication history refinement* of the sorted set of identifiers X_0 if we have

$$\{\alpha(\tilde{c}) : \tilde{c} \in \varrho(c)\} = \{c\}$$

for all $c \in \vec{C}_0$. Since we use an explicit representation of communication histories in our system models, the refinement notion is a simple generalization of our refinement notion for data models.

3.3   Refinement of Black Box Views

A refinement relation for black box system models is defined by a relation between systems. Given two component behaviors $f_0, f_1 \in I \triangleright O$ with the syntactic interface (I, O) the behavior f_1 is called a *black box refinement* of f_0 if for all input histories $i \in \vec{I}$ we have

$$f_1(i) \subseteq f_0(i)$$

We generalize this simple notion of refinement to *interface refinement* as follows. Assume the functions

$$\alpha_1 : \vec{I}_1 \to \vec{I}_0, \varrho_1 : \vec{I}_0 \to P(\vec{I}_1)$$

$$\alpha_2 : \vec{O}_1 \to \vec{O}_0, \varrho_2 : \vec{O}_0 \to P(\vec{O}_1)$$

that define a communication history refinement I_1 for I_0 and a communication history refinement O_1 for O_0, then the black box behavior

$$f_1 \in I_1 \triangleright O_1$$

is called an *interface refinement* of the black box behavior

$$f_0 \in I_0 \rhd O_0$$

if for all input histories $x \in \vec{I}_0$

$$\{\alpha_2(f_1(x)) : x \in \varrho_1(x)\} = f_0(x)$$

Again this is just a straightforward generalization of the concept of data model refinement to the behavior of systems. It allows us to refine systems to systems with a different number of input and output channels, different names and with different sorts that may lead to a different granularity of messages. A simple example is the refinement of a system working with numbers (for instance an adder) into a system working with bits (for more details, see Broy [4]).

3.4 Refinement by Distribution

A distributed system N with interface (I, O) is called a *refinement by distribution* of a black box behavior $f \in I \rhd O$ if $B(N)$ is a refinement of f. $B(N)$ denotes the black box behavior of a system that is defined as described in section 2.5.

3.5 Process Refinement

A process is represented by a special case of a distributed system. So all refinement notions introduced for distributed systems carry over to processes. Hence a process p is a refinement of an action a, if p is a refinement by distribution of the action a. Recall that an action is a special case of a system.

3.6 Glass Box Refinement

Given a distributed system N with a specified black box behavior for all its components, a glass box refinement associates a state machine or a distributed system with a behavior that is a refinement of the specified one. Hierarchical iterated glass box refinement leads to a complete system model.

4 System Views

For the development of large complex systems it is helpful to work with complementary system views. A system view is a projection of a system onto a particular aspect. For a given distributed system we find it useful to work with the following views:

- process views,
- data model and state views,
- black box views (interface views),
- structural views.

Views allow us to concentrate on specific aspects of a system: Given a complete distributed system we define in the following the mentioned views for it.

4.1 Data Model View

For a complete distributed system $N = (C, I, O)$ with syntactic interface (I, O) a data model view provides for each of its components $c \in C$ a data view. Then the state space consists of an assignment that associates a state sort with each component in C. The corresponding state sort can be used to define a state transition system, or, if the component is again a distributed system, a distributed data view can be defined for it.

4.2 Black Box View

Both for state transition systems and distributed systems we have specified a black box view by associating a behavior with them. This provides black box views for all kinds of glass box views of systems that we have considered so far.

4.3 Structural Views

A structural view onto a distributed system N is given by its set of components and the channels connecting them. The structural view allows us to draw a data flow diagram showing the structuring of a system into its subsystems (its components) and their communication connections (channels).

4.4 Process Views

For a distributed system $N = (C, I, O)$ with syntactic interface (I, O) a process view for an input $i \in \vec{I}$ is given by process represented by a distributed system $\tilde{N} = (\tilde{C}, \tilde{I}, \tilde{O})$ consisting of a set $\tilde{C}$ of actions (components). The relation between the distributed system N and the process $\tilde{N}$ is given by two functions

$$\text{act} : \tilde{C} \to C, \text{chan} : H(\tilde{N}) \to H(N)$$

We assume that for each channel $c \in H(N)$ the set of process channels (representing events)

$$\{\tilde{c} \in H(\tilde{N}) : \text{chan}(\tilde{c}) = c\}$$

associated with it is linearly ordered. We assume that for all channels $\tilde{c} \in H(N)$ we have

$$\text{chan}(\tilde{c}) \in I \iff \tilde{c} \in \tilde{I}$$

$$\text{chan}(\tilde{c}) \in O \iff \tilde{c} \in \tilde{O}$$

Further more we assume that $\text{chan}(\tilde{c})$ is in the input or output channels of a component $\tilde{c} \in \tilde{C}$ if $\text{chan}(c)$ is in the input or output channels respectively of the component $\text{act}(\tilde{c})$.

The process $\tilde{N}$ is called a process view for system N with input i if there exists a computation x of N for the input history i such that for every computation $\tilde{x}$ of $\tilde{N}$ the streams associated with x carry the messages occurring in the linear order for the channels of $\tilde{N}$ that are mapped on the respective channels.

5 Conclusion

We have provided a family of mathematical models and concepts that can be used as the core of a mathematical basis for software engineering. Methodological and descriptional concepts of a method can be precisely defined in terms of these models. It is our goal to demonstrate, how simple and straightforward such a mathematical model is. It shows, in particular, that software engineering methods can be provided with a tractable mathematical basis without too much technical overhead.

There are many specific areas where mathematical system modeling can be useful to give more precision to software engineering areas. Examples are software architectures (see Garlan and Shaw [11]), formal methods for the development of large software systems (see Abrial [1]) or systematic program development methods (such as Jones [15]). The structures introduced above can be used, in particular, for the Cleanroom Software Engineering approach propagated in Mills et al. [16].

References

1. J.R. Abrial: On Constructing Large Software Systems. In: J. van Leeuwen (ed.): *Algorithms, Software, Architecture*, Information Processing 92, Vol. I, North-Holland/Elsevier Science Publ., Amsterdam, 1992, pp. 103-119.
2. G. Booch: *Object Oriented Design with Applications*. Benjamin Cummings, Redwood City, CA, 1991.
3. M. Broy: Towards a Formal Foundation of the Specification and Description Language SDL. *Formal Aspects of Computing* 3 (1991) 21-57.
4. M. Broy: (Inter-)Action Refinement: The Easy Way. In: M. Broy (ed.): *Program Design Calculi*. Springer NATO ASI Series, Series F: Computer and System Sciences, Vol. 118,Springer-Verlag, Berlin, 1993, pp. 121-158.
5. M. Broy: Advanced Component Interface Specification. In: Takayasu Ito, Akinori Yonezawa (Eds.). *Theory and Practice of Parallel Programming*, Proc's International Workshop TPPP'94, Sendai, Japan, Lecture Notes in Computer Science, Vol. 907, Springer-Verlag, Berlin, 1995.
6. P. Coad, E. Yourdon: *Object-oriented Analysis*. Prentice-Hall Int. Editions, Englewood Cliffs, NJ, 1991.
7. T. DeMarco: *Structured Analysis and System Specification*. Yourdan Press, New York, NY, 1979
8. E. Denert: *Software-Engineering*. Springer-Verlag, Berlin, 1991.
9. E. Downs, P. Clare, I. Coe: *Structured Analysis and System Specifications*. Prentice-Hall, Englewood Cliffs, NJ, 1992.
10. M. Broy, F. Dederichs, C. Dendorfer, M. Fuchs, T.F. Gritzner, R. Weber: The Design of Distributed Systems - an Introduction to Focus. Technical University Munich, Institute of Computer Science, TUM-I9203, Januar 1992, see also: Summary of Case Studies in Focus - a Design Method for Distributed Systems. Technical University Munich, Institute for Computer Science, TUM-I9203, Januar 1992.
11. D. Garlan, M. Shaw: An Introduction to Software Architecture. In: *Advances in Software Engineering and Knowledge Engineering*. 1993.

12. R. Hettler: Zur Übersetzung von E/R-Schemata nach SPECTRUM. Technischer Bericht TUM-I9409, TU München, 1994.
13. H. Hußmann: Formal foundation of pragmatic software engineering methods. In: B. Wolfinger (ed.), *Innovationen bei Rechen- und Kommunikationssystemen*, Informatik aktuell, Springer-Verlag, Berlin, 1994, pp. 27-34
14. H. Hußmann: Formal Foundations for SSADM. Technische Universität München, Fakultät für Informatik, Habilitationsschrift 1995.
15. C.B. Jones: *Systematic Program Development Using VDM*. Prentice-Hall, 1986.
16. H. Mills, M. Dyer, R. Linger: Cleanroom Software Engineering. *IEEE Software Engineering* 4 (1987) 19-24.
17. W. Reisig: *Petrinetze - Eine Einführung*. Studienreihe Informatik; 2. überarbeitete Auflage (1986).
18. B. Rumpe, C. Klein, M. Broy: Ein strombasiertes mathematisches Modell verteilter informationsverarbeitender Systeme - Syslab-Systemmodell. Technischer Bericht TUM-I9510, Technische Universität München, Institut für Informatik, 1995.
19. M. Wirsing: Algebraic Specification. In: J. van Leeuwen (Ed.): *Handbook of Theoretical Computer Science*, Volume B, chapter 13, Elsevier Science Publ., Amsterdam, 1990, pp. 675-788.

Formulations and Formalisms
in Software Architecture

Mary Shaw and David Garlan

School of Computer Science
Carnegie Mellon University
Pittsburgh, PA 15213, USA

Abstract. Software architecture is the level of software design that addresses the overall structure and properties of software systems. It provides a focus for certain aspects of design and development that are not appropriately addressed within the constituent modules. Architectural design depends heavily on accurate specifications of subsystems and their interactions. These specifications must cover a wide variety of properties, so the specification notations and associated methods must be selected or developed to match the properties of interest. Unfortunately, the available formal methods are only a partial match for architectural needs, which entail description of structure, packaging, environmental assumptions, representation, and performance as well as functionality. A prerequisite for devising or selecting a formal method is sound understanding of what needs to be formalized. For software architecture, much of this understanding is arising through *progressive codification*, which begins with real-world examples and creates progressively more precise models that eventually support formalization. This paper explores the progressive codification of software architecture: the relation between emerging models and the selection, development, and use of formal systems.

1   Status and Needs of Software Architecture

As software systems become more complex, a critical aspect of system design is the overall structure of the software and the ways in which that structure provides conceptual integrity for the system. This level of system design has come to be known as *software architecture* [GS93, PW92].

In an architectural design, systems are typically viewed as compositions of module-scale, interacting components. Components are such things as clients and servers, databases, filters, and layers in a hierarchical system. Interactions between components at this level of design can be simple and familiar, such as procedure call and shared variable access. But they can also be complex and semantically rich, such as client-server protocols, database accessing protocols, asynchronous event multicast, and piped streams.

While it has long been recognized that finding an appropriate architectural design for a system is a key element of its long-term success, current practice for describing architectures is typically informal and idiosyncratic. Usually, architectures are represented abstractly as box and line diagrams, together with accompanying prose that explains the meanings behind the symbols, and provides some rationale for the specific choice of components and interactions.

The relative informality and high level of abstraction of current practice in describing architectures might at first glance suggest that architectural descriptions have little substantive value for software engineers. But there are two reasons why this is not the case. First, over time engineers have evolved a collection of idioms, patterns, and styles of software system organization that serve as a shared, semantically-rich vocabulary between engineers. For example, by identifying a system as an instance of a pipe-filter architectural style an engineer communicates the facts that the system is primarily involved in stream transformation, that the functional behavior of the system can be derived compositionally from the behaviors of the constituent filters, and that issues of system latency and throughput can be addressed in relatively straightforward ways. Thus, although this shared vocabulary is largely informal, it conveys considerable semantic content between software engineers.

The second reason is that although architectural structures may themselves abstract away from details of the actual computations of the elements, those structures provide a natural framework for understanding broader system-level concerns, such as global rates of flow, patterns of communication, execution control structure, scalability, and intended paths of system evolution. Thus, architectural descriptions serve as a skeleton around which system properties can be fleshed out, and thereby serve a vital role in exposing the ability of a system to meet its gross system requirements.

This is, of course, not to say that more formal notations for architectural description and rigorous techniques of analysis are unnecessary. Indeed, it is clear that much could be gained if the current practice of architectural design could be supported with better notations, theories, and analytical techniques. In this paper we explore specification issues in software architecture, with particular attention to the way improvements in the formulation of architectural issues sets the stage for better formalization.

1.1   Current Status

Over the past few years, recognition of the significance of software architecture has led to considerable research and development activity, both in industry and academia. These activities can be roughly placed into four categories.

The first category is addressing the problem of architectural characterization by providing new *architectural description languages*. As detailed later, these languages are aimed at giving practitioners better ways of writing down architectures so that they can be communicated to others, and in many cases analyzed with tools.

The second category is addressing *codification of architectural expertise* [GHJV94, GS93]. Work in this area is concerned with cataloging and rationalizing the variety of architectural principles and patterns that engineers have developed through software practice.

The third category is addressing *frameworks for specific domains* [DAR90, Tra94]. This work typically results in an architectural framework for a specific class of software such as avionics control systems, mobile robotics, or user interfaces. When successful, such frameworks can be easily instantiated to produce new products in the domain.

The fourth category addresses *formal underpinnings for architecture*. As new notations are developed, and as the practice of architectural design is better understood, formalisms for reasoning about architectural designs become relevant. Several of these are described later.

1.2   What Needs to be Specified about Architectures

Architectural design determines how to compose systems from smaller parts so the result meets system requirements. Most system requirements extend beyond functionality to a variety of other properties that matter to the client. Moreover, the correctness of the composition depends at least as much on the component interactions and on the assumptions components make about their execution environment as it does on what the components actually compute.

Accordingly, architectural specifications must address the extra-functional properties of components (structure, packaging, environmental dependencies, representation, and performance), the nature of the interactions among components, and the structural characteristics of the configurations.

Structural Properties. The most significant properties for architectural design deal with the ways components interact, and hence with the ways those components can be combined into systems. The packaging of a component includes the type of component and the types of interactions it is prepared to support. The choice of packaging is often largely independent of the underlying functionality, but components must be packaged in compatible ways if they are to work together smoothly. For example, Unix provides both a sort system call and a sort filter; while they have the same functionality, they are far from interchangeable.

Some common packagings for components and the ways they interact are:

COMPONENT TYPE	COMMON TYPES OF INTERACTION
Module	Procedure call, data sharing
Object	Method invocation (dynamically bound procedure call)
Filter	Data flow
Process	Message passing, remote procedure call
	various communication protocols, synchronization
Data file	Read, write
Database	Schema, query language
Document	Shared representation assumptions

Distinctions of this kind are now made informally, often implicitly. If the distinctions were more precise and more explicit, it would be easier to detect and eventually correct incompatibilities by analyzing the system configuration description. Such checking must address not only local compatibility (e.g., do two components expect the same kinds of interactions), but also global properties (e.g., no loops in a data flow system).

Extra-functional Properties. In addition to functionality and packaging, architectural specifications must be capable of expressing extra-functional properties related to performance, capacity, environmental assumptions, and global properties such as reliability and security [Sha85, MCN92, CBKA95]. Many of these additional properties are qualitative, so they may require different kinds of support from more formal specifications. These other properties include:

time requirements	ease of use
timing variability	reliability
real-time response	robustness
latency	service capacity (e.g., # of clients/server)
throughput	possession of main thread of control
bandwidth	dependence on specific libraries, services
space requirements	conformance to an interface standard
space variability	conformance to implementation standard
adaptability	intended profile of operation usage
precision and accuracy	minimum hardware configuration
security	need to access specialized hardware

For example, this product description specifies the interface between a software product and the operating system/hardware it requires [Com95].

1. IBM or 100% IBM-compatible microcomputer with Intel 80386 microprocessor or higher or 100%-compatible processor.
2. Minimum 4 MB RAM.
3. 3 MB of available space on a hard disk.
4. ISO 9660-compatible CD-ROM drive with 640+ MB read capacity and Microsoft CD-ROM extensions.
5. Microsoft Windows'-compatible printer (not plotter) recommended, with 1.5 MB printer memory for 300 dpi laser printing, 6 MB for 600 dpi.
6. Microsoft Windows'-compatible mouse (recommended).
7. Microsoft Windows'-compatible VGA card and monitor.
8. Microsoft Windows' version 3.1 and MS-DOS version 4.01 or later.

This specification deals with space and with conformance to established standards. The functionality of the product is described (imprecisely) in associated prose and pictures.

Families of Related Systems. In addition to structure and packaging, architectural specifications must also deal with families of related systems. Two important classes of system family problems are:

1. Architectural styles that describe families of systems that use the same types of components, types of interactions, structural constraints, and analyses. Systems built within a single style can be expected to be more compatible than those that mix styles: it may be easier to make them interoperate, and it may be easier to reuse parts within the family.

2. Some systems can accommodate a certain amount of variability: they depend critically on some central essential semantics, and they require certain other support to be present, but do not rely on details. In operating systems, these are sometimes distinguished as policy and mechanism, respectively: for example, it's important for a synchronization mechanism to prevent interference, deadlock, and starvation, but the details of process ordering are incidental.

2   Models and Notations for Software Architectures

Software systems have always had architectures; current research is concerned with making them explicit, well-formed, and maintainable. This section elaborates on the current practice, describes the models that are now emerging and the languages that support some of those models, and discusses the standards that should be used to evaluate new models and tools in this area.

2.1   Folklore and Common Practice

As noted above, software designers describe overall system architectures using a rich vocabulary of abstractions. Although the descriptions and the underlying vocabulary are imprecise and informal, designers nevertheless communicate with some success. They depict the architectural abstractions both in pictures and words.

"Box-and-line" diagrams often illustrate system structure. These diagrams use different shapes to suggest structural differences among the components, but they make little discrimination among the lines—that is, among different kinds of interactions. The architectural diagrams are often highly specific to the systems they describe, especially in the labeling of components. For the most part, no rules govern the diagrams; they appeal to rich intuitions of the community of developers. Diagramming rules do exist for a few specific styles—data flow diagrams and some object-oriented disciplines, for example.

The diagrams are supported by prose descriptions. This prose uses terms with common, if informal, definitions (italics ours):

- "Camelot is based on the *client-server model* and uses remote procedure calls both locally and remotely to provide communication among applications and servers." [S+87]
- "*Abstraction layering* and system decomposition provide the appearance of system uniformity to clients, yet allow Helix to accommodate a diversity of autonomous devices. The architecture encourages a *client-server model* for the structuring of applications." [FO85]

- "We have chosen a *distributed, object-oriented approach* to managing information." [Lin87]
- "The easiest way to make the canonical sequential compiler into a concurrent
  compiler is to *pipeline* the execution of the compiler phases over a number
  of processors. . . . A more effective way [is to] split the source code into many
  segments, which are concurrently processed through the various phases of
  compilation [by multiple compiler processes] before a final, merging pass
  recombines the object code into a single program." [S+88]
- "The ARC network [follows] the *general network architecture* specified by
  the ISO in the Open Systems Interconnection Reference Model. It consists
  of physical and data layers, a network layer, and transport, session, and
  presentation layers." [Pau85]

We studied sets of such descriptions and found a number of abstractions that
govern the overall organization of the components and their interactions [GS93].
A few of the patterns, or styles, (e.g., object organizations [Boo86] and black-
boards [Nii86]) have been carefully refined, but others are still used quite informally, even unconsciously. Nevertheless, the architectural patterns are widely
recognized. System designs often appeal to several of these patterns, combining
them in various ways.

2.2 Emerging Models

Most of the current work on software architecture incorporates models, either
explicit or implicit, of the conceptual basis for software architecture. Some of
this work is directed at refining models; other work implicitly adopts a model
in pursuit of some other goal. Five general types of models appear with some
regularity: structural, framework, dynamic, process, and functional. Of these,
structural and dynamic models are most common. The representative examples
here were discussed at the First International Workshop on Architectures for
Software Systems [Gar95] and the Dagstuhl Workshop on Software Architecture [GPT95].

Structural Models. The most common model views architecture as primarily
structural. This family of models shares the view that architecture is based on
components, connectors, and "other stuff". The "other stuff" in various ways
reaches beyond structure to capture important semantics. Although there is
not as yet consensus on precisely what that semantics is, "other stuff" includes
configuration, rationale, semantics, constraints, style, properties, analyses, and
requirements or needs. As detailed later, structural models are often supported
by architecture description languages. Examples include Aesop, C2, Darwin,
UniCon, and Wright. A shared interchange language, ACME, is being developed.

Framework Models. A second group of models is similar to structural models,
but places more emphasis on the coherent structure of the whole than on describing structural details. These *framework* models often focus on one specific

structure, for example, one that targets a specific class of problems or market domain. Narrowing the focus permits a richer elaboration for the domain of interest. Examples include various domain-specific software architectures (DSSAs), MetaObject Protocols (MOPs), CORBA and other object interaction models, component repositories, and SBIS.

Dynamic Models. *Dynamic* models are complementary to structural or framework models. They address large-grain behavioral properties of systems, often describing reconfiguration or evolution of the systems. "Dynamic" may refer to changes in the overall system configuration, to setting up and taking down pre-enabled paths, or to the progress of computation (changing data values, following a control thread). These systems are often reactive. Examples include the Chemical Abstract Machine, Archetype, Rex, Conic, Darwin, and Rapide.

Process Models. Another, smaller, family, the process models, is constructive, operational, and imperative. These models focus on the construction steps or processes that yield a system. The architecture is then the result of following some process script. Examples include some aspects of Conic and process programming for architecture.

Functional Models. A minority regards architecture as a set of *functional* components, organized in layers that provide services upward. It is perhaps most helpful to think of this as a particular framework.

2.3 Architectural Description Languages

Of the models described in Section 2.2, the structural models are now most prevalent. A number of architecture description languages (ADLs) are being developed to support these models. ADLs typically support the description of systems in terms of typed *components* and sometimes *connectors* that make the abstractions for interaction first-class entities in the language. They often provide a graphical interface so that developers can express architectures using diagrams of the kind that have proven useful. Current ADLs include Aesop [GAO94], ArTek [T+94], Darwin [MK95], Rapide [LAK+95], UniCon [SDK+95], and Wright [AG94].

While all of these ADLs are concerned with architectural structure, they differ in their level of *genericity*. There are three basic levels. Some are primarily concerned with *architectural instances*. That is, they are designed to describe specific systems, and provide notations to answer the questions of the form "What is the architecture of system S?" ArTek, Rapide, and UniCon are in this category.

Other ADLs are primarily concerned with *architectural style*. That is, they are designed to describe patterns, or idioms, of architectural structure. The notations in this category therefore describe families of systems, and answer questions of the form "What organizational patterns are are used in system S?", or "What is the meaning of architectural style T?" Aesop is in this category.

ADLs associated with styles typically attempt to capture one or more of four aspects of style: the underlying intuition behind the style, or the system model; the kinds of components that are used in developing a system according to the pattern; the connectors, or kinds of interactions among the components; and the control structure or execution discipline.

Still other ADLs are concerned with *architecture in general*. They attempt to give meaning to the broader issues of the nature of architecture, and the ways architectural abstractions can provide analytic leverage for system design. Several of these are considered later in this paper.

2.4   Evaluation Criteria

Languages, models, and formalisms can be evaluated in a number of different ways. In this case, the models and the detailed specifications of relevant properties have a utilitarian function, so appropriate evaluation criteria should reflect the needs of software developers. These criteria differ from the criteria used to evaluate formalisms for mathematical elegance.

Expertise in any field requires not only higher-order reasoning skills, but also a large store of facts, together with a certain amount of context about their implications and appropriate use. This is true across a wide range of problem domains; studies have demonstrated it for medical diagnosis, physics, chess, financial analysis, architecture, scientific research, policy decision making, and others [Red88, Sim87]. An expert in a field must know around 50,000 chunks of information, where a chunk is any cluster of knowledge sufficiently familiar that it can be remembered rather than derived. Chunks are typically operational: "in *this* situation, do *that*". Furthermore, full-time professionals take ten years to reach world-class proficiency. It follows that models and tools intended to support experts should support rich bodies of operational knowledge. Further, they should support large vocabularies of established knowledge as well as the theoretical base for deriving information of interest.

Contrast this with the criteria against which mathematical systems are evaluated. Mathematics values elegance and minimality of mechanism; derived results are favored over added content because they are correct and consistent by their construction.

Architecture description languages are being developed to make software designers more effective. They should be evaluated against the utilitarian standard, preferring richness of content and relevance to the application over elegance and minimality. This implies, for example, that these languages should support—directly—the breadth of architectural abstractions that software designers use: data flow (including pipes and filters), object-oriented, functional, state-based, message-passing, and blackboard organizations. The fact that these abstractions could all be expressed using some one of the styles is interesting but not grounds for impeding the choice of abstractions relevant to the project at hand.

3   Progressive Codification

Software specification techniques have often evolved in parallel with our under-standing of the phenomena that they specify.

This development can bee seen in the development of data types and type theory [Sha80]. In the early 1960s, type declarations were added to programming languages. Initially they were little more than comments to remind the program-mer of the underlying machine representation. As compilers became able to per-form syntactic validity checks the type declarations became more meaningful, but "specification" meant little more than "procedure header" until late in the decade. The early 1970s brought early work on abstract data types and the as-sociated observation that their checkable redundancy provided a methodological advantage because they gave early warning of problems. At this time the pur-pose of types in programming languages was to enable a compile-time check that ensured that the actual parameters presented to a procedure at runtime would be acceptable. Through the 1980s type systems became richer, stimulated by the introduction of inheritance mechanisms. At the same time, theoretical com-puter scientists began developing rich theories to fully explain types. Now we see partial fusion of types-in-languages and types-as-theory in functional languages with type inference. We see in this history that theoretical elaboration relied on extensive experience with the phenomena, while at the same time practicing programmers are willing to write down specifications only to the extent that they are rewarded with analysis than simplifies their overall task.

Thus, as some aspect of software development comes to be better understood, more powerful specification mechanisms become available, and they yield better rewards for the specification effort invested. We can characterize some of the levels of specification power:

1. *Capture:* retain, explain, or retrieve a definition
2. *Construction:* explain how to build in instance from constituent parts
3. *Composition:* say how to join pieces (and their specifications) to get a new instance
4. *Selection:* guide designer's choice among implementation alternatives or de-signs
5. *Verification:* determine whether an implementation matches specification
6. *Analysis:* determine the implications of the specification
7. *Automation:* construct an instance from an external specification of proper-ties

When describing, selecting, or designing a specification mechanism, either formal or informal, it is useful to be explicit about which level it supports. Failure to do so leads to mismatches between user expectations and specification power.

Architecture description languages provide a notation for *capturing* system descriptions. Several have associated tools that will *construct* instances from modules of some programming language. At least one technique for design *selec-tion* has been developed [Lan90]. Support for other levels of aspiration is spotty.

No matter how badly we would like to leap directly to fully formal architectural specifications that support analysis and automation, history says we must first make our informal understanding explicit, then gradually make it more rigorous as it matures. In this way the specification mechanisms may be appropriate for the properties that they specify. Application of existing formal methods in inappropriate ways will fail to come to grips with the essential underlying problems.

4   Practice and Prospects for Formalisms

To illustrate the ways in which software architecture is being progressively codified, we now outline some of the formalisms that have been developed for software architecture. The goal here is not to provide a complete enumeration, but rather to indicate broadly the kinds of formalisms that are being investigated by the software architecture research community, and the extent to which those formalisms have been successful.

4.1   Formalisms in Use for Architecture

In order to make sense of the variety of existing formal approaches, it helps to have an organizational framework. One such framework positions architectural formalisms in two dimensional space that follows directly from the distinctions made in previous sections. Along one dimension is the *genericity* of the formalism. As outlined in Sect. 2.3, architectural concerns may relate to (a) a specific system (or architectural instance), (b) a family of systems (or architectural style), or (c) architecture in general. Along the second dimension is the *power* of the formalism. As outlined in Sect. 3, aspirations of different formal notations can vary from system documentation to automated system construction.

In practice, most formalisms address several aspects of this space. For example, a formal notation for architectural styles might be useful both for system construction as well as support verification. In most cases, however, a formalism has at its core a specific problem that it is attempting to address. It is this core that we are most interested in. Here are four core functions in this design space.

Analysis of Architectural Instances. Going beyond the base-level capability of architectural description languages to express specific system designs is the need to perform useful analyses of the designs. To do this requires the association of an underlying semantic model with those descriptions. Several such models have been proposed. These differ substantially depending on the kind of model they consider.

To take four representative examples:

1. Rapide models the behavior of a system in terms of partially ordered sets of events [LAK+95]. Components are assigned specifications that allow the system's event behavior to be simulated and then analyzed. Typical kinds of

analyses reveal whether there is a causal dependency between certain kinds of computations. The presence (or absence) of these causality relationships can sometimes indicate errors in the architectural design.

2. Darwin [MK95] models system behavior in terms of the π-calculus [MPW92]. The flexibility of this model permits the encoding of highly dynamic architectures, while the strong typing system of the π-calculus permits certain static checks. For example, it can guarantee that processes only talk over channels of the correct type, even though the number and connectivity of those channels may change during runtime.

3. UniCon [SDK+95] and Aesop [GAO94] support methods for real-time analysis—RMA and EDF, respectively. These ADLs, and their supporting tools, capture relevant information, repackage it into the formats required by real-time analysis tools, which are then invoked to perform the analyses.

4. Wolf and Inverardi have explored the use of Chemical Abstract Machine notation [BB92] for modelling architectural designs [IW95]. This model also deals well with dynamic behavior of a system, essentially providing a kind of structural rewrite system.

Capture of Architectural Styles. When people refer to a system as being in a pipe-filter style it may not be clear precisely what they mean. While it may be clear that such a system should be decomposed into a graph of stream transformers, more detailed issues of semantics are typically left underspecified, or may vary from system to system. For example, are cycles allowed? Must a pipe have a single reader and a single writer? Can filters share global state?

In an attempt to provide more complete semantics for some specific styles a number of styles have been completely formalized. For example, Allen and Garlan [AG92] provide a formalization of a pipe-filter architectural style, while [GN91] develops a formalization of implicit-invocation architectural style. Both of these use the Z specification language [Spi89]

Generalizing from these examples, Abowd, Allen, and Garlan [AAG93] describe a denotational framework for developing formal models of architectural style (also in Z). The idea of the framework is that each style can be defined using three functions that indicate how the syntactic, structural aspects of the style are mapped into semantic entities. The authors argue that when several styles are specified in this way, it becomes possible to compare those styles at a semantic level. For example, is one style a substyle of another? Does a property of one style hold of another?

A somewhat different approach arises in the context of architectures for specific product families. A number of such "domain-specific" software architectures have been formalized. One of the more prominent is in the avionics domain [BV93]. Here a language, called Meta-H, was developed to capture the architectural commonality among the applications, and to provide high-level syntactic support for instantiating the framework for a specific product. The language was designed to reflect the vocabulary and notations that avionics control systems engineers (as opposed to software engineers) routinely used in their designs.

Verification of Architectural Styles. In many cases architectural descriptions are at a sufficiently abstract level that they must be refined into lower-level architectural descriptions. Typically, the lower-level descriptions are in terms of design entities that are more directly implemented than their abstract counterparts. For example, a system that is described at an abstract level as a dataflow system, might be recast in terms of shared variable communication at a lower (but still architectural) design level.

Moriconi and his colleagues have observed that it is possible to exploit patterns of refinement between different levels of architectural description [MQR95]. For instance, refining a dataflow connector to a shared variable connector involves a stylized transformation of asynchronous reading/writing to synchronized data access.

To capitalize on this observation they have proposed formalisms that encode transformations between architectural styles. In the above example, they might provide a pipe-to-shared-data transformation. The goal is to provide a complete enough system of transformations that machine aided refinement can take place. Moreover, as they note, by factoring out proofs of correctness of refinement at the style (or family) level, they simplify the work needed to carry out the refinement between any two architectural instances written in the respective styles.

Analysis of Architecture in General. When considering architectural design broadly, a number of formal questions arise: What does it mean to have a consistent or a complete architectural description? What is the formal nature of architectural connection?

The Wright specification language represents first steps toward answering these kinds of questions [AG94]. In this language, connectors are viewed as first class entities, defined as a set of protocols. Similarly, interfaces to components are described in terms of the protocols of interaction with their environment. Given this formal basis, it is possible to ask whether a given connector can be legally associated with a given component interface. This amounts to a test for protocol compatibility. Wright protocols are defined as CSP processes [Hoa85], and protocol compatibility can be reduced to a check of process refinement. The result of such a check is a strong guarantee that components interacting over a given connector will never deadlock.

4.2   What's Missing?

Standing back from the specific formalisms currently under development, two salient facts stand out.

First, consistent with the multi-faceted nature of software architecture itself, formalisms for modelling architecture are attempting to address a wide range of different issues. There is both good and bad news in this. The good news is that we are making incremental progress on understanding ways to lend precision and analytic capability to architectural design. The bad news is that the diversity of approaches leads to a fragmented and, in some cases, conflicting set of formal models for architecture. Consequently, no general unifying picture has emerged. And worse, we have no good ways of relating the various models to each other.

Second, existing formalisms address only a small portion of the needs of software architects. By and large, the formal approaches to software architecture have concentrated on the functional *behavior* of architectural descriptions. That is, they typically provide computational models, or ways of constructing them, that expose issues of data flows, control, sequencing, and communication. While useful and necessary, this is only a starting point. In addition—and arguably more important—are the extra-functional aspects of systems, such as performance, reliability, security, modifiability, and so on. Currently we do not know how to provide the necessary calculi for these other kinds of issues, or to relate these systems of reasoning to the existing formalisms for architecture.

5   Current Opportunities

Although the structure of software has been a concern for decades, software architecture has only recently emerged as an explicit focus of research and development. While considerable progress has been made over the last 5-10 years in recognizing the needs of practitioners for codifying, disseminating, describing, and analyzing architectural designs, there remain many, many open problems. Some of these problems might well be solved by better use of formalisms, provided they can bend to the needs of the practice (and not the other way around). Here are some areas that challenge current formalisms; they present promising research opportunities.

5.1   Heterogeneity

Practical systems are heterogeneous in structure and packaging. No matter how desirable it may be for a system to be composed entirely from a single family of compatible components, for most complex systems structural heterogeneity is inevitable. Strict adherence to a single style throughout a system is often impractical, so articulation between styles will be required. Furthermore, components with the desired functionality will often be packaged in different ways. Therefore, we need to find ways to handle packaging incompatibility [GAO95].

Heterogeneity arises from multiple packaging standards, from legacy systems that will not or cannot be rewritten, and from differences in usage within a single standard. At present, many ad hoc techniques are used to compensate for the incompatibility of parts. It would be useful to develop a systematic model that explains these and provides guidance for choosing the appropriate technique for a given situation [Sha95].

5.2   Incomplete and Evolving Specifications

According to conventional doctrine, component specifications are

1. sufficient (say everything you need to know)
2. complete (are the only source of information)

However, architectural elements violate this doctrine. Architectural needs are open-ended, and a designer cannot anticipate all the properties of interest. Specifications are incomplete and evolving. Moreover, gathering specification information incurs costs; even for common properties, completeness may be impractical, and the cost may be prohibitive for uncommon properties. Even worse, interesting properties may emerge after a component is released (e.g., "upward compatible with Fenestre version 4.5") [GAO95].

Notably, we often make progress with only minimal information. Sometime we can take advantage of new information when it comes along. A promising research opportunity is understanding how to make architectural specifications partial, incremental, and evolving. This entails adding new properties, declaring what properties are required for specific kinds of analysis, checking consistency, and propagating new information to improve old analyses. Work on using partial specifications will help [Jac94, Per87], as will a fresh approach that views them as evolving entities rather than static documents.

5.3 Extra-functional Properties

We have already noted the failure of most existing formalisms to handle properties that go beyond the computational behavior of the system. It will be a challenge to find formal systems for reasoning about the kinds of properties listed in 1.2 at an architectural level.

5.4 Multiple Views

Complex specifications require structure, such as different segments for different concerns. However, different concerns also lead to different notations. As indicated in Sect. 4.2, this leads to a multiple-view problem: different specifications describe different, but overlapping issues.

For example, formalisms that are good at accounting for dynamic properties of architectures may not be good for performing static/global analyses. For example, Wright (based on CSP) permits some powerful static checks of deadlock freedom, but does not deal with dynamic creation of processes. On the other hand, Darwin (based on the π-calculus) permits flexible description of dynamic architectures, but is less well-suited to proofs about absence of deadlock.

5.5 Classification and taxonomy

Software designers use a wide variety of styles, which are built up from identifiable types of components and interactions (or connectors). In practice, we see an enormous amount of variation on each of these themes. In order to be support checking and analysis, the specifications must be much more precise than at present. A classification or taxonomy for styles, components, and connectors would be a major step toward declaring and checking these structural types.

6   Research Support

This work reported here was sponsored by the Wright Laboratory, Aeronautical Systems Center, Air Force Materiel Command, USAF, and the Advanced Research Projects Agency, under grant F33615-93-1-1330, by a grant from Siemens Corporation, by National Science Foundation Grant CCR-9357792, and by Federal Government Contract Number F19628-90-C-0003 with Carnegie Mellon University for the operation of the Software Engineering Institute, a Federally Funded Research and Development Center. Some of this material was previously covered in position papers for the First Workshop on Pattern Languages for Programming and the First International Workshop on Architectures for Software Systems.

References

[AAG93]   Gregory Abowd, Robert Allen, and David Garlan. Using style to understand descriptions of software architecture. In *Proceedings of SIGSOFT'93: Foundations of Software Engineering*, Software Engineering Notes 18(5), pages 9–20. ACM Press, December 1993.

[AG92]   Robert Allen and David Garlan. A formal approach to software architectures. In Jan van Leeuwen, editor, *Proceedings of IFIP'92*. Elsevier Science Publishers B.V., September 1992.

[AG94]   Robert Allen and David Garlan. Formalizing architectural connection. In *Proceedings of the Sixteenth International Conference on Software Engineering*, pages 71–80, Sorrento, Italy, May 1994.

[BB92]   G. Berry and G. Boudol. The chemical abstract machine. *Theoretical Computer Science*, (96):217–248, 1992.

[Boo86]   Grady Booch. Object-oriented development. *IEEE Transactions on Software Engineering*, SE-12(2):211–221, February 1986.

[BV93]   Pam Binns and Steve Vestal. Formal real-time architecture specification and analysis. In *Tenth IEEE Workshop on Real-Time Operating Systems and Software*, New York, NY, May 1993.

[CBKA95] Paul Clements, Len Bass, Rick Kazman, and Gregory Abowd. Predicting software quality by architecture-level evaluation. In *Proceedings of the Fifth International Conference on Software Quality*, Austin, Texas, October 1995.

[Com95]   DeLorme Mapping Company. WWW page describing MapExpert product, 1995. URL: http://www.delorme.com/catalog/mex.htm.

[DAR90]   *Proceedings of the Workshop on Domain-Specific Software Architectures*, Hidden Vallen, PA, July 1990. Software Engineering Institute.

[FO85]   Marek Fridrich and William Older. Helix: The architecture of the XMS distributed file system. *IEEE Software*, 2(3):21–29, May 1985.

[GAO94]   David Garlan, Robert Allen, and John Ockerbloom. Exploiting style in architectural design environments. In *Proceedings of SIGSOFT'94: Foundations of Software Engineering*. ACM Press, December 1994.

[GAO95]   David Garlan, Robert Allen, and John Ockerbloom. Architectural mismatch, or, why it's hard to build systems out of existing parts. In *Proceedings of the 17th International Conference on Software Engineering*, Seattle, Washington, April 1995.

[Gar95]   David Garlan, editor. *Proceedings of First International Workshop on Architectures for Software Systems*, Seattle, WA, April 1995. Reissued as Carnegie Mellon University Technical Report CMU-CS-95-151.

[GHJV94]   Erich Gamma, Richard Helm, Ralph Johnson, and John Vlissides. *Design Patterns: Elements of Reusable Object-Oriented Design*. Addison-Wesley, 1994.

[GN91]   David Garlan and David Notkin. Formalizing design spaces: Implicit invocation mechanisms. In S. Prehn, W.J. Toetenel (Eds.), *VDM'91: Formal Software Development Methods*, Conf. Contributions 4th Int. Symp. of VDM Europe, Lecture Notes in Computer Science, Vol. 551, Springer-Verlag, Berlin, pp. 31–44.

[GPT95]   David Garlan, Frances Newberry Paulisch, and Walter F. Tichy, editors. *Summary of the Dagstuhl Workshop on Software Architecture*, Schloss Dagstuhl, Germany, February 1995.

[GS93]   David Garlan and Mary Shaw. An introduction to software architecture. In V. Ambriola and G. Tortora, editors, *Advances in Software Engineering and Knowledge Engineering*, pages 1–39, Singapore, 1993. World Scientific Publishing Company. Also appears as SCS and SEI technical reports: CMU-CS-94-166, CMU/SEI-94-TR-21, ESC-TR-94-021.

[Hoa85]   C.A.R. Hoare. *Communicating Sequential Processes*. Prentice Hall, 1985.

[IW95]   Paola Inverardi and Alex Wolf. Formal specification and analysis of software architectures using the chemical, abstract machine model. *IEEE Transactions on Software Engineering, Special Issue on Software Architecture*, 21(4):373–386, April 1995.

[Jac94]   Michael Jackson. Problems, methods and specialisation (a contribution to the special issue on software engineering in the year 2001). *IEE Software Engineering Journal*, November 1994. A shortened version of this paper also appears in IEEE Software, November 1994, 11(6).

[LAK+95]   David C Luckham, Lary M. Augustin, John J. Kenney, James Veera, Doug Bryan, and Walter Mann. Specification and analysis of system architecture using Rapide. *IEEE Transactions on Software Engineering, Special Issue on Software Architecture*, 21(4):336–355, April 1995.

[Lan90]   Thomas G. Lane. Studying software architecture through design spaces and rules. Technical Report CMU/SEI-90-TR-18 ESD-90-TR-219, Carnegie Mellon University, September 1990.

[Lin87]   Mark A. Linton. Distributed management of a software database. *IEEE Software*, 4(6):70–76, November 1987.

[MCN92]   John Mylopoulos, Lawrence Chung, and Brian Nixon. Representing and using nonfunctional requirements: A process-oriented approach. *IEEE Transactions on Software Engineering*, 18(6), June 1992.

[MK95]   Jeff Magee and Jeff Kramer. Modelling distributed software architectures. In *Proceedings of the First International Workshop on Architectures for Software Systems*. Reissued as Carnegie Mellon University Technical Report CMU-CS-95-151, April 1995.

[MPW92]   R. Milner, J. Parrow, and D. Walker. A calculus of mobile processes. *Journal of Information and Computation*, 100:1–77, 1992.

[MQR95]   M. Moriconi, X. Qian, and R. Riemenschneider. Correct architecture refinement. *IEEE Transactions on Software Engineering, Special Issue on Software Architecture*, 21(4):356–372, April 1995.

[Nii86]   H. Penny Nii. Blackboard systems Parts 1 & 2. *AI Magazine,* 7 nos 3 (pp. 38-53) and 4 (pp. 62-69), 1986.

[Pau85]   Mark C. Paulk. The ARC Network: A case study. *IEEE Software,* 2(3):61–69, May 1985.

[Per87]   Dewayne E. Perry. Software interconnection models. In *Proceedings of the Ninth International Conference on Software Engineering,* pages 61–68, Monterey, CA, March 1987. IEEE Computer Society Press.

[PW92]   Dewayne E. Perry and Alexander L. Wolf. Foundations for the study of software architecture. *ACM SIGSOFT Software Engineering Notes,* 17(4):40–52, October 1992.

[Red88]   Raj Reddy. Foundations and grand challenges of artificial intelligence. *AI Magazine,* 9(4):9–21, Winter 1988. 1988 presidential address, AAAI.

[S+87]   Alfred Z. Spector et al. Camelot: A distributed transaction facility for Mach and the Internet—an interim report. Technical Report CMU-CS-87-129, Carnegie Mellon University, June 1987.

[S+88]   V. Seshadri et al. Semantic analysis in a concurrent compiler. In *Proceedings of ACM SIGPLAN '88 Conference on Programming Language Design and Implementation.* ACM SIGPLAN Notices, 1988.

[SDK+95] Mary Shaw, Robert DeLine, Daniel V. Klein, Theodore L. Ross, David M. Young, and Gregory Zelesnik. Abstractions for software architecture and tools to support them. *IEEE Transactions on Software Engineering, Special Issue on Software Architecture,* 21(4):314–335, April 1995.

[Sha80]   Mary Shaw. The impact of abstraction concerns on modern programming languages. In *Proceedings of the IEEE Special Issue on Software Engineering,* volume 68, pages 1119–1130, September 1980.

[Sha85]   Mary Shaw. What can we specify? Questions in the domains of software specifications. In *Proceedings of the Third International Workshop on Software Specification and Design,* pages 214–215. IEEE Computer Society Press, August 1985.

[Sha95]   Mary Shaw. Architectural issues in software reuse: It's not just the functionality, it's the packaging. In *Proceedings of the Symposium on Software Reuse,* April 1995.

[Sim87]   Herbert A. Simon. Human experts and knowledge-based systems, November 9-12 1987.

[Spi89]   J.M. Spivey. *The Z Notation: A Reference Manual.* Prentice Hall, 1989.

[T+94]   Allan Terry et al. Overview of Teknowledge's domain-specific software architecture program. *ACM SIGSOFT Software Engineering Notes,* 19(4):68–76, October 1994.

[Tra94]   Will Tracz. Collected overview reports from the DSSA project. Loral Federal Systems - Owego, October 1994.

The Oz Programming Model

Gert Smolka

Programming Systems Lab
German Research Center for Artificial Intelligence (DFKI)
Stuhlsatzenhausweg 3, 66123 Saarbrücken, Germany
email: `smolka@dfki.uni-sb.de`

Abstract. The Oz Programming Model (OPM) is a concurrent programming model subsuming higher-order functional and object-oriented programming as facets of a general model. This is particularly interesting for concurrent object-oriented programming, for which no comprehensive formal model existed until now. The model can be extended so that it can express encapsulated problem solvers generalizing the problem solving capabilities of constraint logic programming. OPM has been developed together with a concomitant programming language Oz, which is designed for applications that require complex symbolic computations, organization into multiple agents, and soft real-time control. An efficient, robust, and interactive implementation of Oz is freely available.

1 Introduction

Computer systems are undergoing a revolution. Twenty years ago, they were centralized, isolated, and expensive. Today, they are parallel, distributed, networked, and inexpensive. However, advances in software construction have failed to keep pace with advances in hardware. To a large extent, this is a consequence of the fact that current programming languages were conceived for sequential and centralized programming.

A basic problem with existing programming languages is that they delegate the creation and coordination of concurrent computational activities to the underlying operating system and network protocols. This has the severe disadvantage that the data abstractions of the programming language cannot be shared between communicating computational agents. Thus the benefits of existing programming languages do not extend to the central concerns of concurrent and distributed software systems.

Given this state of affairs, the development of concurrent programming models is an important research issue in Computer Science. A concurrent programming model must support the creation and coordination of multiple computational activities. Simple concurrent programming models can be obtained by accommodating concurrency in the basic control structure of the model. This way concurrency appears as a generalization rather than an additional feature.

The development of simple, practical, high-level, and well-founded concurrent programming models turned out to be difficult. The main problem was the lack of a methodology and formal machinery for designing and defining such models. In the 1980's, significant progress has been made on this issue. This includes the development of abstract syntax and structural operational semantics [17, 27]; functional and logic programming, two declarative programming models building on the work of logicians (lambda calculus and predicate logic); CCS [12] and the π-calculus [13], two well-founded concurrent programming models developed by Milner and others; and the concurrent constraint model [10, 18], a concurrent programming model that originated from application-driven research in concurrent logic programming [21] and constraint logic programming [6].

This paper reports on the Oz Programming Model, OPM for short, which has been developed together with the concurrent high-level programming language Oz. OPM is an extension of the basic concurrent constraint model, adding first-class procedures and stateful data structures. OPM is a concurrent programming model that subsumes higher-order functional and object-oriented programming as facets of a general model. This is particularly interesting for concurrent object-oriented programming, for which no comprehensive formal model existed until now. There is a conservative extension of OPM providing the problem-solving capabilities of constraint logic programming. The resulting problem solvers appear as concurrent agents encapsulating search and speculative computation with constraints.

Oz and OPM have been developed at the DFKI since 1991. Oz [25, 23, 22] is designed as a concurrent high-level language that can replace sequential high-level languages such as Lisp, Prolog and Smalltalk. There is no other concurrent language combining a rich object system with advanced features for symbolic processing and problem solving. First applications of Oz include simulations, multi-agent systems, natural language processing, virtual reality, graphical user interfaces, scheduling, time tabling, placement problems, and configuration. The design and implementation of Oz took ideas from AKL [7], the first concurrent constraint language with encapsulated search.

An efficient, robust, and interactive implementation of Oz, DFKI Oz, is freely available for many Unix-based platforms (see remark at the end of this paper). DFKI Oz features a programming interface based on GNU Emacs, a concurrent browser, an object-oriented interface to Tcl/Tk for building graphical user interfaces, powerful interoperability features, an incremental compiler, and a run-time system with an emulator and a garbage collector.

DFKI Oz proves that an inherently concurrent language can be implemented efficiently on sequential hardware. Research on a portable parallel implementation for shared memory machines has started. More ambitiously, we have also begun work towards a distributed version of Oz supporting the construction of open systems.

This paper describes OPM in an informal manner. Calculi formalizing the major aspects of OPM can be found in [23, 22]. The Oz Primer [25] is an introduction to programming in Oz. Basic implementation techniques for Oz are reported in [11].

2   Computation Spaces

Computation in OPM takes place in a *computation space* 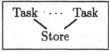 hosting a number of *tasks* connected to a shared *store*. Computation advances by *reduction of tasks*. The reduction of a task can manipulate the store and create new tasks. When a task is reduced it disappears. Reduction of tasks is an atomic operation, and tasks are reduced one by one. Thus there is no parallelism at the abstraction level of OPM.

Tasks can *synchronize* on the store in that they become reducible only once the store satisfies certain conditions. A key property of OPM is that *task synchronization is monotonic*, that is, a reducible task stays reducible if other tasks are reduced before it.

Typically, many tasks are reducible in a given state of a computation space. To obtain fairness, reactivity, and efficiency, a *reduction strategy* is needed to select the reducible tasks qualifying for the next reduction step. *Fairness* ensures that several groups of tasks can advance simultaneously. *Reactivity* means that one can create computations that react to outside events within foreseeable time bounds. The following is an example of a fair and reactive reduction strategy:

> All tasks are maintained in a queue, where the first task of the queue is the one to be considered next for reduction. If it is not reducible, it is moved to the end of the queue. If it is reducible, it is reduced and the newly created tasks are appended at the end of the queue.

We will see later that this strategy is inefficient since its degree of fairness is too fine-grained for OPM. A practical reduction strategy will be given in Section 16.

3   Concurrency and Parallelism

OPM is a concurrent and nonparallel programming model. Concurrency means that one can create several simultaneously advancing computations, possibly synchronizing and communicating. Parallelism means that the execution of several hardware operations overlaps in time. Concurrency can be obtained in a nonparallel setting by interleaving reduction steps. This is typically the case in operating systems that advance several concurrent processes on single processor machines. We can see concurrency as a programming abstraction and parallelism as a physical phenomenon.

The fact that OPM is nonparallel does not exclude a parallel implementation, however. The reason for making OPM concurrent but not parallel is the desire to make things as simple as possible for programmers. In OPM, the semantics of programs does not depend on whether they run on a sequential or parallel implementation. Thus the complexities of parallelism need only concern the implementors of OPM, not the programmers.

4   Synchronization as Logic Entailment

We will now see how OPM realizes monotonic task synchronization. The basic idea is very simple. We assume that a set of logic formulas, called *constraints*, is given. The set of constraints is closed under conjunction, and for constraints a logic entailment relation ("*C* implies *D*") is defined. We also assume that the store of a computation space holds a constraint in a special compartment, called the *constraint store*. The only way the constraint store can be updated is by *telling* it a constraint C, which means that the constraint store advances from S to the conjunction $S \wedge C$. Finally, we assume that it is possible to synchronize a task on a constraint, called its *guard*. A synchronized task becomes reducible if its guard is entailed by the constraint store.

It is easy to see that this synchronization mechanism is monotonic. At any point in time, the constraint store can be seen as a conjunction

$$\mathbf{true} \wedge C_1 \wedge C_2 \wedge \ldots \wedge C_n$$

where $C_1, \ldots, C_n$ are the constraints told so far. The beauty of this arrangement is that the information in the constraint store increases monotonically with every further constraint told, and that the order in which constraints are told is insignificant as far as the information in the store is concerned (conjunction is an associative and commutative operation).

We assume that the constraint store is always satisfiable. Consequently, it is impossible to tell a constraint store S a constraint C if the conjunction $S \wedge C$ is unsatisfiable.

It suffices to represent the constraint store modulo logic equivalence. This means that the synchronization mechanism is completely declarative. It turns out that there are constraint systems for which synchronization as entailment is both expressive and efficient.

Synchronization on a constraint store appeared first in Prolog II [4] in the primitive form of the so-called freeze construct. The idea to synchronize on entailment of constraints is due to Maher [10].

5   Constraint Structures

We now make precise the notions of constraint and entailment. We will also see that the constraint store is the place where information about the values participating in a computation is stored. An important property of the constraint store is the fact that it can store partial (i.e., incomplete) information about the values of variables.

A *constraint structure* is a structure of first-order predicate logic. The elements of a constraint structure are called *values*, and the first-order formulas over the signature of a constraint structure are called *constraints*. We assume that constraints are built over a fixed infinite alphabet of variables. A constraint C

entails a constraint D if the implication $C \rightarrow D$ is valid in the constraint structure. A constraint C *disentails* a constraint D if C entails $\neg D$. Two constraints C and D are *equivalent* if C entails D and D entails C.

The constraint structure must be chosen such that its elements are the values we want to compute with. The values will typically include numbers, ordered pairs of values, and additional primitive entities called names. Values can be thought of as stateless data structures. Note that this set-up requires that values are defined as mathematical entities, and that operations on values are described as mathematical functions and relations.

To ensure that checking entailment between the constraint store and guards is computationally inexpensive, one must carefully restrict the constraints that can be written in the constraint store and that can be used as guards.

We now outline a concrete constraint structure INP. As values of INP we take the integers, an infinite set of primitive entities called *names*, and all ordered pairs that can be obtained over integers and names. We write $v_1|v_2$ for the ordered pair whose left component is the value v_1 and whose right component is the value v_2. Moreover, we assume that the signature of INP provides the following *primitive constraints*:

- $x = n$ says that the value of the variable x is the integer n.
- $x = \xi$ says that the value of the variable x is the name ξ.
- $x = y|z$ says that the value of the variable x is the pair having the value of the variable y as left and the value of the variable z as right component.
- $x = y$ says that the variables x and y have the same value.

An example of a constraint store over INP is

$$x = y \ \wedge \ y = z|u \ \wedge \ z = 3.$$

This constraint store asserts that the value of z is 3, that the value of y is a pair whose left component is 3, and that x and y have the same value. While this constraint store has total information about the value of the variable z, it has only partial information about the values of the other variables. In fact, it has no information about any variable other than x, y and z.

The constraint store above entails the constraint $x = 3|u$ and disentails the constraint $x = 3$. It neither entails nor disentails the constraint $y = 3|5$.

In practice, one uses more expressive constraint structures than INP. The constraint structure CFT [26, 2] offers constraints over possibly infinite records called feature trees. Oz employs an extension of CFT.

6 A Simple Concurrent Constraint Language

We now present a sublanguage OCC of OPM that is also a sublanguage of Saraswat's concurrent constraint model [18]. OCC cannot yet express indeterministic choice, which we will accommodate later (see Section 8).

The store of an OCC computation space consists only of the constraint store. As constraint structure we take INP to be concrete. As tasks we take expressions according to the abstract syntax

$$
\begin{aligned}
E \ ::= \ & C && constraint \\
| \ & E_1 \wedge E_2 && composition \\
| \ & \textbf{if } C \textbf{ then } E_1 \textbf{ else } E_2 && conditional \\
| \ & \textbf{local } x \textbf{ in } E && declaration
\end{aligned}
$$

where C ranges over a suitably restricted class of constraints, and where x ranges over the variables used in constraints. A declaration **local** x **in** E binds the variable x with scope E. *Free* and *bound* variables of expressions are defined accordingly.

An OCC computation space consists of tasks which are expressions as defined above and a store which is a satisfiable constraint. Tasks which are constraints, compositions or declarations are unsynchronized. Conditional tasks synchronize on the constraint store and become reducible only once their guard is entailed or disentailed by the constraint store.

The reduction of a constraint task C *tells* the constraint store the constraint C. We say that such a reduction performs a *tell operation*. If the conjunction $S \wedge C$ of the present constraint store S and C is satisfiable, the reduction of the task C will advance the constraint store to $S \wedge C$. If the conjunction $S \wedge C$ of the present constraint store S and C is unsatisfiable, the reduction of the task C will not change the constraint store and announce *failure*. A concrete language has three possibilities to handle the announcement of failure: to ignore it, to abort computation, or to handle it by an exception handling mechanism.

Reduction of a composition $E_1 \wedge E_2$ creates two tasks E_1 and E_2. Reduction of a conditional **if** C **then** E_1 **else** E_2 creates the task E_1 if C is entailed and the task E_2 if C is disentailed by the constraint store. Reduction of a declaration **local** x **in** E chooses a fresh variable y and creates the task $E[y/x]$ obtained from E by replacing all free occurrences of x with y. A variable is *fresh* if it does not occur in the current state of the computation space.

The expressions of OCC provide basic operations for concurrent programming. Compositions make it possible to obtain several concurrent tasks from a single task. Conditionals make it possible to synchronize tasks on the constraint store. Telling constraints makes it possible to fire synchronized tasks. Declarations make it possible to obtain fresh variables. This will become significant as soon as we introduce procedures. For now observe that two identical tasks **local** x **in** E will reduce to two different tasks $E[y/x]$ and $E[z/x]$, where y and z are distinct fresh variables.

Telling constraints makes it possible to assert information about the values of variables (e.g., $x = 7$). The combination of conditionals and telling makes it possible to access the constituents of nonprimitive values. The task

$$\textbf{if } \exists y \exists z (x = y|z) \textbf{ then } x = u|v \textbf{ else } E$$

will equate the variables u and v to the left and right component of x if x turns out to be pair, and reduce to the task E otherwise. We call this construction a *synchronized decomposition*. To have a convenient notation, we will write

$$\text{if } x_1 \ldots x_n \text{ in } C \text{ then } E_1 \text{ else } E_2$$

as an abbreviation for

$$\text{if } \exists x_1 \ldots \exists x_n \, C \text{ then local } x_1 \text{ in } \ldots \text{ local } x_n \text{ in } (C \wedge E_1) \text{ else } E_2$$

With that we can write the above task as

$$\text{if } y \, z \text{ in } x = y|z \text{ then } u = y \wedge v = z \text{ else } E$$

The reason for having the conditional synchronize symmetrically on entailment and disentailment is that the incremental algorithms for checking entailment automatically also check for disentailment [1, 26]. These algorithms have in fact three outcomes: entailed, disentailed, or neither. The symmetric form of the conditional also has the nice property that it makes negated guards unnecessary since $\text{if } \neg C \text{ then } E_1 \text{ else } E_2$ is equivalent to $\text{if } C \text{ then } E_2 \text{ else } E_1$.

Given a state of a computation space, we say that a variable x is *bound to* an integer n [a name ξ, a pair] if the constraint store entails the constraint $x = n$ [$x = \xi$, $\exists y \exists z (x = y|z)$].

7   First-class Procedures

Every programming language has procedures. Procedures are the basic mechanism for expressing programming abstractions. If provided in full generality, procedures have spectacular expressivity. As is well-known from the lambda calculus, creation and application of nonrecursive functional procedures alone can express all computable functions.

A programming language provides *first-class procedures* if

- procedures can create new procedures,
- procedures can have lexically scoped global variables,
- procedures are referred to by first-class values.

First-class procedures are available in functional programming languages such as Scheme, SML or Haskell. They are typically not available in today's concurrent programming languages although they can provide crucial functionality for concurrent and distributed programming (see the later sections of this paper and also [3]).

In OPM, a *procedure* is a triple

$$\xi : z / E$$

consisting of a name ξ (see Section 5), a *formal argument* z (a variable), and a *body* E (an expression). A procedure binds its formal argument z with scope E.

The *free* or *global* variables of a procedure are defined accordingly. Procedures can actually have any number of formal arguments, but for now we consider only one argument to ease our presentation.

Besides the constraint store, OPM's store has a second compartment called the *procedure store*. The procedure store contains finitely many procedures such that for one name there is at most one procedure. Once a procedure has been entered into the procedure store, it cannot be retracted. Information about the values of the global variables of a procedure is kept in the constraint store. What we call a procedure is often called a closure in the literature.

There are two new expressions for creating and applying procedures:

$$E \ ::= \ \mathbf{proc} \ \{x \ z\} \ E \quad \text{\textit{definition}}$$
$$| \quad \{x \ y\} \qquad\qquad \text{\textit{application}}$$

A definition **proc** $\{x \ z\}$ E binds its *formal argument* z (a variable) with scope E. Definitions are always reducible. The reduction of a definition **proc** $\{x \ z\}$ E chooses a fresh name ξ, tells the constraint store the constraint $x = \xi$, and writes the new procedure $\xi \colon z/E$ into the procedure store.

An application $\{x \ y\}$ must wait until the procedure store contains a procedure $\xi \colon z/E$ such that the constraint store entails $x = \xi$. If this is the case, the application task $\{x \ y\}$ can reduce to the task $E[y/z]$, which is obtained from the body of the procedure by replacing all free occurrences of the formal argument z with the actual argument y, avoiding capturing.

The sublanguage of OPM introduced so far can express both eager and lazy higher-order functional programming [23]. For instance, a higher-order function

$$MkMap \colon (\textit{Value} \rightarrow \textit{Value}) \ \rightarrow \ (\textit{List} \rightarrow \textit{List})$$

returning a list mapping function can be expressed as a binary procedure

```
proc {MkMap F Map}
   proc {Map Xs Ys}
      if X Xr in Xs=X|Xr then
         local Y Yr in Ys=Y|Yr  {F X Y}  {Map Xr Yr} end
      else Ys=Nil fi
   end
end
```

We are now using concrete Oz syntax, where a composition $E_1 \wedge E_2$ is written as a juxtaposition $E_1 \ E_2$. A list $v_1, \ldots, v_n$ is represented as a nested pair $(v_1 | (\ldots (v_n | \nu)) \ldots)$, where ν is a name representing the empty list. We assume that the variable Nil is bound to ν. The procedure MkMap takes a binary procedure F as input and creates a binary procedure Map mapping lists elementwise according to F.

Since our model employs logic variables, there is no static distinction between input and output arguments. The functionality offered by a procedure $\xi \colon z/E$ is simply the ability to spawn any number of tasks $E[y/z]$, where the variable y replacing the formal argument z can be chosen freely each time.

To ease our notation, we will suppress auxiliary variables by means of *nesting*. For instance, we will write

```
{{MkMap F} 1|2|Nil X}
```

as an abbreviation for

```
local Map One Two A B in
    {MkMap F Map}  One=1  Two=2  A=One|B  B=Two|Nil  {Map A X}
end
```

The procedure MkMap actually implements a *concurrent function*. For instance, the task

```
{{MkMap F} A|B|C X}
```

will tell the constraint X=U|V|W, where U, V, and W are fresh variables. It will also create tasks that automatically synchronize on the variables F, A, B, and C and that will compute the values of U, V, and W when the necessary information is available.

The representation of functional computation as concurrent computation has been studied carefully for calculi formalizing the relevant aspects of OPM [23, 16, 15]. The main results include the identification of confluent subcalculi, embeddings of the eager and the lazy lambda calculus, and a correctness proof for the eager embedding. Lazy functional programming can be embedded such that argument computations are shared, a crucial feature of implementations that cannot be modeled with the lambda calculus [9].

OPM combines higher-order programming with first-order constraints. The idea to interface variables and procedures through freshly chosen names appeared first in Fresh [24].

8   Cells

Besides the constraint and the procedure store, OPM's store has a third and final compartment called the *cell store*. A cell is a mutable binding of a name to a variable. Cells make it possible to express stateful and concurrent data structures, which can serve as a communication medium between concurrent agents. There is an exchange operation on cells that combines reading and writing into a single atomic operation, thus providing mutual exclusion and indeterminism as needed for many-to-one communication.

The cell store contains finitely many *cells* $\xi : x$ representing mutable bindings of names to variables. Similar to the procedure store, the cell store contains at most one cell per name. Given a cell $\xi : x$ in the cell store, we say that the cell ξ *hosts* the variable x. The task

```
{NewCell X Y}
```

chooses a fresh name ξ, tells the constraint store the constraint $Y = \xi$, and writes the new cell $\xi : X$ into the cell store. Once a cell has been entered into the cell store, it cannot be retracted. The task

```
{Exchange X Y Z}
```

must wait until the cell store contains a cell $\xi\!:\!u$ such that the constraint store entails $X = \xi$. The task can then be reduced by updating the cell to host the variable Z and telling the constraint store the constraint $Y = u$.

Cells introduce indeterminism into OPM since the order in which multiple exchange tasks for the same cell are reduced is unspecified.

Cells are different from assignable variables in multi-threaded imperative languages. For one thing, OPM ensures mutual exclusion for concurrent exchange tasks for the same cell (since OPM is nonparallel and task reduction is an atomic operation). Moreover, an exchange task combines reading and writing of a cell into a single atomic operation. In the presence of logic variables, this atomic combination turns out to be expressive since one can write a new variable into a cell whose value will be computed only afterwards from the value of the old variable in the cell. This cannot be obtained in an imperative setting since it requires that consumers of a variable are automatically synchronized on the event that the value of the variable becomes known.

9   Ports

Building on cells, we can express complex concurrent data structures with state. The internal structure of such data structures can be hidden by means of procedural abstraction and lexical scoping of variables. We can thus obtain abstract concurrent data types with state.

As a first example we consider ports [8], which can serve as message queues for agents. A *port* is a procedure connected to a stream. A *stream* is a variable S that is incrementally constrained to a list by telling a constraint for every element of the list:

$$S=X_1|S_1, \quad S_1=X_2|S_2, \quad S_2=X_3|S_3, \quad S_3=X_4|S_4, \quad \ldots$$

It is assumed that nobody but the procedure P writes on the stream. An application $\{P\ X\}$ will tell a constraint $S_i=X|S_{i+1}$, where S_i is the current tail of the stream and S_{i+1} is a new variable serving as the new tail of the stream. A port has state because it must remember the current tail of its stream. A port is a concurrent data structure since it allows several concurrent computations to write consistently on a single stream.

The procedure

```
proc {NewPort Stream Port}
   local Cell in
      {NewCell Stream Cell}
      proc {Port Message}
         local Old New in
            {Exchange Cell Old New}  Old=Message|New
         end
      end
   end
end
```

creates a new port Port connected to a stream Stream. The port holds the current tail of its stream in a private cell Cell. Note how lexical scoping ensures that no one but the port can see the cell. Also note that NewPort is a higher-order procedure in that it creates and returns a new procedure Port.

How can we enter two messages A and B to a port such that A appears before B on the associated stream? To make things more interesting, we are looking for a solution making it possible that other concurrently sent messages can be received between A and B (it may take a long time before B is sent).

One possible solution makes assumptions about the employed reduction strategy (see Section 16). Here we will give a solution that will work for every reduction strategy. The basic idea is to model a port as a binary procedure

```
{Port Message Continuation}
```

that will tell the constraint Continuation=Port after Message has been put on the stream [8]. Two messages A and B can then be sequentialized by writing

```
local Continuation Dummy in
    {Port A Continuation} {Continuation B Dummy}
end
```

Such synchronizing ports can be created with

```
proc {NewSyncPort Stream Port}
    local Cell in
        {NewCell Port|Stream Cell}
        proc {Port Message Continuation}
            local New in
                {Exchange Cell Continuation|Message|New Port|New}
            end
        end
    end
end
```

10   Names

Names serve as dynamically created capabilities that cannot be faked. It is often useful to be able to obtain reference to fresh names that do not designate procedures or cells. For this purpose we introduce a primitive task

```
{NewName X}
```

which can be reduced by choosing a fresh name ξ and telling the constraint $X=\xi$. Referring to names by means of variables has the advantage of lexical scoping and also avoids the need for a concrete syntax for names. Using names, lexical scoping, and procedures, sophisticated access control schemes can be expressed.

11   Agents

An agent is a computational abstraction processing messages received through a port. It maintains an internal state and may send messages to other agents. An example of an agent is a queue that can handle concurrent enqueue and dequeue requests.

We assume that the functionality of an agent is given by a procedure

$$Serve: \ State \times Message \ \rightarrow \ NewState$$

describing how the agent serves a message and how it advances its state. The procedure

```
proc {NewAgent Serve Init Port}
   local Stream Feed in
      {NewPort Stream Port}
      {Feed Stream Init}
      proc {Feed Ms State}
         if Message Mr NewState in Ms=Message|Mr then
            {Serve State Message NewState}   {Feed Mr NewState}
         else true fi
      end
   end
end
```

creates a new agent that receives messages through Port and operates as specified by the procedure Serve and the initial state Init. Note that an agent hides the stream queueing its messages.

A queue agent receiving messages through a port Q can be created with

```
local Xs in {NewAgent QueueServe Xs|Xs Q} end
```

where the procedure QueueServe is defined as follows:

```
{NewName Enqueue}
{NewName Dequeue}
proc {QueueServe State Message NewState}
   if First Last in State=First|Last then
      if X NewLast in Message=Enqueue|X then
         Last=X|NewLast  NewState=First|NewLast
      else
         if X NewFirst in Message=Dequeue|X then
            First=X|NewFirst  NewState=NewFirst|Last
         else true fi
      fi
   else true fi
end
```

Messages are represented as pairs Enqueue|X and Dequeue|X, where the variables Enqueue and Dequeue are bound to names identifying the corresponding operations. Using lexical scoping, one can construct contexts in which none or only one of the two operations is visible.

A message Enqueue|X will enqueue X, and a message Dequeue|X will dequeue an item and bind it to X. In case the queue is empty, a dequeue request will wait in a queue of unserved dequeue requests, which is served as soon as an item is entered into the queue. The procedure QueueServe shows that this synchronization idea can be expressed elegantly by means of logic variables.

12 Objects

Objects are a modular programming abstraction for concurrent data structures with state. We model objects as procedures {Object Message} that are applied to messages. A message is a pair MethodName|Argument. When an object is applied to a message, it invokes the requested method with the given argument and advances to a new state. Similar to agents, we assume that the functionality of an object is specified by a procedure

$$Serve: \ State \times \ Message \times \ Self \ \rightarrow \ NewState$$

describing how the agent serves a message and how it advances its state. The argument *Self* is a reference to the object invoking *Serve* making it possible to have a self reference within *Serve* and still share *Serve* between several objects. The procedure

```
proc {NewObject Serve Init Object}
   local Cell in
      {NewCell Init Cell}
      proc {Object Message}
         local State NewState in
            {Exchange Cell State NewState}
            {Serve State Message Object NewState}
         end
      end
   end
end
```

creates a new object Object from a procedure Serve and an initial state Init.

It is straightforward to express classes defining serve procedures in a modular fashion by means of named methods. Methods are modeled as procedures similar to serve procedures. Objects can then be obtained as instances of classes. The states of objects are modeled as finite mappings from attributes to variables, where attributes are modeled as names. Methods can then construct new states from given states by "assigning" variables to attributes. One can also provide for *inheritance*, that is, the ability to construct new classes by inheriting methods and attributes from existing classes. All this is a matter of straightforward higher-order programming. Exploiting the power of lexical scoping and names, it is straightforward to express private attributes and methods.

OPM is a simple and powerful base for expressing concurrent object-oriented programming abstractions. It was in fact designed for this purpose. Concrete programming languages will of course sweeten frequently used programming abstractions with a convenient notation. For a concrete system of object-oriented abstractions and notations we refer the reader to the Oz object system [5, 25].

The reader will have noticed the similarity between agents and objects. We can see agents as active objects. An object can easily be turned into an agent by interfacing it through a port.

13   Distribution

OPM can be extended to serve as a model for distributed programming. Distribution means that a program can spread computations over a network of computers. At the abstraction level of OPM, this can be modeled by assigning a *site* to every task and by assuming that the store is distributed transparently. Moreover, we assume that new tasks inherit the site of the creating task.

We can now see a clear difference between agents and objects. When we send a message to an agent, the message is served at the site where the agent was created (there is a task waiting for the next message sent). When we apply an object to a message, the message is served at the site where the object is applied. In other words, agents are stationary and objects are mobile.

Since OPM has first-class procedures, it is straightforward to express compute servers. Cardelli [3] gives an excellent exposition of distributed programming techniques available in a lexically-scoped language with first-class procedures and concurrent state.

The assumption of a transparently distributed store is not realistic for many applications. It conflicts with the ability to model fault-tolerance, for instance. We have started work on a less abstract model where the store appears as a directed graph whose nodes are situated similar to tasks.

14   Incremental Tell

The tell operation of OCC (see Section 6) is not suitable for a parallel implementation. The reason is that a constraint must be told in a single reduction step. Since telling a constraint (e.g., $x = y$) may involve scanning the entire store, other tell tasks may be blocked for a long time. The problem can be resolved by telling a constraint piecewise. The basic idea is to reduce a constraint task T by keeping the task T as is and by advancing the constraint store from S to a slightly stronger constraint store S' entailed by $S \wedge T$. This amplifying reduction step is repeated until the constraint store entails T, in which case the task T is discarded. Since the constraint store must always be satisfiable, the case where $S \wedge T$ is unsatisfiable needs special care.

To make the incremental tell operation precise, we introduce the notion of a constraint system. A *constraint system* consists of a constraint structure, a set of constraints called *basic constraints*, and, for every basic constraint T, a binary relation $\rightarrow_T$ on basic constraints such that:

1. The basic constraints are closed under conjunction and contain $\perp$ (i.e., false).
2. For every basic constraint T, the relation $\twoheadrightarrow_T$ is well-founded, that is, there exists no infinite chain $S_1 \twoheadrightarrow_T S_2 \twoheadrightarrow_T S_3 \twoheadrightarrow_T \cdots$.
3. If $S \twoheadrightarrow_T S'$, then (i) S' entails S, (ii) $S \wedge T$ entails S', (iii) S is satisfiable, and (iv) S' is unsatisfiable if and only if $S' = \perp$.
4. If T is not entailed by S and both are basic constraints, then there exists S' such that $S \twoheadrightarrow_T S'$.

The *tell reductions* $\twoheadrightarrow_T$ correspond to the visible simplification steps of the incremental algorithms implementing the necessary operations on constraint stores. Such algorithms can be found, for instance, in [1, 26]. Note that the tell reductions may be nondeterministic; that is, for given S and T, there may be different S_1 and S_2 such that $S \twoheadrightarrow_T S_1$ and $S \twoheadrightarrow_T S_2$.

Let S be a satisfiable basic constraint and T a basic constraint. Then the tell reduction $\twoheadrightarrow_T$ satisfies the following properties:

1. S entails T if and only if S is irreducible with respect to $\twoheadrightarrow_T$.
2. S disentails T if and only if every maximal chain $S \twoheadrightarrow_T \cdots$ ends with $\perp$.
3. Let $S \twoheadrightarrow_T \cdots \twoheadrightarrow_T S'$ be a chain such that S' is irreducible with respect to T. Then (i) $S \wedge T$ is equivalent to S' and (ii) $S \wedge T$ is unsatisfiable if and only if $S' = \perp$.

Given a constraint system, we assume that the constraints appearing in expressions and the constraint store are all basic, where the constraints appearing in guards may be existentially quantified. Given a constraint store S and a constraint task T, the *incremental tell operation* is defined as follows: if S is irreducible with respect to $\twoheadrightarrow_T$, then the task T is discarded. Otherwise, choose some basic constraint S' such that $S \twoheadrightarrow_T S'$. If $S' = \perp$, then announce failure and discard the task T; if $S' \neq \perp$, then advance the constraint store to S' and keep the task T.

The canonical constraint system for the constraint structure INP comes with the basic constraints

$$C ::= \perp \mid \top \mid \langle primitive\ constraint \rangle \mid C_1 \wedge C_2.$$

Primitive constraints were defined in Section 5.

As long as failure does not occur, it is not important to know which tell reductions are used. However, if $S \wedge T$ is unsatisfiable and computation can continue after failure (e.g., since there is exception handling), all chains $S \twoheadrightarrow_T \cdots \twoheadrightarrow_T S'$ should only add local information. The notion of "local information" cannot be made precise in general. However, there are straightforward definitions for INP and other practically relevant constraint systems. Here we will just give an example for INP. Given $S \equiv (x = 1|2 \wedge y = u|3)$ and $T \equiv (x = y)$, the tell reduction $\twoheadrightarrow_T$ should only permit two maximal chains issuing from S: $S \twoheadrightarrow_T S \wedge u = 1 \twoheadrightarrow_T \perp$ and $S \twoheadrightarrow_T \perp$.

15   Propagators

The algorithms for telling and checking entailment and disentailment of basic constraints must be efficient. The typical complexity should be constant time, and the worst-case complexity should be quadratic or better in the size of the guard and the constraint store. Consequently, expressive constraints such as $x + y = z$ and $x * y = z$ cannot be written into the constraint store and hence cannot be accommodated as basic constraints. (For nonlinear constraints over integers satisfiability is undecidable (Hilbert's Tenth Problem).)

Nonbasic constraints can be accommodated as tasks that wait until the constraint store contains enough information so that they can be equivalently replaced with basic constraints. For instance, a task $x + y = z$ may wait until there exist two integers n and m such that the constraint store entails $x = n \wedge y = m$. If this is the case, the task can be reduced to the basic constraint $z = k$, where k is the sum of n and m. Nonbasic constraints that are accommodated in this way are called *propagators*.

Another example of a propagator is a Boolean order test for integers:

$$less(x, y, z) \equiv (x < y \leftrightarrow z = \text{True}) \wedge (z = \text{True} \vee z = \text{False}).$$

True and False are variables bound to distinct names. This propagator can reduce to $z = \text{True}$ or $z = \text{False}$ as soon as the constraint store contains sufficient information about the values of x and y.

16   Threads

We now give an efficient reduction strategy for OPM that is fair and reactive (see Section 2). An efficient reduction strategy must make it possible to write programs that create only a moderate amount of concurrency, which can be implemented efficiently on both single and multi-processor architectures.

The example of the Fibonacci function (we use a sugared notation suppressing auxiliary variables)

```
proc {Fib N M}
   local B X Y in
      {Less 2 N B}
      if B=True then {Fib N-1 X}  {Fib N-2 Y}  X+Y=M else M=1 fi
   end
end
```

shows that the naive reduction strategy in Section 2 is impractical: it will traverse the recursion tree of {Fib 5 M}, say, in breadth-first manner, thus requiring exponential space. On the other hand, sequential execution will traverse the recursion tree in depth-first manner from left to right and will thus only need linear space. This difference clearly matters.

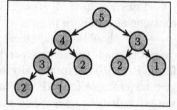

The efficient reduction strategy organizes tasks into threads, where every thread is guaranteed to make progress. Thus fairness is guaranteed at the level of threads. A *thread* is a nonempty stack of tasks, where

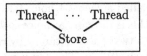

only the topmost task of a thread can be reduced. If the topmost task of a thread is reduced, it is replaced with the newly created tasks, if there are any. If a composition $E_1 \wedge E_2$ is reduced, the left expression E_1 goes on top of the right expression E_2, which means that E_1 is considered before E_2. If the topmost task of a thread is irreducible over the current store and the thread contains further tasks, the topmost task is moved to a newly created thread. A thread disappears as soon as it has no task left.

The outlined reduction strategy tries to be as sequential as possible and as concurrent as necessary. It will execute the task {Fib 5 M} sequentially in a single thread, thus requiring only linear space.

The concurrent execution of an expression E in a separate thread can be forced by writing

local Fire **in if** Fire=1 **then** E **else true fi** Fire=1 **end**

With threads it is straightforward to send messages sequentially through a port. If ports are defined as in Section 9, the simple composition

{Port A} {Port B}

will send A before B provided the store binds Port already to a port.

17 Time

It is straightforward to extend OPM such that tasks can be synchronized on time points. Here we specify a timer primitive

{Sleep T X Y}

which equates two variables X and Y after the time span specified by the variable T has passed. The timer primitive first waits until the store binds T to an integer n. It then stays irreducible for further n milliseconds, after which it can be reduced to the constraint X=Y.

18 Encapsulated Search

Since OPM has constraints and logic variables, it will subsume the problem solving capabilities of constraint logic programming when extended with a nondeterministic choice combinator. However, a completely new idea is needed for encapsulating the resulting problem solvers into concurrent agents.

A nondeterministic choice combinator can be provided as an expression

$$E_1 \text{ or } E_2$$

called a *choice*. Choice tasks can only be reduced if no other task is reducible. If this is the case, a choice can be reduced by *distributing* the computation space into two spaces obtained by replacing the choice with its left and right alternative, respectively. The resulting search tree of computation spaces can be explored with a suitable strategy. If a tell operation announces failure, computation in the corresponding computation space is aborted. The leaves of the search tree are either failed or unfailed computation spaces. Unfailed leaves will contain the solutions of the problem being solved as bindings to certain variables.

While the outlined semantics for nondeterministic choice provides the expressivity of constraint logic programming, distributing the top level computation space is not compatible with the idea of concurrent computation. What we would like to have are concurrent agents to which we can present a search strategy and a problem to be solved and from which we can request the solutions of the problem one by one. This means that the search agent should encapsulate search. It turns out that such a search agent can be programmed with a single further primitive, called a *search combinator*. The search combinator spawns a subordinate computation space and reduces in case the subordinate space fails, becomes irreducible, or is distributed. In the case of distribution, the two alternative local spaces are frozen and returned as first-class citizens represented as procedures. The details of this elaborate construction are reported in [20, 19, 22].

The resulting model is realized in Oz together with further concurrent constraint combinators [20, 19, 14]. Oz gets constraint logic programming out of its problem solving ghetto and integrates it into a concurrent and lexically scoped language with first-class procedures and state. This integration eliminates the need for Prolog's ad hoc constructs and also increases the expressivity of the problem solving constructs.

19   Summary

We have presented a simple and expressive model OPM for high-level concurrent programming. The model is lexically scoped and consists of the concurrent constraint kernel OCC, first-class procedures, and cells providing for concurrent state. It computes with logic variables and constraints and monotonically synchronizes on a declarative constraint store. The constraint store is the exclusive place where information about the values of variables is stored. Dynamically created values called names interface the constraint store with the procedure and the cell store. This way OPM realizes an orthogonal combination of first-order constraints with first-class procedures and stateful cells. We have shown how OPM can express higher-order functions, agents and objects. We have added an incremental tell operation to improve the potential for parallelism. We have also added propagators, threads, and a timer primitive as needed for a practical language. Finally, we have outlined how the model can be extended so that it can express encapsulated problem solvers generalizing the problem solving capabilities of constraint logic programming. Oz translates the presented ideas into an exciting new programming language.

Acknowledgements

The development of OPM and Oz would have been impossible without the combined contributions of the members of the Programming Systems Lab at DFKI. Much inspiration and technical knowledge came from the developers of AKL at SICS, the developers of LIFE at Digital PRL, and the other partners of the Esprit basic research action ACCLAIM.

I'm grateful to Seif Haridi, Martin Henz, Michael Mehl, Joachim Niehren, Andreas Podelski, and Christian Schulte who read and commented on drafts of this paper.

The research reported in this paper has been supported by the BMBF (contract ITW 9105), the Esprit Basic Research Project ACCLAIM (contract EP 7195), and the Esprit Working Group CCL (contract EP 6028).

Remark

The DFKI Oz system and papers of authors from the Programming Systems Lab at DFKI are available through the Web at `http://ps-www.dfki.uni-sb.de/` or through anonymous ftp from `ps-ftp.dfki.uni-sb.de`.

References

1. H. Aït-Kaci, A. Podelski, and G. Smolka. A feature-based constraint system for logic programming with entailment. *Theoretical Computer Science*, 122(1-2):263–283, 1994.
2. R. Backofen. A complete axiomatization of a theory with feature and arity constraints. *Journal of Logic Programming*, 1995. To appear.
3. L. Cardelli. Obliq: A Language with Distributed Scope. In *Proc. 22nd Ann. ACM Symposium on Principles of Programming Languages (POPL'95)*, pages 286–297, 1995.
4. A. Colmerauer, H. Kanoui, and M. V. Caneghem. Prolog, theoretical principles and current trends. *Technology and Science of Informatics*, 2(4):255–292, 1983.
5. M. Henz, G. Smolka, and J. Würtz. Object-oriented concurrent constraint programming in Oz. In V. Saraswat and P. V. Hentenryck, editors, *Principles and Practice of Constraint Programming*, pages 27–48. The MIT Press, Cambridge, MA, 1995.
6. J. Jaffar and M. J. Maher. Constraint logic programming: A survey. *The Journal of Logic Programming*, 19/20:503–582, 1994.
7. S. Janson and S. Haridi. Programming paradigms of the Andorra kernel language. In V. Saraswat and K. Ueda, editors, *Logic Programming, Proc. 1991 Int. Symposium*, pages 167–186. The MIT Press, Cambridge, MA, 1991.
8. S. Janson, J. Montelius, and S. Haridi. Ports for objects. In *Research Directions in Concurrent Object-Oriented Programming*. The MIT Press, Cambridge, MA, 1993.
9. J. Launchbury. A natural semantics for lazy evaluation. In *Proc. 20th Ann. ACM Symposium on Principles of Programming Languages (POPL'93)*, pages 144–154, 1993.

10. M. J. Maher. Logic semantics for a class of committed-choice programs. In J.-L. Lassez, editor, *Logic Programming, Proc. 4th Int. Conference*, pages 858–876. The MIT Press, Cambridge, MA, 1987.

11. M. Mehl, R. Scheidhauer, and C. Schulte. An abstract machine for Oz. In *Proc. 7th Int. Symposium on Programming Languages, Implementations, Logics and Programs (PLILP'95)*. Lecture Notes in Computer Science, Springer-Verlag, Berlin, 1995. To appear.

12. R. Milner. *A Calculus of Communicating Systems*. Lecture Notes in Computer Science, Vol. 92, Springer-Verlag, Berlin, 1980.

13. R. Milner. Functions as processes. *Journal of Mathematical Structures in Computer Science*, 2(2):119–141, 1992.

14. T. Müller, K. Popow, C. Schulte, and J. Würtz. Constraint programming in Oz. DFKI Oz documentation series, DFKI, Saarbrücken, Germany, 1994.

15. J. Niehren. *Funktionale Berechnung in einem uniform nebenläufigen Kalkül mit logischen Variablen*. Doctoral Dissertation. Universität des Saarlandes, Saarbrücken, Germany, December 1994. Submitted.

16. J. Niehren and G. Smolka. A confluent relational calculus for higher-order programming with constraints. In J.-P. Jouannaud, editor, *Proc. 1st Int. Conference on Constraints in Computational Logics (CCL'94)*, pages 89–104. Lecture Notes in Computer Science, Vol. 845, Springer-Verlag, Berlin, 1994.

17. G. D. Plotkin. A structural approach to operational semantics. DAIMI FN-19, Dept. of Computer Science, Aarhus University, Denmark, 1981. Reprinted 1991.

18. V. A. Saraswat. *Concurrent Constraint Programming*. The MIT Press, Cambridge, MA, 1993.

19. C. Schulte and G. Smolka. Encapsulated search in higher-order concurrent constraint programming. In M. Bruynooghe, editor, *Logic Programming, Proc. 1994 Int. Symposium*, pages 505–520. The MIT Press, Cambridge, MA, 1994.

20. C. Schulte, G. Smolka, and J. Würtz. Encapsulated search and constraint programming in Oz. In A. Borning, editor, *Proc. 2nd Int. Workshop on Principles and Practice of Constraint Programming (PPCP'94)*, pages 134–150. Lecture Notes in Computer Science, Vol. 874, Springer-Verlag, Berlin, 1994.

21. E. Shapiro. The family of concurrent logic programming languages. *ACM Computing Surveys*, 21(3):413–511, 1989.

22. G. Smolka. The definition of Kernel Oz. In A. Podelski, editor, *Constraints: Basics and Trends*, pages 251–292. Lecture Notes in Computer Science, Vol. 910, Springer-Verlag, Berlin, 1995.

23. G. Smolka. A foundation for higher-order concurrent constraint programming. In J.-P. Jouannaud, editor, *Proc. 1st Int. Conference on Constraints in Computational Logics (CCL'94)*, pages 50–72. Lecture Notes in Computer Science, Vol. 845, Springer-Verlag, Berlin, 1994.

24. G. Smolka. Fresh: A higher-order language with unification and multiple results. In D. DeGroot and G. Lindstrom, editors, *Logic Programming: Relations, Functions, and Equations*, pages 469–524. Prentice-Hall, Englewood Cliffs, NJ, 1986.

25. G. Smolka. An Oz primer. DFKI Oz documentation series, DFKI, Saarbrücken, Germany, 1995.

26. G. Smolka and R. Treinen. Records for logic programming. *Journal of Logic Programming*, 18(3):229–258, 1994.

27. G. Winskel. *The Formal Semantics of Programming Languages*. Foundations of Computing. The MIT Press, Cambridge, MA, 1993.

Standard Generalized Markup Language: Mathematical and Philosophical Issues [*]

Derick Wood[1]

Department of Computer Science
Hong Kong University of Science & Technology
Clear Water Bay, Kowloon
Hong Kong

Abstract. The Standard Generalized Markup Language (SGML), an ISO standard, has become the accepted method of defining markup conventions for text files. SGML is a metalanguage for defining grammars for textual markup in much the same way that Backus–Naur Form is a metalanguage for defining programming-language grammars. Indeed, HTML, the method of marking up a hypertext documents for the World Wide Web, is an SGML grammar. The underlying assumptions of the SGML initiative are that a logical structure of a document can be identified and that it can be indicated by the insertion of labeled matching brackets (start and end tags). Moreover, it is assumed that the nesting relationships of these tags can be described with an extended context-free grammar (the right-hand sides of productions are regular expressions).
In this survey of some of the issues raised by the SGML initiative, I reexamine the underlying assumptions and address some of the theoretical questions that SGML raises. In particular, I respond to two kinds of questions. The first kind are technical: Can we decide whether tag minimization is possible? Can we decide whether a proposed content model is legal? Can we remove exceptions in a structure preserving manner? Can we decide whether two SGML grammars are equivalent?
The second kind are philosophical and foundational: What is a logical structure? What logical structures may a document have? Can logical structures always be captured by context-free nesting?

1 Introduction

The Standard Generalized Markup Language (SGML) came into being as an ISO Standard [18] in 1987 without fanfare and without hyperbole. It has changed forever the way we view and approach textual documents. Its impact in the textual world is greater than the impact that BNF had in the programming-language community thirty years earlier. The similarity does not end there since SGML is also a metalanguage that we can use to specify grammars. But it is also much more.

---

[*] This work was supported under Natural Sciences and Engineering Research Council of Canada grants.

We explain a little of SGML's intended use and then explore some issues that are raised by the SGML standard. In this way we explore some fundamental issues stemming from the approach taken by SGML's creators.

Each SGML grammar defines a class of structured documents and also a method, called **markup,** of indicating the structure in the documents using interleaved text, called **tags.** When using typesetting systems such as GML, Scribe, LATEX, troff, and TEX [25] authors also interleave. with the source text. typesetting commands specific to the typesetting system; such interleaving is called **procedural markup.** Procedural markup is powerful yet restrictive.

It is now axiomatic that markup should identify the component elements of text; that is, it should be **logical** and **descriptive,** rather than procedural. Such marked-up documents are more useful, because not only can they be typeset by compiling them into, for example, TEX marked-up documents, but also they can be used directly in textual databases and, hence, searched and manipulated. In addition, if the legal markup is defined by some document grammar, then we can communicate a document (and its structure) that is marked up according to a grammar by communicating both the grammar and the marked-up document. The ISO standard for SGML [18] provides a syntactic metalanguage for the definition of textual markup systems. Each SGML-markup system is specified, essentially, by an **extended context-free grammar (ECFG)**that specifies the legal placement and type of the markup in documents. SGML is a syntactic meta-language for document grammars just as BNF, BNF's various extensions, and syntax diagrams are for programming-language grammars.

The most well-known example of the use of SGML is in the World Wide Web. Pages for inclusion in WWW are marked up with HTML (HyperText Markup Language), which is defined by a specific SGML grammar. The explosive growth of WWW has exposed more people to SGML in a day, than were ever exposed to it before. A second example is the CALS initiative of the U. S. Department of Defense; the use of a specific SGML grammar to define a system-independent markup language for contracts, tenders, and other uses. In addition, organizations such as the American Association of Publishers have defined specific SGML grammars for, in their case, the book-publishing industry.

We begin the discussion of SGML by giving a very brief introduction to it by example and by its similarity with ECFGs. In the following sections we survey the status of current research on the issues of content-model unambiguity, DTD equivalence, exceptions, and omitted tag minimization. Lastly, we discuss some philosophical issues of documents, logical structures, and markup.

The work reported here is only a beginning, new standards have been developed that build on SGML; for example, the style specification standard DSSSL [20] and the hypermedia standard HyTime [19, 14]. While SGML and these additional Standards are important attempts to bring order out of chaos, at the same time, it is crucial that they do not add to the chaos. As a theoretician who has become an occasional practitioner, I believe that while taking advantage of these and similar standards, we must also take them seriously enough to investigate them theoretically. Only in this way can we ensure well designed standards that are well defined.

2   An SGML Primer

SGML [18, 16] promotes the interchangeability and application-independent management of electronic documents by providing a syntactic metalanguage for the definition of textual markup systems. An SGML document consists of an SGML prolog and a marked-up document instance. The prolog contains a **document type definition (DTD)**, which is, essentially, an ECFG. An example of a simple SGML DTD is given in Fig. 1.

```
<!DOCTYPE message [
<!ELEMENT message          (head, body)>
<!ELEMENT head             (from & to & subject)>
<!ELEMENT from             (person)>
<!ELEMENT to               (person)+>
<!ELEMENT person           (alias | (forename?, surname))>
<!ELEMENT body             (paragraph)*>
<!ELEMENT subject, alias, forename, surname, paragraph
                           (#PCDATA)> ]>
```

Fig. 1. An SGML DTD for e-mail messages.

The productions of a DTD are called **element type definitions (ETDs)**. The right hand sides of ETDs are extended regular expressions called **content models**. The DTD in Fig. 1 is a DTD for e-mail messages, which consist of a head and a body, in that order; note the use of ',' to mean catenation or followed by. The element head comprises subelements from, to, and subject appearing in any order; note the use of '&' to mean unordered catenation. The element from is defined to be a person, which consists of either an alias or an optional forename followed by a surname; note the use of '|' for alternation and of '?' for an optional item. The element to consists of a nonempty list of persons. The body of a message consists of a (possibly empty) sequence of paragraphs. Finally, the last element definition specifies that the elements subject, alias, forename, surname, and paragraph are unstructured strings, denoted by the keyword #PCDATA.

The structural elements of a document instance (sentences in grammatical terminology) are marked up by enclosing them in matching pairs of **start tags** and **end tags**. A document that is marked up according to the DTD of Fig. 1 is shown in Fig. 2.

We model SGML DTDs with ECFGs. In ECFGs the right-hand sides of productions are regular expressions. Let V be an alphabet; then, the language $L(E)$

```
<message>
  <head>
    <from><person><alias>Boss</alias></person></from>
    <subject>Tomorrow's meeting...</subject>
    <to><person><surname>Franklin</surname></person>
        <person><alias>Betty</alias><person></to>
  </head>
  <body><paragraph>...has been cancelled.</paragraph></body>
</message>
```

Fig. 2. An SGML document instance for the DTD of Fig. 1.

denoted by a regular expression E over V is defined inductively as follows.

$$L(\emptyset) = \emptyset. \qquad\qquad L(\epsilon) = \{\epsilon\}.$$
$$L(a) = \{a\} \text{ for } a \in V. \qquad L(FG) = \{vw \mid v \in L(F), w \in L(G)\}.$$
$$L(F \cup G) = L(F) \cup L(G). \qquad L(F^*) = \{v_1 \cdots v_n \mid n \geq 0, v_1, \ldots, v_n \in L(F)\}.$$

We denote the set of symbols of V appearing in E by $sym(E)$.

An ECFG G consists of two disjoint finite alphabets of **nonterminal symbols** and **terminal symbols,** denoted by N and Σ, respectively, a finite set P of **production schemas,** and a **sentence symbol,** S. Each **production schema** has the form $A \to E$, where A is a nonterminal and E is a regular expression over $V = N \cup \Sigma$. When $\beta = \beta_1 A \beta_2 \in V^*$, $A \to E \in P$ and $\alpha \in L(E)$, we say that the string $\beta_1 \alpha \beta_2$ can be **derived** from string β and denote the derivation by $\beta \Rightarrow \beta_1 \alpha \beta_2$. The **language L(G) defined by an ECFG G** is the set of terminal strings derivable from the sentence symbol of G. Formally, $L(G) = \{w \in \Sigma^* \mid S \Rightarrow^+ w\}$, where $\Rightarrow^+$ denotes the transitive closure of the derivability relation.

Even though a production schema may give rise to an infinite number of ordinary context-free productions, it is well-known that ECFGs and CFGs describe exactly the same languages [33].

SGML DTDs are similar to ECFGs, yet different from them. In particular, content models are more general than regular expressions in that they have the additional operators: '?', '&', and '+'. In a DTD the alphabet V comprises **generic identifiers** that are names of **elements** (nonterminals) and #PCDATA. The language $L(E)$ defined by a content model E is defined inductively as follows:

$$L(a) = \{a\} \text{ for } a \in V. \qquad L(FG) = \{vw \mid v \in L(F), w \in L(G)\}.$$
$$L(F|G) = L(F) \cup L(G). \qquad L(F^*) = \{v_1 \cdots v_n \mid v_1, \ldots, v_n \in L(F), n \geq 0\}.$$
$$L(F\&G) = L(FG|GF). \qquad L(F^+) = \{v_1 \cdots v_n \mid v_1, \ldots, v_n \in L(F), n \geq 1\}.$$
$$L(F?) = L(F) \cup \{\epsilon\}.$$

3   Unambiguous Content Models

The following discussion of unambiguity is based on the work of Brüggemann-Klein and Wood [4, 5, 6, 7, 8, 9].

The SGML standard does not allow arbitrary regular expressions as content models, it says that they should be "unambiguous" in the sense that, using formal language terminology, "a symbol that occurs in a string accepted by the regular expression E must be able to satisfy only one occurrence of this symbol in E without looking ahead in the string." This condition is illustrated by the expression $E = a(b|\epsilon)b$ and the strings ab and abb. After the first symbol a has been matched with the a in the expression E, the second symbol b of the string can either be satisfied by the first or the second b in E, depending on the continuation of the string. So, if the lookahead in the string is confined to the current symbol b, we cannot decide which of the b's in E it should match. Thus, E is "ambiguous" in the sense of the Standard. In this case, there is an equivalent expression $E' = ab(b + \epsilon)$ that is "unambiguous."

The intent of the authors of the Standard is twofold: They wish to make it easier for humans to write and understand expressions that can be interpreted unambiguously and, at the same time, to provide a means of generating parsers that do not have exponential blow up in size. (Such restrictions are familiar in other settings; for example, with vi and grep.) We call these expressions **1-deterministic**, since it is deterministic parsing with one-symbol lookahead that is implied by the standard, rather than unambiguity per se [9, 6, 8, 7]. Indeed, this view is reflected in Annex H of the standard, where the notion is explained, informally, in terms of the nondeterministic finite-state machine with ϵ-transitions obtained from a regular expression. A regular expression is *1-deterministic* if its strings can be recognized deterministically, with one-symbol lookahead, by the corresponding nondeterministic finite-state machine. For example, the lower finite-state machine in Fig. 3 is 1-deterministic, whereas the upper machine in Fig. 3 is not.

Rather than discussing SGML content models directly, we first consider traditional regular expressions. Content models are more general in that they have the additional operators: '?', '&', and '+'.

To indicate different **positions** of the same symbol in an expression, we mark symbols with subscripts. For example, $(a_1|b_1) * a_2(a_3b_2)*$ and $(a_4|b_2) * a_1(a_5b_1)*$ are both **markings** of the expression $(a|b)*a(ab)*$. For each expression E over Σ, a marking of E is denoted by E'. If H is a subexpression of E, we assume that markings H' and E' are chosen in such a way that H' is a subexpression of E'. A **marked expression** E is an expression over Π, the alphabet of subscripted symbols, where each subscripted symbol occurs at most once in E.

The reverse of marking is the dropping of subscripts, indicated by $\natural$ and defined as follows: If E is an expression over Π, then $E^\natural$ is the expression over Σ that is constructed from E by dropping all subscripts. Thus, a marked expression H is a **marking** of expression E if and only if $H^\natural = E$. Unmarking can also be extended to strings and languages: For a string w over Π, let $w^\natural$ denote the string over Σ that is constructed from w by dropping all subscripts. For a lan-

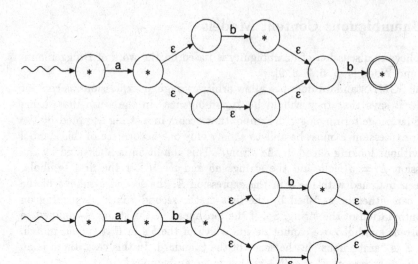

Fig. 3. Thompson's construction [30, 1] for the expression $a(b|\epsilon)b$ that is not 1-deterministic and for the 1-deterministic expression $ab(b|\epsilon)$.

guage L over Π, let $L^\natural$ denote $\{w^\natural | w \in L\}$. Then, for each expression E over Π, $L(E^\natural) = L(E)^\natural$.

Now we can give a concise definition of the SGML notion of unambiguity.

Definition 1. An expression E is **1-deterministic** if and only if, for all strings u, v, w over Π and all symbols x, y in Π, the conditions $uxv, uyw \in L(E')$ and $x \neq y$ imply that $x^\natural \neq y^\natural$. A regular language is **1-deterministic** if it is denoted by some 1-deterministic expression.

In other words, for each string w denoted by a 1-deterministic expression E, there is exactly one marked string v in $L(E')$ such that $v^\natural = w$. Furthermore, v can be constructed incrementally by examining the next symbol of w which must match the next position of v. It is not hard to see that this definition is independent of the marking E' chosen for E. We now give an alternative definition in terms of the pairs of positions that follow each other in a string of $L(E')$.

Definition 2. For each language L, we define the following sets:

$$first(L) = \{b | \text{there is a string } w \text{ such that } bw \in L\},$$

$$last(L) = \{b | \text{there is a string } w \text{ such that } wb \in L\},$$

$$follow(L, a) = \{b | \text{there are strings } v \text{ and } w \text{ such that } vabw \in L, \}$$

for each symbol a, and

$$followlast(L) = \{b | \text{there are strings } v \text{ and } w \text{ such that } v \neq \epsilon \in L \text{ and } vbw \in L\}.$$

Furthermore, for each expression E, we extend the sets to expressions E by defining $first(E)$ to be $first(L(E))$ and similarly for the other sets.

Using these sets we can give an alternative characterization of 1-deterministic expressions that is not difficult to prove.

Lemma 3. *An expression E is 1-deterministic if and only if the following two conditions hold:*

1. *For all x, y in $first(E')$, $x \neq y$ implies that $x^{\natural} \neq y^{\natural}$.*
2. *For all z in $sym(E')$ and x, y in $follow(E', z)$, $x \neq y$ implies that $x^{\natural} \neq y^{\natural}$.*

Glushkov [15] and McNaughton and Yamada [23] were the first to construct finite-state machines from marked expressions using the functions $first$, $last$, and $follow$; the machines they construct are, however, deterministic. Motivated by the work of Glushkov, Book et al. [3] define a nondeterministic finite-state machine G_E, for each expression E, that we call the **Glushkov machine** of E. Pin [26] observes that a finite-state machine for an expression E can be constructed from the $first$, $last$, and $follow$ functions of E as opposed to a marking of E, provided that the language denoted by E is local. Berry and Sethi [2] argue that Glushkov machines are natural representations of regular expressions.

Definition 4. We define the Glushkov machine $G_E = (Q_E, \Sigma, \delta_E, s, F_E)$ of an expression E as follows.

1. $Q_E = sym(E') \cup \{s\}$; that is, the states of G_E are the positions of E' together with a new start state s.
2. $(s, a, x) \in \delta_E$ if $x \in first(E')$ and $x^{\natural} = a$, for some $a \in \Sigma$.
3. $(x, a, y) \in \delta_E$ if $y \in follow(E', x)$ and $y^{\natural} = a$, for some $x \in sym(E')$ and $a \in \Sigma$.
4. $F_E = \begin{cases} last(E') \cup \{s\}, & \text{if } \epsilon \in L(E), \\ last(E'), & \text{otherwise.} \end{cases}$

Book *et al.* [3] established that $L(G_E) = L(E)$. In addition, the following simple observations emerge directly from the definition of the Glushkov machine. Let E be a regular expression; then:

1. The Glushkov machine G_E has no transitions that lead to the start state; that is, it is **nonreturning** [22].
2. Any two transitions that lead to the same state in G_E have identical input symbols.

Using Glushkov machines, we can give another characterization of 1-deterministic expressions that is a direct consequence of Lemma 3.

Lemma 5. *A regular expression E is 1-deterministic if and only if G_E is deterministic.*

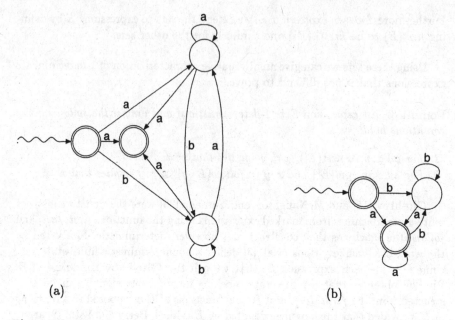

(a)   (b)

Fig. 4. The Glushkov machines corresponding to (a) $(a+b)*a+\epsilon$ and (b) $(b*a)*$.

Fig. 4(a) demonstrates that $(a|b) * a|\epsilon$ is not a 1-deterministic expression. Nevertheless, the language denoted by $(a|b) * a|\epsilon$ is a 1-deterministic language, since it is also denoted by $(b * a)*$, which is a 1-deterministic expression; see Fig. 4(b).

The Glushkov machine G_E can be computed in time quadratic in the size of E, which is worst case optimal [4, 5, 12]. We can also construct the Glushkov machine G_E by induction on E. The inductive definition goes back to Mirkin [24] and Leiss [22]. Recently, Champarnaud has shown that both methods produce the same machine [11]; see also the taxonomy of Watson [32].

We can use the Glushkov machine to test for 1-determinism as follows. During the construction of the machine from an expression E we terminate the construction as soon as we identify two transitions from the same source state that have the same input symbol, but different target states. If we meet two such transitions the expression is not 1-deterministic; otherwise, it is 1-deterministic. We can implement this testing-by-construction algorithm to run in time linear in the size of E.

But what about the 1-determinism of content models? The major difference between regular expressions and content models is that content models have three additional operators: '?', '&', and '+'. They are defined as follows: $E? \equiv E|\epsilon$, $E+ \equiv EE*$, and $E\&F \equiv (EF|FE)$. Clearly, we can remove the operators by using these equivalences to replace them with equivalent expressions; however, the removal of '&' and '+' may change the 1-determinism of the original expression (the removal of '?' does not change the 1-determinism of an expression). For example, $(a?\&b)$ is 1-deterministic, but $(a?b|ba?)$ is not 1-deterministic. Similarly, $(a*|b)+$ is 1-deterministic, but $(a*|b)(a*|b)*$ is not 1-deterministic. Brüggemann-Klein [6, 7] has demonstrated that the approach based on *first*, *last*, and *follow* sets can be modified to avoid the direct computation of the Glushkov machine. This observation is crucial since the corresponding Glushkov machine can have size exponential in the size of the expression (when '&' occurs). For example, the minimal deterministic finite-state machine for the content model $(a_1\&a_2\& \cdots \&a_n)$ has size $\Omega(2^n)$. Similarly, using the preceding equivalence to remove '&' from an expression can also lead to exponential blow up in the size of the expression. To summarize, we have the following result.

Theorem 6. *Given a regular expression or content model, we can decide whether it is 1-deterministic in time linear in its size.*

One important implication of this work is that it has been assumed that SGML DTDs are LL(1); however, this is only the case when the content models are 1-deterministic. Moreover, to construct an LL(1) parser from the DTD in this case means that we need to convert the content models into deterministic finite-state machines and they may have size exponential in the size of the content model.

Lastly, what if an expression or content model is not 1-deterministic? It turns out that the cycle structure of the Glushkov machine (called the **orbit property**) is preserved under minimization when it is deterministic [9, 8]. Thus, if the minimal deterministic machine for a regular expression does not satisfy the orbit property, then the corresponding language is not 1-deterministic. Using this result, it is not difficult to establish that the language of the regular expression $(a|b)*(ac|bd)$ is not 1-deterministic [8] although it is LL(1) since every regular language is LL(1). For example, the following LL(1) grammar generates this language:

$$
\begin{aligned}
S &\rightarrow aC \mid bD \\
C &\rightarrow c \mid aC \mid bD \\
D &\rightarrow d \mid aC \mid bD.
\end{aligned}
$$

The condition can be modified to give a necessary and sufficient condition for a regular language to be 1-deterministic and, hence, give a worst-case exponential-time algorithm to construct a 1-deterministic expression from an expression for a 1-deterministic language.

4   Equivalence

Given two SGML DTDs a natural and fundamental question is whether they are equivalent in some sense [10, 21, 28]. The most basic equivalence is language equality: Two DTDs are equivalent if their languages are the same. For SGML DTDs, because document instances include the start and end tags of the DTD, the basic equivalence is a very strong equivalence: Two SGML DTDs are equivalent if and only if they define exactly the same sets of syntax trees. Moreover, this property holds if and only if the two DTDs have exactly the same elements and the content models of identical elements are language equivalent. Since we can decide language equivalence for content models, we can decide SGML-DTD equivalence.

Although the decidability of SGML-DTD equivalence is of practical interest, SGML-DTD equivalence is too restrictive. For example, if we rename some of the elements in an SGML DTD, then the resulting DTD is not equivalent to the original DTD with respect to the preceding definition of equivalence. Thus, we wish to generalize the notion of equivalence such that it is still decidable, yet can capture such examples. **Structural equivalence** is such an equivalence. Two SGML DTDs are structurally equivalent if, when we replace all occurrences of start and end tags with <> and </>, respectively, in every document instance, the resulting languages are the same. We are, essentially, stripping the element labels from the syntax trees. A result of Thatcher [29] demonstrates, by way of tree machines, that structural equivalence is decidable for ECFGs. Cameron and Wood [10] reprove this result directly for ECFGs. They provide normalizations of two ECFGs such that the resulting grammars are structurally equivalent if and only if they are isomorphic. Although structural equivalence is decidable, the known algorithms take time doubly exponential in the total size of the two grammars. Two open problems are: Prove a nontrivial lower bound for the structural-equivalence problem for ECFGs and determine restricted versions of structural equivalence that are useful for SGML DTDs and investigate their time complexities.

5 Exceptions

SGML allows **exceptions** in content models that modify the corresponding contents. **Inclusion exceptions** allow named elements to appear anywhere within the content, whereas **exclusion exceptions** preclude them from the content. For example, we might want to allow notes to appear anywhere in the body of messages, except within notes themselves. This extension of the DTD of Fig. 1 could be defined by adding an inclusion exception to the EDT of body; namely,

```
<!ELEMENT body              (paragraph)* +(note)>
```

To prevent notes from appearing within notes we could then add the following ETD that has an exclusion exception for note:

```
<!ELEMENT note              (#PCDATA) -(note)>
```

A similar example is the specification of the legal positions for comments in the programs of a programming language. Typically, comments are defined precisely, but their placement is defined informally. The reason is a simple one, the element 'comment' would have to be added everywhere in the right-hand sides of the productions of the programming-language grammar. Such additions make the grammar unreadable and provide a justification for the use of exceptions.

Exclusion exceptions seem to be an especially useful concept, but their exact meaning is unclear from the Standard. We provide rigorous definitions for the meaning of both inclusion and exclusion exceptions and also discuss the transformation of grammars with exceptions to grammars without exceptions. This approach is based on the work of Kilpeläinen and Wood [21] who show that exceptions do not increase the expressive power of SGML DTDs.

Most existing SGML parsers deal with exceptions. The Amsterdam SGML parser [31] handles them in an *interpretive manner*. The names of excluded elements are kept in a stack, which is consulted whenever the parser encounters a new element. Inclusions are handled through the error routine. Whenever an input element that does not match the current content model is encountered, the parser enters its error mode. If the element is an allowed inclusion, the parser calls itself recursively with the included element as the root symbol of the parse.

We *compile* exceptions to produce a DTD that is "equivalent" to the original DTD but does not use any exceptions. In the worst case this transformation may increase the number of elements by a factor that is exponential in the number of the exceptions. An application that requires the elimination of exceptions from content models is the translation of DTDs into static database schemas. This method of integrating text documents into an object-oriented database has been suggested by Christofides *et al.* [13].

The SGML standard requires content models to be unambiguous (or 1-deterministic, see Section 3) and the methods of eliminating exceptions preserve the 1-determinism of the original content models. In this respect exception elimination extends the work of Brüggemann-Klein and Wood [9, 6, 8]. The Standard also gives vague restrictions on the applicability of exclusion exceptions. We propose a simple and rigorous definition of the applicability of exclusions, and present an optimal algorithm for testing applicability.

We first discuss exceptions in the simplified setting of ECFGs (see Section 2) before dealing with the SGML specific problems of how to preserve 1-determinism and how to check the applicability of exclusions.

An **ECFG with exceptions** $G = (N, \Sigma, P, S)$ is similar to an ECFG, but now the production schemas in P have the form $A \to E + I - X$, where I and X are subsets of N. The intuitive idea is that a derivation of any string w from nonterminal A using the production schema $A \to E + I - X$ must not involve any nonterminal in X but w may include, in any position, strings that are derivable from nonterminals in I. When a nonterminal is both included and excluded, its exclusion overrides its inclusion.

We first describe formally the effect of inclusions and exclusions on languages. Let L be a language over alphabet V, and let $I, X \subseteq V$. We define the **language L with inclusions I** as the set

$$L_{+I} = \{w_0 a_1 w_1 \cdots a_n w_n \mid a_1 \cdots a_n \in L, n \geq 0, \text{ and } w_i \in I^* \text{ for } i = 0, \ldots, n\}.$$

Hence, L_{+I} consists of the strings in L interleaved with arbitrary strings over I. The **language L with exclusions X**, denoted by L_{-X}, consists of the strings in L that do not contain any symbol in X. Notice that $(L_{+I})_{-X} \subseteq (L_{-X})_{+I}$, but the converse does not hold in general. We write L_{+I-X} for $(L_{+I})_{-X}$.

We describe formally the global effect of exceptions by attaching exceptions to nonterminals and by defining derivations from nonterminals with exceptions. We denote a nonterminal A with inclusions I and exclusions X by A_{+I-X}. When w is a string over $\Sigma \cup N$, we denote by $w_{\pm(I,X)}$ the string obtained from w by replacing each nonterminal A by A_{+I-X}. Let $\beta_1 A_{+I-X}\beta_2$ be a string over terminal symbols and nonterminals with exceptions. We say that the string $\beta_1\alpha'\beta_2$ can be derived from $\beta_1 A_{+I-X}\beta_2$, denoted by $\beta_1 A_{+I-X}\beta_2 \Rightarrow \beta_1\alpha'\beta_2$, when the following two conditions are met:

1. $A \rightarrow E + I_A - X_A$ is a production schema in P.
2. $\alpha' = \alpha_{\pm(I \cup I_A, X \cup X_A)}$ for some string α in $L(E)_{+(I \cup I_A)-(X \cup X_A)}$.

Finally, the **language L(G) described by an ECFG G with exceptions** is the set of terminal strings derivable from the sentence symbol with empty inclusions and exclusions. Formally, $L(G) = \{w \in \Sigma^* \mid S_{+\emptyset-\emptyset} \Rightarrow^+ w\}$.

Exceptions would seem to be a context-dependent feature: legal expansions of a nonterminal depend on the context in which the nonterminal appears. But exceptions do not extend the expressive power of ECFGs, as we show by presenting a transformation that produces an ECFG that is equivalent to an ECFG with exceptions. The transformation consists of propagating exceptions to production schemas and of modifying regular expressions to capture the effect of exceptions.

Let us first see how to modify regular expressions to capture the effect of exceptions. Let E be a regular expression over $V = \Sigma \cup N$ and $I = \{i_1, \ldots, i_k\}$. We can produce a regular expression E_{+I} from E such that $L(E_{+I}) = L(E)_{+I}$ as follows. (We assume that either E does not contain $\emptyset$ or $E = \emptyset$; otherwise, we can transform E into an equivalent regular expression that satisfies this assumption by applying the rewrite rules $F\emptyset \rightarrow \emptyset$, $\emptyset F \rightarrow \emptyset$, $F \cup \emptyset \rightarrow F$, $\emptyset \cup F \rightarrow F$, and $\emptyset^* \rightarrow \epsilon$.) E_{+I} can be obtained from E by replacing each occurrence of a symbol $a \in V$ by $(i_1 \cup i_2 \cup \cdots \cup i_k)^* a(i_1 \cup i_2 \cup \cdots \cup i_k)^*$, and each occurrence of ϵ by $(i_1 \cup i_2 \cup \cdots \cup i_k)^*$. For a set of excluded elements X we obtain a regular expression E_{-X} such that $L(E_{-X}) = L(E)_{-X}$ by replacing each occurrence of any symbol $a \in X$ in E by $\emptyset$.

An algorithm for eliminating exceptions from an ECFG G with exceptions is given in Fig. 5. The algorithm produces an ECFG G' that is equivalent to G. The correctness of the algorithm is proved by Kilpeläinen and Wood [21]. The nonterminals of G' are of the form A_{+I-X}, where $A \in N$ and $I, X \subseteq N$. A derivation step using a new production schema $A_{+I-X} \rightarrow E$ in P' corresponds to a derivation step using an old production schema for nonterminal A under inclusions I and exclusions X.

The algorithm terminates since it generates at most $2^{2|N|}$ new nonterminals of the form A_{+I-X}. In the worst case the algorithm can exhibit this potentially exponential behavior. As an example consider the following ECFG with exceptions:

$$A \rightarrow (A_1 \cup \cdots \cup A_m) + \emptyset - \emptyset$$
$$A_1 \rightarrow (a_1 \cup A) + \{A_2\} - \emptyset$$

$$N' := \{A_{+\emptyset-\emptyset} \mid A \in N\};$$
$$S' := S_{+\emptyset-\emptyset};$$
$$\Sigma' := \Sigma;$$
$$P'' := \{A_{+\emptyset-\emptyset} \to E + I - X \mid (A \to E + I - X) \in P\};$$
while there is some $(A_{+I_A-X_A} \to E + I - X) \in P''$ for which there
  is such a nonterminal $B \in (sym(E) \cup I) - X$ that $B_{+I-X} \notin N'$
do $N' := N' \cup \{B_{+I-X}\};$
        $P'' := P'' \cup \{B_{+I-X} \to E_B + (I \cup I_B) - (X \cup X_B) \mid$
            $(B_{+\emptyset-\emptyset} \to E_B + I_B - X_B) \in P''\};$
od;
$$P' := \{A_{+I_A-X_A} \to E_A \mid (A_{+I_A-X_A} \to E + I - X) \in P'',$$
        $$E_A = ((E_{+I})_{-X})_{\pm(I,X)};$$

Fig. 5. Elimination of exceptions from an ECFG with exceptions.

$$A_2 \to (a_2 \cup A) + \{A_3\} - \emptyset$$
$$\vdots$$
$$A_m \to (a_m \cup A) + \{A_1\} - \emptyset.$$

The algorithm in Fig. 5 produces production schemas of the form $A_{+I-\emptyset} \to E$ for every subset $I \subseteq \{A_1, \ldots, A_m\}$. We do not know whether this behavior can be avoided; that is, whether it always possible to have an ECFG G' that is (structurally) equivalent to an ECFG G with exceptions such that the size of G' is bounded by a polynomial in the size of G.

We now turn to the compilation of inclusions into content models, giving content models that (locally) realize the effect of the inclusions. The SGML standard describes the basic meaning of inclusions as follows: "Elements named in an inclusion can occur anywhere within the content of the element being defined, including anywhere in the content of its subelements." The description is refined by the rule specifying that "an element that can satisfy an element token in the content model is considered to do so, even if the element is also an inclusion." For example, a content model $(a|b)$ with inclusion a gives baa but does not gives aab. The Standard recommends that inclusions "should be used only for elements that are not logically part of the content"; for example, neither for a nor for b in the preceding example. Since complications occur because of exactly the inclusion of elements that appear in the content model, we have to consider them carefully.

We start by formalizing the effect of inclusions according to the SGML standard. Let L be a language over alphabet V. We need to refer to the first symbol of strings in a language L and to the left quotient of L with respect to some given string. We define the two sets:

$$first(L) = \{a \in V \mid au \in L \text{ for some } u \in V^*\}.$$

and

$$leftq(L, w) = \{u \in V^* \mid wu \in L\}, \text{ for every } w \in V^*.$$

Let I be a subset of V. We define the **SGML effect of inclusions I on language L** as the set

$$L_{\oplus I} = \{w_0 a_1 \cdots w_{n-1} a_n w_n \mid a_1 \cdots a_n \in L, n \geq 0,$$
$$w_i \in (I - first(leftq(L, a_1 \cdots a_i)))^*, i = 0, \ldots, n\} .$$

For example, the language $\{ab, ba\}_{\oplus\{a\}}$ consists of strings $a^k b a^l$ and ba^k where $k \geq 1$ and $l \geq 0$.

The basic idea of compiling the inclusion of symbols $\{i_1, \ldots, i_k\}$ in a content model E is to insert new subexpressions of the form $(i_1 | \cdots | i_k)^*$ in E. Preserving the 1-determinism of the content model requires some extra care however. Consider through an example the complications caused by the $\&$ operator. For example, the content model $E = a?\&b$ is easily seen to be 1-deterministic. A content model that captures the inclusion of symbol a in E should give a string of as after b. A straightforward transformation would produce a content model of the forms $F\&(ba^*)$ or $(F\&b)a^*$, with $a \in first(L(F))$ and $\epsilon \in L(F)$. It easy to see that these content models are not 1-deterministic and that $L(E)_{\oplus a} \neq L(F)$ since $\epsilon \in L(F)$.

Our strategy to handle such problematic subexpressions $F\&G$ is first to replace them by an equivalent subexpression $(FG|GF)$. Notice that this may not suffice, since $FG|GF$ can be ambiguous even if $F\&G$ is 1-deterministic. For example, the content model $(a?b|ba?)$ is ambiguous. To circumvent this problem we define a transformation of a content model E into a content model E° that gives the same strings as E except for the empty string. Moreover, we can now apply the previously mentioned strategy to E° to give a new content model $E_{\oplus I}$ that has the desired properties. These properties can be summarized as follows:

1. E° is 1-deterministic if and only if E is 1-deterministic.
2. The content model $E_{\oplus I}$ is 1-deterministic if E is 1-deterministic.
3. $L(E_{\oplus I}) = L(E^\circ)_{\oplus I} = L(E)_{\oplus I}$.

Thus, for each 1-deterministic content model with inclusions we can construct an equivalent 1-deterministic content model without inclusions.

We now provide a precise definition of the meaning of exclusions, and present an efficient method of checking their validity and of modifying content models to capture the effect of exclusions.

Clause 11.2.5.2 of the SGML standard states that "exclusions modify the effect of model groups to which they apply by precluding options that would otherwise have been available." The exact meaning of "precluding options" is not clear from the Standard. Our first task is therefore to formalize the intuitive notion of exclusion rigorously. As a motivating example consider the exclusion of the symbol b from the content model $E = a(b|c)c$ that defines the language $L(E) = \{abc, acc\}$. Element b is clearly an alternative to the first occurrence of c and we can realize its exclusion by modifying the content model to give $E' = acc$. Now, consider excluding b from the content model $F = a(bc|cc)$. The situation is less clear since b appears in a catenation subexpression. Observe that both E and F define the same language.

Let $L \subseteq V^*$ and $X \subseteq V$. Motivated by the preceding example we define the effect of excluding X from L, denoted by L_{-X}, as the set of the strings in L that do not contain any symbol of X. As an example, the effect of excluding $\{b\}$ from the languages of the preceding content models E and F is $L(E)_{-\{b\}} = L(F)_{-\{b\}} = \{acc\}$. Notice that an exclusion always gives a subset of the original language.

We now describe how we can compute, for a given content model E and a given set of symbols X, a content model $E_{\ominus X}$ such that $L(E_{\ominus X}) = L(E)_{-X}$. The modified content model $E_{\ominus X}$ is 1-deterministic if the original content model E is 1-deterministic. The computation of $E_{\ominus X}$ takes time linear in the size of E.

For the transformation we extend content models with symbols ϵ and $\emptyset$, which are constituents of standard regular expressions. Their addition extends the definition of the language $L(E)$ represented by a content model E with the following two cases:

$$L(\epsilon) = \epsilon. \; L(\emptyset) = \{\emptyset\}.$$

For a content model E, the extended content model $E_{\ominus X}$ is defined inductively as follows:

$$a_{\ominus X} = \begin{cases} \emptyset \text{ if } a \in X, \\ a \text{ otherwise.} \end{cases}$$

$$(FG)_{\ominus X} = \begin{cases} \emptyset & \text{if } F_{\ominus X} = \epsilon \text{ or } G_{\ominus X} = \epsilon, \\ F_{\ominus X} & \text{if } G_{\ominus X} = \epsilon, \\ G_{\ominus X} & \text{if } F_{\ominus X} = \epsilon, \\ F_{\ominus X} G_{\ominus X} & \text{otherwise.} \end{cases}$$

$$(F|G)_{\ominus X} = \begin{cases} F_{\ominus X} & \text{if } G_{\ominus X} = \emptyset, \\ G_{\ominus X} & \text{if } F_{\ominus X} = \emptyset, \\ \epsilon & \text{if } F_{\ominus X} = \epsilon \text{ and } G_{\ominus X} = \epsilon, \\ F_{\ominus X}? & \text{if } F_{\ominus X} \neq \epsilon \text{ and } G_{\ominus X} = \epsilon, \\ G_{\ominus X}? & \text{if } F_{\ominus X} = \epsilon \text{ and } G_{\ominus X} \neq \epsilon, \\ F_{\ominus X}|G_{\ominus X} & \text{otherwise.} \end{cases}$$

$$(F\&G)_{\ominus X} = \begin{cases} \emptyset & \text{if } F_{\ominus X} = \emptyset \text{ or } G_{\ominus X} = \emptyset, \\ F_{\ominus X} & \text{if } G_{\ominus X} = \epsilon, \\ G_{\ominus X} & \text{if } F_{\ominus X} = \epsilon, \\ F_{\ominus X}\&G_{\ominus X} & \text{otherwise.} \end{cases}$$

$$(F?)_{\ominus X} = \begin{cases} \epsilon & \text{if } F_{\ominus X} = \emptyset \text{ or } F_{\ominus X} = \epsilon, \\ F_{\ominus X}? & \text{otherwise.} \end{cases}$$

$$(F^*)_{\ominus X} = \begin{cases} \epsilon & \text{if } F_{\ominus X} = \emptyset \text{ or } F_{\ominus X} = \epsilon, \\ (F_{\ominus X})^* & \text{otherwise.} \end{cases}$$

$$(F^+)_{\ominus X} = \begin{cases} \emptyset & \text{if } F_{\ominus X} = \emptyset, \\ \epsilon & \text{if } F_{\ominus X} = \epsilon, \\ (F_{\ominus X})^+ & \text{otherwise.} \end{cases}$$

The following properties justify the definition of $E_{\ominus X}$:

1. $E_{\ominus X}$ is a content model (that is, $E_{\ominus X}$ does not contain $\emptyset$ or ϵ) if and only if $E_{\ominus X} \notin \{\emptyset, \epsilon\}$.
2. $L(E_{\ominus X}) = \emptyset$ if and only if $E_{\ominus X} = \emptyset$.
3. $L(E_{\ominus X}) = \{\epsilon\}$ if and only if $E_{\ominus X} = \epsilon$.
4. $L(E_{\ominus X}) = L(E)_{-X}$.
5. If E is 1-deterministic, then $E_{\ominus X}$ is 1-deterministic.

As a restriction to the applicability of exclusions the Standard states that "an exclusion cannot affect a specification in a model group that indicates that an element is required." The Standard does not specify how a model group (a subexpression of a content model) indicates that an element is required. A reasonable requirement for the applicability of excluding X from a content model E would be $L(E)_{-X} \not\subseteq \{\epsilon\}$. Note that an ordinary content model cannot denote a language that is either $\emptyset$ or $\{\epsilon\}$. Intuitively, $E_{\ominus X} = \emptyset$ or $E_{\ominus X} = \epsilon$ means that excluding X from E precludes all elements from the content of E. On the other hand, $E_{\ominus X} \notin \{\emptyset, \epsilon\}$ means that X precludes only elements that are optional in $L(E)$. Thus computing $E_{\ominus X}$ is a reasonable and efficient test for the applicability of exclusions X to a content model E.

6   Omitted Tag Minimization

SGML allows us to specify that a tag is optional. It is crucial, however, that when a tag is omitted its position can be uniquely deduced from the context. For example, with the DTD

```
<!ELEMENT S        O -    (a, a?, S?)>
```

the start tag `<S>` is optional. Observe that we have added two fields after the element name, the first one refers to the start tag and the second to the end tag. There are two possible values: '−' meaning cannot be omitted and 'O' meaning may be omitted. Then with the string

<code><S>aaa</S></S></code>,

we do not know whether we should insert the missing `<S>` after the first 'a' or after the second 'a'; that is we do not know whether the fully tagged string should be

<code><S>a<S>aa</S></S></code>

or should be

`<S>aa<S>a</S></S>.`

As with many other features of the Standard, omitted tag minimization is an unfortunate feature. It is clear that it is useful to allow marked-up texts that already exist to have omitted tags; for example LaTeX has the start tag \section but it has no corresponding tag for the end of a section. Thus, there is a good reason for allowing tag minimization, although the implementation of the tag omission leaves much to be desired. Goldfarb's annotations [17] explain the strict rules under which omitted tags can actually be omitted. It is unclear from his discussion whether a tag that is marked for possible omission can be omitted in some documents but not in others. Can we decide whether a tag can always be omitted, sometimes be omitted and in what circumstances, or never be omitted? Currently we are investigating these and related problems.

As a final example of omitted tag minimization, we have a modified version of the e-mail DTD given in Fig. 6. Observe that we may omit the start tag of head and the end tags of from, to, and body. In all document instances we can always deduce the positions of the omitted tags.

```
<!DOCTYPE message [
<!ELEMENT message      - -    (head, body)>
<!ELEMENT head         O -    (from & to & subject)>
<!ELEMENT from         - O    (person)>
<!ELEMENT to           - O    (person)+>
<!ELEMENT person       - -    (alias | (forename?, surname))>
<!ELEMENT body         - O    (paragraph)*>
<!ELEMENT subject, alias, forename, surname, paragraph
                       - -    (#PCDATA)> ]>
```

Fig. 6. The example DTD with omitted tag minimization.

7   Documents, Markup, and Structure

A document is inherently structured at a fine-grained level since it can be defined as a structured collection of marks on a medium (as against a random collection of marks). This definition of a document indicates a truism: structure is in the mind of the author and the reader. The fine-grained concept of structure carries over to coarser-grained levels. For example, this paper has a typical report structure: a footnoted title, author, author's address, abstract, a sequence of sections, and a collection of references. This structure is logical (or descriptive) in that it is independent of content and, hence, of the content's meaning. The logical structure is identified by the author and it can be indicated with markup in general and SGML markup in particular. It is not, however, the only logical structure of this paper. We have a page structure that is defined by the typeset layout of the paper; we have a version structure that indicates the different versions (or revisions) of the paper from its inception to its present form; we have a referential structure that indicates the cross-referencing. There are no footnotes in the body of the paper, but in legal reviews and papers in the humanities they are usually in abundance. *A document can have many logical structures and we cannot always consider only one of them.* The version and report structures are critical structures that need to be maintained in many situations. For example, consider the evolution of a user manual for some system. The user manual will have a report structure and one or two version structures. It is important, in this context, that users be informed of documentation changes for the same version of the system as well as of documentation changes when a new version of the system is distributed.

When faced with a mechanism such as SGML to define markup and markup systems we are invariably led to question its foundations, its raison d'être [27, 28]. Is this method, however attractive and however much used, the most appropriate? Are there similar, yet more widely embracing methods? Is SGML, or something very similar, an inevitable conclusion of the Western history of documents; for example, of manuscripts, books, and electronic documents? Is SGML an irrelevance, in that it is addressing the wrong problem?

We are discussing only textual documents here, although they may be small or large, simple or complex. Punctuation, sentences, and paragraphs are methods of markup (they were introduced in the eighth century) as are the reserved words of Pascal and the use of indentation in displayed Pascal programs. At a completely different level, the start and stop codons that delimit the aminoacid sequences that are genes in chromosomes are also markup (a DNA helix can be viewed as the medium on which the genes are the message). In each of these examples, markup is **embedded** in the text. Although markup need not be embedded (we discuss this issue later in this section), it is often most convenient to have it so and, historically, markup is embedded. Second, the markup is **distinguishable** from the non-markup. For example, punctuation is distinguishable as are start and stop codons and Pascal reserved words. Distinguishability is not necessarily easy to compute; thus, we can only separate Pascal reserved words by parsing a Pascal program. Third, **positioning** is also a feature of these kinds of markup in that none of the markup can be moved without changing a document's structure and meaning. To find a period, which is not associated with an abbreviation or with a decimal number, in the middle of a sentence would produce two sentences were only one was intended.

SGML markup is also embedded, distinguishable, and positioned. In addition, it is **separable, nested, context-free,** and **contiguous.** Separability is stronger than distinguishability in that the markup begins and ends with unique characters. It is nested in that it does not allow markup of the form

<A>...<B>...</A>...</B>.

It is context-free in that its legal nestings and adjacencies are specified with a context-free grammar. Lastly, it is **contiguous** in that it is not interrupted and then resumed. Embedding, distinguishability, and positioning are required properties for the markup of most documents, whereas separability, nesting, context-freeness, and contiguity are not obviously necessary properties. Let us reexamine the latter four properties of SGML markup.

The use of the delimiters '<' and '>' to begin and end tags is not mandated by the SGML standard; we may choose different symbols for them. But, in all cases, we have separability—it is an inherent property of SGML. One reason for requiring this strong version of distinguishability is purely algorithmic—the ease of recognizing tags. Certainly, in a programming language such as ALGOL 60, the markup strings such as while and do can be detected as markup only when a full parse of a program is carried out because a programmer, however unwisely, can use them as variable names. The separation of markup in SGML documents is, in general, more straightforward; it requires only the power of a finite-state transducer. Therefore, separation (or tokenization) is fast.

Nesting and context-freeness are interrelated. SGML DTDs generate nested structures and every context-free language can be viewed as the image of nested structures (the Chomsky–Schützenberger Theorem). But not all nested structures can be obtained in this way. For example, consider a set of documents that exhibit structures of the forms

$$\texttt{<A>}^i \ldots \texttt{</A>}^i \ldots \texttt{<B>}^i \ldots \texttt{</B>}^i,$$

for $i \geq 1$, such that for each $i \geq 1$ there is a document with that structure and, in addition, a substructure of the form $\texttt{<A>}^i$ denotes a string of i copies of $\texttt{<A>}$ interleaved with text. Then, no SGML DTD can specify such markup. Indeed, even with documents of the form

$$\texttt{<A>}^i \ldots \texttt{</A>}^i,$$

where $i = 2^k$, for every $k \geq 0$, is not specifiable with any SGML DTD. The documents in each case are SGML-like, but they are not SGML documents or, to be more precise, they do not form a class of SGML documents. We can always give a DTD for finitely many documents of these forms, but not for **all** of them.

Next, context-freeness while not the most powerful grammatical mechanism has become the standard approach in the programming-language community. The reason is easy to understand; there are fast parsing methods available for context-free grammars and even faster methods for deterministic context-free grammars—SGML DTDs are LL(1).

To summarize, while nesting is an important property it can be too restrictive. The only argument for nesting as the sole bracketed structure in SGML is that, when there are no constraints among the different tags, the structures can be specified by a context-free grammar.

Finally, contiguity is too restrictive. It implies that a string between matching tags $\texttt{<A>}$ and $\texttt{</A>}$, belongs to A and only to A. But take the example of genes once more. Surprisingly, the aminoacid sequence that makes up a gene does not necessarily (indeed rarely) occur as a string; there are usually gaps between the pieces of a gene. A similar example is seen in a conversation. When two or more people are conversing their utterances do not always occur sequentially and con-tiguously, an utterance begins, pauses while another person's utterance begins or continues, the original utterance continues, pauses again, and so on, until it ends. The parts of utterances are interleaved. When expressing this interaction of concurrent processes in a play, the utterances are also noncontiguous. Thus, we obtain structures such as

$$<A>...<:A><B>...<:B></:A>...<:A>...</A>,$$

where I have used `<:A>` as a start-pause tag and `</:A>` as an end-pause tag. In general the structures that we obtain in this way cannot be described by SGML DTDs.

Thus, the answer to the question, "Is this method, however attractive and however much used, the most appropriate?" is a qualified "Yes."

Let us return to the issue of embedding of markup. It is clear that having markup that is not only separable but also is separated from the text can be very useful. It is easier to define multiple markups of the same document; for example, a version markup that tracks the revision structure of a document, a structural markup that captures one of the logical structures of a document, and an annotational markup that provides a scholar's commentary on the text. Hav-ing said this, the issues of markup do not go away. Often markup is an integral part of the text; for example, Pascal's while-do construct and the punctuation in this sentence. We do not want to and often cannot separate the markup from the text.

Lastly, is SGML wrong headed? Is it addressing the wrong problem? In tra-ditional relational databases, data representation is unimportant, rather the semantics of the query language is central. In other words, the same data in two different databases may be represented very differently, but the same query should give the same answer. The data representation should not interfere with the query mechanism. It is possible that we could approach electronic documents in the same way. For example, we could specify a text algebra that abstracts the notion and properties of text, including textual access and modification. Then, such an algebra could serve as a standard interface to higher-level applications. SGML does not specify such an algebra since it does not provide the algebraic operations that are needed. Raymond *et al.* [28] discuss the meta-semantic issues of SGML in more detail and at a higher level.

8   Acknowledgements

The research that I have surveyed is the result of a number of enjoyable and fruitful collaborations over the years with a small group of individuals: Anne Brüggemann-Klein (who introduced me to both typesetting and SGML as re-search areas and has been a continual mentor), Helen Cameron (who lived through my supervision of her PhD research), Pekka Kilpeläinen (who brought me his carefulness and persistence), Darrell R. Raymond (who broadened and continues to broaden my horizons by his readings and reflections), and Frank W. Tompa (who always has had the patience to share his insights into text and his accumulated wisdom of databases). They are responsible for the results and arguments on which this survey is based; however, I alone am responsible for any errors, misdirections, and misinformation.

References

1. A. V. Aho, R. Sethi, and J. D. Ullman. *Compilers: Principles, Techniques, and Tools.* Addison-Wesley Series in Computer Science. Addison-Wesley Publishing Company, Reading, MA, 1986.

2. G. Berry and R. Sethi. From regular expressions to deterministic automata. *Theoretical Computer Science,* 48:117–126, 1986.

3. R. Book, S. Even, S. Greibach, and G. Ott. Ambiguity in graphs and expressions. *IEEE Transactions on Computers,* C-20(2):149–153, February 1971.

4. A. Brüggemann-Klein. Regular expressions into finite automata. In I. Simon, editor, *Latin '92,* pages 87–98, Berlin, 1992. Springer-Verlag. Lecture Notes in Computer Science 583.

5. A. Brüggemann-Klein. Regular expressions into finite automata. *Theoretical Computer Science,* 120:197–213, 1993.

6. A. Brüggemann-Klein. Unambiguity of extended regular expressions in SGML document grammars. In Th. Lengauer, editor, *Algorithms—ESA '93,* pages 73–84, Berlin, 1993. Springer-Verlag. Lecture Notes in Computer Science 726.

7. A. Brüggemann-Klein. Compiler-construction tools and techniques for SGML parsers: Difficulties and solutions. To appear in *Electronic Publishing—Origination, Dissemination and Design,* 1995.

8. A. Brüggemann-Klein and D. Wood. One-unambiguous regular languages. To appear in *Information and Computation,* 1995.

9. A. Brüggemann-Klein and D. Wood. The validation of SGML content models. To appear in *Mathematical and Computer Modelling,* 1995.

10. H. Cameron and D. Wood. Structural equivalence of extended context-free and E0L grammars. Submitted for publication, 1995.

11. J.-M. Champarnaud. From a regular expression to an automaton. Unpublished Manuscript, 1992.

12. C.-H. Chen and R. Paige. New theoretical and computational results for regular languages. Technical report 587, Courant Institute, New York University, 1992. *Proceedings of the Third Symposium on Combinatorial Pattern Matching.*

13. V. Christofides, S. Christofides, S. Cluet, and M. Scholl. From structured documents to novel query facilities. In *Proceedings of the 1994 ACM SIGMOD International Conference on Management of Data,* pages 313–324, 1994. SIGMOD Record, 23(2).

14. S. J. DeRose and D. G. Durand. *Making Hypermedia Work: A User's Guide to HyTime.* Kluwer Academic, Boston, 1994.

15. V. M. Glushkov. The abstract theory of automata. *Russian Mathematical Surveys,* 16:1–53, 1961.

16. C. F. Goldfarb. A generalized approach to document markup. *Proceedings of the ACM SIGPLAN SIGOA Symposium on Text Manipulation,* pages 68–73, June 1981. SIGPLAN Notices of the ACM.

17. C. F. Goldfarb. *The SGML Handbook*. Clarendon Press, Oxford, 1990.

18. ISO 8879: Information processing—Text and office systems—Standard Generalized Markup Language (SGML), October 1986. International Organization for Standardization.

19. ISO/IEC CD 10744: Information Technology—Hypermedia/Time-based structuring language (HyTime), 1991. International Organization for Standardization.

20. ISO/DIS 10179.2: Information processing—Text and office systems—Document style semantics and specification language (DSSSL), 1994. International Organization for Standardization.

21. P. Kilpeläinen and D. Wood. Exceptions in SGML document grammars. Submitted for publication, 1995.

22. E. Leiss. The complexity of restricted regular expressions and the synthesis problem of finite automata. *Journal of Computer and System Sciences*, 23(3):348–354, December 1981.

23. R. McNaughton and H. Yamada. Regular expressions and state graphs for automata. *IRE Transactions on Electronic Computers*, EC-9(1):39–47, March 1960.

24. B. G. Mirkin. An algorithm for constructing a base in a language of regular expressions. *Engineering Cybernetics*, 5:110–116, 1966.

25. J. Nievergelt, G. Coray, Jean-Daniel Nicoud, and Alan C. Shaw. *Document Preparation Systems*. North Holland, Amsterdam, 1982.

26. J.-E. Pin. Local languages and the Berry-Sethi algorithm. Unpublished Manuscript, 1992.

27. D. R. Raymond, F. W. Tompa, and D. Wood. Markup reconsidered. *Principles of Document Processing*, 1992.

28. D. R. Raymond, F. W. Tompa, and D. Wood. From data representation to data model: Meta-semantic issues in the evolution of SGML. *Computer Standards and Interfaces*, to appear, July, 1995.

29. J.W. Thatcher. Characterizing derivation trees of a context-free grammar through a generalization of finite-automata theory. *Journal of Computer and System Sciences*, 1:317–322, 1967.

30. K. Thompson. Regular expression search algorithm. *Communications of the ACM*, 11(6):419–422, 1968.

31. J. Warmer and S. van Egmond. The implementation of the Amsterdam SGML parser. *Electronic Publishing—Origination, Dissemination and Design*, 2:65–90, 1989.

32. B. W. Watson. A taxonomy of finite automata construction and minimization algorithms. Manuscript, 1993.

33. D. Wood. *Theory of Computation*. John Wiley & Sons, New York, NY, 1987.

Avoiding the Undefined by Underspecification

David Gries* and Fred B. Schneider**

Computer Science Department, Cornell University
Ithaca, New York 14853 USA

Abstract. We use the appeal of simplicity and an aversion to complexity in selecting a method for handling partial functions in logic. We conclude that avoiding the undefined by using underspecification is the preferred choice.

1   Introduction

> Everything should be made as simple as possible, but not any simpler.
> —Albert Einstein

The first volume of Springer-Verlag's *Lecture Notes in Computer Science* appeared in 1973, almost 22 years ago. The field has learned a lot about computing since then, and in doing so it has leaned on and supported advances in other fields. In this paper, we discuss an aspect of one of these fields that has been explored by computer scientists, handling undefined terms in formal logic.

Logicians are concerned mainly with studying logic —not using it. Some computer scientists have discovered, by necessity, that logic is actually a useful tool. Their attempts to use logic have led to new insights —new axiomatizations, new proof formats, new meta-logical notions like relative completeness, and new concerns. We, the authors, are computer scientists whose interests have forced us to become users of formal logic. We use it in our work on language definition and in the formal development of programs. This paper is born of that experience.

The operation of a computer is nothing more than uninterpreted symbol manipulation. Bits are moved and altered electronically, without regard for what they denote. It is we who provide the interpretation, saying that one bit string represents money and another someone's name, or that one transformation represents addition and another alphabetization. Our programs define sequences of uninterpreted symbol manipulations, and we elect to construe these as meaningful transformations on data.

How do we justify a belief that a program performs a meaningful transformation —how do we know that it "works"? Few programs produce outputs that are continuous in their inputs, so testing some input-output pairs and generalizing does not work. It is only by deriving, from a program's text, properties satisfied

---
* Supported by NSF grant CDA-9214957 and ARPA/ONR grant N00014-91-J-4123.
** This material is based on work supported in part by ARPA/NSF Grant No. CCR-9014363, NASA/ARPA grant NAG-2-893, and AFOSR grant F49620-94-1-0198.

by the program that we can be convinced that a program works. And how do we derive those properties? Through the use of formal logic —whose proofs, again, are simply uninterpreted symbol manipulations. Thus, uninterpreted symbol manipulation is the key: the computer uses it to execute programs, and we use it to reason about programs.

Logics were not originally intended to be used in this setting. They were intended primarily to formalize thought processes and the implications of employing various deductive apparatus. Logics were tailored to make their *study* easier. Little thought was given to "proof engineering" —the development and presentation of proofs and formalizations of logic that would make using logic easier. But, fueled by the need for programmers to manipulate logical formulas, programming methodologists began developing logics that were suited to use.

Although work on formal correctness of programs began in the late 1960's, the inadequacies of the standard formulations of propositional and predicate logic did not become apparent until the early 1980's. Since the formal logical systems usually taught (e.g. natural deduction) were unwieldy to use, researchers turned to a time-honored technique from mathematics. For decades, substitution of equals for equals —Leibniz's law— has been pervasive among users of mathematics. It allows them to infer new truths from old ones in a simple and efficient way. Why not make such a calculational style available to users of logic? A first cut at an equational logic for computer scientists appeared in the monograph [4]. Three years later, a freshman-sophomore-level text incorporating the approach appeared [5]. The new approach offers hope for a new view of logic and an entirely different method of teaching logic and proof.

One of the principles guiding research by those studying the formal development of programs has been simplicity and uniformity of concept and notation. Tools should be as simple as possible, if they are to be used reliably. Unnecessary distinctions and details should be avoided. For example, a logic should be usable for developing proofs without formal detail and complexity overwhelming. And, the method of proof presentation should lend itself to proof principles and strategies. Engineering and style are legitimate concerns when constructing proofs, just as they are in other creative activities.

In this article, we illustrate the use of simplicity as a goal by discussing the treatment of undefined terms and partial functions in equational propositional logic E and its extension to predicate logic [5]. Partial functions are ubiquitous in programming —some basic mathematical operations are partial (e.g. division), some basic programming operations are partial (e.g. array subscripting $b[n]$), and many functions that arise through recursive definitions are partial. Therefore, a logic for reasoning about programs must handle partial functions.

All treatments of the undefined exploit what logics do well —reason about variables, terms, and predicates that have *a priori* defined values. Some treatments of the undefined involve adding a new value $\perp$ (to represent "undefined") that may be assumed by a variable, term, or predicate. We discuss this approach in Sec. 2. Other treatments rule out writing formulas in which a variable, term, or predicate cannot be evaluated. Approaches along those lines are discussed

---

Table 1. Inference rules of Logic **E**

(1)   **Substitution** $\vdash P \;\longrightarrow\; \vdash P[\nu := Q]$

(2)   **Leibniz** $\vdash P = Q \;\longrightarrow\; \vdash E[\nu := P] = E[\nu := Q]$

(3)   **Transitivity** $\vdash P = Q,\, Q = R \;\longrightarrow\; \vdash P = R$

(4)   **Equanimity** $\vdash P, P \equiv Q \;\longrightarrow\; \vdash Q$

---

in Sec. 3. Finally, the approach we embrace is discussed in Sec. 4: regard all variables, terms, and predicates as being total, but in some cases underspecified.

2   Adding a new constant for undefined

In propositional logic **E** of [5], substitution of equals for equals (Leibniz (2) of Table 1) is the main inference rule. Further, equivalence $\equiv$ [3] plays a more prominent role than is usual in propositional logics. Heavy use is made of the associativity and symmetry of $\equiv$ in order to reduce the number of different theorems that have to be enumerated. For example, the theorem $p \equiv p \equiv true$ can be parsed in several ways: $(p \equiv p) \equiv true$ indicates that $\equiv$ is reflexive, while $p \equiv (p \equiv true)$ and $p \equiv (true \equiv p)$ indicate that $true$ is the identity of $\equiv$. In addition, many problems are more succinctly and easily formalized and have simpler solutions if properties of $\equiv$ are exploited —see e.g. [5].

In fact, the properties of equivalence are so useful that it is unwise to sacrifice them in an extension to handle the undefined. Equivalence should remain an equivalence relation —reflexive, symmetric, and transitive— and should have the identity $true$. In addition, inference rule Leibniz (substitution of equals for equals), along with the others of Table 1, should remain sound.

Consider changing just the model of evaluation of expressions by introducing a third constant $\perp$ to represent an undefined value. Thus, the value of a propositional variable or term in a state is one of $true$, $false$, and $\perp$. Since $p \equiv p \equiv true$ is a theorem of logic **E**, and since $\equiv$ is associative and symmetric, the following must hold:

- $\perp \equiv \perp$ evaluates to $true$ (since $(\perp \equiv \perp) \equiv true$ is a theorem).
- $\perp \equiv true$ evaluates to $\perp$ (since $(\perp \equiv true) \equiv \perp$ is a theorem).
- $true \equiv \perp$ evaluates to $\perp$ (since $(true \equiv \perp) \equiv \perp$ is a theorem).

Now, what should be the value of $\perp \equiv false$?

---

[3] For booleans b and c, $b = c$ and $b \equiv c$ both denote equality. However, in our logic, operator $=$ is handled conjunctionally, i.e. $b = c = d$ is syntactic sugar for $b = c \land c = d$, while $\equiv$ is handled associatively —since in each state, $b \equiv (c \equiv d)$ and $b \equiv (c \equiv d)$ have the same value, the parentheses may be removed. Later, when dealing with predicate calculus, $=$ is regarded as polymorphic and $b = c$ is an (type-correct) expression iff b and c have the same type.

- Suppose $\bot \equiv false$ evaluates to $false$. Then $(\bot \equiv false) \equiv false$ evaluates to $true$ and $\bot \equiv (false \equiv false)$ evaluates to $\bot$, so $\equiv$ would not be associative.

- Suppose $\bot \equiv false$ evaluates to $true$. Then $(\bot \equiv false) \equiv false$ evaluates to $false$ and $\bot \equiv (false \equiv false)$ evaluates to $\bot$, so $\equiv$ would not be associative.

- Suppose $\bot \equiv false$ evaluates to $\bot$. Then $(\bot \equiv \bot) \equiv false$ evaluates to $false$ and $\bot \equiv (\bot \equiv false)$ evaluates to $true$, so $\equiv$ would not be associative.

With every choice of value for $\bot \equiv false$, associativity of equivalence has to be sacrificed.

Other standard logical properties no longer hold as well, when a constant $\bot$ is added. For example, suppose we take the strict approach: the value of an expression is $\bot$ if any of its constituents are $\bot$. Then, the law of the excluded middle, $p \vee \neg p$, and zero of $\vee$, $true \vee p \equiv true$, are no longer valid.

Any way we turn, the logic has to be changed.

Bijlsma [1] gives a model of evaluation that seems to contradict this conclusion. Through formal manipulation, he arrives at the following proposal:

Suppose expression E contains some variables v whose values are $\bot$ in a state s. E evaluates to $true$ in s iff E evaluates to $true$ with all possible combinations of the values $true$ and $false$ for the values of variables v. Similarly, E evaluates to $false$ in s iff E evaluates to $false$ with all possible combinations of the values $true$ and $false$ for the values of v. Otherwise, E evaluates to $\bot$ in s.

For example, $v \vee \neg v$ and $\bot \equiv \bot$ both evaluate to $true$ in all states, but $v \vee \neg w$ does not.

The apparent contradiction of our conclusion and Bijlsma's proposal is explained by our —hitherto implicit— desire for a *compositional* model of evaluation —the value of an expression must be completely determined by the values of its subexpressions. Bijlsma's proposal is not compositional. For example, consider a state in which v has the value $\bot$. Thus, v and $\neg v$ both have the value $\bot$, so we might assume that $v \vee \neg v$ evaluates to $\bot \vee \bot$, which evaluates to $\bot$. However, by Bijlsma's evaluation rule, $v \vee \neg v$ evaluates to $true$.

Each extension of expression evaluation to include $\bot$ compositionally requires extensive changes in the logic. We are not willing to accept changes in the logic if a more suitable alternative for dealing with undefined terms exists.

As the field has explored handling undefined terms, various proposals have been made to extend two-valued logics. Jones and Middelburg [8], for example, developed a typed version of logic LPF of partial functions. Their extension requires an operator that denotes "definedness" and two kinds of equality (weak and strong). Many useful properties in classical logic (eg. excluded middle and associativity of $\equiv$) do not hold. For us, their logic is far too complicated for use.

3   Abortive approaches that avoid undefined

Some approaches to avoiding partial functions assume a typed predicate logic. In a typed logic, every expression has a type, which can be determined syntactically from the expression itself and the types of its primitive constituents (constants, variables, and function symbols). For example, the type of addition $+$ may be $\mathbb{R} \times \mathbb{R} \to \mathbb{R}$. Types provide structure. Also, compilers for typed programming languages offer significant help in uncovering mistakes early, through type checking, and this help could be made available for a typed predicate calculus as well. Further, having type be a syntactic property allows a more implicit use of properties associated with the type than would otherwise be possible in a safe way. If we know that a variable v is of type $\mathbb{Z}$ (integer), we can use properties of integers —rather than reals or complex numbers— in manipulating formulas containing v, without having to list all those properties explicitly in the formula or to give accompanying text explaining the properties being used. The type annotation $v : \mathbb{Z}$ is enough to alert the reader to the properties that can be used.

One approach to avoiding the undefined is to turn partial functions into total functions by restricting the types of their arguments. For example, instead of giving division the type

$$\mathbb{R} \times \mathbb{R} \to \mathbb{R} \quad ,$$

we give it the type

$$\mathbb{R} \times (\mathbb{R} - \{0\}) \to \mathbb{R} \quad .$$

Unfortunately, with this approach, any set can be a type. Therefore, there is no hope of having type be a syntactic property that can be checked mechanically, since the type system is undecidable. This approach is discussed further in [2].

A second approach (which can be used with a typed or an untyped logic) to avoiding the undefined is to view a function $f : B \to C$ as a relation on $B \times C$. Thus, $f.b = c$ is written as $(b, c) \in f$. Function application $f.b$ cannot be written, and just about the only way to refer to a value of a function is in an expression $(b, c) \in f$. To use this form, one must have an expression c for the value of $f.b$, which is awkward if not impossible in many situations. This approach is discussed briefly in [2].

A third approach (which can be used with a typed or an untyped logic) to avoiding the undefined was suggested by Scott [9]: classify all atomic formulas that contain an undefined term as *false*. This means that the law of the excluded middle holds. However, with almost any partial function, we will be able to find conventional laws that no longer hold. For example, the law of trichotomy of arithmetic,

$$x = 0 \ \lor \ x > 0 \ \lor \ x < 0 \quad ,$$

no longer holds, since $x/0 = 0 \ \lor \ x/0 > 0 \ \lor \ x/0 < 0$ evaluates to *false* (terms $x/0 = 0$, $x/0 > 0$ and $x/0 > 0$ are all undefined). This approach therefore seems unworkable.

4   Avoiding undefined through underspecification

Consider avoiding the undefined by using underspecification:

> All operations and functions are assumed to be defined for all values of their operands —they are *total* operations and functions. However, the value assigned to an expression need not be uniquely specified in all cases.

Thus, the value of every (type-correct) expression is defined. We don't have partial functions, we have underspecified functions. Therefore, our logics don't have to deal with undefined values. The propositional and pure predicate logics need not be changed. This approach to handling the undefined is mentioned in [3].

In this approach, division $/ : \mathbb{R} \times \mathbb{R} \to \mathbb{R}$ has to be total, so what should be the value of $x/0$? According to the above principle, we leave it unspecified. The value of $x/0$ could be 2.4 or $20 \cdot x$ or any value in $\mathbb{R}$; we simply don't say what it is.

Axioms and theorems mentioning an underspecified operation $b \circ c$ usually involve an implication whose antecedent describes the set of states in which $b \circ c$ is uniquely specified.[4] In states in which the antecedent is *false*, the expression evaluates to *true*, even though $b \circ c$ evaluates to some (unknown) value. For example, the law $y/y = 1$ should be written as

(5) $y \neq 0 \; \Rightarrow \; y/y = 1$

because y/y is uniquely specified iff $y \neq 0$.

We can prove theorems that rely on such laws in the standard manner. For example, to prove

$$y \neq 0 \Rightarrow x \cdot y/y = x \quad ,$$

we assume the antecedent $y \neq 0$ and prove the consequent:

$$
\begin{aligned}
& x \cdot y/y \\
= \quad & \langle \text{Modus ponens with assumption } y \neq 0 \text{ and (5) yields } y/y = 1 \rangle \\
& x \cdot 1 = x \\
= \quad & \langle \text{Identity of } \cdot \rangle \\
& x
\end{aligned}
$$

---

[4] In some formal systems, a predicate $Dom.\text{'}E\text{'}$ is introduced to represent the set of states in which expression E is uniquely specified. For example, $Dom.\text{'}x/y\text{'}$ denotes $y \neq 0$. Note that Dom is not a function symbol of the logic. Instead, $Dom.\text{'}E\text{'}$ is shorthand for a predicate. To understand the need for quoting the argument of Dom, recall that a function application like $abs.E$ applies function abs to the value of E. For example, $abs(2 - 5)$ evaluates to $abs(-3)$, which evaluates to 3. Thus, $Dom(x/0)$ makes no sense, since it would result in $x/0$ being evaluated. Rather, the argument of Dom is some representation of an expression, and the result is a predicate that describes the set of states in which the expression is uniquely specified.

Using underspecification requires a slight change to the notion of validity. A formula E is *valid* if, for every combination of values that can be assigned to an underspecified term of E, E evaluates to *true* in all states. For example, for $x, y{:}\mathbb{R}$, $x/x = y/y$ is not valid, because one possible value for x/x is 2, one possible value for y/y is 3, and $2 \neq 3$. However, $x/x = x/x$ is valid.

The handling of recursively defined functions has been a concern of several articles that explore the undefined, most notably [2] and [8]. Article [8] introduces the following function $subp$,

$$subp : \mathbb{Z} \times \mathbb{Z} \to \mathbb{Z}$$
$$(\forall i{:}\mathbb{Z} \mid : subp(i, i) = 0)$$
$$(\forall i, j{:}\mathbb{Z} \mid i > j : subp(i, j) = subp(i, j + 1) + 1)$$

and uses proofs of the following property as a leitmotif.

(6) $(\forall i, j{:}\mathbb{Z} \mid : i \geq j \Rightarrow subp(i, j) = i - j)$.

Function application $subp(i, j)$ is normally considered to be defined only if $i \geq j$. However, with the approach of underspecification, $subp(i, j)$ is always defined but its value is unspecified if $i < j$. Property (6) is proved as follows.

We prepare for a proof by induction by manipulating (6). Type annotations for the dummies are omitted.

$$
\begin{aligned}
& (\forall i, j \mid : i \geq j \Rightarrow subp(i, j) = i - j) \\
= \quad & \langle i \geq j \equiv i - j \geq 0 \,;\, \text{Trading; Nesting} \rangle \\
& (\forall i \mid : (\forall j \mid i - j \geq 0 : subp(i, j) = i - j))
\end{aligned}
$$

We prove the last formula by proving

$$(\forall j \mid i - j \geq 0 : subp(i, j) = i - j)$$

for arbitrary i, by induction on natural numbers $i - j$.

Base case. For $i - j = 0$, we have $i = j$. Hence

$$
\begin{aligned}
& subp(i, j) = i - j \\
= \quad & \langle \text{Case } i = j \,;\, \text{Arithmetic} \rangle \\
& subp(i, i) = 0 \quad \text{—Definition of } subp
\end{aligned}
$$

Inductive case. For $i - j > 0$, we assume inductive hypothesis $subp(i, j+1) = i - (j+1)$ and prove $subp(i, j) = i - j$. For arbitrary natural number $i - j$, we have,

$$
\begin{aligned}
& subp(i, j) \\
= \quad & \langle \text{Definition of } subp \rangle \\
& subp(i, j + 1) + 1 \\
= \quad & \langle \text{Inductive hypothesis} \rangle \\
& i - (j + 1) + 1 \\
= \quad & \langle \text{Arithmetic} \rangle \\
& i - j
\end{aligned}
$$

Jones [7] warns that handling undefined through underspecification can lead to difficulties if recursive definitions inadvertently overspecify in such a way that unwanted properties can be deduced. For example, suppose we define $fact.i$: $\mathbb{Z} \to \mathbb{Z}$ by

(7) $fact.i = \textbf{if } i = 0 \textbf{ then } 1 \textbf{ else } i \cdot fact(i - 1) \textbf{ fi}$.

Then, we can use recursive definition (7) to deduce

$$fact(-1) = -1 \cdot fact(-2)$$
$$fact(-2) = -2 \cdot fact(-3)$$
$$\ldots$$

In this case, $fact$ has indeed been overspecified, since $fact(-1) = -fact(-2)$ can be deduced. But the fault lies in the recursive definition rather than in handling undefined using underspecification. The problem can be solved by defining $fact$ so that it indicates nothing about $fact.i$ for negative i :

$$fact.0 = 1$$
$$(\forall i : \mathbb{Z} \mid i > 0 : fact.i = i \cdot fact(i - 1))$$

We conclude that underspecification is the preferred way to deal with undefined terms. With this approach, we can to continue to use simple two-valued logic, with all its nice properties, and still be formal, rigorous, and clear. Only when dealing with a partial function does it become necessary to exert some minimal extra effort, which takes the form of dealing with antecedents that describe the set of arguments for which the partial function is uniquely specified.

References

1. Bijlsma, A. Semantics of quasi-boolean expressions. In Feijen, W.H.J., et al (eds.) *Beauty is Our Business*. Springer-Verlag, New York, 1990, 27–35.
2. Cheng, J.H., and C.B. Jones. On the usability of logics which handle partial functions. In: C. Morgan and J.C.P. Woodcock (eds.). Third Refinement Workshop, pp. 51–69. Workshops in Computing Series, Heidelberg, 1991.
3. Constable, R.L., and M.J. O'Donnell. *A Programming Logic*. Winthrop, Cambridge, Massachusetts, 1978.
4. Dijkstra, E.W., and C.S. Scholten. *Predicate Calculus and Program Semantics*. Springer-Verlag, New York 1990.
5. Gries, D., and F.B. Schneider. *A Logical Approach to Discrete Math*. Springer-Verlag, New York, 1993.
6. Gries, D., and F.B. Schneider. Equational propositional logic. *IPL 53* (1995), 145-152.
7. Jones, C.B. Partial functions and logics: a warning. *IPL 54* (1995), 65–68.
8. Jones, C.B., and C.A. Middelburg. A typed logic of partial functions reconstructed classically. *Acta Informatica 31* (1994), 399–430.
9. Scott, D.S. Existence and description in formal logic. In R. Schoenman (ed.) *Bertrand Russell, Philosopher of the Century*. St. Leonards: Allen and Unwin, 1967, 181–200.

Towards a Theory of Recursive Structures*

David Harel**

Dept. of Applied Mathematics and Computer Science
The Weizmann Institute of Science, Rehovot, Israel
harel@wisdom.weizmann.ac.il

Abstract. In computer science, one is interested mainly in finite objects. Insofar as infinite objects are of interest, they must be computable, i.e., recursive, thus admitting an effective finite representation. This leads to the notion of a recursive graph, or, more generally, a recursive structure, model or data base. This paper summarizes recent work on recursive structures and data bases, including (i) the high undecidability of many problems on recursive graphs and structures, (ii) a method for deducing results on the descriptive complexity of finitary NP optimization problems from results on the computational complexity (i.e., the degree of undecidability) of their infinitary analogues, (iii) completeness results for query languages on recursive data bases, (iv) correspondences between descriptive and computational complexity over recursive structures, and (v) zero-one laws for recursive structures.

1 Introduction

This paper provides a summary of work — most of it joint with Tirza Hirst — on infinite recursive (i.e., computable) structures and data bases, and attempts to put it in perspective. The work itself is contained in four papers [H, HH1, HH2, HH3], which are summarized, respectively, in Sections 2, 3, 4 and 5.

When computer scientists become interested in an infinite object, they require it to be computable, i.e., recursive, so that it possesses an effective finite representation. Given the prominence of finite graphs in computer science, and the many results and open questions surrounding them, it is very natural to investigate recursive graphs too. Moreover, insight into finite objects can often be gleaned from results about infinite recursive variants thereof. An infinite recursive graph can be thought of simply as a recursive binary relation over the natural numbers. Recursive graphs can be represented by the (finite) algorithms, or Turing machines, that recognize their edge sets, so that it makes sense to investigate the complexity of problems concerning them.

---

* A preliminary version of this paper appeared in STACS '94, *Proc. 11th Ann. Symp. on Theoretical Aspects of Computer Science*, Lecture Notes in Computer Science, Vol. 775, Springer-Verlag, Berlin, 1994, pp. 633–645. The main difference is the addition of Section 5.

** Incumbent of the William Sussman Chair of Mathematics.

Indeed, a significant amount of work has been carried out in recent years regarding the complexity of problems on recursive graphs. Some of the first papers were written in the 1970s by Manaster and Rosenstein [MR] and Bean [B1, B2]. Following that, a variety of problems were considered, including ones that are NP-complete for finite graphs, such as k-colorability and Hamiltonicity [B1, B2, BG2, Bu, GL, MR] and ones that are in P in the finite case, such as Eulerian paths [B2, BG1] In most cases (including the above examples) the problems turned out to be undecidable. This is true even for highly recursive graphs [B1], i.e., ones for which node degree is finite and the set of neighbors of a node is computable. Beigel and Gasarch [BG1] and Gasarch and Lockwood [GL] investigated the precise level of undecidability of many such problems, and showed that they reside on low levels of the arithmetical hierarchy. For example, detecting the existence of an Eulerian path is Π_3^0-complete for recursive graphs and Π_2^0-complete for highly recursive graphs [BG1].

The case of Hamiltonian paths seemed to be more elusive. In 1976, Bean [B2] had shown that the problem is undecidable (even for planar graphs), but the precise characterization was not known. In response to this question, posed by R. Beigel and B. Gasarch, the author was able to show that Hamiltonicity is in fact *highly* undecidable, *viz,* Σ_1^1-complete. The result, proved in [H] and summarized in Section 2, holds even for highly recursive graphs with degree bounded by 3. (It actually holds for planar graphs too.) Hamiltonicity is thus an example of an interesting graph problem that becomes highly undecidable in the infinite case.[3]

The question then arises as to what makes some NP-complete problems highly undecidable in the infinite case, while others (e.g., k-colorability) remain on low levels of the arithmetical hierarchy. This was the starting point of the joint work with T. Hirst. In [HH1], summarized in Section 3, we provide a general definition of infinite recursive versions of NP optimization problems, in such a way that MAX CLIQUE, for example, becomes the question of whether a recursive graph contains an infinite clique. Two main results are proved in [HH1], one enables using knowledge about the infinite case to yield implications to the finite case, and the other enables implications in the other direction. The results establish a connection between the descriptive complexity of (finitary) NP optimization problems, particularly the syntactic class MAX NP, and the computational complexity of their infinite versions, particularly the class Σ_1^1. Taken together, the two results yield many new problems whose infinite versions are highly undecidable and whose finite versions are outside MAX NP. Examples include MAX CLIQUE, MAX INDEPENDENT SET, MAX SUBGRAPH, and MAX TILING.

The next paper, [HH2], summarized in Section 4, puts forward the idea of infinite recursive relational data bases. Such a data base can be defined simply as a finite tuple of recursive relations (not necessarily binary) over some countable domain. We thus obtain a natural generalization of the notion of a finite relational data base. This is not an entirely wild idea: tables of trigonometric

---

[3] Independent work in [AMS] showed that perfect matching is another such problem.

functions, for example, can be viewed as a recursive data base, since we might be interested in the sines or cosines of infinitely many angles. Instead of keeping them all in a table, which is impossible, we keep rules for computing the values from the angles, and vice versa, which is really just to say that we have an effective way of telling whether an edge is present between nodes i and j in an infinite graph, and this is precisely the notion of a recursive graph.

In [HH2], we investigate the class of computable queries over recursive data bases, the motivation being borrowed from [CH1]. Since the set of computable queries on such data bases is not closed under even simple relational operations, one must either make do with a very humble class of queries or considerably restrict the class of allowed data bases. The main parts of [HH2] are concerned with the completeness of two query languages, one for each of these possibilities. The first is quantifier-free first-order logic, which is shown to be complete for the non-restricted case. The second is an appropriately modified version of the complete language QL of [CH1], which is proved complete for the case of "highly symmetric" data bases. These have the property that their set of automorphisms is of finite index for each tuple-width.

While the previous topic involves languages for *computable* queries, our final paper, [HH3], summarized in Section 5, deals with languages that express *non*-computable queries. In the spirit of results for finite structures by Fagin, Immerman and others, we sought to connect the computational complexity of properties of recursive structures with their descriptive complexity, i.e, to capture levels of undecidability syntactically as the properties expressible in various logical formalisms. We consider several formalisms, such as first-order logic, second-order logic and fixpoint logic. One of our results is analogous to that of Fagin [F1]; it states that, for any $k \geq 2$, the properties of recursive structures expressible by Σ_k^1 formulas are exactly the generic properties in the complexity class Σ_k^1 of the analytical hierarchy.

[HH3] also deals with zero-one laws. It is not too difficult to see that many of the classical theorems of logic that hold for general structures (e.g., compactness and completeness) fail not only for finite models but for recursive ones too. Others, such as Ehrenfeucht–Fraisse games, hold for finite and recursive structures too. Zero-one laws, to the effect that certain properties (such as those expressible in first-order logic) are either almost surely true or almost surely false, are considered unique to finite model theory, since they require counting the number of structures of a given finite size. We introduce a way of extending the definition of these laws to recursive structures, and prove that they hold for first-order logic, strict Σ_1^1 and strict Π_1^1. We then use this fact to show non-expressibility of certain properties of recursive structures in these logics.

While recursive structures and models have been investigated quite widely by logicians (see, e.g., [NR]), the kind of issues that computer scientists are interested in have not been addressed prior to the work mentioned above. We feel that that this is a fertile area for research, and raises theoretical and practical questions concerning the computability and complexity of properties of recursive structures, and the theory of queries and update operations over recursive data bases. We hope that the work summarized here will stimulate more research on these topics.

2   Hamiltonicity in recursive graphs

A *recursive directed graph* is a pair $G = (V, E)$, where V is recursively isomorphic to the set of natural numbers $\mathcal{N}$, and $E \subset V \times V$ is recursive. G is *undirected* if E is symmetric. A *highly recursive graph* is a recursive graph for which there is a recursive function H from V to finite subsets of V, such that $H(v) = \{u \mid \langle v, u \rangle \in E\}$.

A *one-way* (respectively, *two-way*) *Hamiltonian path* in G is a 1-1 mapping p of $\mathcal{N}$ (respectively, $\mathcal{Z}$) onto V, such that $\langle p(x), p(x+1) \rangle \in E$ for all x.

Bean [B2] showed that determining Hamiltonicity in highly recursive graphs is undecidable. His reduction is from non-well-foundedness of recursive trees with finite degree, which can be viewed simply as the halting problem for (nondeterministic) Turing machines. Given such a tree T, the proof in [B2] constructs a graph G, such that infinite paths in T map to Hamiltonian paths in G. The idea is to make the nodes of G correspond to those of T, but with all nodes that are on the same level being connected in a cyclic fashion. In this way, a Hamiltonian path in G simulates moving down an infinite path in T, but at each level it also cycles through all nodes on that level. A fact that is crucial to this construction is the finiteness of T's degree, so that the proof does not generalize to trees with infinite degree, Thus, Bean's proof only establishes that Hamiltonicity is hard for Π_1^0, or co-r.e.

In [H] we have been able to show that the problem is actually Σ_1^1-complete. Hardness is proved by a reduction (that is elementary but not straightforward) from the non-well-foundedness of recursive trees with possibly *infinite* degree, which is well-known to be a Σ_1^1-complete problem [R]:

Theorem: *Detecting (one-way or two-way) Hamiltonicity in a (directed or undirected) highly recursive graph is Σ_1^1-complete, even for graphs with $H(v) \leq 3$ for all v.*

Proof sketch: In Σ_1^1 is easy: With the $\exists f$ quantifying over total functions from $\mathcal{N}$ to $\mathcal{N}$, we write

$$\exists f \; \forall x \; \forall y \; \exists z \; (\langle f(x), f(x+1) \rangle \in E \wedge (x \neq y \rightarrow f(x) \neq f(y)) \wedge f(z) = x).$$

This covers the case of one-way paths. The two-way case is similar.

We now show Σ_1^1-hardness for undirected recursive graphs with one-way paths. (The other cases require more work, especially in removing the infinite branching from the graphs we construct in order to obtain the result for highly recursive graphs. The details can be found in [H].)

Assume a recursive tree T is given, with nodes $\mathcal{N} = 0, 1, 2, 3, \ldots$, and root 0, and whose *parent-of* function is recursive. T can be of infinite degree. We construct an undirected graph G, which has a one-way Hamiltonian path iff T has an infinite path.

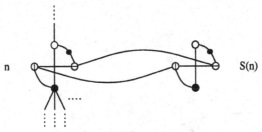

$$n \qquad\qquad S(n)$$

Figure 1

For each element $n \in \mathcal{N}$, G has a cluster of five internal nodes, n^u, n^d, n^r, n^l and n^{ur}, standing, respectively, for *up, down, right, left* and *up-right*. For each such cluster, G has five internal edges:

$$n^l \; \text{---} \; n^d \; \text{---} \; n^u \; \text{---} \; n^{ur} \; \text{---} \; n^r \; \text{---} \; n^l$$

For each edge $n \longrightarrow m$ of the tree T, $n^d \text{---} m^u$ is an edge of G. For each node n in T, let $S(n)$ be n's distance from the root in T (its *level*). Since $S(n) \in \mathcal{N}$, we may view $S(n)$ as a node in T. In fact, in G we will think of $S(n)$ as being n's *shadow node*, and the two are connected as follows (see Fig. 1):[4]

$$n^r \; \text{---} \; S(n)^r \quad \text{and} \quad S(n)^l \; \text{---} \; n^l$$

To complete the construction, there is one additional root node g in G, with an edge $g \text{---} 0^u$.

Since T is a recursive tree and S, as a function, is recursive in T, it is easy to see that G is a recursive graph. To complete the proof, we show that T has an infinite path from 0 iff G has a Hamiltonian path.

(*Only-if*) Suppose T has an infinite path p. A Hamiltonian path p' in G starts at the root g, and moves down G's versions of the nodes in p, taking detours to the right to visit n's shadow node $S(n)$ whenever $S(n) \notin p$. The way this is done can be seen in Fig. 2. Since p is infinite, we will eventually reach a node of any desired level in T, so that any $n \notin p$ will eventually show up as a shadow of some node along p and will be visited in due time. It is then easy to see that p' is Hamiltonian.

---

[4] Clearly, given T, the function $S : \mathcal{N} \rightarrow \mathcal{N}$ is not necessarily one-one. In fact, Fig. 1 is somewhat misleading, since there may be infinitely many nodes with the same shadow, so that the degree of both up-nodes and down-nodes can be infinite. Moreover, $S(n)$ itself is a node somewhere else in the tree, and hence has its own T-edges, perhaps infinitely many of them.

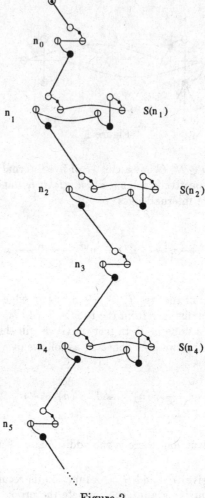

n_0

n_1 $S(n_1)$

n_2 $S(n_2)$

n_3

n_4 $S(n_4)$

n_5

Figure 2

(*If*) Suppose G has a Hamiltonian path p. It helps to view the path p as containing not only the nodes, but also the edges connecting them. Thus, with the exception of the root g, each node in G must contribute to p exactly two incident edges, one incoming and one outgoing.

We now claim that for any n, if p contains the T-edge incident to the up-node n^u, or, when $n = 0$, if it contains the edge between g and 0^u, then it must also contain a T-edge incident to the down node n^d.

To see why this is true, assume p contains the T-edge incident to n^u (this is the edge leading upwards at the top left of Fig. 1). Consider n^{ur} (the small black node in the figure). It has exactly two incident edges, both of which must therefore be in p. But since one of them connects it to n^u, we already have in p the two required edges for n^u, so that the one between n^u and n^d cannot be in p. Now, the only remaining edges incident to n^d are the internal one connecting it to n^l, and its T-edges, if any. However, since p must contain exactly two edges incident to n^d, one of them must be one of the T-edges. $\triangle$

In fact, Hamiltonicity is Σ_1^1-complete even for planar graphs [HH1].

3   From the finite to the infinite and back

Our approach to optimization problems focuses on their descriptive complexity, an idea that started with Fagin's [F1] characterization of NP in terms of definability in existential second-order logic on finite structures. Fagin's theorem asserts that a collection C of finite structures is NP-computable if and only if there is a quantifier-free formula $\psi(\overline{x}, \overline{y}, S)$, such that for any finite structure A:

$$A \in C \Leftrightarrow A \models (\exists S)(\forall \overline{x})(\exists \overline{y})\psi(\overline{x}, \overline{y}, S).$$

Papadimitriou and Yannakakis [PY] introduced the class MAX NP of maximization problems that can be defined by

$$\max_{S} |\{\overline{x}: \ A \models (\exists \overline{y})\psi(\overline{x}, \overline{y}, S)\}|,$$

for quantifier-free ψ. MAX SAT is the canonical example of a problem in MAX NP. The authors of [PY] also considered the subclass MAX SNP of MAX NP, consisting of those maximization problems in which the existential quantifier above is not needed. (Actually, the classes MAX NP and MAX SNP of [PY] contain also their closures under L-reductions, which preserve polynomial-time approximation schemes. To avoid confusion, we use the names MAX Σ_0 and MAX Σ_1, introduced in [KT], rather than MAX SNP and MAX NP, for the 'pure' syntactic classes.)

Kolaitis and Thakur [KT] then examined the class of all maximization problems whose optimum is definable using first-order formulas, i.e., by

$$\max_{S} |\{\overline{w}: \ A \models \psi(\overline{w}, S)\}|,$$

where $\psi(\overline{w}, S)$ is an arbitrary first-order formula. They first showed that this class coincides with the collection of polynomially-bounded NP-maximization problems on finite structures, i.e., those problems whose optimum value is bounded by a polynomial in the input size. They then proved that these problems form a proper hierarchy, with exactly four levels:

$$\text{MAX } \Sigma_0 \subset \text{MAX } \Sigma_1 \subset \text{MAX } \Pi_1 \subset \text{MAX } \Pi_2 = \bigcup_{i \geq 2} \text{MAX } \Pi_i$$

Here, MAX Π_1 is defined just like MAX Σ_1 (i.e., MAX NP), but with a universal quantifier, and MAX Π_2 uses a universal followed by an existential quantifier, and corresponds to Fagin's general result stated above. The three containments are known to be strict. For example, MAX CLIQUE is in MAX Π_1 but not in MAX Σ_1.

We now define a little more precisely the class of optimization problems we deal with[5]:

Definition: (See [PR]) An NPM problem is a tuple $F = (\mathcal{I}_F, S_F, m_F)$, where

- $\mathcal{I}_F$, the set of *input instances*, consists of finite structures over some vocabulary σ, and is recognizable in polynomial time.
- $S_F(I)$ is the space of *feasible solutions* on input $I \in \mathcal{I}_F$. The only requirement on S_F is that there exists a polynomial q and a polynomial time computable predicate p, both depending only on F, such that $\forall I \in \mathcal{I}_F$, $S_F(I) = \{S\colon |S| \leq q(|I|) \land p(I, S)\}$.
- $m_F\colon \mathcal{I}_F \times \Sigma^* \to \mathcal{N}$, the *objective function*, is a polynomial time computable function. $m_F(I, S)$ is defined only when $S \in S_F(I)$.
- The following decision problem is required to be in NP: Given $I \in \mathcal{I}_F$ and an integer k, is there a feasible solution $S \in S_F(I)$, such that $m_F(I, S) \geq k$?

This definition (with an additional technical restriction that we omit here; see [HH1]) is broad enough to encompass most known optimization problems arising in the theory of NP-completeness.

We now define infinitary versions of NPM problems, by evaluating them over infinite recursive structures and asking about the existence of an infinite solution:

Definition: For an NPM problem $F = (\mathcal{I}_F, S_F, m_F)$, let $F^\infty = (\mathcal{I}_F^\infty, S_F^\infty, m_F^\infty)$ be defined as follows:

- $\mathcal{I}_F^\infty$ is the set of *input instances*, which are infinite recursive structures over the vocabulary σ.
- $S_F^\infty(I^\infty)$ is the set of *feasible solutions* on input $I^\infty \in \mathcal{I}_F^\infty$.
- $m_F^\infty\colon \mathcal{I}^\infty \times S_F \to \mathcal{N} \cup \{\infty\}$ is the *objective function*, satisfying

$$\forall I^\infty \in \mathcal{I}_F^\infty, \forall S \in S_F^\infty(I^\infty) \ (m_F^\infty(I^\infty, S) = |\{\overline{x}\colon \psi_F(I^\infty, S, \overline{x})\}|).$$

- The decision problem is: Given $I^\infty \in \mathcal{I}_F^\infty$, does there exist $S \in S_F^\infty(I^\infty)$, such that $m_F^\infty(I^\infty, S) = \infty$? Put another way:

$$F^\infty(I^\infty) = \text{TRUE} \quad \text{iff} \quad \exists S(|\{\overline{x}\colon \psi_F(I^\infty, S, \overline{x})\}| = \infty).$$

Due to the conditions on NPM problems, F^∞ can be shown not to depend on the Π_2-formula representing m_F. This is important, since, if some finite problem F could be defined by two different formulas ψ_1 and ψ_2 that satisfy the condition but yield different infinite problems, we could construct a finite structure for which ψ_1 and ψ_2 determine different solutions.

Here is the first main result of [HH1]:

Theorem: If $F \in \text{MAX } \Sigma_1$ then $F^\infty \in \Pi_2^0$.

A special case of this is:

---

[5] We concentrate here on maximization problems, though the results can be proved for appropriate minimization ones too.

Corollary: For any NPM problem F, if F^∞ is Σ_1^1-hard then F is not in MAX Σ_1.

It follows that since the infinite version of Hamiltonicity is Σ_1^1-complete and thus completely outside the arithmetical hierarchy, an appropriately defined finitary version cannot be in MAX Σ_1. Obviously, the corollary is valid not only for such problems but for all problems that are above Π_2^0 in the arithmetical hierarchy. For example, since detecting the existence of an Eulerian path in a recursive graph is Π_3^0-complete [BG1], its finite variant cannot be in MAX Σ_1 either.

In order to be able to state the second main result of [HH1], we define a special kind of *monotonic* reduction between finitary NPM problems, an *M-reduction*:

Definition: Let A and B be sets of structures. A function $f: A \to B$ is *monotonic* if $\forall A, B \in A$ $(A \leq B \Rightarrow f(A) \leq f(B))$. (Here, $\leq$ denotes the substructure relation.) Given two NPM problems: $F = (I_F, S_F, m_F)$ and $G = (I_G, S_G, m_G)$, an *M-reduction* g from F to G is a tuple $g = (t_1, t_2, t_3)$, such that:

- $t_1 : I_F \to I_G$, $t_2 : I_F \times S_F \to S_G$, and $t_3 : I_G \times S_G \to S_F$, are all monotonic, polynomial time computable functions..
- m_F and m_G grow monotonically with respect to t_1, t_2 and t_3 (see [HH1] for a more precise formulation).

We denote the existence of an M-reduction from F to G by $F \propto_M G$. The second main result of [HH1] shows that M-reductions preserve the Σ_1^1-hardness of the corresponding infinitary problems:

Theorem: Let F and G be two NPM problems, with $F \propto_M G$. If F^∞ is Σ_1^1-hard, then G^∞ is Σ_1^1-hard too.

The final part of [HH1] applies these two results to many examples of NPM problems, some of which we now list with their infinitary versions. It is shown in [HH1] that for each of these the infinitary version is Σ_1^1-complete. Mostly, this is done by establishing monotonic reductions on the finite level, and applying the second theorem above. From the first theorem it then follows that the finitary versions must be outside MAX Σ_1.

Here are some of the examples:

1. MAX CLIQUE: I is an undirected graph, $G = (V, E)$.

$$S(G) = \{Y: Y \subseteq V, \forall y, z \in Y \ y \neq z \Rightarrow (y, z) \in E\}$$
$$m(G, Y) = |Y|$$

The maximization version is:

$$\max_{Y \subseteq V} |\{x: x \in Y \wedge \forall y, z \in Y \ y \neq z \Rightarrow (y, z) \in E\}|$$

MAX CLIQUE$^\infty$: I^∞ is a recursive graph G. Does G contain an infinite clique?

2. MAX IND SET: I is an undirected graph $G = (V, E)$.

$$S(G) = \{Y\colon Y \subseteq V,\ \forall y, z \in Y\ (y, z) \notin E\}$$
$$m(G, Y) = |Y|$$
$$\max_{Y \subseteq V} |\{x\colon x \in Y \wedge \forall y, z \in Y\ (y, z) \notin E\}|$$

MAX IND SET$^\infty$: I^∞ is a recursive graph G. Does G contain an infinite independent set?

3. MAX SET PACKING: I is a collection C of finite sets, represented by pairs (i, j), where the set i contains j.

$$S(C) = \{Y \subseteq C\colon \forall A, B \in Y\ A \neq B \Rightarrow A \cap B = \emptyset\}$$
$$m(C, Y) = |Y|$$

MAX SET PACKING$^\infty$: I^∞ is a recursive collection of infinite sets C. Does C contains infinitely many disjoint sets?

4. MAX SUBGRAPH: I is a pair of graphs, $G = (V_1, E_1)$ and $H = (V_2, E_2)$, with $V_2 = \{v_1, \ldots, v_n\}$.

$$S(G, H) = \{Y\colon Y \subseteq V_1 \times V_2,\ \forall (u, v), (x, y) \in Y,\ u \neq x$$
$$\wedge\, v \neq y \wedge (u, x) \in E_1 \Leftrightarrow (v, y) \in E_2\}$$
$$m((G, H), Y) = k \text{ iff } v_1, \ldots, v_k \text{ appear in } Y,$$
$$\text{but } v_{k+1} \text{ does not appear in } Y.$$

MAX SUBGRAPH$^\infty$: I^∞ is a pair of recursive graphs, H and G. Is H a subgraph of G?

5. MAX TILING: I is a grid D of size $n \times n$, and a set of tiles $T = \{t_1, \ldots, t_m\}$. (We assume the reader is familiar with the rules of tiling problems.)

$$S(D, T) = \{Y\colon Y \text{ is a legal tiling of some portion of } D \text{ with tiles from } T\}$$
$$m(\{D, T\}, Y) = k \text{ iff } Y \text{ contains a tiling of a full } k \times k \text{ subgrid of } D.$$

MAX TILING$^\infty$: I^∞ is a recursive set of tiles T.

Q: Can T tile the positive quadrant of the infinite integer grid?

We thus establish closely related facts about the level of undecidability of many infinitary problems and the descriptive complexity of their finitary counterparts. More examples appear in [HH1].

Two additional graph problems of interest are mentioned in [HH1], planarity and graph isomorphism. The problem of detecting whether a recursive graph is planar can be shown to be co-r.e. Determining whether two recursive graphs are isomorphic is arithmetical for graphs that have finite degree and contain only finitely many connected components. More precisely, this problem is in Π_1^0 for highly recursive trees; in Π_3^0 for recursive trees with finite degree; in Σ_2^0 for highly recursive graphs; and in Σ_4^0 for recursive graphs with finite degree. As to the isomorphism problem for general recursive graphs, Morozov [Mo] has recently proved, using different techniques, that the problem is Σ_1^1-complete.

4   Completeness for recursive data bases

It is easy to see that recursive relations are not closed under some of the simplest accepted relational operators. For example, if $R(x, y, z)$ means that the yth Turing machine halts on input z after x steps (a primitive-recursive relation), then the projection of R on columns 2 and 3 is the nonrecursive halting predicate. This means that even very simple queries, when applied to general recursive relations, do not preserve computability. Thus, a naive definition of a recursive data base as a finite set of recursive relations will cause many extremely simple queries to be non-computable.

This difficulty can be overcome in essentially two ways (and possibly other intermediate ways that we haven't investigated). The first is to accept the situation as is; that is, to resign ourselves to the fact that on recursive data bases the class of computable queries will necessarily be very humble, and then to try to capture that class in a (correspondingly humble) complete query language. The second is to restrict the data bases, so that the standard kinds of queries *will* preserve computability, and then to try to establish a reasonable completeness result for these restricted inputs. The first case will give rise to a rich class of data bases but a poor class of queries, and the second to a rich class of queries but a poor class of data bases. In both cases, of course, in addition to being Turing computable, the queries will also have to satisfy the consistency criterion of [CH1], more recently termed *genericity*, whereby queries must preserve isomorphisms.

The first result of [HH2] shows that the class of computable queries on recursive data bases is indeed extremely poor. First we need some preparation.

Definition: Let D be a countable set, and let $R_1, \ldots, R_k$, for $k > 0$, be relations, such that for all $1 \leq i \leq k$, $R_i \subseteq D^{a_i}$. $B = (D, R_1, \ldots, R_k)$ is a *recursive relational data base* (or an r-db for short) *of type* $a = (a_1, \ldots a_k)$, if each R_i, considered as a set of tuples, is recursive.

Definition: Let $B_1 = (D_1, R_1, \ldots, R_k)$ and $B_2 = (D_2, R'_1, \ldots, R'_k)$ be two r-db's of the same type, and let $u \in D_1^n$ and $v \in D_2^n$, for some n. Then (B_1, u) and (B_2, v) are *isomorphic*, written $(B_1, u) \cong (B_2, v)$, if there is an isomorphism between B_1 and B_2 taking u to v. (B_1, u) and (B_2, v) are *locally isomorphic*, written $(B_1, u) \cong_l (B_2, v)$, if the restriction of B_1 to the elements of u and the restriction of B_2 to the elements of v are isomorphic.

Definition: An *r-query* Q (i.e., a partial function yielding, for each r-db B of type a, an output (if any) which is a recursive relation over $D(B)$) is *generic*, if it preserves isomorphisms; i.e. for all B_1, B_2, u, v, if $(B_1, u) \cong (B_2, v)$ then $u \in Q(B_1)$ iff $v \in Q(B_2)$. It is *locally generic* if it preserves local isomorphisms; i.e., for all B_1, B_2, u, v, if $(B_1, u) \cong_l (B_2, v)$ then $u \in Q(B_1)$ iff $v \in Q(B_2)$.

The following is a key lemma in the first result:

Lemma: If Q is a recursive r-query, then Q is generic iff Q is locally generic.

Definition: A query language is *r-complete* if it expresses precisely the class of recursive generic r-queries.

Theorem: The language of first-order logic without quantifiers is r-complete.

We now prepare for the second result of [HH2], which insists on the full set of computable queries of [CH1], but drastically reduces the allowed data bases in order to achieve completeness.

Definition: Let $B = (D, R_1, \ldots, R_k)$ be a fixed r-db. For each $u, v \in D^n$, u and v are *equivalent*, written $u \cong_B v$, if $(B, u) \cong (B, v)$. B is *highly symmetric* if for each $n > 0$, the relation $\cong_B$ induces only a finite number of equivalence classes of rank n.

Highly symmetric graphs consist of a finite or infinite number of connected components, where each component is highly symmetric, and there are only finitely many pairwise non-isomorphic components. In a highly symmetric graph, the finite degrees, the distances between points and the lengths of the induced paths are bounded. A grid or an infinite straight line, for instance, are not highly symmetric, but the full infinite clique is highly symmetric. Fig. 3 shows an example of another highly symmetric graph.

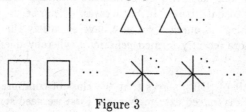

Figure 3

A *characteristic tree* for B is defined as follows. Its root is Λ, and the rest of the vertices are labeled with elements from D, such that the labels along each path from the root form a tuple that is a representative of an equivalence class of $\cong_B$. The whole tree covers representatives of all such classes. No two paths are allowed to form representatives of the same class. We represent a highly symmetric data base B by a tuple

$$C_B = (T_B, \cong_B, C_1, \ldots, C_k),$$

where T_B is some characteristic tree for B, and each C_i is a finite set of representatives of the equivalence classes constituting the relation R_i. We also require that $\cong_B$ be recursive, and that T_B be highly recursive (in the sense of Section 2).

We say that a query Q on a highly symmetric data base is *recursive* if the following version of it, which is applied to the representation C_B rather than to the data base B itself, is partial recursive: whenever $Q(C_B)$ is defined, it yields a finite set of representatives of the equivalence classes representing the relation $Q(B)$.

We now describe the query language QL_s. Its syntax is like that of the QL language of Chandra and Harel [CH1], with the following addition: the test in a

while loop can be for whether a relation has a single representative, and not only for a relation's emptiness. The semantics of QL_s is the same as the semantics of QL, except for some minor technical adaptations that are omitted here. As in [CH1], the result of applying a program P to C_B is undefined if P does not halt; otherwise it is the contents of some fixed variable, say X_1.

Definition: A query language is *hs-r-complete* if it expresses precisely the class of recursive generic queries over highly symmetric recursive data bases.

Theorem: QL_s is hs-r-complete.

The proof follows four main steps, which are analogous to those given in the completeness proof for QL in [CH1]. The details, however, are more intricate.

In [HH2] a number of additional issues are considered, including the restriction of recursive data bases to finite/co-finite recursive relations, completeness of the generic machines of [AV], and BP-completeness.

5   Expressibility vs. complexity, and zero-one laws

One part of [HH3] proves results that relate the expressive power of various logics over recursive structures to the computational complexity (i.e., the level of undecidability) of the properties expressible therein. We summarize some of these, without providing all of the relevant definitions. In the previous section, we mentioned the result from [HH2] to the effect that the very restricted language of quantifier-free first-order relational calculus is r-complete; i.e., it expresses precisely the recursive and generic r-queries. Here we deal with languages that have stronger expressive power, and hence express also non-recursive queries.

There are many results over *finite* structures that characterize complexity classes in terms of logic. One of the most important of these is Fagin's theorem [F1], mentioned in section 2 above, which establishes that the properties of finite structures expressible by Σ_1^1 formulas are exactly the ones that are in NP. This kind of correspondence also holds between each level of the quantifier hierarchy of second-order logic and the properties computable in the corresponding level of the polynomial-time hierarchy.

In order to talk about recursive structures it is convenient to use the following definition, which we adapt to recursive structures from Vardi [V]

Definition: The *data complexity* of a language L is the level of difficulty of computing the sets $Gr(Q_e) = \{(B, u) | u \in Q(B)\}$ for an expression e in L, where Q_e is the query expressed by e, and B denotes a recursive data base (i.e., structure). A language L is *data-complete* (or D-*complete* for short) for a computational class C if for every expression e in L, $Gr(Q_e)$ is in C, and there is an expression e_0 in L such that $Gr(Q_{e_0})$ is hard for C.

Here we restrict ourselves to the consistent, or generic, queries, which are the ones that preserve isomorphisms. In fact, we require that they preserve the isomorphisms of *all* structures, not only recursive ones, under the assumption that there exist oracles for their relations. That is, Q is considiered here to be generic if for all B_1, B_2, if $B_1 \cong B_2$ then $Q(B_1) \cong Q(B_2)$, where $Q(B)$ is the result of applying Q to oracles for the relations in B.

We now provide a very brief description of the main results of this part of [HH3]:

1. First-order logic expresses generic queries from the entire arithmetical hierarchy, but it does not express all of them. For example, the connectivity of recursive graphs is arithmetical, but is not expressible by a first-order formula.

2. The logical formalism E-Σ_1^1, which consists of existential second-order formulas, is D-complete for the complexity class Σ_1^1 of the analytical hierarchy, but there are queries, even arithmetical ones, that are not expressible in E-Σ_1^1. However, over ordered structures (that is, if a built-in total order is added to the vocabulary), all Σ_1^1 properties are expressible in E-Σ_1^1.

3. For $k \geq 2$, a stronger result is proved, analogous to Fagin's result for finite structures: the logical formalism E-Σ_k^1 expresses precisely the generic properties of the complexity class Σ_k^1. This means that every generic query over some vocabulary σ that is expressible by a Σ_k^1 formula over interpreted recursive predicates, is also expressible by an uninterpreted E-Σ_k^1 formula over σ.[6]

4. Monadic E-Σ_1^1, where the second-order quantifiers are restricted to range over unary relations (sets), is D-complete for Σ_1^1, and strict E-Σ_1^1 is D-complete for Σ_2^0.

5. Consider fixpoint logic, which is obtained by adding least fixpoint operators to first-order formulas [CH2, I, Mos]. Denote by FP$_1$ positive fixpoint logic, in which the least fixpoint operator is restricted to positive formulas, and by FP the hierarchy obtained by alternating the least fixpoint operator with the first-order constructs. In finite structures, the FP hierarchy collapses, and a single fixpoint operator suffices [I]. In contrast, for recursive structures FP$_1$ is D-complete for Π_1^1, and hence ¬FP$_1$ (negations of formulas in FP$_1$) is D-complete for Σ_1^1. The data complexity of FP is exactly Δ_2^1, and an example is shown of a query expressible in FP that is hard for both Σ_1^1 and Π_1^1.

The second part of [HH3] deals with 0–1 laws on recursive structures.

If C is a class of finite structures over some vocabulary σ and if P is a property of some structures in C, then the *asymptotic probability* $\mu(P)$ on C is the limit as $n \to \infty$ of the fraction of the structures in C with n elements that satisfy P, provided that the limit exists. Fagin [F2] and Glebskii et al. [GKLT] were the first to discover the connection between logical definability and asymptotic probabilities. They showed that if C is the class of all finite structures over some

---

[6] In the direction going from expressibility in E-Σ_k^1 to computability in Σ_k^1, the second-order quantifiers are used to define a total order and predicates + and *, which, in turn, are used to define the needed elementary arithmetic expression. Each subset of elements must contain a minimum in the defined order, which requires for its definition a universal second-order quantifier. This explains why the result requires $k \geq 2$.

relational vocabulary, and if P is any property expressible in first-order logic, then $\mu(P)$ exists and is either 0 or 1. This result, known as the *0-1 law for first-order logic*, became the starting point of a series of investigations aimed at discovering the relationship between expressibility in a logic and asymptotic probabilities. Several additional logics, such as fixpoint logic, iterative logic and strict E-Σ_1^1, have been shown by various authors to satisfy the 0-1 law too.

A standard method for establishing 0-1 laws on finite structures, originating in Fagin [F2], is to prove that the following *transfer theorem* holds: there is an infinite structure $\mathbf{A}$ over σ such that for any property P expressible in L:

$$\mathbf{A} \models P \text{ iff } \mu(P) = 1 \text{ on } C.$$

It turns out that there is a single countable structure $\mathbf{A}$ that satisfies this equivalence for all the logics mentioned above. Moreover, $\mathbf{A}$ is characterized by an infinite set of *extension axioms*, which, intuitively, assert that every type can be extended to any other possible type. More specifically, for each finite set X of points, and each possible way that a new point $y \notin X$ could relate to X in terms of atomic formulas over the appropriate vocabulary, there is an extension axiom that asserts that there is indeed such a point. For example, here is an extension axiom over a vocabulary containing one binary relation symbol R:

$$\forall x_1 \forall x_2 \left(x_1 \neq x_2 \Rightarrow \exists y \, (y \neq x_1 \wedge y \neq x_2 \wedge \right.$$

$$\left. (y, x_1) \in R \wedge (x_1, y) \notin R \wedge (y, x_2) \notin R \wedge (x_2, y) \in R) \right).$$

Fagin realized that the extension axioms are relevant to the study of probabilities on finite structures and proved that on the class C of all finite structures of vocabulary σ, $\mu(\tau) = 1$ for any extension axiom τ. The theory of all extension axioms, denoted T, is known to be ω-categorical (that is, every two countable models are isomorphic), so that $\mathbf{A}$, which is a model for T, is unique up to isomorphism. This unique structure is called the *random countable structure*, since it is generated, with probability 1, by a random process in which each possible tuple appears with probability 1/2, independently of the other tuples. The random graph was studied by Rado [Ra], and is sometimes called the *Rado graph*.

Now, since all countable structures are isomorphic to $\mathbf{A}$ with probability 1, the asymptotic probability of each (generic) property P on countable structures is trivially 0 or 1, since this depends only on whether $\mathbf{A}$ satisfies P or not. Hence, the subject of 0-1 laws over the class of all countable structures is not interesting. As to recursive structures, which are what we are interested in here, one is faced with the difficulty of defining asymptotic probabilities, since structure size is no longer applicable.

The heart of this part of [HH3] is a proposal for a definition of 0-1 laws for recursive structures.

Definition: Let $\mathcal{F} = \{F_i\}_{i=1}^{\infty}$ be a sequence of recursive structures over some vocabulary, and let P be a property defined over the structures in $\mathcal{F}$. Then the *asymptotic probability* $\mu_{\mathcal{F}}(P)$ is defined to be

$$\mu_{\mathcal{F}}(P) = \lim_{n \to \infty} \frac{|\{F_i|\ 1 \le i \le n,\ F_i \models P\}|}{n}.$$

Definition: Let $\mathcal{F} = \{F_i\}_{i=1}^{\infty}$ be a sequence of recursive structures over some vocabulary σ. We say that $\mathcal{F}$ is a *T-sequence* if $\mu_{\mathcal{F}}(\tau) = 1$ for every extension axiom τ over σ.

As an example, a sequence of graphs that are all isomorphic to the countable random graph $\mathbf{A}$ is a T-sequence. We shall use U to denote one such sequence. Here is another example of a T-sequence: take $\mathcal{F} = \{F_n\}_{n=1}^{\infty}$, where each F_n is a graph satisfying all the n-extension axioms and is built in stages. First take n distinct and disconnected points. Then, at each stage add a new point z for every set $\{x_1, \ldots, x_n\}$ from previous stages and for every possible extension axiom for it, and connect z accordingly.

Definition: Let P be a property of recursive structures. We say that the *0–1 law holds for P* if for every T-sequence $\mathcal{F}$ the limit $\mu_{\mathcal{F}}(P)$ exists and is equal to 0 or 1. The *0–1 law holds for a logic L on recursive structures* if it holds for every property expressible in L.

Here are some of the results proved in [HH3] for this definition of 0–1 laws over recursive structures.

Theorem: The 0–1 law holds for all properties of recursive structures definable in first-order logic, strict E-Σ_1^1 and strict E-Π_1^1. Moreover, if $\mathbf{A}$ is the countable random structure, P is such a property and $\mathcal{F}$ is a T-sequence, then $\mathbf{A} \models P$ iff $\mu_{\mathcal{F}}(P) = 1$.

However, the property of a graph having an infinite clique, for example, is shown not to satisfy the 0–1 law, so that the law does not hold in general for E-Σ_1^1-properties.

As a result of the theorem, a property for which the 0–1 law does not hold is not expressible in first-order logic, strict E-Σ_1^1 or strict E-Π_1^1. In fact, we have the following:

Theorem: Every property on recursive structures that is true in $\mathbf{A}$, but does not have probability 1 on some T-sequence, is not expressible by an E-Π_1^1 sentence or by a strict E-Σ_1^1 sentence.

In way of applying the techniques, we show in [HH3] that the following properties are not expressible by an E-Π_1^1 sentence or by a strict E-Σ_1^1 sentence: a recursive graph having an infinite clique, a recursive graph having an infinite independent set, a recursive graph satisfying all the extension axioms, and a pair of recursive graphs being isomorphic.

Acknowledgements: I would like to thank Richard Beigel, who by asking the question addressed in Section 2, introduced me to this area. His work with Bill Gasarch has been a great inspiration. Very special thanks go to Tirza Hirst, without whom this paper couldn't have been written. Apart from Section 2, the results are all joint with her, and form her outstanding PhD thesis.

References

[AV]   S. Abiteboul and V. Vianu, "Generic Computation and Its Complexity", *Proc. 23rd Ann. ACM Symp. on Theory of Computing*, pp. 209–219, ACM Press, New York, 1991.

[AMS]   R. Aharoni, M. Magidor and R. A. Shore, "On the Strength of König's Duality Theorem", *J. of Combinatorial Theory (Series B)* **54**:2 (1992), 257–290.

[B1]   D.R. Bean, "Effective Coloration", *J. Sym. Logic* **41** (1976), 469–480.

[B2]   D.R. Bean, "Recursive Euler and Hamiltonian Paths", *Proc. Amer. Math. Soc.* **55** (1976), 385–394.

[BG1]   R. Beigel and W. I. Gasarch, unpublished results, 1986-1990.

[BG2]   R. Beigel and W. I. Gasarch, "On the Complexity of Finding the Chromatic Number of a Recursive Graph", Parts I & II, *Ann. Pure and Appl. Logic* **45** (1989), 1–38, 227–247.

[Bu]   S. A. Burr, "Some Undecidable Problems Involving the Edge-Coloring and Vertex Coloring of Graphs", *Disc. Math.* **50** (1984), 171–177.

[CH1]   A. K. Chandra and D. Harel, "Computable Queries for Relational Data Bases", *J. Comp. Syst. Sci.* **21**, (1980), 156–178.

[CH2]   A.K. Chandra and D. Harel, "Structure and Complexity of Relational Queries", *J. Comput. Syst. Sci.* **25** (1982), 99–128.

[F1]   R. Fagin, "Generalized First-Order Spectra and Polynomial-Time Recognizable Sets", In *Complexity of Computations* (R. Karp, ed.), SIAM-AMS Proceedings, Vol. 7, 1974, pp. 43–73.

[F2]   R. Fagin, "Probabilities on Finite Models", *J. of Symbolic Logic*, **41**, (1976), 50 – 58.

[GL]   W. I. Gasarch and M. Lockwood, "The Existence of Matchings for Recursive and Highly Recursive Bipartite Graphs", Technical Report 2029, Univ. of Maryland, May 1988.

[GKLT] Y. V. Glebskii, D. I. Kogan, M. I. Liogonki and V. A. Talanov, "Range and Degree of Realizability of Formulas in the Restricted Predicate Calculus", *Cybernetics* **5**, (1969), 142–154.

[H]   D. Harel, "Hamiltonian Paths in Infinite Graphs", *Israel J. Math.* **76**:3 (1991), 317–336. (Also, *Proc. 23rd Ann. ACM Symp. on Theory of Computing*, New Orleans, pp. 220–229, 1991.)

[HH1]   T. Hirst and D. Harel, "Taking it to the Limit: On Infinite Variants of NP-Complete Problems", *J. Comput. Syst. Sci.*, to appear. (Also, *Proc. 8th IEEE Conf. on Structure in Complexity Theory*, IEEE Press, New York, 1993, pp. 292–304.)

[HH2]   T. Hirst and D. Harel, "Completeness Results for Recursive Data Bases", *J. Comput. Syst. Sci.*, to appear. (Also, *12th ACM Ann. Symp. on Principles of Database Systems*, ACM Press, New York, 1993, 244–252.)

[HH3]   T. Hirst and D. Harel, "More about Recursive Structures: Zero-One Laws and Expressibility vs. Complexity", in preparation.

[I]   N. Immerman, "Relational Queries Computable in Polynomial Time", *Inf. and Cont.* **68** (1986), 86–104.

[KT]   P. G. Kolaitis and M. N. Thakur, "Logical definability of NP optimization problems", *6th IEEE Conf. on Structure in Complexity Theory*, pp. 353–366, 1991.

[MR]   A. Manaster and J. Rosenstein, "Effective Matchmaking (Recursion Theoretic Aspects of a Theorem of Philip Hall)", *Proc. London Math. Soc.* **3** (1972), 615–654.

[Mo]   A. S. Morozov, "Functional Trees and Automorphisms of Models", *Algebra and Logic* **32** (1993), 28–38.

[Mos] Y. N. Moschovakis, *Elementary Induction on Abstract Structures*, North Holland, 1974.

[NR]   A. Nerode and J. Remmel, "A Survey of Lattices of R. E. Substructures", In *Recursion Theory*, Proc. Symp. in Pure Math. Vol. 42 (A. Nerode and R. A. Shore, eds.), Amer. Math. Soc., Providence, R. I., 1985, pp. 323–375.

[PR]   A. Panconesi and D. Ranjan, "Quantifiers and Approximation", *Theor. Comp. Sci.* **107** (1993), 145–163.

[PY]   C. H. Papadimitriou and M. Yannakakis, "Optimization, Approximation, and Complexity Classes", *J. Comp. Syst. Sci.* **43**, (1991), 425–440.

[Ra]   R. Rado, "Universal Graphs and Universal Functions", *Acta Arith.*, **9**, (1964), 331–340.

[R]   H. Rogers, *Theory of Recursive Functions and Effective Computability*, McGraw-Hill, New York, 1967.

[V]   M. Y. Vardi, "The Complexity of Relational Query Languages", *Proc. 14th ACM Ann. Symp. on Theory of Computing*, 1982, pp. 137–146.

Chu Spaces and Their Interpretation as Concurrent Objects

Vaughan Pratt[*]

Dept. of Computer Science
Stanford University
Stanford, CA 94305-2140
pratt@cs.stanford.edu

Abstract. A Chu space is a binary relation $\models$ from a set A to an antiset X defined as a set which transforms via converse functions. Chu spaces admit a great many interpretations by virtue of realizing all small concrete categories and most large ones arising in mathematical and computational practice. Of particular interest for computer science is their interpretation as computational processes, which takes A to be a schedule of events distributed in time, X to be an automaton of states forming an information system in the sense of Scott, and the pairs (a, x) in the $\models$ relation to be the individual transcriptions of the making of history. The traditional homogeneous binary relations of transition on X and precedence on A are recovered as respectively the right and left residuals of the heterogeneous binary relation $\models$ with itself. The natural algebra of Chu spaces is that of linear logic, made a process algebra by the process interpretation.

1   Introduction

Two pressing questions for computer science today are, what is concurrency, and what is an object? The first question is of interest to today's sibling growth industries of parallel computing and networks, both of which stretch our extant models of computation well beyond their sequential origins. The second is relevant to programming languages, where the definition of object seems to be based more on whatever software engineering methodologies happen to be in vogue than on the intuitive sense of "object."

One recent view of computation [Tra95] classifies the extant models under the three headings of logic, networks, and automata. But while this perspective nicely ties together three long-established computational frameworks, it neglects more recent developments such as the recent work of Abramsky on interaction categories as exemplified by the category *SProc* [GN95], and of Milner on the π-calculus [MPW92] and more recently action calculi [Mil93]. Moreover its conception of network is more the channel-connected modules of Kahn [Kah74] than the alternating places and transitions of Petri [Pet62].

---

[*] This work was supported by ONR under grant number N00014-92-J-1974.

Petri nets express the duality of events and states in terms of a "token game" played on a bipartite graph. This bipartiteness is the distinguishing feature of Petri nets, resulting in fine-grained or move-based execution where tokens move alternately between events or transitions and states or places. This is in contrast to the coarse-grained or ply-based execution of transition systems where edges connect states, and schedules where edges connect events.

A popular strategy for controlling the conceptual complexity of large concurrent systems is to decompose them into modules that assemble or compose in mathematically formalizable ways. The basic tool for formalizing the composition of modules is algebra. This motivates the development of process algebras forming a suitable basis for concurrent programming languages. Noteworthy such algebras include Hoare's Communicating Sequential Processes (CSP) [Hoa78], Milner's Calculus of Communicating Systems (CCS) [Mil89], and Bergstra and Klop's Algebra of Communicating Processes (ACP) [BK84, BK89].

The token game does not lend itself well to algebra, a limitation addressed by Nielsen et al [NPW81] with the notion of event structure, which they show to be dual to prime algebraic domains, one kind of Scott domain [Sco76]. This duality is an instance of Stone duality [Sto36], a subject that has matured considerably in half a century [Joh82].

We see the essential elements of concurrency as residing in the topics of Petri nets, event structures, domains, Stone duality, and process algebra.

As the separate chapters of a theory of concurrency, these topics make concurrency something of a jigsaw puzzle. One is then naturally led to ask whether the pieces of this puzzle can be arranged in some recognizable order.

In this paper we review the outcome to date of our recent investigations of Chu spaces as a candidate unifying framework for these aspects of concurrency [Pra92, Pra93, Gup93, GP93, Gup94, Pra94b, Pra95a]. Their simplicity is deceptive, and two years of experience with them have convinced us that they are more than adequately equipped for this role.

Chu spaces are simple, useful, and well-organized. With regard to simplicity, a Chu space is merely a matrix that transforms by deleting and copying columns (antimapping) and identifying and adjoining rows (ordinary mapping). The next section defines this process more precisely in terms of a converse function or antifunction g specifying where the surviving columns were copied from and a forward function f specifying where the resulting rows are to be sent to. These contravariant column manipulations constitute mental preparation of states while the covariant row manipulations constitute physical mapping of points; thus Chu spaces transform by looking before they leap.

With regard to utility, besides the motivating application to concurrent computation, Chu spaces find application in mathematics, where they organize relational structures, topology, and duality into a unified framework [Pra95b]; physics, where they provide a process interpretation of wavefunctions [Pra94a]; and philosophy, where they offer a solution to Descartes' problem of the mechanism by which the mind interacts with the body [Pra95a]. Common to these applications is the construction of "everything" in the domain in question in terms of the interaction of appropriate polar opposites in the domain: in mathematics as the interaction of sets and antisets, in physics as the interaction of particles and waves, in philosophy as the interaction of body and mind. It is a measure of the robustness of the notion of Chu space that none of these applications call for any adjustment to its definition.

With regard to organization, Chu spaces and their transforms form a remarkably well-endowed category, being concrete and coconcrete, self-dual, bicomplete, and symmetric monoidal closed. These properties are expressible concretely as operations on the category corresponding to the operations of linear logic and bringing it as close to being a model of full linear logic as any comparably simple structure. The process interpretation of Chu spaces makes this structure a process algebra interpretation of linear logic. This reinforces the connections previously noticed by Asperti [Asp87] and Gehlot and Gunter [GG89] between linear logic and concurrency in the Petri net setting (Section 4).

2   Definitions

Definition 1. A *Chu space over* a set K is a triple $\mathcal{A} = (A, \models, X)$ consisting of sets A and X and a function $\models : A \times X \to K$, that is, an $A \times X$ matrix whose elements are drawn from K. We write the entry at (a, x) as either $\models(a, x)$ or $a \models x$.

We may view $\mathcal{A}$ as being organized either into rows or columns. When viewing $\mathcal{A}$ by row we regard A as the carrier of a structure and the row indexed by a as the complete description of element a. The *description function* $\widetilde{\models} : A \to K^X$ is the function satisfying $\widetilde{\models}(a)(x) = \models(a, x)$, and assigns to each a its description. We write $\tilde{a}$ for the description of a, namely $\widetilde{\models}(a)$, and $\tilde{A}$ for the set $\{\tilde{a} \mid a \in A\}$ of all rows of $\mathcal{A}$. When the description function is injective (no repeated rows) we say that $\mathcal{A}$ is T_0 (or coextensional).

When viewing $\mathcal{A}$ by column we view A as consisting of locations or variables with values ranging over K, and the column indexed by x as one of the permitted assignments to these variables. The *extension function* $\widetilde{\models} : X \to K^A$ satisfies $\widetilde{\models}(x)(a) = \models(x, a)$; a state $x \in X$ is understood as merely the *name* of an assignment or binding of values to variables. The notations $\tilde{x}$ and $\tilde{X}$ are the evident duals of $\tilde{a}$ and $\tilde{A}$. When the extension function is injective (no repeated columns) we call $\mathcal{A}$ *extensional*. In a nonextensional Chu space two states may name the same assignment.

A Chu space can in this way be seen as a multiset A of rows from K^X and a multiset X of columns from K^A, with "multiset" replaced by "set" when T_0 and extensional. The rows present the physical, concrete, conjunctive, or yang aspects of the space, while the columns present the mental, coconcrete, disjunctive, or yin aspects. We may regard rows and columns as characteristic functions of subsets of respectively X and A, where K is taken to consist of the degrees of membership, with $K = 2 = \{0, 1\}$ giving the ordinary notion of membership, 1 for in and 0 for out.

The Chu space obtained by identifying all pairs x, y of column indices for which $\tilde{x} = \tilde{y}$, and likewise for row indices, is called the *skeleton* of that Chu space. A *normal* Chu space is one satisfying $\tilde{x} = x$ for all $x \in X$ (whence $\tilde{X} = X$), and can be written as simply (A, X), $\models (a, x)$ being definable as $x(a)$. A normal space is automatically extensional but need not be T_0.

The *dual* of Chu space $(A, \models, X)$ is its transpose, notated $(X, \models, A)$ where $\models(x, a) = \models(a, x)$. A *conormal* space is the dual of a normal space, automatically T_0 but not necessarily extensional.

Chu transforms. Just as vector spaces transform via linear transformations and posets via monotone functions, so do Chu spaces transform via Chu transforms, turning the class of Chu spaces into the category $\mathbf{Chu}(\mathbf{Set}, K)$ or just $\mathbf{Chu}_K$.

Definition 2. Given source and target Chu spaces $\mathcal{A} = (A, \models, X)$ and $\mathcal{A}' = (A', \models', X')$, a *Chu transform* $(f, g) : \mathcal{A} \to \mathcal{A}'$ consists of a pair of functions $f : A \to A'$, $g : X' \to X$ satisfying the following *adjointness* condition.

$$\forall a \in A \; \forall x' \in X' \; . \; f(a) \models' x' = a \models g(x').$$

Chu transforms may be understood operationally as "look before you leap," that is, mental preparation followed by physical transformation, with an intermediate Chu space $\mathcal{A}'' = (A, \models'', X')$ representing the result of just the mental preparation. The columns of $\mathcal{A}''$ all appear in $\mathcal{A}$ while its rows all appear in $\mathcal{A}'$. Column x' of $\mathcal{A}''$ appears as column $g(x')$ of $\mathcal{A}$ and row a of $\mathcal{A}''$ appears as row $f(a)$ of $\mathcal{A}'$. Either one of these requirements suffice to determine $\models''(a, x')$ uniquely, as either $\models(a, g(x'))$ or $\models'(f(a), x')$. The adjointness condition is the necessary and sufficient condition for their consistency. This process is illustrated by the following example (which incidentally realizes the projection of the two dimensional vector space over $GF(2)$ onto one axis).

$$
\begin{array}{c}
\begin{matrix} 0\,0\,0\,0 \\ 0\,1\,0\,1 \\ 0\,0\,1\,1 \\ 0\,1\,1\,0 \end{matrix}
\quad
\begin{array}{c} \text{delete cols 2,3} \\ \longrightarrow \\ \text{copy cols 0,1} \end{array}
\quad
\begin{matrix} 0\,0\,0\,0 \\ 0\,1\,0\,1 \\ 0\,0\,0\,0 \\ 0\,1\,0\,1 \end{matrix}
\quad
\begin{array}{c} \text{send rows 2,3} \\ \text{to rows 0,1} \\ \longrightarrow \\ \text{adjoin original} \\ \text{rows 2 and 3} \end{array}
\quad
\begin{matrix} 0\,0\,0\,0 \\ 0\,1\,0\,1 \\ 0\,0\,1\,1 \\ 0\,1\,1\,0 \end{matrix}
\end{array}
$$

Columns 2 and 3 are deleted, and a copy made of columns 0 and 1. Then row 0 is identified with 2 and 1 with 3, and two new rows adjoined (which happen to be rows 2 and 3 of the source but they could have been anything had we not cared whether the target was a vector space). (The intermediate space is not a vector space, but would have been the one-dimensional vector space had we done the row identifying in the first stage and the column copying in the second, a reasonable order.)

The "mental preparation" step therefore consists of deleting some columns and making copies of others. *No new columns are introduced*, so no structure (in the form of disallowed states) is lost. If the target has structure absent from the source, the structure must first be added by deleting columns or the row mapping will not be possible. This gives Chu transforms the character of structure-preserving homomorphisms [Pra95b], with continuous functions then falling out as an obvious special case when analyzed as above. All relational structures are realizable as Chu spaces [Pra93, Pra95b], as are topological spaces [LS91]. These representations can be combined to represent topological relational structures such as topological groups, topological vector spaces (the main *-autonomous category studied in [Bar79]), ordered Stone spaces [Pri70], and so on. More recently (note in preparation) we have shown that every small concrete category C is realizable in $\mathbf{Chu}_K$ where K is the disjoint union of the underlying sets of the objects of C.

3   Process

3.1   Interaction of events and states

This section gives the computational or process interpretation of Chu spaces, in terms of their internal row-and-column structure rather than their external linear-logic structure, the topic of the next section.

We propose to understand computation in terms of the interaction of a pure schedule, understood as a set of concurrent events, with a pure automaton, understood as a set of possible alternative worlds or states, This parallels our proposed interpretations of other phenomena in terms of the interaction of opposites appropriate to those phenomena.

Although computation has a number of facets, a particularly problematic one is concurrency, the search for whose essence led us to the Chu space model. We begin by discussing what is problematic about concurrency.

To cater for concurrency we moved in the 1980's from the traditional state-oriented view of computation that we had embraced in the 1970's to a more event-oriented view. The former understands concurrency in terms of interleaving: concurrent events are those that can happen *in either order*. The latter understands concurrency in terms of independence or asynchrony: concurrent events are those that bear no temporal relationship to each other, happening *without regard for order* as distinct from simultaneous or synchronized events.

The main difference here is that the state oriented view cannot distinguish between mutual exclusion and independence for events that we wish or need to view as atomic. For example, if two children each wish to ride a pony, they are much happier when there are two ponies. One pony offers the choice of two possible sequential behaviors ab or ba. Two ponies dispense with both choice and delay by permitting the single concurrent behavior $a\|b$. Notice that our discussion of the situation is in terms of the rides as atomic actions; we did not say what goes on during the ride in drawing this distinction. The traditional state model cannot draw this distinction because it automatically identifies $a\|b$ and $ab + ba$ when the rides a and b are understood as atomic.

By expressing a behavior as a partially ordered set of events, and a process as a set of possible behaviors, this distinction can now be drawn naturally by representing $a \| b$ as an unordered set of two events constituting one behavior, and $ab + ba$ as two possible behaviors, one for each linear ordering of the two events.

In practice however, people naturally think as much in terms of states as events. What is really needed is a simple connection between the two viewpoints facilitating a smooth passage between them.

Chu spaces address concurrency by admitting their interpretation as processes. The rows and columns of a Chu space are interpreted as respectively the events and states of the process, while the entries of the matrix are interpreted as the interaction of event and state, more specifically as the recording, by the state, of information about the event. Events are regarded as points in time while states are points in information space. Events specify no particular information, though they are associated with incremental changes to information, just as derivatives are associated with no particular position but rather only with incremental changes to position. Dually, states do not exist at any particular moment in time, but rather are associated with incremental changes in time: time passes while one waits in a state, during which (at least for discrete time) no events change status. We distinguish between time as the actual position of events and information as the *knowledge* of those positions.

A Chu space as a process may be viewed either imperatively or declaratively by focusing on the columns or the rows respectively of the representing space.

3.2   Extracting transitions and constraints

The Chu space model of behavior may be usefully contrasted with the traditional imperative transition-based approach as well as with the declarative approach involving temporal (precedence, delay, etc.) constraints between events, as follows (we assume $K = 2$ for simplicity).

The basic component of the imperative approach is the transition, consisting of a pair (x, y) of states whose meaning is that it is *possible* to pass from state x to state y. An automaton is a set of such transitions, which if acyclic may be reflexively and transitively closed to partially order the set X of states.

The corresponding basic component in the event-oriented approach is the precedence constraint, consisting of a pair (a, b) of events whose meaning is that it is *necessary* to perform event a before event b. A schedule is a set of such constraints, acyclic when there is no deadlock and hence transitively closable to partially order the set A of events.

Both these views involve *ongoing motion* between points of the same type, namely states in an information space in the imperative case and events in time in the declarative case. These motions differ with regard to the interpretation of branching, which is understood disjunctively in an automaton (only one path is taken) but conjunctively in a schedule (all constraints must be observed).

The Chu space view involves not ongoing or connected motion but instead recording. A *recording* is a pair (a, x) consisting of an event a and a state x. A Chu space is a set of such recordings. This makes it a bipartite directed graph, namely a binary relation from the set A of events to the set X of states, for which "acyclic" and "transitive" are not usefully definable. In this way Chu spaces capture the fine-grained move-orientation of Petri nets, as opposed to the traditional coarse-grained ply-orientation of transitions and precedence constraints, but with more satisfactory algebra than Petri nets.

What *is* definable for any two binary relations with a common source A is their *right residual*. If $R \subseteq A \times B$ and $T \subseteq A \times C$ then their *right residual* $R \backslash T$, as a relation from B to C, is defined as consisting of those pairs (b, c) such that for all $a \in A$, aRb implies aTc.

Now the right residual $\models \backslash \models$ of the Chu space relation $\models$ with itself yields a binary relation on X. This relation is the largest possible transition relation on X having the property that no transition from x to y can "undo" an event that is recorded in state x as having already happened. It is also the natural "inclusion" or bitwise order on columns, in which $0 \leq 1$, which of course makes it clear that it partially orders X.

The left residual of two relations with a common target is defined dually. If $S \subseteq B \times C$ and $T \subseteq A \times C$, then their *left residual* T/S, as a binary relation from A to B, is defined as consisting of those pairs (a, b) such that for all $c \in A$, bSc implies aTc. The left residual $\models/\models$ yields a binary relation on A, namely the largest possible precedence relation with the property that for every pair (a, b) in the relation, no state has witnessed b without a. This too is a partial order.

The residual-based derivations of ongoing state-state and event-event *motion* in terms of event-state *recording* lifts to more general relationships than the all-or-nothing ($K = 2$) one of possibility of transition and necessity of precedence, a mathematically rich and interesting topic that space and time prevent us from delving into here. To summarize briefly, distances are organized as a *quantale* [Ros90] or complete semilattice monoid. This combines our earlier investigations of purely temporal structures [CCMP91] with our more recent work on time-information duality and Chu spaces in a way that permits the temporal-structure results to be lifted directly, via duality, to information structures such as automata and Scott-style information systems. This generalizes the two-valued generalized metric associated with partial orders to other metrics such as causal-accidental order, strict-nonstrict order, and various notions of real time (*op.cit.* p.187).

3.3   Interpretation as Objects

As an unintended bonus, Chu spaces admit a straightforward interpretation as concurrent objects. Whereas statically sets and antisets are indistinguishable, dynamically they are distinguished by transforming respectively via functions and antifunctions. Noting that the set of states of an automaton forms an antiset, understood as a mental entity, we take an object to be a set, understood as physical. As a conjunctive set, the points of an object coexist, in contrast to a disjunctive antiset of states, the sense in which we consider an object to be concurrent. A collection $A_1, \ldots, A_n$ of objects is concurrent in the sense that its sum or coproduct $\sum_i A_i$ is a concurrent object. In the absence of all constraints (i.e. the set of states of A is K^A), the object is truly concurrent, consisting of independent events. The imposition of constraints creates interferences between events such as conflicts and precedence constraints.

Although the methods of a given class are traditionally viewed as functions performable by objects of that class, in the context of Chu spaces we propose to take as the methods of a Chu space its states, which are just the permitted assignments of values from K to the physical points or locations of the space.

4 Algebra

The previous section examined Chu spaces from the inside in terms of their components. In this section we consider them from the outside, in terms of their language or algebra. The natural language of Chu spaces is linear logic, which appears to us to be as fundamental as any other process language, with Chu spaces giving it a sensible and useful interpretation.

4.1 Chu space interpretation of linear logic

As with Boolean logic there are various choices of basis for the set of all linear logic operations (though none as small as Boolean logic's single NAND operation!). A particularly natural basis, both in its own right and for our process interpretation, consists of four operations and two constants: the additive disjunction *plus*, $A \oplus B$, the multiplicative conjunction (tensor product) *times*, $A \otimes B$, linear negation $A^\perp$, and the exponential or modality *of-course*, $!A$. Associated with plus and times are their respective units or zeroary operations 0 and 1.

When negation is omitted from this list, and $!A$ is interpreted as A, the laws of linear logic expressible in the remaining language are merely those of ordinary number theory. Larry Moss has pointed out to us that this remains true when $A^\ddagger = (!A)^\perp$ is taken as basic in place of $!A$ and interpreted numerically as 2^A (motivations: the axiom $(A \oplus B)^\ddagger = A^\ddagger \otimes B^\ddagger$ can be expressed without negation [Pra93], and the 2^A offers a rationale for Girard's "exponential").

The presence of negation adds a completely new dimension to number theory. To begin with, plus and times and of-course each has its own De Morgan dual, respectively the additive conjunction *with*, $A \& B$, the multiplicative disjunction *par*, $A \otimes B$, and the dual exponential *why-not* $?A$, with the first two having respective units $\top$ and $\bot$. Linear implication $A \multimap B$ is defined as $(A \otimes B^\perp)^\perp$ or $A^\perp \otimes B$, while intuitionistic implication $A \Rightarrow B$ is defined as $!A \multimap B$. None of these operations has a number-theoretic interpretation.

With negation present, the basic operations may be interpreted as acting on Chu spaces as follows. $A^\perp$ is just the dual or transpose of A, $!A$ is the carrier A of A as a Chu space, namely the normal Chu space (A, K^A).

$A \oplus B$ for $A = (A, \models_A, X)$, $B = (B, \models_B, Y)$ is $(A + B, \models, X \times Y)$ where $\models$ is defined by $a \models (x, y) = a \models_A x$, $b \models (x, y) = b \models_B y$. Its unit is $(0, !, 1)$.

With the same A and B, $A \otimes B$ is $(A \times B, \models, |A \multimap B^\perp|)$ whose states are all Chu transforms (f, g) from A to $B^\perp$ (so $f : A \to Y$ and $g : B \to X$) and where $(a, b) \models (f, g)$ is defined equivalently (by the adjointness condition) as either

$b \dashv_B f(a)$ or $a \dashv_A g(b)$. Its unit is the $1 \times K$ normal Chu space whose one row is the identity function on K.

This completes the Chu space interpretation of the basic operations and constants. The interpretations of the derived operations are obtained from their definitions.

4.2 Process interpretation of linear logic

The computational significance of the operations is as follows; we leave negation to the end.

$A \oplus B$ is the asynchronous (noncommunicating or parallel play) concurrent composition of A and B. If A is the process of my eating dinner and I take 47 bites, and B is you taking 53 bites, then $A \oplus B$ is us eating dinner together taking 100 bites in silence, that is, with no interaction. Our possible joint states form the set $X \times Y$ of all possible pairs of our individual states. The associated unit 0 has no events and 1 state, and is as unconstrained as a zero-event process gets.

$A \otimes B$ is the orthocurrence [Pra85, Pra86] or interaction or flow-through of A and B, as with three trains passing through two stations to yield six train-station events. Each event is of the form (a, b) pairing a train with a station. Each state is of the form (f, g) where $f : A \rightarrow Y$ specifies for each train a what state the stations collectively appear to be in as seen from that train, while $g : B \rightarrow X$ does the same for the trains collectively as seen from each station. The associated unit 1 has one event and is completely unconstrained in that it has all states possible for a one-event process, namely K. When A and B realize posets, $A \otimes B$ realizes the poset that is their direct product (same as their tensor product since **Pos** is cartesian closed).

$!A$ consists of the events of A less their constraints, making it a pure set of independent events.

With the operations and constants covered so far (including $A^{\ddagger}$), it is impossible to introduce constraints starting from only unconstrained processes. The only processes are then in effect cardinals, from which follows the completeness of number theory as an axiomatization of the basic operations without negation—any number theoretic counterexample to a nontheorem of number theory becomes a process counterexample making it also a nontheorem of process algebra. (The only awkward part with $A^{\ddagger}$ is to show completeness for number theory of the axiomatization $(A + B)^{\ddagger} = A^{\ddagger} \times B^{\ddagger}$, $0^{\ddagger} = 1$, $1^{\ddagger} = 1 + 1$.)

Negation merely dualizes our point of view, interchanging the qualities of event and state. States become physical entities and events mental, as in an automaton or a computer program where the locations in the text are real and the runtime events must be imagined. Actually running the program undoes the negation; the program itself disappears from physical view, at least in principle, and the runtime events become physical.

Linear implication $A \multimap B$ can be understood as B observing A, a point of view we first developed in [CCMP91]. The definition reveals observation to be equivalent to the interaction $A \otimes B^{\perp}$ of the events of the observed A with the states of the observer B, namely where B records the observations, with the individual recordings of event a of $\mathcal{A}$ in state y of $\mathcal{B}$ as the *recording events* of $\mathcal{A} \otimes \mathcal{B}^{\perp}$. Taking the dual of this then turns the recording events into the states of $\mathcal{A}{-}\!\circ\mathcal{B}$, which is how the recording events should appear to an observer of $\mathcal{B}$ observing $\mathcal{A}$.

5 Universality

The previous sections emphasized the computational or information-processing and behavioral or scheduling interpretation of Chu spaces, our original motivation bringing us to them. In this section we review more briefly three other areas in which Chu spaces seem to offer fundamental insights, namely mathematics, physics, and philosophy.

Mathematics. We have argued elsewhere [Pra95a, Pra95b] that the mathematical universe is constructed from the interaction of polar opposites, specifically sets and "antisets" or Boolean algebras (of the complete and atomic kind when that question arises), in varying proportions.

Chu spaces are in a certain sense the dual of categories. This may be seen from the perspective of universal algebra, which organizes mathematics into three levels of abstraction, elements (numbers, points), structures (groups, topological spaces), and categories of structures (**Grp**, **Top**). This last may be organized as the (superlarge) category **ConCAT** of large *concrete* categories (C, U_C) where $U_C : C \to \mathbf{Set}$ is a faithful functor assigning a set or *carrier* to every object of the large category C.

Category theory reduces this organization to two levels by suppressing the elements of structures and calling the latter merely objects. Elements of objects x of C are recovered when needed as morphisms from T to x for a suitable object T of C, typically C's tensor unit.

Chu spaces also reduce the universal algebra picture to two levels, by suppressing not the elements but instead the boundaries between categories. This viewpoint applies to any category C that concretely and fully embeds a given class of categories; C contains all the objects of all categories in that class, and at least for pairs of objects of C realizing objects from the same category D, the morphisms between those objects in C are exactly those between them in D, in the sense that they consist of the same underlying functions acting on the same underlying sets, by fullness and concreteness.

In addition to this mathematical universality, Chu spaces also have more specialized mathematical uses. For example they permit a more uniform treatment [Pra95b] of the gamut of categories treated by Johnstone under the heading of Stone spaces [Joh82]. Stone duality is poorly understood in computer science, yet is of crucial importance to understanding the relationships between imperative and declarative programming, denotational and operational semantics, and algebra and logic. By simplifying Stone duality to mere matrix transposition, Chu spaces make that subject more accessible.

Physics. The physical universe appears to be constructed from the interaction of particles and waves, an interaction described by quantum mechanics that makes everything a mixture of the two, again in varying proportions. Associating the points of Hilbert space with states and the dimensions (for a given choice of basis) with outcomes of measurements (events) associated to that basis as usual, a wavefunction as a pure state encodes correlations decoded with $\langle\psi|\varphi\rangle$ and $|\psi\rangle\langle\varphi|$, the notation in quantum mechanics for the respective residuals $\psi\backslash\varphi$ and ψ/φ. A mixed state, or mixture of wavefunctions described by a probability density matrix, may be understood as corresponding to a whole Chu space.

Philosophy. Yet another subject amenable to this perspective is the mind-body problem. Descartes proposed in 1637 that the mind interacted with the body. This proposal generated much literature all denying the causal interaction of mind and body and explaining their apparent interaction via various forms of *deus ex machina* (Malebranche, Spinoza, Leibniz), or denial of body (Berkeley) or mind (Hobbes), or the assertion of their equivalence (Russell). Elsewhere [Pra95a] we have applied Chu spaces to an implementation of Descartes' proposal, by taking the causal interaction of mind and body as basic instead of derived and obtaining as its consequences the basic interactions within each of body and mind. We do not see how to obtain the other direction, mind-body interaction from the separate behavior of mind and body, any better than did Descartes' contemporaries.

Viewed at the object level, Chu spaces formalize Russell's solution mathematically by offering dual views of the same Chu space merely by transposition of viewpoint. Viewed at the level of individual interactions within an object however, the solution takes on a new and deeper meaning: mind-body interaction turns out to be the *only* real interaction, body-body and mind-mind interaction are secondary interactions, derivable by residuation, that can be considered mere figments of our imagination as to how the universe interacts with itself.

6   Conclusion

Reflections. Our own interest in linear logic is as a process algebra. But linear logic was developed by a proof theorist, purportedly to tidy up proofs. Why should such different goals lead to the same logic?

Linear logic is a resource sensitive logic in the sense that it disallows weakening (unused premises) and contraction (multiply used premises). Some have taken this to mean that it is a logic for reasoning *about* resources such as time and space in computation. It seems to us however that resource sensitivity in the logic is a dual side effect of resource *neglect* arising from reasoning inside the model, as results with equational logic and categorical reasoning. External reasoning in contrast takes place in the combinatorial world of sets, whose cartesian closed structure renders weakening and contraction sound, and where cardinality tracks resources [Pra95b, §7].

Resource sensitivity is merely a symptom, linear logic is more properly understood as a logic of interaction of polar opposites, with $A\otimes B$ as the interaction operator, $A^\perp$ as the duality "mirror" interchanging opposites, and $!A$ and $?A$ as projecting the domain onto its respective poles. The remaining operator $A\oplus B$

and constant 0 then provide finite coproducts, with duality then yielding finite products (but why not coequalizers etc.?). We have argued [Pra95b] that **Set** and **Set**[op] suffice as poles in mathematical practice, but we acknowledge that there remains considerable room for debate here.

History. The Chu construction takes a symmetric monoidal closed category V with pullbacks and an object k of V and "completes" V to a self-dual category **Chu**(V, k). The details of the construction appear in P.-H. Chu's master thesis, published as the appendix to his advisor M. Barr's book introducing the notion of *-autonomous category [Bar79].

The intimate connection between linear logic and *-autonomous categories was first noticed by Seely [See89], furnishing Girard's linear logic [Gir87] with a natural constructive semantics. Barr then proposed the Chu construction as a source of constructive models of linear logic [Bar91].

The case $V = $ **Set** is important for its combination of simplicity and generality. This case was first treated explicitly by Lafont and Streicher [LS91], where they treated its connections with von Neumann-Morgenstern games and linear logic, observing in passing that vector spaces, topological spaces, and coherent spaces were realizable as games, giving a small early hint of their universality.

Our own interest in Chu spaces was a consequence of attempts to formalize a suitable notion of partial distributive lattice. After arriving at such a notion based on the interaction of ordered Stone spaces and distributive lattices, we found that the resulting category was equivalent to both **Chu**(**Set**, 2) and a full subcategory of **Chu**(**Pos**, 2) for which the description and extension monotone functions of a Chu space were both full, i.e. isometries.

The name "Chu space" (over K) was suggested to the author by Barr in 1993 as a suitable name for the objects of **Chu**(**Set**, K) reifying "Chu construction," which predated Lafont and Streicher's "game." An advantage of "Chu space" is that it requires no disambiguating qualification to uniquely identify it, unlike "game." By analogy with categories enriched in V [Kel82] one might refer to the objects of the general Chu construction **Chu**(V, k) as V-*enriched* Chu spaces.

Acknowledgements

The application of Chu spaces to computation was developed in collaboration with my student Vineet Gupta [Gup94]. Rob van Glabbeek and Gordon Plotkin have separately been invaluable sounding-boards and sources of ideas, and jointly of results [VGP95]. Carolyn Brown, with Doug Gurr, was the first to explore the connection between the Chu construction and concurrency [BG90], and has been a useful source of insights. Dusko Pavlovic has developed a formal sense in which Chu spaces are universal for mathematics, more correctly their couniversality. I am also grateful to H. Andreka, I. Nemeti, I. Sain for the opportunity to present a one-week course on Chu spaces to an attentive audience at their TEMPUS summer school in Budapest in 1994. I am also very grateful to ONR for making it possible to host small two-monthly "Chu sessions" for the past three summers, involving our students along with Rob van Glabbeek and visitors Gordon Plotkin, Carolyn Brown, and this year Dusko Pavlovic and Michael Barr.

References

[Asp87]   A. Asperti. A logic for concurrency. Manuscript, November 1987.

[Bar79]   M. Barr. *-*Autonomous categories*, volume 752 of *Lecture Notes in Mathematics*. Springer-Verlag, 1979.

[Bar91]   M. Barr. *-Autonomous categories and linear logic. *Math Structures in Comp. Sci.*, 1(2):159–178, 1991.

[BG90]   C. Brown and D. Gurr. A categorical linear framework for Petri nets. In J. Mitchell, editor, *Logic in Computer Science*, pages 208–218. IEEE Computer Society, June 1990.

[BK84]   J.A. Bergstra and J.W. Klop. Process algebra for synchronous communication. *Information and Control*, 60:109–137, 1984.

[BK89]   J.A. Bergstra and J.W. Klop. Process theory based on bisimulation semantics. In *Proc. REX School/Workshop on Linear Time, Branching Time and Partial Order in Logics and Models for Concurrency*, pages 50–122, Springer-Verlag, 1989.

[CCMP91] R.T Casley, R.F. Crew, J. Meseguer, and V.R. Pratt. Temporal structures. *Math. Structures in Comp. Sci.*, 1(2):179–213, July 1991.

[GG89]   C. A. Gunter and V. Gehlot. Nets as tensor theories. (preliminary report). In G. De Michelis, editor, *Applications of Petri Nets*, pages 174–191, 1989. Also Univ. of Pennsylvania, Logic and Computation Report Nr 17.

[Gir87]   J.-Y. Girard. Linear logic. *Theoretical Computer Science*, 50:1–102, 1987.

[GN95]   S. Gay and R. Nagarajan. A typed calculus of synchronous processes. In *Logic in Computer Science*, pages 210–220. IEEE Computer Society, June 1995.

[GP93]   V. Gupta and V.R. Pratt. Gates accept concurrent behavior. In *Proc. 34th Ann. IEEE Symp. on Foundations of Comp. Sci.*, pages 62–71, 1993.

[Gup93]   V. Gupta. Concurrent Kripke structures. In *North American Process Algebra Workshop*, Proceedings, Cornell CS-TR-93-1369, August 1993.

[Gup94]   V. Gupta.   *Chu Spaces: A Model of Concurrency*.   PhD thesis, Stanford University, September 1994.   Tech. Report, available as ftp://boole.stanford.edu/pub/gupthes.ps.Z.

[Hoa78]   C.A.R. Hoare. Communicating sequential processes. *Communications of the ACM*, 21(8):666–672, August 1978.

[Joh82]   P.T. Johnstone. *Stone Spaces*. Cambridge University Press, 1982.

[Kah74]   G. Kahn. The semantics of a simple language for parallel programming. In *Proc. IFIP Congress 74*. North-Holland, Amsterdam, 1974.

[Kel82]   G.M. Kelly. *Basic Concepts of Enriched Category Theory*, London Math. Soc. Lecture Notes. 64. Cambridge University Press, 1982.

[LS91]   Y. Lafont and T. Streicher. Games semantics for linear logic. In *Proc. 6th Annual IEEE Symp. on Logic in Computer Science*, pages 43–49, Amsterdam, July 1991.

[Mil89]   R. Milner. *Communication and Concurrency*. Prentice-Hall, 1989.

[Mil93]   R. Milner. Action calculi, or syntactic action structures. In *MFCS'93*, Proceedings, volume 711 of *Lecture Notes in Computer Science*, pages 105–121, Springer-Verlag, 1993.

[MPW92] R. Milner, J. Parrow, and D Walker. A calculus of mobile processes. *Information and Control*, 100:1–77, 1992.

[NPW81] M. Nielsen, G. Plotkin, and G. Winskel. Petri nets, event structures, and domains, part I. *Theoretical Computer Science*, 13:85–108, 1981.

[Pet62]   C.A. Petri. Fundamentals of a theory of asynchronous information flow. In *Proc. IFIP Congress 62*, pages 386–390, 1962. North-Holland, Amsterdam.

[Pra85]   V.R. Pratt. Some constructions for order-theoretic models of concurrency. In *Proc. Conf. on Logics of Programs*, volume 193 of *Lecture Notes in Computer Science*, pages 269–283, Springer-Verlag, 1985.

[Pra86]   V.R. Pratt. Modeling concurrency with partial orders. *Int. J. of Parallel Programming*, 15(1):33–71, February 1986.

[Pra92]   V.R. Pratt. The duality of time and information. In *Proc. of CONCUR'92*, volume 630 of *Lecture Notes in Computer Science*, pages 237–253, Springer-Verlag, 1992.

[Pra93]   V.R. Pratt. The second calculus of binary relations. In *MFCS'93*, Proceedings, volume 711 of *Lecture Notes in Computer Science*, pages 142–155, Springer-Verlag, 1993.

[Pra94a]   V.R. Pratt. Chu spaces: Automata with quantum aspects. In *Proc. Workshop on Physics and Computation (PhysComp'94)*, Dallas, 1994. IEEE.

[Pra94b]   V.R. Pratt. Time and information in sequential and concurrent computation. In *Proc. Theory and Practice of Parallel Programming (TPPP'94)*, Sendai, Japan, November 1994.

[Pra95a]   V.R. Pratt. Rational mechanics and natural mathematics. In *TAPSOFT'95*, volume 915 of *Lecture Notes in Computer Science*, pages 108–122, Springer-Verlag, 1995.

[Pra95b]   V.R. Pratt. The Stone gamut: A coordinatization of mathematics. In *Logic in Computer Science*, pages 444–454. IEEE Computer Society, June 1995.

[Pri70]   H.A. Priestley. Representation of distributive lattices. *Bull. London Math. Soc.*, 2:186–190, 1970.

[Ros90]   K.I. Rosenthal. *Quantales and their applications*. Longman Scientific and Technical, 1990.

[Sco76]   D. Scott. Data types as lattices. *SIAM Journal on Computing*, 5(3):522–587, 1976.

[See89]   R.A.G Seely. Linear logic, *-autonomous categories and cofree algebras. In *Categories in Computer Science and Logic*, volume 92 of *Contemporary Mathematics*, pages 371–382, held June 1987, Boulder, Colorado, 1989.

[Sto36]   M. Stone. The theory of representations for Boolean algebras. *Trans. Amer. Math. Soc.*, 40:37–111, 1936.

[Tra95]   B. Trakhtenbrot. Origins and metamorphoses of the trinity: logic, nets, automata. In D. Kozen, editor, *Logic in Computer Science*, pages 506–507. IEEE Computer Society, June 1995.

[VGP95]   R. Van Glabbeek and G. Plotkin. Configuration structures. In *Logic in Computer Science*, pages 199–209. IEEE Computer Society, June 1995.

Abstracting Unification: A Key Step in the Design of Logic Program Analyses

Maurice Bruynooghe[1], Michael Codish[2] and Anne Mulkers[1]

[1] K.U.Leuven, Department of Computer Science,
Celestijnenlaan 200A, 3001 Heverlee, Belgium
[2] Ben-Gurion University, Department of Mathematics and Computer Science,
P.O.B. 653, 84105 Beer-Sheva, Israel

Abstract. This paper focuses on one of the key steps in the design of semantic based analyses for logic programs — the definition of an abstract
unification algorithm for a given notion of data description. We survey
some of the major notions of data descriptions proposed in the context of
mode and sharing analyses. We demonstrate how a careful and systematic analysis of the underlying concrete unification algorithm contributes
to the design of the abstract algorithm. Several relevant properties of concrete substitutions which influence the design of abstract domains and
algorithms are described. We make use of a novel representation called
abstract equation systems to uniformly represent a a wide range of data
descriptions for such analyses proposed in the literature.

1 Introduction

Abstract interpretation has been established by Cousot and Cousot [17] as a formal basis for program analysis. The essence is captured by the statement: "Abstract interpretation is computation over a non-standard domain of data descriptions". The computation performed during the execution of a logic program consists basically of a sequence of unifications. Similarly, an abstract interpretation-
based program analysis consists of a sequence of unifications over a non-standard
domain of data descriptions. There is more to it however, as concrete computations potentially perform an unbounded number of unifications, thereby accu-
mulating substitutions over an unbounded number of variables. The problems
arising from the unboundedness are solved by abstract interpretation frameworks [5, 6, 10, 18, 24, 31, 33] which are designed in such a way that a safe
approximation of the program behavior — modeled as a fixpoint of a function
over the standard domain of the program — can be obtained in a finite number
of iterations. When applying such a framework to obtain program analyses, an
appropriate domain of data descriptions and a number of primitive operations
must be provided. The key component among these operations is unification in
the domain of data descriptions, called *abstract unification* for short. Many of
the more significant applications of such frameworks to program analysis focus
on characterizing properties of the terms which program variables may be bound
to during executions of the program. Properties of interest include groundness,
freeness, linearity, and sharing — the precise definitions of which will be clarified

below. These properties are useful for a wide range of compiler optimizations, for parallelizing the execution of logic programs as well as for improving the precision of many other types of program analyses. As such, the relevant literature is saturated with proposals for various domains and corresponding unification algorithms which provide the basis for program analyses to obtain information regarding these types of properties. Developing a correct abstraction of unification is for many abstract domains a difficult, if not to say error-prone process [8].

In this paper we discuss some of the major domains of data descriptions and their corresponding abstract unification algorithms. We focus mainly on the issue of ensuring correctness of abstract unification. We develop a setting for analyzing the correctness of abstract unification which is general enough to cover a wide range of analyses described in the literature. We argue that the essential step in developing a correct abstraction is the careful analysis of the underlying concrete unification, we describe several relevant properties of concrete substitutions and their relationship, and finally we unravel the intuitions underlying the abstract unification operation of several abstract domains.

Having argued that computation consists of a sequence of unifications and having pointed out that the problems posed by the unboundedness of the sequences are handled by frameworks, we focus the rest of the paper on abstracting a single unification, which is the key step in the design of a logic program analysis. Section 2 recalls basic concepts about substitutions. Section 3 contains a formulation of abstract unification which is suited as a basis for abstract interpretation frameworks. Section 4 reviews a set of properties of interest for program analyses. In Section 5 the importance of sharing information for both correctness and precision of program analyses is discussed. Section 6 provides a more general formulation of abstract unification that is based on the notion of equation systems. In Section 7, a methodology for developing correct analyses is discussed and the ideas underlying soundness proofs of a few well-known abstract domains are reviewed. In Section 8, a domain of abstract equation systems is described as an illustration of an abstract unification algorithm designed according to this methodology.

2   Preliminaries

We assume the standard notation for logic programs as described for example in [2, 32]. Let Σ be a fixed alphabet of function symbols and Var a denumerable set of concrete variables. The set of terms constructed using function symbols from Σ and variables from Var is denoted Term. The set of variables occurring in a syntactic object s is denoted by $\text{Var}(s)$.

Substitutions are mappings from Var to Term which behave as the identity mapping almost everywhere and which are described by a set of pairs X/t. The domain of a substitution θ is denoted $Dom(\theta) = \{X \mid X\theta \neq X\}$ and $Range(\theta) = \{X \in \text{Var}(Y\theta) \mid Y \in Dom(\theta)\}$ is the range of θ. Unification algorithms produce idempotent substitutions, so we restrict our attention to such substitutions. The composition of two substitutions θ and σ is denoted by $\theta\sigma$ and its effect on an expression is the same as that of first applying θ and then σ. The restriction of a substitution to a set of variables S is $\theta\lceil S = \{X/t \in \theta \mid X \in S\}$. A unifier θ of two terms t and s is a substitution such that $t\theta = s\theta$ and is called relevant if $\mathsf{Var}(\theta) \subseteq \mathsf{Var}(t = s)$ [2].

Program analyses typically focus on properties of a finite set of variables under a (set of) substitution(s). For example, on properties of a clause's variables under the set of substitutions corresponding to the states in which that clause can participate in a resolution step; or the properties of the variables in an atom under the set of its answer substitutions. This finite set of variables of interest is called the *reference domain* and its variables the *reference variables*. Throughout the paper V denotes a reference domain. A preorder with respect to a given reference domain can be defined over substitutions as follows: $\theta \leq_V \sigma$ iff there exists a substitution μ such that $\theta\lceil V = (\sigma\mu)\lceil V$. The preorder on substitutions induces a corresponding equivalence relation on substitutions which is denoted by $\equiv_V$. Note that for every substitution θ, $\theta \equiv_V \theta\lceil V$ and there always exists a substitution σ with $Dom(\sigma) = V$ such that $\sigma \equiv_V \theta$. For example the empty substitution, ϵ, satisfies $\epsilon \equiv_V \{X_1/U_1, \dots, X_n/U_n\}$ where $V = \{X_1, \dots, X_n\}$ is disjoint from $\{U_1, \dots, U_n\}$. For a variable $X \in V$, the properties we focus on in analyses such as freeness, groundness, and sharing with other reference variables are invariant modulo $\equiv_V$. This means that $X\sigma$ and $X\theta$ have identical properties of interest when $\sigma \equiv_V \theta$. Hence, for program analyses we restrict our attention to substitutions modulo $\equiv_V$.

The Martelli-Montanari unification algorithm [35] can be applied to produce idempotent and relevant most general unifiers. We fix a partial function which maps a finite set of equations E to a solved form $mgu(E)$. An idempotent and relevant substitution, which is a most general unifier of E, corresponds to this solved form [2, 28]. A reference to $mgu(E)$ implicitly implies that E is satisfiable. In the following we abuse notation denoting by $mgu(E)$ the solved form of E as well as the corresponding most general unifier. For a substitution θ, we let $eqn(\theta)$ denote the corresponding set of equations (in solved form). For a finite set of equations E and an equation $e \notin E$, we let $e :: E$ denote $\{e\} \cup E$.

3   A General Formulation of Abstract Unification

The concrete operation which is to be mimicked over the abstract domain involves an equation (or set of equations) $s = t$ and a substitution σ. The unification to be performed is between $s\sigma$ and $t\sigma$; the result of the concrete operation is $\mu = \sigma mgu(\{s = t\}\sigma)$. This operation is termed a *unification step* in our setting and its abstract counterpart, *abstract unification*. In the context of a computation, s and t originate from atoms in a program, σ corresponds to a computation state specifying an instance of s and t, while μ is the next computation state. In the context of this paper we will assume that the reference domain, V, includes the variables of s and t. If needed, V can be extended to establish this. Abstractions of operations modifying the reference domain are not considered here. Moreover, as we consider substitutions modulo $\equiv_V$, we will assume that

$Dom(\sigma) \subseteq V$ and that μ is defined as $(\sigma mgu(\{s = t\}\sigma))\lceil V$.

Abstract unification operates on data descriptions. A data description d_{in} describes for a particular analysis relevant properties of the reference variables under a computation state σ. Given a description d_{in} and an equation (or set of equations) $s = t$, abstract unification should provide a description d_{out} expressing a safe approximation of the relevant properties of the reference variables under the new computation state $\mu = (\sigma mgu(\{s = t\}\sigma))\lceil V$ for all σ described by d_{in}.

In the standard framework of abstract interpretation [17, 18] the relation between data and data description is formalized in terms of a *Galois connection*. A Galois connection is a quadruple (C, α, D, γ) where:

1. $(C, \sqsubseteq_C)$ and $(D, \sqsubseteq_D)$ are complete lattices called *concrete* and *abstract domains* respectively;
2. $\alpha : C \to D$ and $\gamma : D \to C$ are monotonic functions called *abstraction* and *concretization functions* respectively; and
3. $\alpha(\gamma(d)) \sqsubseteq_D d$ and $c \sqsubseteq_C \gamma(\alpha(c))$ for every $d \in D$ and $c \in C$.

In practice it is often sufficient to specify only γ (or α). Other frameworks exist that impose less stringent conditions on the domains C, D, and the mappings defining their relationship (see [33] for a discussion). In the setting of the current paper: C is a set of concrete equation systems ordered by set inclusion; γ gives meaning to the data descriptions of D; and γ together with the order of the concrete domain induce an order relation on the abstract domain. A description relation corresponding to the concretization mapping is defined by $d \propto c$ iff $c \in \gamma(d)$.

4   Properties of Interest for Program Analyses

The properties of interest for program analyses characterize the terms a reference variable may be bound to under a (set of) substitution(s). To formalize them, we introduce the concept of variable multiplicity which specifies the number of occurrences of a variable U in a term t under a substitution θ:

– $multiplicity_\theta(U, t) = $ the number of occurrences of U in $t\theta$.

This concept is not useful by itself as it makes reference to variables in the range of θ and as such is not invariant under $\equiv_V$. However, it is the basis for the notion of variable multiplicity for a term t under a set of substitutions Θ:

– $multiplicity_\Theta(t) = max(\{multiplicity_\theta(U, t) \mid \theta \in \Theta, U \in \mathsf{Var}(t\theta)\})$.

Based on the concept of variable multiplicity, two derived concepts are defined:

– $ground_\Theta(t) \Leftrightarrow multiplicity_\Theta(t) = 0$;
– $linear_\Theta(t) \Leftrightarrow multiplicity_\Theta(t) \leq 1$.

Groundness is a very important property and is expressed in almost every abstract domain. Linearity is not so important by itself, but as will be illustrated below, it can be used to increase the precision of abstract unification for other types of information and it is an important component in techniques for occur-check reduction [3, 41, 42].

A second basic predicate concerns the freeness of a term under a substitution θ or set of substitutions Θ:

- $free_\theta(t) \iff t\theta \in \mathsf{Var}$;
- $free_\Theta(t) \iff \forall \theta \in \Theta.\ free_\theta(t)$.

Freeness captures a basic mode property of terms but is notoriously difficult to integrate correctly in an abstract domain [8, 40]. Note that $free_\Theta(t) \rightarrow multiplicity_\Theta(t) = 1$, and hence $free_\Theta(t) \rightarrow linear_\Theta(t)$.

Another important property for program analyses is the notion of sharing between terms under a substitution or set of substitutions as captured by:

- $share_\theta(t_1, t_2) \iff \mathsf{Var}(t_1\theta) \cap \mathsf{Var}(t_2\theta) \neq \emptyset$;
- $share_\Theta(t_1, t_2) \iff \exists \theta \in \Theta.\ share_\theta(t_1, t_2)$.

An important related concept characterizes the independence of terms:

- $indep_\Theta(t_1, t_2) \iff \neg share_\Theta(t_1, t_2)$.

Independence is a very important property in work on AND-parallelization of logic programs [21, 23].

The above notion of sharing is often referred to as *pair sharing* since it specifies the sharing of a pair of terms. Together with groundness and linearity it forms the pair-sharing domain of [9, 42]. A pair $(X, Y) \in V^2$ represents that X and Y may be bound to terms with common variables. A reflexive pair (X, X) represents possibly non-linear bindings. However in [16] reflexive pairs are used to represent possible non-ground bindings. Another useful notion is that of *set sharing* which is specified in terms of sharing groups, which group the variables of the reference domain V sharing a common variable under a substitution. The basic concept, which is not invariant under $\equiv_V$, is

- $sharegroup(\theta, U) = \{ X \in V \mid U \in \mathsf{Var}(X\theta) \}$.

For the purpose of program analysis, sharing groups with respect to arbitrary variables of sets of substitutions are collected, leading to the following derived concept:

- $sharegroups(\Theta) = \left\{ S \left| \begin{array}{l} \exists \theta \in \Theta, \exists U \in \mathsf{Var}. \\ S = sharegroup(\theta, U) \neq \emptyset \end{array} \right. \right\}$.

Sharegroups were first used by Jacobs and Langen [22, 23] and are known as the set-sharing domain. They were also studied and implemented by Muthukumar and Hermenegildo who also extended them with a freeness component [39, 40]. An element of the abstract domain is a set of sets of variables from V [22, 23,

26, 27, 39, 40]. Each set of reference variables S in a description SS is a sharing group expressing that the variables in S can share one or more variables in a substitution described by SS. A singleton set $\{X\} \in SS$ represents that the binding for X may contain a variable that does not occur in bindings to other reference variables.

Interesting properties relating sharing groups with some of the notions introduced above are:

- $\forall X \in V.$

$\quad ground_\Theta(X) \quad \Leftrightarrow \quad \forall S \in sharegroups(\Theta). \ X \notin S;$
- $\forall X, Y \in V.$

$\quad indep_\Theta(X, Y) \quad \Leftrightarrow \quad \forall S \in sharegroups(\Theta). \ X \in S \ \to \ Y \notin S;$
- $\forall t_1, t_2$ such that $\mathrm{Var}(\langle t_1, t_2 \rangle) \subseteq V.$

$\quad indep_\Theta(t_1, t_2) \quad \Leftrightarrow \quad \forall X \in \mathrm{Var}(t_1) \ \forall Y \in Var(t_2). \ indep_\Theta(X, Y).$

Finally, a basic predicate for expressing so-called covering information is introduced. A syntactic object O_1 covers another syntactic object O_2 under a substitution θ if $ground_\theta(O_1) \Rightarrow ground_\theta(O_2)$.

- $covers_\theta(O_1, O_2) \quad \Leftrightarrow \quad \mathrm{Var}(O_1\theta) \supseteq \mathrm{Var}(O_2\theta);$
- $covers_\Theta(O_1, O_2) \quad \Leftrightarrow \quad \forall \theta \in \Theta. \ covers_\theta(O_1, O_2).$

The notion of covering provides an alternative definition for the groundness predicate:

- $ground_\Theta(t) \quad \Leftrightarrow \quad covers_\Theta(\emptyset, t).$

The notion of covering is easily generalized to express implications between other types of properties. For example, in [12], various covering properties are applied to determine nonsuspension for concurrent logic programs. The notion of covering is the basis of the Prop domain [4, 11, 30, 34, 43], where a basic relation $covers_\theta(\langle X_1, \ldots, X_n \rangle, Y)$ is expressed as a propositional formula $X_1 \wedge \ldots \wedge X_n \to Y$.

Sharing groups also encode covering information. As an illustration consider the following example: let

$$sharegroups(\Theta) = \{\{X, Z\}, \{Y, Z\}, \{Y, Z, W\}, \{X\}\}.$$

It follows from the above definitions that for all $\theta \in \Theta$, any variable in $Z\theta$ must occur in either $X\theta$ or in $Y\theta$ and hence $covers_\Theta(\langle X, Y \rangle, Z)$. Similarly, any variable in $W\theta$ or in $Y\theta$ is also in $Z\theta$, hence $covers_\Theta(Z, \langle W, Y \rangle)$. A property useful to extract covering information from a set of sharing groups is the following: Let O be a syntactic object such that $\mathrm{Var}(O) \subseteq V$ and $X \in V$, then

- $covers_\Theta(O, X) \quad \Leftrightarrow \quad \forall S \in sharegroups(\Theta). \ X \in S \to \mathrm{Var}(O) \cap S \neq \emptyset.$

While the above relationship shows that sharing groups capture the covering information expressed in the domain Prop, it does not imply that a set-sharing analysis derives the same covering information as a Prop analysis. Indeed, it is known that the abstract unification for the set-sharing domain may loose covering information which is preserved by the corresponding operation on the Prop domain [15].

Both pair- and set- sharing are related to independence information. However, the corresponding abstract domains are not directly comparable. On the one hand, the pair-sharing domain expresses also linearity information which enables the corresponding abstract unification algorithm to provide more precise independence information. On the other hand, the set-sharing domain captures covering information which helps propagate more precise groundness information. Combining both approaches [13] is often beneficial.

5   On the Importance of Sharing Information

A reader unfamiliar with the area might wonder why the tricky concept of sharing gets so much attention. It is not only because the derived concept of independence plays a crucial role in work on parallelization of logic programs, but because of a fundamental problem regarding correctness and precision of a domain having a mode component but no sharing component. In the following example, we consider such a simple domain which associates one of the modes *ground*, *free*, or *any* with each variable of the reference domain V (mode *any* for X in a data description d does not impose any constraint on $X\theta$ where $\theta \in \gamma(d)$).

Example 1. Let $V = \{X, Y\}$ and consider the unification $X = a$ together with a data description d_{in} which specifies that X and Y are *free*. A substitution σ described by d_{in} is $\{X/U, Y/W\}$. Performing the concrete unification under σ yields $\mu = \{X/a, Y/W\}$, i.e., X becomes *ground* while Y remains *free*. However also $\{X/U, Y/U\}$ is described by d_{in} and the corresponding concrete unification results in $\mu = \{X/a, Y/a\}$, i.e., both X and Y become *ground*. Any correct abstract unification algorithm must provide a data description d_{out} which assigns mode *any* to Y (and in general to any reference variable which is not *ground*). The mode domain of this example is so weak that all freeness information is lost under a single abstract unification involving a non-*free* term.

The problem is less acute if so-called substitution closed domains are used. In such domains, $\sigma \in \gamma(d) \Rightarrow \sigma\theta \in \gamma(d)$ for all θ. A domain assigning modes *ground* or *any* to the variables in the reference domain has this property. In this case, a correct result can be obtained when changing the modes only of those variables directly involved in the abstract unification. Let us reconsider Example 1 in the context of a description d_{in} which assigns mode *any* to both X and Y. Abstract unification for the equation $X = a$, may safely focus only on X providing a description d_{out} which assigns mode *ground* to X. The variable Y remains *any*, which is correct and, with the available information, is the best that is achievable since the abstract operation cannot know whether X and Y are bound to the same term. So, the problem of poor precision remains. Debray [19] was the first to recognize these problems and to point out a flaw in the ad-hoc mode analysis of Mellish [36, 37] that used a domain which was not substitution closed.

Increased precision can be realized by introducing a technique termed reexecution [6, 29] into the framework. A more conventional approach is to enhance the abstract domain with a sharing component. A sufficient condition for not changing the mode of a variable X during an abstract unification is the following: given the description d_{in} and the abstract unification $s = t$, we must guarantee that for every $\sigma \in \gamma(d_{in})$, $\mathsf{Var}(X\sigma) \cap \mathsf{Var}(\{s = t\}\sigma) = \emptyset$, i.e., $indep_\sigma(X, \langle s, t \rangle)$. This implies that $X\sigma = X\mu$ for $\mu = \sigma mgu(\{s = t\}\sigma) \upharpoonright V$ and hence that the mode for X need not change in d_{out}. This motivates the need for sharing analyses.

As mentioned in Section 4, the *share*, *sharegroups*, and *covers* predicates have been used as a basis to express sharing in abstract domains. An extensive discussion of early variable-dependencies analyses can be found in [20].

6   A More General Formulation of Abstract Unification

This section describes a more general setting for abstract unification which covers both traditional analyses such as set-sharing and pair-sharing, as well as more recent ones using abstract equation systems [7, 8, 38]. This setting enables us to break up an abstract unification operation into smaller rewrite steps, much the same as the way the Martelli-Montanari unification algorithm breaks up a concrete unification. This approach facilitates both design and justification of abstract unification algorithms as correctness boils down to showing that the rewriting terminates in a "solved form" and that each rewrite step is correct.

In this approach, an abstract state is a pair $\langle \mathcal{E}, d \rangle$ consisting of a finite set of equations $\mathcal{E}$ and an annotation d typically providing mode and sharing information for some of the variables in $\mathcal{E}$. The description relation $\propto$ associates d with a substitution σ with solved form $eqn(\sigma)$ and $\mathcal{E}$ with a system of equations E. In terms of equations we will write this as $\langle \mathcal{E}, d \rangle \propto E \cup eqn(\sigma)$. In traditional analyses d describes properties of the variables in the reference domain V, $Dom(\sigma) \subseteq V$, $\mathcal{E}$ is a set of equations over the reference variables, and the relation between $\mathcal{E}$ and E is the identity relation. In the solved form of the abstract unification algorithm, the equation component is the empty set of equations, while the annotation d provides the updated properties of the reference variables.

In analyses based on abstract equation systems, a solved form has an equation component AE involving both reference variables as well as *abstract variables* and an annotation component d specifying properties of the abstract variables. So, a solved form is a pair $\langle AE, d \rangle$. The description relation associates such a pair with a set of equations $E \cup eqn(\sigma)$ where E is derived from AE by replacing the abstract variables by variables outside the reference domain and $Dom(\sigma)$ a subset of these newly introduced variables.

Example 2. Consider a set of equations $AE = \{X = f(@_1), Y = @_2\}$, where $V = \{X, Y\}$ and $@_1, @_2$ are abstract variables. The description $d = \{\{@_1\}, \{@_1, @_2\}\}$

is a set-sharing component. A concrete system described by AE obtained by mapping abstract variable $@_1$ to V_1 and $@_2$ to V_2, is for instance $E = \{X = f(V_1), Y = V_2\}$. A substitution described by d is $\sigma = \{V_1/g(U_1, U_2), V_2/h(U_2)\}$. The equation system $E\sigma = \{X = f(g(U_1, U_2)), Y = h(U_2)\}$ gives the bindings of the reference variables. More details about the domain are in Section 8.

Using the abstract equations of [8], consider system $AE = \{X = \perp^+[U, W], Y = \perp[W]\}$. The d-component is implicit in AE and expresses that the first abstract variable $\perp^+[U, W]$ is bound to a non-variable term which can have variables not occurring elsewhere but also variables occurring in the binding of the second abstract variable $\perp[W]$, which can be bound to any term. So for example, mapping $\perp^+[U, W]$ to V_1 and $\perp[W]$ to V_2, a concrete system described by AE is $E = \{X = V_1, Y = V_2\}$ and a substitution described by the annotation is $\sigma = \{V_1/f(g(U_1, U_2)), V_2/h(U_2)\}$. Again $E\sigma = \{X = f(g(U_1, U_2)), Y = h(U_2)\}$ gives the bindings of the reference variables.

Given a description $\langle AE_{in}, d_{in}\rangle$ and a set of equations E, abstract unification starts in a state $\langle E \cup AE_{in}, d_{in}\rangle$ and finishes in a state $\langle AE_{out}, d_{out}\rangle$ where AE_{out} is in an abstract solved form, i.e., a form which exhibits the relevant properties of the reference variables. Under this formalization, abstract unification consists of a sequence of rewrite steps. Each step rewrites a pair $\langle \mathcal{E}_{in}, d_{in}\rangle$ into a pair $\langle \mathcal{E}_{out}, d_{out}\rangle$ such that the following correctness criterion holds:

$$\langle \mathcal{E}_{in}, d_{in}\rangle \propto E_{in} \cup eqn(\sigma) \Rightarrow \exists E_{out}, \mu. \langle \mathcal{E}_{out}, d_{out}\rangle \propto E_{out} \cup eqn(\mu)$$

where $mgu(E_{in} \cup eqn(\sigma)) \equiv_V mgu(E_{out} \cup eqn(\mu))$.

Typically, some rewrite steps are *exact*. This is the case if for every $\langle E_{out}, \mu\rangle$ such that $\langle \mathcal{E}_{out}, d_{out}\rangle \propto E_{out} \cup eqn(\mu)$ there exist E_{in} and σ such that $\langle \mathcal{E}_{in}, d_{in}\rangle \propto E_{in} \cup eqn(\sigma)$ and $mgu(E_{out} \cup eqn(\mu)) \equiv_V mgu(E_{in} \cup eqn(\sigma))$. Typical examples of exact steps are steps which effect only the equation component, e.g. the steps which rewrite $\langle E, d\rangle$ to $\langle mgu(E), d\rangle$ in traditional analyses. These are called preunification steps in [42]. Proving their correctness is a rather trivial affair. In abstract equation systems, other steps are also in this category. In [8], steps leaving all representations of abstract variables (meta-terms in the paper) intact fall in this category.

The more challenging steps, which are the main subject of Section 7 are those which update the annotation component.

7 A Methodology for Developing Correct Analyses

An abstract unification algorithm is designed by mimicking a chosen set of equivalence preserving transitions on concrete equations. The precise transitions chosen depend on the abstract domain but in general include the rewrite rules of the classic Martelli-Montanari unification algorithm. Given a pair $\langle \varepsilon :: \mathcal{E}_{in}, d_{in}\rangle$ the abstract unification algorithm will typically aim to solve or reduce a single abstract equation ε, update the equations $\mathcal{E}_{in}$ and the description d_{in} and then carry on to select another abstract equation in the new system. The abstract

$$\varepsilon :: \mathcal{E}_{in}, d_{in} \quad \varpropto \quad e :: E_{in} \cup eqn(\sigma)$$
$$\downarrow \qquad\qquad\qquad \downarrow$$
$$\mathcal{E}_{out}, d_{out} \quad \varpropto \quad E_{out} \cup eqn(\mu)$$

Fig. 1. Correctness of Abstract Unification.

operation intends to compute a safe approximation of an equivalence preserving transformation (with respect to the reference domain V) from a corresponding $e :: E_{in} \cup eqn(\sigma)$ to $E_{out} \cup eqn(\mu)$. This situation is illustrated in Figure 1.

There are several candidates for such equivalence preserving transformations. A first commonly applied group reduces e to E', possibly updating the equations of E_{in}, but does not affect $eqn(\sigma)$. An example of such a transformation, which also leaves E_{in} intact, is the peeling of an equation $f(t_1, \ldots, t_n) = f(s_1, \ldots, s_n)$ in the Martelli-Montanari algorithm. Another example is a variant of the Martelli-Montanari substitution rule. With $e \equiv x = t$, it applies the substitution x/t on E_{in} but not on $eqn(\sigma)$. Such transformations are typically applied to justify the exact steps mentioned in the previous section. A second group of commonly applied transformations solves the equation $e\sigma$ and applies the result on the remaining equations so that $E_{out} = E_{in}mgu(\{e\sigma\})$ and $\mu = \sigma mgu(\{e\sigma\})|V$. Often, concerns are separated in such a way that $E_{in}mgu(\{e\sigma\}) = E_{in}$. Also, $e\sigma$ typically has no reference variables and can be dropped (it is "absorbed" in $eqn(\mu)$). In the abstract algorithm one applies the result of "solving" ε under d_{in} to the equations in $\mathcal{E}_{out}$ and update d_{out} to describe all possible μ as specified above for all σ described by d_{in}.

Breaking up the abstract unification operator in a number of more simple operators transforming abstract equation systems makes abstract unification a lot easier to understand. As the operators are not necessarily commutative, abstract unification defined this way is not always confluent: the order of applying steps can influence the precision of an analysis. However, this need not reduce precision compared to complex one step operators as the order of applying operators can be controlled. The operations we use below depend only on the properties of the lhs. and rhs. of the selected equation. Other operators, taking the equation apart have to be applied first if properties of components are relevant.

We have observed that the design and the justification of abstract unification algorithms as well as the understanding of the underlying intuition crucially depend on the careful analysis of the relationship between the properties of σ, e, and μ reflected in the abstract domain. We distinguish between *definite* and *possible* properties.

Definite properties are properties such as freeness, groundness and covering information which if d_{out} claims them to hold, must indeed hold in μ. The abstract operation typically considers a case analysis on d_{in} and ε to guarantee that for any corresponding σ and e the property claimed about d_{out} indeed holds for $\mu = \sigma mgu(e\sigma)|V$.

Possible properties are properties such as sharing which if d_{out} claims them to hold might hold in μ. Here it is the careful analysis of concrete unification which relates the assumed property of μ to the properties of σ and e. Since $\langle \varepsilon :: \mathcal{E}_{in}, d_{in} \rangle \propto e :: E_{in} \cup eqn(\sigma)$, the presence of these properties indicates the presence of certain abstract properties in ε, d_{in}. Correctness requires that the abstract operation is designed such that the property assumed in μ indeed shows up in d_{out}.

In the remainder of this section we will carefully unravel the relationships between σ, $e\sigma$, and μ that are the basis for showing correctness of challenging absorbtion steps in a number of well-known domains.

Set-Sharing Analysis The abstract domain used is $\wp(\wp(V))$. The initial assumption is $sharegroups(\{\sigma\}) \subseteq d_{in}$ and the unification problem is $s = t$ with $\mathrm{Var}(\langle s, t \rangle) \subseteq V$. Let $\theta = mgu(\{s = t\}\sigma)$, and $\mu = \sigma\theta \restriction V$. As stated above, it must be proven that, if $S \in sharegroups(\{\mu\})$, then $S \in d_{out}$. We borrow the basic structure of the original soundness proof as presented in [23].

The first part of the proof relates the existence of S in $sharegroups(\{\mu\})$ to the sharing groups of σ and the properties of s and t. Observe that $S \in sharegroups(\{\mu\})$ iff $\exists U. S = sharegroup(\mu, U) \neq \emptyset$. For each such variable U, two cases have to be considered:

1. $U \notin \mathrm{Var}(\langle s\sigma, t\sigma \rangle)$. Since θ is relevant and idempotent, $U \notin \mathrm{Var}(s\sigma\theta)(= \mathrm{Var}(t\sigma\theta))$ and therefore, for $X \in V$, $U \in \mathrm{Var}(X\sigma\theta) \Leftrightarrow U \in \mathrm{Var}(X\sigma)$. Thus $S = sharegroup(\sigma, U)$, i.e., $S \in sharegroups(\{\sigma\})$. Also, since $U \notin \mathrm{Var}(\langle s\sigma, t\sigma \rangle)$, an interesting property of S is: $S \cap \mathrm{Var}(\langle s, t \rangle) = \emptyset$.

2. $U \in \mathrm{Var}(\langle s\sigma, t\sigma \rangle)$ and since θ is relevant and idempotent $U \in \mathrm{Var}(s\sigma\theta)(= \mathrm{Var}(t\sigma\theta))$. The set $SS_s = \{Z \in \mathrm{Var}(s\sigma) \mid U \in \mathrm{Var}(Z\theta)\} \neq \emptyset$ (Figure 2) and similarly $SS_t = \{Z \in \mathrm{Var}(t\sigma) \mid U \in \mathrm{Var}(Z\theta)\} \neq \emptyset$. Since $\mu = \sigma\theta \restriction V$, we have

$$S = \bigcup_{Z \in SS_s} sharegroup(\sigma, Z) \cup \bigcup_{Z \in SS_t} sharegroup(\sigma, Z).$$

Also the following property holds: $\forall Z \in SS_s. \, sharegroup(\sigma, Z) \cap \mathrm{Var}(s) \neq \emptyset$, and $\forall Z \in SS_t. \, sharegroup(\sigma, Z) \cap \mathrm{Var}(t) \neq \emptyset$.

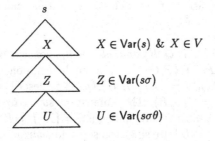

$X \in \mathrm{Var}(s)$ & $X \in V$

$Z \in \mathrm{Var}(s\sigma)$

$U \in \mathrm{Var}(s\sigma\theta)$

Fig. 2. An occurrence of U in $s\sigma\theta$.

For a set-sharing unification algorithm to be sound, it is sufficient to capture both cases, that is, on the one hand to pass on sharing groups $S \in d_{in}$ satisfying the property $S \cap \mathrm{Var}(\langle s, t \rangle) = \emptyset$ to d_{out} and on the other hand to include all unions of sets of sharing groups of which at least one has a non-empty intersection with $\mathrm{Var}(s)$ and at least one a non-empty intersection with $\mathrm{Var}(t)$. For the latter purpose, so-called *set-closure* operations are generally introduced which ensure all such unions are included in d_{out}, with the least possible other spurious unions of sharing groups.

Example 3. Let $V = \{X, Y, P, Q, R, T\}$, $d_{in} = \{\{X, R\}, \{Y\}, \{T, P\}, \{Q, X\}, \{Q\}\}$, $\sigma = \{X/f(W, W, R), Y/U, Q/g(W, B), T/P\}$, and let $s = t$ be the equation $X = f(Y, T, P)$. Then $d_{in} \propto \sigma$ and the unification $s\sigma = t\sigma$ to be abstracted is $f(W, W, R) = f(U, P, P)$. A most general unifier is $\theta = \{W/U, R/U, P/U\}$. The reader can easily check that $sharegroup(\mu, U) = \{X, R, Q, Y, T, P\}$, which is obtained as the union of four sharing groups from d_{in}. On the one hand, as $SS_s = \{W, R\}$, we need $sharegroup(\sigma, W) = \{Q, X\}$ and $sharegroup(\sigma, R) = \{X, R\}$, and on the other hand, as $SS_t = \{U, P\}$, we need $sharegroup(\sigma, U) = \{Y\}$ and $sharegroup(\sigma, P) = \{T, P\}$.

If $ground_\sigma(s)$ (or $ground_\sigma(t)$), then $\mathrm{Var}(s\sigma\theta)(= \mathrm{Var}(t\sigma\theta)) = \emptyset$. In the set-sharing domain, this can be detected if no variable from s (or t) occurs in d_{in}. The abstract algorithm then only needs to capture case 1. above (e.g., $d_{out} = \{S \in d_{in} \mid S \cap \mathrm{Var}(\langle s, t \rangle) = \emptyset\}$). Informally, the groundness information of d_{in} is preserved, the groundness of the variables of s is propagated to the variables of t (or vice versa) and through the (limited) covering information encoded in d_{in} also to some other variables in V.

Further refinements are possible if the set-sharing domain is combined with a mode domain providing linearity and/or freeness information. For instance, by taking into account the following special cases:

- For $U \in \mathrm{Var}(s\sigma\theta)$, if $linear_\sigma(s)$ (resp. $linear_\sigma(t)$) and $indep_\sigma(s, t)$, then SS_t (resp. SS_s) is a singleton set.
- For $U \in \mathrm{Var}(s\sigma\theta)$, if $free_\sigma(s)$ or $free_\sigma(t)$ or $linear_\sigma(\langle s, t \rangle)$, then both SS_s and SS_t are singleton sets. (Note: $linear_\sigma(\langle s, t \rangle) \rightarrow indep_\sigma(s, t)$.)

Based on these observations, the set-closure operations can be optimized [7, 25, 27, 40].

Example 4. Let $V = \{X, P, Q, R\}$ and assume d_{in} consists of both a set-sharing component $\{\{X\}, \{P, R\}, \{P, Q\}\}$ and a mode component $\{X/free, P/any, Q/any, R/free\}$. Then $\sigma = \{P/f(R, U), Q/U\}$ is described by d_{in}. Let $s = t$ be the equation $X = f(P, R)$. The unification $s\sigma = t\sigma$ to be abstracted is $X = f(f(R, U), R)$. A most general unifier is $\theta = \{X/f(f(R, U), R)\}$. For U both $SS_s = \{X\}$ and $SS_t = \{U\}$ are singleton sets and $sharegroup(\mu, U) = \{X, P, Q\}$ is obtained as the union of $sharegroup(\sigma, X) = \{X\}$ and $sharegroup(\sigma, U) = \{P, Q\}$.

The same reasoning has been applied in the domain of abstract equation systems [38] where s and t are terms built from abstract variables and d_{in} expresses the sharing between abstract variables (see Section 8).

Pair-Sharing Analysis The domain used is $\wp(V \times V)$, most often in combination with a groundness component in $\wp(V)$. Let $d_{in} = \langle d_{in}^{share}, d_{in}^{gr} \rangle$. The sharing component d_{in}^{share} is in fact required to be a symmetrical binary relation satisfying the property $d_{in}^{share} \cap (d_{in}^{gr} \times V) = \emptyset$. Again, the unification problem $s = t$ is such that $Var(\langle s, t \rangle) \subseteq V$. The initial assumption is $\sigma \in \gamma(d_{in})$, i.e. $\forall X, Y \in V.\ X \neq Y \& share_\sigma(X, Y) \to (X, Y) \in d_{in}^{share}$ and (following the approach of [42]) $\forall X \in V.\ \neg linear_\sigma(X) \to (X, X) \in d_{in}^{share}$. It must be proven that, if $X \neq Y \& share_\mu(X, Y)$, then $(X, Y) \in d_{out}^{share}$. We borrow the structure of a soundness proof presented in [9].

First note that $share_\mu(X, Y)$ iff $share_\theta(X\sigma, Y\sigma)$. The sharing between $X\sigma$ and $Y\sigma$ under the substitution θ is related to the sharing between X, Y, and the variables of s and t under the initial substitution σ, and can be expressed as follows:

$$share_\theta(X\sigma, Y\sigma) \to share_\sigma(X, Y) \vee \begin{cases} \exists Z_X, Z_Y \in Var(\langle s, t \rangle). \\ share_\sigma(X, Z_X) \ \& \ share_\sigma(Y, Z_Y) \\ \& \ share_\theta(Z_X\sigma, Z_Y\sigma) \end{cases}$$

Note that cases with $X = Z_X$ and/or $Y = Z_Y$ are captured by the above formula. For a pair-sharing unification algorithm to be sound, it is sufficient to capture both parts of the consequent. For the first disjunct, it is sufficient to pass on the pairs $(X, Y) \in d_{in}^{share}$ to d_{out}^{share}. For the second disjunct, abstract unification algorithms generally introduce an operation that computes an appropriate subset of the transitive closure of a binary relation [9, 41]. For example,

$$Compose(s = t, d_{in}^{share}) =$$

$$d_{in}^{share} \cup \left\{ (X, Y) \ \middle| \ \begin{array}{l} \exists Z_X, Z_Y \in Var(\langle s, t \rangle). \\ ((X, Z_X) \in d_{in}^{share} \vee X = Z_X) \ \& \\ ((Y, Z_Y) \in d_{in}^{share} \vee Y = Z_Y) \ \& \\ (Z_X, Z_Y) \in NewShare(s, t) \end{array} \right\}$$

Here, $NewShare(s, t)$ must capture the sharing between the variables of s and t under the substitution μ. For instance, defining $NewShare(s, t) = Var(\langle s, t \rangle) \times Var(\langle s, t \rangle)$ yields a sound abstract unification operation. However, as in the set-sharing case, the algorithm can be refined when using definite groundness and/or linearity information.

For instance, if $ground_\sigma(s)$ (or $ground_\sigma(t)$) is derivable from the groundness component d_{in}^{gr}, the abstract algorithm only needs to capture the first part of the consequent above, e.g., defining $d_{out}^{share} = \{(X, Y) \in d_{in}^{share} \mid X, Y \notin Var(\langle s, t \rangle)\}$ and $d_{out}^{gr} = d_{in}^{gr} \cup Var(\langle s, t \rangle)$. Informally, the definite groundness information of d_{in} is preserved and the groundness of the variables of s is propagated to the variables of t (or vice versa). Since no covering information is encoded in the pair-sharing domain, no further propagation of groundness is possible.

Special properties exploiting linearity enable optimizations in the computation of $NewShare(s,t)$. For instance,

- If $linear_\sigma(\langle s,t\rangle)$, $X, Y \in \mathsf{Var}(\langle s\sigma, t\sigma\rangle)$, and $X \neq Y$, then
  $share_\theta(X,Y) \to (X \in \mathsf{Var}(s\sigma) \leftrightarrow Y \in \mathsf{Var}(t\sigma))$.
  Informally, under the conditions mentioned, X and Y occur on opposite sides of the equation $s\sigma = t\sigma$.
- If $linear_\sigma(s)$, $indep_\sigma(\langle s,t\rangle)$, $X, Y \in \mathsf{Var}(\langle s\sigma, t\sigma\rangle)$, and $X \neq Y$, then
  $share_\theta(X,Y) \to (X \in \mathsf{Var}(t\sigma) \to Y \in \mathsf{Var}(s\sigma))$.

The original pair-sharing analysis [9, 42] incorporated these optimizations.

Example 5. Let $V = \{X, Y, Z, W, R\}$, $d_{in}^{share} = \{(W,X), (R,X)\}$ (for brevity, we use a condensed representation for the symmetrically closed sharing relation), and $d_{in}^{gr} = \{\}$. Then $\sigma = \{X/f(W,R), Z/g(U)\}$ is described by d_{in}. Let $s = t$ be the equation $X = f(Y, Z)$. The unification $s\sigma = t\sigma$ to be abstracted is $f(W, R) = f(Y, g(U))$. A most general unifier is $\theta = \{W/Y, R/g(U)\}$. Without using linearity information, a rough $NewShare(s,t)$ is obtained as $\{(X,X), (Y,Y), (Z,Z), (X,Y), (Y,Z), (X,Z)\}$. Using the linearity and independence information in d_{in}, an optimized $NewShare(s,t)$ is $\{(X,Y), (X,Z)\}$. In the latter case, using *Compose* defined above, the reader can verify that d_{out}^{share} is $\{(W,X), (R,X), (X,Y), (X,Z), (W,Y), (W,Z), (R,Y), (R,Z)\}$. The properties $indep_\mu(W,R)$ and $indep_\mu(Y,Z)$ are captured in the latter case, but would not when using the less optimized definition of $NewShare(s,t)$.

Groundness Analysis Groundness information is derived in both the pair- and set-sharing analyses, but can also be derived on its own in a simple mode domain. The general proof obligation can be formulated as follows: if d_{out} constrains a variable $X \in V$ to be bound to a ground term, then $ground_\mu(X)$ must hold. The first part of a soundness proof relates the groundness information present in d_{out} to the groundness information in d_{in} and particular properties of $s = t$. The second part of the proof then uses $d_{in} \propto \sigma$ and a few obvious properties about the way in which groundness is propagated.

- $\forall X \in V.\ ground_\sigma(X) \to ground_\mu(X)$;
- $ground_\sigma(s) \to \forall Z \in \mathsf{Var}(t).\ ground_\mu(Z)$;
  (and a symmetrical property if $ground_\sigma(t)$).

In the case where (depth-bounded) structural information is derived [16, 38], groundness of subterms may be expressible and can be proven correct using a similar proof strategy.

Freeness and Linearity Analyses Abstract unification algorithms deriving definite freeness and/or linearity information often consist of a case analysis that can be proven correct using a similar scheme as described above. In essence, the proof is based on a set of sufficient conditions for freeness/linearity to be preserved under the application of a most general unifier.

For freeness, for instance, the following properties are intuitively justifiable. For $X \in V$,

- $free_\sigma(X)$ & $free_\sigma(s)$ & $free_\sigma(t) \to free_\mu(X)$;
  (informally, if two variables are being unified, no other variable gets bound to a non-variable term)
- $free_\sigma(X)$ & $indep_\sigma(X, \langle s, t \rangle) \to free_\mu(X)$;
  (informally, free variables that are independent of the terms being unified do not get instantiated to a non-variable term).
- $free_\sigma(X)$ & $free_\sigma(s)$ & $indep_\sigma(X, s) \to free_\mu(X)$
  (and symmetrical for the term t);
  (informally, if one of the terms being unified is a free variable, then other variables independent of that term do not get bound to a non-variable term).

Since these conditions involve independence information, a freeness analysis usually is combined with a sharing analysis in order for non-trivial freeness information to be derivable (e.g., [14, 26, 40]).

The same holds for a linearity analysis. Sufficient conditions for linearity to be derivable are: For $X \in V$,

- $ground_\mu(X) \to linear_\mu(X)$;
- $linear_\sigma(X)$ & $indep_\sigma(X, \langle s, t \rangle) \to linear_\mu(X)$;
- $linear_\sigma(X)$ & $linear_\sigma(s)$ & $indep_\sigma(X, s) \to linear_\mu(X)$
  (and symmetrical for the term t).

Deriving linearity information is particularly useful to enhance set-sharing analysis [7, 25, 27]. It was already intrinsically integrated in the pair-sharing analysis presented by Søndergaard [42].

Covering Analysis The best known abstract domain for deriving covering information is Prop [4, 30, 34, 43], although set-sharing [23] and some other approaches [14] also used this kind of information, primarily to improve groundness analysis.

Useful properties for justifying covering analyses are:

- $\forall X \in \mathsf{Var}(s) : covers_\mu(\mathsf{Var}(t), X)$; and symmetrically
- $\forall X \in \mathsf{Var}(t) : covers_\mu(\mathsf{Var}(s), X)$;
- For $S \subseteq V$, $X \in V$: $covers_\sigma(S, X) \to covers_\mu(S, X)$;
- For $S, T \subseteq V$, $X, Y \in V$:
  $covers_\mu(T, X)$ & $covers_\mu(\{X\} \cup S, Y) \to covers_\mu(T \cup S, Y)$.

8 Abstract Equation Systems

The formulation of abstract unification above and the properties of concrete substitutions are basic means that facilitate the development and justification of analyses that combine the derivation of mode, variable dependencies, and structural information [7, 16]. In particular, the representation has proven useful in the design of correct abstract unification algorithms involving freeness information [8]. By way of example, we illustrate the domain of abstract equation systems [7, 38], which augments the set-sharing domain with a mode component and depth-bounded structural information.

In this approach *abstract* variables are introduced to represent (concrete) terms whose internal structure is hidden by abstraction. We denote by AVar the denumerable set of abstract variables (disjoint from Var). Abstract variables are represented using $@, @_i$, etc. to distinguish them from concrete variables. The set of abstract terms, denoted ATerm, is constructed using function symbols from Σ and variables from AVar. The set of abstract variables occurring in a syntactic object s is denoted AVar(s).

An abstract equation system AE, for reference domain V, is a triplet $\langle \mathcal{E}; \iota; \Delta \rangle$ such that $\mathcal{E}$ is a finite set of equations over Term $\cup$ ATerm with Var($\mathcal{E}$) $\subseteq V$, $\Delta \subseteq \wp(\text{AVar}(\mathcal{E}))$ is a set-sharing component, and $\iota :$ AVar($\mathcal{E}$) $\to \{f, \ell, g, a\}$ is an annotation mapping which indicates for each abstract variable if it corresponds to a *free, linear, ground* or an *arbitrary* concrete term. The set of annotations, $\{f, \ell, g, a\}$ is partially ordered such that $f \preceq \ell \preceq a$ and $g \preceq \ell \preceq a$, corresponding to the intuition that free and ground terms are also linear and that free, linear and ground terms are also arbitrary terms. The abstract equation system is said to be in *solution solved form* if $\mathcal{E}$ contains for each $X \in V$ one equation of the form $X = t$ with $t \in$ ATerm.

Informally, the description relation is defined via an abstract-variable replacement which is a mapping that assigns a concrete variable outside the reference domain V to each abstract variable, and a substitution σ having this set of newly introduced variables V' as domain and all range variables outside both V and V'; moreover, σ should be such that the mode and possible sharing restrictions are met.

Example 6. Let $V = \{X, Y, Z, U\}$ and

$$AE = \langle \left\{ \begin{matrix} X = @_4, Y = @_2, \\ Z = h(@_3, @_1), U = @_1 \end{matrix} \right\} ; \left\{ \begin{matrix} @_1/f, @_2/\ell, \\ @_3/\ell, @_4/a \end{matrix} \right\} ; \left\{ \begin{matrix} \{@_2, @_3\}, \{@_1\}, \\ \{@_1, @_4\}, \{@_4\} \end{matrix} \right\} \rangle.$$

This abstract equation system (in solution solved form) represents many concrete equation systems (and corresponding substitutions). For example,

$$E = \left\{ \begin{matrix} X = V_4, Y = V_2, \\ Z = h(V_3, V_1), U = V_1 \end{matrix} \right\},$$

is represented via the abstract-variable replacement

$$\theta : @_1 \mapsto V_1, @_2 \mapsto V_2, @_3 \mapsto V_3, @_4 \mapsto V_4,$$

and a substitution described by the annotations and sharing component is

$$\sigma : V_1 \mapsto P, V_2 \mapsto f(W), V_3 \mapsto h(W, a), V_4 \mapsto g(P, R, P).$$

The bindings for the reference variables are then obtained from

$$E\sigma = \left\{ \begin{matrix} X = g(P, R, P), Y = f(W), \\ Z = h(h(W, a), P), U = P \end{matrix} \right\}.$$

The abstract unification algorithm consists of a set of rewrite rules that reduce an abstract equation system to solution solved form which clearly exhibits the desired freeness, groundness, linearity, and sharing properties. We illustrate some rewriting steps for reducing a unification problem $s = t, AE_{in}$ to a data description AE_{out}. Below, the annotation mapping ι is represented implicitly by annotating each occurrence of an abstract variable @ with a superscript indicating the value of $\iota(@)$.

Example 7. Let $V = \{X, Y, Z, U\}$, consider an initial data description

$$AE_{in} = \langle \left\{ \begin{array}{l} X = @_4^f, \\ Y = @_2^\ell, \\ Z = h(@_3^\ell), \\ U = @_1^f \end{array} \right\} ; \left\{ \begin{array}{l} \{@_2^\ell, @_3^\ell\}, \{@_1^f\}, \\ \{@_1^f, @_4^f\}, \{@_4^f\} \end{array} \right\} \rangle,$$

and let the equation $s = t$ to be solved be $U = f(Y, Z)$.

In the *preunification phase*, rewriting steps similar to the Martelli-Montanari unification algorithm are applied. The rewriting rules preserve structural information if possible. For instance, the equation component $\mathcal{E}$ of AE_{in} is first applied as a kind of substitution to the equation $U = f(Y, Z)$:

$$\langle \left\{@_1^f = f(@_2^\ell, h(@_3^\ell))\right\}, \langle \left\{ \begin{array}{l} X = @_4^f, \\ Y = @_2^\ell, \\ Z = h(@_3^\ell), \\ U = @_1^f \end{array} \right\} ; \left\{ \begin{array}{l} \{@_2^\ell, @_3^\ell\}, \{@_1^f\}, \\ \{@_1^f, @_4^f\}, \{@_4^f\} \end{array} \right\} \rangle\rangle .$$

The abstract equation is then used as a substitution $\{@_1^f / f(@_2^\ell, h(@_3^\ell))\}$ on $\mathcal{E}$, thereby propagating structural information to the variable $U \in V$.

$$\langle \left\{@_1^f = f(@_2^\ell, h(@_3^\ell))\right\}, \langle \left\{ \begin{array}{l} X = @_4^f, \\ Y = @_2^\ell, \\ Z = h(@_3^\ell), \\ U = f(@_2^\ell, h(@_3^\ell)) \end{array} \right\} ; \left\{ \begin{array}{l} \{@_2^\ell, @_3^\ell\}, \{@_1^f\}, \\ \{@_1^f, @_4^f\}, \{@_4^f\} \end{array} \right\} \rangle\rangle .$$

The sharing and annotation components are only affected in the *absorption phase*. Since freeness and linearity information is available, the optimized set-sharing algorithm can be mimicked here, yielding the final data description:

$$AE_{out} = \langle \left\{ \begin{array}{l} X = @_4^a, \\ Y = @_2^\ell, \\ Z = h(@_3^\ell), \\ U = f(@_2^\ell, h(@_3^\ell)) \end{array} \right\} ; \left\{ \begin{array}{l} \{@_2^\ell, @_3^\ell, @_4^a\}, \\ \{@_2^\ell, @_3^\ell\}, \{@_4^a\} \end{array} \right\} \rangle.$$

The freeness of the abstract variable $@_4$ is not preserved in the absorption step since $@_4$ is possibly dependent (see sharing group $\{@_1^f, @_4^f\}$) on the left-hand side $@_1$ of the equation being absorbed, the right-hand side of which is possibly non-linear (see sharing group $\{@_2^\ell, @_3^\ell\}$).

9   Conclusion

We reviewed a number of analyses using (abstract) equation systems as a common basis to decompose the key abstract operation, namely, unification in the abstract domain, into more simple sub-problems. A modular approach results which eases the design and justification of the analysis. The essential remaining step in developing a correct abstraction is a careful analysis of the underlying concrete unification with respect to the properties of interest. We summarized a collection of properties that have been the basis of several abstract domains described in the literature.

Acknowledgment

We have tried in this paper to present the work of many different authors within a representation of abstract equation systems. We feel that this gives a somewhat unifying view to a field in which many people have made contributions. Discussions and collaborations with many of these authors over the past few years have contributed immensely to this work. We thank them all.

References

1. S. Abramsky and C. Hankin (Eds.). *Abstract Interpretation of Declarative Languages*. Ellis Horwood Series in Computers and their Applications. Ellis Horwood, Chichester, 1987.

2. K. R. Apt. Logic programming. In J. van Leeuwen (Ed.), *Handbook of Theoretical Computer Science, Volume B: Formal Models and Semantics*, pp. 493–574. Elsevier Science Publ., Amsterdam, 1990.

3. K. R. Apt and A. Pellegrini. On the occur-check-free Prolog programs. *ACM Trans. Prog. Lang. Syst.*, 16(3):687–726, 1994.

4. T. Armstrong, K. Marriott, P. Schachte, and H. Søndergaard. Boolean functions for dependency analysis: Algebraic properties and efficient representation. In B. Le Charlier (Ed.), *Static Analysis*, Proc. 1st Int. Symposium (SAS'94), Lecture Notes in Computer Science, Vol. 864, Springer-Verlag, 1994, pp. 266–280.

5. R. Barbuti, R. Giacobazzi, and G. Levi. A general framework for semantics-based bottom-up abstract interpretation of logic programs. *ACM Trans. Prog. Lang. Syst.*, 15(1):133–181, Jan. 1993.

6. M. Bruynooghe. A practical framework for the abstract interpretation of logic programs. *The Journal of Logic Programming*, 10(2):91–124, 1991.

7. M. Bruynooghe and M. Codish. Freeness, sharing, linearity and correctness – all at once. In P. Cousot, M. Falaschi, G. Filè, and A. Rauzy (Eds.), *Static Analysis*, Proc. Third Int. Workshop, Lecture Notes in Computer Science, Vol. 724, Springer-Verlag, 1993, pp. 153–164.

8. M. Codish, D. Dams, G. Filé, and M. Bruynooghe. Freeness analysis for logic programs – and correctness? In D. S. Warren (Ed.), *Proc. Tenth International Conference on Logic Programming*, pp. 116–131, Budapest, Hungary, 1993. The MIT Press, Cambridge MA. Revised version to appear in J. of Logic Programming.

9. M. Codish, D. Dams, and E. Yardeni. Derivation and safety of an abstract unification algorithm for groundness and aliasing analysis. In K. Furukawa (Ed.), *Proc. Eighth International Conference on Logic Programming*, pp. 79–93, Paris, France, 1991. The MIT Press, Cambridge MA.

10. M. Codish, D. Dams, and E. Yardeni. Bottom-up abstract interpretation of logic programs. *Theoretical Computer Science*, 124(1):93–126, Feb. 1994.

11. M. Codish and B. Demoen. Analysing logic programs using "prop"-ositional logic programs and a magic wand. *The Journal of Logic Programming*. (to appear).

12. M. Codish, M. Falaschi, and K. Marriott. Suspension analysis for concurrent logic programs. *ACM Trans. Prog. Lang. Syst.*, 16(3):649–686, May 1994.

13. M. Codish, A. Mulkers, M. Bruynooghe, M. García de la Banda, and M. Hermenegildo. Improving abstract interpretations by combining domains. In *Proc. ACM-SIGPLAN Symp. on Partial Evaluation and Semantics-Based Program Manipulation* (PEPM'93), pp. 194–205, Copenhagen, June 1993. Revised version to appear in *ACM Trans. Prog. Lang. Syst.*

14. A. Cortesi and G. Filé. Abstract interpretation of logic programs: An abstract domain for groundness, sharing, freeness and compoundness analysis. In P. Hudak and N. D. Jones (ed.), *Proc. ACM-SIGPLAN Symp. on Partial Evaluation and Semantics-Based Program Manipulation*, pp. 52–61, 1991.

15. A. Cortesi, G. Filé, and W. Winsborough. Comparison of abstract interpretations. In: W. Kuich (Ed.), *Automata, Languages and Programming*, Proc. 19th Int. Colloquium (ICALP'92), Lecture Notes in Computer Science, Vol. 623, Springer-Verlag, 1992, pp. 521–532.

16. A. Cortesi, B. Le Charlier, and P. Van Hentenryck. Combinations of abstract domains for logic programming. In *Proc. 21st ACM SIGPLAN-SIGACT Symp. on Principles of Programming Languages* (POPL'94), pp. 227–239, Portland, Oregon, 1994. ACM Press.

17. P. Cousot and R. Cousot. Abstract interpretation: A unified lattice model for static analysis of programs by construction or approximation of fixpoints. In *Proc. 4th ACM Symposium on Principles of Programming Languages*, pp. 238–252, Los Angeles, 1977.

18. P. Cousot and R. Cousot. Abstract interpretation and application to logic programs. *The Journal of Logic Programming*, 13(2 and 3):103–179, 1992.

19. S. K. Debray. Static inference of modes and data dependencies in logic programs. *ACM Trans. Prog. Lang. Syst.*, 11(3):418–450, 1989.

20. T. W. Getzinger. The costs and benefits of abstract interpretation-driven Prolog optimization. In B. Le Charlier (Ed.), *Static Analysis*, Proc. 1st Int. Symposium (SAS'94), Lecture Notes in Computer Science, Vol. 864, Springer-Verlag, 1994, pp. 1–25.

21. M. V. Hermenegildo and F. Rossi. Strict and non-strict independent AND-parallelism in logic programs: Correctness, efficiency, and compile-time conditions. *The Journal of Logic Programming*, 22(1):1–45, Jan. 1995.

22. D. Jacobs and A. Langen. Accurate and efficient approximation of variable aliasing in logic programs. In E. L. Lusk and R. A. Overbeek (Eds.), *Proc. North American Conference on Logic Programming*, pp. 154–165, Cleveland, Ohio, USA, 1989.

23. D. Jacobs and A. Langen. Static analysis of logic programs for independent AND-parallelism. *The Journal of Logic Programming*, 13(2 & 3):291–314, 1992.

24. N. D. Jones and H. Søndergaard. A semantic-based framework for the abstract interpretation of Prolog. In Abramsky and Hankin [1], pp. 123–142.

25. A. King. A synergistic analysis for sharing and groundness which traces linearity. In D. Sannella (Ed.), *Programming Languages and Systems*, Proc. Fifth European Symposium (ESOP '94), Lecture Notes in Computer Science, Vol. 788, Springer-Verlag, 1994, pp. 363–378.

26. A. King and P. Soper. Depth-k sharing and freeness. In P. Van Hentenryck (Ed.), *Proc. 11th International Conference on Logic Programming*, pp. 553–568, Santa Margherita Ligure, Italy, 1994.

27. A. Langen. *Advanced Techniques for Approximating Variable Aliasing in Logic Programs.* Ph. D. thesis, University of Southern California, Mar. 1991.

28. J.-L. Lassez, M. J. Maher, and K. Marriott. Unification revisited. In J. Minker (Ed.), *Foundations of Deductive Databases and Logic Programming*, pp. 587–625. Morgan Kaufmann Publishers Inc., Los Altos, 1988.

29. B. Le Charlier and P. Van Hentenryck. Reexecution in abstract interpretation of Prolog. In K. Apt (Ed.), *Proc. Joint International Conference and Symposium on Logic Programming*, pp. 750–764, Washington D.C., 1992. The MIT Press, Cambridge MA.

30. B. Le Charlier and P. Van Hentenryck. Groundness analysis for Prolog: Implementation and evaluation of the domain Prop. In *Proc. ACM-SIGPLAN Symp. on Partial Evaluation and Semantics-Based Program Manipulation* (PEPM'93), pp. 99–110, Copenhagen, June 1993.

31. B. Le Charlier and P. Van Hentenryck. Experimental evaluation of a generic abstract interpretation algorithm for Prolog. *ACM Trans. Prog. Lang. Syst.*, 16(1):35–101, Jan. 1994.

32. J. W. Lloyd. *Foundations of Logic Programming.* Springer Series : Symbolic Computation - Artificial Intelligence. Springer-Verlag, second, extended edition, 1987.

33. K. Marriott. Frameworks for abstract interpretation. *Acta Informatica*, 30(2):103–129, 1993.

34. K. Marriott and H. Søndergaard. Precise and efficient groundness analysis for logic programs. *ACM Lett. Prog. Lang. Syst.*, 2(1-4):181–196, 1993.

35. A. Martelli and U. Montanari. An efficient unification algorithm. *ACM Trans. Prog. Lang. Syst.*, 4(2):258–282, Apr. 1982.

36. C. S. Mellish. The automatic generation of mode declarations for Prolog programs. DAI Research Paper 163, Dept. of Artificial Intelligence, Univ. of Edinburgh, Aug. 1981.

37. C. S. Mellish. Abstract interpretation of Prolog programs. In Abramsky and Hankin [1], pp. 181–198.

38. A. Mulkers, W. Simoens, G. Janssens, and M. Bruynooghe. On the practicality of abstract equation systems. In L. Sterling (Ed.), *Proc. International Conference on Logic Programming*, Kanagawa, Japan, 1995. The MIT Press, Cambridge MA. (To appear.)

39. K. Muthukumar and M. Hermenegildo. Determination of variable dependence information through abstract interpretation. In E. L. Lusk and R. A. Overbeek (Ed.), *Proc. North American Conference on Logic Programming*, pp. 166–188, Cleveland, Ohio, USA, 1989.

40. K. Muthukumar and M. Hermenegildo. Combined determination of sharing and freeness of program variables through abstract interpretation. In K. Furukawa (Ed.), *Proc. Eighth International Conference on Logic Programming*, pp. 49–63, Paris, France, 1991. The MIT Press, Cambridge MA.

41. D. A. Plaisted. The occur-check problem in Prolog. *J. New Generation Computing*, 2(4):309–322, 1984. Also in: *Proc. International Symposium on Logic Programming*, pp. 272–280, Atlantic City, 1984. IEEE Computer Society Press.

42. H. Søndergaard. An application of abstract interpretation of logic programs: Occur check reduction. In B. Robinet and R. Wilhelm (Eds.), *ESOP'86 - European Symposium on Programming*, Proceedings, Lecture Notes in Computer Science, Vol. 213, Springer-Verlag, 1986, pp. 327–338.

43. P. Van Hentenryck, A. Cortesi, and B. Le Charlier. Evaluation of the domain Prop. *The Journal of Logic Programming*, 23(3):237–278, 1995.

Programming Satan's Computer

Ross Anderson and Roger Needham

Cambridge University Computer Laboratory
Pembroke Street, Cambridge, England CB2 3QG

Abstract. Cryptographic protocols are used in distributed systems to identify users and authenticate transactions. They may involve the exchange of about 2–5 messages, and one might think that a program of this size would be fairly easy to get right. However, this is absolutely not the case: bugs are routinely found in well known protocols, and years after they were first published. The problem is the presence of a hostile opponent, who can alter messages at will. In effect, our task is to program a computer which gives answers which are subtly and maliciously wrong at the most inconvenient possible moment. This is a fascinating problem; and we hope that the lessons learned from programming Satan's computer may be helpful in tackling the more common problem of programming Murphy's.

1 Introduction

Cryptography is widely used in embedded distributed systems such as automatic teller machines, pay-per-view TV, prepayment utility meters and the GSM telephone network. Its primary purpose is to prevent frauds being carried out by people forging payment tokens or manipulating network messages; and as distributed client-server systems replace mainframes, it is also being introduced to general systems via products such as Kerberos which let a server identify remote clients and authenticate requests for resources.

As an increasing proportion of gross world product is accounted for by transactions protected by cryptography, it is important to understand what goes wrong with the systems which use it. Here, the common misconception is that a clever opponent will 'break' the cryptographic algorithm. It is indeed true that algorithms were broken during the second world war, and that this had an effect on military outcomes [Welc82]. However, even though many fielded systems use algorithms which could be broken by a wealthy opponent, it is rare for an actual attack to involve a head-on assault on the algorithm.

Surveys conducted of failure modes of banking systems [Ande94] and utility meters [AB95] showed that, in these fields at least, the great majority of actual security failures resulted from the opportunistic exploitation of various design and management blunders.

It is quite common for designers to protect the wrong things. For example, modern prepayment electricity meter systems allow the customer to buy a token from a shop and convey units of electricity to the meter in his home; they replace coin operated meters which were vulnerable to theft. Clearly one ought to prevent tokens — which may be magnetic tickets or suitably packaged EEPROMS — from being altered or duplicated in such a way that the customer can get free electricity. Yet one system protected the value encoded in the token, without protecting the tariff code; the result was that tokens could be produced with a tariff of a fraction of a cent per kilowatt hour, and they would keep a meter running almost for ever.

A lot of the recorded frauds were the result of this kind of blunder, or of management negligence pure and simple. However, there have been a significant number of cases where the designers protected the right things, used cryptographic algorithms which were not broken, and yet found that their systems were still successfully attacked. This brings us to the fascinating subject of cryptographic protocol failure.

2   Some Simple Protocol Failures

In this section, we will look at three simple protocol failures which highlight the improper use of shared key encryption. For a tutorial on cryptographic algorithms, one may consult [Schn94]; in this section, we will simply assume that if Alice and Bob share a string called a *key*, then they can use a shared-key encryption algorithm to transform a *plaintext* message into *ciphertext*. We will assume that the algorithm is strong, in that the opponent (conventionally called Charlie) cannot deduce the plaintext from the ciphertext (or vice versa) without knowing the key. We will write encryption symbolically as

$$C = \{M\}_K$$

Our problem is how to use this mechanism safely in a real system.

2.1   A simple bank fraud

A simple protocol failure allowed criminals to attack the automatic teller machine systems of one of Britain's largest banks. This bank wished to offer an offline service, so that customers could still get a limited amount of money when its mainframes were doing overnight batch processing. It therefore had the customer's personal identification number (PIN) encrypted and written to the magnetic strip on the card. The teller machines had a copy of the key, and so could check the PINs which customers entered.

However, a villain who had access to a card encoding machine discovered that he could alter the account number of his own card to someone else's, and then use his own PIN to withdraw money from the victim's account. He taught other villains how to do this trick; in due course the fraud led to at least two criminal trials, and to bad publicity which forced the bank to move to fully online processing [Lewi93].

Here, the protocol failure was the lack of linkage between the PIN and the account number. In fact, interbank standards call for PIN encryption to include the account number, but the bank's system antedated these standards.

This illustrates the fact that encryption is not as straightforward as it looks. It can be used for a number of purposes, including keeping data secret, guaranteeing the authenticity of a person or transaction, producing numbers which appear to be random, or binding the parts of a transaction together. However, we have to be very clear about what we are trying to do in each case: encryption is not synonymous with security, and its improper use can lead to errors.

2.2   Hacking pay-per-view TV

We will now turn from offline to online systems, and we will assume that our opponent Charlie controls the network and can modify messages at will. This may seem a bit extreme, but is borne out by the hard experience of the satellite TV industry.

Satellite TV signals are often encrypted to make customers pay a subscription, and the decoders are usually personalised with a secure token such as a smartcard. However, this card does not have the processing power to decrypt data at video rates, so we will usually find at least one cryptoprocessor in the decoder itself. Many decoders also have a microcontroller which passes messages between the cryptoprocessor and the card, and these have been replaced by attackers. Even where this is hard, hackers can easily interpose a PC between the decoder and the card and can thus manipulate the traffic.

- If a customer stops paying his subscription, the system typically sends a message over the air which instructs the decoder to disable the card. In the 'Kentucky Fried Chip' hack, the microcontroller was replaced with one which blocked this particular message. This was possible because the message was not encrypted [Mcco93].
- More recently a crypto key was obtained in clear, possibly by a microprobing attack on a single card; as the card serial numbers were not protected, this key could be used to revive other cards which had been disabled.
- In another system, the communications between the decoder and the card were synchronous across all users; so people could video record an encrypted programme and then decrypt it later using a protocol log posted to the Internet by someone with a valid card [Kuhn95].

These attacks are not just an academic matter; they have cost the industry hundreds of millions of pounds.

So in the following sections, our model will be that Alice wishes to communicate with Bob with the help of Sam, who is trusted, over a network owned by Charlie, who is not. In satellite TV, Alice would be the user's smartcard, Bob the decoder, Charlie the compromised microcontroller (or a PC sitting between the set-top box and the smartcard) and Sam the broadcaster; in a distributed system, Alice could be a client, Bob a server, Charlie a hacker and Sam the authentication service.

2.3   Freshening the breath of the wide mouthed frog

Time plays a role in many cryptographic protocols. Often we want to limit our exposure to staff disloyalty and equipment capture, and if system components are given keys which give them access to valuable resources and which have a long lifetime, then revocation can become complicated and expensive.

One common solution is to have each user share a key with an authentication server, Sam. We will write the key which Alice shares with him as K_{AS}, Bob's as K_{BS}, and so on. Now when Alice wishes to set up a secure session with Bob, she gets Sam to help them share a session key (say K_{AB}) which will have a strictly limited lifetime. So if Charlie is caught selling company secrets to the competition, his access can be revoked completely by having Sam delete K_{CS}.

However, many authentication protocols designed for use in this context have turned out to be wrong. One of the simplest is the so-called 'Wide Mouthed Frog' protocol [BAN89], in which Alice chooses a session key to communicate with Bob and gets Sam to translate it from K_{AS} to K_{BS}. Symbolically

$$A \longrightarrow S : \{T_A, B, K_{AB}\}_{K_{AS}}$$
$$S \longrightarrow B : \{T_S, A, K_{AB}\}_{K_{BS}}$$

Here, T_A is a timestamp supplied by Alice, and T_S is one supplied by Sam. It is understood that there is a time window within which Bob will be prepared to accept the key K_{AB} as fresh.

This protocol fails. The flaw is that Sam updates the timestamp from Alice's time T_A to his time T_S. The effect is that unless Sam keeps a list of all recent working keys and timestamps, Charlie can keep a key alive by using Sam as an oracle.

For example, after observing the above exchange, Charlie could pretend to be Bob wanting to share a key with Alice; he would send Sam $\{T_S, A, K_{AB}\}_{K_{BS}}$ and get back $\{T'_S, B, K_{AB}\}_{K_{AS}}$ where T'_S is a new timestamp. He could then pretend to be Alice and get $\{T''_S, A, K_{AB}\}_{K_{BS}}$, and so on.

The practical effect of this flaw would depend on the application. If the users ran the above protocol in smartcards which then passed the session key in clear to a software bulk encryption routine, they could be open to the following attack. Charlie observes that Alice and Bob are setting up a session, so he keeps the session key alive until he can steal one of their smartcards. Indeed, Alice and Bob might become careless with their cards, having thought the message irrecoverable once its plaintext and K_{AB} had been destroyed, and the validity period of the timestamps had expired.

The lesson here is that one must be careful about how we ensure temporal succession and association.

2.4   The perils of challenge-response

Many systems use a challenge-response technique in which one party sends the other a random number, which is then subjected to some cryptographic transformation and sent back. The purpose of this may be to identify someone wishing to log on to a system, or it may play a role similar to that of a timestamp by ensuring freshness in a protocol. In what follows, we will write N_A for a random number challenge issued by Alice.

One widespread application is in password calculators. To log on to a system which uses these, the user first enters her name; the system displays a seven digit challenge on the screen; the user enters this into her calculator, together with a secret PIN; the calculator concatenates the challenge and the PIN, encrypts them with a stored key, and displays the first seven digits of the result; and the user finally types this in as her logon password.

For users logging on to a single system, this is a simple and robust way to avoid many of the problems common with passwords. However, the picture changes when a number of systems are involved, and attempts are made to concentrate the calculator keys in a single security server. For example, consider the following protocol of Woo and Lam, which attempts to let Alice prove her presence to Bob's machine despite the fact that she does not share her key with Bob but with Sam:

$$A \longrightarrow B : A$$
$$B \longrightarrow A : N_B$$
$$A \longrightarrow B : \{N_B\}_{K_{AS}}$$
$$B \longrightarrow S : \{A, \{N_B\}_{K_{AS}}\}_{K_{BS}}$$
$$S \longrightarrow B : \{N_B\}_{K_{BS}}$$

This protocol is wrong. The only connection between Bob's query to Sam, and Sam's reply, is the coincidental fact that the latter comes shortly after the former; this is insufficient against an opponent who can manipulate messages. Charlie can impersonate Alice by trying to log on to Bob's machine at about the same time as her, and then swapping the translations which Sam gives of Alice's and Charlie's replies.

One of us therefore proposed in [AN94] that the last message should be:

$$S \longrightarrow B : \{A, N_B\}_{K_{BS}}$$

However, this is not always enough, as Sam goes not know the name of the host to which Alice is attempting to log on. So Charlie might entice Alice to log on to him, start a logon in Alice's name to Bob, and gets her to answer the challenge sent to him. So we ought to put Bob's name explicitly in the protocol as well:

$$A \longrightarrow B : A$$
$$B \longrightarrow A : N_B$$
$$A \longrightarrow B : \{B, N_B\}_{K_{AS}}$$
$$B \longrightarrow S : A, \{B, N_B\}_{K_{AS}}$$
$$S \longrightarrow B : \{N_B, A\}_{K_{BS}}$$

All this might be overkill in some applications, as someone who could manipulate the network could take over an already established session. Whether there is actually a risk will depend closely on the circumstances.

Anyway, the two lessons which we can learn from this are firstly, that we should be very careful in stating our security goals and assumptions; and secondly, that where the identity of a principal is essential to the meaning of a message, it should be mentioned explicitly in that message.

For more attacks on shared key protocols, see [BAN89] and [AN94].

3. Problems with Public Key Protocols

The shared-key encryption algorithms used in the above protocols are not the only tools we have; there are also public-key algorithms which use different keys for encrypting and decrypting data. These are called the *public key*, K, and the *private key*, K^{-1}, respectively. A public key algorithm should have the additional property that Charlie cannot deduce K^{-1} from K.

The best known public-key algorithm is the RSA scheme [RSA78]. This is straightforward in the sense that the encryption and decryption operations are mutual inverses; that is, $C = \{M\}_K$ holds if and only if $M = \{C\}_{K^{-1}}$. So we can take a message and subject it to 'decryption' $S = \{M\}_{K^{-1}}$, which can be reversed using K to recover the original message, $M = \{S\}_K$.

In this context, the 'decryption' of a message M is usually referred to as its *digital signature*, since it can only be computed by the person possessing K^{-1}, while anybody who knows K can check it. Actually, decryption and signature are not quite the same thing, but we shall postpone discussion of this.

Anyway, if Alice and Bob publish encryption keys KA, KB respectively while each keeps the corresponding decryption key KA^{-1} or KB^{-1} secret, then they can ensure both the integrity and privacy of their messages in the following elegant way [DH76]. To send a message M to Bob, Alice first signs it with her private key KA^{-1} and then encrypts it with Bob's public key KB:

$$C = \{\{M\}_{KA^{-1}}\}_{KB}$$

When Bob receives this message, he can first strip off the outer encryption using his private key KB^{-1}, and then recover the message M by applying Alice's public key KA.

It might be hoped that this technology could make the design of cryptographic protocols a lot easier. Of course, there are a lot of problems which we must solve in a real implementation. For example, how does Bob know that he has received a real message? If Charlie had replaced the ciphertext C with some completely random value C', then Bob would calculate $M' = \{\{C'\}_{KB^{-1}}\}_{KA}$. For this reason, we would usually want to insert redundancy into the message.

Some systems do indeed suffer from a lack of redundancy [AN95]. However, this is not the only thing which can go wrong with a public key protocol.

3.1   The Denning-Sacco disaster

One obvious problem with public key cryptography is that Charlie might generate a keypair K_X, K_X^{-1} and place K_X in the directory with the legend "This is Alice's public key: K_X". So there is still a security requirement on key management, but we have reduced it from confidentiality to authenticity.

One common solution is to use our trusted third party, Sam, as a certification authority (the public key equivalent of an authentication server). Sam would issue each user with a certificate containing their name, public key, access rights (whether credentials or capabilities) and expiry date, all signed with Sam's own secret key (whose corresponding public key we will assume to be well known). We can write

$$CA = \{A, K_A, R_A, E_A\}_{K_S^{-1}}$$

However, public key certificates are not the whole answer, as it is still easy to design faulty protocols using them. For example, one of the first public key protocols was proposed by Denning and Sacco in 1982; it provides a mechanism for distributing conventional shared encryption keys, and runs as follows:

$$A \longrightarrow S : A, B$$
$$S \longrightarrow A : CA, CB$$
$$A \longrightarrow B : CA, CB, \{\{T_A, K_{AB}\}_{K_A^{-1}}\}_{K_B}$$

It was not until 1994 that a disastrous flaw was noticed by Abadi. Bob, on receiving Alice's message, can masquerade as her for as long as her timestamp T_A remains valid!

To see how, suppose that Bob wants to masquerade as Alice to Charlie. He goes to Sam and gets a fresh certificate CC for Charlie, and then strips off the outer encryption $\{...\}_{K_B}$ fromthe third message in the above protocol. He now re-encrypts the signed key $\{T_A, K_{AB}\}_{K_A^{-1}}$ with Charlie's public key — which he gets from CC — and makes up a bogus third message:

$$B \longrightarrow C : CB, CC, \{\{T_A, K_{AB}\}_{K_A^{-1}}\}_{K_C}$$

This failure can also be seen as a violation of the principle that names should be mentioned explicitly within messages.

3.2   The middleperson attack

John Conway pointed out that it is easy to beat a grandmaster at postal chess. Just play two grandmasters, one as white and the other as black, and act as a message relay between them.

The same idea can often be used to attack crypto protocols. For example, one of us proposed in [NS78] that an authenticated key exchange could be carried out as follows. Here we will assume for the sake of brevity that both Alice and Bob already have a copy of the other's key certificate.

$$A \longrightarrow B : \{N_A, A\}_{K_B}$$
$$B \longrightarrow A : \{N_A, N_B\}_{K_A}$$
$$A \longrightarrow B : \{N_B\}_{K_B}$$

This was already known to be vulnerable to a replay attack [BAN89]. However, Lowe has recently pointed out a middleperson attack [Lowe95]. Here, Charlie sits between Alice and Bob. He appears as Charlie to Alice, but pretends to be Alice to Bob:

$$A \longrightarrow C : \{N_A, A\}_{K_C}$$
$$C \longrightarrow B : \{N_A, A\}_{K_B}$$
$$B \longrightarrow C : \{N_A, N_B\}_{K_A}$$
$$C \longrightarrow A : \{N_A, N_B\}_{K_A}$$
$$A \longrightarrow C : \{N_B\}_{K_C}$$
$$C \longrightarrow B : \{N_B\}_{K_B}$$

The fix here is also straightforward: just put the principals' names explicitly in the messages.

3.3   CCITT X.509

Another problem was found by Burrows, Abadi and Needham in the CCITT X.509 protocol [CCITT88]. This is described in [BAN89]; briefly, the idea is that Alice signs a message of the form $\{T_A, N_A, B, X, \{Y\}_{K_B}\}$ and sends it to Bob, where T_A is a timestamp, N_A is a serial number, and X and Y are user data. The problem here is that since the order of encryption and signature are reversed — Y is first encrypted, then signed — it is possible for Charlie to strip off Alice's signature and add one of his own.

We have recently found an even sneakier attack — with many public key encryption algorithms it is possible, given a message M and ciphertext C, to find some key K with $C = \{M\}_K$. The mechanics of this key spoofing attack are described in [AN95]; they depend quite closely on the mathematics of the underlying public key encryption algorithm, and we will not go into them in much detail here[1].

---

[1] Consider for example RSA with a 512 bit modulus. If Alice sends Bob M, and if the modulus, public exponent and private exponent of party α are n_α, e_α and d_α, and if we ignore hashing (which makes no difference to our argument), the signed encrypted message would be $\{M^{e_B} \pmod{n_B}\}^{d_A} \pmod{n_A}$. But since Bob can factor n_B and its factors are only about 256 bits long, he can work out discrete logarithms with respect to them and then use the Chinese Remainder Theorem to get discrete logs modulo n_B. So he can get Alice's 'signature' on M' by finding x such that $[M']^x = M \pmod{n_B}$ and then registering (xe_B, n_B) as a public key.

The effect is that if we encrypt data before signing it, we lay ourselves open to an opponent swapping the message that we thought we signed for another one. In the above example, if Bob wants to convince a judge that Alice actually sent him the message Z rather than Y, he can find a key K' such that $\{Z\}_{K'} = \{Y\}_{K_B}$, and register this key K' with a certification authority.

This provides a direct attack on CCITT X.509, in which Alice signs a message of the form $\{T_A, N_A, B, X, \{Y\}^{e_B} \pmod{n_B}\}$ and sends it to Bob. Here T_A is a timestamp, N_A is a serial number, and X and Y are user data. It also breaks the draft ISO CD 11770; there, Y consists of A's name concatenated with either a random challenge or a session key.

Whether there is an actual attack on any given system will, as usual, depend on the application detail (in this case, the interaction between timestamps, serial numbers and any other mechanisms used to establish temporal succession and association). However, it is clearly a bad idea to bring more of the application code within the security perimeter than absolutely necessary.

In any case, the lesson to be learned is that if a signature is affixed to encrypted data, then one cannot assume that the signer has any knowledge of the data. A third party certainly cannot assume that the signature is authentic, so nonrepudiation is lost.

3.4   Simmons' attack on TMN

False key attacks are not the only protocol failures which exploit the mathematical properties of the underlying algorithms. These failures can sometimes be quite subtle, and an interesting example is the attack found by Simmons on the TMN (Tatebayashi-Matsuzaki-Newmann) scheme [TMN89].

Here, two users want to set up a session key, but with a trusted server doing most of the work (the users might be smartcards). If Alice and Bob are the users, and the trusted server Sam can factor N, then the protocol goes as follows:

$$A \longrightarrow S : r_A^3 \pmod{N}$$
$$B \longrightarrow S : r_B^3 \pmod{N}$$
$$S \longrightarrow A : r_A \oplus r_B$$

Each party chooses a random number, cubes it, and sends in to Sam. As he can factor N, he can extract cube roots, xor the two random numbers together, and send the result to Alice. The idea is that Alice and Bob can now use r_B as a shared secret key. However, Simmons pointed out that if Charlie and David conspire, or even if David just generates a predictable random number r_D, then Charlie can get hold of r_B in the following way [Simm94]:

$$C \longrightarrow S : r_B^3 r_C^3 \pmod{n}$$
$$D \longrightarrow S : r_D^3 \pmod{n}$$
$$S \longrightarrow C : r_B r_C \oplus r_D$$

The lessons to be learned here are that we should never trust in the secrecy of other people's secrets, and that we must always be careful when signing or decrypting data that we never let ourselves be used as an oracle by the opponent.

3.5 The difference between decryption and signature

Nonrepudiation is complicated by the fact that signature and decryption are the same operation in RSA, which many people use as their mental model of public key cryptography. They are actually quite different in their semantics: decryption can be simulated, while signature cannot. By this we mean that an opponent can exhibit a ciphertext and its decryption into a meaningful message, while he cannot exhibit a meaningful message and its signature (unless it is one he has seen previously).

Consider for example another protocol suggested by Woo and Lam [WL92]:

$$A \longrightarrow S : A, B$$
$$S \longrightarrow A : CB$$
$$A \longrightarrow B : \{A, N_A\}_{KB}$$
$$B \longrightarrow S : A, B, \{N_A\}_{KS}$$
$$S \longrightarrow B : CA, \{\{N_A, K_{AB}, A, B\}_{KS^{-1}}\}_{KB}$$
$$B \longrightarrow A : \{\{N_A, K_{AB}, A, B\}_{KS^{-1}}\}_{KA}$$
$$A \longrightarrow B : \{N_A\}_{K_{AB}}$$

There are a number of problems with this protocol, including the obvious one that Bob has no assurance of freshness (he does not check a nonce or see a timestamp). However, a subtler and more serious problem is that Alice never signs anything; the only use made of her secret is to decrypt a message sent to her by Bob. The consequence is that Bob can only prove Alice's presence to himself — he cannot prove anything to an outsider, as he could easily have simulated the entire protocol run. The effect that such details can have on the beliefs of third parties is one of the interesting (and difficult) features of public key protocols: few of the standards provide a robust nonrepudiation mechanism, and yet there is a real risk that many of them may be used as if they did.

So we must be careful how entities are distinguished. In particular, we have to be careful what we mean by 'Bob'. This may be 'whoever controls Bob's signing key', or it may be 'whoever controls Bob's decryption key'. Both keys are written as KB^{-1} in the standard notation, despite being subtly different in effect. So we should avoid using the same key for two different purposes, and be careful to distinguish different runs of the same protocol from each other.

For more examples of attacks on public key protocols, see [AN95].

4 How Can We Be Saved?

We have described the crypto protocols design problem as 'programming Satan's computer' because a network under the control of an adversary is possibly the most obstructive computer which one could build. It may give answers which are subtly and maliciously wrong at the most inconvenient possible moment.

Seen in this light, it is less surprising that so many protocols turned out to contain serious errors, and that these errors often took a long time to discover — twelve years for the bug in Denning-Sacco, and seventeen years for the middleperson attack on Needham-Schroeder. It is hard to simulate the behaviour of the devil; one can always check that a protocol does not commit the old familiar sins, but every so often someone comes up with a new and pernicious twist.

It is therefore natural to ask what we must do to be saved. Under what circumstances can we say positive things about a crypto protocol? Might it ever be possible to prove that a protocol is correct?

4.1   Protocol verification logics

There were some attempts to reduce security claims of specific protocols to the intractability of some problem such as factoring on which the strength of the underlying encryption algorithm was predicated. However, the first systematic approach involved the modal logic of Burrows, Abadi and Needham. Here, we have a series of rules such as

If P believes that he shares a key K with Q, and sees the message M encrypted under K, then he will believe that Q once said M

and

If P believes that the message M is fresh, and also believes that Q once said M, then he will believe that Q believes M

These rules are applied to protocols, and essentially one tries to follow back the chains of belief in freshness and in what key is shared with whom, until one either finds a flaw or concludes that it is proper under the assumptions to believe that the authentication goal has been met. For full details, seen [BAN89].

A more recent logic by Kailar [Kail95] looks at what can be done without making any assumptions about freshness. Its application is to systems (such as in electronic banking) where the question is not whether Q recently said M but whether Q ever said M — as for example in whether Q ever did the electronic equivalent of endorsing a bill of exchange.

Curiously enough, although public key algorithms are based more on mathematics than shared key algorithms, public key protocols have proved much harder to deal with by formal methods. A good example is encryption before signature. This is easy enough as a principle — we normally sign a letter and then put it in an envelope, rather than putting an unsigned letter in an envelope and then signing the flap. It is intuitively clear that the latter practice deprives the recipient of much of the evidential force that we expect a normal letter to possess.

However, encryption before signature can cause serious problems for formal verification. Neither the BAN logic nor Kailar's logic is fooled by it, but more complex tools that try to deal with algorithm properties (such as those discussed in [KMM94]) do not seem able to deal with key spoofing attacks at all.

Another curious thing about formal methods has been that most of the gains come early. The BAN logic is very simple, and there are a number of protocols which it cannot analyse. However, attempts to build more complex logics have met with mixed success, with problems ranging from inconsistent axiom schemes to the sheer difficulty of computation if one has a hundred rules to choose from rather than ten. The BAN logic still has by far the most 'scalps' at its belt.

It is also our experience of using logic that most of work lies in formalising the protocol. Once this has been done, it is usually pretty obvious if there is a bug. So perhaps the benefit which it brings is as much from forcing us to think clearly about what is going on than from any intrinsic mathematical leverage.

4.2   Robustness principles

Another approach is to try to encapsulate our experience of good and bad practice into rules of thumb; these can help designers avoid many of the pitfalls, and, equally, help attackers find exploitable errors. We have given a number of examples in the above text:

- be very clear about the security goals and assumptions;
- be clear about the purpose of encryption — secrecy, authenticity, binding, or producing pseudorandom numbers. Do not assume that its use is synonymous with security;
- be careful about how you ensure temporal succession and association;
- where the identity of a principal is essential to the meaning of a message, it should be mentioned explicitly in the message;
- make sure you include enough redundancy;
- be careful that your protocol does not make some unexamined assumption about the properties of the underlying cryptographic algorithm;
- if a signature is affixed to encrypted data, then one cannot assume that the signer has any knowledge of the data. A third party certainly cannot assume that the signature is authentic, so nonrepudiation is lost;
- do not trust the secrecy of other people's secrets;
- be careful, especially when signing or decrypting data, not to let yourself be used as an oracle by the opponent;
- do not confuse decryption with signature;
- be sure to distinguish different protocol runs from each other.

This is by no means a complete list; more comprehensive analyses of desirable protocol properties can be found in [AN94] and [AN95]. However, experience shows that the two approaches — formal proofs and structured design rules — are complementary, we are led to wonder whether there is some overarching principle, which underlies the success of formal methods in the crypto protocol context and of which the above points are instances. We propose the following:

> **The Explicitness Principle:** Robust security is about explicitness. A cryptographic protocol should make any necessary naming, typing and freshness information explicit in its messages; designers must also be explicit about their starting assumptions and goals, as well as any algorithm properties which could be used in an attack.

This is discussed in greater detail in [Ande94] [AN94] [AN95]. However, there is more going on here than a sloppy expression of truths which are either self evident, or liable one day to be tidied up and proved as theorems. There is also the matter of educating what we call 'commonsense'.

Commonsense can be misleading and even contradictory. For example, we might consider it commonsensical to adhere to the KISS principle ('Keep It Simple Stupid'). However, much erroneous protocol design appears to be a consequence of trying to minimise the amount of cryptographic computation which has to be done (e.g., by omitting the names of principals in order to shorten the encrypted parts of our messages). So one might rather cleave to the description of optimisation as 'the act of replacing something that works with something that almost works, but is cheaper'. Resolving such conflicts of intuition is one of the goals of our research; and both robustness principles and formal methods seem to be most useful when they provide that small amount of support which we need in order for commonsense to take us the rest of the way.

5   Conclusions

We have tried to give an accessible introduction to the complex and fascinating world of cryptographic protocols. Trying to program a computer which is under the control of an intelligent and malicious opponent is one of the most challenging tasks in computer science, and even programs of a few lines have turned out to contain errors which were not discovered for over a decade.

There are basically two approaches to the problem. The first uses formal methods, and typically involves the manipulation of statements such as 'A believes that B believes X about key K'. These techniques are helpful, and have led to the discovery of a large number of flaws, but they cannot tackle all the protocols which we would like to either verify or break.

The complementary approach is to develop a series of rules of thumb which guide us towards good practice and away from bad. We do not claim that these robustness principles are either necessary or sufficient, just that they are useful; together with formal methods, they can help to educate our intuition. Either way, the most important princple appears to be explicitness: this means that, for example, a smartcard in a satellite TV set-top box should not say 'here is a key with which to decode the signal' but 'I have received your random challenge to which the response is X, and Y is a key with which Mrs Smith is authorised to decode the 8 o'clock news using decoder number Z on the 15th June 1995'.

What is the wider relevance? In most system engineering work, we assume that we have a computer which is more or less good and a program which is probably fairly bad. However, it may also be helpful to consider the case where the computer is thoroughly wicked, particularly when developing fault tolerant systems and when trying to find robust ways to structure programs and encapsulate code. In other words, the black art of programming Satan's computer may give insights into the more commonplace task of trying to program Murphy's.

References

[Ande92]   R.J. Anderson, "UEPS - A Second Generation Electronic Wallet", In: Y. Deswarte, G. Eizenberg, J.-J. Quiswater (Eds.) *Computer Security — ES-ORICS 92*, Lecture Notes In Computer Science, Vol. 648, Springer-Verlag, Berlin, 1992, pp. 411–418.

[Ande94]   R.J. Anderson, "Why Cryptosystems Fail", *Communications of the ACM* 37:11 (1994) 32–40.

[AB95]   R.J. Anderson, S.J. Bezuidenhout, "Cryptographic Credit Control in Pre-Payment Metering Systems", in *1995 IEEE Symposium on Security and Privacy*, pp. 15–23.

[AN94]   M. Abadi, R.M. Needham, "Prudent Engineering Practice for Cryptographic Protocols", DEC SRC Research Report no 125, Digital Equipment Corp., June, 1994.

[AN95]   R.J. Anderson, R.M. Needham, "Robustness principles for public key protocols", in: *Advances in Cryptology — CRYPTO '95*, (to appear).

[BAN89]   M. Burrows, M. Abadi, R.M. Needham, "A Logic of Authentication", in *Proceedings of the Royal Society of London A* 426 (1989) 233–271; earlier version published as DEC SRC Research Report no 39.

[CCITT88]   CCITT X.509 and ISO 9594-8, "The Directory — Authentication Framework", CCITT Blue Book, Geneva, March 1988.

[DH76]   W. Diffie, M.E. Hellman, "New Directions in Cryptography", in *IEEE Transactions on Information Theory*, IT-22:6 (1976) 644–654.

[Kail95]   R. Kailar, "Reasoning about Accountability in Protocols for Electronic Commerce", in *1995 IEEE Symposium on Security and Privacy*, pp. 236–250.

[Kuhn95]   M. Kuhn, *private communication*, 1995.

[KMM94]   R. Kemmerer, C. Meadows, J. Millen, "Three Systems for Cryptographic Protocol Verification", in *Journal of Cryptology* 7:2 (1994) 79–130.

[Lewi93]   B. Lewis, "How to rob a bank the cashcard way", in: *Sunday Telegraph*, 25th April 1993, p 5.

[Lowe95]   G. Lowe, "An Attack on the Needham-Schroeder Public-Key Authentication Protocol", preprint, May 1995.

[Mcco93]   J. McCormac, *'The Black Book'*, Waterford University Press, 1993.

[NS78]   R.M. Needham, M. Schroeder, "Using encryption for authentication in large networks of computers", *Communications of the ACM* 21:12 (1978) 993–999.

[RSA78]   R.L. Rivest, A. Shamir, L. Adleman, "A Method for Obtaining Digital Signatures and Public-Key Cryptosystems", *Communications of the ACM* 21:2 (1978) 120–126.

[Schn94] B. Schneier, *Applied Cryptography*, John Wiley & Sons, 1994.

[Simm94] G.J. Simmons, "Cryptanalysis and Protocol Failures", *Communications of the ACM* 37:11 (1994) 56–65.

[TMN89]   M. Tatebayashi, N. Matsuzaki, D.B. Newman, "Key distribution protocol for digital mobile communication systems", in: G. Brassard (Ed.), *Advance in Cryptology — CRYPTO '89*, Lecture Note in Computer Science, Vol. 435, Springer-Verlag, Berlin, 1989, pp. 324–333.

[WL92]   T.Y.C. Woo, S.S. Lam, "Authentication for Distributed Systems", in *IEEE Computer* (January 1992) pp 39–52.

[Welc82] G. Welchman, *The Hut Six Story — Breaking the Enigma Codes*, McGraw Hill, New York, 1982.

Petri Net Models of Distributed Algorithms

Wolfgang Reisig

Humboldt-Universität zu Berlin
Institut für Informatik
Unter den Linden 6
D-10099 BERLIN

Abstract. A framework is suggested for modelling and verifying distributed algorithms. It is based on Petri Nets and Temporal Logic, and focusses on simplicity and readability of proofs.

Specific aspects of this approach include the concept of round based behaviour, and techniques to pick up elementary properties from an algorithm's static display and to master fairness assumptions. Proof rules exploit causal dependencies in runs of distributed algorithms. Some case studies will exemplify the new approach.

1 Introduction

An algorithm is said to be *distributed* if it operates on a physically or logically distributed computing architecture. Distributed algorithms are frequently represented in a programming notation (as in [10] and [14]). Formal semantics, if defined at all, is usually reduced to nondeterministic execution of assignment statements (as in [2] and [1]). Techniques to prove distributed algorithms correct likewise extend the ones corresponding to sequential programs (as in [1]). Additionally, temporal logic has turned out to be useful (as demonstrated in [2] and [5]).

Careful inspection reveals that temporal logic based correctness proofs essentially deal with propositions or predicates on local states, and that they assume actions that synchronously swap a subset of those propositions. Hence it is convenient to employ atomic propositions as local states and synchronized swapping of those propositions as actions. This, of course, is just the basic version of Petri Nets; the modelling technique used in the sequel.

It is meanwhile widely recognized that causal dependencies among events in runs of distributed systems provide valuable information for correctness proofs. Various logics capturing this issue have been suggested (cf. [3], [6], [8]).

Causal dependencies among events are perfectly represented in *concurrent runs* of Petri Nets, as introduced in [9] (cf. also [11]). We will therefore employ this concept in the sequel.

Correctness of algorithms can be proven at different levels of precision. Intuition guided *human proofs* represent one extreme; they are frequently imprecise or incomplete, and their validity is sometimes debatable and a matter of taste. On the other hand, there are machine executable *formal proofs*; such proofs are often too detailed, hard to understand and do not contribute to their reader's intuition and view of an algorithm. Model checking techniques belong to this class of proofs.

There are various ongoing efforts towards providing support for *human formal proofs*, so as to remove the shortcomings of the two modes of expression without loosing their respective qualities. Typical endeavours of this kind include [13] and [16].

This paper suggests a number of integrated notions to represent distributed algorithms and their important properties, and to construct human formal correctness proofs of such algorithms.

2   Basic Notions and Examples

This section provides the fundamental modelling techniques employed in the sequel, beginning with standard terminology of Petri Nets:

As usual, let P and T be two disjoint sets and let $F \subseteq (P \times T) \cup (T \times P)$. Then $N = (P, T, F)$ is called a *net*. Unless interpreted in a special manner, the elements of P, T and F will be called *places*, *transitions* and *arcs*, respectively. We will employ the usual graphical representation of nets, depicting places, transitions and arcs as *circles*, *boxes* and *arrows*, respectively. An arrow $x \to y$ represents the arc (x, y). Fig. 1 shows an (inscribed) net.

The following notations will frequently be used for a net $N = (P, T, F)$: P_N, T_N and F_N denote P, T and F, respectively. By abuse of notation, N often stands for the set $P_N \cup T_N$. Whenever F can be assumed from the context, $^\bullet a$ denotes the set $\{b \in N \mid (b, a) \in F\}$ and $a^\bullet$ the set $\{b \in N \mid (a, b) \in F\}$ for any $a \in N$. Generalized to subsets $A \subseteq N$, let $^\bullet A = \bigcup_{a \in A} {}^\bullet a$ and $A^\bullet = \bigcup_{a \in A} a^\bullet$. For $a, b \in N$ we write $a \prec_N b$ iff $(a, b) \in F^+$ and $a \preceq_N b$ iff $a \prec_N b$ or $a = b$.

Places and transitions frequently denote *local states* and *actions*, respectively. Any subset $a \subseteq P_N$ of local states forms a *global state*. An action t may *occur* in a global state a provided t is *enabled*; i.e. $^\bullet t \subseteq a$ and $(t^\bullet \setminus {}^\bullet t) \cap a = \emptyset$. $eff(a, t) := (a \setminus {}^\bullet t) \cup t^\bullet$ is the *effect* of t's occurrence at a. If t is enabled at a, the triple $(a, t, eff(a, t))$ is a *step in* N, written $a \xrightarrow{t} eff(a, t)$.

As an example, $\{quiet_l, quiet_r\}$ is a global state of the net in Fig. 1. The only action enabled in this state is *act*. Its occurrence then yields the state $\{pending, sent, quiet_r\}$.

Any description of algorithms is usually accompanied by the implicit assumption of *progress*. For example, each execution of a PASCAL program is assumed to continue as long as the program counter points at some executable statement.

The situation is more involved for distributed algorithms. Progress is usually assumed for a majority, but not for all actions. As an example, $quiet_l$ of Fig. 1 may be allowed to remain *quiescent* after finitely many occurrences of *act* (i.e. *act* may eventually stay enabled forever, in contrast to all other actions). This implies Σ_1 always returns to its initial state.

This leads to the following definition of *elementary system nets*, in the sequel denoted by Σ: A net Σ is an *elementary system net (es-net, for short)* iff some global state is distinguished as *initial* (written a_Σ) and each transition $t \in T_\Sigma$

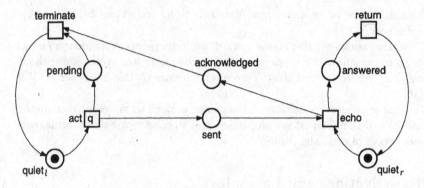

Fig. 1. es-net Σ_1: acknowledged message passing

is assumed either *progressing* or *quiescent*. Places and transitions will then be called *local states* and *actions* of Σ, respectively. A finite or infinite sequence $w = a_0 \xrightarrow{t_1} a_1 \xrightarrow{t_2} \ldots$ of steps is an *interleaved run* of Σ iff $a_0 = a_\Sigma$ and to each progressing action t enabled at some state a_i there exists an index $j \geq i$ with $t_j \in ({}^\bullet t_i)^\bullet$. A global state $a \subseteq P_\Sigma$ is *reachable in* Σ iff there exists an interleaved run $a_0 \xrightarrow{t_1} a_1 \xrightarrow{t_2} \ldots$ of Σ with $a = a_i$ for some index $i \geq 0$. As a further technality we assume *contact freeness* for each $t \in T_\Sigma$ in the sequel: If ${}^\bullet t \subseteq a$ for any reachable state a, then $a \cap (t^\bullet \setminus {}^\bullet t) = \emptyset$.

The initial state a_Σ of Σ is graphically depicted by dots in the corresponding circles. Each quiescent action is inscribed "q". As an example Fig. 1 shows an es-net Σ_1. With $a_{\Sigma_1} = \{quiet_l, quiet_r\}, a_1 = \{pending, sent, quiet_r\}, a_2 = \{pending, acknowledged, answered\}$ and $a_3 = \{quiet_l, answered\}$, the sequence of steps

$$a_{\Sigma_1} \xrightarrow{act} a_1 \xrightarrow{echo} a_2 \xrightarrow{terminate} a_3 \xrightarrow{return} a_{\Sigma_1} \xrightarrow{act} a_1 \tag{1}$$

is *no* interleaved run of Σ_1, as *echo* remains enabled. Skipping the last step however turns (1) into a perfect interleaved run of Σ_1.

The concept of es-nets will be slightly extended in section 10 to cover *fairness* assumptions. In the sequel we assume Σ to denote any es-net.

3   Rounds, Ground States and Concurrent Runs

The issue to be considered next can be motivated by a more thorough investigation of Σ_1. This es-net represents a system of two *sites* l and r (the *left* and the *right* site, respectively), and a communication line that links both sites together. In its *quiet* state, l may spontaneously send a message to r and remains in the state *pending* until the receipt of an acknowledgement. Then l returns to the *quiet* state. Site r upon receiving a message responds with an acknowledgment, turns *answered* and eventually returns *quiet*. This behaviour can be intuitively described in terms of *rounds*. A round starts and ends when both sites are quiet.

The set $\{quiet_l, quiet_r\}$ is therefore said to be a *ground set*. The notion of rounds and ground sets are not entirely trivial, because l may start the $i + 1$st round before r has completed the i-th round, as in

$$a_\Sigma \xrightarrow{act} a_1 \xrightarrow{echo} a_2 \xrightarrow{terminate} a_3 \xrightarrow{act} a_4 \xrightarrow{return} a_1 \qquad (2)$$

with a_1, a_2, a_3 as in (1) and $a_4 = \{pending, sent, answered\}$. This shows that a ground set is not necessarily visible in each interleaved run. This difficulty is due to the arbitrary ordering in (1) and (2) of the independent occurrences of *act* and *return*.

Ground sets can be identified in *concurrent runs*, which represent independent events explicitly. Fig. 2 shows a concurrent run of system Σ_1 (with abbreviated identifiers of Σ_1). The dashed lines denote occurrences of the ground set $\{quiet_l, quiet_r\}$.

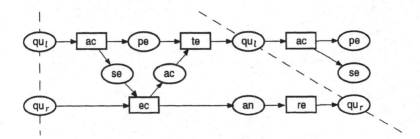

Fig. 2. Concurrent run of Σ_1

A concurrent run is based on *an occurrence net*. Such a net K has three special properties: For each $p \in P_K$, $|p^\bullet| \leq 1$ and $|{}^\bullet p| \leq 1$, the relation $\prec_K$ is a strict partial order (i.e. $a \prec_K b$ implies $a \neq b$) and for each $x \in K$, $\{y \mid y \prec_K x\}$ is finite. An occurrence net K has a *canonical initial state* $a_K = \{p \in P_K \mid {}^\bullet p = \emptyset\}$. Thus K itself can be conceived as an es-net; this will turn out quite useful for technical purposes. Finally, let $max(K) := \{x \in K \mid x^\bullet = \emptyset\}$.

A *concurrent run of an es-net* Σ is an occurrence net K with a labelling function $l : K \to \Sigma$ fulfilling four requirements: Each transition $t \in T_K$ is intended to represent an occurrence of some action $l(t) \in T_\Sigma$, hence $l({}^\bullet t) = {}^\bullet l(t)$ and $l(t^\bullet) = l(t)^\bullet$. The initial state of K is intended to represent the initial state of Σ, hence $l(a_K) = a_\Sigma$. No element of Σ should occur *concurrently to itself*, hence $l(a) = l(b)$ implies $a \preceq_K b$ or $b \preceq_K a$. Finally, no progressing action should remain enabled forever, hence $l(max(K))$ enables quiescent actions only.

The es-net of Fig. 1 admits only one maximal infinite concurrent run, of which Fig. 2 outlines a prefix.

4 Case Study: Ordered Crosstalk and Round Based Mutex

Assume two cooperating sites, l and r. A site *completes a round* each time visiting *quiet*, and is about to begin its next round. Each message sent by a site in its i-th round is to be received by its partner site in its i-th round, too. *Crosstalk* arises when the two sites send each other a message in the same round.

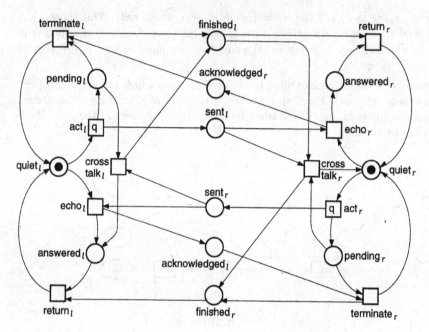

Fig. 3. es-net Σ_2: the ordered crosstalk algorithm

Σ_2 (in Fig. 3) represents this behaviour. It extends Σ_1 (Fig. 1) in two ways: Firstly, site r, like site l may *act* as a sender. Then r remains *pending* until an *acknowledgment* arrives, in which case r *terminates*, sending a *finished* signal and returns to *quiet*. Symmetrically, site l like site r may *echo* a message of r, remaining *answered* until receipt of a *finished* signal, in which case l *returns quiet*. (The above required round policy of messages fails if the *finished* signals are omitted).

The second extension covers the above mentioned case of *crosstalk*. In this case, first l sends a *finished* signal to r, then r sends a *finished* signal to l. (One may suggest the *finished* signals to carry a copy of the originally sent messages, as their concurrent transfer along one line might have corrupted them.)

The es-net Σ_2 exhibits three different types of rounds, and each concurrent run of Σ_2 is just any sequence of those rounds. The left part of Fig. 4 shows the round with sender l and receiver r. The symmetrical case of sender r and receiver l then is obvious. The right part of Fig. 4 shows the crosstalk round.

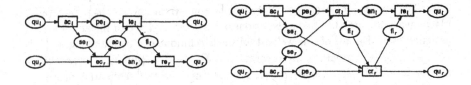

Fig. 4. two rounds of Σ_2

System Σ_2 now serves as a basis for *round based mutual exclusion*, as in Σ_3 of Fig. 5. Site l may spontaneously *apply* for getting critical, by moving from *local*$_l$ to *pend*$_l$. Then l *acts*, i.e. sends a *request* and remains *sent*$_l$ until site r either *grants* l to *enter critical*$_l$ or site r also *requests* to go critical. In this case l goes *critical* along *crosstalk*$_l$. A second component of site l in state *quiet*$_l$ may *echo* a *request* from site r, *granting* r to go *critical*. Notice that site l consists of two synchronized processes, one with states *local*$_l$, *pend*$_l$, *sent*$_l$ and *crit*$_l$, and the other one with states *quiet*$_l$, *sent*$_l$ and *served*$_l$. Site r behaves likewise.

It is not entirely obvious that both sites are never critical at the same time, and that each *pending* site in fact goes eventually *critical*. Formal means will be suggested in the sequel, supporting human formal proofs for this kind of properties.

5   State Properties

Notions and techniques are developed in this section to represent and to prove *state properties* of es-nets, i.e. properties that depend on single states. A typical example is mutual exclusion. The usual propositional formulas over some set P of atoms are employed, constructed over the local states from conjunction $\wedge$, negation $\neg$ etc. A propositional formula constructed over the local states P_Σ of an es-net Σ is a *state formula* of Σ. Given a local state $p \in P_\Sigma$ and a global state $a \subseteq P_\Sigma$ we say p *holds in* a, written $a \models p$, iff $p \in a$. This extends as usual to propositional formulas. Finally, let $\Sigma \models \Box p$ iff for each reachable state a of Σ holds $a \models p$. Mutual exclusion in Σ_3 hence reads $\Sigma_3 \models \Box \neg (crit_l \wedge crit_r)$.

By abuse of notation, for $P = \{p_1 \ldots, p_n\} \subseteq P_\Sigma$ we write $p_1 \ldots p_n$ or just P instead of $p_1 \wedge \ldots \wedge p_n$. We likewise write $\bigvee P$ instead of $p_1 \vee \ldots \vee p_n$. As a technicality, given a concurrent run K of an es-net Σ and a state formula p of Σ, any reachable state a of K is called a *p-state* iff $l(a) \models p$. It is easily shown that $\Sigma \models \Box p$ iff for each concurrent run K of Σ, each state S that is reachable from a_K is a *p*-state.

Proof of state formulas of es-nets is supported by two particularly simple and useful techniques, called *place invariants* and *traps*.

A *place invariant* i assigns to each place $p \in P_\Sigma$ a *weight* $i(p) \in \mathbb{Z}$ such that for each reachable state a of Σ, $\Sigma_{p \in a} i(p) = \Sigma_{p \in a_\Sigma} i(p)$. i is *characteristic* iff $i(p) \in \{0, 1\}$ for all $p \in P_\Sigma$ and $\Sigma_{p \in a_\Sigma} i(p) = 1$. In this case, i will be represented by $\{p \in P_\Sigma \mid i(p) = 1\}$ in the sequel. This implies e.g. $\Sigma \models \Box (p_1 \vee \ldots \vee p_n)$ and

$\Sigma \models \Box(p_1 \rightarrow \neg p_2)$ for each characteristic place invariant $\{p_1, \ldots, p_n\}$. Generally, place invariants are obtained as solutions of a system $\underline{\Sigma} \cdot i = 0$ of linear equations assigned to Σ. Details of this well established technique can be found e.g. in [11].

Typical characteristic place invaraints of Σ_3 are $i_1 = \{quiet_l, sent_l, served_l\}$ and $i_2 = \{local_l, pend_l, sent_l, crit_l\}$, representing the two sequential processes of site l. Less trivial is e.g. $i_3 = \{quiet_l, requested_l, granted_r, granted_l, crit_r, terminated_r\}$.

A *trap* is a subset $P \subseteq P_\Sigma$ of local states such that $P^\bullet \subseteq {}^\bullet P$. Consequently $a_\Sigma \cap P \neq \emptyset$ implies $a \cap P \neq \emptyset$ for each reachable state a. Hence $a_\Sigma \cap P \neq \emptyset$ implies $\Sigma \models \Box \bigvee P$.

A typical trap of Σ_3 is $\{quiet_l, requested_l, granted_r, granted_l, quiet_r, sent_r\}$. Together with some more characteristic place invariants, this trap proves mutual exclusion of $crit_l$ and $crit_r$ in Σ_3, by propositional implication. But generally not all valid state properties can be proven by help of place invariants and traps.

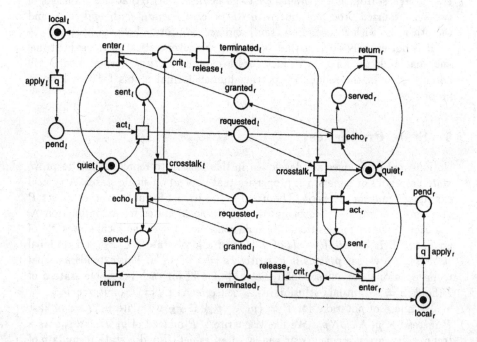

Fig. 5. es-net Σ_3: Round based mutual exclusion

6 Concurrency Based Progress

We are now prepared to deal with *rounds*, *ground sets* and *progress properties* of concurrent systems. To this end we define *causes formulas* $p \triangleright q$ ("p causes q")

built from state formulas p and q. A formula $p \triangleright q$ *holds in a concurrent run* K *of* Σ (written $K \models p \triangleright q$) iff for each reachable p-state S of K there exists a q-state of K that is reachable from S. $p \triangleright q$ *holds in* Σ (written $\Sigma \models p \triangleright q$) iff $p \triangleright q$ holds in each concurrent run of Σ.

Lemma 1. *Let* p, q, r *be state formulas of* Σ. *(i) If* $\Sigma \models \Box(p \to q)$ *then* $\Sigma \models p \triangleright q$. *(ii)* $\Sigma \models p \triangleright p$. *(iii) if* $\Sigma \models p \triangleright q$ *and* $\Sigma \models q \triangleright r$ *then* $\Sigma \models p \triangleright r$. *(iv) If* $\Sigma \models p \triangleright r$ *and* $\Sigma \models q \triangleright r$ *then* $\Sigma \models (p \vee q) \triangleright r$.

7   Pick-up Rules

The previous section introduced means to *represent progress* properties. Now we derive techniques to *prove* this kind of properties.

Assume a set $Q \subseteq P_\Sigma$ of local states. Q gives rise to a formula of the form $Q \triangleright P$ provided Q is *progress prone*, i.e. Q enables at least one progressing action. Then obviously $\Sigma \models Q \triangleright \bigvee_{t \in Q^\bullet} t^\bullet$. In fact, $\Sigma \models Q \triangleright \bigvee_{t \in Q^\bullet} eff(Q, t)$.

As an example, in the net $\Sigma =$

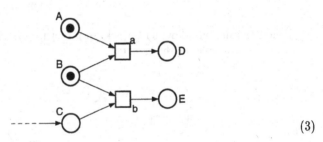

(3)

the set $\{A, B\}$ is progress prone (due to action a) and $\Sigma \models AB \triangleright (D \vee AE)$.

Now assume some $t \in Q^\bullet$ and some $r \in {}^\bullet t \setminus Q$ such that $\Sigma \models \Box Q \to \neg r$. Then t will certainly not occur in any Q-state. Generally Q is said to *prevent* t in T_Σ iff $\Sigma \models \Box Q \to \neg^\bullet t$ and a set U of actions is a *change set* of Q iff Q prevents each $t \in Q^\bullet \setminus U$. Then obviously $\Sigma \models Q \triangleright \bigvee_{t \in U} eff(Q, t)$. The general case is as follows:

Theorem 2. *Let* $Q \subseteq P_\Sigma$ *be progress prone and let* U *be a change set of* Q. *Then* $\Sigma \models Q \triangleright \bigvee_{u \in U} eff(Q, u)$.

Proof outline. Let K be a concurrent run of Σ and let S be a reachable Q-state of K. Let $S_0 = \{s \in S \mid l(s) \in Q\}$. Then $S_0^\bullet \neq \emptyset$, as Q is progress prone. Let t_0 be a smallest (w.r.t. $\prec_K$) transition in $S_0^\bullet$.

There exists a state S_1 of K, reachable from S, with $S_0 \subseteq S_1$ and ${}^\bullet t_0 \subseteq S_1$. With step $S_1 \xrightarrow{t_0} S_2$ of K, the state S_2 is an $eff(Q, l(t_0))$-state, reachable from S. As $l(t_0) \in U$, we are done. $\Box$

In the es-net Σ:

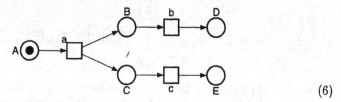

$$(4)$$

$Q = \{B, C\}$ is progress prone. Furthermore, $\Sigma \models \Box B \rightarrow \neg D$. Hence $\{c\}$ is a change set of $\{B, C\}$ and the above Theorem implies $\Sigma \models BC \rhd E$.

As a further example, in Σ_3 the set $q := \{sent_l, requested_l, quiet_r\}$ is progress prone (with $echo_r$). $U = \{echo_r, act_r\}$ is a change set of Q: In fact q prevents $crosstalk_r$, $crosstalk_l$ and $enter_l$. This can be shown by help of characteristic place invariants of Σ_3. Hence we can pick up with the help of Theorem 2:

$$\Sigma_3 \models sent_l requested_l quiet_r \rhd (sent_l requested_l requested_r sent_r)$$
$$\vee (sent_l granted_l served_l) \qquad (5)$$

A further rule will allow us to pick up $p \rhd q$ in the *context* of further local states. As an example, in the es-net $\Sigma =$

$$(6)$$

the valid formula $B \rhd D$ may be picked up in context C, yielding $\Sigma \models CB \rhd CD$. The general case reads as follows:

Theorem 3. *Let* $Q \subseteq P_\Sigma$ *be progress prone and let* U *be a change set of* Q. *Then for each* $R \supseteq {}^\bullet U$ *holds:* $\Sigma \models R \rhd \bigvee_{u \in U} eff(R, u)$.

Proof outline. Let K be a concurrent run of Σ and let S be an R-state of K. Let $S_0 = \{s \in S \mid l(s) \in Q\}$. Then $S_0^\bullet \neq \emptyset$, as Q is progress prone. Let $t_0 \in S_0^\bullet$. Then $l(t_0) \in U$. Hence ${}^\bullet t_0 \subseteq S$. With step $S \xrightarrow{t_0} S_1$ the state S_1 is an $eff(R, l(t_0))$-state. $\qquad\qquad\square$

Quite frequently progressing actions t occur where for $Q := {}^\bullet t$ holds $Q^\bullet = \{t\}$. An example is action b in (5). Q is progress prone in this case and $\{t\}$ is a change set of Q. Hence $P \cup Q \rhd P \cup t^\bullet$, provided $P \subseteq P_\Sigma$ and $P \cap Q = \emptyset$. Hence $\Sigma \models CB \rhd CD$ in (5), with $P = \{C\}$.

Likewise interesting is the special case of $R = {}^\bullet U$ in Theorem 3, yielding

$$\Sigma \models {}^\bullet U \vartriangleright \bigvee_{u \in U} eff({}^\bullet U, u). \tag{7}$$

A typical example shows the es-net $\Sigma =$

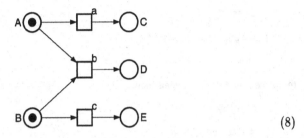

$$\tag{8}$$

The set $Q = \{A\}$ is progress prone (due to a) and $U = \{A\}^\bullet = \{a, b\}$ is a change set of $\{A\}$. With $R = {}^\bullet U = {}^\bullet\{a, b\} = \{A, B\}$ the above Theorem yields

$$\Sigma \models AB \vartriangleright BC \vee D. \tag{9}$$

Notice that (5) can not be derived using Theorem 3.

8   Proof Graphs

Causes-properties can be frequently proved by combining properties that have been picked up according to Theorem 2 or Theorem 3. This can nicely be organized as *proof graphs* (a version of *proof lattices* as introduced in [7]).

A *proof graph for* $\Sigma \models p \vartriangleright q$ is a directed, acyclic, finite graph. All nodes are state formulas of Σ. p is the only node without a predecessor and q the only node without a successor. For each node r and its successor nodes $r_1, \ldots, r_n$, the formula $r \vartriangleright (r_1 \vee \ldots \vee r_n)$ must hold in Σ.

Fig. 6 shows a proof graph. The successors of each node are constructed by help of the above theorems and some characteristic place invariants of Σ_3. As an example, the successors of the inital node are justified by (5).

9   Rounds and Round Based Properties

The notion of *ground set p* has been introduced informally in Section 3 already. Each reachable state causes a p-state. In terms of *causes*-formulas, $p \subseteq P_\Sigma$ is a *ground set of Σ* iff $\Sigma \models true \vartriangleright p$. There is an operational characterization of ground sets which in general does not have to appeal to all reachable states.

Theorem 4. *A set $p \subseteq P_\Sigma$ is a ground set of Σ iff $\Sigma \models a_\Sigma \vartriangleright p$ and for each element u of some change set U of p holds: $\Sigma \models eff(p, u) \vartriangleright p$.*

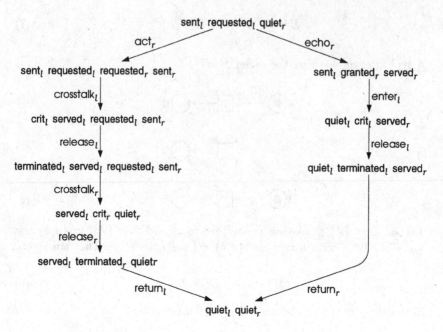

Fig. 6. proof graph for $\Sigma_3 \models sent_l requested_l quiet_r \,\rhd\, quiet_l quiet_r$

As an example we may show that a_{Σ_1} is a ground set of Σ_1: $a_{\Sigma_1} \rhd a_{\Sigma_1}$ holds trivially. The only step starting at a_{Σ_1} is $a_{\Sigma_1} \xrightarrow{act} a_1$(with $a_1, \ldots, a_4$ as in (1)). Proof of $a_1 \rhd a_{\Sigma_1}$ is obtained from the proof graph $a_1 \longrightarrow a_2 \longrightarrow a_3 \longrightarrow a_{\Sigma_1}$. This proves already $\Sigma_1 \models a \rhd a_{\Sigma_1}$ for *each* reachable state a. Notice that the proof graph does without the reachable state a_4 discussed in (2).

As a less trivial example we show that $p = \{quiet_l, quiet_r\}$ is a ground set of Σ_3: The requirement $\Sigma_3 \models a_{\Sigma_3} \rhd p$ is trivial, as $p \subseteq a_{\Sigma_3}$. The set $U = \{act_l, act_r\}$ is a change set of p, because p excludes $echo_l$ due to a characteristic invariant containing both $quiet_r$ and $requested_r$. Action $echo_r$ is likewise excluded. So two properties remain to be shown: i. $\Sigma_3 \models sent_l requested_l quiet_r \rhd p$ and ii. $\Sigma_3 \models sent_r requested_r quiet_l \rhd p$. Property i. has been shown in the proof graph of Fig. 6 already. Property ii. is shown accordingly. Ground states provide a further pick-up rule:

Theorem 5. *Let p be a ground set of Σ and let $q \subseteq P_\Sigma$ with $\Sigma \models \Box q \to \neg p$. Then for each change set U of p holds:* $\Sigma \models q \rhd \bigvee_{u \in U} eff(q, u)$.

Notice that q is not necessarily progress prone. Based on the examples following Theorem 4 and a place invariant of Σ_1 which implies $\Sigma_1 \models \Box pending \to \neg quiet_l$ the above Theorem immediately yields $\Sigma_1 \models pending \rhd quiet_l$. Likewise follows $\Sigma_3 \models sent_l \rhd crit_l$, together with Lemma 1.

10 Fairness

Many distributed algorithms require the assumption of *fairness* for some actions. Experience shows that this is required only for *conflict reduced* actions. $t \in T_\Sigma$ is *conflict reduced* iff for at most one $p \in {}^\bullet t$ holds: $p^\bullet \neq \{t\}$. Then p is called the *conflict place of t*. A concurrent run K *neglects* fairness for some conflict reduced action t iff infinitely many t-enabling global states of K are not followed by any occurrence of t. Fig. 7 shows an example.

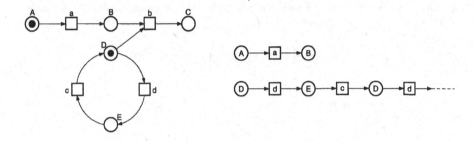

Fig. 7. es-net Σ and a run neglecting fairness

We slightly extend the concept of es-nets by declaring some (progress prone) actions t be *fair*. This means to rule out all runs that neglect fairness for t. More properties of Σ are valid then, some of which can be proven by a very simple pick-up rule.

Theorem 6. *Let $t \in T_\Sigma$ be assumed fair and conflict reduced, with conflict place p. For $Q := {}^\bullet t \setminus \{p\}$ assume furthermore $\Sigma \models Q \triangleright p$. Then $\Sigma \models Q \triangleright t^\bullet$.*

As an example, in Fig. 7 assume fairness for b. This action is clearly conflict reduced, with conflict place D. $\Sigma \models B \triangleright D$ holds due to the place invariant $D + E = 1$ and picked-up $E \triangleright D$. Hence $\Sigma \models B \triangleright C$ by the above Theorem.

A more involved example is the remaining proof for Σ_3 of each *pending* site eventually getting *critical*. We assume fairness for act_l, which intuitively means that the left site does not always *grant* the right site to go *critical*, but eventually *sends* an own *request*. act_l is conflict reduced with conflict place $quiet_l$. $\Sigma_3 \models pend_l \triangleright quiet_l$ follows immediately, because $\{quiet_l, quiet_r\}$ is a ground set, as shown in the previous section. Theorem 6 then implies $\Sigma_3 \models pend_l \triangleright sent_l$ (with Lemma 1). As $\Sigma_3 \models sent_l \triangleright \neg quiet_l$ by the characteristic place invariant $\{quiet_l, sent_l, passed_l\}$, Theorem 4 yields $\Sigma_3 \models sent_l \triangleright crit_l$, with change set $U = \{a_l\}$. Lemma 1 gives the wanted

$$\Sigma_3 \models pend_l \triangleright crit_l. \tag{10}$$

The corresponding property $pend_r \triangleright crit_r$ is proved similarly.

11   Conclusion

The formalism suggested in this paper exploits the structure and nature of concurrent runs. It would be very messy if not impossible to base the notions of rounds and ground sets as well as Theorem 3 on interleaved runs. Experience shows that despite its simplicity the approach presented here suffices for modelling and proving many essential properties of distributed algorithms. It is however far from being complete. Neither place invariants and traps suffice to prove all valid state formulas, nor do the pick-up rules (Section 7) and the proof graphs of section 8 cover all valid causes-formulas. As an example, the formula $ABC \rhd AE \vee CD$ is valid in $\Sigma =$

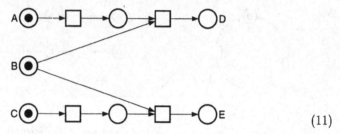

$$(11)$$

but can not be proven in this paper's framework: A further operator is required here, which is sensitive to the *resources* employed in concurrent subruns. Details can be found in [15] and [12].

The logic suggested in [8] represents each concurrent run K as the set of interleaved runs, gained by extending the partial order $\prec_K$ to well-founded total orders. With this transformation, the logic in [8] is more expressive than our combination of state- and causes-properties. It is furthermore complete (hence $ABC \rhd AE \vee CD$ can be derived for (11)).

We would like to however exhaust the possibilities offered by the simple framework presented here until specific applications demand more expressiveness.

The integration of data and the representation of *network* algorithms have not been covered here. The step from elementary system nets, as considered above to system nets that cover *these* aspects corresponds to the step from propositional logic to first order logic. For details we refer to the forthcoming [12].

Acknowledgments

This contribution reports results and experience of a number of people in various projects. This includes the Teilprojekt A3 of the Sonderforschungsbereich 342 based at Technical University of Munich, the ESPRIT II action CALIBAN and the project *Verteilte Algorithmen* funded by Deutsche Forschungsgemeinschaft.

The crosstalk algorithm as well as the crosstalk based mutex algorithm is due to Rolf Walter [15]. Theorem 5, exploiting the notion of rounds, is likewise due to [15]. The fairness rule of Theorem 6 was first published in [4]. All other results

in this contribution have resulted from intensive discussion with Rolf Walter, Ekkart Kindler, Jörg Desel and Dominik Gomm. Many thanks to all of them.

References

1. K.R. Apt, E-R. Olderog: *Verification of Sequential and Concurrent Programs.* Springer-Verlag, Heidelberg 1991.
2. K.M. Chandy, J. Misra: *Parallel Program Design: A Foundation.* Addison-Wesley, Reading, MA 1988.
3. U. Goltz, W. Reisig (Eds.) *Logics for Distributed Systems.* GMD-Studien Nr. 214 Gesellschaft für Mathematik und Datenverarbeitung, St.Augustin 1992.
4. E. Kindler, R. Walter: *Message Passing Mutex.* In: J. Desel (Ed.) Structures in Concurrency Theory, Springer-Verlag, Heidelberg 1995 (to appear).
5. Z. Manna, A. Pnueli: *A Temporal Proof Methodology for Reactive Systems.* In: M. Broy (Ed.) Program Design Calculi, Nato ASI Series, Vol. 118, pp. 287 – 324
6. M. Mukund, P.S. Thiagarajan: *A Logical Characterization of Well Branching Event Structures.* Theoretical Computer Science 96 (1992), 35 – 72
7. S. Owicki, L. Lamport: *Proving Liveness Properties of Concurrent Programs.* ACM Transaction on Programming Languages and Systems 4 (1982) 455 –495
8. D. Peled, A. Pnueli: *Proving partial order properties.* Theoretical Computer Science 126 (1994) 143 – 182
9. C.-A. Petri: *Nonsequential Processes.* Internal Report GMD-ISF-77-5, Gesellschaft für Mathematik und Datenverarbeitung, St. Augustin 1977.
10. M. Raynal: *Distributed Algorithms and Protcols.* J. Wiley & Sons, 1988.
11. W. Reisig: *Petri Nets.* Springer-Verlag, Heidelberg 1984.
12. W. Reisig: *Distributed Algorithms: Modelling and Analysis with Petri Nets.* (to appear)
13. M. Sinzoff: *Expressing program developments in a design calculus of discrete design.* NATO ASI Series 36 (1986) 343 – 356, Springer-Verlag.
14. G. Tel: *Distributed Algorithms.* Cambridge University Press, Cambridge (UK) 1991.
15. R. Walter: *Petrinetzmodelle verteilter Algorithmen: Beweistechnik und Intuition.* Doctoral Dissertation, Humboldt-Universität zu Berlin, 1995.
16. M. Weber, M. Simons, Ch. Lafontaine: *The Generic Development Language Deva.* Lecture Notes in Computer Science, Vol. 738, Springer-Verlag, Heidelberg 1993.

Symmetry and Induction in Model Checking *

E. M. Clarke and S. Jha

Dept of Computer Science
Carnegie Mellon University, Pittsburgh, PA 15213

Abstract. Model checking is a technique for determining whether a finite state-transition system satisfies a specification expressed in temporal logic. It has been used successfully to verify a number of highly complex circuit and protocol designs. A major hurdle in using this approach to verify realistic designs is the state explosion problem. This problem tends to occur when the number of state variables is very large. In this paper we discuss two techniques for handling this problem. The first technique is based on exploiting symmetry in the state-transition graph. We show how to construct a reduced quotient graph that satisfies the same temporal properties as the original graph. The second technique applies to systems that can have an arbitrary number of processes. In this case induction at the process level can be used to avoid the state explosion problem. An invariant process can frequently be found whose correctness implies the correctness of the system. We describe several methods for finding such an invariant process when one exists.

1 Introduction

Temporal Logic Model Checking is a technique for determining whether a temporal logic formula is valid in a finite state system $M = (S, R, L)$, where S is the state space, R is the state transition relation, and L is a function that labels states with sets of atomic propositions. Such a structure is usually called a *Kripke structure* and may have an enormous number of states because of the *state explosion* problem. A system with n boolean state variables can have a state space which is exponential in n. An efficient Model Checking procedure tries to reduce the number of states that are actually explored. In most cases the state space is expressed symbolically in terms of state variables, and the transition relation is represented by a *binary decision diagram* (*BDD*) [4, 6].

---

* This research was sponsored in part by the Avionics Laboratory, Wright Research and Development Center, Aeronautical Systems Division (AFSC), U.S. Air Force, Wright-Patterson AFB, Ohio 45433-6543 under Contract F33615-90-C-1465, ARPA Order No. 7597 and in part by the National Science Foundation under Grant no. CCR-8722633 and in part by the Semiconductor Research Corporation under Contract 92-DJ-294 .

The views and conclusions contained in this document are those of the authors and should not be interpreted as representing the official policies, either expressed or implied, of the U.S. government.

In this paper, we describe techniques for exploiting symmetry to alleviate the state explosion problem. Finite state concurrent systems frequently exhibit considerable symmetry. It is possible to find symmetry in memories, caches, register files, bus protocols, network protocols – anything that has a lot of replicated structure. For example, a ring of processes exhibits rotational symmetry. This fact can be used to obtain a reduced model for the system.

Given a Kripke Structure $M = (S, R, L)$, a symmetry group G is a group acting on the state set S that *preserves* the transition relation R. A symmetry group G acting on the state set S partitions the state set S into equivalence classes called *orbits*. A quotient model M_G is constructed that contains one representative from each orbit. The state space S_G of the quotient model will, in general, be much smaller than the the original state space S. This makes it possible to verify much larger structures.

We also investigate the complexity of exploiting symmetry in model checking algorithms. The first problem that we consider is computing the *orbit relation*, i.e. determining whether two states are in the same orbit or not. This is an important problem because the direct method of computing the quotient model M_G uses this relation. We prove that this problem is at least as hard as the *graph isomorphism problem*. It is also possible to obtain lower bounds on the size of the BDDs needed to encode the orbit relation.

Most of the research done in the area of model checking focuses on verifying single finite-state systems. Typically, circuit and protocol designs are parametrized, i.e. define an infinite family of systems. For example, a circuit design to multiply two integers has the width of the integers n as a parameter. We investigate methods to verify such parametrized designs. The problem of verifying parametrized designs can also be thought of as solving the *state explosion* problem because in this case the state set is unbounded.

The verification problem for a family of similar state-transition systems is to check the correctness of an entire family. In general the problem is undecidable [1]. However, for *specific* families the problem can be solved. Most techniques are based on finding *network invariants* [16, 23]. Given an infinite family $F = \{P_i\}_{i=1}^{\infty}$ and a reflexive, transitive relation $\preceq$, an invariant I is a process such that $P_i \preceq I$ for all i. The relation $\preceq$ should preserve the property f we are interested in, i.e. if I satisfies f, then P_i should also satisfy f. Once the invariant I is found, traditional model checking techniques can be used to check that I satisfies f. We survey various techniques for finding an invariant process.

Our paper is organized as follows: Section 2 contains preliminary definitions. In Section 3 we describe various techniques for exploiting symmetry in model checking. Section 4 gives several techniques for finding invariants for an infinite family of state-transition systems. The paper concludes with some directions for future research in these two areas.

2   Temporal Logic and Model Checking

2.1   Kripke Structures

Let AP be a set of atomic propositions. A Kripke structure over AP is a triple $M = (S, R, L)$, where

- S is a finite set of *states*,
- $R \subseteq S \times S$ is a *transition relation*, which must be total (i.e. for every state s_1 there exists a state s_2 such that $(s_1, s_2) \in R$).
- $L : S \to 2^{AP}$ is a *labeling function* which associates with each state a set of atomic propositions that are true in the state.

Example 1. We consider a simple token ring example which is used throughout the paper. A component process is shown in Figure 1. Each component has three states: n (non-critical section), t (has the token), and c (critical section). There are two visible actions in the process: s (send token), and r (receive token). The process Q is initially in the state t, and the process P is initially in the state n. The semantics of the composition is like CCS [19]. For example, in the composition $Q\|P$, the s action of the left process (Q) is synchronized with the r action of the right process (P). The Kripke structure corresponding to $Q\|P$ is shown in the Figure 2.

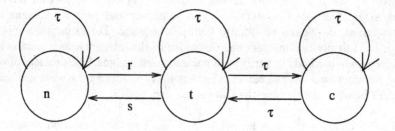

Fig. 1. A process component

2.2   Branching Time Temporal Logic

There are two types of formulas in $CTL^\star$: *state formulas* (which are true in a specific state) and *path formulas* (which are true along a specific path). The state operators in $CTL^\star$ are: **A** ("for all computation paths"), **E**("for some computation paths"). The path operators in $CTL^\star$ are: **G**("always"), **F**("sometimes"), **U**("until"), and **V** ("unless"). Let AP be a set of atomic propositions. A state formula is either:

- p, if $p \in AP$;

2 Temporal Logic and Model Checking

2.1 Kripke Structures

Let AP be a set of atomic propositions. A Kripke structure over AP is a triple $M = (S, R, L)$, where

- S is a finite set of *states*,
- $R \subseteq S \times S$ is a *transition relation*, which must be total (i.e. for every state s_1 there exists a state s_2 such that $(s_1, s_2) \in R$).
- $L : S \to 2^{AP}$ is a *labeling function* which associates with each state a set of atomic propositions that are true in the state.

Example 1. We consider a simple token ring example which is used throughout the paper. A component process is shown in Figure 1. Each component has three states: n (non-critical section), t (has the token), and c (critical section). There are two visible actions in the process: s (send token), and r (receive token). The process Q is initially in the state t, and the process P is initially in the state n. The semantics of the composition is like CCS [19]. For example, in the composition $Q\|P$, the s action of the left process (Q) is synchronized with the r action of the right process (P). The Kripke structure corresponding to $Q\|P$ is shown in the Figure 2.

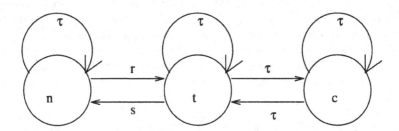

Fig. 1. A process component

2.2 Branching Time Temporal Logic

There are two types of formulas in $CTL^\star$: *state formulas* (which are true in a specific state) and *path formulas* (which are true along a specific path). The state operators in $CTL^\star$ are: $\mathbf{A}$ ("for all computation paths"), $\mathbf{E}$("for some computation paths"). The path operators in $CTL^\star$ are: $\mathbf{G}$("always"), $\mathbf{F}$("sometimes"), $\mathbf{U}$("until"), and $\mathbf{V}$ ("unless"). Let AP be a set of atomic propositions. A state formula is either:

- p, if $p \in AP$;

In this paper, we describe techniques for exploiting symmetry to alleviate the state explosion problem. Finite state concurrent systems frequently exhibit considerable symmetry. It is possible to find symmetry in memories, caches, register files, bus protocols, network protocols – anything that has a lot of replicated structure. For example, a ring of processes exhibits rotational symmetry. This fact can be used to obtain a reduced model for the system.

Given a Kripke Structure $M = (S, R, L)$, a symmetry group G is a group acting on the state set S that *preserves* the transition relation R. A symmetry group G acting on the state set S partitions the state set S into equivalence classes called *orbits*. A quotient model M_G is constructed that contains one representative from each orbit. The state space S_G of the quotient model will, in general, be much smaller than the the original state space S. This makes it possible to verify much larger structures.

We also investigate the complexity of exploiting symmetry in model checking algorithms. The first problem that we consider is computing the *orbit relation*, i.e. determining whether two states are in the same orbit or not. This is an important problem because the direct method of computing the quotient model M_G uses this relation. We prove that this problem is at least as hard as the *graph isomorphism problem*. It is also possible to obtain lower bounds on the size of the BDDs needed to encode the orbit relation.

Most of the research done in the area of model checking focuses on verifying single finite-state systems. Typically, circuit and protocol designs are parametrized, i.e. define an infinite family of systems. For example, a circuit design to multiply two integers has the width of the integers n as a parameter. We investigate methods to verify such parametrized designs. The problem of verifying parametrized designs can also be thought of as solving the *state explosion* problem because in this case the state set is unbounded.

The verification problem for a family of similar state-transition systems is to check the correctness of an entire family. In general the problem is undecidable [1]. However, for *specific* families the problem can be solved. Most techniques are based on finding *network invariants* [16, 23]. Given an infinite family $F = \{P_i\}_{i=1}^{\infty}$ and a reflexive, transitive relation $\preceq$, an invariant I is a process such that $P_i \preceq I$ for all i. The relation $\preceq$ should preserve the property f we are interested in, i.e. if I satisfies f, then P_i should also satisfy f. Once the invariant I is found, traditional model checking techniques can be used to check that I satisfies f. We survey various techniques for finding an invariant process.

Our paper is organized as follows: Section 2 contains preliminary definitions. In Section 3 we describe various techniques for exploiting symmetry in model checking. Section 4 gives several techniques for finding invariants for an infinite family of state-transition systems. The paper concludes with some directions for future research in these two areas.

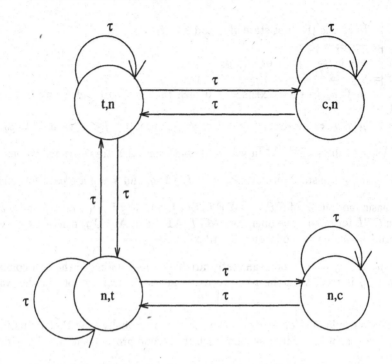

Fig. 2. The kripke structure for $Q\|P$

- if f and g are state formulas, then $\neg f$ and $f \vee g$ are state formulas;
- if f is a path formula, then $\mathbf{E}(f)$ is a state formula.

A path formula is either:

- a state formula;
- if f and g are path formulas, then $\neg f$, $f \vee g$, $\mathbf{X} f$, $f \mathbf{U} g$, and $f \mathbf{V} g$ are path formulas;

$CTL^\star$ is the set of state formulas generated by the above rules.

We define the semantics of $CTL^\star$ with respect to a Kripke structure $M = (S, R, L)$. A *path* in M is an infinite sequence of states $\pi = s_0, s_1, \ldots$ such that, for every $i \geq 0, (s_i, s_{i+1}) \in R$. π^i denotes the *suffix* of π starting at s_i. We use the standard notation to indicate that a state formula f holds in a structure. $M, s \models f$ means that f holds at the state s in the structure M. Similarly, $M, \pi \models f$ means that the path formula f is true along the path π. Assume that f_1 and f_2 are state formulas and g_1 and g_2 are path formulas, then the relation $\models$ is defined inductively as follows:

1. $s \models p \Leftrightarrow p \in L(s)$
2. $s \models \neg f_1 \Leftrightarrow s \not\models f_1$
3. $s \models f_1 \vee f_2 \Leftrightarrow s \models f_1 \text{ or } s \models f_2$
4. $s \models \mathbf{E}(g_1) \Leftrightarrow$ there exists a path π starting with s such that $\pi \models g_1$

5. $\pi \models f_1 \Leftrightarrow s$ is the first state of π and $s \models f_1$
6. $\pi \models \neg g_1 \Leftrightarrow \pi \not\models g_1$
7. $\pi \models g_1 \vee g_2 \Leftrightarrow \pi \models g_1$ or $\pi \models g_2$
8. $\pi \models \mathbf{X} g_1 \Leftrightarrow \pi^1 \models g_1$
9. $\pi \models g_1 \mathbf{U} g_2 \Leftrightarrow$ there exists $k \geq 0$ such that $\pi^k \models g_2$ and for all $0 \leq j < k, \pi^j \models g_1$.
10. $\pi \models g_1 \mathbf{V} g_2 \Leftrightarrow$ for every $k \geq 0$ if $\pi^j \not\models g_1$ for all $0 \leq j < k$, then $\pi^k \models g_2$.

CTL is the subset of CTL^* in which the path formulas are restricted to be:

- if f and g are state formulas, then $\mathbf{X} f$, $f \mathbf{U} g$, and $f \mathbf{V} g$ are path formulas.

The basic modalities of CTL are $\mathbf{EF} f$, $\mathbf{EG} f$, and $\mathbf{E}(f \mathbf{U} g)$, where f and g are again CTL formulas. The operators $\mathbf{AG} f$, $\mathbf{AF} f$ and $\mathbf{A}(f \mathbf{U} g)$ can be expressed in terms of the basic modalities described above.

Example 2. Let c_i be a boolean state variable corresponding to the i-th component. If c_i is true, then the i-th process is in the critical section (in the state c).

- The formula $\mathbf{AG}(c_1 \rightarrow \neg c_2)$ states that it is globally true that if the first process is in the critical section, then the second process is not in the critical section.
- The formula $\mathbf{AG\,AF}(c_1)$ states that along every path the first process is in the critical section infinitely often. Incidentally, this property is not true in the model shown in Figure 2 without assuming some fairness condition.

2.3   Model Checking

The Model Checking problem can be stated as follows:

> Given a a Kripke Structure $M = (S, R, L)$, a state $s \in S$, and a temporal specification f, is it true that $M, s \models f$?

Efficient procedures have been developed to determine if a CTL formula f is true in a Kripke Model M. In [9] an algorithm is given that is linear in the size of the formula f and the model M. A *symbolic model checking algorithm* using *binary decision diagrams (BDDs)* [4] that can handle models with more that 10^{120} states is discussed in [5, 6]. The new algorithm represents transition relations and sets of states by boolean functions given as $BDDs$. This algorithm is based on the standard fixpoint characterization of the temporal operators. For example, $\mathbf{EF} p$ can be expressed by the following least fixpoint equation:

$$\mathbf{EF}\, p = \mu Y \cdot (p \vee \mathbf{EX}\, Y)$$

The set of states satisfying $\mathbf{EF} p$ is computed in an iterative manner. First, the BDD B_0 for all the states satisfying the proposition p is obtained. The $BDDs$

for the successive approximations to the fixpoint are obtained by the following recurrence:

$$B_{i+1} = B_0 \vee \mathbf{EX}\, B_i$$

It can be proved by induction that when the iterative procedure given above terminates, the BDD for all the states satisfying the state formula $\mathbf{EF}\, p$ is obtained. Termination is guaranteed since the set of states is finite.

3   Symmetry

3.1   Definitions

Let G be a permutation group, i.e. bijective mappings acting on the state space S of the Kripke structure M. A permutation $\sigma \in G$ is said to be a *symmetry* of M if and only if it preserves the transition relation R. More formally, σ should satisfy the following condition:

$$(\forall s_1 \in S)(\forall s_2 \in S)\, ((s_1, s_2) \in R \Rightarrow (\sigma s_1, \sigma s_2) \in R)$$

G is a *symmetry group* for the Kripke structure M if and only if every permutation $\sigma \in G$ is a *symmetry* of M. Notice that our definition of a symmetry group does not refer to the labeling function L. Furthermore, since every $\sigma \in G$ has an inverse, which is also a symmetry, it can be easily proved that a permutation $\sigma \in G$ is a symmetry for a Kripke structure if and only if σ satisfies the following condition:

$$(\forall s_1 \in S)(\forall s_2 \in S)\, ((s_1, s_2) \in R \Leftrightarrow (\sigma s_1, \sigma s_2) \in R)$$

Let $\langle g_1, \ldots, g_k \rangle$ be the smallest permutation group containing all the permutations $g_1, \ldots, g_k$. If $G = \langle g_1, \ldots, g_k \rangle$, then we say that the group G is *generated* by the set $\{g_1, \ldots, g_k\}$. It is easy to see that if every generator of the group G is a symmetry of M, then the group G is a symmetry group for M.

Example 3. Consider the Kripke structure M given in Figure 2. Let σ be the transposition $(1, 2)$, which switches the state components corresponding to the first and the second process. There is a transition from state (t, n) to (c, n). There is also a transition from state $\sigma((t, n)) = (n, t)$ to $\sigma((c, n)) = (n, c)$. One can prove that every transition of M is preserved by σ. Therefore, σ is a symmetry for M.

3.2   Quotient Models

Let G be a group acting on the set S an let s be an element of S, then the *orbit* of s is the set $\theta(s) = \{t | (\exists \sigma \in G)(\sigma s = t)\}$. From each orbit $\theta(s)$ we pick a representative which we call $rep(\theta(s))$ with the restriction that $rep(\theta(s)) \in \theta(s)$. Intuitively, the quotient model is obtained by collapsing all the states in one orbit to a single representative state. The formal definition of the quotient model is given below.

Definition 1. Let $M = (S, R, L)$ be a Kripke Structure and let G be a symmetry group acting on S. We define the *quotient structure* $M_G = (S_G, R_G, L_G)$ in the following manner:

- The state set is $S_G = \{\theta(s) | s \in S\}$, the set of orbits of the states in S;
- The transition relation R_G is given by

$$R_G = \{(\theta(s_1), \theta(s_2)) | (s_1, s_2) \in R\}; \tag{1}$$

- The labeling function L_G is given by $L_G(\theta(s)) = L(rep(\theta(s)))$.

Next, we define what it means for a symmetry group G of a Kripke structure M to be an *invariance group* for an atomic proposition p. Intuitively, G is an invariance group for an atomic proposition p if and only if the set of states labeled by p is closed under the application of all the permutations of G. More formally, a symmetry group G of a Kripke structure $M = (S, R, L)$ is an invariance group for an atomic proposition p if and only if the following condition holds:

$$(\forall \sigma \in G)(\forall s \in S)(p \in L(s) \Leftrightarrow p \in L(\sigma s))$$

Example 4. Let c_i be the boolean variable corresponding to the i-th component. If c_i is true, then the i-th process is in the critical section. The proposition *me* (for mutual exclusion) is given below:

$$me = (c_1 \to \neg c_2) \land (c_2 \to \neg c_1)$$

Notice that *me* is *invariant* under the permutation $\sigma = (1, 2)$. Consider the Kripke structure M in Figure 2. The orbits of the state sets are:

$$\{(t, n), (n, t)\} \text{ and } \{(c, n), (n, c)\}$$

We pick the states (t, n) and (c, n) as representatives. The resulting quotient model is shown in Figure 3. Let P^i be the composition of the process P i times. It is not hard to show that the Kripke structure corresponding to $Q \| P^i$ has $2(i + 1)$ reachable states. However, the corresponding quotient model has just two states. Therefore, quotienting can result in considerable savings. In [8] symmetry has been exploited in order to verify a cache-coherence protocol based on the IEEE Futurebus+ standard [14]. For some configurations the BDD sizes were reduced by a factor of 15.

The theorem given below is proved in [8, 13]. The theorem states that if the temporal specification f has only invariant propositions, then f can be safely checked in the quotient model.

Theorem 2. let $M = (S, R, L)$ be a Kripke structure, G be a *symmetry group* of M, and h be a CTL^* formula. If G is an invariance group for all the atomic propositions p occurring in h, then

$$M, s \models h \Leftrightarrow M_G, \theta(s) \models h \tag{2}$$

where M_G is the quotient structure corresponding to M.

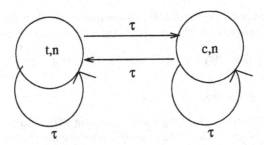

Fig. 3. The quotient model for $Q\|P$

3.3 Model Checking in the Presence of Symmetry

In this section we describe how to perform model checking in the presence of
symmetry. First, we discuss how to find the set of states in a Kripke structure
that are reachable from a given set of initial states using an explicit state representation. In the explicit state case, a breadth-first or depth-first search starting
from the set of initial states is performed. Typically, two lists, a list of reached
states and a list of unexplored states are maintained. At the beginning of the
algorithm, the initial states are put on both the lists. In the exploration step,
a state is removed from the list of unexplored states and all its successors are
processed. An algorithm for exploring the state space of a Kripke structure in
the presence of symmetry is discussed in [15]. The authors introduce a function
$\xi(q)$, which maps a state q to the unique state representing the orbit of that
state. While exploring the state space, only the unique representatives from the
orbits are put on the list of reached and unexplored states. This simple reach-
ability algorithm can be extended to a full CTL model checking algorithm by
using the technique described in [9]. In order to construct the function $\xi(q)$ it is
important to compute the orbit relation efficiently.

   When BDDs are used as the underlying representation, the construction
of the quotient model is more complex. Our method of computing the quotient
model uses the BDD for the orbit relation $\Theta(x,y) \equiv (x \in \theta(y))$. Given a Kripke
structure $M = (S, R, L)$ and a symmetry group G on M with r generators
$g_1, g_2, \cdots, g_r$, it is possible to prove that the orbit relation Θ is the least fixpoint
of the equation given below:

$$\Theta(x,y) \equiv (x = y) \vee (\exists z)(\Theta(x,z) \wedge (z = g_1 y \vee z = g_2 y \cdots \vee z = g_r y)) \qquad (3)$$

   If a suitable state encoding is available, this fixpoint equation can be computed using BDDs [6]. Once we have the orbit relation Θ, we need to compute
a function $\xi : S \to S$, which maps each state s to the unique representative in its
orbit. If we view states as vectors of values associated with the state variables,
it is possible to choose the lexicographically smallest state to be the unique
representative of the orbit. Since Θ is an equivalence relation, these unique representatives can be computed using BDDs by the method of Lin [17].

Assuming that we have the BDD representation of the mapping function ξ, the transition relation R_G of the quotient structure can be expressed as follows:

$$R_G(x, y) = (\exists x_1)(\exists y_1)(R(x_1, y_1) \wedge \xi(y_1) = y \wedge \xi(x_1) = x)$$

3.4 Complexity Issues

The most basic step in performing model checking with symmetry is to decide whether two states are in the same orbit. We now discuss the complexity of this problem. It is often the case that the symmetry group is also given in terms of the state variables. For example, in a two bit adder with inputs x_1, x_2 and x_3, x_4, the permutation $(13)(24)$ is a symmetry because we can exchange the inputs without affecting the result. If we have a permutation σ, which acts on the set $\{1, 2, \ldots, n\}$, then σ acts on vectors in B^n in the following manner:

$$\sigma(x_1, x_2, \cdots, x_n) = (x_{\sigma(1)}, x_{\sigma(2)}, \cdots, x_{\sigma(n)})$$

Given two vectors x and y in B^n and a permutation σ, it is easy to see that $x \neq y$ implies $\sigma x \neq \sigma y$. Therefore, a group G acting on the set $\{1, 2, \cdots, n\}$ induces a permutation group G_1 acting on the set B^n. In other words, *a symmetry on the structure of a system induces a symmetry on the state space of the system.*

Definition 3. Let G be a group acting on the set $\{1, 2, \cdots, n\}$. Assume that G is represented in terms of a finite set of generators. Given two vectors $x \in B^n$ and $y \in B^n$, the *orbit problem* asks whether there exists a permutation $\sigma \in G$ such that $y = \sigma x$.

Theorem 4. The *orbit problem* is as hard as the *Graph Isomorphism* [8] problem.

It can also be proved that the BDD for the orbit relation induced by a transitive group on the components *is exponential in the minimum of the number of component processes and the number of states in one component.* Consequently, exploiting these types of symmetries in symbolic model checking is restricted to examples with a small number of components or where each component has only a few states. An approach which avoids the computation of the orbit relation is described in [8]. Given a Kripke Structure $M = (S, R, L)$ and a set of representatives $Rep \subseteq S$, their approach builds a model M_{Rep} whose state set is Rep. The set Rep can have more than one state from each orbit. This approach does not need the BDD for the orbit relation.

4 Induction in Model Checking

Induction can be used with model checking to verify infinite families of finite state Kripke Structures. For example, consider the infinite family $\mathcal{F} = \{Q \| P^i\}_{i=1}^{\infty}$ of token rings (processes Q and P are defined in Example 1). In this case we are interested in verifying the mutual exclusion property for the entire family $\mathcal{F}$. Formally, the problem can be stated as follows:

Given an infinite family of Kripke Structures $\mathcal{F} = \{M_i\}_{i=1}^{\infty}$ and a temporal specification f verify that all the Kripke Structures in $\mathcal{F}$ satisfy f.

$$\forall i(M_i \models f)$$

In general the problem is undecidable [1]. However, several attempts have been made to verify special classes of infinite families.

4.1 Temporal Logic for Infinite Families

Traditionally, temporal logics specify properties of a single Kripke Structure. These logics have to be extended to specify properties of infinite families of Kripke Structures. Two such logics are discussed below.

In [3] an indexed version of $CTL^\star$ called the *indexed* $CTL^\star$ or $ICTL^\star$ is introduced. The propositions in $ICTL^\star$ are indexed by the natural numbers. Intuitively, if a proposition is indexed by i, it applies to the ith-component process. Let f be an arbitrary $CTL^\star$ formula. Let $f(i)$ be the formula f where all the propositions have been indexed by i. The indexed logic $ICTL^\star$ permits formulas of the form $\wedge_i f(i)$ (the formula f is true in all components) and $\vee_i f(i)$ (the formula f is true in some component). One can also have formulas like $\wedge_{j \neq i} f(j)$ (every component but the i-th component satisfies f) or $\vee_{j \neq i} f(j)$ (some component other than the i-component satisfies f). For example, consider again the infinite family of token rings $\mathcal{F} = \{Q \| P^i\}_{i=1}^{\infty}$. The $ICTL^\star$ formula given below expresses the *mutual exclusion* property for the family $\mathcal{F} = \{Q \| P^i\}_{i=1}^{\infty}$ of token rings.

$$\bigwedge_i \mathbf{AG}(c_i \Rightarrow \wedge_{i \neq j} \neg c_j)$$

In [7] another version of $CTL^\star$ is proposed which replaces atomic propositions by regular expressions. Again consider the family $\mathcal{F} = \{Q \| P^i\}_{i=1}^{\infty}$ and let $S = \{n, t, c\}$. The states in any Kripke Structure in $\mathcal{F}$ can be vectors of arbitrary size whose components are in S. In other words the states of Kripke Structures in $\mathcal{F}$ are strings over the alphabet S, and therefore belongs to $S^\star$. Notice that the regular expression $\{n, t\}^\star c\{n, t\}^\star$ represents the mutual exclusion property for $\mathcal{F}$. The advantage of regular expressions is that they apply to arbitrary sized vectors over S and can characterize states in any Kripke Structure belonging to the infinite family $\mathcal{F}$. The formula given below states the mutual exclusion property:

$$\mathbf{AG}(\{n, t\}^\star c\{n, t\}^\star)$$

4.2 Graph Grammars

An important question in the study of families of Kripke Structures is: How does one generate the infinite family? Most authors consider standard topologies like rings or stars. We present a formalism based on graph grammars which lets us generate many interesting topologies.

Our treatment is based on the material in [22]. A graph over Σ(the *node alphabet*) and Δ(the *link alphabet*) is triplet (N, ϕ, ψ), where N is a finite nonempty *set of nodes*, $\phi : N \rightarrow \Sigma$ is the *node labeling function*, and $\psi \subseteq N \times \Delta \times N$ is the *link labeling function*. Let $\mathcal{G} = \{D | D$ is a graph over Σ and $\Delta\}$; a *graph language* $\mathcal{D}$ over Σ and Δ is a subset of $\mathcal{G}$. A *context-free graph grammar*(CFGG) is a 5-tuple $G = (\Sigma_n, \Sigma_t, \Delta, S, \mathcal{R})$ where the *nonterminal node alphabet* (Σ_n), the *terminal node alphabet* (Σ_t), and the *link alphabet*(Δ) are finite nonempty mutually disjoint sets, $S \in \Sigma_n$ is the *start label*, $\mathcal{R}$ is a finite nonempty *production rules*. Each element in $\mathcal{R}$ is a quadruple $r = (A, D, I, O)$, where

1. $A \in \Sigma_n$;
2. $D = (N, \phi, \psi)$ is a connected graph over $\Sigma = \Sigma_n \cup \Sigma_t$ and Δ; Σ is the *total node alphabet*;
3. $I \in N$ is the *input node*;
4. $O \in N$ is the *output node*.

Given a graph whose nodes are labeled, a new graph is derived using one of the rules of the grammar. We start with a graph with a single node whose label is the start symbol S. During a derivation, a node with label A is replaced by the graph D in some derivation rule (A, D, I, O). Every arc originally entering(exiting) the node labeled by A becomes an arc entering the input node I(output node O).

Example 5. Consider the grammar $G = (\Sigma_n, \Sigma_t, \Delta, S, R)$ with $\Sigma_n = \{S, A\}$, $\Sigma_t = \{P, Q\}$, and $\Delta = \{a\}$. The rules are shown in Figure 4. The grammar generates all rings of the form $Q P^i$. The input nodes have an arrow, and the output nodes are labeled by double circles. Derivation of ring of size 3 is shown

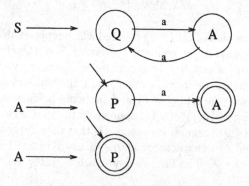

Fig. 4. Rules for the graph grammar

in Figure 5. Consider the second step. Since the node labeled with P is the input node the arc from Q enters P. Similarly, the node labeled A has an arc going out to Q because it is the output node.

Graph grammars can easily be converted into *Network grammars*, i.e. grammars generating infinite families of Kripke structures. For example, if in the

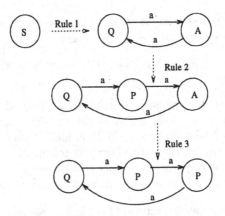

Fig. 5. Derivation of a ring of size 3

example given we interpret P, Q as the processes in Figure 1 and the links as composition operators, we can generate the infinite family $\mathcal{F} = \{Q\|P^i\}_{i=1}^{\infty}$ of token rings. Network grammars have been used by [7, 18, 20] to perform induction at the process level.

4.3   Invariants

Most techniques for verifying families of finite-state Kripke Structures rely on finding an *invariant*. Formally, an invariant can be defined as follows:

Definition 5. Given a family $\mathcal{F} = \{M_i\}_{i=1}^{\infty}$ and a reflexive, transitive relation $\geq$ on Kripke Structures, an *invariant* $\mathcal{I}$ is a Kripke Structure such that $\forall i (\mathcal{I} \geq M_i)$.

The relation $\geq$ determines what kind of temporal property can be checked. Perhaps the most widely used relations are *bisimulation* equivalence ($\cong$) and the *simulation* pre-order ($\succeq$).

Definition 6. Given Kripke Structures $M = (S, R, L, S_0)$ and $M' = (S', R', L', S_0')$ (S_0 and S_0' are the sets of initial states) we say that M *is bisimilar to* M' (denoted by $M \cong M'$) iff there is a *bisimulation equivalance* $\mathcal{B} \subset S \times S'$ that satisfies the following conditions: for every $s_0 \in S_0$ there is $s_0' \in S_0'$ such that $(s_0, s_0') \in \mathcal{B}$, and for every $s_0' \in S_0'$ there exists a $s_0 \in S_0$ such that $(s_0, s_0') \in \mathcal{B}$. Moreover, for every s, s', if $(s, s') \in \mathcal{B}$, then

1. We have that $L(s) = L'(s')$.
2. For every s_1 such that $(s, s_1) \in R$ there is s_1' such that $(s', s_1') \in R'$ and $(s_1, s_1') \in \mathcal{B}$.
3. For every s_1' such that $(s', s_1') \in R'$ there is s_1 such that $(s, s_1) \in R$ and $(s_1, s_1') \in \mathcal{B}$.

Notice that we are assuming that the states in M and M' are labeled by the same atomic propositions. This is not a limitation because, generally, one restricts the labeling function to propositions of interest. The theorem given below states the logic which is preserved by bisimulation equivalence.

Theorem 7. Let $M \cong M'$ and f be a CTL^* formula. Then $M \models f$ iff $M' \models f$ [2].

In [3] a family of token rings is considered. It is shown that a ring of size n ($n \geq 2$) is bisimilar to a ring of size 2. In this case the token ring of size 2 is the invariant $\mathcal{I}$. Let f be an arbitrary CTL^* formula. Using Theorem 7 we have that $\mathcal{I} \models f$ iff f is true in the entire family of token rings. Unfortunately, the bisimulation has to be constructed manually. Moreover, since the equivalence $\cong$ is more stringent than the pre-order $\succeq$, it is harder devise an invariant for $\cong$.

Definition 8. Given Kripke Structures $M = (S, R, L, S_0)$ and $M' = (S', R', L', S'_0)$ (S_0 and S'_0 are the sets of initial states) we say that M *is simulated by* M' (denoted by $M \preceq M'$) iff there is a *simulation pre-order* $\mathcal{E} \subset S \times S'$ that satisfies the following conditions: for every $s_0 \in S_0$ there is $s'_0 \in S'_0$ such that $(s_0, s'_0) \in \mathcal{E}$. Moreover, for every s, s', if $(s, s') \in \mathcal{E}$, then

1. We have that $L(s) = L'(s')$.
2. For every s_1 such that $(s, s_1) \in R$ there is s'_1 such that $(s', s'_1) \in R'$ and $(s_1, s'_1) \in \mathcal{E}$.

The following theorem indicates what kind of temporal formulas are preserved by the simulation pre-order.

Theorem 9. Let $M \preceq M'$ and f be a $\forall CTL^*$ formula. Then $M' \models f$ implies that $M \models f$ [10].

It can easily be shown that the simulation pre-order is *monotonic* with respect to the process composition.

Theorem 10. Let M_1, M_2, M'_1, and M'_2 be Kripke structures such that $M_1 \preceq M'_1$ and $M_2 \preceq M'_2$. Then $M_1 \| M_2 \preceq M'_1 \| M'_2$.

In [16] and [23] the invariant is generated by using the simulation pre-order. We will demonstrate this technique by considering the family of token rings $\mathcal{F} = \{Q \| P^i\}_{i=1}^{\infty}$. First an invariant $\mathcal{I}$ is found such that $\mathcal{I} \succeq \mathcal{I} \| P$ and $\mathcal{I} \succeq P$. The following lemma proves that $\mathcal{I} \succeq P^i$ for all $i \geq 1$.

Lemma 11. If $\mathcal{I} \succeq \mathcal{I} \| P$ and $\mathcal{I} \succeq P$, then $\mathcal{I} \succeq P^i$ (for all $i \geq 1$).

Proof: We prove the result by induction on i. Using the hypothesis, the result is true for $i = 1$. Let $i \geq 2$ and assume that the result is true for $i - 1$. The first equation given below is the induction hypothesis. The second equation follows from the first by composing with process P and using the monotonicity of $\succeq$ with respect to composition.

$$\mathcal{I} \succeq P^{i-1}$$
$$\mathcal{I} \| P \succeq P^i$$

Now using the fact that $\mathcal{I} \succeq \mathcal{I}\|P$, the transitivity of $\succeq$, and the equation given above we get that $\mathcal{I} \succeq P^i \square$.

Therefore, $Q\|\mathcal{I}$ is the invariant for the family $\mathcal{F}$ under the simulation pre-order. Let f be a $\forall CTL^*$ formula. If $(Q\|\mathcal{I}) \models f$, then by Theorem 9 f is true in every Kripke Structure in $\mathcal{F}$. If $Q\|\mathcal{I} \not\models f$, then one has to guess a new invariant. The counterexample generated while checking whether f is true in $Q\|\mathcal{I}$ can be an useful aid in guessing a new invariant.

In [7, 20] the structure of the network grammar is exploited to perform induction at the process level. We will explain these techniques by an example. Consider the following network grammar generating an infinite family of binary trees of depth ≥ 2.

$$
\begin{array}{l}
S \rightarrow \text{root}\|\text{SUB}\|\text{SUB} \\
\text{SUB} \rightarrow \text{internal}\|\text{SUB}\|\text{SUB} \\
\text{SUB} \rightarrow \text{internal}\|\text{leaf}\|\text{leaf}
\end{array}
$$

The symbols root, internal, leaf are the terminal processes. A parity circuit based on this grammar is given in [7]. A representative $rep(\text{SUB})$ is assigned to the non-terminal SUB. This representative must satisfy the following equations:

$$rep(\text{SUB}) \succeq \text{internal}\|rep(\text{SUB})\|rep(\text{SUB}) \tag{4}$$

$$rep(\text{SUB}) \succeq \text{internal}\|\text{leaf}\|\text{leaf} \tag{5}$$

Notice that the two equations correspond to the last two rules in the grammar. Now we prove that $rep(\text{SUB})$ is $\succeq$ than any process derived by the non-terminal SUB. Our proof uses induction on the number of steps in a derivation. We use the symbol $\text{SUB} \overset{k}{\Rightarrow} w$ to denote that w is derived from SUB using k steps. The result is true for $k = 1$ because of the second equation given above. Let w be derived from SUB using $k > 1$ derivations. The process w has the following from:

$$w = \text{internal}\|w_1\|w_2$$

The processes w_1 and w_2 are derived using less than k derivations, so by induction hypothesis we have the following equations:

$$rep(\text{SUB}) \succeq w_1$$
$$rep(\text{SUB}) \succeq w_2$$
$$\text{internal}\|rep(\text{SUB})\|rep(\text{SUB}) \succeq \text{internal}\|w_1\|w_2$$

The third equation follows from the first two using monotonicity of $\succeq$ with respect to the composition operator. Using equation 4 and the equation given above we get that $rep(\text{SUB}) \succeq w$. Therefore, the process $\mathcal{I}$ given below is an invariant (using the partial order $\succeq$) for the infinite family generated by the grammar.

$$\mathcal{I} = \text{root}\|rep(\text{SUB})\|rep(\text{SUB})$$

In [20] a specific process generated by the non-terminal SUB is used as a representative. An abstraction based on the specification is used in [7] to construct a representative. Using these techniques parity tree and token ring designs are verified in [7].

5   Conclusion

We have described techniques for exploiting the inherent symmetry present in the system to perform model checking efficiently. Perhaps, the most important theoretical problem in this area is the exact complexity of the *orbit problem*. Since the BDD for the orbit relation for many interesting symmetry groups is large, it is very important to have techniques which allows multiple representatives from one orbit. One such technique is described in [8], but a considerable amount of research needs to be done in this area. In order for these techniques to become practical, verification tools need to provide facility for the user to specify symmetry groups with relative ease. For example, the user should be able to specify the communication network of the processes and have the system automatically derive the appropriate symmetry group.

Several techniques for finding invariants for infinite families of finite-state Kripke structures are summarized in this paper. Unfortunately, most of these techniques are not completely automatic. Typically, if the method fails, the user has to look at the counterexample and generate a new invariant. Can this process be automated? In other words, can the system use the counterexample to generate a stronger invariant? Another important question is to find pre-orders which incorporate fairness. For example, the simulation pre-order can be defined so that only *fair* paths are considered. Given a fairness condition F we say that $M_1 \succeq_F M_2$ iff every fair path in M_1 has a corresponding fair path in M_2. Can we check $M_1 \succeq_F M_2$ efficiently? If this can be done efficiently, it may be possible to construct invariants which preserve the fairness constraint. Another interesting research area is to find links between symmetry and induction. In [12] arguments based on symmetry are used to reason inductively about rings. Finally, on the practical side, verification tools must be constructed that provide support for finding invariants automatically.

References

1. K. Apt and D. Kozen. Limits for automatic verification of finite-state systems. *IPL*, 15:307–309, 1986.
2. M. Browne, E. Clarke, and O. Grumberg. Characterizing finite kripke structures in propositional temporal logic. *Theoretical Comput. Sci.*, 59:115–131, 1988.
3. M. Browne, E. Clarke, and O. Grumberg. Reasoning about networks with many identical finite-state processes. *Inf. and Computation*, 81(1):13–31, Apr. 1989.
4. R. E. Bryant. Graph-based algorithms for boolean function manipulation. *IEEE Trans. Comput.*, C-35(8), 1986.

5. J. R. Burch, E. M. Clarke, D. E. Long, K. L. McMillan, and D. L. Dill. Symbolic model checking for sequential circuit verification. To appear in IEEE Trans. Comput.-Aided Design Integrated Circuits.

6. J. R. Burch, E. M. Clarke, K. L. McMillan, D. L. Dill, and J. Hwang. Symbolic model checking: 10^{20} states and beyond. In *Proc. 5th Ann. Symp. on Logic in Comput. Sci.* IEEE Comp. Soc. Press, June 1990.

7. E. Clarke, O. Grumberg, and S. Jha. Parametrized networks. In S. Smolka and I. Lee, editors, *Proc. CONCUR '95: 6th International Conference on Concurrency Theory*, Lecture Notes in Computer Science. Springer-Verlag, Aug. 1995.

8. E. Clarke, T.Filkorn, and S.Jha. Exploiting symmetry in temporal logic model checking. In Courcoubetis [11], pp. 450-462.

9. E. M. Clarke, E. A. Emerson, and A. P. Sistla. Automatic verification of finite-state concurrent systems using temporal logic specifications. *ACM Trans. Prog. Lang. Syst.*, 8(2):244-263, 1986.

10. E. M. Clarke, O. Grumberg, and D. E. Long. Model checking and abstraction. In *Proc. 19th Ann. ACM Symp. on Principles of Prog. Lang.*, Jan. 1992.

11. C. Courcoubetis (Ed.). *Computer Aided Verification*, Proc. 5th Int. Conf. (CAV'93), volume 697 of *Lecture Notes in Computer Science*. Springer-Verlag, June 1993.

12. E. Emerson and K. S. Namjoshi. Reasoning about rings. In *Proc. 22nd Ann. ACM Symp. on Principles of Prog. Lang.*, Jan. 1995.

13. E. A. Emerson and A. P. Sistla. Symmetry and model checking. In Courcoubetis [11], pp. 463-477.

14. IEEE Computer Society. *IEEE Standard for Futurebus+—Logical Protocol Specification*, Mar. 1992. IEEE Standard 896.1-1991.

15. C. Ip and D. Dill. Better verification through symmetry. In L. Claesen, editor, *Proc. 11th Int. Symp. on Comput. Hardware Description Lang. and their Applications*. North-Holland, Apr. 1993.

16. R. P. Kurshan and K. L. McMillan. A structural induction theorem for processes. In *Proc. 8th Ann. ACM Symp. on Principles of Distributed Computing*. ACM Press, Aug. 1989.

17. B. Lin and A. R. Newton. Efficient symbolic manipulation of equvialence relations and classes. In *Proc. 1991 Int. Workshop on Formal Methods in VLSI Design*, Jan. 1991.

18. R. Marelly and O. Grumberg. GORMEL—Grammar ORiented ModEL checker. Technical Report 697, The Technion, Oct. 1991.

19. R. Milner. *A Calculus of Communicating Systems*, volume 92 of *Lecture Notes in Computer Science*. Springer-Verlag, 1980.

20. Z. Shtadler and O. Grumberg. Network grammars, communication behaviors and automatic verification. In Sifakis [21], pp. 151-165.

21. J. Sifakis (Ed.). *Automatic Verification Methods for Finite State Systems*, Proc. Int Workshop, volume 407 of *Lecture Notes in Computer Science*. Springer-Verlag, June 1989.

22. P. D. Vigna and C. Ghezzi. Context-free graph grammars. *Inf. and Computation*, 37:207-233, Apr. 1978.

23. P. Wolper and V. Lovinfosse. Verifying properties of large sets of processes with network invariants. In Sifakis [21], pp. 68-80.

Alternating Automata and Program Verification

Moshe Y. Vardi*

Rice University
Department of Computer Science
P.O. Box 1892
Houston, TX 77251-1892, U.S.A.
Email: vardi@cs.rice.edu
URL: http://www.cs.rice.edu/~vardi

Abstract. We describe an automata-theoretic approach to the automatic verification of finite-state programs. The basic idea underlying this approach is that
for any temporal formula we can construct an alternating automaton that accepts
precisely the computations that satisfy the formula. For linear temporal logics the
automaton runs on infinite words while for branching temporal logics the automaton runs on infinite trees. The simple combinatorial structures that emerge from
the automata-theoretic approach decouple the logical and algorithmic components of finite-state-program verification and yield clear and general verification
algorithms.

1 Introduction

Temporal logics, which are modal logics geared towards the description of the temporal
ordering of events, have been adopted as a powerful tool for specifying and verifying
concurrent programs [Pnu77, MP92]. One of the most significant developments in this
area is the discovery of algorithmic methods for verifying temporal logic properties of
finite-state programs [CES86, LP85, QS81]. This derives its significance from the fact
that many synchronization and communication protocols can be modeled as finite-state
programs [Liu89, Rud87]. Finite-state programs can be modeled by transition systems
where each state has a bounded description, and hence can be characterized by a fixed
number of Boolean atomic propositions. This means that a finite-state program can be
viewed as a finite *propositional Kripke structure* and that its properties can be specified
using *propositional* temporal logic. Thus, to verify the correctness of the program with
respect to a desired behavior, one only has to check that the program, modeled as a finite
Kripke structure, is a model of (satisfies) the propositional temporal logic formula that
specifies that behavior. Hence the name *model checking* for the verification methods
derived from this viewpoint. Surveys can be found in [CG87, Wol89, CGL93].

   We distinguish between two types of temporal logics: linear and branching [Lam80].
In linear temporal logics, each moment in time has a unique possible future, while in
branching temporal logics, each moment in time may split into several possible futures.
For both types of temporal logics, a close and fruitful connection with the theory of
automata on infinite structures has been developed. The basic idea is to associate with

---

* Part of this work was done at the IBM Almaden Research Center.

each temporal logic formula a finite automaton on infinite structures that accepts exactly all the computations that satisfy the formula. For linear temporal logic the structures are infinite words [WVS83, Sis83, LPZ85, Pei85, SVW87, VW94], while for branching temporal logic the structures are infinite trees [ES84, SE84, Eme85, EJ88, VW86b]. This enables the reduction of temporal logic decision problems, such as satisfiability, to known automata-theoretic problems, such as nonemptiness, yielding clean and asymptotically optimal algorithms.

Initially, the translations in the literature from temporal logic formulas to automata used *nondeterministic* automata (cf. [VW86b, VW94]). These translations have two disadvantages. First, the translation itself is rather nontrivial; indeed, in [VW86b, VW94] the translations go through a series of ad-hoc intermediate representations in an attempt to simplify the translation. Second, for both linear and branching temporal logics there is an exponential blow-up involved in going from formulas to automata. This suggests that any algorithm that uses these translations as one of its steps is going to be an exponential-time algorithm. Thus, the automata-theoretic approach did not seem to be applicable to branching-time model checking, which in many cases can be done in linear running time [CES86, QS81, Cle93].

Recently it has been shown that if one uses *alternating* automata rather than *nondeterministic* automata, then these problems can be solved [Var94, BVW94]. Alternating automata generalize the standard notion of nondeterministic automata by allowing several successor states to go down along the same word or the same branch of the tree. In this paper we argue that *alternating automata* offer the key to a comprehensive and satisfactory automata-theoretic framework for temporal logics. We demonstrate this claim by showing how alternating automata can be used to derive model-checking algorithms for both linear and branching temporal logics. The key observation is that while the translation from temporal logic formulas to nondeterministic automata is exponential [VW86b, VW94], the translation to alternating automata is linear [MSS88, EJ91, Var94, BVW94]. Thus, the advantage of alternating automata is that they enable one to decouple the logic from the combinatorics. The translations from formulas to automata handle the logic, and the algorithms that handle the automata are essentially combinatorial.

2 Automata Theory

2.1 Words and Trees

We are given a finite nonempty alphabet Σ. A *finite word* is an element of Σ^*, i.e., a finite sequence $a_0, \ldots, a_n$ of symbols from Σ. An *infinite word* is an element of Σ^ω, i.e., an infinite sequence $a_0, a_1, \ldots$ of symbols from Σ.

A *tree* is a (finite or infinite) connected directed graph, with one node designated as the *root* and denoted by ε, and in which every non-root node has a unique parent (s is the *parent* of t and t is a *child* of s if there is an edge from s to t) and the root ε has no parent. The *arity* of a node x in a tree τ, denoted $arity(x)$, is the number of children of x in τ. The *level* of a node x, denoted $|x|$, is its distance from the root; in particular, $|\varepsilon| = 0$. Let N denote the set of positive integers. A *tree τ over N* is a subset of N^*, such that if $x \cdot i \in \tau$, where $x \in N^*$ and $i \in N$, then $x \in \tau$, there is an edge from x to

$x \cdot i$, and if $i > 1$ then also $x \cdot (i - 1) \in \tau$. By definition, the empty sequence ε is the root of such a tree tree. Let $\mathcal{D} \subseteq N$. We say that a tree τ is a $\mathcal{D}$-tree if τ is a tree over N and $arity(x) \in \mathcal{D}$ for all $x \in \tau$. A tree is called *leafless* if every node has at least one child.

A *branch* $\beta = x_0, x_1, \ldots$ of a tree is a maximal sequence of nodes such that x_0 is the root and x_i is the parent of x_{i+1} for all $i > 0$. Note that β can be finite or infinite; if it is finite, then the last node of the branch has no children. A Σ-*labeled tree*, for a finite alphabet Σ, is a pair (τ, T), where τ is a tree and T is a mapping $T : nodes(\tau) \to \Sigma$ that assigns to every node a label. We often refer to T as the labeled tree, leaving its domain implicit. A branch $\beta = x_0, x_1, \ldots$ of T defines a word $T(\beta) = T(x_0), T(x_1), \ldots$ consisting of the sequence of labels along the branch.

2.2   Nondeterministic Automata on Infinite Words

A *nondeterministic Büchi automaton* A is a tuple $(\Sigma, S, s^0, \rho, F)$, where Σ is a finite nonempty *alphabet*, S is a finite nonempty set of *states*, $s^0 \in S$ is an *initial* state, $F \subseteq S$ is the set of *accepting* states, and $\rho : S \times \Sigma \to 2^S$ is a *transition function*. Intuitively, $\rho(s, a)$ is the set of states that A can move into when it is in state s and it reads the symbol a. Note that the automaton may be nondeterministic, since it may have many initial states and the transition function may specify many possible transitions for each state and symbol.

A run r of A on an infinite word $w = a_0, a_1, \ldots$ over Σ is a sequence $s_0, s_1, \ldots$, where $s_0 = s^0$ and $s_{i+1} \in \rho(s_i, a_i)$, for all $i \geq 0$. We define $\lim(r)$ to be the set $\{s \mid s = s_i \text{ for infinitely many } i\text{'s}\}$, i.e., the set of states that occur in r infinitely often. Since S is finite, $\lim(r)$ is necessarily nonempty. The run r is *accepting* if there is some accepting state that repeats in r infinitely often, i.e., $\lim(r) \cap F \neq \emptyset$. The infinite word w is *accepted* by A if there is an accepting run of A on w. The set of infinite words accepted by A is denoted $L_\omega(A)$.

An important feature of nondeterministic Büchi automata is their closure under intersection.

Proposition 1. [Cho74] *Let A_1 and A_2 be nondeterministic Büchi automata with n_1 and n_2 states, respectively. Then there is a Büchi automaton A with $O(n_1 n_2)$ states such that $L_\omega(A) = L_\omega(A_1) \cap L_\omega(A_2)$.*

One of the most fundamental algorithmic issues in automata theory is testing whether a given automaton is "interesting", i.e., whether it accepts some input. A Büchi automaton A is *nonempty* if $L_\omega(A) \neq \emptyset$. The *nonemptiness problem* for automata is to decide, given an automaton A, whether A is nonempty. It turns out that testing nonemptiness is easy.

Proposition 2.

1. [EL85b, EL85a] *The nonemptiness problem for nondeterministic Büchi automata is decidable in linear time.*
2. [VW94] *The nonemptiness problem for nondeterministic Büchi automata of size n is decidable in space $O(\log^2 n)$.*

2.3 Alternating Automata on Infinite Words

Nondeterminism gives a computing device the power of existential choice. Its dual gives a computing device the power of universal choice. It is therefore natural to consider computing devices that have the power of both existential choice and universal choice. Such devices are called *alternating*. Alternation was studied in [CKS81] in the context of Turing machines and in [BL80, CKS81] for finite automata. The alternation formalisms in [BL80] and [CKS81] are different, though equivalent. We follow here the formalism of [BL80], which was extended in [MS87] to automata on infinite structures.

For a given set X, let $\mathcal{B}^+(X)$ be the set of positive Boolean formulas over X (i.e., Boolean formulas built from elements in X using $\land$ and $\lor$), where we also allow the formulas **true** and **false**. Let $Y \subseteq X$. We say that Y *satisfies* a formula $\theta \in \mathcal{B}^+(X)$ if the truth assignment that assigns *true* to the members of Y and assigns *false* to the members of $X - Y$ satisfes θ. For example, the sets $\{s_1, s_3\}$ and $\{s_1, s_4\}$ both satisfy the formula $(s_1 \lor s_2) \land (s_3 \lor s_4)$, while the set $\{s_1, s_2\}$ does not satisfy this formula.

Consider a nondeterministic automaton $A = (\Sigma, S, s^0, \rho, F)$. The transition function ρ maps a state $s \in S$ and an input symbol $a \in \Sigma$ to a set of states. Each element in this set is a possible nondeterministic choice for the automaton's next state. We can represent ρ using $\mathcal{B}^+(S)$; for example, $\rho(s, a) = \{s_1, s_2, s_3\}$ can be written as $\rho(s, a) = s_1 \lor s_2 \lor s_3$. In alternating automata, $\rho(s, a)$ can be an arbitrary formula from $\mathcal{B}^+(S)$. We can have, for instance, a transition

$$\rho(s, a) = (s_1 \land s_2) \lor (s_3 \land s_4),$$

meaning that the automaton accepts the word aw, where a is a symbol and w is a word, when it is in the state s if it accepts the word w from both s_1 and s_2 or from both s_3 and s_4. Thus, such a transition combines the features of existential choice (the disjunction in the formula) and universal choice (the conjunctions in the formula).

Formally, an *alternating Büchi automaton* is a tuple $A = (\Sigma, S, s^0, \rho, F)$, where Σ is a finite nonempty alphabet, S is a finite nonempty set of states, $s^0 \in S$ is an initial state, F is a set of accepting states, and $\rho : S \times \Sigma \to \mathcal{B}^+(S)$ is a partial transition function.

Because of the universal choice in alternating transitions, a run of an alternating automaton is a tree rather than a sequence. A run of A on an infinite word $w = a_0 a_1 \ldots$ is an S-labeled tree r such that $r(\varepsilon) = s^0$ and the following holds:

if $|x| = i$, $r(x) = s$, and $\rho(s, a_i) = \theta$, then x has k children $x_1, \ldots, x_k$, for some $k \le |S|$, and $\{r(x_1), \ldots, r(x_k)\}$ satisfies θ.

For example, if $\rho(s_0, a_0)$ is $(s_1 \lor s_2) \land (s_3 \lor s_4)$, then the nodes of the run tree at level 1 include the label s_1 or the label s_2 and also include the label s_3 or the label s_4. Note that the run can also have finite branches; if $|x| = i$, $r(x) = s$, and $\rho(s, a_i) = $ **true**, then x does not need to have any children. On the other hand, we cannot have $\rho(s, a_i) = $ **false** since **false** is not satisfiable, and we cannot have $\rho(s, a_i)$ be undefined. The run r is *accepting* if every infinite branch in r includes infinitely many labels in F. Thus, a branch in an accepting run has to hit the **true** transition or hit accepting states infinitely often.

What is the relationship between alternating Büchi automata and nondeterministic Büchi automata? It is easy to see that alternating Büchi automata generalize nondeterministic Büchi automata; nondeterministic automata correspond to alternating automata where the transitions are pure disjunctions. It turns out that they have the same expressive power (although alternating Büchi automata are more succinct than nondeterministic Büchi automata).

Proposition 3. [MH84] *Let A be an alternating Büchi automaton with n states. Then there is a nondeterministic Büchi automaton A_{nd} with $2^{O(n)}$ states such that $L_\omega(A_{nd}) = L_\omega(A)$.*

By combining Propositions 2 and 3 (with its exponential blowup), we can obtain a nonemptiness test for alternating Büchi automata.

Proposition 4.

1. *The nonemptiness problem for alternating Büchi automata is decidable in exponential time.*
2. *The nonemptiness problem for alternating Büchi automata is decidable in quadratic space.*

2.4   Nondeterministic Automata on Infinite Trees

We now consider automata on labeled leafless $\mathcal{D}$-trees. A *nondeterministic Büchi tree automaton* A is a tuple $(\Sigma, \mathcal{D}, S, s^0, \rho, F)$. Here Σ is a finite alphabet, $\mathcal{D} \subset N$ is a finite set of arities, S is a finite set of states, $s^0 \in S$ is an initial state, $F \subseteq S$ is a set of accepting states, and $\rho : S \times \Sigma \times \mathcal{D} \to 2^{S^*}$ is a transition function, where $\rho(s, a, k) \subseteq S^k$ for each $s \in S$, $a \in \Sigma$, and $k \in \mathcal{D}$. Thus, $\rho(s, a, k)$ is a set of k-tuples of states. Intuitively, when the automaton is in state s and it is reading a k-ary node x of a tree T, it nondeterministically chooses a k-tuple $\langle s_1, \ldots, s_k \rangle$ in $\rho(s, T(x))$, makes k copies of itself, and then moves to the node $x \cdot i$ in the state s_i for $i = 1, \ldots, k$. A *run* $r : \tau \to S$ of A on a Σ-labeled $\mathcal{D}$-tree T is an S-labeled $\mathcal{D}$-tree such that the root is labeled by the initial state and the transitions obey the transition function ρ; that is, $r(\varepsilon) = s^0$, and for each node x such that $arity(x) = k$, we have $\langle r(x \cdot 1), \ldots, r(x \cdot k) \rangle \in \rho(r(x), T(x), k)$. The run is *accepting* if $\lim(r(\beta)) \cap F \neq \emptyset$ for every branch $\beta = x_0, x_1, \ldots$ of τ; that is, for every branch $\beta = x_0, x_1, \ldots$, we have that $r(x_i) \in F$ for infinitely many i's. The set of trees accepted by A is denoted $T_\omega(A)$. It is easy to see that nondeterministic Büchi automata on infinite words are essentially Büchi automata on $\{1\}$-trees.

Proposition 5. [Rab70] *The nonemptiness problem for nondeterministic Büchi tree automata is decidable in quadratic time.*

2.5   Alternating Automata on Infinite Trees

An *alternating Büchi tree automaton* A is a tuple $(\Sigma, \mathcal{D}, S, s^0, \rho, F)$. Here Σ is a finite alphabet, $\mathcal{D} \subset N$ is a finite set of arities, S is a finite set of states, $s^0 \in S$ is an initial state, $F \subseteq S$ is a set of accepting states, and $\rho : S \times \Sigma \times \mathcal{D} \to \mathcal{B}^+(N \times S)$ is a partial transition function, where $\rho(s, a, k) \in \mathcal{B}^+(\{1, \ldots, k\} \times S)$ for each $s \in S, a \in \Sigma$, and $k \in \mathcal{D}$ such that $\rho(s, a, k)$ is defined. For example, $\rho(s, a, 2) = ((1, s_1) \vee (2, s_2)) \wedge ((1, s_3) \vee (2, s_1))$ means that the automaton can choose between four splitting possibilities. In the first possibility, one copy proceeds in direction 1 in the state s_1 and one copy proceeds in direction 1 in the state s_3. In the second possibility, one copy proceeds in direction 1 in the state s_1 and one copy proceeds in direction 2 in the state s_1. In the third possibility, one copy proceeds in direction 2 in the state s_2 and one copy proceeds in direction 1 in the state s_3. Finally, in the fourth possibility, one copy proceeds in direction 2 in the state s_2 and one copy proceeds in direction 2 in the state s_1. Note that it is possible for more than one copy to proceed in the same direction.

A run r of an alternating Büchi tree automaton A on a Σ-labeled leafless $\mathcal{D}$-tree $\langle \tau, T \rangle$ is a $N^* \times S$-labeled tree. Each node of r corresponds to a node of τ. A node in r, labeled by (x, s), describes a copy of the automaton that reads the node x of τ in the state s. Note that many nodes of r can correspond to the same node of τ; in contrast, in a run of a nondeterministic automaton on $\langle \tau, T \rangle$ there is a one-to-one correspondence between the nodes of the run and the nodes of the tree. The labels of a node and its children have to satisfy the transition function. Formally, r is a Σ_r-labeled tree $\langle \tau_r, T_r \rangle$ where $\Sigma_r = N^* \times S$ and $\langle \tau_r, T_r \rangle$ satisfies the following:

1. $T_r(\varepsilon) = (\varepsilon, s^0)$.
2. Let $y \in \tau_r$, $T_r(y) = (x, s)$, $arity(x) = k$, and $\rho(s, T(x), k) = \theta$. Then there is a set $Q = \{(c_1, s_1), (c_1, s_1), \ldots, (c_n, s_n)\} \subseteq \{1, \ldots, k\} \times S$ such that
   - Q satisfies θ, and
   - for all $1 \leq i \leq n$, we have $y \cdot i \in \tau_r$ and $T_r(y \cdot i) = (x \cdot c_i, s_i)$.

For example, if $\langle \tau, T \rangle$ is a tree with $arity(\varepsilon) = 2$, $T(\varepsilon) = a$ and $\rho(s^0, a) = ((1, s_1) \vee (1, s_2)) \wedge ((1, s_3) \vee (1, s_1))$, then the nodes of $\langle \tau_r, T_r \rangle$ at level 1 include the label $(1, s_1)$ or $(1, s_2)$, and include the label $(1, s_3)$ or $(1, q_1)$.

As with alternating Büchi automata on words, alternating Büchi tree automata are as expressive as nondeterministic Büchi tree automata.

Proposition 6. [MS95] *Let A be an alternating Büchi automaton with n states. Then there is a nondeterministic Büchi automaton A_n with $2^{O(n \log n)}$ states such that $T_\omega(A_n) = T_\omega(A)$.*

By combining Propositions 5 and 6 (with its exponential blowup), we can obtain a nonemptiness test for alternating Büchi tree automata.

Proposition 7. *The nonemptiness problem for alternating Büchi tree automata is decidable in exponential time.*

The nonemptiness problem for nondeterministic tree automata is reducible to the 1-letter nonemptiness problem for them. Instead checking the nonemptiness of an automaton $A = (\Sigma, \mathcal{D}, S, s^0, \rho, F)$, one can check the nonemptiness of the automaton $A' = (\{a\}, \mathcal{D}, S, s^0, \rho', F)$ where for all $s \in S$, we have $\rho'(s, a, k) = \bigcup_{a \in \Sigma} \rho(s, a, k)$. It is easy to see that A accepts some tree iff A' accepts some a-labeled tree. This can be viewed as if A' first guesses a Σ-labeling for the input tree and then proceeds like A on this Σ-labeled tree. This reduction is not valid for alternating tree automata. Suppose that we defined A' by taking $\rho'(s, a, k) = \bigvee_{a \in \Sigma} \rho(s, a, k)$. Then, if A' accepts some a-labeled tree, it still does not guarantee that A accepts some tree. A necessary condition for the validity of the reduction is that different copies of A' that run on the same subtree guess the same Σ-labeling for this subtree. Nothing, however, prevents one copy of A' to proceed according to one labeling and another copy to proceed according to a different labeling. This problem does not occur when A is defined over a singleton alphabet. There, it is guaranteed that all copies proceed according to the same (single) labeling.

As we see later, in our application we sometimes have a 1-letter alphabet Σ, i.e., $|\Sigma| = 1$. It turns out that nonemptiness for alternating automata over 1-letter alphabets is easier than the general nonemptiness problem. Actually, it is as easy as the nonemptiness problem for nondeterministic Büchi tree automata (Proposition 5).

Proposition 8. *The nonemptiness problem for alternating Büchi tree automata over 1-letter alphabets is decidable in quadratic time.*

As we shall see later, the alternating automata in our applications have a special structure, studied first in [MSS86]. A *weak alternating tree automaton* (WAA) is an alternating Büchi tree automaton in which there exists a partition of the state set S into disjoint sets $S_1, \ldots, S_n$ such that for each set S_i, either $S_i \subseteq F$, in which case S_i is an *accepting set*, or $S_i \cap F = \emptyset$, in which case S_i is a *rejecting set*. In addition, there exists a partial order $\leq$ on the collection of the S_i's such that for every $s \in S_i$ and $s' \in S_j$ for which s' occurs in $\rho(s, a, k)$, for some $a \in \Sigma$ and $k \in \mathcal{D}$, we have $S_j \leq S_i$. Thus, transitions from a state in S_i lead to states in either the same S_i or a lower one. It follows that every infinite path of a run of a WAA ultimately gets "trapped" within some S_i. The path then satisfies the acceptance condition if and only if S_i is an accepting set. That is, a run visits infinitely many states in F if and only if it gets trapped in an accepting set. The number of sets in the partition of S is defined as the *depth* of the automaton.

It turns out that the nonemptiness problem for WAA on 1-letter alphabets is easier than nonemptiness problem for alternating Büchi automata on 1-letter alphabets.

Proposition 9. [BVW94] *The nonemptiness problem for weak alternating tree automata on 1-letter alphabets is decidable in linear time.*

As we will see, the WAA that we use have an even more special structure. In these WAA, each set S_i can be classified as either *transient*, *existential*, or *universal*, such that for each set S_i and for all $s \in Q_i$, $a \in \Sigma$, and $k \in \mathcal{D}$, the following hold:

1. If S_i is transient, then $\rho(s, a, k)$ contains no elements of S_i.
2. If S_i is existential, then $\rho(s, a, k)$ only contains *disjunctively related* elements of S_i (i.e. if the transition is rewritten in disjunctive normal form, there is at most one element of S_i in each disjunct).
3. If Q_i is universal, then $\rho(s, a, k)$ only contains *conjunctively related* elements of S_i (i.e. if the transition is rewritten in conjunctive normal form, there is at most one element of Q_i in each conjunct).

This means that it is only when moving from one S_i to the next, that alternation actually occurs (alternation is moving from a state that is conjunctively related to states in its set to a state that is disjunctively related to states in its set, or vice-versa). In other words, when a copy of the automaton visits a state in some existential set S_i, then as long as it stays in this set, it proceeds in an "existential mode"; namely, it imposes only existential requirement on its successors in S_i. Similarly, when a copy of the automaton visits a state in some universal set S_i, then as long as it stays in this set, it proceeds in a "universal mode". Thus, whenever a copy alternates modes, it must be that it moves from one S_i to the next. We call a WAA that satisfies this property a *limited-alternation* WAA.

Proposition 10. *The nonemptiness problem for limited-alternation WAA of size n and depth m over 1-letter alphabets can be solved in space* $O(m \log^2 n)$.

3 Temporal Logics and Alternating Automata

3.1 Linear Temporal Logic

Formulas of *linear temporal logic* (LTL) are built from a set *Prop* of atomic propositions and are closed under the application of Boolean connectives, the unary temporal connective X (next), and the binary temporal connective U (until) [Eme90]. LTL is interpreted over *computations*. A computation is a function $\pi : \omega \rightarrow 2^{Prop}$, which assigns truth values to the elements of *Prop* at each time instant (natural number). A computation π and a point $i \in \omega$ satisfies an LTL formula φ, denoted $\pi, i \models \varphi$, under the following conditions:

- $\pi, i \models p$ for $p \in Prop$ iff $p \in \pi(i)$.
- $\pi, i \models \xi \wedge \psi$ iff $\pi, i \models \xi$ and $\pi, i \models \psi$.
- $\pi, i \models \neg\varphi$ iff not $\pi, i \models \varphi$
- $\pi, i \models X\varphi$ iff $\pi, i+1 \models \varphi$.
- $\pi, i \models \xi U \psi$ iff for some $j \geq i$, we have $\pi, j \models \psi$ and for all k, $i \leq k < j$, we have $\pi, k \models \xi$.

We say that π *satisfies* a formula φ, denoted $\pi \models \varphi$, iff $\pi, 0 \models \varphi$.

Computations can also be viewed as infinite words over the alphabet 2^{Prop}. It turns out that the computations satisfying a given formula are exactly those accepted by some finite automaton on infinite words. The following theorem establishes a very simple translation between LTL and alternating Büchi automata on infinite words.

Theorem 11. [MSS88, Var94] *Given an LTL formula* φ, *one can build an alternating Büchi automaton* $A_\varphi = (\Sigma, S, s^0, \rho, F)$, *where* $\Sigma = 2^{Prop}$ *and* $|S|$ *is in* $O(|\varphi|)$, *such that* $L_\omega(A_\varphi)$ *is exactly the set of computations satisfying the formula* φ.

Proof: The set S of states consists of all subformulas of φ and their negation (we identify the formula $\neg\neg\psi$ with ψ). The initial state s^0 is φ itself. The set F of accepting states consists of all formulas in S of the form $\neg(\xi U \psi)$. It remains to define the transition function ρ.

The *dual* $\overline{\theta}$ of a formula is obtained from θ by switching $\vee$ and $\wedge$, by switching **true** and **false**, and, in addition, by negating subformulas in S, e.g., $\neg p \vee (q \wedge Xq)$ is $p \wedge (\neg q \vee \neg Xq)$. More formally,

- $\overline{\xi} = \neg\xi$, for $\xi \in S$,
- $\overline{\textbf{true}} = \textbf{false}$,
- $\overline{\textbf{false}} = \textbf{true}$,
- $\overline{(\alpha \wedge \beta)} = (\overline{\alpha} \vee \overline{\beta})$, and
- $\overline{(\alpha \vee \beta)} = (\overline{\alpha} \wedge \overline{\beta})$.

We can now define ρ:

- $\rho(p, a) = \textbf{true}$ if $p \in a$,
- $\rho(p, a) = \textbf{false}$ if $p \notin a$,
- $\rho(\xi \wedge \psi, a) = \rho(\xi, a) \wedge \rho(\psi, a)$,
- $\rho(\neg\psi, a) = \overline{\rho(\psi, a)}$,
- $\rho(X\psi, a) = \psi$,
- $\rho(\xi U\psi, a) = \rho(\psi, a) \vee (\rho(\xi, a) \wedge \xi U\psi)$.

By applying Proposition 3, we now get:

Corollary 12. [VW94] *Given an LTL formula φ, one can build a Büchi automaton $A_\varphi = (\Sigma, S, s^0, \rho, F)$, where $\Sigma = 2^{Prop}$ and $|S|$ is in $2^{O(|\varphi|)}$, such that $L_\omega(A_\varphi)$ is exactly the set of computations satisfying the formula φ.*

3.2 Branching Temporal Logic

The branching temporal logic CTL (Computation Tree Logic) provides temporal connectives that are composed of a path quantifier immediately followed by a single linear temporal connective [Eme90]. The path quantifiers are A ("for all paths") and E ("for some path"). The linear-time connectives are X ("next time") and U ("until"). Thus, given a set $Prop$ of atomic propositions, a CTL formula is one of the following:

- p, for all $p \in AP$,
- $\neg\xi$ or $\xi \wedge \psi$, where ξ and ψ are CTL formulas.
- $EX\xi$, $AX\xi$, $E(\xi U\psi)$, $A(\xi U\psi)$, where ξ and ψ are CTL formulas.

The semantics of CTL is defined with respect to *programs*. A program over a set $Prop$ of atomic propositions is a structure of the form $P = (W, w^0, R, V)$, where W is a set of states, $w^0 \in W$ is an initial state, $R \subseteq W^2$ is a total accessibility relation, and $V : W \rightarrow 2^{Prop}$ assigns truth values to propositions in $Prop$ for each state in W. The intuition is that W describes all the states that the program could be in (where a state includes the content of the memory, registers, buffers, location counter, etc.), R describes all the possible transitions between states (allowing for nondeterminism), and V relates the states to the propositions (e.g., it tells us in what states the proposition request is true). The assumption that R is total (i.e., that every state has an R-successor) is for technical convenience. We can view a terminated execution as repeating forever its last state. We say that P is a *finite-state* program if W is finite. A *path* in P is a sequence of states, $\mathbf{u} = u_0, u_1, \ldots$ such that for every $i \geq 0$, we have that $u_i R u_{i+1}$ holds.

A program $P = (W, w^0, R, V)$ and a state $u \in W$ satisfies a CTL formula φ, denoted $P, u \models \varphi$, under the following conditions:

- $P, u \models p$ for $p \in Prop$ if $p \in V(u)$.
- $P, u \models \neg\varphi$ if $P, u \not\models \varphi$.
- $P, u \models \xi \wedge \psi$ iff $P, u \models \xi$ and $P, u \models \psi$.
- $P, u \models EX\varphi$ if $P, v \models \varphi$ for some v such that uRv holds.
- $P, u \models AX\varphi$ if $P, v \models \varphi$ for all v such that uRv holds.
- $P, u \models E(\xi U \psi)$ if there exist a path $\mathbf{u} = u_0, u_1, \ldots$, with $u_0 = u$, and some $i \geq 0$, such that $P, u_i \models \psi$ and for all j, $0 \leq j < i$, we have $P, u_j \models \xi$.
- $P, u \models A(\xi U \psi)$ if for all paths $\mathbf{u} = u_0, u_1, \ldots$, with $u_0 = u$, there is some $i \geq 0$ such that $P, u_i \models \psi$ and for all j, $0 \leq j < i$, we have $P, u_j \models \xi$.

We say that p satisfies φ, denoted $P \models \varphi$, if $P, w^0 \models \varphi$.

A program $P = (W, w^0, R, V)$ is a *tree program* if (W, R) is a tree and w^0 is its root. Note that in this case P is a leafless 2^{Prop}-labeled tree (it is leafless, since R is total). P is a $\mathcal{D}$-tree program, for $\mathcal{D} \subset N$, if (W, R) is a $\mathcal{D}$-tree. It turns out that the tree programs satisfying a given formula are exactly those accepted by some finite tree automaton. The following theorem establishes a very simple translation between CTL and weak alternating Büchi tree automata.

Theorem 13. [MSS88, BVW94] *Given a CTL formula φ and a finite set $\mathcal{D} \subset N$, one can build a limited-alternation WAA $A_\varphi = (\Sigma, \mathcal{D}, S, s^0, \rho, F)$, where $\Sigma = 2^{Prop}$ and $|S|$ is in $O(|\varphi|)$, such that $T_\omega(A_\varphi)$ is exactly the set of $\mathcal{D}$-tree programs satisfying φ.*

Proof: The set S of states consists of all subformulas of φ and their negation (we identify the formula $\neg\neg\psi$ with ψ). The initial state s^0 is φ itself. The set F of accepting states consists of all formulas in S of the form $\neg E(\xi U \psi)$ and $\neg A(\xi U \psi)$. It remains to define the transition function ρ. In the following definition we use the notion of dual, defined in the proof of Theorem 11.

- $\rho(p, a, k) = \mathbf{true}$ if $p \in a$.
- $\rho(p, a, k) = \mathbf{false}$ if $p \notin a$.
- $\rho(\neg\psi, a) = \overline{\rho(\psi, a)}$,
- $\rho(\xi \wedge \psi, a, k) = \rho(\xi, a, k) \wedge \rho(\psi, a, k)$.
- $\rho(EX\psi, a, k) = \bigvee_{c=0}^{k-1}(c, \psi)$.
- $\rho(AX\psi, a, k) = \bigwedge_{c=0}^{k-1}(c, \psi)$.
- $\rho(E(\xi U \psi), a, k) = \rho(\psi, a, k) \vee (\rho(\xi, a, k) \wedge \bigvee_{c=0}^{k-1}(c, E(\xi U \psi)))$.
- $\rho(A(\xi U \psi), a, k) = \rho(\psi, a, k) \vee (\rho(\xi, a, k) \wedge \bigwedge_{c=0}^{k-1}(c, A(\xi U \psi)))$.

Finally, we define a partition of S into disjoint sets and a partial order over the sets. Each formula $\psi \in S$ constitutes a (singleton) set $\{\psi\}$ in the partition. The partial order is then defined by $\{\xi\} \leq \{\psi\}$ iff ξ a subformula or the negation of subformula of ψ. Here, all sets are transient, expect for sets of the form $\{E(\xi U \psi)\}$ and $\{\neg A(\xi U \psi)\}$, which are existential, and sets of the form $\{A(\xi U \psi)\}$ and $\{\neg E(\xi U \psi)\}$, which are universal. ∎

4   Model Checking

4.1   Linear Temporal Logic

We assume that we are given a finite-state program and an LTL formula that specifies the legal computations of the program. The problem is to check whether all computations of the program are legal.

Let $\mathbf{u} = u_0, u_1 \ldots$ be a path of a finite-state program $P = (W, w^0, R, V)$ such that $u_0 = w^0$. The sequence $V(u_0), V(u_1) \ldots$ is a *computation of P*. We say that P *satisfies* an LTL formula φ if *all* computations of P satisfy φ. The *LTL verification problem* is to check whether P satisfies φ.

We now describe the automata-theoretic approach to the LTL verification problem. A finite-state program $P = (W, w^0, R, V)$ can be viewed as a nondeterministic Büchi automaton $A_P = (\Sigma, W, \{w^0\}, \rho, W)$, where $\Sigma = 2^{Prop}$ and $v \in \rho(u, a)$ iff uRv holds and $a = V(u)$. As this automaton has a set of accepting states equal to the whole set of states, any infinite run of the automaton is accepting. Thus, $L_\omega(A_P)$ is the set of computations of P.

Hence, for a finite-state program P and an LTL formula φ, the verification problem is to verify that all infinite words accepted by the automaton A_P satisfy the formula φ. By Corollary 12, we know that we can build a nondeterministic Büchi automaton A_φ that accepts exactly the computations satisfying the formula φ. The verification problem thus reduces to the automata-theoretic problem of checking that all computations accepted by the automaton A_P are also accepted by the automaton A_φ, that is $L_\omega(A_P) \subseteq L_\omega(A_\varphi)$. Equivalently, we need to check that the automaton that accepts $L_\omega(A_P) \cap \overline{L_\omega(A_\varphi)}$ is empty, where

$$L_\omega(\overline{A_\varphi}) = \overline{L_\omega(A_\varphi)} = \Sigma^\omega - L_\omega(A_\varphi).$$

First, note that, by Corollary 12, $L_\omega(\overline{A_\varphi}) = L_\omega(A_{\neg\varphi})$ and the automaton $A_{\neg\varphi}$ has $2^{O(|\varphi|)}$ states. (A straightforward approach, starting with the automaton A_φ and then complementing it, would result in a doubly exponential blow-up, since complementation of nondeterministic Büchi automata is exponential [SVW87, Mic88, Saf88]). To get the intersection of the two automata, we use Proposition 1. Consequently, we can build an automaton for $L_\omega(A_P) \cap L_\omega(A_{\neg\varphi})$ having $|W| \cdot 2^{O(|\varphi|)}$ states. We need to check this automaton for emptiness. Using Proposition 2, we get the following results.

Theorem 14. [LP85, SC85, VW86a] *Checking whether a finite-state program P satisfies an LTL formula φ can be done in time $O(|P| \cdot 2^{O(|\varphi|)})$ or in space $O((|\varphi| + \log |P|)^2)$.*

We note that a time upper bound that is polynomial in the size of the program and exponential in the size of the specification is considered here to be reasonable, since the specification is usually rather short [LP85]. For a practical verification algorithm that is based on the automata-theoretic approach see [CVWY92].

4.2   Branching Temporal Logic

For linear temporal logic, each program may correspond to infinitely many computations. Model checking is thus reduced to checking inclusion between the set of computations allowed by the program and the language of an automaton describing the formula.

For branching temporal logic, each program corresponds to a single "computation tree". On that account, model checking is reduced to checking acceptance of this computation tree by the automaton describing the formula.

A program $P = (W, w^0, R, V)$ can be viewed as a W-labeled tree $\langle \tau_P, T_P \rangle$ that corresponds to the unwinding of P from w^0. For every node $w \in W$, let $arity(w)$ denote the number of R-successors of w and let $succ_R(w) = \langle w_1, \ldots, w_{arity(w)} \rangle$ be an ordered list of w's R-successors (we assume that the nodes of W are ordered). τ_P and T_P are defined inductively:

1. $\varepsilon \in \tau_P$ and $T_P(\varepsilon) = w^0$.
2. For $y \in \tau_P$ with $succ_R(T_P(y)) = \langle w_1, \ldots, w_k \rangle$ and for all $1 \leq i \leq k$, we have $y \cdot i \in \tau_P$ and $T_P(y \cdot i) = w_i$.

Let $\mathcal{D}$ be the set of arities of states of P, i.e., $\mathcal{D} = \{arity(w) : w \in W\}$. Clearly, τ_P is a $\mathcal{D}$-tree.

Let $\langle \tau_P, V \cdot T_P \rangle$ be the 2^{Prop}-labeled $\mathcal{D}$-tree defined by $V \cdot T_P(y) = V(T_P(y))$ for $y \in \tau_P$. Let φ be a CTL formula. Suppose that $A_{\mathcal{D},\varphi}$ is an alternating automaton that accepts exactly all $\mathcal{D}$-tree programs that satisfy φ. It can easily be shown that $\langle \tau_P, V \cdot T_P \rangle$ is accepted by $A_{\mathcal{D},\varphi}$ iff $P \models \varphi$. We now show that by taking the product of P and $A_{\mathcal{D},\varphi}$ we get an alternating Büchi tree automaton on a 1-letter alphabet that is empty iff $\langle \tau_P, V \cdot T_P \rangle$ is accepted by $A_{\mathcal{D},\varphi}$.

Let $A_{\mathcal{D},\varphi} = (2^{AP}, \mathcal{D}, S, \varphi, \rho, F)$ be a limited-alternation WAA that accepts exactly all $\mathcal{D}$-tree programs that satisfy φ, and let $S_1, \ldots, S_n$ be the partition of S. The *product automaton* of P and $A_{\mathcal{D},\varphi}$ is the limited-alternation WAA

$$A_{P,\varphi} = (\{a\}, \mathcal{D}, W \times S, \delta, \langle w^0, \varphi \rangle, G),$$

where δ and G are defined as follows:

- Let $s \in S$, $w \in W$, $succ_R(w) = \langle w_1, \ldots, w_k \rangle$, and $\rho(s, V(w), k) = \theta$. Then $\delta(\langle w, s \rangle, a, k) = \theta'$, where θ' is obtained from θ by replacing each atom (c, s') in θ by the atom $(c, \langle w_c, s' \rangle)$.
- $G = W \times F$
- $W \times S$ is partitioned to $W \times S_1, W \times S_2, \ldots, W \times S_n$.
- $W \times S_i$ is transient (resp., existential, universal) if S_i is transient (resp., existential, universal), for $1 \leq i \leq n$.

Note that if P has m_1 states and $A_{\mathcal{D},\varphi}$ has m_2 states then $A_{P,\varphi}$ has $O(m_1 m_2)$ states.

Proposition 15. $A_{P,\varphi}$ *is nonempty if and only if $P \models \varphi$.*

We can now put together Propositions 9, 10, and 15 to get a model-checking algorithm for CTL.

Theorem 16. [CES86, BVW94] *Checking whether a finite-state program P satisfies a CTL formula φ can be done in time $O(|P| \cdot |\varphi|)$ or in space $O(|\varphi| \log^2 |P|)$.*

Acknowledgements. I am grateful to Orna Kupferman for her careful reading of and comments on this article.

References

[BL80]   J.A. Brzozowski and E. Leiss. Finite automata, and sequential networks. *Theoretical Computer Science*, 10:19–35, 1980.

[BVW94]   O. Bernholtz, M.Y. Vardi, and P. Wolper. An automata-theoretic approach to branching-time model checking. In D.L. Dill, editor, *Computer Aided Verification, Proc. 6th Int. Conference*, volume 818 of *Lecture Notes in Computer Science*, pages 142–155, Stanford, California, 1994. Springer-Verlag, Berlin. full version available from authors.

[CES86]   E.M. Clarke, E.A. Emerson, and A.P. Sistla. Automatic verification of finite-state concurrent systems using temporal logic specifications. *ACM Transactions on Programming Languages and Systems*, 8(2):244–263, 1986.

[CG87]   E.M. Clarke and O. Grumberg. Avoiding the state explosion problem in temporal logic model-checking algorithms. In *Proc. 6th ACM Symposium on Principles of Distributed Computing*, pages 294–303, Vancouver, British Columbia, August 1987.

[CGL93]   E.M. Clarke, O. Grumberg, and D. Long. Verification tools for finite-state concurrent systems. In *A Decade of Concurrency – Reflections and Perspectives (Proc. REX School/Symposium)*, volume 803 of *Lecture Notes in Computer Science*, pages 124–175. Springer-Verlag, Berlin, 1993.

[Cho74]   Y. Choueka. Theories of automata on ω-tapes: A simplified approach. *J. Computer and System Sciences*, 8:117–141, 1974.

[CKS81]   A.K. Chandra, D.C. Kozen, and L.J. Stockmeyer. Alternation. *Journal of the Association for Computing Machinery*, 28(1):114–133, 1981.

[Cle93]   R. Cleaveland. A linear-time model-checking algorithm for the alternation-free modal μ-calculus. *Formal Methods in System Design*, 2:121–147, 1993.

[CVWY92]   C. Courcoubetis, M.Y. Vardi, P. Wolper, and M. Yannakakis. Memory efficient algorithms for the verification of temporal properties. *Formal Methods in System Design*, 1:275–288, 1992.

[EJ88]   E.A. Emerson and C. Jutla. The complexity of tree automata and logics of programs. In *Proceedings of the 29th IEEE Symposium on Foundations of Computer Science*, pages 328–337, White Plains, October 1988.

[EJ91]   E.A. Emerson and C. Jutla. Tree automata, mu-calculus and determinacy. In *Proceedings of the 32nd IEEE Symposium on Foundations of Computer Science*, pages 368–377, San Juan, October 1991.

[EL85a]   E.A. Emerson and C.-L. Lei. Modalities for model checking: Branching time logic strikes back. In *Proceedings of the Twelfth ACM Symposium on Principles of Programming Languages*, pages 84–96, New Orleans, January 1985.

[EL85b]   E.A. Emerson and C.-L. Lei. Temporal model checking under generalized fairness constraints. In *Proc. 18th Hawaii International Conference on System Sciences*, pages 277–288, Hawaii, 1985.

[Eme85]   E.A. Emerson. Automata, tableaux, and temporal logics. In *Logic of Programs*, volume 193 of *Lecture Notes in Computer Science*, pages 79–87. Springer-Verlag, Berlin, 1985.

[Eme90]   E.A. Emerson. Temporal and modal logic. *Handbook of Theoretical Computer Science*, B:997–1072, 1990.

[ES84]   E.A. Emerson and A. P. Sistla. Deciding branching time logic. In *Proceedings of the 16th ACM Symposium on Theory of Computing*, pages 14–24, Washington, April 1984.

[Lam80]   L. Lamport. Sometimes is sometimes "not never" - on the temporal logic of programs. In *Proceedings of the 7th ACM Symposium on Principles of Programming Languages*, pages 174–185, January 1980.

[Liu89]   M.T. Liu. Protocol engineering. *Advances in Computing*, 29:79–195, 1989.

[LP85]   O. Lichtenstein and A. Pnueli. Checking that finite state concurrent programs satisfy their linear specification. In *Proceedings of the Twelfth ACM Symposium on Principles of Programming Languages*, pages 97–107, New Orleans, January 1985.

[LPZ85]   O. Lichtenstein, A. Pnueli, and L. Zuck. The glory of the past. In *Logics of Programs*, volume 193 of *Lecture Notes in Computer Science*, pages 196–218, Brooklyn, 1985. Springer-Verlag, Berlin.

[MH84]   S. Miyano and T. Hayashi. Alternating finite automata on ω-words. *Theoretical Computer Science*, 32:321–330, 1984.

[Mic88]   M. Michel. Complementation is more difficult with automata on infinite words. CNET, Paris, 1988.

[MP92]   Z. Manna and A. Pnueli. *The Temporal Logic of Reactive and Concurrent Systems: Specification*. Springer-Verlag, Berlin, 1992.

[MS87]   D.E. Muller and P.E. Schupp. Alternating automata on infinite trees. *Theoretical Computer Science*, 54,:267–276, 1987.

[MS95]   D.E. Muller and P.E. Schupp. Simulating alternating tree automata by nondeterministic automata: New results and new proofs of the theorems by Rabin, McNaughton and Safra. *Theoretical Computer Science*, 141(1-2):69–108, April 1995.

[MSS86]   D.E. Muller, A. Saoudi, and P.E. Schupp. Alternating automata, the weak monadic theory of the tree and its complexity. In L. Kott, editor, *Automata, Languages and Programming, Proc. 13th Int. Colloquium (ICALP '86)*, volume 226 of *Lecture Notes in Computer Science*, pages 275–283. Springer-Verlag, Berlin, 1986.

[MSS88]   D. E. Muller, A. Saoudi, and P. E. Schupp. Weak alternating automata give a simple explanation of why most temporal and dynamic logics are decidable in exponential time. In *Proceedings 3rd IEEE Symposium on Logic in Computer Science*, pages 422–427, Edinburgh, July 1988.

[Pei85]   R. Peikert. ω-regular languages and propositional temporal logic. Technical Report 85-01, ETH, 1985.

[Pnu77]   A. Pnueli. The temporal logic of programs. In *Proc. 18th IEEE Symposium on Foundation of Computer Science*, pages 46–57, 1977.

[QS81]   J.P. Queille and J. Sifakis. Specification and verification of concurrent systems in Cesar. In *Int. Symp. on programming, Proc. 5th Int. Symposium*, volume 137 of *Lecture Notes in Computer Science*, pages 337–351. Springer-Verlag, Berlin, 1981.

[Rab70]   M.O. Rabin. Weakly definable relations and special automata. In Y. Bar-Hilel, editor, *Proc. Symp. Math. Logic and Foundations of Set Theory*, pages 1–23. North Holland, 1970.

[Rud87]   H. Rudin. Network protocols and tools to help produce them. *Annual Review of Computer Science*, 2:291–316, 1987.

[Saf88]   S. Safra. On the complexity of omega-automata. In *Proceedings of the 29th IEEE Symposium on Foundations of Computer Science*, pages 319–327, White Plains, October 1988.

[SC85]   A.P. Sistla and E.M. Clarke. The complexity of propositional linear temporal logic. *Journal of the Association for Computing Machinery*, 32:733–749, 1985.

[SE84]   R. S. Streett and E. A. Emerson. The propositional mu-calculus is elementary. In J. Paredaens, editor, *Automata, Languages and Programming, Proc. 11th Int. Colloquium (ICALP '84)*, volume 172 of *Lecture Notes in Computer Science*, pages 465–472. Springer-Verlag, Berlin, 1984.

[Sis83]   A.P. Sistla. *Theoretical issues in the design and analysis of distributed systems*. PhD thesis, Harvard University, 1983.

[SVW87] A.P. Sistla, M.Y. Vardi, and P. Wolper. The complementation problem for Büchi automata with applications to temporal logic. *Theoretical Computer Science*, 49:217–237, 1987.

[Var94] M.Y. Vardi. Nontraditional applications of automata theory. In *Theoretical Aspects of Computer Software, Proc. Int. Symposium (TACS'94)*, volume 789 of *Lecture Notes in Computer Science*, pages 575–597. Springer-Verlag, Berlin, 1994.

[VW86a] M.Y. Vardi and P. Wolper. An automata-theoretic approach to automatic program verification. In *Proceedings of the First Symposium on Logic in Computer Science*, pages 322–331, Cambridge, June 1986.

[VW86b] M.Y. Vardi and P. Wolper. Automata-theoretic techniques for modal logics of programs. *Journal of Computer and System Science*, 32(2):182–21, April 1986.

[VW94] M.Y. Vardi and P. Wolper. Reasoning about infinite computations. *Information and Computation*, 115(1):1–37, 1994.

[Wol89] P. Wolper. On the relation of programs and computations to models of temporal logic. In *Temporal Logic in Specification, Proc.*, volume 398 of *Lecture Notes in Computer Science*, pages 75–123. Springer-Verlag, Berlin, 1989.

[WVS83] P. Wolper, M.Y. Vardi, and A.P. Sistla. Reasoning about infinite computation paths. In *Proc. 24th IEEE Symposium on Foundations of Computer Science*, pages 185–194, Tucson, 1983.

Reasoning about Actions and Change with Ramification

Erik Sandewall

Department of Computer and Information Science
Linköping University
S-58183 Linköping, Sweden
email: erisa@ida.liu.se

Abstract. The *systematic approach* to nonmonotonic logics of actions and change attempts to identify, for each proposed logic, what is its *range of applicability* relative to a precise definition of *intended models*. The article describes the concepts and methods that are used in this approach, and examples of assessed range of applicability for a few of the previously proposed logics in the case of strict inertia. The article also presents some new results, where the same systematic approach is applied to the case of chronicles with *inertia and ramification*.

1 The Systematic Approach to Actions and Change

The class of problems being addressed here will first be defined in abstract terms, and will then be discussed from a more applied point of view.

1.1 Logics of Actions and Change

A *chronicle* is a description, using logical formulae, of a number of actions, their general effects, and observations of some properties of the world while the actions are being performed. In simple cases, a chronicle consists of the following kinds of formulae:

action statements, for example $D(20, 25, make\text{-}coffee)$, saying that the current agent performs the act of making coffee from time 20 to time 25;

observations, for example $H(25, coffee\text{-}hot)$, saying that there is hot coffee at time 25;

action laws, for example $D(s, t, make\text{-}coffee) \Rightarrow H(t, coffee\text{-}hot)$, saying that if coffee is made from time s to time t, then hot coffee exists at time t;

timing statements, for example $t_2 < t_4 - 1$, relating the values of two expressions using temporal constants. Such statements are useful when the timepoint arguments of D and H are constant symbols and not explicit timepoints (for example, t_2 rather than 25).

The letter D stands for *Do* and H for *Holds*. To accommodate multi-valued properties, we consider the general form of H to be $H(t, f, v)$, saying that the "feature" f has the value v at time t. Then $H(t, p)$ is an abbreviation for $H(t, p, T)$

for the case where p can only have the value T or F[1]. The terms *feature* and *property* will be used synonymously here.

In more complex cases, chronicles may contain observations that refer to multiple timepoints, action statements that refer to conditional or composite actions, and other ontologies for time such as branching time. Also, action symbols and features/properties may have objects as arguments, for example

$$H(25, stateof(tralite4), \texttt{Green}),$$

expressing that the state of traffic light number 4 is Green at time 25. Logics whereby one can express and reason about chronicles are called *logics of actions and change*.

1.2   Research Problem

The notation for chronicles that is suggested by these examples can of course be understood as the language of a first-order logic. The central research problem for logics of actions and change is that *the set of intended models for a chronicle does not agree with the set of Tarskian models as provided by first-order logic*, henceforth referred to as *classical models*. The main research task is therefore to find and to analyze suitable complements to the machinery of classical logic whereby intended and actual model sets agree, so that one obtains all the intended conclusions and only them.

The research problem and the research task can of course be equivalently formulated in terms of the "set of conclusions" instead of the "set of models". Possible conclusions from a given chronicle include derived facts (syntactically similar to observations) about the state of the world at other times or in other properties than those that were directly observed.

Different variants of this research problem are obtained by varying the assumptions that lead to the mismatch between intended and classical models. The basic assumption is *inertia* or "no change without a known reason". In the simplest case it means that actions only change those properties of the world which are indicated in the action law, whereas other properties remain constant. This simple case is referred to as *strict inertia*. Less trivial cases are obtained e.g. if certain static constraints are known for the state of the world, and if it is then necessary to assume that actions cause additional changes, besides those indicated by the action law, in order that the situation resulting from a particular action shall satisfy the static constraints. This case is referred to as *ramification*, and it will be addressed towards the end of the present article.

Non-deterministic actions pose particular problems in the context of the inertia assumption. One way of dealing with them is to introduce an additional *occlusion predicate* $X(f, t)$, expressing that the value of the feature f may change during the timestep $[t-1, t]$.

---

[1] In earlier publications I wrote $D(s, t, E)$ as $[s, t]E$, and $H(t, f, v)$ as $[t]f \doteq v$.

1.3 Applications

The research on logics for actions and change has its origin in artificial intelligence, where it is historically known under the name of the "frame problem" [4]. Two kinds of uses have been foreseen in A.I. One is for *common-sense reasoning* based, in particular, on information given in natural language. Statements about actions and about the state of the world at different times are commonplace in natural-language text, and understanding them is one essential aspect of understanding the text as a whole.

The other usage is for *cognitive robotics*, that is, for allowing an intelligent robot to reason about its own actions and its effects, as well as about the effects of natural events and of actions taken by other robots in the same habitat. In this case, the actions are implemented as programs in the robot controller system, and reasoning about the actions is a particular kind of reasoning about programs. It is particular in the sense that one reasons not only about the program itself, but also about spontaneous events in the world where the robot (and indirectly, the program) is set to operate.

The notation for chronicles that was exemplified above allows one to characterize the duration of an action in terms of metric time. The consequent side of an action law is not restricted to specifying the final result of an action; it may also characterize the duration of the action (as a constraint on the combination of s and t), and the state of the world at intermediate points during the execution of the action. Logics of actions and change are therefore potential candidates for reasoning about *hard real-time* programs. However, that aspect has not been investigated very much yet, and will not be addressed in the present article.

Typically, one wishes action laws to be as compact as possible, so ideally they should only have to specify some of the changes that are due to an action, leaving other resulting changes to be inferred by logical means. This topic is closely related to the *update problem* in databases.

1.4 Use of Preferential Nonmonotonic Logics

The standard approach in this research is to use *nonmonotonic logics*. The following notation will be used. Let Υ be a chronicle, represented as a set of logical formulae of the kinds exemplified above. Then $[\Upsilon]$ will refer to the set of classical models for Υ, and $Mod(\Upsilon)$ will refer to the set of intended models. A *unary selection function* is a function from a set of models to a subset of that set. A selection function S is *correct* for a chronicle Υ iff $Mod(\Upsilon) = S[\Upsilon]$. Selection functions are therefore the primary instrument for reconciling intended and classical model sets.

A *preference relation* is a strict partial order on models. Many simple cases of selection functions can be defined directly in terms of a preference relation $\ll$, so that the set of selected models is

$$Min(\ll, [\Upsilon]),$$

meaning the set of $\ll$-minimal classical models. More sophisticated selection functions can be obtained in the following fashions:

Binary selection functions: the premises are divided into two *partitions*, so that the chronicle Υ is in fact a pair $\langle \Upsilon_1, \Upsilon_2 \rangle$. The set of classical models is defined by

$$[\langle \Upsilon_1, \Upsilon_2 \rangle] = [\Upsilon_1] \cap [\Upsilon_2],$$

and the set of selected models is defined as

$$S([\Upsilon_1], [\Upsilon_2]),$$

where S is a function which maps two sets of models to a subset of their intersection.

Reformulation: the set of selected models is defined as

$$[G(\Upsilon)],$$

where G is a *reformulation function*, that is, a syntactic transformation on the set Υ of formulae which satisfies $G(\Upsilon) \supseteq \Upsilon$. The goal of reducing the set of models is achieved by minimization in the case of filtering, and by adding more formulae to the originally given set, in the case of reformulation.

Combinations and generalizations of the methods described so far, that is, minimization, k-ary selection functions, and reformulation. In particular, it is possible and often useful to let a chronicle consist of more than two partitions, corresponding to the use of a k-ary selection function.

One particular use of binary selection functions is for *filtering*, where the set of selected models for $\langle \Upsilon_1, \Upsilon_2 \rangle$ is

$$Min(\ll, [\Upsilon_1]) \cap [\Upsilon_2].$$

1.5   Entailment Methods and Range of Applicability

In earlier publications [6, 5, 8], I have argued that the appropriate question with respect to a method based on a non-monotonic logic is not "is it correct", but "what is its range of applicability". In other words, one identifies the set of conditions that must be satisfied by a chronicle Υ in order that the set of selected models according to the given entailment method shall agree with the set of intended models for the same chronicle. I refer to this as the *systematic approach* to the study of applied non-monotonic logics.

The reasons for analyzing the range of applicability should be fairly evident. One is not always interested in finding and using the method with the largest range of applicability: it is to be expected that there are some methods with a fairly narrow range of applicability, but which allow more efficient implementation. If such a method exists, and its range of applicability does include those chronicles that may arise in a given application, then one will be happy to use that method for the application at hand.

The range of applicability may be significantly improved through the use of the following concepts. A *pretransformation* $\mathbf{G}$ is a mapping from chronicles to chronicles such that $Mod(\Upsilon) = Mod(\mathbf{G}(\Upsilon))$. An *entailment method* is a pair

$\langle \mathbf{G}, S \rangle$ where $\mathbf{G}$ is a pretransformation and S is a selection function whose arity corresponds to the structure of the chronicle. If S is unary, then an entailment method $\langle \mathbf{G}, S \rangle$ assigns the set $S[\mathbf{G}(\Upsilon)]$ of models to each chronicle Υ. It is *correct* for the chronicle Υ iff

$$S[\mathbf{G}(\Upsilon)] = Mod(\Upsilon).$$

Similarly, if S is a binary selection function, and $\mathbf{G}(\langle \Upsilon_1, \Upsilon_2 \rangle) = \langle \Upsilon_1', \Upsilon_2' \rangle$, then $\langle \mathbf{G}, S \rangle$ is correct for $\langle \Upsilon_1, \Upsilon_2 \rangle$ iff

$$S(\langle [\![\Upsilon_1']\!], [\![\Upsilon_2']\!] \rangle) = Mod(\langle \Upsilon_1, \Upsilon_2 \rangle).$$

Pretransformations may be used, for example, for adding timing statements which exclude concurrent execution of actions, if the intended models only allow sequentially executed actions.

In order to identify the range of applicability for an entailment method, one needs the following formal tools:

an underlying semantics, providing a formal definition of the set of intended models corresponding to each chronicle;

a taxonomy of chronicles, providing a "coordinate system" whereby one can characterize the range of applicability.

In the earlier publications I have defined the underlying semantics and the taxonomy for the case of strict inertia, together with precise formulations of the syntax and of the classical semantics, which are of course also needed.

The *purpose of the present paper* is to give an introduction to the systematic approach. I shall first *summarize* some of the earlier results, and describe the *conceptual framework* within which they have been developed. After that, I present some *new results* concerning generalizations to the case of inertia with ramification.

2   The Precise Structure of Chronicles

Ordinary logic analyzes what conclusions can be drawn from an unstructured set of premises (axioms). Since logics of actions and change tend to need partitioned premises, we introduce a general framework for accommodating such partitioning. Formally, a *chronicle in* $\mathcal{K}$ is a tuple

$$\langle \mathcal{K}, \mathtt{Diw}, \mathrm{SCD}, \mathrm{OBS} \rangle$$

where $\mathcal{K}$ is a code indicating the epistemological assumption of *complete knowledge about the actions* that accompanies the chronicle, $\mathtt{Diw}$ is a *world description* containing e.g. action laws, SCD is a set of formulae for the *schedule* characterizing the actions and their temporal relationships using action statements and timing statements, and OBS is a set of *observations* as introduced above.

The world-description component of the scenario is again a tuple whose first element characterizes the type of world. For the case of strict inertia, the world description will be assumed to be a twotuple $\langle IA, LAW \rangle$, were again **IA** is a code indicating the ontological assumption of strict inertia, and LAW is the set of action laws. A more general class of world descriptions is formed as threetuples $\langle IAD, LAW, DCS \rangle$, where **IAD** is a code for inertia with ramification, LAW is as before, and DCS is a set of *static domain constraints* of the general form

$$\forall t[\alpha],$$

where α is an expression formed only using the H predicate, and with t as the first argument. The following is an example of a static domain constraint:

$$\forall t[H(t, f_4, F) \Rightarrow H(t, f_6, G)],$$

where of course F must be a possible value for the feature f_4, and G must be a possible value for the feature f_6. This domain constraint says that in any state where f_4 has the value F, f_6 must have the value G.

The epistemological code $\mathcal{K}$ and the ontological codes **IA** and **IAD** belong to a broader reportoire of codes for characterizing epistemological and ontological assumptions. Each choice of assumptions and codes is associated with its own definition of intended models and, therefore, its own analysis of range of applicability for entailment methods.

The standard use of domain constraints is for ramification: the action law is supposed to specify the "essential" changes that are due to the action, and other changes are obtained implicitly as the (or a) minimal set(s) of additional changes that must be assumed in order to avoid getting into a state that violates some of the domain constraints.

The special case where DCS is the empty set reobtains strict inertia: since there are no domain constraints, there is never any reason to force additional value changes, so the only changes of feature values are those that are expressly stated in the action laws for expressly known actions. Therefore, a world description $\langle IA, LAW \rangle$ is equivalent to one of the form $\langle IAD, LAW, \rangle$.

For simplicity, we address only the "propositional" case where feature symbols f and action symbols E appear without arguments. In many applications it is necessary to reason about multiple objects with similar properties, for example several cars that move in the same environment, as well as actions that take one or more objects as arguments. However, this case is very often only "quasi-propositional" in the sense that each chronicle binds the object domain to a specific, finite size. The action laws need to be specified for arbitrary object domains, since they should be reusable in several chronicles, but reasoning about a particular chronicle is still essentially propositional. In [5] we have worked out the relatively straight-forward details of this generalization.

¿From a formal point of view, action laws will be understood as definitions of abbreviations, and not as first-class logical formulae. The action law in the introductory example,

$$D(s, t, \textit{make-coffee}) \Rightarrow H(t, \textit{coffee-hot}),$$

simply states that e.g. the action statement

$$D(20, 25, make\text{-}coffee)$$

is an abbreviation for

$$H(25, coffee\text{-}hot).$$

The purpose of dealing with action statements and action laws in this way is to avoid the need of saying, in formulae, that there are no other actions besides those stated in SCD. If LAW is a set of action laws in this sense, and SCD is a set of action and timing statements, then LAW[SCD] will represent the result of expanding all formulae in SCD using the definitions in LAW. From the point of view of a selection function, a $\mathcal{K}$-**IA** chronicle therefore contains two premise sets, LAW[SCD] and OBS. Its classical model set is [LAW[SCD]] ∩ [OBS]. An entailment method $\langle \mathbf{G}, S \rangle$ for $\mathcal{K}$-**IA** chronicles assigns

$$S([\![\text{LAW}'[\text{SCD}']]\!], [\![\text{OBS}']\!])$$

as the set of selected models for a given chronicle

$$\langle \mathcal{K}, \langle \mathbf{IA}, \text{LAW} \rangle, \text{SCD}, \text{OBS} \rangle,$$

provided that

$$\langle \mathcal{K}, \langle \mathbf{IA}, \text{LAW}' \rangle, \text{SCD}', \text{OBS}' \rangle = \mathbf{G}(\langle \mathcal{K}, \langle \mathbf{IA}, \text{LAW} \rangle, \text{SCD}, \text{OBS} \rangle).$$

Similarly, an entailment method $\langle \mathbf{G}, S \rangle$ for $\mathcal{K}$-**IAD** chronicles requires S to be ternary, and assigns

$$S([\![\text{LAW}'[\text{SCD}']]\!], [\![\text{OBS}']\!], [\![\text{DCS}']\!])$$

as the set of selected models for a given chronicle

$$\langle \mathcal{K}, \langle \mathbf{IAD}, \text{LAW}, \text{DCS} \rangle, \text{SCD}, \text{OBS} \rangle,$$

provided that

$$\langle \mathcal{K}, \langle \mathbf{IAD}, \text{LAW}', \text{DCS}' \rangle, \text{SCD}', \text{OBS}' \rangle = \mathbf{G}(\langle \mathcal{K}, \langle \mathbf{IA}, \text{LAW}, \text{DCS} \rangle, \text{SCD}, \text{OBS} \rangle).$$

3   Trajectory Semantics

The *underlying semantics* for a class of chronicles defines the set of *intended models* for chronicles in that class. We shall first define it for $\mathcal{K}$-**IA** chronicles, and later generalize it to $\mathcal{K}$-**IAD** chronicles.

3.1 Simple IDS Worlds

A similarity type σ is a mapping from feature symbols to the set of possible values for the feature. The set of feature symbols f that are defined by a given σ will be written $\mathcal{F}_\sigma$. A *state* for a given similarity type σ is a mapping which to each feature symbol f assigns a corresponding value i.e. a member of $\sigma[f]$. The set $\mathcal{R}_\sigma$ for given σ is the set of possible states for σ.

Let also $\mathcal{E}$ be a set of *action symbols*, like *make-coffee* in the trivial example. A *complete trajectory* v is a finite non-empty sequence of states in $\mathcal{R}_\sigma$. A *simple IDS world* is a mapping W from $\mathcal{E} \times \mathcal{R}_\sigma$ to non-empty sets of complete trajectories.

A *finite history* from time 0 to n (now) is a mapping from integers in the interval $[0, n]$ to complete states.

A *simple IDS game* is played between an *ego* and a simple IDS world, in the following fashion. At each step in the game, there is an integer *current time* n and a *current history* h which is a mapping from the closed interval $[0, n]$ to $\mathcal{R}_\sigma$. Initially, the current time is 0, the current history assigns some initial state to 0, and the ego has the move. Each time the ego has the move, it may choose to invoke an action, i.e., a member of $\mathcal{E}$, or to do nothing. If the ego invokes an action E at time n with the current history h, the world's move is to select some trajectory $v \in W(E, h(n))$, that is, one of the trajectories that the world admits for the present state of the world, $h(n)$, and the currently chosen action E. The world then increases n by the length of v, and concatenates v at the end of h. If the ego chooses not to make any move, then the world defines $h(n + 1)$ as $h(n)$ and increases n by 1. In either case the move is then returned to the ego.

This definition of a world and of the ego-world game is a specialization, with a trivial reformulation, of how those concepts were defined in [5]. Note that the definition of simple IDS worlds is a straight-forward variant and generalization of finite-state automata, with the following specific properties:

- Structured states, since a state is assumed to be a vector of "state variables".
- Non-determinism: several "moves" are possible for the world.
- Metric time: the result of an action is a sequence of states rather than a single state.

The game is open to choice both for the ego (which has a choice of actions at each step) and for the world (which may have more than one trajectory for a given action and starting state). Different choices result in different games. Each game results in an (infinite) *history* H, that is, a mapping from the non-negative integers to states in $\mathcal{R}_\sigma$. An *interpretation* is a pair $\langle M, H \rangle$, where M assigns values to temporal constant symbols, and H is a history. The truth of an observation or a timing statement in an interpretation is defined in the obvious way. An action statement $D(s, t, E)$ is said to *be satisfied* in an interpretation $\langle M, H \rangle$ iff there is some game that results in the history H, and the action E was invoked at time $M[s]$ in that game, and the world then selected a trajectory of length $M[t] - M[s]$. A set of action statements is said to be satisfied in an interpretation $\langle M, H \rangle$ iff there is some game, resulting in H, such that all the given action statements and no others are satisfied for $\langle M, H \rangle$ in that game.

The set of *intended models* $Mod(\Upsilon)$ for a given **IA** chronicle

$$\Upsilon = \langle \mathcal{K}, \langle \mathbf{IA}, \text{LAW} \rangle, \text{SCD}, \text{OBS} \rangle$$

is defined as the set of those interpretations $\langle M, H \rangle$

- which are obtained from a game between a world W which is correctly characterized by LAW, and an arbitrary ego, from an arbitrary starting state; and
- which satisfy all the observations in OBS and all the timing statements in SCD; and
- where the set of action statements in SCD is satisfied.

A chronicle contains a world description based on action laws LAW, but the definition of intended models for such a chronicle uses the ego-world game, where the world is defined as a mapping W assigning sets of trajectories to action symbols. It remains to relate the action-law characterization LAW and the trajectory characterization W of a world. The important difference, of course, is that the action law only specifies those features that *change* in the course of the action, or even a subset of them, whereas the trajectory is constructed out of complete states and therefore specifies the new values for all the features in $\mathcal{F}$.

3.2   World Descriptions for Strict Inertia

In order to define how action laws LAW correctly characterize a world W, we shall complement *logical world descriptions* which consist of logic formulae, with *set-theoretic world descriptions*. In either case, a world description is a more compact version of the original trajectory characterization. There are straightforward ways of relating worlds (W) and set-theoretic world descriptions, and the latter are in turn related (by a simple syntactic transformation) to action laws in the logical world description.

We first consider world descriptions of type **IA**, that is, world descriptions which are based on an assumption of strict inertia. First some auxiliary definitions. If $F \subseteq \mathcal{F}_\sigma$, then a *partial trajectory* for F is a finite nonempty sequence of partial states each of which is defined exactly for the features in F. A *world description* for **IA**, then, is a tuple

$$\langle \mathbf{IA}, \textit{Infl}, \textit{Rtrajs} \rangle,$$

where **IA** is a code indicating the type of world description, *Infl* ("influenced features") is a mapping which for each combination of action symbol and starting state returns a subset of $\mathcal{F}$, and *Rtrajs* ("reduced trajectories") is a mapping from action symbols times states such that $\textit{Rtrajs}(E, r)$ is a non-empty set of partial trajectories for $\textit{Infl}(E, r)$.

Let $r \ddagger F$ be the partial state obtained from the total state r and the set F of features by restricting r so that it is only defined for members of F. Also, let $v \ddagger F$ be the partial trajectory obtained from the total trajectory v by restricting each element to F. For a given, simple IDS world W and a given function $Infl$, the *corresponding* **IA** world description $\langle \mathbf{IA}, Infl, Rtrajs \rangle$ is obtained by choosing

$$Rtrajs(E,r) = \{v \updownarrow Infl(E,r) \mid v \in W(E,r)\},$$

that is, by restricting each trajectory in $W(E,r)$ to those features indicated in $Infl(E,r)$.

Let $\oplus$ be the override operator, so that if r is a total state and r' is a partial state, then $r \oplus r'$ is the total state assigning the same value as r' whenever defined, and otherwise the value assigned by r. If r is a total state and v' is a partial trajectory, then $r \oplus v'$ is the total trajectory defined similarly.

Now, if W is a simple IDS world, and the world description $\langle \mathbf{IA}, Infl, Rtrajs \rangle$ is formed from W, then this world description *conserves* W iff

$$W(E,r) = \{r \oplus v' \mid v' \in Rtrajs(E,r)\},$$

that is, if one can take the partial trajectories in $Rtrajs(E,r)$, extend every partial state in each of those trajectories by assigning, for each feature that does not have a value, the value that it has in r, and if one then gets back the original world W.

Evidently, for a given W, if $Infl$ is chosen so that it at least contains all members f of $\mathcal{F}_\sigma$ which change their value in some trajectory in $W(E,r)$, then the corresponding world description $\langle \mathbf{IA}, Infl, Rtrajs \rangle$ conserves W.

Let a world W be given, and choose a corresponding world description $\langle \mathbf{IA}, Infl, Rtrajs \rangle$ which conserves W. In [5] we defined, in syntactic terms, the transformation from such a world description to an equivalent world description of the form $\langle \mathbf{IA}, \text{LAW} \rangle$, where LAW is a set of action laws as exemplified in section 1 here. We say that $\langle \mathbf{IA}, \text{LAW} \rangle$ *correctly characterizes* a world W iff it is formed, in the way defined in [5], from a world description that conserves W.

3.3   Summary of transformations

The successive shifts of representation that were described above can be summarized as follows.

1. Start with a world $W(E,r)$.
2. Select a suitable $Infl$ function for W.
3. Construct $Rtrajs$ from W and $Infl$, and obtain the set-theoretic world description $\langle \mathbf{IA}, Infl, Rtrajs \rangle$. Require that it conserves W.
4. Convert it to the corresponding logical world description $\langle \mathbf{IA}, \text{LAW} \rangle$, where the action laws in LAW are considered as abbreviations.
5. Use the logical world description (repeatedly) in chronicles of the form

$$\Upsilon = \langle \mathcal{K}, \langle \mathbf{IA}, \text{LAW} \rangle, \text{SCD}, \text{OBS} \rangle.$$

6. The set of intended models $Mod(\Upsilon)$ for such a chronicle is defined using W, SCD, and OBS.

7. The set of selected models for the chronicle according to an entailment method $\langle \mathbf{G}, S \rangle$ is defined as $S([\text{LAW}'[\text{SCD}']], [\text{OBS}'])$, where $\mathbf{G}$ transforms SCD to SCD$'$, and similarly for the others. The particular $\mathbf{G}_{\text{seq}}$ used below adds some more formulae to SCD, and leaves the other components unchanged.

This definition is usable even if Υ is given, so that one starts in step 5, since the previous steps are reversible. A given LAW identifies a corresponding W uniquely.

4   Simple Approaches to Strict Inertia

4.1   Preference-Order Compatibility

For the characterization of range of applicability, we need the following concepts. If r is a state and v is a trajectory of length j, then $r; v$ is the trajectory of length $j+1$ obtained by adding r as the first element in v. (In other words, the semicolon is used as a "cons" operator).

Let $\ll_m$ be a preference relation on interpretations $\langle M, H \rangle$ which is well-defined even if H is a finite history, and which is always false when comparing histories of unequal length. We wish to use $\ll_m$ for comparing members of $Rtrajs(E, r)$, but there is a technical problem since $\ll_m$ compares interpretations and not trajectories.

Technically, therefore, M_0 is defined as a placeholder valuation which assigns the value 0 to every temporal constant symbol. The *corresponding model function* for a world W is defined by

$$Cmf(E, r) = \{\langle M_0, (r; v) \rangle \mid v \in W(E, r)\}.$$

More general versions of *Cmf* will appear later on, so this is just the simplest case for the purpose of introduction. It works as follows: for given E and r we construct one interpretation for each trajectory in $W(E, r)$, but we prefix it with r, and add a harmless M component. Then, a simple IDS world W is said to be *m-compatible* iff

$$I \not\ll_m I'$$

whenever I and I' are two members of $Cmf(E, r)$ for some E and r. It follows at once that strictly deterministic worlds, defined as those where $W(E, r)$ is a singleton for each combination of E and r, are m-compatible for arbitrary $\ll_m$.

4.2   Prototypical Chronological Minimization, PCM

The method of prototypical chronological minimization (PCM) is a slightly corrected variant of an entailment method that was first proposed by Kautz [2] and Shoham [9]. The preference relation $\ll_{\text{pcm}}$ is defined so that $\langle M, H \rangle \ll_{\text{pcm}} \langle M', H' \rangle$ iff $M = M'$ and there is some $\mathbf{t}$ such that

1. $H(t) = H'(t)$ for all $t < \mathbf{t}$;
2. $\text{Diff}(H(\mathbf{t} - 1), H(\mathbf{t})) \subset \text{Diff}(H'(\mathbf{t} - 1), H'(\mathbf{t}))$;

where
$$\text{Diff}(r, r') = \{f \mid r[f] \neq r'[f]\},$$
that is, the set of features where r and r' differ. The entailment method PCM for $\mathcal{K}$-**IA** is defined as $\langle \mathbf{G}_{seq}, S_{pcm} \rangle$, where $\mathbf{G}_{seq}$ adds sequentiality premises to the schedule part of the given chronicle, and
$$S_{pcm}(A, B) = Min(\ll_{pcm}, A \cap B).$$

Assessment: it was proved in [6] that PCM is correct for all chronicles Υ satisfying the following three assumptions:

- The world represented in the LAW part of Υ must be PCM-compatible.
- The world represented in the LAW part must also be *equidurational*, meaning that the set of possible durations of an action must be independent of the starting state.
- The OBS partition may not contain any observations for times other than 0.

We notice that if $\langle$**IA**, *Infl, Rtrajs*$\rangle$ is formed from and conserves W, then W is PCM-compatible iff *Rtrajs* is. The first and second requirements are *ontological* ones, in the sense that they are requirements on the world that is involved in the scenario. It was proved in [5] that these two requirements are not only sufficient but also necessary, in the sense that for any world W that does not satisfy both of these requirements, there exists some schedule Υ using W for which PCM does not give the intended set of models.

The third requirement is *epistemological*, in the sense that it specifies restrictions on our knowledge about the world rather than on the world itself. It is sufficient but not necessary.

All three requirements are undesirable from the point of view of practical usage. The third requirement can be removed using the technique of *filtering*. This is the topic of the next subsection.

4.3 Prototypical Chronological Minimization with Filtering, PCMF

The entailment method PCMF for $\mathcal{K}$-**IA** is defined as $\langle \mathbf{G}_{seq}, S_{pcmf} \rangle$, where $\mathbf{G}_{seq}$ is as before, and
$$S_{pcmf}(A, B) = Min(\ll_{pcm}, A) \cap B.$$
It was proved in [6] that PCMF is correct for all chronicles Υ satisfying the first two assumptions for the correctness of PCM, that is,

- The world represented in the LAW part of Υ must be PCM-compatible.
- The world represented in the LAW part must also be *equidurational*, meaning that the set of possible durations of an action must be independent of the starting state.

It was also shown that these requirements are necessary as well as sufficient. The removal of the third requirement of PCM means that PCMF is also applicable for *postdiction* and not only for prediction. Postdiction arises e.g. in diagnostic reasoning.

5   Strict Inertia with Occlusion

5.1   Occlusion

The restriction of PCM-compatibility is harmless for deterministic actions, but it excludes many cases of nondeterministic actions. Several methods have been proposed for lifting this restriction. One such technique is to use *occlusion*, which means effectively that the *Infl* component of the set-theoretic world description is represented explicitly in the models, so that it is also accessible for preference relations and selection functions. The following is an outline of how the framework of the previous section has to be revised for this purpose.

The definition of an interpretation is revised so that it is a triple $\langle M, H, X \rangle$, where the first two components are like before, and the third component is a mapping from features times timepoints to truth-values. The formulation of the action laws for a given world description $\langle IA, Infl, Rtrajs \rangle$ is revised so that if an action statement $D(s, t, E)$ applies in an interpretation $\langle M, H, X \rangle$, and the feature f is a member of $Infl(E, H(s))$, then $X(f, u)$ is forced to be true for every u in the interval $[s + 1, t]$. The intention is that if $X(f, u)$ is true then one makes an exception from the principle of inertia so as to allow a change in the value of f between time $u - 1$ and time u.

This extension of the structure of classical models makes it possible for preference relations and selection functions to use their X component. At the same time, there is a structural mismatch since intended models still have the simpler structure $\langle M, H \rangle$. We therefore introduce the coercion function Ci such that

$$Ci(W) = \{\langle M, H \rangle \mid \exists X [\langle M, H, X \rangle \in W]\}.$$

An entailment method $\langle G, S \rangle$ is then defined to be correct for a chronicle Υ of the usual $\mathcal{K}$-**IA** structure iff

$$Ci(S([\![LAW[SCD]]\!], [\![OBS]\!])) = Mod(\Upsilon).$$

The remaining technical details of this machinery can be found in [5]. Notice that action laws can only force $X(f, u)$ to be true at certain points; they can not force it to be false at all other points. Therefore, one needs some other device, such as minimization, in order to avoid X being true at unintended points.

5.2   Chronological Minimization of Occlusion and Change, CMOC

The entailment method CMOC for $\mathcal{K}$-**IA** (chronological minimization of occlusion and change) makes use of occlusion in order to eliminate the restrictions limiting nondeterminism. The preference relation $\ll_{cmoc}$ is defined so that $\langle M, H, X \rangle \ll_{cmoc} \langle M', H', X' \rangle$ iff $M = M'$ and there is some t such that

1. $H(t) = H'(t)$ and $X(t) = X'(t)$ for all $t < t$;
2. Either of the following holds:
    (a) $X(t) \subset X'(t)$, or

(b) $X(t) = X'(t)$, and
$$\text{Diff}(H(t-1), H(t)) - X(t) \subset \text{Diff}(H'(t-1), H'(t)) - X(t).$$

Here, $X(t)$ represents the set of those features f for which $X(f, t)$ is true. The effect of $\ll_{cmoc}$ is to chronologically minimize changes in *unoccluded* features. The entailment method CMOC is defined using filtering as $\langle \mathbf{G}_{seq}, S_{cmoc} \rangle$, where $\mathbf{G}_{seq}$ is like before, and
$$S_{cmoc}(A, B) = Min(\ll_{cmoc}, A) \cap B.$$

The assessment of this entailment method is as follows. It was proved in [6] that CMOC is correct for all equidurational chronicles, and that this requirement is not only sufficient but also necessary, in the same sense of necessary as for PCM.

5.3 Other Entailment Methods

A number of other entailment methods have been assessed in [5]. Some of them involve pretransformations that are more complex than $\mathbf{G}_{seq}$; others involve more complex preference relations. Their assessments often involve preference-order compatibility or other similar constraints.

6 Inertia with Ramification

The framework that has been described so far will now be extended to the case of inertia with ramification. These are new results.

6.1 World Descriptions for Inertia with Ramification

A logical world description for a world with ramification is $\langle \mathbf{IAD}, \text{LAW}, \text{DCS} \rangle$, that is, a threetuple as already specified above. Here LAW is a set of action laws of the same kind as for the **IA** case, and DCS is a set of static domain constraints. The corresponding set-theoretic formulation of an **IAD** world description is now introduced as a tuple $\langle \mathbf{IAD}, \textit{Infl}, \textit{Rtrajs}, \mathcal{R}_C, \textit{Dep} \rangle$, where the first three components are like before. $\mathcal{R}_C$ is a subset of $\mathcal{R}_\sigma$, and is intended as the set of states which are acceptable in view of the static domain constraints. Thus, $\mathcal{R}_C$ is effectively the set of models for DCS, but represented simply as states and without the temporal dimension.

Furthermore, *Dep* is a function from action symbols times states to sets of features, such that $Dep(E, r)$ and $\textit{Infl}(E, r)$ are disjoint sets. It is intended that $Dep(E, r)$ shall contain those features whose values are determined by the static domain constraints, so that the changes in these features need not be specified by the action laws and should not be subject to minimization.

The functions *Infl* and *Dep* together divide $\mathcal{F}$ into three partitions:

occluded features: members of $\textit{Infl}(E, r)$;
dependent features: members of $Dep(E, r)$;
remanent features: not members of either $\textit{Infl}(E, r)$ or $Dep(E, r)$.

In rough terms, dependent features correspond to the "non-frame" features of Kartha and Lifschitz, and occluded features correspond to their "frame, released" features [1]. For a more precise comparison, and for a motivation for the use of these partitions, please refer to [7].

In the case of **IA**, we were able to replace a world W by a world description $\langle \text{IA}, \text{LAW} \rangle$ that conserved W, and then use the world description as the basis for the logical treatment. Therefore, the step from W to the world description was independent of the preference relation. This is not the case for **IAD** world descriptions: the basic idea here is to allow, for a given W, a function $Infl(E, r)$ which is so restrictive that it omits some features which actually change their values in some trajectories in $W(E, r)$, but to rely on the static domain constraints and the minimization of change for recovering the lost information.

We write $\mathcal{R}_C^*$ for the set of all (finite) trajectories and (infinite) histories consisting exclusively of states in $\mathcal{R}_C$. A world W is said to *preserve* a set $\mathcal{R}_C \subseteq \mathcal{R}_\sigma$ iff $W(E, r) \subseteq \mathcal{R}_C^*$ for every $r \in \mathcal{R}_C$ and every action symbol E.

Let $\mathcal{R}_C$ and a world W preserving $\mathcal{R}_C$ be given. For given functions $Infl$ and Dep of the kinds defined above, the *corresponding* **IAD** world description is the fivetuple

$$\langle \textbf{IAD}, Infl, Rtrajs, \mathcal{R}_C, Dep \rangle,$$

where $Rtrajs$ is obtained from W just like before, by restricting all trajectories to their occluded features. Formally,

$$Rtrajs(E, r) = \{v \ddagger Infl(E, r) \mid v \in W(E, r)\}.$$

In the corresponding logic-formula variant of the world description,

$$\langle \textbf{IAD}, \text{LAW}, \text{DCS} \rangle,$$

DCS is obtained from $\mathcal{R}_C$, and LAW is obtained from the other components in such a way that interpretations have the form $\langle M, H, X, Y \rangle$, where M, H, and X are like before, and Y is analogous to X but for the Dep component. Thus, $Y(f, t)$ shall be true iff the feature f is a member of $Dep(E, r)$ where E is being executed at time t. The definition of the coercion function Ci is adjusted accordingly.

Intended models are defined like before, using W. Selection functions for $\mathcal{K}$-**IAD** shall take three arguments, and assign

$$S([\text{LAW}[\text{SCD}]], [\text{OBS}], [\text{DCS}])$$

as the set of selected models for a given chronicle $\langle \mathcal{K}, \langle \textbf{IA}, \text{LAW}, \text{DCS} \rangle, \text{SCD}, \text{OBS} \rangle$. Clearly [DCS] consists of the infinite members of $\mathcal{R}_C^*$.

6.2   Preferential Conservation

The preferential conservation concept combines the functions of "conservation" and "compatibility" which were used for **IA** ontology. The basic idea is that a world description is m-conservative for a given W iff one can reconstruct the originally given world using minimization with the preference relation $\ll_m$. Notice that it is the combination of a world and a world *description* (that is, essentially, a set of action laws for the world) that is m-conservative, and not the world itself.

The specifics are as follows. Let

$$\text{Diw} = \langle \mathbf{IAD}, \textit{Infl}, \textit{Rtrajs}, \mathcal{R}_C, \textit{Dep} \rangle$$

be a world description corresponding to a world W that preserves $\mathcal{R}_C$. For each combination of E and r, we are to construct two sets of finite models, each finite model being a tuple $\langle M, H, X, Y \rangle$ where H is a history for a finite interval $[0, k]$ of time. The given world description is m-conservative iff those two sets are equal.

The first set is defined using a generalization of the corresponding model function Cmf. If F is a set of feature symbols, $F^\bullet$ is a function such that $F^\bullet(f, t)$ is true iff $f \in F$, for arbitrary integer $t > 0$. Then the function Cmf is adapted to read

$$Cmf(E, r) = \{ \langle M_0, (r; v), \textit{Infl}(E, r)^\bullet, \textit{Dep}(E, r)^\bullet \rangle \mid v \in W(E, r) \}.$$

Comparing this to the old definition in Subsection 4.1, we notice that the new one depends on Diw and not only on W.

Secondly, for given Diw with the structure indicated above, we define the *expanded trajectories function* as

$$Xtf(E, r) = \{ \langle M_0, (r; v), Infl(E, r)^\bullet, Dep(E, r)^\bullet \rangle \mid$$

$$v \ddagger Infl(E, r) \in Rtrajs(E, r) \wedge v \in \mathcal{R}_C^* \}.$$

In other words, as we went from W to *Rtrajs* by removing the values for all features outside $Infl(E, r)$, we now go back by allowing those features to vary freely within only the constraints of $\mathcal{R}_C$. It follows at once that

$$Cmf(E, r) \subseteq Xtf(E, r)$$

for every E and r. We say that the given world description is m-*conservative* for a given world iff

$$Cmf(E, r) = Min(\ll_m, Xtf(E, r))$$

for all E and r. This means that the preference relation $\ll_m$ is able to recover the information that was lost when W was "projected" to obtain *Rtrajs*. Notice that the property of being m-conservative is a property of the world *description*, and not of the world itself, since it depends on the choice of *Infl*, $\mathcal{R}_C$, and *Dep*.

6.3   Chronological Preferential Entailment

The entailment methods MRC and MRCC are natural generalizations of CMOC allowing ramification. MRC stands for *Minimal Remanent Change*, and MRCC stands for *Minimal Remanent Change with Changeset-partitioning*; they are defined as follows. The preference relation $\ll_{mrc}$ is defined so that

$$\langle M, H, X, Y \rangle \ll_{mrc} \langle M', H', X', Y' \rangle$$

iff $M = M'$ and there is some t such that all of the following hold:

1. $H(t) = H'(t)$, $X(t) = X'(t)$, and $Y(t) = Y'(t)$ for all $t < \mathsf{t}$.
2. Either of the following holds:
   (a) $X(\mathsf{t}) \subset X'(\mathsf{t})$;
   (b) $X(\mathsf{t}) = X'(\mathsf{t})$ and $Y(\mathsf{t}) \subset Y'(\mathsf{t})$;
   (c) $X(\mathsf{t}) = X'(\mathsf{t})$, $Y(\mathsf{t}) = Y'(\mathsf{t})$, and
       $\mathtt{Diff}(H(\mathsf{t}-1), H(\mathsf{t})) - R(\mathsf{t}) \subset \mathtt{Diff}(H'(\mathsf{t}-1), H'(\mathsf{t})) - R(\mathsf{t})$,
       where $R(t) = X(t) \cup Y(t)$.

Then MRC is defined as $\langle \mathbf{G}_{seq}, S_{mrc} \rangle$ using

$$S_{mrc}(A, B, C) = Min(\ll_{mrc}, A \cap C) \cap B.$$

The preference relation $\ll_{mrcc}$ is defined in a similar fashion, except that the last subitem in the definition is

- $X(\mathsf{t}) = X'(\mathsf{t})$, $Y(\mathsf{t}) = Y'(\mathsf{t})$, $H(\mathsf{t}) \ddagger X(\mathsf{t}) = H'(\mathsf{t}) \ddagger X(\mathsf{t})$, and
  $\mathtt{Diff}(H(\mathsf{t}-1), H(\mathsf{t})) - R(\mathsf{t}) \subset \mathtt{Diff}(H'(\mathsf{t}-1), H'(\mathsf{t})) - R(\mathsf{t})$.

The selection function S_{mrcc} and the entailment method MRCC itself are defined as analogous with MRC.

The basic idea in these two entailment methods is to do chronological minimization of changes in remanent features, while not minimizing changes in occluded or dependent features. Changes in occluded features are supposed to be specified by the action laws, and are not to be minimized. This is instrumental for dealing systematically with nondeterministic actions.

Changes in dependent features are forced by the domain constraints, and are also not subject to minimization in these methods. One might think that minimization of changes in dependent features is harmless, since such features are typically completely determined by the values of other features. However, well-known scenario problems such as the Aunt Agatha Livingroom [10] and the Double Switch scenarios [3] have shown that one may obtain unintended tradeoffs between changes in remanent and in dependent features, thereby introducing unintended selected models.

These two entailment methods give the same result for strictly deterministic actions. They differ for non-deterministic actions, where MRCC will minimize changes in remanent features separately for each outcome in occluded features, whereas MRC will minimize changes in remanent features jointly for all outcomes in occluded features.

The MRC entailment method is a generalization of the defined semantics for the language $\mathcal{AR}_0$ by Kartha and Lifschitz [1].

The assessment proofs for PCM and CMOC can easily be adapted to show that MRC is correct for equidurational chronicles containing MRC-conservative world descriptions, and similarly for MRCC. Neither one of MRC-conservativeness or MRCC-conservativeness subsumes the other, since it is easy to construct a world description that is MRC-conservative but not MRCC-conservative, and vice versa [7].

The case of strictly inert world descriptions can be obtained easily, by choosing $Dep(E, r) = $ for all E and r, and $\mathcal{R}_C = \mathcal{R}_\sigma$. It is trivial that every strictly inert world description that conserves a world W is MRC- and MRCC-conservative for W. Therefore, every world has *some* MRC- and MRCC-conservative description, which can be obtained by including sufficiently many features in $Infl(E, r)$. In particular, if one includes all features whose values may change in the course of the action, strict inertia is obtained, and both MRC- and MRCC-conservation is achieved trivially. From a practical point of view, however, one presumably wishes to keep $Infl(E, r)$ as small as possible, in order to make the corresponding action law as compact as possible.

In this context, it was demonstrated in [7] that for single-timestep actions, MRCC has an interesting monotonicity property: if

$$\langle \mathbf{IAD}, Infl, Rtrajs, \mathcal{R}_C, Dep \rangle$$

is an MRCC-conservative world description corresponding to a world W, $Infl'$ satisfies $Infl(E, r) \subseteq Infl'(E, r)$ for all E and r, and $Rtrajs'$ is formed from $Infl'$, then

$$\langle \mathbf{IAD}, Infl', Rtrajs', \mathcal{R}_C, Dep \rangle$$

is also MRCC-conservative with respect to W. (The generalization to actions with arbitrary finite duration seems to be straight-forward). This result means that if one starts with the full world W and gradually reduces the extent of $Infl$, then the resulting world descriptions are at first MRCC-conservative, but if one reaches a point where the world description is not MRCC-conservative, and one then continues to reduce the extent of $Infl$, one will never again get back to an MRCC-conservative world description. MRC does not have the same monotonicity property.

In other words, the concept of a "smallest MRCC-conservative $Infl$ function" is well defined for each choice of W, $\mathcal{R}_C$, and Dep. This result is of interest since in practice, one likes to involve as few features as possible in the action laws. It would be convenient to have an algorithm which takes a specification of W and obtains, in the form of action laws, the smallest MRCC-conservative action laws by minimizing the extent of $Infl$. The monotonicity result means that it is meaningful to look for such an algorithm.

7   The Systematic Approach: Current Developments

In this paper, I have tried to present, in very condensed form, the *conceptual framework* that is used in the *systematic approach* to logics of actions and change.

The complete presentation of that framework can be obtained in the monograph
[5]. The basic approach is presently being extended in a number of directions,
allowing for concurrency, ramification, faulty observations, etc. There is also considerable work on implementation methods for some of the assessed entailment
methods. The present paper has only showed current work in one direction,
namely for ramification.

An up-to-date overview of the state of the art in this research can be obtained
from the following WWW page:

```
http://www.ida.liu.se/labs/rkllab/groups/FF/
```

which contains an overview of current results and links to current articles.

References

1. G. Neelakantan Kartha and V. Lifschitz. Actions with indirect effects (preliminary
   report). In *International Conference on Knowledge Representation and Reasoning*,
   pages 341–350, 1994.
2. H. Kautz. The logic of persistence. In *Proc. 6th National Conference on Artificial
   Intelligence*, AAAI-86, pages 401–405, 1986.
3. V. Lifschitz. Restricted monotonicity. In *Proc. 11th National Conference on
   Artificial Intelligence*, AAAI-93, pages 432–437, 1993.
4. J. McCarthy and P. Hayes. Some philosophical problems from the viewpoint of
   artificial intelligence. In *Machine Intelligence, Vol. 4*, pages 463–502. Edinburgh
   University Press, 1969.
5. E. Sandewall. *Features and Fluents. The Representation of Knowledge about Dynamical Systems. Volume I.* Oxford University Press, 1994.
6. E. Sandewall. The range of applicability of some non-monotonic logics for strict
   inertia. *Journal of Logic and Computation*, 4:5 (1994) pp. 581-615.
7. E. Sandewall. Systematic comparison of approaches to ramification using restricted
   minimization of change. Technical Report LiTH-IDA-R-95-15, IDA, 1995.
8. E. Sandewall and Y. Shoham. Non-monotonic temporal reasoning. In D.M. Gab-
   bay, C.J. Hogger, and J.A. Robinson (Eds.), *Handbook of Logic in Artificial Intelligence and Logic Programming*, Vol. 4: Epistemic an Temporal Reasoning, Oxford
   Science Publ., Clarendon Press, Oxford, 1995, pp. 439-498.
9. Y. Shoham. *Reasoning about Change*. The MIT Press, 1988.
10. M. Winslett. Reasoning about actions using a possible models approach. In *Proc.
    7th National Conference on Artificial Intelligence*, AAAI-88, pages 89–93, 1988.

Trends in Active Vision

Jan-Olof Eklundh

Computational Vision and Active Perception Laboratory (CVAP)
Department of Numerical Analysis and Computing Science
KTH (Royal Institute of Technology), S-100 44 Stockholm, Sweden
Email: joe@bion.kth.se

Abstract. Active, or animate, computer vision regards the visual process as an active and task-oriented process over time. It also emphasizes the strong ties between perception and action that one can observe among seeing creatures. This paradigm has emerged over the past decade, and the article reviews its background, as well as progress made and noticeable trends. Although progress so far is limited, both concerning theoretical foundations and practical implementations, the field addresses key issues about seeing systems. Active vision is therefore likely to have substantial impact on our understanding of computational vision as well as of intelligent agents.

1 Introduction

"What does it mean to see? The plain man's answer (and Aristotle's too) would be to know what is where by looking. In other words, vision is the process of discovering from images what is present in the world and where it is". This is the definition of what seeing means that the late David Marr gave in the beginning of his seminal book "Vision" (Marr 1982), which has had a great influence on research in both biological and computational vision. However, such a definition does not capture the fact that we generally use vision to guide our activities and that it hence has a strong tie to behavior. Both our acquisition of visual information, i.e. what we look at, and what information we explicitly extract is largely dependent on the task at hand, be it to move from one point to another, to grasp something or to look for an object. Hence, we use vision in our interaction with the environment, and we do so in an active and purposive manner: we direct our gaze, we track and attend to features and events selectively on the basis of our needs and goals. Over the past decade research in computer vision has emphasized such aspects. Nelson (1991) appropriately noted that: "...In its broadest form this theme states that understanding the phenomenon of intelligence and discovering how to produce an artificial one must proceed in the context of behavior. Applied to machine vision, this theme has produced a paradigm variously referred to as animate, behavioral, or active vision..."

Several arguments for and against such a view have been forwarded, in computer vision as well as in artificial intelligence. We will only repeat these in passing, while elaborating on the question of what computer vision research is really about. The main purpose of this paper is to highlight the accomplishments made during ten years of research in active vision.

2   Computer Vision and Seeing

The aim of biological vision research is obvious: to study and acquire an understanding of existing visual systems. However, computer vision research has a less clear goal. Probably most researchers would subscribe to the idea that we want to understand and develop principles for computer-based seeing systems. Of course, others would say that they study computational principles for biological vision, but that places the effort in the realm of biological vision and must again be related to the study of *such systems*.

In any case there is a wide variety of vision systems in nature, from highly specialized ones to others with very general functionalities. In the same sense one could talk about machine vision systems of many types. They could be designed to solve very specific problems, like dedicated systems for visually guided autonomous navigation or robot manipulation.

Alternatively, they could be systems using vision in a large number of different tasks and under highly varying circumstances, like we observe among the primates. While it in the former case would be natural to design the systems deriving the constraints from the task at hand, approaches with different emphasis have been advocated in the latter case.

Until the past few years the prevailing view was that the recovery of scene structure in terms of surfaces and volumes and their properties was a key step towards general purpose vision. In reaction to this so-called reconstructionist approach, Aloimonos (1990), stressed the purposiveness of perception, while Ballard (1991) and others put the behaviors in focus, arguing that general purpose capabilities could be obtained by combining such behaviors, e.g. in a layered architecture in the spirit of Brooks (1991), or by adding components of learning. Others still have explicitly focused on seeing systems that combine the flexibility and performance of the human visual system. It is important to note that unless we specify the capabilities and behaviors of the system we aim at (note, there exists no such system), it is unclear what sensor structure it should have and what activities it should be engaged in. If human vision is the yardstick by which performance is measured then anthropomorphic features become essential. On the other hand a system capable of, say, catching moving prey aided by vision, e.g. mimicking a frog catching flies, can also be of interest. However, our understanding of such behaviors is useful to machine vision only if it can be applied together with other desirable behaviors.

Vision, as we observe it in nature, is trivially active, both because it is tied to action and in the sense that it has to respond to dynamical changes in the world surrounding the visual agent. However, as argued by Pahlavan *et al.* (1993), this does not by itself exclude the interest or use of "passive" or "reconstructionist" approaches. It is true that for most of the tasks we want to solve using vision all but a small fraction of the potentially available visual information is irrelevant. Nevertheless, this does not imply that active vision is the only way to address these problems. At the same time the importance of the active vision approach follows from a methodological argument: if we want to study computer-based seeing systems it is natural to study them in the context of active and purposive behaviors, because this is how the only seeing systems we know about, the biological ones, function.

As explained in the cited paper, such a perspective puts constraints on what information is available, on the possible algorithms and on what should be computed. A more elaborate analysis of the same type of problems, although from a different viewpoint, has been presented by Tsotsos (1995). Notwithstanding that, many problems remain at the level of computational theory, as Marr expressed it.

To summarize one can say that active or animate vision is the appropriate methodology for the study of computer vision, but nevertheless more traditional approaches are needed to address competence problems about what information is available and how it can be computed.

3   Implementing Active Vision Systems

The emerging interest in vision as an active process and the importance of its embodiment naturally led researchers to consider issues on control of perception, and also to actually build systems. Another reason for this development is of course that the field is empirical, and that computational models require experiments to uncover their predictive power. Without controllable systems working with feedback from a dynamically changing environment such experiments are in practice not possible. Gibson (1950) noted that, "...The normal human being, however, is active. His head never remains in a fixed position for any length of time except in artificial situations. If he is not walking or driving a car or looking from a train or airplane, his ordinary posture will produce some changes of his eyes in space. Such changes will modify the retinal image in a quite specific way." (Gibson 1950, p.117)

For these reasons, considerable efforts have over the past decade been spent on developing head-eye systems and studying problems of gaze control. Although this work has been severely limited by current technology and therefore resulted in solutions far from the versatility found in biological (head-eye) systems, it has provided an important enabling technology. In this section we will discuss some aspects of these efforts and point to important issues to be addressed.

3.1   Head-Eye Systems

The first attempts to design head-eye systems, e.g. Krotkov (1989), aimed at systems that could "look" following the observation by Gibson.

However, the underlying idea was still to reconstruct the environment by fusing monocular and binocular cues and real-time issues were not considered. Ballard and his co-workers (see Brown 1988) and Clark and Ferrier (1988), on the other hand, directly addressed the problem of controlling how the system could direct and hold its gaze on points in the world on the basis of what it saw. Hence, control problems and real-time characteristics became central. Ballard

and Ozcandarli (1988) in particular emphasized that a system capable of binocularly fixating a point in 3 dimensional space had immediate access to object
centered representations (at least near the fixation point), which addressed a
classical problem in computer vision. The gaze control problem has ever since
been central in active vision research, but Ballard's claim has hardly yet been
materialized in systems capable of knowing what they see.

More principled approaches to design head-eye systems have been presented
recently. Pahlavan and Eklundh (1992) present a system inspired by the human
oculomotor architecture, with redundant degrees of freedom, controlled through
constraints imposed by so-called primary ocular processes. Murray *et al.* (1992)
argue from a robotics point of view, by listing the tasks to be executed and
the performance needed, and from that derive constraints on kinematics of the
system. We will discuss these methods for gaze control further in the next subsection.

The technology of head-eye systems, though far from satisfying all needs,
is fairly well-known, and advanced as well as simple plants are commercially
available. Future developments will likely be dependent on general technology
advances in sensors, actuators and computers, and on possible market needs,
such as in surveillance.

3.2   Gaze Control

Seeing creatures are capable of controlling their gaze. There are two main functions of gaze control: to bring new parts of the scene into specific parts of the
field of view (e.g. foveation in humans), and to stabilize some part by holding
gaze on it for some time. Carpenter describes this elegantly: "...Different species
vary considerably in how much they can see at any given moment. The horse,
for example, can see almost all round its head, and, given an adequate system
for stabilization of the retinal image, it is not obvious that it would ever need to
make any other kinds of eye movements at all. The reason that it does is that it
cannot see equally well in all parts of its field." (Carpenter 1988, p6)

In computer vision changes due to observer locomotion form an established
topic in the study of time varying imagery, e.g. for motion tracking and segmentation, but gaze control became of interest only with the advent of systems for
active vision. The needs for shifting and holding gaze certainly exist in active
machine vision both to achieve stabilization and to deploy limited computational
resources, even if non-uniform retinas and foveal-peripheral organization are not
used. We will now discuss progress in gaze control and what impact it has had
on the development of "seeing robots".

Having moving cameras, like in the head-eye systems mentioned, necessitates
some control mechanism for acquiring visual data in a meaningful way. Therefore, it is not surprising that the first attempts to develop active vision systems
built upon well-known ideas of automatic control, see e.g. Clark and Ferrier
(1988), and Brown (1990a, 1990b). Such models had since long been applied
to human vision, in particular by Robinson (1968), but even if the work was
unavoidable, it provided limited new knowledge to active machine vision. The

application of Kalman filters or lattice filters for shifting and holding gaze was of course not aimed at deriving visual information from the scene. Notwithstanding that, such control approaches have been quite powerful in applications of visual servoing, especially for vehicle guidance, as demonstrated by Dickmanns and his co-workers (1988) and Thorpe *et al.* (1992).

Of greater importance to robot vision is the work on gaze control that more directly involves visual cues. In primate vision such oculomotor adjustments can be categorized as

- optokinesis (whole image stabilization)
- smooth pursuit (foveal stabilization)
- vergence
- saccades

Computer vision researchers have in particular considered the three first of these mechanisms. How to drive saccades is still largely an open issue.

Ballard and Ozcandarli (1988) and Ballard (1991) advocated the importance of motion parallax and kinetic depth to derive scene geometry in relation to the fixation point.

Such techniques are today well established, but have yet to be applied to actually inferring something from the scene. Pahlavan and Eklundh (1992) and Pahlavan (1993) stressed the importance of separating movements providing motion parallax from those that don't (e.g. the pure eye movements in man). This approach allows a system to be driven by binocular disparities and monocular cues such as blur and image motion in an integrated manner, in analogy to what is observed in man. Other approaches, like e.g. Murray *et al.* (1992) and Andersen and Christensen (1994) have employed 3 dimensional motion information to hold gaze. Few of these models actually derive scene characteristics while looking at the dynamic environment. An exception is a recent approach by Mayhew (1995) that derives depth from binocular stereo by fixating points in the surrounding scene.

Although gaze holding is essential for a system to establish a stable view from which e.g. properties of what it is looking at can be extracted, gaze shiftings are maybe even more important. A major reason for this is that the world is so rich on information that a task dependent interactive sampling of it is essential also for a system with very high computational power and a very large memory, see Aloimonos (1993) and also Ullman (1987).

In technical terms state-of-the-art active vision systems can perform saccadic gaze shifts with both high speed and accuracy. The knowledge about mechanisms for driving them is however limited. Reactive techniques, e.g. based on observing that something is moving into the field of view, have been presented by Uhlin *et al.* (1995) and Murray *et al.* (1993). Active techniques based on preprogrammed desired behaviors have also been proposed, see e.g. Rimey and Brown (1994). However, the intricate relations between a human observer's tasks and intentions and his way to fixate, that were first demonstrated in the seminal work by Yarbus (1967), although often cited, have had little actual impact on machine vision. This should not be surprising, since the issue really involves the entire problem of intentionality, will and maybe behaviors as a whole. The insight that this is an important issue clearly exists, and work such as that Rao and Ballard (1995) forms the first steps towards applying it in machine vision.

In summary, there is now ample knowledge about how to make an active vision system direct and hold gaze in a dynamic environment. Incidentally, most techniques rely mainly on retinal cues. It is well-known from biology that extraretinal cues, such as from the vestibular system in humans, and from the motor systems, are important especially for a moving observer. How such cues can be integrated and if they should be precise, or just represent e.g. heading, or the fact that the observer is moving, remain open problems. Some attempts to model gaze shifts in active machine vision show promise. However, the more far-reaching questions about how to use active gaze to perceive the world and guide actions have been addressed only to a limited extent. Advances in robot vision depend critically upon such developments.

4   Visual Sensors

At this point it is appropriate to discuss the sensors used in active vision. Most research has been performed using conventional cameras, using computer controlled motors to drive focus, iris and zoom and standard framegrabbers to get digital images. An interesting observation is that mechanical eye (camera) movements then hardly are motivated (see the quotation from Carpenter above). In particular, such systems have no foveal-peripheral structure, like that of the human eye. It is doubtful if limitations in computer hardware warrant the complex function of an oculomotor system. The human eye has centrally a resolution corresponding to about 100 cycles per degree and a field of view of around 180°. With the same resolution over the whole field a scaled version of the entire visual system would need a brain weighing several tons. Hence, the decreasing resolution towards the periphery seems ecologically necessary, in this case.

Researchers in machine vision have addressed the issue by constructing foveated sensors, e.g. Sandini and Tistarelli (1992) and Schwartz and his colleagues (see Wallace et al. (1994)). Much of this work has been based on a log-polar mapping of the retinal plane, which has some interesting features like being conformal and representing rotations as shifts. These efforts are indeed promising. However, they are not yet meeting the requirement of combining high resolution with a wide field of view, that seems essential for a system capable both of form vision and, say, navigation during ego-motion (information about the latter is manifested peripherally).

In other work, in particular by Burt and others (see e.g. Burt 1988), it has been suggested that similar properties can be obtained by employing multiscale sampling tapering off away from the region of interest. This is in principle possible, but still leaves us with the optical problem of acquiring a wide field of view allowing high resolution sampling the whole range.

Since fixational eye or camera movements also serve the purpose of giving the observer a clear view of static and moving objects while moving, technical implementations of oculomotor mechanisms nevertheless have a role to play.

5 Visual Front-Ends

Linear filtering techniques in early vision form a predominant theme in computer vision since the 1970's. With inspiration from the physiological studies of Campbell and Robson, (see e.g. Campbell and Robson 1968), and Hubel and Wiesel (see e.g. Hubel and Wiesel 1968), such approaches have been advocated for several reasons. One is of course that they provide a framework for image feature detection, analogous to what can be observed in primate vision. A second reason, of greater importance to active vision, is that they also provide a framework for direct computations of scene characteristics, like surface orientation, binocular disparities and optic flow components, as shown by Jones and Malik (1992), and Gårding and Lindeberg (1993), to name a few. This work focuses on the computation of local image deformations caused by projection effects or arising due to variations in view points or motion. In other research, e.g. Rao and Ballard (1995) have applied a similar foundation to guide eye movements while e.g. Edelman (1993) has employed it for model indexing in recognition. The latter problem is seemingly beyond the scope of what we are discussing, but we will later argue that it is quite relevant also in active vision.

There is an on-going scientific debate on whether linear filtering models provide an appropriate foundation for the early stages of computational vision models. There is also a discussion of direct versus indirect perception and of representation in vision. It would in this context lead too far to review these arguments. However, surveying the trends in active vision it seems highly likely that filtering techniques will play great role in the coming years. There are in particular two reasons for that. First, there exists substantial knowledge of what can be computed in such a framework. Secondly, and maybe even more importantly, these techniques allow high performant and inexpensive realizations in hardware. Hence, they can already today be used to implement real-time vision systems. Issues of whether such models are overly simplistic, or, if other techniques, for instance based on neural networks, can perform the same computations, does not change that. Approaches founded on the notion of a visual-front-end, such as presented in Koenderink and van Doorn (1990), or a set of steerable filters as described by Freeman and Adelson (1991), obviously perform well enough to be used in the study of "seeing systems" in the foreseeable future.

6 Visually Guided Behaviors

The proponents of active computer vision in the late 1980's stressed the ties between perception and action, see e.g. Nelson (1991) and Ballard (1991). These links were of course already obvious to those who studied intelligence in nature.

Also in fields such as artificial intelligence and robotics this perspective was common at the time. However, the models and techniques for perception employed in the latter fields were, and often still are, far too simple to encompass the intricacies of visual perception. Hence, such work only in part apply to computational vision.

More relevant to active computer vision is the work on neural modeling of visually guided behaviors and sensori-motor control performed by e.g. Arbib and his colleagues, see Arbib (1987), Arbib and Liaw (1995). The architectural and behavioral aspects of that research will likely be important to computer vision. However, the visual functions are also in this case quite simple, for instance for discrimination of moving and non-moving blob-shaped objects, and of small and large blobs. Moreover, the set of tasks and behaviors is still quite small. It is an open question whether and how such models can be scaled up to large systems capable of many different behaviors and functioning under the varying circumstances, as envisioned for seeing robots. A similar debate concerns also the layered architecture approach to intelligent robots proposed by Brooks (1991). Tsotsos (1995) argues that scaling might be untractable. In contrast to Ramachandran (1990), who suggests that vision is based on "a bag of tricks", these architectural attempts at least form principled approaches.

There is a large range of other efforts on behaviorally guided vision, based on high level models of behaviors. Examples involve purposive adjustments of viewpoints, as in Kutulakos and Dyer (1994) and selective analysis of the visual field based on high level knowledge and statistical inferences, as in Rimey and Brown (1994). See also Crowley and Christensen (1995) for a general treatment of control of perception. Such techniques may well be useful in given applications, when the set of tasks is limited, but the systems need to be tailored to the tasks a priori. Their implications on our understanding of behavioral vision seem limited. More interesting in this context is maybe systems that also are capable of learning and have memory. Rao and Ballard (1995) propose a model for driving saccades in that spirit. Much remains to be done before such models will provide competent vision systems, but including learning seems quite natural.

7   Animate Vision in a Rich Environment

In computer vision there exists a wealth of theories and methods for deriving information about a scene from images of it. These are mainly competence theories, addressing what can be computed and what the needed information is. Such models are generally of a minimalistic nature. An extreme example concerns the computation of the structure of a rigid object from K points on it observed in n images. This puts much emphasis on the derivation of these $k \times n$ features in a stable manner.

In complex environments it is difficult to predict what can be observed at a particular instant of time. Hence, an animate vision system must be capable of using many types of information and multiple cues. Moreover, since both the contexts and the tasks may vary, it could even be reasonable to include several algorithms to compute the same scene characteristic. Notably, it has been suggested that humans may apply different mechanisms for stereopsis in different tasks (Mallot 1995).

As a consequence, it is important to consider animate vision from a systems perspective. Such approaches still lack solid theoretical foundations but will likely form a topic for research in the future.

It can in fact be argued that for a system capable of using what the world offers, the complexity of the environment is an asset, while an approach based on a (small) given set of cues may have difficulties in deriving these cues for the same reason. Segmentation, grouping and figure-ground problems have, not surprisingly, constituted recurrent themes in computer vision research. An example of how such problems may be manageable in animate vision is given in Uhlin and Eklundh (1995). That work deals with a mobile observer, capable of detecting, binocularly fixating, and holding gaze on independently moving objects. What constitutes an object is defined by its sticking out from its neighborhood, by differences in motion or disparities.

Fig. 1. A realtime sequence of images (every 24th frame is shown) from a moving robot binocularly fixating the moving person. The white X denotes a point estimated to be fixed with respect to the target, while the white square is fixed relative to the background.

Fig. 2. Resulting target pixels as extracted by the system (after integration and update) from the sequence shown in Figure 1.

Hence, what the observer sees is a lump of materia. When fixating this lump the observer can conceivably use any distinguishing feature to derive whatever information is relevant, e.g. about its motion for avoiding it, or something that aids in recognizing what it is. See Figure 1 and 2 for an example.

A few remarks can be made about this example. Certain features are used to subtract the background motion, or segment the disparities. What is useful to characterize this "thing" is in a sense independent of the figure-ground segmentation. A textured object moving against a background with the same texture, can be masked out using motion, but hardly based on the texture. Nevertheless, the texture may precisely be the property that makes it possible to identify what object it is, when it is stabilized. In other cases completely different features may be distinguishing on the object, while rather inconspicuous in the scene as whole.

This example is fairly simple and involve only few cues. However, by using 3 dimensional cues early and including gaze holding, it points to a way of bridging the gap between techniques for pictorial vision (on the stabilized object) and active vision. Moreover, such an approach fits well with current theories that visual recognition is view-based. Here is an approach providing such views. It can be expected that future work in active vision will be concerned with such systems oriented techniques using multiple cues. Methodologies for tying them to sets of active and reactive behaviors are still lacking and more competent animate vision systems may still be far away.

8 Conclusion

In this article we have presented the field of active, or animate vision, which has emerged in computer vision over the past decade. Arguing that perception has strong ties to behavior, and that perception is a continuous process over time, researchers have proposed approaches that capture these aspects. Much effort has so far been spent on developing systems capable of controlling their gaze. Only limited progress has been made on applying such techniques to actually derive perceptual information. Similarly, the behaviors displayed by existing systems are quite simple. Nevertheless, since perception, as we can observe it in nature, is an active process for guiding behaviors, there are strong methodological arguments for considering computer perception in an analogous way. Although progress may be slow, both theoretically and for practical implementations, we foresee that this will be an important research area in the next decade, with potentially great impact on robotics as well as on the study of intelligent agents.

9 Acknowledgements

The author wants to thank Kourosh Pahlavan and Tomas Uhlin for valuable discussions on the topic of the article, and for helping in the preparation of the manuscript. This work has been supported by a grant from the Swedish Research Council for Engineering Sciences. This support is gratefully acknowledged.

References

1. Aloimonos, Y., Purposive and Qualitative Active Vision, *Proc. DARPA Image Understanding Workshop* (1990), pp. 816-828.
2. Aloimonos, Y. (Ed.), *Active Perception*, Lawrence Erlbaum Associates, Hillsdale, NJ. (1993).
3. Andersen, C.S. and Christensen, H.I., Using Multiple Cues for Controlling an Agile Camera Head, *Proc. Workshop on Visual Behaviors*, IEEE CS Press. (1994), pp. 97–101.
4. Arbib, M.A., Levels of Modeling Visually Guided Behavior (with peer commentary and author's response), *Behavioral and Brain Science* 10 (1987) 407–415.
5. Arbib, M.A. and Liaw J-S., Sensorimotor Transformations in the World of Frogs and Robots, *Journal of Artificial Intelligence* 72 (1995) 53–79.
6. Ballard, D.H., Ozcandarli, A., Eye Fixation and Early Vision: Kinetic Depth, *Proc. 2nd ICCV*, Tampa, FL (1988), pp. 524-531.
7. Ballard, D.H., Animate vision, *Journal of Artificial Intelligence* 48 (1991) 57–86.
8. Brooks, R.A. (1991), Intelligence without representation, *Journal of Artificial Intelligence* 47 (1991) 137–160.

9. Brown, C.M., *The Rochester Robot*, TR-257, Department of Computer Science. University of Rochester, Rochester, NY (1988).

10. Brown, C.M., Gaze Control with Interaction and Delay, *IEEE Transactions on Systems, Man and Cybernetics* 20 (1990a) 518–527.

11. Brown, C.M., Perception and Cooperation in Gaze Control, *Biological Cybernetics* 63 (1990b) 61–70.

12. Burt, P.J., *Smart Sensing in Machine Vision*, Academic Press, New York, NY (1988).

13. Campbell, F.W. and Robson, J.G., Application of Fourier Analysis to the Visibility of Gratings, *Journal of Physiology* 197 (1968) 551–556.

14. Carpenter, R.H.S., *Movements of the Eyes*, Pion Limited, London, second edition (1988).

15. Clark, J.J. and Ferrier, N.J., Modal Control of an Attentive Vision System, *Proc 2nd ICCV*, Tampa, FL (1988), pp. 514-523.

16. Crowley, J.L. and Christensen, H.I. (Eds.), *Vision as Process*, Springer-Verlag, Berlin (1995).

17. Dickmanns, E.D. and Graefe, V., Dynamic Monocular Machine Vision, *Machine Vision and Applications* 1 (1988) 223–240.

18. Edelman, S., Representing Three-dimensional Objects by Sets of Activities of Receptive Fields, *Biological Cybernetics* 70 (1993) 37–45.

19. Freeman, W.T. and Adelson, E.H., The design and Use of Steerable Filters, *IEEE Transactions on Pattern Analysis and Machine Intelligence* 13 (1991) 891–906.

20. Gårding, J. and Lindeberg, T., Direct Computation of Shape cues Based on Scale-Adapted Spatial Derivative Operators, *International Journal of Computer Vision* (1995) (to appear).

21. Gibson, J.J., *The Perception of the Visual World*, Houghton Mifflin. Boston, MA (1950).

22. Hubel, D.H. and Wiesel, T., Receptive Fields and Functional Architecture of Monkey Striate Cortex, *Journal of Physiology* 160 (1968) 106–154.

23. Jones, D.G. and Malik, J., A Computational Framework for Determining Stereo Correspondences from a Set of Linear Spatial Filters, in: G. Sandini (Ed.), *Computer Vision – ECCV '92*, Proc. 2nd European Conference on Computer Vision, Lecture Notes in Computer Science, Vol. 588, Springer-Verlag, Berlin (1992), pp. 395–410.

24. Koenderink, J.J. and van Doorn, J.J., Receptive Field Families, *Biological Cybernetics* 63 (1990) 291–298.

25. Krotkov, E.P., *Active Computer Vision by Cooperative Focus and Stereo*, Springer-Verlag. Berlin (1989).

26. Kutulakos, K.N. and Dyer, C.R., Recovering Shape by Purposive Viewpoint Adjustment, *International Journal of Computer Vision* 12 (1994) 137–172.

27. Mallot, H., *Personal Communication* (1995).

28. Marr, D., *Vision*, W.H. Freeman, New York (1982).

29. Mayhew, J.E.W., *Personal Communication* (1995).

30. Murray, D.M., Du, F., McLauchlan, P.F., Reid, I.D., Sharkey, P.M. and Brady, J.M., Design of Stereo Heads, in: Blake, A. and Yuille, A. (Eds.). Active Vision, the MIT Press, Cambridge, MA (1990), pp. 155–172.

31. Murray, D.M., Du, F., McLauchlan, P.F., Reid, I.D. and Sharkey, P.M., Reactions to Peripheral image Motion Using a Head/Eye Platform, *Proc. Fourth International Conference on Computer Vision*, Berlin (1993), pp. 403–409.

32. Nelson, R.C., Vision as intelligent behavior – an introduction to machine vision. research at the University of Rochester, *International Journal of Computer Vision* 7 (1991) 5–10.

33. Pahlavan, K. and Eklundh, J-O., A Head-Eye System - Analysis and Design, *Computer Vision Graphics and Image Processing: Image Understanding* 56 (1992) 41–56

34. Pahlavan, K., *Active Robot Vision and Primary Ocular Processes*, Dissertation. Royal Institute of Technology, Stockholm (1993).

35. Pahlavan, K. Uhlin, T. and Eklundh, J-O., Active vision as Methodology, in: Aloimonos, Y. (Ed.), *Active Perception*, Lawrence Erlbaum Associates, Hillsdale, NJ. (1993)

36. Rao, R.P. and Ballard, D.H., Learning Saccadic Eye Movements Using Multiscale Spatial Filters, in: Tsauro, G., Touretzky, D. and Leen, T. (Eds.). *Advances in Neural Information Processing Systems* 7, the MIT Press, Cambridge, MA (1995).

37. Rimey, R.D. and Brown, C.M., Control of Selective Perception Using Bayes nets and Decision Theory, *International Journal of Computer Vision* 12 (1994) 173–208.

38. Uhlin, T., Nordlund, P., Maki, A. and Eklundh, J-O., Towards an Active Visual Observer, *Proc. 5th ICCV*(1995), pp. 679–686.

39. Uhlin, T. and Eklundh, J-O., Animate Vision in a Rich Environment, *Proc. IJCAI-95*, Montreal (1995) (to appear).

40. Ullman, S., *Visual Routines. Readings in Computer Vision*, Morgan-Kaufmann Publishers, Los Altos, CA (1987), pp. 298–328.

41. Ramachandran, V.S., Interactions Between Motion, Depth, Color and Form, the Utilitarian Theory of Perception, in: Blakemore, C. (Ed.). *Vision: Coding and Efficiency*, Cambridge University Press, New York, NY (1990), pp. 346–360.

42. Robinson, D.A., The Oculomotor Control System: A Review, *Proceedings of the IEEE* 56 (1968) 1032–1049.

43. Sandini, G. and Tistarelli, M., Vision and Space Variant Sensing, in: Wechsler, H. (Ed.), *Neural Networks for Perception*, Academic Press, New York, NY (1992), pp. 398–425.

44. Thorpe, C. Herbert, M., Kanade, T. and Shafer, S., The new Generation System for the CMU Navlab, in: Masaki, I. (Ed.), *Vision-based Vehicle Guidance*, Springer-Verlag, Berlin (1992), pp. 30–82.

45. Tsotsos, J.K., Behaviorist intelligence and the scaling problem, *Journal of Artificial Intelligence* 75 (1995) 135–160.

46. Wallace, R.S., Ong, P.W., Bederson, B.B. and Schwartz, E.L., Space Variant Image Processing, *International Journal of Computer Vision* 13 (1968) 71–90.

47. Yarbus, A., *Eye Movements and Vision*, Plenum Press, New York, NY (1967).

Computational Machine Learning in Theory and Praxis*

Ming Li[1] and Paul Vitányi[2]

[1] Computer Science Department, University of Waterloo,
Waterloo, Ontario N2L 3G1, Canada.
Email: mli@math.uwaterloo.ca
[2] CWI and University of Amsterdam,
Kruislaan 413, 1098 SJ Amsterdam, The Netherlands
Email: paulv@cwi.nl

Abstract. In the last few decades a computational approach to machine learning has emerged based on paradigms from recursion theory and the theory of computation. Such ideas include learning in the limit, learning by enumeration, and probably approximately correct (pac) learning. These models usually are not suitable in practical situations. In contrast, statistics based inference methods have enjoyed a long and distinguished career. Currently, Bayesian reasoning in various forms, minimum message length (MML) and minimum description length (MDL), are widely applied approaches. They are the tools to use with particular machine learning praxis such as simulated annealing, genetic algorithms, genetic programming, artificial neural networks, and the like. These statistical inference methods select the hypothesis which minimizes the sum of the length of the description of the hypothesis (also called 'model') and the length of the description of the data relative to the hypothesis. It appears to us that the future of computational machine learning will include combinations of the approaches above coupled with guaranties with respect to used time and memory resources. Computational learning theory will move closer to practice and the application of the principles such as MDL require further justification. Here, we survey some of the actors in this dichotomy between theory and praxis, we justify MDL via the Bayesian approach, and give a comparison between pac learning and MDL learning of decision trees.

1 Introduction

In the past three decades, the art of machine learning has evolved from two opposed ends: from the pure theoretical approach there have emerged theories

* The first author was supported in part by NSERC operating grant OGP-046506, ITRC, and a CGAT grant. The second author was supported by NSERC through International Scientific Exchange Award ISE0125663, and by the European Union through NeuroCOLT ESPRIT Working Group Nr. 8556, and by NWO through NFI Project ALADDIN under Contract number NF 62-376.

hat are getting closer to practice; from the applied side *ad hoc* theories have
arisen that often lack theoretical justification. However, there is also a sound
body of methods, often statistics based, which are widely applied in practical
situations.

It is the purpose of this article to examine part of this situation. On the one
hand we follow the thread of inductive inference and pac learning; from the other
end we examine an approach related to statistics, Bayesian reasoning, and MDL.
It appears to us that the future of computational machine learning will involve
combinations of these approaches coupled with guaranties with respect to used
time and memory resources. It is clear that computational learning theory will
move closer to practice and the application of principles such as MDL require
further justification. In this paper, we justify certain applications of MDL via
the Bayesian approach.

It is not always realized that most of traditional statistics is about computational learning. It is always involved with algorithms to obtain the general from
the particular. Not only is this approach to machine learning mathematical, but
also very much applied. A novel approach in statistical learning is based on minimum description length of hypotheses and data together—one way to express
the so-called MDL principle.

A general task of statistical learning is to select the most plausible hypothesis from among all possible hypotheses in the light of experimental evidence.
The classic method to do so is Bayes' rule. The problem with applying Bayes'
rule is that one requires the prior probabilities of the possible hypotheses first.
Unfortunately, it is often impossible to obtain these.

One way out of this conundrum is to require inference of hypotheses to be
completely data driven. The MDL approach, [28, 20], embodies this idea. MDL
is usually presented as justified in and of itself by philosophical persuasion.
We give a derivation for MDL from Bayes' rule, identifying similarities and
differences, and give a comparison of pac learning criteria and MDL algorithms
for the practical topic of decision tree learning. The MDL discussion in this paper
consists for the most part of preliminary results of ongoing work.

2   Learning In The Limit

Following E.M. Gold, [7], we are given an effective enumeration of partial recursive functions $f_1, f_2, \ldots$. Such an enumeration can be the functions computed by
Turing machines, but also the functions computed by finite automata. We want
to infer a particular function f. To do so, we are presented with a sequence of
examples $D = e_1, e_2, \ldots, e_n$, containing elements (possibly with repetitions) of
the form

$$e = \begin{cases} (x, y, 0) \text{ if } f(x) \neq y, \\ (x, y, 1) \text{ if } f(x) = y. \end{cases}$$

For $n \to \infty$ we assume that D contains all elements of the displayed form.

To infer a function, Gold proposed the method of *induction by enumeration*.
We eliminate all functions which are inconsistent with D from left to right in

the enumeration of functions, up to the index of the first consistent function. Each step we receive a new example e, set $D := D, e$, and repeat this process. Eventually, when we meet a function in the enumeration which is identical to f, such an enumeration process converges, and the function will not change any more. This deceptively simple idea has generated a large body of sophisticated literature, see [1] for a survey.

The Gold model apparently only partially captures human learning, even as an idealized model. It requires the learner to identify a function precisely while this clearly does not happen in human practice. It also requires the machine to identify the target function with certainty. This again is not generally (or mostly not) required in practice. That is, this model is less relevant to practice since its goal is too high. Moreover, for almost all nontrivial concepts it takes exponential time to find the *first* concept that is consistent with the data at each new example (as required by the identification in the limit procedure) and it takes forever to converge.

3   Learning In Polynomial Time and Examples

The Gold paradigm ignores the time requirement. Clearly, adding significant (like polynomial) time restrictions directly to the inductive inference model make almost all functions, except for a few trivial ones not learnable. The next step towards a 'feasible' learning theory was taken by L. Valiant in 1984, [26].

Modeling practical learning by putting some time bound on the learning process implies that not all examples can turn up. This means it is impossible to infer a concept precisely, and therefore we can only hope to learn the concept approximately. But we also have to account for where the examples originate. We could be presented with unrepresentative examples for the concept to be inferred. Valiant assumes that the examples are drawn randomly from a sample space according to a probability distribution. The approximation between the target concept and the learned concept can be expressed in the probability of the set of examples on which the two concepts disagree.

We give a short description of the pac-model in the simplest case. The sample space S contains *examples*. A *concept* c is a subset of S. A *concept class* C is a set of concepts.

Consider a concept class C. For each concept $f \in C$ and example $v \in S$,

$$f(v) = \begin{cases} 1 \text{ if } v \text{ is a positive example of } f \\ 0 \text{ if } v \text{ is a negative example of } f. \end{cases}$$

The learning algorithm draws an examples from the sample space S according to a fixed but unknown probability distribution P. Each example in the sample comes with a label 'Positive' or 'Negative'.

A concept class C is *pac-learnable* (probably approximately correct learnable) iff there exists a (possibly randomized) learning algorithm A such that, for each $f \in C$ and ϵ $(0 < \epsilon < 1)$, algorithm A halts in a finite number of steps and examples, and outputs a concept $h \in C$ which satisfies the following. With probability at least $1 - \epsilon$,

$$\sum_{f(v) \neq h(v)} P(v) < \epsilon.$$

A concept class is *polynomially pac-learnable* iff it is pac-learnable and the learning algorithm always halts within time and number of examples $p(l(f), 1/\epsilon)$, for some polynomial p, where $l(f)$ is the length of a given binary program to compute f.

Subsets of natural numbers, the set of finite automata, and the set of Boolean formulas are all examples of concept classes. It turns out that none of the above classes is known to be polynomial time pac-learnable. The classes that are known to be polynomial time pac learnable include for example k-DNF which is the set of DNF formulas such that each term contains at most k variables.

In the past decade, following the introduction of the pac model, more negative (nonlearnability) results were proved than positive (learnability) results. Although the pac model has relaxed the requirements from the Gold model by allowing learning approximately and only with high probability instead of with certainty, it seems that we are still asking for too much. In practical learning situations, the class of probability distributions is often restricted; the learner usually is allowed to ask questions; there are may even be helpful teachers. Great efforts have been made to improve the pac-model to be more close to practical situations. New models are proposed to allow the learner to ask various kinds of questions, to have good teachers [1], to learn under a restricted class of distributions [11].

4   Learning With MDL

The previous models were mainly about formal 'criteria' for learning such as learning in the limit and pac learning. The notion of learning by enumeration is an algorithm for learning, albeit a very nonpractical one. Similarly, the MDL principle is an algorithmic paradigm that is widely applied. That is, it is widely applied at least in spirit; to apply it literally may run in computational difficulties since it involves finding an optimum in a exponentially large set of candidates as noted for example in [12]. Yet in some cases one can approximate this optimum, [27, 30].

A practice oriented theory like MDL, although often lacking in justification, apparently works and is used by practitioners. The MDL principle is very easy to use in some loose sense, but it is hard to justify. A user of the MDL principle does not need to *prove* that the concept class concerned is learnable, rather he needs to choose a concept that can be described shortly and without causing too many errors (and he needs to balance these two things). In this section, we will describe the MDL principle and establish its justification from first principles.

4.1   Bayesian Reasoning

Consider a situation in which one has a set of observations of some phenomenon, and also a (possibly countably infinite) set of hypotheses which are candidates to explain the phenomenon. For example, we are given a coin and we flip it 100 times. We want to identify the probability that the coin has outcome 'head' in a single coin flip. That is, we want to find the bias of the coin. The set of possible hypotheses is uncountably infinite if we allow each real bias in $[0, 1]$, and countably infinite if we allow each rational bias in $[0, 1]$.

For each hypothesis H we would like to assess the probability that H is the 'true' hypothesis, given the observation of D. This quantity, $\Pr(H|D)$, can be described and manipulated formally in the following way.

Consider a sample space Ω. Let D denote a sample of outcomes, say experimental data concerning a phenomenon under investigation. Let $H_1, H_2, \ldots$ be an enumeration of countably many hypotheses concerning this phenomenon, say each H_i is a probability distribution over Ω. The list $\mathcal{H} = \{H_1, H_2, \ldots\}$ is called the *hypothesis space*. The hypotheses H_i are exhaustive and mutually exclusive.

For example, say the hypotheses enumerate the possible rational (or computable) biases of the coin. As another possibility there may be only two possible hypotheses: hypothesis H_1 which says the coin has bias 0.2, and hypothesis H_2 which puts the bias at 0.8.

Suppose we have *a priori* a distribution of the probabilities $P(H)$ of the various possible hypotheses in $\mathcal{H}$ which means that $\sum_{H \in \mathcal{H}} P(H) = 1$. Assume further more that for all $H \in \mathcal{H}$ we can compute the probability $\Pr(D|H)$ that sample D arises if H is the case. Then we can also compute (or approximate in case the number of hypotheses with nonzero probability is infinite) the probability $\Pr(D)$ that sample D arises at all

$$\Pr(D) = \sum_{H \in \mathcal{H}} \Pr(D|H)P(H).$$

From the definition of conditional probability it is easy to derive **Bayes' formula**

$$\Pr(H|D) = \frac{\Pr(D|H)P(H)}{\Pr(D)}. \tag{1}$$

The prior probability $P(H)$ is often considered as the learner's *initial degree of belief* in hypothesis H. In essence Bayes' rule is a mapping from *a priori* probability $P(H)$ to *a posteriori* probability $\Pr(H|D)$ determined by data D.

Continuing to obtain more and more data, this way the total inferred probability will concentrate more and more on the 'true' hypothesis. We can draw the same conclusion of course, using more examples, by the law of large numbers. In general, the problem is not so much that in the limit the inferred probability would not concentrate on the true hypothesis, but that the inferred probability gives as much information as possible about the possible hypotheses from only a limited number of data. Given the prior probability of the hypotheses, it is easy to obtain the inferred probability, and therefore to make informed decisions. However, in general we don't know the prior probabilities. The following MDL approach in some sense replaces an unknown prior probability by a fixed 'universal' probability.

4.2   Minimum Description Length

A relatively recent method in statistics was developed by C. Wallace [28, 29], who called the principle involved *Minimum Message Length* and J. Rissanen [18, 20] who named it *Minimum Description Length* leading to *stochastic complexity* [22]. In accordance with Occam's dictum, it tells us to go for the explanation that compresses the data the most.

Definition 1. Given a sample of data, and an effective enumeration of theories, the MDL principle is to select the theory which minimizes the sum of

- the length, in bits, of the description of the theory; and
- the length, in bits, of data when encoded with the help of the theory.

Intuitively, with a more complex description of the hypothesis H, it may fit the data better and therefore decreases the misclassified data. If H describes all the data, then it does not allow for measuring errors. A simpler description of H may be penalized by increasing the number of misclassified data. If H is a trivial hypothesis that contains nothing, then all data are described literally and there is no generalization. The rationale of the method is that a balance in between seems required. However, straightforward application of the idea may lead to obviously false results in pathological cases.

Example 1. Suppose we want to determine the probability of success p of a Bernoulli process $(p, 1-p)$ (a coin with probability p of coming up heads) through a data sample consisting of a sequence of independent coin flips. Now assume the contrived example that we set hypothesis H (bias p expressed in binary expansion) and data D (a sequence of h(ead)s and t(ail)s) as

$$H_p := p = 0.r_1 \ldots r_n$$
$$D := s_1 \ldots s_n.$$

Let the hypothesis $H = 0.1$ (in binary, so the bias is $1/2$) be both the true one and the most likely one to lead to outcome D. Let $D = s_1 \ldots s_n$ be a random typical outcome of fair coin tosses. Such an outcome will have about the same number of heads and tails. But straightforward application of the MDL principle selects H_p with $p = 0.s_1 \ldots s_n$.

4.3   Derivation of MDL from Bayes' Rule

Here, we present a rigorous analysis of a pure version of MDL. While this does not rigorously prove anything about applied MDL, the relations with Bayesian inference we establish for pure MDL are corroborated by empirical evidence for applied MDL as in [14, 24, 3].

How to derive MDL from first principles, *in casu* Bayes' rule as given by Equation 1? In the latter equation we are only concerned with maximizing the term $\Pr(H|D)$ over H. Taking the negative logarithm at both sides of the equation, this is equivalent to *minimizing* the expression $-\log\Pr(H|D)$ over H:

$$-\log\Pr(H|D) = -\log\Pr(D|H) - \log P(H) + \log\Pr(D).$$

Since the probability $\Pr(D)$ is constant under varying H, this means we want to find H which minimizes:

$$-\log\Pr(D|H) - \log P(H). \tag{2}$$

Because of space limitations, we refer the reader to [12] for all definitions and analysis of auxiliary notions. This way we also do not deviate from the main argument, do not obstruct the knowledgeable reader, and do not confuse or discourage the reader who is as yet unfamiliar with Kolmogorov complexity theory.

To obtain the MDL principle it suffices to replace the probabilities involved in Equation 2 by the so-called *universal probability* $\mathbf{m}(\cdot)$. The analysis of the *conditions* under which this substitution is *justified*, or, conversely, how application of MDL is equivalent to Bayesian inference using *admissible* probabilities, is deferred to the next section.

$$\log P(H) = \log\mathbf{m}(H) + O(1), \tag{3}$$
$$\log\Pr(D|H) = \log\mathbf{m}(D|H) + O(1).$$

According to [12],

$$-\log\mathbf{m}(H) = K(H) \pm O(1),$$
$$-\log\mathbf{m}(D|H) = K(D|H) \pm O(1),$$

where $K(\cdot)$ is the prefix complexity. Therefore, using the substitution of Equation 3 we can replace the sum of Equation 2 by the sum of the minimum lengths of effective self-delimiting programs which compute descriptions of H and $D|H$. That is, we look for the H that minimizes

$$K(D|H) + K(H), \tag{4}$$

which is the code-independent, recursively invariant, absolute form of the MDL principle.

We mention that the term $-\log\Pr(D|H)$ is also known as the *self-information* in information theory and the negative log-likelihood in statistics. It can now be regarded as the number of bits it takes to redescribe or encode D with an ideal code relative to H.

In [5] (see also [12], Theorem 3.5 on p. 195) it is proved that symmetry of information holds for individual objects in the following sense

$$K(H, D) = K(H) + K(D|H, K(H)) + O(1)$$
$$= K(D) + K(H|D, K(D)) + O(1). \tag{5}$$

Since it is not more difficult to describe some object if we get more conditional information, we have $K(D|H, K(H)) \leq K(D|H) + O(1)$. Thus, by Equation 5 the quantity in Equation 4 satisfies

$$K(H) + K(D|H) \geq K(H, D) + O(1) \geq K(D) + O(1).$$

For the trivial hypothesis $H_0 = D$ or $H_0 = \emptyset$ we find

$$K(H_0) + K(D|H_0) = K(D) + O(1).$$

At first glance this would mean that the hypothesis H_{mdl} which minimizes the sum of Equation 4 could be set to D or $\emptyset$, which is absurd in general. However, we have only derived the validity of Equation 4 under the condition that Equation 3 holds. The crucial part of our justification of MDL is to establish precisely when Equation 3 is valid, which is the main thrust of this paper.

4.4   The Rôle of Universal Probability

It is well known, see for example [12], that the so-called Shannon-Fano code for an ensemble of source words distributed according to probability Q is a prefix code E_Q with $l(E_Q(x)) = -\log Q(x)$ satisfying

$$\sum_x Q(x)l(E_Q(x)) = \min_E \{\sum_x Q(x)l(E(x)) : E \text{ is a prefix code}\} + O(1).$$

Therefore, without any restrictions Equation 2 is equivalent to

$$E_{\Pr(\cdot|H)}(D) + E_P(H).$$

To satisfy restriction Equation 3 we *can simply assume* that the prior probability $P()$ in Bayes' rule Equation 1 is $\mathbf{m}()$. Whether this can be justified or not is a question which we address later.

However, we *cannot assume* that the probability $\Pr(\cdot|H)$ equals $\mathbf{m}(\cdot|H)$. Namely, as explained at length in Section 4.1, probability $\Pr(\cdot|H)$ may be totally determined by the hypothesis H. Depending on H therefore, $l(E_{\Pr(\cdot|H)}(D))$ may be *vastly* different from $K(D|H)$ indeed. This holds especially for 'simple' data D which have low probability under assumption of hypothesis H.

Example 2. Let us look at a simple example evidencing this discrepancy. Suppose we flip a coin of unknown bias n times. Let hypothesis H and data D be defined by:

$$H := \text{Probability 'head' is } 1/2$$
$$D := \underbrace{hh\ldots h}_{n \text{ times '}h\text{'(ead)s}}$$

Then we have $\Pr(D|H) = 1/2^n$ and

$$l(E_{\Pr(\cdot|H)}(D)) = -\log \Pr(D|H) = n.$$

In contrast,

$$K(D|H) \leq \log n + 2\log\log n + O(1).$$

However, the theory dealing with randomness of individual objects states that under certain conditions $-\log \Pr(D|H)$ and $K(D|H)$ are close.

First, assume that $\Pr(\cdot|\cdot)$ is a recursive function. That is, it can be computed to any required precision for each argument D and conditional H. Then we can appeal to the following known facts, [12]. Firstly, it is known that $\mathbf{m}(D|H) \geq 2^{-K(\Pr(\cdot|H))} \Pr(D|H)$. Therefore,

$$\log(\mathbf{m}(D|H)/\Pr(D|H)) \geq -K(\Pr(\cdot|H)) \geq -K(H) + O(1). \tag{6}$$

The last inequality arises since from H we can compute $\Pr(\cdot|H)$ by assumption on $\Pr(\cdot|\cdot)$. Secondly, for D which are sufficiently *random* with respect to the distribution $\Pr(\cdot|H)$ (with respect to H therefore) in the sense of Martin-Löf one can show, [12], pp. 228-229, that

$$\log(\mathbf{m}(D|H)/\Pr(D|H)) \leq 0. \tag{7}$$

The overwhelming majority of D's is random in this sense because for each H we have

$$\sum_D \Pr(D|H) 2^{\log \mathbf{m}(D|H)/\Pr(D|H)} = \sum_D \log \mathbf{m}(D|H) \leq 1,$$

since $\mathbf{m}(\cdot|H)$ is a probability distribution. For D's which are random in the appropriate sense, Equations 6, 7 mean by Equation 3 that

$$K(D|H) - K(\Pr(\cdot|H)) \leq -\log \Pr(D|H) \leq K(D|H).$$

Above, by assuming that the *a priori* probability $P(H)$ of hypothesis H is in fact the universal probability we obtained $-\log P(H) = \mathbf{m}(x)$. However, we do not need to make this assumption. For recursive $P(\cdot)$, we can analyze the situation when H is random in the required sense with respect to $P(\cdot)$. The first inequality below holds since $\mathbf{m}()$ majorizes $P()$ this way; the second inequality expresses the assumption of randomness of H,

$$\mathbf{m}(H) \geq 2^{-K(P)} P(H)$$
$$\log(\mathbf{m}(H)/P(H)) \leq 0.$$

Then,

$$K(H) - K(P) \leq -\log P(H) \leq K(H). \tag{8}$$

Altogether we find

$$K(D|H) + K(H) - \alpha(P,H) \leq -\log \Pr(D|H) - \log P(H) \leq K(D|H) + K(H), \tag{9}$$

with $\alpha(P,H) = K(\Pr(\cdot|H)) + K(P)$ and we note that $K(\Pr(\cdot|H)) \leq K(H) + O(1)$. We call this formula the **Fundamental Intequality (FI)** because it describes the fundamental relation between Bayes' Rule and MDL, and it is left for us to interpret it.

4.5   Validity Range of FI

We begin by stressing that our arguments validate the bounds in Equation 9 only in case simultaneously H is P-random and D is $Pr(\cdot|H)$-random. What is the meaning of this?

H is P-random means that the true hypothesis must be 'typical' for the prior distribution P in the sense that it must belong to all effective majorities (sets on which the majority of P-probability is concentrated). In the [12] it is shown that this is the set of H's such that with high P-probability $K(H) \approx -\log P(H)$. In case $P(H) = \mathbf{m}(H)$, that is, the prior distribution equals the universal distribution, then for *all* H we have $K(H) = -\log P(H)$, that is, all hypotheses are random with respect to the universal distribution..

Let us look at an example of a distribution where some hypotheses are random, and some other hypotheses are nonrandom. Let the possible hypotheses correspond to the binary strings of length n, and P is the uniform distribution which assigns probability $P(H) = 1/2^n$ to each hypothesis $H \in \{0,1\}^n$. Then $H = 00\ldots0$ has low complexity $K(H) \leq \log n + 2\log\log n$. However, $-\log P(H) = n$. Therefore, by Equation 8, H is not P-random. If we obtain H by n flips of a fair coin however, then with overwhelming probability we will have that $K(H) = n + O(\log n)$ and therefore $-\log P(H) \approx K(H)$ and H is P-random.

D is $Pr(\cdot|H)$-random means that the data are random with respect to the probability distribution $Pr(\cdot|H)$ induced by the hypothesis H. Therefore, we require that the sample data D are 'typical' that is 'randomly distributed' with respect to $Pr(\cdot|H)$. If, for example, $H = (\mu, \sigma)$ induces the Gaussian distribution $Pr(\cdot|(\mu, \sigma)) = N(\mu, \sigma)$ and the data D are concentrated in a tail of this distribution, like $D = 00\ldots0$, then D is atypical with respect to $Pr(\cdot|H)$ in the sense of being non-random because it violates the $Pr(\cdot|H)$-randomness test Equation 7.

4.6   If Optimal Hypothesis Violates FI

The only way to violate the Fundamental Inequality is that either D is not $Pr(\cdot|H)$-random and by Equation 7, $-\log Pr(D|H) > K(D|H)$, or that H is not P-random and by Equation 8, $-\log P(H) > K(H)$. We give an example of the first case.

We sample a polynomial $H_2 = ax^2 + bx + c$ at n arguments chosen uniformly at random from the interval $[0, 1]$. The sampling process introduces Gaussian errors in the function values obtained. The set of possible hypotheses is the set of polynomials. Assume that all numbers involved are of fixed bounded precision.

Because of the Gaussian error in the measuring process, with overwhelming probability the only polynomials H_{n-1} which fit the sample precisely are of degree $n - 1$. Denote the data by D. Now this hypothesis H_{n-1} is likely to minimize $K(D|H)$ since we have just to describe the n lengths of the intervals between the sample points along the graph of H_{n-1}. However, for this H_{n-1} data D is certainly not $Pr(\cdot|H_{n-1})$-random, since it is extremely unlikely, and

hence untypical, that D arises when sampling H_{n-1} with Gaussian error. There-
fore, Equation 7 is violated which means that $-\log \Pr(D|H_{n-1}) > K(D|H_{n-1})$
contrary to what we used in deriving the Fundamental Inequality. With prior
probability $P(\cdot) := \mathbf{m}(\cdot)$, which means $-\log P(\cdot) = K(\cdot) + O(1)$, this moreover
violates the Fundamental Inequality.

In contrast, H_2 will show the data sample D random to it in which case the
Fundamental Inequality holds. Now what happens if H_{n-1} is the true hypothesis
and the data sample D by chance is as above? In that case the Fundamental
Inequality is violated and Bayes' Rule and MDL may select very different hypotheses as the most likely ones, respectively.

4.7 If Optimal Hypothesis Satisfies FI

Suppose the H that minimizes either $-\log \Pr(D|H) - \log P(H)$ (selection accord-
ing to Bayes' Rule) or $K(D|H) + K(H)$ (selection according to MDL) satisfies the
Fundamental Inequality. This condition restricts the set of *admissible* hypotheses
with the result that not necessarily *a priori* holds $K(D|H) + K(H) \approx K(D)$ for
some minimizing trivial admissible hypothesis (like $H = \emptyset$ or $H = D$ which are
not admissible). When moreover $\alpha(P, H)$ as in Equation 9 is small, then Bayes'
Rule and MDL select the same optimizing hypothesis. The smallness of $\alpha(P, H)$
means that both the prior distribution P is simple, and that the probability
distribution $\Pr(\cdot|H)$ over the data samples induced by hypothesis H simple. In
contrast, if $\alpha(P, H)$ is large, which means that either of the mentioned distri-
butions is not simple, for example when $K(\Pr(\cdot|H)) = K(H)$ for complex H,
then there may be some discrepancy. Namely, in Bayes' Rule our purpose is to
maximize $\Pr(H|D)$, and the hypothesis H which minimizes $K(D|H) + K(H)$
also maximizes $\Pr(H|D)$ up to a $2^{-\alpha(P,H)}$ multiplicative factor. Conversely, the
H that maximizes $\Pr(H|D)$ also minimizes $K(D|H) + K(H)$ up to an additive
term $\alpha(P, H)$. That is, with

$$H_{\text{mdl}} := \text{minarg}_H\{K(D|H) + K(H)\} \qquad (10)$$
$$H_{\text{bayes}} := \text{maxarg}_H\{\Pr(H|D)\}$$

we have

$$2^{-\alpha(P,H)} \leq \frac{\Pr(H_{\text{mdl}}|D)}{\Pr(H_{\text{bayes}}|D)} \leq 1 \qquad (11)$$
$$\alpha(P, H) \geq K(D|H_{\text{mdl}}) + K(H_{\text{mdl}}) - K(D|H_{\text{bayes}}) - K(H_{\text{bayes}}) \geq 0.$$

4.8 What MDL Does

We can now assess what prior distributions and assumptions about the relation
between the data sample and selected hypothesis MDL assumes. That is, how we
can translate MDL in terms of Bayes' Rule. Identifying application of MDL with
application of Bayes' rule on some prior distribution P we must assume that the
Fundamental Inequality is satisfied for H_{mdl} as defined in Equation 10. This

means that H_{mdl} is P-random for the used prior distribution P. One choice to guarantee this is to choose

$$P(\cdot) := \mathbf{m}(\cdot)(= 2^{-K(\cdot)}).$$

This is a valid choice even though $\mathbf{m}$ is not recursive, since the latter requirement arose from the requirement that $\mathbf{m}(\cdot)/P(\cdot)$ be enumerable, which is certainly guaranteed by choice of $P(\cdot) := \mathbf{m}(\cdot)$. This choice of prior distribution over the hypotheses is an objective and recursively invariant quantified form of Occam's razor: simple hypothesis H (with $K(H) \ll l(H)$ have high probability, and complex or random hypothesis H (with $K(H) \approx l(H)$) have low probability, see [12]. This choice of prior distribution is most convenient, since the randomness test $\log \mathbf{m}(H)/P(H) = 0$ for *each* hypothesis H. This means that all hypotheses H are random with respect to distribution $\mathbf{m}(\cdot)$, see [12].

With prior $P(\cdot)$ set to $\mathbf{m}(\cdot)$, and the Fundamental Inequality satisfied, it follows that D must be $\mathrm{Pr}(\cdot|H_{\mathrm{mdl}})$-random. With the chosen prior, and given data sample D, this restriction is therefore the only constraint on the range of hypothesis from which we can choose H_{mdl}. Hence we can interpret MDL as an application of Bayes' Rule with as prior distribution the universal distribution $\mathbf{m}(\cdot)$ and selection of a hypothesis H_{mdl} which shows the given data sample random to it in the precise sense of $\mathrm{Pr}(\cdot|H_{\mathrm{mdl}})$-randomness of individual objects as developed in [12].

Since the notion of individual randomness incorporates all effectively testable properties of randomness, practical application of MDL will select the simplest hypothesis which balances the $K(D|H)$ and $K(H)$ and also shows the data sample D random (as far as we are able to tell) with respect to the selected hypothesis H_{mdl}.

This is the 'reason' why the hypothesis selected by MDL is not simply the one which perfectly fits the data. With some amount of overstatement on can say that if one obtains perfect data for a true hypothesis, then MDL interprets these data as data obtained from a simpler hypothesis subject to measuring errors. Consequently, in this case MDL is going to give you the *false simple* hypothesis and *not* the *complex true* hypothesis.

– That is, MDL only gives us the true hypothesis if the data satisfies certain conditions relative to the true hypothesis. Stated differently: there are only data and no true hypothesis for MDL. The principle simply obtains the hypothesis which is suggested by the data and it is assumed that the data are random with respect to the hypothesis. For proper application of MDL assuming a true underlying hypothesis one must also assume that the data are not completely perfect.

5   Applying MDL

Unfortunately, the function K is not computable, [12]. In this paper we will not address the question which encoding one uses in practice, but refer to references [20, 17, 28, 30, 27]. For practical applications one must settle for easily computable approximations.

In statistical applications, H is some statistical distribution (or model) $H = P(\theta)$ with a list of parameters $\theta = (\theta_1, \dots, \theta_k)$, where the number k may vary and influence the (descriptional) complexity of θ. (For example, H can be a normal distribution $N(\mu, \sigma)$ described by $\theta = (\mu, \sigma)$.) Each parameter θ_i is truncated to fixed finite precision. The data sample consists of n outcomes $\mathbf{y} = (y_1, \dots, x_n)$ of n trials $\mathbf{x} = (x_1, \dots, x_n)$ for distribution $P(\theta)$. The data D in the above formulas is given as $D = (\mathbf{x}, \mathbf{y})$. By expansion of conditional probabilities we have therefore

$$\Pr(D|H) = \Pr(\mathbf{x}, \mathbf{y}|H) = \Pr(\mathbf{x}|H) \cdot \Pr(\mathbf{y}|H, \mathbf{x}).$$

In the argument above we take the negative logarithm of $\Pr(D|H)$, that is,

$$-\log \Pr(D|H) = -\log \Pr(\mathbf{x}|H) - \log \Pr(\mathbf{y}|H, \mathbf{x}).$$

Taking the negative logarithm in Bayes' rule and the analysis of the previous section now yields that MDL selects the hypothesis with highest inferred probability satisfying $\mathbf{x}$ is $\Pr(\cdot|H)$-random and $\mathbf{y}$ is $\Pr(\cdot|H, \mathbf{x})$-random.

Learning Polynomials. In biological modeling, we often wish to fit a polynomial f of unknown degree to a set of data points D such that it can predict future data y given x. Even if the data did come from a polynomial curve of degree, say two, because of measurement errors and noise, we still cannot find a polynomial of degree two fitting all n points exactly. In general, the higher the degree of fitting polynomial, the greater the precision of the fit. For n data points, a polynomial of degree $n - 1$ can be made to fit exactly, but probably has no predictive value. In general, we are either given the sampling position $\mathbf{x}$, or we restrict the viable models to those for which $\mathbf{x}$ fairly covers the range of arguments with typical behavior. That is, we do not want $\mathbf{x}$ to be bunched together in one corner of the representative domain. This means that we can treat the term $-\log \Pr(\mathbf{x}|H)$ as a constant. Hence, applying MDL we look for $H_{\mathrm{mdl}} := \mathrm{minarg}_H \{K(\mathbf{y}|H, \mathbf{x}) + K(H)\}$.

Let us apply the MDL principle where we describe all $(k - 1)$-degree polynomials by a vector of k entries, each entry with a precision of d bits. Then, the entire polynomial is described by

$$kd + O(\log kd) \text{ bits.} \tag{12}$$

(We have to describe k, d, and account for self-delimiting encoding of the separate items.) For example, $ax^2 + bx + c$ is described by (a, b, c) and can be encoded by about $3d$ bits. Each datapoint (x_i, y_i) which needs to be encoded separately with precision of d bits per coordinate costs about $2d$ bits.

To apply the MDL principle we must trade the cost of hypothesis H (Equation 12) against the cost of describing $\mathbf{y}$ with help of H and $\mathbf{x}$. As a trivial example, suppose the $n - 1$ out of n datapoints fit a polynomial of degree 2 exactly, but only 2 points lie on any polynomial of degree 1 (a straight line). Of course, there is a polynomial of degree $n - 1$ which fits the data precisely (up to precision). Then the MDL cost is $3d + 2d$ for the 2nd degree polynomial, $2d + (n - 2)d$ for the 1st degree polynomial, and nd for the $(n-1)$th degree polynomial. Given the choice among those three options, we select the 2nd degree polynomial for all $n > 5$. For a more sophisticated approach accounting for the average encoding cost of exceptions assuming they are Gaussian distributed, see [20].

Learning Decision Trees. Let us compare the application of MDL and of pac-learning for a widely used and practical problem like learning decision trees. Before proceeding, recall that pac-learning is not an algorithmic method, but rather a formal criterion to determine whether a given algorithm has performed satisfactory within that criterion. In contrast, the MDL principle is a method for designing algorithms. Theoretical approaches worry whether certain formal requirements like those for pac-learning of certain problems can be achieved or not for any algorithm within certain time bounds. As a consequence pac-learning certain concept classes often results in essentially tautological statements where any algorithm that selects an hypothesis consistent with the data satisfies the pac-learning criterion. Algorithmic approaches like MDL worry whether the algorithms satisfy certain performance guaranties or give practically acceptable performance.

A *decision tree* defined on $\{0, 1\}^n$ is a binary tree T, each of whose internal nodes is labeled with one of n *attributes*, and whose leaves are labeled by the *class value* 0 or 1. The value of T on an input vector is obtained by traversing the tree from the root to the appropriate leaf as follows: at each internal node choose the left or right descendant depending on whether the input bit corresponding the attribute of that node is 0 or 1, respectively. See [12], page 313 for a concrete example.

Decision trees are the key concept in learning systems such as ID3 [16] and CART [2], and have found use in many applications. There is a large amount of machine learning literature on learning decision trees (see, for example, [15, 16, 17]). However, the learnability of decision trees remains at this time of writing one of the most prominent open questions in learning theory. Other than heuristic learning algorithms using principles such as minimum description length and maximum entropy, the theoretically best learning algorithm [4] pac-learns a decision tree using $O(n^{\log n})$ time and samples.

Learning decision trees in the pac sense from labeled examples usually requires finding the approximately smallest decision tree with high probability. For some time, it has been open that whether or not the decision version of computing the smallest decision tree is NP-complete. Recently, the following results were obtained in [8].

1. The decision version of computing the minimum decision tree is NP-complete.
2. In general a target decision tree cannot be approximated in polynomial time by decision trees using data consisting of labeled examples to within a factor

of $2^{\log^\delta n}$ for $\delta < 1$, unless NP is contained in DTIME$[2^{\text{polylog} n}]$.

This gives evidence that it may be not possible to learn decision trees by any algorithm in polynomial time satisfying the pac model requirements.

Due to its practical importance, heuristic algorithms to learn decision trees are rife. M. Wax and J. Rissanen [23] and Quinlan and Rivest [17] applied the MDL principle to learn decision trees as follows.

We are given a set of data, possibly with noise, representing a collection of examples. Each example is represented by a data item in the data set, which consists of a tuple of *attributes* followed by a binary *class value* indicating whether the example with these attributes is a positive or negative example. A consistent decision tree can be viewed as a classification procedure of the data. The internal nodes in the tree are *decision nodes*. Each such node specifies a test of a particular attribute; the possible answers are labeled on the arcs leaving the decision node to the two descendant nodes. A leaf of the tree specifies a class to which the object that passed the attribute tests and arrived at this leaf belongs. Given a set of data, we can construct many different decision trees of various sizes which agree with the data. Some data, for example noisy data, may not obey the predicting rule defined by the decision tree. We usually have a choice between using a small *imperfect* tree which classifies some data falsely or a big *perfect* tree which correctly classifies all given data.

The aim is in general to construct a decision tree that has the smallest error rate in classifying future data. Is the *smallest perfect decision tree* really a good predictor? It turns out that in *practice* this is not the case. Due to the presence of noise or inadequacy of the given attributes, selecting a perfect decision tree 'overfits' the data and gives generally poor predictions. Many *ad hoc* rules have been suggested and used for overcoming this problem.

The MDL principle appears to provide a solution and generally works well in practice. Essentially, given the data sample *without* the class values, we look for a reasonably small tree such that most data are correctly classified by the tree. We encode the inconsistent data as exceptions. We minimize the sum of

- the number of bits to encode a (not necessarily perfect) decision tree T, that is, the model which gives the $-\log P(H)$ term; and
- the number of bits to encode (describe) the examples (x_i, y_i) in the sample $(\mathbf{x}, \mathbf{y})$ that are inconsistent with T, given the entire data sample $\mathbf{x}$ without the class values $\mathbf{y}$. This gives the $-\log P(\mathbf{y}|H, \mathbf{x})$ term.

Now a coding method must be provided. This is important in applications, since it determines where the optimum is. If the encoding of trees is not efficient, then we may end up with a very small tree (with relatively large depth), and too many examples become exceptions. An inefficient encoding of the exceptions would result in overly large trees. In both cases, the prediction of unseen data is affected. Quinlan and Rivest encode a tree by making a depth-first traversal. At each internal node, write down the attribute name in some self-delimiting form followed by its edge label. At a leaf write down the class value. If the tree is not perfect, then the data that do not fit in the tree are encoded separately as exceptions (in some economical way using the provided total data sample without the class values).

Apparently, there is a problem of 'subjectivity' of encoding. More efficient ways of encoding the model (tree) may result in a larger decision tree, and more efficient methods of encoding the exceptions may result in a smaller decision tree. Quinlan and Rivest have observed that the decision trees their algorithm produced were slightly smaller than they should be. This suggests that the *model cost* is too high, that is, the model is encoded using too many bits per parameter. These trees were found by direct comparison. Nohre, [13], has described a tree pruning algorithm for binary trees to model Markov processes for data compression. This method finds the MDL subtree starting from an arbitrarily large tree. Rissanen in [22] has demonstrated how to use a sharper formula for *stochastic complexity* in applying Nohre's algorithm to overcome the tendency of producing too small decision trees. All these MDL style algorithms are reported to be quite competitive with other learning algorithms for decision trees.

6 Alternative MDL-Like Principle

In the above interpretation of MDL we essentially look for a hypothesis H minimizing $K(D|H) + K(H)$. This always satisfies

$$K(D|H) + K(H) \geq K(D).$$

Another interpretation of MDL is sometimes useful, and in fact used in [6] to recognize on-line handwritten characters. In the new approach the idea is that we we define $E := D - D_H$, where D_H is the data set classified according to H. We want to minimize

$$K(H, E) \approx K(H) + K(E|H)$$

over H. That is, E denotes the subset of the data sample D which are *exceptions* to H in the sense of being 'not covered' by H. We want to find H such that the description of H and the exception data E *not covered* by H is minimized. Note that in this case always

$$\min_{H}\{K(H) + K(E|H)\} \leq K(\emptyset) + K(D) = K(D),$$

in contrast to the standard interpretation of MDL above. This incarnation of MDL is not straightforwardly derived by our approach above. We may interpret it that we look for the shortest description of an accepting program for the data consisting of a classification rule H and an exception list E. While this principle sometimes gives good results, application may lead to absurdity as the following shows.

In many problems we our data sample D consists of only positive examples. Suppose we want to learn (a grammar for) English language, given a corpus of data D. Here, data D can be the Bible or an even larger sample like the so-called 'Brown Corpus'. Then, according to our new MDL rule the best hypothesis is the trivial grammar H generating *all* sentences over the alphabet. Namely, this grammar gives $K(H) = O(1)$ independent of D and alsp $E := \emptyset$. Consequently,

$$\min_{H}\{K(H) + K(E|H)\} = K(H) = O(1),$$

which is absurd.

References

1. D. Angluin, Computational learning theory: survey and selected bibliography, *Proc. 24th Ann. ACM Symp. Theory of Computing*, 1992, pp. 319-342.
2. L. Breiman, J. Friedman, R. Olshen and C. Stone, *Classification and Regression Trees*. Wadsworth International Group, Belmont, CA, 1984.
3. W. Buntine, Personal communication, September 1994.
4. A. Ehrenfeucht and D. Haussler, Learning decision trees from random examples. *Proc. 1988 Workshop on Comp. Learning Theory*, Morgan-Kaufmann, 1988, pp. 182-195.
5. P. Gács, On the symmetry of algorithmic information, *Soviet Math. Dokl.*, 15 (1974) 1477-1480. Correction: ibid., 15 (1974) 1480.
6. Q. Gao and M. Li, An application of minimum description length principle to online recognition of hand-printed alphanumerals, *11th International Joint Conference on Artificial Intelligence*, Morgan Kaufmann, 1989, pp. 843-848.
7. E.M. Gold, Language identification in the limit, *Inform. Contr.* 10 (1967) 447-474.
8. T. Hancock, T. Jiang, M. Li, and J. Tromp, Lower bounds on learning decision lists and trees. in: E.W. Mayr, C. Puech (Eds.), *STACS 95*, Proc. 12th Annual Symp. Theoret. Aspects of Comput. Science, Lecture Notes in Computer Science, Vol. 900, Springer-Verlag, Heidelberg, 1995, pp. 527-538.
9. A.N. Kolmogorov, Three approaches to the quantitative definition of information, *Problems Inform. Transmission* 1:1 (1965) 1-7.
10. M. Li and P.M.B. Vitányi, Inductive reasoning and Kolmogorov complexity, *J. Comput. Syst. Sci.* 44 (1992) 343-384.
11. M. Li and P. Vitányi, A theory of learning simple concepts under simple distributions, *SIAM J. Computing* 20:5 (1991) 915-935.
12. M. Li and P.M.B. Vitányi, *An Introduction to Kolmogorov Complexity and its Applications*, Springer-Verlag, New York, 1993.
13. R. Nohre, *Some Topics in Descriptive Complexity*, Ph.D. Thesis, Linköping University, Linköping, Sweden, 1994.
14. D. MacKay, pp 59 in *Maximum Entropy and Bayesian Methods*, Kluwer, 1992. (Personal communication W. Buntine.)
15. J. Mingers, An empirical comparison of selection measures for decision-tree induction. *Machine Learning* 3 (1989) 319-342.
16. J.R. Quinlan, Induction of decision trees, *Machine Learning* 1 (1986) 81-106.
17. J.R. Quinlan and R. Rivest, Inferring decision trees using the minimum description length principle, *Inform. Computation* 80 (1989) 227-248.
18. J. Rissanen, Modeling by the shortest data description, *Automatica-J.IFAC* 14 (1978) 465-471.
19. J. Rissanen, Universal coding, information, prediction and estimation, *IEEE Transactions on Information Theory* IT-30 (1984) 629-636.

20. J. Rissanen, *Stochastic Complexity and Statistical Inquiry*, World Scientific Publishers, 1989.
21. J. Rissanen, Stochastic complexity, *J. Royal Stat. Soc., series B* 49 (1987) 223-239. Discussion: ibid., pp. 252-265.
22. J. Rissanen, Stochastic complexity in learning, in: P. Vitányi (Ed.), *Computational Learning Theory*, Proc. 2nd European Conf. (EuroCOLT '95), Lecture Notes in Artificial Intelligence, Vol. 904, Springer-Verlag, Heidelberg, 1995, pp. 196-210.
23. J. Rissanen and M. Wax, Algorithm for constructing tree structured classifiers, US Patent No. 4719571, 1988.
24. J. Segen, *Pattern-Directed Signal Analysis*, PhD Thesis, Carnegie-Mellon University, Pittsburgh, 1980.
25. R.J. Solomonoff, Complexity-based induction systems: comparisons and convergence theorems, *IEEE Trans. Inform. Theory* IT-24 (1978) 422-432.
26. L.G. Valiant, A Theory of the Learnable, *Comm. ACM* 27 (1984) 1134-1142.
27. V. Vovk, Minimum description length estimators under the universal coding scheme, in: P. Vitányi (Ed.), *Computational Learning Theory*, Proc. 2nd European Conf. (EuroCOLT '95), Lecture Notes in Artificial Intelligence, Vol. 904, Springer-Verlag, Heidelberg, 1995, pp. 237-251.
28. C.S. Wallace and D.M. Boulton, An information measure for classification, *Computing Journal* 11 (1968) 185-195.
29. C.S. Wallace and P.R. Freeman, Estimation and inference by compact coding, *J. Royal Stat. Soc., Series B*, 49 (1987) 240-251. Discussion: ibid.,252-265.
30. K. Yamanishi, Approximating the minimum description length and its applications to learning, Manuscript, NEC Research Labs, New Jersey, 1995.
31. A.K. Zvonkin and L.A. Levin, The complexity of finite objects and the development of the concepts of information and randomness by means of the theory of algorithms, *Russian Math. Surveys* 25:6 (1970) 83-124.

Fuzzy Sets as a Tool for Modeling

Ronald R. Yager

Machine Intelligence Institute
Iona College
New Rochelle, NY 10801

Abstract. A introduction to the basic concepts of fuzzy set theory is first provided. We next discuss some ideas from the theory of of approximate reasoning. As we shall see it is this theory, which uses fuzzy sets as its primary representational structure, that provides a formal mechanism for reasoning with uncertain information. Finally we discuss the technology of fuzzy systems modeling. This technology has provided the bases for most of the current generation of applications of fuzzy set theory.

1. Introduction

The concept of a fuzzy set was originally introduced by Zadeh in 1965 [1]. In [32] Dubois, Prade and Yager provide a collection of readings of seminal articles in this field. While lack of space prevents us from covering the whole spectrum of this field it is worth noting some of the pioneering contributors. Hans Zimmermann of Germany provided some of the earliest applications of fuzzy set theory and made important contributions to the development of fuzzy mathematical programming. The work of Didier Dubois and Henri Prade of France on fuzzy arithematic and possibility theory is also worth noting. Other early contributors from France were Elie Sanchez and Bernadette Bouchon-Meunier. In Spain the work of Enric Trillas and Llorence Valverde on the logical underpinnings has proven to be very useful. The Linz workshops on fuzzy mathematics lead by Peter Klement of Austria, Ulrich Hohle of Germany and Robert Lowen of Belgium provided an important forum for explorations of the connection between classical mathematics and fuzzy set theory. In England the pioneering work of Abe Mamdani on fuzzy logic control and the work of James Baldwin and Richard Tong are worth noting. Constantin Negoita and Dan Ralescu, originally from Romania, wrote one of the earliest books in this field. Janusz Kacprzyk of Poland investigated the use of fuzzy sets in complex decision making environments. Any discussion of the history of this field requires a special acknowledgement of the contribution of the researchers in Japan. We particularly note the contribution of Michio Sugeno whose work on fuzzy modeling and fuzzy measures has proven very important. Toshiro Terano and Kiyoji Asai provided imortant leadership direction for other Japanese researchers. James Bezdek and Enrique Ruspini of the United States made seminal contributions to the development of fuzzy clustering and classification. Among other pioneering contributors from North

America we note Abraham Kandel and George Klir of the United States and Madan Gupta and Burhan Turksen of Canada.

Formally fuzzy set theory can be seen as a mathematical structure which extends the idea of a classic set by allowing partial membership rather than be restricted to only the yes or no choice of classic set theory. In this spirit many fuzzy extensions of classic mathematical disciplines have been developed and studied. However, the primary motivation behind Zadeh's seminal work was to provide a tool for the representation of the type of uncertainty that is prevalent in the definition of concepts used by people in describing, discussing and thinking about the world. In this spirit fuzzy set theory provides an important tool for use in the construction of computer based intelligent systems by providing a means for representation and manipulation of knowledge. Here we describe a number of aspects of fuzzy set theory related to its use in this endeavor. We first introduce some basic concepts from the formal theory. We next discuss some ideas from the theory óf of approximate reasoning. As we shall see it is this theory, which uses fuzzy sets as its primary representational structure, that provides a formal mechanism for reasoning with uncertain information. Finally we discuss the technology of fuzzy systems modeling. This technology has provided the bases for most of the current generation of applications of fuzzy set theory. Central to the use of this theory is the exploitation of the tolerance for imprecision and uncertainty in achieving solutions to complex problems.

2. Basic Foundations of Fuzzy Set Theory

As originally introduced by Zadeh a fuzzy subset generalizes the concept of a subset by allowing partial membership. In the following we introduce some of the basic ideas associated with the theory of fuzzy subsets and the related field, the theory of approximate reasoning. Further details can be found in any of the texts now appearing [2, 3].

Definition: Assume X is a set serving as a universe of discourse. A fuzzy subset F of X is associated with a characteristic function

$$F: X \to [0, 1].$$

In the framework of fuzzy set theory the characteristic function is usually called the membership function associated with the fuzzy subset. The terminology stresses the idea that for each x, $F(x)$ indicates the degree to which x is a member of F. The important thing to emphasize is that the membership grades are in the unit interval rather simply in the set $\{0, 1\}$ as is the case for an ordinary subset. A typical example of a fuzzy set is $\{\frac{1}{a}, \frac{0.4}{b}, \frac{0.7}{c}, \frac{1}{d}, \frac{0.2}{e}\}$. In this representation the denominator is the element and the numerator is the membership grade.

The first order of business in developing fuzzy set theory was the extension of the basic operations on sets to this new environment. In extending these operations it is required that they collapse to the ordinary set operations in the case when the membership grades are only 0 and 1.

In [1] Zadeh suggested the following definitions associated with the operations of intersection, union and negation of fuzzy subsets. Assume A and B are fuzzy subsets of X:

    1. $A \cap B = D$, where D is a fuzzy subset of x such that
$$D(x) = \text{Min} [A(x), B(x)]$$
    2. $A \cup B = E$, where D is a fuzzy subset of x such that
$$E(x) = \text{Max} [A(x), B(x)]$$
    3. $F = \overline{A}$ where
$$F(x) = 1 - A(x).$$

Quit early in the development of this field it was suggested, especially for the intersection and the union, that the operations originally introduced by Zadeh where not the only possible way of defining the union and intersection of fuzzy subsets. For example it is possible to define
$$D(x) = A(x) B(x)$$
$$E(x) = A(x) + B(x) - A(x) \cdot B(x)$$
In [4] we suggested that one can select as the definition of intersection and intersection any member of the parameterized families where $P \in (0, \infty)$

For intersection: $D(x) = 1 - \text{Min} [1, ((1 - A(x))^P + (1 - B(x))^P)^{1/P}$

For union: $E(x) = \text{Min} [1, ((A(x)^P + (B(x))^P)^{1/P}]$

Other parameterized families defining intersection and union have been suggested in the literature [3].

A most comprehensive framework for formalizing the operations of intersection and union on fuzzy subsets was provided with the introduction of the concepts of t–norm and t-conorm [5, 6]. A *t-norm* T is a binary mapping
$$T: [0, 1] \times [0, 1] \to [0, 1]$$
such that it satisfies
    1. *Commutativity:* $T(a, b) = T(b, a)$
    2. *Monotonicity:* $T(a, b) \geq T(c, d)$ if $a \geq c$ and $b \geq d$
    3. *Associativity:* $T(a, T(b, c)) = T(T(a, b), c)$
    4. *One Identity:* $T(a, 1) = a$

Using the idea of a t-norm we can express a general intersection operation
$$D = A \cap B$$
where
$$D(x) = T(A(x), B(x))$$
A *t-conorm* S is a binary mapping
$$S: [0, 1] \times [0, 1] \to [0, 1]$$
which satisfies the first three properties above but replaces four with
    4' *Zero Identity:* $S(a, 0) = a$.
Using the t-conorm we can express a general union operator
$$F = A \cup B$$
where
$$F(x) = S(A(x), B(x)).$$
A natural extension of the idea of a fuzzy subset is the concept of a fuzzy relationship. A fuzzy relationship on the spaces $X_1, X_2, ..., X_n$ is defined as a fuzzy subset of the cartesian product space $X_1 \times X_2 \times ... X_n$.

3. Linguistic Values and Approximate Reasoning

A fundamental concept that plays a significant role in many of the successful applications of fuzzy set theory is the idea of a linguistic value. Assume V is a variable taking its value in the set X. For example, if V is the temperature, then X is the set of possible temperatures. The usual way to represent information about this variable is by statements of the form V is x where x is some value from the space X for example, V is 50°. In many situations our knowledge about the variable V is not so precisely known but involves some uncertainty. For example, we may know the temperature is *about 50°* or is *very high*. We shall call such types of information a linguistic value. Thus in this environment our information is of the form V is $\mathcal{A}$ where $\mathcal{A}$ is a linguistic value. It should be pointed out that the type of specific information typical associated with a the assignment of a value to a variable can be seen as a special case of these linguistic values. Using the concept of a fuzzy set we can formally represent a linguistic value, such as *about 50°*, as a fuzzy subset A over the space of possible temperatures. In this representation for any $x \in X$, A(x) would indicate the compatibility of the value x with the concept we are representing by the fuzzy subset A. Alternatively we can view A(x) as the possibility [7, 8] that the temperature is x given the knowledge that temperature is *about 50°*. Another view in this same spirit is one in which we view the linguistic value $\mathcal{A}$ as putting some constraints on the possible values for the temperature given the knowledge about the temperature, these constraints are carried by fuzzy subset A. A special case are worth noting. If we have no knowledge about the value of the variable we represent this as V is X where X is the base set of V, thus we see all values are possible.

Given the knowledge about the value of some variable a natural question we may be interested in is the determination of the validity of some other statement about the variable. For example, if we know the temperature is *about fifty degrees* we may ask is it cold or is the temperature greater then 70°. In many cases, the existence of some uncertainty in our knowledge about the value of a variable precludes us from providing a yes or no answer to these kinds of questions. For example, if we know the temperature is between 50-60 degrees while we can easily answer yes to the question is the temperature more then 40 degrees and no to the question is the temperature greater than 70°. we can't easily answer the question is the temperature more than 55°. In order to address this issue two surrogate measures are introduced. The first of these is called the measure of possibility [7, 8], which provides a kind of optimistic answer. The second of these, called the measure of certainty [7, 8] provides a pessimistic measure. We shall now formally describe these measures. Assume we have the information that V is A, where A is a fuzzy subset over the domain of V. Consider now the question as to whether V is B is true. The possibility of B being true is defined as

$$\text{Poss}[V \text{ is } B / V \text{ is } A] = \text{Max}_X[A \cap B]$$

and the certainty of B being true is defined as

$$\text{Cert}[V \text{ is } B / V \text{ is } A] = 1 - \text{Max}_X[A \cap \overline{B}].$$

We note that Dubois and Prade [8] have studied these concepts in considerable detail. In general $\text{Poss}[V \text{ is } B / V \text{ is } A] \geq \text{Cert}[V \text{ is } B / V \text{ is } A]$, and the $\text{Truth}[V \text{ is } B / V \text{ is } A]$

$\in$ [Cert[V is B/V is A], Poss[V is B/V is A]]. A number of special cases are worth noting. If Cert[V is B/V is A] = 1 then this corresponds to yes (true). If Poss[V is B/V is A] = 0 this corresponds to no (false). If Poss[V is B/V is A] = Cert[V is B/V is A] = α then Truth[V is B/V is A] = α.

The theory of approximate reasoning which was introduced by Zadeh [9, 10] provides a tool which enables us to reason using the kinds of imprecise information described above. This theory is very much in the spirit of the constraint propagation methodology used in other areas of artificial intelligence. The reasoning mechanism used in this theory consists of a three step process. The first step is a translation process in which we provide a representation of our knowledge in terms of fuzzy relationships. The second step involves a conjunction of these fuzzy relationships to form a complete fuzzy relationship which is a representation of our total knowledge. The third step is the use of the projection principle to obtain the value of any variable of interest. In the following we briefly describe the basic ideas of this reasoning mechanism. In [2] we provide a formulation of this reasoning process which relates it to the deductive reasoning mechanism used in the classic logic. As a matter of fact we show that binary logic can be viewed as a special case of this more general theory.

The primary elements of an AR system are a collection of variables V_1, V_2, ..., V_n called the atomic variables and an associated collection of sets X_1, X_2, ..., X_n called the respective base sets. Essentially X_k provides the set of allowable values for V_k. A joint variable is any collection of atomic variables such as V_1, (V_1, V_2), (V_1, V_2, V_5). A proposition in this system is a statement of the from

$$V \text{ is } M$$

where V is a joint variable and M is a fuzzy relationship on the cartesian product of the base sets of the atomic variables making up the joint variable. As noted previously a proposition essentially provides a constraint on the allowable values for the joint variable.

The translation rules of fuzzy logic provides a mechanism for taking natural language statements and representing them as propositions in the theory of approximate reasoning. In the following we shall describe some of the basic translation rules used in the theory of approximate reasoning.

In the following we shall use V to indicate the variable John's height and U to indicate the variable Mary's age. We shall also use A and B to indicate the fuzzy subsets tall and young.

Statement: John is tall.
  Translation: V is A

Statement: John is not tall.
  Translation: V is B
where B(x) = (1 - A(x)).

Statement: John is very tall.
  Translation:[1] V is S

where $S(x) = (A(x))^2$.

Statement: John is <u>sort of tall</u>.
  Translation: V is D
where $D(x) = (A(x))^{1/2}$.

Statement: John is tall <u>is α certain</u>.
  Translation: V is R
where $R(x) = Max[(1 - \alpha), A(x)]$.

Statement: John is tall and Mary is young.
  Translation: (V, U) is M
where $M(x, y) = Min[A(x), B(y)]$. We note that here M is a fuzzy relationship specifying the possible pairs of values for John's height and Mary's age.

Statement: John is tall or Mary is young.
  Translation: (V, U) is G
where $G(x, y) = Max[A(x), B(y)]$.

Statement: If John is tall then Mary is young.
  Translation: (V, U) is H
where $H(x, y) = Max(\overline{A}(x), B(y))$. Again we emphasize that H is a fuzzy relationship specifying the possible pairs of values for John's height and Mary's age.

In [11] Zadeh describes in considerable detail the translation of many other types of statements from natural language. Among these are statements such as

John is <u>tall is likely</u>

which involves a probabilistic qualification. Another type of statements involving what Zadeh calls a quantification is a statement of the form

Most tall men are very intelligent.

The important point to emphasize is that the theory of approximate reasoning provides a large collection of rules for translating many different types of natural language statements into formal representations which can be manipulated, as described in the following, in order to be able to make deductions from our knowledge base. While classic logic also provides a machinery for translating natural language into formal representations it doesn't provide as rich a repaitoire.

Once having obtained the translation of natural language statements into a collection of propositions in the language of the theory of approximate reasoning the next step is to combine these statements to obtain an overall constraint on the knowledge space. The basic rule for implementing this task is the conjunction principle.

Assume $P_1, P_2, ..., P_q$ are a collection of propositions each of the form

$$V^i \text{ is } N_i$$

---

[1] This and the following translation rule can be see as default definitions and other possible definitions can be used in different contexts.

where V^i is a joint variable. The conjunction of these propositions is a proposition

$$V \text{ is } N$$

where V is the union of the variables in the V^i and

$$N(z) = \text{Min}[N_i(z)].$$

In the above z is an element in the cartesian product space of the variables in V. A simple understanding of this principle can be had when we view each proposition as a constraint on the allowable values for the associated variables. In this view the conjunction principle is seen a requirement that all constraints imposed by the individual propositions must be satisfied. In the above the resulting proposition, V is N, is the total effect of all the restrictions imposed by the individual pieces of knowledge we have and as such constitutes a manifestation of our knowledge base, thus we can view V is N as our knowledge base.

The final step in the reasoning process is to deduce the value of any particular atomic variable V_j from our In particular we say that the deduced information about the variable V_j is

$$V_j \text{ is } A_j$$

where A_j is a fuzzy subset on the base set of V_j, X_j, defined such that

$$A(x_j) = \underset{\substack{\text{for z} \\ \text{such that the} \\ j^{th} \text{ component} \\ \text{of z is } x_j}}{\text{Max}} N(z)$$

Actually this process is a special case of an application of what is called the entailment principle [12]. While a full discussion of this idea is beyond the scope of this short introduction the basic idea of this important principle is that from specific information we can deduce less specific information. This principle is a generalization of the observation that if I know that Mary's age is between 40 and 50 I can also say that Mary is between 30 and 50.

The following simple example illustrates a simple but important application of the theory of approximate reasoning..

Example. Consider we have the following two premises

P1: If V is A then U is B

P2: V is D

We assume A and D are fuzzy subsets of X and B is a fuzzy subset of Y.
Translating P1 we get

$$(V, U) \text{ is } E$$

where E is a fuzzy subset of $X \times Y$ when

$$E(x, y) = \overline{A}(x) \vee B(y).$$

Translating P2 we get

$$V \text{ is } D.$$

Conjuncting these two propositions we get

$$(V, U) = F$$

where

$$F(x, y) = (\overline{A}(x) \vee B(y)) \wedge D(x) = (\overline{A}(x) \wedge D(x)) \vee (B(y) \wedge D(y))$$

Finally over inferred value for V is

$$V \text{ is } H$$

where

$$H(x) = \text{Max}_y \, F(x, y) = (1 - \text{Certainty}[A/D]) \vee B(x)$$

We see that if we absolutely certain about the validity of A given D, Certainty[A/D] = 1, (A is true), then we conclude that

$$H = B$$

and the rule has completely fired. At the other extreme if Certainty[A/D] = 0, (A is false) then we get $H(x) = 1 \vee B(x) = 1$ and hence $H = X$ and we have obtained no information regarding U. Finally if Certainty[A/D] = α, we have a partial certainty then

$$H(x) = \alpha \vee B(x)$$

and we get a partial firing of the rule.

In the preceding we have very briefly introduced the theory of approximate reasoning and provided an account of it as one in which propositions are viewed as imposing constraints on the allowable values of variables. In this spirit one can begin to get an understanding of the process of deduction in this system as being closely related to the solution of a nonlinear programming.

4. Fuzzy Systems Modeling

One area where fuzzy set theory and the the theory of approximate reasoning has found considerable applications is in the domain of fuzzy systems modeling [2, 13, 14]. The applications of this approach has been particularly noteworthy in the development of fuzzy logic controllers. Many of these applications have provided early examples of what in the future will be a very important domain of computer science, **"things that think"**

We consider a system as shown in figure #1. In this system V is the input variable and U is the output variable, they respectively take their values from the sets X and Y which are subsets of the real line.

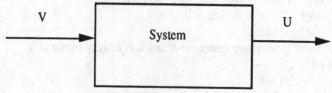

Figure #1 Typical System

A fuzzy system model (FSM) provides a representation of the complex input/output relationship of the system by partitioning the input space into fuzzy regions and then associating with each of these regions a output value that is itself a fuzzy subset [2]. Formally the partitioning is accomplished be representing our knowledge of the system in terms of rules of the form

$$\text{If V is } A_i \text{ then U is } B_i \qquad i = 1, 2, ..., n$$

where A_i and B_i are fuzzy subsets defined over their domains of discourse, X and Y. Typical of these types of rules are statements of the form

If V is *small* then U is *close to* 20

If V is *median* then U is *close to* 40

If V is *large* then U is *close to* 90.

It is required that the rules completely cover the space X in the sense that for any x in X there exists at least one A_i such that $A_i(x) \neq 0$. The basic structure of the fuzzy system model was suggested by Zadeh [15] and the first application of the FSM technology was done by Mamdani and his group [16-19]. In [20, 21] the editors provide a number of interesting applications of this technology.

Generally in using an FSM we are given a specific input value for the variable V and desire to use the model to determine a specific value for the output variable U. With the aid of the theory of approximate reasoning a specific simple algorithmic type procedure has been developed for implementing this task, this procedure is called FSM reasoning. We now describe this procedure. For a given input $V = x^*$ the following four step process is used to determine the output of the system [22]:

1. Find the degree of firing of each rule, λ_i

2. Determine the effective output of each of the rules, denoted U is F_i (F_i is a fuzzy subset)

3. Aggregate the individual rule outputs to obtain an overall output, U is F

4. Defuzzify F to obtain a crisp value y^* from the space Y

We now describe each of these steps in more detail.

In the first step we simply obtain the membership grade of x^* in the fuzzy subset A_i, thus $\lambda_i = A_i(x^*)$. In some environments the input variable may be a joint variable, $V = (V_1, V_2, ..., V_n)$. In this situation $A_i = A_{i1} \times A_{i2} \times ... A_{in}$ where each A_{ij} is a fuzzy subset. In this case the input is an n-tuple $x^* = (x_1^*, x_2^*, ..., x_n^*)$ and

$$\lambda_i = A_i(x^*) = \text{Min}_j (A_{ij}(x_j^*)).$$

In the second step the determination of the effective output of reach rule is accomplished by calculating the fuzzy subset F_i having membership grade

$$F_i(x) = T(\lambda_i, B_i(x))$$

where T is a t-norm operator. In most applications the two most often used t-norm operators are the min and the product

$$F_i(y) = \text{Min} [\lambda_i, B_i(y)]$$

$$F_i(y) = \lambda_i B_i(y).$$

For a number of computational considerations it is more effective to use the product and hence we assume this step is accomplished bé the product.

The original proposal for aggregating the individual rule outputs, step 3, suggested by Mamdani was based upon the use of Max operator,

$$F(y) = \text{Max}_i [F_i(y)].$$

However, most recent applications use an additive formulation in this step,

$$F(y) = \sum_{i=1}^{n} F_i(y).$$

The reason for this choice, as discussed by Kosko [14], is based upon the fact that this allows a kind of reinforcement if more then one rule says the same thing. Also the use of an additive model leads to computationally easier forms during the process of learning the rules.

The defuzzification step involves the use of F to determine the effective output of the system, y^*. The usual method for accomplishing this task is to calculate the center of area of F,

$$y^* = \frac{\sum_y F(y) \cdot y}{\sum_y F(y)}$$

In many applications of fuzzy modeling, following the work of Takagi and Sugeno [23], , the consequent fuzzy subset is often replaced by a singleton value which may be function of the input, that is we have as our consequent

$$U \text{ is } y_i$$

where $y_i = a_i + bx^*$.

The use of this formulation for the consequent along with a choice of multiplication to implementation step 2, and addition to implement step 3, leads to a simple form for the output of fuzzy system

$$y^* = \sum_{i=1}^{n} w_i y_i \qquad \qquad \textbf{(I)}$$

where

$$w_i = \frac{\lambda_i}{\sum_{j=1}^{n} \lambda_j}.$$

In [1] Yager and Filev called this the direct fuzzy reasoning method (DFR). In using this method the process of finding the output of a fuzzy system model becomes simply a two step process.

(1) Calculate $\lambda_i = A_i(x^*)$

(2) Calculate y^* from **I**

Essentially we see that the output of a fuzzy model becomes the weighted average of the consequent of each rule weighted by the firing level.

In using the fuzzy system modeling technology a key issue is the construction of the rule base. That is, some means must be provided for obtaining the rules that are used to model the system. In [2] Yager and Filev discuss three fundamental ways of obtaining the rules used in the fuzzy system model. In the first method, which we call the direct method, one obtains the rules directly from a expert in the field. In this approach a dialog between the system builder and expert is used to obtain the rules. We note that this approach is very much in the spirit of the knowledge engineering methods used in expert systems. The early examples of fuzzy systems models were all build using this approach.

The second method for obtaining the rules is based upon a complete reliance on input/output data about the system. Using this approach we use the input/output data to generate the rules associated with a system. These approaches generally use a clustering type method. One clustering method used in this environment is the mountain method introduced in [24-27]. Another very popular method is the fuzzy c-means [28].

The basic idea in using these methods is as follows. We apply a clustering technique such as the mountain method to the data. Using the clustering technique we find a collection of cluster centers, (x_i, y_i). Then each of the cluster centers is used as a focus of a fuzzy rule such as

If V is "about x_i" then U is "about x_i."

In these rules the fuzzy sets are usually represented as exponential fuzzy subsets of the form

$$A_i(x) = \exp{\frac{1}{2}(\frac{x - x_i}{\sigma_i})^2}$$

a turning step, using a gradient accent method, such as that used in the back propagation algorithm, is then applied to refine the fuzzy subsets used in the rule base. In [26] Yager and Filev describe such an approach in complete detail. Chiu [27] also discusses an application of the mountain clustering methodology for learning the rules. Other approaches to learning the rules directly from the data have been suggested in the literature using neural networks [14, 29].

The third approach to obtaining the rules in a fuzzy systems model, called the template method, has been discussed in [30]. This approach is based upon work initially done by Tong [31] and Kosko [14]. The template approach lies between the complete data driven approaches and the direct approach. It uses both data and expert information to obtain the rules. In this method an initial collection of linguistic values, called the templates are provided. These template values which form a partitioning of each input and output space are generally provided by an expert and are a reflection of the experts language for describing the environment which we are attempting to model. In addition we have a collection of observations about the system, input-output pairs (x_k, y_k)

Let $B_1, B_2, ..., B_s$ be a collection of templates, linguistic values represented as fuzzy subsets, that partition the input space and let $D_1, D_2, ..., D_t$ be a collection of templates that partition the output space. It is then assumed that each pair of template values forms a potential rule, $R(B_i, D_j)$, of the form if V is B_i then U is D_j. The data is now used to select from these potential rules the actual rules. Essentially each piece of data is assigned to a particular potential rule based upon the data falling into the partition described be the rule, that is the data (x_k, y_k) is assigned to the potential rule $R(B_i, D_j)$ if x_k is in B_i and y_k is in D_j. Then those potential rules which have a significant number of data points assigned to them becomes the actual rules in the rule base. More details on this approach can be found [30].

5. Conclusion

In the preceding we have provided a very brief introduction to some aspects of fuzzy set theory. For those interested, three edited volumes of original readings in the field are available. The first [10] is a collection of notable papers by L.A. Zadeh, the founder of the field. The second [32], edited by Dubois, Prade and Yager, in addition to providing a collection important original readings contains a comprehensive annotated bibliography. The edited volume [33] is devoted to papers in the area of fuzzy pattern recognition.

References

1. Zadeh, L. A., "Fuzzy sets," *Information and Control* 8, 338-353, 1965.
2. Yager, R. R. and Filev, D. P., *Essentials of Fuzzy Modeling and Control*, John Wiley: New York, 1994.
3. Klir, G. J. and Bo, Y., *Fuzzy Sets and Fuzzy Logic: Theory and Applications*, Prentice Hall: Upper Saddle River, NJ, 1995.
4. Yager, R. R., "On a general class of fuzzy connectives," *Fuzzy Sets and Systems* 4, 235-242, 235-242, 1980.
5. Klement, E. P., "Characterization of fuzzy measures constructed by means of triangular norms," *J. of Math. Anal. & Appl.* 86, 345-358, 1982.
6. Weber, S., "A general concept of fuzzy connectives, negations and implications based on t-norms," *Fuzzy Sets and Systems* 11, 115-134, 1983.
7. Zadeh, L. A., "Fuzzy sets as a basis for a theory of possibility," *Fuzzy Sets and Systems* 1, 3-28, 1978.
8. Dubois, D. and Prade, H., *Possibility Theory : An Approach to Computerized Processing of Uncertainty*, Plenum Press: New York, 1988.
9. Zadeh, L. A., "A theory of approximate reasoning," in *Machine Intelligence*, Vol. 9, Hayes, J., Michie, D., & Mikulich, L.I. (eds.), New York: Halstead Press, 149-194, 1979.
10. Yager, R. R., Ovchinnikov, S., Tong, R. and Nguyen, H., *Fuzzy Sets and Applications: Selected Papers by L. A. Zadeh*, John Wiley & Sons: New York, 1987.
11. Zadeh, L. A., "PRUF--a meaning representation language for natural languages," *International Journal of Man-Machine Studies* 10, 395-460, 1978.
12. Yager, R. R., "The entailment principle for Dempster-Shafer granules," *Int. J. of Intelligent Systems* 1, 247-262, 1986.
13. Yager, R. R., Sugeno, M., Nguyen, H. T. and Tong, R. T., *Theoretical Aspects of Fuzzy Control*, John Wiley & Sons: New York, 1995.
14. Kosko, B., *Neural Networks and Fuzzy Systems*, Prentice Hall: Englewood Cliffs, NJ, 1991.
15. Zadeh, L., "Outline of a new approach to the analysis of complex systems and decision processes," *IEEE Trans. Systems, Man, and Cybernetics*, SMC-3, 28-44, 1973.
16. Mamdani, E. H., "Application of fuzzy algorithms for control of simple dynamic plant," *Proc. IEEE* 121, 1585-1588, 1974.
17. Mamdani, E. H. and Assilian, S., "An experiment in linguistic synthesis with a fuzzy logic controller," *Int. J. of Man-Machine Studies* 7, 1-13, 1975.
18. Mamdani, E. H. and Baaklini, N., "Prescriptive method for deriving control policy in a fuzzy logic control," *Electronic Lett.* Ii, 625-626, 1975.

19. Mamdani, E. H., "Advances in the linguistic synthesis of fuzzy controllers," *Int. J. of Man-Machine Studies* 8, 669-678, 1976.

20. Sugeno, M., *Industrial Applications of Fuzzy Control*, North-Holland: Amsterdam, 1985.

21. Yen, J., Langari, R. and Zadeh, L. A., *Industrial Applications of Fuzzy Logic and Intelligent Systems*, IEEE Press: New York, 1995.

22. Yager, R. R. and Filev, D. P., "On a flexible structure for fuzzy systems models," in *Fuzzy Sets, Neural Networks and Soft Computing*, edited by Yager, R. R. and Zadeh, L. A., Van Nostrand: New York, 1-28, 1994.

23. Takagi, T. and Sugeno, M., "Fuzzy identification of systems and its application to modeling and control," *IEEE Transactions on Systems, Man and Cybernetics* 15, 116-132, 1985.

24. Yager, R. R. and Filev, D. P., "Learning of fuzzy rules by mountain clustering," *SPIE Conference on Applications of Fuzzy Logic Technology*, Boston, 246-254, 1993.

25. Yager, R. R. and Filev, D. P., "Approximate clustering via the mountain method," *IEEE Transactions on Systems, Man and Cybernetics* 24, 1279-1284, 1994.

26. Yager, R. R. and Filev, D. P., "Generation of fuzzy rules by mountain clustering," *Journal of Intelligent and Fuzzy Systems* 2, 209-219, 1994.

27. Chiu, S. L., "Fuzzy model identification based on cluster estimation," *Journal of Fuzzy and Intelligent Systems* 2, 267-278, 1994.

28. Bezdek, J., *Pattern Recognition with Fuzzy Objective Function Algorithms*, Plenum: New York, 1981.

29. Pedrycz, W., *Fuzzy Sets Engineering*, CRC Press: Boca Raton, FL, 1995.

30. Yager, R. R. and Filev, D. P., "Template based fuzzy systems modeling," *Journal of Intelligent and Fuzzy Systems* 2, 39-54, 1994.

31. Tong, R. M., "Synthesis of fuzzy models for industrial processes- some recent results," *Int. J. of General Systems* 4, 143-163, 1978.

32. Dubois, D., Prade, H. and Yager, R. R., *Readings in Fuzzy Sets for Intelligent Systems*, Morgan Kaufmann: San Mateo, CA, 1993.

33. Bezdek, J. C. and Pal, S. K., *Fuzzy Models for Pattern Recognition*, IEEE Publications: New York, 1992.

Information Retrieval and Informative Reasoning

C.J. van Rijsbergen

Department of Computing Science
University of Glasgow
Glasgow   G12 8RZ
Scotland
U.K.

Abstract This is a brief account of some of the formal models underlying recent research in information retrieval. In particular I discuss the central role that uncertain implication plays in viewing retrieval as a form of inference. There is some hope that a paradigm borrowed from quantum mechanics may lead to a unified model, that is, a framework within which the different formal models can be expressed.

1. Introduction

Information Retrieval has been a bit of a Cinderella subject, claimed by the Library and Information Science community and viewed with a certain amount of suspicion by the Computer Science community (why not solve it by DB technology?[1]), but as part of computing its roots go back to at least before World War II when Robert Fairthorne (Walker,1974) was speculating about the use of computing machinery to enhance the retrieval of bibliographic records. The physical storage of large amounts of information on electronic media has ceased to be a major problem, hence the emphasis in IR on the *retrieval* of the stored information. The arrival of electronic storage devices that will comfortably handle data sets in the terabyte range has allowed researchers and developers to concentrate on the searching, retrieval, browsing and display of multi-media information.

What is the Information Retrieval problem? Why is it not enough to say: 'Just store it and when you need it just find it, and retrieve it!' In fact as long ago as in Plato's day the IR problem was already apparent. I quote (paradoxically):

> 'And how will you enquire, Socrates, into that which you do not know?...if you find what you want, how will you ever know that this is the thing which you did not know?...a man cannot enquire either about that which he knows, or about that which he does not know: for if he knows, he has no need to enquire; and if not, he cannot; for he does not know the very subject about which he is to enquire.'
> Meno, Plato

---

[1] But see the work of Harper and Walker(1992).

The storage step is now easy; finding the right information and looking at it is a different matter. A user interested in a item of information, first has to ask for it. In IR asking for it means constructing a query which may be a natural language statement, a tune, a picture, a bit of image, etc. This query is formulated to reflect or represent what the user is interested in, and ultimately intended to lead to items that the user wishes to explore, read, think about, absorb etc. The process is one of locating information for further examination.

2. The Haystack Analogy

In practice the number of items[2] in the repository of items likely to be of interest to a user is small, hence one is dealing with the computation of very rare events. It is like looking for a needle in a haystack, this simple analogy to a haystick will give one some idea of the early models that were proposed for solving the IR problem. If one were given the problem of finding a needle in a haystack one would very quickly find a way to do it. To begin with one would think about the problem in the following way:

1. the thing I am looking for is rare, so a random
    search is likely to be useless
2. its characteristics are very different from the
    things I do not want (hay)
3. I can exploit this difference if I know more
    about it, I could use a magnet or burn down
    the stack.

Now imagine that the same problem was faced by a Martian who knows nothing about the properties of metal, for example that it is resistant to fire and attracted by magnets. How would such a creature proceed? Well, the Martian's situation is not very different from users faced with a large information store: they know that there is likely to be an item of interest but it is one amongst millions which are of no interest. To take a random sample does not help much for in the case of the haystack it would produce only hay, from which we infer that the needle is not made of straw! We need to find out more about the item looked for, a Martian would consult our knowledge about needles. In the case of IR the user would express a query which when processed would return items likely to be like the ones sought and it is precisely the charateristics of the items returned that could be used to continue the search. The approximate response of the IR system will give clues about the nature of the items sought. It is important to emphasise that what is retrieved is not a random sample.

3. The QM Analogy

The haystack analogy is a very simple one, and indeed does correspond to some retrieval models. Another analogy which is far more sophisticated and leads into more recent IR models, is one based on the quantum mechanical paradigm. The theory of quantum mechanics is mainly concerned with observables and state vectors. It is possible to reduce the QM analysis to one in which the observables are simple 'yes'/'no' questions about the state of a system. Moreover the answer to such a binary question

---

[2] I will treat objects, items and documents interchangeably.

has associated with it a probability of being either yes or no in any state. If one now thinks of the states as documents in an information space and observables as simple queries then the analogy is complete. In fact the properties of simple observables are such that they form a structure, a non-boolean lattice, which gives rise to a logic: quantum logic. The same can be said for IR, instead of the physics we have the semantics of the query terms, and these can also give rise to a non-classical logic. It is interesting that in quantum logic one of the central questions is how to specify an appropriate conditional for the logic; similarly in defining an IR logic the central issue appears to be what the semantics of the conditional will look like. For confirmation of this common concern one should compare the work in a paper by Hardegree(1976) in quantum mechanics with that of Van Rijsbergen(1989) in IR; both conclude that an appropriate implication is the Stalnaker conditonal.There is a further correspondence and this arises through the Hilbert space respresentation for state vectors, in this an observable can be thought of as a subspace and the quantum logic as operations on subspaces. In IR we often represent our documents as points in a high dimensional vector space and indeed the Boolean logic of queries corresponds to set-theoretic operations, it may be that the Hilbert space formalism is more appropriate for IR , if so, it would give a concrete example of a non-boolean logic (Beltrametti and Cassinelli, 1981). Finally, in quantum mechanics it is possible to express the states and observables as projectors on Hilbert Space; this is analogous to expressing documents and queries in terms of index terms each of which can be seen as a projector.

4. Feedback and Iteration

How does the IR problem differ from the DB problem? In databases it is assumed that the user can specify completely and accurately the data items of interest. In the relational technology this means asserting a logical combination of attribute values to be satisfied. Any item not satisfying the query in this way is assumed to be of no interest. In IR such an approach simply will not work. Given a logical combination of keywords the chances are that no item will satify it, or that too many will! In either case the answer (the set of items) is not the end of the story. A null answer does not mean that there are no items of interest, nor does a large set as response mean that all the retrieved items are of interest. How does IR get around this problem? The main solution rests on an iterative approach to retrieval, using feedback to focus the search. Conceptually one attempts to locate the *relevant* items in the store and proceeds to iteratively discover the attributes of such relevant items so that they can be retrieved.

    In statistical terms looking for a rare item is not easy, the literature on signal detection has established that. In terms of the haystack analogy, starting a search might consist of taking a random sample, since this is the time honoured way of estimating properties subject to randomness, but in doing so you are likely to find nothing. To start the iteration one needs to use clues which are likely to tell you something about the items sought.These clues are used to retrieve relevant documents: documents relevant to the information need of the user. The usual way of accomplishing this is to match a query against each document in a large store. The underlying assumption is that closely matching documents are likely to be relevant. These matching strategies make extremely simple assumptions about the relationships between the index terms appearing in both queries and documents Once such items have been identified their properties can be used to improve the search. In other words once a relevant item has been found (because the user says so) one assumes that other relevant items are like it and feedback will lead to further relevant items. There are other ways of enhancing retrieval by exploiting the relationships between pairs of documents and pairs of index terms: the first is *document clustering*, the second is *query expansion*.

Document clustering takes its cue from Numerical Taxonomy (Sneath and Sokal, 1973). In this latter area many techniques were invented to measure similarity between objects on which to base a classification of objects. Towards the end of its heyday I think it was agreed that a 'universal' way of measuring similarity could be based on an information measure. In this context objects are described by attributes each of which can be as complex as a probability function, the similarity between two objects is then a function of *the extent to which one attribute contains information about another*. The information from different attributes is agregated. Many similarity measures used in numerical taxonomy and in IR are special cases of this more general information theoretic one. To exploit the similarity between documents one assumes that closely associated documents tend to be relevant to the same requests. On the basis of this asumption ducument classifications can be used to improve retrieval (Van Rijsbergen, 1979).

Similarly query expansion can used to improve retrieval. The basis of such a process can be summarised as follows. If an index term is good at discriminating relevant documents from non-relevant documents then any closely associated index term is likely to be good at this. Hence to enhance the retrieval performance it is necessary to identify closely associated index terms (Van Rijsbergen, 1977). Such associations are frequently measured in terms of some kind of information measure: the idea being that if two terms were linked closely in an information-theoretic sense then this indicated a close semantic association from the point of view of establishing relevance. This is similar to claiming that a high correlation between variables implies a causal link, which is manifestly false. Measuring associations through the strenghth of their statistical association (even in terms of information) is like measuring the extent to which terms are co-extensive. Such an association hypothesis implies that if terms are strongly co-extensive then they are about the same thing. In general this is false and demonstrates once again that 'aboutness' or 'information content' has first order intentionality as Dretske(1981) would put it. Nevertheless exploitation of associations between index terms continues to attract research, the belief is that by refining the measurement of such associations useful information can be discovered that will lead to better retrieval performance.

5. Retrieval as Inference

In the last few years a new way of looking at the IR problem has been explored: retrieval is modelled as a form of inference. It is simplest to explain this in terms of textual objects. A document is seen as a set of assertion or propositions and a query is seen as a single assertion or proposition[3] Then, a document is considered relevant to a query if it implies the query. The intuition here is that when say q is implied by Δ then Δ is assumed to be about q. Another reason for being attracted to this view of things is

---

[3] In this paper I will not distinguish between assertions and propositions.

that it captures a notion of information containment. When $A => B^4$ then the information that B is contained in A e.g. A = 'is a square' contains B = 'is a rectangle'. Hence by seeking that which *implies* the query we are seeking that which is *about* the query and that which contains the information specified by the query.

Although I have represented retrieval as logical inference it is not enough. Basing retrieval on strict logical consequence has the major disadvantage that typically a query is not implied by any documents (of course, this is similar to the failing of Boolean retrieval). Nevertheless it is possible to extend and modify the implication retaining the idea of inferring the query but making it less strict. For this we move to the idea of *partial entailment, degree of provability,* or *plausible inference* as it is variously called.

There is an extensive literature on partial entailment going back to at least Leibniz. The intuition is that we are able to assess the degree to which a proposition is entailed by a set of other propositions. So if we have a set Δ , then $\Delta \longrightarrow q$ is measurable. One of the ways is through calculating the conditional probability $P(q|\Delta)$. Another way is to evaluate $\Delta \longrightarrow q$ as a conditional whereby we measure the extent to which Δ has to be augmented so that $\Delta \longrightarrow q$ will go through This latter approach has a much debated history, for example Ramsey in the 1930's (Mellor,1976) already stated:

> 'To evaluate a conditional, first hypothetically make the minimum
> revision of your stock of beliefs required to assume the antecedent.
> Then evaluate the acceptability of the consequent on the basis of
> this revised body of beliefs.'

This statement has become widely known as the Ramsey test (e.g Gardenfors, 1988) My application of it is slightly different. Perhaps an example will help. Given a query about 'Programming Languages' $(=q)$ and a document described by 'Fortran' $(=\Delta)$, then the document would be considered relevant because $\Delta \longrightarrow q$. On the other hand consider q = 'Reasoning under uncertainty' and a document Δ = 'probabilistic logic'. Here it is not obvious that $\Delta \longrightarrow q$, what to do? The Ramsey test motivates the following, augment Δ in some minimal way until $\Delta + d\Delta \longrightarrow q$. The measure of $d\Delta$ can then be used to give a measure of $\Delta \longrightarrow q$.

This modification of Ramsey can be summarised as follows:

> Given any two sentences Δ and q; a measure of the uncertainty
> of $\Delta \longrightarrow q$ relative to a given data set is determined by the minimal
> extent to which we have to add information to the data set to
> establish the truth of $\Delta \longrightarrow q$.

This principle, if I may call it that, is not as unusual as one would think. For example, if you have (in propositional logic) A and B and you wish to derive B from A, then $B \supset A$ is the logically *weakest* information you can add to A to derive B: $A, B \supset A \vdash B$; and modus ponens is a well accepted rule of inference. Of course

---

[4] At this point nothing is said about the nature of the implication.

logically weakest is not the same as minimal in information-theroretic terms but see Sober(1975) for a closely allied concept of minimum extra information. For furhter details of this approach the reader should consult my earlier work and that of others (Nie, 1990, Bruza, 1993, and Lalmas and Van Rijsbergen, 1992).

The above approach has much in sympathy with evidential reasoning, that is, given that q constitutes the evidence/clues for the identity of a relevant document D, then we can interpret P(q|D) or P(D|q) as the strenght of evidential support.

6. Vector Space and Probabilistic Models

Possibly the most complete and satisfactory models for IR that have been described in the literature over the last 20 to 30 years are the vector space and probabilistic models for retrieval. These models are very abstract and assume a considerable data reduction of the objects in the domain of application before they can be used. The vector space model assumes that documents and queries can be represented as points in a high dimensional vector-space and that relevance is measured by a query's proximity to documents in that space. The probabilistic model assumes that one can estimate P(relevance|document). This is done by assuming that the document is a random vector and that relevance is a property whose probability for any unknown document can be estimated by using sample information from a set of known documents(Van Rijsbergen, 1979). The model can be shown to be optimal with respect to quality of retrieval if the documents are retrieved in their order of probability of relevance(Robertson, 1977). Under both models most of the semantics associated with the documents and queries is lost, in fact, it is replaced by absence/presence index terms or frequency counts of those terms.

The basis for Probabilistic Retrieval is the celebrated Bayes' Theorem:

$$P(H|e) \propto P(e|H)P(H)$$

or $$P(H|e) = \frac{P(e|H)P(H)}{P(e)}$$

since $$\sum_H P(H|e) = 1 .$$

The usual interpretation of the symbols is that H is a hypothesis (one of several) which is supported (or otherwise) by some evidence e . P(H|e) is interpreted as the probability that H is true given certain evidence e. Bayes' Theorem is a form of belief revision in that P(e|H), P(H), and P(e) are probabilities associated with propositions (or events) *before* e is actually observed and P(H|e) is the probability of H *after* e has been observed.   The notation used to express this is especially opaque because the same P(.) is used for the prior and posterior probabilities.   In fact P(H|e) would be better written as $P_e(H)$ indicating that we now have a *new* probability function P_e . A further difficulty with this approach is that the evidence e has to be certain at observation, that is, cannot be disputed once it is observed, which implies that $P_e(e) = 1$. The fact that in general a conditional probability can only take into account an exact and certain proposition, or event, as its basis for revising the probability in the light of observation, is a source of some difficulty.   In IR we use the Bayesian approach by calculating $P_q(R|d)$ through $P(R|x)$ where x is some representation of the document assumed to be certain.   This means that the description x is assumed to be true of the document, or *in* the document, depending on one's point of view.   In many cases this is not fully appropriate, as the description, or representation x may be subject to uncertainty itself at the time of observation.

Let us examine the calculation of $P(R|x)$ in a little more detail: let x be a set of independent variables $x_1, ... x_n$., then

$$\frac{P(R \mid x)}{P(\overline{R} \mid x)} = \frac{P(x \mid R)\, P(R)}{P(x \mid \overline{R})\, P(\overline{R})} \qquad\qquad P(R) = 1 - P(\overline{R})$$

and

$$\log \frac{P(R \mid x)}{P(\overline{R} \mid x)} = \log \frac{p_1(x_1)}{q_1(x_1)} + \log \frac{p_2(x_2)}{q_2(x_2)} \;\cdots\cdots$$

$$+ \log \frac{p_n(x_n)}{q_n(x_n)} + \log \frac{P(R)}{P(\overline{R})}$$

where
$$P(x \mid R) = p_1(x_1)\, p_2(x_2) \cdots p_n(x_n)$$
$$P(x \mid \overline{R}) = q_1(x_1)\, q_2(x_2) \cdots q_n(x_n)\;.$$

Thinking now of the values of the individual variables x_i as applied to a particular document as bits of evidence in support of R or not-R, the support will rise or fall as

$$\log \frac{p_i(x_i)}{q_i(x_i)}$$

increments or decrements the overall support. Remember that p_i and q_i have to be estimated; they are not given *ab initio*. The interpretation of one of the evidential weights e.g.

$$\log \frac{p_i(x_i=1)}{q_i(x_i=1)}$$

is not entirely obvious. $p_i(x_i = 1)$ decodes to: if the document d *were* relevant, p_i is the probability that x_i *would* be true, or present. We are calculating the probability because we are observing a document with x_i true. There is room for confusion, x_i is true and yet we ask for the probability that x_i is true. It is like observing a '6' on a dice and asking what was the probability governing that chance event happening. In addition it is very likely that the observation itself is uncertain. In IR we assign index terms with a degree of certainty. So for example, a component of a document representation, x_i, might only be true of, apply to, the document with a certain probability. This way of viewing indexing was explored early by Maron and Kuhns(1960). Adopting such a view makes the application of Bayes' Theorem less obvious, one should not identify the probability of relevance with $P(R|x_i)$ since x_i is now not certain, and its degree of uncertainty needs to be taken into account. Therefore other ways of conditionalising must be found.

7. Kinematic IR (Crestani and Van Rijsbergen, 1995)

The probabilistic model is in some ways a precursor of the logic-based model that views retrieval as inference. The form of inference in the former case is Bayesian Inference. In its original formulation the model is used to estimate the probability of relevance given some *simple-minded properties of documents* . A more recent approach is to estimate the probability of relevance on the basis of a logical relationship between a document Δ and a query q. This can be captured formally as follows:

$$P^*(rel) = P(rel|\Delta—>q)P^*(\Delta—>q) + P(rel|{\sim}(\Delta—>q))P^*({\sim}(\Delta—>q))$$

In this expression one calculates the probability of relevance based on the evidence that Δ entails q and one assumes that the entailment is partial where the strength of the entailment is measured by P^*. This way of conditioning is based on the approach of Jeffrey(1983); he made a strong case for generalising Bayes' Theorem to handle cases of uncertain evidence. He introduced his method of conditionalisation through a now famous example. Imagine one inspects a piece of cloth by candlelight and one gets the impression that it is green, although it might be blue, or even violet. If, G, B, and V are the propositions involved, then the outcome of the observation might be that the degrees of belief in G, B or V are .7, .25, and .05, whereas *before* observation the degrees of belief were .3, .3, .4 . In symbols we would write

$$P(G) = .3, \qquad P(B) = .3, \qquad P(V) = .4$$
$$P^*(G) = .7, \qquad P^*(B) = .25, \qquad P^*(V) = .05$$

Here P is a measure of the degree of belief before observation, and P* the measure after observation. As Jeffrey puts it, the 'passage of experience' has led P to be revised to P*. In Bayesian terms $P^*(x) = P(x|e)$ where e is a *proposition*, but Jeffrey rightly claims that it is not always possible to express the passage of experience as a proposition. Given that one has changed one's degree of belief in some propositions G, B, and V as shown above, how are these changes to be propagated over the rest of the structure of one's beliefs? For example, suppose saleability A of the cloth depends on the colour inspection in the following way:

$$P(A|G) = .4 \qquad P(A|B) = .4 \qquad P(A|V) = .8$$

Prior to inspection

$$P(A) = P(A|G) P(G) + P(A|B)P(B) + P(A|V)P(V)$$
$$= 4 \times .3 + .4 \times .3 + .8 \times .4 = .56$$

After inspection Jeffrey proposes:

$$P^*(A) = P(A|G)P^*(G)+P(A|B)P^*(B)+P(A|V)P^*(V),$$
$$= .4 \times .7 + .4 \times .25 + .8 \times .05 = .0485$$

known as *Jeffrey's rule of conditioning*

It is valid whenever $P^*(A|E_i) = P(A|E_i)$ where E_i is a partition of the sample space. This differs from Bayesian conditioning which would use $P^*(G) = 1$, or $P^*(B) = 1$, or $P^*(V) = 1$ and so revise $P(A)$ to $P^*(A) = P(A|X)$ when X = G, B, or V. Thus Bayesian conditioning can be seen as a special case of Jeffrey conditioning.

In this example the conditioning event is a simple property, namely colour, in what was proposed earlier, $\Delta \longrightarrow q$ is a logical relationship. The machinery required to calculate the relevant probabilities is not so simple and I suggest the reader consult , for example, Van Rijsbergen(1992) or Wong and Yao(1995). It is interesting that this complex expression defaults to some of the esarlier models under certain assumptions. Assume that Δ is empty then

$$P^*(Rel) = P(Rel \mid q) P^*(q) + P(Rel \mid \bar{q}) P^* (\bar{q}).$$

In the classical case $P^* (q) = 1$ implies $P^*(Rel) = P (Rel \mid q)$ whereas $P^* (\bar{q}) = 1$ implies $P^*(Rel) = P (Rel \mid \bar{q})$. Boolean retrieval would judge that

$$P^* (q) = 1 \implies P(Rel \mid q) = P^* (Rel) = 1$$
$$P^* (q) = 0 \implies P(Rel \mid q) = P^* (Rel) = 0$$

8. Conclusion

This paper has given a brief sketch of how uncertain implication can be modelled in Information Retrieval. There appear to be a number of ways of doing this as is well illustrated by the literature. I would conjecture that by adopting the 'quantum mechanical paradigm' all these different ways may well be unified into the one model.

9. References

1. P.D. Bruza, Stratified Information Disclosure: A synthesis between hypermedia and information retrieval, PhD thesis, University of Nijmegen (1993).

2. E.G. Beltrametetti and G. Cassinelli, *The logic of quatum mechanics*, Addison-Wesley:London (1981).

3. F. Crestani and C.J. van Rijsbergen, Probability kinematics in information retrieval, *Proceedings of the Eighteenth Annual ACM SIGIR Conference on Research and Development in Information Retrieval*. Seattle,July, 291-299 (1995).

4. F. Dretske, *Knowledge and the flow of information*, The MIT Press: Cambridge (Mass.) (1981).

5. P. Gardenfors, *Knowledge in flux: Modelling the dynamics of epistemic states*, The MIT Press:London (1988).

6. G.M. Hardegree, The conditional in quatum logic, In P.Suppes (ed.) *Logic and Probability in Quatum Mechanics*, Reidel:Dordrecht, 55-72 (1976).

7. D.J. Harper and A.D.M. Walker, ECLAIR: an extensible class library for information retrieval, *The Computer Journal*, **35**, 256-267 (1992).

8. R.C. Jeffrey, *The Logic of Decision*, 2nd Edition. University of Chicago Press: Chicago (1983).

9. M. Lalmas and C.J. van Rijsbergen, A logical model of information retrieval based on situation theory, *Proceedings 14th Information Retrieval Colloquium*, Lancaster, 1-13 (1992).

10. M.E. Maron and J.L. Kuhns, On relevance, probabilistic indexing and retrieval, *Journal of the ACM*, **7**, 216-244 (1960).

11. D.H. Mellor (Ed.), *Foundations: Essays in philosophy, logic, mathematics and economics: F.P. Ramsey*, Routledge & Keegan Paul: London (1976).

12. J. Nie, Un modele de logique general pour les systemes de recherche d'informations. Application au prototype RIME. PhD Thesis, University Joseph Fourier, Grenoble (1990).

13. S.E. Robertson, The probability ranking principle in IR.   *Journal of Documentation*, **33**, 294-304 (1977).

14. C.J. van Rijsbergen, A theoretical basis for the use of co-occurence data in information retrieval, *Journal of Documentation*, **33**, 106-119 (1977).

15. C.J. van Rijsbergen, *Information Retrieval*, Second Edition. London:Butterworths (1979).

16. C.J. van Rijsbergen, A non-classical logic for Information Retrieval. *The Computer Journal*, **29**, 481-485 (1986).

17. C.J. van Rijsbergen. Towards an Information Logic. In N. Belkin and C.J. van Rijsbergen (eds.) *Proceedings of the Twelfth Annual ACM SIGIR Conference on Research and Development in Information Retrieval*. New York:ACM, 77-86 (1989).

18. C.J.van Rijsbergen, Probabilistic retrieval revisited, *The Computer Journal*, **35**, 291-298 (1992).

19. P.H.A. Sneath and R.R. Sokal, *Numerical Taxonomy*, W.H. Freeman: San Francisco (1973).

20. E. Sober, *Simplicity*, Clarendon Press: Oxford (1975).

21. P.B. Walker, Robert Arthur Fairthorne: An appreciation, *Journal of Documentation*, **30**, 127-138 (1974).

22. S.K.M. Wong and Y.Y. Yao, On modelling information retrieval with probabilistic inference, *ACM Transactions on Information Systems*, **13**, 38-68 (1995).

Database Transaction Models

Gottfried Vossen

Universität Münster, Institut für Wirtschaftsinformatik,
Grevenerstraße 91, D-48159 Münster, Germany

Abstract. The transaction concept provides a central paradigm for correctly synchronizing concurrent activities and for achieving reliability in database systems. In transaction modeling and processing, theory and practice influence each other a lot, and over the years the transaction concept has undergone a considerable evolution from a pure implementation vehicle to a powerful abstraction concept. This survey deals with conceptual issues in designing transaction *models*, and with approaches to specify correctness of concurrent transaction executions (schedules). As will be described, there is a vastly uniform methodology for putting these aspects to work, which is illustrated by examples ranging from simple reads and writes to semantically rich operations. In addition, the survey covers novel transaction models, whose goal is to adequately support a variety of requirements arising in modern database applications.

1   Introduction

A core functionality of a database system is to allow users shared access to databases, and to simultaneously provide a certain degree of fault tolerance [43]. In the 1970s, the *transaction concept* [18] emerged as a tool to serve both purposes. The basic idea underlying this concept (commonly known as the "ACID principle") is to consider a given program that wants to operate on a database as a logical unit (Atomicity), to require that it leaves the Consistency of the database invariant, to process it as if the database was at its exclusive disposal (Isolation), and to make sure that program effects survive later failures (Durability). In particular, operations cast into the logical brackets of a transaction are no longer required to keep a database consistent at an individual basis, but only at the end of the transaction; hence, inconsistent intermediate states are acceptable.

There are two issues to be dealt with in order to put this to work: The *concurrency control problem* is to provide synchronization protocols which allow an efficient and correct access of multiple transactions to a shared database; the *recovery problem* is to provide protocols that can react to certain types of failures automatically and in the right way. Both problems have mostly been studied separately, although they are not independent of each other [46]. The typical result of looking at one of them is a criterion which has to be met by transaction executions in order to be considered "correct"; today, there are numerous correctness notions, many of which are obtained using a uniform methodology which is described in Sect. 2. Examples of how to apply the methodology in various distinct contexts are provided in Sect. 3. After that, a survey of generalizations which have been proposed and studied over the years is given in Sect. 4. We emphasize that we do *not* look at protocols here, but at *models* which have to be designed and studied before protocols can be developed.

The transaction model that underlies most system implementations is extremely simple amd primitive (see Sect. 3.1). It justs looks at read and write operations applied to pages in storage, and disregards any semantics of the underlying application program. Therefore, a new goal, which essentially emerged in the 1980s, became to capture and to exploit *semantic* information when modeling and when processing transactions. Moreover, as database applications evolved, the transaction concept was discovered as an abstraction mechanism which is powerful already, but which needs to be adapted and extended when previously irrelevant issues enter the picture. A look at advanced transaction models, proposed in response to this requirement, is taken in Sect. 5. Due to space limitations, we sometimes just provide hints to the literature we consider most relevant for the topic in question.

2   A Methodology for Devising Transaction Models

We begin our discussion of traditional and more recent technical issues related to database transactions from the point of view of a system for which the concurrency control problem as well as the recovery problem are to be solved. The "program" that needs to be gone through for providing efficient solutions to both problems is roughly as follows:

1. First, a suitable *model* of transactions and their *executions* (called histories or *schedules*) is needed (where typically the latter is implied by the former).
2. Then an appropriate notion of *correctness* for schedules needs to be established.
3. Finally, *protocols* need to be devised which àre capable of automatically generating correct schedules (since we will not discuss protocols in this paper, the interested reader is referred to [9, 19, 30, 44]).

The correctness issue is the most crucial one, since it should ideally capture both correct synchronization *and* reliability, and it must be suited for a *dynamic* situation in which the transactions to be processed are not fully known in advance. If, as done frequently, a static setting is considered first (in which complete knowledge of the transactions under consideration is available), it must be ensured that the results obtained easily transfer to the dynamic case.

To put the above program to work, the following is a common procedure:

1. Fix a notion of *database object* as well as *operations* applicable to such objects.
2. Transactions can then be described as (finite, totally ordered) sequences (or, which is sometimes more appropriate, as partial orders) of such operations.

3. For (statically) given transactions, a *complete schedule* is simply an element of their shuffle product, representing an interleaved execution of the transactions' operations; for a dynamic setting, a *schedule* is a prefix of a complete one.

4. Define a notion of *conflict* for operations from distinct transactions occurring in a given schedule, and consider a (complete) schedule correct if it is (conflict-) *serializable*, i.e., (conflict-) equivalent to a serial schedule for the transactions in question.

5. In addition to synchronization correctness, pick an appropriate criterion capturing reliability (e.g., one that excludes dirty-read situations).

An agreement seems to exist in the world of transactions that *serializability* is a good approach for describing when a schedule represents a correct synchronization. Indeed, if an individual transaction preserves the consistency of a given database, which is typically easy to test, then the same holds for any *serial* execution of several transactions. Now serializability just requires *equivalence to seriality*, and notions of serializability typically differ in their underlying equivalence relation. We will say more about this in what follows. However, it has to be kept in mind that reliability is generally *not* subsumed by serializability, so that something additional is needed to this end.

Another agreement seems to be that *conflict-based* correctness criteria are a good choice. Intuitively, such a criterion considers that two operations from distinct transactions are *in conflict* in a given schedule if their execution order is relevant for determining whether that schedule is equivalent to a schedule known to be correct (e.g., a serial one). As will be discussed in the next section, depending on the semantic information taken into account, conflicts (and the commutativity of operations) are defined differently.

3   Sample Realizations

We now present two examples of how the methodology described in the previous section can be applied. The first is the traditional *read/write model* of transactions, the second is a more recent one in which the operations represent *updates* on a *relational* database.

3.1   The Read/Write Model

The best known transaction model considers database objects to be pages in memory which can be read or written in one atomic operation; thus, transactions in this model are *sequences of read and write operations*, thereby abstracting from all kinds of computations that a user program might execute in main memory or in its buffer. This model is justified by the fact that database programs, when executed, are treated by the underlying operating system like any other program; hence, they reside in main memory, are subject to execution scheduling, and are assigned buffer space to manipulate data and to create results. However, transactions frequently access *secondary* memory via read and write operations, and since multiple transactions may access identical locations there, it is the read and write operations that need to be synchronized.

Transactions and schedules. Let a database be a (countably infinite) set $D = \{x, y, z, \ldots\}$ of objects (e.g., pages); then a *transaction* has the form $t = p_1 \ldots p_n$, where each p_i is of the form $r(x)$ ("read x") or $w(x)$ ("write x") for some $x \in D$. A *complete schedule* for a (finite) set T of transactions is an element of the shuffle product of T, i.e., an ordering of all operations of the transactions which respects the order of operations specified by the individual transactions. Additionally, it contains a termination step for each transaction following its last data operation; such a step states whether a transaction finally *commits* (i.e., ends successfully) or *aborts* (i.e., is canceled prior to successful termination). If t_i appears in the schedule, a commit [abort] is indicated by c_i [a_i], resp. Two steps from distinct transactions are *in conflict* in a given schedule, if they operate on the same database object and at least one of them is a write.

Notice that, in this model, transactions (and schedules) are purely *syntactic* objects, just describing the sequencing of data accesses performed by a database program, how these are interleaved, and what eventually happens to each transaction (but not what the underlying program does to the database as a state transformation). A common assumption in traditional concurrency control theory is that the *semantics* of transactions are not known. As a consequence, only a *Herbrand semantics* can be defined for schedules, as described, for example, in [22, 44].

The following is a complete schedule for four transactions, in which t_0, t_2 and t_3 are committed and t_1 is aborted:

$$s = w_0(x)r_1(x)w_0(z)r_1(z)r_2(x)w_0(y)c_0r_3(z)w_3(z)w_2(y)c_2w_1(x)w_3(y)a_1c_3$$

Conflicts exist, for example, between t_0 and t_2 on x, or between t_1 and t_3 on z (the latter would be considered irrelevant since t_1 is aborted). A serial schedule for the same transactions would be $s' = t_0t_2t_1t_3$. Notice that in general there exist $n!$ serial schedules for n transactions.

Serializability and reliability. We next look at some notions of serializability for schedules in the read/write model. Recall that serializability means equivalence to seriality, so what we actually look at are distinct notions of schedule equivalence. Following [29], two schedules are *final-state equivalent* if they have the same Herbrand semantics; a schedule is *final-state serializable* (in the class FSR) if there exists a serial schedule for the given transactions which is final-state equivalent to the schedule under consideration. The notion of *view serializability* [48] (or the class VSR) seems intuitively more realistic, since it emphasizes the fact that equivalent schedules should have, at all points in time, the same view on the database. *Conflict-based* serializability for the read/write model (or the class

CSR) is more restricted, but enjoys a number of interesting properties, most importantly that membership in CSR can be tested in linear time (in the number of unaborted transactions), while testing membership in VSR is NP-complete.

The *conflict relation* conf(s) of a schedule s consists of all pairs of steps (a, b) from distinct, unaborted transactions which are in conflict in s, and for which a occurs before b. If s and s' are two schedules for the same transactions, s and s' are *conflict equivalent*, denoted $s \approx_c s'$, if conf(s) = conf(s'), i.e., all pairs of conflicting operations appear in the same order in both schedules. Finally, a complete schedule s is in CSR if $s \approx_c s'$ for some serial s'. For example, for the sample schedule s above conf(s) = conf($t_0 t_2 t_1 t_3$) (= conf($t_0 t_2 t_3$)) holds, so $s \in$ CSR.

An easy test for membership of a schedule s in CSR is to look at the *conflict graph* $G(s) = (V, E)$ of s, whose set V of nodes consists of those transactions from s which are not aborted, and for which $(t_i, t_j) \in E$ if some step from t_i is in conflict with a subsequent step from t_j. As shown in [16], a schedule s is in CSR iff $G(s)$ is acyclic.

As mentioned above and discussed in more detail in [22], pure serializability is not sufficient as a correctness criterion for schedules in the presence of failures. It turns out that *closure properties* of schedule properties (especially closure under commit operations and under taking prefixes) are of particular relevance, and that membership in the class CSR enjoys them, i.e., for each schedule $s \in$ CSR, the projection (defined straightforwardly) of any prefix of s onto the transactions committed therein is also in CSR (whereas neither membership in VSR nor in FSR is closed in this sense). However, to ensure that a failure of transactions cannot cause the Herbrand semantics of committed transactions to change, a schedule must also be *recoverable* (in the class RC) in the sense that at no time a committed transaction has read a ("dirty") value written by an uncommitted one. Ultimately, a *correct* schedule is one that is both (commit) serializable *and* recoverable. The latter can be strengthened in various ways, for example so that *cascading aborts* are avoided (class ACA) or that *strictness* (class ST) is achieved [22, 44].

More on correctness. We next sketch other, more recent notions related to serializability and to reliability; what is interesting to note here is that, while the read/write model and its classical serializability notions have been around for about 20 years, new discoveries keep being made in this field, and some recent additions to the knowledge about the read/write model are even pretty significant.

A typical example of a notion to which the latter remark applies is *order-preserving* conflict serializability (class OCSR), which intuitively requires that in schedules which are conflict equivalent, non-overlapping transactions do not get rearranged (with this additional requirement, OCSR $\subset$ CSR). While the notion is as old as conflict serializability itself, a systematic study of it appeared only recently in [2, 3].

A further restriction of CSR is established by the following condition: A

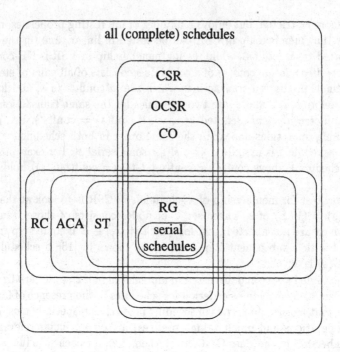

Fig. 1. Excerpt from the landscape of schedule classes.

schedule s enjoys the property of *commitment ordering*, or is in the class CO, if for any pair of committed transactions t_i and t_j occurring in s, where $i \neq j$, the following holds: If operation $p_i(x)$ from t_i occurs in s before conflicting operation $q_j(x)$ from t_j, then c_i also occurs before c_j in s. In other words, in a CO schedule, conflict ordering determines commit ordering. It is easily seen [33, 34] that CO $\subseteq$ CSR, and the schedule $s = r_1(x)w_2(x)c_2c_1$ shows that this inclusion is strict. Moreover, CO $\subset$ OCSR, as can be verified straightforwardly. We mention that the CO property, phrased here in terms of the traditional read/write model only, is of particular relevance in the context of multidatabases (see below).

For reliability, there have also been recent additions of criteria. The first we mention is *rigorousness* [12], which intuitively requires a correct placement of termination operations not only for write-read conflicts (as done by RC and ACA) or write-write conflicts (as done by ST), but also for read-write conflicts. Schedules is the resulting class RG have the important new property that they are both conflict serializable and strict; hence, schedule correctness can now be made precise in terms of *one* condition instead of two.

Figure 1 summarizes the relationships between the various classes of schedules we have mentioned so far.

3.2 A Model of Relational Updates

We now look briefly at another transaction model, originally introduced in [1] for studying dynamic aspects of relational databases. In this model, the basic *operations*, to be executed atomically, are insertions of single tuples, and deletions or modifications of sets of tuples (satisfying a given condition), all applied to the relations in a given database. *Transactions* are sequences of such operations, representing a bunch of updates a user wants to be executed in ACID fashion; due to the types of operations involved, we call them IDM transactions. As before, *schedules* represent interleavings of several transactions, and two operations from distinct transactions are *in conflict* if they do not commute. Serializability, in particular final-state as well as conflict-based serializability, can again be defined via an appropriate equivalence to serial schedules; details can be found in [40].

Notice that what we have just described follows exactly our methodology from Sect. 2. However, the model now under consideration differs significantly from the read/write model in that it carries semantic information, and this can now be exploited. Indeed, since the semantics of each individual update operation can be made formally precise, we can define and reason about the *effect* of transactions and of schedules. As investigated in [40], the implications of this are manifold. For example,

1. there is a host of schedule classes between the conflict serializable and the final-state serializable ones which have a polynomial-time membership test, or
2. while testing unrestricted serializability is NP-complete as in the read/write model, it becomes polynomially decidable if modify operations do not appear in transactions.

More importantly, the IDM model allows for an entirely new notion of schedule correctness which has nothing to do with equivalence to seriality. To indicate the idea behind this new notion, consider a relation TA that keeps track of teaching assistants and which has attributes Name and Course. Suppose the following two transactions are issued:

1. Hire(Joe, DBMS), on behalf of the instructor of the database class, would first remove all existing entries about Joe, and then insert the fact that Joe is now a TA for the DBMS course.
2. Fire(Joe), on behalf of the department's chairman who wants to get rid of Joe, would simply delete the relevant tuple.

A scheduler based on serializability would produce an execution which is equivalent either to Hire; Fire or to Fire; Hire; in both cases, one of the two users would not be satisfied. So a more appropriate approach seems to be to *reject* the concurrent execution of these transactions, since their "goals" are incompatible. In [41], this is made precise via the criterion of *goal-correctness* for schedules; a scheduler observing this condition would not execute the Hire and Fire transactions if they are submitted concurrently.

4   Generalizations

We now survey a number of extensions and generalizations, in particular for the read/write model, that have been investigated in recent years. As should have become clear from the exposition so far, there are three central ingredients in a world of transactions which can conceptually be altered:

1. the correctness criterion for schedules,
2. the underlying database model, or
3. the transaction (and schedule) model.

Basically all extensions and generalizations of what we have described so far can be classified according to these issues, and whether their modifications touch one issue in isolation or in combination with others. Two major categories can be identified:

1. Correctness of schedules in the traditional setting, i.e., read/write transactions on untyped databases;
2. departure from the classical (ACID) transaction model.

We describe examples of what falls into the former category next and turn to advanced or extended transaction models in the next section.

New notions of correctness. For the read/write model, [32] proposes *predicatewise serializability* (PWSR), whose idea is that if the database consistency constraint is in conjunctive normal form, it can be maintained by enforcing serializability only with respect to data items which share a disjunctive clause. For example, in a database with two objects x and y, suppose consistency is defined by two conjuncts one of which is over x, the other over y. Now consider the following schedule:

$$s = r_1(x)w_1(x)r_2(x)r_2(y)w_2(y)r_1(y)w_1(y)c_1c_2$$

Due to the cyclic conflict between t_1 and t_2, $s \notin$ CSR, but s is PWSR since it can be decomposed into the two schedules $s_1 = r_1(x)w_1(x)c_1r_2(x)c_2$ and $s_2 = r_2(y)w_2(y)c_2r_1(y)w_1(y)c_1$, each of which is even serial. The PWSR notion is actually more general and can be applied in a variety of other contexts as well [23].

Motivated by the fact that there are uniform conditions (such as RG) for schedule correctness capturing both serializability and reliability, a new and fruitful attempt in that direction was started in [37] and later continued in [5]. (This even provided a theoretical underpinning for the observation made in [46] that concurrency control and recovery cannot be treated in isolation, but influence each other.) Unifying the theory of concurrency control and recovery is here based on the idea of making recovery operations, so far implicit in an abort, *explicit* in a given schedule, using inverse writes which undo previous writes of a transaction to be aborted. The result is an *expanded* schedule in which all transactions terminate successfully (but some are without effect). Next, an expanded schedule can be treated like an ordinary schedule, relative to a notion of conflict which integrates inverse writes; moreover, it can eventually be reduced to a (possibly trivial) serial schedule using straightforward manipulation rules. If the latter is the case, the original schedule is *reducible*; if the same holds for each of its prefixes, it is *prefix-reducible* or in the class PRED. As an example, consider

$$s = r_1(x)w_1(x)r_2(x)w_2(x)a_2a_1.$$

Expanding s by inverse writes for each abort yields

$$s' = r_1(x)w_1(x)r_2(x)w_2(x)w_2^{-1}(x)c_2w_1^{-1}(x)c_1.$$

s' can be reduced to the trivial serial schedule c_2c_1 by eliminating $w_2(x)$ and its adjacent inverse, dropping the reads, commuting c_2 with its right neighbor, and finally eliminating $w_1(x)$ and its (now adjacent) inverse. It follows that s is reducible.

As shown in [37], members of PRED are both in CSR and in RC; conversely, PRED is a superset of CSR ∩ ST. [5] provides an alternative description of PRED, called *serializability with ordered termination* (SOT). [42] extends this theory to semantically rich operations.

Other untyped database models. A generalization based on an alternative database model is the assumption that database objects are no longer updated in place, but write operations create new object *versions*. The result, a *multi-version* database, has a number of interesting applications; for example, concurrency control protocols can be relaxed, and recovery mechanisms can be made more flexible. Transactions now need to be assigned versions to read; proper version assignment is the major correctness issue in this context. The theory of multi-version concurrency control goes back to [7, 24] and was further developed in [31, 21]; however, it was discovered only recently that the total number of versions which can be simultaneously be stored has a serious impact on schedule correctness [27].

Other modifications of the original database model assume that the database is no longer centralized, but (homogeneously) *distributed*. This requires a modified transaction model, in which transactions (and hence schedules) are *partial orders* of steps; details are, for instance, in [13]. A special case of a distributed database is that data objects get *replicated* in several locations [8]. More recently, the database community has taken interest in *heterogeneous* (distributed) databases, which roughly are federations of multiple, autonomous databases. Multi-database transactions perform read or write accesses at one or more local database, and may there get into intrinsic conflicts with transactions which are local to this database. A survey of concurrency control theory in this context is [11].

5   Advanced Transaction Models

During the past 15 years, the scope of database applications has grown tremendously, from purely business-type and record-based applications such as banks or reservation systems to highly technical applications such as computer-aided design (CAD) in a multi-media, object-based, and networked environment. This has brought along a host of new requirements to adequate transaction support, and the answer to this from the database world has been a great variety of advanced transaction models. For developing these models, two insights are of central importance: First, a transaction is basically — at least in the read/write world — a logical *implementation vehicle*, since it has associated with it the ACID properties (and these are not built-in, but have to be provided by the underlying implementation). Second, however, a transaction is an *abstraction concept*; indeed, even the read/write abstracts from all the details of a user application, and retains read and write operations only. Thus, there are two basic features advanced models can bring along:

1. Further operational abstractions, and
2. a departure from strict ACID.

For the former, many options are available, including providing *more* operations, providing *higher-level* operations, providing more *execution control* within and between transactions, or providing more transaction *structure*. Structure, in turn, can refer to *parallelism* inside a transaction, it can refer to *transactions inside other transactions*, or it can even refer to *transactions plus other operations* inside other transactions. In essence, the goal thus is to enhance the expressive power of the transaction concept, and to do so in such a way that not only complex or long-running activities, but also structured collections of such activities can be modeled adequately.

For example, consider a trip planning activity consisting of flight reservations, car rentals, and hotel bookings. It *is* reasonable to perform this activity within transaction brackets, in order to make sure that all data sets accessed are finally consistent again, and that inconsistent intermediate states can be tolerated. However, the three types of reservations can be made in parallel, since they will most likely access distinct databases; they can even be performed as subtractions inside the entire trip reservation which could abort autonomously (e.g., if all hotels in some place are fully booked).

Complex activities might also involve another novel aspect, namely the fact that there might be operations which cannot be undone. For example, if I cancel a flight reservation and decide to book it again, *undoing* the cancellation would mean rebooking brings back the old seat, which cannot be expected. Thus, the second book operation would only *compensate* for the former, but not exactly undo it. Compensation is an important issue in many applications, and hence has to be accounted for in transactional support.

The second aspect above, departure from pure ACID, means that for many applications today ACID transactions are too restrictive. Again consider the trip reservation: If a flight from Berlin to Rome is desired at a certain day, the transaction may state that a particular airline should be tried first, but another would do as well in case the first one has no more seats available. Thus, the transaction would not be atomic, since not all operations will get executed. More generally, it would be desirable if the ACID properties could be switched on and off in an application-dependent fashion, and that a user can interactively control how a transaction is actually performed. For another example, consider a design activity in a CAD environment, such as car or VLSI design. Typically, design is a long-running and evolutionary activity, which even requires group interaction and cooperation. A design transaction t lasting for days cannot be executed isolated from other transactions, since that would now imply that others get access to the objects on which t operates only after t has finished.

As an aside, we mention two proposals for treating *long-running* (read/write) transactions, e.g., in CAD. While it is difficult to capture in a transaction *model* whether a transaction quantitatively contains just a few or very many operations (i.e., whether it is supposed to run within milliseconds or will last for hours or even days), the introduction of additional operations can help to describe solutions to the problem that a long transaction eventually blocks others for long periods. For serializability, the concept of *altruistic locking* [36] is relevant here, while for reliability the notion of *partial strictness* [39] seems appropriate.

In the remainder of this section, we present a sample of proposals which have been made in recent years in this context. A good introduction to the subject is [15], which presents, among others, *split/join transactions* for long-running, open-ended activities with unpredictable development and interaction with other activities, *flex transactions* and *polytransactions* for multidatabase environments, or the *ConTract model* for defining and controlling long-lived, complex computations beyond pure transactions. Surprisingly, serializability has vastly survived as a correctness criterion for executions even in advanced transaction models, although these models typically comprise semantic information that would render other criteria feasible; on the other hand, serializability appears more refined in many advanced models.

Typed databases. With the advent of abstract data types (ADTs) and object models in databases, operations on *typed* databases as the basic building blocks of transactions have gained considerable interest. The foundations of a concurrency control theory for ADTs go back to [38]. With respect to correctness of executions, it appears appropriate to take the properties of ADT operations, return values delivered by such operations, and generally state information into account [45]; in particular, commutativity of operations can now be made *state-dependent*. An interesting correctness criterion called *orderability* was recently proposed in [4]; it takes semantics of objects and transactions into account, and defines operation semantics via pre- and postconditions, which are predicates involving object states as well as input and output values. In object-oriented databases, an appropriate view is that transactions consist of method invocations which can recursively call other methods, so that a nested structure arises naturally; a corresponding theory is developed in [20].

Nested transactions. As indicated earlier, a departure from the flatness of transactions is motivated by a number of considerations, e.g., by the fact that a database management system is commonly organized as a hierarchy of functional layers or layers of abstraction; a transaction concept could then be made available at distinct layers of this hierarchy. Also, complex activities cannot always be modeled adequately with standard flat transactions. A more flexible interaction with a database is achievable if flat transactions are replaced by *nested* ones. As indicated by the trip planning example above, the basic idea is to allow transactions to contain other transactions as *subtransactions*, thereby giving transactions a tree structure whose leaves are elementary operations, but whose other nodes all represent transactions. If a subtransaction appears atomic to its parent, it can be reset without causing the parent to abort too. Furthermore, if subtransactions are isolated from each other, they can execute in parallel. Two prominent special cases of nested transactions are *closed* ones, in which subtransactions have to delay their commit until the end of their root transaction, and *open* ones in which subtransactions are allowed to commit autonomously. If all leaves in a transaction tree are of the same height, *multilevel* transactions result, in which the generation of subtransactions can be driven by the functional layers of the underlying system, and in which a generalized notion of serializability is obtained in a layer-by-layer fashion. The theory of nested transactions, initiated in [28], has been studied and developed intensively in recent years [6, 15, 20, 23, 25, 26, 47].

Frameworks for customizing transaction facilities. While the advanced transaction models which have been proposed in recent years all have their particular benefits, user or application developers frequently have requirements which are not met by a single model. This situation has produced the quest for *customizable* transaction models, which are available today in the form of *frameworks* for specifying and analyzing advanced transaction models. Such frameworks typically provide a number of transaction primitives which facilitate the formal description of transactional properties, and thus the synthesis of dedicated transaction models. Examples of such frameworks are *ACTA* [14] and *ASSET* [10]; both have successfully been used, for example, for realizing nested transactions and their correct executions. Another example is *TSME* [17], which provides both a specification language for extended transactions and a programmable transaction management mechanism.

Transactional workflows. Customized transaction management can ensure the correctness and reliability not only of traditional transaction-based applications in which a particular functionality (e.g., relaxed atomicity or isolation, cooperation) is required. It can additionally support applications in which transactions are grouped together with non-transactional operations into a logical unit. At present, there is a high interest is implementing and managing activities which have been modeled as dynamic *processes*, in particular as *business processes*. Such activities, which typically involve the coordinated execution of a number of tasks on a variety of processing entities, are called *workflows*; *transactional* workflows are workflows in which transactions play a central role as an execution, synchronization, and reliability vehicle for individual tasks [35]. However, traditional transaction models and management are of limited use here, since, for example, such models may ensure predefined properties (such as ACID) which are not required by the application in question; furthermore, transaction management is tailored towards processing entities which are database systems. Customization, as provided by frameworks like ASSET or TSME, is then considered an appropriate solution, although we here enter into an area of current research in which final solutions are yet to be seen.

6   Conclusions

The transaction concept was originally perceived in the database field as a universal tool for the secure execution and synchronization of activities inside and between databases. In this survey we have tried to touch upon the most relevant *logical* issues related to database transactions. What started out as an *implementation concept* has over time taken a second role; today the transaction concept is also widely used as an *abstraction mechanism*. Since this mechanism turns out to be applicable at vastly arbitrary *levels* of abstraction, what has been learned about its implementation remains valid, and even continues to evolve. We have tried to indicate that there are general concepts for designing conceptual transaction models. Also worth mentioning is that fact that there is a high interest in re-using the transaction concept in contexts other than databases.

References

1. Abiteboul, S., Vianu, V.: Equivalence and optimization of relational transactions. *J. ACM* 35 (1988) 70–120.
2. Agrawal, D., El Abbadi, A.: Locks with constrained sharing. In: *Proc. 9th Annual ACM Symp. on Principles of Database Systems*, 1990, pp. 85–93.
3. Agrawal, D., El Abbadi, A., Lang, A.E.: The performance of protocols based on locks with ordered sharing. *IEEE Trans. Knowledge and Data Engineering* 6 (1994) 805–818.
4. Agrawal, D., El Abbadi, A., Singh, A.K.: Consistency and orderability: semantics-based correctness criteria for databases. *ACM Trans. Database Systems* 18 (1993) 460–486.
5. Alonso, G., Vingralek, R., Agrawal, D., Breitbart, Y., El Abbadi, A., Schek H.-J., Weikum, G.: Unifying concurrency control and recovery of transactions. *Information Systems* 19 (1994) 101–115.
6. Beeri, C., Bernstein, P.A., Goodman, N.: A model for concurrency in nested transaction systems. *J. ACM* 36 (1989) 230–269.
7. Bernstein, P.A., Goodman, N.: Multiversion concurrency control — theory and algorithms. *ACM Trans. Database Systems* 8 (1983) 465–483.
8. Bernstein, P.A., Goodman, N.: Serializability theory for replicated databases. *J. Computer and System Sciences* 31 (1985) 355–374.

9. Bernstein, P.A., Hadzilacos, V., Goodman, N.: *Concurrency Control and Recovery in Database Systems*. Addison-Wesley Publishing Comp., Reading, MA, 1987.

10. Biliris, A., Dar, S., Gehani, N., Jagadish, H.V., Ramamritham, K.: ASSET: A system for supporting extended transactions. In: *Proc. ACM SIGMOD Int. Conf. on Management of Data*, 1994, pp. 44–54.

11. Breitbart, Y., Garcia-Molina, H., Silberschatz, A.: Overview of multidatabase transaction management. *The VLDB Journal* 1 (1992) 181–239.

12. Breitbart, Y., Georgakopoulos, D., Rusinkiewicz, M., Silberschatz, A.: On rigorous transaction scheduling. *IEEE Trans. Software Engineering* 17 (1991) 954–960.

13. Cellary, W., Gelenbe, E., Morzy, T.: *Concurrency Control in Distributed Database Systems*. North-Holland, Amsterdam, 1988.

14. Chrysanthis, P.K., Ramamritham, K.: Synthesis of extended transaction models using ACTA. *ACM Trans. Database Systems* 19 (1994) 450–491.

15. Elmagarmid, A.K.: *Database Transaction Models for Advanced Applications*. Morgan Kaufmann, San Francisco, CA, 1992.

16. Eswaran, K.P., Gray, J.N., Lorie, R.A., Traiger, I.L.: The notions of consistency and predicate locks in a database system. *Comm. ACM* 19 (1976) 624–633.

17. Georgakopoulos, D., Hornick, M., Krychniak, P., Manola, F.: Specification and management of extended transactions in a programmable transaction environment. In: *Proc. 10th IEEE Int. Conf. on Data Engineering*, 1994, pp. 462–473.

18. Gray, J.: Notes on data base operating systems. In R. Bayer, R.M. Graham, and G. Seegmüller (Eds.): *Operating Systems — An Advanced Course*. Lecture Notes in Computer Science, Vol. 60, Springer-Verlag, Berlin, 1978, pp. 393–481.

19. Gray, J., Reuter, A.: *Transaction Processing: Concepts and Techniques*. Morgan Kaufmann, San Francisco, CA, 1993.

20. Hadzilacos, T., Hadzilacos, V.: Transaction synchronization in object bases. *J. Computer and System Sciences* 43 (1991) 2–24.

21. Hadzilacos, T., Papadimitriou, C.H.: Algorithmic aspects of multiversion concurrency control. *J. Computer and System Sciences* 33 (1986) 297–310.

22. Hadzilacos, V.: A theory of reliability in database systems. *J. ACM* 35 (1988) 121–145.

23. Korth, H.F., Speegle, G.: Formal aspects of concurrency control in long-duration transaction systems using the NT/PV model. *ACM Trans. Database Systems* 19 (1994) 492–535.

24. Lausen, G.: Formal aspects of optimistic concurrency control in a multiple version database system. *Information Systems* 8 (1983) 291–301.

25. Lynch, N., Merritt, M.: Introduction to the theory of nested transactions. *Theoretical Computer Science* 62 (1988) 123–185.

26. Lynch, N., Merritt, M., Weihl, W., Fekete, A.: *Atomic Transactions*. Morgan Kaufmann, San Francisco, CA, 1994.

27. Morzy, T.: The correctness of concurrency control for multiversion database systems with limited number of versions. In: *Proc. 9th IEEE Int. Conf. on Data Engineering*, 1993, pp. 595–604.

28. Moss, J.E.B.: *Nested Transactions: An Approach to Reliable Distributed Computing*. MIT Press, Cambridge, MA, 1985.

29. Papadimitriou, C.H.: The serializability of concurrent database updates. *J. ACM* 26 (1979) 631–653.

30. Papadimitriou, C.H.: *The Theory of Database Concurrency Control*. Computer Science Press, Rockville, MD, 1986.

31. Papadimitriou, C.H., Kanellakis, P.C.: On concurrency control by multiple versions. *ACM Trans. Database Systems* 9 (1984) 89–99.

32. Rastogi, R., Mehrotra, S., Breitbart, Y., Korth, H.F., Silberschatz, A.: On correctness of non-serializable executions. In: *Proc. 12th ACM SIGACT-SIGMOD-SIGART Symp. Principles of Database Systems*, 1993, pp. 97–108.

33. Raz, Y.: The principle of commitment ordering, or guaranteeing serializability in a heterogeneous environment of multiple autonomous resource managers using atomic commitment. In: *Proc. 18th Int. Conf. on Very Large Data Bases*, 1992, pp. 292–312.

34. Raz, Y.: Serializability by commitment ordering. *Inf. Proc. Letters* 51 (1994) 257–264.

35. Rusinkiewicz, M., Sheth, A.: Specification and execution of transactional workflows. In W. Kim (ed.): *Modern Database Systems*. Addison-Wesley Publishing Comp., Reading, MA, 1995, pp. 592–620.

36. Salem, K., Garcia-Molina, H., Shands, J.: Altruistic locking. *ACM Trans. Database Systems* 19 (1994) 117–165.

37. Schek, H.J., Weikum, G., Ye, H.: (1993). Towards a unified theory of concurrency control and recovery. In: *Proc. 12th ACM SIGACT-SIGMOD-SIGART Symp. Principles of Database Systems*, 1993, pp. 300–311.

38. Schwarz, P.M., Spector, A.Z.: Synchronizing shared abstract types. *ACM Trans. Computer Systems* 2 (1984) 223–250.

39. Soisalon-Soininen, E., Ylönen, T.: Partial strictness in two-phase locking. In: G. Gottlob, M.Y. Vardi (Eds.), *Database Theory - ICDT '95*, Proc. 5th Int. Conference, Lecture Notes in Computer Science, Vol. 893, Springer-Verlag, Berlin, 1995, pp. 139–147.

40. Vianu, V., Vossen, G.: Conceptual level concurrency control for relational update transactions. *Theoretical Computer Science* 95 (1992) 1–42.

41. Vianu, V., Vossen, G.: Static and dynamic aspects of goal-oriented concurrency control. *Annals of Mathematics and Artificial Intelligence* 7 (1993) 257–287.

42. Vingralek, R., Ye, H., Breitbart, Y., Schek, H.-J.: Unified transaction model for semantically rich operations. In: G. Gottlob, M.Y. Vardi (Eds.), *Database Theory - ICDT '95*, Proc. 5th Int. Conference, Lecture Notes in Computer Science, Vol. 893, Springer-Verlag, Berlin, 1995, pp. 148–161.

43. Vossen, G.: Databases and database management. In: E.G. Coffman, J.K. Lenstra, A.H.G. Rinnooy Kan (Eds.): *Handbooks in Operations Research and Management Science*, Vol. 3: *Computing*. North-Holland, Amsterdam, 1992, pp. 133–193.

44. Vossen, G., Groß-Hardt, M.: *Grundlagen der Transaktionsverarbeitung*. Addison-Wesley, Bonn, 1993.

45. Weihl, W.: Local atomicity properties: modular concurrency control for abstract data types. *ACM Trans. Programming Languages and Systems* 11 (1989) 249–282.

46. Weihl, W.: The impact of recovery on concurrency control. *J. Computer and System Sciences* 47 (1993) 157–184.

47. Weikum, G.: Principles and realization strategies of multilevel transaction management. *ACM Trans. Database Systems* 16 (1991) 132–180.

48. Yannakakis, M.: Serializability by locking. *J. ACM* 31 (1984) 227–244.

Multimedia Authoring Tools:
State of the Art and Research Challenges

Dick C.A. Bulterman and Lynda Hardman

CWI: Centrum voor Wiskunde en Informatica, Kruislaan 413, 1098 SJ Amsterdam
E-Mail: {Dick.Bulterman, Lynda.Hardman}@cwi.nl

Abstract: The integration of audio, video, graphics and text on the desktop promises to fundamentally challenge the centuries-old model of the printed document as the basis for information exchange. Before this potential can be realized, however, systems must be devised that enable the production and presentation of complex, inter-related media objects. These systems are generically called multimedia authoring tools. In this article, we consider the development of multimedia authoring tools, examine the current state of the art, and then discuss a set of research challenges that need to be addressed before the full potential of multimedia output technology can be effectively utilized to share information.

1 Introduction

The encoding and distribution of information has been a problem that has kept much of mankind busy since its beginnings. Perhaps the most significant milestone in this activity was the development of the written word, which allowed spoken communication to be reliably reproduced and distributed under a measure of control of its originator. The technology available for producing written documents remained relatively constant until a few hundred years ago, when significant refinements in the means for creating and distributing documents began to take place. Fig. 1 summarizes some of these refinements, including the printing press, the postal service, the development of newspapers (the catalyst for current wide-scale literacy), the xerographic copier and, more recently, the combination of computer-based page composition systems with the com-

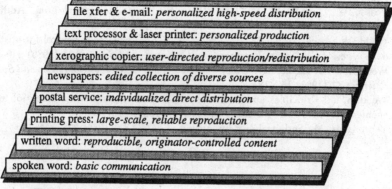

Figure 1. Significant developments in text processing and distribution.

puter network and laser printer. Each of these developments addressed specific user needs to make text-based information processing more effective, reliable, reproducible and broadly-available.

During the past five years, an enormous increase in computer processing speed and a dramatic reduction in the cost of intelligent peripheral devices have created the potential to augment and even replace text as the standard form of information exchange. These developments have been grouped under the generic name of *multimedia*. Unlike the user-driven development of text processing facilities, much of the growth of multimedia has resulted from the relatively independent development of the underlying output technology. This has led to a gap between a computer's ability to process and present information and the user's ability to create and manage documents that exploit the power of the technology available.

The problem of creating and managing multimedia information is not trivial. Consider the introduction of audio to the desktop: in spite of a lifetime of experience in producing and processing spoken information, 'audio e-mail' has not developed as a natural alternative to text-based electronic mail. The major drawback is not the lack of familiarity with the medium, but rather the lack of integrated authoring and editing tools that enable a broad class of users to access the technology and to create messages that can be easily shared with others. The creation and editing problems include the ability to visualize, rearrange and refine documents. These problems are compounded when several media must be manipulated together and when media are used that require specialized training before they can be used for general information exchange.

In the following paragraphs, we review the development of applications that support the construction and presentation of multimedia documents. Section 2 reviews the building blocks used by authoring systems, including media object creation and document distribution technologies. Section 3 discusses the current state of the art for supporting multimedia authoring, including authoring paradigms and an extended example. Section 4 concludes with a discussion of topics that need to be addressed in the development of next-generation authoring systems.

2 Media Objects and Multimedia Data Distribution

A *multimedia document* can be viewed as an activity specification that can be used to coordinate the runtime presentation of a collection of *media objects*, where each media object can contain one or more media items, of one or more types. *Multimedia authoring systems* provide a mechanism for defining a multimedia document based on an underlying multimedia information model. The development of multimedia authoring systems encompasses many of the problems and challenges of generalized multimedia data manipulation: data objects must be created, often using special-purpose tools; they must be integrated into a coherent presentation, usually requiring some form of media synchronization; the presentation must be defined in a form that allows distribution to various types of target environments; and the presentation must be 'maintainable' over its commercial or intellectual life-time.

The structure of media objects determines the level of information combination, placement and presentation granularity available to the document author. Consider the abstraction of a document fragment in Fig. 2. Here two choices of object organization are illustrated. On the left side we see a pointer from the document to a composite media object that contains a video sequence, a static illustration, a text overlay and an accompanying soundtrack. The composite object, with dependencies resolved at its source, is fetched and delivered to the processor hosting the presentation. (We ignore for the moment issues of network vs. local access, or encoding in particular formats for particular storage media.) On the right side of the illustration the document references four separate media objects, each of which is individually fetched and sent to the processor. Clearly, the use of composite media objects reduces the burden on the document specification: it only needs to identify the object and provide high-level access control, since the relationships *among* the items are captured within the object definition. The use of a collection of separate object provides extra flexibility—for example, we can choose run-time substitution of objects to tailor the presentation for, say, a multi-lingual audience—at the expense of extra complexity within the document and document presentation system.

2.1 Individual Media Object Definition and Manipulation

Current multimedia data object creation tools are the result of the historical development of a number of separate tools and systems to develop and manipulate separate and distinct types of data. Low-cost graphics adapters have allowed high-resolution bit-mapped displays to become commonplace; low-cost signal processing chips have allowed stereo audio adapters to be integrated into many low- and medium-cost computers; digital cameras and integrated video processing chips have brought full-motion video to the desktop; and inexpensive high-density storage devices such as the CD-ROM have enabled the efficient distribution of the massive amounts of digital data that are generated for and by the above devices.

Where text and drawing systems can usually integrate data creation and editing, data for most other types of media are first created using a capture tool and then refined using an editing tool. Capture and editing are typically done outside the scope of the authoring tool, although some degree of interaction between editing and authoring is often required. Created media objects can be stored as totally separate entities (like

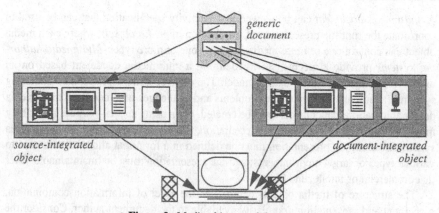

Figure 2. Media objects and documents

user files) or they can be integrated into multimedia databases or file servers. The temporal access constraints of multimedia data usually require special-purpose file- or database-servers to manage storage and delivery of media objects.

Representative capture/editing tools are: [2S] and [2] for video, [9S] and [29] for audio and [1S] and [4S] for image data. A survey of multimedia data servers is given in [15]. A general overview of encoding and delivery aspects of networked multimedia is given in earlier publications in the LNCS series (614, 712 and 846).

2.2 Integrating Separate Objects into a Common Document

Authoring multimedia documents—whether static in structure or dynamically created at runtime—essentially consists of collecting and presenting media objects in a author-desired order, with some degree of navigation control available to the end user. While the degree of composition of each media object will influence the complexity of the authoring/presentation environment, the user-level management of the authoring process remains the most critical element in applying multimedia technology.

Authoring systems are programs that assist the user in managing the creative task of specifying the placement and relative order of media object events. The development of authoring systems can be broadly classified into three generations, each of which are discussed below. Note that the migration of multimedia technology from high-end to low-end systems has had the result that each of the generations are not defined in terms of a time period, but rather in terms of a collected body of facilities available to users at different times on different classes of computing systems.

In identifying breaks in generations, three types of evolutionary change can be identified: changes in the portability/distributability of documents, changes in basic multimedia technology supported within documents and changes in user facilities to access documents. (These parallel the evolutionary forces supporting change in text-based system development.) Performance changes—such as more video frames per second or high audio quality—are not considered to indicate fundamental changes in authoring system functionality.

G_0: **First generation authoring systems.** The distinguishing characteristics of G_0 include authoring systems that are highly processor-architecture dependent, relying on a high-degree of sophistication of special-purpose graphics and/or audio hardware, with minimal user support for general document browsing. While multimedia is often seen as a new field within computer science, examples of G_0 authoring systems have been present on high-end computing systems and workstations for decades. Representative examples include programs that support air traffic control systems, where real-time graphics and alpha-numeric data are displayed together with static background images, or text formatting systems, where pictures and text integrated into a single print file. More recently, systems like [5S] and [21] provided authoring support that is typical of G_0. Some of these systems provide experimental hypertext navigation support.

G_1: **Second generation authoring systems.** In G_1, the first evidence of portability of multimedia documents—albeit to a limited degree—is available, often within family members of a particular hardware/software architecture. Support for representation-based document navigation and browsing facilities (that is, navigation/browsing based on the implementation of an object rather than its content) are also included, such as document fast-forward/rewind. In some systems, commercial support for content-based navigation (hyper-links) is also provided, but almost always limited to text data or static images. In G_1 systems, media objects are usually 'leaf nodes': they are treated as self-contained entities with little support for document-level object embedding. The presentation metaphor remains based on a page-by-page model rather than on a single continuous presentation. User input facilities are usually limited to coarse navigation control. Representative examples of G_1 systems are [3S], [10S], and [28].

G_2: **Third generation authoring systems.** These systems represent the current generation of commercially-available multimedia authoring systems. They have some degree of multi-platform presentation support, enabling basic sharing of documents between Apple Macintosh and IBM PC (compatible) computers. (Support is also available for UNIX workstations, although typically only in research prototype systems.) A limited amount of client-server networking is supported, although most systems rely on local copies of data to provide the required levels of presentation performance. Broad support is available for *de facto* standard output devices, although only rudimentary support is available for emerging standard document and object formats. Representation-based browsing is widely supported, and some systems allow support for content-based searching for dynamic media as well as text/images. Examples and properties of G_2 systems are described in more detail in the next section. In section 4, we consider the needs of characteristics of future generation authoring support.

3 Multimedia Authoring: The State of the Art

This section discusses the major characteristics of current-generation (G_2) authoring systems. We begin with a discussion of development paradigms for authoring and then give an example of the facilities available in an advanced G_2 system.

3.1 Approaches To Authoring Multimedia Documents

Four general paradigms exist for multimedia authoring systems:
- *graph-based authoring,* describing a presentation's control flow;
- *timeline-based authoring,* describing a presentation's data flow relative to a common time axis;
- *program-based authoring,* using a text-based specification to describe the positions and timings of individual objects; and
- *structure-based authoring*, which groups objects based on presentation content.

We outline the basic properties and describe representative systems using each paradigm in the following sections. (Note that many authoring environments provide a mixture of paradigms; in our discussion, we classify systems under the dominant paradigm used.)

Graph-based authoring systems. This approach uses a schematic diagram of the control flow interactions among multimedia objects, as illustrated in Fig. 3. Graphs can be informal or formal. Informal graphs are used to give a global illustration of the order-

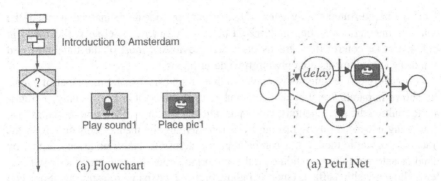

(a) Flowchart   (a) Petri Net

Figure 3. Examples of graph-based authoring paradigms.

ing of relatively coarse object interactions. Formal graphs also illustrate object interactions, but they additionally provide a mechanism for "proving" or determining properties of the presentation based on the semantics of the graph.

Graph-based authoring can provide very powerful presentation descriptions. For all but the simplest documents, however, both informal and formal graphs suffer from a 'complexity explosion' once the size of the presentation grows beyond that found in a simple document. In order to manage this complexity, sophisticated user interface systems are required that allow the user to zoom-in or zoom-out of a presentation. This limits the utility of the approach, especially in the case of informal graphs: here, there is typically no added value of the graph itself aside from an ordering mechanism; once the presentation becomes so complex that it fills multiple physical or screen pages, the integrated view of a presentation is lost. For formal graphs, this added complexity is offset by the results generated from the graph formalism, but even here, the complexity of the description typically limits the use of such models to special-purpose authoring needs such as synchronization analysis.

Graph-based mechanisms also have the disadvantage that detailed interactions among data objects are difficult to describe. For example, in Fig. 3(a), an audio and picture object are shown occurring "at the same time". Suppose that we instead want the audio to start first and then, after a lead-in period, have the picture presented. At one level, the audio and picture are presented in parallel (as shown), but at a more detailed level, the interaction among the items becomes quite complex. Such as relationship can be modelled by the fragment of Fig. 3(b) that is enclosed in the dotted-line box: the bottom node represents the audio fragment, with above it a period of delay followed by the picture. (Note that a similar approach could have been used in the flowchart, at the expense of more detail). In both cases, however, it would be difficult to describe even more detailed relationships, such as: *display the picture when a phrase 'pretty picture' is spoken in the audio object*. It is also difficult to model hyper-navigation behavior in this type of system.

Examples of flowchart-based authoring paradigms are reviewed in [24]. An example of a recent Petri-net-based authoring system is [5]. An example of a hybrid system is Eventor [13], which uses CCS (Calculus of Communicating Systems) as an underlying formal specification mechanism, while providing a flowchart-like user interface. (Eventor also incorporates timeline graphs, as discussed in the following section.)

Timeline-based Authoring Systems. These systems provide a schematic diagram of the dataflow interactions among multimedia objects. A generic timeline is illustrated in Fig. 4. Unlike control flow graphs discussed previously, most of the timeline-based authoring environments use only informal descriptions.

The nature of the timeline is similar to that of a musical score: a number of events are shown in parallel relative to a common axis. This metaphor is especially appropriate to multimedia presentations, with their inherent use of parallel, time-based events. Authoring is carried out by placing icons representing the media items on one of the tracks at a specific time. Items can be stretched across several time frames (either by hand or automatically, depending on the authoring system). Some timeline-based systems allow transition effects (such as fading, blurring, or spatial transposing of objects) to be specified as timeline properties. The granularity of the timeline can be tied to the granularity of the system clock or it can be a user-scalable logical time reference. (Logical clocks ease problems of porting systems, but they do not guarantee that a particular presentation will be able to be presented on all systems.)

The primary advantage of the timeline is that it provides an intuitive ordering of object events. The potential disadvantages with timeline-based authoring systems include the side effects of object editing, run-time control, and presentation navigation. Object editing can be a problem if changes made to individual objects are not correctly integrated back to the presentation timeline. For example, if the start time or duration of a media item is changed (e.g. by editing the data belonging to the item) then the relative positions of other objects on the same or related timelines may also need to change. Such changes are rarely automatic (that is, the 'correct' choice depends on the semantics of the presentation rather than the structure of the timeline); this can require substantial changes in a document. Presentation control involves the imposition of a higher-level control structure on a document (such as a pause facility or the ability to integrate user feedback into the presentation). The control problem of timeline authoring is often solved by introducing a special control track; such a track can be used to define meta-operations such as grouping common presentation elements or indicating when pauses should be inserted in a presentation.

A third problem is presentation navigation. By adjusting a logical time pointer, most timeline systems allow an end-user to jump to specific parts of a presentation. While this type of 'fast-fowarding' or 'fast rewind' in intuitively obvious, the resulting

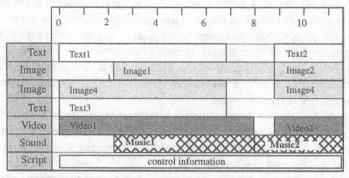

Figure 4. Example of a timeline-based authoring paradigm.

behavior is not: if the time pointer in Fig. 4 is moved to time '2', it is not clear if all objects defined at that time are activated, or only new objects starting at or after the new time. (If one views a video tape as a multi-channel timeline, then an 'activate all' model is used. For computer-based presentations, this is much more difficult since each of the composite items need to be independently started and run up to the time indicated by the time pointer.) Navigation problems in timeline result from the use and manipulation of data representations rather than information object contents.

Three example timeline-based systems are Director [8S], Integrator [31] and MAEstro [12]. Of these, perhaps the most widely-used is Director, which was designed for creating animation-based presentations. Graphics, text and video objects can be placed on a timeline, or score as it is termed in the system. The timeline is divided into separate frames, whose speed of playing is determined by the current tempo, where the tempo can be changed at any frame. An object has a position in each frame, and the author can describe a path for the object to follow through a series of frames.

Programming-based authoring systems. Both graph- and timeline-based authoring paradigms make use of illustrations to describe the interaction among media items in a presentation. While this is appropriate for high-level interaction, it is less appropriate for detailed descriptions of complex system behavior. As is illustrated in Fig. 5, a programming-based system gives an author low-level facilities for specifying the components, their timing, layout and interactions within a presentation. The programming effort can range from rapid prototype languages (typically referred to as scripts), through object-based library models, to detailed, low-level extensions to—or replacements of—existing programming languages.

Programming-based approaches can be used to model and manipulate individual media objects or they can be used to coordinate/orchestrate previously created (or dynamic) objects, or both. This has the advantage that rich interaction facilities can often be provided and that at least rudimentary content-based decisions can be made at runtime to guide the presentation of the document. This flexibility comes at a significant price: the definition of the document can be tedious, the portability of a particular document may be limited and the expressive power of the programming interface will be limited by the underlying operating or transport mechanism to provide the control primitives required by the programming interface.

While the programming model appeals to specialists, it is unclear if this model will be accepted by the general multimedia community. Just as there is a trend away from

```
set win=main_win
set cursor=wait
clear win
put background "pastel.pic"
put text "heading1.txt" at 10,0
put picture "gables.pic" at 20,0
put picture "logo.pic" at 40, 10
put text "contents.txt" at 20,10
set cursor=active
```

Figure 5. Example of a programming-based authoring paradigm.

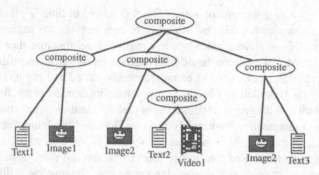

Figure 6. Example of a *structure-based* authoring paradigm.

programming-based text formatters (such as *troff* and *TeX*) to more WYSIWYG text and drawing systems (such as [6S] or [10S]), it may be that programming-based authoring will be reserved for special-purpose documents with critical performance constraints [7S]. Although authoring and object editing systems will be implemented using a hierarchy of programming languages, the user interface to these tools will not be based on the programming paradigm.

Structure-based authoring systems. The three types of authoring paradigms discussed up to this point share a common characteristic: they define documents in terms of the placement and activation of groups of media objects. As is illustrated in Fig. 6, another approach is to separate the definition of the logical structure of a presentation and the media objects associated with a document. In a structure-based document view, the advantages of structured/composite design approaches used in software engineering can be transferred to the multimedia domain. This approach delays the binding of data to documents, allowing an author to develop (and also edit) a presentation outline.

Text-based documents are often developed in terms of a *beginning-middle-end* model, in which the document and often individual sections are constructed in terms of an introduction, the main text body and a summary. Entire documents can then be created in a top-down or bottom-up fashion (or some mixture of the two). Navigation within a document is typically related to its logical structure; detailed reference or content associations can be found locally while more general references are often found further away from a particular point in the document. In multimedia documents, there is usually also a locality of interaction between media objects: synchronization constraints are defined among items that are structurally related more often than items that are farther apart in the document structure.

The definition of a document in terms of an explicit logical structure can be used to partition tasks among several clusters of authors and assist in resource allocation during presentation. The ease with which a document can be edited and maintained also is increased when the author has a good view of the logical relationships between items. Unfortunately, a single structure-based view is typically not sufficient to describe all of the timing and interactions requirements of detailed sections of a presentation. As a result, structure-based authoring is usually combined with other techniques to produce an entire document [20]. We give an example of this in the following section.

3.2 An Example Hybrid Authoring Environment: CMIFed

Several hybrid systems exist that combine the features of graph-, timeline-, programming- and structure-based editing. Three examples are CMIFed [30], Mbuild [17] and MET++ [1]. Of these, we look at CMIFed—which forms the core of the ESPRIT-IV authoring environment CHAMELEON [10]—in more detail to demonstrate the integration of techniques into a full-scale authoring environment.

CMIFed was designed to provide authors with a rich environment for structured viewing and manipulation of a presentation. The authoring tasks are split into three separate but closely communicating views of the presentation: the *hierarchy* view, the *channel* view and the *runtime* (or *player*) view. The hierarchy view gives the author structure-based control of the presentation. This structure can be created top down or bottom up, allowing the author to group existing media items together, or to define completely empty structure to be filled in later. The channel view is a modified timeline presentation, which describes timing information and logical resource usage. Control flow information is overlaid directly onto the channel view by using a series of synchronization constraint descriptors (called *synchronization arcs*.) The player allows the runtime view of the document to be presented, and allows user navigation using the link structure of the Amsterdam Hypermedia Model [18]. Note that no explicit programming-based view is used with CMIFed.

A presentation is composed by defining the structure of the presentation, and assigning the appropriate media items to the structure. At present, media items are of four basic types: text, still images, audio and video. Media items are created using external editor(s), available directly from within the authoring environment.

The hierarchy view for structure-based editing. The hierarchy view (Fig. 7) is the primary authoring window, providing a means of displaying and manipulating the document structure. The document has a hierarchical structure whose leaf nodes are the media items which are played in the presentation, and whose non-leaf nodes are composite nodes containing a collection of other composite nodes and/or media items. The hierarchical structure is represented in the hierarchy view as an embedded block structure. During the authoring phase, each media item in the structure diagram is assigned to a *channel*, a logical output device which is mapped by the player at runtime to a physical output device—i.e. an area on the screen or a loudspeaker.

In order to allow the author to specify timing constraints in a convenient manner, two types of composition are supported—parallel and sequential. This enables the author to group media items together to be played either at the same time or one after the other. The author does not need to specify any timing information at this point, since this is deduced from the hierarchical structure and the durations of the nodes within the structure. (Timing constraints *can* be added later—see the description of the channel view below). In Fig. 7(b) the two boxes *Places*, and *contents button* are played in parallel; the three smaller boxes nested inside the *Places* box are played one after the other. The duration of a composite node is derived by the system. The duration of a serial composite node is the sum of the durations of its children; that of a parallel composite node is the duration of the longest child. When a node has no explicit duration, for example a textual title, it is presented for the duration of its parent.

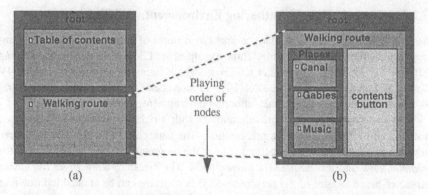

(a) The large boxes indicate different levels of structure of the presentation. The *Table of contents* part is played before *Walking route*. The small white box next to a component's name indicates that the node containing it has embedded structure not currently being shown.

(b) A zoomed-in view of the *Walking route* scene. The *Places* node contains three children each with nested structure. The right-hand box represents a text media item (a leaf node of the hierarchical structure).

Figure 7. CMIFed hierarchy view, showing top level structure of the Amsterdam tour.

The channel view for timeline-based logical resource allocation. While the hierarchy view provides a means of organizing the structure of a presentation, it provides only an indirect way of specifying logical resource use. To provide the author with an explicit time representation of the document and control of the available resources the *channel view* illustrates the media items mapped onto the available logical resources (channels). A representation of the channel view is shown in Fig. 8. By supplying this extra layer above the physical resources the author is able to describe the presentation in a system-independent way. It is up to the player software, optimized for a particular hardware configuration, to interpret the logical channels and assign the media items to the available physical output devices. A single document can be played on heterogeneous environments by adapting the players, not the document itself.

The channel view shows the timing relations derived from the structure defined in the hierarchy view. The media items making up the presentation (the leaves of the hierarchical structure) are shown with their precise durations and timing relationships. If the author changes the timing in any part of the presentation, via either the hierarchy or channel views, a new channel view is derived to reflect the change.

As well as providing a device-independent description of a media item's display characteristics, channels allow the author to include, for example, multiple languages (spoken or written) within one presentation rather than having to recreate the complete presentation for each language. The player allows the reader to dynamically select which language to listen to, by selectively turning channels on or off.

Creating hyperlinks. Presentations can be made interactive by providing choice points. This can be done via the use of scripts, but this leads to a navigation structure

that is difficult to maintain. In order to give the author better control over the navigation structure, the *contexts* facility of the Amsterdam Hypermedia Model is used for
anchor and link object grouping [19]. Creating links in a multimedia presentation is not
just a matter of creating a link to a single object, but also requires support for linking to
collections of items incorporating timing relations.

The CMIFed player. The player interprets the system-independent specification of the
multimedia presentation (in terms of the presentation's structure, logical resource allocation and timing constraints) and plays the presentation on the available hardware.
This process is described in detail in [30]. The player provides facilities, such as start,
pause and stop, for the author or end-user to control the playing of the presentation.

From the authoring perspective, the player is closely integrated with the hierarchy
and channel views. The player also allows users to select which channels should be
played, for example to select one of a number of voice-overs in different languages.

At a low level of operation, the player converts data formats of the different media
types at runtime, saving the author from having to go through tedious conversion procedures. Similarly, re-scaling the window size for the presentation is a simple operation. The window containing the channels can be scaled and the channels within will
scale automatically.

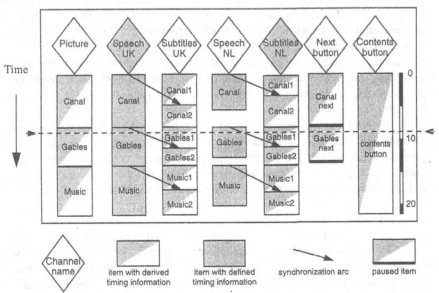

The diamonds at the top of the figure show the channel names (inactive channels are
shaded). The media items assigned to the channels are represented as boxes beneath the
diamonds. The height of a box represents its duration. A fully-shaded box has its duration
explicitly defined, either through its data type, for sound and video, or through the author
assigning a specific duration. A box with a shaded triangle has inherited its duration from
its parent in the presentation's structure.

Figure 8. Channel View for the *Walking route* sequence.

4 Research Challenges for Future Generations

Within the research community, several projects are underway that expand and augment present G_2 commercial approaches to providing multimedia authoring support. As with other advancements, the primary challenges that exist include improved distribution support (making documents more portable to create an attractive return on authoring investment), improved hyper-media information associations within a document (allowing full-function content-based navigation to be provided for generic media), improved media object support (allowing data to be dynamically tailored to the capabilities of the presentation environment), and support for automatic generation of document structure. We highlight a representative sample of projects that address these challenges in the following paragraphs.

4.1 Author-Once Model

Text documents (and, to a lessor degree, drawings and illustrations) benefit from using the printed page as a common model upon which to base generic authoring. Once a document is created, it can be mechanically transformed for presentation on computer screens, loose sheets of paper, books, overhead transparencies, etc., with little extra effort. Unfortunately, there is no such unifying model for multimedia. Still, the basis of multimedia authoring should be to produce a single representation of a document that can be shared among various types of presentation environments. In the multimedia case, this variety can be restricted to electronic documents, but it should span high-end to low-end computers, from fully-equipped engineering workstations to relatively simple portable computers. In supporting this heterogeneity, the guiding philosophy should be to transform a single document to fit the available presentation environment rather than creating separate versions of a document for each environment. We call this an *author-once* approach.

One approach to supporting this model is to define a 'standard' intermediate form, such as HyTime [22], [27] or MHEG [23], [26]. A player/program to interpret/execute standard formats on all types of platforms could then be defined. Several research projects currently exist to produce such players, although to date they have been developed in isolation from integrated authoring systems. Another approach is to define a rich document model, with explicit object resolution priorities and synchronization models that allow an author to express constraints on media object presentation. Such a model—which would encode author intentions in addition to object dependencies—could then be used to guide the instantiation of a general document on a particular hardware platform. This approach has been used in the design of CMIFed and is used implicitly in the development of document synchronization and navigation architectures ([6], [14]).

4.2 Hyper-Everything

One of the primary advantages of electronic documents (whether mono- or multimedia) is an ability to rapidly search through the information and to provide content-based, non-linear means of information navigation. In current multimedia systems, conventional hypertext facilities have been expanded to incorporate keyword-based references to audio, video and picture data. In future systems, the ability to search and 'link' pieces of information will need to become significantly more universal. While the models that support hyper-information are reasonably well understood [16], [18], methods for physically creating links and then activating them need to be improved to non-text media. The associations that are created will need to span collections of related data items and provide support for conditional activation based on the runtime state of a complex document [4], [9].

4.3 Finding and Integrating Adaptive Media Objects

Where the author-once model advocates reuse and tailoring of documents, the development of adaptive media objects supports reuse and tailoring of data items. Given the high cost of producing quality audio, video, graphic and even text data—plus the need to protect owner copyright as an incentive to increasing the number of data objects available—three aspects of object integration into documents needs to be supported: locating a particular object from an object store, extracting the relevant portion of the object for use in a particular document and transforming the representation of the fragment to meet the dynamic needs of the runtime presentation environment. The first two aspects are being addressed by research projects rooted in database systems and content-based information modelling [11], [32], [33].

Once integrated into a document, object adaptability can allow an object to be presented on a variety of systems, under a variety of hardware and performance constraints by being able to transparently transform its presentation format to the needs of the system and the users to which it is being presented. For example, a picture might be replaced by a text description depending on network resources or presentation hardware limitations; this is done to a limited degree in the Netscape Navigator World-Wide Web browser [11S]. Another type of translation may be to select one of several natural or artificial language encodings, such as substituting Dutch audio for English audio for users in the Netherlands, or for substituting computer-generation audio for text[1] [8].

4.4 Automated Document Structure Generation

Along with support for the selection and integration of media objects, further authoring support can be provided by (partially) automating the process of structural definition of the document itself. Examples of this from the intelligent interface community include [3] and [25]. A major extension to this effort is the incorporation of temporal constraints among the media objects included in the document. An approach we are investigating is to specify the subject matter to be conveyed to an end-user along with knowledge of the user's task as input to a structure generation system. Based on these constraint specifications, a document structure is generated for combining appropriate media items into coherent groups with derived temporal and layout presentation specifications.

---

1. An extreme example of this for the CMIFed environment was the development of a translation routine that mapped text to Morse code.

5 Conclusions

To date, the integration of multimedia capabilities on the desktop has been made possible by technological advances in processor and peripheral architectures. At some point, the emphasis will need to shift to new application and systems support tools to give the user real control over the flow of information to and through computers. We anticipate that the user requirements for more effective control over electronic information flow through local systems and across international networks will ultimately motivate new languages where fundamental support will exist for parallel, time-constrained data interaction and new operating systems will need to be defined that allow content-based, multi-stream I/O coordination, both in the context of a distributed information model that allows data to be shared and author/publisher rights to be protected.

It is difficult to predict the impact of improved electronic communication on future societies; in the short term, however, it is clear that unless grade schools integrate required drawing, video production and public speaking as adjuncts to reading and writing into the standard curriculum, creating multimedia documents will remain the domain of specialists. While there is an increase of using multimedia in teaching, teaching the skills required for effectively producing multimedia documents for general communication is in its infancy.

The capabilities of current architectures and the needs of current users should serve as a starting point in the development of authoring systems and media manipulation tools. In a sense, we are only at the stage of developing quill pens and indelible ink— and then only pens and ink that write on very limited types of paper. The emphasis for new generations of multimedia authoring systems should be geared to defining reliable means of encoding and saving information for future use. Reflecting back on the development of text-based communication, it is clear that a number of developments are still required to improve the quality, reliability, availability and cost-effectiveness of multimedia documents.

6 References

6.1 Articles

1   P. Ackermann, "Direct Manipulation of Temporal Structures in a Multimedia Application Framework," in Proceedings *Multimedia '94*, San Francisco, pp. 51 - 58, Oct 1994.

2   T. G. Aguierre Smith, "Parsing Movies in Context," in Proc. Summer *USENIX* Conference, Nashville, TN, pp. 157 - 167, 1991.

3   E. André and T. Rist, "The Design of Illustrated Documents as a Planning Task," in *Intelligent Multimedia Interfaces*, ed. Mark T Maybury, AAAI Press/MIT Press, ISBN 0-262-63150-4, pp. 94-116, 1993.

4   B. Arons, "Hyperspeech: Navigating in Speech-Only Hypermedia," in Proceedings *Hypertext '91* (Third ACM Conf. on Hypertext), San Antonio TX, pp. 133-146, Dec. 1991.

5   R. Botafogo and D. Mossé, "The MORENA Model for Hypermedia Authoring and Browsing," Proc. IEEE Int. Conf. on Multimedia Computing and Systems, Washington, D.C., pp. 40-49, May 1995,

6   M. C. Buchanan and P. T. Zellweger, "Automatic temporal layout mechanisms," in Proceedings *ACM Multimedia '93*, Anaheim CA, pp. 341-350, Aug 1993.

7   D.C.A. Bulterman, G. van Rossum and R. van Liere, "A Structure for Transportable, Dynamic Multimedia Documents," in Proc. Summer *USENIX* Conference, Nashville, Tennessee, pp. 137-155, 1991.

8   D.C.A. Bulterman, "Specification and Support of Adaptable Network Multimedia," ACM/Springer *Multimedia Systems*, 1(2), pp. 68-76, September 1993.

9   V.A. Burrill, T. Kirste & J.M. Weiss, "Time-Varying Sensitive Regions in Dynamic Multimedia Objects: A Pragmatic Approach to Content-Based Retrieval from Video," *Information and Software Technology*, 36(4), Butterworth-Heinemann, pp. 213-224, April 1994.

10   CHAMELEON: An Authoring Environment for Adaptive Multimedia Documents, CEC ESPRIT-IV Project 20597, 1995.

11   M. Davis, "Media Streams: An Iconic Language for Video Annotation," *Cyberspace*, 84(9), (Norwegian Telecom Research), pp. 49-71, 1993.

12   G.D. Drapeau and H. Greenfield, "MAEstro — A Distributed Multimedia Authoring Environment," in Proc. Summer 1991 *USENIX* Conference, Nashville, TN, pp. 315-328. 1991.

13   S. Eun, E.S. No, H.C. Kim, H. Yoon and S.R. Maeng, "Eventor: An Authoring System for Interactive Multimedia Applications," *Multimedia Systems* 2(2), pp.129 - 140, 1994.

14   K. Fujikawa, S. Shimojo, T. Matsuura, S. Nishio and H. Miyahara, "Multimedia Presentation System 'Harmony' with Temporal and Active Media," in Proc. Summer 1991 *USENIX* Conference, Nashville, TN, pp. 75-93, 1991.

15   D. J. Gemmell, H.A. Vin, D.D. Kandlur, P.V. Rangan and L.Rowe, "Multimedia Storage Servers: A Tutorial," IEEE Computer, 28(5), pp. 40-49, May 1995.

16   Frank Halasz and Mayer Schwartz, "The Dexter Hypertext Reference Model," *Communications of the ACM*, 37 (2), pp. 30 - 39, Feb. 1994 (Also NIST Hypertext Standardization Workshop, Gaithersburg, MD, January 16-18 1990.)

17   R. Hamakawa and J. Rekimoto, "Object Composition and Playback Models for Handling Multimedia Data," *Multimedia Systems* 2(1), pp. 26-35, 1994.

18   L. Hardman, D.C.A. Bulterman and G. van Rossum, "The Amsterdam Hypermedia Model: Adding Time and Context to the Dexter Model," *Communications of the ACM*, 37 (2), pp. 50 - 62, Feb. 1994.

19   L. Hardman, D.C.A. Bulterman and G. van Rossum, "Links in Hypermedia: The Requirement for Context," in Proceedings *ACM Hypertext '93*, Seattle WA, pp. 183-191, 1993.

20   L. Hardman, G. van Rossum and D.C.A. Bulterman, "Structured Multimedia Authoring," in Proceedings *ACM Multimedia '93*, Anaheim CA, pp. 283 - 289, Aug. 1993.

21   M.E. Hodges, R.M. Sasnett and M.S. Ackerman, "A Construction Set for Multimedia Applications," *IEEE Software*, 6(1), pp. 37-43, Jan. 1989.

22   ISO, "HyTime. Hypermedia/Time-Based Structuring Language," ISO/IEC 10744:1992.

23   ISO, "MHEG. Information Technology Coded Representation of Multimedia and Hypermedia Information Objects (MHEG) Part 1: Base Notation (ASN.1), ISO/IEC CD 13552-1:1993, Oct 15 1994.

24   J.F. Koegel and J.M. Heines, "Improving Visual Programming Languages for Multimedia Authoring," *ED-MEDIA '93*, World Conference on Educational Multimedia and Hypermedia, Charlottesville, Virginia, pp. 286-293, June 1993.

25   R. Macneil, "Generating Multimedia Presentations Automatically Using TYRO, The Constraint, Case-Based Designer's Apprentice," in Proceedings: *IEEE 1991 Visual Language Workshop*, pp. 74-79, 1991

26   T. Meyer-Boudnik and W. Effelsberg, "MHEG Explained," *IEEE MultiMedia*, 1(4), pp. 26-38, Spring 1995.

27   S.R. Newcomb, N.A. Kipp and V.T. Newcomb, "HyTime: The Hypermedia/Time-Based Document Structuring Language," *Communications of the ACM*, 34(11), pp. 67-83, 1991.

28   R. Ogawa, H. Harada and A. Kaneko, "Scenario-Based Hypermedia: A Model and a System," in Proceedings: *ECHT '90* (First European Conference on Hypertext), INRIA France, pp. 38-51, Nov. 1990.

29   S. Travis Pope and G. van Rossum, "Machine Tongues XVIII: A Child's Garden of Sound File Formats." *Computer Music*, 19(2), pp. 25-63, 1995.

30   G. van Rossum, J. Jansen, K.S. Mullender and D.C.A. Bulterman, "CMIFed: A Presentation Environment for Portable Hypermedia Documents," in Proceedings *ACM Multimedia '93*, Anaheim CA, pp. 183-188, Aug. 1993.

31   A. Siochi, E.A. Fox, D. Hix, E.E. Schwartz, A. Narasimhan, W. Wake, "The Integrator: A Prototype for Flexible Development of Interactive Digital Multimedia Applications," *Interactive Multimedia*, 2(3), pp. 5-26, 1993.

32   H. Wittig and C. Griwodz, "Intelligent Media Agents in Interactive Television Systems," Proc. IEEE Int. Conf. on Multimedia Computing and Systems, Washington, D.C., pp. 182-189, May 1995.

33   H. Zhang, Y. Gong, S. Smoliar, "Automatic Parsing of News Video," Proc. First IEEE ICMS, Boston, 1994.

6.2 Software

1S   Adobe Systems, Inc., "Adobe Photoshop 3.0." URL:http://www.adobe.com/

2S   Adobe Systems, Inc., "Adobe Premiere." URL:http://www.adobe.com/

3S   Apple Computer Corp., "HyperCard." URL:http://www.apple.com/

4S   J. Bradley, "XV," University of Pennsylvania. Available via anonymous ftp: ftp.cis.upenn.edu:pub/xv

5S   IBM Corp., "AVC: Audio Visual Connection," User's Guide, 1990.

6S   Frame Technology Corp, "FrameMaker 5.0." URL:http://www.frame.com/

7S   Kaleida Labs, Inc., "ScriptX." URL:http://www.kaleida.com/

8S   Macromedia, Inc., "Macromedia Director 4.0 for Windows." 1994.
URL:http://www.macromedia.com/

9S   Macromedia, Inc., "Macromedia SoundEdit 16." 1993
URL:http://www.macromedia.com/

10S   Microsoft Corp., "Microsoft Word 6.0." 1994. URL:http://www.microsoft.com/

11S   Netscape Comm. Corp, "Navigator 1.1," 1995. URL:http://home.mcom.com/

Computational Models for Distributed Multimedia Applications

Thomas Käppner and Ralf Steinmetz

IBM European Networking Center, Vangerowstr. 18, D-69115 Heidelberg
Mail: {kaeppner, steinmetz}@vnet.ibm.com

Abstract: The paper surveys recent work on abstractions for distributed multimedia applications. The essential questions are: How can multimedia applications express their computational requirements with respect to the data and its processing? What is the role of time and quality of service? What tasks should be delegated to a multimedia system's layer being an extension of the operating system and how could data handling multimedia applications work with such a layer? We discuss these issues reviewing several systems and architectures that have been proposed.

1 Introduction

Early in the nineties the term continuous media has been coined [1] for those data types that incorporate an inherent temporal dimension. In addition to digital audio and video, animation, formatted music encodings and continuously sampled scientific data are covered by this definition. In contrast, the traditional data types, as text and graphics, without such temporal dependencies, are called discrete media.

After years of research and development on multimedia systems the term multimedia is still very widely interpreted. Literally 'multimedia' means 'many media'. From a computing perspective, a medium is a means of communication between humans and computers. In consequence, systems that process text and graphics are sometimes referred to as multimedia systems. We believe that rather than counting quantities of media to define a multimedia system, the qualities of media must be taken into account. For the purpose of this paper we use the following notion [34]:

> A multimedia system is characterized by the integrated, computer-controlled generation, manipulation, presentation, storage, and communication of independent discrete and continuous media.

According to this definition, multimedia applications combine the processing of discrete and continuous media. Experience has shown that the difficulty of developing multimedia applications depends on the support provided by the underlying computing platform, a support that is necessary, since the characteristics of continuous media make a development from scratch particularly difficult:

- Since audio and video data must be continuously presented to the user, data of a movie must be processed in real-time during its presentation. In an interactive application the user interface must be served concurrently, i.e., in general multiple independent threads are simultaneously active.
- The temporal dependencies of continuous media require that applications have an

awareness of time, e.g. data must be read timely from hard disk to be presented. Time sources and timing conditions must be evaluated to determine the next processing steps. Synchronization is necessary for the correct presentation of single and multiple related streams of continuous media.

- The application of coding and compression algorithms decreases the amount of memory needed to store continuous media. Applications rather control these complex processing steps than perform them themselves. The most prominent encoding formats of continuous media are defined in international standards and must be understood by application developers in order to correctly process the data.

- Digital video is generated by special digitization hardware, audio devices are needed to convert between the analog and the digital representation for the purpose of recording and playback. In general, devices and drivers are tailored to the platform and operating system, which inhibits the development of portable multimedia applications. Replacing any underlying continuous media device, even with a functionally-equivalent component from another vendor, often requires reimplementing a substantial part of the application. Moreover, device access is exclusive in most cases, i.e., several multimedia applications can not simultaneously write data to a device.

Distribution and communication are important aspects for all multimedia applications, some of them are even inherently distributed: The purpose of teleconferencing and CSCW applications is the communication between participants who are separated spatially or temporally.

In distributed systems multimedia applications can leverage resources such as data and devices remotely. In contrast, in stand-alone systems every special device, such as a broadcast television receivers or a CD mass storage system, must be installed locally. Since the amount of storage needed for digital audio and video easily exceeds the capacities of local hard disks, continuous media should be stored on specialized file servers that are able to support the sustained data rates during read and write operations. The access to such services of distributed systems introduces another set of issues for multimedia application development:

- Network access must be programmed explicitly, since well-known mechanisms of distributed systems like remote procedure calls are not applicable to the transport of continuous media.

- Since transport requirements of continuous media are different from those of traditional data types, special communication protocols are being developed to supplement existing protocol stacks. As multimedia applications combine discrete and continuous media, they must integrate both types of communication.

- Generally, distributed systems are heterogeneous with regard to the underlying hardware and operating systems. For multimedia applications this heterogeneity is especially hard to overcome.

These issues of multimedia application development have formed the conviction that generic support from the computing platform will be necessary, if integrated distributed continuous media is to become a reality. Such support is established by a system extension that we will refer to as a multimedia platform. In the past system extensions for multimedia have already been introduced as products, being able to support applications locally [25, 19, 26]. However, the development of multimedia platforms in an open distributed environment is still the subject of active research. This paper introduces a review of this work by clarifying demands on the computational models of multimedia platforms in Section 2. These demands are taken as criteria to evaluate in Section 3 a selection of systems and architectures that have been proposed in the past. Section 4 introduces a computational model in which abstractions are structured along orthogonal dimensions. Finally, Section 5 gives an outlook and concludes the paper.

2 Requirements for Computational Models of Multimedia Platforms

It is evident that multimedia applications should be portable, easy to program, and efficient. However, we want to clarify this notion, in order to provide a set of criteria for the evaluation of multimedia platforms. The topic of this paper are the computational models as provided by multimedia platforms and used by applications. Their expressiveness and power is the focus of the following set of requirements, which are marked for later reference, e.g. (CR1), and classified by their necessity:

- A requirement that *must* be satisfied contains a necessary function for multimedia applications and is viewed as an obligation.
- A requirement that *should* be satisfied contains a desirable function for multimedia applications and is viewed as a recommendation.

CR1: *A multimedia platform must support the development of a wide variety of multimedia applications.*

Multimedia applications can be classified into categories with different requirements like teleconferencing, editing, animation, and speech recognition and synthesis. Editing for example, demands a different granularity of data access than teleconferencing. On the other hand data streams enabling the communication between humans have distinctive requirements with regard to end-to-end delay. Platforms for continuous media should provide generic support for many, possibly all, different kinds of applications.

CR2: *The level of abstraction an application is programmed at, should be adaptable to its requirements [20].*

Although applications belong to the same category, they may have to deal with multimedia data in different ways. A simple editor for mailing might not want to control the format in which audio and video is recorded or played back. A professional system for editing commercials will support special effects and might need in-depth knowledge of the data and its format. In principle, simple applications should be easy to develop. The computational model of a multimedia platform should offer a hierarchy of abstractions, which allow the development of applications at a level that hides irrelevant details, yet offers the necessary means to keep control.

CR3: *A multimedia platform must support applications in a distributed system.*

Applications need access to data and resources of the distributed system and there should be no principal difference between remote and local access. However, while in prominent window systems [31] the location of resources and the network are transparent to applications, many multimedia applications, due to their inherent distribution, have a need to address and access components on remote locations explicitly.

CR4: *The notion of time should be made explicit in the computational model of a multimedia platform.*

Many applications need an awareness of time, since their processing depends on time, or they combine continuous and discrete media in a presentation. Time services should be flexibly definable by the application in order

- to choose time references such as a clock or a stream of data
- to modify resolution and offset of a time reference to make it compatible with other notions of time.
- to receive information about the course of time synchronously and asynchronously.

CR5: *Applications must be able to establish and control streams of continuous media.*

Since audio and video data are represented as a sequence of digital information units, continuous flow of these units is a prerequisite for the processing of continuous media [17]. Controlling streams of continuous media is very illustrative and should be part of the computational model [33]. Operations like *Start* and *Stop* facilitate dynamic user interactions. The set of available operations depends on the way the data is generated. For instance if data is read from a hard disk, a larger degree of control (e.g. *Rewind, FastForward*) will be possible, than if data was recorded from a microphone.

CR6: *Applications must be able to choose the quality of service for a data stream.*

The quality a user can expect from a data stream is determined by a set of parameters that we refer to as its quality of service (QoS). In addition to the format, the quality of service of the stream includes the following aspects:

- Importance for the application
- Preemptability
- Behavior in case of resource unavailability
- Delay between source and sink
- Error characteristics
- Reservation of resources
- Cost

The quality of service determines the treatment and scheduling of streams once they are established. Distinguishing classes of QoS enables a multimedia platform to adapt the mechanisms that support a stream to the demands of the application.

CR7: *Applications must be able to express relations between several streams.*

Relations of logical or temporal nature exist for example between the audio and video tracks of a movie. Temporal relations, so-called synchronization relationships are necessary to preserve the meaning of the combined presentation. Logical relation are used for instance to atomically establish and control several streams.

CR8: *A multimedia platform must provide access to data processing components that are independent of the underlying hardware.*

Several processing steps, e.g. digitization, compression, and decompression require additional adapter cards or built-in hardware devices, which are accessed by libraries that are generally specific for the operating system and hardware. If the processing of continuous media is made available in a hardware independent manner, applications will stay robust in the face of the replacement of adapter cards or even the complete hardware platform. Such generic processing components have been referred to as devices [2, 7, 3], even when their functionality does not require hardware support.

CR9: *Applications must be able to obtain information about installed devices and their characteristics during run-time.*

When applications are developed independently of a specific hardware platform, they have to query the characteristics of a particular installation in order to utilize their capabilities. For instance, conference applications will query devices for supported formats to negotiate the format of audio and video streams. Characteristics of a device that are to be queried include:

- the number, type, and format of data streams a device is capable to process,
- the kinds of events, a device generates,
- special operations and presentation specific attributes a device supports, such as volume, contrast, saturation.

CR10: *A multimedia platform must provide the option of accessing continuous media data directly.*

Controlling streams and devices is a way to supervise the flow of continuous media through the system without touching the data itself. While this has been sufficient for many applications in the past, to an increasing degree, applications are beginning to analyze data to extract content information, convert, and present it in unforeseen ways. To the extent that such processing is not provided by generic devices. applications must access the data to implement it themselves.

CR11: *A multimedia platform should provide devices for the transport of data streams over communication networks.*

Continuous media has different transport requirements from the traditional discrete data types (e.g. real-time transport, multicast). New protocols that provide this functionality are being developed [12, 13, 32] but are not yet widespread. Access to communication networks can be provided consistently by a transport device. By mapping parameters and emulating functions such devices could integrate a multitude of existing communication platforms.

CR12: *A multimedia platform should provide devices for the storage of continuous media data.*

There is already a multitude of formats for the storage of continuous media in files and the problems of providing storage services that scale many streams and large files are not yet solved. A device that models storage services for continuous media data can shield the application from further developments in these areas.

CR13: *A multimedia platform should facilitate the explicit allocation and release of resources needed for operations.*

The success of an operation can only be guaranteed, if necessary resources can be allocated for it. Only if allocation and release of resources are independent operations, the time at which they are carried out can be controlled by applications. For instance, after stopping a data stream an application might want to keep resources for that stream allocated, in order to ensure that the following restart operation would be successful. Explicit allocation of resources can decrease the latency of operations by splitting off and preparing the rather time consuming resource allocation process.

3 Available Multimedia Platforms and Services

This section evaluates the extent to that existing multimedia platforms satisfy the requirements of applications as defined in Section 2.

3.1 VOX

Work at Olivetti Research Center [7, 8] had the goal to provide programmers with all resources for speech applications in an easy, effective, and flexible way. The result is a client/server architecture, where applications have access as clients to a so-called VOX server, which controls all hardware and software components required for speech processing.

The LAUD (Logical AUdio Device) is the main abstraction inside the VOX server offering basic functions like switches, amplifiers, microphones, and telephones (CR8). LAUDs offer two kinds of interfaces: Control Ports receive commands and send events, whereas Audio Ports are characterized by direction (input/output) and the type of data they transport. Data is modeled as analog signals (line level, Mike, RJ11) which shows that VOX was targeted to the control of analog components rather than to providing an integrated digital system. Digital data is only used for storage: LAUDs for recording and playback have several attributes to describe data in digital formats including encoding, sample rate, and sample size.

LAUDs are considered as building blocks, which can be assembled to higher level components, so-called CLAUDS (Composite LAUD), by connecting their input and output ports. Functions of CLAUDS could be e.g., answering machine or preamplified microphones.

The VOX server interface, as visible to clients, is independent of its location, so access to the server is called network transparent. However, data streams can not be established between servers residing on different hosts in the network (CR3). Moreover, the application can directly access data, because data is always flowing inside a CLAUD (CR10).

3.2 XMedia

The XMedia architecture [3] was developed at Digitals's Western Software Lab. The design is based on main concepts of the X Windows System [31] and VOX: As in X Windows, a protocol defines commands and events for client-server interactions. Clients can establish connections to several servers and servers can hold connections to several clients. A library provides the clients with a procedural protocol interface. Higher level functional blocks are offered by a toolkit (CR8).

Similar to LAUDs in VOX there are Virtual Devices (VD) in XMedia that abstract basic functions of audio processing from the underlying hardware. An application specifies attributes when creating a VD. When the VD is activated, the server maps its attributes to capabilities of physical devices, in order to select a physical device for the application.

As in VOX, virtual devices can be composed by building a tree structure that is called Logical Audio Device. Connections combine output and input ports of VDs to model data flow. In contrast to VOX, the data can be represented as analog and digital signals in XMedia. Data flow is not restricted to the server, but the application can access data via the protocol interface (CR10), which facilitates a limited distribution of data: An application can receive data from one server and send it to another. However, direct connections between servers are impossible (CR3).

3.3 ACME

Work at University of California at Berkeley dealt with abstractions for continuous media (ACME) [2] and their integration in a distributed environment. As in VOX and XMedia there is a hierarchy of abstractions in ACME (CR8):

- Physical Devices (PDev) represent the underlying hardware and belong to one of four classes: audio input, audio output, video input, and video output, which shows that ACME is the first system that includes support for the medium video (CR1).
- Logical Devices (LDev) are created by applications specifying a PDev and other attributes including the data format to be used. Several LDevs may share one PDev: For audio output the data of all LDevs is digitally combined by the server and processed by the PDev; input data is forwarded to all LDevs.
- Sequences of stored data units are called Strands, combinations of several Strands are Ropes. These abstractions facilitate an easy access to stored data (CR12). The processing of a Rope, e.g. a video with a related audio track, is supported by a so-called combined LDev (CLDev). To create a CLDev the application must specify a list of PDevs, that is capable of processing the single strand's audio and video data.

There is more support for distribution of data in ACME than in XMedia and VOX: Data streams can flow between applications and servers (CR10) and between several servers (CR3). Special protocols for continuous media are considered important by the authors, however, for their implementation they use the common transport system TCP/IP, which does not support multicast functionality (CR11).

3.4 AudioFile and NCDaudio

The systems AudioFile [24] and NCDaudio [27] have several common aspects: They are organized in a client/server architecture and are designed similar to the X Windows System. Both systems support only audio, they are in the public domain and have been ported to several UNIX-based environments.

In AudioFile digital audio signals can either flow from application to server to be played back on an output device or they can be transported from an input device of the server to the application. Because of this simple model, all important information of a data stream, e.g. direction, data encoding, physical device, can be determined by a simple abstraction called audio context (AC). The audio context is one parameter of the most important operations AFPlay and AFRecord that transport blocks of audio data from application to server and vice versa. Interactions with stored data are not supported by the server, an application must manage these on its own (CR12).

AudioFile expresses time information explicitly: AFRecord and AFPlay use time parameters that specify the time at which data is recorded and played back. Data is buffered within the server to reduce real-time constraints on the application. However, applications must ask the server for its notion of time to play the data (CR4). Audio-File offers no further time services and the synchronization of data streams must be implemented by applications. However, since time information of the server depends on the clocks of physical devices, they can not be related to other events, from e.g. a window system or another audio server.

NCDaudio introduces some concepts in addition to those implemented in Audio-File: A Flow is a combination of physical devices similar to the CLOUDs in XMedia (CR8). A Bucket represents stored data inside the server. Buckets can be created from files (CR12), from application's data or from a sink of a Flow. In contrast to AudioFile, these concepts enable applications to model data flow inside the NCDaudio server without the need to touch them.

Both systems do not support real-time processing by special mechanism of resource management and therefore can not guarantee the functionality during overload situations. Clients and servers communicate via TCP/IP without separate data connections (CR11). Experience with AudioFile over wide area networks shows that this transport system is not well suited for real-time data transport. Nevertheless, AudioFile is the most widespread system applied for audio processing today, for which the main reasons are its free availability for several system environments and the utilization of internet protocols.

3.5 Touring Machine

In the late eighties several multimedia applications were developed at Bellcore, that model the character of informal or work group meetings [29][28]. The fact that these applications were written directly on top of the operating system limited their flexibility and motivated work on the Touring Machine System [5], which was designed as a generic platform for multimedia applications.

The model of the Touring System is derived directly from group applications: Applications communicate via so-called sessions, in which they control local sources and sinks of potential data streams such that direct access to remote devices is impossible (CR3). While a session is created, the characteristics of data streams are negotiated by applications. Once they agree, the system tries to map the communication topology onto the network in order to establish audio and video streams.

Streams are flowing between so-called ports, characterized by direction and medium, the latter being audio or video. First the Touring Machine was restricted to analog media, however an extended version supports digital data streams additionally [4]. By specifying a port only partly, applications can indicate that the system may complement the specification to make the ports of a stream compatible. Ports are connected by connection objects, which can express point-to-point and multi-point connections (CR11).

3.6 University of Lancaster

At the University of Lancaster the demands of multimedia applications for the standardization of distributed systems were investigated within the scope of Open Distributed Processing (ODP). The Advanced Networked Systems Architecture (ANSA [6]), being the closest available implementation of the ODP standard, was used as a basis for multimedia system service development [10]. One part of ODP, the 'Computational Viewpoint', describes the relation between service providers and service users in an object model. Service providers export interfaces to a trader, that consist of signatures and associated attributes; Service users specify the desired services with attribute predicates to the trader, which will establish a binding between the parties, if it can identify a suitable service (CR9).

The multimedia system services contain abstractions for process components and data [35]: Devices represent physical devices, stored data or software processes (CR8). Using a device, a chain can be created, representing a sequence of pointers to data objects. The interface of a chain contains operations to move the current read/write position, indicating a model tailored to stored data (CR12). However, the abstraction also covers sources like cameras and microphones. All aspects of data flow with regard to a device are represented by the interfaces of so-called endpoints, which can be created by chains. Attributes of an endpoint consist of the rate at which data objects flow through an endpoint and their type, specified in abstract terms like RGB_Video and PCM_Audio. More detailed parameters of the data formats are not accessible for an application.

Streams can be established between endpoints of devices. Embedding system services in ANSA facilitates the distribution of devices transparent for the application. Characteristics of streams contain quality of service parameters (CR6). However, the implementation contains no mechanisms that guarantee the compliance with the specification. Recent work in Lancaster shows how quality of service can be expressed more comprehensively [9] (CR6) and how such model can be supported by a resource management being implemented as an extension of the Chorus micro kernel [11].

3.7 Further Object Models

Several computational models have been introduced, partially without the goal to provide a complete multimedia platform. The most relevant of them are built within object oriented frameworks and are summarized in the following section.

At the University of Geneva multimedia applications have been built as groups of processing components [15, 16]. Processing components are called active objects, that produce and consume multimedia data (CR8). Data is defined as finite sequences of multimedia values that must be produced and consumed with a fixed rate. The data types are structured by an class hierarchy that includes time-dependent and time-independent data. Data types are classified by semantic aspects (audio, music, video, scene) and by the syntax of the data (NTSC, PAL).

Active objects can be sources, sinks and filters of multimedia values and they are placed in a class hierarchy, in which they can represent analog devices and software processes that offer the basic methods *Start* and *Stop*, in order to control the processing of data. Two axes are distinguished for the time internal and external to each object. Times of several objects can be related to each other and methods facilitate the conversion of times between time axes, in order to synchronize starting points of active objects (CR4). Components are configured to composite objects by means of special connection objects. Composite objects are handled and controlled like simple objects.

With regard to its expressional power the model is at a similar level as VOX and XMedia. Its additional contributions lie in the modeling of simple synchronization relations (CR7) and the concept of reusable components represented in object hierarchies.

In the related CINEMA system [30], components are configured in so-called clock hierarchies that define relationships of control and temporal synchronization. Synchronization is not constrained to start-times of streams but is supported continuously, after streams have been established. Relationships between clocks can be changed dynamically during run-time.

In [14] a data and object model is proposed by which applications can be programmed in a hardware-independent fashion (CR8). At the highest layer the object model is composed of four basic functions: Perception, writing to mass storage, reading from mass storage and presentation. Devices like microphones and speakers can be built by simple inheritance. Complex functions can be modeled by multiple inheritance. The data model distinguishes between audio and video and provides data structures to access data at different levels (CR2):

```
Audio_list  = LIST OF Track;
Track       = SEQUENCE OF Sector;
Sector      = ARRAY [m] OF Sample;
```

Data formats, like those defined by different compression algorithms, are not visible to the programmer. The authors assume that data formats are converted by the system transparently to the programmer.

Samples, sectors, and tracks have associated starting point and duration to express the time dependence of data (CR4). All samples of a sector and all sectors of a track have equal duration, i.e., their time parameters are predefined. In contrast, the starting time of a track can be modified by the application.

A request for Technology by the Interactive Multimedia Association (IMA) has been responded by Hewlett Packard, IBM, and SunSoft introducing an object model [18] that should enable the development of multimedia applications in heterogeneous distributed systems. Like the approaches described above, devices are structured by object hierarchies. The object technology is used in order to facilitate extensibility and a uniform interfaces to devices (CR8). Data is described by a hierarchy of format objects. In contrast to [14], direct access to data is not possible, instead data flow is modeled by stream objects (CR10). Quality of service aspects are associated with stream objects and can be specified by applications at a relatively low level as throughput, delay, delay jitter (CR6). The complete encapsulation of data streams within the platform yields the development of teleconferencing applications in a peer-to-peer architecture impossible (CR1).

4 A Canonical Model for Multimedia Abstractions

The examination of existing computational models for multimedia applications reveals that they separate various aspects of multimedia computing, however they do not do it consistently. Almost all provide separate abstractions for multimedia data and the way it is processed. The processing is modeled by a device, with ports or endpoints through which data of a specific type may flow. In contrast, other aspects like time are not represented independently in some models, which results, e.g. in [14], in a replication of time representations at the various layers of the data model (cf. Section 3.7). In order to avoid such inconsistencies, we propose a canonical model in which different aspects of multimedia computing are expressed explicitly and independently.

The canonical model is a method of structuring the aspects of multimedia computing along the dimensions time, data, quality, and operations. Abstractions within this model are one-dimensional in the sense, that they represent notions that are confined to only one dimension. There are special binding mechanisms to express relations between abstractions. Hence, programming with the canonical model is a two-phase process: Applications (1) specify their requirements using individual abstractions independently and (2) build relationships between abstractions resulting in a global view of their computational requirements. The replication of information is avoided, since specifications are reusable, i.e., they can be used in several relationships. For instance, an application can define a time axis and bind it to several clocks, which in turn are used to control operations.

The decomposition into dimensions results in another advantage: The complex global view of computational requirements is divisible into more easily comprehensible 'sub-models', which capture various aspects of development and run-time of applications (see Figure 1).

- The definition of data formats together with the nominal time defines the timing conditions of data, which form the data model.
- Operations on objects can have time parameters in order to control the time of their execution. The relations of operations and time are referred to as the application's activity model.
- When streams are established within a multimedia platform, operations are carried out periodically on the data. The quality determines whether special mechanisms have to be applied for synchronization or to handle overload situations. Due to its importance for resource management, this set of relations is called the resource model.

The canonical model can also be viewed as a meta-model for the API of multimedia platforms. According to this meta-model we have designed and implemented the Distributed Multimedia Object Services (DMOS) [23, 21, 22]. DMOS is based on the CORBA architecture, a framework for distributed cooperating objects. In the following sections the computational model of DMOS is taken as an example to further illustrate the individual dimensions of the canonical model.

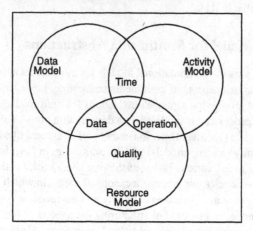

Fig. 1: Dimensions of Multimedia Abstractions with Sub-Models

4.1 Time

Applications use expressions of time to control their own operations and those that are executed within a multimedia platform. In DMOS there are two object classes that express notions of time: *LogicalTimeSystem* (LTS) and *Clock*. A LTS defines the resolution and speed at which time advances in relation to wall clock time. The resolution enables the application to adapt time expressions to any time coordinate system it might have to use, such as samples or bytes of a data stream. The attribute 'speed' provides a method of changing the notion of real-time for all objects bound to a LTS.

A *Clock* object is bound to a LTS, i.e., the LTS determines how time advances in a *Clock*. Applications can read and set actual time values and can start and stop the clock by appropriate methods. An event mechanism delivers events to the application either periodically, relatively, or absolutely with regard to the *Clock's* time and facilitates event-based synchronization of discrete data with continuous media.

4.2 Data

The data dimension contains the specification of data that is processed by the multimedia platform. Descriptions of data types are organized in a class hierarchy with the common ancestor class *Format*. A special format, the *AbstractFormat*, allows applications to specify the data as a tuple of type and quality, independent of the exact data encoding. The type of an *AbstractFormat* can be Audio, Video, or AudioVideo and its quality one of Low, Medium, and High. Abstract formats are mapped onto the other format classes, after a negotiation process, in which the supported formats of all devices that have to process a stream are taken into account.

Other format classes, e.g. *ADPCMFormat*, *MPEG1Format*, and *DVIPLVFormat*, contain parameters that are specific to the encoding of the data. Applications can use these detailed formats with the risk, that a format or even a particular setting might not be supported on a platform at run-time.

4.3 Quality

Qualities of a stream apart from data format and time are covered by the quality dimension. Note that its definition differs from the term *quality of service*, which, as generally defined, includes all aspects perceptible by a service user and covers several dimensions of the canonical model. Qualities in DMOS are defined by the single class *Quality* containing the following attributes:

- Service Commitment: The support the multimedia platform gives for processing multimedia data can be chosen from four values: Guaranteed, Statistical, Scalable, and Best-effort. The value determines the mechanisms applied for resource reservation and scheduling.
- Synchronization parameters: These attributes contain the end-to-end delay and other parameters controlled by intra-stream and inter-stream synchronization mechanisms.
- Importance: This value, expressed on a scale from 1 to 10, specifies the relative priority that a stream has for the application. For all but streams with guaranteed service commitment, this priority is evaluated to determine an order of streams that must degrade their quality when an overload situation occurs.
- Error characteristics are specified for data corruption as Ignore, Discard, Receive, Correct, and for data loss as Indicate and Correct (see e.g. [12] for the interpretation of error specifications in a continuous media transport protocol)
- Cost: Without associated costs there is little motivation to choose any other than the highest quality parameters. A cost parameter is a means to experiment with tariff models in order to adapt the mix of applications and continuous media streams to a level the underlying platform can support.

4.4 Operations

There are two levels of processing covered by this dimension: In DMOS the data is processed by *Devices* that are operated by applications. If, however, an application must do special processing on the data (cf. OD4) it can subclass any of the device classes to access the data directly. Data enters and leaves devices through *Ports*, which are created on a device with a specified *Format* (see Section 4.2). *Devices* are combined by *Connection* objects between *Ports*, a *Connection* can represent filtering of data and transport over communication networks.

Streams are created by adding *Connections*; a *Stream* eventually controls all *Devices* that belong to added *Connections*, building a topology of a directed graph. Since one ancestor of the *Stream* class is the *Clock*, (1) the *Stream* is bound to an LTS that defines its time axis and (2) it inherits methods for starting and stopping triggered by its own and other *Clock*'s time. An application binds a *Quality* to a *Stream* in order to activate the specified attributes for it. *Streams* can be combined to a *StreamGroup* in order to control several related *Streams* together.

5 Conclusion

The characteristics of continuous media make special system support necessary for the development of distributed multimedia applications. Such system support is offered by multimedia platforms that provide a computational model to express requirements with regard to multimedia data and its processing in a distributed system. In this paper we have presented a list of requirements for these computational models. We have surveyed recent work on multimedia platforms in order to evaluate their computational models in face of this list of requirements. One conclusion of the evaluation is that several different aspects of multimedia computing have been mixed into abstractions by various systems, a fact that results in inflexibility of the models or even implicit interdependencies between abstractions. This result motivated our proposal of a canonical model of multimedia abstractions, in which abstractions belong to separate dimensions each covering a different aspect of multimedia computing. Abstractions are structured along the dimensions time, data, quality, and operations and can be flexibly related to each other by special binding methods. We believe that this structuring is functionally complete in the sense that all kinds of applications could be developed on top of such model, however, the provision of higher level services could make development of applications for specific areas even more convenient.

6 References

1.   D. P. Anderson, "Metascheduling for Continuous Media", ACM Transactions on Computer Systems, vol. 11, no. 3, pp. 226-252, August 1993.

2.   D. P. Anderson, R. Govindan, and G. Homsy, "Abstractions for Continuous Media in a Network Window System", Proceedings of International Conference on Multimedia Information Systems, pp. 273-298, Singapur, 1991.

3.   S. Angebranndt, R. Hyde, D. H. Luong, N. Siravara, and C. Schmandt, "Integrating Audio and Telephony in a Distributed Workstation Environment", Proceedings 1991 Summer Usenix Conference, pp. 59-74, Nashville, Tennesse, USA.

4.   M. Arango, M. Kramer, S. L. Rohall, L. Ruston, and A. Weinrib, "Enhancing the Touring Machine API to Support Integrated Digital Transport", Proceedings of the Third International Workshop on Network and Operating System Support for Digital Audio and Video, pp. 176-182, San Diego, California, USA, November 1992.

5.   M. Arango, L. Bahler, P. C. Bates, M. Cochinwala, D. Cohrs, R. Fish, G. Gopal, N. Griffeth, G. E. Herman, T. Hickey, K. C. Lee, W. E. Leland, C. Lowery, V. Mak, J. Patterson, L. Ruston, M. Segal, R. C. Sekar, M. P. Vecchi, A. Weinrib, and S-Y. Wuu, "The Touring Machine System", Communication of the ACM, vol. 36, no. 1, pp. 68-77, January 1993.

6.   Architecture Projects Management Ltd., "The Advanced Networked Systems Architecture Reference Manual Release 01.00", A.P.M Cambridge Ltd., Poseidon House, Castle Park, Cambridge CB3 0RD, UK, March 1989.

7.   B. Arons, C. Binding, K. Lantz, and C. Schmandt, "A Voice and Audio Server for Multimedia Workstations", Proceedings of Speech Tech '89, May 1989.

8. B. Arons, C. Binding, K. Lantz, and C. Schmandt, "The VOX Audio Server", Second IEEE International Workshop on Multimedia Communications, Ottawa, Ontario, August, 1989.

9. A. Campbell, G. Coulson, and D. Hutchison, "A Quality of Service Architecture", ACM SigComm Computer Communications Review, vol. 24, no. 2, pp. 6-27, Association for Computing Machinery, New York, April 1994.

10. G. Coulson, G. S. Blair, N. Davies, and N. Williams, "Extensions to ANSA for Multimedia Computing", Computer Networks and ISDN Systems, vol. 25, pp. 305-323, 1992.

11. G. Coulson, G. S. Blair, and P. Robin, "Micro-kernel Support for Continuous Media in Distributed Systems", Computer Networks and ISDN Systems, vol. 26, pp. 1323-1341, 1994.

12. L. Delgrossi, C. Halstrick, R. G. Herrtwich, and H. Stuettgen, "HeiTP: A Transport Protocol for ST-II", Proceedings of GLOBECOM' 92, Orlando, Florida, USA, December 1992.

13. D. Ferrari, A. Banerjea, and H. Zhang, "Network Support for Multimedia: A Discussion of the Tenet Approach", TR-92-072, International Computer Science Institute, Berkeley, California, USA, Oktober 1992.

14. J. C. Fritzsche , M. Boerger, and H. Braun, "An Abstract View on Multimedia Devices in Distributed Systems", Proceedings of Computer Networks, Architecture and Applications (IFIP), pp. 27-39, Trivandrum, India, Oktober 1992.

15. S. Gibbs, "Composite Multimedia and Active Objects", Proceedings of Object Oriented Programming Systems Languages and Applications, pp. 97-112, Phoenix, Arizona, USA, Oktober 1991.

16. S. Gibbs, "Application Construction and Component Design in an Object-Oriented Multimedia Framework", Proceedings of the Third International Workshop on Network and Operating System Support for Digital Audio and Video, pp. 394-398, San Diego, California, USA, November 1992.

17. R. G. Herrtwich and L. Wolf, "A System Software Structure for Distributed Multimedia Systems", Proceedings of the Fifth ACM SIGOPS European Workshop, Le Mont Saint-Michel, France, September 21-23, 1992.

18. Hewlett Packard, Industrial Business Machines, and SunSoft, "Multimedia System Services", Response to Request for Technology: Working Document, Interactive Multimedia Association, July 1993.

19. E. Hoffert, M. Krueger, L. Mighdoll, M. Mills, J. Cohen, D. Camplejohn, B. Leak, J. Batson, D. van Brink, D. Blackketter, M. Arent, R. Williams, C. Thorman, M. Yawitz, K. Doyle and S. Callahan, "QuickTime: An Extensible Standard for Digital Multimedia", Proceedings of the Thirty Seventh IEEE Computer Society International Conference COMPCOM, pp. 15-20, San Francisco, California, USA, 24-28 February, 1992.

20. T. Käppner, D. Hehmann, and R. Steinmetz, "An Introduction to HeiMAT: The Heidelberg Multimedia Application Toolkit", Proceedings of the Third International Workshop on Network and Operating System Support for Digital Audio and Video, pp. 362-373, San Diego, California, USA, 12-13 November 1992.

21. T. Käppner and L. C. Wolf, "Media Scaling in Distributed Multimedia Object Services", Proceedings of 2nd International Workshop on Advanced Teleservices and High-Speed Communication Architectures, Heidelberg, 26-28 September, 1994.

22. T. Käppner, F. Henkel, M. Müller, and A. Schröer, "Synchronisation in einer verteilten Entwicklungs- und Laufzeitumgebung für multimediale Anwendungen", Gesellschaft für Informatik (GI) Jahrestagung, Hamburg, August/September 1994.

23. T. Käppner, F. Henkel, A. Schröer, and M. Müller, "Eine verteilte Entwicklungs- und Laufzeitumgebung für multimediale Anwendungen", Kommunikation in Verteilten Systemen, Chemnitz, February 1995.

24. T. M. Levergood, A. C. Payne, J. Gettys, G. W. Treese, and L. C. Stewart, "AudioFile: A Network-Transparent System for Distributed Audio Appplications", Proceedings 1993 Summer USENIX Conference, August 1993.

25. Microsoft Corporation, "Microsoft Windows: Multimedia Programmer's Reference", Microsoft Press, 1991.

26. S. M. Miller, S. K. Singhal, R. A. Smith, and B. Q. Nguyen, "OS/2 Multimedia: MMPM/2 Programming Support", TR 29.1560, IBM Programming Systems, Cary, NC, USA, December 1992.

27. Network Computing Devices, "NCDaudio, V2.0 Overview and Programming Guide", Part Number 9300237, April 1993.

28. J. F. Patterson, R. D. Hill, A. L. Rohall, and W. S. Meeks, "Rendezvous; An Architecture for Synchronous Multi-user Applications", Proceedings of the Conference on Computer Supported Cooperative Work '90, pp. 317-328, Los Angeles, California, USA, Oktober 1990.

29. R. W. Root, "Design of a Multi-Media System for Social Browsing", Proceedings of the Conference on Computer Supported Cooperative Work '88, pp. 25-38, Portland, Oregon, USA, September 1988.

30. K. Rothermel, I. Barth, and T. Helbig, "CINEMA - An Architecture for Configurable Distributed Multimedia Applications", in *Architecture and Protocols for High-Speed Networks*, ed. O. Spaniol, A. Danthine, and W. Effelsberg, pp. 253-271, Kluwer Academic Publishers, 1994.

31. R. W. Scheffler and J. Gettys, "The X Window System", ACM Transactions on Graphics, vol. 5, no. 2, pp. 79-109, April 1986.

32. H. Schulzrinne, S. Casner, R. Frederick, and V. Jacobson, "Internet Draft: RTP: A Transport Protocol for Real-Time Applications", Work in Progress, Internet Engineering Task Force, March 1995.

33. R. Steinmetz and T. Meyer, "Modelling Distributed Multimedia Applications", International Workshop on Advanced Communication and Applications for High-Speed Networks, München, 16-19 March 1992.

34. R. Steinmetz and K. Nahrstedt, *Multimedia: Computing, Communications, and Applications*, Prentice Hall, New York, July 1995.

35. N. Williams, G. S. Blair, G. Coulson, and N. Davies, "A Support Platform for Distributed Multimedia Applications", Intelligent Tutoring Media, vol. 3, no. 4, pp. 117-126, November 1992.

Hypermedia Systems as Internet Tools

Hermann Maurer

Institute for Information Processing and
Computer Supported New Media,
Graz University of Technology, Graz/Austria
email: hmaurer@iicm.tu-graz.ac.at

Dedicated to the visionary of hypertext, T.H. Nelson.

Abstract. In this paper we start from the fact that Internet is the largest information and communication system the world has ever had ... but also the most chaotic one. We explain that "a posteriori" tools are too weak to solve the problem; we claim however that second generation hypermedia system that can be considered "a priori" techniques can go a long way to help. We then discuss one such archetypical system Hyper-G, developed at our institute, in some detail. Hyper-G has been discussed from different points of view before e.g. in [Andrews et al 1995 a,b] and readers familiar with the important features of Hyper-G may initially want to ship this part (Chapter 2). We then discuss a number of pragmatical, ethical and legal issues and propose novel approaches that are a mixture of technical and organisational measures.

In a nutshell we argue that emerging "information hubs" are crucial for the usefulness of Internet; that Internet needs techniques that allow mild legislative actions to control some undesirable features of Internet; and that some of the copyright nightmares connected with trying to market electronic material can at least be partially solved using second generation hypermedia systems and suitable charging mechanisms.

1   Introduction

The steady growth of the Internet [Fenn et al 1994] has made resource discovery and structuring tools increasingly important. Historically first was the introduction of various dictionary servers, Archie [Deutsch 1992] being probably the first and most prominent. As an alternative to having servers that need constant updating, WAIS [Kahle et al 1992] introduced a powerful search engine permitting full-text searches of large data-bases and returning a ranked list, the ranking based on a heuristic approach. Although directory servers like Archie (to locate a database) and search engines like WAIS (to locate a desired item in that database) alleviated the problem of finding information in the Internet somewhat, it soon became apparent that other techniques would also be necessary.

The most important such technique is to emphasise the a-priori organisation of information, rather than try to search for information in a universe of completely different databases. Two efforts in this direction have proved particularly successful: *Gopher*, originally developed at the University of Minnesota [Alberti et al 1992] and [McCahill and Anklesaria, 1995a] and the *World-Wide Web* (WWW or W3, originally developed at CERN in Geneva [Berners-Lee et al. 1992] and [Berners-Lee et al. 1994].

In both cases information is stored in a simple structured fashion on servers, and can be accessed via clients, with clients available for most major hardware platforms.

Information in Gopher was originally structured in a hierarchical fashion using menus, an access technique which, though simple to use, has many well-known weaknesses. Information in W3 is structured in documents; documents are linked together according to the hypertext-paradigm (see [Conklin 1987], [Tomek et al. 1991] and [Buford-Koegel 1994] and [Nielsen 1995] for a general and thorough discussion of hypertext and hypermedia). *Anchors* within documents are associated with *links* leading to other documents. Although many stand-alone systems using the hypertext-metaphor have emerged since the introduction of HyperCard on the Mac in 1987, W3 can claim to be the first wide-spread hypertext system whose component servers are accessible via the Internet.

W3 servers are easy to install and clients are available on all major platforms. All software is free and sources are available. The node-link technique for navigating and finding information is quite appealing at least for small to medium amounts of data, and the mix of media makes the use of W3 aesthetically pleasing. All this has contributed to the proliferation of W3, – the success of W3, the number of of its proponents and freaks, and its publicity even in non-scientific publications like TIME magazine may create the impression that W3 is the solution for most information needs and will remain the dominating system for the foreseeable future.

The reality is different, however. Whilst W3 is undoubtedly a big step forward compared to pre-W3 times, experience shows that much functionality required for sizable applications is missing from W3. In this sense, W3 should be considered a first generation networked hypermedia system. More advanced "second generation" hypermedia systems are required to cope with the problems currently being encountered on the Web. To give one example, while pure node-link navigation is satisfactory in small systems it tends to lead to confusion and disorientation, if not chaos, when applied to large amounts of data. For substantial applications, some additional structuring and searching facilities are clearly required [Conklin 1987], [Maurer et al. 1994b]. Similarly, the necessity to keep links separate from rather than embedded in, documents as is the case in W3 has already been demonstrated in the pioneering work on Intermedia at Brown University [Haan et al. 1992].

Thus, although W3 has been successful to the extent that nowadays all modern hypermedia systems are called "systems serving the Web" the time to go from W3 as first generation hypermedia system a step forward to second generation systems has come. W3 developers are doing so by adding functionality and introducing "intelligent agents" and executable code (Hot Java); the Gopher team has done so by incorporating links, multimedia, and 3D into Gopher [Mc-Cahill 1995b]; and a team at Graz University of Technology has spent some 100 person years to develop what might well be the first widely available hypermedia system of a second generation, Hyper-G.

Before describing some aspects of the functionality of Hyper-G in the following section in comparison with W3, two important points must be made. First, the comparison is not to belittle W3 or to glorify Hyper-G, but to clarify why certain facilities are needed. Second, despite the fact that we do not mention Gopher much in what follows, Gopher is alive and doing well. Indeed, some of the original followers of Gopher who got sucked in by W3's success, are returning ruefully to Gopher that now offers structure and links, thus resembling Hyper-G in a number of important ways. With the increased cooperation between the Gopher team in Minnesota, the W3 teams of CERN, INRIA and NCSA, and the Hyper-G team in Graz, users are going to have a good choice of compatible systems.

2   WWW and Hyper-G

In this section we explain some of the properties of first generation hypermedia systems, using W3 as the most prominent example. We contrast them with those of Hyper-G [Andrews et al. 1995a,b,] and [Kappe et al. 1993], the first second generation system.

Information in a hypermedia system is usually stored in "chunks". Chunks consist of individual documents which may themselves consist of various types of "media". Typically, a document may be a piece of text containing a picture. Each document may contain links leading to (parts of) other documents in the same or in different chunks. Typical hypertext navigation through the information space is based on these links: the user follows a sequence of links until all relevant information has hopefully been encountered.

In W3, a chunk consists of a single document. A typical document consists of textual information and may include pictures ("inline images") and the (source) anchors of links. Anchors can be attached to textual information and inline images, but not to parts of images, although this is possible using scripting and so-called "forms" that can be used to prepare "clickable maps". Links may lead to audio or video clips which can be activated, but cannot emanate from such documents. The textual component of a document is stored in so-called HTML format, a derivative of SGML.

In Hyper-G the setting is more general. Chunks, called "clusters" in Hyper-G terminology, consist of a number of documents. A typical cluster might, for example, consist of five documents: a piece of text (potentially with inline images), a second piece of text (for example in another language, or a different version of the same text, or an entirely different text), a third piece of text (the same text in a third language perhaps), an image and a film clip. Anchors can be attached to textual information, to parts of images (without scripting), and even to regions in a film clip or objects within a 3D model. Links are not part of the document but are stored in a separate database. They are both typed and bidirectional: they can be followed forward (as in W3) but also *backwards* so that references *to* a particular document become directly accessible. The textual component of a document is usually stored in HTF format, also a derivative of SGML, and HTML 3.0, the newest verson of the W3 data protocol will be supported by Hyper-G by September 95.

Multiple pieces of text within a cluster allow Hyper-G to handle multiple languages in a natural way. It also elegantly handles the case where a document comes in two versions, a more technical (or advanced) one and one more suitable for the novice reader. As in W3, pictures can be treated as inline images, as separate documents, or both (a low resolution inline image pointing to a high quality external image).

Hyper-G provides full support for PostScript documents, including hyperlinking facilities and high-quality PostScript viewers. Almost all wordprocessing packages are capable of producing PostScript files as output and can thus be used to prepare data for Hyper-G. Also, PostScript files allow the incorporation of pictures and formulae; they offer the user the possibility to view documents exactly as if they were printed (given high enough resolution screens), giving Hyper-G the necessary professionalism for high quality electronic publishing of journals, books, and manuals.

For one of the major applications of Hyper-G, the *Journal of Universal Computer Science* [Maurer et al. 1994], semi-automatic text extraction and link generation tools allow articles submitted in PostScript form to be presented side-by-side with fully searchable, interlinked hypertext. The use of standard compression techniques allows the PostScript files to be compacted to about the same size as equivalent HTF and HTML files. In addition to the usual types of documents found in any modern hypermedia system, Hyper-G also supports 3D objects and scenes with embedded hyperlinks in VRML, the virtual reality modeling language, a de facto 3D-standard supported by SGI. The native X-Windows client for Hyper-G (Harmony) provides four different ways to navigate within such 3D models. Finally, Hyper-G allows the use of documents of a "generic" type, permitting future extensions and the encapsulation of documents otherwise incompatible with Hyper-G.

Let us turn to the discussion of the philosophy of links in W3 versus Hyper-G. The fact that links are bidirectional and not embedded in the document, has a number of very important consequences. Firstly, links relating to a document can be modified without necessarily having access rights to the document itself. Thus, private links and a certain amount of customisation are possible. (We will come back to this very important issue later.) Secondly, when viewing a document it is possible to find all documents referring to the current one. This is not only a desirable feature as such, but is of crucial importance for being able to maintain the database. When a document is deleted or modified, all documents referring to it may have to be modified to avoid the "dangling link syndrome". Hyper-G offers the possibility of automatically notifying the owner of a document that some of the documents that are being referred to have been changed or deleted, an important step to "automatic link maintenance". Thirdly, the bidirectionality of the links allows the graphic display of a *local map* showing the current document and all documents pointing to it and being pointed at, an arbitrary number of levels deep. Finally, the fact that links can have types can be used to show to the user that a link just leads to a footnote, or to a picture, or to a film clip, or is a counter argument or supporting argument of some claim at issue: typed links enhance the perception of how things are related and can be used as tool for discussions and collaborative work. They can be also used for version control.

Navigation in W3 is performed solely using the hypertext paradigm of anchors and links. It has become a well-accepted fact that structuring large amounts of data using only hyperlinks such that users don't get "lost in hyperspace," is difficult to say the least. W3 databases are large, flat networks of chunks of data and resemble more an impenetrable maze than well-structured information. Indeed every W3 database acknowledges this fact tacitly, by preparing pages that look like menus in a hierarchically structured database. Items are listed in an orderly fashion, each with an anchor leading to a subchapter (subdirectory). If links in W3 had types, such links could be distinguished from others. But as it is, all links look the same: whether they are "continue" links, "hierarchical" links, "referential" links, "footnote links", or whatever else.

In Hyper-G not only can have links a type, links are by no means the only way to access information. Clusters of documents can be grouped into collections, and collections again into collections in a pseudo-hierarchical fashion. We use the term "pseudo-hierarchical" since, technically speaking, the collection structure is not a tree, but a directed acyclic graph. A collection can have more than one parent: an impressionist picture X may belong to the collection "Impressionist Art", as well as to the collection "Pictures by Manet", as well as to the collection "Museum of Modern Art".

The collection hierarchy is a powerful way of introducing structure into the database. Indeed many links can be avoided this way [Maurer et al. 1994b], making the system much more transparent for the user and allowing a more modular approach to systems creation and maintenance. Collections, clusters and documents have titles and attributes. These may be used in Boolean queries to find documents of current interest.

Finally, Hyper-G provides sophisticated full-text search facilities. Most importantly, the scope of any of such searches can be defined to be the union of arbitrary collections, even if the collections reside on different servers (we will return to this important aspect of Hyper-G as a distributed database below).

Note that some W3 applications also permit full-text search. However, no full-text search engine is built into W3: the functionality is bolted "on top". However, adding functionality on top of W3 leads to the "Balkanisation", or the fragmentation of W3, since different sites implement missing functionality in different ways. Thus, to stick to the example of the full-text search engine, the fuzzy search employed by organisation X may have a different syntax and yield entirely different results from the fuzzy search employed by organisation Y, much to the bewilderment of users.

Actually, the situation concerning searches in W3 is even more serious. Since documents in W3 do not have attributes, no search is possible on such attributes; even if such a search or a full-text search is artificially implemented, it is not possible to allow users to define the scope of the search due to the lack of structure in the W3 database. Full-text searches in W3 always work in a fixed, designated part of the W3 database residing on one particular server. As was mentioned before, over 12,000 W3 servers are currently installed, and are accessible over Internet. There is, however, little or no coherence between these servers: users wanting to search for an item on a number of W3 servers have to initiate a new search for each server. This problem is compounded by W3's limited support for access-rights.

In contrast, Hyper-G is a distributed database: servers (independent of geographical location) can be grouped into collections, with the "hyperroot" at the very top. Users can focus the scope of searches to arbitrary sets of collections on arbitrary servers. Hyper-G provides various types of access rights and the definition of arbitrarily overlapping user groups, hence different groups can work within the same server without fear of interfering with someone else's data. To be more concrete, suppose 10 departments within a university intend to operate a W3 database. If they operate one server together and if all want to input their own data, the data of department X is not (easily) protected from any kind of access or change by department Y! Hence the tendency would be to operate 10 different servers. (Indeed, there are many more W3 servers than there are sites, clearly demonstrating this phenomenon.) However, if the 10 departments operate 10 different servers and a user from outside wants to look up a person without knowing the department, the user is forced to query all of the servers, one after the other.

Hyper-G, being a distributed database with well-defined access rights of fine granularity, offers a much more satisfactory solution. The 10 departments operate a single server, different users have different access rights. Not only can department X not influence the information of department Y, certain parts of the database may have even their read access restricted to certain groups or even to single individuals (private collections). Continuing the example, suppose an outside user looks for a certain person. Accessing the Hyper-G servers operated by the 10 departments with a full-text search will find the information, assuming it is present. However, suppose the departments insist on each operating their own Hyper-G server: by simply defining a collection "Servers of this University", a single Hyper-G search will still examine all ten databases (assuming they are all in a LAN or on the Internet). Even now, the servers offer possibilities not available without proper access control: members of the departments may keep some information just for themselves, or for a group they collaborate with, etcetera.

Hyper-G may be accessed anonymously by anyone. However, users having an account on a particular Hyper-G server may *identify* themselves with name and password to gain access to their account and any additional access rights associated with it. Identified users have a "home collection" on the server where personal documents can be kept (similar to a home directory on a Unix machine) and a personal view of the information space maintained (pointers to the information most important for them). Since home collections reside on the server rather than being maintained locally (like hotlists in W3), they are not dependent on using a particular client on a particular machine.

If one has access to a local Hyper-G server, all accesses to other Hyper-G servers, but also W3 and Gopher servers are routed through the local Hyper-G server. Documents retrieved once are automatically cached (for all users of that server), so they will no longer be retrieved from the remote database next time around. A scalable flooding algorithm ensures that cached documents are automatically updated [Kappe 1995]. Although recent W3 servers also support caching, the consistency of cached documents cannot be guaranteed.

The acceptance of a hypermedia system is certainly not only dependent on deep technical features, but above all on the information content and the ease of use. Due to the fact that large hypermedia systems tend to lead to disorientation, second generation hypermedia systems have to try very hard, both at the server and at the client end, to help users with navigational tools. Some navigational tools, like the structuring and search facilities have already been described; others, such as maps, history lists, specific and personal collections can also be of great help and are available in Hyper-G; a particular speciality of the Harmony client is a 3D browser whose "information landscape" depicts collections and documents (according to their size) as blocks of varying size spread out across a three-dimensional landscape, over which the user is able to fly.

First generation hypermedia systems like W3 have traditionally been seen mainly as (simple) information systems. Most applications currently visible support this view: very often W3 servers offer some pleasantly designed general information on the server-institution, but only rarely does the information go much deeper. If it does, usually a "hybrid" system is used, W3 with some add-ons using the scripting interface of W3.

It is our belief that hypermedia systems acting as simple information systems, where one or more people put information to be read by other users, do not offer much potential: they will disappear into obscurity sooner rather than later. To ensure the success of a hypermedia system, it must allow users also to act as authors, allow them to change the database, create new entries for themselves or other users, create a personal view of the database as they need it, and, above all, allow the system to be used also for communication and cooperation.

First generation hypermedia systems almost entirely lack support for such features. Emerging second generation hypermedia systems are bound to incorporate more and more features of the kind mentioned; Hyper-G provides a start. First generation hypermedia systems like W3 have traditionally been seen mainly as (simple) information systems. Most applications currently visible support this view: very often W3 servers offer some pleasantly designed general information on the server-institution, but only rarely does the information go much deeper. If it does, usually a "hybrid" system is used, W3 with some add-ons using the scripting interface of W3.

The native Hyper-G clients Amadeus and Harmony are designed to allow the easy import of data into the server. They are also designed to allow point-and-click link generation: select the source anchor location with a mouse-click, select the destination anchor with a mouse-click and confirm that a link should be created.

Hyper-G supports annotations (with user-definable access rights): in contrast to some W3 clients which also allow annotations which are then kept locally, Hyper-G annotations become part of the database, i.e. are also available when working with other clients, or from another user account or machine. Annotations can themselves be annotated; the network of annotations can be graphically displayed using the local map function of Harmony. Thus, the annotation mechanism can be used as the basis of (asynchronous) computer-conferencing, and has been successfully employed in this fashion. The client-server protocol in W3 is "static" in the sense that the server can only react to requests by the client, but cannot become active itself. In Hyper-G the client-server protocol is "active" in the sense that the server can contact the client: this can be used for example to send update notification to a client, and provides the first (rudimentary) possibilities for client-client communication for synchronous communication, conferencing and cooperation.

We believe that many of the features discussed in the area of computer supported cooperative work [Dewan 1993] will eventually be incorporated into second generation hypermedia systems. This approach is also planned for Hyper-G. Some of the most widely used functions of the Internet are file transfer (FTP) and electronic mail. Hence, second generation hypermedia systems have to support both FTP and particularly email. Without leaving their hypermedia environment, users must be able to edit, send, and receive email. Email should automatically be presorted by criteria such as subject, author, date, etcetera. Related pieces of email can be linked together, the local map feature presenting a good graphical overview of the flow of the email discussion pertaining to a certain subject. The hypermedia system should also have the possibility to send mail with delays or on certain dates to act as reminder and as an active personal scheduler. A number of relevant ideas are collected in [Kappe et al. 1993b] and are currently under implementation for Hyper-G.

As will have become clear from the above discussion, first generation hypermedia systems such as W3 do not have enough functionality to serve as unified basis for substantial multi-user information systems with a strong communicational component.

Hyper-G is a first attempt to offer much more basic functionality, yet to continue the path started by W3 and remain fully interoperable with W3 [Andrews et al. 1995b]. Any W3 and Gopher client can be used to access any Hyper-G server; a Hyper-G client may, through a Hyper-G server, access any W3 or Gopher server, indeed providing "free" caching as a by-product. The compatibility of Hyper-G with W3 and Gopher actually goes much further: tools to import complete W3 and Gopher databases into Hyper-G without manual intervention are in preparation. Thus, users of W3 and Gopher can migrate up to an environment allowing all kinds of searches, access control, etcetera, without being forced to abandon their current database or their favourite client.

3   Pragmatical, Ethical and Legal Issues

Each of the three major hypermedia systems: Gopher, W3 and Hyper-G discussed above, allow to access a vast body of information. It has been pointed out that this information is sufficiently scattered and unstructured that finding what one is interested in is, to say the least, difficult. Second generation hypermedia systems like Hyper-G and other modern tools ease the problem a bit, but much further work is required. This further work concerns both technical and organisational aspects.

One of the issues is the need for powerful *information hubs*. To explain this point, it is useful to consider a historical analogy. After the invention of the printing press by Gensfleisch zu Laden (often called Gutenberg) in Mainz/Germany in 1450, neither books nor journals were the major products produced by the new machines, but rather a chaotic plethora of leaflets, posters and the like. It took more than a generation to establish a number of substantial organisations that would act as information broker, by bundling information for a certain clientele into journals, newspapers, books, etcetera. Note that those organisations (publishing houses and news agencies) started to employ a significant body of personnel (editors, lectures, authors, journalists, investigating agents, ...) to collect and pre-select material. Depending on taste, readers would choose one source over another, much as it is still true today: some prefer to read Time Magazine, others US Today! In an age where all types of information (text, pictures, audio and video clips) can be manipulated at will (see e.g. [Maurer 1995]) and thus cannot be trusted as such, it becomes critical to know the source of the material and to know how far this source can be relied on.

It is our claim that information in Internet-based hypermedia systems today resembles the chaotic plethora of leaflets and posters of the 1480's: new kinds of publishing organisations providing "information hubs" and pre-selecting and validating materials are needed, and are indeed starting to be visible. Services like America Online (or European and local counterparts such as Styria Online that are in their formative stages) are typical examples.

Such information hubs have a dual role. First, they make information much easier to find, by collecting and bundling it: by topic and according to the taste of readers. Second, they make information much more useful by assuring a certain uniformity, quality and timeliness.

Some visionaries see hypermedia systems on the Internet as having the potential for a gigantic revolution by making everyone a publisher. Noting that other mediatools such as photocopying machines have not turned all persons into authors or publishers either, we believe that such visions are exaggerated. And if those visions were to become true, how would we be able to find information and be able to determine its reliability? We think that organisations operating "information hubs" will have to play a major role. This does not mean that information on the net will be as static as in print: users may well be able to choose their profile, organize their own archives or participate in discussions, etcetera, thus exploiting the interactivity and the communication component of the Internet.

Due to our belief that "information hubs", i.e. electronic publishing houses, will be necessary, we can follow Odlyzko's arguments [Odlyzko 1994] about the demise of printed technical journals, but not the belief that this also leads to the demise of publishers. We rather believe in approaches like J.UCS (see *http://hyperg.iicm.tu-graz.ac.at/CJUCS_root*) and [Maurer et al. 1994a] for references.

The second major issue is not how easy it is to find information, but whether everyone should indeed be able to access everything. In all countries, the freedom of what one reads and what one publishes is limited to some degree by local or national laws. There are laws to protect the young from material considered harmful to them (like pictures violating certain sexual tabus) and mosts countries have laws that prohibit the distribution (sometimes even ownership) of certain types of information. In the author's home country Austria, the list of "offensive" items includes some types of pornography and depicting or describing acts of violence against women (violence against men is OK, however!). It also includes material that is considered blasphemous, is trying to foster "civil disobedience" or racism, supports anyone of a long list of ideas spread in the Third Reich, etcetera, etcetera. Austria is no exception: every country has such laws, and they differ widely from country to country. World-wide hypermedia systems on the Internet "undermine" those laws by making material available in a country whose laws make such material illegal, yet the originators can often not even be prosecuted beyond national boundaries.

We strongly believe that Internet must not be allowed to undermine existing laws. This is not because the laws at issue are necessarily good (indeed many might as well be abolished or ignored), but it is because not heeding the laws can damage Internet badly, even mortally.

In a number of places (we are explicitly aware of this happening in New Zealand, Australia, and the USA) concerned citizens have asked for legislative action to make sure that Internet does not lead to access of "illegal" information. Legislators - not aware of better alternatives - have drafted laws whose passage would virtually kill Internet. Note that the U.S. Public Policy Committee of ACM (USACM) chaired by Barbara Simons has fought with much effort against the Communications Decency Act proposed by Senators Exon and Gorton in February 1995, and in the end it has been able to avert the worst (making server operators not responsible for material forwarded through their servers), at the same time still prohibiting "obscene, lewd, lascivious, filthy, or indecent" communications even between consenting adults (see *http://info.acm.org*). Note that while this one threat to Internet has just been avoided, the Anti-Indecency Internet Censorship Bill introduced by Senators Dole and Grassley is going to be the next battle to be fought to preserve some freedom on the Internet.

It is perhaps appropriate to mention one more typical example. There is a strong push in Austria to give all schools (and schoolchildren via workstations in the schools) access to Internet. We believe that such a measure would backfire: as soon as teachers and parents realise what suddenly becomes available to their children, the demand for laws to curtail Internet will be as strong as in the USA and elsewhere. We thus believe that, before Internet is made available to the general public, techniques have to be developed that allow a *disciplined use* of the Internet, if legislators so desire.

Without the knowledge of such techniques, it is likely that laws will be passed that will virtually eliminate world-wide hypermedia systems that we are just starting to witness, and other uses of the Internet. With the knowledge and the dissemination of suitables techniques and self-imposed discipline, laws curtailing the Internet may never become an issue, and if they do, versions of laws will hopefully be passed that will still be acceptable to most of us. Putting it differently: if we continue to preach that computer networks are the final solution to complete freedom of censorship, we will even eliminate the large amount of freedom we could enjoy if we are "reasonable".

The situation described above is one of the reasons why the Web Society (see *http://info.websoc.at*) has been founded recently (to obtain more information see the URL mentioned or send an email to websoc@websoc.at). The Web Society will support the "efficient and disciplined use of the Web". "Efficient" means that modern tools and hypermedia systems, and organisational techniques for better information location (and "information hubs" are one example) will be endorsed and encouraged. "Disciplined" means that the Web Society believes that the Internet cannot be free of some rules if it is to survive.

The Web Society is against central censorship, yet believes that techniques that allow to control what specific user groups can obtain, have to be developed. There are three main reasons for this:

- if it is not done, Internet is not suitable for general public use, as outlined earlier, and will eventually be curtailed by strict laws;
- if it is not done, companies (at least where charges are volume based) will not be keen to have employees use Internet, much the same way as companies are not keen on providing all employees with the possibility to conduct unlimited long distance telephone conversations;
- if it is done, the "control" also allows to weed out all those tens of thousands of Web sites that contain only minute amounts of information.

Observe that SurfWatch ("Protect your kids on the Net!" is their main slogan) (*http://www.surfwatch.com*) is one commercial enterprise that allows to impose some kind of control by incorporating into a Web viewer a list of blacklisted sites that (if users take a subscription!) is updated automatically and regularly.

We do not believe that incorporating such a tool in a viewer is the best solution: it is easy to circumvent it by installing another viewer; yet, it is a first attempt.

Another, probably more promising approach is currently being tested at one of the top highschools in Graz, Austria. There, a proxy-server is installed (also convenient for caching) in whose router a list of permissible addresses of computers is installed. Teachers can change this list any time they want; only computers on the list can be accessed, and the list may vary from user group to user group. Thus, younger students may be allowed to access only a shorter list than older ones; some addresses may be temporarily added to the list for one of the user groups for a specific project, etcetera. This approach works with a "white-list" rather than a "black- list" (but a black list could also be used); the main difference is that the software is part of the router and hence no viewer or other technique (like FTP) can bypass this mechanism. Thus, this is a fairly tamper-proof way to limit access.

Of course, illicit material is not restricted to hypermedia systems or FTP files; it is also contained in newsgroups. Thus, controlling newsgroups will also have to be addressed at some stage. Among other proposals it has been suggested to replace newsgroups by structured discussions in hypermedia systems: this may kill two birds with one stone. First, mechanisms to control hypermedia systems would automatically apply to this new kind of newsgroup. Second, discussions (due to their hyperlinked structure) may well be more valuable than the linear lists of contributions in today's set-up.

"Disciplined use" of the Internet also involves one further thorny issue: to what extent should anonymous contributions be allowed on the Internet? Again, the Web Society takes a liberal position, yet within reason, to which we also subscribe. To be specific, there are servers that allow to post messages anonymously in a way that the originator cannot be traced: we do not believe that such complete anonymity should be permitted, let alone supported: in addition to material violating laws in the sense mentioned earlier, now the particularly dangerous threat of defamation and libel with no possibility for corrective actions arises. On the other hand, some topics are better discussed anonymously. In [Flinn et al. 95] it is argued that in all such cases "level 3 anonymity" is most suitable: users register with a pen-name, the association of pen-name and real identity encrypted in such a fashion that users are assured complete anonymity, unless a court order is issued (due to the violation of some laws) to reveal the real identity. To further reassure individuals, the keys for decryption can be held in multiple escrow, so that no single party can determine the real identity of a pen-name.

In connection with multi- and hypermedia systems, questions of intellectual property, of electronic copyright, etcetera, keep emerging. In [Lennon et al. 1994] it has been argued that exclusive electronic rights for works of arts will be more precious in the future than the originals, and hence sale and export of such rights should be strictly controlled. However, the very control of electronic copyrights for non-textual material (like pictures) is preventing some potentially very important multimedia undertakings: note that none of the famous encyclopedias like the Encyclopedia Britannica, Meyer or Brockhaus, etcetera, come in electronic form with pictures: the publishing companies own the right to print the pictures, but not to use them electronically. Yet re-negotiation of rights for some 20.000 pictures for electronic publishing is estimated to cost some 3 million (!) US dollars, making the multimedia production a fairly expensive enterprise.

In few areas the interests of users and of the owners of information clash as much as they do in the hypermedia arena. An example will illustrate the situation. Surely what a university instructor wants is that hypermedia material from hundreds of sources (that has been purchased under some licensing agreement) is available on a university server and can now be *customised* by the instructor as desired.

"Customizing" usually means taking pieces from various sources, combining them together with maybe material created by the user and then offer it to students as set of "electronic lecture notes". This kind of situation is a copyright nightmare, it seems. Yet it really is not, if the right approach is taken akin to what Ted Nelson proposed many years ago. (For a recent edition of some of Ted Nelson's ideas see [Nelson 1987]).

It is curious that Hyper-G, together with a special licensing mechanism, is close to Ted Nelson's vision and does indeed offer a reasonable solution. At a point in time where Ted Nelson is attacked in [Wolf 1995], it is fitting to dedicate this paper to Ted Nelson, to a man with imagination and vision, a man who has been inspired many of us ... hence the note at the beginning of this paper.

However, let us now return to a rough description of the scheme that one can implement using Hyper-G that does indeed resolve parts of the copyright versus customisation nightmare.

When electronic material is sold over networks some charging mechanisms are necessary. Assuming that users identify themselves with some username/password combination, charging mechanisms typically are:

(1) by time,
(2) by volume,
(3) by number of accesses,
(4) by subscription.

Note that in cases (1) – (3) there is some potential danger to the user (if others manage to get access to the username/password – something fairly easy to do on the Internet), and that (4) is dangerous to the publisher: persons may allow friends to use their username/password, resulting in many more readers than paid subscribers. Thus, (1) – (3) requires sophisticated security mechanisms (see e.g. [Posch 1995]) to protect users, (4) requires additional mechanisms to protect publishers.

An alternative is to use pre-paid accounts that e.g. allow a fairly liberal, yet limited number of accesses. This is a mix of essentially (3) and (4) that offers a number of advantages: Even if the username/password is detected by others, it is only of limited use and can cause only limited damage (by illegally "exhausting" the pre-paid sum). Thus, the consumer is better protected in this mode, hence complicated security measures are not that essential. The publisher is also protected: users who pass on their username/password are welcome to do so. After all, whatever use they or friends make of the material offered has been pre-paid. This latter technique has e.g. been used with the electronic version of the ED-MEDIA'95 proceedings, see *http://hyperg.iicm.tu-graz.ac.at/Cedmedia*.

All of the above assumes that the information resides on only a few servers in the Internet and that users access these servers. We consider this assumption unrealistic for two reasons. First, world-wide access to Internet nodes is often painfully slow. Second, if large numbers of users access a server, it and Internet connections to it will be overloaded unless complex counter-measures are taken.

For this reason we have been propagating for some time that electronic material should reside in local servers, with Internet used to update the material, but users accessing the local (library) servers. This approach taken in J.UCS (see [Maurer et al. 1994a], [Calude et al. 1994]) improves performance for users and also allows publishers a new way of selling information: they sell for each server a license for "at most n simultaneous users", where n can be arbitrary. Typically, a university library could start with $n=1$ and increase n as necessary (i.e. if the material is popular enough that often more than a single user wants to access it at the same time). Note that "same time" is really a parameter that can be adjusted by publishing companies: it means "an electronic book accessed by a person is blocked for other persons for m minutes" (values of m that we have actually experimented with are between 3 and 10 minutes).

Observe in passing that connection - less protocols such as *http* in W3 are not well-suited for this approach, since persons accessing a book block keep themselves from accessing it again shortly thereafter. This is one of the many reasons why a connection-oriented protocol is built into Hyper-G.

The above charging regime is easy to administer for publishers, and allows to install electronic material on a network for all users of the network at low cost (a single license), yet upgrading is easy. Note that the upgrades can even be system supported. Suppose the license is set to "20 users at a time" and the system monitors that usage is increasing steadily and peaks of 19 simultaneous users become more and more frequent; then the system can alert the librarian to buy additional licenses. Indeed variants are possible: no limit to the number of simultaneous users is fixed, but the charges for some electronic material are made to depend on the "average number of simultaneous users".

We now come to the main point. Using second generation systems like Hyper-G and a version of above charging regime, it is possible to customize material from various sources without violating copyright restrictions. This is so, because customisation in systems such as Hyper-G is done by linking, not by copying, very much in the spirit of Nelson's Xanadu proposal.

To be concrete, suppose on a server a number of books from various publishers have been installed, each booked for some number of simultaneous users. An instructor wanting to customise information by taking material from various books and combining it (potentially integrating own material) can do so in Hyper-G by not copying the material but by adding links that are only visible to a specific group, e.g. the group of intended students. This is depicted in a small example in Figure 1.

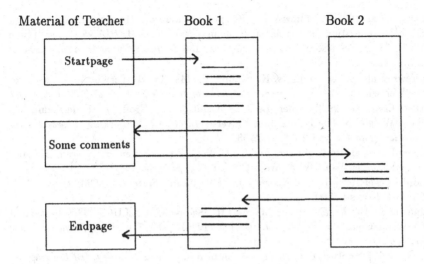

Figure 1

The arrows in Figure 1 present links created by the teacher and are only visible to the intended usergroup.

Note that the teacher has thus combined the information on the "Startpage" with a section of Book 1, followed by "Some comments", a section in Book 2, a further section in Book 1 and some material on the "Endpage". Even if Book 1 and Book 2 are from different publishers, no copyright violation occurs. If many students use the material as customised, Book 1 will be accessed more often then Book 2, hence the number of licenses for Book 1 may have to be increased, as should be the case.

Thus, holding electronic material in LAN's and using systems such as Hyper-G, customisation is not only possible but can be done without any infringement on copyrights. In a way what the proposed set-up does is to implement Nelson's vision of "world-wide publishing using transclusion" [Nelson 1987] in a local environment.

4   Summary

In this paper we have discussed hypermedia systems as tools for using the Internet. We have tried to show that second generation hypermedia systems such as Hyper-G and simple organisational measures can eliminate many of the pitfalls and problems we currently often encounter when using the Internet.

References

[Alberti et al. 1992] Alberti,B., Anklesaria,F., Lindner,P., McCahill,M., Torrey,D., Internet Gopher Protocol: A Distributed Document Search and Retrieval Protocol; FTP from boombox.micro.umn.edu , directory pub/gopher/gopher_protocol.

[Andrews et al. 1995a] Andrews, K., Kappe, F., Maurer, H., Schmaranz, K., On Second Generation Hypermedia Systems; *Proc. ED-MEDIA'95*, Graz (June 1995), 75-80. See also *J.UCS* 0,0 (1994),127-136 at *http:///www.iicm.tu-graz.ac.at /Cjucs_root*.

[Andrews et al. 1995b] Andrews, K., Kappe, F., Maurer, H., Serving Information to the Web with Hyper-G; *Computer Networks and ISDN Systems* 27 (1995), 919-926.

[Berners-Lee et al. 1992] Berners-Lee, T., Cailliau, R., Groff, J., Pollermann, B., WorldWideWeb: The Information Universe; *Electronic Networking: Research, Applications and Policy* 1,2 (1992),52-58.

[Berners-Lee et al. 1994] Berners-Lee, T., Cailliau, R., Luotonen, A., Nielsen, H.F. and Secret, A., The World-Wide Web; *C.ACM* 37 (8) (1994), 76-82.

[Buford-Koegel 1994] Buford-Koegel, J., *Multimedia Systems*; ACM Press, SIG-GRAPH Series (1994).

[Calude et al. 1994] Calude, C., Maurer, H., Salomaa, A., J.UCS: The Journal of Universal Computer Science; *J.UCS* 0,0 (1994) 109-117 at *http://www.iicm. tu-graz.ac.at/Cjucs_root*.

[Conklin 1987] Conklin, E.J., Hypertext: an Introduction and Survey; *IEEE Computer* 20 (1987), 17-41.

[Dewan 1993] Dewan,P., A Survey of Applications of CSCW Including Some in Educational Settings; *Proc. ED-MEDIA'93*, Orlando (1993), 147-152.

[Deutsch 1992] Deutsch, P., Resource Discovery in an Internet Environment-the Archie Approach; *Electronic Networking: Research, Applications and Policy* 1,2 (1992), 45-51.

[Fenn et al. 1994] Fenn, B., Maurer, H., Harmony on an Expanding Net; *ACM Interactions* 1,3 (1994), 26-38.

[Flinn et al. 1995] Flinn, B., Maurer, H., Levels of Anonymity; *J.UCS* 1,1 (1995), 35-47.

[Haan et al. 1992] Haan, B.J., Kahn, P., Riley, V.A., Coombs, J.H., Meyrowitz, N.K., IRIS Hypermedia Services; *C.ACM* 35,1 (1992), 36-51.

[Kahle et al. 1992] Kahle, B., Morris, H., Davis, F., Tiene, K., Hart, C., Palmer, R., Wide Area Information Servers: An Executive Information System for Unstructured Files; *Electronic Networking: Research, Applications and Policy* 1,2 (1992), 59-68.

[Kappe et al. 1993] Kappe, F., Maurer, H., Scherbakov, N., Hyper-G – a Universal Hypermedia System; *Journal of Educational Multimedia and Hypermedia* 2,1 (1993), 39-66.

[Kappe and Maurer 1993] Kappe, F., Maurer, H., From Hypertext to Active Communication/Information Systems; *J.MCA* 17,4 (1994), 333-344.

[Kappe 1995] Kappe, F., A Scalable Architecture for Maintaining Referential Integrity in Distributed Information Systems; *J.UCS* 1,2 (1995), 84-104.

[Lennon et al. 1994] Lennon, J., Maurer, H., They Just Sold New Zealand; *NZ Science Monthly*, (March 1994), 6-7.

[Marchionini et al. 1995] Marchionini, G., Maurer, H., The Role of Digital Libraries in Teaching and Learning; *C.ACM* 38,4 (April 1995), 67-75.

[Maurer et al. 1994a] Maurer, H., Schmaranz, K., J.UCS – The Next Generation in Electronic Journal Publishing; *Proc. Electronic Publ. Conference*, London (November 1994), in: *Computer Networks for Research in Europe* 26, Supplement 2-3 (1994), 63-69.

[Maurer et al. 1994b] Maurer, H., Philpott A. and Sherbakov, N., Hypermedia Systems without Links. *J.MCA* 17,4 (1994), 321-332.

[Maurer 1995] Maurer, H., Wichtig ist nur die Quelle; in: 'Der Tod als Hilfe' oder 'Die andere Seite des Berges', *OVG Vienna* (1995), 190 - 193.

[McCahill and Anklesaria, 1995a] McCahill, M.P. and Anklesaria, F.X., *J.UCS* 1,4 (1995), 235-246.

[McCahill 1995b] McCahill, M.P., Design for a 3D Spatial User Interface for Internet-Gopher; *Proc. ED-MEDIA '95*, Graz/Austria (1995), 35-40.

[Nelson 1987] Nelson, T.H., *Literary machines*; Edition 87.1, 702 South Michigan, South Bend, IN 46618, USA (1987).

[Nielsen 1995] Nielsen,J., *Hypertext and Hypermedia*; Academic Press (1995).

[Odlyzko 94] Odlyzko, A., M., Tragic Loss or Good Riddance? The Impending Demise of Traditional Scholarly Journals; to appear in: *Electronic Publishing Confronts Academia: The Agenda for the Year 2000*; (Peek.,R.P., Newby,G.B., eds.) MIT Press (1995);see also *J.UCS* 0,0 (1994), 3-53 at *http://www.iicm.tu-graz.ac.at/Cjucs_root*.

[Wolf 1995] Wolf, G., The Curse of Xanadu; *Wired* (June 1995), 138-202.

Biographies Contributing Authors

This section contains short biographies of all authors who have contributed to this anniversary volume of the Lecture Notes in Computer Science.

Leonard M. Adleman is the Henry Salvatori Professor of Computer Science at the University of Southern California. Prior to joining USC, he was on the faculty of the Mathematic Department of MIT. His research interests include algorithmic number theory, complexity theory, cryptography, molecular computation and immunology.

Pankaj K. Agarwal is Associate Professor in the CS Department of Duke University. He received his Ph.D. in Computer Science from the Courant Institute of Math. Sciences, New York University, in 1989. His research interests include computational and combinatorial geometry, graph algorithms, graphics, and robotics. He is the author of *Intersection and Detection Algorithms for Planar Arrangements*, and a co-author of *Combinatorial Geometry* and of *Davenport-Schinzel Sequences and Their Geometric Applications*. He was awarded a National Young Investigator Award in 1992.

Ross Anderson is a Senior Research Associate at the University of Cambridge, where he received his M.A. (in Mathematics and Natural Sciences) and Ph.D. (in Computer Science). He is a chartered mathematician and a chartered engineer, and has worked in a number of fields from avionics to medical systems. For the last ten years, his interests have centered on cryptography and computer security. He is particularly interested in the engineering aspects of security mechanisms, such as their performance and reliability. He has served on the program committees of Crypto and Oakland, and was the programme chair of the 1993 Workshop on Fast Software Encryption, a conference series which he initiated. He is also the editor of 'Computer and Communications Security Reviews'.

Anuchit Anuchitanukul is a Ph.D. candidate in the CS Department at Stanford University. His research interests are program synthesis and formal verification.

Zhaojun Bai is an associate professor at the University of Kentucky in Lexington, KY. His major research interests include numerical linear algebra, parallel numerical computation and software development. He was involved in the design and implementation of numerical linear algebra software package LAPACK.

Thomas Beth (1949) has studied Mathematics, Physics, and Medicine. He received his diploma in Mathematics in 1973 from Universität Göttingen and was awarded a DAAD fellowship in mathematics at the Mathematics Department of Ohio State University. He received the Dr. rer. nat. from the Universität Erlangen in 1978, where he worked in the Department of Computer Science (Institut für Mathematische Maschinen und Datenverarbeitung) until he obtained the degree of Dr. Ing. habil. in the area of Informatics in 1984. He was subsequently appointed Professor of Computer Science at the University of London and Head of the Department of Computer Science and Statistics at the Royal Holloway College, from where he headed back to Germany for taking a chair in 'Informatik' at the Universität Karlsruhe, in Europe's largest Department of Computer Science. In 1988 he was also appointed Director of the newly-founded European Institute for System Security (E.I.S.S.). In the past decades since his appointment at Karlsruhe he has built up the Institut für Algorithmen und Kognitive

Systeme (IAKS) jointly with his colleagues Hans-Hellmut Nagel and Jacques Calmet. He has been visiting professor at King's College (London), Universität Innsbruck (Austria), and the University of Wollongong (Australia). Beth has published several books in different areas, amongst which are: *Design Theory* jointly with Jungnickel and Lenz, *Kryptographie* jointly with Hess und Wirl, and a monograph on methods of fast Fourier transforms, *Verfahren der schnellen Fourier Transformation*. These publications are accompanied by many volumes of lecture notes in computer algebra, coding theory and system security. More than 120 research papers in and around the essential areas of Computer Science, Mathematics and Electrical Engineering have been published. He has been editor of the Journal of Cryptology, AAECC, the Journal of Designs, Codes and Cryptography, Surveys of Mathematics for Industry, and the Journal of Computer Security. His current research interests include cryptography, applied algebra and computer algebra with its applications in signal processing, optical algorithms, microtechnology, and most recently quantum computing.

Gilles Brassard was born in Montréal, Canada, in 1955. He received a Masters degree from the Université de Montréal in 1975 and a Ph.D. from Cornell University in 1979, both in Computer Science. He returned to the Université de Montréal as faculty member in 1979. After one year as Visiting Associate Professor at the University of California, Berkeley, in 1984-85, he was promoted to the rank of Full Professor at the Université de Montréal in 1988. He spent his sabbaticals as Visiting Professor or Visiting Researcher at the CWI (Amsterdam, 1987), the late Philips Research Laboratory (Brussels, 1988), the École Polytechnique Fédérale (Lausanne, 1988), the École Normale Supérieure (Paris, 1994) and the University of Wollongong (Australia, 1995). He was Program Chair for Crypto '89 (Santa Barbara, 1989) and Program Committee Member for Crypto '88 (Santa Barbara, 1988) and for the IEEE Conference on Structures in Complexity Theory (Boston, 1992). He has been Editor-in-Chief for the Journal of Cryptology since 1991 and he is on the editorial board of Design, Codes and Cryptography. He is the author of three books that have been translated into 7 languages. He was awarded the E.W.R. Steacie Memorial Fellowship and the Prix Urgel-Archambault, both in 1992, and the Steacie Prize in 1994. He is interested in all aspects of cryptology, and particularly its information-theoretic foundations, zero-knowledge protocols and unconditionally-secure cryptography. His main interest is in quantum information theory, which lies at the confluent of computer science and quantum mechanics. In particular, he is among the pioneers of Quantum Cryptography and Quantum Teleportation, and he has contributed to the field of Quantum Computing.

Manfred Broy is full professor of Computing Science at the Technical University of München. His research interests are software and systems engineering, comprising both theoretical and practical aspects. This includes system models, the specification and refinement of system components, specification techniques, development methods, advanced implementation languages, object-orientation, and quality assurance by verification. He is leading a research group working on a number of industrial projects that try to apply mathematically-based techniques and to combine practical approaches to software engineering with mathematical rigour. Broy is the organizer of the Marktoberdorf Summer Schools on Foundations of Programming. He published a four-volume introductory course to Computing Science (in German). He is main editor of Acta Informatica and editor of Information and Software Technology, Distributed Computing, Formal Aspects in Computer Sciences, and the Journal of Universal Computer Science. Broy is a member of the European Academy of Science. In 1994 he received the Leibniz Award by the Deutsche Forschungsgemeinschaft.

Maurice Bruynooghe obtained a degree of Engineer in Computer Science at the K.U. Leuven and a Ph.D. from the same University in 1979. The subject of his thesis was logic programming. In 1983, he became a research associate of the Belgian National Fund for Scientific Research and started a Logic Programming group at the K.U. Leuven. Currently, he is research director of the same Fund and part-time professor at the K.U. Leuven. He worked on implementation techniques for Prolog, on intelligent backtracking techniques for Prolog and for solving combinatorial search problems, on program transformation techniques, on abstract interpretation of logic programs, on planning and temporal reasoning, and on inductive logic programming. He published in many conference proceedings and journals, including ACM ToPLaS, Artificial Intelligence, and Machine Learning. He participated in the Programme Committees of several conferences and workshops, including IJCAI95, and several Logic Programming Conferences and was Programme Chair of META90, PLILP92, PLILP93 and ILPS94. Since 1991, he is Editor-in-Chief of the Journal of Logic Programming.

Dick Bulterman is project leader of the Multimedia Kernel Systems group at the CWI in Amsterdam, where he is senior researcher and research group leader. He received his Sc.M. (1977) and Ph.D. (1981) in Computer Science from Brown University. From 1980-1988, he was an assistant professor of engineering at Brown, working in the Laboratory for Man/Machine Systems. Since joining CWI in 1988, he has held teaching appointments at the University of Amsterdam and the University of Utrecht, as well as visiting appointments at Brown University. He also held a visiting professorship at the University of Delft in 1985. His current research interests include multimedia authoring systems and studying the direct architectural implementation of multimedia specifications. Bulterman is on the editorial board of Multimedia Tools and Applications, as well as Springer/ACM's Multimedia Systems. He is a member of Sigma Xi, the IEEE Computer Society and the ACM.

Edmund M. Clarke received a B.A. degree in mathematics from the University of Virginia, Charlottesville, VA, in 1967, an M.A. degree in mathematics from Duke University, Durham NC, in 1968, and a Ph.D. degree in Computer Science from Cornell University, Ithaca NY, in 1976. After receiving his Ph.D., he taught in the Department of Computer Science at Duke University for two years. In 1978 he moved to Harvard University, Cambridge, MA, where he was an Assistant Professor of Computer Science in the Division of Applied Sciences. He left Harvard in 1982 to join the faculty in the Computer Science Department at Carnegie-Mellon University, Pittsburgh, PA. He was appointed Full Professor in 1989. In 1995 he became the first recipient of the FORE Systems Professorship, an endowed chair in the School of Computer Science. His interests include software and hardware verification and automatic theorem proving. Clarke has served on the editorial boards of Distributed Computing and Logic and Computation and is currently an editor-in-chief of Formal Methods in Systems Design. He is on the steering committees of two international conferences, Logic in Computer Science and Computer-Aided Verification. He is a member of the Association for Computing Machinery, IEEE Computer Society, Sigma Xi, and Phi Beta Kappa.

Michael Codish received his Ph.D. in Computer Science from the Weizmann Institute of Science in 1991. He is a permanent member of the Department of Mathematics and Computer Science at Ben-Gurion University since 1993. In the past seven years he has been involved in an extensive study of abstract interpretation and its application to logic languages. This study spans both theoretical and practical work, including applications to various types of logic languages (sequential, constraint, concurrent). In the course of this study he has published related papers in ACM ToPLaS, in Information and Computation, in the Journals of Logic and Computation, Logic Programming, and New Generation Computing, and Theoretical Computer Science.

David Day is a Visiting Professor of Mathematics at the University of Kentucky (1994-1995) in Lexington, KY. He specializes in algorithms for matrix computations.

James Demmel received his B.S. degree in Mathematics from the California Institute of Technology in 1975, and his Ph.D. in Computer Science from the University of California at Berkeley in 1983. He was at the Courant Institute of Mathematical Sciences, New York University, before returning to Berkeley in 1990 where he now works in the Computer Science Division and the Mathematics Department. He works in numerical analysis, especially numerical linear algebra, and parallel computing. He is on the design teams for LAPACK and ScaLAPACK. He has won numerous prizes, most recently the J.H. Wilkinson Prize in Numerical Analysis and Scientific Computing, in 1993.

Jack Dongarra holds a joint appointment as Distinguished Professor of Computer Science in the Computer Science Department at the University of Tennessee (UT) and as Distinguished Scientist in the Mathematical Sciences Section at Oak Ridge National Laboratory (ORNL) under the UT/ORNL Science Alliance Program. He specializes in numerical algorithms in linear algebra, parallel computing, use of advanced-computer architectures, programming methodology, and tools for parallel computers. Other current research involves the development, testing and documentation of high quality mathematical software. He was involved in the design and implementation of the software packages EISPACK, LINPACK, the BLAS, LAPACK, ScaLAPACK, Netlib/XNetlib, PVM/HeNCE, MPI and the National High-Performance Software Exchange; and is currently involved in the design of algorithms and techniques for high performance computer architectures. He has published numerous articles, papers, reports and technical memoranda, and has given many presentations.

Jan-Olof Eklundh worked in computer vision at the National Defence Research Institute in Stockholm and the Computer Vision Laboratory of the University of Maryland, after obtaining his degree in mathematics at Stockholm University in 1969. In 1982 he became an Associate Professor at the Royal Institute of Technology (KTH) in Stockholm, where he founded the Computer Vision and Active Perception Laboratory. In 1986 he became a Professor in Computer Science, in 1993 Vice Dean, and in 1995 Dean of the School of Electrical Engineering and Information Technology, KTH. Eklundh is a member of the Royal Swedish Academy of Engineering Science and of the Swedish Research Council for Engineering Science. He is a founding member of the European Vision Society, 1992, as well as of the Swedish Association of Image Analysis in 1976. He serves on the editorial boards of several journals, including the Int. Journal of Computer Vision, Computer Vision: Image Understanding, Image and Vision Computing, and the Journal of Mathematical Imaging and Vision. His research interests cover a broad range of topics in computational vision and robotics, especially active visual machine perception with relations to human vision, behavioral aspects of perception, and autonomous systems.

Rainer Feldmann received his Ph.D. from the University of Paderborn in 1993. His research interest is massively parallel game-tree search. In 1995, he received the Novag award for the best work on computer chess in the years 1993/1994.

David Garlan is an Assistant Professor of Computer Science in the School of Computer Science at Carnegie Mellon University. His research interests include software architecture, the application of formal methods to the construction of reusable designs, and software development environments. Garlan heads the ABLE project, which focuses on the development of languages and environments to support the construction of software system architectures. Before joining the CMU faculty, Garlan worked in the Computer Research Laboratory of Tektronix, Inc., where he developed formal, architectural models of instrumentation software. Further information is available at URL http://www.cs.cmu.edu/ garlan/

Ralph Gasser received hist Ph.D. from the ETH Federal Institute of Technology in Zurich in1995. His research interests are: exhaustive search, combinatorial optimization and software engineering. His recent work includes the development of a workbench for studying retrograde analysis techniques and solving Nine Men's Morris.

David Gries received his B.A. from Queens College in 1960, M.S. from Illinois in 1963, and Dr. rer. nat. from the Munich Institute of Technology in 1966 (all in mathematics). After three years as assistant professor at Stanford, he left (because Stanford had no weather) for Cornell (where he has experienced weather for 26 years). He served as Chair of Computer Science in 1982–87. Gries is known for his texts *Compiler Construction for Digital Computers* (1971), *An Introduction to Programming: a Structured Approach* (1973, with Dick Conway), and *The Science of Programming* (1981), and *A Logical Approach to Discrete Math* (1993, with F.B. Schneider). He is co-managing editor of Springer-Verlag's Texts and Monographs in Computer Science series, a main editor of Acta Informatica, and a managing editor of Information Processing Letters. He was a Guggenheim Fellow in 1984–85 and is a Fellow of the AAAS. For his contributions to education, he received the IEEE Computer Society's 1994 Taylor L. Booth Award, the 1991 ACM SIGCSE award, and the AFIPS education award in 1985. He was co-recipient of the 1976 ACM Programming Languages and Systems Best Paper award. He served as Chair of the Computing Research Association during its formative years 1987–89 and received its Service Award in 1991.

Ming Gu holds a joint appointment as a Morrey Assistant Professor in the Department of Mathematics at the University of California at Berkeley and as a Hans Lewy Fellow in the Mathematics Department at Lawrence Berkeley National Laboratory. His research interests are in numerical linear algebra, its applications, parallel computing, numerical optimization, linear systems control theory, and complexity theory. For a list of his recent publications, see the URL http://http.cs.berkeley.edu/ minggu/reports/reports.html

Sridhar Hannenhalli is currently a Ph.D. candidate in the Department of Computer Science and Engineering at the Pennsylvania State University. He received his B.Techn. degree in Computer Science and Engineering from the Institute of Technology, Banaras Hindu University, Varanasi, India, in 1990 and his M.S. degree in Computer Science from the University of Central Florida, Orlando. His current research interest concerns the application of graph-theoretic techniques to the analysis of Genome rearrangements and to sequencing by hybridization.

Lynda Hardman is a researcher in the Multimedia Kernel Systems group at the CWI in Amsterdam. Here she developed the Amsterdam Hypermedia Model. She also investigated authoring systems for multi- and hypermedia and collaborated on the hypermedia authoring system CMIFed. After graduating with honours in mathematics and natural philosophy (that is, Physics) in 1982 from Glasgow University, Hardman began her computing career at ICL (International Computers Ltd.). She later joined OWL (Office Workstations Ltd.), where she became the development manager for Guide (the first hypertext authoring system for personal computers). Her interests in the problems associated with navigating in hypertext documents led her to become a research assistant at the Scottish HCI Centre at Heriot-Watt University, Edinburgh. She continued the hypertext navigation work, along with work on data models for hypermedia at OWL as part of a European research project. Her current research interests include improving authoring environments for hypermedia documents destined for heterogeneous platforms. Lynda serves on the editorial board of the Hypermedia Journal. She is a member of the ACM and of the British Computer Society, and a Chartered Engineer.

David Harel is the William Sussman Professor of Mathematics at the Weizmann Institute of Science in Israel. He was chairman of its Department of Applied Mathematics and Computer Science from 1989 to 1995. He is also co-founder of i-Logix, Inc., Andover, MA, and the inventor of the language of statecharts. He received his Ph.D. from MIT in 1978, and has spent two years at IBM's Yorktown Heights research center, and sabbatical years at Carnegie-Mellon and Cornell Universities. His research interests are in computability and complexity theory, logics of programs, theory of databases, automata theory, visual languages and systems engineering. He received ACM's 1992 Karlstrom Outstanding Educator Award, and the best paper award in the 1988 Int. Conf. on Software Engineering. His book, *Algorithmics: The Spirit of Computing*, was the Spring 1988 Main Selection of the Macmillan Library of Science. He is a Fellow of the ACM and of the IEEE.

Maurice Herlihy received the A.B. degree in Mathematics from Harvard University, and the M.S. and the Ph.D. degrees in Computer Science from MIT. From 1984 to 1989 he was a faculty member in the Computer Science Department at Carnegie Mellon University. From 1989 to 1994 he was a member of research staff at Digital Equipment Corporation's Cambridge Research Laboratory. In 1994, he joined the faculty at Brown University. His research interests encompass practical and theoretical aspects of highly concurrent computation.

Somesh Jha received a B.Tech. degree in Electrical Engineering from the Indian Institute of Technology, New Delhi, India, in 1985, and a M.S. degree in Computer Science from Pennsylvania State University, University Park, PA, in 1987. He is currently pursuing a Ph.D. degree in Computer Science at Carnegie Mellon University, Pittsburgh, PA. After receiving his M.S., he was a consultant from 1987-1991. During this time he consulted for IBM, AT&T, and UPS. His interests include software and hardware verification, distributed systems and stochastic finance.

Thomas Käppner received his M.Sc. (Dipl.-Inf. Univ.) in Computer Science from the University of Erlangen-Neurenberg. He was a visiting scientist at the multimedia lab of the University of California at San Diego in 1991, working on networked storage systems for multimedia data. He joined the IBM European Networking Center in 1992 to participate in projects on multimedia transport systems and collaborative multimedia applications. His current research interests include support platforms for distributed multimedia applications.

Andreas Klappenecker studied Informatics at the Universität Karlsruhe, where he received his Diplom degree in 1994. His decision to stay in Karlsruhe as a research assistant was based on the multi-functionality of his room: office and sauna in summer. Currently, he is working on his Ph.D. thesis in algebraic wavelet analysis at the Fakultät für Informatik. His research interests include wavelet analysis, data compression, image processing, and VLSI design.

Ralf Klasing received his Ph.D. from the University of Paderborn in 1995. His research interests include graph embedding and communication algorithms in interconnection networks.

Ming Li is a professor of Computer Science at the University of Waterloo. He received his Ph.D. from Cornell University in 1985. He is a coauthor of the book *An Introduction to Kolmogorov Complexity and Its Applications* (Springer-Verlag, 1993). He is currently on the editorial boards of the Journal of Computer and System Sciences, the Journal of Computer Science and Technology, and the Journal of Combinatorial Optimization. His research interests are in Theory of Computing, Kolmogorov Complexity, Machine Learning, and Computational Biology.

Reinhard Lüling is a Ph.D. candidate in the Computer Science Department at the University of Paderborn. His research interests include load balancing, graph partitioning and architectures of massively parallel systems.

Zohar Manna is a Professor of Computer Science at Stanford University. He received his Ph.D. from Carnegie-Mellon University. He is the author of the textbook *Mathematical Theory of Computation* (McGraw-Hill, 1974) and co-author of the textbooks *The Temporal Logic of Reactive and Concurrent systems: Specification* (Springer-Verlag, 1991), *The Deductive Foundations of Computer Programming* (Addison-Wesley, 1993), and *Temporal Verification of Reactive Systems: Safety* (Springer-Verlag, 1995). His research interests include: automated deduction; the specification, verification and systematic development of reactive and real-time systems; and automatic and machine-supported verification systems. He is supervising the STeP (Stanford Temporal Prover) project.

Fabian Mäser received his Diploma in Computer Science at the ETH Zürich in 1993. His research interest include: heuristic search methods, combinatorial game theory, and retrograde analysis.

Hermann Maurer received his Ph.D. in Mathematics from the University of Vienna 1965. He was Assistant and Associate Professor for Computer Science at the University of Calgary in 1966–1971, Full Professor for Applied Computer Science at the University of Karlsruhe in 1971-1977, and Full Professor at the Graz University of Technology since 1978. In addition, he is director of the Research Institute for Applied Information Processing of the Austrian Computer Society since 1983, chairman of the Institute for Information Processing and Computer Supported New Media since 1988, and director of the Institute for Hypermedia Systems of Joanneum Research since April 1990. He was an Adjunct Professor at Denver University 1984–1988. and became Professor for Computer Science at the University of Auckland, New Zealand, starting Feb. 1, 1993, Adjunct Professor since October 93. Maurer is the author of eleven books and over 400 scientific contributions, holder of a patent for an optical storage device, referee for a number of journals and publishing companies, editor of a series of research papers, member of the board of various institutions. His main research and project areas include: languages and their applications, data structures and their efficient use, telematic services, computer networks, computer assisted instruction, computer supported new media, hypermedia systems and applications, and social implications of computers.

Bill McColl received his B.Sc. in 1973 and his Ph.D. in 1976, both in Computer Science. Since 1977 he has held a number of academic appointments in the U.K. He has also been a Visiting Professor of Computer Science in Japan and a Senior Visiting Scientist at research centers in the United States, Canada and the Netherlands. He is currently a member of the Programming Research Group at Oxford University, a Fellow of Wadham College, and Chairman of Oxford Parallel - a major centre for parallel computing at Oxford. His research interests include scalable computing, programming languages and computational complexity.

Knut Menzel received his Ph.D. from the University of Paderborn in 1995. His research interests include methods for 3D image generation and its parallelization on various hardware platforms.

Torsten Minkwitz studied Informatics at the Technische Universität Braunschweig in 1987 and then went to the Universität Karlsruhe, where he received his Diplom degree in 1991. He interrupted his studies in 1988 to go to the University of Texas at Austin as a Fulbright scholar to study Linguistics for a year. After returning, he participated in Computational Linguistics research at the Universität Heidelberg. To escape unclear semantics and baroque syntax, he made his way back to Computer Science and received a Dr. rer. nat. in 1993 at the Universität Karlsruhe. From 1992-1995 he was Fellow of the Graduiertenkolleg "Beherrschbarkeit komplexer Systeme" sponsored by Deutsche Forschungsgemeinschaft at the Universität Karlsruhe. In 1995 he was a visiting scholar at the University of Sydney. Since summer 1995 he is working for Deutsche Telekom AG in Bonn. Minkwitz's research is in computational group theory and algorithms in signal processing. In working with the group of T. Beth at IAKS, he has developed a method to automatically derive fast algorithms for several signal transforms.

Burkhard Monien is Professor of Computer Science at the University of Paderborn. He received his Ph.D. from the University of Hamburg in 1969. After having worked at the Institutes for Applied Mathematics and for Computer Science at the University of Hamburg, he was appointed as Associate Professor at the Department of Computer Science of the University of Dortmund in 1975. Since 1977 he has been full professor at the University of Paderborn. His research interests include theoretical questions (design of efficient algorithms, theory of interconnection networks, complexity theory) and practical problems concerning the efficient use of parallel systems (mapping, load balancing, parallel implementations of algorithms). He has published more than 100 papers in most of the well-known Computer Science conferences and journals. Burkhard Monien was a member of the program committees of many important international conferences, program chair of the Symp. on Theoretical Aspects of Computer Science (STACS) in 1986 and 1989 and of the Int. Colloquium on Automata, Languages and Programming (ICALP) in 1991. He served as Dean of the Computer Science departments in Dortmund and Paderborn and as Vice-President of the University of Paderborn. He is a member of the Council of the Heinz-Nixdorf-Institute in Paderborn and Head of the Paderborn Center for Parallel Computing, PC^2. In 1992, he was awarded the Leibniz research prize of the German Research Association (DFG) together with Friedhelm Meyer auf der Heide, also from the University of Paderborn.

Anne Mulkers obtained a degree in mathematics (1982), informatics (1984), and a Ph.D. in informatics (1991), all at the K.U. Leuven. Since 1984 she has been working as a research assistant at the Department of Computer Science at the K.U. Leuven. Her research interest concerns the implementation and analysis of logic programming languages. Specific research topics include abstract interpretation of Prolog for the applications of compile-time garbage collection, and type- and mode analysis. She published in ACM ToPLaS and her Ph.D. on liveness analysis for logic programs appeared in the Lecture Notes in Computer Science series (Springer-Verlag).

Shin-ichi Nakano was born in Karuizawa, Japan, on July 27, 1962. He received the B.E. and M.E. degrees from Tohoku University, Sendai, Japan, in 1985 and 1987, respectively. He joined Seiko Epson Corp. in 1987 and Tohoku University in 1990. He received the Dr.Eng. degree from Tohoku University, Sendai, Japan, in 1992. He is currently a Research Associate of Department of System Information Sciences, Graduate School of Information Sciences, Tohoku University. From 1994 to 1995 he was on leave at University of California at Riverside, California, CA. His areas of research interest are combinatorial algorithms, graph theory and graph drawings. Dr. Nakano is a member of the Institute of Electronics, Information and Communication Engineers of Japan, the Information Processing Society of Japan, the Japan Society for Industrial and Applied Mathematics, ACM and IEEE.

Roger Needham is Professor of Computer Systems and Head of the Computer Laboratory in the University of Cambridge. He obtained his Ph.D. from Cambridge in 1961 and has been on the faculty of Cambridge University since 1963. He led the team which completed the Titan Multiple-Access System in 1967, and that which designed the CAP computer and its operating system in the 1970's. In the 1980's he led the Cambridge contribution to Project Universe, which interconnected local area networks by satellite. In between these activities he has worked intermittently on security and authentication for many years. He was elected to the Royal Society in 1985, and the Royal Academy of Engineering in 1993. He is currently Chairman of the School of Technology in the University of Cambridge.

Jurg Nievergelt received a Diploma in Mathematics from ETH in 1962, and a Ph.D. in Mathematics from the University of Illinois in 1965. From 1965-77 he was on the faculty of Computer Science at the University of Illinois at Urbana-Champaign, from assistant professor to full professor. Since 1975 he is professor of Computer Science at ETH Zurich. On leave from ETH 1985-89, he was Kenan Professor and Chairman of the Computer Science Dept. at the Univ. of North Carolina at Chapel Hill. His visiting appointments include NTT's Yokosuka Electrical Communications Lab, Visiting IBM Professor at Keio University, and Visiting Professor at the National University of Singapore. He is a Fellow of ACM, IEEE and AAAS. His research interests include:

algorithms and data structures, interactive systems, user interfaces, heuristic and exhaustive search, parallel computation.

Takao Nishizeki was born in Sukagawa, Japan, on February 11, 1947. He received the B.E., M.E., and Dr.Eng. degrees from Tohoku University, Sendai, Japan, in 1969, 1971, and 1974, respectively, all in electrical communication engineering. He joined Tohoku University in 1974, and is currently Professor of Graduate School of Information Sciences. From 1977 to 1978 he was on leave at Mathematics Department of Carnegie-Mellon University, Pittsburgh, PA. His areas of research interest are combinatorial algorithms, VLSI routing, graph theory, network theory and computational complexity. He has published over 100 papers in these areas. He is a coauthor of two books *Planar Graphs: Theory and Algorithms* (North-Holland, 1988) and *Discrete Mathematics* (Asakura, 1989), and is a co-editor of three books: *Graph Theory and Algorithms* (Springer-Verlag, 1980), *Discrete Algorithms and Complexity* (Academic Press, 1987), and *Algorithms* (Springer-Verlag, 1990). Nishizeki is a member of the Information Processing Society of Japan, the Institute of Electronics, Information and Communication Engineers of Japan, the Japan Society for Industrial and Applied Mathematics and the Association for Computing Machinery. He is a Fellow of IEEE, a Vice Chair of Information Systems Society of IEICE, and an Editor of the journal Algorithmica.

Armin Nückel studied Informatics at the Universität Karlsruhe, where he received his Diplom degree in 1989. Since then he is working as a research assistant at the Universität Karlsruhe. His research interests include algebraic and algorithmic system design and VLSI architectures. Currently, he is working on his Ph.D. thesis concerning the generation of VLSI-architectures based on the structural analysis of algebraic systems.

Pavel Pevzner is currently an Associate professor of Computer Science and Engineering at the Pennsylvania state university. He was a postdoctoral research associate in the Dept. of Mathematics at the USC from 1990 to 1992. Prior to that, he was first a scientist and then a senior scientist at the Laboratory of Mathematical methods, Institute of Genetics of Microorganisms, Moscow, USSR. Pevzner received his Ph.D. degree in Mathematics and Physics from the Moscow Institute of Physics and Technology. Pevzner is organizer and/or chair of numerous conferences including the First World Congress in Computational Medicine and Biotechnology, Third International Conference on Bioinformatics and Supercomputing and two workshops for DIMACS Computational Molecular Biology Year. He is a member of the Editorial Board of the Journal of Computational Molecular Biology and was a guest Editor for Computer Genetics: Bio Systems. His research interests are in the area of computational molecular biology, including optimization of DNA sequencing chips and additional biochemical experiments for sequencing by hybridization, software for sequencing by hybridization and combinatorial methods for gene recognition and analyzing genome rearrangements.

Vaughan Pratt received his B.Sc. and M.Sc. from Sydney University in 1967 and 1970, and his Ph.D. from Stanford in 1972. He taught in EECS at MIT for ten years before transferring to Stanford's Computer Science Department, where he presently has the rank of professor. He has diverse research interests, publishing in computational linguistics, algorithms, logics of programs, computer graphics, and concurrency, and lectures frequently at conferences and summer schools in theory, AI, and systems. He introduced Dynamic Logic in 1976, initially as a logic of sequential programs but now popular in philosophy as a logic of human language and behavior. At MIT he was co-founder and president of Research and Consulting Inc, a consortium of MIT computing professors. While on sabbatical at Stanford he managed the Sun workstation project after its founder Forest Baskett left for PARC. He participated in the founding of Sun Microsystems, where he designed Pixrect, Sun's primary device-independent graphics interface. He designed the Sun logo and the Stanford Computer Forum logo.

Nicholas J. Radcliffe is the a director of Quadstone Ltd., a company specialising in decision support, including optimisation, large-scale data analysis and traffic planning. He combines this position with a Visiting Professorship in Mathematics at the University of Edinburgh, and a directorship of the Institute for Policy Analysis and Development, a think-tank on sustainability. Prior to his present appointment, Radcliffe ran the Information Systems Group at Edinburgh Parallel Computing Centre, where he was responsible for commercial applications of parallel processing. He received his Ph.D. in Theoretical Physics from the University of Edinburgh in 1990. Radcliffe's research interests include stochastic search and non-linear optimisation, with a focus on evolutionary methods, as well as the wider fields of complex adaptive systems and sustainability. He is the author (with A. M. H. Clayton) of *Sustainability: A Systems Approach* and (with P. D. Surry) of *The Reproductive Plan Language RPL2*. Radcliffe serves on the program comittee of several conferences (ICGA, FOGA, PPSN, ESA, is on the editorial board of the journals Neural Computing and Application (NCAF) and Evolutionary Computing and is referee for numerous other journals. He is a member of the Council of the International Society for Genetic Algorithms (ISGA).

Sergio Rajsbaum received a degree in Computer Engineering from the National University of Mexico (UNAM) in 1986, and a Ph.D. in Computer Science from the Technion, Israel, in 1991. Since then he has been a member of the Institute of Mathematics of UNAM, doing research in sequential and distributed algorithms, clock synchronization, petri nets, and graph theory. He was a visiting scientist at the Laboratory for Computer Science of MIT and at the Cambridge Research Laboratory of DEC.

Wolfgang Reisig is a Professor of Computer Science and Managing Director of the Computer Science Institute of Humboldt-University at Berlin. Prior to joining Humboldt-University he was a Professor at Technical University of Munich and a project manager at GMD Bonn. His research interests include distributed algorithms, specification and correctness of distributed systems and Petri Nets. His book on *Petri Nets* has been published in various languages.

Thomas Römke is research assistant and Ph.D. candidate at the Paderborn Center for Parallel Computing PC^2. His research interests are programming frames for parallel applications.

Axel Ruhe is Professor of Numerical Analysis in the School of Mathematical and Computing Sciences at the Chalmers University of Technology and the University of Göteborg in Sweden. He is chairman of the steering committee for a research program in computational methods for super- and parallel computer systems for NUTEK (Swedish National Board for Industrial and Technical Development), board member of ITM (Swedish institute of applied mathematics) and was previously a member of the board for Physics and Mathematics of NFR (Swedish Natural Sciences Research Council). His works deal primarily with numerical computation of eigenvalues for matrices, first numerical treatment of matrices with very ill- conditioned eigenproblems and composite Jordan normal form, then large symmetric pencils arising from mechanical vibration problems, the Spectral transformation Lanczos algorithm, later Rational Krylov algorithms, and the use of eigenvalue methods to predict singularities and bifurcations of nonlinear systems of equations. For more information see the URL: http://www.cs.chalmers.se/ ruhe

Erik Sandewall is Professor of Computer Science at Linköping University, Sweden. He received his Ph.D. from Uppsala University, Sweden, in 1969. He is the author of the research monograph *Features and Fluents. The Representation of Knowledge about Dynamical Systems* (Oxford University Press, 1994). His research interests are in knowledge representation and cognitive robotics. Sandewall is a member of the Swedish Academy of Sciences and the Swedish Academy of Engineering Sciences, and a Fellow of the American Association for Artificial Intelligence. He was a program co-chair of the International Conference on Knowledge Representation and Reasoning in 1991, and the general chair of the same conference in 1994.

Fred B. Schneider received an M.S. (1977) and Ph.D. (1978) from SUNY Stony Brook in Computer Science. When he received his B.S. in CS and EE from Cornell in 1975, he resolved never to come back and never to work in academia. Three years later, he returned as assistant professor of Computer Science and has been there ever since. He served as associate chair and director of the department's undergraduate programs from 1991–1993. Schneider's research concerns concurrent programming, particularly for fault-tolerant, real-time, and distributed systems. He has developed logics for reasoning about system behavior as well as algorithms and systems for this setting. Schneider is a Fellow of the AAAS and ACM. From 1983–1988, he served on the College Board Committee for Advanced Placement in Computer Science. He is the managing editor of Distributed Computing, co-managing editor of Springer-Verlag's Texts and Monographs in Computer Science series, and a member of the editorial boards of Annals of Software Engineering, High Integrity Systems, Information Processing Letters, IEEE Transactions on Software Engineering, and ACM Computing Surveys.

Ulf-Peter Schroeder is a Ph.D. candidate in the CS Department at the University of Paderborn. His research interests include graph theory and graph embedding.

Micha Sharir is Nizri Professor of Computational Geometry and Robotics in the Department of Computer Science at the School of Mathematical Sciences of Tel Aviv University. He received his Ph.D. in Mathematics from Tel Aviv University in 1976. His research interests include computational and combinatorial geometry and their applications, motion planning, and other topics in robotics. He is an author of over 200 research papers, and is also a co-author of *Davenport-Schinzel Sequences and Their Geometric Applications*. He is a Visiting Research Professor at the Courant Institute of Mathematical Sciences, New York University, where he was also an Associate Director of the Robotics Lab. He was awarded a Max-Planck Research Prize (jointly with Emo Welzl) in 1992, and is a Director of a newly established Minerva Center in Geometry at Tel Aviv University.

Mary Shaw is the Alan J. Perlis Professor of Computer Science and Associate Dean for Professional Programs, and a member of the Human Computer Interaction Institute at Carnegie Mellon University. She has been a member of this faculty since completing the Ph.D. degree at Carnegie-Mellon in 1972. Her research interests in Computer Science lie primarily in the areas of programming systems and software engineering, particularly software architecture, programming languages, specifications, and abstraction techniques. From 1984 to 1987 she served as Chief Scientist of CMU's Software Engineering Institute. She had previously received a B.A. (cum laude) from Rice University and worked in systems programming and research at the Research Analysis Corporation and Rice University. In 1993 Shaw received the Warnier prize for contributions to software engineering. She is a Fellow of the IEEE and of the American Association for the Advancement of Science. She is a member of the Association for Computing Machinery, the Society of the Sigma Xi, and the New York Academy of Sciences. She serves on Working Group 2.4 (System Implementation Languages) of the International Federation of Information Processing Societies. Further information is available at URL http://www.cs.cmu.edu/ shaw/

Hava T. Siegelmann specializes in biologically motivated information processing systems, including neural networks and evolutionary algorithms, as well as in alternative models of computation (such as analog, distributed, and stochastic dynamics) that are relevant to natural systems. Siegelmann received her B.A. from the Technion (Summa Cum Laude) in 1988, her M.Sc. from the Hebrew University in 1992, and her Ph.D. from Rutgers University (where she was on a Fellowship of Excellence) in 1993, all in Computer Science. Currently, she is an assistant professor on the faculty of Industrial Engineering and Management at the Technion. Siegelmann is a 1995-1997 ALON Fellow (Israeli Presidential Young Investigator). She has published in a variety of prestigious journals, including Science, Theoretical Computer Science, and the Journal of Computer and Systems Science, and has given numerous invited talks.

Gert Smolka is Professor of Computer Science at the Universität des Saarlandes at Saarbrücken and Head of the Programming Systems Lab of the DFKI. He received his Dr.rer.nat. in Computer Science in 1989 from the Universität Kaiserslautern. He is a member of the executive committee of the European Network of Excellence in Computational Logic and served on many international programming committees. Gert Smolka has published papers on computational logic, logic programming, type systems, knowledge representation and reasoning, formalisms for computational linguistics, constraints, concurrency, and programming languages and systems. Since 1991, Gert Smolka is leading the design and implementation of Oz, the first concurrent language combining a rich object system with advanced features for symbolic processing and problem solving. He and his group have now begun work towards a distributed version of Oz supporting the construction of open systems.

Lawrence Snyder received a bachelor's degree from the University of Iowa in mathematics and economics, and in 1973 he received a Ph.D. from Carnegie Mellon University in Computer Science. He was a visiting scholar at the University of Washington in 1979–80 and joined the faculty permanently in 1983 after serving on the faculties of Yale and Purdue. During 1987–88 he was a visiting scholar at MIT and Harvard, and in 1994–95 was a visiting professor at the University of Sydney. Snyder's research has ranged from the design and development of a 32 bit single chip (CMOS) microprocessor, the Quarter Horse, to proofs of the undecidability of properties of programs. He created the Configurable Highly Parallel (CHiP) architecture, the Poker Parallel Programming Environment, and is co-inventor of Chaotic Routing. He is a co-developer of the Take/Grant Security Model and co-creator of several new algorithms and data structures. He is inventor of the CTA, co-designer of Phase Abstractions and the ZPL programming language.

Luc Steels is chairman of the Computer Science Department of the University of Brussels (VUB) and director of the VUB Artificial Intelligence Laboratory. He formerly worked at the MIT AI laboratory and at the Schlumberger-Doll Research Labs, mostly in the fields of message passing systems, knowledge representation, and knowledge engineering. Since 1985 he has focused on both autonomous robots and the adoption of mechanisms from dynamical systems theory and biology. Steels has published about 100 papers and 10 books, including textbooks on LISP and knowledge systems, as well as monographs, conference proceedings and edited collections of papers.

Ralf Steinmetz manages the multimedia department at the IBM European Networking Center, Germany. There he initiated the first activities on networked multimedia issues in 1988. Since then he was in charge of a multimedia laboratory, he was the leader of the whole OS/2 multimedia transport system development and subsequently he was in charge of several application and application support projects. At the same time he has worked in academia by supervising numerous thesis and lecturing at the Universities of Mannheim and Frankfurt on several issues in Computer Science. He wrote the first technical in-depth book on multimedia systems published in German 1993, a second restructured -now coauthored- English book appears in 1995. In 1994 he received his "Habilitation" at the Computer Science Department of the University of Frankfurt. Before joining IBM, Ralf Steinmetz worked as software engineer in the ISDN and multimedia workstations development activities of Philips Kommunikations Industrie in Siegen, Germany. Ralf Steinmetz studied electrical engineering with the focus on communications at the University of Salford, England, and at the Technical University of Darmstadt, Germany, where he received the M.Sc. (Dipl.-Ing.) degree in 1982. He received his Ph.D. (Dr.-Ing.) in 1986 working in the area of Petri-Nets and concurrent programming languages. He wrote the first book on the programming language OCCAM in German. Ralf Steinmetz is associate editor-in-chief of the IEEE Multimedia Magazine. He has served as editor and member of the editorial advisory board of several journals. He was the co-program chair of the first IEEE Multimedia Conference. Ralf Steinmetz has served as chair, vice-chair and member of numerous program and steering committees of multimedia workshops and conferences. He is member of acm, GI, ITG, and senior member of IEEE.

Patrick Surry is a Ph.D. candidate in the Dept. of Mathematics and Statistics at the Univ. of Edinburgh and works part-time for Quadstone Ltd, a company specialising in decision support, including optimisation, large-scale data analysis and traffic planning. His research interests include representational issues in stochastic search, particularly evolutionary methods. Previously trained in applied mathematics, he also spent several years at the Edinburgh Parallel Computing Centre where he was chief architect of the representation-independent, parallel, evolutionary computing language RPL2.

Mario Tokoro is Professor and Head of the Computer Science Department at Keio University. He is also the Director of the Sony Computer Science Laboratory, since its establishment in 1988. He received Ph.D. in E.E. from Keio University, Yokohama, Japan in 1975. He was Visiting Assistant Professor at the University of Waterloo and Carnegie-Mellon University in 1979 and 1980, respectively. His main interest is in computational paradigms, especially in relation to Open and Distributed Systems. He is the author of many technical papers and a few books in Computer Architectures, Computer Networks, Operating Systems, Object-Oriented Systems, and Multi-Agent Systems.

Tomás E. Uribe is a Ph.D. candidate in the CS Department at Stanford University. His main research interests are automated deduction and formal verification. He is a member of the development team for STeP, the Stanford Temporal Prover.

Keith van Rijsbergen was born in Holland in 1943 and was educated in Holland, Indonesia, Namibia and Australia. He took a degree in mathematics at the University of Western Australia. As a graduate he spent two years tutoring in mathematics while studying Computer Science. In 1972 he completed a Ph.D. in Computer Science at Cambridge University. After almost three years of lecturing in information retrieval and artificial intelligence at Monash University he returned to the Cambridge Computer Laboratory to hold a Royal Society Information Research Fellowship. In 1980 he was appointed to the chair of Computer Science at University College Dublin; from there he moved in 1986 to the Glasgow University where he is now. Since about 1969 his research has been devoted to information retrieval, covering both theoretical and experimental aspects. His current research is concerned with the design of appropriate logics to model the flow of information. He is also involved with the Esprit project FERMI concentrating on the design and specification of a logic for IR incorporating a notion of uncertainty. He is a member of the management board for IDOMENEUS, a network of excellence in IR and DB, and a participant in MIRO, a working group on multimedia information retrieval. A recent research interest is automatic speech processing for IR. He is a fellow of the Royal Society of Edinburgh, the Institution of Electrical Engineers, and a Member of the British Computer Society. In 1993 he was appointed Editor-in-Chief of The Computer Journal. He is a member of the Advisory Committee (Beirat) for GMD in Germany, a director of the Turing Institute and Itext Ltd. He is also the author of a well-known book on Information Retrieval. (http://www.dcs.gla.ac.uk/Keith/preface.html)

Moshe Y. Vardi is a Noah Harding Professor of Computer Science and Chair of Computer Science at Rice University. Prior to joining Rice University, he was at the IBM Almaden Research Center, where he managed the Mathematics and Related Computer Science Department. His research interests include database theory, finite-model theory, knowledge-theory, and protocol specification and verification. Vardi received his Ph.D. from the Hebrew University of Jerusalem in 1982. He is the recipient of three IBM Outstanding Innovation Awards. Vardi was the program chair of the 6th ACM Symp. on the Principles of Database Systems (1987), the 2nd Conf. on Theoretical Aspects of Reasoning about Knowledge (1988), and the 8th IEEE Symp. on Logic in Computer Science (1993). He is currently an editor of the Chicago Journal for Theoretical Computer Science, Information and Computation, the Journal of Computer and System Sciences, and the SIAM Journal on Computing.

Paul Vitányi is Professor of Computer Science at the University of Amsterdam and Senior Researcher at the CWI in Amsterdam. In each affiliation he heads the research group on Algorithms and Complexity. He received his Ph.D. from the Free University of Amsterdam. He has been Visiting Professor at the University of Copenhagen, York University, the University of Waterloo, and Research Associate at MIT. He is the author (with Ming Li) of the textbook *An Introduction to Kolmogorov Complexity and Its*

Applications (Springer-Verlag, New York, 1993). He has recently been program committee member or program chair of conferences in theory of computation, structural complexity theory, distributed algorithms, machine learning, computational machine learning, and physics and computation. His research interests range over these topics. Recently he was invited speaker at "Inductive Logic Programming" (1994), "Workshop on Algorithms and Data Structures" (1995), and "Symposium on Mathematical Foundations of Computer Science" (1995). He is editor of several scientific journals including Distributed Computing, Mathematical Systems Theory, Information Processing Letters, Parallel Processing Letters, guest editor of the Journal of Computer and System Sciences on a volume on computational machine learning, and member of the Scientific Board of the 'Encyclopaedia of Mathematics', Reidel (1987 –).

Henk A. van der Vorst is a professor of Numerical Analysis and Computational Science at the Mathematics Department of Utrecht University. His current research interests include iterative solvers for linear systems, large sparse eigenproblems, overdetermined systems, and the design of algorithms for parallel computations. Van der Vorst received a Ph.D. in applied mathematics from the University of Utrecht in 1982 for a thesis on the effects of preconditioning. Together with Meijerink, he proposed in the mid-1970s the so-called Incomplete Choleski Decompositions and the ICCG method, which are still widely used for solving certain types of discretized partial differential equations. More recently he suggested the methods Bi-CGSTAB, GMRESR (with K. Vuik), and the Jacobi-Davidson method for eigenvalue problems (with G. Sleijpen). Henk van der Vorst co-authored the book *Solving Linear Systems on Vector and Shared Memory Computers*, and on the Templates for iterative methods for (sparse) linear systems. He authored and co-authored numerous papers on iterative methods and parallel linear algebra.

Gottfried Vossen received the M.Sc. degree (Dipl.-Inform.), the Ph.D. degree (Dr. rer. nat.), and the German Habilitation, all in Computer Science, from the Technical University of Aachen, Germany, in 1981, 1986, and 1990 respectively. He is professor of Computer Science and Director of the *Institut für Wirtschaftsinformatik* at the University of Münster, Germany, after having held various visiting positions in the USA and in Germany from 1986 to 1991, and the position of an associate professor at the University of Giessen, Germany, from 1991 to 1993. His research interests include theoretical and practical issues as well as applications of object-oriented database systems, in particular models for data and objects, database design, database languages, transactions, and integration of databases into scientific applications. He is an author of *Data Models, Database Languages and Database Management Systems* (Addison-Wesley, 1991), a co-editor of *Query Processing for Advanced Database Systems* (Morgan Kaufmann, 1994), and an author/co-author/co-editor of nine more books in German. He is chairman of the German GI information systems special interest group (EMISA), on the editorial advisory board of *Information Systems*, and an advisory textbook editor for *International Thompson Publishing* in Germany.

Jiří Wiedermann was born in 1948. In 1971 he graduated from the Faculty of Natural Sciences of Comenius University in Bratislava, Slovakia. Since then he was employed in the Institute of Informatics and Statistics, Bratislava, lastly as the chairman of the Division of Applied Informatics. He also lectured at Comenius University during that time. In 1981 he received his Ph.D. degree from the Czechoslovak Academy of Sciences, Prague and in 1992 a Dr. of Sciences degree from Comenius University, Bratislava.

In 1993, after the split of Czechoslovakia, he moved from Bratislava to Prague, in the Czech Republic. Here he has been with the Institute of Computer Science of the Academy of Sciences of the Czech Republic, serving as Vice-Director and Head of the Department of Theoretical Informatics. He also lectures at the Dept. of Computer Science of the Faculty of Mathematics and Physics of Charles University, Prague. His research interest include complexity theory of sequential and parallel computations, and the design and analysis of efficient algorithms and data structures for the respective machine models. He is the author of more than 70 papers in the above mentioned fields.

Christoph Wirth received his Diploma in Computer Science at the ETH Zürich in 1993. His research interests include: game theory (focus on chess endgames), and application design. He developed the commercial Smart Chess Board database software.

Derick Wood is a Professor of Computer Science at Hong Kong University of Science & Technology and a Full Professor of Computer Science at the University of Western Ontario, Canada. Prior to joining these two universities, he was a Full Professor in the Department of Computer Science, University of Waterloo, from 1982 to 1992. His research interests include document processing, symbolic computation of formal-language-theory objects, computational biology, algorithms, data structures, formal language theory, and computational geometry. He has published widely in these areas and has written two textbooks, *Theory of Computation* (Wiley) and *Data Structures, Algorithms, and Performance* (Addison-Wesley).

Ronald R. Yager is Director of the Machine Intelligence Institute and Professor of Information Systems at Iona College. He received his undergraduate degree from the City College of New York and his Ph.D. from the Polytechnic Institute of Brooklyn. He has served at NSF as program director in the Information Sciences program. He was a visiting scholar at Hunter College of the City University of New York. He was a NASA/Stanford fellow. He was a research associate at the University of California, Berkeley. He has served as a lecturer at the NATO Advanced Study Institute. He is a research fellow of the Knowledge Engineering Institute, Guangzhou University, China. He is on the scientific committee of the Fuzzy Logic Systems Institute, Iizuka, Japan. He is co-president of the International Conference on Information Processing and Management of Uncertainty, Paris. He is editor and chief of the International Journal of Intelligent Systems. He also serves on the editorial board of a number of other journals including Neural Networks, the Journal of Approximate Reasoning, Fuzzy Sets and Systems and the International Journal of General Systems. He has published over 300 articles and fifteen books. His current research interests include information fusion, multi-criteria decision making, uncertainty management in knowledge based systems, fuzzy set theory, fuzzy systems modeling and control, neural modeling and nonmonotonic reasoning.

Xiao Zhou was born in Shanghai, China, on April 30, 1963. He received the B.E. degree from the East China Normal University, Shanghai, China, 1986. He received the M.E. and the Dr.Eng. degree from Tohoku University, Sendai, Japan, in 1992 and 1995, respectively. He is currently a Research Associate of Education Center of Information Processing, Tohoku University. His areas of research interest are combinatorial algorithms, graph theory and computational complexity. He is a member of the Information Processing Society of Japan.

Author Index

Lecture Notes in Computer Science

For information about Vols. 1–926

please contact your bookseller or Springer-Verlag

Vol. 961: K.P. Jantke, S. Lange (Eds.), Algorithmic Learning for Knowledge-Based Systems. X, 511 pages. 1995. (Subseries LNAI).

Vol. 962: I. Lee, S.A. Smolka (Eds.), CONCUR '95: Concurrency Theory. Proceedings, 1995. X, 547 pages. 1995.

Vol. 963: D. Coppersmith (Ed.), Advances in Cryptology - CRYPTO '95. Proceedings, 1995. XII, 467 pages. 1995.

Vol. 964: V. Malyshkin (Ed.), Parallel Computing Technologies. Proceedings, 1995. XII, 497 pages. 1995.

Vol. 965: H. Reichel (Ed.), Fundamentals of Computation Theory. Proceedings, 1995. IX, 433 pages. 1995.

Vol. 966: S. Haridi, K. Ali, P. Magnusson (Eds.), EURO-PAR '95 Parallel Processing. Proceedings, 1995. XV, 734 pages. 1995.

Vol. 967: J.P. Bowen, M.G. Hinchey (Eds.), ZUM '95: The Z Formal Specification Notation. Proceedings, 1995. XI, 571 pages. 1995.

Vol. 968: N. Dershowitz, N. Lindenstrauss (Eds.), Conditional and Typed Rewriting Systems. Proceedings, 1994. VIII, 375 pages. 1995.

Vol. 969: J. Wiedermann, P. Hájek (Eds.), Mathematical Foundations of Computer Science 1995. Proceedings, 1995. XIII, 588 pages. 1995.

Vol. 970: V. Hlaváč, R. Šára (Eds.), Computer Analysis of Images and Patterns. Proceedings, 1995. XVIII, 960 pages. 1995.

Vol. 971: E.T. Schubert, P.J. Windley, J. Alves-Foss (Eds.), Higher Order Logic Theorem Proving and Its Applications. Proceedings, 1995. VIII, 400 pages. 1995.

Vol. 972: J.-M. Hélary, M. Raynal (Eds.), Distributed Algorithms. Proceedings, 1995. XI, 333 pages. 1995.

Vol. 973: H.H. Adelsberger, J. Lažanský, V. Mařík (Eds.), Information Management in Computer Integrated Manufacturing. IX, 665 pages. 1995.

Vol. 974: C. Braccini, L. DeFloriani, G. Vernazza (Eds.), Image Analysis and Processing. Proceedings, 1995. XIX, 757 pages. 1995.

Vol. 975: W. Moore, W. Luk (Eds.), Field-Programmable Logic and Applications. Proceedings, 1995. XI, 448 pages. 1995.

Vol. 976: U. Montanari, F. Rossi (Eds.), Principles and Practice of Constraint Programming — CP '95. Proceedings, 1995. XIII, 651 pages. 1995.

Vol. 977: H. Beilner, F. Bause (Eds.), Quantitative Evaluation of Computing and Communication Systems. Proceedings, 1995. X, 415 pages. 1995.

Vol. 978: N. Revell, A M. Tjoa (Eds.), Database and Expert Systems Applications. Proceedings, 1995. XV, 654 pages. 1995.

Vol. 979: P. Spirakis (Ed.), Algorithms — ESA '95. Proceedings, 1995. XII, 598 pages. 1995.

Vol. 980: A. Ferreira, J. Rolim (Eds.), Parallel Algorithms for Irregularly Structured Problems. Proceedings, 1995. IX, 409 pages. 1995.

Vol. 981: I. Wachsmuth, C.-R. Rollinger, W. Brauer (Eds.), KI-95: Advances in Artificial Intelligence. Proceedings, 1995. XII, 269 pages. (Subseries LNAI).

Vol. 982: S. Doaitse Swierstra, M. Hermenegildo (Eds.), Programming Languages: Implementations, Logics and Programs. Proceedings, 1995. XI, 467 pages. 1995.

Vol. 983: A. Mycroft (Ed.), Static Analysis. Proceedings, 1995. VIII, 423 pages. 1995.

Vol. 984: J.-M. Haton, M. Keane, M. Manago (Eds.), Advances in Case-Based Reasoning. Proceedings, 1994. VIII, 307 pages. 1995.

Vol. 985: T. Sellis (Ed.), Rules in Database Systems. Proceedings, 1995. VIII, 373 pages. 1995.

Vol. 986: Henry G. Baker (Ed.), Memory Management. Proceedings, 1995. XII, 417 pages. 1995.

Vol. 987: P.E. Camurati, H. Eveking (Eds.), Correct Hardware Design and Verification Methods. Proceedings, 1995. VIII, 342 pages. 1995.

Vol. 988: A.U. Frank, W. Kuhn (Eds.), Spatial Information Theory. Proceedings, 1995. XIII, 571 pages. 1995.

Vol. 989: W. Schäfer, P. Botella (Eds.), Software Engineering — ESEC '95. Proceedings, 1995. XII, 519 pages. 1995.

Vol. 990: C. Pinto-Ferreira, N.J. Mamede (Eds.), Progress in Artificial Intelligence. Proceedings, 1995. XIV, 487 pages. 1995. (Subseries LNAI).

Vol. 991: J. Wainer, A. Carvalho (Eds.), Advances in Artificial Intelligence. Proceedings, 1995. XII, 342 pages. 1995. (Subseries LNAI).

Vol. 992: M. Gori, G. Soda (Eds.), Topics in Artificial Intelligence. Proceedings, 1995. XII, 451 pages. 1995. (Subseries LNAI).

Vol. 993: T.C. Fogarty (Ed.), Evolutionary Computing. Proceedings, 1995. VIII, 264 pages. 1995.

Vol. 994: M. Hebert, J. Ponce, T. Boult, A. Gross (Eds.), Object Representation in Computer Vision. Proceedings, 1994. VIII, 359 pages. 1995.

Vol. 995: S.M. Müller, W.J. Paul, The Complexity of Simple Computer Architectures. XII, 270 pages. 1995.

Vol. 996: P. Dybjer, B. Nordström, J. Smith (Eds.), Types for Proofs and Programs. Proceedings, 1994. X, 202 pages. 1995.

Vol. 997: K.P. Jantke, T. Shinohara, T. Zeugmann (Eds.), Algorithmic Learning Theory. Proceedings, 1995. XV, 319 pages. 1995.

Vol. 998: A. Clarke, M. Campolargo, N. Karatzas (Eds.), Bringing Telecommunication Services to the People – IS&N '95. Proceedings, 1995. XII, 510 pages. 1995.

Vol. 999: P. Antsaklis, W. Kohn, A. Nerode, S. Sastry (Eds.), Hybrid Systems II. VIII, 569 pages. 1995.

Vol. 1000: J. van Leeuwen (Ed.), Computer Science Today. XIV, 643 pages. 1995.

Vol. 1004: J. Staples, P. Eades, N. Katoh, A. Moffat (Eds.), Algorithms and Computation. Proceedings, 1995. XV, 440 pages. 1995.

Vol. 1005: J. Estublier (Ed.), Software Configuration Management. Proceedings, 1995. IX, 311 pages. 1995.

Vol. 1006: S. Bhalla (Ed.), Information Systems and Data Management. Proceedings, 1995. IX, 321 pages. 1995.

Vol. 1008: B. Preneel (Ed.), Fast Software Encryption. Proceedings, 1994. VIII, 367 pages. 1995.